DATE DUE

			PRINTED IN U.S.A.

Poetry
Criticism

Guide to Gale Literary Criticism Series

For criticism on	Consult these Gale series
Authors now living or who died after December 31, 1959	*CONTEMPORARY LITERARY CRITICISM (CLC)*
Authors who died between 1900 and 1959	*TWENTIETH-CENTURY LITERARY CRITICISM (TCLC)*
Authors who died between 1800 and 1899	*NINETEENTH-CENTURY LITERATURE CRITICISM (NCLC)*
Authors who died between 1400 and 1799	*LITERATURE CRITICISM FROM 1400 TO 1800 (LC)* *SHAKESPEAREAN CRITICISM (SC)*
Authors who died before 1400	*CLASSICAL AND MEDIEVAL LITERATURE CRITICISM (CMLC)*
Black writers of the past two hundred years	*BLACK LITERATURE CRITICISM (BLC) AND BLACK LITERATURE CRITICISM SUPPLEMENT (BLCS)*
Authors of books for children and young adults	*CHILDREN'S LITERATURE REVIEW (CLR)*
Dramatists	*DRAMA CRITICISM (DC)*
Hispanic writers of the late nineteenth and twentieth centuries	*HISPANIC LITERATURE CRITICISM (HLC)*
Native North American writers and orators of the eighteenth, nineteenth, and twentieth centuries	*NATIVE NORTH AMERICAN LITERATURE (NNAL)*
Poets	*POETRY CRITICISM (PC)*
Short story writers	*SHORT STORY CRITICISM (SSC)*
Major authors from the Renaissance to the present	*WORLD LITERATURE CRITICISM, 1500 TO THE PRESENT (WLC)*
Major authors and works from the Bible to the present	*WORLD LITERATURE CRITICISM SUPPLEMENT (WLCS)*

ISSN 1052-4851

R

Poetry Criticism

*Criticism of the Works
of the Most Significant and Widely
Studied Poets of World Literature*

VOLUME 25

Laura A. Wisner-Broyles
Editor

The Gale Group

DETROIT • SAN FRANCISCO • LONDON • BOSTON • WOODBRIDGE, CT

STAFF

Laura Wisner-Broyles, *Editor*

Debra A. Wells, *Assistant Editor*

Maria Franklin, *Permissions Manager*
Kimberly F. Smilay, *Permissions Specialist*
Kelly Quin, *Permissions Associate*
Sarah Chesney, *Permissions Assistant*

Victoria B. Cariappa, *Research Manager*
Cheryl L. Warnock, *Research Specialist*
Patricia T. Ballard, Wendy Festerling, Tamara C. Knott,
Tracie A. Richardson, Corrine Stocker, *Research Associates*
Timothy Lehnerer, Patricia Love, *Research Assistants*

Mary Beth Trimper, *Production Director*
Dorothy Maki, *Manufacturing Manager*
Cindy Range, *Buyer*

Randy Bassett, *Imaging Database Supervisor*
Robert Duncan, Michael Logusz, *Imaging Specialists*
Gary Leach, *Graphic Artist*
Pamela A. Reed, *Imaging Coordinator*

Library of Congress Catalog Card Number 88-641014
ISBN 0-7876-3073-X
ISSN 1052-4851

Printed in the United States of America

10 9 8 7 6 5 4 3 2 1

Contents

Preface vii

Acknowledgments xi

Preface

A Comprehensive Information Source on World Poetry

Poetry Criticism (PC) provides substantial critical excerpts and biographical information on poets throughout the world who are most frequently studied in high school and undergraduate college courses. Each *PC* entry is supplemented by biographical and bibliographical material to help guide the user to a fuller understanding of the genre and its creators. Although major poets and literary movements are covered in such Gale Literary Criticism Series as *Contemporary Literary Criticism (CLC)*, *Twentieth-Century Literary Criticism (TCLC)*, *Nineteenth-Century Literature Criticism (NCLC)*, *Literature Criticism from 1400 to 1800 (LC)*, and *Classical and Medieval Literature Criticism (CMLC)*, *PC* offers more focused attention on poetry than is possible in the broader, survey-oriented entries on writers in these Gale series. Students, teachers, librarians, and researchers will find that the generous excerpts and supplementary material provided by *PC* supply them with the vital information needed to write a term paper on poetic technique, to examine a poet's most prominent themes, or to lead a poetry discussion group.

Coverage

In order to reflect the influence of tradition as well as innovation, poets of various nationalities, eras, and movements are represented in every volume of *PC*. Each author entry presents a historical survey of the critical response to that author's work; the length of an entry reflects the amount of critical attention that the author has received from critics writing in English and from foreign critics in translation. Since many poets have inspired a prodigious amount of critical explication, *PC* is necessarily selective, and the editors have chosen the most significant published criticism to aid readers and students in their research. In order to provide these important critical pieces, the editors will sometimes reprint essays that have appeared in previous volumes of Gale's Literary Criticism Series. Such duplication, however, never exceeds fifteen percent of a *PC* volume.

Organization

Each *PC* author entry consists of the following components:

- **Author Heading:** the name under which the author wrote appears at the beginning of the entry, followed by birth and death dates. If the author wrote consistently under a pseudonym, the pseudonym will be listed in the author heading and his or her legal name given in parentheses in the lines immediately preceding the Introduction. Uncertainty as to birth or death dates is indicated by question marks.

- **Introduction:** a biographical and critical essay introduces readers to the author and the critical discussions surrounding his or her work.

- **Author Portrait:** a photograph or illustration of the author is included when available.

- **Principal Works:** the author's most important works are identified in a list ordered chronologically by first publication dates. The first section comprises poetry collections and book-length poems. The second section gives information on other major works by the author. For foreign authors, original foreign-language publication information is provided, as well as the best and most complete English-language editions of their works.

- **Criticism:** critical excerpts chronologically arranged in each author entry provide perspective on changes in critical evaluation over the years. All individual titles of poems and poetry collections by the author featured in the entry are printed in boldface type to enable a reader to ascertain without difficulty the works under discussion. For purposes of easy identification, the critic's name and the publication date of the essay are given at the beginning of each piece of criticism. Unsigned criticism is preceded by the title of the journal in which it originally appeared. Publication information (such as publisher names and book prices) and parenthetical numerical references (such as footnotes or page and line references to specific editions of a work) have been deleted at the editor's discretion to enable smoother reading of the text.

- **Explanatory Notes:** introductory comments preface each critical excerpt, providing several types of useful information, including: the reputation of a critic, the importance of a work of criticism, and the specific type of criticism (biographical, psychoanalytic, historical, etc.).

- **Author Commentary:** insightful comments from the authors themselves and excerpts from author interviews are included when available.

- **Bibliographical Citations:** information preceding each piece of criticism guides the interested reader to the original essay or book.

- **Further Reading:** bibliographic references accompanied by descriptive notes at the end of each entry suggest additional materials for study of the author. Boxed material following the Further Reading provides references to other biographical and critical series published by Gale.

Other Features

- **Cumulative Author Index:** comprises all authors who have appeared in Gale's Literary Criticism Series, along with cross-references to such Gale biographical series as *Contemporary Authors* and *Dictionary of Literary Biography*. This cumulated index enables the user to locate an author within the various series.

- **Cumulative Nationality Index:** includes all authors featured in *PC,* arranged alphabetically under their respective nationalities.

- **Cumulative Title Index:** lists in alphabetical order all individual poems, book-length poems, and collection titles contained in the *PC* series. Titles of poetry collections and separately published poems are printed in italics, while titles of individual poems are printed in roman type with quotation marks. Each title is followed by the author's name and the volume and page number corresponding to the location of commentary on specific works. English-language translations of original foreign-language titles are cross-referenced to the foreign titles so that all references to discussion of a work are combined in one listing.

Citing *Poetry Criticism*

When writing papers, students who quote directly from any volume in the Literary Criticism Series may use the following general formats to footnote reprinted criticism. The first example pertains to material drawn from periodicals, the second to material reprinted from books:

[1]David Daiches, "W. H. Auden: The Search for a Public," *Poetry* LIV (June 1939), 148-56; excerpted and reprinted in *Poetry Criticism*, Vol. 1, ed. Robyn V. Young (Detroit: Gale Research, 1990), pp. 7-9.

[2]Pamela J. Annas, *A Disturbance in Mirrors: The Poetry of Sylvia Plath* (Greenwood Press, 1988); excerpted and reprinted in *Poetry Criticism*, Vol. 1, ed. Robyn V. Young (Detroit: Gale Research, 1990), pp. 410-14.

Comments Are Welcome

Readers who wish to suggest authors to appear in future volumes, or who have other suggestions, are cordially invited to contact the editors.

Acknowledgments

The editors wish to thank the copyright holders of the excerpted criticism included in this volume and the permissions managers of many book and magazine publishing companies for assisting us in securing reproduction rights. We are also grateful to the staffs of the Detroit Public Library, the Library of Congress, the University of Detroit Mercy Library, Wayne State University Purdy/Kresge Library Complex, and the University of Michigan Libraries for making their resources available to us. Following is a list of the copyright holders who have granted us permission to reproduce material in this volume of *PC*. Every effort has been made to trace copyright, but if omissions have been made, please let us know.

COPYRIGHTED EXCERPTS IN *PC,* VOLUME 25, WERE REPRODUCED FROM THE FOLLOWING PERIODICALS:

The American Book Review, v. 16, April-May, 1994. (c) 1994 by The American Book Review. Reproduced by permission.—**American Poetry Review,** v. 13, July/August, 1984 for an interview with N. Scott Momaday by Joseph Bruchac. Copyright (c) 1984 by World Poetry, Inc. Reproduced by permission of the author.—**The Bloomsbury Review,** v. 13, July-August, 1993 for a review of In the Presence of the Sun: Stories and Poems, 1961-1991 by Scott Edward Anderson. Copyright (c) by Owaissa Communications Company, Inc. 1993. Reproduced by permission of the author. —**Callaloo,** v. 18, 1995. Copyright (c) 1995 by Charles H. Rowell. Reproduced by permission of The Johns Hopkins University Press.—**Colloquia Germanica,** v. 26, 1993 for "Anticolonialism in Heine's 'Vitzliputzli'" by John Carson Pettey. (c) A. Francke AG Verlag Bern, 1993. All rights reserved. Reproduced by permission of the author.—**Eighteenth-Century Studies,** v. 10, Spring, 1977. (c) 1977 by The American Society for Eighteenth-Century Studies. Reproduced by permission.—**ELH,** v. 57, Summer, 1990; v, 62, Summer, 1995. Copyright (c) 1990, 1995 by The Johns Hopkins University Press. All rights reserved. Both reproduced by permission.—**The French Review,** v. LVII, April, 1984. Copyright 1984 by the American Association of Teachers of French. Reproduced by permission.—**The Hollins Critic,** v. 1, December, 1964. Copyright 1964 by Hollins College. Reproduced by permission.— **Journal of English and Germanic Philology,** v. LXV, January, 1966. (c) 1966 by the Board of Trustees of the University of Illinois. Reproduced by permission.—**L'Esprit Créateur,** v. XXXII, Spring, 1992. Copyright (c) 1992 by L'Esprit Créateur. Reproduced by permission.—**Modern Philology,** v. 93, February, 1996. (c) 1996 by The University of Chicago. Reproduced by permission of the University of Chicago Press.—**The Nation,** New York, v. 187, July 5, 1958. (c) 1958, renewed 1986 The Nation magazine/ The Nation Company, Inc. Reproduced by permission.— **The New Criterion,** v. 6, April, 1988 for "The Trials of a Poet" by Robert Richman. Copyright (c) 1988 by The Foundation for Cultural Review. Reproduced by permission of the author.—**The New York Times Book Review,** October 28, 1945. Copyright 1945 by The New York Times Company. Reproduced by permission.—**Papers on Language & Literature,** v. 17, Fall, 1981; v. 25, Fall, 1989. Copyright (c) 1981, 1989 by The Board of Trustees, Southern Illinois University at Edwardsville. Both reproduced by permission.—**Philological Quarterly,** v. 75, Fall, 1996 for "When a Sparrow Falls: Women Readers, Male Critics, and John Skelton's Phyllyp Sparowe" by Celia R. Daileader. Copyright (c) 1996 by The University of Iowa. Reproduced by permission of the author.—**Poetry,** v. LXXI, March, 1948 for "The Power and the Hazard" by Stephen Spender. Copyright 1948, renewed 1976 by the Modern Poetry Association. Reproduced by permission of the Editor of Poetry and the Literary Estate of Stephen Spender./ v. XCVI, June, 1960 for "On the Road: or the Adventures of Karl Shapiro" by Leslie Fiedler. (c) 1960, renewed 1988 by the Modern Poetry Association. Reproduced by permission of the Editor of Poetry and the author.—**Romanian Review,** No. 6, 1986. Reproduced by permission.—**The Sewanee Review,** v. 54, Autumn, 1946; v. 97, Winter, 1989. Copyright 1946, renewed 1974, 1989 by The University of the South. Both reprinted with the permission of the editor.—**The South Carolina Review,** v. 14, Fall, 1981. Copyright (c) 1981 by Clemson University. Reproduced by permission.—**South Dakota Review,** v. 18, Summer, 1980. (c) 1980, University of South Dakota. Reproduced by permission. —**The Southern Review,** Louisiana State University, v. XI, Summer, 1975 for "N. Scott Momaday's Angle of Geese" by John Finlay./ v. XIV, January, 1978 for "The Art and Importance of N. Scott Momaday" by Roger Dickinson Brown. Copyright, 1975, 1978, by the authors. Both reproduced by permission of the authors.—**Studies in English Literature,** v. XVII, Summer, 1977; v. 32, Summer, 1992. (c) 1977, 1992 William Marsh Rice University. Both reprinted by permission of the Johns Hopkins University Press.—**Studies in Philology,** v. LXII, January, 1965.

PHOTOGRAPHS AND ILLUSTRATIONS APPEARING IN *PC*, VOLUME 25, WERE RECEIVED FROM THE FOLLOWING SOURCES:

Aimé Césaire
1913-

(Full name Aimé Fernand Césaire) West Indian poet, dramatist, and essayist.

INTRODUCTION

Césaire is recognized as a major Caribbean poet and dramatist. Best known for his surrealist poem *Cahier d'un retour au pays natal,* he is also acknowledged as "The Father of Negritude." Defining negritude as "the affirmation that one is black and proud of it," Césaire urged blacks to reject assimilation into white culture and honor instead their racial heritage, a belief that permeates his poetry and essays.

Biographical Information

Césaire was born in 1913 to a poor family on the island of Martinique in the French West Indies. Under the tutelage of his grandmother, he learned to read and write by age four. When he was eleven, he enrolled at Lycée Schoelcher, a leading school in Martinique's capital, Fort-de-France. Upon graduating in 1931, Césaire received a scholarship to study in Paris. While enrolled at the École Normale Supérieure, he, along with Léopold Sedar Senghor and Léon-Goutran Damas, founded *L'étudiant noir,* a student magazine dedicated to uniting blacks and promoting pride in black culture. Although they produced only five or six issues, his involvement with the magazine was vital to the development of negritude. After the publication of *Return to My Native Land* in 1939, he returned to Martinique and immersed himself in politics, serving as mayor of Fort-de-France and as a member of the French National Assembly. Césaire has continued to compose poetry as well as drama and essays, but has written less frequently in recent years due to an increasingly busy political career.

Major Works

Although each of his works has received favorable reviews, none has matched the success of Césaire's first poem, *Return to My Native Land.* Consisting of three movements and covering sixty-six pages, the poem is considered the original statement on negritude, moreover, it evinces the basic tenets of the acceptance of one's blackness and the rejection of white assimilation. The first movement surveys the demoralizing effects of colonialism on Martinique, the second chronicles Césaire's struggle to

free himself from white culture, and the third celebrates negritude.

Critical Reception

As observed by commentators, Césaire's poetic language strongly shows the influence of French surrealists of the 1930s. Like the surrealists, he endeavored to free his writing from the conventions of French literature. Unlike them, however, he infused his poetry with angry images and bitter invectives against Western culture. Some critics see his poetic language as a form of literary violence marked by jarring images and forceful rhythms that assault the reader. Some commentators, in addition to admiring its literary finesse, also praise *Return to My Native Land* for its universal appeal. The poem speaks to people of all color and nationality, they contend, because Césaire's struggle for self-acceptance is a struggle shared by all people. Today, his concept of negritude forms the foundation for black movements across the world. Whether consciously or unconsciously, many black leaders have adopted Césaire's negritude as their rallying cry.

PRINCIPAL WORKS

Poetry

Les armes miraculeuses 1946
*Cahier d'un retour au pays natal [Return to My Native
    Land]* 1947
Soleil cou coupé 1948
Corps perdu 1949
Ferrements 1960
Cadastre 1961
State of the Union 1966
Noria 1976
moi, laminaire . . . 1982
The Collected Poetry 1983
Non-Vicious Circle 1985
La poésie [Poems] 1994

Other Major Works

Discours sur le colonialisme [Discourse on Colonialism]
    (essay) 1950
Et les chiens se taisaient (drama) 1956
Lettre à Maurice Thorex [Letter to Maurice Thorex] (let-
    ter) 1956
*La Tragédie du roi Christophe [The Tragedy of King
    Christophe]* (drama) 1963
Une saison au Congo [A Season in the Congo] (drama)
    1966
*Une tempête: d'après "La tempête" de Shakespeare,
    Adaptation pour un théâtre nègre [A Tempest: After
    "The Tempest" by Shakespeare, Adaptation for the
    Negro Theatre]* (adaptation) 1969

CRITICISM

Edward A. Jones (essay date 1970)

SOURCE: "Aimé Césaire," in *Voices of Négritude: The
Expression of Black Experience in the Poetry of Senghor,
Césaire & Damas,* Judson Press, 1970, pp. 53-62.

[*In the following essay, Jones discusses the defining characteristics of Césaire's work.*]

In her excellent book on Aimé Césaire and his works, in
the *Poètes d'Aujourd'hui* series, Lilyan Kesteloot apprais-
es the extraordinary talent of this Afro-French, West Indian poet as follows:

> Je ne vois pas dans l'histoire de la littérature française
> une personnalité qui ait à ce point intégré des éléments
> aussi divers que la conscience raciale, la création
> artistique et l'action politique. Je ne vois pas de

personnalité aussi puissamment unifiée et à la fois aussi
complexe que celle de Césaire. Et c'est là, sans doute,
que réside le secret de l'exceptionnelle densité d'une
poésie qui s'est, à un degré extrême, chargée de toute
la cohérence d'une vie d'homme.[1]

I do not see in the history of French literature a
personality who has so highly integrated such diverse
elements as racial consciousness, artistic creation, and
political action. I do not see any personality so
powerfully unified and at the same time so complex as
that of Césaire. And, without doubt, therein resides
the secret of the exceptional density of a poetry which
has, to an extreme degree, taken on itself all the
coherence of a man's life.

Paying eloquent tribute to Césaire's rare poetic gifts in his
Préface to Césaire's first major collection, **Cahier d'un
retour au pays natal**, the "high priest" of French surrealistic poetry, André Breton, who discovered Césaire during
a visit to Martinique, has this to say in that Preface, titled
"Un grand poète noir" [To a Great Black Poet]:

> Et c'est un noir qui manie la langue française comme
> il n'est pas aujourd'hui un blanc pour la manier. Et
> c'est un noir celui qui nous guide aujourd'hui dans
> l'inexploré, établissant au fur et à mesure, comme en
> se jouant, les contacts qui nous font avancer sur des
> étincelles. Et c'est un noir qui est non seulement un
> noir mais *tout* l'homme, qui en exprime toutes les
> interrogations, toutes les angoisses, tous les espoirs et
> toutes les extases et qui s'imposera de plus en plus à
> moi comme le prototype de la dignité.

> A black man it is who masters the French language as no
> white man can today. A black man it is who guides us
> today through unexplored lands building as he goes the
> contacts that will make us progress on sparks. A black
> man it is who embodies not simply the black race but *all*
> mankind, its queries and anxieties, its hopes and ecstasies
> and who will remain for me the symbol of dignity.[2]

Just who is this black poet who has elicited such flattering
appraisals from persons best equipped to appreciate his
genius? To understand Césaire's complexities and the
magnitude of his anger, we are reminded by his biographer that one must understand the island which gave birth
to him: Martinique, in the French West Indies, where
dazzling luxury and wealth on the part of the few (whites)
are in sharp contrast with the abject poverty of the masses
(blacks)—where hunger, disease, and ignorance stalk the
land—where former slavery and present-day exploitation
have combined to crush the black masses of the population. This is especially true of Martinique, where Aimé
Césaire was born in 1913, ". . . a miniature house which
lodges in its guts of rotten wood dozens of rats, as well as
the turbulence of my six brothers and sisters, a tiny cruel
house whose intransigence infuriates the last days of the
month . . .". . . *une maison minuscule qui abrite en ses
entrailles de bois pourri des dizaines de rats et la turbulence de mes six frères et soeurs, une petite maison cruel-
le dont l'intransigeance affole nos fins de mois . . .").[3] His

family was, however, in the "middle" (*moyen*) on the scale of local wretchedness, his father being, for a time at least, an "employee of the lower-echelon government" (*petit fonctionnaire*) in the town of Basse-Pointe.

Even worse than the material poverty afflicting the island was the spiritual and moral bankruptcy resulting from years of domination and exploitation: the complete resignation, loss of the will to resist, and the despair and constant fear of hunger, unemployment, and the like. Moreover, a color elite had developed among non-whites, which further aggravated the real blacks.

Thanks to native intelligence, industry, and promise, Césaire was to be sent to France to pursue his secondary and higher education. The former was acquired at the Lycée Louis-le-Grand, in Paris, where he met and began his lifelong friendship with Léopold Senghor. He then attended the Sorbonne and the École normale supérieure, the teacher-training school where to be admitted is an enviable distinction. Like Senghor, he graduated from both and was *agrégé* in literature. It was while Césaire was at the École normale supérieure, in 1935-1936, that this writer met him and introduced him to Sterling Brown via his poetic collection, *Southern Road.* Some years later, Césaire was to become mayor of Fort-de-France, capital of Martinique. After entering politics, he was elected delegate (*délégué*) to the Assemblée nationale in Paris; and in 1946, like Senghor, he was a member of the Assemblée constituante which framed the Constitution for the Fourth Republic in France (1946-1958).

Césaire's bitterness attracted him to the Communist party, a recognized political party in France's multi-party set-up, which he later abandoned. Ultimately, his ardent Communist activities made him somewhat unpopular among literary circles in France, where he still lives with his wife and daughter and continues to write.

A co-founder of *L'Étudiant Noir* in Paris, Césaire was also one of a group of Communist and surrealist West Indian students who founded in 1932 a magazine known as *Légitime Défense.*

Thus this black poet who, in the eyes of another great poet, possesses qualities of soul and genius which brought the two men together in a deep and abiding friendship also possesses a universality of interest and appeal which makes him the voice not only of his native Martinique but of all mankind. Indeed, Césaire's song is a social lament which elicits a ready response from all those who suffer from social, economic, and political injustices.

First of all, Césaire is a poet: he is essentially a singer of songs. His native sense of rhythm and his power to transform into poetry the commonest and even the ugliest aspects of life make of him a truly great poet. To quote André Breton again:

> . . . la poésie de Césaire, comme toute grande poésie et tout grand art, vaut au plus haut point par le pouvoir de transmutation, qu'elle met en oeuvre et qui consiste,

> à partir des matériaux les plus déconsidérés, parmi lesquels il faut compter les laideurs et les servitudes mêmes, à produire on sait assez que ce n'est plus l'or la pierre philosophale mais bien la liberte.

> Césaire's poetry, like any great poetry or art, draws its supreme value from its power of transmutation which consists in taking the most discredited materials, among which daily squalor and constraints, and ultimately producing neither gold nor the philosopher's stone any longer but freedom itself.[4]

Césaire's poetry, whose rhythm is suggestive of the weird and mysterious beat of the tom-tom, is replete with the exotic and luxuriant beauty inspired by the flora and fauna of the tropics. It excels in colorful and vivid imagery.

Behind the exquisite beauty of Césaire's verse there is a profound and prophetic meditation on the social injustices of which his people, especially in Martinique, are victims. The bard of Martinique sings of the wretchedness of colonial peoples and bemoans their exploitation by a handful of European parasites, who, frequently in defiance of the law, set themselves up as cruel, inhuman masters of an unhappy people forced to resign themselves to a status of virtual slavery. He sings of the evils of this system of colonization as they manifest themselves in the daily life and activities of his native island—in poverty, miserable housing, poor health, ignorance, superstition, and prejudice. He sings of ". . . the hungry West Indies, pitted with smallpox, dynamited with alcohol, stranded in the mud of this bay, in the dirt of this city sinisterly stranded" *(". . . les Antilles qui ont faim, les Antilles grêlées de petite vérole, les Antilles dynamitées d'alcool, èchouès dans la boue de cette baie, dans la poussière de cette ville sinistrement échouées").*[5]

Césaire's major work, for our purposes, at lest, is his ***Cahier d'un retour au pays natal,*** written in Paris in 1939 on the eve of the poet's return to his native Martinique after completing his work at the École normale supérieure. This work was published in the review *Volonté* in 1939, but it did not attract attention until it was republished by Bordas in 1947. As the young poet makes ready to return to his native soil after a highly successful academic sojourn in Paris, he is haunted by the real and tragic vision of the West Indies inflicted with hunger, disease, alcoholism, and moral turpitude—fruits of a despicable, though doomed, system of economic exploitation and social abuse. He thinks particularly of his native city:

> Au bout du petit matin, cette ville inerte et ses au-delà de lèpres, de consumption, de famines, de peurs tapies dans les ravins, de peurs juchées dans les arbres, de peurs creusées dans le sol, de peurs en dérive dans le ciel, de peurs amoncelées et ses fumerolles d'angoisse.

> At the end of the dawn, this inert city, with its lepers, consumption, famines, fears hidden in ravines, fears perched in trees, fears sunk in the soil, fears drifting in the sky accumulations of fears with their fumeroles of anguish.[6]

These conditions with which the poet's hometown is afflicted invariably breed social vices and warp human personality and destroy human souls. The poet reflects:

> Au bout du petit matin, l'échouage hétéroclite, les puanteurs exacerbées de la corruption, les sodomies monstrueuses de l'hostie et du victimaire, les coltis infranchissables du préjugé et de la sottise, les prostitutions, les hypocrisies, les lubricités, les trahisons, les mensonges, les faux, les concussions— l'essoufflement des lâchetés insuffisantes, l'enthousiasme sans ahan aux poussis surnuméraires, les avidités, les hystéries, les perversions, les arlequinades de la misère, les estropiements, les prurits, les urticaires, les hamacs tièdes de la dégénérescence. Ici la parade des risibles et scrofuleux bubons, les poutures de microbes très étranges, les poisons sans alexitère connu, les sanies de plaies bien antiques, les fermentations imprévisibles d'espèces putrescibles.[7]

> At the end of the dawn, the odd stranding, the exacerbated stench of corruption, the monstrous sodomies of the offering and the sacrificer, the dauntless prows of prejudice and stupidity, the prostitutions, the hypocrisies, the lubricities, the treasons, the lies, the frauds—the concussions, the breathlessness of half-hearted cowards, the smooth enthusiasms of budding bureaucrats, the avidities, hysterias, perversions, the harlequinades of misery, the injuries, itchings, urticarias, the dreary hammocks of degeneracy. Here the parade of contemptible and scrofulous bubos, the gluttony of very strange microbes, the poisons for which there are no known alexins, the pus of very ancient wounds, the unforeseeable fermentations of species destined to decay.[8]

Further in his dream of his return home, M. Césaire depicts the advent of Christmas in his native city. His reminiscences on this most beautiful of all Christian celebrations are all the more vivid because of the contrasts which they evoke between the economic extremes of the city. He announces the approach of Christmas in high poetic images:

> Et le temps passait vite, très vite.

> Passés août où les manguiers pavoisent de toutes leurs lunules, septembre l'accoucheur de cyclones, octobre le flambeur de cannes, novembre qui ronronne aux distilleries, c'était Noël qui commençait.

> And quickly, time went by.

> From August, when the mango-trees were decked with lunulas, to September, midwife of hurricanes, to October, incendiary of sugar canes, then November, purring in the distilleries, and suddenly Christmas was there.[9]

Then he depicts the joy that reigns habitually in the city at Christmas time:

> . . . et le bourg n'est plus qu'un bouquet de chants, et l'on est bien à l'intérieur, et l'on en mange du bon, et l'on en boit du réjouissant et il y a du boudin, celui étroit de deux doigts qui s'enroule en volubile, celui

large et trapu, le bénin à goût de serpolet, le violent à incandescence pimenteé, et du café brûlant et de l'anis sucré et du punch au lait, et le soleil liquide des rhums, et toutes sortes de bonnes choses qui vous imposent autoritairement les muqueuses ou vous les distillent en ravissements, ou vous les tissent de fragrances, et l'on rit, et l'on chante. . . .

> . . . the little town is now only a bouquet of songs: you are well inside, you have good things to eat, wine to drink, and there are sausages, one kind is thin as two fingers tightly wound, the other big and dumpy, the soft kind tastes of thyme, the strong of red-hot spice, there is burning coffee and sugary anise, punch with milk, and the liquid sun of rum, and all sorts of good things which despotically work on your mucous membrane, distilling delights or weaving fragrances, and you laugh and sing. . . . [10]

But all these good things associated with the celebration of Christmas were reserved for the fortunate few in Basse-Pointe, the poet's native city. The observance of Christmas in the poet's own family contrasted sharply with the affuence and abundance of good things *(bonnes choses)* described above. He remembers his family abode, rat-infested and dilapidated in an ill-smelling, unsanitary street, as the scene of a laborious mother tirelessly pedaling a Singer sewing machine in order to feed her numerous brood, while his indolent, irascible, and sickly father sat idly by. To such people, Christmas was hardly any different from any other day. The poet remembers this scene in these words:

> Au bout du petit matin, une autre petite maison qui sent très mauvais dans une rue très étroite, une maison minuscule qui abrite en ses entrailles de bois pourri des dizaines de rats et la turbulence de mes six frères et soeurs, une petite maison cruelle dont l'intransigeance affole nos fins de mois et mon père fantasque grignoté d'une seule misère, je n'ai jamais su laquelle, qu'une imprévisible sorcellerie assoupit en mélancolique tendresse ou exalte en hautes flammes de colère; et ma mère dont les jambes pour notre faim inlassable pédalent, pédalent de jour, de nuit, je suis même réveillé la nuit par ces jambes inlassables qui pédalent la nuit et la morsure âpre dans la chair molle de la nuit d'une Singer que ma mère pédale, pédale pour notre faim et de jour et de nuit.[11]

> At the end of the dawn, there is another tiny house stinking in the narrow street, a miniature house which lodges in its guts of rotten wood dozens of rats, as well as the turbulence of my six brothers and sisters, a tiny cruel house whose intransigence infuriates the last days of the month and my fantastic father chewed by a certain ailment, I never discovered what, my father whom an unanticipated sorcery makes drowsy with melancholy sweetness or exalts to the high flames of anger; and my mother, whose limbs, in the service of our tireless hunger, pedal, pedal, day and night, I am even awakened at night by those tireless limbs which pedal the night, by the bitter punctures in the soft flesh of the night made by the Singer machine my mother pedals, pedals for our hunger day and night.[12]

As the time for the poet's return approaches, he takes inventory of the rupture, which has developed during his stay in France, between him and his people, not only the relatives in the smelly little house but also all men of color similarly situated, and he seeks to repair that rupture. The first step in the process of repair is to destroy his refound cowardice *(lâcheté retrouvée)* which revealed itself to the poet one day when, on a Paris tramway, he had renounced his racial allegiance and solidarity with "a comical and ugly Negro" *(un nègre comique et laid)* whose presence was a source of embarrassment to the poet in the occidental setting so unsympathetic with this comical Negro (an incident described earlier). This impetuous and thoughtless decision was foolish, the poet concludes, and he must accept all that is characteristic of even the most backward of his people, all that has been imposed upon them by years of disease, poverty, and ignorance. All this he must accept as his heritage, and he must identify himself fervently with the cause and fate of Negroes. This he does:

"*J'accepte, j'accepte tout cela . . . [toute cette Négritude]. . . .*"[13] He accepts the bad along with the good, but he does it in the conviction that the future holds a promise of liberation, of complete and real freedom for his people and for all peoples. He believes that the conquest of liberty has only begun: ". . . but the work of man has only begun . . . and there is room for all at the rendez-vous of conquest" ("*. . . l'oeuvre de l'homme vient seulement de commencer . . . et il est place pour tous au rendez-vous de la conquête*").[14]

The Negro, Césaire believes, is destined to have a part in mankind's liberation from "this serfdom of our time," a liberation of mind and body. As a poet, M. Césaire is resolved to fight for the former, and as a politician he is in the thick of the struggle for social and economic liberation. In his poem **"A l'Afrique"** he looks into his poetic crystal ball and foresees a pestilence that will depopulate the West, and he exhorts the peasants, with a philosophy suggestive of Voltaire's "cultivate your garden" *(cultivez votre jardin),* to continue to strike the earth, identifying himself with the toilers of the land, the tillers of the soil.

The caustic candor and cutting irony of the selection that follows point up the characteristic rage of Césaire when he is forced to defend blacks against the whites who have victimized them, reduced them to a status of social and economic inferiority, and then castigated them for being "inferior," for not having excelled as inventors, discoverers, explorers, philosophers, scholars, and so forth.

> Ceux qui n'ont inventé ni la poudre ni la boussole
> ceux qui n'ont jamais su dompter la vapeur ni
>   l'électricité
> ceux qui n'ont exploré ni les mers ni le ciel
> mais ils savent en ses moindres recoins le pays de
>   souffrance
> ceux qui n'ont connu de voyages que de
>   déracinements
> ceux qui se sont assoupis aux agenouillements
> ceux qu'on domestiqua et christianisa
> ceux qu'on inocula d'abâtardissement

> tam-tams de mains vides
> tam-tams inanes de plaies sonores
> tam-tams burlesques de trahison tabide[15]

> Those who invented neither powder nor compass
> those who never tamed steam or electricity
> those who did not explore sea or sky
>   but they know in their innermost depths
>   the country of suffering
> those who knew of voyages only when uprooted
> those who are made supple by kneelings
> those domesticated and Christianized
> those inoculated with degeneracy
> tom-toms of empty hands
> tom-toms of sounding wounds
> burlesque tom-toms of treason.[16]

The **Cahier d'un retour** is above all a song, a lament, perhaps the greatest lyrical creation of our time. No lesser than M. André Breton has characterized it as "the greatest lyrical monument of our times" *("le plus grand monument lyrique de ce temps").*[17]

Truly, M. Césaire, equipped with all that he could learn from the white man and his civilization, belongs, at least as far as his literary genius is concerned, body and soul to the vast collectivity of the proletariat, to the millions of laborers whose voice he becomes as he sings their joys and sorrows, their tribulations and aspirations. And Césaire's voice is in truth, as M. Breton has described it, "beautiful as nascent oxygen" *("belle comme l'oxygéne naissant").*[18]

As Lilyan Kesteloot puts it, **Le Cahier** is a decisive date in the birth of black consciousness, and it has for twenty years served as a standard for the revolutionary youth of colonized countries,"[19] whether in Africa or the West Indies or elsewhere. It may well be studied by black youth today in their efforts to set the current struggle in historical perspective. Alioune Diop characterizes this work as "the sum-total of Negro revolt against European history" *("la somme de la révolte nègre contre l'histoire européenne").*[20]

At once an epic and a lyrical poem, it defies classification as a poetic creation. Like the medieval literary form *(chante-fable),* there is an alternation of verse with prose passages. It is unique, resembling only itself. Its surrealism is often hard to penetrate and to interpret. But where its social commentary is clear—which often it is not, thanks to surrealistic verbiage—it is a scathing denunciation of European colonialism and an eloquent apology for the dignity of man and his equality with all his fellowmen.

Notes

[1] Lilyan Kesteloot, *Aimé Césaire* (Paris: Editions Pierre Seghers, 1962), p. 9.

[2] André Breton, "Preface: Un grand poète noir," in A. Césaire, *Cahier d'un retour au pays natal* [Return to my native land], tr. Emile Snyder (Paris: Présence Africaine, 1956), pp. 14-15.

[3] Aimé Césaire, *Cahier d'un retour au pays natal* [Return to my native land], tr. Emile Snyder (Paris: Présence Africaine, 1956), pp. 50-53.

[4] André Breton, *op. cit.,* pp. 18-19.

[5] Césaire, *Cahier d'un retour au pays natal,* pp. 30-31.

[6] *Ibid., pp.* 34-35.

[7] *Ibid.,* pp. 39, 41.

[8] *Ibid.,* pp. 38, 40.

[9] *Ibid.,* pp. 44-45.

[10] *Ibid.,* pp. 46-47.

[11] *Ibid.,* pp. 51, 53.

[12] *Ibid.,* pp. 50, 52.

[13] *Ibid.,* p. 137.

[14] *Ibid.,* pp. 138-141.

[15] Césaire, *Cahier d'un retour au pays natal,* p. 111.

[16] *Ibid.,* p. 110.

[17] André Breton, *op. cit.,* pp. 16-17.

[18] *Ibid.,* pp. 26-27.

[19] Translated from Kesteloot, *Aimé Césaire,* p. 25.

[20] *Ibid.*

Hilary Okram (essay date 1976)

SOURCE: "Aspects of Imagery and Symbolism in the Poetry of Aimé Césaire," in *Yale French Studies,* No. 53, 1976, pp. 175-96.

[*In the following essay, Okram examines the relationship between Césaire's imagery and his West Indian heritage.*]

If Aimé Césaire's poetry is difficult to understand, as every student of his works is well aware, it appears to me that the difficulty comes principally from three basic factors. Briefly, these are Césaire's use of highly sophisticated vocabulary that bears witness to his solid literary education, his fixation for tortuous parataxic sentence structure and, what on the surface would appear to be, his cavalier penchant for discordant and disparate images and symbols as vehicles for poetic enunciation. The combination of these characteristics gives rise to poetry that is exceedingly personal in form and overtones despite the poet's avowed posture as the voice of the collective conscience of his people. Another consequence of this poetic aesthetics is

that the reader emerges from Césaire's poetry with the distinct impression of having "felt" and "sensed" rather than "understood" what was intended to communicate.

It appears to me that this rather knotty poetic démarche is not the vainglorious exercise of a young man whose learning has gone into his head but rather reveals the psychological trauma which the poet had to scale in order to verbalize his vision and thought. I am strongly persuaded that Césaire's poetic idiosyncracies, especially his search for and use of uncommon vocabulary, are symptomatic of his own mental agony in the search for an exact definition of himself and, by extension, of his people and their common situation and destiny. The torments and agonies of this quest are reflected not only in the tortuous and intractable syntax of his poetry but also in the rarity of the vocabulary that attempts to capture and objectify that definition. Similarly, every image and symbol, no matter how far-fetched or seemingly unrelated, but that contributes even ephemerally towards this definition by its suggestiveness and or association of ideas, is exploited to the utmost.

This quality of Césaire's imagery and symbols has led students of his poetry to draw a parallel between his poetry and those of his French Surrealist forerunners. And André Breton's salute to Césaire's ***Cahier d'un retour au pays natal*** as "nothing but the greatest lyrical monument of our times"[1] has only gone to bolster the belief that to understand the character of Césaire's imageries and symbols one must drink deep from the fountain of *The Manifesto of Surrealism.*

Césaire, for his part, of course, does not deny his admiration for and the possible influence on him of the surrealists and the symbolists before them. But it appears unsatisfactory to me to explain the entire character of Césaire's imageries and symbols as the result of the influence of these European predecessors. To get to the root of the character of Césaire's symbols and images we must attempt to penetrate that sacred domain of the mind and psyche in which every image and symbol is born. In a word, we must attempt to fathom the various layers of what Léopold Sédar Senghor calls the poet's subjectivity.[2]

What then does Aimé Césaire's subjectivity reveal? From reading his poetry and contemplating his personal use of imageries and symbols one arrives at the conclusion that Aimé Césaire, among the best of our poets of French-expression, has, if I may paraphrase Senghor, assimilated but has not been assimilated. In other words, it is clear from his use of symbols and imagery, that despite years of alienation and acculturation he has continued to live in the concrete reality of his Negro-subjectivity. The late Janheinz Jahn, alluded to this phenomenon when in an article, "Rythmes et styles dans la poésie africaine," presented before the 1963 Dakar conference on African literature, he asserted that the main difference between African poets and their European contemporaries is the ". . . non-European stylistic processes that arise from African traditional poetry . . ."[3] Although Jahn limited himself to discerning the influence of traditional African rhythmic patterns on the works of our contemporary poets in the absolute neglect of the influence of that same poetic tradition on the character and quality of the images they employ, he did at least make the all important point, namely: that our writers of today, no matter in what European language they write, cannot be divorced from their African roots.

Our poets, therefore, are hybrids who live in two worlds: the world of their Judeo-Christian education and environment; and the world of their African traditions and values. Years of slavery, colonialism, assimilation and acculturation have attempted to re-enforce the former but have scarcely weakened the latter. As Aimé Césaire so succinctly put it in *Et Les Chiens se taisaient.* "In vain have they whitewashed the foot / of the tree, / the sap underneath cries out . . ."[4] It is within this context therefore that we have to view Césaire's poetry in general and his use of symbols and imagery in particular.

And if it is true, as Césaire asserts, that the wonder of poetry comes from the "marvelous contact of internal and external totality seen imaginatively,"[5] then it is safe to conclude that his poetic démarche includes a plunge into his black subjectivity to objectify certain qualities which in conjunction with the external world serve as the vehicle for expressing what Jean-Paul Sartre aptly describes in "Orphée Noir" as the realities of "the being in the black world."[6] And Negro subjectivity, Léopold Sédar Senghor tells us, reveals, among other qualities, a synthetic reasoning process which attempts to unify every phenomenon, being and object by discovering the links that bind them to one another and to man. By contrast Greco-Roman subjectivity perceives the external world through analytical reasoning which separates man from nature in order to control and dominate it. Césaire seems to endorse this view of black subjectivity when in *Cahier d'un retour au pays natal* he says this of the black race:

truly the elder sons of the world
porous to all the breath of the world
fraternal space of all the breath of the world
bed without drain of all the waters of the world
spark of the sacred fire of the world
flesh of the flesh of the world
panting with the very movement of the world
tepid dawn of ancestral virtues.

And in *Et Les Chiens se taisaient,* using the symbol of the Architect and the Rebel to represent the white man and the black revolutionary leader respectively, Césaire puts these words in the mouth of the Rebel to describe white subjectivity and what happens when that subjectivity brings its full weight to bear on the external world:

Architect deaf to things, clear like the tree
but closed like an armor every step of yours
is a conquest and a spoliation and a
   misinterpretation
and an outrage. . . .
Architect, Orcus without a gate and without a star
without a source and without a budding

Architect of the tail of the peacock, of the step of
cancer, of the blue speech of mushroom and steel
Beware of yourself

It is my view that the unique qualities and seemingly disparate character of Césaire's imagery and symbols come from the role played in his poetry by his Negro subjectivity. And if his poetry attains the height of "memorable speech" the reason is to be found in the imaginative relationships he establishes between that subjectivity, defined as thought-reality, and objective reality defined as the observable and tangible phenomena of his world. Since our examination of Césaire's use of symbols and imagery is based on this premise, a word or two on what constitutes Césaire's subjectivity and the external evidence of his universe will not be out of place.

Césaire has always referred to himself metaphorically as a bastard whose mother is Africa and whose run-away father is France and who has, in consequence, clung stubbornly to the mother that suckled and nourished the infant. He therefore sees himself as an African, a black African, who has never tired of deepening his lien with his black mother. As he says through the Rebel:

I ask for no forgiveness.
With my heart I have raised the ancient gem
the old tinder deposited by Africa in the
very depth of me.

Césaire's subjectivity therefore is first and foremost black African subjectivity for as he tells us "my country is the 'night lance' of my Bambara ancestors," whose affective participation in and synthesis with the "very movement of the world" constitutes their cardinal philosophical essence.

As for the external realities of his universe, Césaire bears the following witness:

My memory is encircled with blood.
My memory is girdled with corpses . . .

                                    [*Cahier*]

And they sold us like beasts, and
they counted our teeth . . . and they
felt our pouches and they examined
the gloss or wrinkle of our skin
and they felt our pulse and they
weighed us and underweighed us
and they slipped around our neck
of tamed beast the necklace of
servitude and sobriquet.

                                    [*Et les Chiens*]

The above is Césaire's representation of the slavery, servitude and dehumanization of his ancestors that preceded the era of current French colonization of his native Martinique. This is the background that explains the present plight of Césaire's island-home which he describes as "flat, tripped by its common sense, inert, out of breath under the geometric weight of its eternally renewed cross, at odds with its fate, mute, baffled, unable to grow in the manner of the pith of this land, lopped, reduced, at odds with its fauna and flora." That then is the socio-historical reality of Césaire's immediate universe. On the other hand is the geophysical reality of Martinique with its relief of the surrounding sea, hills, valleys, rivers and lakes; an abundance of forests, leaves, grass and flowers. In a word, the geographic realities of Martinique with its suffusion of fauna and flora and varied topography and weather conditions make up another aspect of Césaire's universe.

Césaire's use of imagery and symbols, as vehicles for poetic expression, comes from the relationship he establishes, under the guiding hand of his synthetic Negro subjectivity (that binds and synthesizes), between the various elements that make up the socio-historical and geo-physical milieu in which he lives. To see what happens when this type of alchemy takes place we shall examine his manipulation of an object that has a kind of pervasive presence in the island, namely the sea. Césaire uses the sea as a paradigm to express various and sometimes antithetical thoughts and realities. This is understandable because, in a sense, the Caribbean sea is synonymous with Martinique since without that sea there would be no island that goes by that name. Thus literally the sea makes the island what it is and Césaire therefore exploits the sea-symbol in a variety of ways to depict in what light he sees his island-home at a given time.

In a poem **"Les Pur-Sang"** (The Thoroughbreds) the sea, as a symbol, is used to depict what Césaire considers to be the moribund state of the island:

> and the sea forms a necklace of silence
> around the land
> and the sea sipping up the sacrificial peace
> where our voices rattle in confusion, (the sea)
> motionless with strange pearls and the silent
> maturation of abyss
> In silence
> the land makes a silent bulge into the sea
> And behold the land alone,
> Without tremor and without shimmering
> without sprouting of roots
> and without the perforation of insects . . .[8]

The sea, as a symbol to portray the decadence of the island, is used again in another poem, **"Débris,"** but in this instance (and due to the implied metamorphic qualities of the sea) new dimensions are added to the initial impression of wretchedness created in **"Les Pur-Sang."** In **"Débris"** we have this:

> Shit is the sea without allele which opens its fans
> and causes its nuts to rustle it is the sea which
> lays all its chromosomal cards on the table it is
> the sea which imprints a river of flocks and tongues
> under the palm of lethal lands

> (*Les Armes*)

In **"Les Pur-Sang,"** as in **"Débris,"** the sea creates the ambiance within which and in which the central thematic of the poems is expressed. In **"Les Pur-Sang"** the sea

serves as a central symbol whose dull, inanimate physical state is a mirror in which the night-moribund state of Césaire's nativeland is reflected. It is precisely because the sea is silent that the land has remained silent. It is because the sea in its immobility seems to grip the island in a strangulating embrace that the islanders themselves seem immobile and unconcerned about their fate while their agony matures and ripens. It is because the sea has not vomited its "strange pearls" of storm and turbulence that the land has remained without tremor or glimmer of light. It is because the sea has not washed away the bulge of silence that the land makes into it that there is neither the sprouting of roots nor destructive insects to gnaw away at the suicidal peace that comes in the wake of the people's abandonment of their responsibility to themselves. The impression rightly is created that the sea is impregnated with potential force which it has failed to channel into kinetic energy just as the Martinican has in himself the wherewithal to change his socio-economic condition but which wherewithal he has never known nor cared to master.

In **"Débris,"** on the other hand, the potential vitality of the sea is completely undermined for here the sea is presented as struck with a kind of genetic abnormality which accounts for its uselessness. The sea is "shit" because it is bereft of allele which, according to Mendel's law of genetic selection, gives every organism its unique characteristic. Lack of allele results in premature death. The sea, which has no character of its own, no secret of its own (lays all its chromosomal cards on the table) and which is predestined to die precociously becomes a symbol to portray both the lack of racial pride and distinction on the part of the black Martinican (without allele) and his lack of any secret nefarious scheme whatsoever against his white oppressor (lays all of its chromosomal cards on the table). Like a flock of sheep the black population wanders about aimlessly. Like the nuts that rustle in the useless wind its voice takes issue with the inconsequential. The black Martinican, therefore like this useless sea, is apparently predestined to vanish from the surface of the lethal lands that are the West Indies.

The symbol of the sea, as used in these two poems, already suggests the interjection into the poetic process of Césaire's subjectivity. The impression is created that there are different kinds of seas. But we know that the sea, as a body of water, cannot at one time be an inanimate object as in **"Les Pur-Sang"** and at another a living object as in **"Débris."** A third dimension is added to the sea-symbol later in **"Les Pur-Sang"** when Césaire says:

> Ah
> The last of the last suns is setting
> Where will it set if not in me?
> As everything was dying
> I enlarged, I enlarged myself—like the world—
> and my conscience larger than the sea!
> Last sun.
> I am exploding. I am fire, I am the sea
> The world is coming apart. But I am the world . . .

Here the sea is the symbol of the poet himself. Its vastness which encompasses the six continents in one firm embrace is seen as a replica of the poet's conscience. In fact the poet's conscience is larger than the sea. It is without prejudice and encompasses every continent. The sun, and not the sea, is the symbol of everything that is unacceptable and whose demise has been wrought by fire (image of the poet himself) which consumes and purifies. The poet is the sea which gathers in its bosom all that has been cleansed and purified just as he is the fire that consumes and purifies. Hence fire and sea become symbols to depict not only the wreckage of the old order but also the regeneration and fraternal concordance of the world that will come in its wake. The poet at this point can say: "But I am the world." That it to say that he is the quintessence of the world purified and united.

Césaire's poetic imagery is characterized by its multivalence which derives from his Negro African subjectivity. When for instance he declares that he is the world he is in no way enunciating a simple algebraic equation, where although x and y are given initially as representing different realities or quantities, we can, by manipulating some given data, arrive at a solution in which x is equal to y. In algebra the initial quantitative difference between x and y is taken for granted but when Césaire says that he is the sea no such difference is implied. He is simply asserting a philosophical truth of Negro African ontology according to which every object both living and non-living shares in the vital force of life. As Father Placide Temples tells us in *Bantu Philosophy,* "Human beings considered outside of the ontological hierarchy of the interaction of forces is inexistent in Bantu conception."[9] Every object, seen on the philosophical level, is a link in the unbroken chain of the unifying vital force.

The multivalent character of the objects that constitute Césaire's images and symbols comes, therefore, from the amount of vital force they possess at a given time for, as is clear from Fr. Temple's study, the vital force of every object is capable of increase or decrease under the influence direct or indirect of a higher being. The sea in the first part of **"Les Pur-Sang"** and **"Débris"** can be seen as having suffered a decrease in its vital force and therefore has lost the power to influence the land. But when the vital force of the sea is on the ascent as in the later section of **"Les Pur-Sang"** it becomes the very symbol of the poet who sees in its largeness and clarity the vastness and purity of his love for mankind.

The essential unity of all things which is apparent in Bantu philosophy of existence permeates Césaire's imagery. In consequence, Western prosodic clichés such as metaphor, simile, allegory and personification, when seen as mere equations and transference of attributes completely fail to explain the complexity of his images. When, for instance, Césaire says:

> I grow, like a plant
> without remorse and without bulking
> towards the unknotted hours of day
> pure and sure like a plant

> without crucifixion
> towards the unknotted hour of evening
> ("Les Pur-Sang," *Les Armes*)

he is not just comparing the growth of the plant with his own deepening awareness of himself and of he world around him but also, and more importantly, he sees his own ontological involvement in the vital force of the plant which causes it to become more properly a plant.

Césaire's imagery is so informed by this philosophical truth that objects considered inanimate in other cultures and philosophies arise in his poetry as animate objects full of energy and dynamism which, according to circumstances, are either on the rise or on the decline. Smoke like the sea or the sun is infused with force. Again in **"Les Pur-Sang"** smoke, in a state of diminished vital force, serves as a symbol to show the temporary gloom that hangs over all things and the near-despair of the poet:

> The greyness of things oozes before my eyes
> weighs down my ham, lazes horribly along my arm
> I, Mine
> smoke
> smoke
> of the earth

Here the poet's entire universe is a universe of smoke. But what kind of smoke? Smoke whose vital force has been greatly diminished as witness the impunity with which its accumulation of greyness parades before the protagonist, weighs down his ham, and lingers along his arm, and so renders him temporarily ineffectual.

But when, in a poem like **"Prophétie,"** smoke is full of force and dynamism, its movement is swift and purposeful. It vanishes to become one with the air that bears the poet's voice and revolt:

> I watch
> smoke rushes headlong like a wild horse on the
> fore-front of the scene hems briefly the lava of
> its fragile peacock-like tail and then rending its
> shirt pierces its breast with a stab and I watch it
> in British Isle in small islands in jagged rocks
> melt gradually into the lucid sea of air
> where prophetically bathe
> my voice
> my revolt
> my name

The same philosophical concept of vital force enables us to explain Césaire's use of imagery drawn from the animals, plants and topography of his native land. Since these objects are an integral part of the island, they exercise mutual influence on one another, on the island and on its human pupulation. In fact Césaire recognizes a direct relationship between the animals and plants that make up the wild life of Martinique and the lot of its human population. In *Et Les Chiens se taisaient* for instance the Rebel's lady-lover asks him rhetorically:

Beautiful sweet friend without us will the
ungrateful sky be populated with unsealed
hawks without us will the pearl-oysters under
the cover of time appease with their dormant
gestures the meandering of the obscure injury?
Beautiful sweet friend without us will the wind
go off stripping plants of their bloom groaning
towards the arched expectation?

Here, of course, it is easy to see that it is the action of
the Rebel and his lady-lover that seem to have dictated
the triumphant gestures of the unsealed hawks, the pearl-
oysters and the wind. As a general rule however it is the
people who are called upon to heed these supposed lower beings and learn from them. The reason seems to be
evident for, whereas the plants and animals, the hills and
valleys, the wind, the sea and the marshes have retained
their primal force and character, the people have gone
off seduced by the denigrating bait of an alien culture
that is "demonstratively tearing away our sonorous petals in the campanular rain of blue blood" (**"Conquête de
l'aube,"** *Les Armes*), and that has rendered the "negro
each day more base, more cowardly, more sterile, less
profound, more exteriorized, more separated from himself, more shrewd with himself, less immediate with himself . . ." (*Cahier*). Is it any wonder then that Césaire
should call upon himself and his people to turn to these
animals and plants as a source of inspiration and guidance? Thus in an exchange of invocations between the
five cavaliers in *Et Les Chiens se taisaient* we have this
sudden appeal to the plants and animals to guide the
people:

FIRST CAVALIER: Stammering ferns, guide us

SECOND CAVALIER: Dry speech of grasses, guide us

THIRD CAVALIER: Heart-broken grass-snakes, guide us

FOURTH CAVALIER: Glow-worms, cry of flint, guide us

FIFTH CAVALIER: Guide us, oh guide us, blind aloes,
thundering vengeance armed for a century . . .

These plants and animals are not only guides. They are
indeed the alter-ago and a reflection of the inviolate primitive character of the people. Césaire, recognizing this fact,
identifies himself completely with them. Thus in **"Barbare"** for instance, Césaire identifies himself with the
spitting viper, the wall-gekko, the horned toad, and the
worm lizard whose combined poison and nuisance-value
are sufficient to kill or drive his oppressors insane:

Barbarian
the single article
barbarian the tapaya
barbarian the white Amphisbeana
barbarian I the spitting viper
who from my putrifying flesh arouse myself
suddenly flying gekko
suddenly fringed gekko
and cling so tightly to the sources of your strength

that to forget me you will have to throw to
the dogs the hairy flesh of your chests . . . [10]

Similarly Césaire summons all the beasts of his nativeland
not to abandon him in his travail of taking possession of
the enemies' sources of strength. Thus, in the poem **"De
Mes Haras,"** he celebrates the accustomed strength he
once drew from them:

Time of lightning, time of lightning, calm beasts,
frantic beasts, time of lightning, time of lightning
frail beasts, toilsome beasts of old you ran
from the stables of the sky through nostrils and
foam to my voice
and these beasts were of all colors
of every trot and of every bay.[11]

In like manner Césaire invokes the plants:

Parasitic plants, poisonous plants, burning plants,
canibalistic plants, incendiary plants, true plants
veers out in large chunks your unforeseen curbs
                                          (*Et Les Chiens*)

In his poetry these plants and animals feature basically as
nefarious agents whose sole intent is to bring about the
demise of Césaire's island-home as it is presently constituted:

the big market towns came to graze in the
grassy uppermost retreats
then harassed excessively by mosquitoes
held out their muzzle towards the black waters
thoroughly infected by mangrove roots . . .
                                    (**"Fantômes,"** *Ferrements*)

Indeed, these plants and animals serve basically as images
to communicate the revolutionary ardor of the poet. Accordingly "the forest remembers that the last word can
only be the flaming cry of the bird of ruins in the bowl of
storm" (**"Chevelure"**); and "the baobab is our tree that
feebly moves arms so dwarfish that you would think it an
idiotic giant" (**"Chevelure"**), and "cassias on the hiccup-
jolted chest of an island adultrous to its roots" (**"Présence,"**
Cadastre).

Through a conjuration of images drawn from the fauna
and flora of his nativeland, Césaire creates the impression of a veritable revolt in which unfortunately the human
population stands out as a pitiable foil. Something therefore has gone amiss if that essential unity of all things so
characteristic of Negro-African philosophy and so present
in Césaire's subjectivity is lacking in the people. It is
then the role of Césaire, the educator of his people, to
lead the people back to their true personality in order for
them to see in the gestures of these plants and animals
the rebellion that they should be leading against their
oppressors. Thus in *Et Les Chiens se taisaient*—a veritable allegory in the classical sense of the word—Martinique, through a sudden awakening of conscience wrought
by the poet, is transformed into one of these dangerous
insects:

The island sinks its claws of poisonous spider on the
filth of baracoons

Until such an awakening is achieved the extant volcanic
hills of Northwestern Martinique serve as imagery to reflect the temporary lassitude of the people. In *Cahier d'un
retour au pays natal,* for instance, by a kind of Baudelairean correspondence, the inertia of the Martinican population is borne out in:

The hill on all fours before bulimia, lying in
wait for lightnings and mills, slowly vomiting
its human fatigue, the hill alone, its blood
drained, the hill bandaged with shadows,
The hill with rivulets of fear . . .

But who would have thought that after "lying on all fours"
for more than fifty years, Mount Pelée would suddenly erupt
in 1902 to change both the life and topography of the towns
of Saint Pierre, Mourne Rouge, Ajoupa-Bouillon and surrounding localities? Thus perhaps the present inertia of the
people is only temporary and Césaire foresees their imminent revolt in the imagery of future Mount Pelées:

On this most fragile bulge of earth whose
grandiose future out-paces in a humiliating
manner the volcanoes will salvo the bear water
will carry off the ripe stains of the sun and
nothing will be left but a lukewarm bubbling
pecked by sea-birds.

It is clear, therefore, that through the use of imagery and
symbols drawn from the fauna, flora and topography of
his native land, Césaire is at once able to portray what
obviously is to him the suicidal complacency of the people, their future awakening and the rebellion he expects of
them if they are to throw off the yoke of oppression and
find true liberty and freedom.

A word or two are in order here on the type of imagery
with which Césaire portrays the world of the white oppressor of his race. First, the cities of Europe and continental North America, as do the artifacts of Western
technological civilization—cathedral, sky-scraper, stained-
glass, steel, concrete—stand out in Césaire's poetry as
images to depict the exploitation of the black race by the
white race. Thus in *Cahier d'un retour au pays natal*
Césaire identifies some of these cities and cultural artifacts in order to circumscribe the position in which the
black man finds himself in the scheme of things:

AND I said to myself Bordeaux and Nantes and
Liverpool and New York and San Francisco
not a bit of this world that does not bear
my fingerprint and my calcaneum on the back
of skyscrapers and my filth in the glitter of
jewels . . .

And later in *Et Les Chiens se taisaient* the picture is supplemented with this:

a treasure, it's I who reclaim from them my
stolen treasure,

London, Paris, New York, Amsterdam
I see them all gathered around me like stars,
like triumphal moons
and I want with my evil eyes, my rotten breath,
my fingers of a blind man on the lock, to
calculate, ah calculate under their calm, and
their dignity and their balance and their movement
and their noise and their harmony and their
   measure,
what it has been required
of my nervousness
of my panic
of my cries of the eternal tramp and of the beads
of sweat of my sweating face to do this, my son . . .

These cities and their wealth and jewels and skyscrapers
suddenly lose their charm because they were built on the
inhuman exploitation of other races, especially the black
race whose people

know only the voyage of uprooting
. . . who went to sleep on their knees
. . . who were domesticated and christianized
. . . who were inoculated with degeneration.
                                                      (*Cahier*)

It is against the backdrop of the inhuman degradation of
the black man, amidst the opulence of the world of his
white oppressors that the full symbolic representation of
the white civilization is appreciated. Thus in *Et Les Chiens
se taisaient* the Echo, forewarning us of the imminent death
of the Rebel, describes the white man and his world in
these words:

Blue eyed architect
I defy you
beware of yourself architect for it the Rebel dies
it will not be without having made it clear to all
that you are the builder of a world of pestilence
   beware of yourself architect
   Who appointed you? In what night did you
exchange
   the compass for the dagger?
   architect deaf to things, clear like the tree
   but closed like an armour every step of yours
   is a conquest and a spoliation and a
misrepresentation
   and an outrage
   For sure the Rebel is about to leave the world,
your world
   of rape where the victim is by your grace
   a brute and impious
   architect Orcus without a gate and without a star
   without a source and without a budding architect
   of the tail of the peacock, of the step of cancer,
   of the blue speech of mushroom and steel
beware of
   yourself

By representing the white man as an architect, and later as
Orcus, that demon of the underworld who frightens little

children, Césaire is able to give free vent to his feelings about his oppressors. First we have the arrogant self-esteem of the white man (architect of the peacock tail): his cold, inhuman and destructive inflexibility (architect of the tread of cancer, of the blue speech of mushroom and steel). Next the architect is represented as Orcus, a demon that thunders up and down in his infernal domain that allows no exit, no regeneration and no illumination. The imagery of Orcus allows Césaire to direct his critical shafts against the moribund state of white civilization whose arrogance and egotism will not allow it to open itself to the humanizing and rejuvenating influences of other civilizations and cultures.

I am strongly persuaded that Césaire's poetic idiosyncrasies, especially his search for and use of uncommon vocabulary, are symptomatic of his own mental agony in the search for an exact definition of himself and, by extension, of his people and their common situation and destiny.

—Hilary Okram

To complement this view of the white world and present European civilization and mentality as essentially inimical and, at best, passive to other cultures and civilizations, Césaire takes recourse to the animal world in which predatory birds, carrion animals, venomous insects and all species of poisonous and dangerous sea animals and plants serve as symbols to describe Europe. Thus in **"La Parole aux Oricous,"** the African vulture, the dog and the poisonous spider serve as the central symbols to define Europe:

> You Oricous to your whirling ripping positions
>   above
> the forest and up to the very carven whose door is
> a triangle
> whose keeper is a dog
> where life is a calyx
> whose virgin is a spider
> whose exceptional lode is a lake from which to
> arise upon the
> contrapuntal path of the stormy water spirits
>   **(*Cadastre*)**

The nuisance that these vultures, with their eternal ripping and whirling, make of themselves transforms life into solid grief—calyx—for others. Even the most "innocent" of white men is depicted as the spider that perpetually weaves its web to entangle its prey. The stormy water-spirits of other cultures beat, albeit in vain, against the hard inflexible rhythm of white cultural hegemony, a hegemony that has maintained its sway thanks to its ever present watchdog and despite what obviously are its disastrous effects on humanity. That this hegemony no longer serves any

useful purpose is evident in the imagery and symbols with which Césaire communicates the desuetude of Europe and the folly of its cultural narcissism:

> Europe splinter of casting
> Europe low tunnel from which oozes a dew of
>   blood
> Europe old dog Europe barouche for transporting
>   worms
> Europe threadbare tattoo Europe your name is a
> raucous chuckling and a deadened shock.
>   **("Aux Ecluses du vide,"** *Cadastre*)

By symbolically representing Europe as "splinter of casting," "low tunnel from which oozes a dew of blood," etc., Césaire effectively communicates the atrophy of European civilization and, by innuendo, mocks its claim to universality.

To images and symbols drawn from the world of his immediate environment Césaire adds images and symbols built out of both African and European myth and mythology. To appreciate Césaire's use of mythology as vehicle for effective poetic communication it is essential to recall Pierre Albouy's assertion that "there is no literary myth without the regeneration that resuscitates it in an age in which it shows itself best apt to express the proper problem of that age . . ."[12]

It is within the context of the palingenesis of myths and mythology that Césaire's use of them is an apposite poetic mode to articulate the realities of the human condition of the black man. Thus, for instance, Christopher Columbus, that emblem of the triumph of European age of discovery, that personification of European spirit of adventure whose arrival at the shores of the American continent opened the new world to the old, becomes in Césaire's poetry a villain, the inaugurator of the odious slave trade:

> Is it you Columbus? Captain of slave-ships? Is it
> you old pirate, old privateer?
> the night is enlarged with debris
> Columbus, Columbus
> Answer, do answer me . . .
>   (*Et Les Chiens*)

Why the desecration of the apparently sacred image of Columbus? A reasonable answer is that for Césaire, as the spokesman of the black man whose ancestors were forcibly transported to the new world as slaves, the discovery of the new world was, in fact, the beginning of a calvary. To Césaire, therefore, Columbus the "discoverer" of the New World, as Europe would have us believe, is at the origin of all the evils associated with the hunting down of slaves in Africa and their subsequent obnoxious transportation across the Atlantic and enslavement in plantations in the Americas. He is, by extension, responsible for the oppression that the descendants of slaves suffer today. The heroism associated with Columbus in European thought, mentality and mythology is completely destroyed in Césaire's presentation, and a new interpretation, more germane to the experience of the black man, takes its place.

In the same vein Césaire makes myths of historical characters whose lives and deeds serve as symbols to articulate cherished attitudes, hopes and convictions. Accordingly, Toussaint Louverture is mythified in *Cahier d'un retour au pays natal* and becomes not just the leader of insurgents against slavery and French colonization in Haiti but also the symbol of the true rebel who revolts, even at the cost of his own life, against all forms of oppression. Toussaint is described as:

> A man who fascinates the white hawk of white
>   death
> A man alone in the sterile sea of white sand an
> old nigger standing upright against
> the waters of the sky
> Death describes a shining circle above his head
> death stars gently above his head,
> death, driven mad, breathes in the ripe
> sugar-cane plantation of his arm
> . . . shall not the splendor of this blood burst
>   forth?

In the same way Louis Delgrès "the last defender of the freedom of blacks in Guadeloupe, killed during the capture of Matouka on May 28, 1802," appears in Césaire's poetry as the symbol of the poet-warrior. The Larousse Dictionary tells us further about this man; that "without any illusion about the certain outcome of a struggle he accepted, without having provoked it, he distinguished himself by his chivalrous courage. He was seen seated in the embrasure of the cannon, a violin in his hand, braving the bullets of General Richepanse, the commander of that odious expedition; a new Tyrataeus, he was seen playing his instrument to animate his soldiers."

In Césaire's poetry Delgrès becomes the symbol of the poet-warrior, the clairvoyant, the standard bearer, the town-crier who with his voice sustains the struggle for a sure and better future for a people who have known throughout history nothing but pain, humiliation and oppression:

> I celebrate Delgrès who stubborn at the ramparts
> for three days strode up and down the blue height
> of dream
> propelled beyond the sleep of the people
> for three days sustaining sustaining with the fragile
> contexture of his arms
> our sky of crushed pollen

(*Ferrements*)

Like Toussaint Louverture and Louis Delgrès before them, King Christopher[13] and Patrice Lumumba[14] are mythified to become symbols of the martyr who willfully and joyfully makes the supreme sacrifice for the greater good and ultimate freedom of his country. The historical details leading to this martyrdom are inconsequential insofar as they have been subjected to that palingenesis that makes the resultant myth relevant to the times in which and about which the author writes. Thus, in a kind of an apotheosis of Lumumba, Césaire, ignoring historical niceties of some of his protagonist's actions which, at any rate are purely academic, calls him ". . . a man of imagination; always

above the present situation and, by that same token, a man of faith; he is also the man of Africa; the muntu, the man who, at one and the same time, participates in the vital force (the ngolo) and is the man of "verb" (the nommo). Through this man whose stature seems to have designated him for *myth,* the whole history of a continent and of a humanity is played out in an exemplary and symbolic manner . . ."[15]

Just as Lumumba's life and death reenact the entire history of post-colonial Africa, thanks to the myth that Césaire has built around him, so also the invocation of ancient African empires and cities serves as a symbol to give the lie to the supposed primitivism of precolonial Africa. Thus in *Cahier d'un retour au pays natal,* Césaire asserts with an ironic twist:

> And I laugh at my old childish imaginings
> No, we have never been Amazons of the king of
> Dahomey, nor princes of Ghana with eight thousand
> camels, nor doctors at Timbuctoo when Askia the
> Great was king, nor architects at Djenne, nor
> Madhins, nor warriors . . .

In his poetry Césaire goes beyond the simple celebration of the greatness that was Africa to make her the symbol of his own search for cultural rebirth:

> With my heart I have brought up the ancient silex
> The old tinder deposited by Africa inside of me . . .

(*Et Les Chiens*)

Why this spiritual return to Africa? It is because Africa is:

> Land, forge and silo, land directing our routes
> It is here that a truth, silencing the
> tinsel of the old cruel glare, is bethought

(**"Pour saluer le tiers monde,"** *Ferrements*)

It is clear then that Africa is not only the rampart that protects the poet from the arrogance of white cultural hegemony and the resultant political and economic domination but also is the source of strength and energy with which to fight back.

It is pertinent to emphasize Césaire's use of African cities, empires, legends and civilization as symbols. If in some of his symbols and imagery, Africa features subliminally because it is the source of the Negro-subjectivity that gives them their internal cohesion and relevance, in others Africa emerges concretely in response to the poems' structural and thematic imperatives. It does appear therefore that through the symbols and imagery he employs, Césaire shows himself as a man no longer torn by the agonizing imperatives of two conflicting cultures but as a man whose conscious and subsconscious minds merge in their singular focus on Africa as the matrix of his poetic enunciation and source of personal definition.

Notes

[1] Breton, André, "Un grand poète noir" in *Cahier d'un retour au pays natal* (Paris: Ed. Présence Africaine, 1971). Article written in 1943.

[2] Senghor, Leopold, "L'Esthétique négro-africaine," in *Liberté I* (Paris: Le Seuil, 1964), pp. 202-217.

[3] Jahn, Jahneiz, "Rythmes et styles dans la poésie africaine," *Présence Africaine* (August-October, 1963).

[4] Césaire, Aimé, *Et Les Chiens se taisaient* (Paris: Ed. Présence Africaine, 1956), p. 38. The translation is the author's.

[5] Cesaire, Aimé, *L'Art poétique,* eds. Jacques Charpier and Pierre Seghers (Paris: Ed. Seghers, 1956), p. 703.

[6] Sartre, Jean-Paul, "Orphée noir," in *Anthologie de la nouvelle poésie africaine et malgache* (Paris: P.U.F., 1948), p. XXXIX.

[7] Césaire, Aimé, *Cahier d'un retour au pays natal,* p. 72. Translations of quotes from this text are a blend of two previous translations by Emile Snyder (1971) and John Berger and Anna Bostock (1969) with a few touches by the author. All other translations are the author's.

[8] Césaire, Aimé, "Les Pur-sang," *Les Armes miraculeuses* (Paris: Gallimard, 1970), p. 11.

[9] Tempels, Placide, *La Philosophie bantoue* (Paris: Ed. Présence Africaine, 1949), p. 71.

[10] Césaire, Aimé, "Barbare," *Cadastre* (Paris: Le Seuil, 1961), pp. 56-57.

[11] Césaire, Aimé, *Ferrements* (Paris: Le Seuil, 1960), p. 40.

[12] Albouy, Pierre, *Mythes et mythologie dans la littérature française* (Paris: Armand Colin, 1969), p. 9.

[13] Césaire, Aimé, *La Tragédie du roi Christophe* (Paris: Ed. Présence Africaine, 1963).

[14] Césaire, Aimé, *Une Saison au Congo* (Paris: Le Seuil, 1967).

[15] *Ibid.,* back cover.

Emile Snyder   (essay date 1976)

SOURCE: "Aimé Césaire: The Reclaiming of the Land," in *Exile and Tradition: Studies in African and Caribbean Literature,* edited by Rowland Smith, Longman & Dalhousie University Press, 1976, pp. 31-43.

[*In the following essay, Snyder offers an overview of the major themes of Césaire's verse.*]

Take a cruise to the French-speaking Caribbean, a cruise skilfully organised by your local travel agency so that what you will see there will match the expectations of the travel folders. You will stay at a Hilton-type hotel and be entertained at night by local musicians; you will go on a guided tour in the interior and drive so fast that the memories you retain of the people will be images of colourful bandannas wrapped around the heads of women, shapes moving gracefully in the sunlight, a waving of hands and the smiles of children. And you will return home rhapsodising to your friends about the paradise which is Martinique. Surely—you will be inclined to say—all this nonsense about colonialism and neocolonialism must be insidious propaganda pro-pounded by misguided radicals. And not even once will you have guessed at the reality of life in Martinique: the physical and mental misery of the people, their sense of despair at an unchanging situation, their loss, over the years, of pride, of colour, of self.

This bleaker image of Martinique—the other side of the advertised coin—faced Aimé Césaire from his birth, undermining his childhood, festering during his adolescence, and bursting open like a neglected sore just as he was about to depart from Martinique 'with rapture'. But in the most closeted chambers of his consciousness memories awaited, restless for the poems which would deliver them and exorcise them.

Beginning with ***Return to my Native Land (Cahier d'un retour au pays natal,*** 1939) that long epic, dramatic and lyrical poem which André Breton called 'nothing less than the greatest lyric monument of the epoch', the painful memories began to emerge. Césaire recalled his mother working late at night to improve the family earnings:

> . . . I am even awakened at night by
> those tireless limbs which pedal the night, by the
> bitter puncture in the soft flesh of the night
> made by a Singer machine my mother pedals,
> pedals for our hunger.[1]

Césaire evoked his island:

> At the end of the dawn, flowered with frail
> creeks, the hungry West Indies, pitted with
> smallpox, dynamited with alcohol, stranded in
> the mud of this bay, in the dirt of this city
> sinisterly stranded.

And the apparent passivity of his Martinique brothers:

> In this inert city, this brawling crowd which
> so astonishingly by-passes its cry, its motion,
> its meaning, calm, passive to its true cry, the
> only cry you want to hear for it is all the city can
> say, because the sound inhabits some refuge of
> shadow and pride in this inert city, going by its
> cry of hunger, of grief, of revolt, of hate, this
> crowd so strangely blabbing and mute.

And in prose Césaire ridiculed his secondary school friends, the sons of the mulatto bourgeoisie, aping the white world, and fuelled by what Frantz Fanon called the drive for 'lactification':

> I was literally choking amid these Blacks
> who thought of themselves as white.

Already by 1939 Césaire was instinctively fusing with the history of the race the more immediate, existential conditions of his own life.

How do you accept, act upon, and transform such a past if not by speaking against it, if not by trying to raise 'the good drunken cry of revolt'? How do you validate your existence, record for yourself and for your posterity a plot of land in the world register (*cadastre*), if not by trudging back along the ancestral path to return to the source— Africa, the matrix, the point of embarkation for the black diaspora and the irreversible moment of parturition? You must sail back to the 'homeland', the family names, the genealogies which almost dissolved in the wake of the slavers' ships.

For Césaire the Orphic voyage was to pass through Paris. It was there, as a student at the Ecole Normale, that he met Léopold Sédar Senghor from Senegal (and later he was to say that the first time he met Senghor he began to think of himself as an African), that he befriended the poet Léon Damas from French Guiana, and that he merged with the African and Caribbean students attending the classrooms of the Sorbonne and sharing thoughts while sitting at the cafés on the Boulevard Saint Michel. An elite group? Yes indeed, but what poet, what novelist, what intellectual has not willingly or unwillingly at some point been co-opted into the intelligentsia class, by reason of his education and the privilege of having to till the stacks of a library rather than the furrows of an improverished land? An elite group, yes, but one intent upon denouncing the mystifications of the colonial reality (including the ambiguity of its own situation as an acculturated class), and asserting something of its own specificity as black men among men.

The 'Negritude' movement was launched, Césaire coining the word for the first time in **Return to my Native Land**, Senghor refining the theory, Alioune Diop providing with his review *Présence Africaine* (furthering the pioneering work of *Légitime Défense* and *L'étudiant Noir*) the voice or vehicle for keeping alive the palaver among black men, for defining 'the originality of African culture', for promoting 'its insertion into the future concert of nations'.

Césaire's contribution, over the years, took many forms. As a polemicist, in *Discours sur le colonialisme* (1950) he attacked the arrogant premises on which western intellectuals asserted the so-called superiority of western culture; as an historian, in *Toussaint Louverture* (1961), he rehabilitated the historical figure of the great Haitian patriot; as a playwright, he embarked upon a dramatic trilogy centred on black heroes in the world because, as Césaire once said to Lylian Kesteloot 'we need heroes of our own'. His first real play, *La tragédie du roi Christophe* (1963), focused upon the forceful figure of the Haitian ruler, Henri Christophe. *Une saison au Congo* (1967) depicted the martyrdom of Patrice Lumumba and the rape of the Congo by foreign powers. To close the trilogy Césaire is said to be projecting a play on Malcolm X. In addition to his literary career, Césaire entered Martinique's politics, serving for years as mayor of Fort-de-France. He also joined the French Communist Party to which he adhered for over a decade, resigning from it in 1956 and putting forth the reasons for his defection in a brilliant letter addressed to Maurice Thorez, the then titular head of the party.[2]

But poetry has remained for Césaire the most cherished, the most exacting, and the most intimate way to conciliate his anger with his love, his despair with his dreams, his sense of his own blackness with his yearning for an anonymous and universal presence in a future fraternal world. Poetry has always been for Césaire the 'miraculous weapons', *les Armes Miraculeuses*, as the title of his volume of 1964 announced.

Refusing the facile exoticism of the previous generation of black poets writing in French (despite the fact that his vocabulary drives the reader to a variety of dictionaries), eschewing the simple statement (for Césaire once said that there was a world of difference between a political pamphlet and a poem), Césaire adopted the nightmarish visions of a Lautréamont or Rimbaud, the convoluted syntactical subtleties of a Mallarmé, and followed the hermetic plunges of the Surrealists into the reservoir of the unconscious.

But for him so much of Surrealism was only a matter of technique. For Césaire's visions coagulated into precise images of the indignities and tortures suffered under the colonial system, and into counter-images of anticipated liberation which would bring about the flowering of love and the reconciliation of man with the universe. Moreover, the syntactical meanders of Césaire's poems do not stem from a *précieux* mind. They reflect his intentions to record the tortuous labour of memory grappling with lost landmarks. They, at the same time, underline the dialectic project which is political in nature and often stated at the onset by the very titles of the poems. Thus Césaire, although technically heir to the Surrealist tradition, stands ideologically poles apart from it. Nothing in his poetry is gratuitous. The imagination is not allowed to wander aimlessly for self-gratification. Each poem is in itself a project, a praxis—in the Sartrian sense of the word—carefully mapped out by a sense of urgency and of responsibility. The dialectic moves from the awareness of a tragic racial past to the lucid recognition of the present horror, compelling the poet forward to revolt in the name of a desired transcendence. The movement is from awareness to revolt and to love.

Let us trace this dialectic in '**Raving Mad**', one of the most poignant poems from his early volume, *Soleil Cou Coupé* (1948) salvaged in the recapitulative text of *Cadastre* (1961).[3]

Raving Mad

Greetings to you birds slicing through and scattering
    the circle of
    herons
and the genuflexion of their resigned heads
in a sheath of white down
Greetings to you birds who peck open the true belly
    of the swamp
and the chieftain's chest of the setting sun

Greetings to you raucous cry
    resinous torch

in which mingle the trails
of rain ticks and white mice

Raving mad I greet you with my ravings whiter
than death

Simple open sea
I welcome my future hour
when each word each gesture will liven
your face like that of a blond goat
foraging in the intoxicating vat of my hand

And then then
my good leech
then the beginning of time
then the end of time
and the erect majesty of the original eye.

It is twilight. The poet imprisoned in his anger, contemplates a circle of herons. They stand there, outlined in the sunset, on one leg, the other leg doubled back under the knee, and their heads lowered into their bodies. And the poet perceives in this attitude of the herons a symbol of the resignation of his black brothers under colonial subjugation. This resignation is expressed ironically—for Césaire's poetry is frankly anti-Christian—through the image of penitents in genuflexion before the altar:

and the genuflexion of their resigned heads
in a sheath of white down.

But all of a sudden a flock of small birds traverse the circle of herons and the herons, frightened, take flight. All the birds (small birds joined by the herons) taking off towards sunset are for Césaire messengers of hope. In Césaire's bestiary almost all birds are symbols of liberation on the way.

The poet greets three times these harbingers of freedom, anticipating his own freedom. He follows the birds as far as his eyes can see. They lose themselves in the swamp. But, by poetic transposition, this swamp, his dusk, now become the mediation for a psychic plunge into the past, into Césaire's collective past which he relates to Africa by the warlike personification of nature: 'and the chieftain's chest of the setting sun'.

And it is no longer the 'raucous cry' of the birds which the poet greets but his own recovered voice now asserting itself. For he is now going to be able to 'raise with stiffness the great black cry so that the foundations of the world will be shaken' ('d'une telle raideur le grand cri nègre que les assises du monde en seront ébranlées'), a project he will set for himself in his dramatic monologue *Et les chiens se taisaient* (1956). The imagination of the poet carries him into the most secret recesses of the bush— (and of the past)—; it is there that life pulses with real intensity: 'rain ticks and white mice'.

Césaire begins to feel free at last from his psychic torture. Having recovered a sense of his roots, he also recovers his personal and collective voice which he now uses to vilify his oppressors: 'Raving mad I greet you with my ravings whiter than death?' Note that for Césaire, as for Damas, the colour white always has a negative connotation, being synonymous with physical death, spiritual atrophy, and cultural decadence: manichaean principle in French black poetry (not always adhered to by Senghor!) which tends to counter-balance the opposite manichaeanism of western poetry where the colour white has been associated for centuries with notions of virginity, purity, spirituality and strength: 'Raving mad I greet you with my ravings whiter than death.'

Moment of supreme arrogance, of supreme liberation when the poet's whole being coheres with his anger. Now Césaire can go beyond his anger, surpass it, and channel it towards a higher synthesis:

I welcome my future hour
when each word each gesture will liven
your face like that of a blond goat
foraging in the intoxicating vat of my hand.

The last movement of the poem, an oceanic movement (for Césaire is an oceanic poet always conscious of the presence of the ocean lapping his small island: he once referred to Martinique as a 'dandruff speck on the surface of the ocean') prefigures universal fraternity. But this leap toward the 'future hour' of freedom is also a return to a primal unity: return to simplicity ('simple open sea'), and to the harmony of man with the universe. Freedom will express itself through the now possible gestures of love between man and women, the sensual communication:

When each word each gesture will liven
your face like that of a blond goat
foraging in the intoxicating vat of my hand.

Beautiful image, that of a woman whose angular face, bathed in the golden colour of sunset, is being intimately, almost domestically, caressed by the loving hand of the poet!

Without freedom there cannot be, for Césaire, any possibility of loving. But with the advent of freedom the cycle is completed, the 'beginning of time' and 'the end of time' fuse into a myth of fertility, the frankly phallic image of the triumphant sun, the old Egyptian symbol of power and fecundity: 'the erect majesty of the original eye'.

Critics have often remarked upon the tone of violence in the poetry of Césaire. It should be seen, however, that violence for Césaire is only the second term of the dialectic, the moment of negativity in the Hegelian sense. True, by comparison with his manifested anger, Césaire's final leap into love and tenderness is verbalised quietly—a muted lyricism—in the poems. Often a single verse reveals it, as if the poet overwhelmed by his newly discovered treasure finds himself too shy to share it with the rest of the world. In *Return to my Native Land*, referring to his pregnant wife but without naming her or his child precisely, he simply wrote:

and you, O star, will draw lemuridae from
your foundation with the unfathomable sperm
of man
     the not dared form (my italics)

In Césaire's poetry images of renaissance through love
counter-balance images of violence and destruction. Examples abound in the volume **Cadastre**. In '**Millibars of
the storm**' he wrote:

Dream let's not yield
among the hooves of frenzied horses
a tearful noise groping towards the immense wing
   of your eyelid.

In '**Chevelure**', at the conclusion of the poem, he invoked
the loving woman:

and you
abode of my insolence of my tombs of my
   whirlwinds
mane bundle of lianas fervent hope of shipwrecks
sleep softly on the meticulous trunk of my embrace
   my
woman
my fortress.

In '**The Wheel**', after having recalled ancestral miseries:

but you minutes will you not wind onto your spool
   of life
the lapped up blood
the art of suffering sharpened like tree stumps by
   the knives
of winter,

he prophesised the rebirth of nature enhanced by the loving face of his woman:

the doe drunk with thirst
bringing to my unexpected wellstones your
   face of an unmasted schooner
your face
like a village asleep in the depth of a lake
and which is reborn to the realm of green and
to the fruitful year.

A rebirth 'to the realm of green and to the fruitful year',
that is the key to Césaire's most private obsession. His
anthropomorphisation of nature which he carries to a near
frisson of eroticism reflects his desire to reintegrate himself into the very minute manifestations of the vegetable
mineral and animal world. There is, in his poetry, a rich
catalogue—indeed an encyclopaedia—of flora and fauna.
A brief repertoire of his images should include plants,
shrubs, flowers, such as a 'silphium-lascinatum' cassia,
monk's hood ('aconit napel'), solandra, albizzia, umbel
and terrebela—to name only a few—and trees such as a
ceiba, kaelcedra, cassia, manchineel, baobab, and flamboyant. Césaire reflects the preoccupation of the botanist,
bent as he is to avoid the 'vulgar' terms in preference for
the Latin names which embody the genus of the species.

His bestiary is just as impressive. It not only includes
known birds, fishes and insects, such as a toucan, macaw,
aras, gekko (lizard), scollopendra (centipede), remora
(sucking fish), medusa-aurelia (jellyfish), shark, dolphin,
but it also includes fossilated forms of life and mythical
ones: the lailape, a gigantic fossil carnivorous dinosaur,
the amphisbaena, a serpent in classical mythology, and the
griffin, half-animal, half-human creature said to have kept
watch over the tombs of the Egyptians. Finally the poems
seem embedded into the earth, drawing their strength from
the mineral eternity; numerous are the references to clay,
laterite, dacite, chromium, mercury, and so on.

This constant obsession with the botanical, zoological, and
geophysical world (overwhelming by far the human *personae* of his poems) might lead us to think that Césaire has
spent his formative years with his head buried in specialised
scientific dictionaries. The documentation alone is shattering. Are we dealing here with a poet conceitedly flashing his
esoteric erudition? Jacqueline Sieger, in an interview with
Césaire in *Afrique* (No. 5, October 1961), asked him about
this seemingly *recherché* aspect of his poetry:

One feels that you are searching for the erudite word
and soon this gives to your poetry an impression of
esoterism;

to which Césaire answered:

It is true that the language of my poems is very precise;
it is because I have wanted, above all, to *name* things.
If I want to speak of a certain tree, I say a palm tree,
of a certain flower, an hibiscus. And why not? The
French poet, in his turn, does not speak of flowers but
of the rose or of the violet.

             (my own translation)

Césaire's precise nomination of the natural world has a
political implication—political because racism attempts to
disfranchise a man from his geographical roots, indeed
perhaps from the earth itself. In *Anti-semite and the Few*,
J. P. Sartre, considering the situation of the Jew in France,
remarked that anti-semitism aimed at questioning the very
legitimacy of the Jew's presence on French soil and within
the context of French history. Are not his roots—hence his
biology, his culture and his allegiance—in Odessa or in
some other extra-territorial places, would the racist say?
Thus racism (all forms of racism) attempts to *deterritoria-
lise* its victim who becomes reduced to beg acceptance as
an alien or to seek to assimilate in the hope of disappearing
from this monstrous illegitimacy fostered upon him.

Similarly Césaire, the son of uprooted African slaves, is
first compelled to react against this curse. Naming the
world in its totality is one way of claiming for himself an
unchallenged plot (a *cadastre*) from which he cannot be
disfranchised. Africa, the Africa which Césaire evokes at
times in idealised terms (and which is not the Africa of
Africans but the Africa of a Caribbean grandchild), is but
a passage to a more lasting—Moses-like—homeland which
is the universe itself! Naming the Nile, the Niger, the cities of Timbuktu or Uagadougou, is for Césaire like setting

road signs along the homeward journey. But in the final analysis Africa is not enough for Césaire, for the centuries of colonialism have *disfranchised* him from that original homeland. In **Return to my Native Land** he wrote:

> No, we have never been amazons of the king of Dahomey, nor the princes of Ghana with eight hundred camels, nor wise men of Timbuktu under Askia the Great; nor architects in Djene, nor *mahdis* nor warriors. Under our armpits, we do not feel the itch of those who bore the lance. And since I have sworn to hide nothing of our history (I who admire nothing so much as the lamb chewing his afternoon shadow), I want to declare that we were from the very first quite pitiful dishwashers, shoeshiners without scope and, at best, rather conscientious sorcerers whose only incontestable achievement has been the endurance record under the lash.

Hence, nothing short of the whole undifferentiated earth can be his homeland; but Césaire feels that even that birthplace has been vitiated by racism, by human stupidity and hatred. It is therefore necessary to restructure poetically this ideal birthplace of man, beginning with an apocalyptic disaster (one of his poems is entitled **'Tangible Disaster'**) and followed by a loving reconstruction. Césaire, a sort of self-appointed Noah figure, gathers lovingly all the beasts, birds, insects, saps, to shelter them from moral deluge. And then, having done so, Noah becomes Thor, the god of thunder and lightning, raining retribution upon the wicked. And the sky and the sun remain the only witness to this apocalypse which is a genesis in reverse. Césaire's poetry abounds with 'convulsive sky', 'exploded stars', 'splitting craters', 'braziers of flames', and 'primal debris'. Purification through fire from which even extinct volcanoes find renewed strength. The poem **'Crusades of Silence'** ends with the terrifying vision of Chimborazo, the volcanic mountain in the Andes, awakening once more to its original potential: 'Chimborazo though extinct still devours the world'.

In this poetic destruction of the universe there is a refusal to accept the world as handed down from an official version of Genesis because, to Césaire, those who may have written it as well as those who pretend to derive moral commandments from it, are immoral people. Genesis, and the natural reproductive cycle which Césaire loves so much, and to which he returns constantly through the images of water, ovaries, tadpoles, seeds in germination, *should* in his mind have led to the full blossoming of man in a fraternal world. However, already in the official Genesis Césaire finds himself and his black brothers cast out. That is why he said with irony 'Don't mind me, I am of before Adam', meaning not only that ideally he wishes to antedate a creation which has gone foul, but that in that Christian version of creation, starting with Adam, his own black forefathers had already been damned.

Léon Damas, the French Guiana poet, has expressed a similar attitude in a bitter poem entitled 'Against our love which asked for nothing more':[4]

> Against our love
> which dreamed of living in a free space
> which dreamed of living its own life

> of living a life
> which would be
> neither
> shameful
> nor leprous
> nor faked
> nor partitioned
> nor haunted
> they have invoked NOAH
> and NOAH called upon SHEM
> and SHEM called upon JAPHET
> and JAPHET referred it to NOAH
> and NOAH called upon METHUSELAH
> and METHUSELAH once again took out of the
>   arsenal
> all the tinsel rags
> all the taboos
> all the warning lights of prohibitions

> Beware
> Now dangerous
> Detour
> Game-preserves
> Private property
> Guarded domain
> No trespassing
> Dogs and Niggers forbidden on the lawn
> (my own translation).

Politics and metaphysics are inseparable for Césaire. For the imbalance in human rapports (racism) has upset the innate balance of the universe. Nature henceforth re-enacts, in the poet's mind, the drama of human beings enslaved through hatred and stupidity. In an early poem, **'Les Pur-Sangs'**, from **Les Armes Miraculeuses,** Césaire paralleled man's enslavement with the deterioration of the harmonised forces of the universe:

> the earth no longer makes love with the sun
> the earth no longer rubs its cheek against the stars'
>   clusters;

but as the poet finds a way to free himself from the yoke of servitude, as he begins to grow

> . . . like a plant
> without remorse and without stumbling
> toward the loosened hours of the day,

the earth too begins to regain its original composure:

> And the earth began to breathe beneath the gauze of
>   mists
> And the earth stretched. A loosening came
> upon its knotted shoulders. In its veins
> a crackling of fire

Cosmic eroticism (and Sartre wrote in *Orphée Noire* that Césaire 'vegetalises, animalises sea and sky and stone') is his disguised love for the earth; it is at the same time the expression of his anguish at feeling *disfranchised* from it through centuries of racism. Tree-forms, laterite-forms, fossilated and organic forms become the only tenable *cadastre* of a man whose very race has been uprooted. In the already mentioned interview with Jacqueline Sieger, Césaire clarified his position:

> But I am an African poet! I feel very deeply the uprooting of my people. Critics have remarked upon the recurrence of certain themes in my works, in particular plant symbols. I am in fact obsessed by vegetation, by the flower, by the root. There is nothing gratuitous in that, it is linked with my situation, that of a black man exiled from his native soil. It is a psychological phenomenon from which I have never freed myself and which I feel to the point of nausea. It is as if I was hearing, in the most intimate part of my sensibility, the echoes of the lapping of the waves, the tossing which the slaves felt in the holds of the slave ships. The tree, profoundly rooted in the soil, is for me the symbol of man who is self-rooted, the nostalgia of a lost paradise. (My own translation)

Césaire's *cri de coeur* is first directed to his black brothers, but it does not stop there. It extends itself to all men who, in some ways, have been humiliated, have suffered injustices, are seeking for redress and for peace. André Breton, perhaps the first to have understood the universal impact of Césaire's indignation, summarises it in this manner:

> What to my mind makes this indignation priceless, is that it transcends at every moment the anguish felt by a Negro because of the fate of Negroes in modern society and, indistinguishable from that felt by all poets, artists and true thinkers, while furnishing Césaire with a special fund of verbal genius, embraces the more generally determined condition of man today, in all its intolerable and also infinitely improvable aspects.

The dialectic of Césaire's poetry, in short, synthetises the potentially *précieux* aesthetics of Surrealism with the political thrust of humanistic and existential ideology, the past and present with the future, and the experience of a unique individual with the universal condition of man.

Notes

[1] The quotations from *Return to my Native Land* are from my own translations in the bilingual edition, *Return to my Native Land,* Paris, Présence Africaine, 1971.

[2] *Lettre à Maurice Thorez,* Présence Africaine, 1956.

[3] *Cadastre,* Edition du Seuil, 1961.

[4] Léon Damas, 'Névralgies', *Présence Africaine,* 1965.

Ronnie Leah Scharfman (essay date 1980)

SOURCE: "The Subject and the Intimate Other: Woman as *Tu*," in *"Engagement" and the Language of the Subject in the Poetry of Aimé Césaire,* University of Florida Press, 1980, pp. 65-73.

[*In the following essay, Scharfman provides a semantic analysis of the role of women in Césaire's poetry.*]

> . . . là où les femmes rayonnent de langage. . . .
>
> Aimé Césaire, **"Prophétie"**

[In *Cahier*] the textual intervention of woman as "tu" can have major consequences for the subject's definition of itself. Woman is an essential figure in Césaire's poetry, and there are certain lyrical texts that could qualify as "love poems." But in speaking of woman here, we are not addressing an erotic, archetypal, or even potentially political figure. We are concerned, rather, with examining the signifier that represents her, the "tu" that appears in tandem with the speaking subject itself. The presence of the "tu" is often what makes it possible for the subject to delineate itself, to delimit itself in discourse. In reading Césaire we are justified in wondering if "je" is here, can "tu" be far behind? Within the context of the colonial dialectic of otherness, the "tu" represents a different kind of other, a double, an alter ego, literally, another self. This is why we choose to call it "the intimate other." This dual relationship, what Lacan calls the Imaginary, has its own characteristics and its own problems. If the "je" and the "tu" form a couple, this does not necessarily protect the subject from certain forms of alienation, as when Sartre states, "autrui me vole mon monde." The focal point of the readings in this chapter, however, is the constitutive role that the "tu" plays for the subject wherever their dialectical relationship is dramatized.

The major source of reflection that informs our analysis of this relationship is found in Benveniste's *Problèmes de linguistique générale,* in the section entitled "L'homme dans la langue." In Benveniste's discussion, one of the salient characteristics of the "je-tu" relationship is a linguistic complicity, what he calls a "corrélation de personnalité." This binds the first and second person together in discourse, since "'tu' est nécessairement designé par 'je' et ne peut être pensé hors d'une situation posée à partir de 'je.'" Moreover, since Benveniste defines subjectivity as a fact of discourse, it follows that the couple "je-tu" can exist only as actualized within each instance of discourse. Last, although the two form a unit because of their "corrélation de personnalité," and because their properties are reversible, they are not equal or symmetrical. A specific opposition obtains between the two. Self-consciousness proceeds by contrast, by positing the "tu" as difference. The difference is that "'ego' a toujours une position de transcendance à l'égard de 'tu'; néanmoins, aucun des deux termes ne se conçoit sans l'autre; ils sont complémentaires, mais selon une opposition 'intérieur/extérieur'."

Thus, the subject and the other must be defined by each other, dialectically, and always within discourse. The ramifications of this analysis for our problematic will be illustrated by the three readings that follow. Usually, in Césaire's poems, "je" and "tu" are the signifiers for man and woman. But as we shall see in another poem, "Hors des jours étrangers," the "people" can be the signified of the "tu." It is no less an intimate other, but it poses its own problems, which will be discussed in the appropriate chapter.

The unique nature of subjectivity that is founded in discourse requires that the subject must reestablish and restate itself anew each time it appropriates language for itself. In Césaire's quest for being, each poem becomes the difficult scene of a different formulation of subjectivity. Since identity necessitates an acknowledgment of difference, the "tu" to which many of the poems are addressed, and in function of which the subject is defined, will also be endowed with a specificity that varies with each poem. In the three texts that follow, one taken from each of Césaire's three major collections of poetry, the nature of the relationship between the "je-tu," and the textual space that it deploys, are so compelling as to preclude, momentarily, the larger issue of *engagement*. And yet the exploration of the "je" and the "tu" is not an anomaly in a static situation. It is a dialectical way station which is the condition of the subject's positing that other relation of otherness, the "je-vous," or the "nous-vous" of the colonial situation. It is therefore necessary to include such an examination here.

In the first poem, **"Le Cristal automatique"** (*Les Armes miraculeuses*), the positing of the "tu" functions as a dramatization of the communicational need that subtends human desire.[1] Lacanian theory explains the close relationship that exists between desire and language. One always speaks to or for someone, to or for something. In the same way, desire is always desire for. Both are based on the notion of absence, of "manque."[2] In this sense, the dialectical dialogue between "je-tu" is the source of the poem itself. The subject modulates between projecting the desired object and striving toward recognition by her or fusion with her, on the one hand, and being thrown back from her toward a clearer self-definition, on the other.

In the repeated initial "allo allo" of the poem, we immediately recognize the familiar verbal formula used in telephone conversation. It evokes certain associations: distance, absence, a desire to communicate, here versus there, a reaching out from one interlocutor to another. However, the form of this prose poem is problematic. It continues in one long, unpunctuated run-on sentence of sorts, a monologue in the guise of a dialogue, which has significance in terms of the nature of the "je-tu" relationship as it is mapped out in this poem. The other, the "tu," is posited rhetorically in the beginning of the poem in a peculiar way. The subject preempts the question that she will presumably ask by answering it first, "pas la peine de chercher, c'est moi." This ellipsis of the question foreshadows a later ellipsis in the poem. The absent question is central to the poem. It is the question of identity, "who is it?" The subject is compelled to disallow the articulation of the question and to answer it at the same time. The absent question sets in motion the whole chain of signifiers that characterize the "moi" versus the "toi." It also reveals a strangely self-referential aspect of what is nominally a desire for the other. The subject defines itself first, without looking or listening, as it were. And the only indication it gives us initially of the presence of the other is

based on an absence. Moreover, we have only to look at the poem's disposition on the page to realize that it is defending against this absence, that it runs on in a desperate effort to make a block of words that huddle together, filling in all the gaps, never letting the "tu" get a word in edgewise. The only graphic chink in the fortress of black printed signifiers comes, not surprisingly, after the first "c'est toi," where we have an ellipsis, a blank, a zero, a "trou dans le discours." This is followed by "c'est toi, ô absente." In the poem **"Séisme"** (*Ferrements*), the poet asks, "Essayer des mots? Leur frottement pour conjurer l'informe . . . ?"

And yet the "tu," by her very absence, is what motivates the discourse. "Pour penser à toi j'ai déposé tous mes mots au monts-de-piété." This phrase is an oxymoron, since there is no thought without words. But one could read this as a desire on the part of the subject to revert to that prelinguistic moment, to a time of fusion, of reunification, of presence. We have further evidence for this point of view in the image of "le pain et l'alcool de tes seins," where the breasts are depicted as a source of nourishing delirium, where the desire to assimilate, to incorporate, is not only an erotic one but also one that implies a throwback to the mother-child symbiosis, to a time before linguistic codes and telephone wires, to a time before separation. Associated with the breast is "l'envers clair de la terre," there where "je voudrais être."

In fact, the entire poem is structured around the associative poles designated by "je" and "tu." The subject articulates a "tu" that is an inverted form of itself. "C'est moi" is associated with "nuit," "mort," "noyé," "pluie." "C'est toi," on the contrary, is related to "journée blonde," "l'envers clair de la terre," "baigneuse," "l'accroissement du cristal," "l'aube," "le maguey éblouissant." The effort to reconcile the two poles, his negative, hers positive, passes through desire, imagination, and the future tense, which is the sign for hope in Césaire: "je voudrais être," "dans ma tête," "quand viendra l'aube, c'est toi qui poindras." Furthermore, the "moi" defines itself as "l' homme des cavernes," that is, a hollow, a concavity, a darkness, in opposition to the "toi" who, although or because absent, is imagined paradoxically as "plénitude," convex breast, "accroissement du cristal," and is associated with the concreteness of "les îles" and "la terre," as opposed to the "moi" that is drowning.

We are left with what seems to be a contradictory reading of this text: the "tu," desired for the illusion of projected plenitude, is conspicuously absent, whereas the "moi" seems caught in its own sterile web, automatically repeating the formula "allo allo," which should imply communication but instead seems to indicate absence of anything but its own echo. What there is, the series of "il y a" in the poem, is undesirable. One might also extrapolate that if the "tu" were present, and, with her, dawn and the future, the present, that is, the subject and its night, would have to disappear and, with it, possibly the text also. Perhaps this threat of disappearance explains the ambivalence of the subject's desire for the "tu," invoking her yet underscoring her absence.

One might also look to the title of the poem for some clarification of this ambiguity. The word "automatique" of the title never reappears in the body of the text per se, but its self-referentiality illuminates the automotivation pointed out. As for "le cristal," it is repeated as part of the first definition of the "tu," in "l'accroissement du cristal, c'est toi." As noted, what actually accumulates on the page is three dots, signifiers of nothing, of absence. Could "cristal" then be a figure for *écriture?* Both contain a hidden *cri.* The association then of the term *écriture automatique* with the title of this poem seems inevitable. The stream-of-consciousness form of the text, the unwonted associations of images within it, its placement in the collection **Les Armes Miraculeuses**, all attest to its relation to the surrealistic poetic praxis.

"L'accroissement du cristal" also approaches "la cristallisation" in the Stendhalian sense of the term, being that phenomenon by which signs are read through the distorting lens of desire until they crystallize around the desired love object, thus giving her an imaginary form.[3] "Cristal" also connotes wireless, by synecdoche, the crystal being that substance used as a corrective to regulate oscillatory current. Without concluding, then, we can at least suggest that there is a connection between "l'accroissement du cristal," the accumulation of the written words of the signifying chain that is the prose poem, and the analogous spoken word with its desire for immediacy conveyed by the telephone metaphor. All of these seem to converge in the "toi," both written and oral in form. She is absent as a dialoguing interlocutor from the verbal conversation because the subject has chosen to exclude her. The subject, which is *hic et nunc* in the text, prefers to keep the "tu" there and future. For absence need not only be threatening; it can also be a substitutive possibility. The text takes over the conversation, and the subject can experience the liberating effect of imagining the other without losing itself.

The second poem, **"Totem"** (*Cadastre*), articulates a completely different aspect of the "je-tu" relationship.[4] It is a poem not of absence but of obstruction. At first reading the text reveals this strange contradiction: a blatant absence of subject pronouns amidst a preponderance of possessive adjectives. Further, the possessive adjectives designating the "tu" far outnumber those for the first person. Some preliminary questions already suggest themselves: what is the difference between, on the one hand, having and being, and, on the other, saying that the "tu," the more sharply delineated of the two persons, constitutes a whole by virtue of the sum of her parts?

The "moi" is roaming the page in search of a linguistic space in which to intervene in the poem as a true grammatical subject. It never, in fact, succeeds in constituting itself as such, although it travels widely, back and forth, "de loin en proche de proche en loin." For that matter, the "toi" does not ever attain real grammatical status as subject either. According to Benveniste, this is tantamount to nonexistence, and the anguished atmosphere of the poem resides in this struggle for existence.

Where, then, is the troubling element in the text, the constraining, oppressive force that prevents the subject from constituting itself? What is responsible for the web of anxiety that is woven into this texture such that a subject cannot affirm itself? "détresse"-"trahison"-"destructrice"-"venin"-"naufrage"-"captive"-"abîme"-"piétinez"-"sanglots"-"silence."

The distorted, ambiguous syntax of the one real sentence with proper grammatical subject in the first part of the poem, and the doubt expressed by its verbal form (conditional, negative, interrogative), leads us to posit the question of the status of the titular "totem." If we read that sentence as "comment le totem buvant dans la gloire de ma poitrine un grand coup de vin rouge et de mouches ne bondirait-il pas d'étage en étage de détresse en héritage au sommet des buildings sa tiédeur de cheminée et de trahison?" certain tensions become evident which help delimit the framework within which and against which the subject/text is attempting to articulate itself. In a reversal of the usual ethnological connotations, the "totem" somehow is defined by the "moi." Yet what the "moi" can offer is ambivalent: "un coup de vin rouge et de mouches"; what the "totem" derives is equally worrisome: "sa tiédeur de cheminée et de trahison." The chain by which this is transmitted, a cynical, mock-progression from concrete "étage" to emotional "détresse" to historical "héritage," and the uncertainty expressed by the verb, whose form contradicts the usual assertive connotation of "bondir," all add to the poem's anxious atmosphere. We are faced with a poetic crisis, a modulation between affirmation and negation, freedom and constraint, phallic thrust and frustration or, worse, castration. The "totem," that hereditary emblem that should guarantee the subject's ability to insert itself into a chain of being and meaning, functions here as a disarticulating force, an alienating, castrating, symbolic father.

The "tu" is looked to as a source of possible mediation, as a liberation from these inhibitions. But Benveniste's category of correlation should already warn us that the "tu" cannot have any more sure claim to existence than the "je." The "tu" is trapped into identification by simile, "comme." The best that can be effected through positing the other is to emphasize her potential in language, to somehow squeeze a different signified out of the signifier, to extract "distraction" from "destructrice," to distill "vin" from "venin," to salvage "rire" from the wreck of "naufrage," and so on. These images are, indeed, intensely beautiful. But it is mere poetic desire, willing its creation into existence, like Michelangelo's trying to free his slaves from the stone. Words are not action. A cruel self-mockery attests to the arbitrariness of this enterprise, underlying the poem from the first, as the text opens under the aegis of the "sistre des circoncis" (an ancient music hovering just short of castration), and the "soleil hors moeurs," that Césairian symbol par excellence of strength, here unintelligibly out of control. The subject doubts its very ability to assert itself. "Gloire" is first declared as self-value in "vin rouge," then reduced to the humiliation of self-hatred in "mouches." In this tenuous state the "moi" asks the woman as other to testify in some way to its existence, but she is, as we have seen, equally impotent. The subject cannot even see itself in her "regard," which remains captive behind closed eyelids. And the signifier, the potential for metaphor, the "comme" that attempted to constitute the "tu," proves to be a gratuitous, inhibiting god, which justifies the call to destruction toward the end of the poem: "chevaux du quadrige piétinez la savane de ma parole vaste ouverte."

By the last sentence, the spatial options for the subject to move in have been severely reduced—so much so that the other disappears completely: the "tu" is no longer designated in any way. The presence of the subject might conceivably be deduced from "sanglots" but quickly self-effaces, in an ending worthy of Beckett, into "silence" and "nuit." Is there perhaps a hidden Oedipal murder mystery in **"Totem"**?

Is **"Totem"** a figure carved out of the subject's desire to individuate from and identify with the "tu," simultaneously, in language? In the case of this poem, such desire is impotent to effect a unified, total image, either of the "je" or, and consequently, of the "tu." Language, the other available tool, functions as an ambiguous, double-edged sword here, which disarticulates "je" and "tu" even as they strain to constitute themselves. It leaves only features strewn across the page like so many word-corpses after a struggle. And yet this dismemberment forms the "totem," and the poem, a strikingly subjective "totem" to be sure. In this sense, the discourse projects a third element that is external to the "je" and the "tu," Benveniste's "non-personne, il," and whose menacing, paternal presence seems to detract from the resources that should ordinarily be available to the subject. The "totem" has appropriated the poem, and perhaps the subject, too, instead of the subject appropriating the "totem."

Not all of Césaire's poems that attempt to incorporate the intimate other end in the land of hushed defeat of **"Totem,"** however. Different geographies provide a more fertile space in which the subject and the "tu" may insert themselves more successfully. Such is the case of the third poem that we will discuss . . . **"Intimité marine."**[5] In this text, we are far from the paralysis experienced by the subject in **"Totem."** On the contrary, the "marine" of the title is indicative of the flowing movement that characterizes this poem and of the possibilities of reflection and exchange that allow the subject to constitute itself.

Significantly for our purposes, it is the "tu" that is addressed repeatedly in the first part of the poem. She is immediately endowed with the strength to be the grammatical subject of several sentences. Yet she does not speak in the first person: her presence as "tu" implies the "je" of the speaking subject that defines her as such. If we look closely at these definitions, we see that they proceed by negation: "tu n'es pas" rather than "tu es." This form is ambiguous. On the one hand, as a form of litotes, it implies the opposite: "you are not this," in the sense of "you cannot be reduced to merely this because you are actually limitless." On the other hand, it can be read thus: "you are not this—but I cannot say what or who you are." What "tu" is not is either a confining shelter ("toit" and there is an aural pun here, too, "toi" which emphasizes a breaking down of the usual barriers of definition) or a suffocating death ("tombe"), but rather, by inference, a powerful force

bursting out of and transcending limitation, as in the androgynous, container-contained "silo/ventre" image. Neither is the "tu" static, having resolved all conflict ("une paix"). The sharp, alliterative "k" sounds and the interaction of assonances in "courroux," "couteaux," and "coraux" reaffirm the existence of an active, aware presence. A constant sense of potential force seems to hover around the "tu."

It is at this point that the "moi" enters the poem, although not yet as a defined subject pronoun. "Je" does not become the actual subject of the text until the second part of the poem. What is so important here is the "moi" in relation to the "toi." The "tu" is temporarily but lucidly qualified as none other than the projection and externalization of the desire of the "moi": "D'ailleurs en un certain sens, tu n'es pas autre que l'élan sauvage de mon sang" and, even more revealingly, "qu'il m'est donné de voir." It is what the subject sees of itself reflected in the other that gives it the force to constitute itself into a subject. The image coincides with what Fanon calls the muscular dream of the oppressed man in *Les Damnés de la terre.* And it is illuminated by Lacan's discussion of the infant's construction of sense of self by means of his mirror image, in the essay "Le stade du miroir."[6] For Lacan, however, it must be remembered that the resulting sense of self is Imaginary in the etymological sense, that is, based on image, "manque," not "realité," and therefore alienating. Such a reading would account for the threatening presences of "tombe," "funèbre," and "morsure" (read also "mort sure").

In spite of these potential menaces, the self becomes the subject in the second part of the poem with triumphant elation. The transition to this second moment in the text was made, as we have seen, through the mirror—"il m'est donné de voir," now transformed grammatically to "je me vois." In many ways, these two parts of the text are inverted mirror images of each other, reflecting and echoing one another and dependent upon each other for their existence. This relationship bears out Benveniste's reflections concerning the dialectical nature of the "je-tu" couple in language. "Je" could not be metamorphosed into the now active subject, realizing its own powers, had the potential in "tu" to be constructed into a subject not been previously conceded.

In fact, the first expressions that the "je" chooses to describe its newly found self, while appropriately phallic in terms of sexual imagery, are direct phonic quotations of the insistent, aggressive "k" sounds we found repeated in connection with the "tu." This links the "je" and the "tu," but it is also the first and last appearance of the "tu" in the second part of the poem. From here on, the subject breaks away and stands on its own, in a joyous declaration of animal strength. Many of the verbs here are reflexive, the acts self-referential, as in "je me vois," "je m'enroule," "je me déroule," "je me brise." This breaking away seems to render the other unnecessary. While sexually we might say that this represents a regression to an onanistic equivalent—and one cannot help but note the orgasmic rhythm of the sentence "Je frappe, je brise, toute porte je brise et hennissant, absolu, cervelle, justice, enfance je me brise"—on other levels this narcissistic acceptance of self signifies an optimistic assertion of self-discovery and independence. The "je" has found its "vrai cri" and is able to call upon all sorts of sources and resources now available to it, as if magically freed, for the first time. These include not only sheer animal force but categories of thought, morality, personal history: "absolu," "justice," "cervelle," "enfance." The "je" can play with signifiers because they have already been experimented on the "tu." Thus, "je ne tombe pas" derives from "tu n'es pas une tombe," and "je me brise" can be risked because "tu ignores tout silo dont tu n'éclates le ventre."

If the "tu," the intimate other, has been eclipsed, it is because she has fulfilled her function as imaginary alter ego permitting the subject to articulate itself.

As the subject is constituted anew in each poem, so is the couple "je-tu," and we have discussed only three ways out of many in which the relationship can be posed. It must be mentioned, although it should seem obvious, that the attraction of the "je-tu" couple is so powerful for Césaire because the nature of the binding has great metaphorical value as well. Thus, in the title poem of *Ferrements*, for instance, the chains that unite the subject and the intimate other are also linked to those of slavery:

> tiens-moi bien fort aux épaules au reins esclaves . . .
>
> . . . . .
>
> où nous deux dans le flanc de la nuit gluante
>   aujourd'hui
> comme jadis
> esclaves arrimés de coeurs lourds
> tout de même ma chère tout de même nous cinglons
> à peine un peu moins écoeurés aux tangages

In this way, the linguistic enactment of the subject's relationship to the "tu" opens onto the possibility of pointing beyond itself and cannot be read in a static fashion. Even if the "tu," once posed, is transcended, she offers the subject the vital momentary illusion that its utterances have overcome fragmentation, and this permits the subject to continue its poetic explorations.

Notes

[1] Césaire, "Le Cristal automatique," in *Les Armes miraculeuses* (2d ed.; Paris: Editions Gallimard, 1970), p. 39. This poem and others of Césaire's texts that are discussed here and in the remainder of this study are reproduced in the Appendix.

[2] Jacques Lacan, "Au-delà du principe de réalité," quoted in Xavière Gauthier, *Surréalisme et sexualité*, p. 320.

[3] Stendhal, *De l'Amour*.

[4] Césaire, "Totem," *Cadastre*, trans. Emile Snyder and Sanford Upson, bilingual ed. (Paris: Editions du Seuil, 1961), pp. 29-30. See Appendix. See also Catherine Lowe, "Vers une lecture de 'Totem' d'Aimé Césaire." Her study of this text inspired my own, for which I am grateful.

[5] Césaire, "Intimité marine," *Ferrements*, p. 50.

[6] Jacques Lacan, "Le stade du miroir comme formateur de la fonction du Je," in *Rarits I*, pp. 89-97.

Maxine G. Cutler (essay date 1981)

SOURCE: "Aimé Césaire's 'Barbare': Title, Key Word, and Source of the Text," in *Teaching Language Through Literature*, Vol. XXI, No. 1, December, 1981, pp. 3-13.

[*In the following essay, Cutler contends that "a study of the extraordinary power of Césaire's language will serve as a key to the poem's meaning as well as an introduction to the emotionally charged themes of black poets writing in French."*]

Black poetry from Africa and the Caribbean has become the focus of interest in courses ranging from "Black Studies" to studies of Francophone literature in general. Black poets are as varied as the countries from which they come but they all share common concerns with the black man's alienation and suffering. Singing songs of despair and revolt, of nostalgia and hope, they bring new vocabulary and images to the poetic canon and express the complex black experience in frequently unfamiliar forms. Aimé Césaire's **"Barbare"** is typical of many poems of social protest and revolt but the constant motifs of black poetry achieve passionate formulation within the poem. A study of the extraordinary power of Césaire's language will serve as a key to the poem's meaning as well as an introduction to the emotionally charged themes of black poets writing in French.

In **"Barbare,"** an unrhymed free verse poem from the Surrealist work **Soleil cou-coupé**,[1] Césaire unleashes the generative power of the word *Barbare* to create a poetic text *and* re-create man. Césaire's belief in the power of the Word to create reality and in the power of poetry to change life stems from two widely different traditions which fuse in the Sorbonne-educated Martiniquan. On the one hand, the tradition of French poetry since Baudelaire, Mallarmé, and Rimbaud has been to escape from a conventional vision of the world and to create a new and more authentic universe by means of "l'alchimie du verbe." Surrealism, with which Césaire had a brief but important association in the 1940's, carried the mystique of language to the frontiers of the Absolute by attempting to bring forth the *surréel* through automatic writing. André Breton emphasizes the importance of that "opération qui tendait à restituer le langage à sa vraie vie . . . il faut que le nom *germe* pour ainsi dire, sans quoi il est faux." As Breton also recognized, the power of language to name and create has been part of all cultures. "L'esprit qui rend possible, et même concevable, une telle opération n'est autre que celui qui a animé de tout temps la philosophie occulte et selon lequel . . . l'énonciation est à l'origine de tout. . . ."[2] Especially in the magical rites of African religion, Césaire discovered language as invocation and incantation which explains his penchant for nomination:

En nommant les objets, c'est un monde enchanté, un monde de "monstres" que je fais surgir sur la grisaille mal différenciée du monde; un monde de "puissances" que je somme, que j'invoque et que je convoque . . . à interpréter à l'africaine.[3]

While African tradition is less strong in Césaire's poetry than in the poetry of Léopold Senghor whose ancestors never left the continent, African sources nonetheless inform Césaire's rhythms, images, and symbols[4] and the African belief in verbal magic underlies Césaire's concept of poetry as "magie, magie."[5]

For Césaire, founder of *négritude* in 1934 together with Léon Damas and Senghor, the function of poetry is clearly defined. It must sound a call to the black man to assume his blackness and the racial consciousness of *négritude* which is, in the words of Césaire, ". . . conscience d'être noir, simple reconnaissance d'un fait qui implique acceptation, prise en charge de son destin noir, de son histoire et de sa culture."[6] To this end, **"Barbare"** becomes a rallying cry but only when its etymological and historical meanings have been negated and reinterpreted since, in a context of cultural relativism, *barbare* is always a pejorative term denoting the Other. From the Greek âÜñâáñïö meaning "foreign," it signified to Ancient Greeks one living outside the pale of Hellenic civilization, i.e., someone non-hellenic and therefore primitive and brutal. For Romans, the term pertained to one outside the Roman Empire, hence an outsider who was uncivilized and uncultured. For Christians of the Middle Ages, it referred to one outside the pale of Christian civilization, i.e., the Saracen or heathen. As applied depreciatively to foreigners, *barbare* as both substantive and adjective expressed the negative function of the hyphenated prefix of *non*-Hellenic, *non*-Roman and *non*-Christian and articulated the prejudices of the dominant culture against uncivilized, uncultured, and therefore less than human (sub-human) ethnic groups.

Contemporary Western civilization has done no less. In *Race and History* Claude Lévi-Strauss describes the persistent "ethnocentric attitude" of modern man who uses *sauvage* in the same sense as *barbare*:

> Underlying both these epithets is the same sort of attitude. The word "barbarous" is probably connected etymologically with the inarticulate confusion of birdsong, in contra-distinction to the significant sounds of human speech, while "savage"—"of the woods"— also conjures up a brutish way of life as opposed to human civilization. In both cases, there is a refusal to admit the fact of cultural density; instead, anything which does not conform to the standard of society in which the individual lives is denied the name of culture and relegated to the realm of nature.[7]

Although the enlightened eighteenth century heard Rousseau's defense of primitivism and the "noble savage," the dominant belief in progress perpetuated conventional notions about nature. Even when Voltaire, who was hardly a supporter of primitivist theory, used *barbare* in *Alzire ou*

les Américains to describe the Spanish conquerors and not the natives, he reversed only the target of the insult and not the meaning of the word. By attaching the epithet to the Europeans, Voltaire attacked their un-Christian attitude in forcing Christianity upon the New World:

> Les Espagnols sont craints, mais ils sont en horreur:
> Fléaux du nouveau monde, injustes, vains, avares,
> Nous seuls en ces climats nous sommes les barbares.
> *Alzire*, I, 1

Savage, primitive, brutal, and cruel are extended depreciative synonyms of the original cultural definitions of *barbare* and connote the *non*-human *in*human instincts of the barbarian. In the conflict between nature and culture in which nature has been debased by the higher pretensions of culture, Césaire's **"Barbare"** denies the status quo and asserts the power of the Word to restore value to natural forces and revitalize the realm of nature.

Barbare

C'est le mot qui me soutient
    et frappe sur ma carcasse de cuivre jaune
    où la lune dévore dans la soupente de la rouille
    les os barbares
5 des lâches bêtes rôdeuses du mensonge

Barbare
    du langage sommaire
    et nos faces belles comme le vrai pouvoir
operatoire
    de la négation

10 Barbare
    des morts qui circulent dans les veines de la
terre
    et viennent se briser parfois la tête contre les
murs de nos oreilles
    et les cris de révolte jamais entendus
    qui tournent à mesure et à timbres de musique

15 Barbare
    l'article unique
    barbare le tapaya
    barbare l'amphisbène blanche
    barbare moi le serpent cracheur
20 qui de mes putréfiantes chairs me réveille
    soudain gekko volant
    soudain gekko frangé
    et me colle si bien aux lieux mêmes de la force
    qu'il vous faudra pour m'oublier
25 jeter aux chiens la chair velue de vos poitrines

tapaya: a type of tropical lizard.
    amphisbène: a type of blind and limbless lizard
    with indistinguishable head and tail.
    gekko: a type of nocturnal lizard with adhesive
    pads on toes. Some have fringe-like scales.

As a title, **"Barbare"** commands our attention and brings to mind the dictionary definitions and cultural connotations that flow logically from the word. Unquestionably, they are all pejorative but paradoxically, the first line of the poem states the meliorative value of "le mot" and anticipates the conversion of the word's negative meanings into positive ones as the text unfolds. Through the power of its multiple meanings, *Barbare* as title, key word, and organizing element of the poem calls forth images which reflect semantic oppositions that the poem must resolve. In the poetic process *Barbare* is transformed from a term of insult to one of inspiration.

From the first line the poem is clearly focused upon *le mot.* Both syntactic and metrical structures combine to emphasize it in its terminal position in the short monosyllabic independent clause. The peculiarly French turn of phrase *c'est . . . qui*[8] places stress upon *le mot* and its functions (*me soutient/ et frappe*) and sets forth the paradoxical effects of the word that both "supports" and "strikes" the speaker (*me*) who is intimately connected to *mot* by alliteration and symmetrical placement on either side of the relative. By a striking example of what Roman Jakobson has called "Poetry of Grammar," referring to the poetic resources of grammatical tropes,[9] *mot* and speaker are placed in a subject-object relationship with *mot,* the antecedent of *qui,* as protagonist acting upon a *moi* which has been reduced by syntax to an object. The grammatical pattern inverts common usage of animate agent —> transitive verb —> inanimate goal and, by reversing animate and inanimate classes of nouns, endows *mot* with dynamic vitality even as it characterizes the speaker as its passive recipient. This passivity becomes flagrant in the synecdoche of l. 2 which substitutes a lifeless carcass for the live speaker.

Heavily charged with associations of death and decay, *carcasse* injects a note of sordid realism into the poem and at the same time actualizes the "non-human human" connotation of *barbare.* Literally, *carcasse* denotes the skeleton of a dead animal; figuratively, it refers contemptuously to the dead body of a human and by extension describes a lifeless impotent being, devoid of human dignity and unworthy of the human species. Because of its literal and figurative meanings, *carcasse* unites different semantic categories of animation/inanimation and animality/humanity within one signifier and engenders parallel descriptive systems—both with pejorative meanings—of dead animality on a literal level and degraded humanity on a moral level.

Césaire's poem "Barbare" proclaims the primacy of nature and the black man and the absolute power of the incantatory Word to liberate and transform—in the text and in the world.

—*Maxine G. Butler*

However, because of the genitive link (*de*) with *cuivre jaune, carcasse* does not function independently. It is part of a compound expression which transforms the realistic *carcasse* into a metaphor recalling similar clichés of language and literature in which semantic oppositions are united oxymoronically:[10] *coeur de bronze* (popular), *coeur d'airain* (Racine, *Esther*), *corde d'airain* (Hugo, *Feuilles d'automne* xl). Fragility (*coeur, corde*) and hardness (*bronze, airain*) are linked inseparably in tropes which have long since lost their shock value and the semantic value of their component parts. *Coeur de bronze* and *coeur d'airain* have lost their concreteness to metaphors for cruelty. *Corde d'airain* which Hugo promised to add to his lyre is a metaphor for the virile-sounding poetry of political engagement. The lexical substitution of *carcasse,* a pejorative metonym of *coeur,* and *cuivre jaune* within the same syntactic structure recalls the worn-out stereotypes through repetition of the initial phoneme [k] to the point of cacophony, but concrete language transforms the cliché into a new effective image. *Cuivre jaune* transmits its vibrant (*corde d'airain*) strength (*coeur de bronze, d'airain*) to the inert carcass and initiates the conversion of negative into positive values within the poem. *Carcasse de cuivre jaune* is a verbal paradox which exemplifies the paradox of *le mot* that both "uplifts" and "beats down" (l. 1). The oxymoron unifies negative values implicit in *carcasse* with positive meanings associated with *cuivre jaune,* a valuable metal in the paradigm of metals. By replacing the poetic *airain* or the prosaic *bronze, cuivre jaune* introduces a new alloy into a stereotyped expression but novelty or realism would be equally satisfied by *laiton,* the common word for brass. *Cuivre jaune* has the advantage over *laiton* of not only alliteration but more importantly, its use as a generic term (*cuivre*) for a brass instrument. As a synecdoche for orchestral brass, *cuivre jaune* transforms *carcasse* into a musical instrument. Like Victor Hugo's *corde d'airain,* Césaire's *carcasse de cuivre jaune* will resonate forcefully, producing sounds and images under the pressure of the word that is now an active force. Even its phonetic shape with three *c*'s, a sibilant, and at least two pronounced mute *e*'s (*carcasse de cuivre jaune*) gives aural prominence to the image. Overdetermined by intertextual associations and formal stylistic devices, the image tends toward symbolic interpretation and becomes an emblem of the poet.

In the first stanza *carcasse de cuivre jaune* generates only negative markers. Gleaming brass is countered by rust—the rust of a garret (*soupente*) beneath a tin roof which recalls the dilapidated native shacks of the Caribbean. Physical decay prevails (*la lune dévore . . . les os*). Against the lunar landscape of l. 3 which functions as a metaphor for spiritual death in Césaire's solar universe, beneath a devouring moon instead of life-giving sun, *barbares* makes its first appearance within the text of the poem. A plural descriptive adjective linked to lifeless, dry, skeletal remains (*os carcasse*) and linked by alliteration to *bêtes* whose transferred epithet it is in fact (*les os . . . des bêtes [barbares]*), *barbares* is subsumed into the long grammatically complex sentence which carries over the entire first stanza. Together with *lâches* which precedes *bêtes* for emphasis, *barbares* brings a moral dimension to *bêtes* and activates its figurative meaning. Like *carcasse, bêtes* (beasts/beast-like humans) unites different semantic categories of animality/humanity and repeats the non-human connotations of the title. Moral decadence becomes the equivalent of death and physical decay in the final word of the stanza. *Mensonge* sums up the immoral "hypocrisie collective," the "mensonge principal à partir duquel prolifèrent tous les autres" that Césaire condemned in his *Discours sur le Colonialisme.*[11] By alliteration with *mot* and *me, mensonge* clearly stands in an antithetical relationship to both the purity of the word and the integrity of the *moi.* In its prominent position at the end of the sentence and stanza, *mensonge* completes the chain of negative meanings and associations which connote the rotten beast-like, dehumanized state of the black man in colonial "civilization."[12]

In reply to *mensonge, Barbare* resounds like a trumpet call to arms at the beginning of stanza 2, filling out the short first line with its two syllables, one echoing the other and contrasting with the polysyllabic lines of stanza 1. Metrically and syntactically independent and capitalized as in the title, the title word becomes an energizing force within the poem and dominates the three remaining stanzas through anaphora. As in the first stanza, *le mot* focuses upon itself, calling forth *du langage sommaire* which cuts through the obfuscations of complex grammatical structure to declare *le vrai pouvoir opératoire/de la négation.* By a systematic negation of the language, syntax, and rhythms of stanza 1, *Barbare* reverses its own negative connotations. *Du langage sommaire* is one of two paratactic nominal phrases in the shortest stanza of the poem. The syntactic and metrical changes signal semantic change with *Barbare* now linked to *belles* by alliteration, thus reversing its shameful alliance with *bêtes.* Through summary language, the vehicle of true communication, the solitary lifeless *moi* becomes solidary with the community of *nous: ma carcasse > nos faces.* Together they oppose the paralyzing *mensonge* of stanza 1 with a new and original image of physical beauty that is allied to truth (*vrai*) and resembles the abstract power of negation. The unconventional simile, *comme le vrai pouvoir opératoire/ de la négation,* has been segmented for emphasis, producing an effect similar to enjambment by giving prominence to the phrase in l. 9. The first part of the simile is remarkable for its phonetic patterning. *Comme le vrai pouvoir opératoire* reinforces its verbal power through alliteration ([v] [r] [p]), assonance ([. . .] [wa]), and internal rhyme (*pouvoir/ opératoire*) which repeat vocalic and consonantal features of the stanza as well as the phonetic shape of the key word. Related phonemes prolong the sounds of *Barbare* into the stanza: [b>p] and [ar>Ér>er>war] producing som*m*aire, *b*elles, *p*ouv*o*ir o*p*é*ra*toire. The strong phonetic patterning of l. 8 and approximate end-rhymes of ll. 6, 7, and 8—the only example of sustained rhyming in the poem—set off the contrasting non-rhyming *négation* in l. 9 and underline, together with meter and syntax, the importance of negation to black revolt. By negating the truth and value of the dominant white culture, the black man denies both his master and the master-slave relationship that has reduced him to a "bestial being."[13] Underlying the racial consciousness of *négritude* is the defiant refusal of the white man's world. On a symbolic level, it is the negation of illegitimate power by the true power of the Word.

The Word blares forth at the beginning of stanza 3 and sustains the high rhetorical tone which marks Césaire's verse. Like the trumpet on the Day of Judgment, *Barbare* resounds and summons the dead to stand together with the living in the struggle against oppression. Called up by the Word, the dead become animated through active verbs of motion (*circulent, viennent se briser*) and through regular rhythmic patterns which are icons of movement. Three of the stanza's six lines are approximate alexandrines with prescribed stresses and almost parallel hemistichs which contrast with the irregular verse lines of the poem and especially with l. 12.[14]

> 11 des morts qui circulent // dans les veines de la terre 5 // 7

> 13 et les cris de révolte // jamais entendus 6 // 5

> 14 qui tournent à mesure // et à timbres de musique 6 // 7

The even metrical pattern and musical vocabulary of ll. 13 and 14 beat out steady rhythms of revolt but movement is blocked (*viennent* is counteracted by *se briser*) or circular. *Circulent* and *tournent* evoke the endless rounds of past generations of rebels and their frustration in making themselves heard: *les cris de révolte* jamais *entendus.* Literally their cries fall upon deaf ears. Césaire renews the well-established cliché of frustration, *la tête contre les murs,*[15] by adding a physical precision—*de nos oreilles*—to the worn-out image making it literal once again. *De nos oreilles* restores vigor to the metaphor at the same time that it adds another concrete notation to a text that includes *ma carcasse* and *nos faces.* The renewed cliché is emphasized by meter in the distended twelfth line of at least seventeen syllables. Clashing rhythmically with the well-proportioned, almost classical alexandrines of the stanza, line 12 underlines the anguish and frustration of past generations that must be remembered and redressed. Césaire brings the powerful memory of humiliated slaves to the present struggle and gains strength from identity with all blacks, past and present, in the cause of freedom.

The incantatory power of *Barbare* increases in the last stanza with four repetitions in five lines. While the first two lines repeat the metrical pattern of stanzas 2 and 3 with *Barbare* isolated on the first line from the conjured nouns, lines 17-19 conjoin epithet and noun and impose a metrical pattern of ascending rhythm through syllable gradation: l. 15, 2 syllables; l. 16, 4 syllables; l. 17, 6 syllables; l. 18, 7 syllables; l. 19, 8 syllables. The expanding rhythms and insistent, frequent repetitions of *Barbare* create a tone of urgency as one exotic animal after another is called into being through the magic of incantation. Grammatical parallelism, which underlies the litanical structure of invocation, draws all conjured nouns into a semantic relationship.[16] *L'article unique* signals a return to the singular number of stanza 1 but stands in contrast with that stanza's negative imagery. Singularity is not just a grammatical category: it is a logical notion of individuality as well as a value judgment. Unusual, extraordinary, superior, *l'article unique* stands in positional equivalence with *le tapaya, l'amphisbène blanche* and *moi le serpent cracheur* and confers its positive connotations upon the exotic fauna of the Antilles. But exoticism for its own sake holds no interest for Césaire:

> . . . disons que si je *nomme* avec précision (ce qui fait parler de mon *exotisme*), c'est qu'en nommant avec précision, je crois que l'on restitue à l'objet sa valeur personnelle (comme quand on appelle quelqu'un par son nom); on le suscite dans sa valeur unique et singulière; on salue sa valeur de force, sa *valeur-force.*

> . . . En les nommant, flore, faune, dans leur étrangeté, je participe à leur force; je participe de leur force.[17]

Summoning, invoking, convoking *à l'africaine,* the poet (*moi*) participates in the animal force that *re*vitalizes, *re*stores, and *re*news. Wedged in between the incantatory Word and *le serpent cracheur, moi* is transformed by apposition into the serpent that Césaire has made his personal emblem in his poetry.[18] As the only dangerous animal in Martinique, the serpent represents the poet's aggression; by its molting, it embodies the process of renewal so vital to the defeated black man of stanza 1. Signifying resurrection, the serpent and its reptilian variants—*le tapaya* and *l'amphisbène*—become symbols of the *moi* and vehicles of black revolt. Invoked by repeated calls of *Barbare,* reptiles, which are universal archetypes of pure energy, dominate stanza 4 and assert the primacy of the elemental primitive forces of nature.

Césaire's characteristic nominal style is replaced by a long relative clause (ll. 20-25) which develops the *moi-serpent* metaphor and, gathering momentum, culminates in a final explosion of aggression. The inversion of *de mes putréfiantes chairs* and the unusual position of the polysyllabic *putréfiantes* before its noun emphasize allusions to rotting and decay in stanza 1 as well as the symbolic meaning of *putréfiantes.* Here, however, the accent is on *me réveille* which has acquired special relief at the end of the verse line and out of the nuclear subject-verb order. Indeed, the self's awakening as a primitive aggressive force is aptly symbolized by the molting process of the serpent shedding its skin to renew its vitality. The tenor of the metaphor (*moi*) awakens to the aggressivity, strength, and danger of yet another frightening reptile—the gecko. Its sudden metamorphosis in two short parallel disyllabic lines (22, 23) underlines the changing frightening features of the gecko—*volant, frangé*—which prepare the brutal assault of the last three lines. For the first time *moi>serpent>gekko* confronts *vous* directly, and only when they are locked together (*me colle*) in mortal combat. An unexpectedly vague periphrasis (*aux lieux mêmes de la force*) instead of Césaire's usual precision suggests the totality of the attack. Incantation turns to prognostication as the future imperative announces a threat that is both an attack on the Other as well as an assault on the dominant culture. For in the last line of the poem Césaire has couched his declaration in the popular form of cliché, but a cliché

that he violates for his own subversive purposes. By modifying an established linguistic syntagm, Césaire symbolically rejects both the language and the society that produced it.[19] In its original form, *c'est bon à jeter aux chiens* is a figurative expression of condescension and contempt which would describe the scornful attitudes of the white ruling class toward blacks. In the context of this poem, its literal meaning would be activated by *carcasse,* a decaying worthless body and an appropriate antecedent of *ce (c'est).* The cliché would then describe only too well the abuse of the black race at the hands of whites who literally and figuratively throw rotten flesh (*carcasse*/black man) to the dogs. Since *chien* in Césaire's lexicon almost always refers to the watchdog (*chien de garde, molosse*) of the white overseer[20] and thus is a metonym of the slave driver, *chiens* would reinforce the symbolic meaning of the expression. But, by using negation as a means to power as he promised in stanza 2, Césaire reverses the meaning of the cliché by substituting a different object for the verb *jeter.* Prominently placed after both verb and indirect object, *la chair velue de vos poitrines* has the shock value of a brutal visual image which forces a literal interpretation of the renewed expression. Repeated *v*'s underline *vous* as the target of a "barbaric" act, but one that is self-inflicted. *Vous,* the oppressors, will destroy yourselves in the struggle—skinned men are dead men—but the gecko, a metaphor of the resurrected black man, will triumph. The cliché has been negated to signify its opposite. Articulated in strongly marked rhythms of the romantic trimeter (*jeter aux chiens // la chair velue // de vos poitrines*), the last line exploits resources of meter and sound to achieve effective poetic closure.[21]

Negation is fundamental to Césaire's racial aesthetic as it is inseparable from *négritude.* In his well-known preface, *Orphée noir,* Sartre points to negativity as the distinctive feature of black poetry:

> Destructions, autodafé du langage, symbolisme magique, ambivalence des concepts, toute la poésie moderne est là, sous son aspect négatif. Mais il ne s'agit pas d'un jeu gratuit. La situation du noir, sa "déchirure" originelle, l'*aliénation* qu'une pensée étrangère lui impose sous le nom d'assimilation, le mettent dans l'obligation de reconquérir son unité existentielle de nègre. . . . Il s'agit donc pour le noir de mourir à la culture blanche pour renaître à l'âme noire. . . . [22]

By negation of traditional cultural definitions, *Barbare* reverberates across the stanzas and operates its magic transformations. Emerging from syntactic ties with dead animality in stanza 1, *Barbare* exercises its vocative function at the head of each stanza, calling forth the powerful forces of nature to restore inert, impotent forms to life. Like a bugle (*cuivre*) blowing reveille,[23] *Barbare* awakens dying men to rebirth and revolt. The degrading identification of blacks and beasts is the very basis of the resurrection. In the final reversal of the poem, *Barbare*'s non-human inhuman connotations become positive attributes as ferocious beasts become metaphors of the poet. Drawing vital energies from the animal kingdom, *moi serpent>gekko* embodies elemental primitive power that assures the triumph of natural forces. In the conflict between nature and culture, the dominant white culture is defeated through subversion of its values: its truth is declared *mensonge* and *Barbare* connotes the highest praise. Césaire's poem **"Barbare"** proclaims the primacy of nature and the black man and the absolute power of the incantatory Word to liberate and transform—in the text and in the world.

Notes

[1] (Paris: K éditeur, 1948). Césaire has taken as his title Apollinaire's striking image of spiritual death in the last line of "Zone" (*Alcools*, 1913). For Césaire the image effectively evokes the tragedy of the black race, its enslavement and alienation.

[2] *Du Surréalisme en ses oeuvres vives* (1953) in *Manifestes du Surréalisme* (Paris: Gallimard, 1973), pp. 181-2.

[3] Lettre à Lilyan Kesteloot in Lilyan Kesteloot, *Aimé Césaire* (Paris: Editions Seghers, 1962), p. 198.

[4] Janheinz Jahn, "Sur la littérature africaine," *Présence Africaine*, 48 (1963), pp. 151-162.

[5] Lettre, p. 199.

[6] Quoted in L. Kesteloot, *Les Ecrivains noirs de langue française: naissance d'une littérature* (Bruxelles: Université libre de Bruxelles, 1963), pp. 114-5.

[7] (Paris: Unesco, 1961), p. 11.

[8] Maurice Grevisse, *Le Bon Usage*, 7ᶜ éd. (Gembloux: Editions J. Duculot, 1961), pp. 162, 446-7.

[9] "Poetry of Grammar and Grammar of Poetry," *Lingua*, 21 (1968), pp. 597-609.

[10] The important role of the cliché in literature has been analyzed as a form of intertextuality (Julia Kristeva, *Sèméiotikè: Recherches pour une sémanalyse* [Paris: Seuil, 1969], p. 255), as a mark of literariness (Michael Riffaterre, "Fonction du cliché dans la prose littéraire," *Essais de stylistique structurale* [Paris: Flammarion, 1971], p. 173), and as a sign of poeticity (M. Riffaterre, *Semiotics of Poetry* [Bloomington and London: Indiana University Press, 1978], pp. 31-42). In particular, "Fonction du cliché" examines the formal structure of the cliché, its potential for renewal, and its expressive function in literature. See also Laurent Jenny, "Structure et fonctions du cliché," *Poétique* 12 (1972), pp. 495-517.

[11] 3ᶜ éd. (Paris: Présence Africaine, 1955), p. 8.

[12] Césaire, *Discours:* "Et je dis que de la *colonisation* à la *civilisation*, la distance est infinie; que de toutes les expéditions coloniales accumulées, de tous les statuts coloniaux élaborés, de toutes les circulaires ministérielles expédiées, on ne saurait réussir une seule valeur humaine" (p. 10).

[13] Alexandre Kojève, *Introduction to the Reading of Hegel*, ed. Allan Bloom, trans. James H. Nichols, Jr. (New York: Basic Books, 1969), p.

[16] In his first chapter, "In Place of an Introduction," Kojève explicates Hegel's analysis of the master-slave relationship which is at the center of human History. Hegel distinguishes two opposed concrete-forms of Consciousness: "autonomous Consciousness for which the essential-reality is Being-for-itself [*Wesen*]. The other is dependent Consciousness for which the essential-reality is animal-life, i.e., given-being for an other-entity [*sein*]. The former is the *Master*, the latter—the Slave" (id.).

[14] Since contemporary free verse disregards traditional rules of meter as well as rhyme, metrical analysis of modern French poetry is always a problem because of the problematical value of the mute *e*. Meter, which is determined by the number of syllables in a line, will vary depending upon whether the mute *e* is counted as a syllable as in traditional verse (except, of course, before a vowel and at the end of a line) or is omitted as in the rhythms of conversational discourse. For the purpose of my analysis, I am omitting the mute *e* at the caesura so that the hemistich may end on a strong accent as in traditional versification.

[15] The use of this cliché in poetry brings to mind Paul Eluard's "La Tête contre les murs," *Les Yeux fertiles* (1936) where frustration is expressed through uncharacteristic images of revolt and violence. The capital role of the cliché in Surrealism is a function of automatic writing and has its most complete expression in Eluard's *152 Proverbes mis au goût du jour* written in collaboration with Benjamin Péret. Césaire may be using the "telescoping" techniques of automatic writing which fuse two or more expressions into one. Here the cliché of frustration appears to fuse with the wartime admonition of silence: "les murs ont des oreilles," thereby producing a new linguistic form.

[16] Jakobson, "Poetry of Grammar": ". . . in poetry similarity is superimposed on contiguity, and hence 'equivalence is promoted to the constitutive device of the sequence.' Hence any noticeable reiteration of the same grammatical concept becomes an effective poetic device" (p. 602).

[17] Lettre, pp. 197-8.

[18] Kesteloot, *Aimé Césaire*, p. 46.

[19] Pierre Parlebas, "Le Synthème dans les *Paroles* de Prévert," *Poétique*, 28 (1976), pp. 496-510, relates Prévert's linguistic transgressions to social protest. Using the term *synthème* coined by André Martinet to distinguish a collocation of *mots figés* from a collocation of *mots libres* (*syntagme*), Parlebas concludes: "Indiscutablement, les défigements et surfigements des synthèmes visent à contester les hiérarchies établis dans la société" (p. 510).

[20] Kesteloot, *Aimé Césaire*, p. 38.

[21] For a comprehensive analysis of the techniques of closure, see Barbara Herrnstein Smith, *Poetic Closure: A Study of How Poems End* (Chicago: University of Chicago Press, 1968).

[22] Léopold Sédar Senghor, éd., *Anthologie de la nouvelle poésie nègre et malgache de langue française* (Paris: Presses universitaires de France, 1969), p. xxiii.

[23] The *cuivre > clairon* progression may well have its intertext in Rimbaud's famous "Lettre du Voyant" (à Paul Demeny): "Si le cuivre s'éveille clairon . . . ," *Oeuvres complètes*, éd. Rolland de Renéville et Jules Mouquet, Bibliothèque de la Pléiade (Paris: Gallimard, 1954), p.

270. Césaire shares Rimbaud's view of the poet as the instrument of occult powers: "Alors *quid* de la poésie? Il faut toujours y revenir: surgie du vide intérieur, comme un volcan qui émerge du chaos primitif. C'est notre lieu de force; la situation éminente d'où l'on somme; magie; magie" (Lettre, p. 199).

Janis L. Pallister (essay date 1991)

SOURCE: "The Poetry Collections," in *Aimé Césaire*, Twayne Publishers, 1991, pp. 29-41.

[*In the following essay, Pallister offers a thematic and stylistic analysis of Césaire's verse.*]

Les Armes miraculeuses

In 1944 Aimé Césaire published another collection of poetry, *Les Armes miraculeuses*, comprised of poems even more hermetic and more revolutionary than *Cahier d'un retour au pays natal*. Bertrand Visage asserts that with this collection Césaire's poetry becomes more complex, the poet now having found in surrealism—and in his friendship with André Breton—a stimulus to take more risks in associating of images.[1] These images, Visage claims, are more hazardous, but they are always sustained by the obsession of the tom-tom, the taste for rhythm, the mixture of verse and prose. The collection is marked, too, he says, by semantic ambiguity.[2]

The collection's very title showed that the "new negritude" had taken up its arms, its weapons, and that the struggle had at that point assumed a new tone of aggression and resistance. This recueil included the dramatic poem *Et les chiens se taisaient*, which Eshleman refers to as the coda of the collection. Like the recueils of the French Renaissance, this one contains interrelated poems and must therefore be taken as a whole. The titular poem is, incidentally, carefully examined from a structural point of view by John Erickson, who claims that it "valorizes the power of the word, or, more precisely, the revolutionary power of the poetic discourse."[3]

Person and persona are again problematic, as in *Cahier d'un retour au pays natal*, perhaps even more so. The author, the agent, seems absent. Who is speaking and in the name of whom? The themes of the island "prison," of the ills and oppression of colonialization, against which is pitted the theme of rebellion—coming in many forms, or having many weapons—again surface. These themes, expressed through surrealist (or, as some prefer, magic realist) and automatist techniques, include allusions to the German occupation of French territories as a type of any colonial "occupation," and they present the idea that poetry is the principal miraculous weapon. Poetry is "enlisted" in the negritude "cause" like a shield or coat of arms, sometimes impenetrable, but also like a spear or any weapon able to pierce colonialism and racism, the arch enemies. Moreover, the volume traces the mythic and heroic journey of the poet-narrator-warrior in his battle against the "elements."

As a meditation on poetry, this convulsive and militant collection opens with a warning, **"Avis de tirs"** ("Warning: shots will be fired" or "Warning: heavy artillery is to be shot off in the vicinity"). These shots, directed at many of the same ills targeted in the *Cahier*, truly delineate the tensions of the postwar era, with its occupations, power struggles, and disregard for the conditions of the down-and-out. The work also entails veiled references to the tensions inherent in the writing process. One of the most remarkable poems in the collection from this point of view is **"Batouque,"** which uses the Luso-Brazilian name for black dances of Brazil as something of a "call to arms." Césaire repeats this word 30 times or more to establish a sort of rhythmical *mise en relief* that structures the poem and epitomizes the oppression suffered by the colonized Martiniquais. But that is not all, for as Aliko Songolo shows, the act of dancing this dance defies the established social order, and thus the word, and the dance, represent rebellion.[4] **"Batouque"** has been the object of many studies and commentaries: Songolo, of course, gives it ample space, but it is also examined by A. James Arnold and Bernadette Cailler[5] and is the object of a comparison with Gaston Miron in an important article by Eloise Brière.[6] (Césaire returns to the Batuque [as he then spells it] in **"Le verbe marronner, . . . à René Depestre,"** from the 1976 collection *Noria*.)

Gregson Davis has aptly said that *Les Armes miraculeuses* "refract[s] the harsh realities of life in a colonial outpost under the shadow of the Vichy government." But the collection is also obscure and hermetic, perhaps because there is an unresolved tension between its themes and the metaphoric-associative approaches used to express these themes. Clayton Eshleman and Annette Smith liken *Les Armes miraculeuses* to a "trampoline that resists penetration at the same time it affords an exhilarating 'ride'." Despite this obscurity, however, a couple of the poems are accessible. **"Perdition,"** like several poems in the collection, offers a prophesy, while the title poem **"Les Armes miraculeuses"** speaks to the ancestral cultural load that is to be recovered: the birds, says the speaker, will sing the Congolese lullaby that the "soudards" (ugly white colonial soldiers) have made him "unlearn." The poem asserts, then, the rich human activity that lies buried in prehistory and that must be taken into account.

"Le Grand Midi" (**"High Noon"**) is easily the collection's most stunning poem. Césaire uses the *pirogue* motif of *Cahier d'un retour* and intertextually echoes Rimbaud, carefully rescribing the Frenchman's verse for his own purposes. Describing a feeling of incapacity and hesitation followed by decision and resolve, this poem is also a prereading of *Et les chiens se taisaient*. It seems to be Le Rebelle of *Et les chiens* who is saying out of a victimized agony:

> Qui fêle ma joie? Qui soupire verse le jour?
> Qui conspire sur la tour?
> Mon sang miaule
> des cloches tintent dans mes genoux . . .

> (Who cracks my joy? Who sighs toward light?
> Who conspires on the tower?

My blood howls like a cat
and bells clang in my knees . . .)[7]

But the persona of his poem (described as "Fragments")
resolves not to wait. (Why wait?) Instead, in the closing
movements he cries out, like the poet of *Cahier d'un
retour,* "Arrière! je suis debout." It is time to act! Therefore, he says, "Je marcherai . . . je pars je pars . . . j'avance
plus sûr et plus secret et plus terrible que l'étoile pourris-
sante" ("I shall march . . . I am on my way; I am on my
way . . . I advance, more certain, more secret and more
terrible than the rotting star"). **"Le Grand Midi"** can well
be regarded as a bridge poem between *Cahier d'un retour* and *Et les chiens se taisaient.*

Soleil cou coupé

In 1948 Césaire published *Soleil cou coupé,* a title with
an obvious debt to Apollinaire. Eric Sellin suggests that
the image in this collection evokes the rising sun that has
been cut off from the horizon.[8] Thomas Hale goes on to
note that the images of the sun used here also flow from
those in Rimbaud as well as in Paul Claudel, especially in
his *Tête d'or* (Hale 1978, 13-16). Hale points out that it
is not just the images but their impact on the universe that
is at play here, for the imagery conveys the idea of seasonal cycles, of weather modifications, of the sun's metaphorical power as judge of mankind. Indeed, he contends, the sun is virtually deified; this solar god is associated with the poet's desire to return to his origins. Equally
interesting is that in this collection, as Hale points out, the
poet's earlier surrealist inclinations are somewhat less
marked: the poems are less hermetic and more optimistic.
(Can this optimism be linked to the political successes
that Césaire was then experiencing, in which departmen-
talization was realized and seemed—at least momentarily—to promise a better standard of life for the Caribbean
Francophone islands? Hale seems to think so.)

Soleil cou coupé originally contained the poem **"A
l'Afrique" ("To Africa"),** which might point to the direction Césaire's poetry was to take. This poem first appeared (with one stanza that was ultimately suppressed) in
1946 in the journal *Poésie 46*; it reappeared with slight
revisions in the 1971 revised edition of *Les Armes miraculeuses* as **"Prophesy,"** a poem "in which a contemplative speaker bears witness to a surreal transformation of
his Caribbean seascape" (Arnold). The poem was again
reprinted in *Cadastre,* with some "crude and vulgar blasphemy" omitted. The important thing to collect from all
this is that the revised texts of **"A l'Afrique"** demonstrate
the extent to which Césaire ultimately abandoned a mythic
model of human experience—an Africa of the heart. His
revisions carefully restore to history what once had been
mere myth. But leaving aside the question of infinite revisions, which make the particular edition one selects of
prime importance, the message of *Soleil cou coupé* is one
of self-sacrifice and mutilation, themes well-illustrated in
"Lynch I."

In **"Le Coup de couteau du soleil dans le dos des villes
surprises"** we again have prophesy, preceded by three

visions that, as Arnold shows, have passages from Revelation and Saint Matthew as important intertexts. Arnold's
analysis is flawed, however, by his comparing translations
of Césaire's text to those of the King James version of the
New Testament. A comparison of Césaire's original language with passages from the Catholic version of the
Apocalypse in French would be more valid and every bit
as revealing. Regardless, the reader is referred to this
section in Arnold for a thorough study of the structure and
meaning of this central poem, which may well be an index
to Césaire's religious perspectives. Rejecting the God of
the Christians, he shifts to a modernist version of the Earth
Mother, the alchemical-surrealist woman, Omphale, a
chthonic goddess or nocturnal giant, an archaic female
divinity of the underworld. Into this are woven allusions
to Vever, the mandala of voodoo, which is the very definition of religious syncretism. But as one may gather by
a syncretic summation of various critical viewpoints (Arnold, Cailler, et al.) and from the text itself, the poem
conveys the idea that the black heart of negritude replaces
Christ, that Nommo replaces Logos, and that the sun as a
natural force subverts the role of God as a supernatural
agency in the life of man. This is an anti-Catholic poem,
vividly illustrating the effect of personal creativity as it
confronts the monoliths of colonial society, namely the
Catholic church. Similar replacements occur in **"Lynch
I,"** where the lynched man replaces the crucified Christ.

Like *Cahier d'un retour* and especially *Les Armes miraculeuses, Soleil cou coupé* is the record of a spiritual journey, enlisting more intensely than the other two the support of African animism and a fully articulated system of
metaphors, including the Cesairean "bestiary" often discussed by scholars. Like the other two the collection is an
assertion of the primacy of poetry as the principal logos,
as the sun that purifies as it undergoes transformation and
transforms. The power of the word is evident in the tremendous language play apparent in the collection's title,
Soleil cou coupé, and in the play of words in **"Le Coup
de couteau."** By the interplay of these two titles we see
that the sun is both a passive and an active force. These
plays on language are hardly new to Césaire; a good example from *Les Armes miraculeuses* is found in **"Jour et
nuit,"** with the marvelous play of the words *terre* and *ver(s):*
"de terre de ver cherchent parmi terre et vers."

Corps perdu

The title poem of *Corps perdu* (1949) is not without its
references to the surrealist view of life and the human
body as fragmented. Yet despite this scattering, the umbi-
licus—a central and unifying agent—is quite present here,
as it is in much African art. The idea of possible unification through centrality and natural phenomena is not new
to Césaire: in **"Le Coup de couteau"** the primal woman
is called, among other things, Omphale. Janheitz Jahn finds
"Corps perdu" concerned with and expressive of the Ntu
philosophy, which involves the total relationship of all
things and beings.

Corps perdu refers not only to the scattered and mutilated
race but also and more specifically to the poet's body—

Osiris-like, orphic. And within this cluster of symbols we must include too the concept of the tragic, sacrificial poet who labors, Hercules-like, as a representative of the people, the collectivity. (So here we would recall that Omphale was also the name of the mistress who purchased Hercules as a slave; but, while present in the original version, this European resonance is excluded in *Cadastre*.) *Corps perdu* evokes the scattering of the race, the diaspora. Thus the island as a place of alienation and isolation recurs, but the island is also the place of restoration. The phoenix symbol seen in Césaire's previous work recurs in this collection—and not without bearing on the restoration motif—specifically in **"Dit d'errance" ("Song of Wandering")**.

As he had done in *Soleil cou coupé*, Césaire constructs more open poetry in *Corps perdu*, but he also begins to question the concept of Africa as Paradise Lost, especially in **"Dit d'errance,"** in which the poet says he is bringing low the trees of paradise. Césaire adopts the image of the volcano, which, as Hale points out, will become a major metaphor in his poetry. Yet we should also note the important poem **"Ton portrait,"**[9] which is reminiscent of Langston Hughes and which vividly announces Christophe's apostrophe to the river in *La Tragédie du roi Christophe*. No metaphor is more characteristic of Césaire, except perhaps the escaped slave pursued by dogs, an image we encountered in the *Cahier* and will again in *Et les chiens se taisaient*.

The most famous poem of *Corps perdu* is probably the first, **"Mot,"** often reprinted and commented on. Its power and violence are uncommon, even for Césaire. In some respects it is the Césaire poem most reminiscent of the slight style adopted by Damas, although the tone is certainly Césaire's. The "word" of the poem is *nègre* or *Negro*, which has a wide field of meanings that include hatred, pain, suffering, hangings. This word, like a spasm or hiccup, vibrates in the gullet, especially when pronounced in French. It is like the claw of the tiger, the shattering sound of bullets, or the tearing of taffeta. The lynchings and the poisoned arrows endured by the black ironically recall the Christian martyrdom of Saint Sebastian. But dualism is present here. If the word sounds ugly and stinging when lashed out by a white, it nonetheless is like a "roll of thunder in the summer" that comes from the liberties the blacks are now taking as their own, and as a matter of course. *Nigger* becomes *black*: both meanings are contained in the French word. The word *nègre* or *nigger* is like an exfoliating stigma, and, as Davis puts it, the manner in which Césaire turns the negative word back on the user, making of it a sonorous challenge, reminds us of **"Barbare"** from *Soleil cou coupé*. The word *nègre* additionally functions to pinpoint the poet's relationship to words as they are read and spoken—verbal icons, to use an oxymoron. Within the context of this poem, which Arnold compares to passages of Valéry's *Cimetière marin*, Césaire reiterates the theme of the poet-priest who must submit to the "vibrating arrow" and become the scapegoat of the community.

In his conclusion to a discussion of this collection, Arnold finds that *Corps perdu* as a title "has a profoundly ambig-

uous resonance." And although Arnold finds many possible meanings for the expression, including the notion that the body must be lost in order to be reborn (as was certainly true in the myth of the phoenix—a privileged metaphor for Césaire, according to Kesteloot and Kotchy), he never once appears to relate the concept of the lost body to the myth of Orpheus, surely as pertinent as the Egyptian tale of Osiris, whose tragic fate Arnold recalls in his minute and statistical analysis. (It was clear, of course, in the original edition, that the "elle" in the **"Dit d'errance"** referred to Isis; it is therefore only by analogy that one should incorporate the story of Orpheus into the references to Osiris. The story of Orpheus is the story of Césaire.)

Ferrements

The year 1960 saw the publication of *Ferrements*, whose central image replaces the concept of armor as an iron or steel coat with that of the iron chains of slavery. The collection focuses on the future (*devenir*) rather than the present (*être*), however, and it again introduces the theme of the renaissance of the black race, symbolized by the phoenix. This collection communicates a message of hope to the oppressed through such metaphors of fertility as pollen and ripe fruit. The poems function in terms of antithetical or dialectical configurations, such as doubt versus certainty, servitude versus freedom, anguish versus hope. As with many of Césaire's works, this collection contains such classical allusions as the Promethean myth (in **"Ferment"**), which shows how the poet challenges the Sun, seen as an eagle devouring his liver. Perseus is invoked in **"Me centuplant Persée"**: playing on the words *perce, transperce,* and *Persée*, the poet shows how perseverance and *attente*—important "arms" of the negritude program—ripen him for battle; the poet, like a tree, shows the rings of the years that have recorded all the "volcanoes."

The tree image, which becomes a full-blown metaphor in Césaire's plays, recurs here, as do the vampires or cannibals of the *Cahier*[10] and the dog imagery of the *Cahier* and *Et les chiens se taisaient*. The primary tropes of the collection, however, are the roll of the seasons and the sense of *attente* and preparation.

Time is an essential subject of *Ferrements*. Whereas in *Cahier d'un retour* we may have felt time as a pressure—the poet and his people being in a hurry for change, for revolution—here time, conditioned by sun and moon, is viewed (especially in **"Comptine"**) as a molding process, in which that *lente patience* which is an attribute of negritude brings the race to a sufficient state of ferocity. **"Hors des jours étrangers"** exhorts the race to come into its own, to evolve its "own head," to cease to be the toy at other men's carnivals, the scarecrow in their fields. The speaker encourages the people to overthrow their oppressors and disenfranchisers through their tears and their rage, which will be like a salubrious storm. Ronnie Scharfman studies the spatio-temporal problems of this poem at length and appears to see it as a fitting example of Césaire's *poésie engagée*. "The whole ambition of this text," she writes, "aims at liberation through reversing the existing alienated order." We cannot, strictly speaking, say that a "text" has "ambition," yet the poet does indeed marshal the Marxist ideology of leveling and fresh construction as liberating measures, just as Scharfman implies.

The major metaphors and themes of Césaire's poetry collections are commitment, decolonization, and revolution, and all seek to liberate the individual, the race, and poetic creativity.

—*Janis L. Pallister*

While the first half of *Ferrements,* as Hale correctly observes, deals with slavery and the sad past of the race, the second half looks to future action. Hale judiciously notes that one not only finds all of Césaire's preferred images—island, volcano, birds, animals, trees, and the sun—but also "for the first time" a series of elegies consecrated to Louis Delgrès, Paul Eluard, Emmet Till, and the black labor leader Albert Cretinoir. Yet in a very real sense one might justifiably argue that the *Cahier* already contained such an elegy in memory of Toussaint Louverture. These elegiac poems tend to fall into the second half of the volume and are therefore apt to be allied with an optimism through a sense of leadership or at least of action not present in the first section. The brevity and highly accessible symbolism of the little African-style poem **"Small Song for Crossing a Big River"** do not diminish its effectiveness; rather, the little song, taken from the Yoruba, attenuates the optimism of the second half, for the ending speaks of the great palm trees' force as stifled by the huge burden (of the storm, or the wind).

Lilyan Kesteloot and A. James Arnold have extensively commented on the poems of *Ferrements*: both see the collection as the result of a new poetics. Arnold, who recalls Kesteloot in his analysis, finds that the 48 poems display considerable stylistic diversity and that the collection as a whole has three voices. It in fact contains songs of combat and songs of praise, the latter reminding us somewhat of the African praise song in structure and especially in intent. Of these, the poems **"Africa"** and **"Salute to Guinea."** are notable: they can be said to express Césaire's praise at what he sees to be an end of colonialism in Africa, the arrival of the African nations at Hegelian wholeness and solidarity. Arnold contends that in this collection the dialectical process of history is, for Césaire, more Hegelian than Marxist. (Césaire, however, might today view the so-called decolonized situation somewhat differently.) The reader would do well to examine Césaire's essay "The Political Thought of Sékou Touré" in conjunction with his poem **"Salute to Guinea."** The essay clarifies Touré's rejection of communism—as much as capitalism—as a Western *ideology* or philosophy; it shows how he willed a restitution of African and specifically Guinean values and social institutions in his decol-

onization program. Touré's rejection of Western rationalism and insistence on self-determination as a moral imperative and psychological necessity is in harmony with the goals of Césaire. This exposé of the Guinean leader, who is represented here as anything but the dictator Western circles perceive, portrays him as a man to be admired.

In other poems in this collection the topos of the mutilated hero is transferred to the suffering people. Arnold specifies that the collection sometimes manifests the Nietzschean notion of the redeemer hero, but a hero whose contribution is conditioned by the prerequisite that his sacrifice not be a purely social one: this is tied to the idea of the poet whose quest is at once poetic, spiritual, and, coincidentally, social. (Social because with the negritude poets we never encounter *l'art pour l'art* but always, as with such other art forms as sculpture, music, architectural appointments, and dance, a creation at once aesthetically pleasing and functional.)

Cadastre

Cadastre, containing two previously published recueils—*Soleil cou coupé* and *Corps perdu*—was published by Seuil in 1961. In his study of *Cadastre,* Jacques Chevrier finds that the collection, which delineates what he calls a painful combat or struggle, has no "schéma d'ensemble," no "dramatic progression." Rather, it is a nebulous gathering of themes and images that constitute "keys" the reader must patiently count and decode. We find metaphors pertaining to suffocation, struggle, and victory; we sense opacity, a fixation with imperfection or lack, while a decomposed Europe is depicted through imagery of petrification and rot. On occasion, says Chevrier, a corrective is added. To Chevrier's charge that the volume lacks cohesion we might respond by noting that we are dealing here with two distinct volumes and that it was more Césaire's intention to "clean up" his early poems than to present a recueil in which the individual pieces relate to one another or present a singular dramatic thrust. His modifications of *Soleil cou coupé* in particular are extensive. Hale concludes that despite Césaire's apparent intention to minimize the excesses of surrealism in *Corps perdu* by modifying *Cadastre,* "the collection does not lose its Surrealist nature."

From *Cadastre* comes one of Césaire's most famous poems, **"Exvoto pour un naufrage."** Kesteloot finds this poem one of the most transparent, one of the most thematically, lexically, and syntactically lucid. Although the poet sings in a style reminiscent of a *griot* or cult slave preceding the cortege of a black king, the piece contains a strong dose of that irony so characteristic of Césaire, for here the king is The White Man of South Africa. Use of the tom-tom again supplies the rhythms evoking the Black Man's word, so "enigmatic for foreigners." In the opening lines the white supervisor searches for diamonds that the miners may have cached in their mouths or anuses before leaving the mine, but then the poem moves through a highly condensed series of metaphors, alluding to the "three souls of the poet," at once the heart, brain, and liver as identified by the Caribbean Indian and also the three civilizations (i.e., Indian heart, European brain, and African liver). Especially striking are the allusions to the African culture hero Chaka, to the question mark of the scorpion (perhaps Africa, in mystical geography), and to the most famous "surrealist" image of all, "beau comme une machine à coudre sur une table d'opération" ("beautiful like a sewing machine on an operating table"), which perhaps harks back to the Singer of the poet's mother. After this comes a series of "flash" images that show the diminished power and greatness of the "king," no longer a healer who cures tuberculosis but instead one who gives it, he himself being sick, infected, and doomed to die. All here is dirisible, says the persona, who invites the reader-spectator to laugh. Kesteloot's detailed, sugestive analysis is excellent.

Noria

"Le verbe marronner," one of Césaire's most frequently cited poems, is found in *Noria,* which consists of previously published pieces. *Noria* first appeared in the *Oeuvres complètes* in 1976. "Le verbe marronner" is dedicated to the great Haitian poet René Depestre. One of the most important things Césaire is conveying here is that for him poetry must always be functional, must always be at the service of revolution. No matter how much people may not like it, he seems to be saying, "le fond conditionne la forme" ("the content of the poem dictates and conditions its form"). This position considerably distances Césaire from the continental Parnassian and symbolist poets' espousal of art for art's sake. It makes of Césaire not only a consummate surrealist—for the surrealists espoused the notion that art, while not being polemical, should serve revolution[11]—but also a true African in his aesthetics. Central to this poem is the play on the word *marronner* ("to maroon, to abandon, to give something a chestnut color"; to pull the chestnut out of the fire, and alluding also to the fugitive slave). Derived from American Spanish *cimarrón* (wild, unruly) and from the Old Spanish *cimarra* (thicket), the word has been fused with the French word *marron,* derived from Italian *Marrone* (a chestnut color), to create multiple associations and meanings. (The verb form is similarly used in the *Cahier*: "mon audace marronne.")

Moi, laminaire

In the preface to his most recent poetry collection, *Moi, laminaire* (1982; translated roughly as *I, ever-present, ever-entwining sea tangle*), Césaire tries to bring together familiar but irreconcilable realities, which might include time and nontime, past and future, north and south, east and west, life and death, fervor and lucidity, sun and shadow, mountain and mangrove, the sound of body and the halt. Using such polarities as a vehicle for poetic expression is hardly new to Césaire, nor is it original, although Bernadette Cailler[12] fixes on "Crevasses" ("Fissures"), intending to show these opposites as a source of tension, both poetic and political, because they are not to be resolved and therefore result in a vicious circle, a situation with no exit. In "Crevasses," she writes, "it seems that the nadir of the place of reverie has been privileged in this collection, as if it were a point that is closer to survival than to resurrection, closer to the fleeing moment than to eternity, a marginal-point, a lagoon-like retreat where a constellation of terms moves about exploring the efficacy of the hollow, of the wound, of the scratch, of the toothbite" (Cailler, my translation). She seems to find the same phenomena at work in both **"Calendrier lagunaire"** and **"Ça, le creux."** **"Crevasses"** portrays that vicious circle of which I just spoke, the circle being an entanglement of sorts that leaves the narrator, after 300 years of climbing, not only still not at the top of the hill but confronted by fissures into which he might or must fall. Some consider the circle "non-vicious" (Davis, after Césaire himself), but I think it likely that Césaire is working as he often does with dialectical rather than antithetical constructions. Imagistically, the chameleon-hornbill cluster suggests the basic but dialectical conflict between order and chaos: both are constant, neither will win. Cailler's analysis is very complex and somewhat hazy as she seeks to translate the images of the serpent, vine, and bird of prey, as well as what she calls "unidentified" insects that sting a "nonidentified" narrator into everyday meanings. (The sting of the insects reminds us of Antoine Bolamba, who calls them good because they sting but do not suck the blood, as would a white colonist.)[13] The best part of Cailler's short piece about **"Crevasses"** comes toward the end, when she suggests that Césaire is communicating the notion that the epic grandeur of his own past, like the past of the race, is not present in these texts (i.e., there is no longer the possibility of a poetic ego or of such a leader as Toussaint or Le Rebelle).

The major metaphors and themes of Césaire's poetry collections are commitment, decolonization, and revolution, and all seek to liberate the individual, the race, and poetic creativity. Césaire announced many of these themes and metaphors in the *Cahier* and was to take them up as part of his permanent literary baggage in his plays, the first of which was *Et les chiens se taisaient.*

Notes

[1] Bertrand Visage, in Beaumarchais's *Dictionnaire des litteratures de langue française* (Paris: Bordas, 1984), 400-401. It is hard to understand why Visage speaks of a mixture of prose and poetry; more accurately, we have "prose poems" throughout. Césaire's surrealism is beautifully epitomized in Jean-Claude Michel's *Les Ecrivains noirs et le surréalisme* (Sherbrooke, Canada: Editions Naaman, 1982), especially chapter 4, where he studies Césaire's poetic language, surrealist *art poétique,* verbal automatism, poetic image, and individuality and originality. He concludes with comments on negritude.

Senghor has clarified the role of images in negritude poetry in at least two important essays, "Comme les lamantins vont boire à la source" (in *Poèmes* [Paris: Seuil, 1973]) and "Dialogue sur la poésie francophone" (in *Elegies majeures* [Paris: Seuil, 1979]). In these pieces Senghor explains that the analogical image of Francophone negritude poetry has no function until it becomes rhythm. He also traces the history of poetry as vision and shows that, since the Renaissance, French poetry has not been characterized by vision; rather, poetry as vision comes from the Greek or Mediterranean tradition and is therefore linked to Africa. While Western discourse, which is enlisted for French poetry, is premeditated, African poetry arises from inspiration. Additionally, what counts for today's Francophone poets is the *object* of the poem, and this object is an ontological vision of the universe, of man in the universe. Senghor's concept of image, of poetry as vision, and the notion of object in that vision is quite applicable to Césaire's work, even though the latter is not, strictly speaking, African.

[2] On the vast array of images, see Keith Louis Walker, *La Cohésion poétique de l'oeuvre césairienne* (Paris: Editions Jean-Michel Place, 1979); hereafter cited in the text.

[3] John Erickson, "Le Discours révolutionnaire dans *Les Armes miraculeuses*," in *Aimé Césaire, ou l'athanor d'un alchimiste,* 53-62; hereafter cited in the text.

[4] Aliko Songolo, *Aimé Césaire, une poétique de la découverte* (Paris: L'Harmattan, 1985), 108; hereafter cited in the text.

[5] Bernadette Cailler, *Proposition poétique: Une lecture de l'oeuvre d'Aimé Césaire* (Sherbrooke, Canada: Editions Naaman, 1976), 73; hereafter cited in the text.

[6] Eloise Brière, "Poésie québécoise et situation coloniale," *Revue francophone de Louisiane* 2, no. 1 (Spring 1988): 9-18.

[7] *Les Armes miraculeuses* (Paris: Gallimard, 1970), 52; hereafter referred to in the text as *AM.* The translation here is my own.

[8] Eric Sellin, "*Soleil cou coupé,*" *Romance Notes* 14, no. 1 (Autumn 1972): 13-16; hereafter cited in the text.

[9] *Corps perdu,* in *Cadastre* (Paris: Seuil, 1961), 83.

[10] *Ferrements* (Paris: Seuil, 1960), 32; hereafter referred to in the text as *F.*

[11] Breton's interest in revolution, and even in failed revolutionary heroes like Henri Christophe and Patrice Lumumba, is studied by Anna Balakian in "André Breton's *Les Etats généraux:* Revolution and Poetry," *French Review* 62, no. 6 (May 1989): 1008-16.

[12] Bernadette Cailler, "Crevasse,' métaphore vive du texte," in *Aimé Césaire ou l'athanor d'un alchimiste,* 97-102; hereafter cited as in the text.

[13] Antoine Bolamba, *Esanzo,* trans. Jan[is] Pallister (Sherbrooke, Canada: Editions Naaman, 1977), 42. All the great themes of negritude are found in this collection, as Senghor states in his Introduction. Expressed in "metalanguage" (the language of the sacred), these poems by the Congolese Bolamba, like those of Césaire, express humanism, poetic and political revolt, and revolt against rationalism.

E. Anthony Hurley (essay date 1992)

SOURCE: "Link and Lance: Aspects of Poetic Function in Césaire's *Cadastre*—An Analysis of Five Poems," in *L'Esprit Créateur*, Vol. XXXII, No. 1, Spring, 1992, pp. 54-68.

[*In the following essay, Hurley examines Césaire's search for identity as a black poet within the French literary tradition.*]

It would be difficult to examine the notion of poetic function in relation to Aimé Césaire without taking into consideration the tension and ambivalence of Césaire's situation as a black intellectual and as a poet, functioning within a profoundly alienating white French socio-cultural context. On the one hand, as a black man, and particularly as a black Martinican-Frenchman, Césaire is constantly confronted by identity issues, grounded in the unhealed and perhaps unhealable wound of slavery, of colonization, and of relatively forced assimilation into an alien culture, as well as in potential isolation and separation within the black/African diaspora. As a poet and black intellectual, Césaire serves as the voice of a leader for an audience and a people (fellow Blacks) on whom he depends and to whom he is inextricably linked for the integration of his identity. Césaire's situation therefore suggests the tension of a poetry that would tend to function simultaneously inwardly and outwardly, personally and politically, as both link and lance: as a link for exploring identity issues, a means of searching and solidifying, of facilitating and articulating identity; as a lance, a weapon of personal and political liberation, but also an instrument to open the festering wound of alienation and self-hatred in order to create hope and healing.

At the same time, Césaire is a citizen of France, albeit black and Martinican, writing poetry in the French language within an established French literary tradition with its own socio-symbolic order. While Césaire's awareness as an educated black man might tend to incline him towards consciously or unconsciously rejecting or subverting the French social order, he does not become "un-French," and both his use of the French language and his renown as a French (Caribbean) writer would tend to validate, and contribute to the survival of, the French social order to which he belongs.

A discussion of poetic function in relation to Césaire should therefore take into account the peculiarities of his French Caribbean situation and the ambivalence of his relationship to a metropolitan French literary tradition. The term poetic function itself, however, though part of the rhetoric of the Western sociocultural tradition, tends to be somewhat elusive. Its meaning, for the purposes of this study, may be said to lie within the parameters of two modern critical and linguistic approaches, advanced by Kristeva and Jakobson. Kristeva's approach captures the irony of Césaire's position vis-à-vis metropolitan French society. She posits a revolutionary and subversive function for poetry or poetic language within the context of a socio-symbolic order; poetry thus serves paradoxically both to transform the social order and to ensure its survival:

Dans cet ordre socio-symbolique ainsi saturé sinon déjà clos, la poésie—disons plus exactement le langage poétique—rappelle ce qui fut depuis toujours sa fonction: introduire, à travers le symbolique, ce qui le travaille, le traverse et le menace. Ce que la théorie de l'inconscient cherche, le langage poétique le pratique à l'intérieur et à l'encontre de l'ordre social: moyen ultime de sa mutation ou de sa subversion, condition de sa survie et de sa révolution. . . . [1]

Kristeva's approach in relating poetry to the context of a social order shares linkages with Jakobson's analysis of linguistic communication. Jakobson identifies six constituent factors in linguistic processes: "destinateur," "destinataire," "message," "contexte," "code," and "contact." He relates poetic function to emphasis placed on the "message" itself: "l'accent mis sur le message pour son propre compte est ce qui caractérise la function poétique du langage. . . ."[2] Césaire's poetry indeed necessarily emphasizes the "message," since it serves as a concrete manifestation of a communication link between poet and self and poet and people. In this study, therefore, poetic function will refer to the role of the poet and of the poem in relation to the sociopolitical context within which the poet writes.

The interpretation of Césaire's poetry as revolutionary, in relation to the nature and direction of the poet's communication, was suggested, long before the articulations of Jakobson and Kristeva, by Aristide Maugée, Césaire's close friend, fellow Martinican and co-contributor to the early 1940s Martinican journal, *Tropiques*. In a 1942 article, Maugée suggests aspects of the functions of Césaire's poetry that will become almost clichés in the years that follow: the poem as liberation, as verbal magic, as a means of exploring and discovering inner truths. He asserted:

> [Césaire] façonne des mots nouveaux, crée des images nouvelles pour exprimer la nuance exacte de sa perception, trouve des sonorités neuves pour libérer son chant intérieur.
>
> Magie du son. Sortilège du Verbe.
>
> [. . .] par la désintégration du réel, le poète recherche un monde nouveau: un monde de beauté et de vérité.
>
> Où le trouvera-t-il sinon dans la profondeur de sa conscience?[3]

Moreover, Césaire himself, in his 1943 article in *Tropiques,* "Maintenir la poésie," had indicated that poetry as he conceived and practiced it had a deliberately subversive function, in relation to the existing social order:

> Se défendre du social par la création d'une zone d'incandescence, en deça de laquelle, à l'intérieur de laquelle fleurit dans une sécurité terrible la fleur inouïe du "Je"; [. . .] conquérir par la révolte la part franche où se susciter soi-même, intégral, telles sont quelques-unes des exigences qui [. . .] tendent à s'imposer à tout poète [. . .].
>
> Ici poésie égale insurrection [. . .][4]

Césaire's poetics have perhaps been most comprehensively articulated in "Poésie et connaissance,"[5] in which he established an opposition between poetic and scientific processes of knowledge, affirming the superiority of the poetic process as a means of true cosmic knowledge. Césaire thus aligned himself with the revolutionary adventures of poets like Baudelaire, Rimbaud, Mallarmé, Lau-tréamont, Apollinaire and Breton. "Poèsie et connaissance" ended with a summary of Césaire's poetics, expressed in seven propositions, the first of which asserts that "la poésie est cette démarche qui par le mot, l'image, le mythe, l'amour et l'humour m'installe au cœur vivant de moi-même et du monde" (169).[6]

Césaire's explicit alignment with these luminaries of modern French poetry has opened the door for Euro-centered critical approaches to his own poetry. Such approaches, however well meaning, however brilliantly executed, feed into the same dilemma from which Césaire as a French Caribbean writer has tried so courageously to escape: absorption into a socio-politico-cultural entity that has, through slavery, colonization, and assimilation, consistently denied a voice to him and his people. French Caribbean poets like Césaire are necessarily characterized by the problem of cultural identity, including the struggle of separation from France, and their textual voice is grounded in the geographical and sociocultural reality of the French Caribbean. Because of the peculiar situation of such poets, in terms of the dynamics of geography, language, history, and culture, it is inevitable that the signs of this situation will be literally inscribed in the texts produced. If these signs are unrecognized or ignored, much of the "significance" of the literary work will be missed.

Moreover, any approach to Césaire's poetry and indeed to the literature of the Caribbean that ignores the existence of an authentic and valid voice which compensates for an orality lost or repressed over the last few centuries will inevitably fall short of determining the profound significance of the literature.

No analysis of French Caribbean literature is ultimately meaningful if it does not directly engage the problematic of cultural identity with which every Caribbean writer is confronted. Approaches to Caribbean texts through the mediation of European theories tend to devalue and deny the pivotal thrust of French Caribbean literary production, which is ultimately to proclaim and assert its validity as an authentic cultural manifestation.

A problem arises, however, for, while it may be inappropriate to rely on Euro-centered critical approaches to explicate French Caribbean poetry, there is a lack of alternative approaches sensitive to this problematic. Since critical practice necessarily has political implications, there is a need for critical activity by scholars sensitive enough to the challenge posed by the special situation of French Caribbean letters not to adopt the easier task of imposing a traditional, metropolitan critical framework on French Caribbean texts, but to seek to develop approaches which will support the evolution of a French Caribbean literary canon on its own terms.

The investigation which follows centers on the notion of poetic function in Césaire's *Cadastre,* with specific reference to five poems. *Cadastre,* published in 1961 by Seuil, is the re-edition of poems from two previously published collections, *Soleil cou-coupé* of 1948 and *Corps perdu* of 1950, with some of the original poems omitted and others revised.[7] Césaire's poetic practice in this collection has been analyzed by A. James Arnold, who has sought to reconcile contrasting modernist and negritude approaches to Césaire. Arnold's assertion of a paradox in the negritude movement in that it "simultaneously cultivated a rhetoric of protest and an intensely subjective poetics," which colors his readings of Césaire's poems, suggests a practical and unreconciled separation between "lyrical" and "polemical" functions in Césaire's poetry not borne out by the texts themselves. Ronnie Scharfman, who has also produced penetrating analyses of many of Césaire's poems, seeks to address and supplement "the absence of a problematic that could simultaneously articulate the difficulties of Césaire's poetic discourse and its political *engagement*."[8] Scharfman consequently reads each text "as an enactment of some conflict by or for the subject." While her analyses are consistently insightful, she has, by defining Césaire's genius as the "textualization of marginality," and by imposing European critical approaches on Césaire's poetic practice, perhaps underestimated the importance of the relationship existing between Césaire and his chosen "others."

As the title of this collection (*Cadastre*) suggests, the poet is concerned with making a survey—taking an inventory of his situation as a black man and as a poet. The poems suggest the tension implicit in the ambivalence of the relationship between the poet and the social order within which he functions, and serve to concretize the message of liberation. As mentioned earlier, Césaire's poetry operates in two directions simultaneously, inwardly and personally, and outwardly and politically: inwardly, the poetry serves as a vehicle for the poet to explore and resolve issues of personal identity and liberation, and as a means of personal salvation; outwardly, the poetry operates as a means of communicating with his people and with the supporters of the alienating social order, and as a means of affirmation, education, disalienation, and even of subversion.

Linking these two functions which represent the personal and political thrusts of Césaire's poetry is a connecting function which may be identified as creative, concerned with the poet's exploitation of the magical and prophetic potential of poetry. By a close textual reading that resists the temptation to assimilate the poetry into a predetermined European theoretical model, and that refrains from considering the poetry as other than what it is (French Caribbean poetry), I propose to illustrate the specific ways in which these functions operate. I shall attempt to answer the following questions: What voices speak within the poem? What are the roles and characteristics of the poetic voice? Whom does the poet address within the poem? How does the poem link poetic voice, addressee and context?

Magique

The title of this opening poem of the collection anticipates the magical metamorphosis which occurs at the end of the poem: the repositioning of "un dieu noir." This metamorphosis takes place against a background of natural phenomena, an overcast sky in which only a thin slice of blue is visible ("une lèche de ciel"), and high winds ("vous bêtes qui sifflez"), which are characteristic of the destructive "tornade." The island, "ce quignon de terre," is represented as virtually dead, "cette morte," threatened by and at the mercy of the "bêtes" and the "fougères" that are shown to be already "libres." The metaphors signify a geopolitical context of conflict, between "vous bêtes" and "cette morte"; between "vous libres fougères" and "les roches assassines"; between "les conques," suggestive of the island, and "leur destin"; even between the implies light of "midi" and the darkness associated with "les étoiles." Césaire suggests here a conflict between forces of oppression and destruction and other forces with an impulse toward liberation. The struggle takes place on an island, but one that shares a situational bond of worthlessness with other islands, in that they are "englouties comme un sou," and "oubliées comme un sou."

Against this background, the poetic voice identifies itself through the plural "nous" of line 14 ("mol glissement des grains de l'été que nous fûmes"). This is significantly a communal identity, with an already realized potential for regeneration and metamorphosis. The poet also assumes the roles of "bouche," of "suffète des îles englouties," and of "prophète des îles oubliées," attempting to communicate with an audience, designated as "vous bêtes" and "vous libres fougères." The context evoked, within which this communication takes place, is that of "l'île," "cette morte," featuring "roches assassines" and "conques trop vastes pour leur destin."

Césaire's poetic practice cannot be anything but revolutionary, as it operates harmoniously both inwardly and outwardly, linking and lancing, exploring, attacking, cutting, binding and healing all at once.

—E. Anthony Hurley

The voice of the poet in this situation attempts to transcend the limitations of the island: "la bouche aux parois du nid." The poet assumes the role of responsible leadership, that of "suffète," but also that of "prophète" announcing the future of his people. Through the vision and the prophecy of the poet, the dead island, "cette morte," is restored to life; through the poetic activity implicit in the poem a metamorphosis takes place, "ce mol glissement des grains d'été que nous fumes."

The hope of change is implicit throughout the poem. For, even in the midst of the atmosphere of menace and danger, signs of hope appear: the "lèche de ciel" bore within itself signs of good weather to come; the "étoiles" suggest not only darkness, but also light, with associations of good fortune, "trèfles au ciel," and vitality, "gouttes de lait chu." Hope is at the heart of the "message" of this poem: the restoration of the divinity of the black man ("réadjustent un dieu noir mal né de son tonnerre").

The poem functions as a means of concretizing this hope, and of articulating the poet's prophetic voice, his sense of responsibility and leadership. It illustrates the identity dilemma confronting the French Caribbean poet. The poet as a linking voice magically emerges out of the silence historically imposed on Blacks in a neo-colonial situation. It is essentially through the poem that the "black" voice acquires validity.

Couteaux midi

In the first part of this poem, the subjective presence of the poet appears in the possessive and object pronouns of "ma foi," "mes paroles," "mes cris," "mes crocs de poivre," "mes lèvres," and "m'absente." The poet is evoked as a disembodied voice and mouth, involved in a dialogue, as the questions "Ils tirent à blanc?" and "Midi?" (posed five times) indicate. The poetic replies to the questions are always an affirmative "oui," which suggests the validity of the propositions advanced.

These propositions relate to the activities of blacks, and specifically to what the poet suggests occurs "quand les Nègres font la Révolution." He intimates, with evident irony, playing on common connotations of "blanc" and "noir," that "ils tirent à blanc," and supports the validity of the paradox by explaining that "le blanc est la juste force controversée du noir qu'ils portent dans le cœur." The text suggests that the poet considers this an abortive, pseudo-revolution, doomed from the start by its own endemic contradictions, equivalent to a whitewashing process taking place under a pseudo midday sun, so pale in comparison to the tropical sun that it is to be greeted only with derisive laughter: "[. . .] les cornettes des sœurs de Saint Joseph de Cluny qu'elles lessivent sous les espèces de midi dans la jubilation solaire d'un savon tropical."

The poet, struck by the contrast between these two different noons, explores the significance which the tropical noon holds for him. He suggests that it provides a natural avenue of escape from the muzzling of his voice and limitations of a complacent and comfortable life: "Midi qui disperse dans le ciel la ouate trop complaisante qui capitonne mes paroles et où mes cris se prennent." The poetic voice shifts to a more assertive and affirmative mode, corresponding to the graphic shift from the common noun, "midi," disdain for which is suggested by "espèces de," to the proper "Midi." This contrasting "Midi" is invested with capacities which stand in opposition to the other "midi": the capacity for a presence affirmed even in darkness ("amande de la nuit"), and the capacity for speech ("langue"). This "Midi," too, is associated with the sensitivity that comes from emotional and social humiliations: "qui porte sur son dos de galeux." This "Midi" is suggestive of courageous patience and endurance and of the potential for creating movement: "met sur toutes les lignes de toutes les mains les trains." It is this "Midi" which, significantly, makes possible a break with the (white) world ("Midi somptueux qui de ce monde m'absente").

The attitude and activities of the poet change with the movement within the poem away from "ce monde." The poetic voice enters into full presence as the poem assumes a poetic "form" in the middle section of the poem. The poet becomes active and assumes the voice of revolt—a revolt so complete it embraces the extremes of "doux" and "dur":

> Doux Seigneur!
> durement je crache. Au visage des affameurs,
> au visage des insulteurs, au visage des
> paraschites et des éventreurs. Seigneur dur!
> doux je siffle; je siffle doux . . .

The chiasma signals the parallelism of the roles of poet ("je") and "Seigneur," as the poet moves from rebellion to acceptance. This new attitude is presented by the poet as indicative of his identity, characterized by wounds, but founded on dignity and commitment: "Oh! je tiens mon pacte / debout dans mes blessures où mon sang bat contre les fûts." The poetic identity includes solidarity with others of his race and the poetic voice sends a message of hope and humanitarianism, bringing into existence, at the end of this section, the day of a new revolution that transcends hatred:

> [. . .] c'est le jour,
> un jour pour nos pieds fraternels
> un jour pour nos mains sans rancunes
> un jour pour nos souffles sans méfiance
> un jour pour nos faces sans vergogne

The final short prose section, which continues the discussion of the opening section, links the role of the poet to that of "les sorciers," suggesting the involvement of both poet and sorcerer in harnessing powers of potential ferocity and in creatively exploiting intimacy with the dark forces of nature: "l'intime férocité des étoiles."

The poet, in this poem, suggests a contrast, implicit in the title, between violent physical pseudo-revolution ("couteaux") and the lucidity ("Midi") of true revolt. The poet moves beyond embracing violence, to transform the lance-"couteau" into a kind of magic wand, as he assumes the role both of prophet predicting a future of hope, dignity and love, and of sorcerer, using materials supplied by his brother "Nègres" to participate in the creative activity of the cosmos. Once again, the poem becomes the connecting link between past and future, a hopeful echo of the "lost" black voice in the present of the French Caribbean.

Barbare

The poetic voice makes itself heard from the first line of the poem, in "C'est le mot qui me soutient," immediately suggesting the nature of the relationship between the poet and "le mot," which functions as a source of needed support for the poet. The poet is represented metonymically as "ma carcasse," on whom "le mot," as voice, strikes to produce sound and, by extension, life. In the second and third stanzas, the voice of the poet becomes identified and fused with the voices of others, sharing with them "nos faces belles" and "nos oreilles," within the context of the word that introduces and dominates even visually those two stanzas—"Barbare." In the final stanza, the poet fully assumes the identity of "barbare" and at the same time that of "le serpent cracheur," as he addresses a "vous," whose physical presence is indicated in "la chair velue de vos poitrines."

Contrast and conflict between the barbarian group which includes the poet and the other hairy-chested group are clearly indicated by the text. The poem thus sends a message of revolt, different from "les cris de révolte jamais entendus." The revolt in the poem involves investing a word with pejorative and insulting resonances with an aura of primitive nobility and power. The resonance of the word "barbare" is a reminder of psychological debasement, represented metaphorically in the text as the rusting effect of noon on the poet's carcass, in which ironically only true barbarism, characterized by cowardice and dishonesty, is being destroyed:

> C'est le mot qui me soutient
> et frappe sur ma carcasse de cuivre jaune
> où la lune dévore dans la soupente de la rouille
> les os barbares
> des lâches bêtes rôdeuses du mensonge.

In the second stanza, the poet suggests the magical power of language to affirm the validity and beauty of "nos faces"—an attitude of rejection which bears within itself the power of creation. In the following stanza, the poet uses the word "barbare" as a reminder of the past suffering and present condition of people who have been characterized as dead, but who are yet the life-blood of the earth, reminiscent of the situation of black South African miners: "des morts qui circulent dans les veines de la terre." **"Barbare"** is used also as a reminder of a spirit of revolt concealed behind a façade of dance and music: "et les cris de révolte jamais entendus / qui tournent à mesure et à timbres de musique."

The poet exploits the regenerative potential intrinsic in the word "barbare," so that it is represented as the magical and beautiful principle of life concealed in savage and reptilian forms normally regarded as loathsome ("amphisbène," "serpent," "gekko"), and with which he completely identifies: "Barbare moi." It is this vital principle that enables the poet to metamorphose ("qui de mes putrifiantes chairs me réveille") and adopt an attitude of direct and violent revolt ("me coller [. . .] aux lieux mêmes de la force").

Through the use of the explicit and implicit "barbare"-"moi"-"poète" linkage, the poem itself functions as the theatre where a subversive linguistic revolution takes place, and as the means by which the word "barbare" achieves a truly healing significance. The poet, by appropriating and transforming the various implications of the word, validates the cultural perspective of the French Caribbean.

Mot[9]

The poet refers to himself directly only in the first two shorter sections of this poem. At the beginning of the poem, the poet's "moi" serves as the point of departure for the poem, as the context, as source or sender, and as receiver of this word: "Parmi moi/de moi-même/à moi-même/ [. . .] en mes mains." At the beginning of the second section, the poet becomes a voice of hope: "j'aurai chance hors du labyrinthe." Soon afterwards, however, the poet becomes the object to be acted upon, at the mercy of, increasingly possessed by, the word ("me prendre," "me pendre," "que me clouent"). After this point, the poet virtually disappears from the poem as a self-referential voice. No further explicit references to a "moi" appear. The only direct indication of a subjective presence occurs in "savez-vous," while the vibration of the word "nègre" gathers momentum and dominates the remainder of the poem.

The word, unspecified at the opening of the poem, is lodged deep in the poet's psyche, inseparable from the poet's identity,[10] and is evoked as a vital instinct, an automatic impulse of revolt: "le rare hoquet d'un ultime spasme délirant." The word becomes active and vibrates ("vibre") more and more throughout the poem. It is this vibration that gives the poet hope of escaping from the "labyrinthe" of his present situation. Hence, his willingness to submit to the emotional vibration, translated into a series of circular images that indicate the poet's delirium of magical possession, as he assumes the role, suggested by Arnold, of poet-priest and scapegoat at the center-stake of the voodoo temple: "au beau poteau-mitan des très fraîches étoiles."

As the poem develops, the poet's "moi" is possessed by the word "nègre," which assumes an independent force of its own, evoking and conjuring, to the rhythm of a drum, images of humiliations, lynchings, horrible sufferings of mothers and children, and the burning of black bodies. The evocation of these horrors produces its own metamorphosis; the word "nègre," vibrating in the poet's unconscious, magically emerges as a symbol of resistance and revolt, of virility and dignity, successful beyond all expectation in obtaining liberty: "dru savez-vous/du tonnerre d'un été/que s'arrogent/des libertés incrédules."[11]

The whole poem, therefore, concretely represents the transformation of the poetic "moi" into "le mot nègre," from the first to the second half of the poem, under the influence of a literal vibration within the poem itself. Hence, the poem functions as the arena within which this creative and liberating transformation takes place. The vibration of the word "nègre" within the poem has implications for the pivotal dilemma of French Caribbean writers. This poetic vibration counteracts the attempts at cultural silence and repression imposed on Blacks and becomes a manifestation of life, freedom, and creativity. The vibrant "mot" is the symbol of the authentic French Caribbean voice.

Dit d'errance[12]

This poem, the poem with which *Cadastre* ends, illustrates the use of the poem as a means of both clarifying the poet's own identity and providing a catalyst, the poem itself, for other blacks, universally, to explore and validate their own identity as black people in a white-dominated society.

For the poet, there is a fusion between inner exploration and outward political commitment to his island and his people. At the beginning of the poem, he assumes the microcosmic mantle of all suffering humanity and of all alienation from self:

> Tout ce qui jamais fut déchiré
> en moi s'est déchiré
> tout ce qui jamais fut mutilé
> en moi s'est mutilé

This personal alienation is associated with an alienation in cosmic terms and necessitates a search for the other half of the identity: "au milieu de l'assiette de son souffle dénudé / le fruit coupé de la lune toujours en allée / vers le contour à inventer de l'autre moitié."

The reappraisal of the past that follows suggests only limited meaningful successes ("à peine peut-être certain sens") and even the possibility of having been led astray: "quand d'aucuns chantent Noël revenu / de songer aux astres / égarés." At this point, the poetic voice appears overwhelmed by a sense of failure, of lamentation: "tout est du tout déchu"; "j'ai bien en tête la saison si lacrimeuse." Indeed, the dominant characteristic of one part of the poet's fragmented identity, represented by his past experience of slavery, seems to be silence:

> Ciel éclaté courbe écorchée
> de dos d'esclaves fustigés
> peine trésorière des alizés
> grimoire fermé mots oubliés
> j'interroge mon passé muet

As the poet evokes the island which is part of his identity, "île de sang," the island, like every island, is represented as sharing in the same condition of alienation and loss as the poet himself: "île maljointe île disjointe / toute île appelle / toute île est veuve." The loss for the island, as it is for the poet, is related to separation from the source of identity, Africa, represented by the civilizations of Bénin and Ifé, and his rhetorical question, in the name of all alienated Africans ("nous"), suggests his own doubt of ever being able to heal this breach: "tendrons-nous toujours les bras?"

The apostrophe that follows ("ô déchiré") may be read as an address to the poet's wounded and divided self, as he conjures up an image of triumphant reunification and healing, which leads him to a new state of consciousness, in which he assumes the priestly mantle of hope: "J'ai inventé un culte secret / mon soleil est celui que toujours on attend."

The poet adopts another role, that of lover ("corps féminin île retrouvée"), which becomes fused with his role as plaintive prophet ("moi sybille flébilant"). When he turns again to look back on his (shared) childhood past ("mes enfances"), the painful memories of communal failure with

which he identifies ("j'ai vu un oiseau mâle sombrer") produce in him a sense of disillusionment: "je regarde le plus bas de l'année."

The poet's rather depressing impression of his past life, his doubts about his identity and his role, about whether he is indeed agent or victim, and about the validity of his concern with issues of black identity, are translated into lucid, self-reflexive ironic wit: "serais-je jouet de nigromance?" This question echoes the ambivalence of the title, "Dit d'errance," which suggests (in "errance") a lack of certainty on the part of the poet. As a result, however, of the process of rigorous self-examination and the awareness of identity linkages to Africa and his native island, the image of the "pierre" emerges to suggest both fixity and power, and the poem ends on a triumphant note, with the poet adopting the active, heroic role of lance:

> Or mieux qu'Antilia ni que Brazil
> pierre milliaire dans la distance
> épée d'une flamme qui me bourrelle
> j'abats les arbres du Paradis.

The foregoing analyses highlight certain aspects of poetic function in the poems: the relationship between the poet and a social order characterized by "vous"; the various roles assumed by the poet; the "messages" sent by the poem; and the general function of the poem itself. In *Cadastre* as a whole, the dominant roles adopted by the poet are those of leader and of voice: the leader and voice of revolt, the voice of prophecy and hope; the magician who protects the integrity and destiny of a people; even the scapegoat leader who endures and articulates the sufferings of his people in order to guarantee their survival and eventual triumph.

The poems presuppose a context of alienation from self, of loss of identity, dignity, nobility, beauty and power, of divisiveness and inhumanity. Within this context, which is in fact the social order in which the poem itself functions, the poetic act becomes an affirmation of contrary values. The constant "message" sent by the poems is one of hope: hope in the restoration of the dignity and divinity of the black man, hope in the triumph of humanitarianism, hope in the validity of true revolt.

Although references to an opposing "vous" occur, their relative rarity and indirectness, when compared to the references to a "moi" or a "nous," would tend to suggest that communication is directed not so much to the representatives of the oppressive and alienating social order but rather to the poet's self and to the group with whom the poet chooses to identify. This also tends to suggest that some of the implications of Scharfman's analysis,[13] informed by Benveniste, are problematical. This factor, the direction of Césaire's communication, invests Césaire's poetry with a "revolutionary" function that is radically different from that discussed by Kristeva, who pointed to poetic language functioning paradoxically and unconsciously both to subvert and at the same time to maintain a social order, specifically the bourgeois technocratic structure of late nineteenth-century France. Césaire's poetry, in my view, deliberately transgresses such considerations. I see, furthermore, no separation in Césaire's poetic practice between the rhetoric of protest and subjective poetics, as Arnold suggests.

Indeed, the peculiarity of Césaire's situation, a poet with the problematical cultural identity of an educated Black, while at the same time a non-French Martinican Frenchman, gives a new significance to the term revolutionary. His poetic practice cannot be anything but revolutionary, as it operates harmoniously both inwardly and outwardly, linking and lancing, exploring, attacking, cutting, binding and healing all at once. This multifaceted revolutionary function of poetry, related to a need to affirm and protect the threatened integrity of identity, has remained a constant in Césaire's poetry. At the same time, Césaire has retained his conception of the poet as leader and prophet for a people. In a recent interview, discussing a poem entitled **"Dyâli,"** which he had written in honor of his longtime friend and colleague, Léopold Sédar Senghor, Césaire explains: "'**Dyâli**' autrement dit 'le diseur de parole', le 'poète' [. . .]. Le Dyâli c'est aussi celui qui montre le chemin [. . .]."[14]

Césaire himself, by his continued literary and political activity, has also been showing the way. What he has shown, what his poetry shows by its very existence and by its function as a literary artifact, both within the context of and in opposition to the mainstream socioliterary order of metropolitan France, is that French Caribbean poetry exists. Césaire's poetry proclaims its own identity as an authentically distinct cultural manifestation which is essentially Caribbean.

Notes

[1] Julia Kristeva, *La Révolution du langage poétique* (Paris: Seuil, 1974) 9.

[2] Roman Jakobson, *Essais de linguistique générale,* trans. Nicholas Ruwet (Paris: Minuit, 1963), 218.

[3] Aristide Maugée, "Aimé Césaire Poète," *Tropiques* 5 (avril 1942): 14-15.

[4] *Tropiques* 8-9 (octobre 1943): 7-8.

[5] Aimé Césaire, "Poésie et connaissance," *Tropiques* 12 (janvier 1945): 157-70. A recent translation by A. James Arnold appears as "Poetry and Knowledge" in Aimé Césaire, *Lyric and Dramatic Poetry 1946-82* (Charlottesville: University Press of Virginia, 1990), xlii-lvi. (See the review of Patrick Mensah, end of this issue.)

[6] The five elements of this proposition have been used by Bernadette Cailler as the basis of an often illuminating analysis of Césaire's poetry in *Proposition poétique: une lecture de l'oeuvre d'Aimé Césaire* (Québec: Sherbrooke, 1976). Césaire's poetic practice, however, does not conform to such a neat formulation.

[7] For a discussion of changes from the original collections to the revised edition, see A. James Arnold, *Modernism and Negritude: The Poetry and Poetics of Aimé Césaire* (Cambridge, Mass.: Harvard University Press, 1981), 191-251.

[8] Ronnie Leah Scharfman, *"Engagement" and the Language of the Subject in the Poetry of Aimé Césaire* (Gainesville: University of Florida Press, 1987), 1-2.

[9] For informative and penetrating readings of this poem see Arnold, *Modernism* 224-29, and Scharfman *Engagement,* 85-92.

[10] As Scharfman correctly points out: "'mot' comes to be substituted for 'moi' as the subject of the poem," *Engagement* 85-86. However, her interpretation of the "i" as a castration figure seems somewhat strained.

[11] Scharfman accurately suggests that the ending of the poem attests "to the successful binding of the subject with the ideals of negritude: poetic reinvention utilized to reveal black solidarity and identity," *Engagement* 92.

[12] For a detailed reading of this poem, see Arnold, *Modernism* 242-51.

[13] See Scharfman, *Engagement,* Chap. 3: "The Subject and the Intimate Other: Woman as 'Tu,'" 65-73.

[14] Charles H. Rowell, "C'est par le poème que nous affrontons la solitude-Une interview avec Aimé Césaire," *Callaloo* 12.1 (Winter 1989): 52.

Clarisse Zimra (essay date 1992)

SOURCE: "On Ancestral Ground: Heroic Figuring in Aimé Césaire," in *L'Esprit Créateur,* Vol. XXXII, No. 1, Spring, 1992, pp. 16-30.

[*In the following essay, Zimra explores Césaire's treatment of the past in his work, in particular his use of the Ancestor figure.*]

Qui et quels nous sommes?

Admirable question.

It is hardly an exaggeration to say that contemporary Caribbean writers are obsessed with the past, an obsession made manifest by a recurring textual figure, that of the Ancestor. Both proponents and opponents of the tenets of Negritude, from Senghor to Soyinka, have tended to see the figure as heroic. In the Caribbean text, the ancestral trope plunges into an imaginary past predicated on collective history in order to gain access to a common future. Edouard Glissant calls it "a prophetic reading of the past" (preface to *Monsieur Toussaint*). But, as he also cautions in *Le Discours antillais,* this textual strategy may well elide an alienating present and prolong a self denying cultural stasis that renders political action impossible.[1]

The sociological approach still predominates, whether among critics (I. F. Case's damning Césaire's inability to write about contemporary Martinique) or writers (Daniel Maximin condemning Glissant's unwillingness to do likewise as "evasiveness").[2] It would appear that the Caribbean corpus, a literature initially triggered by specific historical conditions, must always return to its ideological origins. This may account in no small part for the uneasy dance between myth and history in the Caribbean corpus, a feature particularly prominent in the Cesairean topos of the ancestral quest.

The question of the Ancestor remains a constant of Caribbean literature after Césaire as well. It took Maryse Condé a considerable African detour before she could trust herself to face her own "mangrove swamp." Her first novel stages this alienation with maximum impact when the child asks, "what were we before" and the Caribbean father refuses to entertain the notion that there may have been a past "before." Whether plaintive (in Condé's *Hérémakhônon),* wistful (in Léon Damas's *Hoquet*: "Désastre / parlez-moi du désastre / parlez-m'en"), or defiant (in Maximin's *L'Isolé soleil*: "Il nous faut drageonner nos pères"), the child's insistent question is the textual sign of a never-ending tug of war between the mythical and the historical dimension. From Derek Walcott's sobering words on selective amnesia in "The Muse of History,"[3] to Glissant's gradual evisceration of his once admirable "Negator," the question triggers an imaginery projection backward that must locate its object in an immemorial past before any move forward. ***Cahier d'un retour au pays natal*** is exemplary in this.

In the wake of the ***Cahier,*** the poet had taken his stand. Fresh from the shock of his Haitian tour, Césaire delineated in the 1945 "Poésie et connaissance" his poetics of Caribbean authenticity as the weaving of the private, obsessional, self with the collective, ancestral, unconscious. But, as the whole *Tropiques* adventure made clear, it was a genetic unconscious nonetheless radically grounded in a specific moment:

> Ce qui émerge, c'est le fonds individuel. Les conflits intimes, les obsessions . . . Tous les chiffres du message personnel . . .

> Ce qui émerge aussi, c'est le vieux fonds ancestral. Images héreditaires, que seules peut remettre à jour, aux fins de déchiffrement, l'atmosphère poétique . . .
> (*Tropiques* XII, Jan. 1945)

The poet starts with the retrieving of long forgotten selves buried deep within the collective memory. However, the very conditions of such a plunge are historically determined, as the ***Cahier*** finds time and again.[4] At the time this was written, diving into the unconscious and recovering the African past seemed feasible, if not identical, projects. Thus, Suzanne Césaire in "Léo Frobénius et le problème des civilisations": ". . . l'Afrique ne signifie pas seulement pour nous un élargissement vers l'ailleurs, mais approfondissement de nous mêmes" (*Tropiques* 1, avril 1941). The young rebels of Martinique, looking at Price-Mars's example on the next island, had every reason to be optimistic. The final movement of the ***Cahier,*** going downward and inward in order to expand outward and upward ("ailleurs"), attempts to answer the challenge it poses somewhat ironically for itself: "Qui et quels nous sommes? / Admirable question."[5] Close to half-a-century lat-

er, in his 1982 preface to ***moi, laminaire*** Césaire would reconsider this poetic project and answer it otherwise, raising over his whole corpus the ghost of blind, self-deluded, limping Oedipus, torn between east and west, reason and imagination, past and present, myth and history: "Ainsi va toute vie. Ainsi va ce livre, entre soleil et ombre, entre montagne et mangrove, entre chien et loup, claudiquant et binaire."[6]

My contention here is simple: it is against Césaire's definitions of the ancestral ground that much of subsequent Caribbean literature measures itself, whether deliberately or not. To give but one example, Condé's paradigmatic "what were we before" destabilizes the solid ground of Césaire's earlier "who and what we are." To his glorious African depth sounding, she opposes a version of Walcott's radical amnesia, the surface of a blank Caribbean wall. Césaire's last work, *laminaire,* moves away from a unified, collective mythical dimension into a fragmented, tentative, historical consciousness, halfway between his glorious past soundings and Condé's radical negation. A clear understanding of the ancestral permutations in the Cesairean corpus, in turn, gives us a clearer sense of the writers who have followed in his footsteps.

For the Negritude generation, Caribbean history consisted of a before and after, a reading often modeled after the paradigmatic metaphor of western intervention in the Caribbean, Shakespeare's *Tempest,* turned upside down. It was a frankly oppositional move, whose binary dance of difference was not always stable. Within this world, Césaire's Ancestor has remained a cipher of polarization both from within and from without, the trope of the Other's otherness. It represents the black self as non-white invading and engaging the white discourse; yet, it is also polarized within itself in a kind of mirroring effect oscillating between Caliban, the primal autonomous being, wild and free, and Toussaint, the all too willing victim of white cunning sacrificed on the altar of nationalism. In the Cesairean corpus, Caliban and Toussaint are sometimes figures of opposition and sometimes of complementarity, the Rebel borrowing from each.[7] Toussaint, the ghost erased from white history books spitting up his lungs in Napoleon's dank cell, is a figure that the 1930s ***Cahier*** seeks simultaneously to reclaim for history, as the origin of black historical consciousness in the Caribbean, and turn into tragic myth, a dead hero greater than any one of his living descendants. As original presence on the primeval shore, Shakespeare's imaginary cannibal who at the end of *Une Tempête* sings his African freedom is a figure of myth too; for Césaire's 1969 play pointedly ends before the test of history begins. Or rather, with Prospero's final descent into lifeless impotence, colonial history has ended but postcolonial liberation has yet to begin. Conversely, from the 1946 oratorio to the 1956 play, the symbolic trajectory of *Et les chiens se taisaient* seems to move away from myth into more factual history. Yet, the successive versions of *Chiens,* down to the latest one in 1974,[8] show clearly that neither dimension is relinquished. Trying to connect the corpus's fluctuations to the writer's own, critics have spent an inordinate amount of ink on the relationship between the poet and the politician. Given Césaire's highly ob-

41

lique, deliberately opaque, style and the complexity of the issue itself, it is impossible to separate the strands neatly, even when the poet leaves the realm of openly creative writing for the more sobering arena of the political essay. In their biblical echoes, with their eternal present tense, the famous concluding words of *Toussaint Louverture*: "Au commencement est Toussaint Louverture," do indicate how hard it is for the Caribbean imagination to separate history from myth in excavating the ancestral ground.[9]

In the Caribbean text, the absence of the Ancestor is everywhere. It represents simultaneously the inheritance and the eviscerating of a particularly obsessive sentimental reading of European Romanticism, from *Bug-Jargal* onward. The inversion of the false white father who refuses to acknowledge his mulatto progeny (from Séjour to Fanon, Capécia to Manicom), that of the defeated black father who could not protect his (from Thouret to Lacrosil, Condé to Schwarz-Bart), subtend Negritude's vision of an individual liberation that must precede the collective one at the risk of death—to follow Césaire's rough unfolding in the *Cahier.* What Ronnie Scharfman sees through Lacanian categories as the salient feature in the *Cahier,* "the binding of desire with violence,"[10] signals the inadequation of the child-self to the intended father-Ancestor, perhaps because of the inadequacy of the model. The temptation—or the trap—is to posit a Negritude self as a phallic father indeed, but a better one. The famous, defiant passage on those who have invented nothing, a "how to" for black self-refashioning, briefly gives in to that urge, before transcending it in an epistemological shift. Among other things, the *Cahier* is also a warning on the simplistic danger of a binary oppositional vision.

In the justly famous and always moving shift, the shackled poetic self frees itself in a series of powerful kinetic images, starting with the simple standing *up* hand in hand with the beloved island; or rather hand in fist. For the child's tiny *open* hand, the gesture of trust, is engulfed by the giant knotted fist, a gesture of protection that triggers the total immersion downward into "la négraille," the nigger-scum, a plunge into a historically anchored collective self that prepares the illimited, unanchored self-hurtling upward of ritual rebirth. Reversing the initial roles, this now gigantic self leads, the tiny "mote-dust" of a country follows, each led ever upward by the ascending Dove: "monte, / Colombe / monte / monte / monte / Je te suis . . .".

The very intensity of this final prayer courts a realization ever deferred.[11] Although it seeks to inscribe the autonomous black self in the text by establishing a clear line to an authentic Ancestor, the *Cahier* fails to maintain a stable ancestral figuring, as does Césaire's next dramatization of the question, *Et les chiens se taisaient.* The Rebel attempting to sound his deeper African self must choose something or someone other than the false historical fathers, whose judgment he refuses by appealing to the African gods, primitive Greece dovetailing primeval Africa: "Pourquoi aurais-je peur du jugement de mes dieux? qui a dit que j'ai trahi?"[12] As Suzanne Césaire had implied, the only way into the authentic self is through myth, a choice that signals a characteristic turning away from

contemporary reality. The blood shed is called "communiel" and the emphasis kept firmly on the collective outcome.[13] At the end of *Les Chiens,* the redoubling of motifs marks the fully mythical dimension: as the Ancestor of a new people, the Rebel becomes his own ancestor as well. But such outcome is still far in the future, as implied by the subjunctive mode, a vision rather than a fact: "que de mon sang oui, de mon sang / je fonde ce peuple."

The ideological gap between the two versions has usually been attributed to Césaire's own ideological fluctuations at the time.[14] In this case, the autobiographical does not satisfactorily account for the fact that neither version chooses either mythical or historical dimension clearly. It might be more fruitful to look at the successive versions as modulating an ancestral question that has no fixed answer, given Césaire's habitually constant (rather than consistent) refiguring of symbols.

A precise scene connects the *Cahier* to *Les Chiens,* matrix whence all ancestral figuring flows. It is that of the blood baptism, the first step toward a Caribbean definition of self. In *Les Chiens,* the execution of the cockroach-eyed master, who, given the realities of plantation life, could well be the executioner's father, is claimed as the moment that ushers in the authentic self: "Que de sang au fond de ma mémoire (. . .) Je frappai, le sang gicla. C'est le seul baptême dont je me souvienne aujourd'hui." The execution that occurs out of the frame, off camera, before the beginning of *Les Chiens,* makes its symbolic significance possible. In *Le Cahier,* the phrase had appeared but had been undercut by a failure of nerve, the memory of rebellions eventually drowned in the master's liquor that made betrayal possible (as, we are told, Mackandal's was):

> Que de sang dans ma mémoire. Dans ma mémoire sont des lagunes, elles sont couvertes de têtes de morts . . .
>
> Ma mémoire est entourée de sang. Ma mémoire a sa ceinture de cadavres!
>
> et mitrailles de barils de rhum génialement arrosant
>
> nos révoltes ignobles . . .

Of course, the Rebel, too, has been betrayed by his own. However, *Le Cahier* reworks otherwise the theme of betrayal that is historically intertwined with the theme of constant uprisings, offering a historical ancestor that makes positive self-refiguring possible. To the dishonorable betrayal of Mackandal by his own people, his inebriated co-conspirators, to the dishonorable betrayal of the Rebel by his own people, cowards afraid of white revenge, *Le Cahier* opposes an honorable counter-example, that of Toussaint kidnapped under the flag of truce by a dishonorable enemy:

> Ce qui est à moi
> c'est un homme seul emprisonné de
> blanc
> c'est un homme seul qui défie les cris
> blancs de la mort blanche
> (TOUSSAINT, TOUSSAINT LOUVERTURE)

C'est un homme que fascine
l'épervier blanc de la mort blanche . . .
La splendeur de ce sang n'éclatera-t-elle point.

Retrieved from the silence of white history, the dying man is made to belong to black (rather than white) depth consciousness in a movement that answers violence with murder. **"Ce qui est à moi"** has been triggered by the gory sequence of the Middle Passage ("Et je me dis Bordeaux et Nantes et Liverpool et New York et San Francisco . . . / terres rouges, terres sanguines, terres consanguines"), a sequence that is but the prelude to the Césairean leitmotiv that connects several works ("que de sang dans ma mémoire"). This leitmotiv, in turn, introduces the sequence of the father-master's execution by the son-slave and signals the birthing of the true Caribbean now free, as in *Les Chiens,* to claim the Ancestor of his choice: himself. Thus, *Le Cahier* and *Les Chiens* present what looks like a joint version of positive self-birthing.

Critics have abundantly commented on the fact that, in the description of Toussaint's white death, Césaire operates an epistemological reversal. Deconstructing western values, the upending of color categories gives a heightened emotional impact to this scene of remembering that, in turn, makes the execution of the master possible. But it is, as well, a remembering of the contingency of defeat. In self-defeated Haiti, the fulgurant splendor of this sacrificial blood has yet to explode. Toussaint remains here trapped and his death in exile is further mocked by Christophe's own failure soon to come—as Césaire's next play was to explore, a political failure triggered by his people's failure of imagination (or, one might say more gently, their human frailties). By analogy, a pall is thrown over the true outcome of the Rebel's sacrifice (it, too, happens off camera and cannot be witnessed by us). Thus, the exaltation of the future tense, subtly undermined by the negative-interrogative form ("La splendeur de ce sang n'éclatera-t-elle point"), as in the final subjunctive wish of the Rebel ("que de mon sang . . . je fonde ce peuple"), remains the sign of "a dream deferred." To wish it to happen is to acknowledge that it has not and, simultaneously, to fear that it may not.

Yet again myth seems to surge through the palimpsest of history, since the self-birthing voice who acknowledges Toussaint as Ancestor in a baptism of blood is, so nakedly, that of Caliban. The "ce qui est à moi" of *Le Cahier* is Caliban's response to Shakespearean Prospero's boast: "this thing of darkness is mine." The claim of common humanity makes Prospero unable or unwilling to relinquish moral responsibility for his acts, a position of liberal humanism that may hide the darker imperialist urge upon which Césaire's 1969 *Une Tempête* will eventually "signify" (to use Gates's fashionable term).

Une Tempête: Adaptation de 'La Tempête;' de Shakespeare pour un théâtre noir may well hark back to a more ancient mode; that of *Les Chiens*. It is as if the limitations of history, as confronted in the intervening plays, *Christophe* and *Une Saison au Congo,* were to be replayed as myth, but a postlapsarian myth now put through the process of degradation by the recent "years of African independence." If we hear Caliban distinctly proclaiming "U'huru," at the beginning of the play, we can no longer see him at the end. The son of Sycorax sings himself in the Other's language ("la liberté, ohé, la liberté"), and we can barely make it out. Is it feebly heard because Caliban's own resolve—and, therefore, its exemplary quality—has weakened? Or is it feebly heard because we hear it through Prospero's own weakening physical and spiritual condition? Césaire leaves us with this ambivalence.

It is likewise with the white death, Toussaint's trope. Presented as the silenced collective history that must be reclaimed through the power of the imagination, it is immediately absorbed as a potentially mythical figuring of the past in *Le Cahier*—albeit one trailing historical contingencies in its turbulent wake. The famous "what is mine" sequence constructs an analogue between Haiti and Martinique, the past and the present, the humiliated niggerscum and the emerging black self eager to inscribe otherwise the very past the white memory has appropriated. The binary temptation persists, a hint that the poetic self has a hard time moving out of the subject/object, myth/history trap when excavating the ancestral ground.

> **My contention here is simple: it is against Césaire's definitions of the ancestral ground that much of subsequent Caribbean literature measures itself, whether deliberately or not.**
>
> **—*Clarisse Zimra***

One can excavate this ancestral ground otherwise, and go back to the hortatory quotation cited above: "La splendeur de ce sang n'éclatera-t-elle point?" The future tense of spurted blood expressed the wish for the moment of explosive self-baptism, hallowed by another image of spurted blood, the Master's execution ("le sang gicla," a recurrent image in the Césairean corpus), when the slave, by taking back his rightful name, that of Rebel, is giving birth to himself. This moment of fulgurant birthing connects us to that other constant of Césaire's poetic landscape, the volcano, cipher of physical as well as spiritual liberation, and anchors us back, squarely, on Caribbean soil.

With the natural imagery of the Caribbean landscape comes a fairly consistently polarized bestiary. To give but one instance, the positive thoroughbred ("pur sang," with its punning on racial purity as well as "bad blood," including that of the Rimbaldian variety), drawing on the boundless primeval freedom in the mythical time before time, is usually opposed to the negative mangy dog, steel jaws tearing the flesh of the runaway slave, drawing on the direct experience of a recent, historical past. As we observed before in Césaire, the outside polarization is often mirrored inside, within the same image cluster. For instance, *Les Chiens* is able to play on both registers, master's mastiffs and cynocephalic gods. Its signifying downward dive through Ancient religions (Egyptian or Greco-Roman) retrieves the positive god of a former consciousness: the psychopomp who presides over a different poetic passage, Anubis/Cerberus. Moreover, in the expanding doubling constitutive of myth, the dog-faced god is, often, also pictured as the monkey-faced god, willing mediator between the human and the divine. As the Yoruba trickster Eshu, his pranks emphasize the unpredictable nature of the human connection to the divine but never severs it. As the flying Anuman of India, he is the harbinger of the Word, who brings knowledge, culture and, above all, writing to the human species. He is, as well, the giant laughing Monkey-God carved into the stone of pre-Columbian temples all over the Mexican peninsula.[15] A common symbol runs through all these avatars, one that, tapping the collective memory of the folktale, fuses myth and history without contradiction within the only syncretic ancestral trope that is uniquely Caribbean.

"**Beau sang giclé**" is an homage to the folktales rescued from oblivion in the pages of *Tropiques* by way of Lafcadio Hearn. Although the poem appears in *Ferrements* (1960), it clearly harks back, in its elusive imagery of a beheading, to the 1948 *Soleil cou coupé,* the collection that is usually considered Césaire's most "surrealistic," the critics' perplexed stamp of good housekeeping in the face of a violently fragmented subject. It is also connected to the earlier collection born of the war years, *Les Armes miraculeuses,* through two image clusters; first, the famous machete stab of the opening, a sort of beheading, and, second, the sacred bird: "Le grand coup de machète du plaisir rouge en plein front . . . quand mourir avait le goût du pain et la terre et la mer un goût d'ancêtre et cet oiseau qui me crie de ne pas me rendre . . .." The sacred bird of non-surrender, often depicted with phoenix-like qualities, reappears throughout the corpus; to wit, the *Cahier*'s prayer ("pour que revienne le temps de promission / et l'oiseau qui savait mon nom"), or, in *Corps perdu,* "**Dit d'errance**" ("Par le soleil d'un nid coiffé / où phénix meurt et renaît.") By threading the fairly constant images of sacrificial dismemberment and/or beheading throughout Césaire's poetry, one may discern the patterns of sadistic torture that make up a universe where apocalyptic, yet primeval, beasts roam at will; a fusion of the before-time and the after-time characteristic of myth. It does not take great acumen to read the political referent in the myth, such descriptions also matching standard practices of slave torture. By connecting them to birds, one arrives at something more.

"**Beau sang giclé**" is built on a famous folk subtext, but one probably undecipherable without some help for the non-Caribbean. The poem illustrates the story of Yé, who shot the sacred bird in order to feed his starving family: here, too, the political signifier keeps floating up to the surface on the mythical signified. *Tropiques* considered the Afro-Caribbean folk tradition an integral element of political resistance and made little mystery of it, a fact which eventually led to its being banned:

Un tambour. Le grand rire du Vaudou descend des mornes. Combien, au cours des siècles, de révoltes

ainsi surgies! Que de victoires éphémères! Mais aussi, quelles défaites! Quelles répressions! Mains coupées, corps écartelés, gibets, voilà ce qui peuple les allées de l'histoire coloniale. Et rien de tout cela n'aurait passé dans le folklore? Vous connaissez le conte de Colibri. ("Introduction au folklore martiniquais," *Tropiques* IV, janvier 1942)

Césaire (and Ménil) obligingly provide the folk connection between the story of Yé and "**Conte Colibri.**" In a multiplicity of crisscrossing references, firmly connected by the central image of a beheading, the story of Yé spills into the tale of Colibri. The drum and the drum-bird stand for the primal Maroon, Caliban's last avatar. An obvious reference to the maroon's mode of communication, the drum functions both as an ontological metaphor (for instance, the vaudo ceremony in *Christophe* III), and the poem as sample of the counter-poetics of "marronnage"; what Césaire wittily defined for Depestre in their famous friendly quarrel, "Réponse à Depestre, poète haïtien," as a symbolic system where nothing is what it seems.[16]

Dismemberment connects the poem to *Les Chiens*. It also connects the tale of Colibri to that of Yé's sacred bird[17]:

Beau sang giclé

tête trophée membres lacérés
dard assassin beau sang giclé
ramages perdus rivages ravis . . .

       Ô assassin attardé
l'oiseau aux plumes jadis plus belles que le passé
exige le compte de ses plumes dispersées.

On one level, the poem can be read as a riddle on the fact of colonization, predicting a successful revolt, if not revolution. The "standing nigger-scum" ("elle est debout la négraille") force the defeated colonizer, once triumphant trophy hunter, now defeated murderer, to acknowledge its dignity ("exige le compte de ses plumes dispersées"). On another level, Yé who would feed his children the body of the fallen god is replaying both those West African rituals of which Frazer and Freud made so much; and which, in their Mediterranean transformations, René Girard sees as the non-western foundations of our western beliefs—Christ's ritual sacrifice and "flesh-and-blood" communion embracing both. Willingly shedding his own "communial blood," the Rebel of *Les Chiens* is, among others, a (counter)version of Christ. On yet another level, the poem stages an allegorical replay of the Rebel's betrayal by his own people. If the ignorant trophy hunter may be compared to the ignorant betrayers of the oratorio, he has nonetheless committed a sacreligious crime for which he must atone; as, by inference, must they. The criticism of the betrayal is here muted, since Yé (metonym for the poorest "nigger-scum") was trying to feed his children (take charge of the people and so continue the Rebel's task). By forcing them to reconstitute its body, the sacred bird of Negritude is leading them to the self-awareness ("ever more beautiful than before") that precedes collective action. As usual with Césaire, any close-reading eventually proceeds in "expanding rings," to use Rilke's metaphor.

For it is the image of Afro-Caribbean consciousness that brings into the poem's semantic interplay its twin folktale, that of Colibri—not so coincidentally, the other Hearn selection reproduced by Césaire and Ménil. "**Conte colibri**" is the story of the hummingbird who fights a succession of monsters sent by a jealous god to steal the bird's magic drum. When the last monster, Poisson-Armé, presents himself, a badly-wounded Colibri, "spurting blood," knows that he must die but gallantly accepts the challenge:

—Mon dernier combat, dit Colibri qui tomba mort.

Pouesson-Armé, en toute hâte, ramassa un grand coutelas qui traînait par là, coupa la tête de Colibri, la mit sous la pierre de taille dans la cour de la maison. Alors, seulement, il prit le tambour et l'emporta.

(*Tropiques*, IV)

In "**Beau sang giclé**," the "trophy head" is the clue that Colibri and the sacred bird of the past are one. Like Osiris's and Orpheus's, Colibri's head must be severed after death to prevent reincarnation. But, as with Orpheus, the head buried in the house yard is immortal, drawing a perpetual potential reincarnation from Caribbean soil/self. The connection between the chtonic forces of the soil and the Rebel (who, sprawled on the ground, anoints his nape with crumbling earth), was made rather forcefully in the 1946 version of *Les Chiens*. Colibri may well be the Rebel's totem. We already know that it is Christophe's.

As Pestre d'Almeida has shown, parts of the pre-Columbian myth of the hummingbird correspond to aspects of the Ancient Phoenix as well as to the Aztec Hummingbird God; the latter represented the rising sun, the dawning of a new age—a particularly potent cluster in Césaire. In this overlapping of cultural traditions, Césaire has found the perfect syncretic Ancestor; and, as such, the model of the authentic Afro-Caribbean self: the eternal "bird of no surrender."

With its incredibly fast beating heart, the hummingbird is a living drum. And we remember that it is the sacred drum that Poisson-Armé stole from Colibri: in other words, along with his life, that which defined him, his self. Pushing the metaphor, one might also add, his music, his poetry, his language; or, in biblical terms, his Word. The tale of Colibri is that of an ontological murder. But it enfolds a possible rebirth. For, if Colibri did not, in the folktale, come back to life, Yé's magic bird did.

Colibri was a frame of reference in the Césairean corpus every time the questions of ontological and historical authenticity were raised. With *moi, laminaire* . . . , whose lower capped title is significant (all poems have lower capped titles as well), Césaire operates a bitter eviscerating:

rien de tout cela n'a la force d'aller bien loin
essoufflés

ce sont nos oiseaux tombant et retombant
alourdis par le surcroît de cendres des volcans

("éboulis")

The once fertile, revolution-nurturing landscape is now dry ashes. We can measure the depth of despair in this image of sterility and death for a man who once described himself as volcanic, "homme péléen," and praised the other pelean giant of Caribbean history, Louis Delgrès who blew himself to bits on Matouba and who, like Césaire, was born on Basse-Terre. We have passed from the gigantic realm of an all embracing, all-creating, explosive imagination birthing an all-expanding consciousness (the sorcerer's incantations that create a new world and a new people) to a contracting, almost imploding universe. The poetic self, a figure of mythical resilience, once Phoenix-like in its stubborn Colibricourage, is now confronting historical contingency, "limping," Oedipus-like, between self-knowledge and its reverse, self doubt: "Ainsi va toute vie. Ainsi va ce livre, entre soleil et ombre, entre montagne et mangrove, entre chien et loup, claudiquant et binaire." A shrunken giant wonders about his choice of ancestors: "j'ai tiré au sort mes ancêtres" ("ibis-anubis"). The Ancient myths that so empowered him are now inoperative, reduced to arbitrary choices.

The heroic self has been reduced to a non-self, a modest life form that cannot stand separate from its marine environment for long, but sometimes manages self-consciousness, to "inhabit one of my wounds one minute at a time":

j'habite de temps en temps une de mes plaies
chaque minute je change d'appartement
et toute paix m'effraie
            ayant craché volcan mes entrailles d'eau vive
            je reste avec mes pains de mots et mes
    minerais secrets

j'habite donc une vaste pensée

("**calendrier lagunaire**")

The fragmented, tentative consciousness is all too aware of its vulnerability, yet tenaciously clinging to the hope of resurgence with a serenity born of experience at the end of a long life ("algues"):

la relance
        se fait
                algue laminaire

This is Colibri's last incarnation: limited and modest in its acts yet keeping the epic dream alive ("une vaste pensée"). In its last reincarnation, Césaire-Colibri acknowledges that his mission has not changed, and so finally answers the "admirable question," but this time without irony:

il n'est pas question de livrer le monde aux assassins d'aube . . .
une nouvelle bonté ne cesse de croître à l'horizon[18]

("**nouvelle bonté**")

Somehow, this last incarnation is infinitely more touching, in its limitations, and stubborn hope, than the wildest of the Rebel's visions. Until we remember that, in Césaire's syncretic pantheon, Oedipus enfolds the smiling, limping figure of Legba-Eshu, cunning messenger of the gods, the liminal deity who never gave up. And so, infinitely refracted, the iconic figure of Colibri.

Notes

[1] Edouard Glissant, "La Dépossession," *Le Discours antillais* (Paris: Seuil, 1981), 84.

[2] Frederick Ivor Case, "Le Théâtre d'Aimé Césaire," *La Revue romane* 10 (1975). Maximin, unpublished interview by Clarisse Zimra, 29-30 March 1991.

[3] *Is Massa Day Dead?*, ed. Orde Coombs (New York: Doubleday, 1974).

[4] Cf. René Depestre's sobering analysis of the contradiction inherent in Breton's a-historical championing of Césaire as a true surrealist, "André Breton en Haïti," in *Bonjour et adieu à la Négritude* (Paris: Laffont, 1980), 227-35.

[5] Aimé Césaire, *The Collected Poetry*, eds. Clayton Eshleman and Annette Smith (Berkeley: University of California Press, 1983) 50. Cited in the text as *CP*.

[6] Aimé Césaire, *moi, luminaire . . .* (Paris: Seuil, 1982), 9.

[7] I am fully aware that I have so far paid no attention to the chronology of these works. But, as the reworking of *Et les chiens se taisaient* would indicate, these ancestral figures represent momentary positionings in an imaginary continuum, which they roam at will. Witness Césaire's continued reworking of certain image clusters throughout his corpus.

[8] Actually, since the 1990 Virginia translation was made from a later stagescript, it is technically, the latest version of them all.

[9] Aimé Césaire, *Toussaint Louverture: La Révolution française et le problème colonial* (Paris: Club français du livre, 1960), 282.

[10] Ronnie Scharfman, *"Engagement" and the Language of the Subject in the Poetry of Aimé Césaire* (Gainesville: University of Florida Press, 1980), 59.

[11] I do follow James Arnold's lead, who calls this self "the leader-lover" in *Modernism and Negritude: The Poetry and Poetics of Aimé Césaire* (Cambridge: Harvard University Press, 1981), 154; but I put more emphasis on the putative aspect of the leadership role, emphasized by the imperative forms at the end; not to mention that "the lasso of stars" that the new poetic self follows may strangle as well as pull up, and even strangle as it pulls upward. Unafraid of "the great black hole" in which it prepares to dive, the poetic self may still find itself forever trapped in its "motionless veerition."

[12] Aimé Césaire, *Et les chiens se taisaient* (Paris: Présence Africaine, 1956), 33.

[13] Although the term disappears from the 1956 version, the tragic agon does not. Arnold makes a good case for the syncretic aspect of the work, drawing on Poggioli's notion of "agonism" (introduction to *Lyric*

and Dramatic Poetry by Aimé Césaire. Charlottesville: University of Virginia Press, 1990, xxx), to establish the connection with an Ancient Egypt that would enfold Césaire's rather vague and certainly idiosyncratic understanding of African history by way of Frobenius (as evinced in Suzanne's essay on Frobenius) and of classical "agon" by way of Nietzsche. Case, "Eléments de civilisations égyptienne, grecque et romaine dans *Et les chiens se taisaient*," in *Soleil éclaté*, ed. J. Leiner (Tübingen: Gunter Naar, 1984), 69-80, has painstakingly identified all possible references to the Egyptian Book of the Dead. An excellent comparative myth analysis of the two versions is found in Lilian Pestre de Almeida's "Les deux textes de *Et les Chiens se taisaient*" in *Œuvres et Critiques* III-IV (Automne 1979): 203-12.

[14] To attribute the shift to Césaire's increasing dissatisfaction with, and subsequent break from, the Communist Party in 1956 oversimplifies the relationship between the "idealistic" poet and the politician beset by "concrete realities." For example, Rodney Harris: "Césaire a perdu une partie de son idéalisme et se bat contre des difficultés concrètes," in *L'Humanisme dans le théâtre de Césaire* (Sherbrooke: Naaman 1973), 51.

[15] This aspect of harbinger/bearer of the Word is not lost on another contemporary poet, Octavio Paz, who, like Césaire but more openly, practices what he calls a poetics of "convergences" in *The Monkey Grammarian* (New York: Seazer Books, 1981).

[16] Aimé Césaire, "Réponse à Depestre, poète haitien," *Présence africaine*, (avril-juin 1955): 113.

[17] Cailler's splendid close reading of the poem rightly points out a binary, oppositional cadence that carries mixed ideological implications and makes it impossible to arrive at a stable meaning: for he who is victorious (the trophy bearer) is also a complacent murderer, whose unforgivable sin is clearly set off by the typography ("ô assassin attardé"). *Proposition poétique: Une lecture de l'oeuvre d'Aimé Césaire* (Sherbrooke: Naaman, 1976).

[18] This may be the last incarnation of "Beau sang giclé," a counter echo to the first heroic stirring of implacable Negritude: "l'aube sur sa chaîne mord féroce à naître." This is not to say that *laminaire* is unheroic. There are enough "pelean" poems to show that Césaire has lost none of his vigor. But the overall voice, and the Caribbean poetic persona, nonetheless, show signs of unmistakable lassitude.

Mireille Rosello (essay date 1993)

SOURCE: "One More Sea to Cross: Exile and Intertextuality in Aimé Césaire's *Cahier d'un retour au pays natal*," in *Yale French Studies*, No. 83, 1993, pp. 176-95.

[*In the following essay, Rosello compares the theme of exile in Maryse Condé's "Notes on a Return to the Native Land" and Césaire's early poem.*]

> l'exil s'en va ainsi dans la mangeoire des astres
>   portant de malhabiles
> grains aux oiseaux nés du temps
>   —**"Birds"** in *Ferrements*

The people of Martinique and Guadeloupe will perhaps never recover from their exile, will perhaps never even succeed in defining it.[1] Exile will thus be, for a long time to come, the raw material of the texts of Aimé Césaire, Edouard Glissant, Maryse Condé, and of many others. Like their books, these writers, born in the Antilles and educated in metropolitan France, fall outside the traditional classifications in anthologies of literature, eluding the canon which does not know what place to assign them. Although retrieved by the hegemony and placed among marginal categories (Caribbean texts, Francophone texts, Black literature), the works of Martinican and Guadeloupean writers will always be elsewhere, but an elsewhere that one will choose at times to appropriate and assimilate: Martinique and Guadeloupe, departments of France, Aimé Césaire, "great Black poet."[2] Whatever the label imposed upon these texts, it is clear that the canon violates them when they are reduced to the "Oneness" of "French," "Francophone," "Black," or even "Antillean" culture, when it minimizes the differences that separate them from the traditions within which they are classified. The dubious privileges accompanying literary fame and recognition cannot offset the loss of a vital part of their multiple identity.

The study of the "theme" of exile will relieve none of this pain. Exile here does not yet have a satisfactory definition, it is not resolved by a "return" to the "land." Texts which "come from" the islands and which "return" there are stricken not by Exile but by a *series* of exiles; they suffer from an impossible departure and return, they are marked by the ambiguity of an eternal movement of "detours."[3] For Edouard Glissant, "retour" and "détour" thus become inseparable, and the quasi-homonymy of these two words invites us to look towards language to find what might be a possible definition of a "native land" for writers in the Antilles.

When Glissant writes that the Martinican who decides to leave his island "n'emporte pas sa patrie à la semelle de ses souliers" [does not take along the homeland on the soles of his shoes] (*Discours Antillais*), he suggests in effect that exile has a link, often obscured, with the language one uses, in this case with French, whose clichés and proverbs are incompatible with the lived experience of Antilleans. We will see how with Césaire, the French language becomes the object of appropriation and is transformed into a strategic instrument of resistance. We do well, however, to remember that for Antillean writers of French language and culture, every unexplored intertextuality risks being an unfortunate missed opportunity: the monolithic French Language is not necessarily equipped to talk about a "land" that is not one, about a "native land" that is not an origin, about a "return" that would only be another departure and a new detour, about joyous departures that are transformed into unhappy exiles and become little by little the acceptance of "wandering,"[4] about an infinite and irremediable exile. I will use two texts as examples, because from them was born the intuition that, among certain Antillean writers, the notion of exile is the result of a long process of recognition, and that often it is only a posteriori that a voluntary and wished-for departure is reinterpreted as a disaster—an agonizing separation, but one that is overshadowed by an Antillean culture imagined as nothing-ness, a void.

. . . . .

In 1939, Césaire, who from then on would consider himself an "exile" in Paris, finished **Notebook of a Return to the Native Land**.[5] Forty years later, Maryse Condé, having returned to Guadeloupe after a "detour" through Europe and Africa, borrowed from Césaire the essence of his title and spoke of her exiles in an essay entitled "Notes on a Return to the Native Land." The two titles resemble each other, recall each other, echo each other. An example of a problematic intertextual dialogue, is Maryse Condé's title a reference-homage to the father of Négritude, to the Master of Antillean literature whom the novelist recognizes henceforth as her own? Does this title signal the end of a literary exile and the adoption of a cultural homeland? It appears that both elements coexist, and that the title may also be a pastiche, a disabused wink at a pathetic (literary) history that does not allow writers to change problematics, that condemns them to an unending repetition; it is paradoxical, at the exact moment when Condé alludes to a Césairian "native land" which might constitute a possible origin, to choose as a theme the absence of origin, and thus the difficulty of "return."

From generation to generation, Antillean writers who have gone to study and work in France have had in common the perception that their initial departure was *not* an exile—indeed, the opposite seems true. Maryse Condé describes her adolescence as long years of boredom, and speaks of her island-*"rison"* and of the "mer qu'on ne regardait que pour avoir le désir de *s'échapper des Antilles"* [the sea one looked at only to have the desire to *escape* from the Antilles] (my emphasis). "Le pays natal se réduisait pour nous à un décor, le décor d'un constant ennui" [The native land was reduced for us to a setting, the setting of constant boredom]. "Donc, quand j'ai quitté la Guadeloupe, . . . j'avais l'impression que j'allais enfin commencer à vivre" [Thus, when I left Guadeloupe, . . . I had the impression that I was finally going to begin to live]. This first voluntary departure is euphorically described as the end of a confinement, as a liberation. One may be surprised that Maryse Condé's remembrances echo Césaire's own declarations, when he asserts to Lilyan Kesteloot: "J'ai quitté la Martinique avec volupté" [I left Martinique with exquisite delight][6]. At this stage, as if the Césairian experience had not entered into the Condé's History, there is no origin. The concept itself of exile seems impossible to forge. The place from which exile could possibly be defined has been completely annihilated by the colonial situation. Literally, the native land has been erased:

> Si on m'avait demandé à ce moment-là "Qu'est-ce que ton pays natal?" Je n'aurais *rien eu à dire;* j'aurais dit que c'était peut-être deux ou trois palmiers à côté de la mer qui *encadraient* le *vide le néant.* [my emphasis]

> If someone had asked me at that time "What is your native land?" I would have had *nothing* to say; I would have said that it was maybe two or three palm trees next to the sea framing *nothingness,* the void.

The native land is a "nothingness," a "void," and therefore in leaving, Martinicans and Guadeloupeans leave nothing towards which they could eventually return. It is only later, *retrospectively,* that Antillean intellectuals can rediscover a "homeland" by representing the people of the Antilles as already exiled—uprooted from Africa and from themselves. It is thus striking to discover that the two texts of Maryse Condé and Aimé Césaire, although separated by a literary generation, take up the same problematic in almost exactly the same terms. In 1987, Condé speaks of her adolescence as a period during which the Antilles are not *representable.* Condé confesses that in 1954, the date of her first departure, "[elle n'avait] jamais entendu prononcer le nom d'Aimé Césaire" [She had never heard the name of Aimé Césaire]. For her, everything happens as though the Négritude movement and the publication of *Tropiques* had gone unnoticed.[7] What is remarkable in Condé's narrative is the persistent impression that she has no literary past from her native soil. Even Césaire, to whom she owes her title, is discovered after her departure, in metropolitan France. The "native land" is a silence, it is peopled by words which could be hers: it has "nothing to say." No precursor existed for her, and oddly, her text resembles Césaire's own in which he admits that Antillean literature did not exist for him as he prepared to leave Paris ("Quand je suis rentré à la Martinique, qu'est-ce que je connaissais? La littérature française: Rimbaud, Claudel, Baudelaire" [When I returned to Martinique, what did I know? French literature: Rimbaud, Claudel, Baudelaire]).[8] The recognition of exile will thus be paradoxical since the "land" is not the idealized homeland towards which nostalgia turns. Césaire and Condé will undergo in Paris the experience of their foreignness, of their alienation, of a negative exile in relation to a metropolitan community which excludes them but they will not know where to place their loyalty, their sense of belonging, their return. Maryse Condé says: "La première découverte que je fais, c'est que je ne suis pas française" [The first discovery I made, is that I am not French]. It is only after having arrived in Paris that Condé joins the itinerary of the authors of the preceding generation and begins to suspect that the island was in fact already exiled from its African origin. Nonetheless, even this origin is henceforth mythic and illusory; tempted by the "great Black womb," she realizes that it does not want her[9] and that the return to the Black continent is, as Glissant says, "un espoir raturé," [a deleted hope]. Under these conditions, "return" emerges as the only possible choice, but by elimination, by violence. The political and literary awakening which results from contact with France also renders return the only possible strategy for an author determined to participate in the birth of an Antillean nation and writing. Condé insists that it required "bravery" on her part to accept to return to this prison she had left, to what Césaire had described as "ces quelques milliers de mortiférés qui tournent en rond dans la calebasse d'une île . . . l'archipel arqué comme le désir inquiet de se nier" [these few thousand death-bearers who mill in that calabash of an island . . . the archipelago arched with an anguished desire to negate itself] (*Collected Poetry, Notebook*).

The result is that one has the impression that the return to the land resolves nothing, that the departure for Martinique and Guadeloupe are logical political decisions, but that strangely, for Antillean writers, the "return to the native land" is yet another form of exile. Exile here is perceived as a permanent gap, no longer between the speaking subject and a clearly identified cultural or national identity, but between the "I" and the community within which that "I" temporarily finds itself (speaking). Every displacement, every attempt to return, every new departure renders the "I" more and more aware of the gap, of his or her difference. The revealing element of this incessant exile, of this return constantly deferred, is thus the meeting of the "I" and a community by which he or she tries to become adopted, which he or she tries to recognize as a homeland; this repeated endeavor could be compared to what Glissant calls "mise en Relation" [putting into Relation].

. . . . .

With Césaire, this "mise en Relation" is accomplished by the poetic word. The ***Notebook of a Return to the Native Land*** is not, like the "Notes" of Maryse Condé, an autobiographical narrative in prose which retraces after the fact the steps leading to an awareness of exile. A prophetic vision of what will be the return, this long poem allows the "I" to anticipate the same discoveries as those of the narrator of "Notes on a Return to the Native Land." In the ***Notebook,*** the "mise en Relation" is achieved by the confrontation of the poetic language of the "I" and the language of the community within which he finds himself. The passage I will examine here, which critics customarily call the streetcar scene, seems to me an extraordinary moment of textual putting into relation, a moment of awareness in which the narrator becomes hyperconscious of manipulating a language and a culture which also manipulate him. The "I," at first tempted by the recourse to assimilate (here an individual solution), is two steps away from enclosing himself in his unconscious exile, and risks becoming irrevocably "other." But this episode also coincides with the discovery of a solution, a moment of illumination for the narrator who remembers and tells the story.

I would like to show that in this passage, a reference to "L'Albatros" by Baudelaire which at first seems to slip its way into the poem as though by accident, is immediately picked up, unmasked, and systematically explored by the "I" who refuses to obscure the work of language, which is capable in turn of serving and harming him, of enriching and impoverishing him, of including and excluding him, of liberating and oppressing him. I cite one following the other the poem by Baudelaire and the meeting between the narrator and a "grouchy nigger" in a Parisian streetcar:

> Souvent, pour s'amuser, les hommes d'équipage
> Prennent des albatros, vastes oiseaux des mers,
> Qui suivent, indolents compagnons de voyage,
> Le navire glissant sur les gouffres amers.
>
> A peine les ont-ils déposés sur les planches,
> Que ces rois de l'azur, maladroits et honteux
> Laissent piteusement leurs grandes ailes blanches
> Comme des avirons traîner à côté d'eux

Ce voyageur ailé, comme il est gauche et veule
Lui, naguère si beau, qu'il est comique et laid!
L'un agace son bec avec un brûle-gueule
L'autre mime, en boîtant, l'infirme qui volait!

Le Poète est semblable au prince des nuées
Qui hante la tempête et se rit de l'archer;
Exilé sur le sol aux milieux des huées
Ses ailes de géant l'empêchent de marcher.[10]

Often, to pass the time on board, the crew
will catch an albatross, one of those big birds
which nonchalantly chaperone a ship
across the bitter fathoms of the sea.

Tied to the deck, this sovereign of space,
as if embarrassed by its clumsiness,
pitiably lets its great white wings
drag at its sides like a pair of unshipped oars.

How weak and awkward, even comical[11]
this traveller but lately so adroit—
onc deckhand sticks a pipestem in its beak,
another mocks the cripple that once flew!

The Poet is like this monarch of the clouds
riding the storm above the marksman's range;
exiled on the ground, hooted and jeered, he cannot
  walk because of his
great wings.

                                        [Baudelaire]

Et moi, et moi, moi qui chantais le poing dur.
Il faut savoir jusqu'où je poussai la lâcheté. Un soir
  dans un tramway en face de moi, un nègre . . .
La misère on ne pouvait pas dire, s'était donné un
  mal fou pour l'achever. . . .
Et l'ensemble faisait parfaitement un nègre hideux,
  un nègre grognon, un nègre mélancolique, un
  nègre affalé, ses mains réunies en prière sur un
  bâton noueux.

Un nègre enseveli dans une vieille veste élimée. Un
  nègre comique et laid et des femmes derrière moi
  ricanaient en le regardant
Il était COMIQUE ET LAID,
COMIQUE ET LAID pour sûr.
J'arborai un grand sourire complice . . .
Ma lâcheté retrouvée!

                                [Césaire, *Collected Poetry*]

And I, and I,
I was singing the hard fist
You must know the extent of my cowardice.
One evening on the streetcar facing me, a nigger . . .
Poverty, without any question, had knocked itself out
to finish him off. . . .
And the whole thing added up perfectly to a
  hideous nigger, a grouchy nigger, a melancholy
  nigger, a slouched nigger, his hands joined in
prayer on a knobby stick. A nigger shrouded in an
  old threadbare coat.
A comical and ugly nigger, with some women

behind me sneering at
him.
He was COMICAL AND UGLY,
COMICAL AND UGLY for sure.
I displayed a big complicitous smile . . .
My cowardice rediscovered!

                                        [*Collected Poetry*]

For M. a M. Ngal, "this scene takes root in the daily colorfulness of the Latin Quarter. It was really lived."[12] Although Ngal devotes an entire chapter of his study on Césaire to the "school of foreign maturities," concentrating especially on an inventory of philosophical and literary influences, he does not read the streetcar scene as an example of intertextuality.[13] Classified under the rubric "other sources," this passage is considered one of the scenes that depict "the collective experience of the 'nigger' in time and space." I would like to suggest that the "comical and ugly nigger" underlines what is problematic in the rewriting of a space-time "nigger" when one writes in French. This scene which Ngal considers "banal" does not escape the problems of literary influences. To the contrary, it shows how these influences are problematic: this passage from the *Notebook* is the meeting of the "grouchy nigger" and the narrator, but also the meeting between the writing of Césaire and that of Baudelaire. The episode puts into relation two black men but also two poets, two discourses. It also puts into relation the space-time of individuals and the space-time of writing. It enables us to witness the creation of the production of communities in formation, of the resulting conflicts, and of the manifold choices occasioned by these manifold meetings.

The streetcar scene is written around a Baudelairian reminiscence that abruptly becomes aware of being a quotation: not only is a "textual dialogue" established (Cailler), but also the text catches itself in a blatant (and dangerous) use of "sources," "origins." This awareness is closely tied to the referential context of the scene and makes the Baudelairian reference coincide with a moment in which the poet confesses an (auto)betrayal. The progressive modification of this connection with the other's poetry becomes a political act; the poem masterfully demonstrates that intertextuality is not limited to a problem of literary form, but touches in addition a community much larger than the restricted circle of critics. The putting into relation of two complicitous or rival texts serves at the same time to create boundaries between communities of readers and to put these boundaries into question, to underscore the differences and similarities between the readers and characters of the *Notebook,* to create networks of belonging and exclusion in relation to which the poet (and the reading "I") must define their place, their nostalgia, their exile.

The work of putting into relation follows three stages that correspond to three successive references to the same poem by Baudelaire: "A comical and ugly nigger, with some women behind me sneering at him. / He was COMICAL AND UGLY, / COMICAL AND UGLY for sure." The repetition of the same adjectival phrase avoids obscuring the process of putting into relation, which would otherwise risk transforming the poem into a passive intertextual assimilation on the part of the black poet (recognizing the distinction Léopold Senghor established between "to assimilate" and "to be assimilated").

The first appearance of the phrase "comical and ugly" creates a simple and binary world in which the "grouchy nigger," grotesque and scorned, is contrasted with the sneering women with whom the poet identifies. At this point in the narrative, the narrator presents us with the "nigger" isolated from everyone else, and who no longer has anything in common with the assimilated poet, both supportive and an accomplice of the women, unaware of any tie he may have with the wretched character he curiously eyes. The tie between the poet and his race has been cut by the language he uses. The adjectives "comical and ugly," to which no punctuation marks draw our attention, at first infiltrate the poem without the narrator noticing that they are a "ready-made," part of the language and culture; the Baudelairian reference at first appears without any signs of quotation, without distance, irrevocably absorbed by the word that the poet thinks he is speaking, but that in fact speaks him. Part and parcel of the language called French, the reference could quite easily at this stage remain obscure, without requiring the poet here to claim that he has drawn his inspiration from the restricted community of "étudiants français plus ou moins cultivés" [more or less cultured French students][14] among whom he could feel at home. Readers will not suffer from a feeling of incompetence if they do not identify "comical and ugly" as a quotation. Some will probably have the intuition of an intertextual moment without the sense of the passage becoming irremediably obscure for all that if the vague memory does not become clearer. Every Francophone can be satisfied with understanding the expression which is, like the narrator's language, perfectly assimilated.

Césaire finds a homeland only in the acceptance of his own exile. He is Black, Creole, Martinican, Antillean, he is elsewhere, forever.

—Mireille Rosello

This reference, which is not necessarily one, demonstrates the theoretical possibility of cultural "assimilation" that certain researchers consider impossible,[15] but of course renders it extremely problematic; for how can one delight in this form of assimilation since the expression "comical and ugly" is used to oppress him whom I have just constructed as "other": the Black, the poor Black, he who from now on has nothing more in common with the poet, and who is treated as an object of curiosity and derision. By choosing these two adjectives, the "I" excludes himself from a whole group of wretched and grouchy "niggers" to which he absolutely refuses to belong. He has mastered the language of the colonizer sufficiently well to be able to consider his words an origin without quotation, a free message without ties. In contrast, for example, to

the tradition of African-American slave narratives, whose authors often use the authority of a well-known or powerful white to support the truthfulness of their account, Césaire does not need to cite Baudelaire to talk about a "comical and ugly nigger." But at the very moment at which he has the impression of possessing language, language possesses him since it forces him to convey the ideology of which it is the carrier. The more the poet appropriates this language, the more he makes it his own, the more quotation marks, that is, an awareness of distance, are absent, and the more he exiles himself from this people of grouchy niggers with whom he no longer recognizes the slightest affinity, the slightest resemblance. The first appearance of the reminiscence is probably accompanied by the same "exquisite delight" as the first departure for Paris—the poet undergoes an exile of which he is not conscious, his foreignness has become alienation. The sign of this alienation is a moment of the "verbal delirium" which Mudimbe discusses,[16] of the gap between ideology and the speaking subject which Glissant, Fanon[17] and Sartre denounce in their theoretical works. In "Black Orpheus," Sartre notes that school teaches the "Negro" not just the words "black" and "white," but rather the existence of a hierarchic coupling: "en le livrant au nègre, l'instituteur lui livre par surcroît cent habitudes de langage qui consacrent la priorité du blanc sur le noir" [in passing it to the Negro, the instructor gives him [her] in addition a hundred habits of language which consecrate the priority of white over black.][18] If a certain social stratum manages to achieve assimilation, it must have adopted "l'idéologie donnée avec l'enseignement. Elle deviendra vite le véhicule de la pensée officielle" [the ideology given with schooling. It will quickly become the vehicle of official thought] (Glissant). Exile consists then in being from nowhere, in being only the "vehicle," the point of passage of a language, in losing oneself as Edouard Glissant claims:

> Comment ne pas voir qu'une communauté ainsi accoutumée à l'emploi des mots qui pour elle et si visiblement ne correspondent à aucune réalité sinon projetée en phantasmes, peu à peu *se perd* dans un usage irréel, et par conséquent irresponsable des mots.

> How can one not see that a community thus accustomed to using words which for it, only so obviously, correspond to no reality, if not one projected in fantasy, little by little loses itself in an unreal, and consequently irresponsible, usage of words. [Glissant, My translation]

If the first appearance of the reminiscence is an integral part of the language of the poet and ideologically influences the rest of his text, the second stage of the work of "mise en Relation" is a *revelation* in the sense that photographers use the term: an image appears suddenly there where before nothing was visible. "COMICAL AND UGLY" stand out from here on in capital letters which do not explicitly acknowledge the status of quotation but graphically represent a moment of awareness; for us, the two adjectives are henceforth unavoidable, hypervisible, we can no longer ignore them. The two words demand our attention as though their enlargement corresponded to the moment at which they suddenly became audible for the poet as elements foreign to his own language.

The capital letters establish a distance, a difference between the one who blames the "grouchy nigger" and the speaking subject. From now on, the "I" will be forever distanced from the group with which he had been trying to identify. Not that the poet is seeking to refute responsibility for his judgment, but a foreign presence appears around which alliances will establish themselves.

By accentuating the reference invisible up till then, by graphically admitting that these two adjectives are out of the ordinary, the poet accomplishes a doubly subversive act; he voluntarily exiles himself from words which he had thought were his own and from the reassuring ideology which made of him an assimilated member of society. In representing, through his poetic language, a moment of awareness, in putting us in presence with the moment at which he realizes that he is quoting, he admits first that he was taken in by what he thought was his own language, he sets himself apart, on the outside, he makes Baudelaire, this canonized white poet, the origin of his discourse. The narrator discovers that he is alienated, that another speaks in his place. The textual "mise en Relation" "separates the poet from a universe that he erroneously thought was his."[19] And suddenly, the meaning of the whole passage is altered, as if by magic: all at once, the meaning of the two adjectives is enriched and transformed, because the context has changed, and because the reference to "the Albatross" has modified the forces present. This passage of the poem seems to me to offer a remarkably economical representation of a moment of awareness, which, for Césaire, had perhaps lasted for years. The conclusions of the Négritude movement, notably the decision no longer to permit colonialist ideology to contaminate poetic language, the search for an authentic Black voice, are distilled here into a moment of revelation which can act as a founding myth. The Baudelairian intertext, even if it is perceived as a text testifying to colonial power, thus becomes liberating.

The nigger suddenly becomes a positive image, that of a free and majestic bird, misunderstood by the crewmen who "to pass the time" have exiled it far from the natural habitat to which it was marvelously adapted. The streetcar becomes similar to the "deck" of the ship, and suddenly appears as a last resort compared to the aerial space the albatross masters. A first connection becomes clear between the grouchy nigger and the poet: like him, the poet is an exiled "winged traveller" who has crossed the seas on the decks of boats of men. Without bringing in racial solidarity, which the colonial situation has perhaps irremediably destroyed or rendered impossible to define, the text forces the poet to perceive resemblance where before he had only wanted to see the incongruous presence of the comical and ugly Other. Departure, voyage, and winged traveller take on an entirely new meaning, painting a portrait in which the "I" is forced to recognize himself. In an interview with Daniel Maximin, Césaire described the **Notebook** as the "departure," "le grand coup d'aile, il y a Icare qui se met des ailes et qui part" [the great flapping of wings, Icarus is there putting on his wings and leaving].[20] Two identical images refer henceforth to the wretched Black and to the poet, the textual putting into relation that at first oppressed the unassimilated Black now turns

ironically against the poet who sought to exile himself voluntarily. In spite of all the efforts of the assimilated narrator to distinguish himself, it becomes clear that he cannot ignore the fate that the "crewmen" thrust upon the albatross because he himself is part of the race of winged travellers. At present, two groups face each other, and it is impossible to ignore that their relationship is marked by a violence before which the poet cannot remain neutral. It is clear that the two groups confront one another in a tragic struggle that cannot leave the poet (literally) in/different: he must resign himself to choosing his homeland, he must see himself as "albatross" or "member of the crew" and the choice is no longer so easy as when it was a question of allying himself with the "women" who made fun of the grouchy nigger, because the image has overturned the valorization. Paradoxically, in becoming aware of the reference, that is, of the fact that language exiles him, speaks in his place, the "I" also discovers that this same language forces him to make a choice he did not know existed. The women with whom he had exchanged a great complicitous smile are no longer a group whose privileges it is flattering to share; they are transformed into contemptible and hateful "members of the crew."

Conversely, the Antillean context enriches the reading of Baudelaire's poem with new historical references that give a more tragic meaning to the presence of the sailors. In proposing to the reader the association between the albatross and the nigger "finished off by poverty," the text invites a comparison between the generic ship and the slave ships that haunt Césaire's poetry: "le navire lustral [qui s'avance] impavide sur les eaux écroulées" [the lustral ship [advancing] fearlessly on the crumbling water] is also the reminder of the first voyage, the first exile, the first wrenching away: "le négrier craque de toute part . . . Son ventre se convulse et résonne . . . L'affreux ténia de sa cargaison ronge les boyaux fétides de l'étrange nourisson des mers!" [the slave ship cracks everywhere . . . its belly convulses and resounds. . . . The ghastly tapeworm of its cargo gnaws the fetid guts of the strange suckling of the sea!]. Thus for a second time the poet crosses the sea, and the "pastime" of the crew members, like the "sneering" of the women and the poet, appear to be criminal violence. The hidden story of the first exile returns to haunt the text. The awareness of the reference thus has the consequence of forcing the narrator to accept that his identification with the women makes him guilty of an ignoble violence towards this "winged traveller" who, like him, has crossed the sea. The textual putting into relation forces him to recognize his own situation as an exile and the seriousness of the choice he makes in placing himself among the laughers.

All the more so since his laugh is marked by an enormous irony, an irony that the third repetition of "COMICAL AND UGLY" brings sharply into evidence: the third stage of textual "mise en relation" is no longer simply a more or less invisible reminiscence (an unconscious exile) or an oppressive reference (an unhappy exile), but the discovery of new alliances, of new relations of force, of new readings. In taking up for the third time the expression "comical and ugly," the text completely isolates it from the rest of the poem: "COMICAL AND UGLY for sure." Placed in apposition, without a noun, without a verb, the two adjectives seem apprehended by a narrative moment whose lucidity becomes superiority. The "for sure" can be read as an ironic illumination, the moment when the poet abruptly discovers another meaning in the parallel between the Albatross and the grouchy nigger.

Because not only does the image of the Albatross oppressed by the members of the crew underscore the alienation of the narrator who thought he would easily be able to side with the sailors, but also Baudelaire's poem enables us to push the parallel even further; the link between this wretched Black and the "I" becomes abruptly clearer, more complex, if we understand that the "grouchy nigger albatross" is also the symbol of the Poet. This "winged traveller" "tied to the deck" is not simply the exile who has lost his native land—he is also the narrator himself, insofar as he calls himself a poet. Therefore, it is not only because he makes himself the accomplice of the colonizers that the narrator may regret his laugh, but also because without knowing it, he has been making fun of himself. It is an image of himself that the narrator-Poet suppresses, without knowing that he has made himself both henchman and victim, again the Baudelairian "héautontimoroumenos." He was "sneering" at himself. All his superiority caves in here, all alliances between "the assimilated," between "intellectuals," are ferociously denounced as illusory. In refusing to face his "désolidarisation," the poet is reduced to oppressing himself, not as a poor and ignorant man, not even as a Black, but as a Poet. The textual dialogue thus forces him to recognize that when he seeks to withdraw from class and racial solidarity (there is nothing in common between a "cultivated French student" and a "nigger finished off by poverty"), he repudiates in fact the Poet, "this monarch of the clouds." The textual putting into Relation reveals to him the extent of what Glissant calls "derision." The Antillean poet is "Exilé ou malade. Malade de cette absence dont le signe est si intarissable à établir: un palmarès de la dérision." [Exiled or sick. Sick because of this absence whose sign is so inexhaustible to establish: a prize list of derision].

The "I" who just discovered that he himself was guilty of oppressing the Other by the intermediary of a reference, was in fact falling into a paradoxical trap; ironically, the Baudelairian adjectives he used to poke fun at the "comical and ugly nigger" are in fact taken from a poem that, at the outset, pleaded in favor of the damned Poet, misunderstood by the crowd.

The reference to the poem by Baudelaire is therefore not necessarily a reactionary gesture forcing the poet to side with the colonizer. Certainly there is danger in speaking the language of the other, in assimilating it without questioning the quality of the relation uniting the "I" with the groups that form around him when he speaks French. Language may become the place of voluntary or unconscious exile, the place from which the poet renounces his own because he has transformed the world into violent binaries where only the oppressed, "winged travellers," and the oppressors, "members of the crew," any longer

exist. But this passage illustrates the moment at which thought understands that there is a future far from this duality that resembles, to the point that it is difficult to tell them apart, the colonial situation as described by Fanon: a manicheanism without hope. The narrator need not choose between two equally detestable alternatives, cowardice or poverty, and will thus never be reduced to producing this parody of literature against which the journal *Tropiques* had declared war early in the century: "Littérature de hamac, littérature de sucre et de vanille. Tourisme littéraire. Guide bleu et CGT. Poésie, non pas" [Hammock literature, literature of sugar and vanilla. Tourist literature. Blue Guide and CGT. Poetry, not at all.][21]

The danger here would be what Glissant calls "mimetic annihilation," which would be the pure and simple disappearance of a "homeland" other than Occidental culture and values. To the contrary, the inevitable intertextuality becomes textual "Entrée en Relation," and the dialogue established little by little between the discourse of the "I" and the discourse of others becomes in itself a land that here makes the Poet a perpetual exile, but an exile conscious of his condition, capable of solidarity towards those whom he resembles. Of course this abstract "homeland" does not at all solve the problems confronting Antillean poets, nor does it prevent the poet from feeling exiled from his people of prosaic sailors or his position from making him suspect (rightly or wrongly) of an unbearable elitism. But at least this work of textual putting into relation offers proof that the poet can, in spite of the danger of assimilation, speak his own language, his own French. Sartre, describing the black/white hierarchy that forces the black poet to condemn himself, writes in "Black Orpheus":

> Dès qu'il ouvre la bouche, il s'accuse, à moins qu'il ne s'acharne à renverser la hiérachie. Et s'il la renverse en français, il poétise déjà: imagine-t-on l'étrange saveur qu'auraient pour nous des locutions comme "la noirceur de l'innocence" ou "les ténèbres de la vertu"?

> Let him open his mouth and he condemns himself, except insomuch as he sets himself to destroy the hierarchy. And if he destroys it in French, he poetizes already; let one imagine the strange savor which terms such as "the blackness of innocence" or the "shadows of virtue" would have for us.

By putting his poetic word and language into Relation, Césaire goes even further than what Sartre proposed: he is not happy simply to invert the valorized metaphors separating whites and blacks, he calls into question the systems of inclusion and exclusion that make of some either exiles or full citizens. The narrator of the *Notebook* discovers the power of alternating between his language and that of the other. This contact obviously necessitates a perpetual wandering, but also provides the means of becoming aware of exile and of perceiving its tragedy. To claim the homeland of the "members of the crew" is quickly an untenable situation, and would also be an inhuman price to pay for the end of exile (and the scene reminds us that no one is immune from these moments of "cowardice"). This passage from the *Notebook* may thus be read as an allegory of the difficult process of recognizing the Negritude that presides over the creation of the text in its entirety; it is at once a warning against the deceitful "cowardice" constantly lying in wait for the narrator but also the discovery of the possibility of choice, of what Ronnie Scharfman calls his "engagement."[22] Textual relationality can be a strategy at the service of the "grouchy nigger" and grant him the power that language would like to take away from him. Despite the dangers of seeing oneself transformed into a passive vehicle of official ideology, "Un homme qui possède le langage possède par contrecoup le monde exprimé et impliqué par ce langage. On voit où nous voulons en venir: il y a dans la possession du langage une extraordinaire puissance" [A man who possesses language possesses as an indirect consequence the world expressed and implied by this language. My point may already be seen: there is extraordinary power in the possession of language]. In ascertaining the role that Baudelaire's language plays in his own poem, the narrator of the *Notebook* ran the risk of discovering that he has perhaps no other homeland than Relation, that is, an exile, that he remains a "winged traveller" incapable of walking. Certainly, the "return" to the "native land" is an indispensable step that redeems the temptation of "sneering." The "j'ai longtemps erré et je reviens vers la hideur désertée de vos plaies" [I have wandered for a long time and am returning towards the deserted hideousness of your wounds], keeps alive the hope that solidarity towards the grouchy nigger is possible in the name of a homeland of suffering and oppression. But the moments of textual putting into relation remind the poet that his words express above all this multiple I to which the French language had denied him access. In an interview with Jacqueline Leiner, Césaire tries to define his work as a poet:

> mon effort a été *d'infléchir* le français, de le transformer pour exprimer disons: "ce moi, ce moi-nègre, ce moi-créole, ce moi martiniquais, ce moi-antillais." C'est pour cela que je me suis plus intéressé à la poésie qu'à la prose et ce *dans la mesure ou c'est le poète qui fait son language.*

> My effort has been to *bend* French, to transform it so that we can say: "this I, this Black I, this Creole I, this Martinican I, this Antillean I." That is why I was more interested in poetry than in prose, *to the extent that the poet creates his own language.*

The poet finds a homeland only in the acceptance of his own exile. He is Black, Creole, Martinican, Antillean, he is elsewhere, forever.

> Partir
> Comme il y a des hommes-hyènes et des hommes-
>   panthères, je serais
> un homme-juif,
> un homme-cafre
> un homme-hindou-de-Calcutta
> un-homme-de-Harlem-qui-ne-vote-pas
> To go away.
> As there are hyena-men, and panther-men,
> I would be a jew-man

> a Kaffir-man
> a Hindu-man-from-Calcutta
> a Harlem-man-who-doesn't-vote

"Il y a encore une mer à traverser / oh encore une mer à traverser" [There still remains one sea to cross / oh still one sea to cross], he writes at the end of the *Notebook.* And his complaint seems to have rendered possible (and just as problematic) the conclusion of Maryse Condé, who at the end of her "Notes on a Return to the Native Land" asked a question without answer:

> Etre Antillais, finalement, je ne sais toujours pas très bien ce que cela veut dire! Est-ce qu'un écrivain doit avoir un pays natal? Est-ce qu'un écrivain doit avoir une identité définie? Est-ce qu'un écrivain ne pourrait pas être constamment errant, constamment à la recherche d'autres hommes? Est-ce que ce qui appartient à l'écrivain, ce n'est pas seulement la littérature, c'est-à-dire quelque chose qui n'a pas de frontières?

> To be Antillean, finally, I still don't quite know what that means! Does a writer have to have a native land? Does a writer have to have a defined identity? Couldn't a writer constantly be wandering, constantly searching for other men? Is that which belongs to a writer not something more than literature, that is, something without boundaries?

Notes

[1] It is arbitrary and useless here to try to put into operation a clear-cut difference between "exiles," "émigrés," "expatriates," etc. . . . What the French Antillean leaves is neither a country nor a homeland in that the islands are French territories. Nonetheless, writings resulting from this displacement betray the same anguish that Edward Said describes when he analyzes individuals deported by the will of a totalitarian state in his essay entitled "Reflections on Exile," *Granta* 13 (Autumn 1984): 157-72. While the exile's hope of return, although generally illusory and forever deferred, remains the longed-for solution to their distress, Martinicans and Guadeloupeans who leave for metropolitan France are not yet in a position, at first, to idealize the "native land" they voluntarily abandoned. In addition, exile is not necessarily geographic and the Martinicans and Guadeloupeans who remain in their "native" land may very well suffer from the syndrome of exile. The diglossic situation that always forces the speaking subject to situate him/herself in relation to a language and culture can serve as a symbol of this perpetual gap in relation to an inaccessible home. For a discussion of the terms that attempt to classify rigorously the misery of different forms of exile, see the text by Robert Nixon, "London Calling: V. S. Naipaul and the License of Exile," *The South Atlantic Quarterly* 87.1 (Winter 1988): 1-38, in which he analyzes "the medley of terms—exile, emigrant, émigré, expatriate, refugee, and homeless individual" that may be used.

[2] The title that André Breton gives to the preface of the 1947 edition of *Notebook of a Return to the Native Land,* "Un grand poète noir" in *Cahier d'un retour au pays natal* (Paris: Présence Africaine, 1983), 77-87, reduces Aimé Césaire's identity to a racial composite. It is true that in 1947 it was crucial not to obscure the element that was used as a pretext for the oppression of various groups tossed together under the heading "Black," but Breton's formulation makes of Césaire a cultural "man without a home."

[3] On this subject see the chapter of the first book of Edouard Glissant's *Discours antillais* (Paris: Seuil, 1981), 28-37, entitled "Retour et Détour" ["Return and Detour"].

[4] Maryse Condé, "Notes sur un retour au pays natal" in *Conjonction: revue franco-haïtienne*. Supplément to 176 (1987), 23. All translations are mine when no published translations are indicated in the notes.

[5] I will use Clayton Eshleman and Annette Smith's translation from the bilingual edition *Aimé Césaire: The Collected Poetry* (Berkeley: University of California Press, 1983).

[6] Lilyan Kesteloot, *Aimé Césaire* (Paris: Seghers, collection poètes d'aujourd'hui, 1962), 18.

[7] Retrospectively, here again she refers the reader back to Frantz Fanon's analysis in *Peau noire, masques blancs* (Paris: Seuil, Collection Points, 1952) concerning the difficulty Antillean writers encounter in gaining access to noncanonical works. See especially the chapter "L'Expérience vécue du Noir" (88-114).

[8] Jacqueline Leiner, "Entretien avec Aimé Césaire" in *Tropiques* I, 1-5 (April 1941-April 1942), 8.

[9] See the novel *Hérémakhonon* (Paris: Editions 10/18, 1976), which recounts this "detour" through Africa, and Françoise Lionnet's analysis of this novel: "Happiness Deferred: Maryse Condé's *Hérémakhonon* and the failure of Enunciation" in *Autobiographical Voices* (Ithaca: Cornell University Press, 1989).

[10] Charles Baudelaire, *Les Fleurs du Mal*. With translations by Richard Howard (Boston: David R. Godine, Publisher, 1982), 11-12, my emphasis.

[11] The translation of this sentence does not allow the reader to fully appreciate the complexities of Césaire's work of appropriation: for the sake of more accurate comparison, I suggest: "This winged traveller, how awkward and weak he is! Formerly so splendid, how he is comical and ugly"

[12] In regard to this, Ngal cites the interview he had with Aimé Césaire in 1967: "Some of it is lived. . . . He was a guy who used to hang around the Latin Quarter. His name was Hannah Charley. A very strange man, half crazy . . . but who was also half philosopher, half bum, who often visited the Latin Quarter and questioned every black student. He had moments of prosperity and moments of poverty. He was originally from Guadeloupe. The scene doesn't only refer to him, I had to mix in other people," quoted in Mbwil a Mpaang Ngal, *Aimé Césaire: un homme à la recherche d'une patrie* (Dakar: Les Nouvelles éditions africaines, 1975), 203.

[13] Ngal has researched the echoes that are produced for a "French student" between Césaire's texts and canonical texts. A system of correspondences is established between Césaire, Rimbaud, Claudel, Saint-John Perse, Péguy, the surrealists, etc. . . . Other essays, notably Jean Bernabé's "La Négritude césairienne et l'occident" in *Négritude africaine, négritude caraïbe: les littératures d'expression française*, Acts of the colloquium that took place at Paris-Nord University (Paris 13), 26 27 January 1973, Centre d'études francophones (Paris: Editions de la Francité, 1973) seek to propose "intertextual dialogues" between the works of Césaire, Corneille, and Giraudoux, for example, as described in Bernadette Cailler's *Proposition poétique: une lecture de l'oeuvre d'Aimé Césaire* (Paris, Québec: Naaman, 1976), 32. And in her chapter entitled "Le Mot ou une écriture en situation," Cailler seeks in addition to define the *nature* of the tie that links related texts. For her, the language of "Négritude poets" is proof of "an intertextuality of particularly dense writing in which knowledge and refusal, abandon and revolt are intimately intertwined" (ibid).

[14] Césaire himself describes himself at that time: "I was subjected to the same influences that all more or less cultured French students were subjected to at that time," quoted in Leiner, 8.

[15] Albert Memmi, in *Portrait du colonisé* (Paris: Petite bibliothèque Payot, 1973), maintains on the contrary that assimilation is not only undesirable for obvious ideological reasons, but is also quite simply impossible because in reality, the colonizer does not want it at all. See the chapter entitled "Impossibilité de l'assimilation" (153-55).

[16] See especially, *L'Odeur du père. Essai sur les limites de la science et de la vie en Afrique noire* (Paris: Présence africaine, 1982). In this essay, Mudimbe masterfully describes the delirium from which the discourse of the Occidental who attempts to describe the Other suffers, but also the delirium of the discourse of the African who talks about his/her own continent. The idea of a "separating distance" which would serve as a sign of the cultural gap within a discourse is to be related to Césaire's poem and to the poetic representation of the awareness of a textual putting into Relation.

[17] The very first chapter of *Peau noire, masques blancs* is devoted to the relationship between the "Black and language." "To speak," writes Fanon, "is essentially to assume a culture, to bear the weight of a civilization" (13). The metaphor of the burden is remarkably significant in the context of Césaire's poem in which the Albatross tries in vain to take flight.

[18] Jean-Paul Sartre, *Black Orpheus*, trans. S. W. Allen (Paris: Gallimard, 1969), 27.

[19] Aliko Songolo, *Aimé Césaire, une poétique de la découverte* (Paris: L'Harmattan, 1985), 45.

[20] Daniel Maximin, "Aimé Césaire: la poésie, parole essentielle" in *Présence Africaine* 126 (1983), 11.

[21] Suzanne Césaire, "Misères d'une poésie: John-Antoine Nau" in *Tropiques* 1, 4.4 (January 1942), 50.

[22] See Ronnie Scharfman's *"Engagement" and the Language of the Subject in the Poetry of Aimé Césaire* (Gainesville: University of Florida Press, 1987). The conclusion of this study stresses the multiplicity of positions that what the author calls "the subject" can occupy in Césaire's works: "poet, victim, slave, universe, spokesman, nigger, island. The other can be language, oppressor, master, lover, people, poem, country" (12).

Hedy Kalikoff (essay date 1995)

SOURCE: "Gender, Genre and Geography in Aimé Césaire's *Cahier d'un retour au pays natal*" in *Callaloo*, Vol. 18, No. 2, 1995, pp. 492-505.

[*In the following essay, Kalikoff delineates the gender construction of the poem and challenges its reputation as "epic" and "heroic."*]

Aimé Césaire's **Cahier d'un retour au pays natal** is one of the acknowledged master-pieces of francophone Caribbean literature. A great work seems to require a great man, a hero who can act and speak for an entire people, and indeed the period *Cahier* inhabits in Caribbean literary history has been referred to as an era of "Heroic Negritude" (Arnold). There is scarcely any scholarship on the long poem which does not refer to it as "epic" and "heroic." What I would like to argue, however, is that these terms are inappropriate, for two reasons.[1] First, they function to smooth out the disruptive quality of the poem by couching it in comfortably traditional categories of genre. And second, since the epic hero is always male and the trajectory of his journey has traditionally been gendered as masculine,[2] these generic labels also serve to thwart discussion of the poem's figuration of gender by suppressing the role the feminine plays and reading the poem's figuration of masculinity as "natural." This ends up lending false coherence to the lyrical subject, suggesting an easily identifiable, active narrator moving through time and space, a notion *Cahier d'un retour* defies.

When one examines the way that the poem's complex imagery is gendered, one arrives at a point of reversal of terms, where what was once masculine (the sun) becomes feminine (the moon) and vice versa. This reversal is eventually overturned, yet a fundamental ambiguity remains and is never fully resolved. The poem's ending is both an attempt to rewrite the binary oppositions of masculine and feminine, vertical and horizontal, sun and moon, and a call to transcend a debilitating collective history. By unsettling this symbolic structure—what amounts to a "colonial Imaginary," in Althusserian terms—the poem unsettles the ideology which strove to justify the wrenching history of the African diaspora.

Once the poem undermines its own binary imagery and starts to sketch in a third term, one can see that what has been viewed as a sort of phallic negritude, where "negritude as phallus . . . revalorizes the black man" (Scharfman), is nothing of the sort. The imposition of such Lacanian terms on the text leads to a reading of colonization and decolonization where the former is figured as emasculating and the latter as "rephallicizing." What I would like to do is to provide a reading which both illuminates the construction of gender in the poem, and shows how attempts to fit the poem into traditional generic concepts (hero and epic) and Lacanian structures (by way of Althusser and Fanon) unintentionally serve to preclude any possibility for female decolonization and to oversimplify the poem's obscurities. By drawing out the ambiguities of the poem's conclusion I hope to show just how ambitious the poem's decolonizing impulse is, and how difficult its project.

A. James Arnold has called Aimé Césaire's *Cahier* "the epic of negritude," referring to Ezra Pound's definition of an epic as "a long poem with history in it." This definition is indeed a terse one, as Arnold writes, yet no matter how minimalist Pound's definition may be, it cannot denude the epic of its heroic proportions. This view is certainly not Arnold's alone. Aliko Songolo (in *Aimé Césaire: Une Poétique de la Découverte*) also calls the speaker of the poem "le poète-héros," not only upholding the notion of heroism but also eliding the distinction between the poet

and the speaker of the poem. Indeed, this is one of the temptations *Cahier* poses. Césaire himself is such an extraordinary figure that his biography occasionally casts a shadow over interpretations of the poem. Yet this urge to read a hero into the work, in light of the textual evidence, is difficult to accept, particularly when one considers Ronnie Scharfman's convincing point that Césaire's poetry "is permeated not only with a sense of the arbitrariness of language but also with doubts as to the very possibility of mediating between the individual and the collective." Certainly the subject of the poem sometimes *yearns* to be the voice of the people, to be their leader, to singlehandedly decolonize them. However, this posture is not a constant one, and much of the poem strikes intensely personal, idiosyncratic notes which belie the stance of a public, heroic figure. As Eileen Julien has pointed out, the epic form is not one used by women writers, precisely because of its masculinist characteristics: "This hierarchic form is tied to nationalistic agendas and military might, which have been and continue to be, for the most part, provinces of patriarchy."

The world of the epic does not resemble that of *Cahier,* despite moments where heroism is invoked. As Mikhail Bakhtin has written,

> [t]he epic past is absolute and complete. It is as
> closed as a circle; inside it everything is finished,
> already over. There is no place in the epic world
> for any openendedness, indecision, indeterminacy.

However, indeterminacy, openendedness, and a constant interrogation of the past are important characteristics of Césaire's long poem. In a more recent example of scholarship on epic, and one perhaps more appropriate to literature of the African diaspora, Isidore Okpewho shows that "the hero is quite simply a comprehensive symbol of the ideals of human society and the dangers attendant upon such exaggerated expectations." The epic hero has a dual role: as champion of his community he is both a "man of the people" and a superior, noble creature endowed with supernatural powers. This comprehensive duality should not be mistaken for anything like the constant shifts and struggles of the poem's lyrical voice, for the epic hero's conflicts are the expression of a coherent identity, replete with biography and praise-singers. Nor should the mythic tone and historical references characteristic of Césaire's poem be read as evidence of epic qualities:

> History for the [traditional oral] artist is both what has
> actually happened and what is fabled to have happened.
> For him myth has considerable historical value; because
> it has been told all too often, it bears the stamp of
> truth.

What is so extraordinary and powerful about Césaire's poem is precisely that it is a story which had not previously been told. And in Césaire's case, this story is being told on the page; it is an extremely *written* text whose frequently esoteric vocabulary and imagery take it far from traditional oral art forms even while sometimes invoking them. If anything it is the notion of epic that Césaire interrogates in this poem, and this is perhaps a good example of the way that some colonial and postcolonial texts appropriate traditional genres in order to reinvent them.

When we turn from these theorists and critics to look at the poem's rhetoric, there is even more reason to avoid these generic labels, however casual their use may be. Perhaps one of the most frequently quoted lines from *Cahier* is one which places the poet in the position of lighting the way for his people, leading them to freedom:

> Je viendrais à ce pays mien et je lui dirais: / . . . / "Ma bouche sera la bouche des malheurs qui n'ont pas de bouche, ma voix, la liberté de celles qui s'affaissent au cachot du désespoir."

Only if this line is taken out of context could the subject of *Cahier* be seen as speaking continually and successfully as a representative for and of his people. The text itself resists this stance. Not only explicitly, as in **"Mon héroïsme, quelle farce,"** but in the way that the passage above is phrased and presented. It is written in the conditional mood and, more importantly, it is placed within quotation marks. When the narrator says he would speak for "you" ("c'est pour vous que je parlerai"), it seems in retrospect to be a naive hope or intention, deflated upon actual arrival in the "pays natal." The triumphant cry, "Et voici que je suis venu!" is followed immediately by the vision of "cette vie clopinante devant moi, non pas cette vie, cette mort . . ." and the word "mort" will be repeated five times in this one stanza. This is a devastating rebuke of the fantasy that "ma bouche sera la bouche des malheurs qui n'ont pas de bouche." Scharfman points out the possibility that in this passage the subject is taking on a Christ-like voice and "by quoting itself as if it were already poetry or gospel, the subject reveals itself as having been confined by a kind of textual grandiosity."

This moment of grandiose fantasy is quite different from what Okpewho has described as the typical immodesty of the epic hero: "[T]he hero has an exaggerated notion of his worth. He claims precedence above everyone else, his elders included, and expects others to recognize his greatness." The subject of *Cahier* only briefly imagines himself as a savior-figure before coming face to face with the morbid landscape of his island, "où la grandeur piteusement échoue." In traditional epic, there is no such bracing self-mockery.[3]

Daniel Maximin's novel *L'Isolé soleil* explicitly invokes *Cahier* as an important intertext, both responding to and reinterpreting Césaire's work, and for this reason I would like to use the novel as another way to comment on the poem. One of the characters in *L'Isolé soleil* explains why a female reader might be frustrated with heroic epic: "Si on écoute nos poètes, nos révolutionnaires, nos romanciers et leurs historiens, la seule fonction des femmes noires serait d'enfanter nos héros." It is precisely this question as to the "fonction des femmes noires" in *Cahier* which will lead us into an examination of the way the poem manipulates gendered imagery.

From the opening moments of *Cahier,* what is female appears in the text as a symbol of duplicity: "Puis je me tournais vers des paradis pour lui et les siens perdus, plus calme que la face d'une femme qui ment." A few lines later the phrase "menteusement souriante" will point the reader back to the first mention of "mensonge" and the lying, smiling female face will be established as a trope. This smile provokes the lyrical "je" of the poem into outrage: "on voit encore des madras aux reins des femmes des / anneaux à leurs oreilles des sourires à leurs bouches / des enfants à leurs mamelles et j'en passe: / ASSEZ DE CE SCANDALE!". It becomes clear that the poem's narrator is referring to the smiling face of the "doudou," the stereotypical *mulâtresse* in her cheerful, French-loving mode about whom the song "Adieu foulards, adieu madras" was written. The speaker's disdain and anger appear to be focused at the perpetuation of this stereotype. However, this may also be an instance of scorn towards the women who, in the complicated colonial history of the French Caribbean, were able to raise their social status through sexual relations with white slaveowners.[4] This moment of hostility perhaps prefigures Frantz Fanon's (in)famous critique of Caribbean women who attempt to "lighten the race" by bedding white men.

The notion of duplicitousness, then, is linked to the image of degraded sexuality, and the imagery which is gendered as female in the poem is inscribed along a horizontal line. The *mulâtresse* is the woman who represents lying down with the colonizer for survival. The city is marked as a degraded landscape, passive, horizontal, mute. "Cette ville plate-étalée" is associated with the powerless, faceless crowd which is in turn associated with "une femme." In a circular series of comparisons, the subject is as calm as the lying face of a smiling woman, and smiling, scandalous women are like the city which is laid out flat and passive as the body of a woman, and in this city there is a crowd which is silent and incomprehensible as a woman who would order a hypothetical rain not to fall. Occasionally, what is horizontal is not passive and degraded but warm and fertile as the earth: "toi terre tendue terre / saoule / terre grand sexe levé vers le soleil / . . . la terre où tout est libre / et fraternel, ma terre."

The instability of the figuration is not limited to female symbols alone. The poem lurches and leaps back and forth from a dismal, colonized notion of "islandness" to moments of exalted joy in a pattern which has been described as having three large movements or three acts. Within these larger movements are smaller reversals, ascents and falls.[5] The figuration changes according to the transformations of the subject's viewpoint. At its lowest point, the female is the city, the impoverished hybrid of urban modernism and colonialized squalor—flattened, sprawled, prostrated. In its antithesis, the female represents fertility. Both of these extremes are on a horizontal axis, whether positive or negative, whether they signify fertility or passivity.

Not surprisingly, then, what is vertical is usually gendered as male. I would like to focus on one primary and persistent figure of the masculine, "le soleil"—a conventional male symbol in traditional poetic imagery as well as in this poem.

The sun appears on the first page as cursed and venereal, a force on high, looking down on the colonized island. This is a gaze which inscribes an invisible vertical line, like a plumb line dropped from the sun to the island, surveying it authoritatively as a policeman would (". . . arpentée nuit et jour d'un sacré soleil vénérien"). The metaphorics of verticality are immediately in play here, embodied by conflicting symbols, the most famous of which is the reference to "mes profondeurs à hauteur inverse du vingtième étage" or as one of the translations puts it, "in my depths height-deep" (Eshleman and Smith). There is a constant up-and-down movement, a vertical axis which is masculinized as one realizes that the speaker's voice is always a male voice. The sun, meanwhile, is infected by an illness, a malady of the colonizer, apparently the result of a contagious coupling, and the implication is that "la terre" or "la ville" has been infected by a diseased phallus.

> It is easy to call *Cahier* an epic: it is a vast, complex and unwieldy text. To refer to it as a "long poem" seems somehow to slight its power.
>
> —*Hedy Kalikoff*

In the second movement of the poem, with the introduction of the one-word sentence "Partir," the register changes. The sun is refigured. The earth, as we have seen, is the female sex raised towards the phallic sun, "la mentule de Dieu," and the sun now has the capacity not to infect but to fertilize, to turn golden that which is under its light. The sun will be represented as diseased once again in the poem—"Au bout du petit matin le soleil qui toussotte et crache ses poumons"—but this time the illness is tubercular. These shifts do not end here. Just before the beginning of the third movement, when the speaker calls to the sun with its curly hair like that of a black man ("Ange Soleil, Ange frisé du soleil"), he is asking it to help him affect a leap beyond the self disgust which had permeated the preceding section. This is the pinnacle of the sun as symbol, the moment when it is personified and, most importantly, made into a black angel to help the subject ascend skyward, out of the depths of his colonized state. The vertical axis, at its most inspired, transcendent moments, stands for power, hope and independence. At its most negative it represents the diseased phallus, the colonial gaze, the surveillance and oppression of the colonizer, and the fall downward to despair.

Once the figural structure is established in the first half of the poem, the language and tone shift in a wave of ambiguous imagery. The gendered figures of sun and moon are reversed, changed back again, and then upset completely, plunging the poem into periods of instability and culminating in a profoundly obscure ending.

The major turning point comes at the famous, much-quoted section about the black man in the streetcar, "le nègre grand comme un pongo." This is the lowest moment for the "je" of the poem. He has just described the slave market under the guise of a horse market, rejected the notion that a glorious African past holds any hope, and evoked the despair in the hulls of slave ships. In a city streetcar, the speaker of the poem sees a hideous and pathetic black man and smiles along with the white women who sneer at him. Once he realizes his complicity with the disdain of the white gaze, he is as low as he can go, mired in self-hatred, "[c]omme cette ville dans la crasse et dans la boue couchée." He becomes completely prostrate, identifying for the first time in the poem with the horizontal position which has up to now been gendered as female.

The poem's narrator remains flattened until the imagery of the poem starts to signal the advent of a new order: "je tremble maintenant du commun tremblement que / notre song docile change dans le madrépore." The madrépore is a particularly telling figure to use here. As Samuel Weber has pointed out, it is a term which has caused confusion: "Le madrépore, dont on a longtemps cru qu'il appartenait à la flore, est le site d'une erreur: son origine n'est pas végétale mais animale." The madrépore is a symbol of ambiguity and uncertainty, and it announces that the categories in the poem are shifting, the subject doubling and changing.

This is followed by several androgynous figures where masculine and feminine coexist side by side. When the word "silo" appears ("silo où se préserve et mûrit ce que la terre a de plus / terre"), we have a symbol whose shape is phallic and yet whose function is womblike, to house ripening grain until it is mature (Scharfman). In the passage, "ma négritude n'est pas une pierre . . . ," the speaker seems to take on a masculine identity again:

> ma négritude n'est ni une tour ni une cathédrale / elle plonge
> dans la chair rouge du sol / elle plonge dans la chair ardente du
> ciel / elle troue l'accablement opaque de sa droite patience.

Yet, in this one passage, the text both denies an upright phallic shape ("ni une tour ni une cathédrale") and reaffirms it ("sa droite patience") while reiterating a vertical movement from the earth to the sky, from a high tower to deep down in the soil. The earth here is red flesh being penetrated by "ma négritude," yet because "négritude" is feminine in French, the masculine movement of the speaker is expressed by a feminine pronoun: "*elle plonge* dans la chair rouge du sol."

The litany of flora and fauna which follows this places the narrator in the role of a Noah figure who "gathers lovingly all the beasts, birds, insects, saps, to shelter them from moral deluge" (Snyder). This is indeed the new beginning which the narrator had anticipated, both as the beginning of the end of the world and a rebirth of the self, a self-birthing.

At the end of this section the imagery becomes explicitly sexual:

viennent les ovaires de l'eau où le futur agite ses
   petites têtes /
viennent les loups qui pâturent dans les orifices
   sauvages du
corps à l'heure ou à l'auberge eliptique se /
   rencontre *ma lune*
et *ton soleil.* (my emphasis)

Embedded in this passage is the startling reversal of symbols already referred to—at this moment the speaker no longer identifies himself with the masculine sun. He is the moon, and the "tu" of the poem is the sun. For the first time in the poem, masculine and feminine axes are realigned. This new identification continues through the next few stanzas. In the line, "Calme et berce ô ma parole l'enfant . . . ," the speaker appropriates a maternal posture. When he addresses himself to the light—" ô fraîche source de la lumière"—he is speaking *to* the sun, the source of light whose supply will replenish him in his new identity as moon reflecting light.

On the next page, the symbols of the sun and the moon are explicitly restored to their conventional figuration and the sun becomes male once again: "le coeur mâle du soleil," "la féminité de la lune au corps d'huile." In this stanza, there is a celebration of the notion of reconciliation. However, this realignment and "close concordance" are never so neat and unambiguous as they first seem.

We have seen the gendered imagery suddenly reverse itself, going through a period of change heralded by a metaphorics of instability and androgyny. While the images seem to revert to their initial pattern, there is an element of ambiguity which never goes away. Masculinity is now insisted upon as the speaker of the poem seems to be trying to construct his own identity. This notion of renewal, restructuring and rethinking is underlined by the emphasis on geography. The "je" of the *Cahier* in redefining himself must also redraw the map of the world since his identity is so closely affiliated with the fragmented, volcanic islands, with the far-flung history of the diaspora, the middle passage, and the triangle inscribed by Africa, France and Martinique.

Now the speaker of the poem seems particularly muscular, sending up a "viril" prayer, asking for the faith of a sorcerer, for powerful hands, for the temper of a sword. He runs through the gamut of masculine roles, desiring to be "le frère . . . le fils . . . l'amant de cet unique peuple." The insistence and repetitiveness of the male imagery, the very foregrounding of the speaker's virility, signals that the constitution of the subject as masculine is in process, that he is trying singlehandedly to forge a new self, upright and masculine, capable of resisting oppression.

When the speaker of the poem intones an ironic and vituperative list of the outrages that he accepts, he includes his own geography, his own version of the world: "mon originale géographie aussi; la carte du / monde faite à mon usage . . .". "Originale" here suggests a trajectory back to the beginning when earth, sun and moon were in their appropriate places. Yet original also signifies *new,*

something never seen before. Not only is the narrator's version of the world new, it is also eccentric and strange—the third meaning of the word "original" in French. The speaker of the poem is remaking the map of the world and of the universe as well. The very horizon is coming undone ("l'horizon se défait, recule et s'élargit"), the sun becomes a toy ball ("saute le soleil sur la raquette de mes mains") and this former symbol of masculine power is no longer adequate ("l'inégal soleil ne me suffit plus").

The speaker's explicit virility and sense of power intensify until they reach perhaps their most blatant image: "Et voici soudain que force et vie m'assaillent comme un taureau . . .". With swords and sorcery at his command, embodied with the force of a bull, the speaker sounds just like a hero leading his people: "Et nous sommes debout maintenant, mon pays et moi . . .". The poem rushes forward and upward towards its resolution, and with the constant vertical imagery and the insistence on standing and rising, "heroic negritude" does indeed seem implacably phallic.

Standing upright is a metaphor for resistance and survival in the poem, which makes the vertical axis the more strongly privileged one in the figurative scheme. This has led some critics to read the poem's symbolic structure in Lacanian terms:

> The image of negritude as phallus serves several functions for the subject. As a corrective device, it revalorizes the black man, symbolically castrated throughout the text by the forces of oppression. It is the perfect metaphor for the desired union between the subject and primal forces in nature. (Scharfman)

Lacan's notions about phallic power and castration in language are tempting ones to put to use here. But this is a temptation which should be resisted, for several reasons.

Lacan's conception of the phallus is a way of describing the subject's relation to language. The phallus is a signifier: "c'est le signifiant destiné à désigner dans leur ensemble les effets de signifié, en tant que le signifiant les conditionne par sa présence de signifiant." The effects of the signified are that man's needs are alienated due to their expression in language. To be castrated in language is a condition of subjectivity; it implies that the speaking subject is incapable of expressing need in such a way that it can be satisfied.

The notion that language precedes the subject and that the subject is constructed through language but cannot master language has become a commonplace of post-structuralist theory. It is important to keep in mind that this alienation in language is as true for the colonizer as it is for the colonized. The alienation of those who are deprived of a political speaking voice under the conditions of colonization is quite different from the lack of mastery over language which is at the heart of subjectivity. To use a profoundly linguistic concept as a metaphor for a political one is, in this case, to risk attributing a kind of mastery to the colonial powers which would place colonial discourse at the mythic "center" of discourse; it would phallicize colonization by endowing it with complete control over language, with the absolute power to generate meaning as though colonial discourse stood somehow outside of language. Yet, "hegemony is a fragile and difficult process of containment," writes John Frow. "Further, there are historically quite distinct degrees of coherence of the 'dominant ideology.'" If the colonizing subject were not castrated in language, the dominant ideology would then be perfectly coherent.

Fredric Jameson's long article on Lacan which serves as his attempt to reconcile psychoanalytic and Marxist schools of criticism does seem, as Scharfman notes, particularly helpful in the context of Césaire's *Cahier*. Jameson's intent in "Imaginary and Symbolic in Lacan" is to find a way of reading which would mediate "between social phenomena and what must be called private, rather than even merely individual, facts." He does this by relying on Althusser's definition of ideology as the "'representation' of the Imaginary's relationship of individuals to their Real conditions of existence." It is within representations of the Imaginary relationship of the colonized to the conditions of colonization that a historically grounded notion of alienation can be examined through the Symbolic order of language.

The real sticking point of Lacanian theory for feminist writers and theorists is the use of masculine terminology to represent ideas that are supposed to be gender-neutral. Lacan refers to the phallus as not being reducible to "l'organe, pénis ou clitoris, qu'il symbolise," suggesting that the phallus can refer to both male and female bodies. Yet this distinction between the phallus and the penis which Lacanians insist on is surely a tenuous one since it refuses to recognize the way these terms are inseparably associated by a larger culture within which individuals are powerless to dictate meaning. Merely willing it so will not strip the phallus of its male connotations. As Jane Gallop puts it, these Lacanian "attempts to remake language to one's own theoretical needs, as if language were merely a tool one could use, bespeaks a very un-Lacanian view of language." Gallop goes on to say that,

> as long as the attribute of power is a phallus which can only have meaning by referring to and being confused with a penis, this confusion will support a structure in which it seems reasonable that men have power and women do not.

If the purpose of figuring negritude as phallus is to revalorize the black man, one has to ask then where this schema leaves the question of female oppression, female resistance and decolonization and if this reading of negritude does not empower "the black man" in a way which seems "reasonable" while leaving female decolonization aside as a nonissue. But, does *Cahier d'un retour* really figure negritude as phallus? Do the rising tone and ecstatic imagery, the "arousal of ethnic consciousness" (Arnold) at the end of the poem, imply that the poem is, in fact, getting an erection?

If we look closely at the last pages of the poem, the powerful mounting rhythm is seen to be subtended by explosive imagery which insists on the mediatedness of this vertical movement. The axes which have structured the poem's imagery are erupting as the tension and tone intensify. The repeated images of verticality are interladen with an angry irony, palpable in the repetition of the heavy phrase "c'était un très bon nègre," and in the question, "Tenez, suis-je assez humble?" which both tend to weigh down the poem's final flight.

When the last lines of the poem finally appear, they are so idiosyncratic and inaccessible that the text ends on a note not of reconciliation but of obscurity, forcing a reconsideration of what came before. The last line of the text reads: "et le grand trou noir où je voulais me noyer l'autre lune / c'est là que je veux pêcher maintenant la langue maléfique de la nuit et son immobile verrition." In three different translations of the poem, the rendering of the last few words varies from "unmoving flick" to "motionless veerition" and "immutable truth."[6] None of these makes the meaning of the last lines any clearer since Césaire ends the poem with a neologism:

> Césaire's great lyric about finding a voice, about returning to native ground, strands us, finally, with a made-up, Latinate, abstract-sounding question mark of a word. So much for expectations of direct, immediate linguistic "authenticity." With Césaire we are involved in a poetics of cultural *invention*. (Clifford)

It is difficult, then, to agree that "dans le troisième acte, le poète reconcilié avec luimême et avec son pays conduit son peuple vers la liberté désirée" (Songolo). At the end of the poem the sun is no longer adequate for the speaker, and he addresses himself to the wind. Bind me to the soil, he asks the wind, strangle me with your lasso of stars to the sky. Rise, dove, rise rise rise. Despite the exuberant upward movement, bounding and strangulation are perplexing images to use to express reconciliation and liberation.

The ending of the poem might be read instead not only as a "poetics of cultural invention" but as the attempt to constitute a decolonized subjectivity under a different Imaginary scheme. To return to Althusser's very Lacanian conception of ideology, if the poem maps out an ideology which might be called negritude and in doing so decenters what I would conceptualize as a "colonial Imaginary," then what is its own Imaginary scheme?

To answer that question, I find it most useful to turn to the work of Luce Irigaray who has written lengthy critiques of Lacanian psychoanalytic theory and shown what a non-phallocentric Imaginary might look like, while still relying on Lacan's ideas. The most relevant aspect of Irigaray's work here is her insistence that Western philosophy is based on the "logic of sameness." Psychoanalysis, starting with Freud, has defined sexual difference according to phallic logic:

> Partie prenante d'une idéologie qu'il ne remet pas en cause, [Freud] affirme que le "masculin" est le modèle sexuel, que toute représentation de désir ne peut que s'y étalonner, s'y soumettre. (Irigaray)

By this masculine standard, the clitoris is a smaller version of the penis, and the little girl is a "little man." This, of course, allows women to be viewed as the same as men, but inferior. Extending this logic to wider philosophical terms, "[c]ette domination du logos philosophique vient, pour une bonne part, de son pouvoir de *réduire tout autre dans l'économie du Même*" (her emphasis). This economy of the same is the engine which powers colonial discourse and colonial self-justification. When the standard of measure is the white European male, the resulting philosophy holds that Africans, including Africans of the diaspora, fall far short of that standard, which, not coincidentally, makes them ripe for the "civilizing mission." From the insistent oppression of this colonial discourse stems what Fanon calls the "psychoexistential" inferiority complex of blacks, the internalization of racist ideology. Fanon's stated aim was to analyze the complex in order to destroy it.

Césaire, who was of course a great influence on Fanon, also has this destructive impulse as an aim; his text is linguistically disruptive in the same sense that Irigaray's is: "Irigaray attempts to disrupt symbolic discourse . . . by reimagining the female Imaginary" (Herrmann). Césaire's poem with its eruptive, disruptive, denunciatory power aims to explode colonial discourse, the phallogocentric system on the other side of which lies a new map of the world, a different Imaginary. When the speaker of the poem associates himself with the masculine sun, he is filling in the role the colonizer had played. He is not upsetting the structure, but changing the players. In the historical context of the poem's production, this is an extraordinary move. However, as Irigaray puts it, "si [le] projet visait simplement à renverser l'ordre des choses—admettons même que cela soit possible . . . —l'histoire reviendrait finalement encore au *même*" (my emphasis). Césaire goes further than a reversal of terms: when the sun is removed from its privileged position, the rigid vertical-horizontal structure crumbles. The wind, which the speaker of the poem addresses throughout the last passage, serves as a new metaphor, one which, in this poem, defies being categorized or even defined since it can be felt but not touched, heard but not seen, spoken to as if it were listening:

> . . . enroule-toi, vent, autour de ma nouvelle croissance / pose-toi sur mes doigts mesurés / je te livre ma conscience et son rythme de chair / . . . / je te livre mes paroles abruptes / dévore et enroule-toi / en t'enroulant embrasse-moi d'un plus vaste frisson / embrasse-moi jusqu'au nous furieux / embrasse, embrasse NOUS. . . .

Is the wind a voice which can be heard around the world? Is it a reference to oral culture and oral art? A non-material response to the aggressive sharpness of colonizing technology? A holy spirit? A form of resistance which does not imply phallic logic?

It is the "radical indeterminacy"[7] of the poem's final stretch which the reader is left with at the end, yet the outlines of something new are sketched in. The poem's troublesome conclusion, with its complexity of image and language, introduces a third and perhaps mediating term, suggesting a new Imaginary which remains to be fully articulated. If

we return to *L'Isolé soleil* for a moment, it is interesting to see the way that Maximin reiterates a Caribbean landscape of three elements and insists on the triangularization of meaning and desire: the sun, the volcano and the sea make up the three terms in Maximin's geography. Towards the end of the book "la voie lactée" joins "le soleil" and "la mer" in a more feminized version of the threesome. This figuring and refiguring of three terms includes the play of characters who often comprise two men and a woman, reinscribing the threesome who founded *Tropiques,* Léon Damas, Aimé Césaire, and Suzanne Césaire. Maximin insists on the inclusion of a third term and of a female voice in what I would like to read as a novelistic continuation of Césaire's long poem. It is part of *L'Isolé soleil*'s power that it recognizes the movement from two to three terms in **Cahier,** the triangularization of its imagery.

The poem's emphasis on vertical movement and insistence on masculinity should not, then, be read literally as the epic outpouring of a phallic leader, but rather as an attempt to subvert colonial discourse through reimagining the colonial Imaginary. The poem's blatant sexual images and gendered landscapes prove to be unstable and disruptive, suggesting a reading of the poem's masculinity that highlights its constructedness rather than its depiction of a natural process.

Negritude has long been subject to controversy. Heralded as a pan-Africanist response to colonialism by some, it has been derided as essentialist, globalizing and falsely idealist by others. Eventually, the topic lost some of its argumentative bite; with the distance of time, negritude has been viewed in its historical specificity. As Clarisse Zimra has noted, "the quest which [negritude] expresses was defined, primarily, according to the socio-political terms of the 1930s."

If negritude may be many things to many people, it has surely always been male, from the nearly exclusive maleness of its participants to the supposedly phallic logic of its symbolic order. The question of whether there is a "negritude in the feminine mode," as Zimra puts it, has started to receive its share of scholarly attention. But the classics of negritude, including Césaire's **Cahier,** have remained strangely untouched. While critics cannot ignore the explicit sexuality of Césaire's metaphors, the construction of both female and male in the text and the significance of gender for the work as a whole has itself been a fairly uncharted landscape.

The issues of female oppression and female decolonization tend to be silent spaces in the poem. After all, when the narrator allies himself with other oppressed people— "je serais un homme-juif / un homme-cafre / un homme-hindou-de Calcutta / un homme-de-Harlem-qui-ne-vote-pas"—the major omission on the list of sufferers is "un homme-femme." This is not to say that this absence undermines the text's extraordinary artistic power nor its force as a tool for "decolonizing the mind." However, this is something which stands to be remarked on, particularly if the text is to be taken as *the* epic of negritude, the blueprint for resistance and liberation.

If colonialism was an emasculating experience, how were the "always-already castrated" affected by it? Yet, colonialism was not of course literally emasculating; it has been figured as such, as the strongest mode of disempowerment some writers can imagine. Exactly what is missing from this schema is a different Imaginary. What the poem attempts to do in fact is to refigure the schema. The upsetting of the binary order and the introduction of the elements of a new one are crucial to the poem's revolutionary power.

It is easy to call *Cahier* an epic: it is a vast, complex and unwieldy text. To refer to it as a "long poem" seems somehow to slight its power. Yet, we need to foreground its unwieldiness, since the poem's difficult form is one of the ways in which it bespeaks an unresolved historical struggle.

To try to disinvest *Cahier* of its heroic status is not to try to weaken the effect of the poem. As Trinh T. Minh-ha points out in another context, to posit a poet(-hero) lighting the way for his people is to suggest a liberation of the masses where "the masses are regarded as an aggregate of average persons condemned by their lack of personality or by their dim individualities to stay with the herd." One of Maximin's characters reiterates this point: "Quelle prétention chez tous ces écrivains mâles ou ces héros de romans. . . . Et tous ces moi-je toujours seuls face au peuple silencieux." The poem without its epic status and without a hero might not end in as clean and powerful a reconciliation as some of its readers might like, but it ends with the movement of struggle towards resolution. To deprive the poem of its final obscurity and struggle is to underestimate the difficulty of its project.

Notes

[1] This paper came out of discussions with Richard D.E. Burton. My thanks to Richard, and to David Labiosa, Hubert Rast and Ronnie Scharfman for their comments on earlier versions.

[2] Teresa de Lauretis shows how the male figure is traditionally associated with narrative movement and the female with narrative closure or static image in the chapter "Desire in Narrative."

[3] Okpewho uses examples of epics from Russian, African, Latin and Greek traditions, among others.

[4] This situation led to the differential treatment of free colored males and free colored females, enmiring mulatto women in sexual relations which exploited them while at the same time gave them access to white power. Richard D.E. Burton has demonstrated the importance of this history for understanding the gendered symbolism of political discourse in Martinique.

[5] Scharfman has adeptly traced the multiple shifts of the subject's voice and position in her chapter, "The Subject of the *Cahier*."

[6] In translations by Eshleman and Smith, Snyder, and Abel and Goll.

[7] "Radical indeterminacy" is what James Clifford calls the "essence of neologism" (177).

Works Cited

Arnold, A. James. *Modernism and Negritude: The Poetry and Poetics of Aimé Césaire.* Cambridge: Harvard University Press, 1981.

Bakhtin, Mikhail. *The Dialogic Imagination.* Trans. Caryl Emerson and Michael Holquist. Austin: University of Texas Press, 1987.

Burton, Richard D.E. "'Maman-France Doudou': Family Images in French West Indian Colonial Discourse." *Diacritics* 23 (1993): 69-90.

———. *La Famille coloniale: La Martinique et la mere patrie, 1789-1992.* Paris: L'Harmattan, 1994.

Césaire, Aimé. *Cahier d'un retour au pays natal.* Paris: Présence Africaine, 1983.

———. *Return to My Native Land.* Trans. Emil Snyder. Paris: Présence Africaine, 1968.

———. *Aimé Césaire: The Collected Poetry.* Trans. Clayton Eshleman and Annette Smith. Berkeley: University of California Press, 1983.

———. *Cahier d'un retour au pays natal: Memorandum on my Martinique.* Trans. L. Abel and Y. Goll. New York: Brentano's, 1947.

Clifford, James. *The Predicament of Culture: Twentieth-Century Ethnography, Literature and Art.* Cambridge: Harvard University Press, 1988.

De Lauretis, Teresa. *Alice Doesn't.* Bloomington: Indiana University Press, 1984.

Fanon, Frantz. *Peau noire, masques blancs.* Paris: Editions du Seuil, 1952.

Frow, John. *Marxism and Literary History.* Cambridge: Harvard University Press, 1986.

Gallop, Jane. *Thinking through the Body.* New York: Columbia University Press, 1988.

Herrmann, Anne. *The Dialogic and Difference: "An/Other Woman" in Virginia Woolf and Christa Wolf.* New York: Columbia University Press, 1989.

Irigaray, Luce. *Ce sexe qui n'en est pas un.* Paris: Les Editions de Minuit, 1977.

Jameson, Fredric. "Imaginary and Symbolic in Lacan: Marxism, Psychoanalytic Criticism, and the Problem of the Subject." *Yale French Studies* 55-56 (1978): 338-95.

Julien, Eileen. *African Novels and the Question of Orality.* Bloomington: Indiana University Press, 1992.

Lacan, Jacques. "La signification du phallus." *Ecrits II.* Paris: Editions du Seuil, 1971.

Maximin, Daniel. *L'Isolé soleil.* Paris: Editions de Seuil, 1981.

Okpewho, Isidore. *The Epic in Africa: Toward a Poetics of the Oral*

Performance. New York: Columbia University Press, 1979.

Scharfman, Ronnie. *'Engagement' and the Language of the Subject in the Poetry of Aimé Césaire.* Gainesville: University of Florida Press, 1980.

Snyder, Emile. "Aimé Césaire: The Reclaiming of the Land." *Exile and Tradition: Studies in African and Caribbean Literature.* London: Longman Group, 1976.

Songolo, Aliko. *Aimé Césaire: Une Poétique de la Découverte.* Paris: Editions L'Harmattan, 1985.

Trinh, T. Minh-ha. *Woman, Native, Other: Writing Postcoloniality and Feminism.* Bloomington: Indiana University Press, 1989.

Weber, Samuel M. "Le Madrépore." *Poétique* 13 (1973): 28-54.

Zimra, Clarisse. "Negritude in the Feminine Mode: The Case of Martinique and Guadeloupe." *The Journal of Ethnic Studies* 12 (1984): 53-77.

Aimé Césaire with Annick Thebia Melsan (interview date 1997)

SOURCE: "The Liberating Power of Words," in *The Unesco Courier,* May, 1997, pp. 4-7.

[*In the following interview, Césaire discusses his political and poetic ideology.*]

MELSAN: *The usual way of trying to place you is by reference to various things such as time and place, writing, poetry and its different categories, political action and so on, but how would you place yourself?*

CÉSAIRE: That's a terribly difficult question to answer but, well, I'm a man, a man from Martinique, a coloured man, a black, someone from a particular country, from a particular geographical background, someone with a history who has fought for a specific cause. It's not very original but, broadly speaking, my answer would be that history will say who I am.

You are from the north of Martinique. . . .

I've always had the feeling that I was on a quest to reconquer something, my name, my country or myself.

That is why my approach has in essence always been poetic. Because it seems to me that in a way that's what poetry is.

The reconquest of the self by the self.

And what is your preferred instrument for that purpose?

I think words are the essential instrument! For a painter it would be painting! For a poet it is words!

I think it was Heidegger who said that words are the abode of being. There are many such quotations. I believe it was René Char, in his surrealist days, who said that words know much more about us than we know about them.

I too believe that words have a revealing as well as a creative function.

Revealing, creative . . . exploratory, perhaps?

Exploratory is very well put! It's the plummet dropped in the water, the homing device that brings the self back up to the surface.

You have often said that the black person's first words, after the long years of silence, are bound to be revolutionary words. Does that mean that poetry is "revolutionary" as well?

Yes, it is revolutionary because it is the world turned upside down, ploughed up, transmuted.

When the review *Tropiques* came out in Martinique under the occupation in 1941, in the middle of the world war, like a plunge into the contradictory wellsprings of the West Indian soul, a stark glimpse into the depths of colonial alienation, it was truly a cultural revolution.

And when the Vichy censor banned *Tropiques* in 1941 with the comment that it was revolutionary, he showed himself to be a very good critic. It's true! It was a cultural revolution.

We were carrying out a kind of Copernican revolution. There was good reason to be surpised! And the Martiniquais were themselves surprised as they stood revealed to themselves. It was a strange encounter!

It modified quite a number of values.

Which ones?

We are by definition complicated beings. That is the general rule for any society but one that is particularly applicable in the case of societies where complex layers of sediment have been laid down as a result of the inequalities of colonial life. Not everything was negative, far from it. The hybridization of which we are the outcome has achievements and positive values to its credit wherein the West and Europe also had their share. There was, as I say, a positive side, the effects of which were only belatedly felt by the non-Europeans but which are undeniable and in which we are simultaneously agents and partners—and, I should add, sometimes the beneficiaries as well. The Abbé Grégoire[1], Victor Schoelcher[2] and all those who spoke out and still speak out, who campaigned for human rights without distinction of race and against discrimination, these were my guides in life. They stand forever as representatives of the West's great outpouring of magnanimity and solidarity, an essential contribution to the advancement of the ideas of practical universality and human values, ideas without which the world of today would not be able to see its way forward. I am forever a brother to them, at one with them in their combat and in their hopes.

You made an important speech in Geneva in 1978, at the event called "Geneva and the Black World", in which you said: "The effective power of poetry, with its two faces, one looking nostalgically backward, the other looking prophetically forward, with the redeeming feature of its ability to redeem the self, is the power of intensifying life". Was your **Cahier d'un retour au pays natal**, *published in 1939, just such a primary utterance?*

Yes, that is how I see it: a new starting-point, a real start—there are many false starts in life.

But I think that was, for me, the real start.

Disinterring memories, all that was buried, bringing it back, presenting it so that it bursts forth fully formed upon the world—I think this sends an important signal. To express, not suppress, the force of one's reaction, to wield reinvigorated words as a miraculous weapon against the silenced world, freeing it from gags that are often imposed from within.

How does one set about "ungagging" the world?

I simply believe in the redeeming power of words.

Is that enough to deal with the human condition and the way it repeatedly slides out of control?

Probably not, not without love and humanism.

I really do believe in human beings. I find something of myself in all cultures, in that extraordinary effort that all people, everywhere, have made—and for what purpose?

Quite simply to make life livable!

It is no easy matter to put up with life and face up to death.

And this is what is so moving.

We are all taking part in the same great adventure.

That is what is meant by cultures, cultures that come together at some meeting-point.

You invented the term "negritude", which has been the mortar holding together a historic movement. Does not the assertion of negritude carry with it the risk of separating you from others, from "non-blacks"?

We have never regarded our specificity as the opposite or antithesis of universality. It seemed to us—or at least to me—to be very important to go on searching for our identity but at the same time to reject narrow nationalism, to reject racism, even reverse racism.

Our concern has always been a humanist concern and we wanted it to have roots.

We wanted to have roots and at the same time to communicate.

I think it was in a passage in Hegel emphasizing the master-slave dialectic that we found this idea about specificity. He points out that the particular and the universal are not to be seen as opposites, that the universal is not the negation of the particular but is reached by a deeper exploration of the particular.

The West told us that in order to be universal we had to start by denying that we were black. I, on the contrary, said to myself that the more we were black, the more universal we would be.

It was a totally different approach. It was not a choice between alternatives, but an effort at reconciliation.

Not a cold reconciliation, but reconciliation in the heat of the fire, an alchemical reconciliation if you like.

The identity in question was an identity reconciled with the universal. For me there can never be any imprisonment within an identity.

Identity means having roots, but it is also a transition, a transition to the universal.

Fire, one of the main life forces?

Yes, as you say, fire.

There is an obvious fiery quality in my poetry, but why? I belong to this island. . . . Why this obsession in my poetry? It is not something that I deliberately seek. I am aware—everyone is aware—that the volcano is out there. It is earth and it is fire.

Fire is not destructive. The volcano is not destructive except in an indirect way. It is a cosmic anger, in other words, a creative anger, yes, creative!

We are far removed from that romantic idyll beneath the calm sea. These are angry, exasperated lands, lands that spit and spew, that vomit forth life.

That is what we must live up to. We must draw upon the creativity of this plot of land! We must keep it going and not sink into a slumber of acceptance and resignation. It is a kind of summons to us from history and from nature.

How, then, do you explain the fact that your "primary utterance" was expressed in the language of the colonial power, of colonialism?

I have no problem with that.

It was not something I wanted, but it happens that the language I used was the language I had learned at school. That didn't bother me in the slightest, it didn't in any way come between me and my existential rebellion and the outpouring of my innermost being. I bent the French language to my purposes.

Nature and history have placed us at the cross-roads of two worlds, of two cultures if not more. There is the

African culture, which I see as being below the surface; and precisely because it is below the surface, overlooked, treated with contempt, it needed to be expressed, to be brought out alive into the light.

But the other culture was the obvious one, the one we were conscious of from books and from school, and which was also ours, an integral part of our individual and collective destiny.

And so I have tried to reconcile those two worlds, because that was what had to be done. On the other hand, I feel just as relaxed about claiming kinship with the African griot and the African epic as about claiming kinship with Rimbaud and Lautréamont—and through them with Sophocles and Aeschylus!

But what does the African griot think when he sees the tragic events unfolding in Rwanda or Zaire and the pall of hopelessness hanging over Africa, the Africa of which you dreamed so often while you campaigned for decolonization?

I have never harboured any illusions about the risks of history, be it in Africa, in Martinique, in the Americas or anywhere else. History is always dangerous, the world of history is a risky world; but it is up to us at any given moment to establish and readjust the hierarchy of dangers.

I saw that very clearly as early as 1966, at a time when great hopes had been aroused by the accession of many countries to independence. Indeed, I spoke out about this at the opening seminar of the World Festival of Black and African Arts in Dakar in April 1966, before an assembly of African dignitaries who were new to their jobs and, it must be admitted, unclear in their minds about the world and the power relationships in it, about themselves and about their irreversible responsibility.

I have the words of my speech of 6 April 1966 here in front of me. This is what I said:

"Africa is under threat, threatened by the impact of industrial civilization, threatened by the internal dynamism of Europe and America. You may ask why we should talk of threats when there is no European presence in Africa, when colonialism has disappeared and Africa has become independent.

"Unfortunately, Africa will not get off so lightly. The disappearance of colonialism does not mean that the danger of African culture disintegrating has also disappeared. The danger exists and everything contributes to it, whether the Europeans are there or not: economic development, modernization, political development, higher school attendance rates, education, urbanization, the integration of Africa into the world network of relationships, and so on and so forth. In short, just at the moment when Africa is truly being born into the world, it is in greater danger than ever of dying unto itself. That does not mean it should not be born into the world. It does mean that in opening itself up to the world it should keep its eyes wide open to the

dangers and that, in any event, the shield of a merely political independence, political independence unaccompanied and unsupplemented by cultural independence, would in the long run prove to be the most unreliable of shields and the most untrustworthy of safeguards. On top of that there has been political irresponsibility, and the whole gamut of cynicism has been run through! Fortunately, however, there have also been shining examples of the greatness of Africa, such as Nelson Mandela. Africa is experiencing the human adventure, and I am prepared to wager that the vital force of eternal Africa will once more inspire the song of the griot.

What about the Marxist Utopia to which you subscribed in 1946 and which you condemned before the Budapest crisis in your Letter to Maurice Thorez, in which you set out your reasons for breaking with the Communist Party?

It is true that, like so many of my contemporaries, I believed in what turned out to be a false Utopia. I am not at all ashamed about this. In the postwar context it expressed a heartfelt enthusiasm, a spiritual yearning.

But it was very soon followed by disappointment, a feeling of being manipulated, a conviction that one was being lied to and, as I said at the time, an unbearable awareness of "the collapse of an ideal and the poignant illustration of the failure of a whole generation". I felt an irresistible need not to keep silent and, regardless of the prevailing conformism, to break away at whatever risk to myself from the then all-powerful framework of the Marxist apparatus. It was part of my ontological choice as a human being aware of the non-negotiable responsibility that goes with a consciously accepted identity.

In Discours sur le colonialisme (1950), you said that "nobody can colonize with impunity, there is no innocent colonization. There will be a heavy price to pay for reducing humanity to a monologue".

Yes, I am deeply convinced that universal civilization has a great deal to lose by reducing whole civilizations to silence.

I think it would greatly impoverish human civilization if the voices of African, Indian and other Asian cultures were to fall silent. If the globalization we are now being offered were to reduce the dialogue of cultures to a monologue, it would create a civilization doomed to languish and decline. I believe in the importance of exchange, and exchange can only take place on the basis of mutual respect.

Is it still relevant, in 1997, to think in terms of combat?

We are always, all of us, warriors. The war takes different forms at different times, but there are always things to rebel against. One is always in rebellion against something, things that are unacceptable, things I will never accept. That is the inevitable way of the world, probably for everyone. There are things with which I cannot come to terms. I cannot accept that a people be stifled or that Africa be obliterated, I cannot resign myself to such things.

I desire—passionately—that peoples should exist as peoples, that they should prosper and make their contribution to universal civilization, because the world of colonization and its modern manifestations is a world that crushes, a world of awful silence.

At the age of eighty-four, Aimé Césaire, well over half a century after **Retour au pays natal,** *are you still faithful to your belief in the urgent relevance of poetry?*

Of course I am. I no longer have the same elemental energy, or the same strength, but I stand by it, I have not reneged on it.

Is poetry still effective today? Will it always be?

At any rate, it is for me the fundamental mode of expression, and the world's salvation depends on its ability to heed that voice. It is obvious that the voice of poetry has been less and less heeded during the century we have lived through, but it will come to be realized more and more that it is the only voice that can still be life-giving and that can provide a basis on which to build and reconstruct.

Wouldn't you say that underlying the poetic dimension of your work there is always a purpose, an ethical aim?

Yes indeed, there is an ethical aim underlying everything. From the time of the **Cahier d'un retour au pays natal** onwards, a concern for humankind emerges, a searching for the self but also a searching for fellowship and universality, a searching for human dignity, which I believe to be the bases of ethics.

And yet this century has not been one where ethics has triumphed, has it?

Certainly not, but one must speak out, whether one is heeded or not; we hold certain things to be fundamental, things that we cling to. Even if it means swimming against the tide, they must be upheld.

What we seek is reconciliation, to be in league with the cosmos, in league with history, to be in keeping with ourselves.

In other words, poetry is for me a searching after truth and sincerity, sincerity outside of the world, outside of alien times. We seek it deep within ourselves, often despite ourselves, despite what we seem to be, within our innermost selves.

Poetry wells up from the depths, with explosive force.

The volcano again.

No doubt I have reached the moment of crossing the great divide but I face it imperturbably in the knowledge of having put forward what I see as essential, in the knowledge, if you like, of having called out ahead of me and proclaimed the future aloud.

That is what I believe I have done; somewhat disoriented though I am to find the seasons going backwards, as it were, that is how it is and that is what I believe to be my vocation.

No resentments, none at all, no ill feelings but the inescapable solitude of the human condition. That is the most important thing.

Notes

[1] Henri Grégoire (1750-1831), French ecclesiastic and politician, a leader of the movement in the Convention for the abolition of slavery. *Ed.*

[2] French politician (1804-1893), campaigner for the abolition of slavery in the colonies, Deputy for Guadeloupe and Martinique. *Ed.*

FURTHER READING

Biography

Pallister, Janis L. *Aimé Césaire.* New York: Twayne Publishers, 1991, 149 p.
  Critical and biographical study of Césaire.

Criticism

Arnold, A. James. *Modernism and Negritude: The Poetry and Poetics of Aimé Césaire.* Cambridge: Harvard University Press, 1981, 318 p.
  Discusses Césaire and his poetry, focusing on social, political, historical, and literary contexts.

Davis, Gregson. Introduction to *Non-Vicious Circle: Twenty Poems of Aimé Césaire,* by Aimé Césaire, translated by Gregson Davis, pp. 3-28. Palo Alto: Stanford University Press, 1984.
  Brief biography of Césaire, focusing on his literary life.

Dayan, Joan. "The Figure of Negation: Some Thoughts on a Landscape by Césaire." *The French Review* LVI, No. 3 (February 1983): 411-23.
  Contends that Césaire "disposes and arranges concrete images, diverse and conflicting, into an unexpected tableau, which both reveals the present and initiates its transformation."

Knutson, April Ane. "Negritude and Surrealism, Marxism and Mallarmé: Ideological Confusion in the Works of Aimé Césaire." *Ideology and Independence in the Americas.* Minneapolis: MEP Publications, 1989, pp. 47-64.
  Examines Césaire's ideology and determines how it affects his work.

Morot-Sir, Edouard. "The Savage Humor of Aimé Césaire." *Soleil éclaté,* edited by Jacqueline Leiner. Tübingen: Gunter Narr Verlag, 1984, pp. 303-26.
  Explores the role of humor in Césaire's verse.

Scharfman, Ronnie Leah. *"Engagement" and the Language of the Subject in the Poetry of Aimé Césaire.* Gainesville: University of Florida Press, 1980, 133 p.

> Provides a stylistic and linguistic reading of Césaire's verse.

—————. "Repetition and Absence: The Discourse of Deracination in Aime Césaire's 'Nocturne d'une nostalgie'." *The French Review* LVI, No. 4 (March 1983): 572-78.

> Scharfman states: "By giving a close reading of Césaire's poems 'Nocturne d'une nostalgie,' I hope to initiate a new series of questions concerning the poetic discourse of deracination."

Additional coverage of Césaire's life and career is contained in the following sources published by The Gale Group: *Contemporary Literary Criticism,* Vols. 19, 32, 112; *Black Literature Criticism,* Vol. 1; *DISCovering Authors: Multicultural Authors Module; DISCovering Authors: Poets Module; Black Writers,* Vol. 2; *Contemporary Authors,* 65-68; *Contemporary Authors New Revision Series,* Vols. 24,43; *Major 20th-Century Authors.*

John Dryden
1631-1700

English poet, critic, playwright, and translator.

INTRODUCTION

Regarded by many scholars as the father of modern English poetry and criticism, Dryden dominated literary life in England during the last four decades of the seventeenth century. By deliberately and comprehensively refining language, Dryden developed an expressive, universal diction which has had a profound impact on the evolution of speech and writing in the English-speaking world. Although initially famous for his comedies and heroic tragedies, among Dryden's other accomplishments are critical essays as well as translations of works by Virgil, Chaucer, and Boccaccio. Today he is also highly regarded for his satirical and didactic poems, notably *Absalom and Achitophel, The Hind and the Panther,* and *Religio Laici.* In poems such as these, Dryden displayed an irrepressible wit and forceful line of argument which later satirists adopted as their model.

Biographical Information

The eldest son of a large, socially prominent Puritan family, Dryden was born in Aldwinkle, Northamptonshire. Little is known about his early years, except that as a young boy he received a classical education at Westminster School through a royal scholarship. While there he published his first poem, *Upon the Death of the Lord Hastings,* commemorating the life of a schoolmate who had recently died of smallpox. In 1650 Dryden began attending Trinity College, Cambridge, where he earned a bachelor of arts degree. Shortly afterward his father died, leaving him to oversee the affairs of his family and of his own small estate. Dryden's activities and whereabouts during the next several years are unknown; in 1659, however, following the death of Oliver Cromwell, Lord Protector of England, Dryden returned to writing and published *Heroique Stanzas,* a group of complimentary verses which portray Cromwell as architect of a great new age. In the following years, Dryden continued to publish politically oriented poems, of which the most notable are *Astraea Redux* and *Annus Mirabilis: the Year of Wonders, 1666.* The former, which celebrated the exiled Charles II's restoration to the English crown, incited condemnation in later years from those who charged Dryden with political inconsistency and selfish motivation. Since then, historians have argued that Dryden maintained throughout his life a belief in religious tolerance and moderate gov-

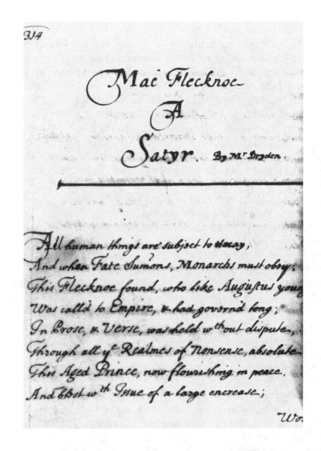

ernment and switched allegiance from the republicans to the royalists in keeping with the majority of the English people.

In 1663, following his marriage to Lady Elizabeth Howard, Dryden debuted as a playwright, a career which at the time held the most financial promise for an aspiring writer in England. His first play proved unsuccessful, but later endeavors, in particular *The Indian Emperour* (1665), were popular and established Dryden's reputation in drama, a field which he increasingly dominated during the next fifteen years. In 1668 Dryden became poet laureate of England, and shortly thereafter, received the title of historiographer royal. In 1685, during the first year of the reign of Catholic monarch James II, Dryden converted to Catholicism. He did not renounce this conversion after the abdication of James or with the accession in 1689 of Protestant rulers William and Mary. Dryden died in London in 1700 and was buried in Westminster Abbey. Throughout the years, Dryden's detractors have focused on his shifts from Protestantism to Catholicism and from republicanism to monarchism as proof of the poet's flair for political expediency. Generally, however, Dryden is recognized as someone who in his time was an extremely popular literary figure, who believed in religious moderation, and who influenced heavily the tastes of his age.

Major Works

Apart from the encomiums or complimentary poems of his early years, Dryden is well-known for his satirical verse. The Popish Plot (1678-81), a thwarted attempt by the Earl of Shaftesbury and others to exclude Charles's Catholic brother, James, from his right of succession to the throne, provided Dryden with the topic for what critics consider his greatest work, *Absalom and Achitophel,* a satirical attack on Shaftesbury and his confederates. This work inaugurated a phase of satirical and didactic verse which directly influenced the development of Augustan poetry in the next century, especially that of Alexander Pope. The poem was followed in 1682 by *Mac Flecknoe,* a mock-heroic poem which was directed at the poet Thomas Shadwell, a literary antagonist of Dryden. Allied to *Absalom and Achitophel* in tone, *Mac Flecknoe* displays Dryden's mastery of rhythm and cunning verbal attack. The same year there also appeared a shorter, more serious satiric poem titled *The Medall,* which again was aimed at Shaftesbury.

Political and religious matters repeatedly overlapped in Dryden's time, an era much vexed with the question of whether Protestant or Roman Catholic monarchs were the legitimate rulers of Britain; accordingly, Dryden also began to address religious issues in his poetry. *Religio Laici; or, a Layman's Faith* (1682) appeared when Whig plots to assassinate King Charles II were being formed. In this didactic poem, which also contains religious and metaphysical insights, Dryden advocated a compromise between Protestant Anglican exclusivism and Roman Catholic belief in absolute papal authority, articulating the king's stance in favor of religious toleration. Dryden's later, allegorical poem, *The Hind and the Panther* (1687), a three-part work written in beast-fable form, was published after the poet's conversion to Catholicism, but like *Religio Laici,* it argues for moderation between the two churches. Dryden's odes represent his final poetic period. They include *A Song for St. Cecilia's Day, 1687,* and *Alexander's Feast.* Today, they are widely anthologized, and they attest to Dryden's skill at incorporating musical composition into his poetry.

Critical Reception

The eighteenth-century English author Samuel Johnson regarded Dryden as a poet who crystallized the potential for beauty and majesty in the English language by effectively shaping rough words into refined verse. Dryden first began developing his poetic style while writing his early, laudatory verses, experimenting as he wrote them with the traditional hexameter form. Although recognized for their artistic promise and innovation, these poems have since been faulted for misplaced or excessive conceits and sim-

iles. Ultimately, the best of this early poetic period is represented by *Annus Mirabilis,* an inspirational, heroic treatment of the great fire in London and of the Anglo-Dutch naval war. Years later, with *Absalom and Achitophel,* Dryden displayed his mastery of the heroic couplet and the suitability of his streamlined verse for political satire. Cloaked in allusive language and based on the biblical story of King David's rebellious son, this mock-heroic poem addresses the explosive political climate of the time through a string of character portraits, narrative, and speeches. Dryden's portrayals of Charles II, an inveterate philanderer; his illegitimate son Monmouth, who planned to dethrone his father; and Shaftesbury, the chief orchestrator of the Popish Plot; are admired by critics not only for their liveliness but for the judicious manner in which they are presented. Scholars have remarked that the relentless movement of the poem, its delightful yet pointed commentary on the crucial situation, and its timeless appeal establish it as one of the highest achievements in the heroic couplet form. That Dryden was an exemplary poet of public events and was able to infuse even the most ordinary incident with dignified, original art is not disputed. However, his poems have been charged with displaying a disturbing impersonality. Nevertheless, several modern critics have detected a clear, confessional tone in Dryden's later poems, *Religio Laici* and *The Hind and the Panther.* Although the theological viewpoints in them are disparate, critics have observed that both these works forcefully document the poet's personal reactions to the political milieu as well as to the power of religious faith in his era.

PRINCIPAL WORKS

Poetry

Upon the Death of the Lord Hastings 1649
Heroique Stanzas 1659
Astraea Redux. A Poem on the Happy Restoration & Return of his Sacred Majesty Charles the Second 1660
Annus Mirabilis: The Year of Wonders, 1666 1667
Absalom and Achitophel 1681
Mac Flecknoe; or, A Satire upon the True-Blew-Protestant Poet, T. S. 1682
The Medall. A Satyre against Sedition 1682
The Second Part of Absalom and Achitophel [with Nahum Tate] 1682
Miscellany Poems 1684
Sylvae: or, The Second Part of Poetical Miscellanies 1685
Threnodia Augustalis 1685
To the Pious Memory of the Accomplisht Young Lady Mrs. Anne Killigrew 1686
The Hind and the Panther. A Poem in Three Parts 1687
A Song for St. Cecilia's Day, 1687 1687
Examen Poeticum: Being the Third Part of Miscellany Poems 1693
Alexander's Feast 1697

Fables Ancient and Modern; Translated into Verse, from Homer, Ovid, Boccace, & Chaucer: with Original Poems (includes adaptations and translations) 1700

Other Major Works

The Wild Gallant (drama) 1663

The Indian Queen [with Sir Robert Howard] (drama) 1664

The Rival Ladies (drama) 1664

The Indian Emperour (drama) 1665

Sir Martin Mar-All [with the Duke of Newcastle] (drama) 1667

The Tempest; or, The Enchanted Island [with Sir William Davenant, from William Shakespeare's *The Tempest*] (adaptation) 1667

Of Dramatick Poesie* (criticism) 1668

Tyrannick Love (drama) 1669

The Conquest of Granada by the Spaniards [in two parts] (drama) 1670-71

Marriage à-la-Mode (drama) 1672

Aureng-Zebe (drama) 1675

All for Love; or, The World Well Lost (drama) 1677

The State of Innocence, and the Fall of Man [from the poem *Paradise Lost* by John Milton] (dramatic adaptation) 1677

Troilus and Cressida; or, Truth Found Too Late [from William Shakespeare's *Troilus and Cressida*] (adaptation) 1679

The Duke of Guise [with Nathaniel Lee] (drama) 1682

Don Sebastian, King of Portugal (drama) 1689

King Arthur: or, The British Worthy (drama) 1691

The Works of Virgil (translation) 1697

The Letters of John Dryden (letters) 1942

*This work is commonly referred to as *Essay of Dramatic Poesy*.

CRITICISM

David M. Vieth (essay date 1965)

SOURCE: "Irony in Dryden's Ode to Anne Killigrew," in *Studies in Philology,* Vol. LXII, No. 1, January 1965, pp. 91-100.

[*In the following excerpt, Vieth argues that in his* To the Pious Memory of the Accomplisht Young Lady Mrs. Anne Killigrew, *Dryden has not written a conventional ode of praise, but created instead an elegy that is both gently mocking and affectionate.*]

In the current revival of interest in Dryden and his contemporaries, much attention has been given to his ode **To the Pious Memory Of the Accomplisht Young Lady Mrs Anne Killigrew.** Extensive and illuminating analyses have been contributed by Ruth Wallerstein ["On the Death of Mrs. Killigrew: The Perfecting of a Genre"] E. M. W. Tillyard [*Five Poems, 1470-1870*], and Arthur W. Hoffman, whose recent book, *John Dryden's Imagery,* devotes more space to the Killigrew ode than to any of Dryden's other poems. All three critics interpret the ode as essentially a performance in terms of tradition, ritual, manners, and decorum—that is, as an attempt to say exactly what a Restoration poet was expected to say concerning the death of a fashionable young lady. In so doing, these critics have viewed the ode, not primarily as a product of the Augustan sensibility, but in light of its kinship with poetry of the earlier seventeenth century such as Donne's *Anniversaries,* Cowley's Pindaric odes, and Milton's minor poems. The special value of Hoffman's presentation is that it traces Dryden's implied characterization of Anne Killigrew as a Christian nun, as a classical poetess elevated to the status of a divine muse, and ultimately as a saint-like and Christlike figure of incarnation, atonement, and redemption.

When a poem has been discussed so thoroughly and so well, it may seem that little could be added. Yet Dryden has, I believe, relied upon more than a pretentious display of literary conventions to disarm the common-sense resistance of his readers—particularly his Augustan readers, who, with the many-sided awareness typical of the period in which they lived, might well have been skeptical of the extravagant praise that is lavished upon Anne. Throughout the poem, the picture of Anne is lightly etched with an irony which implicitly concedes that she may not have been an apotheosized being, after all, but only an ordinary, though attractive, girl. This irony is almost automatically latent in the mode of hyperbole which pervades the poem, but it is also reinforced at crucial points by ambiguities in phrasing, imagery, and tone which must have been deliberate on Dryden's part.

Recognition of the irony in the Killigrew ode entails no disagreement with the general interpretations advanced by earlier critics: it is merely an added dimension that enriches the poem. Nor should its importance be overemphasized: it remains always secondary to the ritual celebration of Anne's personal and artistic merits. In the concluding three stanzas I discover no irony apart from the prevailing hyperbole, while in the first four stanzas the irony is barely discernible without reference to the central portion of the poem, where it is most prominent. To be sure, earlier critics have not been entirely unaware of the irony in some passages. Tillyard found it "hard to feel warmly about the political metaphor in stanza six," and he argued uneasily that line 146, "What next she had design'd, Heaven only knows," would not have had the "absurdity" in the seventeenth century that it has in the twentieth (p. 50). Hoffman describes the same line as "skillfully edged by the phrasing with a playful tone" (p. 114), and he acknowledges that "to the modern eye" lines 75-76 "may appear inverted" (p. 107). But instead of seeing these lurking ironies as purposeful, Tillyard and Hoffman tend to explain them away.

The function of the irony is best understood in relation to Hoffman's account of Anne as an implied figure of incarnation and atonement. Tillyard stressed the dichotomy in the poem between Anne's heavenly and earthly guises (pp. 50-51); Hoffman distinguishes more elaborately between the "movement of praise" of Anne as incarnation and the "mournful elegiac movement" for her in her mortal dimension:

> Because of the dual nature of the object of praise in the ode *To Anne Killigrew,* the elegiac movement is

simply a phase of the total movement and is a limiting frame only for the object as person; in its other aspect. as transfigured being and incarnate principle, the object of praise from the beginning surmounts death and mourning. (p. 92)

The irony in the poem is part of the "limiting frame." It enforces a double focus, requiring that Anne be seen simultaneously not only as a potentially divine figure of atonement but as conceivably no more than an average, even if charming, mortal. Read with this bifocal vision, individual passages yield multiple meanings which are frequently opposed to one another yet everywhere functional.

Tillyard observed that the first four stanzas form an introduction to the "body" of Dryden's ode (p. 51); Hoffman explores in greater detail how they gradually and tactfully establish Anne as a figure of incarnation and atonement, building to a preliminary climax near the end of stanza four:

> What can we say t' excuse our *Second Fall?*
> Let this thy *Vestal,* Heav'n, attone for all!

Appropriately, since the development of Anne into an apotheosized figure is the main business of these stanzas, the irony remains relatively muted. After the climax in stanza four, however, the irony is more noticeable, as in the last line of the stanza:

> Her Wit was more than Man, her Innocence a
> Child!

In the context of Anne's possible divinity, this line has the meaning Hoffman assigns to it: "In her wit that is *more than Man* she is like Christ the Redeemer, and in her innocence like the Christchild" (p. 102). Applied to Anne as ordinary mortal, however, the line suggests something engagingly freakish about her poetical disposition: she bubbles over with childish precocity, but her experience of life is so shallow that she can scarcely write knowledgeably on any subject. Later in the poem, line 146 is similarly double-edged:

> What next she had design'd, Heaven only knows . . .

If Anne is a celestial being, her plans were so transcendent that heaven alone could comprehend them. If she was merely a mortal, the line implies that she was girlishly scatterbrained.

Ironic qualification is most insistent in stanzas five through seven—fittingly so, since these stanzas portray Anne's earthly career most directly. Stanza five opens with two examples (the italics are mine):

> *Art she had none,* yet wanted none:
> For Nature did that Want supply . . .

> Such Noble Vigour did her Verse adorn,
> *That it seem'd borrow'd,* where 'twas only born.

Both examples employ the same type of syntactical ambiguity. Momentarily, each sentence seems to be completed in an unfavorable sense. Then, as one reads on, the thought unfolds into a favorable meaning, but once the qualification has been injected, it lingers as an ironic connotation. In the primary and favorable sense of the two passages, Anne in her nature as divine muse has no need of the art which ordinary poets must labor to acquire, and her works necessarily reflect the "Noble Vigour" of the past poets whose transmigrating soul she shares. In their secondary sense, the examples hint that her writing is undisciplined and even plagiarized. Dryden here makes literary capital out of the standard situation in which an American college freshman produces a sentence fragment by prematurely inserting a period as soon as his thought appears to be complete.

Stanza five continues (again the italics are mine):

> Her Morals too were in her Bosome bred
> By great Examples daily fed.
> What in the best of Books, her Fathers Life, she
> read.
> *And to be read her self she need not fear . . .*

In the primary and favorable sense of this last line, Anne's life and poetry were infused with such purity that they can survive any moral test. In the secondary, ironic sense, however, her poems are so trivial that no one would bother to read them. The stanza concludes:

> Ev'n Love (for Love sometimes her Muse exprest)
> Was but a *Lambent-flame* which play'd about her
> Brest:
> Light as the Vapours of a Morning Dream,
> So cold herself, whilst she such Warmth exprest,
> 'Twas *Cupid* bathing in *Diana's* Stream.

As Christlike figure of incarnation and as classical goddess of virginity, Anne could write of sexual love without being sullied by its earthly impurities. But in terms of the underlying irony, she is a foolish young lady writing imitatively of experiences which she does not know at first hand. The imitative character of Anne's love poetry is further suggested by the phrase *"Lambent-flame,"* which was a cliché of epic language during the Augustan period, and which is conspicuously italicized in the two authoritative texts of 1686 and 1693. So familiar was this cliché that nearly a decade earlier, Dryden could burlesque it in the "lambent dullness" which plays around Shadwell's face in *Mac Flecknoe* For readers who remember the earlier poem, the use of the cliché in the Killigrew ode carries doubly ironic force.

Stanza six, recounting Anne's excursion into the sister art of painting, initiates the military and political metaphor which Tillyard found "hard to feel warmly about." Tillyard's response was accurate, for the image is partially pejorative. In her "ambitious" designs on the realm of painting, Anne teeters on the brink of Christian pride and classical hybris: also, she justifies her conquest with flimsy pretexts, she apparently enlists a fifth column (*"Cham-*

ber of Dependences"), and she overcomes by force rather than merit. Evidently the province of painting did not wish to be conquered but could do nothing to avert the disaster. For many of Dryden's readers, the image must have called up uncomfortable associations with Louis XIV's wars of aggression:

> Born to the Spacious Empire of the *Nine*,
> One would have thought, she should have been content
> To manage well that Mighty Government:
> But what can young ambitious Souls confine?
>   To the next Realm she stretcht her Sway,
>   For *Painture* neer adjoyning lay,
> A plenteous Province, and alluring Prey.
> *A Chamber of Dependences* was fram'd,
> (As Conquerors will never want Pretence,
>   When arm'd, to justifie the Offence)
> And the whole Fief, in right of Poetry she claim'd.
> The Country open lay without Defence . . .

Translating from vehicle back to tenor, the lines depict an eager but ignorant girl who thought to master painting before she had taken proper pains with her poetry. They conjure up an amusing vision of Anne, Jackson Pollock-like, splashing paint in all directions. The military metaphor is sustained through the end of the following stanza, where ironic overtones are likewise evident:

> To such Immod'rate Growth her Conquest rose,
> That Fate alone its Progress could oppose.

Here the operative word is "Immod'rate." Guilty of violating the classical principle of "nothing to excess," Anne is punished by a classical "Fate."

Stanza six then describes Anne's painting more specifically:

> Her Pencil drew, what e're her Soul design'd,
> And oft the happy Draught surpass'd the Image in her Mind.

Besides insinuating that Anne's successes were happy accidents, these lines trigger a hostile question: what image, if any, was in her mind? In the next passage, which enumerates the subjects Anne chose, the ironic point seems to be that her efforts were conventional and derivative: she painted just what everyone else in the seventeenth century had painted. This implication is strengthened by the meter, whose obtrusively regular beat recalls the way a child repeats a nursery rhyme by rote:

> The *Sylvan* Scenes of Herds and Flocks,
>
> And fruitful Plains and barren Rocks,
>
> Of shallow Brooks that flow'd so clear,
>
> The Bottom did the Top appeer;
>
> Of deeper too and ampler Flouds,
>
> Which as in Mirrors, shew'd the Woods;

> Of lofty Trees with Sacred Shades,
>
> And Perspectives of pleasant Glades,
>
> Where Nymphs of brightest Form appear,
>
> And shaggy Satyrs standing neer,
>
> Which them at once admire and fear.

The stanza is rounded off with two ambiguous lines:

> So strange a Concourse ne're was seen before,
> But when the peopl'd Ark the whole Creation bore.

In their primary and adulatory sense, as Hoffman notes, these lines credit Anne with Godlike creativity. But the comparison of her paintings to the contents of Noah's ark, together with the key word "strange," also suggests that they are a grotesque hodgepodge.

Instances of irony in the first four stanzas, though less striking than in stanzas five through seven, are nonetheless present. As is true elsewhere in the poem, the tone of hyperbole constantly holds ironic possibilities. In stanza three, the posture of the heavens at the birth of Anne is almost too good to be true: even the "most Malicious" planets are "in Trine." In stanza four, the abject apology for the "steaming Ordures" of the Restoration stage implies something prudish about the person addressed. Similar hints of irony in the first two stanzas are supported by the use of conditional constructions which, in their note of polite hesitation, tacitly qualify the eulogy by opening up meanings opposite to those urged by direct statement. In stanza one, it is uncertain whether Anne's soul inhabits a planet, the region of the fixed stars, or the empyrean; thus she may be in none of these exalted places. In stanza two, it is uncertain whether her soul originated by "Traduction" from her father or by transmigration from the great poets of antiquity; thus there may be a less flattering explanation.

In stanza three, the ironic effect of the conditional mode is maintained by gestures of concession (the italics are mine):

> *May we presume to say,* that at thy Birth,
> New joy was sprung in Heav'n, as well as here on Earth.

But perhaps we may *not* presume to say this.

> *For sure* the Milder Planets did combine
> On thy Auspicious Horoscope to shine . . .

"For sure" protests too much.

> And then *if ever,* Mortal Ears
> Had heard the Musick of the Spheres!

But *has* the music of the spheres ever been audible to humans? (One thinks of Swift's Laputians.)

> And if no clust'ring Swarm of Bees

On thy sweet Mouth distill'd their golden Dew,
   'Twas that, such vulgar Miracles,
   Heav'n had not Leasure to renew . . .

Possibly there was no miracle because Anne's birth was in no way extraordinary.

Two final examples of irony may be noticed in the first stanza. One passage anticipates the later portrayal of Anne as the enthusiastic but bungling amateur. Like a music student who practices too many hours a day, she is advised, in avuncular accents, that in heaven there is no hurry:

   What ever happy Region is thy place,
   Cease thy Celestial Song a little space;
   (Thou wilt have Time enough for Hymns Divine,
     Since Heav'ns Eternal Year is thine.)

This is followed by a left-handed compliment:

   Hear then a Mortal Muse thy Praise rehearse,
     In no ignoble Verse;
   But such as thy own voice did practise here . . .

"No ignoble" is noncommittal, nor does Dryden's assumed modesty concerning his own verses offer much guarantee of the quality of Anne's.

As the foregoing discussion has suggested, Dryden's ode to Anne Killigrew, far from being a frigid exercise in the manipulation of early seventeenth-century conventions, shapes those conventions into a vital expression of the Augustan sensibility. If its ancestors include Donne's *Anniversaries,* its descendants are such masterpieces of ironic eulogy as Pope's *Epistle to Augustus.* It is both traditional in seventeenth-century terms and gentlemanly in the best eighteenth-century manner. And, being of two ages, it is also for all time. Anne is the Christ, the divine potential, in every man. At the same time, the irony in the poem makes her real as a person, thereby universalizing the poignancy of her mortality: because she is human, she is imperfect, and because she is imperfect, she can be loved. I am reminded, perhaps subjectively, of that chef-d'oeuvre of twentieth-century elegies, *Bells for John Whiteside's Daughter.* Though the opposed attitudes that are held in tension in Dryden's poem are not the same as in Ransom's, the technique is analogous, and the emotional impact is comparable. What the ode on Anne Killigrew communicates above all is *affection.* In a clumsy paraphrase, it says something like this: "When we consider Anne objectively, we know that she was not a great poet or great painter, but we love her as much as if she were." In such terms Dryden's poem very nearly earns Dr. Johnson's accolade as "undoubtedly the noblest ode that our language ever has produced."

Bessie Proffitt (essay date 1970)

SOURCE: "Political Satire in Dryden's *Alexander's Feast,*" in *Texas Studies in Literature and Language,* Vol. XI, No. 4, 1970, pp. 1307-16.

[*In the following excerpt, Profitt asserts that* Alexander's Feast *should not be assessed simply for its qualities as a musical ode, but also regarded as a pointed "attack" on King William III.*]

The contention of this paper is that *Alexander's Feast* is not only the zenith of the Restoration ode for music but also a well-hidden attack upon William III. If Dryden's ode is an attack upon William, it may be rescued from the accusation of jingling to which such poetry is subject. Mark Van Doren reflects this attitude when he suggests that "perhaps [*Alexander's Feast*] is only immortal ragtime." If this Cecilian ode is more than "immortal ragtime," it must have a greater unity and depth of meaning than is imparted by its musical subject and undeniably musical verse. But the ode, although a continuous narrative in relation to Timotheus and Alexander, is so episodic that it tends to defy interpretation. Both Alan Roper and Earl Miner have the uneasy feeling that *Alexander's Feast* is, in some way, connected with William III. Nevertheless, the ode's lack of a strictly sustained pattern of images with a one-to-one correspondence—for example, Alexander as William III and Darius as James II—has prevented either critic from further developing his insight. *Alexander's Feast* develops its attack upon William, not through an image pattern, but rather through the theme of illegitimacy and illegality which pervades the ode.

This theme springs from the implications contained in the tale of Timotheus and Alexander. The story, which had been used since the Middle Ages, is singularly effective; not only does it give Dryden a continuous narrative upon which to construct his ode, but, as an account connected with an actual person, it has the further advantage of possessing its own depths of meaning. Dryden could have drawn upon these depths for the complex, hidden satire in his poem. As his image patterns succeed one another, it will be noted that they produce a cumulative effect. Far from being a flattering portrait of the conquering Macedonian monarch and an appreciative glance at Bacchus phrased in intricate and beautiful verse, the ode repeats its theme of illegality and illegitimacy over and over. And behind the façade of beauty lurks the blighting shadow of bloodshed and violence, which is manifest in the account of the burning of Persepolis and is hidden in the story of Bacchus. Because the ode seems to depend for its development upon a consistent theme rather than upon a sustained pattern of images, Alan Roper, who senses that there are political implications in the poem, is able to see only that in Stanza 4 Alexander may represent William III and Darius may represent James II. As Roper points out, it is certain that Dryden compared William III to Alexander in his epistle to his kinsman, John Driden, and it seems possible that he may have done so in *Alexander's Feast.*

Nearly every critic who comments at any length upon this ode mentions Dryden's letter to his sons, in which he tells of his troublesome commission to write the ode for the St. Cecilia's Day celebration. But most critics stop at this point; they ignore the following portion of the letter, which illuminates Dryden's personal attitude at the time of composition toward a king whom he, as a Tory, could never consider a legal monarch. This monarch had also caused Dryden to suffer financial difficulties; in his letter, Dryden apparently is replying to the advice of his sons to attempt some measure of reconciliation with the government.

> I remember the Counsell you give me in your letter: but dissembling, though lawfull in some Cases, is not my talent: yet for your sake I will struggle with the plain openness of my nature, & keep in my just resentments against that degenerate Order. . . . I never can repent of my Constancy; since I am thoroughly perswaded of the justice of the laws, for which I suffer.

There can be no doubt that Dryden detested the government and that he believed William of Orange to have no legal right to England's throne. Perhaps Dryden was not a royalist of the old "divine right" persuasion, but he had a horror of the disruption of proper order, and, obviously, he could not be expected to concede that William was the rightful king of England.

The relatively flat, one-dimensional style of *Alexander's Feast* suggests that the ode may develop on more than one level. For example, the well-known chorus of Stanza 1 affirms a half-truth so blatantly that the reader is virtually invited to supply an ironic qualification:

> None but the Brave
> None but the Brave
> None but the Brave deserves the Fair.
>
> (ll. 13-15)

Thus it may be well to look below the surface for additional significance. When the various episodes are subjected to close scrutiny, they assume meanings strikingly different from those of their clever musical surface. *Alexander's Feast* can be read as a pleasant bit of virtuosity, but, as Earl Miner observes, much of its praise of Alexander is ironic. Dryden seems to have depended upon the context of the classical allusions and upon the multiple meanings and associations of words to develop an ironic second level on which he could attack William III, and this level can be detected by a close examination of the details of *Alexander's Feast*.

In the first stanza Dryden gives the setting and characters of the poem, but there are ironies which are not immediately apparent hidden within the graceful language. Perhaps the first hint that the ode may be concerned with William comes in line 6, where Dryden places Alexander's "Peers" around his throne. "Peers" immediately summons up the image of English lords rather than Macedonian nobles; it is a peculiarly and thoroughly English word. The incongruity of "Peers" forces attention back to the beginning allusions of the poem, which then take on additional import. Because William's victory over Louis XIV had occurred in the preceding year, a contemporary reader or listener would be very apt, consciously or unconsciously, to make an association between William and Alexander. Further, in the light of such phrases as "God-like

Heroe" (l. 4) and their associations, "Persia won" may refer not only to the more immediately obvious parallel with William's victory over Louis, but also to William's ascent of the English throne; the words seem to carry a double meaning. And the choice of Alexander to represent William, too, could have a double significance; for, like Alexander, William is a courageous and victorious man, even though in Dryden's eyes he is no more a king than the "God-like Heroe" is a god. The peculiar crowns worn by the "Peers" also hint at the possibility of another level of interpretation; these "Peers" are crowned with roses and myrtles. Although these flowers, often worn at Greek banquets, add an extra touch of lush beauty, they can also serve as symbols. Among other things, the rose is a symbol of England, a fact which reinforces the impression that the "Peers" are English lords. And the myrtle is associated with Venus. Hence, these crowns can both establish the setting as England and carry out a theme of a venal and illegal alliance. For Thaïs was one of the Athenian *hetairai* whose favors were sold to the highest bidder. Can Dryden be passing judgment on his fellow Englishmen by personifying them as Thaïs? He apparently was not concerned with a particular courtesan, for he asked Tonson to change the name of Lais in the manuscript to Thaïs, who, though she was not Alexander's mistress, actually accompanied his army on its Eastern campaign. Since Alexander and Timotheus were not contemporaries, Dryden's condescension to history seems relatively unimportant; he was interested in the venal and illicit nature of the alliance.

There is further possible commentary on William and his right to the throne in other terms used in this stanza. After the slaying of Darius, Alexander married Statira, the daughter of Darius, and the Sogdian princess Roxane, to give a greater appearance of legality to his sovereignty over the Persian Empire. Is this, perhaps, the significance of the word "Eastern"? If so, this word has many implications. For one, since Thaïs only seems "like" an Eastern bride, there is an immediate intimation of illegality, of something outside the law. But "Eastern" possibly could convey another message, for it was through his marriages to Statira and Roxane that Alexander could give himself the regality and ceremony of a Persian king. And it was through his marriage to Mary that William of Orange ascended the English throne. William refused to divide the crown with Mary, whose claim was far greater than his own, although even she had no true claim as long as James and his infant son lived. But William was a brave and resourceful man, and the venal English were only too happy to have such a man as monarch.

The story of Alexander's half-god parentage (Stanza 2), ostensibly an extreme compliment to Alexander, continues the theme of illegality and illegitimacy, while drawing additional parallels between Alexander and William. Alexander's mother, Olympias, declared that he had been fathered by Jove. While this paternity, if true, would certainly have made Alexander a semideity, it would also have destroyed his right to Philip's throne. Indeed, Alexander's succession was doubted, after a violent quarrel with Philip. A further parallel, though slightly twisted, between Alexander and William seems to be involved here.

Like James, Philip of Macedon had a second wife and an infant son who had strong claims upon the throne. Olympias secured Alexander's succession by either slaying this wife and son or having them slain. Thus the apparently gracious compliment to Alexander implies illegal possession of the Macedonian throne, even while it seems to bestow supernaturality on Alexander. Of course, Alexander's divinity has already been denied by the phrase "God-like Heroe" (l. 4). Moreover, there are connotations of a counterfeit coin, or sovereign (cf. *The Medall*), in *"bely'd"* (l. 28) and "stamp'd an Image of himself, a Sov'raign of the World" (l. 33). Both as the result of an inflated ego and as a political maneuver, Alexander had demanded to be worshiped as a god. It seems very possible that Dryden is equating William with Alexander. For William, too, occupies a throne illegally, and he demands respect as a sovereign—a sovereignty which, like Alexander's divinity, is not real, but false, even though he does possess certain royal qualities. The foolish crowd admires the lofty sound of Alexander's divinity—sound, note, not substance—and pays the expected homage. Gratified, this king assumes the god, that is, takes on the role of a rightful monarch, very graciously affects to nod, and seems—but only seems—to shake the spheres. A. W. Verrall notes that the see-sawing motion in these lines is a mockery of majesty, and a very real mockery it seems in the light of the ironic meaning of the words.

Nor can the submerged implications in the song of Bacchus (Stanza 3) be ignored. Although Bacchus usually is associated with the pleasure of wine, there is a darker side to his story. For Bacchus established a new religion in Greece, much as William attempted to establish Calvinism in England; the word "Triumph" (l. 49) seems to establish a connection between Alexander, fresh from his triumph over Persia, and Bacchus. The god comes "Flush'd with a purple Grace" (l. 51), and purple can be symbolic of royalty as well as of wine and the flush caused by overindulgence. Rather than implying that the "jolly God" is the well-favored god of wine, the lines seem to hint that he wears the royal purple by the gift of the people, for "grace" can also refer to a freely given, unmerited gift. Although the Greek rulers feared the violence of the worship of Bacchus, he was welcomed by the crowds, just as William was received by the foolish English. Bacchus was not a harmless god; once in power, he exacted his worship by cunning and force; hence, purple may also signify bloodshed. Considering the manner in which Bacchus compelled men to worship him, "honest" (l. 52) is an example of extreme irony. Nor could William, the "butcher of Glencoe," who occupied a throne not rightfully his, be termed "honest."

The strangely religious tone is carried further in the succeeding lines. "He comes, He comes" (l. 53) has religious overtones, and "Ordain" (l. 55) is too solemn a word for the revelry which, ostensibly, was introduced into Greece by Bacchus. His "Blessings" (l. 56) were not, however, unmixed joy, for the crowds at the Bacchanalia became literally savage beasts who tore their victims limb from limb. Therefore, it can be wondered what kind of joys Bacchus has "ordained," and how much of a "treasure"

are his "Blessings." Dryden seems to be indulging in a subtle, ironic attack upon a cruel, illegal monarch and religious innovator, and upon the gullible, savage English mob which welcomed him.

The following stanza (4) purportedly shows the power of music to excite Alexander to rage; however, "Thrice He routed all his Foes; and thrice He slew the slain" (l. 68), although to some degree an heroic convention, is reminiscent of the Battle of Agincourt in *Henry V* (Act 4, scenes 6, 7). In *Henry V* the speech on Alexander's madness at another feast is put into the mouths of Fluellen and Gower, who are comparing Henry V to Alexander. Since these history plays are Shakespeare's commentary upon the usurpation of the English throne and the disruption of order which resulted from this usurpation, it seems more than coincidental that the scenes from *Henry V* and the fourth stanza of *Alexander's Feast* should be so closely parallel. Further, though Henry V is not a legal king, he is a great man, like both William and Alexander. Once again, there seems to be an allusion to the illegality of William's occupation of the throne. This allusion is made more emphatic by Alexander's defiance of heaven and earth (l. 71); a usurper would be defying heaven and earth, for he would be disrupting both natural and supernatural order.

The story of Alexander and Darius is concrete enough to give a certain amount of one-to-one correspondence, and the development of a consistent theme seems to indicate that the comparison of William to Alexander is sustained beyond this stanza. The suitability of the legend of Darius and Alexander to Dryden's purpose is obvious. Darius was deserted, betrayed, and slain by his own men. Clearly, James's situation parallels that of Darius, although James was not slain by his men, but was allowed to escape. By following the classical outline Dryden could avoid any contemporary criticism. The possible political correspondence is clear, although the plight of Darius may even to a degree refer to Dryden himself, who felt that he had been deserted by those whom he had believed trustworthy.

Does Alexander pity Darius, or is the joylessness of the "Victor" (l. 84) due to his own waning popularity? The "various Turns of Chance" (l. 86) do not seem to belong to Darius alone. Dryden could have camouflaged his examination of William's reaction to his loss of popularity by having Alexander weep for Darius' ill fortune. William had encountered the Whigs' lack of respect for the monarchy and had realized that the Tories did not accept him as their ruler. Although William was the king de facto, Parliament took care to limit his power. This limitation was an irritant to William, and, like "Philip's Warlike Son" (l. 2), he was engaged in a constant struggle for more power.

And in Stanza 5 Dryden seems to be advising through Timotheus that William cease his power struggle at home and his wars abroad. After all, William is not a true king; he is but the recipient of a crown given him by the "Gods" (l. 106). Moreover, when Timotheus terms war "Toil and Trouble" (l. 99), he would seem to be censuring Alexander's, or William's, much criticized series of wars. Too,

"Toil and Trouble" echoes the witches' song in *Macbeth* (IV.i.1-38), a play concerned with usurpation. Thus this phrase reinforces the theme of illegitimacy and illegality. In the following line Timotheus sings, "Honour is but an empty Bubble" (l. 100). This expression also appears in Samuel Butler's satire of Puritanism, *Hudibras* (II, ii, 385), and Jaques in *As You Like It* (II.vii.152) employs the same concept in relation to the soldier. *As You Like It,* too, is concerned with usurpation, and Dryden is said to have condemned the crown's ingratitude to Butler, whose situation resembled his own. The quantity of these allusions would seem to indicate that the similarities are not accidental.

And again there is a reference to an undeserved crowning, "So Love was Crown'd, but Musique won the Cause" (l. 108). Perhaps this line alludes to the widespread criticism of William's wars and to the control which Parliament exercised over him. If not, why should William gaze with pain upon Thaïs, the cause of his care? Surely, as a courtesan, she will fulfill his desires. If Alexander represents William, his care could be the fickleness of the venal English. Their arbitrariness caused William much care, and, at last, he was forced to accede to the demands of Parliament, to become a "vanquish'd Victor" (l. 115). Alexander, also, experienced unrest both among his Macedonians and among the Persians, and was forced to surrender to the demands of his men.

William's forced surrender to Parliament was as much a rude awakening as the literal awakening of Alexander, who is summoned to battle in behalf of the "Grecian Ghosts" (Stanza 6). There is an ambiguous quality to Timotheus' account of the rising Furies and the Grecian Ghosts' quest for vengeance, which suggests that the Furies' anger may be directed at Alexander and the Ghosts. Although the Furies avenge bloodshed, their primary function is the avenging of kindred blood and the maintaining of natural order; for example, they pursue Orestes more because he has slain his *mother* than because he has murdered someone. William's queen, Mary, was the daughter of the symbolically slain James II. And, even though Darius was not related to Alexander, his murder represents a disruption of natural order. There are ironic hints that the Grecian Ghosts (l. 138) are "Inglorious" (l. 140) in more ways than a mere lack of burial. Their unburied state suggests a lack of respect for them by their fellow Greeks, who would normally have made extraordinary efforts to bury their honorably slain comrades, so that they could descend to their rest; only criminals were left unburied. The Ghosts' very lack of burial suggests something truly inglorious about them, and Alexander is linked to them by being "as awak'd from the Dead" (l. 129). It is possible that the Grecian Ghosts are the unburied corpses of the regicides and even the exhumed and mutilated bodies of Cromwell and Ireton; their heads, elevated on stakes, would, even in 1697, have been in the public consciousness. If the Ghosts are Cromwell, Ireton, and the regicides, they would be the enemies of an ordered monarchy.

The burning of Persepolis unites both the religious conflicts and the disruption of natural order which would follow if the Grecian Ghosts actually are Cromwellians. Persepolis was the capital of the Achaemenidae, who believed themselves the vicegerents of God. This concept would have been familiar to anyone who, like Dryden, did not believe in deposing a lawful monarch. Thus the parallel between James II and Darius would be drawn even more clearly. For Darius was a member of the royal house of Persia, the Achaemenidae, and, by this reason, God's vicegerent; and James was the rightful king of England and, by this reason, God's vicegerent. Although Dryden was not a strict adherent to the "divine right" theory of kingship, he does seem to have accepted the basic theory. If the Persians represent a belief that is contrary to that of the Constitutionalists, obviously their temples are to hostile gods. If, then, the Grecian Ghosts are the Constitutionalists and Alexander is the usurping William, the burning of Persepolis implies the defeat of the "divine right" faction. Too, "Zeal" (l. 147) has overtones of Calvinism. Thaïs, who lights Alexander to his prey, becomes like another Helen. If Thaïs represents the English people, likening her to Helen raises another image of illegality. For Helen became the wife of two men, just as England rightfully belongs to James, but is possessed by William.

The role of Timotheus is somewhat ambiguous, but his defeat by St. Cecilia would represent a hoped-for triumph for Christianity and proper order. If *Alexander's Feast* is considered purely as an ode for music, Timotheus becomes a personification of the power of music. If, on the other hand, the ode is political in nature, Timotheus may in a sense symbolize Parliament. Just as Parliament can control William, so Timotheus can control Alexander. And it was Parliament that "rais'd a Mortal to the Skies" (l. 169)—that is, asked William to ascend the English throne. The allusion to St. Cecilia was a necessary feature of the genre within which Dryden was working, but Dryden made this required element into a further comment upon the illegal possession of a crown. Samuel Johnson saw the implications, although he did not fully understand them: "The conclusion is vicious; the musick of Timotheus, which 'raised a mortal to the skies,' had only a metaphorical power; that of Cecilia, which 'drew an angel down,' had a real effect; the crown therefore could not reasonably be divided."

Ostensibly, the crown to which the ode refers is that of music; however, it also may refer to the English crown. The Christian St. Cecilia may represent the power of the rightful possessor of the crown, who, if he comes, can easily defeat the pagan manipulator of power. Further, the idea that the "sweet Enthusiast" will enlarge the "former narrow Bounds" (ll. 163—164) connotes a more satisfactory approach to religion.

Alexander's Feast appears to be constructed in geometric form, like the 1687 ode [Dryden's *A Song for St. Cecilia's Day*]. In the later poem, however, Dryden seems to have tended toward the concentric pattern common in ancient literature. This structure, which places the most important section of a composition in its center, can be found in the *Iliad* and in the Bible, for instance, in the gospels of St. Matthew and St. John. In *Alexander's Feast,*

Stanza 4, on the death of Darius, seems to be the stanza of greatest importance, and it is precisely in the center of the ode. Stanzas 3 and 5 are concerned with mixed blessings: in Stanza 3 the "Blessings" of Bacchus contain hints of violence which is directed toward the people, whereas in Stanza 5 the "Good the Gods" have provided to Alexander also implies the imposition of an irritating restraint upon his propensity to violence. Stanzas 2 and 6 emphasize usurpation and the destruction of God's vicegerent: in Stanza 2 Alexander is assuming both a royalty and a divinity which are called into question, and the burning of Persepolis, home of the Achaemenidae (Stanza 6), indicates an illegal destruction of the capital of God's vicegerents. Stanza 1 has already shown that the royalty which Alexander obtains by the dstruction of Darius and the Achaemenidae is purely illusory, and in Stanza 7 the fundamental weakness of illusory royalty is demonstrated by St. Cecilia's victory over Timotheus. Thus even the structure of the ode places emphasis on the violent and illegal nature of Alexander's victory over Persia and his assumption of a throne and a divinity which are not rightfully his.

Douglas Murray (essay date 1977)

SOURCE: "The Musical Structure of Dryden's *Song for St. Cecilia's Day,*" in *Eighteenth-Century Studies,* Vol. 10, No. 3, Spring 1977, pp. 326-34.

[*In the following excerpt, Murray uses seventeenth-century music theory to demonstrate how the stanzas in Dryden's* Song for St. Cecilia's Day, 1687, *conform to classical music modes in order to produce such emotional effects as love, patriotism, and mourning.*]

No one questions that the *Song for St. Cecilia's Day, 1687* is a well-structured lyric, but Dryden's critics have reached no consensus on exactly why its internal stanzas are arranged as they are. Alastair Fowler and Douglas Brooks have suggested that stanzas iii-vi depict the four humors—"choleric, melancholic, phlegmatic, and sanguine." Jay Arnold Levine argues that these same four stanzas represent both the four primeval elements from which God created the cosmos and the traditional four parts "of full instrumental music." Earl Miner posits that the whole poem falls into a chronological or historical order, with the exception of St. Cecilia's organ, which must enter the scene out of proper historical sequence in order to be climactic. Of course, all of these suggestions may be simultaneously valid: Manfred Bukofzer has cogently demonstrated that a single chorus from a Bach cantata contains at least five distinct levels of meaning, and baroque poetry such as *Song for St. Cecilia's Day* may exhibit a similar complexity. But to these previous explanations must be added another, one which should enhance our conception and appreciation of the lyric: Dryden, in keeping with his subject matter, used musical theory, especially the widely accepted theory of the modes, as the structural basis for his *Song.*

The first critic to glimpse something of the subtle musicality of Dryden's construction was Jay Levine, who noted that, like a musical scale, the *Song* moves from harmony to harmony. Music is circular: a scale moves upward from the tonic—the initial note—to the octave, which is the most perfect concord possible with the original pitch. Likewise, *Song for St. Cecilia's Day* moves from the establishment of harmony in the first stanza to the paradoxical creation of a higher and more perfect harmony in the "Grand Chorus," which represents a "return to the note of divine harmony in the first line and thus completes the celestial circle or octave." So the poem with its eight stanzas refers metaphorically to the eight notes of a scale running, say, from C to c. But Levine explains only the first and last stanzas of the ode in terms of musical theory. He does not examine the musical structure of stanzas ii-vii, metaphorically the notes of the scale between the tonic and its octave. Dryden's basic scheme with these middle stanzas is this: he has associated each stanza with the mode traditionally beginning upon the note which that stanza represents, carefully matching each stanza with the effect of its corresponding mode.

Plato, Aristotle, and practically every other writer about music since them had expounded a theory of the modes. Basically, modes are types of musical scales; in different modes the half and whole steps fall at different places, each mode theoretically producing a characteristic effect upon the passions of the listener. The most famous Greek modes were the Dorian, Phrygian, Lydian, and Mixolydian; medieval musical theorists associated these modes with the characteristic interval patterns of the white-note octave scales beginning on d, e, f, and g respectively. By the seventeenth century, musical theorists were notating the modes as these same four white-note scales, Dorian beginning on d, Phrygian on e, and so on. The first recognition of our major and minor scales as independent modes came with the publication of Heinrich Glarean's *Dodecachordon* in 1547; these modes, the Ionian and Aeolian, consisting of the white-note keyboard scales extending from c and a, became increasingly popular throughout the Renaissance. During the baroque era, this familiar major-minor system largely replaced the older modal theories, but information about the modes persisted long after their usefulness had ended: John Playford wrote in his *Introduction to the Skill of Musick* that "Of these Moods [the 'five Moods used by the *Grecians*'], though of little use among us, there is scarce any author that has wrote of Musick but do give some account of them." Sometimes, as in Denis Gaultier's *La Rhétorique des Dieux,* a manuscript collection of lute pieces compiled between 1664 and 1672, the word "mode" is synonymous with the concept of key, and the traditional effects of the modes are transferred to the various keys.

The salient fact about the modes—for the poets, at least—was their much-discussed effects. The idea of the modes, therefore, could blend well with baroque art, one of whose governing ideals was *Affektenlehre*—the theory that art should both portray and excite the human emotions. Dryden, as a man of his age, was interested in the artistic portrayal of the passions, and the affective properties of the musical modes must have had a strong appeal to his aesthetic consciousness.

Now we must examine Dryden's use of modal tradition in his **Song.** Moving up the major scale from unison or perfect harmony—the harmonious stanza i—we come to the second tone of the scale, which in the C major scale is, of course, d. The Dorian mode begins on the note d, and Dryden has well matched stanza ii with the traditional effect of this mode. According to John Playford,

> The *Dorick Mood* consisted of *sober slow Tun'd Notes* (Counterpoint) . . . as is set forth in my late Book of Musick of four Parts to the Psalms and Hymns used in our Churches, Printed in *Folio,* 1671. This Mood has its name from *Doria* . . . ; and being solemn, moveth to Sobriety and Godliness.

Jubal's performance in stanza ii of Dryden's **Song** produces the expected Dorian effect:

> What Passion cannot MUSICK raise and quell!
>   When *Jubal* struck the corded Shell,
>   His list'ning Brethren stood around
>   And wond'ring, on their Faces fell
>   To worship that Celestial Sound.
> Less than a God they thought there cou'd not dwell
>   Within the hollow of that Shell
>   That spoke so sweetly and so well.
> What Passion cannot MUSICK raise and quell!
>
>   (16-24)

Jubal's music is religious, promoting awe and godliness—emotions often associated with Dorian counterpoint.

The mode whose compass consists of the white-note keyboard scale form E to e is the Phrygian. Socrates in Plato's *Republic* identifies this mode as that which "would fittingly imitate the utterances and the accents of a brave man who is engaged in warfare." Playford agrees, writing that

> The *Phrygian Mood* was a more warlike and couragious [sic] kind of Musick, expressing the Musick of Trumpets and other Instruments of old, exciting to Arms and Activity, as *Almans,* and the like. . . . Many Historians have written of its rare Effects in warlike Preparations. . . .

Charles Butler, in *The Principles of Music,* identifies the trumpet, fife, and drum as Phrygian instruments. Dryden's correlation of the Phrygian effect with stanza iii is too patent to need comment:

> The TRUMPETS loud Clangor
>   Excites us to Arms
> With shrill Notes of Anger
>   And mortal Alarms.
> The double double double beat
>   Of the thundering DRUM
> Cryes, heark the Foes come;
> Charge, Charge, 'tis too late to retreat.
>
>   (25-32)

To discover the associations of the Lydian mode, one need not go to volumes of music theory. This mode of sensu-

ality and voluptuousness captured the poetic imaginations of Spenser and Milton, both of whom included references to it in major works. In *The Faerie Queene,* Spenser paints the following picture of Castle Joyous, home of sexual delight and sensual pleasure:

> So was that chamber clad in goodly wize,
>   And round about it many beds were dight,
>
>   . . . . .
>
> And all was full of Damzels, and of Squires,
>
>   . . . . .
>
> And *Cupid* still emongst them kindled lustfull
>   fires.
>
> And all the while sweet Musicke did diuide
>   Her looser notes with *Lydian* harmony. . . .
>
>   (3.1.39-40)

In *L'Allegro* Milton commands,

> And ever against eating Cares
> Lap me in soft *Lydian* Airs,
> Married to immortal verse,
> Such as the meeting soul may pierce
> In notes, with many a winding bout
> Of linked sweetness long drawn out,
> With wanton heed, and giddy cunning,
> The melting voice through mazes running;
> Untwisting all the chains that tie
> The hidden soul of harmony.
>
>   (135-44)

Socrates' well-known comments in *The Republic* add another dimension to the Lydian tradition: he there identifies the Lydian mode as "dirgelike" as well as "soft," "convivial," and "lax." Dryden, in **Song for St. Cecilia's Day,** apparently combined the idea of voluptuousness with that of the threnody to produce his fourth stanza, in which

> The soft complaining FLUTE
> In dying Notes discovers
> The Woes of hopeless Lovers,
> Whose Dirge is whisper'd by the warbling LUTE.
> (33-36)

The effect of the Mixolydian mode, consisting of the white-note octave scale from G to g, is difficult to characterize. Seventeenth-century English volumes did not comment upon this mode, and Dryden consequently had little access to information concerning it. According to Aristotle, Mixolydian music is "sad and grave." It is of "a woeful and quiet character," eminently suitable for the chorus in a tragedy. Further light is shed upon the effect of this mode by reference to Abraham Bosse's "douze desseins" in Denis Gaultier's aforementioned volume of lute pieces, *La Rhétorique des Dieux.* Gaultier explains

> . . . comme chacun de ces modes est propre à exciter

certaines passions, & qu'ils sont propre à certains chants, l'on a representé dans chacun les actions que le mode fait naistre, les Instruments tant anciens que modernes qui luy sont plus convenables, & mesmes l'on a observé d'y faire l'Architecture conforme à ces modes, en chacun desquels se trouve sur tout un Luth avec un Livre ouvert où le mode est notté.

Bosse's Mixolydian "dessein" associates this mode with human love: Cupid, having dropped his arrows, provides music for two lovers; another Cupid-like figure plays the virginal; an elevated statue of Cupid dominates the scene. Of course, Dryden probably did not know this contemporary manuscript, but both Bosse and Dryden were products of similar traditions. At any rate, it appears that Dryden, having read Aristotle and having been exposed to the contemporary aphrodisiac effect of the Mixolydian mode, combined these two distinct effects into a third, containing the ideas of tragedy, despair, and love:

> Sharp VIOLINS proclaim
> Their jealous Pangs, and Desperation,
> Fury, frantick Indignation,
> Depth of Pains, and height of Passion,
>   For the fair, disdainful Dame.
>
> (37-41)

The mode corresponding to our minor scale is the Aeolian, extending from A to a. Playford writes,

> The *Æolick Mood,* was that which was a more Airy and soft pleasing sound . . . : Which Musick by its variety and delightfulness, allayeth the Passions, and charmeth the Affections into a sweet and pleasing temper; such as was that enchanting Musick of the Harp, provided for King *Saul,* I *Sam.* 16. *That* Saul *was refreshed, and the evil Spirit departed from him.*

Likewise, the music from St. Cecilia's organ in stanza vi calms the destructive passions of stanzas iii-v:

> But oh! what Art can teach
>   What human Voice can reach
> The sacred ORGANS praise?
> Notes inspiring holy Love,
> Notes that wing their heav'nly ways
>   To mend the Choires above.
>
> (42-47)

The Swiss Heinrich Glarean, whose *Dodecachordon* appeared in 1547, relates another bit of information which links the Aeolian mode with Dryden's stanza vi: he writes that

> the Romans were so fond of the Aeolian mode that, when the first church musicians of Rome thought of using songs in churches for the ears of the congregation, they employed this mode first, but very moderately and temperately.

Considering this, it is historically fitting that a Roman saint like Cecilia should produce her music in the Aeolian

mode. But since English writers on music failed to include this fact in their works, it was perhaps unknown to Dryden.

Some theorists described a Locrian mode beginning on b, but this scale was primarily hypothetical. Glarean, one of the most thorough of the theorists, slights it because, as he says, pieces "rarely end on it." No native English volume of music theory provided this mode with a characteristic effect. Perhaps, in terms of the scalar structure of the **Song,** Dryden merely meant his readers to realize that, just as b is the penultimate note of the scale, the note which automatically leads upward to c, so Cecilia's music is the closest possible earthly approach to "heav'nly Harmony," the type of melody which may provide a link to that higher and more perfect music. Such a linkage, at any rate, does take place in stanza vii: there Cecilia's ardor leads to a momentary union of heaven and earth.

Through the use of musical theory as a structural principle, Dryden was able to present much in the short span of a lyric. The cosmos, both at its beginning and at its disintegration, is founded upon harmony: in the beginning, God created a perfect heaven and earth; and, according to Christian eschatology, the future destruction of our world is to be followed by His construction of a "new heaven and new earth." The scalar structure of Dryden's **Song** emphasizes this, the tonic and the octave symbolizing the once and future perfect harmonies. But now, in the time between the original creation and the future re-creation, between the tonic and its octave, sounds the "music" of man's passions, symbolized by the audible *musica instrumentalis* of the modes. And this music of the passionate modes, often so chaotic, so mundane, so limited, seems to sound in dissonance with the great cosmic harmony composed by God in stanzas i and viii. But yet the modal scales consist of the same notes which comprise the familiar C major scale; they are only arranged in different sequences. When one realizes this, he sees in **Song for St. Cecilia's Day** the familiar *discordia concors* theme: the passionate modes, at first glance out of step with the music of the great C major scale, are merely varied arrangements of those very notes which, in the "correct" order, comprise that most orderly of scales. Here, Dryden presents his readers with the paradoxical view that the extravagant baroque passions are, after all a part of the universal order. The passions and the modal music which excites them merely characterize the intervening historical era between the harmony of God's first creation and the higher harmony of His future re-creation. One needs only to keep in mind the musical structure of **Song for St. Cecilia's Day** to realize that the phrase "All discord, harmony not understood" is thematic in more than one English masterpiece.

K. W. Gransden (essay date 1977)

SOURCE: "What Kind of Poem is *Religio Laici?*" in *Studies in English Literature,* Vol. XVII, Summer 1977, No. 3, pp. 397-406.

[In the following excerpt, Gransden suggests that Dryden regarded his poem Religio Laici *as a satire in the classical tradition: one that would instruct his audiences rather than criticize or ridicule them.]*

It is natural that recent critics of the **Religio Laici** have been more concerned to analyze Dryden's moral and theological position than to consider the poem's literary ancestry. Yet such an examination may be more than a sterile exercise in "influences," for it can illuminate Dryden's entire technique as a moral poet. Moreover, the two approaches are more fully complementary than is perhaps always realized. The moral position which Dryden takes up is one to which the genre he was writing in was traditionally accommodated. Further, an understanding of the poem's ancestry, which I shall approach through Dryden's own translations of the relevant classical poetry, emphasizes—what is again not always sufficiently appreciated—that his purpose in writing the poem was not primarily theoretical, but strongly practical.

Dryden's moral position in the poem has been clarified by a number of modern critics, notably E. J. Chiasson in "Dryden's Apparent Scepticism in **Religio Laici**," as belonging to "that tradition of Christian humanism which had, in varying degrees and with varying speculative and practical emphases, been common to patristic, medieval and renaissance Christendom." In the *Life of Plutarch* which he published in 1683 (the year after **Religio Laici**) Dryden had specifically attacked the "*Pyrrhonians,* or grosser sort of *Scepticks,* who bring all certainty into question." Extreme skepticism denies the existence of that "common ground" which Dryden in the *Religio* seeks to define and hold. In the *Life of Plutarch* Dryden maintains that "the Wise-men in all Ages, have not much differ'd in their opinions of Religion; I mean as it is grounded on human Reason: For Reason, as far as it is right, must be the same in all Men." The same point is made in the *Religio:* "Canst *Thou,* by *Reason,* more of *God-head* know/ Than *Plutarch, Seneca,* or *Cicero?*" The emphasis in both passages is on the concept of reason: of course we can know more of godhead, but only because we have access to revelation, while those who lived in what Donne in his third satire called "the first blinded age" of pagan moral philosophy did not. The combination in a single poem of a personal declaration of belief together with instruction on how to achieve happiness is first authoritatively established in Roman verse satire, to which genre Dryden's poem belongs. But the nature of this satiric tradition is complex, and there is some reason to believe that Dryden himself had not fully mastered it when he published the **Religio.** His own translations from Latin verse all appeared after 1682, though this is not, of course, to say that he was not previously familiar with the originals. But one particular discrepancy in Dryden's own account of the **Religio** and his later views on Latin verse satire is important. Dryden says in the preface to the **Religio** that it is in the style of Horace's *Epistles.* He also says, "The Expressions of a Poem, design'd purely for Instruction, ought to be Plain and Natural, and yet Majestick." Yet when, in 1693, in the *Discourse on the Original and Progress of Satire,* he sets out his mature views on satire, he does not conceal his dislike of Horace with his "perpetual grin" and his preference for Persius and Juvenal. Horace, he says, writes in a "low familiar style," while Persius and Juvenal are "sublime and majestic." In fact, almost the only Horatian feature of the **Religio** is its "throwaway" ending, a literary joke which is often felt to be at variance with, and to undercut, the rest of the poem.

In the *Discourse on Satire* Dryden praises Juvenal and Persius. The former is praised for preserving the rule that one should keep to "one principal Instructive Point," "one Precept of Moral Virtue," and should caution the reader against one particular vice or folly. "Other Virtues, subordinate to the first, may be recommended . . . and other Vices or Follies may be scourg'd. . . . But he is chiefly to inculcate one Virtue, and insist on that."

Dryden's admiration of Persius is expressed in one of the most eloquent tributes ever paid by one poet to another. It is in particular a tribute to a kind of moral seriousness and steadfastness: Persius "sticks to his one Philosophy: He shifts not sides, like *Horace* . . . Nor declaims like *Juvenal* against Vices. . . . Persius is everywhere the same. . . . There is a Spirit of sincerity in all he says." It seems clear that, from the standpoint of Dryden's subsequent and mature views on Roman satire, **Religio Laici** turned out to be a rather un-Horatian poem. Both its style and its urging of "one principal instructive point" place it in a literary tradition quite different from Horace's—a tradition of which Persius and Juvenal are the best-known representatives but whose origins are to be found in the work of another Latin poet whom Dryden translated even before he translated Persius and Juvenal—Lucretius.

Before we consider Lucretius as the founder of a tradition of satirical writing which was developed by Persius and Juvenal rather than Horace, we should note that it was the tenth satire of Juvenal (the "vanity of human wishes") which Dryden most admired: it is this poem above all of Juvenal's, and particularly its concluding peroration, which is in tone and spirit most Lucretian, for both are homiletic rather than "satirical" in the narrow and commonly adduced sense. Moreover, Juvenal's tenth satire is itself much indebted to Persius' second, as Dryden noted in the argument to his version of Persius. (One of Dryden's greatest strengths as a critic is his sense of literary tradition and continuity.) Dryden quotes with approval, in his *Discourse,* Gilbert Burnet, Bishop of Salisbury, who regarded the satires of Persius, together with Juvenal's tenth, as "Store-Houses and Magazines of Moral Virtues." Dryden's encomium of Persius must now be quoted at greater length:

> Satire is of the nature of Moral Philosophy; as being instructive: He therefore, who instructs most Usefully, will carry the Palm. . . . The Philosophy in which *Persius* was Educated, and which he professes throughout his whole Book, is the Stoick: The most noble, most generous, most beneficial to Humane Kind, amongst all the Sects, who have given us the Rules of Ethiques, thereby to form a severe Virtue in the Soul; to raise in us an undaunted Courage, against the assaults of Fortune . . . to be always Happy, while we possess our Minds, with a good Conscience. . . . I will not

lessen this Commendation of the Stoick Philosophy, by giving you an account of some Absurdities in their Doctrine, and some perhaps Impieties, if we consider them by the Standard of Christian Faith: *Persius* has faln into none of them. . . . *What he teaches, might be taught from Pulpits, with more profit . . . than all the nice Speculations of Divinity, and Controversies concerning Faith. . . . Here is nothing propos'd but the quiet and tranquillity of Mind.* . . .

Dryden's last remark anticipates one made by Byron about the tenth satire of Juvenal: "I should think it might be redde with great effect to a man dying without much pain, in preference to all the stuff that ever was said or sung in churches."

It is clear from the quotations given above that the satirical tradition which Dryden most valued had as its chief aim, not to mock or castigate men, but to instruct them. Now it is true that Horace's *Epistles,* which are more reflective than his earlier *Satires* or *Sermones,* do contain much instructive matter. But their tone is wayward and their philosophical standpoint inconsistent, being now Stoic, now Epicurean: Horace actually boasts of this, saying that he will conform to no single doctrine but will keep an open mind. He remains subjective and uncommitted in his judgments. It is this which gives his poetry its unique autobiographical charm. Even his most orthodox *sententiae* are delivered in a tone of unmistakable *eironeia:* "uirtus est uitium fugere et sapientia prima/stultitia caruisse." But it is precisely these elements in Horace's poetry which are most alien to the purpose and manner of *Religio Laici.* Its magisterial authority and didactic purpose are proclaimed strongly throughout: "Thus have I made my own Opinions clear." Stylistically, Dryden places his poem in the "Horatian" tradition of the "low style" "as fittest for discourse and nearest prose"; yet it has escaped no admirer of the poem that certain passages in it, notably of course the opening lines (but also 152-167, 184-211), are written in a style, "majestic and divine," than which nothing less might appropriately set forth the God whose eternal laws the poem celebrates.

This discrepancy in tone between the expository and the emotional parts of the poem itself conforms to an established tradition of didactic poetry, and indeed of all ancient rhetoric. The low style was suited to exposition and information, and was used primarily for rational persuasion; the grand style was used to express emotional conviction; the former sought to carry the hearer by argument, the latter to sweep him off his feet.

The use of a mixture of styles to convey a moral message itself goes back to a popular homiletic tradition, that of the diatribe, in which philosophy was made palatable to the ordinary man. The most famous ancient exponent of the diatribe was Bion, whose wit was praised by Horace. A feature of the diatribe was that, as in a Platonic dialogue, there was an interlocutor or butt, whose objections were usually prefaced by the Greek word meaning "he says," and were then promptly demolished. This feature survives in the objectors of the *Religio:* "Oh but says one,

Tradition set aside . . ." (l. 276). There is no doubt that the immediate ancestor of the satirical tradition in which Persius and Juvenal wrote was Lucretius. Not only does his *De Rerum Natura* consist of a mixture of styles, the "low" expository and the "high" emotional; but he also, like Persius and Juvenal, was concerned to put forward, with all the moral fervor at his command, a single, consistent philosophy which he believed would make men saner and happier if it were universally adopted. The *De Rerum Natura* is a didactic epic, not a satire; its aim, that is, is practical. But unlike other didactic epics, though its aim is practical its subject is not. Lucretius was not teaching about farming or astronomy, but about "the nature of things." His poem includes much scientific exposition, for he was a believer in the atomic theory of Democritus, to which his master Epicurus gave allegiance. But the section of his poem which primarily concerns us is to be found in the third book. This ends with a long and eloquent *consolatio* designed to prove that man should not fear death. The aim of the *consolatio* was to encourage and fortify men against the contingencies of life by bringing together arguments which would console and comfort them. Naturally such arguments, to have any effect, must carry a strong emotional content; the writer must himself fervently believe what he preaches, and this is as true of pagan homiletic as of Christian sermons.

The emotional power of the conclusion of Juvenal's tenth satire is to be explained by the fact that it belongs, like the end of Lucretius III, to the tradition of the *consolatio.* Dryden himself translated the end of Lucretius III and included it in his *Sylvae* (1685). If we now examine the *Religio* in the light of Dryden's Lucretius and Juvenal we shall find significant affinities of tone, phrase, and intention.

The theme of Juvenal's tenth satire is that, since we cannot know the future, all our hopes, fears, and desires are based on false reasoning: "quid enim ratione timemus/aut cupimus?" or as Dryden rendered it, "How void of Reason are our Hopes and Fears!" This idea reappears in the *Religio* as "Heav'n from humane Sense/Has hid the secret paths of *Providence*" (ll. 186-187). Similarly, Lucretius in his third book seeks to convince man that he has nothing to fear (or to hope for) after death. But the stripping away of men's illusions and delusions can be a bleak process. "Human kind cannot bear very much reality." It is precisely for this reason that the technique and practice of the *consolatio* becomes relevant. For when you have taken away the illusions, what is left? Compare these passages from the concluding perorations of the *Religio* and Juvenal X:

> What then remains? Are we depriv'd of Will?
> Must we not Wish, for fear of wishing Ill?
> Receive my Counsel, and securely move;
> Intrust thy Fortune to the Pow'rs above,
>
> . . . . .
>
> Yet, not to rob the Priests of pious Gain,
> That Altars be not wholly built in vain;

Forgive the Gods the rest, and stand confin'd
To Health of Body, and Content of Mind. . . .
                                        (Juvenal X. 533-549)

What then remains, but, waving each Extreme,
The Tides of Ignorance and Pride to stem:
Neither so rich a Treasure to forgo;
Nor proudly seek beyond our pow'r to know?
Faith is not built on disquisitions vain;
The things we *must* believe, are *few,* and *plain:*
But since men *will* believe more than they *need:*
And every man will make *himself* a Creed:
In doubtful questions 'tis the safest way
To learn what unsuspected Antients say. . . .
                                        (R. L. 427-436)

The *consolatio* of Lucretius and Juvenal depended upon the enthronement of reason, man's highest faculty, above superstition. In producing a Christianized version of these consolations, Dryden had to enthrone faith above reason. But though the doctrine is thus changed, the rhetorical modes of inculcating it are not. Even the famous opening image, in which faith is the sun to reason's moon and stars, is a rhetorical commonplace which occurs in Lucretius III, where Epicurus is said to have excelled all men, *stellas exortus ut aetherius sol,* or in Dryden's rendering, "As does the midday sun the midnight star." The figure also occurs in Donne's third satire, where truth is seen as self-evident yet incomprehensible, "like the Sunne, dazling, yet plaine to all eyes"; Dryden himself uses it again in *The Hind and the Panther,* in a well-known passage in which he argues that, if reason can be subordinated to faith, one should have even less trouble with the senses:

Can I my reason to my faith compell,
And shall my sight, and touch, and taste rebell?
Superior faculties are set aside,
Shall their subservient organs be my guide?
Then let the moon usurp the rule of day,
And winking tapers shew the sun his way. . . .

The common ground in all these passages is the search for a true guide to conduct: above all, this guide, when found, will give to man, amid a babble of confusing propaganda, what he most needs: contentment and peace. In the same way, Rochester's *Satyr Against Reason and Mankind,* for all its "Byronic" coat-trailing, has a serious didactic purpose: to argue that a vaunted rationality can confuse man's mind with too much speculation. Nevertheless, Rochester's poem called forth an immediate broadside response, an "Answer to the Satyr Against Mankind," in which Rochester's definition of reason is corrected by arguing that, if one has to choose between reason and sense, reason is "the less obnoxious and the surest guide."

The error of the rationalist is that he assumes reason has the same status in the age of faith or revelation as it had when its only rival in the field of apperception was the senses. The debate between reason and sense, a common topic in the Renaissance, is dramatized in Persius' third satire. Persius invents here an objector to the higher life, a bluff centurion who rejects reason and accepts only the

evidence of the senses: "quod sapio satis est mihi." He of course is the typical objector of the diatribe, introduced only to have his arguments rejected later. By a witty paradox, Rochester turns the debate between reason and sense upside down, attacking man for preferring erring reason to sure instinct; he is able to do this because it was a Christian commonplace that human reason can be deceived—Milton bases *Paradise Lost* on this premise. At the same time, Rochester's use of paradox produces some disconcerting, if brilliant, inversions. Thus he puts into the mouth of an objector to his antirationalist thesis a splendid *defence* of reason which we are emotionally surprised to feel is going to have to be overruled:

Reason, by whose aspiring influence
We take a flight beyond material sense,
Dive into mysteries, then soaring pierce
The flaming limits of the universe,
Search heav'n and hell, find out what's acted there,
And give the world true grounds of hope and fear.

This passage is closely modeled on some lines of Lucretius (I.72-77) describing how Epicurus solved the mysteries of the universe.

In the **Religio** Dryden describes various pre-Christian versions of the highest good, including that of the sensualists: his description is closely modeled on that of the sensualist in Persius' third satire:

But 'tis in vain: the Wretch is drench'd too deep;
His Soul is stupid, and his Heart asleep:
Fatten'd in Vice; so callous, and so gross;
He sins, and sees not; senseless of his Loss.
Down goes the Wretch at once; unskill'd to swim;
Hopeless to bubble up and reach the Water's Brim.
 (Persius III. 59-64)

In *Pleasure* some their glutton Souls would steep;
But found the Line too short, the Well too deep;
And leaky Vessels which no *Bliss* cou'd keep.
                                        (R. L. 33-35)

Again, in Lucretius III the voice of nature reproaches man for complaining about his mortality:

If all the bounteous blessings I cou'd give
Thou hast enjoy'd, if thou hast known to live,
And pleasure not leak'd thro' thee like a Seive,
Why dost thou not give thanks. . . .

In this passage, Nature addresses man as "ungrateful wretch, thou vain, thou mortal thing. . . ." In the **Religio,** Dryden reproaches man for trying to soar to heaven by his own strength rather than God's, and calls him "Vain, wretched Creature."

The central thesis of all these didactic homilies may be formulated thus: what man most wants—truth, certainty, peace—he is least able to discover:

Thus, *Anxious Thoughts* in *endless Circles* roul,
Without a *Centre* where to fix the *Soul:*

In this wilde Maze their vain Endeavours end:
How can the *less* the *Greater* comprehend?

(*R. L.* 36-39)

Eternal troubles haunt thy anxious mind,
Whose cause and cure thou never hop'st to find;
But still uncertain, with thy self at strife,
Thou wander'st in the *Labyrinth* of life.

(Lucretius III. 267-270)

The poet's aim is to comfort man in his bewilderment and to show him how to achieve "true grounds for hope and fear." Dryden's urging of public peace over private reason demands to be explained as a piece of practical consolation: as a theoretical position it is bound to seem unsatisfactory:

'Tis some Relief, that points not clearly known,
Without much hazard may be let alone:
And, after hearing what our Church can say,
If still our Reason runs another way,
That private Reason 'tis more Just to curb,
Than by Disputes the publick Peace disturb.
For points obscure are of small use to learn:
But *Common quiet is Mankind's concern.*

(*R. L.* 443-450)

We recall that in his praise of Persius Dryden wrote that "Here is nothing propos'd but the quiet and tranquillity of Mind." Tranquillity is similarly proposed by Juvenal at the end of his tenth satire as the reward of man if only he will trust Providence and Prudentia (Wisdom) rather than Fortune (the private god each man seeks to deify for his own individual ends): "semita certe/tranquillae per uirtutem patet unica uitae."

The same distinction between private reason and public wisdom is made by Dryden again in **The Hind and The Panther,** I, 62-69:

What weight of antient witness can prevail
If private reason hold the public scale?

. . . . .

O teach me to believe Thee thus conceal'd,
And search no farther than thy self reveal'd.

If Dryden seems to some modern readers to be overstating his case, it is because he senses how easily the past, traditional wisdom, can be threatened and undermined. Religious, social, and political stability are closely linked in his thinking as in that of his classical predecessors. His conservatism, with its emphasis on quietism, outward conformity, avoidance of extremes, derives massive and valuable support from his literary classicism. The "unsuspected ancients" are of course the fathers of Christianity, but the phrase also invites us to consider the literary tradition on which Dryden's sense of a proper order so much depends. It is in this respect that the **Religio** affirms Dryden's literary as well as his religious adherence. Not only its form and structure, but its rhetorical techniques also,

are modeled on just those Latin poems which could underwrite, with their immense prestige, his own urging of a sane and healthy approach to "the nature of things" and which could give to the commonplaces in which he rests a majesty and sublimity they might otherwise lack.

Jerome Donnelly (essay date 1981)

SOURCE: "Fathers and Sons: The Normative Basis of Dryden's *Absalom and Achitophel,*" in *Papers on Language & Literature,* Vol. 17, No. 4, Fall 1981, pp. 363-80.

[*In the following excerpt, Donnelly demonstrates that in* Absalom and Achitophel, *Dryden relied upon humanist and Aristotelian theories to defend Charles's fitness as a monarch without condoning Charles's behavior as a man.*]

The most widely accepted readings of **Absalom and Achitophel** view Dryden's attitude toward his monarch and patron, the hero and central character of his poem, as one of almost unreserved admiration. Unfortunately, these readings seem to begin with the assumption that it would have been unthinkable for Dryden to give complete support to Charles in his role as monarch and to place him at the heroic center of the poem while withholding support from and even criticizing his behavior as a man. It is the purpose of this study to show that the poem expresses just such an attitude and that to understand the normative basis of **Absalom and Achitophel** requires seeing the characters in terms of their relationships, their natural contiguity, and against a background of the Aristotelian and humanist ideas upon which Dryden draws in the poem.

To establish a basis for discussion, it will be helpful first to single out difficulties of interpretation fostered by some of the best-known approaches. While modern scholarship and criticism have vastly improved our understanding of Dryden's work, they have often created new problems. In the case of **Absalom and Achitophel,** distorted readings have accrued from studies which (1) place too great an emphasis on esoteric sources of minor importance but which, simply because they are esoteric, require extended elaboration and thus acquire an undue quantitative significance, or (2) examine character portraits detached from their poetic framework, or (3) derive interpretations by focusing on isolated lyric passages instead of taking a more comprehensive view relating them to the rest of the work. One of the standard articles on the poem, Ruth Wallerstein's "To Madness Near Allied: Shaftesbury and his Place in the Design and Thought of *Absalom and Achitophel,*" suffers from the first and second of these difficulties by highlighting the influence of esoteric works and commentators on them, thus creating an exaggerated sense of their importance. In many respects an excellent piece of scholarship, Wallerstein's study begins by commenting on the importance of the Aristotelian background, but then leaves Aristotle to focus on Jerome Cardan's theory of psychology as the key to understanding Achitophel, whose character in turn Wallerstein regards as the basis for understanding the entire poem. This approach unfortunately results in an examination of Achitophel without sufficient consideration of his poetic context and of his relationship to other important characters, and neglects the importance of the main Aristotelian tradition in favor of the exposition of Cardan. In either case, understanding of the poem is distorted. No less than the Judeo-Christian scriptural tradition upon which the poem's allegory and typology are based, and infinitely more than Cardan's curious psychology, the Aristotelian philosophical tradition—political, physical, ethical—inheres in the structure of the poem.

The third difficulty is one which besets much modern criticism: attaching undue importance to isolated passages. This has happened in the case of the ten introductory lines of **Absalom and Achitophel** which comment on David's (Charles') promiscuity, a passage which has probably had almost as much critical attention devoted to it as anything in the poem. Earl Miner has discussed these lines at length in what must now be the most widely read interpretation ["Some Characteristics of Dryden's use of Metaphor," *Studies in English Literature* 2 (1962): 309-20]. According to his view, the introductory passage comprises the strategy whereby Dryden anticipates the potential charge of Charles' promiscuity by directly referring to the issue of his infidelity at the very outset of the poem. By this strategy Dryden reverses potential criticism of the king so that David (Charles) emerges as "wittily praised for what 'Nature prompted.'" Rather than criticizing the king, this passage implies, according to Miner, that Dryden's praise is unreserved, that these lines actually contribute to the construction of the king's heroic character.

This interpretation is most convincing when the opening passage is isolated from the rest of the work, which is essentially how Miner examines these introductory lines, commenting on them without reference to anything else in the poem. When regarded as part of the entire span of the poem, however, this interpretation is not nearly so convincing. The passage is witty and seems to praise what would ordinarily be a vice; as an opening rhetorical stratagem anticipating and undercutting a potential rejoinder to a Whig attack on Charles, the lines do a masterful job. Granting that the passage does all of these things, however, to assert, as Miner does, that in these lines Dryden is actually praising Charles' behavior as something "unusually admirable" is to attach too definite a meaning to a passage whose virtue lies in its deliberate ambiguity. Rather than establishing a moral norm for royal behavior, the passage both deftly undercuts any attack on the king's personal life, first, by appropriating and making ironic use of the very same Biblical allegory originally used by the Whigs themselves, and second, by holding in ambiguous suspension the question of ethical propriety. Only when the ambiguity of these lines is resolved in the totality of the poem does it become clear that Dryden, while defending Charles' monarchy against the rebel faction, is not blindly uncritical, but rather that Dryden reveals through the poem's dynamic structure his disapproval of the king's promiscuity.

The opening lines do not raise the issue of promiscuity simply to blunt an enemy weapon. Indeed, the issue is not raised to be dismissed; the theme of illegitimacy as the result of promiscuity dominates much of the poem and is highlighted at poetic cruxes by means of scriptural and topical allusions and images which suggest sexual impropriety. Further, Dryden not only criticizes, he finally reveals an ethical heroic norm as an alternative, a norm just as explicit as the positive political norm of authority he places in the mouth of David at the conclusion of the poem.

The treatment of political legitimacy and succession parallels a concern with progeny, and the introduction of the allegorical rulers, David and Michal, immediately takes up this theme by referring to his ability to beget children: "*Israel's* Monarch . . . Scatter'd his Maker's Image through the Land" (7-10). He refers to her inability to conceive: "*Michal* . . . A Soyl ungratefull to the Tiller's care" (11-12); and emphasizes the fact of having been begotten: "Of all this Numerous Progeny was none / So Beautifull, so brave as *Absolon*" (17-18). Concern with paternity, along with inheritance, is a matter which, as Christopher Ricks has shown, recurs throughout Dryden's poetry. Yet, in no other poem of Dryden's is this concern so central to the meaning, and these opening references set in motion the development of a theme which pervades the description of characters and their dramatic relationships. Dryden goes beyond pointing to the fact of Absalom's illegitimacy; he speculates as to the effect of his begetting on Absalom's subsequent behavior:

> Whether, inspir'd by some diviner Lust,
> His Father got him with a greater Gust;
> Or that his Conscious destiny made way
> By manly beauty to Imperiall sway.
> Early in Foreign fields he won Renown,
> With Kings and States ally'd to *Israel's* Crown:
> In Peace the thoughts of War he coud remove,
> And seem'd as he were only born for love
>
> [19-26]

all of which David enjoys with "His Youthfull Image in his Son renew'd" (32). Dryden thus emphasizes the inheritance of paternal characteristics in the son not limited simply to physical features, but also including inclinations of temperament and behavior. This inheritance includes the "byast Nature" (79) of fallen man which leans toward sin, transmitted to all from generation to generation, as well as the transmission of individual character disposition from parent to child, so that even the apparent praise of Absalom as "And seem'd as he were only born for love" becomes ambiguous.

In addition to invoking the doctrine of the general inheritance of original sin in the Judeo-Christian tradition, Dryden complements it by drawing on the theory of particular inheritance in Aristotle's natural philosophy. In the Aristotelian view, generational inheritance of physical and psychological traits is one manifestation of a meaningful universe, and behind the ideas of Cardan or the specific political views of Bodin and Filmer is the Aristotelian tradition with which these Renaissance thinkers, as well as Restoration poets like Dryden, were familiar. This exoteric tradition, disseminated and shared by such Roman writers as Cicero, and which had spread with the infusion of rediscovered works and a quickened scholarly interest, is manifest in the texture of ideas as they operate in the poem. Whatever skeptical turns of mind were fashionable during the Restoration, the basic Aristotelian tradition was deeply woven in the fabric of intellectual tradition.

Aristotle's political theory grows out of his view that an observable order exists in the universe; it inheres in physical nature, in social relationships toward which men naturally tend, and in ethics and politics which men may develop as an extension of natural order. Even changes in phenomena, instead of being signs of imperfection and disorder in reality, could be signs of order by exhibiting repetition and continuity. Basic Aristotelian notions, his theory of substances as composed of matter and form, his theory of the ethical mean, his theory of political structure and hierarchy—all of which testified to an interrelated order in the universe—remained part of the inherited stock of ideas.

The description of begetting in the poem, of the inability of the royal couple to conceive an heir, along with the transmission of likeness, bears the stamp of the Aristotelian tradition. Likenesses of related things and transmission of characteristics are basic to Aristotle's system, and it is thus axiomatic that "for the things of which the generations are good things are themselves also good; and if they are themselves good, so also are their generations." The same holds true if "their generations are bad things, they themselves are also bad things." Such generational propriety is part of the order of things; Achitophel, from his disordered perspective, sees this order as a sinister plot, as "Natures trick to Propagate her Kind" (424). The notion of inherited disposition of character inheres in the poem even more fundamentally by reference to an Aristotelian, hylomorphic physics. This theory of matter and form, when applied to procreation, as in Aristotle's *On the Generation of Animals,* attributes the form of the progeny to the male role in generation and associates the material element with the female contribution. The "youthful image" which David sees renewed in his son, Absalom, is that form transmitted in procreation. Aristotle compares this generational transmission of form in living creatures to the form a craftsman achieves: "the shape and the form are produced from the carpenter through the movement in the matter . . . similarly the male's nature. . . ." Conversely, "it is the female that contains the matter. . . ." Dryden invokes this application of hylomorphism in generation, only shifting the image from carpentry to agriculture—to the farmer scattering seed and tilling the soil. As "Soyl," the queen is the proper source of matter to be joined with the king's form, or "Image," latent in the farmer's seed, yet the royal matter and form have failed to unite in an act of generation (her "Soyl ungrateful to the Tiller's care"). David's subsequent turning from his proper matter, his wife, and his siring of "several Sons" from "several Mothers" (13-14) has the effect that, instead of the propriety of the king's form mixed with his queen's matter, "No True Succession" (16) attends this progeny. Absalom is quite aware of this as he laments his illegitimacy—which he expresses in terms suggesting matter and form; his "large [royal] Soul" is disproportionate to the material matter and, consequently, he does not participate in but is only contiguous to succession:

> I find, I find my mounting Spirits Bold,
> And *David's* Part disdains my Mothers Mold.
> Why am I Scanted by a Niggard Birth?
> My Soul Disclaims the Kindred of her Earth.
>
> [367-70]

But Absalom cannot will away his matter, "her Earth," and he knows that refusing his responsibility to obey his king and father is to risk "a Godlike Sin" (372).

The sin Absalom contemplates is, of course, a double rebellion which is at once a son's disobedience of his father and a subject's disloyalty to his king. Just as the process of generation is based on Aristotle's philosophy of nature, so this linking of monarchic and paternal roles finds an explicit foundation in Aristotelian political thought. Analogous to the spiritual foundation for obedience in scripture, Aristotle's *Politics* provides a secular basis in the repeated comparison of the rule of a king over his subjects to that of a father over his children. Indeed, for Aristotle, social and political organizations have their roots in the family structure. The Aristotelian position emphasizes the value of the family unit and family affection as well as the propriety of paternal authority. David's intertwined roles as king and father have their counterpart in Aristotle's often repeated view that a father's "rule over his children is like that of a monarch over his subjects." This Aristotelian view emphasizing the normative propriety of father and son relationships thus serves Dryden by accentuating the dislocation of Absalom's status both as an illegitimate son and as the result of an improper combination of matter and form.

However critical this relation between David and Absalom, the importance of continuity is incipient and becomes increasingly manifest with the appearance of other characters. Thus, Achitophel's encouragement to revolt is not only political but generational. His attempts to become the paternal adviser of Absalom also imply a neglect of his own progeny. Achitophel's son has no role in the poem, but reference to him is important in working out the norms of the satire, and thus the narrator digresses to point to the son as an indication of the begetter's corruption. Achitophel's own corrupt nature is indicated in his person by a lack of proportion between matter and form, his soul (or form) having "fretted the Pygmy Body to decay" (157). Corruption has generated corruption, and the same disproportion has passed on to Achitophel's own progeny, that "unfeather'd, two Leg'd thing, a Son" (170), a puny opposite to the "manly" Absalom, who has inherited so many brilliant qualities from his father. The cynical point of this commonplace definition used to describe Achitophel's son is that it omits reference to man's form—his rational soul. Indeed, Achitophel's son, though legitimate, seems lacking human form, his matter "born a shapeless Lump, like Anarchy" (172), thus bearing the stamp of the "Turbulent," Satanic willfulness of the sire. Here, as elsewhere,

Dryden is building satire on what was public knowledge or gossip; as H. T. Swedenberg has noted regarding these lines, Shaftesbury was unusually short, and his son was of sickly body from birth. Progeny again reveals something of the nature of the parent; this time, though, a thoroughly corrupt character has engendered corruption. Ironically, Achitophel has fathered what he most desires: anarchy. However, evil cannot disrupt what has no order to begin with, so Achitophel must turn in another direction, towards the not yet corrupted Absalom, whose own energy lacks a proper goal in kingship since his illegitimacy has left him with a yearning instilled by the kingship of his father's form but without the solid foundation of a legitimate mother's matter. David's (Charles') sexual impropriety has bred generational disorder, itself a condition of vulnerability which Achitophel sees as a potential source of further disorder extending to society and the state.

The theme of sexual disorder as leading to further corruptions is grotesquely evident in several of the portraits of Achitophel's co-conspirators. In addition to presenting the rebel faction as a group of money-grubbing religious zealots, a subtler motif of allusion plays through the portraits of this group, one to which Dryden's contemporaries' ears were better attuned than modern readers', since it is based on biographical information or gossip about the real-life figures, as well as on the scriptural association of the allegorical counterparts. Many of these allusions underscore the connection between political corruption and deviation from an implied sexual norm. Just as Dryden wittily alludes to Charles' womanizing, he obliquely refers to a similar predilection in Buckingham, who manifests an instability grown to madness. Infidelity itself is too stable a pastime for Zimri (Buckingham), and only after his quickly succeeding roles as "Chymist, Fidler, States-Man, and Buffoon" (550) does he turn to "Women, Painting, Rhiming, Drinking" (551). Like Charles, to whose siring of bastard progeny Dryden alludes, Buckingham has sired "ten thousand freaks that dy'd in thinking." Since the biblical Zimri was a licentious figure, he makes an especially appropriate allegorical counterpart to Buckingham. As Swedenberg notes, Zimri was guilty of "brazenly appearing before Moses and the people with a Midianite woman and taking her into his tent," an allusion which would remind readers of the parallel in Buckingham's own flagrant relationship with the Countess of Shrewsbury. The fact that Buckingham's adultery yielded a child who died soon after birth again serves Dryden in suggesting an illustration of imperfect progeny resulting from an illegitimate union. Zimri's instability implies a proportional imbalance of soul and matter, paralleled by his unlawful (and thus disordered) sexual behavior, both of which are signified by the fatal end of Buckingham's bastard progeny.

Other conspirators, either singly or in pairs, exhibit various forms of sexual disorder. Immediately following the picture of Buckingham, whose reputation for lust has been accentuated by the Biblical parallel with Zimri, Dryden presents "the well hung *Balaam* and cold *Caleb* free" (574), where linking by syntactic parallelism implies an antithesis of sexual excess and defect. Scriptural allusion supports syntax; the Biblical Balaam of the second Epistle of

Peter is associated with lust (excess) which contrasts with Caleb's implied impotence (defect). James Kinsley's identification of Caleb as Lord Grey—who appeared indifferent to Monmouth's involvement with Lady Grey—reinforces the suggestion of this defect. Like Balaam's lust, Caleb's indifference also signals deviation from a sexual mean.

More than all the minor characters, the figure of Corah (Titus Oates) underscores the notion of disorder, an imbalance of matter and form resulting from an illegitimate sexual union. The rumors of Oates' illegitimacy ring in the reference to this birth as "base," which suggests bastardy as well as low birth. In an attempt to disguise his humble background, Oates had equipped himself with a fraudulent coat of arms, and as Dryden comments ironically, "By that one Deed Enobles all his Bloud" (641). The mock-heroic irony of "one Deed Enobles" suggests a parallel with the attempts to have Monmouth's birth declared legitimate; like Absalom (Monmouth), Oates has unlawfully attempted to surmount his origins. The unblessed and illegitimate union of Oates' progenitors has in his case passed to the progeny in a manifestation of unremitting sexual corruption. George McFadden has suggested that identification of Oates with the Biblical Corah links him not only with rebelliousness against the legitimate authority of Israel but also with the sexual perversion of Sodom and Gomorrah, a connection which would recall to Dryden's contemporaries reports of Oates' own behavior and dismissal for sodomy from his position as ship's chaplain (see Swedenberg.)

The lack of fidelity in marriage and the illegitimacy of offspring represent a breakdown of an orderly succession and the substitution of Fortune. Achitophel thrives in such a disordered environment. His conspiratorial band is bred out of social and moral disorder. Rumors of Popish plots serve him well; similar to Oates' fraud regarding his lineage, Achitophel's political lies are an attempt to destroy the order of truth and history in hopes of building political rule on a foundation of chance and fortune. If he cannot alter the legal succession, he will call on luck or the stars. Just such an ironic reference in connection with Corah,

> What tho his Birth were base, yet Comets rise
> From Earthy Vapours ere they shine in Skies,
>
> [636-37]

recalls the words with which Achitophel launches his temptation of Absalom:

> Auspicious Prince! at whose Nativity
> Some Royal Planet rul'd the Southern sky. . . .
>
> [230-31]

Seemingly innocuous flattery, these lines preface an argument which ultimately becomes successful in convincing Absalom to rebel.

The successful temptation of Absalom is promised on this appeal to Fate and Fortune as compensating for ethical and legal claims to the throne. Achitophel's speech moves cleverly from this initial mention of the "Royal Planet" to suggest the implications:

> Heav'n, has to all allotted, soon or late,
> Some lucky Revolution of their Fate:
> Whose Motions, if we watch and guide with Skill,
>
> . . . . .
>
> . . . Our Fortune rolls. . . .
>
> [252-56]

Seizing Fortune, Achitophel argues, will only be the act of a true son, since, he tells Absalom, "Old *David,* from whose Loyns you spring," had "dar'd, when Fortune call'd him, to be King" (262-63). Thus, Achitophel glibly reduces David's kingship from an expression of divine will and law to a whim of Fortune. The introduction of Fortune is especially revealing since it evokes the Renaissance tradition of the opposition of *Virtus-Fortuna* which in turn was based on a similar classical, ethical tradition. According to this tradition, steadfastness to *Virtus* enables men to resist the power of *Fortuna.* Alberti, who discusses this opposition in his dialogue, *The Family,* is particularly concerned to argue that maintenance of virtue is more than a matter affecting individuals; the practice of virtue applies to generations, and only if and when family virtue is lost does Fortune then triumph over succeeding generations, causing family honor and even family existence to dwindle and die (see Skinner,)

Using the appeal to Fortune as simultaneously furnishing support to Absalom's hopes and as undermining the status of his father's kingship, Achitophel presents for Absalom a picture of David as an aging king, no longer popular, and who, falling from glory "like the Prince of Angels from his height, / Comes tumbling downward with diminish'd light . . ." (273-74). Achitophel, in keeping with his character as a type of Satan, has here performed an inversion of values and has thus provided what appears to be a further sanction for Absalom's quest of the crown. The dramatic irony in these lines—an irony which escapes tempter and tempted—is that Lucifer's own disastrous revolt involved just such a presumptuous attempt to seize Fortune and subvert the divine order in heaven. Like the ancient pagans, Achitophel has in effect deified Fortune and thus set himself in opposition to classical and Christian *Virtus* as well as to divine providence (Cf. Skinner.)

The strength of this appeal to Fortune derives from the fact of Absalom's illegitimate birth which, in turn, reflects on David's failure to observe steadfastness in the virtue of chastity in marriage. This state of affairs makes it easier for Achitophel to rationalize for Absalom how usurping the throne would only be following in his father's footsteps "when Fortune call'd" (263), and he makes the appeal to Absalom all the more tempting by couching his argument in buried sexual imagery in hopes that the son shares his father's lustful proclivities. In each of his temptation speeches, Achitophel likens the seizure of power to a sexual conquest. The first speech draws on the appeal to Fortune presented in the image of a temptress:

> if unseiz'd, she glides away like wind;
> And leaves repenting Folly far behind.
> Now, she meets you, with a glorious prize,
> And spreads her Locks before her as she flies.
>
> [258-61]

The appeal to lust is reinforced in Achitophel's second speech when he compares the king's attitude to "women's Leachery" (472) and urges Absalom to "commit a pleasing Rape upon the Crown" (474). The spirit of this appeal to lust as part of an inducement to rebellion has its counterpart in II Samuel, where Achitophel urges Absalom to visit David's concubine (16: 20-23). The inducement also exhibits Achitophel's "great wit," his canniness in realizing that the son shares the same natural inclination upon which the king has already acted. It is the genius of Achitophel's Satanic cunning to capitalize on this disposition in Absalom, the unexpected way in which the king's "Image in his Son renew'd" (32), and this inherited weakness, combined with Absalom's pride (inherited from his fallen first parents), result in his decision to rebel. Dryden, in placing an evil but highly persuasive argument in the mouth of Achitophel and in depicting the son's character as inherited from the father, is nonetheless insistent on Absalom's free choice in becoming the center of rebellion. In words that could have been written specifically as a comment on Absalom's situation, Etienne Gilson has remarked that "no man can fall a victim to his own genius unless he has genius; but those who have none are fully justified in refusing to be victimized by the genius of others." While this is essentially Dryden's view, he has mitigated the circumstances, so that because of Absalom's inherited natural inclination and because of the great, persuasive wit of Achitophel, Absalom's choice is not entirely malevolent; he is still the king's beloved son and "'tis Juster to Lament him, than Accuse" (486).

Thus, Dryden uses the flattering Davidic allegory in such an open, obvious manner that reservations suggested by ambiguity are rendered inconspicuous and easily glossed over. However, modern critical preoccupation with metaphoric structure (which includes allegory and typology) should not allow these metonymic, natural contiguities to become obscured. No matter how important the relation of historical figures to their Biblical counterparts, the structural arrangement of father and son pairs is also essential to working out the values inherent in the poem. Absalom's fall is set against a background consisting of more than Biblical allegory and typology. The Aristotelian tradition of matter and form, generation, and the ethical mean is integral to the working out of character relationships and ideas in the poem. The flawed relationships between father and son are structured to reveal ethical criticism of the king, partly as his behavior is revealed in a disposition he bequeathes to his progeny. In turn, the son's deficiencies—his lack of propriety, balance, and order—are heightened in the depiction of those with whom Absalom has allied himself, the "Male-contents" who display all manner of excess and defect in sexual disorder. But Dryden not only presents these departures from the ethical norm, he makes the norm itself explicit, using the same Aristotelian concept of natural inclination transferred from parent to progeny in human generation.

In keeping with traditional satiric structure, Dryden with-holds this norm until the latter part of the poem (just as he withholds the royal, political norm until David's final speech). The Barzillai passage expresses this moral norm. Strangely, it is probably the least discussed passage in the entire work, even though the relationship between father and son presented in these lines climaxes the progeny theme in presenting the poet's conception of the ideal. Even the most intensive studies of Dryden's poetry or of this par-ticular poem either ignore or make only a passing nod at this dramatic crux, at best comparing only two of the three father-son relationships. Miner compares the off-spring of Achitophel with Absalom and concludes that the differ-ence between the sons implies that "the king's natural promiscuity is infinitely preferable to this perversion [i.e. the son of Achitophel] of nature." Such a reading ignores the climactic father-son pair which shows what Dryden in fact regards as "infinitely preferable." There is nothing ambiguous about the unrestrained praise lavished on Barz-illai whose magnanimity includes the perfection of lineage in the begetting of progeny implicitly contrasting with those presented earlier.

> His Bed coud once a Fruitfull Issue boast:
> Now more than half a Father's Name is lost:
> His Eldest Hope, with every Grace adorn'd,
> By me (so Heav'n will have it) always Mourn'd,
> And always honour'd, snatcht in Manhoods prime
> By'unequal Fates, and Providences crime:
> Yet not before the Goal of Honour won,
> All parts fulfill'd of Subject and of Son;
> Swift was the Race, but short the time to run.
>
> [829-37]

Like David, Barzillai could boast a "Fruitfull Issue" (829), now reduced from six, to one remaining son. More impor-tant, however, is the fact that Barzillai's (Ormonde's) issue was the fruit of his marriage, a propitious blend of matter and form, legitimately coming from "His Bed." In confor-mity with the Aristotelian dictum that the rule of kings over subjects is like that of fathers over sons, Barzillai's son (the Earl of Ossory) is eulogized as the ideal progeny: "all parts fulfill'd of Subject and of Son" (836), which Absalom (Monmouth) has failed to be. The disproportion of Ab-salom's form and matter, his "large soul," too large for the soil of his body, and the converse, that of Achitophel's "unfeather'd, two legg'd thing," a body lacking sufficient soul, give way to a perfect blend of matter and form in a son, all of whose "parts" are fulfilled:

> Oh Narrow Circle, but of Pow'r Divine,
> Scanted in Space, but perfect in thy Line.
>
> [838-39]

Adorned "with every Grace" (831), he equals Absalom in appearance and bravery, but unlike him, Ossory has sac-rificed his life as a faithful subject. Like the king, Barz-illai has lost a son, but in a noble death, not to rebellion and Achitophel. The brief span of Ossory's life, his "Nar-row Circle," suggests the wheel of fortune, but this is now a Fortune triumphed over by *Virtus,* "the Goal of Honour won." The "Line" of the circle has been cut short by an

early death, but the perfection of the life is implied by the image of the circle.

The emphatic rhyme word, "Line," with which the couplet concludes implies an order of perfection over and above that of individual virtue. Indeed, the entire passage does more than praise the separate characters of Ormonde and Ossory; the unreserved praise is directed at the perfection of lineage, the "Line" reaching from father to son and the perfection of the son as an index of a disposition to virtue in the father. This father-son combination climaxes the earlier double portrait presentations, making natural con-tiguity rather than individual, isolated character control the values of the poem. The relationship between Barzillai and his son is one founded on chastity—his issue resulting from lawful and sacramental marriage. In the Aristotelian scheme, Absalom represents the excess, Achitophel's son the defect, and Barzillai's son the mean, a balance of matter and form, an emblem of ideal generation perfect in virtue, and thus the presentation of this final father-son relation-ship serves as the moral norm of the poem. Dryden height-ens the passage, as Reuben Brower has noted, applying to Ossory "the words originally spoken by Aeneas on the anniversary of Anchises' death." The Virgilian echoes of a heroic father-son relation further emphasize the ideal character of the Ormonde-Ossory pairing in these most impassioned lines in the poem and the only passage in which intensity of feeling causes the narrator to express his own emotion in the first person (831-63). Such terrible events as the early, violent death of Barzillai's son appear to be the work of "unequal Fates, and Providences crime" (834) and make it seem "as Heaven our Ruine had design'd" (848). Yet, in choosing to follow his father's noble exam-ple, the now dead son had become a model of virtue. Working to preserve the social and political authority in harmony with his king and father, he has contributed to that common good toward which divine providence aims. Now, as his "disencumbred Soul / Mounts up" (850-51) to heav-en, he has also achieved a personal good in union with God, the ultimate end of divine providence. Having achieved immortality, the sainted hero may continue his good work as "from thence" he can enlist "kindred legions . . . To aid the guardian Angel of [his] King" (852-53). Finally, the death of Barzillai's son offers to David an example of self-less magnanimity on the part of both son and father.

This consideration of Barzillai (Ormonde) and his late son is followed by the description of the king's party which serves, of course, as a favorable reflection on the king, all the more so since the description of the David-Absalom relationship is separated from this passage by almost 800 lines. The implicit comparison, though, however subtly separated from the beginning of the poem, can hardly reflect favorably on the king. Along with Hushai and the loyal supporters of legal succession, Barzillai and his son, in particular, epitomize magnanimity and its transmission from parent to progeny. Even in death, the son becomes a testament to the prevalence of virtue as the result of conformity with natural and sacramental law.

From this perspective, the ambiguity of the opening lines of the poem give way to normative clarity. The introductory passage of the poem cannot be read in isolation, whatever its disarming and conciliatory effect or however much in these lines Dryden may seem to make the king's profligacy appear "unusually admirable." The action of the poem does not consist of a narrative of events; it consists of a gradual revelation of a political situation grounded in ethical norms. The apparent dismissal of Charles' (David's) promiscuity in the opening lines is witty, but the moral question does not immediately disappear, and Dryden does not get the matter "over with at once," as Miner has argued (115). The off-handed, parenthetical, "for who from faults is free?" (35), is finally answered in a moving passage where both character and the ordered relationship of characters are, in fact, exhibited as free from fault. Absalom's "byast Nature [which] leans" (79) toward rebellion against the political and successional order is correspondingly David's violation of the order of chastity in marriage. Insofar as David (Charles) has violated this order, he has jeopardized the concomitant political order whose foundation, according to the Aristotelian tradition, resides in the order of the family and which holds as analogous the authority of fathers and monarchs. The contrasts between the sets of characters do not imply condemnation of Charles; he remains basically virtuous, like his Old Testament counterpart who remained God's anointed despite repeated transgressions. Whatever his flaws, like David, Charles remains the dynastic embodiment of God's Will. David's closing speech implies that the example of Barzillai and the virtue of the king's "small but faithful Band" (914) has fortified his resolve to act righteously and to co-operate with God's providential order rather than his own natural inclination. Thus, he acknowledges that for too long the doting "Father did the King asswage" (942) and that, as monarch, he has a duty "to Rule" (946) since "Kings are publick Pillars of the State" (953). As a consequence the king avers,

> If my Young *Samson* will pretend a Call
> To shake the Column, let him share the Fall.
>
> [955-56]

Yet, David will not abandon his role as parent:

> But oh that yet he would repent and live!
> How easie 'tis for Parents to forgive!
> With how few Tears a Pardon might be won
> From Nature, pleading for a Darling Son!
>
> [957-60]

With these words, David assumes his proper roles as monarch and father. Following in earthly imitation of his heavenly Father's infinite mercy, he tempers his sense of justice with a capacity for love and forgiveness.

It is likely that the tradition regarding the origin of *Absalom and Achitophel* has inclined scholars to begin with the assumption that if Dryden wrote the poem in order to influence events in favor of the king, his attitude must have been one of unremitting approval as well as allegiance. Such an assumption would not necessarily be correct in itself. Phillip Harth has convincingly dispelled the myth that the origin of *Absalom and Achitophel* stems

from a request by the king in an attempt to influence Shaftesbury's jury. Harth argues that the "tradition that either Dryden or his patrons ever imagined that a poem could have the slightest influence on such a contest must be dismissed as an improbable fiction." Indeed, except for a bookseller's puff on the title page in an edition conveniently published after the deaths of both Charles II and Dryden, there is no evidence that Dryden wrote the poem at the king's request.

Nor is there any reason to conclude from his implicit criticism of Charles that there is any duplicity about Dryden's attitude. *Absalom and Achitophel* is not an instance of Dryden having "Alexander'd up," or subtly condemning a reigning king as he was to do later to William III in *Alexander's Feast.* In *Absalom and Achitophel,* Dryden consistently upholds ethical and political ideas, and his presentation of Ormonde-Ossory as the embodiment of the ethical norm implies that not only family difficulties but serious political problems may result from ethical failings. The poem is complex but highly consistent. George DeForest Lord has drawn attention to the importance of the use of the Old Testament as amalgamating the present and the past in the poem (162-63). The father-son relationships work the same way on a smaller and secular scale to show how past acts cast shadows on the present. The Aristotelian conception of character passing to the progeny of succeeding generations is admirably suited to emphasizing the effect of that past on the present.

Anne Barbeau Gardiner (essay date 1989)

SOURCE: "Divine and Royal Art: History as Hand-Formed Artwork in Dryden's *Threnodia Augustalis* (1685)," in *Papers on Language & Literature,* Vol. 25, No. 4, Fall 1989, pp. 398-424.

[*In the following brief excerpt, Gardiner reflects on the "political context" of* Threnodia Augustalis, *observing that Dryden constructs the poem to reassure the English public that far from being sinister, the transfer of power from the dying Charles II to his brother James was both legitimate and divine.*]

Although many poets wrote elegies on the occasion of Charles II's death and a number of them added congratulatory poems to the new king, none managed to mourn Charles and welcome James in such a seamless design as John Dryden did in *Threnodia Augustalis.* In this poem Dryden meditates on the nature of history, showing it as an artwork wrought both by a wise king and by Providence. . . .

. . . . .

Dryden began writing his elegy in February 1685, when the English were in the throes of anxiety about their new king; in the first stanza, the king's death is compared to the end of the world. David Hume notes that many had attributed every "hard measure" since 1683 to the counsels of James, and Sir John Dalrymple observes that now the exclusionists expected "little mercy from a King to whom they had shewn none when he was a subject." The nation's mood was grim. Here was a man on the throne whom most of the English had been willing, only four years before, to banish for life because of his religion. Commons had approved the Exclusion Bill of 1680 that rendered all who supported James's right to the throne "incapable of pardon but by act of parliament."

Dryden addresses this fear by portraying James as another Hercules and Aeneas, one too dedicated to the public good to stop for revenge. He makes the central moment of the poem, in stanza 8, a drama of reconciliation between James and England at the deathbed of the late king. Dryden also alludes to the reassuring declaration of 6 February, when James told the privy council, immediately after his royal brother's death, that he would preserve the established government in church and state. The council had this declaration printed in the *London Gazette,* and public thanks poured in from all parts of England. One Tory writer thought James had entered a "Caution for his Good Behaviour" and had shown the nation he had too much a "sense of his own Greatness" to be a "Vassal" to the Pope. Dryden alludes to the declaration when he assures the English that James II's "Truth" has always been kept "inviolate," and that "For him to Promise is to make it Fate" (486-87).

Such reassurance was needed, for between the king's death and the advertising of Dryden's poem in mid-March, an accurate account of Charles II's deathbed conversion to Catholicism had been published: *A True Relation of the late King's Death.* Besides this alarming pamphlet, anonymous letters appeared in the houses of mayors and of "all great men that are accounted zealous protestants," warning them to "stand their guard" lest they be "overwhelm'd with popery," since the late king "died a papist" and a "papist succeeds him." A crisis seemed imminent, for Narcissus Luttrell reported that three days after the death of Charles, Mary of Modena was rumored to be "with child." Ralph Thoresby believed that the great sorrow over Charles II's death was due to the "gloomy prospect of popery," and he resolved to start attending services in the Church of England, since it was the "strongest bulwark against Popery, and a union of Protestants absolutely necessary." John Evelyn reproached the late king for not speaking in his final hours about the national Church "now falling under the government of a Prince suspected for his religion," and a few days later he blamed the new king for hearing Mass in his palace "to the great griefe of his subjects," and for letting "Romanists" swarm at court so that "every body" grew "Jealous to what this would tend." In this context, Dryden's stressing James II's mission to achieve international glory for England may be meant to deflect suspicion of him on religious grounds.

The political context for this ode includes the rumors that James had poisoned Charles II. The duke of Monmouth, on 15 November 1680, had accused his uncle James, in Lords, of intending to murder the king. After 1688, Gilbert Burnet and James Welwood insinuated that James had poisoned his brother. Dr. Raymond Crawfurd examines the eyewitness accounts, the medical records, and the autopsy reports, in *The Last Days of Charles II* (1909), and finds no evidence of foul play. He concludes the king died of a chronic kidney ailment. Like Dalrymple before him, Crawfurd thinks Burnet distorts the evidence badly, especially in claiming that Dr. Thomas Short, the Catholic physician whom Dryden praises so warmly in *Threnodia,* was poisoned himself to keep him quiet about the king's death. Roger North, a key witness to the events of 1685, disputes Burnet's claim:

> Dr. *Short,* one of the Physicians of the Consult, said that *the King had not fair Play for his Life.* Of which Words the natural Construction was that the methods used, did him more Hurt than Good; and if he had been let alone, and nothing done to him, Nature had had its Course; which the Doctor might probably mean by *fair play.* And so was the Opinion of Dr. *Stokeham,* who might have used the same words as he expressed the same thing.

North adds that Dr. Short died in the Fall of 1685 attended by all the eminent physicians of London, not one of whom believed him to be poisoned.

Dryden may be responding to the rumors when he stresses the tender friendship between the royal brothers right from the title page, where the epigraph alludes to Nisus and Euryalus. This passage is not from the fifth book of the *Aeneid,* where Nisus helps his friend to win the footrace, but from the ninth book, where the two friends unite in a perilous enterprise to serve the public good. At the exact center of the ode in stanza 8, also, Dryden compares the love of the brothers to that between two persons of the Trinity, making any suspicion of murder absurd.

A final element in the political context for **Threnodia Augustalis** is the belief that the timing of Charles II's death was so favorable to James that foul play could not be ruled out. The enemies of James believed there was a plan afoot, which Charles II had devised, to restore [his illegitimate son] Monmouth and to banish James to Scotland. Sir John Dalrymple, a Whig himself, found no solid evidence of such a plan, and recently J.P. Kenyon, after sifting the evidence, has dismissed this alleged plan to restore Monmouth as having no foundation in fact. Kenyon believes the pro-Dutch policy of late 1684, which James himself approved, has been misunderstood as a turn toward Monmouth. Although Charles did meet Monmouth on 30 November 1684, as arranged by Lord Halifax, father and son were not reconciled. Eyewitnesses at the death of Charles II heard the king bless all his children by name, except Monmouth. Dryden alludes to this crucial omission of Monmouth's name from the king's last benediction in stanza 8: "Those, for whom love cou'd no excuses frame, / He graciously forgot to name" (244-45). Dryden assures the English in stanza 7 that James was the dying king's explicit choice for a successor: he received a bequest of the "supream command" (228) from the hand of Charles II, having been found worthy to take up the burden of rule.

Helen M. Burke (essay date 1990)

SOURCE: "*Annus Mirabilis* and the Ideology of the New Science," in *ELH*, Vol. 57, No. 2, Summer 1990, pp. 307-34.

[*In the following excerpt, Burke contends that in* Annus Mirabilis, *Dryden glorifies the "new" or practical science of his era and in the process, anticipates the advent of the more "materialistic" and "republican" enlightenment that was to dominate the final half of the eighteenth century.*]

In an article on Dryden and the issue of human progress, Earl Miner comments that the poet's degree of enthusiasm for the new science is a "knotty problem." Though he notes that Dryden "probably wrote more progress-pieces than any other of our poets," Miner argues that Dryden's attitude to progress was, at best, qualified; one "really significant fact," Miner notes, is that the poet "wrote no Cowleyan ode on the Royal Society, as he surely would have, if he had placed his strongest hopes in the new science." Here I will suggest that both the extent of Dryden's interest in the new science and his attitude to it can be understood by a reading of his longest poem, *Annus Mirabilis*. At approximately the center of *Annus Mirabilis*, there is, of course, Dryden's well-known "Apostrophe to the Royal Society":

> This I fore-tel, from your auspicious care,
>> Who great in search of God and Nature grow:
> Who best your wise Creator's praise declare,
>> Since best to praise his works is best to know.
>
> O truly Royal! who behold the Law,
>> And rule of beings in your Makers mind,
> And thence, like Limbecks, rich Idea's draw,
>> To fit the levell'd use of humane kind.

(165-66)

That Dryden should adopt this complimentary attitude to the newly formed society is not surprising. As Phillip Harth points out, the poet's intellectual formation took place in Trinity, Cambridge in the 1650s, where Bacon's ideals and spirit still held sway, and where enthusiasm for the new philosophy was high. Some of the men teaching at Cambridge during this time (Isaac Barrow, John Ray) and many of Dryden's fellow students (John Mapletoft, Thomas Allen, Francis Willughby and Walter Needham) were later to become fellows of the Royal Society. Dryden was also a fellow until October 29, 1666, and even though he had been dropped from the rolls (for nonpayment of dues) by the time he was writing *Annus Mirabilis*, he still, as the above passage suggests, regarded the work of the society as important and praiseworthy.

But this overt vote of confidence in the achievement of the recently founded Royal Society must be understood as only one expression of the poem's wider interest in the new science and its achievement. One source of the wonder in *Annus Mirabilis*, I will argue, is the very power of the "arts" or technology to effect progress. As the poem explicitly indicates, it is by means of technological advances in the areas of warfare and navigation that England will finally achieve its goal of mastering nature and of gaining access to the world and its wealth. "The beauteous Arts of Modern pride" (296), Dryden prophesizes, will finally transform London and, by extension, the destiny of England. By making this new technology a central focus, the poem is celebrating the achievement of the new science, a science that was deeply concerned with the practical application of its studies.

On a deeper structural level, the poem could be said to articulate the tensions inherent in the development of a coherent ideology of science and the difficulties of incorporating a new natural philosophy into existing symbolic structures. Recent studies of the history of science show that the ideology of the new mechanical science was forged only through the gradual modification of materialistic philosophies to suit hegemonic interests. As Margaret Jacob demonstrates, the moderate *virtuosi* and divines of the 1650s and 60s were deeply engaged in working out a synthesis of old and new natural philosophies, a synthesis which would reject the potentially radical impulses implicit in the philosophies of Descartes, Hobbes and the recently revived Epicureanism, while still retaining some of the basic mechanistic premises of these philosophies. Robert Boyle, for example, in response to the threat of occultism and materialism was, at this time, working out his corpuscular philosophy, his version of what Jacob calls "a Christianized Epicurean atomism" which acknowledges the atomistic nature of the universe but sees God as determining the path of the atom. Order is thus maintained in an unstable universe. The young Newton, influenced by the churchman, Isaac Barrow, was attempting a similar reconciliation in his *De gravitatione et aequipondio fluidorum* (1664-68) in which he attempted to modify Cartesian notions of space and matter to fit Christian orthodoxy, divesting corporeal substances of any property which belonged to the divine being while simultaneously affirming the dependence of all that is created on the Creator. The quest of both these scientists, as Robert Markley points out, is for "a single system of representation that articulates their equally strong devotions to experimental philosophy and Christian theology."

Annus Mirabilis, I will suggest, attempts a similar reconciliation of conflicting natural philosophies, although it operates not through expository persuasion but through poetic figures. In its use of the tropes of war and fire, the poem creates two different paradigms of man's relation to the natural world. On the one hand, the poem proclaims the dominance of spirit over matter, of the imperial subject over the inanimate world, a transcendence achieved (as it was for the Christian *virtuosi*) through *techne*, the "art" which is both technology and a process of representation. On the other hand, through the narrative of the Great Fire of London, the poem also proclaims the irreducibility of nature and the limitations of the rational subject in relation to the exterior animated world. Though this narrative is enclosed in the dominant story of man's triumph over the world, *Annus Mirabilis*, by acknowledging the existence of an alternate paradigm of nature, delimits the conditions of possibility for Restoration science. It indirectly discloses what this science seeks to forget, revealing what Christopher Hill calls the "dialectical element in scientific thinking, a recognition of the 'irrational' (in the sense of the mechanically inexplicable)" which was lost in the triumph of the mechanical philosophy.

But if this poem is concerned with scientific thinking, it is therefore, by necessity, equally concerned with theological and political thinking. Theories of matter in the seventeenth century, as Jacob points out, were never ideologically neutral. Newton's belief that there was "an analogy between the world natural and the world politic" was representative of his age, and theories of the nature of the universe, consequently, were understood to have social, political and theological ramifications. If, for example, matter was thought to be able to move by its own innate force, as the revived Epicurean atomism claimed, or if the atheistic materialism of Hobbes was accepted, then God ceased to rule nature and the established order was jeopardized. As Jacob explains, "the separation of God from Creation, creature from creature, of matter from spirit, so basic to Christian orthodoxy and such a powerful justification for social hierarchy and even for absolute monarchy, crumbles in the face of animistic and naturalistic explanation. God does not create *ex nihilo;* nature simply is and all people (and their environment) are part of this greater All."

To the minds of conservatives like Dryden in the "restored" order of the 1660s, such atheistic explanations of the physical universe were patently threatening. The radical implications of such theories had already become apparent during the Revolution, and churchmen like Isaac Barrow feared a return to what they perceived as the social anarchy of this period. The Hobbesian world, for Barrow, was a holocaust in which the church would founder and its sectarian enemies would collide and burn like "prodigious meteors" creating "anarchy, emulation, and strife." It is such a possibility, I suggest, that the section on the Great Fire also opens up. The trope of the fire recovers not only a repressed scientific paradigm but also a repressed theological and social paradigm. It effects a spiritual and political tracing, recreating a configuration of power in which the church and the king are inoperative and in which the social body asserts itself against the divine right of kings.

On a superficial level, it is clear that the poem is immersed in the scientific discourse of its day, reflecting both its beliefs and concerns. Dryden's understanding of the role of science is very much in keeping with contemporary thinking. The "Apostrophe to the Royal Society" follows immediately on the "Digression concerning Shipping and Navigation" (155-165), which traces the ever-increasing sophistication of navigational technology, thus placing the research of the society firmly in the context of technological development. It is clear from the narrational sequence that there is no disjunction between the search for theoretical knowledge as "science"—knowing the "Law / And rule of beings" (166)—and the search for a navigational technology which would permit "a more exact mea-

sure of Longitude" (Dryden's note on "instructed ships" [163]). Both science and art (the latter used to describe the agency of progressive change in navigation, "Art, / Makes mighty things from small beginnings grow" [155]) are seen to have the same utilitarian function; navigational technology functions to transform the universe into "one City" where "some may gain, and all may be suppli'd" (163), just as pure research transmutes "rich Idea's . . . To fit the levell'd use of humane kind" (166).

This utilitarian emphasis is evident in much of the scientific thinking of the day. As Charles Webster explains in his extensive study of science in the pre-Restoration period, there was no essential split between science and technology in the minds of many seventeenth-century scientists. In the Baconian concept of natural philosophy, Webster explains, "science, perfect knowledge of the inner workings of nature was the ultimate goal, but this knowledge could be best attained through the investigation of the arts which related to everyday life. The value of knowledge in this area would be proved by its capacity to yield socially beneficial rewards." As Bacon himself puts it, in his study of the works of creation, "Truth and utility are here the very same things." Under the new regime of 1660, this Baconian ideal was still espoused, though there was a changing perception of which arts were the most useful. As Hunter points out, Restoration scientists took an unprecedented interest in naval and military technology (interregnum scientists, by contrast, displayed little interest in these areas). In 1664, for example, when a special committee was set up by the Fellows of the Royal Society to study "mechanics," two of its particular interests were gunnery and nautical innovations.

That Dryden also emphasizes these new arts is not a sheer coincidence. The description he gives of his poetic endeavors in the "Account" of *Annus Mirabilis* to Sir Robert Howard, would suggest rather the degree to which he is making these new technologies his explicit focus:

> In general I will only say, I have never yet seen the description of any Naval Fight in the proper terms which are us'd at Sea; and if there be any such in another Language, as that of *Lucan* in the third of his *Pharsalia,* yet I could not prevail my self of it in the *English;* the terms of Arts in every Tongue bearing more of the Idiom of it then any other words. We hear, indeed, among our Poets, of the thundring of Guns, the smoke, the disorder and the slaughter; but all these are common notions. And certainly as those who, in a Logical dispute, keep in general terms, would hide a fallacy, so those who do it in any Poetical description would vail their ignorance. (1:45)

His argument here for the use of a more technical language ("proper terms which are us'd at Sea") to describe sea battles, and his rejection of the more traditional general description which he equates with an attempt to hide "ignorance," would also suggest that he is consciously trying to achieve the objectivity that was the ideological project of the new scientists. Dyden's contempt for the traditional "common notions" of poets is similar to Thomas Sprat's contempt for the language of the old philosophy. In the last sentence of his *History of the Royal Society,* Sprat, the official historian of the Royal Society, writes: "While the Old could only bestow on us some barren Terms and Notions, the New shall impart to us the uses of all the *Creatures,* and shall inrich us with all the Benefits of *Fruitfulness* and *Plenty.*" Accepting, as we have seen, a similar utilitarian emphasis, Dryden also espouses an ideal of converse between socially disparate groups, in the interest of acquiring accurate data. In the "Account," he writes:

> For my own part, if I had little knowledge of the Sea, yet I have thought it no shame to learn: and if I have made some few mistakes, 'tis onely, as you can bear me witness, because I have wanted opportunity to correct them, the whole Poem being first written, and now sent you from a place, where I have not so much as the converse of any Sea-man. (1:45)

This sentiment is symptomatic of what Hunter describes as the realignment of European intellectual life in the seventeenth century, "the conviction growing since the Renaissance that intellectuals should involve themselves in practical matters traditionally considered beneath them" (99). One obvious manifestation of this impulse was the History of Trades program. This encyclopedic project undertaken by the Royal Society had as its goal the acquisition of technological and industrial data in order to render it more useful, a goal that would necessarily involve closer interaction between different social and economic groups. The new scientific inquiry, as Robert Boyle says, "may enable gentlemen and scholars to converse with tradesmen, and benefit themselves (and perhaps the tradesmen too) by that conversation." In finding it "no shame" to learn the language of marine technology and in acknowledging the desirability of collecting precise data from a "Sea-man," Dryden is thus displaying his awareness of contemporary scientific trends and implicitly establishing himself as part of the scientific community.

It is precisely this scientific orientation that Samuel Johnson found most offensive in this poem, and his critique is illuminating because it indicates a clear recognition of the poem's scientific emphasis. Johnson attacks Dryden for his refusal to speak "an universal language," for his violation of the rule that a subject such as navigation, drawn from "arts not liberal," arts that are "far removed from common knowledge," should be "sunk in general expressions." To demonstrate what he considered to be an inappropriately specialized language, Johnson reproduces, in his *Lives of the Poets,* the following three stanzas in which Dryden described the repairing of the fleet (146-48), using the technical terms Johnson disapproved of:

> So here some pick out bullets from the side,
>   Some drive old *okum* thro' each *seam* and rift:
> Their left-hand does the *calking-iron* guide
>   The rattling *mallet* with the right they lift.

> With boiling pitch another near at hand
>   (From friendly Sweden brought) the *seams instops:*

> Which, well laid o'er, the salt-sea waves withstand,
>   And shake them from the rising beak in drops.

> Some the *gall'd* ropes with dauby *marling* bind,
>   Or sear-cloth masts with strong *tarpawling* coats:
> To try new *shrouds* one mounts into the wind,
>   And one below, their ease or stiffness notes.

Though Johnson considers Dryden's attempt to integrate technology and poetry a failure, he clearly acknowledges the originality of Dryden's attempt. "Battles have always been described in heroick poetry," Johnson comments, "but a sea-fight and artillery had yet something of novelty. New arts are long in the world before poets describe them; for they borrow every thing from their predecessors, and commonly derive very little from nature or from life." Dryden's attempt to describe these "new arts" is acknowledged even if, in Johnson's opinion, the poem "does not fully answer the expectation raised by such subjects and such a writer" (1:314).

But it is not only because of its subject matter and diction that this poem forms part of the discourse of the new science. The dominant narrative of the poem is also the narrative of the new scientific quest, related in a tale of military and commercial conquest. The "Digression" and "Apostrophe" (155-166) mentioned above, which Dryden specifically places outside the frame of his narrative, provide the scientific agenda, the thematic summary of the drama which the poem enacts.

> The Ebbs of Tydes, and their mysterious flow,
>   We, as Arts Elements shall understand:
> And as by Line upon the Ocean go,
>   Whose paths shall be familiar as the Land.

> Instructed ships shall sail to quick Commerce;
>   By which remotest Regions are alli'd:
> Which makes one City of the Universe,
>   Where some may gain, and all may be suppli'd.
>   (162-63)

A thinking subject, the Cartesian *ego cogito* ("We . . . shall understand") imposes himself through technology ("instructed ships") upon nature ("the Universe") turning it into a product for human consumption ("where some may gain, and all may be suppli'd"). And a transformation is effected in the nature of matter and space whereby what was fluid, unbounded and multifaceted will become solid, circumscribed and unified: the "mysterious flow" will become transmuted into "paths . . . familiar as the Land"; the ocean or "open Sea" (160) will be striated "by Line"; the many diverse "Regions" of the "Universe" will be converted into "one City."

These stanzas fit perfectly with the epistemological model of classical science. As Gilles Deleuze and Felix Guattari note, this epistemology, which they call "Royal Science," is distinguished by "a theory of solids" to the concurrent exclusion of fluids; a privileging of homogeneity, "the stable, the eternal, the identical, the constant," over heterogeneity; a concept of space as "striated" rather than unbounded; and a "theorematic" procedure belonging to "the rational [*de l'ordre des raisons*] rather than to the irrational order." Inherent in this mode is the impulse to objectify and represent nature as stable and controllable, an impulse that Heidegger equates with the genesis of modern science and the inauguration of the "new" in world history, and which he relates to Cartesian metaphysics. "We first arrive at science as research," Heidegger says, "when and only when truth has been transformed into the certainty of representation. What is to be is for the first time defined as the objectiveness of representing, and truth is first defined as the certainty of representing in the metaphysics of Descartes."

However, the Cartesian model only partly explains the epistemology that governs *Annus Mirabilis*. Dryden too wishes (as we see in stanzas 162 and 163) to valorize a science that allows us to represent being with certainty, to render it stable and knowable, but the English poet (unlike the continental *philosophes*) also wishes to locate his epistemology within a framework of traditional religious and political beliefs. The work of the new scientists is to detect the "rule of beings" and to function "like Limbecks," transmuting fluids, "rich Idea's," into something that can be of "use," Dryden tells us in stanza 166, taking up many of the images from the "ocean" stanzas cited above (162-63). But the scientific operation is now fixed very specifically within monarchical and Christian contexts. The society which performs the scientific experiment on nature works under the charter and the patronage of a king and is thus a "truly Royal" society, while the "beings" which are the object of the experiment are ultimately contained within the "Makers mind" (166). Scientific knowledge has to be integrated into a conceptual framework of human and divine order, and it is important finally only because it is the ultimate act of worship, "since best to praise his works is best to know" (165).

A close reading of what I am calling the first section of the poem, stanzas 1-154, reveals such an integration of science with traditional power structures, an integration achieved through the imaginative conflation of the military with the scientific enterprise. In the stanza immediately following the "Apostrophe" is a retrospective interpretation of the Anglo-Dutch war that frames this event in a scientific context. War, we are told, is but a necessary preliminary to the progress of science, a stage that has to be gone through to clear the way for science's greater achievement: "But first the toils of war we must endure, / And, from th'Injurious *Dutch* redeem the Seas" (167). But while the military struggle and the achievement of science are clearly differentiated here, this rigid distinction is undercut through the poem's imagery. The king, who is the military leader of this first section, is also represented as the scientist in action.

The opening stanzas of *Annus Mirabilis* establish the primacy of the royal subject and the association between science, military undertaking, and monarchy. Charles is represented as the one who controls reality through what he sees, through his theory (as in the Greek *theorein:* to

look at or behold). The importance of this gaze as a controlling device is overtly established in the later passages on science: the moment when technology will make "one City of the Universe" will also be the longed-for moment of total cosmic power, when the whole of creation will be contained within one all-encompassing perspective, one epistemology:

> Then, we upon our Globes last verge shall go,
>   And view the Ocean leaning on the sky:
> From thence our rolling Neighbours we shall know,
>   And on the Lunar world securely pry.
>
>   (164)

The above stanza suggests that this moment of totalization will be accomplished in the future, as the culmination of technological progress. However, in the opening stanzas of the poem, we already see such an epistemology at work. The description of the political real—the English threatened by the commercial greed of the Dutch and by the imperial ambitions of the French (stanzas 1-9)—is contained in the king's "gen'rous mind" (11). It is his interpretation, his retrospective gaze, which gives meaning to the flow of ships and goods: "This saw our King; and long within his breast / His pensive counsels ballanc'd too and fro" (10). In this and in the following stanzas (11-14), we see the *ego cogito* giving form to content, distributing reality in terms of dialectical oppositions that balance "too and fro" (10): freedom and oppression (10); pleasure and pain (11); gain and loss (12); peace and war (12).

But the king is not cast as a mere rationalist or theoretician. He is rather the *virtuoso,* the experimental scientist who proceeds according to an orderly inductive methodology. Bacon described the importance of gathering and organizing data as the basis for true scientific work, distinguishing such a procedure from "mere groping": the "true method of experience," he says, "first lights the candle, and then by means of the candle shows the way; commencing as it does with experience duly ordered and digested, not bungling or erratic, and from it deducing axioms, and from established axioms again new experiments." It is this process the king follows, proceeding from observation through general axioms to experiment:

> He, first, survey'd the charge with careful eyes,
>   Which none but mighty Monarchs could
> maintain;
> Yet judg'd, like vapours that from Limbecks rise,
>   It would in richer showers descend again
>
> At length resolv'd t'assert the watry Ball,
>   He in himself did whole Armado's bring:
> Him, aged Sea-men might their Master call,
>   And choose for General were he not their King.
>
>   (13-14)

The imaginative connection between the scientific experiment and the military undertaking is clearly established here, and, as the above stanza suggests, it is Charles who is the "Master" of the action. The fact that others actually conduct the "experiment" does not negate the primacy of the role of the king. Like many of the actual scientists of the Royal Society, the king delegates to others the menial mechanical tasks, but, as the poem insists, he remains the cognitive power behind the undertaking. His mind contains and receives the aggression of his rivals; when France joins with the Dutch against the English, the French show a hatred "which *Charles* does with a mind so calm receive / As one that neither seeks, nor shuns his foe" (41). It is the king, we are reminded after the Battle of Lowestoft and the Attempt at Bergen, who bears ultimate responsibility: "He without fear a dangerous War pursues, / Which without rashness he began before" (45).

The military leaders thus are portrayed as extensions of the royal "we," one line, one blood with him. In the Duke of York's case, the literal relationship is emphasized in the stanza celebrating the first victory at Lowestoft. "Thus Heav'n our Monarch's fortune did confess, / Beginning conquest from his Royal Race" (19). In the case of Prince Rupert and the Duke of Albemarle, the war's most important generals, the kinship line is figurative. Charles is their metaphorical father, and they are his creations, "with equal pow'r he does two Chiefs create" (47). The purely subordinate role of these two leaders is emphasized in stanza 53, in which their strictly instrumental function is described in imagery that reinstates the notion of the scientific experiment:

> Diffusive of themselves, where e'r they pass,
> They make that warmth in others they expect:
> Their valour works like bodies on a glass,
> And does its Image on their men project.
>
> (53)

As this stanza suggests, the generals are not so much human beings as parts of the war technology that implements the will of the royal subject. They are part of the machinery of the ship, nautical instruments for the king's use: "It seems as every Ship their Sovereign knows, / His awful summons they so soon obey" (15). The importance of technology in the war is constantly emphasized. It is because of a technological imbalance that the war starts in the first place. Holland's "thriving Arts," as the first line explains, led to her maritime supremacy; like Carthage, she grew "mighty in her Ships," and by means of them she "swept the riches of the world from far" (5). The outcome of the battle is also often determined by marine technological superiority, as stanzas 59-60 emphasize: we are told that the make of the ships on each side affected the outcome of the fighting, "and as the built, so different is the fight" (60), a fact validated by historians who note that a reliance on smaller and more lightly armed ships was one of the reasons for the Dutch failure in this war. Each encounter ends with an account of the state of the "Ship," and success or failure of the outcome is measured on this basis. After the Battle of Lowestoft, the Dutch ships are "shatter'd' (23), and English victory is assured. At Bergen, the outcome is indecisive and both sides suffer "Shipwrack" (35). During the Four Days Battle, the outcome fluctuates: the first day ends with the Dutch dreaming in terror of being "shipwrack'd" (71), the second day with the "burning ships" (102) of the English. On the third day,

the swelling numbers of English ships predict their victory, but the battle ends on the fourth day, with the enemy ships of both sides lying "helpless" (130).

Though the king is not directly engaged in the above naval action, it is clear that he is the force behind the technological deployment. Just as the action of the war is prefaced by the image of the king thinking, and by a specific analogy to a scientific experiment (13), so this action is also finally encompassed by a similar representation of the king as scientist, assessing the success of his experiment and repairing his technology for future use. The Four Days Battle ends with the king, now represented as a miner, checking to see if the transmutation of liquid into gold has yet taken place, an activity reminiscent of his earlier undertaking, his prediction that the "vapours" in the limbecks would change into "richer showers" (13).

> As those who unripe veins in Mines explore,
>   On the rich bed again the warm turf lay,
> Till time digests the yet imperfect Ore,
>   And know it will be Gold another day:
>
> So looks our Monarch on this early fight,
>   Th'essay, and rudiments of great success,
> Which all-maturing time must bring to light,
>   While he, like Heav'n, does each days labour bless.
>
> (139-40)

That Dryden should use a mining image to replace the earlier alchemical one is not surprising. As Webster points out, minerals were considered by many to be in a fluctuating condition in the earth, naturally evolving towards the state of gold. The study of mineralogy and metallurgy was thus considered a part of a continuum of scientific research which aimed at gaining access to treasure, whether it be gold or other "fruits" of the earth. As Sir John Pettus, one of Hartlib's associates, explained earlier in the century, the study of mineralogy and metallurgy would lead to "the Study of Geography, Hydrography and other Sciences, thereby to learn the Wonders of the Land and Deeps; insinuating also to us the richest Minerals, Plants, and Precious Stones." Following these studies would come the study of rivers and the sea, whereby "the Art of Navigation is known and improv'd, and Merchandizing thereby encouraged."

Dryden seems to see scientific research, navigation, and mining as similarly related, and by his imposition of the mining imagery on the activity of war he further suggests the similarity between military aggression and this kind of scientific exploitation. However, at the end of this first section, he returns to the dominant image of the ship as the embodiment of technological achievement, and in the detailed description of naval technology to which Johnson objected, he celebrates both the complexity and skill involved in this art. As is consistent with the procedure throughout this passage, he attributes this technological expertise to the king. In the section entitled, "His Majesty repairs the Fleet" (142-150), the idea of the king as *virtuoso* is again reinforced. As the section title implies, the king is the subject of the action: the repairing is "Royal work" (144), though others actually perform the mechanical tasks. The engagement of the king is further emphasized in stanza 149, in which we see Charles personally handling the ships' military equipment—the cannons, gunpowder and artillery:

> Our careful Monarch stands in Person by,
>   His new-cast Canons firmness to explore:
> The strength of big-corn'd powder loves to try,
>   And Ball and Cartrage sorts for every bore.
>
>   (149)

It is in the passage on the *Loyal London* (151-154), however, that we see figured most clearly the synthesis of science with monarchy that this poem works to realize. This ship, with its clearly magical and illusionary qualities (the weaver who equips her is "charm'd" by her [152], and "she seems a Sea-wasp flying on the waves" [153]) most ideally embodies the achievement of technology in both the military and commercial arenas. On the one hand, the *Loyal London* represents the best of military technology, the technology that has helped Charles in the war against the Dutch: she is the fire ship, "warlike in her length," equipped with "guns of mighty strength" (153); her "sanguine Streamers seem the floud to fire" (152). On the other hand, by her obvious wealth and grandeur, she foretells the achievement of technology in the commercial field; she is "like a rich Bride," riding on her shadow "in floating gold" (151), an anticipation of the merchant ship, the "instructed ships" which "shall sail to quick Commerce" (163). It is this "martial Present," this technological miracle, "piously design'd" (154), which is given the king, a gift "built, fitted and maintain'd to aid him bring" (154). Technology and its achievement in both military and commercial areas, these stanzas suggest, serve the monarchy.

This passage on the *Loyal London* thus summarizes in symbolic terms the ideal reconciliation of science and kingship which the first section of the poem articulates in more detailed form. Dryden's object is to make the new science a "royal" science, just as he does in his earlier poem **"To my Honour'd Friend, Dr. Charleton,"** where, as Earl Wasserman has argued, "the ultimate objective . . . is to celebrate the Stuart reign insofar as it is confirmed by the providential correspondence of political developments and the progress of the new science." In appropriating science for monarchy, this earlier poem and *Annus Mirabilis* are following the same ideological agenda as Sprat's *History,* a work that also places the monarchy at the center of the scientific enterprise. The "favour of the *King,* and the *Royal Family,*" Sprat says, "ought to be esteem'd the very *life,* and soul of this *undertaking*" (133). It could be argued that in following this ideological agenda, Dryden's poem, no less than Sprat's work, is part of the scientific historiography which served to establish the myth that the Royal Society had its origins in the Restoration, and not, as historiographers of science now believe, in the Puritan Revolution.

But if this passage on the *Loyal London* serves to summarize the first section of the poem, it also has an important

function in relation to the poem's remainder, a function it acquires through its identification of the "Ship" with London. The *Loyal London* is given to the king by the "Loyal City" (154) as an emblem of the city's willingness to assist Charles. Symbolically, the ship and the city thus become one. This identification of the metropolis with the scientific undertaking is not original. We find this idea explicitly elaborated in Sprat, who, after listing the "advantages" enjoyed by London (its location, its diverse population) concludes: "It is, as the *Poets* describe their *house of Fame,* a City, where all the noises and business in the World do meet: and therefore this honour is justly due to it, to be the *constant* place of *residence* for that *Knowledge,* which is to be made up of the Reports, and Intelligence of all Countreys" (87-88). But in establishing the ship/city correlation, Dryden is doing more than reiterating an accepted perception of the correspondence between the development of the metropolis and the development of science. He is also setting up the connection that allows him to move imaginatively from the Anglo-Dutch war to the Great Fire of London, his second subject. The fire ship of the first section becomes the ship/city on fire in the second, in which the paradigm of royal science is gradually undone. The ship/city is unmoored from sovereign control; the "Chymick flame" (293) destroys existing symbolic structures and the royal subject is rendered impotent before irreducible forces.

As in the first part of the poem, the scientific paradigm evokes a corresponding political and religious paradigm. When bodies (both men and natural bodies) move of their own accord, God's function as Prime Mover, by implication, is no longer necessary. This is a correlation made directly by the young Newton at this time, as he seeks to construct an alternative to Aristotelian matter theory because of its potential heretical implications: "Indeed," Newton writes, "however we cast about we find almost no other reason for atheism than this notion of bodies having, as it were, a complete absolute and independent reality in themselves." In **Annus Mirabilis,** this theological apprehension is made indirectly through the political apprehension that when bodies move independently, kings are no longer functional. The possibility that is rendered symbolically in the imaginative conjunction of the ineffective king and the raging and vital fire is of a revolutionary social and spiritual order, a world turned upside down.

The shift to a different conceptual paradigm is only gradually apparent. Stanzas 167-208, which describe the preparation for the St. James's Day Fight and the fight itself, would seem, at first, to belong thematically with the first section of the poem. Like the opening section, these stanzas also focus on the maritime war with the Dutch. But in this section the king is displaced as "Master" of the ship, the "stable, the eternal, the identical, the constant" royal subject giving way to a volatile heterogeneity, a plurality represented by the "Sea-men" (178) who first image the concept of a natural and political body that refuses its assigned place in the traditional order.

The emergence of a new kind of subject is first apparent in the increasing sense of bodily density, of mass. In stanzas 170-85, there is a gradual widening of the definition of who "we" are, a gradual broadening of the term "English" (170). While in the first section of the poem a "royal we" mastered the action of the ship—the king, and his substitutes, the Duke of York, Prince Rupert and the Duke of Albemarle—the emphasis is now on a more amorphous, less unified subject. The conventional Homeric roll call of heroes (171-76) creates an initial sense of a crowd, a sense reinforced in the image of the anonymous "thousands" with which this roll call ends:

> Thousands were there in darker fame that dwell,
>   Whose deeds some nobler Poem shall adorn:
> And, though to me unknown, they, sure, fought
>   well,
>   Whom *Rupert* led, and who were *British* born.
>
> (176)

That this image of the anonymous seaman is equated with a different conceptual order soon becomes obvious. The seaman's discourse is not the balanced articulation of the royal subject who keeps long "pensive counsels" (10) before he asserts himself, but a non-reflective, inarticulate scream: "Now Anchors weigh'd, the Sea-Men shout so shrill, / That Heav'n and Earth and the Wide Ocean rings" (178). Allusions to the British fleet as a "gathering storm" (179) and to their appearance as "Ghosts" (185) reinforce the notion that the seamen represent that which disrupts the rational order.

The relation of this disruptive force to royal power is also made clear. In the Saint James's battle itself, though the "adverse Admirals" finally square off to decide the victory (187), it is this newly emergent entity, the seaman, who is the force behind the deployment of military power:

> The distance judg'd for shot of every size,
>   The Linstocks touch, the pond'rous ball expires:
> The vig'rous Sea-man every port-hole plies,
>   And adds his heart to every Gun he fires.
>
> (188)

It is after the St. James's Day victory, however, that this other conceptual order is fully described, and a direct relation established between it and political and religious disruption. In the reflective passage that immediately follows the description of the victory, there is a shift from the present celebration to the memory of past mistakes by "our Fathers" (199). England erred in helping Holland to rebel against Philip the Second of Spain: "*England,* which first, by leading them astray, / Hatch'd up Rebellion to destroy her King" (198). In the historic context in which this poem was written, the theme of a misguided rebellion by "our Fathers" against a king would, of course, suggest the recent civil war in which rebellion actually destroyed a king, in which the ship of state was indeed temporarily controlled by the common man.

This theme of subversion, of the destroyed king, is related to a paradigm of knowledge that both recalls and displaces that outlined in stanzas 162 and 163:

> In fortunes Empire blindly thus we go,
>   And wander after pathless destiny:

> Whose dark resorts since prudence cannot know
>   In vain it would provide for what shall be.
>
> (200)

The hegemonic gaze here is now no longer operative. The assurance of the "Line" is replaced by a wandering trajectory; the solid and stable "paths . . . familiar as the Land" by the unbounded and uncertain "pathless destiny"; plenitude, where "all may be suppli'd," by lack, "in vain it would provide for what shall be"; identity, "one City of the Universe," by difference: "dark resorts". The description recalls a Lucretian view of life, which sees men "wandering aimlessly in a vain search for the way of life" or, as Dryden's own translation of these lines goes, "bewilder'd in the Maze of Life, and blind."

It is this other conceptual order, this other natural, political, and theological paradigm, which the rest of this section of the poem (202-208) and the section on the Great Fire put into operation. The action of the "conquering Navy" (202) after victory is emblematic of this other structure. Unlike the "Royal" science which enunciates itself in straight lines—the battle ships of both sides are "born each by other in a distant Line" (57) while the later commercial ships are visualized as going "by Line upon the Ocean" (162)—this other order expresses itself in a waywardness and impulsiveness; it "Way-lays" enemy ships, and gains "new wealth without their care" (202). The use of the term "Leviathan"—"So, close behind some Promontory lie / The huge Leviathans t'attend their prey" (203)—with its Hobbesian overtones, reinforces the association between the marauding fleet and a materialistic and godless state of nature. The burning and looting represent a state of nature where, to use Hobbes's words, there is no "*finis ultimus,* utmost aim, nor *summum bonum,* greatest good," but only the "continual progress of the desire from one object to another." The "destructive Fires" which the conquering navy sends out destroy the goods that were the object of commercial trade, so that wealth no longer circulates, "out-bound ships at home their voyage end" (204). The new economy is based solely on self-interest and the gratifying of personal desire:

> Our greedy Sea-men rummage every hold,
>   Smile on the booty of each wealthier Chest:
> And, as the Priests who with their gods make bold,
>   Take what they like, and sacrifice the rest.
>
> (208)

The relation of the seamen's action to the political model of the commonwealth is implicit. Here, the control over the economic "Chest" passes into the hands of the common man, as many of the radical sectaries proposed it should, believing, as did Gerrard Winstanley, that "true freedom lies in the community in spirit and community in the earthly treasury." The comparison of the ship looters to blasphemous priests also recalls the many nonorthodox religious sects that made "bold" with the traditional teaching of the established church, and the popular iconoclasm of the 1630s and 40s which resulted in the destruction of sacred objects (altar rails, statues, ecclesiastical documents, for example) (Hill, 29). The interregnum destruction of churches is directly recalled later on in the poem with the allusion to the desecration of St. Paul's Cathedral (273-75). For a contemporary audience, the seaman would also suggest the dispute raging between gentlemen captains and "tarpaulins" during the 1660s on the issue of who should rule at sea. Halifax, writing on the issue at this time, explicitly relates the dispute to the more general question of government. "The Navy," he argues, "is of so great importance that it would be disparaged by calling it less than the life and soul of government." Moreover, he equates dominance by "Tarpaulins" with the notion of a commonwealth: "In case the Officers be all Tarpaulins, it would be in reality too great a tendency to a Commonwealth."

The section on the Great Fire of London that immediately follows the "Burning of the Fleet in the Vly" is a more extensive configuration of this other paradigm that subverts sovereign meaning at the natural, political and spiritual levels. The fire is at once self-activated matter in motion, the revolutionary forces that destroyed the crown, and the philosophy that undoes providential order.

Like the atoms Dryden later describes in **Religio Laici,** which "leapt into *Form,* (the Noble work of *Chance*)" (311), the fire originates in a "deep quiet, from what source unknown," (217) and then similarly "leaps up" (222) into being. The fire recalls the unbounded Lucretian universe, a universe where natural forces are not contained: it "breaks out" (214) from its unknown background; it is "prodigious" (215); it moves from "mean buildings" to "open streets" (215); it "breaks" (219) out of a "close-pent room" (218), as if it were "too great for prison" (219); it "scapes" its "narrow jail, / And makes small out-lets into open air" (220). In its movement, it also replicates the atomistic universe where matter is in a state of irreducible flux. With its wave-like motion, the "restless Tyde" (235) of the fires evades control, flying "in unctuous vapours" (246) or "in a shining sheet" (247) above ground, or creeping underground, and "climbing from below" (247).

The association between this natural chaos and political subversion is established both within the text and contextually. Other writers at the time made the imaginative connection between fire and political anarchy. In his poem celebrating the Restoration, for example, Cowley uses fire to describe the interregnum period. During that period, *"Ignis Fatuus,"* Cowley writes, misled the country; the *"fiery Tayl"* of a comet inflamed the country and proved "fatal to our *Monarchy.*" Much later, in 1691, Dryden explicitly relates fire and civil war. Praising Halifax, he comments that that politician's counsels "were the Means of preventing a Civil War, and of extinguishing a growing Fire which was just ready to have broken forth among us." References within this section also clearly suggest that the fire is being used as a metaphor for populist government. The reference to the fire's obscure origin, "his birth, perhaps, some petty Village hides / And sets his Cradle out of Fortune's way" (213), and the comparison of the fire to a "dire Usurper" who rules with "lawless sway" (213) clearly recall Cromwell and the dissenting forces led by him. The restless mobility of the fire is suggestive of the New Model Army, which Hill calls "the supreme example

of social mobility" in the already mobile period of the interregnum (58). Explicitly described in military terms, the fire rolls up and down the town as the New Model Army rolled up and down the country:

> At first they warm, then scorch, and then they take:
>   Now with long necks from side to side they feed:
> At length, grown strong, their Mother fire forsake,
>   And a new Collony of flames succeed
>
> To every nobler portion of the Town,
>   The curling billows roul their restless Tyde:
> In parties now they straggle up and down,
>   As Armies, unoppos'd, for prey divide.
>
> (234-35)

Like the sectaries, the fire also has levelling impulses. The "*Hydra* like" fire with its "hundred heads" (249) effects the breakdown of social hierarchy and the redistribution of wealth:

> The rich grow suppliant, and the poor grow proud:
>   Those offer mighty gain, and these ask more.
> So void of pity is th'ignoble crowd,
>   When others ruine may increase their store.
>
> As those who live by shores with joy behold
>   Some wealthy vessel split or stranded high;
> And, from the Rocks, leap down for shipwrack'd Gold,
>   And seek the Tempest which the others flie.
>
> (250-51)

The re-appearance of a ship analogy here—the poor people who take advantage of the fire are compared to those who take advantage of storms to prey on wrecked ships—thematically units the "ignoble crowd" with the seamen discussed above. The burning of the fleet and the Great Fire of London are imaginatively connected as images of the praxis of a radical social order—where self-directed forces rule, where traditional hierarchy is undone, where the "Ship" is deprived of its lawful "Owners" (252).

The absence of epistemological and ontological certainty which this absence of authority creates is reflected in the errancy of the fire. Instead of the stability of "paths . . . familiar as the Land" (162), the poem now depicts "burning Lab'rinths" (257), the metaphorical space of Hobbes' *ignes fatui,* which are the consequences of abandoning sovereign meaning. In his chapter on "Reason and Science" in *Leviathan,* Hobbes writes:

> To conclude, the light of human minds is perspicuous words, but by exact definitions first snuffed and purged from ambiguity; *reason* is the *pace;* increase of *science,* the *way;* and the benefit of mankind, the *end.* And, on the contrary, metaphors, and senseless and ambiguous words, are like *ignes fatui;* and reasoning upon them is wanderings amongst innumerable absurdities; and their end, contention and sedition, or contempt. (45-46)

The fire, in its wanderings, creates such "innumerable absurdities." In its trajectory, it undoes the "Line" (162), attacking and laying waste the socio-political semiotic system that gives coherence to society: the economic institution, "the *Lombard* Banquers and the *Change*" (236); the legal institution, "the *Tow'r*" (237); and the religious institution, *"Paul's"* (275). It also disrupts the family and destroys the home (255-59), so that the "Infant" is no longer fed, "and meets, instead of milk, a falling tear" (259). Its ultimate target, however, is the institution that gives coherence to all the rest—the institution of kingship itself: "But the main body of the marching foe / Against th'Imperial Palace is designed" (237).

Against this assault, the king stands helpless, an acknowledgment of the limitations of the *ego cogito,* of the sovereign "I" / eye. When the fire appears, the king "wants the pow'r to meet it" (214): he is "the slumbering King" (224), the king surrounded by darkness: "Near as he draws, thick harbingers of smoke / With gloomy pillars, cover all the place" (239). Though he repeats the scientific procedure of the early part of the poem—he "behold[s]" (242), "directs" (243), "orders" (243), "sees" (244) and "lay[s] waste" (244)—all his work is "lost labour" (253). He applies the intellectual process, "all the long night he studies their relief, / How they may be suppli'd, and he may want" (261), but is forced to acknowledge his impotence. The analogy to burning parchment in the king's prayer for divine assistance, "like flying shades before the clowds we show, / And shrink like Parchment in consuming flame" (266), effectively figures the destruction of the traditionally inscribed symbolic order, a destruction that was described by Winstanley in similar terms, when he notes that "the old world . . . is running up like parchment in the fire."

The fire, then, represents the *furor* that threatens civilizations, causing the breakdown of law, the disruption of order. But this breakdown, as the poem acknowledges, also has the function of liberating what lies outside the traditional order, a liberation expressed in the image of ghosts of traitors and witches returning to dance about the fire:

> The Ghosts of Traitors, from the *Bridge* descend
>   With bold Fanatick Spectres to rejoyce:
> About the fire into a Dance they bend,
>   And sing their Sabbath Notes with feeble voice.
>   (223)

As Keith Thomas points out, the sectarians really did bring magic into vogue in a new way, the rise in popular magic during the interregnum often being associated with the practice of enthusiastic religion. But the recurrence of the "witch" image in association with the fire also suggests an equation between it and the liberation of a suppressed other. The fire, by destroying the traditional symbolic order and the efficacy of the king/father, provides an imaginative space where *mater*/matter expresses itself. The loss of the paternal function allows for the return of the maternal, viewed here as terrifying and horrible:

> Thus, to some desert plain, or old wood side,
>   Dire night-hags come from far to dance their

round:
> And o'r brode Rivers on their fiends they ride,
>   Or sweep in clowds above the blasted ground.
>   (248)

Other passing references to the flames as *"Turks"* (246) or *"Hydra*-like" (249) further reinforce this association between the fire and the pagan, the monstrous, the feminine—all that is associated with the illegitimate, that which flies in the King's "Sacred Face" (239).

It is this vision of a godless, kingless, fatherless universe, of a chaotic nature, that is closed off by the miracle, the "more then natural change" (283) brought about by the divinely constructed "Extinguisher" (281). Spirit in matter is, as it were, extinguished and sinks with the flames "into a sleep" (282) the moment God is lined up on the side of the king. This alignment occurs in stanzas 280-87, where God and king become metaphoric substitutes for each other. Stanzas 280-82, in which God first surveys the situation and then dips his glass into "firmamental waters" (281), recall and repeat the earlier stanzas discussed above, where the king, cast in the image of the scientist, decides to "assert the watry Ball" (14). But here God becomes the mechanic par excellence, using technology, the "hollow chrystal Pyramid" (281) (Samuel Johnson rightly notes the "unexpectedly mean" imagery here [1:340]) to master a recalcitrant nature. Conversely it is the king who "God's own place suppli'd" in relation to "the empty"; he is the "Father of the people" who gives them their "daily bread" (286).

With this alliance between monarchy and providence once again established, order is restored in the world. As the image from falconry suggests, a wild and dangerous nature is tamed: God "hoods the flames that to their quarry strove" (281). The *ignes fatui* that threatened the palace of the king are now domesticated, reduced to the "little *Lares*" (282), *lares familiares,* benevolent spirits of the hearth. This submission of nature is further represented by the analogy to the cyclic return of the seasons (284) and the yielding of the earth of its fruit: the "tender blade peeps up to birth, / And straight the green field laugh with promis'd grain" (284).

The submission of London subsequent to this restoration is a more complex image of this process, whereby the principle of order is restored and the natural world is rendered passive. The "Cities request to the King not to leave them" imaginatively reconstitutes a "Loyal London" (the people, we are told, "have not lost their Loyalty by fire" [289]). Thus the ship/city, the metaphor for science, is once again moored to the principle of social and spiritual order. This anchoring in turn permits the emergence of the new London, the realization of the dream of a truly royal science. The desire articulated in the first section of the poem of transmuting "rich Idea's / To fit the levell'd use of humane kind" (166), the hope that "the yet imperfect Ore . . . will be Gold another day" (139), is imaginatively fulfilled in the vision of the new London that emerges from the scientific laboratory:

> Me-thinks already, from this Chymick flame,
>   I see a City of more precious mold:

> Rich as the Town, which gives the *Indies* name,
>   With Silver pav'd, and all divine with Gold.
>
>   (293)

This vision of "a City of more precious mold" dominates the end of the poem as we move from London as process to London as product. The *Loyal London,* as we have seen in the stanzas that describe the ship, is an emblem of the riches of the merchant ship as well as the warship, and this commercial aspect of "loyal London" is now developed. The idealized city of the last stanzas is nature as consumable commodity, being transformed into being-for-us, a universe reduced to "One City of the Universe, / Where some may gain, and all may be suppli'd" (163). As a feminized and passive "Maiden Queen" (297), London's role is to put an end to errancy, to provide certainty, a shore where men come to "unlade" themselves and "depart no more" (300). As a "fam'd Emporium" (302), she is the path which bounds the "mysterious flow" (162) and makes the ocean *"British"* (302).

But even while nature is thus objectified and this triumph of certainty proclaimed, the effect is undermined by the strange conflation of shores that takes place at end of the poem. In the final stanzas, the English city becomes indistinguishable from the foreign countries, the "Eastern Quarries" (3), which war and commerce seek to conquer. In her riches and attractiveness, London becomes a type of the "Spicy shore," of the "Eastern wealth" which is the object of the militaristic and commercial quest. The equation between the non-European world and London is explicit. The city is "rich as the Town which gives the *Indies* name" (293), and the exotic riches of foreign countries are now associated with her shore: "The East with Incense, and the West with Gold" (297). Her "wealthy Coast" (302), and not the coasts of Africa or the Indies, is now the target of both the "vent'rous Merchant" (300) and "Pyrats" (302). The poem thus inadvertently discloses the inherent tendency of rationalism, of which Restoration science is one expression, to return only to what it already knows, the autonomy of consciousness, as Levinas puts it, finding itself "in all its adventures, returning home to itself like Ulysses, who through all his peregrinations is only on the way to his native island." The final stanza suggests this kind of redoubling in the image of the ship rounding the Cape:

> Thus to the Eastern wealth through storms we go;
>   But now, the Cape once doubled, fear no more:
> A constant Trade-wind will securely blow,
>   And gently lay us on the Spicy shore.
>
>   (304)

Dryden, in *Annus Mirabilis,* traces a voyage out that ends only on his native shore, an epistemological and scientific quest that doubles back to find only its point of origin, the old world of God and King.

In conclusion, it could be said that *Annus Mirabilis* (re)creates the symbolic synthesis of the new science with conservative statist and religious forces, a synthesis which, Jacob explains in her discussion of Newtonianism, sustained post-civil-war English society and eventually enabled the settlement of 1688. On a broader historical level, the poem gives expression to the newly emerging ideology of conservative liberalism, that "amalgam of possessive individualism, philosophic and scientific rationalism, authoritarian statism, and natural law market economics," which, Michael Ryan argues, "has served so well as the philosophy of the capitalist class." Latitudinarian social theory, of which, I believe, *Annus Mirabilis* is a reflection, is an early articulation of this ideology, an ideology which justified political and economic imperialism by tying it to a Christianized mechanical philosophy.

On the other hand, *Annus Mirabilis* operates to reveal what exceeds the symbolic synthesis it articulates: it demonstrates the limits of its own ideology of nature, of science and, by extension, of power. As Pierre Macherey notes, it is by means of the work of art that we can escape the domain of lived ideology which always asserts itself as a "false totality" which is "unable to reflect the limitation of its own limits." Because art produces ideology as "a determinate image," it necessarily reveals its constructed and contradictory nature so that even works (like *Annus Mirabilis*) that purport to adopt a clearly ideological position work as much against as in favor of their own position. The effect is never cultural reproduction but is rather cultural ideology "broken, and turned inside out in so far as it is transformed in the text from being a state of consciousness. Art, or at least literature, because it naturally scorns the credulous view of the world, establishes myth and illusion as *visible objects.*" In the fire section and in the final passage on the new London, Dryden inadvertently turns the ideology of the new science inside out, revealing what this discourse represses or repeats in order to maintain its coherence and political viability. In thus articulating difference—the potential for different paradigms of nature and thus for different theological and social paradigms—it could be said that Dryden also indirectly sets the stage for the emergence of other social and epistemological formations, that he gestures toward that more "radical enlightenment," materialistic and republican in emphasis, which was to shake European culture in the second half of the eighteenth century.

Alberto Cacicedo (essay date 1992)

SOURCE: "Seeing the King: Biblical and Classical Texts in *Astraea Redux,*" in *Studies in English Literature,* Vol. 32, No. 3, Summer 1992, pp. 407-27.

[*In the following excerpt, Cacicedo argues that as a depiction of the Restoration, Dryden's poem* Astraea Redux *is not servile as critics have suggested, but that instead it relies upon analogies from the bible and from classical works to provide a realistic view of King Charles as well as of the contemporary political climate under which he was obliged to rule.*]

Panegyric as it is, Dryden's *Astraea Redux* has been the object of much critical scorn. Samuel Johnson articulated the problem clearly when he said that "In the meanness and servility of hyperbolical adulation, I know not whether, since the days in which the Roman emperors were deified, he [Dryden] has ever been equaled." Twentieth-century critics, although taking into account the historic event celebrated in the poem and acknowledging the honest "exultation of an England restored to its monarch" that the poem expresses, nonetheless find Dryden trapped "between ludicrous exaggeration and the majestic assertion of high ideals." The poem may be interesting as a sociological or historical document, or because of its place in Dryden's canon as his earliest sustained effort in the heroic couplet; but surely no critic can take seriously a poem whose typical modes are exaggeration and lofty sentiment. If the poem does indeed oscillate between those two poles, it deserves critical obscurity.

Not surprisingly, given such opinions, critics view *Astraea Redux* in a rather condescending manner. K.G. Hamilton mentions the poem only in reference to that much-lamented line, "An horrid Stillness first invades the ear" (line 7). Paul J. Korshin damns the poem with faint praise when he writes that the reader of the poem "is being instructed that a typological code (a rather simple one, it happens) is in operation." If the poem is fully contextualized, however, it becomes clear that such condescension is not warranted. As Arthur Hoffman recognizes, "Just beneath the surface of compliment are perilous rocks upon which kings have foundered." Those rocks include the suggestion, presented only to be withdrawn, of the millenarian potential of Charles's restoration as well as the political realities by which Charles is translated from a millenarian, metahistorical redeemer to a limited, simply historical one. As I see it, *Astraea Redux* does not oscillate between the ludicrous and the sublime; rather, the poem presents a very clear-eyed image of Charles, his historical significance to England, and the political constraints within which he will be obliged to reign. Central to that presentation is the "typological code" of the poem, perhaps simple but nonetheless producing a complex understanding of the Restoration.

To understand *Astraea Redux* one must first understand its place as one of the poems written for the Restoration. In the general outpouring of joy at the return of Charles II from exile, poets played a significant part. As Leonard Lichfield, the printer of Oxford University's contribution to the barrage of verse written for the Restoration, puts it,

> Nor can we yet give o're; great *CHARLES* his Name
> Inspire's us all with a Poetique flame.
>
> (lines 1-2)

The offerings of the "Poetique flame" come in a great many forms. The City of London's official welcome to Charles, for instance, was an ornate pageant, part of which includes poetic speeches delivered by the allegorical figures of Time, Truth, and Fame, the purport of which is that Charles's return renews time, establishes truth, and reanimates fame. Of course, not all the poems were so ceremonial in purpose or effect. In "The Countrey-mans Vive Le Roy," an anonymous broadside ballad in the form

of a dialogue "between Dick a Plough-man, and Jack a Shephard," Jack urges Dick to go

> To Mother *Mabs* old tipling-house
> Where we will take a smart carouse
> Of her brown nappy Stuff, till we
> Are full of Ale and Loyalty.
>
> (lines 91-94)

The economic aspct of the Restoration was also a source of much poetic joy. In "Song xxxix. On the Kings returne," one of three songs on the Restoration included in Alexander Brome's *Songs and Other Poems,* Brome relishes England's "redemption" from the involuntary offerings exacted by the governments of the Interregnum:

> And when *Civil* wars were past
>   They civil *Government* envade;
> To make our taxes, and our slavery last,
>   Both to their *titles,* and their *trade.*
>
> (lines 11-14)

Brome's economic interest is seconded in the anonymous *The Purchasers Pound,* in which the poet pictures the return, not so much of Charles, monarchy, and due order, but of the "stole goods [that finally] restor'd are" (line 189).

Despite the unevenness of the poems, the evident differences of their approaches to the Restoration, and the variety of subjects that they address, almost without exception the verses written for Charles's return record the people's amazement at the political changes of 1660. The poets of 1660 were keenly aware of the point made forcibly by John Evelyn: "your [Charles's] Virtues are superior to all that passd before you; so is the conjuncture, and the steps by which you are happily ascended to it, Miraculous, and all together stupendous." Evelyn's language suggests the way in which Charles's return was popularly conceived—a miracle, either unparalleled in history or paralleled only by the most significant of historical events. So, Evelyn's religious language is turned allegorical by the tippling Dick and Jack of "The Countrey-mans Vive Le Roy," who understand that Charles's return means that "flocks will now with safety feed, / . . . / Free from the danger of the beast" (lines 43-45). The fact, of course, was that Charles's restoration meant also the restoration of the pre-Civil Wars religious establishment—for instance, the recovered goods envisioned in *The Purchasers Pound* are all ecclesiastical. Dick and Jack in effect give the restoration of due and proper religion a clearly millenarian turn.

The millenarian implication of "The Countrey-mans Vive Le Roy" is, to say the least, not unusual in the poetic output of 1660. Time after time, in poems as rough as "The Countrey-mans Vive Le Roy" or as deeply considered as *To the King, Upon His Majesties Happy Return,* by "a Person of Honour," poets attempt to picture or figure Charles, to see him in all the fullness of his significance to English history and to history itself. Indeed history is one of the recurring means by which poets attempt to give Charles his proper significance in all of his functions. Readers are constantly being told that Charles is like this great man or that great man. More often than not, however, the poems find in Charles an apocalyptic historical significance, as a consequence of which Charles is presented as Christ returned. As the "Person of Honour" says,

> Twice has the World been trusted in a Barque;
> The New, the *Charles* contain'd, the Old, the Ark;
> This bore but those who did the World re-build,
> But that bore You, to whom that World must yeild.
>
> (lines 63-66)

Thomas Mayhew agrees, for Charles brings

> those Tidings, which none other might;
> Tidings of peace on Earth, which the most High
> Committed onely to his Embassy:
> For Heav'n decreed no Mercy to dispence,
> But through the Conduct of his Influence?
>
> (lines, 151-55)

In comparison to such poems, Dryden's *Astraea Redux* is not unusually adulatory.

Steven Zwicker argues that Dryden's "abrupt shift of [political] loyalties from *Heroique Stanzas* to *Astraea Redux*" is not as significant as Dryden's movement from the "profound uncertainty" of 1659 to a new assurance in 1660 about how the problems of the nation might be resolved. Like many of his contemporaries, in fact, Dryden in *Astraea Redux* is attempting to present as comprehensive an image of Charles and of his significance as is possible, but he is also aware of the danger of falling into what the anonymous author of *A Glimpse of Joy* calls "Anthropolatry" (line 38). Consequently, Dryden works mightily *not* to overreach himself. It is not an easy task to accomplish, particularly because Charles's return is not only a secular restoration of rightful government but also the restoration of "true" religion. It is, in fact, in representing the religious significance of Charles's return that poets struggle and, often, fail. In *Rebellion's Downfall,* for instance, John Quarles focuses so closely on the parallel between England and Old Testament Israel that he suggests that Charles's Restoration is a return to a pre-Christian dispensation. By contrast, the Charles that Dryden presents works within a Christian milieu and is, potentially, of metahistorical importance. But Dryden does not fall into the opposite problem, of presenting Charles as, for instance, Arthur Brett does in *The Restauration,* a completely metahistorical figure:

> Great Charles unto large Empire born,
> Has had his Crown made all of Thorn;
> Now hee'l have one of better Stuffe,
> If Lumbard-street have Gold enough.
>
> (lines 113-16)

The rhythm and diction of the passage qualifies the statement that Brett makes, but nonetheless it is clear that *his* Charles transcends the merely human and approaches the divine, as if he were in fact Christ come again to end history.

What makes *Astraea Redux* unusual in the context of other poems written for the Restoration is the self-consciousness of its efforts to present and limit Charles's potential. Dryden cannot fully represent Charles's religious significance by figuring him in typological terms, as an Old Testament character, nor can he fully represent Charles's limitations by figuring him in antitypological terms, as Christ come again. To mediate between type and antitype, Dryden includes a second, classical context to figure Charles. The relationship between the biblical and classical contexts is difficult to determine, however. Stephen Zwicker, for example, begins his comments on the poem by emphasizing the classical element. After two paragraphs, however, Zwicker turns his attention to the means by which Dryden makes Charles into a Christic figure, and the biblical, typological element dominates to the end of the analysis, where Zwicker off-handedly remarks that "the poem closes with . . . a reference to Charles's nativity star, and a Virgilian welcome to a new golden age." It is the apparent interchangeability of the two figural contexts that leads Paul Korshin to categorize Dryden's use of typology in *Astraea Redux* as simple on the one hand and "abstracted" on the other, a kind of "nonvisual iconography" meant to suggest, to those able to read the signs, the connections between the historic present and the biblical past. Dryden uses biblical types, says Korshin, merely to situate Charles and the Restoration within a historical continuum. Classical figures, which serve the same function, are according to Korshin therefore not different in kind from biblical figures.

Korshin's argument has its roots in the Renaissance tradition of reading classical myth as a confused, post-Babel rendering of biblical wisdom and prophecy. In the Preface to *Religio Laici,* indeed, Dryden himself argues that "what *Socrates* said of him [God], what *Plato* writ, and the rest of Heathen Philosophers of several Nations, is all no more than the Twilight of Revelation, after the Sun of it was set in the Race of *Noah*" (*Works,* 2:100). As Korshin emphasizes, moreover, it was not only pagan philosophers who were made to yield Christian wisdom: "the search for typological parallels to Christianity in pagan mythology continued virtually unabated" from the first to the seventeenth centuries. Speculation on the meaning of pagan myth led to moralized versions of classical texts, of course. As humanists applied allegorical modes of reading more and more consistently to the myths, moreover, they "discovered in mythology something other and much greater than a concealed morality: they discovered religious teaching—the Christian doctrine itself." The discovery of Christian ideas in classical mythology leads to precisely the leveling of the two traditions that Korshin and Allen trace so effectively. In the mid-seventeenth century, however, in matters of Christian doctrine and theology, the leveling has yet to occur. Even in the groups most prone to affirming the intersection of the two traditions, in fact, theological ideas still force the separation of Christian from pagan. So the Cambridge Platonist John Smith argues that ancient Platonists had available to them a methodology by which to recover religious truth from pagan myth, and he affirms that the Platonists of old were perfectly correct to prize "The true Metaphysical and Contemplative man": nonetheless, "by the *Platonists* leave such a *Life* and *Knowledge* as this is, peculiarly belongs to the true and sober Christian who lives in Him who is *Life* itself, and is enlightened by Him who is *Truth* itself." In effect, Christian truth appropriates pagan method and idea to show the superiority of the biblical approach. Not surprisingly, Smith ends his discourse with the language of biblical typological exegesis.

The best known instance in the seventeenth century of the "contamination of pagan and Christian material," as Don Cameron Allen says of *Comus,* is in Milton's poetic practice. So, in *Paradise Lost,* the Satanic legions include

> Th' *Ionian* gods, of *Javan's* Issue held
> Gods, yet confessed later than Heav'n and Earth,
> Their boasted Parents.
>
> (1:508-10)

And yet, "On the Morning of Christ's Nativity" gives a far better sense of Milton's idea of how pagan myth and Christian dispensation are connected:

> The Oracles are dumb,
> No voice or hideous hum
>   Runs through the arched roof in words deceiving.
> *Apollo* from his shrine
> Can no more divine,
>   With hollow shriek the steep of *Delphos* leaving.
> No nightly trance, or breathed spell,
> Inspires the pale-ey'd Priest from the prophetic cell.
>
> (lines 173-80)

The impotence of the silenced pagan gods is reflected in their absence from Milton's doctrinal and political analyses. *The Reason of Church Government* illustrates the point, albeit from a relatively conservative point of view. In chapter three of the work, Milton argues that prelacy imitates the "ministry which engendered to bondage the sons of Agar" and so is simply

> a cancelling of that birthright and immunity which Christ hath purchased for us with his blood. . . . For the ministration of the law, consisting of carnal things, drew to it such ministry as consisted of carnal respects, dignity, precedence, and the like. . . . If the religion be pure, spiritual, simple, and lowly, as the Gospel most truly is, such must the face of the ministry be.

In the next two chapters Milton shows that the prelatical form of government depends on a misreading of type and antitype. The "type of priest is taken away by Christ's coming," he says, and consequently the "right of jurisdiction . . . must descend upon the ministers of the gospel equally." Milton's language focuses entirely on the analysis of biblical types, and uses the analysis to inform his politics and ecclesiology.

Milton's use of biblical typology for such doctrinal and political analyses is typical of even more radical theoreti-

cians of sainthood, who argued for a jurisdiction distributed to *all* believers, again on typological grounds. So, Richard Sibbes, examining the relationship between Old Testament types, Christians, and Christ, finds that the Old Testament Israelites "could not see the drift and scope of his [Moses'] ministry, by reason of the types and shadows, which was 'the veil he put upon his face.'" For Christians, however, "the gospel in the spirit and efficacy of it cometh home to their hearts, and taketh off 'the veil that is upon their hearts' also," so that "this ministry of the gospel . . . will 'change' them even 'into the image of Jesus Christ, and carry them on still in that image and likeness, from one degree of glory to another.'" There is no indication at all in Sibbes's work of a similar doctrinal application to classical figures. Indeed, Sibbes's argument depends heavily on the language of image and likeness rooted in biblical texts.

The popular expression of such a perspective on typology, found in the sermons and tracts addressed to the common people, also depends on biblical typology simply because it implodes Sibbes's careful language of "image and likeness," so that the Christian believer becomes an antitypical counterpart of Christ himself. An extreme but not rare formulation of such a perspective is found in the works of John Saltmarsh, one of the leading ministers in the New Model Army. Saltmarsh argues that the "Kingdom of Christ" is "a company of godly gathered by his owne Spirit, having their Lord and Saviour in the midst, confederated by an holy and sacramental paction, ruled by the law of his Will and Spirit; obeying his commands, whether in silent inspirations, or louder exhortations." That Saltmarsh conceives of this "kingdom of Christ" literally as the New Jerusalem of Revelation, and so conceives of the "godly gathered" as antitypes of Old Testament figures, is made clear in his *Sparkles of Glory.* Before the fall, says Saltmarsh, man "being the glorious and bright *sum* or *whole* of the [first] *Creation,* was a *figure* and type of the *Son of God,* Jesus Christ." With man's disobedience and fall, however, the first creation became "but *earthly* or *fleshly* in the *Spirits* account, and as it stands in distinction to the second *Creation,* or new man, or *Lord* from heaven." The second creation, the world of the spirit, is Christ, "that *glory*" of God in which "the *Father* is revealed." But Christ represents more than a revelation of the world of the spirit. He is God as well as spirit, and so can work upon the souls of men and bring them to sit within the circle of eternity while they are still in this earthly life: "The *Sons of men* taken into this *glory* of the *Son of God,* are that new or second Creation, that *new Jerusalem,* which came down from God, the *city of the living God,* the *spirits* of *just men* made *perfect,* the *new creature,* the *heavenly men.*" There is, in effect, no need to wait for the millennium. Saltmarsh argues that the "saints" of the Civil Wars are identical to Christ, antitypes in themselves. For him, the political liberties of the Interregnum follow from the perfection of the "heavenly men."

Arguments such as Saltmarsh's, based on specifically biblical typology, were not rare in the Interregnum. As a consequence, for Dryden and for those who read his poems in 1660, biblical typology is not only a familiar linguistic code: it is a code fraught with the danger of millenarian enthusiasm. In *Astraea Redux,* indeed, Dryden is very conscious of the dangers implicit in adulation that overreaches itself and presents Charles as the inaugurator of the millennium. Classical types, because they support Christian superiority generally but do not favor one doctrinal perspective over another, are not burdened with the political baggage of the Civil Wars and Interregnum. For Dryden and his contemporaries, biblical and classical figures are very different in kind.

From its beginning, *Astraea Redux* presents classical and biblical imagery in so intimately connected a fashion that each allusive context becomes the essential completion of the other. To see the full scope of the collaboration one must remember that Dryden seeks to present the full pattern of Charles's exile and return. With that in mind, one sees that, in the first verse paragraph, exile is presented in classical terms, whereas return appears in biblical terms. Dryden borrowed the description of Britain as "a World divided from the rest" (line 2) from Virgil's First Eclogue, in which Meliboeus complains about the exile of rustics during the reign of Augustus Caesar. That reference leads to the development of more general classical images of exile. Charles's exile becomes parallel to Jove's exile,

> when the bold *Typhoeus* scal'd the sky
> And forc'd great *Jove* from his own Heaven to fly.
> (lines 37-38)

The "Rabble" (line 43), which Dryden conceives to be the agent of Charles's exile, is in turn likened to Typhoeus in his expression as a natural force, "Winds at Sea" (line 44), and to

> our painted Ancestours . . .
> Ere Empires Arts their Breasts had Civiliz'd.
> (lines 47-48)

As Dryden then explains (lines 76-78), while in exile, Charles learns the arts of government with which he—like Julius Caesar, the civilizer of those "painted Ancestours"—will be able to tame the British rabble. From the point of view of the pattern of exile and return, the problem with the reference, of course, is that Caesar is not exiled as Charles—or Jove for that matter—is, and that the civilizing of the "painted Ancestours" does not suggest the return of a rightful monarch to his alienated throne. Indeed, the classical figuration that begins with the likening of Charles to Jove and the people of England to Typhoeus dies, so to speak, with Jove still in exile.

Return and restoration do not appear in *Astraea Redux* until the poem's biblical context is made explicit:

> Thus banish'd *David* spent abroad his time,
> When to be God's Anointed was his Crime;
> And when restor'd made his proud Neighbours rue
> Those choise Remarques he from his Travels drew.
> (lines 79-82)

The explicit biblical reference here also brings overtly to the surface the biblical allusive context that has been present in the poem from the beginning. England's division from the rest of the world, after all, depends on the fact that it is at war while "Now with a general Peace the World was blest" (line 1). Dryden grounds that peace in the historical here and now of 1660, when Europe seemed miraculously peaceful after the adventurism of Charles X of Sweden (lines 9-12) and as a result of the mutual wooing of France and Spain that culminated in the marriage of Louis XIV to the Infanta Maria Theresa (lines 13-18). But the line also suggests the historically key "general Peace" of the *Pax Romana,* first established under Augustus Caesar, to whom the allusion to Virgil's First Eclogue refers us, and into which Christ was born.

Parallels between Christ and Charles follow in the rest of the first verse paragraph. Charles, for instance, "Was forc'd to suffer for Himself and us" (line 50). He endured his "Banishment," moreover, like those whose "Souls reach Heav'n while yet in Bodies pent" (lines 59-60), that is to say, like Ezekiel and Elijah, both types of Christ, and ultimately like Christ himself. Raised thus high "above his Banishment," Charles can legitimately be likened to "That Sun . . . / . . . [which] mov'd along the skies" (lines 60-62). In the context of the poem's references to Charles's martyred father, the commonplace quibble on sun/son becomes emphatic in the poem and takes a millenarian turn: Charles II will make good the execution of Charles I much as the militant Christ of the second coming will make good the execution of the suffering Christ of the first coming. The relationship is complicated by the fact that Charles II also suffers—so, for instance, the poet considers Charles's exile much as a good Christian must consider Christ's travails on earth:

> How shall I then my doubtful thoughts express,
> That must his suff'rings both regret and bless.
> (lines 71-72)

Whether to the suffering or to the militant Christ, however, Christic references abound in the first verse paragraph.

Many of the Christic references arise from the same lines as do the classical references. The impression that the double context of the imagery gives is that the England of 1660 is much like the Palestine of Christ's time. It might follow, therefore, that a man who is typically related to Old Testament figures—as Charles in the first verse paragraph is connected with David by means of their common experiences of exile and restoration—and who is also given Christ-like characteristics could well be figured as antitype. In the words of Saltmarsh, Charles could be considered one of the *"just men* made *perfect"* who, in his political role as king, is the redeemer himself. Dryden allows the suggestion to be present in the poem, and in doing so hints at Charles's potential for being a metahistorical redeemer, Christ come again in the end times of 1660. And yet, Dryden is very careful to give sharp limits to Charles's redemptive potential. It is clear that Charles does not come like the avenging Christ of Revelation: no "raging floods" are his, but rather the "kindly heat of lengthned day" (lines 134-36). More importantly, Dryden demonstrates that Charles's political success is bought at the price of his spiritual, redemptive potential. Charles's "future rule" is "To bus'ness ripened by digestive thought" (lines 89-90): he is transformed by his historical context into a politician, significant in English history, of course, and perhaps in European history as well—but certainly not of metahistorical importance. The "digestive thought," moreover, is likened to the art of painting, in particular the optical illusion of "Proportion" produced, after much practice, by "a Masters hand" (lines 91-92).

The artifice of Charles's "future rule" is part of a series of images in the poem, all associated with erroneous perception. The "Vulgar" who rebel against monarchy in the first place are "gull'd into Rebellion" by their "designing Leaders" (lines 31-33). The "Rabble" who then rule in the place of due government are like the "painted Ancestours" eventually civilized by Caesar's "Arts" and so made pliable to empire (lines 43-48). The victorious rabble is "cous'ned" when it perceives "That Sun," the apparently fallen Charles, as its reflection "Within the water" while in fact it "mov'd along the skies" (lines 61-62). The gullibility of the people continues even after the political tide has turned. So, the "blessed change" that the people experience in Charles's return is effected "as wise Artists mix their colours" so that

> Black steals unheeded from the neighb'ring white,
> Without offending the well-cous'ned sight.
>
> (lines 125-30)

The people are gulled again, this time into believing that the return of Charles is something that they desire in an unforced, inartificial way. In fact, Charles—"The Prince of Peace" (line 139), as Dryden, echoing Isaiah 9:6, calls him at this point with what must be considered a good dose of irony—was eager to make the people know his worth, and so "took care . . . That we should know it [i.e. his worth] by repeated pray'r" (lines 141-42). Charles's political "wisdom," moreover, is matched by General Monk's method of preparing the Restoration. Monk too is an artist, whose

> Pencils can by one slight touch restore
> Smiles to that changed face that wept before.
>
> (lines 157-58)

He too performs his actions on the basis of "wisdom," "the well-ripened fruit of wise delay" (line 170).

Like the "bus'ness" to which Charles is "ripened" during his exile, Monk's "wise delay" allows him to seem to do one thing while in fact he accomplishes something very different. The result of Monk's stratagems, of course, is Charles's return itself, the subject of *Astraea Redux.* Here too Dryden's language picks up the imagery of artifice and erroneous perception, but now applied to Charles himself:

> Behold th'approaching cliffes of *Albion;*
> It is no longer Motion cheats your view,
> As you meet it, the Land approacheth you.
>
> (lines 251-53)

The final irony of the imagery of erroneous perception is that, now that Charles too is cheated by his perceptions, the people come to see him as what he can no longer be, a millenarian redeemer:

> That Star that at your Birth shone out so bright
> It stain'd the duller Suns Meridian light,
> Did once again its potent Fires renew
> Guiding our eyes to find and worship you.
>
> (lines 288-91)

The language of perception is by this point in the poem so evidently fraught with ambiguity, that the millenarian implication of these lines is made null and void. The classical coda of the poem, invoking as it does "Time's whiter Series" (line 292) and the "times like those alone / By Fate reserv'd for Great *Augustus* Throne!" (lines 320-21), on the one hand returns the poem to the classical imagery with which it begins—in some sense it rounds off the reference to Augustus in the allusion to Virgil's First Eclogue: but in doing so, it also sets the biblical, millenarian references of the poem at an ironic distance, and avows the political rather than spiritual character of Charles's return.

Politically speaking, of course, Charles's mastery of the arts of government is an absolute necessity. Without those arts he would be like Julius Caesar without "Empires Arts," incapable of civilizing the Typhoeus-like rabble of England. Charles will, after all, govern a "too too active age" which seems to be "govern'd by the wild distemper'd rage / Of some black Star infecting all the Skies"; but it is precisely the political wisdom of Charles's mastery that "Made him at his own cost like *Adam* wise" (lines 111-14). For Dryden's purposes, the highly ambiguous character of the reference to Adam is crucial: Adam is, of course, a biblical type, and so suggests the potential importance that Charles has in God's universal scheme; but given the context of the reference, it would be impossible to make Charles in any way antitypical. On the contrary, Charles is likened to Adam at a point in Adam's career that makes it impossible to see him as pure, spiritual, or redemptive. The reference also puts in a less than flattering context all of the "wisdom" of artifice that Charles, and Monk as well, have deployed in the course of maneuvering towards the Restoration.

The "wisdom" of Charles is a mark of the political reality into which he descends from his potential as millenarian redeemer. But while the decline of Charles from his potential to his reality—in short, the restoration of Charles—is conveyed in terms of the biblical imagery itself, beyond the first verse paragraph the political reality as such is presented in terms of the poem's classical imagery. Sandwiched between the reference to Adam in his post-lapsarian, "wise" condition and the ironic reference to Charles as "The Prince of Peace," for instance, comes an allusion to the sea race episode from the *Aeneid* (5:138-372). The part of the episode to which Dryden makes specific reference involves the crucial point in the race, when Cloanthus

> to the seas . . . holds his hands,
> And succour from the wat'ry pow'rs demands:

"Gods of the liquid realms, on which I row!
If, giv'n by you, the laurel bind my brow,
Assist to make me guilty of my vow!
A snow-white bull shall on your shore be slain;
His offer'd entrails cast into the main,
And ruddy wine, from golden goblets thrown,
Your grateful gift and my return shall own."

(5:303-11)

The "wisdom" of Cloanthus's prayer is emphasized by the fact that, up to that point, Mnestheus, his rival, was close enough so that both he and Cloanthus might well have "shar'd an equal prize" (5:302). Cloanthus's "guilt," then, is not only the debt that he owes the gods of the sea, but also the willingness to politicize the race in order to have himself crowned victor without actually meriting the prize. Similarly, the mercy that Charles will show to the rebels whom he has by indirection conquered is presented in classical terms:

Suffer'd to live, they are like *Helots* set,
A vertuous shame within us to beget.

(lines 205-206)

One must remember that *Astraea Redux* does not radically separate classical from biblical figures. On the contrary, the two sets of images work together, sometimes arising from the same lines, in order to present Charles's potential and reality as complexly and fully as possible. In *Exultationis Carmen*, Rachel Jevone might serve as a point of contrast to *Astraea Redux*. Like Dryden, Jevone presents Charles in relation to biblical and classical imagery, to which she adds a significant number of natural images not associated with either allusive context. Classical and natural imagery predominates in the first two-thirds of the poem, where Jevone develops the circumstances that surround Charles and his return. Indeed, for most of the poem Jevone refers the reader interchangeably to classical figures or to natural images. At one point Jevone writes of "The Deities of *Pontus* flowing stream" (line 56) that calmed the Channel during Charles's voyage from Holland to Dover; later, the same Channel crossing is presented in terms that do not involve any classical figures:

Loe how the late revolted Sea obeys,
How gladly it the Billows prostrate lays
Before Your Royal Navy, proud to bring
Three widow'd Kingdoms their espoused King!

(lines 96-99)

The two passages are in effect interchangeable, the "Deities" being simply a mode of expressing the natural phenomenon described more fully in the second passage. Jevone intends the reference to Pontus to be read exactly as are the floral references to the various countries in which Charles spent periods of his exile: England is the royal oak, France the lily, Spain the olive, etc. Natural and classical images both are simply emblematic.

The same is not true of Jevone's presentation of Charles himself, where classical and biblical imagery come into sharp conflict. In representing Charles, Jevone sometimes invokes classical imagery that likens Charles to the great men of classical antiquity. For instance, she calls Charles a "Milde *Caesar*, born of Heav'nly Race" (line 13), and later says that Caesar and Charles are each a "Terrestrial God, offspring of Heaven" (line 122). The sense of "Heav'nly" and "Heaven" in these passages is problematic, however, particularly because "Heaven" also appears as part of the later biblical imagery of the poem. The reader is therefore left in doubt about the nature of the heaven from which Caesar and Charles descend: is the image intended to be emblematic, like Pontus and the oak, or does it bear a more profound sense? In the case of Charles the ambiguity is compounded by Jevone's insistence that his ancestors "Long since outshin'd the golden *Phoebus* far," and that Charles himself is

The living Image of our Martyr'd King,
For us His People freely suffering.

(lines 16-17)

The language here is redolent with Christic significance, ambiguous because of the classical context in which it appears, but tending towards the exaltation of Charles.

One can argue that Jevone is attempting to perform the same tightrope act that Dryden carries off in *Astraea Redux*. If so, however, the final third of *Exultationis Carmen* demonstrates how easily a poet can slip from the high wire. The exaltation of Charles in the poem culminates when Jevone focuses on the effect of the Restoration on the people of England and on Charles himself. Englishmen

as C[or]ps inanimate lay,
Till You (*Our Breath*) repaired our decay.

(lines 126-27)

The revivification of the human clay, already suggesting a typical—perhaps antitypical—task for Charles, leads to an extended metaphor in which Charles's effect on his people is paralleled to Phoebus's effect on all the earth, *"Tellus,"*

when with glorious Lamp he views,
Earth after Winter,
[And] tender grass renews.

(lines 128-31)

Here Apollo seems to serve an emblematic role much like that of Pontus. But where Apollo's effect is a natural one, Charles's is a supernatural one, "Enlightning all to bring forth Fruits Divine" (line 133).

The character of those "Fruits," moreover, is clearly millenarian. As a result of the Restoration, Jevone says, Charles's "Fates"

have reacht the skies,
And from the appeased Deity brought down
T'adorn Your Sacred Temples many a Crown,

all of them descended from the true "Heaven of Heavens" (lines 136-41). Significantly, the number of the crowns is five, and their sequence invites a millenarian reading. The first three crowns represent Charles's heavenly glory, then his spiritual virtue, then his people's love for him.

The Fourth's compleat by Your high Charity,
Which hath subdu'd and pardon'd th' enemy.
The Fifth shall shine with Gold and Jewels bright,
Upon Your Head, *O Monarch!* our Delight;
Where the Almighty grant it flourish may,
Until in Heaven You shine with Glorious Ray.

                                        (lines 146-51)

Although relatively indirect, to ears accustomed to the language of the "saints," Jevone's reference to the fifth monarchy must be evident. Certainly Jevone's depiction of post-Restoration England is, indeed, frankly millenarian:

    Leap for joy ye Beasts of every Plain
    Behold Your King (the Lion) comes to Reign.

                                        (lines 166-67)

Jevone struggles with precisely the same problem that Dryden does: how does one see the king aright? What is the limitation of his significance? At what point does the construction of the king's significance overstep the bounds of reasonability and invite a millenarian reading that in effect subverts the authority of the secular ruler? For Jevone as for Dryden, the method by which the significance of the king is presented revolves around two major sets of images, one classical and the other biblical. In the case of Jevone, however, the biblical imagery, coming at the end of the poem, overwhelms the classical, so that the reader ends the poem concluding that Charles's return in fact represents the beginning of the millennium.

It is precisely such a suggestion, fraught with dangers as it is, that Dryden does not allow to stand in *Astraea Redux*. The "simple code" of the poem manages to suggest that the millennium—expected every day in 1660 and into 1666, that "year of wonder," though it might be—must be resolutely discounted, must be transformed into political reality. To do otherwise is to be like the "Zealous Missions" who pervert religion by allowing the typical "shadow" to "invade" the antitypical "substance" (lines 191-94). The classical context of *Astraea Redux* is presented in intimate connection with its biblical context specifically to demonstrate the limits of typology applied to contemporary figures. Indeed, for even the zealots, the "Heaven" that they imitate turns out to be a classical one: the

        horses hoofs that beat the ground,
    And Martial brass, bely the thunders sound.

                                        (lines 196-98)

Ambitious though their self-conception is, the zealots offer a mere pale imitation of Jove's weapon. Charles returned is, finally, Jove taming a political Typhoeus with the proper tools: not apocalypse, but politic wisdom.

Susan C. Greenfield   (essay date 1995)

SOURCE: "Aborting the 'Mother Plot': Politics and Generation in *Absalom and Achitophel*," in *ELH*, Vol. 62, No. 2, Summer 1995, pp. 267-93.

[In the following excerpt, Greenfield observes that a marked ambiguity in Dryden's poem Absalom and Achitophel *reflects the confusion and changing attitudes toward sexual biology, succession, and the monarchy which occurred during his era.]*

Although critics have discussed the connections between fatherhood and kingship in *Absalom and Achitophel,* nobody has yet attended to the poem's less obvious, but equally important and politically-charged representations of maternity. *Absalom and Achitophel* begins and ends with references to mothers: the opening describes how, despite the queen's infertility, the lustful David has still managed to create "several Mothers" (13), and the poem concludes with David's stunning image of a "Viper-like" destruction of the "Mother Plot" against him (1013). Indeed, the shift between these framing images of maternity is a central mechanism in the poem's royalist resolution. For if the text initially suggests that David has so actively turned women into mothers that he bears at least some responsibility for the birth of the rebel son, it ends by transferring the blame for the insurrection onto the Mother Plot, as if only the female power of generation threatens familial and political order and must be suppressed. The shift works because by the time David redeems himself in his speech, the poem's emphasis on his promiscuity has been effaced by increasing references to a feminine sexual desire and productivity so dangerous that the king appears politically reliable by contrast.

Before considering the poem closely it is useful to review the cultural—and specifically political and medical—context for its familial and sexual details. Much has been written about the way the king was viewed as the ultimate patriarch of a family of subjects. But to appreciate Dryden's attack on maternity, it is also important to recognize that the most popular patriarchal political theory of the period—best articulated in Sir Robert Filmer's *Patriarcha* (1680)—was fundamentally structured around the erasure of the mother. In trying to prove that "the first kings were fathers of families" and that "kings now are the fathers of their people," for instance, Filmer points out that "the law which enjoins obedience to kings is delivered in the terms of 'honour thy father' . . . as if all power were originally in the father."

As Locke later suggests time and again in his *Two Treatises of Government* (1690), Filmer is clearly manipulative here, "for God [actually] says, *Honour thy Father and Mother;* but our Author . . . leaves out *thy Mother* quite, as little serviceable to his purpose." Locke here is neither especially interested in biblical accuracy nor in the question of women's rights but rather in the dynamics of political rhetoric. Arguing against unconditional and exclusive monarchal authority, he understands that in general the paternal argument can work only if the role of the mother is denied, because to acknowledge her would suggest that the fathering-king does not have an inherent right to unilateral control. It thus logically follows that to introduce the idea of mother is to disrupt the patriarchal justification of kingship:

> It will but very ill serve the turn of those Men who
> contend so much for the Absolute Power and Authority

of the *Fatherhood* . . . that the *Mother* should have any share in it. And it would have but ill supported the *Monarchy* they contend for, when by the very name it appeared that the Fundamental Authority from whence they would derive their Government of a single Person only, was not plac'd in one, but two Persons joyntly.

Critics have pointed out that this is hardly a feminist argument since Locke "uses the mother's 'equal Title' as a *reductio ad absurdum* to refute the derivation of political from parental authority." That is, he uses her to prove the inherent separateness of parenthood and state. Nevertheless, it is worth noting how, by concentrating on the threat maternity poses to any conservative understanding of monarchy, Locke ironically demonstrates the mother's political utility.

The *Two Treatises,* composed during the 1680s but published anonymously nearly a decade after **Absalom and Achitophel,** did not have a direct influence on the poem. But, as Steven Zwicker suggests, Locke's and Dryden's texts are usefully read in relation to each other (as well as to Filmer's *Patriarcha*) "as contemporary rhetorical and political events, as competing interpretations of the origins of government, the nature of royal authority, and the political meaning of paternity and patriarchy." Locke is particularly useful in the context of the present discussion about maternity because he articulates an implicit tension in patriarchal theory that was already long evident, clarifying one position about motherhood in an ongoing debate about the relationship between political and familial power. In both *De Cive* (1642) and *Leviathan* (1651), for instance, Hobbes had already implied that fatherhood could not be the ultimate grounds upon which sovereignty is based because "the originall Dominion over *children* belongs to the *Mother*. . . . The birth followes the belly." If in many political systems the father acquired control over the mother and young, that was simply the consequence of "Civill Law[s]" that privileged him, resulting from the fact that "for the most part Common-wealths have been erected by the Fathers, not by the Mothers of families." Thus, paternal power was a sign of conquest but not unquestionable governmental entitlement. Fully understanding that any successful argument about the mother's natural authority could dismantle his defense of monarchy, Filmer challenged Hobbes in his *Observations Concerning the Originall of Government* (1652) by countering: "But we know that God at the creation gave the sovereignty to the man over the woman, as being the nobler and principal agent in generation."

Significantly, Filmer here promotes not just the idea of paternal power, but also a specific theory of conception, maintaining that the father plays the more active role in generation and refusing "any acknowledgement of the capacity and creativity that is unique to women." Hobbes was not alone in deconstructing such arguments by suggesting that the mother was the more important creator. John Hall in his *Of Government and Obedience as They Stand Directed and Determined by Scripture and Reason* (1654) reminds his readers that the mother "hath part of her own substance imployed in nourishment of the young whilst it is within her." And Locke is even more explicit:

For no body can deny but that the Woman hath an equal share, if not the greater, as nourishing the Child a long time in her own Body out of her own Substance. There it is fashion'd, and from her it receives the Materials and Principles of its Constitution; And it is so hard to imagine the rational Soul should presently Inhabit the yet unformed Embrio, as soon as the Father has done his part in the Act of Generation, that if it must be supposed to derive any thing from the Parents, it must certainly owe most to the Mother.

There is something else at stake here in addition to the problem of governmental succession. Whether or not the authors were deliberately referring to specific medical theories (and Locke, originally trained in medicine, may well have been), the contrast between their accounts of generation is also characteristic of contemporary scientific debates. Filmer's emphasis on paternal agency evokes the then still popular Aristotelian notion that the female contributes the matter or passive principle in conception and the male the efficient or active one that creates the movement necessary for the embryo to develop. Like a sculptor "the male model[s] or mould[s] this [female] material into a form like itself." Aristotle himself explains: "the female always provides the material, the male that which fashions it. . . . While the body is from the female, it is the soul that is from the male."

In his pathbreaking *De Generatione Animalium* (1651), William Harvey challenged Aristotle's emphasis on female subordination and argued that both the mother and father provided the efficient cause of generation. It is unclear exactly how much influence he believed the female primordium had, but Harvey did argue that the material carried by the mother contained its own "power to develop," that was then ignited by the semen (by contagion, not direct contact). Harvey also suggested that the womb functioned as a kind of brain that "conceived" the fetus like an idea, but this was not necessarily evidence of maternal power since Harvey considered the uterus an independent organism and also believed that the fetus's life did not depend on the mother's. Those scientists who, unlike Harvey, favored preformation theory (believing that the offspring existed fully formed at conception) were much more willing to credit a single parent with the power to shape the child, insisting that "only one sex could donate the true embryo." By the end of the seventeenth century there were two competing groups in this category of thinkers: the ovists, who argued that the whole embryo existed preformed in the ovary, and the animalculists, who claimed the same for the sperm.

Locke's account of generation blends and revises a number of these medical theories. He never questions the Aristotelian idea that the woman supplies the matter for the embryo, but Locke does insist that it is primarily the work of pregnancy—and not the act of the sperm—that fashions the female material into a child. Contesting both the notion that the father gives the soul, and those who had begun to claim that the embryo exists fully formed in either the sperm or the egg, Locke emphasizes the process of development, reasoning that because the embryo grows in the mother, she most influences the child's outcome.

Despite their very different scientific assumptions, both Filmer and Locke, like Hobbes and Hall, assume that discourses about the body and state overlap, and they recognize that any representation of conception is thus a political act. This sense of integration was obviously influenced by their own system of government, figured in the body of a ruler who passed his power through genetic descent. At the same time, though, recent historical events—most importantly the execution of Charles I—had proved that the royal succession could be broken. The classic seventeenth-century patriarchalism that linked monarchal and paternal procreative power would not endure. As Carole Pateman explains, "Filmer's father . . . stands *at the end* of a very long history of traditional patriarchal argument in which the creation of political society has been seen as a masculine act of birth." In challenging the logic of a political theory based on paternal procreation, Locke's arguments articulate and anticipate permanent changes in the understanding of the origin of government.

Absalom and Achitophel is situated at the crossroads of this change. As he seeks to develop a pragmatic and contemporary defense of monarchal authority, Dryden appropriates and discards various procreation narratives along the way, moving from a story of paternal conception reminiscent of Filmer's, to an account of maternal creativity that anticipates Locke's. When Dryden finally abandons the model of patriarchal generation at the end of the poem, he, like Locke, marks the cultural turn against the traditional emphasis on masculine birth as well as his own wariness of the role of paternity in political argument. But unlike Locke's work, Dryden's narrative is designed to support the king, and more specifically, to resolve the generative problems posed by Monmouth's bid for the throne. Because the poem recounts the details of the Exclusion C sis, which, after all, involved an illegitimate son's challenge to the promiscuous king who had conceived him, the paternal control of conception is necessarily associated, not with the king's authority, but rather with his vulnerability. David is ultimately acquitted of his role in this generative act when maternal creative power, far from signalling a Lockean need to reconsider the origin of government, emerges as the primary and most dangerous source of any challenge to the status quo. For Dryden it is the very variety and ideological flexibility of accounts of generation that make them useful, and he shapes and reshapes conception to suit his changing narrative needs.

Absalom and Achitophel is centrally organized around the connection between generation and politics because the challenge to the king's authority comes from his illegitimate son. One of the main questions throughout is: who is to blame for producing the unlawful child who, in turn, helps produce the unlawful plot against David? As I have already suggested, the answer varies as Dryden moves towards an increasingly misogynistic conclusion.

At the opening, however, it seems that David has, at least in part, conceived his own problems. Most obviously, because he is so "Promiscuous" (6) and has sired bastard children "through the Land" (10), David has encouraged his own destruction, illicitly producing a population that has little reason to support a system of privileges based on legitimacy and hereditary succession. As Howard Weinbrot suggests, "David makes his own rebellion by propagating his own lawlessness in his lawless son and lawless nation." Absalom is especially dangerous because David has overindulged and failed to discipline him, encouraging the favored son to expect rights and opportunities he does not legally deserve.

But the problems of generation in the beginning of the poem are also specifically related to the way David makes mothers at the same time that he does children. We learn first that Michal, the royal wife, is barren because her "Soyl [is] ungratefull to the Tiller's care," but next:

> Not so the rest; for several Mothers bore
> To Godlike *David,* several Sons before.
> But since like slaves his bed they did ascend,
> No True Succession could their seed attend.
>
> (13-16)

Precisely because it is confusing, this passage is enormously important as it generates a variety of ways to interpret David's culpable behavior and the problem of female desire. In many respects Dryden at first seems remarkably sensitive to the mothers, reflecting what James Winn has described as his "more than occasional insight into the hard lot of . . . women." But this insight is, as Winn notes of other works, also balanced by Dryden's tendency to lapse into misogynistic conventions. Ultimately, the competing readings available at the beginning of *Absalom and Achitophel* are telescoped, so that by the end only the standard negative implications about female sexuality persist.

Let me unpack the various angles of interpretation initially available by beginning with the "several Mothers." A quick reading suggests simply that their problematic status is the source of the trouble with "True Succession"; based on earlier lines, it seems that because the women were not brides but slaves or concubines, their children cannot be kings. But this explanation is not entirely precise. The passage specifically emphasizes the sexual moment when the several Mothers ascended David's bed "*like* slaves" (15; emphasis added). We are not told that the women *were* slaves, and a careful reading of the opening reveals that some may have actually been among David's many wives (9). Zwicker points out that "the line suggests not just a technical category but sexual slavery or slavishness." Indeed, the stress is on the means by which the mothers came to bed: if they entered like slaves, perhaps they were forced to lie with the king. At best, there is no indication that the women actively wanted to be there or that David had any interest in making their experience enjoyable. From this perspective, the problem of succession has as much to do with the way the mothers were impregnated as it does with their status, the implication being that it is because the women were passive objects of David's desire and possibly even victims of rape that their children are not fit for royalty.

Lest this emphasis on the importance of female desire seem anachronistic, we need only recall that until the middle of the eighteenth century, it was widely believed that female pleasure and orgasm were necessary for conception. Thus, a seventeenth-century audience would likely have made a connection between the mothers' sexual experiences and their success in generation. Dryden himself need not have been concerned with the question of women's sexual rights to have been interested in the reproductive implications of female pleasure. Nevertheless, despite this medical context, the poetic reasoning at first seems illogical because even if a woman enjoyed having sex with David she could not necessarily produce a king.

But the illogic of the association does not negate the emphasis on David's disinterest in arousing female desire and on his capacity to be abusive. It is worth noting, for instance, that the reference to Absalom's murder of Amnon, which follows a few lines later (39), specifically alludes to rape; in the biblical story, Absalom kills Amnon (his half brother) for raping their sister, Tamar. The narrator in Dryden's poem condemns Absalom's behavior, but nevertheless uses the attack on the brother to foreshadow Absalom's attack on his father. This, plus the fact that Amnon was also the king's son, invites us to consider the resemblance between Amnon and David—even to wonder if Absalom, who has killed his brother for having offended his sister, may have reason to object to his father's treatment of his mother.

In the context of this layered allusion to David's problem with female desire, the earlier description of how Michal's "Soyl" is "ungratefull" to David's "care" reads not simply as an account of the queen's infertility, but also as a satiric comment on her own sexual experience with the king. Michal is clearly distinguished from the "several Mothers" and Tamar, for there is no indication that she has been raped. But given David's apparent neglect of the importance of female sexual feeling, as well as his notorious philandering, she too may have little reason to be grateful in bed. Perhaps, when it comes to lovemaking, the "Tiller's care" is simply inadequate. For those seventeenth-century readers who assumed that conception depended on female orgasm, such sexual insensitivity could explain Michal's infertility. In order to prevent barrenness, "the man was . . . obliged to ensure the woman's satisfaction." Modern readers have assumed that the burden of infertility lies with Michal, but David's preoccupation with other women, inattention to female desire and possible willingness to employ force, suggest that it is just as likely that he has failed to perform his sexual duty to please—and thereby impregnate—his wife.

The connection between female pleasure and conception becomes much more complicated when read in relation to the "several Mothers." On the one hand, the seemingly illogical suggestion that the several Mothers have not emitted the "seed" of "True Succession" because they were brought "like slaves" to David's bed makes sense if we interpret it as another account of the relationship between female desire and successful generation. One might argue that the mothers produce incomplete children because they

were not active and willing participants in the sexual experience. From this perspective, the passage anticipates the description of Achitophel's son who is born deformed because he was conceived during a particularly clumsy and inadequate act of intercourse (170-72); the quality of lovemaking marks the quality of the product.

On the other hand, though, if the connection between female orgasm and generation is taken literally, then regardless of the means by which they came to David's bed, the several Mothers must have enjoyed themselves; otherwise they could not have proved fertile. Granted, there were medical theories that challenged the insistence on the need for female orgasm, and, as Laqueur notes, "counter-evidence must have been readily at hand that women frequently conceived without it." Perhaps David's women became mothers against their will. But such a reading needs to be balanced by the fact that well into the eighteenth century, a woman's pregnancy could be used to disprove an accusation of rape, for it was still widely believed that, as Richard Burn put it in his 1756 *Justice of the Peace,* "a woman can not conceive unless she doth consent." According to this logic, the several Mothers wanted what they got, an implication that anticipates Achitophel's oft-noted suggestion that the King, like all women, secretly longs to be raped (471-74; discussed in more detail below). Such reasoning even revises my earlier account of Michal's infertility. For using this lens, one can argue that the problem with the royal wife is that David has singled her out and treated her with too much "care." If, like the several Mothers, Michal had been abused in the way women secretly desire, perhaps she too would have conceived.

The competing readings available here serve both a political and narrative purpose. The poet exposes the king and acknowledges the problem of his self-indulgent promiscuity, something necessary to gain credibility with an audience that would have been well aware of Charles's sexual faults. But Dryden also protects David by leaving open the possibility that the main culpability lies elsewhere—that the production of a rebellious population, and specifically of an illicit son, was fueled primarily by maternal, not monarchal, desire. At this point, however, the balance of responsibility is unclear, and the irresolution generates useful suspense.

If anything, the case against David remains stronger. The king's apparent indifference to female desire, for instance, is highlighted by his contrasting indulgence of Absalom: "To all *his* wishes Nothing he deny'd, / And made the Charming *Annabel* his Bride" (33-34; first emphasis added). These lines continue to draw attention to the problematic objectification of women (the gift of *Annabel* indicates the extent to which Absalom has been spoiled), while also introducing a homoerotic twist. Pointedly contrasting with his neglect of women, the account of the king's excessive interest in pleasing his son (in this case sexually) highlights David's disorientation. He gazes at the boy with "secret Joy" because in Absalom David sees "His Youthfull Image . . . renew'd" (32), and this narcissistic investment emphasizes the king's attraction to a body that is the same as his own.

The stress on David's physical similarity to Absalom is important for another reason as well because it suggests that as a father he has exerted greater control over the act of conception, corroborating the argument that he is responsible for producing the political problem embodied in the son. In general, stressing what Filmer describes as the man's "principal agen[cy] in generation," the poem begins by offering an Aristotelian account of fertilization, showing how the king ignites or works on female matter to shape his progeny. If he has failed effectively to heat the queen's soil, David has nevertheless fruitfully imparted his "vigorous warmth" (8) throughout the land. In keeping with later animalculist theories that suggested that the full embryo existed in the sperm, the beautiful Absalom seems to have sprung complete from his father's seed. Apparently bearing no relationship to his mother, Absalom is strictly the product of his father's great desire and activity, perhaps even "inspir'd" by David's "diviner Lust" and gotten "with a greater Gust" (19-20).

But importantly, then, in contrast to the way Filmer celebrates and links male generative and governmental control, Dryden here exposes the political problems of masculine conception. For if David has determined the development of his son, then the father is ultimately the source of the troubles that ensue. As with Achitophel, David's control of procreation is a dangerous one. Granted, when we learn about Achitophel's act of fatherhood it is clear that he is considerably less successful than David; Achitophel has, in fact, failed appropriately to conceive. His son is an "unfeather'd two Leg'd thing," "born a shapeless Lump, like Anarchy" because he was "Got, while his [father's] Soul did hudled Notions try" (170-72). But, as different as their sexual acts may have been and as different as their children now appear, both David and Achitophel seem unilaterally to have begotten a political problem.

It is not until Absalom himself speaks, that this account of paternal conception begins to be redefined and the idea of the mother's participation is clearly introduced. The moment marks the point at which the poem begins to develop an increasingly more direct attack on maternal culpability. Tempted by Achitophel's call for him to seek the political privileges he is denied, Absalom memorably exclaims:

> Yet oh that Fate Propitiously Enclined,
> Had rais'd my Birth, or had debas'd my Mind;
> To my large Soul, not all her Treasure lent,
> And then Betray'd it to a mean Descent.
> I find, I find my mounting Spirits Bold,
> And *David's* Part disdains my Mothers Mold.
> Why am I Scanted by a Niggard Birth?
> My Soul Disclaims the Kindred of her Earth.
>
> (363-70)

On the one hand, Absalom's account of his own production repeats the earlier Aristotelian model, stressing how the mother gives the matter and the father creates action and soul. As before, the mother here is associated with "Earth" and the physicality of birth; in addition to the "Soul," the father bequeathes the "Mind" and "Spirits." Importantly, however, in contrast to the opening of the poem, this passage also rebalances the generational model in much the same way that Harvey did by suggesting that the female parent's contribution is at least as important as the male's to the development of the child: thus, "*David's* Part" is evenly balanced by "my Mothers Mold," the latter an arresting formulation since it suggests that the mother has the power to shape her offspring and conflicts with the way David sees the child as an image of himself. Indeed, what torments Absalom is the extent to which *he* sees his mother in himself—the extent to which he feels that, as one of her "Kindred," he is indelibly marked by a "mean Descent." Absalom longs to rise out of this maternal boundary but, frustratingly, cannot.

In a number of ways, the narrator encourages us to agree with Absalom's account of maternal influence. We are told that, when tempted by Achitophel's promise of power, Absalom is "Half loath, and half consenting to the Ill, / (For Royal Blood within him struggled still)" (313-14), meaning that when he agrees to rebel Absalom is influenced by his ignoble part, the mother's half. Such intimations would, for a seventeenth-century audience, have been strengthened by the scandalous history of Monmouth's mother, Lucy Walter, a woman rumored to have been a whore of "mean Descent." She died (perhaps of venereal disease) shortly after Charles rather forcibly removed their young son from her care. Not all of the rumors were true, but Lucy was well-known for her affairs, and she created considerable trouble for the king, which Monmouth would later compound.

In addition to evoking memories of Monmouth's actual mother, the narrator reinforces Absalom's account of maternal influence by associating him with Milton's Eve throughout the seduction scene. As Frank Ellis points out, "Dryden would not forget that it is Eve whom Satan deceives" and he creates here "an androgynous Monmouth" marked by an effeminate beauty to dramatize the connection. Winn makes similar associations, suggesting that Monmouth's resemblance to Eve "casts doubt on his authenticity as a hero" and that "the plot to settle the succession on [him] . . . is like [her] false dream." So too, as with Satan and Eve, the serpentine Achitophel "sheds his Venome, in . . . words" (229) that ultimately flatter and provoke the initially resisting child to turn against the father and reach for the "Fruit . . . upon the Tree" (250-51). The desire Achitophel arouses in Absalom is framed as a feminine one, linked to that experienced by Milton's "general Mother." And the danger Absalom poses, intensified by the rumors that Monmouth's mother was a whore, shifts attention away from the critique of the king's sexual excesses and towards the earlier intimation that the political problem is the consequence of feminine longing.

Like the description of David's eagerness to please his son, the interaction between Absalom and Achitophel can also be read as a homoerotic one, but whereas his father once indulged him, Achitophel is seducing Absalom to satisfy his own needs. Ironically oblivious to the various ways in which he has been feminized, Absalom himself is attracted by Achitophel's false promise of greater masculinity. Achitophel begins by assuring Absalom that if he dares to seize the temptress Fortune he can enjoy a kind of sexual conquest reminiscent of his father's:

> Now, now she meets you, with a glorious prize,
> And spreads her Locks before her as she flies.
> Had thus Old *David,* from whose Loyns you spring,
> Not dar'd, when Fortune call'd him, to be King,
> At *Gath* an Exile he might still remain.
>
> (260-64)

Reminding the son of his own debt to David's sexual fertility and invoking an image of exclusive paternal generation that has already proved problematic (Absalom springs from David's "Loyns"), Achitophel encourages Absalom to imitate his father and gain the advantage of sexual dominance. Next, he changes his strategy and puts David in Fortune's position, arguing that the King himself is the feminine figure Absalom must conquer. After twice describing David as "Naked" (280, 400) and stressing that he lacks "Manly Force" (382), Achitophel famously urges Absalom to commit "a pleasing Rape upon the Crown" (474), suggesting that the king "by Force . . . wishes to be gain'd / Like womens Leachery, to seem Constrain'd" (471-72). This description does the trick: "And this Advice above the rest, / With *Absalom's* Mild nature suited best" (477-78).

If the "Mild" Absalom is really moved by the idea that he will be doing what his father wants, it is notably the image of rape that persuades him to act. Evoking the opening allusion to the king's capacity to rape and Achitophel's demand that he ravish Fortune like his father before him, the passage suggests that Absalom is driven to become his father's sexual replacement, perhaps hoping that he can exert the very force against David that David has so magnificently displayed; or, that he can reverse the abusive act that injured his birth by becoming his father's abuser. In either case, rape, according to Achitophel, is productive, an implication that plays off the opening example of the prolific "several Mothers" brought like slaves to David's bed. Apparently consumed by the evidence of his father's virility, Absalom needs to imagine the king as an effeminate figure he can dominate in order to recreate himself.

But Absalom's fantasy of masculine grandeur proves simply ironic, first because the rape he and Achitophel imagine performing is pointedly homoerotic, and second, because throughout the scene Absalom is actually the one who, like Eve and the whorish Lucy Walter, is being seduced. When he thinks he will become most virile, the son is really the reverse. The contrast highlights David's genuine manliness, reminding us that Achitophel's account of the king's effeminacy is just as much a ploy as his description of Absalom's machismo, and that although David may have been too eager to please his son, he is nevertheless the man who has not only demonstrated the potential to rape, but also done so with women. So too, Achitophel's efforts to paint David as old and impotent are ironically balanced by the narrator's earlier assurance that Achitophel is actually the one who "Refuse[s] his Age the needful hours of Rest" (166). He may have an

impact on Absalom, but Achitophel cannot function successfully enough in bed with a woman to generate a well-shaped child. The accumulating evidence of the sexual differences between David and these men begins to reconfigure the implications of the king's behavior; David's aggressive promiscuity with women is no longer necessarily a problem so much as a mark of his masculine authenticity. And it is in keeping with his virility that far from wishing "by Force . . . to be gain'd" (471), David ultimately proves instead that he is "not Good by Force" (950).

But if Achitophel's description of how women secretly long to be raped finally fails to define the king's position, it nevertheless is gradually validated as an accurate account of feminine sexual desire, a turn that revises the opening emphasis on women's passivity and possible victimization. Not only does Absalom demonstrate a feminine readiness to be seduced, but the crowd, which he (now playing the role of a man) in turn seduces, is lecherously interested in his overtures. Aroused by his good looks, the people open themselves to Absalom and thoroughly enjoy his penetration. As "He glides unfelt into their secret hearts" his "words" are "easy" and "fit," "slow" and "sweet" (693-97). In this context, the accounts of how "govern'd by the *Moon,* the giddy *Jews*" "By natural Instinct" often "change their Lord" (216-19) and are apt to leave themselves "Defensless, to the Sword / Of each unbounded Arbitrary Lord" (761-62) read as further evidence of the people's sexual exposure and whorish willingness to be raped.

Some of David's enemies are also marked by their capacity to be "Seduc'd" (498) and especially by their effeminacy. Zimri (standing for Buckingham who had a notorious affair with the Countess of Shrewsbury) may seem as fertile as the king, but the "ten thousand freaks that dy'd in thinking" (552) that he sires signal his failures of conception and resemble Achitophel's monstrous son. Demonstrating what Weinbrot characterizes as an "impotence of which Charles is free," Zimri may be "Stiff in Opinions" but he performs "every thing by starts, and nothing long" (547-48). And like the fickle and whorish Jews, he too is influenced by the feminine "Moon" (549). Corah (Titus Oates) is just as bad. Although he stands "Erect," Corah's "Monumental Brass" only proves his masculine inauthenticity (633), especially because it was well known that Oates had been dismissed from his office as chaplain for the navy after committing sodomy while on ship.

Like Monmouth, Oates was also rumored to be illegitimate and, echoing the description of Absalom's development from and desire to rise above maternal matter, Corah's "base" birth originates in "Earthy Vapours" though he seeks to "shine in Skies" (636-37). The implicit return to the problem of the maternal prepares us for the later account of Barzillai's son (the Earl of Ossory), Dryden's "conception of the ideal" male child, whose legitimate birth and noble death enable him to be free of matter in a way Absalom and Corah cannot. Unlike Absalom, torn between "*David's* Part" and his "Mothers Mold" (368), Barzillai's child fulfills "All *parts* . . . of Subject and of Son" (836; emphasis added), suggesting that he reflects his father more completely than the divided Absalom. The passage as a whole, however, does not so much endorse a paternal model of generation as establish the advantages of escaping feminine origins. When Ossory dies

> Now, free from Earth, thy disencumbered Soul
> Mounts up, and leaves behind the Clouds and Starry
>   Pole
> From thence thy kindred legions mayst thou bring
> To aid the guardian Angel of thy King.
>
> (850-53)

In echoing Absalom's earlier longing to escape his mother's influence—"I find my mounting Spirits Bold . . . / . . . My Soul Disclaims the Kindred of her Earth" (367-70)—the lines define the essential difference between the men. Where Absalom is grounded in the maternal earth, Ossory's soul can mount above it. Ultimately his "kindred" transcends the feminine.

When David reappears in the finale he seems to have reaped some of Ossory's advantages without even having to die. Demonstrating the true superiority of a Godly ruler, he is closer to heaven than ordinary mortals and suddenly free of earthly faults. Originally "inspir'd by some diviner Lust" (19) David now speaks "from his Royal Throne by Heav'n inspir'd" (936). He thus bears a greater resemblance to his "Maker" than he did when he was self-indulgently scattering his own image throughout the land. Nevertheless, the difference between the legitimate Ossory and the illegitimate Absalom, and thus between the virtuous Barzillai and the promiscuous David, remains. As if recognizing the problem of his reputation, David pointedly reconfigures his history of sexual indulgence in his speech, completing the poem's attack on maternal desire and danger, and finally proving that he is not responsible for generating the child of disorder (though he may be guilty of the lesser charge of having raised Absalom "up to all the Height his Frame coud bear" [962] and thus of having given him a false sense of potency). Even as he resolves the initial problem of the poem, then, Dryden leaves open the possibility that David, like Achitophel, is simply developing a rhetorical strategy that is necessary for his own survival.

Part of David's strategy is to emphasize his phallic advantage, magnified now for readers by the contrasting effeminacy of his enemies. Unlike Zimri, for instance, who is "nothing long" (548), David's "Manly [temper] can the longest bear" (948). And he is prepared to exercise his potency on the "Factious crowds" (1018)—to "rise upon 'em with redoubled might: / For Lawfull Pow'r is still Superiour found, / When long driven back, at length it stands the ground" (1023-25). David here defines governmental repression in terms of his lawful right to phallic conquest, and in so doing, reverses the opening intimation of his lawless capacity for sexual abuse.

But David's defense of his phallic authority cannot, in itself, solve the problem of the conception of Absalom and the Plot. Fully to extricate himself, the king still needs to prove that the burden of desire and generation lies else-where. He is at an advantage with the reader because the text has increasingly emphasized the problem of the people's desire. In addition to the crowd's prostitution before Absalom discussed above, the opening describes how the Jews "led their wild desires to Woods and Caves, / And thought that all but Savages were Slaves" (55-56). At the conclusion David is finally convinced "That no Concessions from the Throne woud please" (925). And when the narrator defends hereditary succession, he specifically insists that the reason subjects should never be given the right to choose their own ruler is that "Then Kings are slaves to those whom they Command, / And Tenants to their Peoples pleasure stand" (775-76). In weighting the problem of desire with the populace, the text interestingly reconceptualizes the whole issue of slavery. If it begins by questioning David's enslavement of women, the poem subsequently stresses the savagery of a people in need of control and suggests that the king had better play the part of "Master" (938) lest he himself become a slave. Given Charles's central role in sponsoring the Royal African Company, these passages arguably serve a colonialist purpose, functioning to support England's expanding empire and role in the slave trade.

But by shifting the onus of desire away from the king, the passages also prepare the reader for David's ultimate attack on maternal longing and responsibility. First David links the petitioners' pretended interest in his approval of their choice of king to the way "*Esau's* Hands suite ill with *Jacob's* Voice" (982), recalling another biblical mother who, like Eve, plotted to undermine the father. After all, Jacob deceives Isaac in Genesis 27:13 only because Rebekah urges him to do so, assuring him that "Upon me be thy curse."

Next, David insists that, as with Absalom, he has been far too indulgent with his people—and especially with his enemies in Parliament—who are "Unsatiate as the barren Womb or Grave; / God cannot Grant so much as they can Crave" (987-88). Developing a wonderful counterpart to the opening possibilities that Michal is barren either because he has neglected her needs for sexual arousal or because he has not delivered the force she secretly wants, David instead figures his subjects' ravenous longing as the result of their feminine infertility. The problem is not that he has in some way failed to satisfy feminine desire, but rather that such longing is so uncontrollable that nothing he could have done would have produced a solution. Bearing no relationship to the king's own behavior, the empty womb becomes the driving force of the revolt, reminding us that if only the queen had been fertile all might be well.

David's final maternal image completes the reconfiguration of the "several Mothers." Adopting an opposite strategy than the one above, the king now blames his problems on feminine fertility as he anticipates his enemies' self-destruction by exclaiming:

> By their own arts 'tis Righteously decreed,
> Those dire Artificers of Death shall bleed.
> Against themselves their Witnesses will Swear,

Till Viper-like their Mother Plot they tear:
And suck for Nutriment that bloody gore
Which was their Principle of Life before.

(1010-15)

Originally unrelated to the rebel son, the mother here becomes the plot against the king, her pregnant body the bloody incubator of revolt. Compared with the description of Achitophel's and Zimri's children, the birth of the vipers is the most monstrous of all, in part because here, for the first time, the mother alone provides the "Principle of Life." Having moved from a paternal to a joint parental model of generation, the poem ends, ironically, with the same emphasis on the power of pregnancy Locke would later endorse: the offspring "is fashion'd [in the mother's womb], and from her it receives the Materials and Principles of its Constitution." But unlike Locke, Dryden figures maternal generation as the ultimate horror. His emphasis evokes not Harvey's or the ovists' accounts-of the importance of the egg so much as an ancient and enduring myth about pregnant mothers. Mounting embryological research had done little to erode the widespread belief that a woman's mental state and desires could affect and distort the child in her womb, even turning it into a monster. It was assumed that frustrated maternal longings could mark and injure the fetus, and, as one eighteenth-century gynecological textbook explained, any excessive feeling might "impress a *Depravity* of Nature upon the Infant's *Mind,* and *Deformity* on its *Body.* Suggesting that the development and birth of the vipers is the result of a Mother *Plot,* Dryden's image exonerates the father by emphasizing the gestatory danger of a certain kind of intensive maternal thinking.

Moreover, according to ancient lore about vipers and in keeping with theories about monstrous births, the progeny here is specifically the product of the mother's excessive desire. As Swedenberg points out, in addition to recalling Spenser's Error and Milton's Sin, the description of the viper is based on popular fables about the beast itself. One mid seventeenth-century account explains that when vipers couplate the male puts his "head into the mouth of the female, who is so insatiable in the desire of that copulation, that when the male hath filled her with his seed-genital . . . she biteth" off his head and kills him. As a result, the young she conceives, "in revenge of their fathers death, do likewise destroy their mother, for they eate out her belly, and by an unnatural issue come forth." If there were any question at the beginning, the answer is now unmistakable: the female not only wants sex, she is utterly voracious, and the offspring that result are marked by her hunger. The depiction of the viper completes David's acquittal, dramatizing the uncontrollable danger of maternal sexuality and his own victimization as father. Far from producing the plot, David has fallen prey to it. The comfort, however, lies in the certain knowledge that he will be avenged when his rebels turn against their mother, and, in destroying her body and consuming their own placenta, effectively abort themselves. Beautifully, even these vipers will participate in the father's defense.

Because it recalls the way he developed the plot by shedding words of "Venome" (229), the image of the viper also completes the attack on Achitophel's manliness by associating him with a monstrous mother. Now the earlier description of his "shapeless Lump" (172) of a son has a different ring. Swedenberg suggests that the word Lump refers "to the soulless body or to the primordial matter of chaos." Perhaps, then, Achitophel has not simply failed in his paternal mission to shape his progeny and give it a soul; perhaps the child remains a form of chaotic maternal material because that is actually all he has to offer.

Tearing out of their mother's belly, the vipers are the last in a series of images suggesting that those associated with the plot have grown too large for the containment of the body. From the opening, the plot itself is a raging fever, boiling the blood so that it "bubbles o'r" (136-39) and "Foam[s]" (141) out of physical boundaries. Similarly, Absalom's "warm excesses . . . / Were constru'd Youth that purg'd by boyling o'r" (37-38). And Achitophel cannot stay inside himself, for his "fiery Soul . . . working out its way, / Fretted the Pigmy Body to decay" (156-57). It is in keeping with such details that, at the end of the poem, David finally recognizes the way the people, bearing the "Wound" of a "foment[ing] . . . Disease" (924-26) cannot be placated or restrained. The recurring ideas of blood, disease and interior pressure, concluding in the final description of the viper birth, construe the revolt itself as the inevitable rupture of a swelling pregnancy. And the discussions of how the "Plot [that] is made" (751) is designed to persuade people that they "have a Right Supreme / To make their Kings" (409-10; see also 795) read in this context as warnings about the danger of offering the subjects any kind of gestatory power. If the populace believes that Kings are made, not designated—if it assumes the right to create a ruler—then like the mother viper, it too will become the breeder of chaos.

Dryden's dismissal of the theory of patriarchal procreation reflects a larger political trend. Pateman suggests "the classic patriarchalism of the seventeenth century was the last time that masculine political creativity appeared as a paternal power or that political right was seen as father-right"; Dryden's poem might then be read as marking the end of an ideal, the moment when the generative father-king is no longer a viable image. So too, the attack on maternity anticipates the misogynist implications that, according to Pateman, shaped the contractual body born out of the impotent father—the "body of the 'individual'" whose form is "very different from women's bodies. His body is tightly enclosed within boundaries, but women's bodies are permeable, their countours change shape and they are subject to cyclical processes. All these differences are summed up in the natural bodily process of birth." Among other things, Dryden's explosive mother viper proves that the female cannot contain political rights.

But the familial images in *Absalom and Achitophel* are also specifically related to the particular details of the Exclusion Crisis and Dryden's determination to support the king. Given the nature of Monmouth's role, Dryden could not have depended on traditional patriarchal theory to defend the monarch even if he had wanted to, because it appeared in part to be Charles's act of fatherhood that threatened his position as king as well as the endurance of royal succession. To emphasize Filmer's conception of how a ruler, especially one who promiscuously generated a rebellious son, "had, by right of fatherhood, royal authority over [his] children" and subjects would simply have highlighted the irony of the situation.

The poem's attack on maternity instead enables the king to rise by virtue of contrast. Locke's debate with Filmer suggests that, whether or not it was explicitly acknowledged, the fatherly model of kingship was sustained by denying the role of motherhood in the family. "That the Mother too hath her Title" Locke cautions, "destroys the Sovereignty of one Supream Monarch." Dryden clearly capitalizes on this rhetorical tension between motherhood and monarchy, though for political reasons much different from Locke's. Unable to rely on David's paternity as proof of his right to govern, he turns to the other parent and proves her worse. Demonstrating that to introduce the mother into the governmental model is to invite disaster and effectively "Physick [the] Disease into a worse" (810), Dryden argues that the mother must be erased for a stable kingship to be maintained and in so doing upholds one of the most basic premises of patriarchal theory.

By insisting on the mother's primary role in conception, the poem can end by disposing of the notion that David (or Charles) was sexually responsible for making his own chaos. Maternal productivity, the consequence of a feminine desire that far outstrips David's own, is the ultimate danger. And David's virtue is marked by his removal from all aspects of the process of generation. The king proves stable both because he suggests that his blood did not create the child of blood, and because he rises above average mortals, becoming someone who is not (and should never be) bred or made by them, someone whose origins are fundamentally dissociated from the feminine earth.

But perhaps what is in the end most compelling about the politics of generation in *Absalom and Achitophel* is the variety of narratives about sexuality and the family that emerge before this conclusion. Dryden develops a model of maternal generation in order to defend the royalist tradition as best he can under the circumstances, but because he has adopted and discarded other models along the way, the work ultimately reflects the ideological flexibility of a familial political theory that could be shaped to suit various purposes. At a time when the traditional emphasis on patriarchal procreation was on the wane, when the inevitability of royal succession had long been subject to doubt, and when there was no uniform scientific account of the creation of the human body, any political defense that depended on the image of governmental generation was necessarily unstable and open to rhetorical play. If Dryden ends with an account of maternal monstrosity and a non-procreative monarchy that solves the problem with which his poem began, he also proves in the process the ease with which his own structure could be dismantled—especially because the questions of who comes next and how are still unresolved.

Margery A. Kingsley (essay date 1996)

SOURCE: "'High on a Throne of His Own Labours Rear'd': *Mac Flecknoe,* Jeremiad, and Cultural Myth," in *Modern Philology,* Vol. 93, No. 3, February 1996, pp. 327-51.

[*In the following excerpt, Kingsley asserts that Dryden's intention in writing* Mac Flecknoe *was to warn England against the cultural, moral, and political "chaos" that was being created by irresponsible and sloppy writers.*]

Ironically, scholars have had little to say about *Mac Flecknoe,* the Restoration's great nightmare vision of cultural anarchy, despite the fact that John Dryden, poet laureate, historiographer royal, and "the father of English criticism," has long stood as the central figure for the formation of a literary culture in late seventeenth-century England. One of Dryden's most virulent satires, *Mac Flecknoe* defies the very critical constructions of eighteenth-century decorum and neoclassical balance and proportion which he himself championed, and as a result it is often bypassed as an anomaly by prominent studies of his career. At the same time, the obtrusiveness and accessibility of the poem's topical political and theatrical references have led literary historians to mine *Mac Flecknoe* for the scholarly equivalent of "local color," dismembering it as needed and utterly divorcing the poem's political and literary content from its poetic structure. Even the best of critics have tended to read it one topical reference at a time, and often only in passing; more often it is represented as the petty manifestation of personal and professional resentment or the "historically significant" precursor of a later satiric tradition. Thus this immensely popular poem has remained oddly enigmatic, widely known and read yet surprisingly resistant, or so it would seem, to strenuous critical exploration on its own terms.

Yet despite the implications of this critical strip-mining, Dryden's poem does not merely reflect contemporary cultural and political institutions, nor is its representation of those institutions independent of its poetic strategies. For *Mac Flecknoe* is, we might say, "about" theater, and like the theater it depicts, it is essentially performative—persistently materializing the texts it represents. The titular identification of "the true-blue-protestant poet, T.S." as the object of satiric attack emphasizes theater, rather than monarchy, as the poem's informing discourse (the tenor of its metaphor), and effectively frames the poem in the confines of the stage. Flecknoe's kingdom is, in fact, the stage presided over by its playwright-king, and its limits are those of the theater: the stage itself is associated with "the walls which fair Augusta bind" (line 64). [All references to *Mac Flecknoe* are taken from *The Works of John Dryden,* ed. H. T. Swedenberg, Jr. (Los Angeles, 1972), 2:54-60, with line references given in the text.] Within this world, text, like script, is literally formed into solid substance: Shadwell's productions clog the streets like refuse, and the subjects who flock to his coronation are books transformed into men by Dryden's own figures of speech.

The point, however, is not merely that text, as the literary product of an explicit commercial order, takes on a physical being in this poem, for *Mac Flecknoe* also argues that literary representation determines the very institutions—political and cultural—from which society is formed. Margaret Doody and Michael Seidel have argued that the poem reflects late seventeenth-century political attitudes toward imperialism and succession, respectively, but *Mac Flecknoe* is also clearly concerned with depicting the textual origins of political authority itself. The symbol of Flecknoe's authority is a pile of his own "labours"—at once literary and excremental (line 107)—and his incompetence as a playwright is realized at the social and political level in his failure as a king: Dryden insistently relates the decline of the kingdom he depicts to the inability of its monarchs to "represent" their state on the stage, embodying poor script in the form of an imperfect world. Moreover, while George McFadden has suggested that the poem puts forth a set of coherent literary standards in its attack upon poor writing in general, Dryden clearly sees those cultural standards—which he implicitly claims to maintain in his own poem—as the only hope for the restoration of order to a chaotic society. Within the poem disorder springs primarily from dull poetry and tautological poets, while the ability to establish order comes (if only in Dryden's own poetic project) with the literary amelioration brought about by satire.

Thus *Mac Flecknoe,* I would argue, offers a powerful and coherent myth of the creation (and destruction) of social, political, and cultural order as Dryden depicts a state that is formed, however badly, by text—a state decaying through the transformation of the human word that both sinks in bathos to the physicality of material remains and enacts excrescence in a grotesque parody of metaphysical transcendence. As a text engaged in both political and literary criticism, Dryden's poem is above all interested in the laws (political, aesthetic, and often religious) that regulate literary production, social institutions, and the metamorphic process that binds text and society together. It is thus with these laws that this article will be concerned, both as *Mac Flecknoe* seeks to sustain them, asserting its own myth-making as the authority by which they are maintained, and as the poem (in its obsessive representation of the violation of those laws) often threatens to collapse into chaos itself. In the process it offers a glimpse of Dryden's own anxieties concerning the relationship between literary product and social institution—registering one seventeenth-century recognition of the complexities and potential dangers inherent in the social text.

The notion of the metamorphosis of the word and of the efficacy of the text in creating social order was hardly new to Dryden. It was in fact a popular image among radical writers of the 1640s, 1650s, and 1660s, many of whom described the revelation of God's Word as a kind of theater. It is a trope whose principal source seems at first glance unlikely for a Restoration Tory, later to be Catholic, however, for as we shall see it was grounded in the language of prophecy and in the jeremiad, that particular prophetic genre so popular with seventeenth-century Quakers which both calls a nation "to repent for violation of its covenant with God" and threatens its imminent destruction if it does not. Yet Dryden would later locate the origins of satire in the Roman equivalent of the English jeremiad, developed by actors who "were first brought from Etruria to Rome, on occasion of a pestilence, when the Romans were admonished to avert the anger of the gods by plays." Those players, he would claim, "with a gross and rustic kind of raillery, reproached each other with their failings" by assuming the role of the castigating prophet.

Nor was the rhetoric of divine judgment strange to Dryden in the 1670s. He had used it earlier in *Annus Mirabilis,* and however petty, self-interested, and aggressively unspiritual *Mac Flecknoe* may be, Shadwell is after all the "last great prophet of tautology" (line 30). Furthermore, we are told his reign had been "prophesied long since" by "ancient Dekker" (line 87). Thomas Dekker, a playwright famously ridiculed by Ben Jonson, was also the author of pamphlets that proclaimed the destruction of England for its manifold sins under titles like "Gods Tokens of his fearful Judgements." If Shadwell is "a scourge of wit, and flail of sense" (line 89), he is equally the long-awaited judgment upon his people and upon himself. Within *Mac Flecknoe,* moreover, the words of the prophet Shadwell (who is also one of "Gods Tokens") form the very fabric of Dryden's own satire (or raillery); for while Flecknoe is, for instance, figured as John the Baptist, "sent before but to prepare [the] way" for a Christlike Shadwell (line 32), he is also, quite in spite of himself, Jeremiah denouncing the false priest, speaking an inspired truth which he need not comprehend.

Yet the point of the jeremiad in Dryden's poem is not simply another formulation of satire, although complaint and satire have traditionally been linked by literary criticism. For that particular prophetic form also provides a crucial model for the transformation of text into social order by way of the relationships it formulates among the Word of God, the speech of the prophet, and the maintenance of social boundaries through enforcing the law and punishing those who transgress. Although, as Nigel Smith has shown, imagined relationships between the Word and the prophetic text proliferated wildly in the religious turmoil of the mid-seventeenth century, it is nevertheless fair to say that even late in the century one of the basic assumptions of the jeremiad held the prophetic utterance, as the Word, to guarantee its own efficacy and realization. God's prediction of destruction, if unheeded, inevitably became destruction, and thus the book of Jeremiah, for instance, was read by the late Renaissance as the fulfillment and execution of Mosaic law, the utterance which effected punishment for transgression of the law, and so created and substantiated a kind of religious and social hegemony by denouncing both false prophets and bad rulers.

For some late seventeenth-century radicals this formulation of the prophetic text meant the ability to re-create social order in God's image. For royalists less eager to accept the potentially anarchic implications of the divine inspiration of the prophet, the prophetic mode was adopted as a ritualized vocabulary of obedience and an instrument of cultural control; as part of the regular liturgical cycle the text of Jeremiah was used on days like November 5 and January 30 to commemorate traumatic threats to the political status quo: "The aldermen of Cambridge, and thousands of other loyal Englishmen like them, were giving thanks for a 'miracle of resurrection' of church and state [after the civil wars], the most admirable of 'the wonderful revolutions and intricate riddles of God's providence' in which the hand of God could be seen 'punishing us justly for our sins, yet relieving us mercifully from our sufferings.'" For Dryden, at least in **Mac Flecknoe,** the fact that the jeremiad was read and used as the embodiment of social order dictated by "the law"—as, that is, the interpretation, application, and practical fulfillment of a theoretical model—means that it is precisely the ability of the monarch/prophet/playwright to establish and stage the distinction between order and transgression that constructs (or destroys) the state. As the word becomes "real," the failures of the monarch and his representations to maintain a certain literary standard, imposed by Dryden himself, are revealed in the process of physical decay to which, the opening lines of the poem suggest, the original imperfections of man universally subject him and his works. And it is precisely the insistence of Flecknoe upon blessing when he should, we feel, be castigating or at least lamenting (like Jeremiah after the destruction of Jerusalem), imposing in some way the structure of the law, that ultimately dictates the excremental future of his kingdom, while it dooms him to the underworld/privy and the "Hell" of the restoration stage. Collapse, chaos, and revolution are all suggested as social repercussions of the improvident efforts of the prophet/playwright, as Dryden assesses the social impact of literary representation.

To suggest that we should read **Mac Flecknoe** as a myth of political and cultural formation (or deformation), loosely in the tradition of Hobbes's *Leviathan* but based on a specifically prophetic formulation of the relationship between text and social order, is not to remove the poem from its traditional grounding in the specifics of both Tory politics and the political and economic battles of the London stage, however; if anything, the opposite is true. Whether Dryden wrote **Mac Flecknoe** in 1678, the year which G. Thorn-Drury long ago suggested as the date of the poem's composition, or somewhat earlier, as more recent critics have tended to argue, its satire was very much the product of a turbulent decade—one whose problems were of a piece throughout, though much like **Mac Flecknoe** itself they achieved their fullest public articulation only at its end. The poem's claims concerning the process of social formation reflect a period when both jeremiad and the associated lament were deeply enmeshed in contemporary economic, political, and theatrical debates, and it is to these issues that I now wish to turn.

As we have seen, the prophetic provides one layer of metaphoric language within Dryden's poem. The economics of poetic production offers another, and **Mac Flecknoe**'s treatment of the literary marketplace proves to be very much tied to the politics of complaint in the late 1670s. Flecknoe's kingdom is overwhelmingly ordered (or

disordered) by a market economy; in the anarchic world of **Mac Flecknoe** both theatrical and poetic product are linked inextricably to a commercial order and a process of production that is inevitably destructive, leading to bad text and thus to a bad state. Theater is joined to brothel: the "Nursery" in Flecknoe's kingdom is a place for training both young actors and young prostitutes. Text is meant for sale: at Shadwell's coronation, his subjects/works emerge from "dusty shops" in the commercial streets of London. Moreover, just as these associations with the literary marketplace are negative, the process of production in this system yields only excrement. Confirming Jean Baudrillard's claim that the process of artistic production in a capitalist society inevitably alienates the product from the act of creation, the productions of Shadwell and Flecknoe are dead, dismembered, and essentially meaningless: "scattered limbs," "Martyrs of pies, and relics of the bum" (lines 99, 101), and of course the ubiquitous fecal matter of Flecknoe's kingdom. Here at least, excretion embodies both production and alienation, effectively equating them. Text itself is cut off from both integration and interpretation, shredded and unread—salvageable only, the poem implies, by the strict enforcement of critical laws rather than market values.

Yet the 1670s also saw a reaction against jeremiad and lament primarily on the basis of Whiggish economic progressivism—a reaction that often led to the association of complaint with Tory conservatives. Typical of the objections against complaint was a pamphlet (attributed to John Houghton) entitled *England's Great Happiness or A Dialogue Between Content and Complaint Wherein Is demonstrated that a great part of our Complaints are causeless* (1677). At first glance, this author sounds much like many royalists who had attacked radical Jeremiahs during the civil wars on the grounds of their autonomous claims to divine inspiration, warning his reader in "The Author to his book" that

> You must take care, you don't ill fare
>   From those men that are furious
>
>   . . . . .
>
> Against all things that reason brings
>   To contradict their humours;
> And scarce are pleas'd, unless they're eas'd
>   By spreading forth false rumours.

The author's rejection of these "false rumours" quickly goes beyond problems of religious skepticism, however, to challenge the central identification between complaint and national prosperity that had traditionally defined the jeremiad. Where earlier writers had often insisted, as Sacvan Bercovitch does regarding the American jeremiad, that national destiny hinged upon self-flagellation in the name of divine providence, here the figure of Content quotes liberally from biblical texts against murmuring and urges Complaint to "remember that you are a rational creature, don't make your own and others [*sic*] lives uncomfortable by refusing to enjoy those Blessings Providence hath heaped upon you. Insisting that those blessings viewed by fanatics and sectarians as "great Complaints," when "rightly considered are some of our main temporal advantages . . . [a] great encrease whereof would make us so rich as to be the envy of the whole world," this pamphlet then suggests that complaint has been outmoded by a new construction of national prosperity based on trade, self-interest, and the individual accumulation of wealth. Content openly declares that he judges all things purely by individual interest; an overconcern with divine providence would here seem to retard rather than advance the nation. Tossing aside issues that had been a mainstay of religious radicalism during the 1650s and 1660s—luxury and excessive living on the part of the rich, the enclosure acts, mismanagement of national resources, and ill treatment of the poor—the author speaks for a great many in Restoration England who had tasted imperial power under Cromwell and were eager for a new age in which a combination of laissez-faire economics and imperial politics could leave behind the vocal misgivings of radical sectarians.

Despite this progressivist rejection of complaint, however, both jeremiad and lament experienced a revival throughout the 1670s which culminated in the anxiety surrounding the Popish Plot and the Exclusion Crisis. Often explicitly opposing an overemphasis upon commercial prosperity, pamphlets and ballads asserted the right to complain in a political environment where men were again prepared to risk violence and conflict in the name of political interest after the relative calm of the early 1660s. As early as 1668, the postscript to *Vox & Lachrymae Anglorum, or The True Englishman's Complaint* threatened that "if [Clarendon's] Practise justify our Fears, / He'll set's again together by the Ears." Often these texts used God's judgment as an analogue to and an excuse for a purely human show of force, while their claims to interpret the law (both divine and human) and set the boundaries of social acceptability served to historicize and institutionalize the absolute and essentially arbitrary terms of contemporary political conflict. A lord mayor's proclamation of 1679, for example, uses the logic of divine judgment to rationalize threatened violence:

> The Lord Mayor having taken into his serious Consideration the many dreadful Afflictions, which this City hath of late years suffered, by a raging plague, a most unheard of devouring fire, and otherwise: And justly fearing that the same have been occasioned by the many hainous crying Sins and Provocations to the Divine Majesty: And his Lordship also considering the present dangers of greater mischiefs and misery which seem still to threaten this City, if the execution of the Righteous Judgements of God Almighty be not prevented by an universal timely Repentance and Reformation: he hath therefore thought it one duty of his Office . . . first, to pray and perswade all and every the Inhabitants thereof to reform in themselves and families all Sins and Enormities whereof they know themselves to be guilty: And if neither the fear of the Great God nor of his Impending Judgements shall prevail upon them, he shall be obliged to let them know, that as he is their Chief Magistrate, he ought not to bear the Sword in vain.

The city's security from divine punishment is ultimately determined by an appeal to law that is represented principally as a use of force, and the purely human swipe of the magisterial sword both averts and ultimately replaces the greater fiery sword so often depicted as the symbol of God's vengeance.

Much as this proclamation translates the terms of divine order into the representation of a predominantly legal division between ruler and ruled (or obedient and unruly), complaint also became a means of establishing the laws, so to speak, of party politics, particularly among moderate to conservative Anglican supporters of the monarchy. Attacks upon the duke of Buckingham dating from the early 1670s defined opposition to him in terms of his earlier "treason," reminding readers that he had "[sworn] Allegiance to the rotten Rump," and was now "re-killing dead Kings by monstrous Slanders." Similarly, a 1679 broadside ballad entitled simply *The Lamentation* explains the politics of the Popish Plot as a reconfiguration of the basic divisions of the civil wars:

> Great *Charles,* we do lament thy Fate,
> For thou the Object art of late
> Of Popish and of factious Hate.
> These Winds from distant Quarters come,
> From North and South, *Scotland* and *Rome;*
> Yet both Concentre in thy Doom.
>
>   . . . . .
>
> Each of them Plots to have the Sway,
> And struggle only, that it may
> Be brought about in their own way.
>
> 'Tis neither Love nor Loyalty,
> That make Phanaticks talk so high
> 'Gainst Popish Plots and Treachery,
>
> For they'l rejoyce at *Charles'* Fall,
> And hope, once more, to have at all;
> If Common-Wealth they could Recal.
>
> The Papists hope will ne're be gone,
> While they can set the Factions on,
> And by them get their business done.

This "lament" over the king's projected fate—which threatens to repeat that of his father, for whom the Restoration was exhorted to "weep . . . for the Murther of a Father, the Father of our People and Country," as "the Prophet *Jeremiah's* grief swelled to that height as to wish his *head all waters,* and his *eys a fountain of tears, that he might weep day and night for the slain of the Daughter of his People*"—cements the royal genealogy of father and son in suggesting the equally continuous descent of their enemies. The ballad goes on to insist that the safe negotiation of present political division depends utterly upon its representation in terms of past polarities. Thus lament in this broadside suggests the absolute, unchangeable, nonnegotiable nature of party opposition, while ultimately containing that opposition in its claim to properly identify the source of the threat to the king; it rejects the confounding of political oppositions to embrace a rigidly and historically defined polarity between Whig and Tory which offers to preserve political order and social harmony in the face of threatened chaos, paradoxically symbolized by Shaftesbury and the emergent Whig party.

Similarly, in *Mac Flecknoe,* the claims of the prophet to realize a viable legal order form the basis of what can only be described as a politics of culture. If Flecknoe's (Shadwell's) kingdom decays because the economic transformation of the word into text fails to fulfill the dictates of the law, even as it forms the substance of the kingdom, the true prophecy of Flecknoe resides in the satiric strategy of Dryden's poem as it executes the arbitrary, exclusionary law of literary criticism which draws an absolute disjunction between aesthetic and transgressive, wit and dullness, and articulates a distinction (relatively new to the late seventeenth century) between popular and polite cultures. These distinctions are represented in terms of political division: Shadwell is the "true-blue protestant poet." And just as Flecknoe asserts explicitly literary criteria—stupidity, dullness, and "thoughtless majesty" (line 26)—for rulership, he also describes the maintenance of literary standards in terms of the arbitrary use of force, as had the lord mayor's proclamation: Shadwell's duty is to "wage immortal war with wit" (line 12).

Yet as *The Lamentation* suggests, it is precisely that elaborated difference in Dryden's poem between the divine efficacy of jeremiad and the human execution of satire that necessitates some form of textual arbitration. In *Mac Flecknoe* for instance, it generates the paradox that has frustrated so many Dryden scholars, for while Dryden establishes refinement as a criterion for literary judgment and accuses Shadwell of transgressive crudeness, Dryden's own verse revels in these very faults. The rules of neoclassical criticism leave little to say about Flecknoe's description of the progress of the "new Arion":

> Echoes from Pissing Alley Sh——call,
> And Sh——they resound from Aston Hall.
> About thy boat the little fishes throng,
> As at the morning toast that floats along.
>
> (Lines 47-50)

The problem, after all, with human law as the earthly reflection of divine law is its arbitrariness and potential inaccuracy when subject to the vagaries of political and personal interest. This is a difficulty of which the late seventeenth century was acutely aware, and one which brings us back, albeit circuitously, to the conceptions of theater in the 1670s and their relations to the religious, political, and economic matter of Dryden's poem.

Theater, as we have seen, was a popular seventeenth-century metaphor for divine revelation, parodied, for instance, in the beginning of Robert Herrick's *Poor Robins Vision* as the speaker complains of his vision that "this Tragedy was so long a playing." It had also been used as a figure for the political arena. Sources ranging from Samuel Pepys's *Diary* to Andrew Marvell's *Rehearsal Transprosed* suggest the perceived interrelation of monoarchy and theater, as well as a specific politics of that analogy; if the

royalist Pepys praises the spectacle of restored monarchy, the nonconformist Marvell worries about the power of the player-king from his "Horatian Ode" through the *Rehearsal Transprosed.* In the 1670s, however, theater also came to be regarded as an answer to the very problem of the arbitration of human law that is so clearly raised by Dryden's aesthetics, and it is to that context that we now turn.

As the terms of legal transgression were both politicized and humanized, the arbitrary nature of the interpretation of divine or "universal" law became particularly evident to seventeenth-century Englishmen who lacked an easy faith in either God's signs of displeasure or the interpretive power of human institutions: "For, as a late *Author* well observes, *Every Opinion makes a Sect; every Sect, a Faction; and Every Faction (when it is able) a War, and every such War is the Cause of God.*" Jean-François Lyotard has suggested that all of history is a series of propagandistic statements that must be arbitrated in order for meaning to be determined, and the late seventeenth century regarded divine judgment in remarkably similar terms. Typical of an age obsessed by almanacs, wonders, and "providential histories" was Simon Ford's *A Discourse Concerning God's Judgements* (1678). Working carefully against traditions that read the world as organized by a divine grammar, Ford seeks in effect to provide a strictly human grammar by which to interpret God's judgments, the signs of transgression; to this end he divides those judgments into two kinds, law (words) and dooms (execution), and then concludes that human law (or, for Ford, the human word) is often but not always the execution of God's judgment: "We too often render our selves guilty of *prophaning God's Name* (of which his great works are a considerable part) by stamping our own fond conceits with his *Image* and *Superscription.*" Rejecting both the erected wit and the metaphysical potential of human language as a form of false coinage. Ford provides a code of instructions for reading God's judgments in the story of an unfortunate man who seems to have died from gangrene. Interpretation becomes a system of exchange that like any monetary system is subject to both the regulations of official coinage and the possibility of counterfeit, and thus seems dependent upon the authority to mint, without ever being fully insured or reliable. With this caution Ford lays down a series of conditions by which those judgments may (in all probability) be known; they must be greater than anything man can inflict, and relate to some identifiable crime, and although the application of judgments is best made privately "in our own Bosoms," the public confession of a criminal is a good sign that his destruction is God's punishment and that the human word has successfully represented the divine will according to a meaningful syntax of crime and punishment.

Ford's text exemplifies the Restoration attempt to portray a system capable of comprehending the signs of transgression. The fact that he focuses upon those signs rather than upon the definition of sin suggests that for him and others like him the violation of either divine or human law is significant primarily as the mechanism by which the signs of its own being are produced—signs which, as we have seen, ultimately go on to generate or inform a social order.

In the *Discourse,* wrongdoing becomes the means by which God's judgments are to be known since it precipitates the providential signs that must be interpreted: a crime and preferably a criminal's confession are the best means of identifying God's judgments, themselves the sign of human trespass. Transgression, for Ford, is not merely represented as that against which the social order is defined; rather, it becomes the source of a symbolic order that ensures human order by bringing crime and punishment into a social syntax.

As a partial result of this interpretive dilemma (and the attitude toward wrongdoing which it necessitates), the stage emerged during the 1670s as a forum for arbitrating the competing claims of false prophets and misguided lamenters on one hand and the politics of the succession on the other. The stage was an arena (some argued) neither political or religious which could serve as a locus for reconciliation and the creation of a stable hegemony. As early as "An Essay of Dramatic Poesy" (1668). Dryden had invoked the Aristotelian commonplace of tragic irony or poetic justice as a criterion for good drama, suggesting that the audience expected the play to provide such a judgment. In his *Tragedies of the Last Age,* first published in 1677, Thomas Rymer argues the moral superiority of drama over history on the grounds that poetic justice is potentially more perfect and thus more instructive than the seeming vagaries of divine providence. He writes of those past poet/playwrights that "finding in History, the same *end* happen to the *righteous* and to the *unjust, vertue* often opprest, and *wickedness* on the Throne: they saw these particular *yesterday-truths* were imperfect and unproper to illustrate the *universal* and *eternal truths* by them intended. Finding also that this *unequal* distribution of rewards and punishments did perplex the *wisest,* and by the *Atheist* was made a scandal to the *Divine Providence.* They concluded, that a *Poet* must of necessity see *justice* exactly administered, if he intended to please." Earthly politics, Rymer concedes, often seem unfair and imperfect; more important, perhaps, they provide the opportunity for those (atheists) motivated by religious interest to question and confuse man's interpretation of the workings of providence. Drama, on the other hand, freed from the restrictions of history, has the power to clarify the perplexing evidence of divine judgment by seeing "*justice* exactly administered"; it serves as a higher interpretive truth, determining (or overdetermining) the link between crime and punishment that Ford found so problematic. For Rymer, a strong exponent of the Restoration belief that drama was meant to teach by example, the perfected and *"eternal truths"* of the playwright serve as the most effective pedagogy. Thus, he implies, the privileged arena of the stage can most effectively heal the "real" political and religious evils of oppression and wickedness that have already been amended within the text, returning order and stability to the state.

While Rymer's analysis provides a theoretical model to explain the privileged position of the stage in Restoration society, a broadside of 1679 entitled *A New Satyricall Ballad Of The Licentiousness of the Times* points pragmatically to the stage as the only locus of truth amid the chaos of libels and false prophetic claims which, it asserts, characterize Restoration politics:

The devil has left his puritanical dress,
And now like a Hawker attends on the Press,
That he might through the Town Sedition disperse,
In Pamphlets, and Ballads, in prose and in Verse

. . . . .

They howl and they yowl aloud through the whole
  Town,
The rights of Succession and Claims to the Crown,
And snarling and grumbling like Fools at each
  other,
Raise Contests and Factions betwixt Son and
  Brother.

. . . . .

But it is not enough to see what is past,
For these very Men become Prophets at last,
And with the same eyes can see what is meant,
To be Acted and done in the next Parliament.

. . . . .

Petition the Players to come on the Stage,
There to represent the vice of the Age,
That people may see in Stage looking-Glasses,
Fools of all sorts, and those pollitick Asses.

. . . . .

Men may prate and may write, but 'tis not their
  Rimes,
That can any way change or alter the Times,
It is now grown an Epidemical Disease,
For people to talk and to write what they please.

For this author, the theater reveals the folly of politically interested prophetic claims through the elevation of the mimetic ("Stage looking-Glasses") over the supposedly inspired word, as the language of the ballad sets true vision—the recognition of vice in public spectacle—against politically interested assertions of privileged sight. Moreover, this preference for the spectacle of the theater seems grounded in the idea that truth will be revealed in a human embodiment of vice on the stage (as opposed to the prophetic embodiment of the Word) that is simply not available to the printed word. Written text has become, in its battle over political signifiers ("the rights of Succession and Claims to the Crown"), a prelinguistic chaos of "snarling and grumbling" entirely divested of meaning and motivated primarily by the economic interest of the Hawker/devil. Thus just as Dryden located the origins of Roman satire in the theatrical exorcism of vice, here the accurate enactment of sedition, divorced from a market economy and thus from self-interest, will rid London of the "Epidemical Disease" of false argument that, through the transformation of the devil from puritan to balladmonger, has come to replace the complaint of earlier religious radicals and Dissenters. If the potential of the stage is somewhat undercut by the last stanza, and by the ballad form itself, theater nevertheless remains the only hope for the restoration of order.

All this is not to say that the theater was somehow immune from the discourse of political propaganda, or that anyone at the time thought it was; in fact it was one of the principal means for publicly disseminating propaganda, both royalist and Whig. Precisely because of its public political engagement, the privileging of the stage as (quite literally) an apolitical theater of judgment, shown in the *New Satyricall Ballad,* is extremely important to understanding both **Mac Flecknoe** and the need to subject theatrical production to a form of critical arbitration which ultimately drives the poem. Both Rymer and the author of the *New Satyricall Ballad* suggest that the actor replaces the prophet as the fulfillment of the law; the law itself is essentially Aristotelian, as in the case of Rymer's translation, or it is satiric, replicating the theater's judicial strategies in its own insistence upon the right to judge. **Mac Flecknoe** too, although clearly not theater but poetry, comments upon the capacity of the theater to pass judgment and simultaneously authorizes its own judicial role by appealing to the theatrical sign, the represented and representing body, as we shall now see.

Like the idea of the metamorphosis of the word, a belief in the capacity of theater to affect real social structures was hardly new to Dryden. Sir John Davenant, for example, had argued for the effectiveness of heroic drama as a means of regulating social order in his "Preface to *Gondibert.*" Yet **Mac Flecknoe** is perhaps the Restoration's most memorable and comprehensive statement of that theme, and it is certainly much more than an echo of earlier formulations. This satire of Dryden's is not, as critics have so often claimed, "about" literary standards or literature in its most general terms of wit, imagination, and dullness; the poem's terms are certainly more widely applicable and are primarily concerned with theater as an arena for the arbitration of political and religious opposition. Early in the poem, the stage is equated with a Christian place of judgment. Describing "Barbican," the literal boundaries of Flecknoe's kingdom, Dryden writes:

> From its old Ruins Brothel-houses rise,
> Scenes of lewd loves, and of polluted joys.
> Where their vast Courts the Mother-Strumpets keep,
> And, undisturbed by Watch, in silence sleep.
> Near these a Nursery erects its head,
> Where Queens are form'd, and future Hero's bred;
> Where unfledg'd Actors learn to laugh and cry,
> Where infant Punks their tender Voices try,
> And little *Maximins* the Gods defy.
>
> (Lines 70-77)

Here the stage and the brothel are conflated by physical proximity, as Dryden maps out the geography of the kingdom he creates, and by the interweaving of metaphor in the passage: "Queens" and "Punks" are actresses, but also prostitutes, and both professions are linked by the political vocabulary that metaphorizes them. At the same time, amid this spatial and metaphorical confusion, these lines echo Cowley's description of an underworld

> Beneath the Dens where *unfletcht Tempests* lye,
> And Infant *Winds* their tender *Voices* try,

> . . . . .
>
> Beneath th'eternal *Fountain* of all Waves,
> Where their vast *Court* the *Mother-waters* keep,
> And undisturb'd by *Moons* in Silence sleep.

This allusion, in turn, identifies "Dens" with brothels and hence with theater, suggesting that "Hell" is located precisely where, in one sense, it was—beneath the Restoration stage. The stage becomes a locus of judgment for Dryden.

The same figurative association of theater and hell is realized at the end of the poem, as the stage becomes a poetic mechanism for separating the goats from the sheep, enacting a final satiric judgment against both Flecknoe and Shadwell.

> For *Bruce* and *Longville* had a *Trap* prepar'd,
> And down they sent the yet declaiming Bard.
> Sinking he left his Drugget robe behind,
> Born upwards by a subterranean wind.
> The Mantle fell to the young Prophet's part,
> With double portion of his Father's Art.
>
> (Lines 212-17)

In this passage describing the final flatulent fall of the aging monarch, the reign and the prophecies of Flecknoe are theatrically arbitrated in two different senses. The last comment on the reign of that Zedekiah and false prophet proceeds through theatrical allusion, since the trap is the one prepared for Sir Formal in *The Virtuoso;* yet the function of the throne/stage/privy/hell that forms the trap is to identify Flecknoe's worth (or lack of it) as king, prophet, and playwright. Moreover, as the trap is sprung upon the "yet declaiming" monarch, succession becomes confused with political revolution. The natural order, as always in **Mac Flecknoe,** gives way before the unnatural, and thus the event seems to offer an equally pertinent comment on Shadwell's status as a "young Prophet" and a "true-blue-protestant poet."

While representing this theatrical judgment, **Mac Flecknoe,** like the more general cast of the fight between Dryden and Shadwell, sustains its concern with the poet's own right and authority to arbitrate political opposition. *The Medal of John Bayes* (1682), presumed to be the immediate impetus for Dryden's official acknowledgment of his authorship of **Mac Flecknoe,** insisted on Shadwell's prophetic status in trying to "avert those Plagues which we deserve," and attacked Dryden and the Tories on precisely the matter of the right to judge: "'Tis you who in your Factious Clubs vilifie the Government, by audaciously railing against *Parliaments.* . . . If anything could make the King lose the love and confidence of his people, it would be your unpunished boldness, who presume to call the *Freeholders* of England the Rabble, and their *Representative* a Crowd, and strike at the very Root of all their Liberty. . . . Who made ye Judges in Israel?" It is this question that **Mac Flecknoe** implicitly answers through its primary metaphors. As the playwright takes on the part of king and prophet, and as Dryden uses the principal analogy of political rule and succession to describe both Shadwell's and Flecknoe's pretenses to literary greatness, the analogous realms of politics and prophecy become subject to the same forms of critical legislation as the drama itself.

Thus Flecknoe's opening speech, another kind of judgment that rationalizes his choice of a successor, figures Shadwell's poetic ability in terms of politics and prophecy.

> . . . Sh——'s genuine night admits no ray,
> His rising Fogs prevail upon the Day:
> Besides his goodly Fabrick fills the eye,
> And seems design'd for thoughtless Majesty;
> Thoughtless as Monarch Oakes, that shade the plain,
> And, spread in solemn state, supinely reign.
> *Heywood* and *Shirley* were but Types of thee,
> Thou last great Prophet of Tautology:
> Even I, a dunce of more renown than they,
> Was sent before but to prepare thy way.
>
> (Lines 23-32)

Here the mock-heroic comparisons of Shadwell to monarch and prophet ridicule his literary abilities, but Dryden's particular use of the mock-heroic effectively corrupts the vehicle of his metaphor as well as its tenor. Shadwell's "Majesty"—as well as his poetry—is "thoughtless," the oaks that symbolize his rule are lethargic, if not fallen (over), and his prophecies are senseless repetition. Shadwell is a bad king and a false prophet precisely because he is a bad playwright: dull, tautological, and pedantic. Thus Dryden implies that the act of critically regulating the drama authorizes his poem's claim to legislate both political and religious institutions, as it emphatically does in its final lines.

As a myth of the formation of social structure, *Mac Flecknoe* insists that both religious and political order, represented by the roles of king and prophet, are a function of literary production. Arbitrated by the theater that both literally and figuratively marks the boundaries of Flecknoe's society, these orders are formed through the mimetic process; as metaphors for theater, they are subject to the same legislation as the sign itself. For Dryden, however, this is not a cultural authority based upon a structure of rigid signifiers, an analogue to the essentially political force of the prophetic word, and thus a source of exclusion, oppression, or damnation in a system organized by cultural hegemony. Baudrillard has said of parody that it "makes obedience and transgression equivalent" and thus "cancels out the difference upon which the law is based." Much the same might be said of Dryden's conception of satiric theater, in part because of the unusual relationship drawn between signifier and signified. Because the actor who represents crime or vice also serves as a means of vitiating that crime, theater becomes a medium in which the signs of transgression inevitably function as judgments upon themselves, not by association or analogy but by a principle of identity inherent in the dual nature of the signifier. As such, the sign does not merely fulfill the law, replacing both the word of the prophet and the executive function of government, nor does it serve, like Ford's "grammar," as a means of replicating and ordering itself

as sign. Rather, represented as literary product and literary icon, the signifier embodies the transgressive; it can create social order only as it serves to figure both crime and punishment, and thus only as it is itself inherently unstable. Paradoxically, the violation of the law becomes the sign of the authority of the signifier.

Thus while *Mac Flecknoe* itself is not theater, and so cannot present the embodiment of the visual icon in the way that live performance can, the iconographic structures of the poem do closely parallel the theater's investment in symbol as Dryden replicates the authoritative structure of the double signifier. Throughout the poem, acts of transgression produce material signs which function as instruments of justice because of their inadequacy to the heroic world with which they are compared. At his coronations Shadwell is invested with the symbols of office:

> In his sinister hand, instead of Ball,
> He place'd a mighty Mug of potent Ale;
> *Love's Kingdom* to his right he did convey,
> At once his Sceptre and his rule of Sway;
>
>   . . . . .
>
> His Temples last with Poppies were o'erspread,
> That nodding seem'd to consecrate his head.
>
> (Lines 120-27)

While these are the symbols of power in a mock-heroic universe, suited to that world because they represent the sins rather than the valor of its hero; in their mock-heroic employment they execute judgment through the very comparisons which that form implies. Shadwell's implied gluttony, drunkenness, sloth, and opium addiction lead to the "goodly Fabrick," itself a sign of his transgression, which both condemns him as an ascetic prophet and destines him for "thoughtless majesty" (line 26). Likewise, Flecknoe's supposed poverty as a dramatist produces *Love's Kingdom,* here the thoroughly useless scepter of anarchy, which implies, in its failure as a heroic sign, the punishment of decay and social disintegration.

More pervasively, the inferior poetry of Heywood, Shirley, Ogilby, and of course Shadwell himself produces the material of the kingdom over which that monarch will rule, ridiculing and punishing him through the comparison of that kingdom to the Rome of Augustus Caesar and through the conflation of privy, brothel, and hell. At Shadwell's coronation,

> No *Persian* Carpets spread th'Imperial way,
> But scatter'd Limbs of mangled Poets lay;
> From dusty shops neglected Authors come,
> Martyrs of Pies, and Reliques of the Bum.
> Much *Heywood, Shirly, Ogleby* there lay,
> But loads of *Sh——*almost choakt the way.
> Bilk't *Stationers* for Yeomen stood prepar'd,
> And *H——*was Captain of the Guard.
> The hoary Prince in Majesty appear'd,
> High on a Throne of his own Labours rear'd.
>
> (Lines 98-107)

Flecknoe's own productions form the throne that is the symbol of his office and the scaffold that becomes the site of the final judgment of his reign, opening into the hell of his eventual punishment. At the same time, the scatological humor of the passage, also realized in the material productions of Flecknoe's "Labours," performs the present-tense judgment of Dryden's own satire, enacting "justice" on the writings of Shadwell and Flecknoe as well as their politics.

Thus the emphasis on the symbol's materiality simultaneously empowers and degrades it, much as the actor's embodiment of the character of vice both represents and condemns. Its presence as object allows it to serve both as a locus for (product of/sign of) sin, while its referential function as part of the larger mock-heroic text permits it to expose that very vice: Flecknoe's texts are both his greatest crime and his greatest curse. As the word of the prophet effected punishment by being both the Word of God and, when unheeded, the justification for God's wrath, the strength and efficacy of this judgment lie ultimately in its implied inevitability. Sins create a system of signs, the signs of transgression, as it were, which, as Rymer had suggested, precipitate an inevitable, dramatic succession of punishment.

On the one hand, this conception of the satiric signifier suggests that Dryden's investment in the exclusionary nature of critical law may not be as great as it is usually taken to be; like the theatrical sign that arbitrates social order by representing transgression, the law that regulates literary culture is based on a fundamental instability which Dryden readily accepts. Critics long endorsed the notion that Dryden, "[preferring] cerebral to physical humor," attacked Shadwell for his crudity in an attempt to establish a polite, balanced, and decorous English verse; more recently, Laura Brown has sought to reconcile that perceived refinement with the poem's scatological humor in her description of a schizophrenic Dryden whose "ideology can be seen to belie his own experience as well as the realities of his age." But Dryden's use of gross materiality in *Mac Flecknoe* is a crucial means of embodying vice (poor writing) within the logic of the poem; without it the kind of arbitration which Dryden proposes would be impossible. Within his aesthetic sensibility the grotesque and the real, as those terms function to describe Dryden's essentially symbolic use of the dross of material substance, play an important role because of their dual nature within the poem as physical detail and symbolic signifier. They are, to reiterate for emphasis, both that which the logic of the poem defines as transgressive and, quite literally, the signs of transgression that ensure its detection and punishment.

Nevertheless, *Mac Flecknoe* is not only concerned with how text creates society but also with how culture itself is structured. If Dryden eagerly adopts strategies that he himself defines as crude and farcical, his attack on Shadwell for "selling bargains" does exhibit a determined appeal to laws of literary criticism, laws opposing the market economy that produces the text of Flecknoe's kingdom and thus the kingdom itself. The problem with theater in Flecknoe's kingdom is that it has become a form of prostitution and a process of excretion that render the product meaningless except as an object for sale. Flecknoe's offhand criticism of Ben Jonson—"Where sold he Bargains, Whip-stitch, kiss my Arse / Promis'd a Play and dwindled to a Farce?" (lines 180-81)—suggests the extent to which Dryden's critical attack on Shadwell is also a repudiation of an economic order which abandons literary greatness (represented throughout *Mac Flecknoe* by the figure of Jonson) in favor of monetary success. It might be argued that, as a personal attack, the aesthetic claims of the poem can be disregarded as so much personal and political propaganda. But if Dryden's attack was personal, he was also using it to engage a new and significant description of cultural division, according to which the term "scribbler" (like the incendiary cry of "Papist") was used to denote an absolute, arbitrary, and exclusionary difference of opinion, all the while that the wide prevalence of plagiarism, imitation, unauthorized editions, and the sordid curse of writing for hire made such distinctions virtually impossible to draw. Shadwell refers to Dryden as a "Hired Libeller" and a plagiarist, Dryden calls Shadwell a "kilderkin of wit" (line 196), and we find ourselves, rather like Ford, in search of a grammar to arbitrate this exchange and interpret the signs of transgression which each proposes.

Nonetheless, we can, I think, regard *Mac Flecknoe*'s appeal to a critical structure which it itself fails to uphold, as well as Dryden's criticism of a literary marketplace of which he was a part, as results of an ambivalence concerning the production of the "material image" itself. If Ford worries about the possibility of the counterfeit sign of transgression, Dryden is just as concerned with the possible miscarriage of production (with, i.e., excretion) in an age in which materialism meant not only self-interest but Whiggishness and the opposition to traditional moral economies on which authority could be based, as shown in *A Dialogue Between Content and Complaint*. *Mac Flecknoe* repeatedly reflects Dryden's own fear that the very image that links transgression and punishment in his poem will ultimately be left meaningless by the process that creates it. Over and over again, the link between crime and punishment proceeds through a logic of creation or emanation; Shadwell's gluttony, as we have seen, produces the bulk that is both the evidence of his transgression and the manner of his punishment, and his ignorance produces the play that is the symbol of his lack of efficacy or authority. At the same time, however, the materialization of the sign (especially in the form of literary text) always threatens to leave it dismembered, alienated, and ultimately without signification in the world of Dryden's poem—a mere pile of "reliques," "scatter'd Limbs," and human waste. The problem with the real, the material, the grotesque—which are not identical, but certainly linked as aesthetic terms in *Mac Flecknoe*—is, as localized in the problem of the poem's "indecorum," that these always threaten to be merely the transgression which they embody, rather than the loci of a symbolic logic of transgression and punishment. Describing the grotesque in graphic detail and using the terms of excrement and mutilation, as Dryden does throughout *Mac Flecknoe,* repeatedly incurs the charge of crudity.

Thus if *Mac Flecknoe* is a poem which argues that symbol and text create both structure and order, it is not entirely comfortable with the relationship between the transgression of that order and the linguistic structures that the poem proposes. Dryden's text is perpetually threatened by the chaos and decay it describes, and it continually teeters on the verge of a collapse into the realm of expletive "snarling and grumbling." At times, the grotesque image seems to overwhelm the poem altogether:

> With whate'er gall thou sett'st thy self to write,
> Thy inoffensive Satyrs never bite.
> In thy fellonious heart, though Venom lies,
> It does but touch thy *Irish* pen, and dyes.
> (Lines 199-202)

The final exhalation that marks the simultaneous conclusion of sentence, couplet, and image suggest that Shadwell's "*Irish* pen," more deadly than venom, destroys not only his own satire but the continuity of Dryden's poem as well. At other times, Shadwell's poetic faults materialize in Dryden's own verse, becoming the fabric of the poetry through a satiric imitation whose ability to compel judgment depends wholly on its recognizability as bad prosody.

> St. *Andre's* feet ne'er kept more equal time,
> Not ev'n the feet of thy own *Psyche's* Rhime:
> Though they in number as in sense excell;
> So just, so like tautology they fell,
> That, pale with envy *Singleton* forswore
> The lute and Sword which he in Triumph bore.
> (Lines 53-58)

Moreover, with his much broader sense of the dangers posed by the satiric symbol, Dryden also seems to understand that his use of the transgressive figure threatens the stability of the metaphorical structures that hold his poem together. If the dual nature of the symbol allows, even necessitates, a place for the grossly material, a depicted breakdown in the metaphorical structure of the poem suggests that an inability to distinguish signifier from signified threatens the symbolic (and political and cultural) order through the process of exchange that renders Shadwell's kingdom a world of commodities, of lifeless material and thus of remains and excrement. Ostensibly, of course, *Mac Flecknoe* uses the political (as well as the prophetic) as means for commenting upon the process of literary production and establishing political distinctions between good king and bad king, good writing and hack scribbling. But just as politics itself can be analogized, as we have seen, in terms of representation, the tenor and vehicle of Dryden's metaphor are easily reversible. This is as much a poem about politics as it is about theater; and by a somewhat perverse logic, interchangeability suggests an explanation of what is really wrong with Shadwell's kingdom, as political, theatrical, and prophetic are all leveled (or razed) by the processes of production and consumption that commodify and reify everything they can. Here prostitutes are actresses, but they are also queens, and Shadwell rises from the brothels as the prince "by ancient Dekker prophesied long since" (line 87). Yet this multiplicity does not bind these realms in stable analogies; rather, it threatens to destroy them all, for, as the logic of the poem constantly reminds us, the prostitute is neither good actress nor good queen, nor is a brothel the appropriate cradle for a great prince. A bad playwright is not a competent king, in part because he is drawn to produce garbage (or incendiary propaganda) to make a living. Thus it is that *Mac Flecknoe* exhibits a desire to retreat into the rhetorical structures of the political and arbitrary—and into satire, the assertion of the right to profess a thoroughly human judgment. The exchanges to which both bodies and texts are subject render them gross and material, potentially able to defy the symbolic order they create, through their lowness escaping the analogies between political, cultural, and religious orders which, for Dryden, organize both the poem and the world.

Thus Dryden insists upon a literary criticism structured as law, a system of regulation, like Ford's in proposing a mechanism for correctly interpreting the signs of transgression, unlike Ford's in claiming the ability to correctly arbitrate those signs. Thus too *Mac Flecknoe* can tell us much, not only about Dryden's own conceptualization of aesthetics but also about the growing frequency and urgency of depictions of the division between high and low culture in this period. While Dryden's poem is only one example of this emergent formulation, as a response to a world in which he perceives even theater as subject to the same control that threatened to destroy all political and religious order in the face of unbridled self-interest, *Mac Flecknoe* does suggest the extent to which critical legislation sought vainly to impose a set of distinctions upon a rampant and uncontrollable economy of literary production in which all such distinctions were superfluous, or meaningless, or both. The poem also, I think, says something about the mechanisms of cultural hegemony in the late 1670s and early 1680s. If representation defined the dynamics of political and religious division (as in *The Lamentation*), then a desire to impose some system of order in the face of political chaos, intrigue, and suspicion is certainly understandable, if ultimately untenable. Perhaps the greatest irony of *Mac Flecknoe* as well as its greatest success is the simultaneous institutionalization of a political distinction between popular and polite and a conception of the literary marketplace as part of a symbiotic system of literary production and standards.

FURTHER READING

Criticism

Barnard, John. "Dryden: History and 'The Mighty Government of the Nine.'" *The University of Leeds Review* 24 (1981):13-42.

> Discusses how in his poetry Dryden pointedly directed his audience toward historical and political events rather than the universal themes preferred by the later Romantics.

Benson, Donald R. "Space, Time, and the Language of Transcendence in Dryden's Later Poetry." *Restoration: Studies in English Literary Culture, 1660-1700* 8, No. 1 (Spring 1984): 10-16.

Compares the scientific theories of Newton against Dryden's later spirituality as seen in such poems as *The Hind and the Panther.*

Blake, David Haven Jr. "The Politics of Commercial Language in Dryden's *Annus Mirabilis.*" *Criticism* XXXIV, No. 3 (Summer 1992): 327-48.

Identifies in *Annus Mirabilis* Dryden's preoccupation with commerce and its lack as the result of the wars of the period as well as the devastating fire in London.

Brown, Laura. "The Ideology of Restoration Poetic Form: John Dryden." *PMLA* 97, No. 3 (May 1982): 395-407.

Discounts the claims of Dryden as a great poet, but argues that his method and his place in history paved the way for the great poets of later eras.

Budick, Sanford. *Dryden and the Abyss of Light: A Study of* Religio Laici *and* The Hind and the Panther. New Haven: Yale University Press, 1970, 272 p.

Looks closely at Dryden's two religious poems in light of the Restoration Period during which they were written and in the context of Dryden's personal feelings about his religious conversion.

Bywaters, David. "The Problem of Dryden's *Fables.*" *Eighteenth-Century Studies* 26, No. 1 (Fall 1992): 29-55.

Speculates upon Dryden's purpose for publishing the *Fables,* which includes translations but also original poems, and argues that the work's continuity lies partly in its criticism of William III.

Carnochan, W. B. "Dryden's Alexander." In *The English Hero, 1660-1800,* edited by Robert Folkenflik, pp. 46-60. Newark: University of Delaware Press, 1982.

Suggests that like King William III, whom he was meant to symbolize, Dryden's Alexander in *Alexander's Feast* is a mass of contradictions.

Chiasson, Elias J. "Dryden's Apparent Scepticism in *Religio Laici.*" *Harvard Theological Review* LIV, No. 3 (July 1961): 207-21.

Argues that rather than showing Dryden's scepticism, the poem *Religio Laici* reveals the poet's Anglican Christian humanism.

Clingham, Gregory J. "Johnson's Criticism of Dryden's Odes in Praise of St. Cecilia." *Modern Language Studies* XVIII, No. 1 (Winter 1988): 165-80.

Analyzes Samuel Johnson's general admiration for Dryden's works in light of Johnson's more specific assessments of the language and music of two of Dryden's odes.

Cotterill, Anne. "Parenthesis at the Center: The Complex Embrace of *The Hind and the Panther.*" *Eighteenth-Century Studies* 30, No. 2 (Winter 1996-97): 139-58.

Analyzes the heavily allusive and allegorical language of *The Hind and the Panther* as Dryden strove both to communicate with his audience and protect himself.

Cousins, A. D. "Heroic Satire: Dryden and the Defence of Later Stuart Kingship." *Southern Review* XIII, No. 3 (November 1980): 170-87.

Defines the term, "heroic satire" and explains how *Absalom and Achitophel, Mac Flecknoe,* and *The Medall* qualify as heroic satires.

Daly, Robert. "Dryden's Ode to Anne Killigrew and the Communal Work of Poets." *Texas Studies in Literature and Language* XVIII, No. 2 (Summer 1976): 184-97.

Tries to account for the greatness of this particular poem with the apparent mediocrity of its subject matter—the poet Anne Killigrew, herself.

Ellis, Frank H. "'Legends no Histories' Part the Second: The Ending of *Absalom and Achitophel.*" *Modern Philology* 85, No. 4 (May 1988): 393-407.

Argues that while *Absalom and Achitophel* is "propaganda for the 'True Succession'" of James II, though it does not resort in the end to slavish flattery.

Fujimura, Thomas H. "The Personal Element in Dryden's Poetry." *PMLA* 89, No. 5 (October 1974): 1007-23.

Asserts that Dryden's personality "with all its virtues and faults" shows itself clearly and consistently in his poems.

——. "Dryden's Poetics: The Expressive Values in Poetry." *JEGP* LXXIV, No. 2 (April 1975): 195-208.

Argues that Dryden not only chose his poetic diction carefully, but that he selected it for its "expressive" or emotional and imaginative effect as well as for its rhetorical power.

Gardiner, Anne Barbeau. "Dryden's *The Medall* and the Principle of Continuous Transmission of Laws." *CLIO* 14, No. 1 (Fall 1984): 51-70.

Regards *The Medall* as, in part, the poet's rumination on English law and history and describes these as interests which were typical to Dryden.

——. "*Religio Laici* and the Principle of Legal Continuity." *Papers on Language & Literature* 20, No. 1 (Winter 1984): 29-46.

Argues that Dryden asserts that "the Bible is a set of written laws to be interpreted . . . according to precedent" rather than according to the interpretive needs of rebels.

Griffin, Dustin. "Dryden's 'Oldham' and the Perils of Writing." *Modern Language Quarterly* 37, No. 2 (June 1976): 133-50.

Regards Dryden's "To the Memory of Mr. Oldham" as an autobiographical poem if it is seen as the poet's meditations on his own mortality.

Hammond, Paul. "Flecknoe and *Mac Flecknoe.*" *Essays in Criticism* XXXV, No. 4 (October 1985): 315-29.

Suggests reasons why Dryden chose to use in particular the bad seventeenth-century poet Flecknoe to lampoon his enemy Thomas Shadwell.

Jose, Nicholas. "Dryden and other Selves." The *Critical Review,* No. 25 (1983): 102-14.

Discusses Dryden's capacity for writing through other personas or "selves": in his translations, epistles, satires, dedications, etc.

Kenshur, Oscar. "Scriptural Deism and the Politics of Dryden's *Religio Laici.*" *ELH* 54, No. 4 (Winter 1987): 869-92.

Argues that *Religio Laici* is not as preoccupied with religion as many critics believe, but that it is instead much more concerned with the "maintenance of public order" and obedience to authority.

Love, Harold. "Shadwell, Flecknoe and the Duke of Newcastle: An Impetus for *Mac Flecknoe.*" *Papers on Language & Literature* 21, No. 1 (Winter 1985): 19-27.

Discusses the significance of the fact that the three objects of satire in *Mac Flecknoe*—Thomas Shadwell, Richard Flecknoe, and James Shirley—also shared William Cavendish, Duke of Newcastle, as their patron.

Luckett, Richard. "The Fabric of Dryden's Verse." *Proceedings of the British Academy* LXVII (1981): 289-305.

Uses the word "fabric" to describe the manner in which Dryden succeeds in drawing all the separate parts of a poetic work into a unified whole.

Madsen, Valden. "Dryden's Forgotten Ode: A Reading of *Threnodia Augustalis.*" *Concerning Poetry* 15, No. 2 (Fall 1982): 1-15.

Analyzes the ways in which *Threnodia Augustalis* both memorializes the dead king, Charles II, and attempts to prepare the way for a smooth transition for his successor, James II.

Maurer, A. E. Wallace. "The Form of Dryden's *Absalom and Achitophel,* Once More." *Papers on Language & Literature* 27, No. 3 (Summer 1991): 320-37.

Examines the numerous labels which critics have applied to *Absalom and Achitophel* (including epic, classical oration, allegory, and satire) and discusses the validity of each.

McKeon, Michael. *Politics and Poetry in Restoration England: The Case of Dryden's* Annus Mirabilis. Cambridge: Harvard University Press, 1975, 336 p.

Offers a close reading of *Annus Mirabilis* within its historical context, as well as a discussion of the manner in which twentieth-century critics deal with the question of politics within poetics.

Miller, Rachel. "Physic for the Great: Dryden's Satiric Translations of Juvenal, Persius, and Boccaccio." *Philological Quarterly* 68, No. 1 (Winter 1989): 53-75.

Argues that Dryden expressed his adamant disapproval of the monarchs William and Mary through his satirical translations of classic texts in lieu of the original poetic satires he was accustomed to writing before their ascension.

Miner, Earl. *Dryden's Poetry.* Bloomington: Indiana University Press, 1967, 354 p.

"Discusses the assumptions, ideas, and techniques of Dryden's major poetry, including not only his nondramatic work but also his plays . . . and his translations. . . ."

Pohli, Carol Virginia. "Formal and Informal Space in Dryden's Ode, *To the Pious Memory of . . . Anne Killigrew.*" *Restoration: Studies in English Literary Culture, 1660-1700* 15, No. 1 (Spring 1991): 27-40.

Discusses the meaning behind the dialectal structure of Dryden's elegy to the young, inexperienced poet and daughter of his friend, Dr. Henry Killigrew.

Quinsey, K. M. "Sign-post Painting: Poetry and Polemic in Dryden's *The Medall.*" *Restoration: Studies in English Literary Culture, 1660-1700* 16, No. 2 (Fall 1992): 97-109.

Argues that instead of resorting to the standard assessment of *The Medall* as an inferior version of *Absalom and Achitophel,* critics should give *The Medall* its due as a different type of polemical poem.

Quinsey, Katherine M. "*Religio Laici?* Dryden's Men of Wit and the Printed Word." In *The Wit of Seventeenth-Century Poetry,* edited by Claude J. Summers and Ted-Larry Pebworth, pp. 199-214. Columbia: University of Missouri Press, 1995.

Asserts that while the central subject of *Religio Laici* is "the nature of religious authority," the poem nevertheless deals with the debate on wit typical to the seventeenth century.

Reverand, Cedric D., II. *Dryden's Final Poetic Mode: The* Fables. Philadelphia: University of Pennsylvania Press, 1988, 239 p.

Examines Dryden's *Fables* (works which he translated in his later years into English from Greek, Italian, and Middle English) and argues for their importance as part of Dryden's poetic achievements.

Shaheen, Abdel-Rahman. "'Two Beasts Talking Theology': John Dryden's *The Hind and The Panther.*" *CLA Journal* XXIX, No. 2 (December 1985): 185-96.

Argues that *The Hind and The Panther* works as a complex, occasionally humorous poetic fable defending the sincerity of Dryden's conversion to Catholicism and trying to reconcile it with Anglicanism.

Sloman, Judith. *Dryden: The Poetics of Translation.* Toronto: University of Toronto Press, 1985, 265 p.

Argues that Dryden's translations of ancient and non-English poetry are not simply transliterations but imaginative "recreations."

Swedenberg, H. T., Jr. *Essential Articles for the Study of John Dryden.* Hamden, CT: Archon Books, 1966, 587 p.

Publishes examples of essays on Dryden's works, including general surveys and discussions of his plays, poetry, and criticism.

Tamer, Nanette C. "'These Are the Joys': Poetic Effects and the Idea of Poetry in Dryden's Translations from Horace." *Classical and Modern Literature* 15, No. 3 (Spring 1995): 215-22.

Compares and contrasts Horace's and Dryden's individual poetic theories as revealed through Dryden's translations of Horace's *Odes.*

Van Doren, Mark. *John Dryden: A Study of His Poetry.* Bloomington: Indiana University Press, 1963, 298 p.

Looks at Dryden's poetic history, including his early years, his lyric and narrative poems, and his poetic reputation.

Weinbrot, Howard D. "'Nature's Holy Bands' in *Absalom and Achitophel:* Fathers and Sons, Satire and Change." *Modern Philology* 85, No. 4 (May 1988): 373-92.

Argues that the poem is not only satirical but didactic: gently criticizing Charles II in order to improve him.

Wilson, Gayle Edward. "'Weavers Issue,' 'Princes Son,' and 'Godheads Images': Dryden and the *Topos* of Descent in *Absalom and Achitophel.*" *Papers on Language & Literature* 28, No. 3 (Summer 1992): 267-82.

Discusses the importance of the *topos* or motif of "descent" in *Absalom and Achitophel,* and how this same *topos* is used to praise the rightful heirs and vilify the pretenders.

Zwicker, Steven N. *Dryden's Political Poetry: The Typology of King and Nation.* Providence: Brown University Press, 1972, 154 p.

Argues that Dryden's understanding of history was an important factor in his political-poetry writing.

——. *Politics and Language in Dryden's Poetry: The Arts of Disguise.* Princeton: Princeton University Press, 1984, 248 p.

Close study of the symbols, imagery, allegorics, and metaphors that are found in Dryden's political poetry.

Heinrich Heine
1797-1856

(Born Harry Heine) German poet, essayist, critic, journalist, editor, dramatist, novella and travel writer.

INTRODUCTION

Heine is one of the outstanding literary figures of nineteenth century Europe. He is best known for his *Buch der Lieder* (1827; *Heinrich Heine's Book of Songs*), a collection of love lyrics which were, in time, set to music by Franz Schubert, Robert Schumann, and other composers. Because of his Jewish background he was frequently reviled by European anti-Semites and his works were censored during the period of Nazi hegemony in Germany. In the contemporary era, Heine has been recognized as the first major poet to adopt a humorous, ironic tone, which pervades his poetry, prose, and commentaries on politics, art, literature, and society.

Biographical Information

Heine was born in Düsseldorf into a Jewish household, the poor relations of a larger, wealthy family. His early years were greatly influenced by his uncle, Salomon Heine, a successful and influential banker who financed Heine's education. In 1819, Heine was sent to study law at the University of Bonn, where he showed a growing interest in literature and history and studied under the famous critic August Wilhelm Schlegel, who introduced him to the ideas of the German Romantic School. He completed his courses at the University of Göttingen and received his law degree in 1825. In that same year he changed his name from Harry to Heinrich and converted to Protestantism, a practical measure done because of anti-Semitic laws in nineteenth-century Germany. In 1831 Heine emigrated to Paris, where he remained in self-imposed exile for most of his life. From the mid-1830s through the rest of his life, he suffered with increasing illness from venereal disease, and in the spring of 1848 he became completely paralyzed and partially blind. Confined to what he called his "mattress grave," Heine lived in constant pain, yet was intellectually alert until his death in 1856.

Major Works

Heine began his literary career while still a student, publishing his first book of poetry, *Gedichte* (*Poems*), in 1822. His next published work, *Tragödien nebst einem lyrischen Intermezzo* (1823), which contains his only attempt at drama, was considered unimportant at the time of its pub

lication and largely ignored. However, with the publication of his third volume of poetry, *Book of Songs,* Heine became one of the most popular German poets of his day. The work established his preeminence as a lyric poet, and has long remained the basis of his international reputation. This early poetry reflects the influence of Romanticism in its emphasis on love and despair, as well as in its pervasive tone of reverie. But *Book of Songs* also abounds with realism, skepticism, wit, and irony. Critics of the work acknowledge that Heine did not share the positive world view of such German Romantics as Johann Wolfgang von Goethe and Friedrich Schiller, and that he lacked faith in the ability of poetry to overcome the alienation of modern life. *Book of Songs* thus represents Heine's rejection of the German Romantic tradition and is thought to mark the beginning of the post-Romantic movement in German literature. Following a long hiatus from poetry in which Heine focused his attention on prose works related to politics, religion, society, and art, the first of two long, satirical poems *Deutschland: Ein Wintermärchen* (1844; *Germany: A Winter's Tale*) appeared, followed by *Atta Troll: Ein Sommernachstraum* (1847; *Atta Troll*). These poems blend history with political and literary satire, defying generic classification. Regarded as among Heine's most powerful and compelling poetry, *Romanzero* (1851; *Romancero*) and the posthumously published *Letzte Gedichte und Gedanken* (1869; *Last Poems*), date from late in his career. In these works, Heine frequently returns to the lyrical form of his earliest poetry. These poems vividly describe a man preparing for death, which he alternately fears and welcomes as a refuge. With their self-mocking, ironic tone, they capture the full range of Heine's tenderness and delicacy as well as his pain and terror, and are considered the fullest expressions of his poetic genius.

Critical Reception

Although Heine was one of the most influential and popular poets of the nineteenth century, critical response to his work has varied over the years. His writings have met with both admiration and disapproval in his native land, where his ruthless satires and radical pronouncements made him appear unpatriotic and subversive to his contemporaries. His religion consistently worked against him: he was ostracized as a Jew among Germans, but when he converted to Protestantism, both Jews and Christians assailed him as an opportunist. All of Heine's works were banned in 1835 and he was at one time forbidden to return to Germany. During the 1930s and 1940s, the Nazis tried to erase Heine's name from German history. They destroyed his grave, banned his books, and when they found that they could not eliminate his famous poem "Die Lorelei" from the collective memory of the German people, they attributed it to an unknown author. Heine's reputation has fared better outside Germany, but while his lyric poetry is widely praised, his ironic and satiric writings have only recently met with critical acclaim. The complexity and variety of his views have often made him an outcast—those who appreciated the politically militant poet of the 1840s in some cases resented his later, more conservative work. The only portion of Heine's oeuvre to be accepted by all critical factions remains the *Book of Songs*.

PRINCIPAL WORKS

Poetry

Gedichte [*Poems*] 1822
Tragödien nebst einem lyrischen Intermezzo (drama and poetry) 1823
Buch der Lieder [*Heinrich Heine's Book of Songs*] 1827
Deutschland: Ein Wintermärchen [*Germany: A Winter's Tale*] (essay and poetry) 1844
Neue Gedichte [*New Poems*] 1844
Atta Troll: Ein Sommernachtstraum [*Atta Troll*] 1847
Romanzero [*Romancero*] 1851
Letzte Gedichte und Gedanken [*Last Poems*] 1869
The Poems of Heine, Complete 1878

Other Major Works

Reisebilder. 4 vols. [*Pictures of Travel*] (travel sketches) 1826-31
Französische Zustände [*French Affairs: Letters from Paris*] (essays) 1833
Zur Geschichte der neuern schönen Literatur in Deutschland [*Letters Auxiliary to the History of Modern Polite Literature in Germany*] (essay) 1833
Der Salon. 4 vols. [*The Salon; or, Letters on Art, Music, Popular Life and Politics*] (criticism, poetry, unfinished novels, essays, and letters) 1834-40
Zur Geschichte der Religion und Philosophie in Deutschland [*Religion and Philosophy in Germany*] (essay) 1835
Shakespeare's Mädchen und Frauen [*Heine on Shakespeare: A Translation of His Notes on Shakespeare's Heroines*] (criticism) 1839
Heinrich Heine über Ludwig Börne [*Ludwig Börne: Recollections of a Revolutionist*] (criticism and fictional letters) 1840
Der Doktor Faust: Ein Tanzpoem, nebst kurosien Berichten über Teufel, Hexen und Dichkunst [*Doktor Faust: A Dance Poem, Together with Some Rare Accounts of Witches, Devils and the Ancient Art of Sorcery*] (ballet scenario) 1851
Der Verbannten Götter [*Gods in Exile*] (novella) 1853
Vermischte Schriften. 3 vols. (poetry, novella, ballet scenario, and essays) 1854
Heinrich Heines sämtliche Werke. 12 vols. [*The Works of Heinrich Heine*] (poetry, essays, ballet scenario, criticism, novella, unfinished novels, travel sketches, and memoirs) 1887-90
Heinrich Heines Familienleben [*The Family Life of Heinrich Heine*] (letters) 1892
Briefe. 6 vols. (letters) 1950-51

CRITICISM

Stuart Atkins (essay date 1957)

SOURCE: "The Evaluation of Heine's *Neue Gedichte*," in *Wächter und Hüter: Festschrift für Hermann J. Weigand,* edited by Curt von Faber du Faur, Konstantin Reichardt, and Heinz Bluhm, Department of Germanic Language, Yale University, 1957, pp. 99-107.

[*In the following essay, Atkins surveys critical opinion of Heine's relatively neglected* Neue Gedichte.]

One of the great curiosities of German literary history is the division of opinion which has long prevailed on the subject of Heine's stature as a poet. Outside the German-speaking world Heine may properly be named in the same breath with Goethe or Rilke, for an overwhelming majority of non-German critics, even those knowing something of his complex character and personality, have agreed and continue to agree that Heine is a lyric poet of incontestable greatness.[1] Yet Emil Ermatinger, writing in Switzerland between 1943 and 1946, has classed him among

"Forcierte Talente," moralistically condemned him for a "Wurzellosigkeit" for which he can hardly be held ultimately responsible, and concluded his discussion of him with these disparaging observations:

> "Heine ist, nach Goethe, sicherlich der meistgelesene und geliebte deutsche Lyriker des neunzehnten Jahrhunderts gewesen. Dass er das war, ist ein Zeichen für den langsamen seelischen Zerfall jener Zeit."[2]

That Ermatinger's is no outmoded or peculiarly provincial viewpoint is clear from the importance—or, better, non-importance—assigned to Heine in H. O. Burger's recent *Annalen der deutschen Literatur,* where W. Baumgart, disparaging him as an egocentric with an exhibitionistic "Publikumsbewusstsein," tells us, "Das Buch der Lieder enthält bereits den ganzen Heine, mit allen Vorzügen, nur noch nicht allen Unarten."[3] Given this premise, it is not surprising that Heine's lyrics are passed over in complete silence in Burger's own discussion of German letters from 1832 to 1842 (a period of which it is said, "Die Höhe grosser Lyrik erreichen wir wieder mit den *Gedichten* Friedrich Hebbles," a poet with whom only Eichendorff, Mörike and Droste-Hülshoff are named as of comparable stature) and that in his account of 1843-1850 Heine's *Neue Gedichte* are conveniently disposed of as a collection containing "neben Natur- und Liebesliedern und Romanzen eine Abteilung 'Zeitgedichte'."[4]

Although moral sensibility and chauvinistic prejudices have at times been important factors in determining the German estimate of Heine, I think it can be shown that the innate shortcomings of biographical and—to a lesser extent—literary-historical criticism have played the decisive rôle in the process which has as it were reduced him to a poet of secondary importance for many twentieth-century German readers and critics. A brief survey of typical evaluations of Heine's *Neue Gedichte,* the only one of his three great collections of poems about which opinion seems predominantly unfavorable, will serve to make clear the workings of this process; at the same time it will permit me to select from what seem irreconcilably diverse opinions based upon apparently irreconcilable premises certain uncontradicted facts and certain critical constants that may perhaps together constitute a more solid basis for evaluation of Heine's total poetic achievement than has yet been successfully established.

Of the cycle **"Neuer Frühling"** Max J. Wolff declared that it contains "eininge von Heines besten und zartesten Liedern," but that "als Ganzes bleibt er hinter den früheren Zyklen zurück. Es ist zu viel Virtuosität darin." And after noting that "die besten Lieder . . . entstammen einer sehr frühen Zeit und sind im unmittelbaren Anschluss an die 'Heimkehr', ja noch vor ihr verfasst worden," he concluded: "Sie bieten keine Klänge, die nicht schon im *Buch der Lieder* angeschlagen wären; neu ist . . . höchstens der Ton der Missmut, die ihren Abschluss bildet."[5] His comments on **"Verschiedene"** and **"Zeitgedichte"** are on the whole even less favorable and have their counterparts in many other biographies and biographical-critical sketches; they may be subsumed under H. G. Atkins' view that *Neue*

Gedichte would not have added very greatly to Heine's reputation as a poet if his production had ceased with their appearance" and that, although some of them are "in execrably bad taste," "only when we come to the '**Zeitgedichte**' do we find the important new note of the whole collection."[6] But even so devoted an admirer of Heine as Ernst Elster chose thus to explain why *Neue Gedichte* had not achieved the same popularity as *Buch der Lieder* or *Romanzero*:

> der zarte Duft und die Anmut der ersten Sammlung hat sich hier verflüchtigt, und es fehlt noch der wilde Schmerzensklang, die Weltanklage und der grelle Farbenreiz der letzten. Sie [i.e., *Neue Gedichte*] stehen in der Mitte von beiden, deuten vielfach noch auf die frühere Dichtweise zurück, lassen aber schon manche Züge der späteren Kunst Heines erkennen.[7]

And for what Elster has offered a biographical-historical explanation, Ernst Alker has even given a teleological-historical one, declaring that "die *Neuen Gedichte* . . . sich nicht recht durchsetzen konnten, vor allem deswegen, weil sie in vieler Beziehung eine Abschwächung und Wiederholung des *Buch der Lieder* und einen matten Vorklang zum *Romanzero* darstellten."[8]

If it is patent nonsense for a collection of poems not to have achieved popularity because it was inferior to a collection that had not yet appeared to rival it, it is nevertheless seriously disturbing that influential interpreters of Heine should disagree about what would seem an objectively determinable fact, viz., whether there are "neue Klänge" in the cycle **"Neuer Frühling"** or not. Although Geneviève Bianquis, admiring its delicate perfection, was constrained to admit that "ce qu'on peut reprocher à ce recueil charmant, c'est qu'il manque de nouveauté" and even declared, "Le poète a beau n'être plus l'adolescent timide épris d'une cousine, il n'ose encore faire entendre que de tendres plaintes et des soupirs résignés,"[9] her German counterpart Helene Herrmann insisted that in **"Neuer Frühling"** Heine used the forms and techniques of earlier cycles

> in einem anderen Sinne . . . , den die neue Stimmung verlangte: Heine gibt sich nämlich nicht mehr als den Leidensbewussten, Tiefenttäuschten, er ist vielmehr skeptisch heiter, melancholisch überlegen. Kein Byronscher Trotz mehr, der sich auflehnt, aber auch kein allzu weiches Lamentieren, das in Spott umschlägt. Überhaupt kein auffallendes Nebeneinander der Gefühle mehr, vielmehr ein selbstverständliches und wohllautendes Ineinander.[10]

It was obviously in full awareness of such conflicting views that Rodolfo Bottachiari concluded his careful analysis of the same group of poems by insisting on "l'organicità lirica di questo ciclo, che a me pare eccessivamente trascurato e a torto giudicato soltanto come une pura e semplice ripetizione di vecchi motivi."[11]

But Bottachiari himself became a moralist-biographer when he turned to **"Verschiedene,"** of which he said, "Ora è [la sensualità di Heine] soltanto cronaca biografica di trascorsi lascivi."[12] Elster, more cautious, conceded that "selbst der Duldsame fühlt sich befremdet oder erschrocken, wenn Heine ihn in dieser Abteilung . . . gleich mit einem knappen Dutzend seiner Geliebten bekannt macht. . . . Und wenn sie noch liebenswürdig geschildert wären . . . ! . . . Sie sind meist ziemlich geistlos und in der Regel treulos . . . und die übergrosse Wirklichkeitsnähe, in der sie erscheinen, wird ihnen gefährlich."[13] Although it would be interesting to demonstrate that *Treue* was not the virtue of the heroine(s) of ***Buch der Lieder,*** it is perhaps sufficient to balance Elster's remarks with a statement by R. M. Meyer:

> die **"Verschiedenen,"** die er hier besingt—man hat es ihm grausam verdacht, obwohl man es jahrhundertelang den Ovid und Horaz verzieh, wenn sie die lockersten Liebchen feierten—werden zumeist so wenig greifbar, wie die konventionell stilisierte "Geliebte" des Buches der Lieder.[14]

And it is possible to balance Wolff's "Unmoralisch mögen die Gedichte sein, aber die Hauptsache ist, dass sie unmoralisch wirken, weil sie unkünstlerisch sind, weil sie in dem persönlichen Erlebnis stecken bleiben,"[15] with Mme. Bianquis'

> On aurait tort cependant de prendre ces poésies galantes pour une confession pure et simple. Il y a beaucoup d'art dans la composition de ces médaillons. . . . Les estampes plus légères dont s'est épouvantée la pudeur allemande . . . nous font tout au plus sourire. . . . Ces héroïnes auxquelles on a reproché leur basse extraction et leurs manières vulgaires nous semblent bien naïves et sans vices. . . . Ces accents libertins ne déparent nullement une poésie qui a d'autre part . . . chanté tous les moments de l'amour idéal, éthéré, tendre ou mélancolique.[16]

The poems dealing with what Gottfried Keller, in *Der Apotheker von Chamounix,* unkindly called "die Totenmädchen von Paris" (although some obviously had English and German prototypes) seemed neither novel nor scandalous to Charles Andler, who observed:

> Volontiers [les Allemands] se croient les héritiers des Grecs, mais ils n'osent être des païens. Dès que Gœthe publia ses admirables *Elégies romaines,* ce fut une levée de boucliers, parmi une critique composée surtout de pasteurs. Heine n'a pas atteint Gœthe en hardiesse, et ne l'a pas atteint en plasticité non plus. Imaginons cet être passionné, tenaillé par une douleur tenace, renouvelée. Comment évitera-t-il la tentation du désespoir, du suicide, si ce n'est par la consolation charnelle? Il n'y a là rien que de jeune, peut-être d'un peu vulgaire, mais d'humain. Les Anciens savaient sauver cette vulgarité des "amours diverses" par la perfection de la forme. Gœthe s'y est essayé et Heine après lui.[17]

But whereas Andler saw the difference between Goethe and the Heine of **"Verschiedene"** as one of two different types of artistic genius, Fritz Friedländer, in an admirable monograph on Heine and Goethe, came to the equally plausible conclusion that, despite the sharp distinction between Heine's satiric-ironic outlook and Goethe's "Weltfrömmigkeit," in ***Neue Gedichte***

> trifft Heines Tonfall die grosse lyrische Form der kleinen Lieder Goethes; er beherrscht mit souveräner Gebärde das Arsenal der metaphorischen und allegorischen Vorstellungen; wiederum rollt in dem Zyklus "Verschiedene" das Eros-Thema in unerschöpflichen Variationen an uns vorüber, während die prächtigen Zeitgedichte . . . das Niveau der plastischen Anschaulichkeit Goethes innehalten.[18]

By this point the reader has no doubt been tempted to cry, despairingly, "Quot homines tot sententiae" and "A plague on all your critics." Yet if he looks back through the opinions I have cited it will quickly become clear to him that the poems of ***Neue Gedichte*** have on the whole inspired favorable reactions when critics have simply examined their effectiveness as poetic statements, and that they have been less favorably judged when critics—sometimes the same ones—have read them as fragments of a presumedly literal autobiography or as unscrupulous falsifications of biographical truth. And the more biographers have concerned themselves with Heine's moral and poetic development and minimized the external details of his life, the more valid or at least more critically useful seem to have been their comments on this collection and its several parts. Thus Jules Legras, one of the few interpreters of Heine to have considered the group **"Verschiedene"** superior to the cycle **"Neuer Frühling"** (it has the virtue of not being "insipide . . . dans son ensemble"), suggested that "Verschiedene représentait peut-être pour Heine une parodie du Buch der Lieder, ou tout au moins du désespoir amoureux qui domine ce recueil"[19]—an interpretation which, regardless of his own somewhat negative evaluation of ***Neue Gedichte,*** has the virtue of in fact insisting that this collection is somehow distinct in character from its more popular predecessor. That there may be, moreover, a measure of truth in his suggestion seems confirmed by Heine's expression, as early as 1830, of the desire to find a new poetic style.[20]

Wider recognition that the poems of **"Neuer Frühling"** represent more than minor variations on the substance and style of **"Lyrisches Intermezzo"** and **"Heimkehr,"** and that those of **"Verschiedene"** are not experiments in poetic realism (Heine never included the experimental ***An Jenny,*** beginning "Ich bin nun fünfunddreissig Jahr alt," in this group, and he wisely excluded from it a goodly number of equally witty and equally bitter poems whose effectiveness depends primarily on their realistic tones), might contribute much to the establishment of Heine's full poetic stature both in Germany and elsewhere. H. Herrmann made an important contribution, therefore, when she emphasized that poems of *both* of these cycles

> erinnern zuweilen an Rokokopoesie. Es liegt aber keine Nachahmung vor, sondern ein Hineinfinden in die Art eines solchen Stils auf Grund ähnlicher Erlebnisse, wie die, welche diesen Stil hervorgebracht hatten. . . . Das Misstrauen in die Dauer der Gefühle zeitigt eine Art

Rokokophilosophie: Sinn für den Reiz des Vergänglichen in Gefühlen und Situationen, Vertrauen in die Unermesslichkeit des Moments und überlegene Freiheit dem eigenen Fühlen gegenüber, dem man ebenso wie dem fremden misstraut.[21]

That Heine was actually conscious of his poems' affinities with Rococo verse seems evident, however, from his use of *In Gemäldegalerien,* the twelfth and last poem of "Neuer Frühling" in 1831, as *Prolog* to the expanded cycle published in 1844: the motif of cupids binding a hero with chains of flowers is patently pre-romantic and should have compelled more readers than have so far done so to evaluate in a non-romantic frame of literary reference the poems that follow *Prolog.* And H. Herrmann in a sense confirmed this when she observed that

in den sprachlichen Mitteln drückt sich der Charakter der neuen Dichtung Heines besonders stark aus. Das was wir das Rokokohafte nannten, tritt hervor in der Scheu vor schwerwiegenden Worten, aber ganz anders als in der Zeit des *Intermezzos* und der *"Heimkehr".* Das kindlich Lallende, das jene Dichtung suchte, wird verschmäht. Alle Bezeichnungen für Lust und Schmerz, alle Gefühlsworte der Liebe sind gedämpft, ins Heitere gewendet; die Worte "zärtlich," "Zärtlichkeit," "verliebt," früher selten genug, werden jetzt häufig. Ja, in einer preziös-archaisch wirkenden Weise wendet Heine das Wort "zärtlich" auch auf die körperliche Erscheinung an. . . .

Yet, writing when the only important form of the lyric was still generally held to be the "romantic" one, she could but conclude that the lyrics of *Neue Gedichte* represented a transition "von dem Stil des *Intermezzo,* von diesem etwas blutlosen Stil einer Epigramm- und Stimmungslyrik hinüber zu dem Spätstil, der ganz mit Leben, Farbe, Bewegung gesättigt ist."[22]

Now that it is once more possible, even in Germany, to recognize that other non-romantic types of the lyric than those represented by ode and elegy may embody positive literary values, the biographical readings of "Neuer Frühling" and the literally realistic interpretations of "Verschiedene"—Wolff's "Der Dichter schildert seine Strassen- und Zufallsbekanntschaften mit tagebuchartiger Genauigkeit"[23]—should finally be superseded by sounder, more objective criticism. I therefore venture to prophesy that the author of *Neue Gedichte* will ultimately be acknowledged as the creator and only nineteenth-century German master of a form of serious anacreontic verse for which few close analogues might be found in the long history of *poésie galante.* And that this creation of his resulted from conscious artistic effort, was no chance consequence of literary-historical forces larger than himself, would seem to be proclaimed by the otherwise strange presence of six—later seven—*Schöpfungslieder* in the section "Verschiedene." For although this group of poems has been condemned as mediocre, I think unjustly, by critics as diametrically opposed in their approach to Heine's work as Wolff and Barker Fairley, it is at least an effective and witty announcement that Heine shared the great Baroque poets' view that any subject could be made,

by a great creator, the medium of universally meaningful poetic statement: "Der Stoff," declares its Lord, "gewinnt erst seinen Wert / Durch künstlerische Gestaltung."

If the question of the novelty of the motifs and symbols of *Neue Gedichte* be disregarded—although there is more novelty than most critics have conceded[24]—, it should still, I believe, be possible to recognize that this collection represents an achievement very different from, yet no less meritorious intrinsically than, that of *Buch der Lieder.* In forms of the romantic and Heinesque-romantic lyric "Neuer Frühling" develops the timeless and universal theme of man's sense of the transitoriness of things and feelings with an impersonality of tone patently absent in both earlier and later lyric cycles by Heine. (This impersonality is particularly evident in the function assigned to dreams in the cycle: in "Lyrisches Intermezzo," in "Heimkehr," and again in "Lamentationen" *Träume* are immediate personal experiences in present time, but here they are either illusions at once recognized as such—"Hab' ich nicht dieselben Träume / Schon geträumt von diesem Glücke?"—or symbols of pessimism and disillusionment, as in "Ernst ist der Frühling, seine Träume / Sind traurig" and in "Spätherbstnebel, kalte Träume, / Überfloren Berg und Tal.") This general theme, traditionally associated with the Baroque sonnet and the ode, is developed in a new mode and with brilliant variations in "Verschiedene" (how important it was to Heine that it receive full emphasis is especially clear if the *Clarisse* of *Neue Gedichte* is compared with that of *Salon* 1; not only have poems too vigorous in tone been excised, but the little group ends with the newly added lines, "Nur wissen möcht' ich: wenn wir sterben, / Wohin dann unsre Seele geht? / Wo ist das Feuer, das erloschen? / Wo ist der Wind, der schon verweht?"), then is treated in "Romanzen" with reference both to erotic situations clearly not involving the poet personally and to non-erotic ones, finally to be illustrated by the transitory emptiness of contemporary German political life as poetically mirrored in "Zeitgedichte."

The charge of frivolity brought against Heine the author of *Neue Gedichte* would be strictly applicable to him if he were merely a late-born Rococo poet. But his scepticism is surely more pessimistic than it is frivolous, and in this collection he might be said to voice Baroque despair in a nineteenth-century secular-nihilistic form. In a masterly profile of German literature during the Restoration, an essay in which equal attention is paid to the stylistic and intellectual-historical facets of that literature, Friedrich Sengle has, like H. Herrmann, made much of the similarities between Heine's writing and that of the Enlightenment. Instead of depreciating Heine's achievements in the realm of what she called "Epigramm- und Stimmungslyrik," however, he claims—with considerable justness, I think—that Heine

hat das in dieser Zeit absterbende Epigramm alter Art durch neue Kleinformen der "Lyrik" ersetzt. . . . Aber seine Sprache hält in besonders reiner Weise den alten Instrumentalcharakter fest. . . . Der elegante Spötter . . . verkleidet sich so dicht mit einer Maske, dass sein eigentliches individuelles Gesicht, so sehr diese

Feststellung der heutigen Auffassung widersprechen mag, kaum zu erkennen ist. . . . Er steht dem Rokoko, auch seinen modernen Erneuerungen, näher als dem echten Realismus. . . . Wenn das Ausland immer noch den Romantiker Heine verehrt und Deutschland wegen seines innigeren Verhältnisses zur deutschen Sprache den Pseudoromantiker verachtet, so verstellen sich beide den Weg zu einer gerechten Einordnung und Einstufung.[25]

At least one literary historian has, then, established a frame of reference in which Heine's total poetic achievement can be judged with greater critical objectivity than was ever possible before. Perhaps his example will encourage biographers and interpretative critics to examine Heine's works with new eyes and so offer evaluations of their significance less mutually contradictory than those I have shown to be explicit and implicit in even a small sampling of critical opinion on so relatively neglected a work as *Neue Gedichte*.

Notes

1 "Ce qui est incontestablement grand en lui, c'est le poète." Geneviève Bianquis, *Henri Heine L'Homme et l'œuvre* (Paris, 1948), p. 169.—A survey of German critical opinion since Scherer (1883) is offered by Harry Slochower, "Attitudes towards Heine in German Literary Criticism," *Jewish Social Studies*, III (1941), 355-74.

2 *Deutsche Dichter 1700-1900, Eine Geistesgeschichte in Lebensbildern* (Frauenfeld, 1948-49), II, 327-34.

3 (Stuttgart, 1952), p. 603 f.

4 p. 664.

5 *Heinrich Heine* (München, 1922), p. 476 f.

6 *Heine* (London, 1929), p. 182 and 187 ff.

7 Heine, *Werke*, 2.Ausgabe (Leipzig, n.d.), I, 267.

8 *Geschichte der deutschen Literatur von Goethes Tod bis zur Gegenwart* (Stuttgart, 1949-50), I, 97.

9 *Henri Heine*, p. 74.

10 Heine, *Werke*, ed. H. Friedemann *et al.* (Berlin, *etc.*, n.d.), I, 27.

11 *Heine* (Torino, 1927), p. 183.

12 p. 187.

13 Heine, *Werke*, 2.Ausg., I, 269.

14 Richard M. Meyer, *Die deutsche Literatur des 19. und 20. Jahrbunderts*, ed. H. Bieber, 7.Auflage (Berlin, 1923), p. 106.

15 *Heinrich Heine*, p. 478.

16 *Henri Heine*, p. 76-78. Jules Legras, in *Henri Heine Poète* (Paris, 1897), similarly asserted that in "Verschiedene"—and in this respect he

opposed the cycles to *Buch der Lieder*—there is not "une seule strophe dont un lecteur modeste puisse être effarouché" (p. 210 f.).

17 *La Poésie de Heine* (Lyon and Paris, 1948), p. 118 f.

18 *Heine und Goethe* (Germanisch und Deutsch, H.7—Berlin and Leipzig, 1932), p. 64 f.

19 *Henri Heine Poète*, p. 207.

20 So I would interpret the remarks reported in Ludolf Wienbarg's "Erinnerungen an Heinrich Heine in Hamburg" (cited *Gespräche mit Heine*, ed. H. H. Houben [Frankfurt a.M., 1926], p. 180): "Ich bin in eine Manier hineingeraten, von der ich mich schwer erlöse. Wie leicht wird man Sklave des Publikums. Das Publikum erwartet und verlangt, dass ich in der Weise fortfahre, wie ich angefangen bin; schrieb ich anders, so würde man sagen: das ist gar nicht Heinesch, Heine ist nicht Heine mehr."

21 Heine, *Werke*, ed. Friedemann, I, 26.

22 Heine, *Werke*, I, 29-31 passim.

23 *Heinrich Heine*, p. 480.

24 Novel features of *Neue Gedichte* not mentioned above include (I) the grouping of sub-cycles to constitute one lyric cycle (a point not noted in her discussion of "Verschiedene" by U. Belart, *Gehalt und Aufbau von Heinrich Heines Gedichtsammlungen* [Sprache und Dichtung, H.38-Bern, 1925]); (2) the extensive use of fables and fable motifs; (3) conscious echoes of Graeco-Latin elegiac poetry (perhaps not only in several "Romanzen," but also in the use of *Philomele* instead of *Nachtigall* in "Neuer Frühling" and of classical-historical allusion in "Zeitgedichte"); (4) the autonomous anthropomorphization of nature and (5) the apparent avoidance of the real comparison in "Neuer Frühling," as pointed out by Alexander Pache, *Naturgefühl und Natursymbolik bei Heinrich Heine* (Hamburg and Leipzig, 1904), p. 46 ff.

25 "Voraussetzungen und Erscheinungsformen der deutschen Restaurations-literatur," *Deutsche Vierteljahrsschrift*, XXX (1956), 291.

Margaret A. Rose (essay date 1978)

SOURCE: "The Idea of the 'Sol Iustitiae' in Heine's *Deutschland. Ein Wintermärchen*," in *Deutsche Vierteljahrs Schrift für Literaturwissenschaft und Geistesgeschichte*, December, 1978, pp. 604-18.

[*In the following essay, Rose examines Heine's use of pagan and Christian imagery in* Deutschland: Ein Wintermärchen—*a poetic satire of volatile German politics in the 1840s.*]

It has been assumed, that, in *Deutschland. Ein Wintermärchen* of 1844, Heine eschewed the symbols of Midsummer as well as the carnivalistic laughter of *Atta Troll. Ein Sommernachtstraum* of 1843. Yet astral myth motifs abound in his "Winter's Tale," as in the earlier "Midsummer Night's Dream," and it might also be claimed that they are treated with no less irony in the latter.[1] Heine begins his satirical "Wintermärchen" by parodying the promise of a better world beyond that of Germany, and the material world as such—the utopian "Entsagungslied" of the "Harfenmädchen." But this song of a better world in another time and place, which functions as an opiate and soporiphic for those not able to change the present, is also contrasted with a new "song"—or at least the promise of it—for a new earthly society. The satire thus proceeds to relate the false consciousness of the "Entsagungslied" to the reality of its social context, but also to contrast both with the opinions and dreams of the narrator. Images and figurae connected with the invincible sun gods of astral myths, with the idea of the birth of a new world, and with the Judaic-Christian concept of a Messiah who will both introduce the new and judge the old, are interwoven with Heine's own judgements on the Germany of Friedrich Wilhelm IV and on the opposition offered to it by the Republicans and "Tendenzdichter" already satirised in *Atta Troll*. Because of this, the astral motifs in the "Winter's Tale" must also function as an ironic comment on the importance of the earlier celebration of the powers of the sun in the work of the Young Germans, and in Heine's own enthusiastic praise for the July Revolution in the 1830's. In the *Wintermärchen* these symbols of light, and of rebirth, shine from the darkness of Winter, and, forming an ironic sub-text to the work, cannot be ignored. Yet little has been said of their significance, or of their interconnection with the numerous Messiah figures who appear in the work. This paper will attempt to investigate this area, and relate it to Heine's comments of the censorship of the time and to the role of the satirist as both judge and victim of that institution.

Hegel's *Philosophie der Geschichte* had opened by describing the course of the sun from East to West as a metaphor for the progress of Reason and the consciousness of Freedom from the Orient to Germany. But, following the July Revolution in 1830, Heine's Jacobin court jester, Kunz von den Rosen, had announced that the sun would now rise in the West. This for Heine was not Germany but Paris, the New Jerusalem and birth-place of the Revolution. *Deutschland. Ein Wintermärchen* of 1844 is, however, written in more sceptial times, and—while the old vision of a new and sensualistic Utopia opposes the Spartan ideals of the Republicans of 1844—Liberty, and French liberalism, are also shown to have tripped up: Liberty has twisted her foot, and the sun now rises on a Winter scene. Nothing—not even the French, or Liberty herself—are free from its revealing gaze, or from the poet's satire. The new song Heine had spoken of in the *Stadt Lucca*, in the **"Nachtrag"** of 1830, had even then consisted of a mixture of enthusiasm and mockery ("Sterne der Begeisterung und Raketen des Spottes"—Elster, III, 402), but now the latter is turned against the utopian opposition to the forces of reaction, as well as against those forces themselves.

Deutschland. Ein Wintermärchen begins in the month of November, just prior to the period when the mid-winter solstice of mid-December was celebrated. And as Shakespeare's *Winter's Tale* had turned tragedy into comedy—the image of the waning of the sun at mid-winter may also

be taken as an image of the prelude of a new period of growth. The Roman Saturnalia, held between December 17th and 23rd, to initiate the rebirth of the waning sun, are also thought to have been models for Christian carnivals such as the Lord of Misrule festival, and (like the satire used by Heine in both his "Sommernachtstraum" and "Wintermärchen") show the world in a topsy-turvy state before the symbolic death and renewal of the sun. Here we have an ancient model for the interconnection of astral mythology and satire as developed by Heine in his *Wintermärchen*. Both the satirical reversal of the power of the old world (by the "Raketen des Spottes") and the new utopian song for the birth of a better society (the "Sterne der Begeisterung") mirror the carnivalistic process of burying the old sun and initiating the new.

But, more than this, the introduction of pagan astral motifs into Christian eschatology is also mirrored in Heine's juxtaposition of pagan and Christian elements in his satire, and of figures such as the "sol invictus" and "sol iustitiae" with Christ. Mithras, the Indo-Iranian god of light, had been celebrated as a "sol invictus" in Roman festivals. E. O. James writes that he was seen as an "invincible god of celestial light, who never grew old, died or lost his vigour—he was at once the creator of the world and the inaugurator of the new order destined to last forever—the first and final cause of things, the upholder of justice and truth."[2] This then was a figure to call on when invoking the rebirth of the new sun at mid-winter. December 25th, as a date for the rebirth of the sun at the solstice of mid-winter, had been celebrated as the birth-date of Mithras. Later, when taken as the birthdate of Christ, the Christian Messiah was called the new and true sun, the "true light of the world." The incarnation of that light in the world had for Heine in the 1830's—as for the Saint-Simonians, and for Young Germans such as Mundt—served as a metaphor for the "rehabilitation of the flesh" and the birth of a new sensualistic Revolution. The juxtaposition of Christian and pagan astral myths in *Deutschland. Ein Wintermärchen* introduces other elements to complicate the interpretation of Heine's secularisation of Christian eschatology. One of these is, as we shall see, the need to satirise the misuse of that eschatology by his contemporary "Tendenzdichter."

The synthesis of astral myths with Judaic-Christian figurae was, as Erwin Panofsky has shown, revived in the Renaissance. In his essay on "Albrecht Dürer and Classical Antiquity" Panofsky comments, for example, on the significance of Dürer's synthesis of Apollo as "Helios Pantokrator," or "sol invictus" with the figure of Christ in his woodcut "The Resurrection." It is a synthesis of particular significance, of course, for the poet who, as Heine, could take Apollo as his muse. But yet another figure from pagan iconography united with Christ was that of the "sol iustitiae"—the sun as judge[3] and here Heine found a muse for his satire. Dürer presents the "sol iustitiae" in a work of 1498 with scales and a sword[4]—an image attached by Heine to the figure of Christ as judge (and to the satirist) at the conclusion of the *Wintermärchen*. Earlier it is also suggested in the folk-song of the "Sonne als klagende Flamme." Panofsky also explains that this synthesis is more usual than that of Christ and the "sol invictus" in Christian art:

> The Church itself sanctioned the union between Christ and the Sun from the very beginning; but in doing so, it opposed to, and finally substituted for, the cosmological sun-god a moral one: the *sol invictus* became a *sol iustitiae,* the "Never-Vanquished Sun" a "Sun of Righteousness".[5]

The title of "Sol Iustitiae" had also been given to the promised Messiah in the book of Malachi. The verse quoted by Panofsky as "Et orietur vobis timentibus nomen meum Sol Iustitiae" occurs at the conclusion of the Old Testament in the *Lutherbibel*:

> Euch aber, die ihr meinen Namen fürchtet, soll aufgehen die Sonne der Gerechtigkeit und Heil unter ihren Flügeln. (Maleachi 3, 20)

Significantly, it follows the description of punishment by fire and suggests, therefore, a judge like that post-figured in the Apocalypse. In the Apocalypse itself the transfigured Christ, coming as judge, is described in the following imagery:

> Und er hatte sieben Sterne in seiner rechten Hand, und aus seinem Munde ging ein scharfes zweischneidiges Schwert, und sein Angesicht leuchtete wie die helle Sonne.

One might also suggest that this picture had—apart from Renaissance juxtapositions of the Hellenist sol iustitiae with Christ—led to the association of the sun with Christ the Judge becoming a common-place.

As suggested earlier, the synthesis of Christ with Apollo was, however, less common in Christian iconography before the Renaissance. Panofsky argues,[6] that Dürer united the figures of the resurrected Christ and the pagan "sol invictus" after having "converted the Apollonian sun-god into an Adam—transformed him into the resurrected Christ in several prints and permitted the analogy between the Saviour and 'Phoebus' to be stressed in a poem printed on the back of them." The latter part of the poem is strikingly similar to the key given his Altarpiece, "Kreuz im Gebirge," by Heine's contemporary, C. D. Friedrich:

> On this day the all-seeing Sun, affixed to the cross, hidden and dying when the sun set in darkness, splendidly reappeared when it rose.

Heine's more sceptical portrait of the crucified Christ reflects, however, a waning of belief in the promised rebirth of the sun, which mixes in the work with criticism of the forces of reaction. Hegel's *Philosophy of History* had, as a "theodicy," made a connection between the incarnation and death of Christ and the progress of Reason as a sun across the world. The Young Hegelian secularisation of this theodicy had not, however, captured Heine's imagination. Though he wrote in 1844 in the *Briefe aus Deutschland* that he had been the first to recognize the secret revolutionary nature of Hegelian philosophy, he also emphasised his belief in a sensualistic rather than a republican revolution. Thus too Heine's cynical portrait of both sun and Christ, the incarnated Logos, in Caput XIII, reflect a growing scepticism about the Hegelian "theodicy."

In the *Elementargeister* of 1837 Heine had condemned the Renaissance failure to revive the spirit of Hellenism in its true sensualistic form. In *Deutschland. Ein Wintermärchen* Heine's scepticism about the fate of the sensualistic Revolution (of the Dantonist tradition) is shown in his criticism of the new "Robespierrian" Messiahs of the 1840's. Related to such contemporary figures, as well as to older ideas, the figures of the "sol invictus" and the "sol iustitiae" are treated in diverse, sometimes apparently conflicting ways in the *Wintermärchen.* Sometimes they function as masks for Heine's persona, and, at other times, as a characterisation of his targets. Similarly, the related symbols of fire, flame, the sword, and the axe appear within the opposing metaphorics of Revolution and Restoration. And while it sometimes functions to indicate the similarity between the aims of the Prussian State and the national Republicanism of the Tendenzdichter and Republicans attacked in *Atta Troll* and the *Zeitgedichte,* this ambiguity also serves to reflect the complex nature of Heine's sympathy for the principle of a sensualistic Revolution which must also bring some destruction.

While the Hellenistic celebration of a "sol invictus" is reflected in Heine's wish for "ein neues Lied" the more terroristic, spiritualistic figure of the "sol iustitiae" reflects the need for destruction as well as rebirth in the establishment of the new utopia. As this need is created by Heine's targets it is perhaps ironically appropriate that the destructive element in Heine's satire should also borrow its metaphors from the iconography of its targets—the "christlich-nationalistisch" tradition.

The historical context of Heine's work—the period 1843/4—saw the tightening of censorship in Friedrich Wilhelm IV's Prussia, an upsurge of a new Romantic revival of mediaevalism, expressed by the monarch's own ultramontanist philosophy (which was given concrete form in the renewal of plans for the rebuilding of the Cologne Cathedral), and related radicalisation of the Republican "Tendezdichtung" which Heine had already attacked in *Atta Troll.* In poems such as **"Unsere Marine"** Heine had also pointed to the similarity between the nationalism of Republicans and Ultramontanists.

Thus the targets in Heine's *Wintermärchen* are, as in his "Sommernachtstraum," numerous. But from the very opening attack on Prussiar Zollverein, censor, and false religious consciousness, Heine's satire is accompanied by the spirit of his "new song." In that song for an earthly utopia—his "Hochzeitskarmen"—Heine also takes up a biblical topos, that of Jacob's star, which also introduces the opposition between true and false utopias which is to underlie most of the astral myths used in his work.

> Ein Hochzeitkarmen ist mein Lied,
> Das bessere, das neue,

In meiner Seele gehen auf
Die Sterne der höchsten Weihe—

Begeisterte Sterne, sie lodern wild,
Zerfliessen in Flammenbächen—
Ich fühle mich wunderbar erstarkt,
Ich könnte Eichen zerbrechen.

The image of Jacob's star (also used by Heine in **"Katharina"** I of the *Neue Gedichte*) is taken from 4. Mose 24, 17:

Ich sehe ihn aber nicht jetzt, ich schaue ihn aber nicht von nahe. Es wird ein Stern aus Jakob aufgehen und ein Zepter aus Israel aufkommen und wird zerschmettern die Fürsten.

This eschatological motif has been interpreted as a promise of David, forefather of Mary, the mother of Christ, and of a Messiah who—like Barbarossa of whom later Heine speaks—would be both Messiah and King. Yet throughout *Deutschland. Ein Wintermärchen* Heine's persona, the "ich," who speaks of feeling the strength to break oaks, contrasts with the historical manifestations of the "sol iustitiae" of whom he talks.

Above all it is the contrast of the censor as judge to the poet as satirist on which Heine concentrates in his *Wintermärchen.* In 1831, in his Introduction to "Kahldorf über den Adel," Heine compared the censorship of the press to the terror of the guillotine (Elster, VII, 284 and 600), as Karl Marx was to later in 1842 when condemning the "Terrorism" of the new Prussian censorship laws. Again in 1844, following his meeting with Marx in Paris and the strengthening of the Press censorship which had contributed to Marx's departure from Germany, Heine uses the images of judgement axe and scissors—in the *Wintermärchen*—to condemn censorship in Prussia. But in the chapters set in Cologne a part of his persona also carries the "Henkersbeil," attributed in satire and caricature to the censor, to use against both the "obscuranti" of the Restoration and their Republican, and equally terroristic opposition.

The flames of the auto-da-fe of books and men of which Heine's traveller is reminded in Cologne, the "home of obscurantism," represent an inversion of the cleansing flames of the sun of astral mythology. But in the concluding chapter, Kaput XXVII, in the poet's warning to the King, that the poet can send him to hell-fires worse than those promised by Christ the Judge, these flames take on again the symbolism of eschatological renewal. Yet while the poet's judgement of his judges turns the status quo upside down, it ironically also leaves us with a picture of the all-pervading character of the Terror, and of the ambivalent mixture of death and renewal in the saturnalia, satire, and Revolution. Norman O. Brown's words in *Love's Body* could just as well apply to Heine's problem in using of parody and satire to attack censorship:

Freedom is poetry and taking liberties with words, breaking the rules of normal speech, violating common sense. Freedom is violence.

While Liberty represents in Heine's works freedom from censorship, it also represents the use of tools to bring this about which (like parody and satire) violate and destroy norms. It still contrasts, however, in all its ambiguity, to the castrating character of the censor's treatment of the writer; for its purpose, like that of the saturnalia, is to renew.

Heine's ambivalent attitude toward the figure of the Messiah as judge is given concrete form in Caput 6, in which the "Doppelfigur" of "Gedanke" and "Tat," "Rhetor" and "Liktor" turns against the symbols of mediaevalism and Restoration in Germany, the three Kings of the "Kölner Dom." These followers of the star which had pointed to the new Messiah (significantly concealed from the terroristic *census*[7] taken by Herod to find his "rival monarch") are destroyed as representing all that has (like the modern censor) worked against the establishment of the earthly utopia. In their place in the Cologne Cathedral (rather than as searchers after the star) they represent both the Restoration as a retrograde revival of the union of Church and State, and a mediaeval antithesis to the principle of Reason.

The form taken by poet's judgement on these representatives of Friedrich Wilhelm IV's Ultra-Montanist period is, ironically, that of the Passover. Pesach, symbolical in Christian exegesis as the prefiguration of the salvation of man through the crucifixion of Christ, the sacrificial Lamb, becomes in this chapter a vehicle of the poet's revenge on obscurantism. Heine's persona is accompanied through Cologne by his "double." This companion, who is to put his thoughts into action, and to make the Word flesh, carries a "Richtbeil" and describes himself as a "Liktor." Symbolic of death, his axe introduces the figure of the Old Testament Judge, but the image is to be found in Matthew (3, 10) as well as in the prophetic books such as Jesaja 10, 15. As Liktor the Double recalls again the figure of the terroristic census-taker, as well as that of the censor in contemporary caricature, but is also an image of the incautious, spiritualistic revolutionary. The Word is "made Flesh" by his action, but (as Heine had also written in *Lutezia*) now it is also made to bleed.

In Chapter 7 the Tribune walks through the streets of Cologne with his Liktor, marking the doors of the houses with the blood from his heart. The bleeding heart recalls the symbol for the martyred Christ of the Pelican, but that image of salvation is ironically juxtaposed with that of the avenging God of the Old Testament, and with the destruction of the first-born of Egypt, when the persona marks the door-posts of the (Christian) inhabitants of Cologne "im Vorübergehen" with the blood from his breast. Exodus 12, 22 ff is used as the biblical model for the scene—but Heine has telescoped the two actions described in those verses into one in combining the Israelites' marking of their door-posts so that they would be passed over and spared by the Lord, with the marking of those to be slaughtered. Heine's "Vorübergehen" does not spare the inhabitants of Cologne but marks them for death and the verb of the biblical account ("to pass over") becomes the adverbial phrase "in passing." The Christ-like Messiah (defined as such by the images of sacrificial lamb and pelican) is shown in the role of judge of his own "chosen people": it is this ambivalence which characterises Heine's own satire against Germany, but it also clearly attacks the attitude of righteousness of the Restoration. Significantly, the sun is missing from this eschatological scene: not only is Passover a moon festival, but the moon is covered by the black steeds which are found in Sacharja 6, 1 ff and which designate midnight, the time when the Lord had brought down his plagues onto Egypt (2. Mose 12, 29).

The sword and the axe are images of the destructive aspect of the eschatological moment, and when the Liktor's axe strikes down the Three Kings it again results in injury to its Tribune. Not only are sword and axe, like the guillotine, used to caricature the censor at the time, they are also attributes, in verses such as those of the "Tendenzdichter" Herwegh, of the revolutionaries of 1840. When, in Chapter XII, the narrator is confronted by the more radical German revolutionaries, his ironic stance reflects caution in the face of a terroristic reaction to the Restoration.

The radicals appear in "concrete" form as the wolves which confront the poet, as Hermann did Varus in the Teutoburger Wald, and as the poet Dante is confronted by evil in Canto 1 of the *Inferno*, a work which is echoed in several ways in the *Wintermärchen*. The eyes of the wolves are like "Lichter in der Dunkelheit," and though this metaphor may recall the opposition of von Hutten to the "Dunkelmänner" of Cologne, or to the revolutionary South German Illuminati of the 18th Century, it is also suggested that the light of their eyes is not—as the sun's is—sufficient to dispel the darkness. The "ausgehungerte Stimmen" also suggest that the glint of their eyes reflects not so much the light of Reason, but the spiritualist's hypocritical hungering after material satisfaction.

It is no wonder then that the traveller takes up again the role of Tribune, and argues, in a parody of revolutionary rhetoric, that he is—despite the sheep-skin he wears to warm himself—not a sheep.[8] He is, of course, neither sheep nor wolf, and his denial that he is no "Schwärmer" for the sheep from whom he dissociates himself, introduces the ironic image of the crucified Christ (the sacrifical lamb) in Kaput XIII. In Kaput XII the traveller had ironically alluded to the warning of the "Bergpredigt" (Matt. 7, 15) to avoid false prophets who come in sheep's clothing when describing himself as a wolf in sheep's wool. His warning was of course misunderstood by the wolves, for whom wolves (as false prophets) are relatives, and the Tribune's easy escape from them further reflects the lack of reason behind their bright eyes. Heine also criticises a lack of caution in Christ himself in the next Chapter, describing him also in the terms used by radicals such as the pre-Communist Weitling to make of him a prototype of the modern, anti-capitalist Revolutionary. This Christ is also identified with by Heine when he is named as "mein armer Vetter." The identification is, nevertheless, ambiguous, indicating both sympathy and scepticism, for it recalls both Heine's sympathetic characterisation of Christ as critic of the status quo in the *Stadt Lucca*, and Börne's ironic references to Christ's Jewish heritage (see Elster, VII, 122), as well as Heine's use of the irony to describe Spinoza as a martyr for the right to free speech in Book 2 of *Zur Geschichte der Religion und Philosophie in Deutschland.* Though there is little of the spiritualistic Republican to be found in the picture of the "dying sun" which Heine gives in his portrait of the crucifed Christ, he is characterised as the prototype of the modern "Menschheitsretter" as well as a cousin to the poet, the defender of free speech, and, thus, as a threat to the censor who bears some resemblance to Christ in his other role as "Sol Iustitiae."

The chapter opens with an ironic comment on the hopelessness of the sun's apparent attempt to light all sides of the earth at once. This is not only an ironic and self-parodistic reference to Heine's use of the sun as a symbol of his hope in the Revolution of 1830—but may be taken as a comment on the problem of establishing both Liberty and Unity—Freiheit und Einheit—in Germany. Heine saw the failure to solve this problem as having led to an emphasis on unification at the expense of liberation in both conservative and Republican parties in the 1840's, and many of his "Zeitgedichte" criticise both camps as sharing the same, retrograde concern.

Irony appears also to give way to cynicism in the *Wintermärchen* when the sun finally lights up the wayside crucifix showing the Messiah crucified. C. D. Friedrich's explanation (like Dürer's) of the crucified Christ as mediator between the old world and the new paradise is replaced by the explanation that the crucified Messiah serves as a warning to all other would-be "Menschheitsretter." Ironically it is the "Bergpredigt," which Heine's "Tribune" has just used to save himself from the radical and atheistic wolves, which is now given as an example of Christ's lack of caution in speaking out against Church and State. Heine then ironically suggests that the modern censor may have saved the Messiah by forbidding the publication of such dangerous tracts. Again the equation between guillotine and censorship is made, by suggesting that the one can substitute for the other—and it is clear that the price of salvation from death in this case would be a silence which would also have eliminated the Messiah from history.

Heine's Christ, the dead "sun" lit by the rising natural sun, is sympathetically mocked as a "Schwärmer," the defender of human rights (including freedom of speech), taken by Lamennais, Cabet, Weitling, and other radicals as a prototype of the anti-capitalist:

> Geldwechsler, Bankiers, hast du sogar
> Mit der Peitsche gejagt aus dem Tempel—
> Unglücklicher Schwärmer, jetzt hängst du am Kreuz
> Als warnendes Exempel

In the 18th Century the term "Schwärmer" had been applied by Lessing to the prophets of the Third Testament,[9] such as Joachim di Fiore, but more recently, in 1835, the Young Hegelian D. F. Strauß had described Christ as a "Schwärmer," on account of the trust placed by him in his father and his lack of independent action.[10] It is ironic that Heine's use of the word serves to juxtapose the Young Hegelian condemnation of the orthodox image of Christ with the contemporary Republicans' heterodoxical support of Christ as a prototype of the anti-capitalist. Heine has connected the Left Hegelians to the Republicans in *Atta Troll*, when Atta Troll the Republican had condemned the atheism of Feuerbach and Bauer, and simultaneously proven himself to be one with them in his image of God as a terroristic, blasphemous beast, here Heine again appears to suggest that inconsistency exists in the arguments of those offering radical opposition to the union of Church and State.

But Heine's own attitude appears to be ambivalent. He too acknowledges the revolutionary nature of the "Bergpredigt,"[11] and connects its anti-materialist lessons with the condemnation of the money-changers which "Tendenzdichter" like Herwegh had taken as authority for their condemnation of pre-capitalism. Weitling had called Christ the "first Communist," and in the poem "Zuruf" of 1841 Herwegh celebrated the Christ of Matthew 21, 12 as a prefiguration of the new Messiah who was still to come:

> Junge Herzen, unverzagt
> Bald erscheint der neue Täufer,
> Der Messias, der die Käufer
> Und Verkäufer aus dem Tempel jagt.[12]

Karl Beck was amongst the many "Tendenzdichter" to use the image,[13] but Heine's ironical warning to the historical Christ must also be taken as having the function of warning those living socialists—the "young suns" of the Revolution—of the consequences of their own radical complaints. Heine's arguments against their "Schwärmerei" differ from that put forward by Marx in the *Deutsche Ideologie* of 1845/6, which quoted liberally from Heine's *Wintermärchen*—Heine having sent a copy to Marx in 1844. There Marx condemned the "Bergpredigt" parable of the lilies in the field as "schwärmerisch" and naive in preaching the avoidance of the realities of the production of material history:

> "Sehet die Lilien auf dem Felde." Ja sehet die Lilien auf dem Felde, wie sie von den Ziegen verspeist, von dem Menschen ins Knopfloch verpflanzt werden, wie sie unter den unkeuschen Liebkosungen der Viehmagd und des Eseltreibers zusammenknikken![14]

Heine's Messiahs had not been condemned for their avoidance of the material realities of production, or ignorance of the interconnection of production and exchange, as much as for their incautious utopianism, and for actions which prove counter-productive to the cause of Liberty, such as the tightening of controls such as censorship, which followed their breaking of the existing press laws, and which restricted Heine's own opportunities for criticism.

Heine's consistent rejection of the older figures of Christian eschatology, and of astral mythology, includes the figure of Barbarossa—a Messiah figure he had already condemned in *Ludwig Börne* as a hero of the Restoration lacking both reality and decisiveness. In many old Third Testament writings Barbarossa had, however, been taken as a figuration of the Messiah-King.[15]

Heine introduces the legend of Barbarossa with the refrain "Sonne, du klagende Flamme," of the folk-tale of justice done to a murdered girl by the sun who searches out her murderers. It is clearly an astral-legend, and evokes the figures of both the "sol invictus" and the sun as judge, the "sol iustitiae." Other such legends can be found in the collections of folk-tales made at that time: one example is "Die klare Sonne brings an den Tag" in Grimms *Märchen*. The refrain serves first of all as an introduction, and then as a contrast to the legendary chiliastic figure of Barbarossa: but in the narrator's dream which follows he appears not as the mythological hero of a new Testament, nor as the secular leader of a new German Empire, but as a miserly autocrat, apparently incapable of taking action, and believing in the same values expressed by the three Kings of the "Kölner Dom." And whereas the legend of the sun as "klagende Flamme" describes how the sun had revealed those responsible for the murder of a young girl, Barbarossa is said to be unable to find the murderers of "Jungfrau Germania." As the model for Friedrich Wilhelm IV's "parody" of the mediaeval Holy Roman Empire, Barbarossa is a Messiah treated with both caution and irony by Heine.

Again in a dream[16] the narrator sees the Prussian reality as destroying the promise of a new world. Dreaming that he is being attacked by the Prussian eagle, the narrator describes himself as Prometheus—the hero who had stolen the fire of heaven and braved the lightning of Jove: (The cartoon caricaturing the ban on Marx's *Rheinische Zeitung,* as the Prussian eagle's attack on Prometheus, uses a similar image.) The dream fades with the crowing of the Gallic cock, yet another symbol of the new dawn and the liberating Revolution in Heine's work (as in his Introduction to "Kahldorf über den Adel" and in *Ludwig Börne*), and used later by others, including, again, Marx.[17]

The "klagende Flamme" of the sun—like that of the poet's satire—is one which does not, like the Terror, destroy without renewing life. While the burning of Hamburg is described as cleansing it of the past, in the same chapter (Kaput XXI) Heine uses the image of St. Just's Terror to characterise the vision of the future which confronts the narrator when he is given a glimpse into the bowl of Charlemagne's throne by Hammonia. Here eschatology is ironically secularised as scatology, and sensualism made grotesque. The new "wedding song" promised earlier in the *Wintermärchen* has become farce. Liberty cannot, in the face of continuing censorship, be seriously considered by Heine as having been realised in 1844, and the conclusion of the work reflects this fact.

Thus the mood is sombre in Kaput XXVIII, where Heine secularises both negative and positive images of the "sol iustitiae" in translating them into images of the poet's judgement on his society. In his Introduction to *Don Quixote* of 1837 Heine had already described the poet in the role of sol iustitiae. There he painted Cervantes in heroic colours as handsome and strong, perspicacious and dangerous to those who conceal the truth, and a ray of sunlight to the good:

> Den Gutenwar sein Blick ein Sonnenstrahl, der ihr Inneres freudig erhellte; den Bösen war sein Blick ein Schwert, das ihre Gefühle grausam zerschnitt.

Here the attributes of Christ the Judge of the Apocalypse—of sword and sun—were given the satirist as the creator of both critical and sensualistic verse or prose. For Heine Cervantes and Shakespeare (who are also both alluded to in the *Wintermärchen* in various ways) were sons of the sun-god Apollo: for Heine good satire was both poetic and sensualistic. And the poet's judgement of society which Heine speaks of at the conclusion of *Deutschland. Ein Wintermärchen* is, like the art of Cervantes, described as cutting like a sword through the hearts of evil, while—for the just—it is to bring the new sun, promised earlier by the vision of the "lodernde Sterne," and a sensualistic revolution. Thus, though the mood of the conclusion is sombre, Heine also promises a reversal of the status quo.

This status quo is indeed attacked in the conclusion of Caput XXVIII, when Friedrich Wilhelm IV is warned of maltreating living poets, and promised a hell-fire worse than that warned of in Matthew, and comparable to that described by Dante in the *Inferno*:

> Beleidge lebendige Dichter nicht,
> Sie haben Flammen und Waffen,
> Die furchtbarer sind als Jovis Blitz,
> Den ja der Poet erschaffen.

This last "demythologizing" line (though it may also recall the image of God as the author of the Book of Life) translates the astral symbols of flame and sword into metaphors for the poet's criticism. But whereas the reference to Dante's *Inferno* casts again a sombre light over Heine's satire, it also recalls the figure of Satan, inverted and standing on his head, who—as Northrop Frye has pointed out[18]—may be taken as a symbol of the passing of tragedy into satire and irony—modes which, though they belong (like tragedy) to the "Winter" of the soul, also belong to the rejuvenating, carnivalistic world of the saturnalia, and to the world turned upside down. And—as in the saturnalia—Heine now shows us an inverted world, in which the judged include the King and his State as well as the censor, while the role of judge has been taken over by the poet-satirist. Yet, still, we see, in Heine's continued use of the figurae of astral mythology, the hand of the censor forcing explicit criticism "underground" into the covert languages of metaphor and irony.

The return of the crucified Christ as resurrected Judge (the sol iustitiae) does not appear to indicate a rebirth of the new sun, or the figure of the sol invictus: it is again only in the poet's satire, if anywhere, that such a rebirth is suggested. The Winter sun still shines less brightly in Germany than promised by her old and new Messiahs, the subjects of Heine's criticism. Heine's scepticism about the liberating nature of Revolution is still present at the conclusion of the work, despite the renewing fiction of the saturnalia. Satire—though fighting the "Winter" of tragedy—must still remind us of the forces of repression which have made it necessary.

In that the role of the sol iustitiae is taken over by the poet himself at the conclusion of the *Wintermärchen,* the fate of the saturnalia and the rebirth of the sun become to some extent dependent on him. In view of this fact it is important to also consider the role played by the breakdown in Heine's health at the time, and his use of metaphors in other works to describe this—metaphors which can be found again in the astral metaphors of *Deutschland. Ein Wintermärchen.* Most striking amongst those related to the waning powers of the sun, are those which can also be said to relate to the gradual loss of eyesight which Heine had suffered from the end of the 1830's. Metaphors relating to this fact are of several different kinds.

Ironically, Heine's birthday, on December 13th, is celebrated by the Christian Church as the feast of St. Lucy, patron of all those with afflicted eyes. Reference to Dante's *Inferno* at the conclusion of the *Wintermärchen* may also remind us that it is in Canto II of the *Inferno* that St. Lucy appears—with Mary and Beatrice—as a Divine Grace who will guide and protect the poet. And St. Lucy's day is of course also celebrated as a mid-Winter feast by candlelit processions and the lighting of a candle to burn until the 12th Night of Christmas.

Heine's letter to Marx in 1844, with which he sent a copy of *Deutschland. Ein Wintermärchen,* speaks of the continuing affliction to his eyes, of which he had complained earlier, as in a letter to Campe of 1841. Hubert Arbogast,[19] who suggests that Heine's illness had begun to afflict him in 1837, also draws attention to a one-act "Mysterium" set in the time of Guizot's Ministry in 1841, in which he argues that Heine identifies himself with the "blinded eagle" who has flown too close to the sun. Without going into Arbogast's interpretation of that work, it can be suggested that Heine's loss of sight is not irrelevant to an understanding of the *Wintermärchen.* S. S. Prawer in discussing the "Sommernachtstraum," *Atta Troll,* has spoken of how Heine transferred the illness he suffered in the Pyrenees in 1841 to the "Tendenzbär" Atta Troll in the conclusion of the work. Similarly it can be suggested that Heine has transferred much of his own loss of sight, and the consequent "darkening" of the sun in his world to the elements which have darkened Germany's Winter—to, that is, the metaphorical blindess of the Republicans and "Tendenzdichter," as well as to the "obscuranti" of the Restoration, and to their heroification of such figures as Barbarossa in his underground cavern. The poet who appears at the conclusion of the work represents nothing of the blindness and darkness he has come to judge. Given however, the process of transference, we may assume that this illness has played some role in the view of the sombre Winter scene which concludes the satire. As sol iustitiae the satirist himself represents the sun to which others are blind. Thus it may be said that Heine has not only transferred the illness of the blinded eagle of the "Mysterium" of 1841 to Prussia, and to its Republican opposition, but has changed his role from that of the blinded eagle to that of the sun itself, to his muse Apollo.

Heine's use of Astral motifs in his work is both highly structured and "polyphonic." His critical contrast of the false utopias and failed messianism offered by the Restoration on the one hand, and by its radical opposition on the other, must be seen to be part both of his own "saturnalian" condemnation of these alternatives and of his attempt to write a new but ironically self-conscious song for the future Germany.

Notes

[1] I have discussed the carnivalistic and "tendentious" forms of satire in Hein's *Atta Troll. Ein Sommernachtstraum* in an article published in *AUMLA*, 43 (1975), 33-49.

[2] E. O. James, *Seasonal Feasts and Festivals* (1963), p. 195, and see also p. 230.

[3] Erwin Panofsky, *Meaning in the Visual Arts* (1970), p. 298.

[4] Op. cit., p. 307. The figure of Sol with scales and sword had been used in illustrations to the Zodiac.

[5] Op. cit., p. 302.

[6] Op. cit., p. 303.

[7] I am indebted to Professor Sidney Monas for pointing out that the etymology of the word "censorship" can be taken back to the Roman census-taker, and for other thoughts on the subject of censorship. I would also like to thank Professor Ian Donaldson for his helpfull discussion of several other points.

[8] Hans Kaufmann's well-known and important analysis of the "Wintermärchen" overlooks, however, this level of irony.

[9] Lessing, *Erziehung des Menschengeschlechts*, paragraphs 87 and 90.

[10] D.F. Strauss, *Das Leben Jesu* (1835, reprint 1969), I, 493 and 494. The criticism of Christ as a "Schwärmer" is also to be found in Gutzkow's *Wally, die Zweiflerin* of the same year. See reprint (1965), p. 271.

[11] Ernst Bloch comments on the eschatological idea of an immanent Revolution in the "Bergpredigt" in his *Prinzip Hoffnung* (1959), p. 561.

[12] Herwegh, *Werke*, ed. Hermann Tardel (1909), p. 65.

[13] See Antal Madl, *Politische Dichtung in Österreich* (1830-48) (1969), p. 113 on Beck: "Ein Bild aus dem Neuen Testament als Jesus die Krämer aus dem Tempel vertreibt, kehrt in seinen Gedichten mehrmals wieder." Beck came under attack as a True Socialist in Marx and Engels' *Deutsche Ideologie* in 1845/6.

[14] Marx/Engels *Gesamtausgabe*, I/V, 456.

[15] Norman Cohn, *The Pursuit of the Millennium* (1962), p. 103. Bar-

barossa's messenger, the raven, is also the bird shown together with the sun-god Apollo.

[16] In *Lutezia*, Elster, VI, 402 Heine claimed that Hegel had told him, "Wenn man die Träume aufgeschrieben hätte, welche die Menschen während einer bestimmten Periode geträumt haben, so würde einem aus der Lektüre dieser gesammelten Träume ein ganz richtiges Bild vom Geiste jener Periode aufsteigen."

[17] See Marx' 1843 "Introduction to the Critique of the Hegelian Philosophie of Right."

[18] See Northrop Frye, *Anatomy of Criticism* (1957), p. 239.

[19] Hubert Arbogast, "Ein erblindender Adler. Bemerkungen zu einem unbekannten Manuskript Heines," *Jahrbuch der Deutschen Schillergesellschaft*, 13 (1969), 47-61.

Hanna Spencer   (essay date 1982)

SOURCE: *Heinrich Heine,* Twayne Publishers, 1982, 173 p.

[*In the following excerpt, Spencer explores the popular lyric poems of Heine's* Buch der Lieder.]

The collection through which Heine's poems have achieved this world renown, entitled simply and appropriately ***Buch der Lieder*** [***Book of Songs***], was published by Hoffmann und Campe in Hamburg in 1827. The book contains poems Heine wrote beginning at age sixteen, although the majority originated between 1821 and 1824, that is, two to five years after he had left Hamburg and his muse. It is divided in chronological order into sections entitled **"Junge Leiden"** [Young Sorrows], **"Lyrisches Intermezzo"** [Lyric Intermezzo], **"Heimkehr"** [Homecoming], **"Aus der Harzreise"** [Songs from the Harz-Journey], and two sections called **"Nordsee"** [North Sea].

The book first attracted only moderate attention, but from 1837 onward its popularity soared. In its thirteenth edition at the time of the author's death, ***Buch der Lieder*** became the most widely read book of poetry in world literature, establishing the fame of its author and the wealth of its publisher, to whom Heine had sold it for a pittance. Indeed, so great was the popularity of ***Buch der Lieder*** that it overshadowed Heine's other, more mature and superior work, or at least delayed its appreciation. The broad public which the poet of ***Buch der Lieder*** so successfully wooed would have been shocked and repelled by the views that Heine actually held, while many of those who might have appreciated the more problematic and sophisticated "other" Heine turned away from the poet whose name was synonymous with ***Buch der Lieder.***

The format, tone, and style of ***Buch der Lieder*** is that of the folksong. Despite—or because of—his adherence to the simple forms and metric lines of the conventional four-line stanza, Heine achieved a distinctive voice surprisingly early. For, by and large, Heine's poetry owes much of its unique appeal to the subtle tension and interaction between the seemingly natural, homespun format and the flashes of his agile, sophisticated mind. Still, modern readers of the *Buch der Lieder* may well wonder what captivated the imagination of readers for a century. They will find in it much that seems mannered and derivative—especially in the early sections—and throughout, they will encounter verses that are flawed and weak, glib and trivial, and many that seem unbearably sentimental. The thought of facing 240 poems of which all but a handful deal with unrequited love may lead us to ask with Heine, albeit in a different context than he had in mind:

> Anfangs wollt ich fast verzagen,
> Und ich glaubt, ich trüg es nie;
> Und ich hab es doch getragen—
> Aber fragt mich nur nicht, wie?[1]
>
> (1:38)

(At first I almost despaired and thought I could not bear it; yet I did—but do not ask me how.)

Yet when we pause to scrutinize these lines, glib and facile as they seem, like an entry for an album which, in fact, they originally were, we find that even they tell us something about Heine's craft. We note the easy melodious rhythm, the syntactic simplicity along with a talent for the mot juste: "verzagen" has a certain tentative, poetic flavor; "getragen" is more subtly effective than the anticipated "ertragen" would have been; we note the rising crescendo inherent in the second "und"; and, finally, the turn in the last line when the all-too-easy rhythmic flow is halted to introduce the suggestive question. Moreover, this poem achieves a certain poignancy, as the penultimate of nine songs and the only one compressed into one stanza within a cycle that tells the usual bittersweet tale. Heine had a knack for arranging his independently conceived poems so that they complemented and enhanced each other in content, rhythm, and mood, to form a larger whole.

Early in the *Buch der Lieder,* amid a mixed lot of cliché-ridden tales which for the most part team love with death, we encounter two ballads of extraordinary power. **"Die Grenadiere"** has become an international favorite in the setting of Robert Schumann in which the strains of the Marseillaise underscore the climactic ending. But the verses retain their impact even if one blocks out the memory of Schumann's tune. Two returning soldiers of Napoleon's defeated Grand Army reveal a simple, unconditional loyalty to their immortal hero, whose presence shines through with almost mythic force. It is noteworthy that here, in one of his first poems, Heine has combined the traditional genre with a topic of current interest: in 1813—Heine tells us that he wrote the ballad when he was sixteen—Napoleon was still very much in the news. While borrowing from tradition—echoes of the Scotch ballad "Edward" are clearly discernible[2]—Heine already shows his own touch. Such lines as "Der eine sprach: Wie weh wird mir/ Wie brennt meine alte Wunde" ("One of them said: oh, what grief comes over me—how my old wound is burning") exemplify his penchant for presenting an abstract concept (grief) through concrete, sensual experience and his skill in making the experience palpable: here, for instance, the alliteration reinforces the semantic content of "weh" and "Wunde."

An even more dazzling example of Heine's early artistry is the ballad **"Belsazar,"** which used to provide a trusty showpiece for recitalists in days long past. The biblical tale of the blasphemous challenge to Jehovah originally is told in the Book of David (V), but it is likely that Heine's immediate source of inspiration was Byron's version of "Belshazzar." Lord Byron, discoverer of new worlds of suffering, was Heine's admired model in many ways. Scene and mood are established with a few strokes, in a perfect blend of sound and sense, starkly contrasting the nocturnal stillness in the town below with the riotous goings-on in the king's palace. Note the verbal economy which is maintained throughout the poem:

> Die Mitternacht zog näher schon;
> In stiller Ruh' lag Babylon.
>
> Nur oben in des Königs Schloss,
> Da flackert's, da lärmt des Königs Tross.
>
> (1:52)

(Midnight was slowly coming on;
In silent rest lay Babylon.

But above in the palace of the king,
There is the blaze of torches and the noise of the
   king's gang.)

After Belsazar's brazen challenge to Jehovah the tension mounts, beginning with the anxiety that suddenly grips the king himself, followed by the deafening silence of his men and finally, the spine-chilling writing on the wall. By the choice of words and the blend of rhythm, image, and sound the poet does not so much describe as physically reproduce the scene. The hand really appears and writes on the wall:

> Doch kaum das grause Wort verklang,
> Dem König ward's heimlich im Busen bang.
>
> Das gellende Lachen verstummte zumal;
> Es wurde leichenstill im Saal.
>
> Und sieh! und sieh! an weisser Wand
> Da kam's hervor wie Menschenhand;
>
> Und schrieb, und schrieb an weisser Wand
> Buchstaben von Feuer, und schrieb und schwand.
>
> (1:53)

(No sooner was the gruesome word spoken
When the king's heart secretly filled with dread.

The shrill laughter suddenly stopped;
Deadly silence filled the hall.

Behold, behold! On the white wall
A thing appeared like a human hand;

And wrote and wrote on the white wall
Letters of fire, and wrote and was gone.)

In contrast to the biblical source as well as to Byron's poem, both of which dwell on the interpretation of the Mene Tekel, Heine invented his own ending, a "man-made" ending so to speak, leaving the reader to ponder its implications with regard to human relations: "Belsazar ward aber in selbiger Nacht / Von seinen Knechten umgebracht" ("Belsazar, however, in the selfsame night / was put to death by his own horde"). According to Heine's own recollection, this ballad was also written when he was not quite sixteen. And it may or may not be a coincidence that the topic anticipates Heine's later concerns and his announcement, in quite different tones, of the death of Jehovah.

With **"Lyrisches Intermezzo"** and **"Heimkehr"** we come to the poems with which Heine's name is most commonly identified. Here he developed some of his most characteristic features: his flair for epigrammatic brevity and suggestive terseness that leaves room for the reader's imagination, his vivid imagery, his musical phrasing, his unexpected ironic turns and brilliant quips. Among these poems we find many of Heine's most renowned gems. In all the world's literature, they have invited the greatest number of musical settings; of the approximately five thousand songs that have been made of Heine's poems, the majority by far is based on verses from the middle period of **Buch der Lieder,** pieces which he wrote when he was between twenty-four and twenty-seven years of age.

Heine never made a secret of the care and deliberation that went into his work. Yet the very charm of his poetic style lies in its seeming artlessness and easy grace. His language flows so naturally that the meaning rather than the binding meter appears to dictate the word order. Rhyme and meter do not seem strained or restraining but have a heightening effect. In his best pieces, each line is a perfect blend of content and expression, and with their melodious cadences the words themselves seem to make music. Take, for example, the poem which opens the cycle, **"Intermezzo No. 1"**:

Im wunderschönen Monat Mai,
Als alle Knospen sprangen,
Da ist in meinem Herzen
Die Liebe aufgegangen.

Im wunderschönen Monat Mai,
Als alle Vögel sangen,
Da hab ich ihr gestanden
Mein Sehnen und Verlangen.

                                                        (1:72)

(In the lovely month of May
When all the buds were bursting.
'Twas then that in my heart
Love sprang up.

In the lovely month of May,
When all the birds were singing,

'Twas then that I confessed to her
My longing and my yearning.)

The attempt to render this little poem in English makes one realize just how meager is its intellectual content and, conversely, how intricate and magical (pronounce: untranslatable) the fusion of the various lyrical elements which produce its effect. It consists of two sparse quatrains of similar structure, each containing a statement which in turn is made up of two parts. The most obvious feature, shared by the two stanzas, is their first line which sounds like a mellifluous, perhaps somewhat old-fashioned formula—a refrain positioned at the beginning—suggesting the sweetness and recurrent renewal of spring. This seemingly swift-footed tetrameter with masculine ending is followed by three trimetric lines with feminine endings.[3] The resulting effect is a sense of slowing down, of a waiting for something more significant to happen, and the content confirms it: springtime reigns not only outdoors but within the heart of the lyrical "I." The smooth-running phrase is filled with meaning, and the general, natural phenomenon is transformed into something unique and personal.

But, apart from rhythm and meter, how is this crescendo of feeling achieved? Each of the two stanzas contains a statement about two events which are linked by coincidence. But what the syntax presents as a temporal relationship turns out, by way of image, to be a relationship of another kind. "Als alle Knospen sprangen" ("when all the buds were bursting"): No translation can do justice to the effect of the explosive onomatopoeia (kn, sp, spr, ng) of this line, especially in contrast to the mellow and softly undulating one that preceded it: spring's awakening is physically converted into language. "Da ist in meinem Herzen die Liebe aufgegangen." "Aufgehen" is a rather commonplace word which is used in connection with many things, but "Liebe" ("love") is not one of them: it means "to open" as a door might open, or "to rise" as the sun or dough rises. And it means to come up, as a seedling comes up. Of course, herein lies the creative spark of the poem. Before our mental eye we see the human heart suddenly transform itself into a bud and simultaneously we recognize the heartlike quality of the bursting buds; human love becomes part of a natural, elementary force, participant in the universal rite of spring.

The second quatrain seems to run parallel to the first. Again the alluring phrase rolls prettily along, followed by "als alle Vögel sangen": in context, even this sturdy cliché exudes a childlike simplicity. Again the natural event and the human experience turn out to be not merely simultaneous events but of the same quality. Once again, what is implied is not so much a comparison as an equation. But this time, the equation does not quite balance. Something new is added which introduces the difference between singing creatures and the human lover. The subtle turn occurs with the reference to her ("ihr"). That it takes two to be in love is not much of a novelty. Novel, however, is the manner in which the reference is made, almost inadvertently, through the dative of a pronoun: not as "dir," which the verse would have equally allowed and which would have been the conventional way, but which also—

and that is of course the crux of the matter—would have invited this "du" into the poem. No, the focus does not shift even for a moment from the lyrical "I" at its center. What the rhythms and imagery of these two stanzas have led up to, what moreover all the rhymes have prepared us for, is the lover's "Sehnen und Verlangen," which fills the last line and which seems to linger on after the poem has ended.

What began as a celebration of harmonious unity with nature has turned into its opposite, a feeling of loneliness and deprivation in the midst of a blossoming world. There is none of the exuberance that emanates from the passage in Goethe's famous "Mailied":

> O Mädchen, Mädchen
> Wie lieb ich dich
> Wie blinkt dein Auge
> Wie liebst du mich!

> (Sweetheart, sweetheart, how I love you! How your eyes shine, how you love me!)

Note that Goethe's joyous declaration was ushered in by a stanza that in essence has the same semantic content as Heine's:

> Es dringen Blüten
> Aus jedem Zweig
> Und tausend Stimmen
> Aus dem Gesträuch

> (Buds press forth from every branch and thousand voices [sing out] from the bush).

With Heine, love is never a partnership, never the shared, fulfilling and mutually enriching experience conveyed by Goethe, but it always results in an even deeper isolation. Heine's capacity for inventing different modes of presenting the lament of the aching heart seems inexhaustible. In one of the best known (**"Lyrisches Intermezzo No. 33"**), the lone pine tree in the barren north yearns for the palm in the distant, torrid south. Besides embodying, to the point of absurdity, hopeless love and extreme isolation, this poem also exemplifies Heine's view of the universe in which Eros reigns supreme:

> Ein Fichtenbaum steht einsam
> Im Norden auf kahler Höh'.
> Ihn schläfert; mit weisser Decke
> Umhüllen ihn Eis und Schnee.

> Er träumt von einer Palme,
> Die, fern im Morgenland,
> Einsam und schweigend trauert
> Auf brennender Felsenwand.

(1:85)

> (A fir-tree stands lonely
> Far north on barren height.
> It drowses; ice and snow
> Envelop it with a white blanket.

> It dreams of a palm-tree
> Which far away in the Orient
> Mourns lonely and mute
> On a sunparched cliff.)

Instead of the parodies which this pining pine tree and the silently mourning palm would seem to invite, numerous imitations have been stimulated by it and it provided the lyrics for no less than 121 musical settings.[4] It is, by the way, one of the few poems which objectivizes the theme without the presence of the lyrical "I." This is also true in the case of the lotus flower in love with the moon (**"Lyrisches Intermezzo No. 10"**). Prompted by the information that the lotus closes its bloom in sunlight, Heine depicts her dreamily awaiting her lover the moon, being awakened by him, and revealing her "friendly" beauty to his sight, and finally, in an even more suggestive third stanza, glowing and trembling with desire. Such are the purely tonal effects of these lines that even a reader who knows no German will appreciate its sensuality:

> Sie blüht und glüht und leuchtet,
> Und starret stumm in die Höh';
> Sie duftet und weinet und zittert
> Vor Liebe und Liebesweh.

(1:76)

> (She blooms and glows and shines
> And silently gazes upward;
> Full of fragrance, she weeps and trembles
> With love and loving woe.)

To present the female as the loving partner is not exactly Heine's habit, and even in this instance the point of view is not really that of a woman: clearly the lotus flower, paragon of purity, modesty, and beauty yet exuding affectionate devotion and exotic sensuousness, is the product of a man's wishful thinking. For Heine, it is almost always the man who is endowed with a passionate heart, while the object of his longing and cause of his perennial grief and frustration is the distant, heartless, inscrutable beauty. She is a Sphinx, a vampire, a marble statue, a siren. She is the "Loreley."

The poem which popularly goes by this name, **"No. 2"** in the cycle **"Heimkehr"** (where it appears untitled), has, in the setting of Friedrich Silcher, achieved the status of a folksong comparable to Goethe's "Heidenröslein" (or in English to Robert Burns's "Auld lang syne"). It is so beloved and so much felt to be part of German folksong heritage that even in Hitler's Germany, when the name of the Jew Heine was unmentionable, the "Loreley" could not be left out of songbooks. It was accompanied by the note "author unknown." How Heine would have savored the irony of it all as well as the implicit compliment!

"Loreley," meaning "elfin rock," was the name associated with a cliff in the Rhine valley (between Bingen and Koblenz) in the vicinity of some hazardous reefs. Clemens Brentano had transformed it into "Lore Lay" and given the name to a woman whose tragic death near the treacherous rock he described in a ballad of that name. Other contemporary poets picked up the theme, among them Joseph von Eichendorff, who in "Waldgespräch" made her into a demonic wood nymph, and Count Otto Heinrich von Loeben, whose ballad "Der Lurleyfels" thematically is very similar to Heine's. Anyone interested in comparing two treatments of essentially the same subject, one eminently forgettable and the other a masterpiece, should read Count Loeben's "Der Lurleyfels" and compare it with Heine's poem, which runs:

> Ich weiss nicht, was soll es bedeuten,
> Dass ich so traurig bin;
> Ein Märchen aus alten Zeiten,
> Das kommt mir nicht aus dem Sinn.
>
> Die Luft ist kühl und es dunkelt,
> Und ruhig fliesst der Rhein;
> Der Gipfel des Berges funkelt
> Im Abendsonnenschein.
>
> Die schönste Jungfrau sitzet
> Dort oben wunderbar,
> Ihr goldnes Geschmeide blitzet,
> Sie kämmt ihr goldenes Haar.
>
> Sie kämmt es mit goldenem Kamme,
> Und singt ein Lied dabei;
> Dat hat eine wundersame,
> Gewaltige Melodei.
>
> Den Schiffer im kleinen Schiffe
> Ergreift es mit wildem Weh;
> Er schaut nicht die Felsenriffe,
> Er schaut nur hinauf in die Höh.
>
> Ich glaube, die Wellen verschlingen
> Am Ende Schiffer und Kahn;
> Und das hat mit ihrem Singen
> Die Loreley getan.
>
> (1:103)

(I don't know what it means that I am so sad; I can't get out of my mind a tale from olden times. The air is cool and it is growing dark, and the Rhine flows peacefully; the peak of the mountain sparkles in the evening sunshine. The fairest maiden sits up there, wonderfully, her golden jewelry glitters, she combs her golden hair. She combs it with a golden comb, and sings a song the while; it has a wondrous, powerful melody. The boatman in his little boat is seized with wild woe; he does not see the rocky reefs, he only looks up to the heights. I believe the waves finally swallow the boatman and his boat; and that the Loreley has done with her singing.)

Even without the sentimental strains of Silcher's tune, the words seem to sing. The trimetric lines with crossed rhymes, feminine cadenzas alternating with masculine ones, make up six quatrains, each of which forms a closed unit— with the exception of the two middle ones which, not accidentally, belong together. Throughout, structural elements seem to fuse perfectly and naturally with image and sound, each stanza weaving its own particular spell. In the

first it is mainly the broken syntactical awkwardness which reinforces the vague melancholy and groping uncertainty evoked by the haunting memory of "ein Märchen aus uralten Zeiten." Next, the view shifts from the subjective mood, the mindscape, to the external scene. Twilight is descending on the calmly flowing river. The uncertain rhythm gives way to smoothly flowing lines which, with their dark vowels, physically convey what the words say, finally coming to rest on the one majestic noun that almost takes up the whole last line of the stanza: "Abendsonnenschein." With this our gaze has lifted to perceive "die schönste Jungfrau." Having somehow materialized out of the glowing radiance, she unmistakably sits there, triply endowed with objects of gold as befits the fairytale figure, all three of them—jewels, hair, and comb—feminine attributes that are now brought into play in a stunningly simple, commonplace, and yet exquisitely feminine act: the lady combs her hair. The reiteration, "Sie kämmt es mit goldenem Kamme," leads into the next stanza and thus into the siren's song. Moreover, it underscores the repetitive quality of the stroking motion itself, with the hint of hypnotic fascination and sexual lure, at the same time connoting narcissistic aloofness. Similarly evocative are the allusions to the song itself. Presently the view is again lowered to the river, to show the devastating effect of it all on the man in the small boat who is now mentioned for the first time. The circle is finally completed with the return to the "I" with which it began: "Ich glaube die Wellen verschlingen." The initial question has been answered, and the haunting tale has been recreated, as it were, before our eyes. Only at the very end does the spell receive a name, and the untitled poem the title under which it was to be remembered, making Loreley an archetype of the forever elusive one whose beauty is matched by the coldness, if not the evil, within.

Break of Mood

Heine's talent for establishing mood with a few vivid strokes was matched only by his flair for breaking it. The sudden change of mood became a characteristic feature of the ***Buch der Lieder,*** known as *Stimmungsbrechung.* In its early form it had ensued from the dream situation, when fantasy inevitably ended with a return to reality. But from ***Lyrisches Intermezzo*** onward, this awakening takes on many guises that are symptomatic of that tension between nostalgia and disillusion, romantic sentiment and critical judgment, emotion and intellect which inform Heine's entire work and being. In effect it usually means that his sense of humor asserts itself. Readers come to expect the tongue-in-cheek punch lines and ironic reversals as quintessential Heine. It should be noted that Heine's irony does not fall into the category of "Romantic irony" associated with other poets of the era. Unlike the ironic flights of the Romantics which allow them to escape from reality, Heine's irony has precisely the opposite effect; it bursts the idealistic bubble by confrontation with reality:

> Die Jahre kommen und gehen,
> Geschlechter steigen ins Grab,
> Doch nimmer vergeht die Liebe,
> Die ich im Herzen hab.

Nur einmal noch möcht ich dich sehen,
Und sinken vor dir aufs Knie,
Und sterbend zu dir sprechen:
"Madame, ich liebe Sie!"

                    (1:117; **"Die Heimkehr, No. 25"**)

(The years keep coming and going,
Generations pass to the grave,
But never the love will perish
Which in my heart I have.

Just once more I'd like to see you
And sink upon my knee
And speak to you while dying:
"Madame, ich liebe Sie.")

What prompts the reader's chuckle in the first place is of course the deflating last line with its startling shift—a linguistic shift that cannot be duplicated in English—from the intimate *du* of the first seven lines to the tamely formal address of "Madame" with *Sie* instead of the climax which we were led to expect. This shift in speech levels denotes the incongruity between the grandiloquently idealized "eternal" passion and the rather mannered and lean relationship on which it had fed, revealing a world of difference between illusion and reality. In presenting this love in such obviously hyperbolic terms, Heine exposes its hollow bathos and histrionic posturing. In mocking maudlin sentiment, he mocks not only contemporary poetic trends but also himself.

Ein Jüngling liebt ein Mädchen,
Die hat einen andern erwählt,
Der andre liebt eine andre,
Und hat sich mit dieser vermählt.

Das Mädchen heiratet aus Ärger
Den ersten besten Mann,
Der ihr in den Weg gelaufen;
Der Jüngling ist übel dran.

Es ist eine alte Geschichte,
Doch bleibt sie immer neu;
Und wem sie just passieret,
Dem bricht das Herz entzwei.

                    (1:88; **"Lyrisches Intermezzo, No. 39"**)

(A young man loves a girl
Who has chosen another;
This other one loves another
And has married her.

The girl in vexation
Marries the first man
Who comes her way;
The young man is up against it.

It is an old story,
But it remains ever new;
And when it happens to someone
His heart breaks.)

The *Stimmungsbrechung* in this poem has a diametrically opposite effect. Here the unadorned summary of the plain facts, the cheerfully galloping meter, the colloquial idiom and carefree tone, all combine to make light of the old predicament—up to the last two lines, that is, when the right of feeling is reaffirmed.

Heine's touch can at times be so subtle that the ironic undertones may be—and indeed have been—overlooked. In pieces that nineteenth-century readers (including the composers) took at face value, modern readers can frequently savor an ironic intent and sophistication that eluded his contemporaries. To give just one example: I am convinced that poem **"No. 14"** in **"Die Heimkehr,"** "Das Meer erglänzte weit hinaus" [The sea shone far into the distance], which sounds hopelessly maudlin when taken literally, actually contains a parodistic inversion of Goethe's ballad "Der Fischer" to which its second stanza unmistakably alludes. (Compare: "Der Nebel stieg, das Wasser schwoll". . . "Aus deinen Augen, liebevoll", and the reference to a "Fischerhaus" in the beginning.) Both poems involve a man by the water's edge and a "damp lady" that draws him to his watery doom. But the fatal waters in the peculiarly Heinesque version flow from the lady's eyes. Does he mean to provide a more realistic interpretation of the liquid element's demonic power?

A return visit to Hamburg in 1823 inspired one of the key poems of the cycle **"Die Heimkehr,"** about the man who visits the deserted house of his former beloved. It is a powerful poem about suffering revisited, embodied in his agonizing former self, the man shut out from love and home whom the lyrical "I" encounters under his sweetheart's window. The concept of the divided self does not, of course, originate with Heine. "Zwei Seelen wohnen, ach, in meiner Brust" ("Two souls, alas! dwell in my breast"), Goethe had said in *Faust,* and in the Romantic era the theme of the double was a familiar one, notably in the formulation of E. T. A. Hoffmann, from whom Heine may have borrowed the image of the ghostlike companion. But it was probably Heine's poem, unforgettably set to music by Franz Schubert, which gave the term "Doppelgänger" European currency.

Still ist die Nacht, es ruhen die Gassen,
In diesem Hause wohnte mein Schatz;
Sie hat schon längst die Stadt verlassen,
Doch steht noch das Haus auf demselben Platz.

Da steht auch ein Mensch und starrt in die Höhe,
Und ringt die Hände, vor Schmerzensgewalt;
Mir graust es, wenn ich sein Antlitz sehe—
Der Mond zeigt mir meine eigne Gestalt.

Du Doppelgänger! du bleicher Geselle!
Was äffst du nach mein Liebesleid,
Das mich gequält auf dieser Stelle,
So manche Nacht, in alter Zeit?

                    (1:115; **"Die Heimkehr, No. 20"**)

(The night is still, the streets are at rest,
My darling used to live in this house;

She has long since left town,
But the house still stands in the same place.

A man stands there too and stares up,
And wrings his hands in agony;
I shudder when I see his face—
The moon shows me my own features.

You double-ganger! pale fellow!
Why do you ape my love-pain
Which tormented me in this very place
On so many a night in times gone by?)

"North Sea"

Reading *Buch der Lieder* today, one cannot help but marvel at this amazing phenomenon of thematic monotony—the critic Gerhard Storz calls it "monstrous"[5]—coupled with such a seemingly inexhaustible wealth of variations. Each poem a self-contained unit, almost always bound internally by finely wrought antithesis, yet all of them, by clever arrangement, bonded together through links of association or contrast. One of the early pieces is about *Minnesänger,* the medieval troubadours. Clearly, this is a label Heine wished to apply to himself—he actually did so in his letters—thus placing his preoccupation with Eros into an ancient and highly respected European tradition.[6] Still, no one was more aware of the ridiculousness of the eternal love plaint than the poet himself.

"Teurer Freund! Was soll es nützen,
Stets das alte Lied zu leiern?
Willst du ewig brütend sitzen
Auf den alten Liebeseiern?

Ach! das ist ein ewig Gattern,
Aus den Schalen kriechen Küchlein,
Und sie piepsen und sie flattern,
Und du sperrst sie in ein Büchlein."

(1:127)

("Dear friend! What use is it
To grind out the same old tune?
Do you want to go on hatching
Those old love-eggs?

What a never ending clucking!
Out of the shells crawl little chicks
And they chirp and they flutter
And you lock them into a little book".)

Even within the *Buch der Lieder* one can discern Heine's progressive attempts to free himself from the shackles of the love theme and the format of the folksong. One new concern which begins to emerge in the longer poems that follow **"Die Heimkehr"**—a concern which will assume great prominence in his later opus—has to do with religion. **"Donna Clara"** is a biting satire on anti-Semitism. When his friends found this poem amusing, the poet expressed surprise: he, for once, was not amused. More or less oblique allusions to the topic of religion are also contained in **"Götterdämmerung"** [Twilight of the Gods],

"Almansor," **"Die Wallfahrt nach Kevlaar"** [Pilgrimage to Kevlaar], and, most explicitly, **"Bergidylle"** [Mountain Idyll].

The breakthrough in content and form which Heine evidently sought was achieved in a cycle of twenty-two poems entitled **"Die Nordsee"** [North Sea] which makes up the last part of *Buch der Lieder*. They are rhapsodic hymns that were inspired by the poet's encounters with the sea. (Beginning in 1823, as already mentioned, he vacationed on the isle of Norderney to cure his headaches.) But the thematic focus on the seascape was novel not only for Heine: it is said that he "discovered" the sea for German literature, much as Albrecht Haller had discovered the majesty of the Alps.

The experience of the ocean's elemental power, grandeur, and beauty seems to have opened fresh perspectives and vistas and unleashed an exuberant surge of feeling in Heine. Others made use of free verse before him. Klopstock's famed odes had been succeeded (and surpassed) by the hymnic masterpieces of the young Goethe, and in Heine's own time Ludwig Tieck brought free verse into vogue. Yet once again Heine develops a distinctive note. In his inimitable way he uses the freedom of free verse to create rhythmic and tonal effects that sensually convey the ebb and flow, the roar and music of the surf. In marked contrast to the simple idiom of his folksongs, he now produces high-flown rhetoric and compounds descriptive epithets with a Homeric ring, in line with the mythological topics which he introduces. It is mythology with a difference, however, as Heine presents his own irreverent interpretation of the familiar classical figures. His deities of antiquity do not stand for eternal and universal absolutes— quite the opposite. He shows them as exiles, deposed and replaced by Christian gods (the plural is his), and he means to infer the relative and changing validity of all religious "truths." One of the key poems which makes this point explicit is entitled **"Die Götter Griechenlands"** [The Gods of Greece] and uses Schiller's poem of the same title as point of reference and departure.

The hymnic tone does not preclude the use of *Stimmungsbrechung* or the treatment of humorous and even burlesque topics. In fact, just as some of Heine's seemingly simple songs achieve their particular piquancy by sophisticated nuances, so the exalted format when superimposed on commonplace topics produces hilarious effects, which were not appreciated by all of Heine's readers.

Throughout these poems, one can hear and feel the sea, not by itself but always in relation to the reflecting, questing man at the center whose loneliness and vulnerability (and sometimes fatuity) it throws into relief:

Fragen

Am Meer, am wüsten, nächtlichen Meer
Steht ein Jüngling-Mann,
Die Brust voll Wehmut, das Haupt voll Zweifel,
Und mit düstern Lippen fragt er die Wogen:
"O löst mir das Rätsel des Lebens,

Das qualvoll uralte Rätsel,
Worüber schon manche Häupter gegrübelt,
Häupter in Hieroglyphenmützen,
Häupter in Turban und schwarzem Barett,
Perückenhäupter und tausend andre
Arme, schwitzende Menschenhäupter—
Sagt mir, was bedeuter der Mensch?
Woher ist er kommen? Wo geht er hin?
Wer wohnt dort oben auf goldenen Sternen?"

Es murmeln die Wogen ihr ew'ges Gemurmel,
Es wehet der Wind, es fliehen die Woklen,
Es blinken die Sterne, gleichgültig und kalt,
Und ein Narr wartet auf Antwort.

(1:207)

Questions

The sea, the midnight, the desolate sea
Where a young man stands,
His head full of doubts, his breast of sorrows,
And with bitter lips he questions the ocean:

"O solve me the riddle of being,
The painful, primordial riddle,
Whereover so many heads have been cudgelled,
Heads in hieroglyphic bonnets,
Heads in turbans and scullcaps of black,
And heads in perukes, a thousand other
Heads of poor men who drudged and sweated—
Tell me, what purpose has man?
From whence does he come here? And whither
    goes?
Who lives above there, beyond where the stars
    shine?"

The billows are murmuring their unending murmur,
The breezes are blowing, the cloudbanks are flying,
The stars are blinking, indifferent and cold,
And a fool awaits his answer.[7]

In 1827, Heine was glad to have found in Hoffmann und Campe a publisher who was willing to bring out in one book all the poems that had been published here and there, in the volume **Gedichte,** in journals, as a "lyrical interlude" between the tragedies *William Ratcliff* and *Almansor* (which, for all the energy, enthusiasm, and hope he invested in them, never did catch on), or in the two volumes of *Reisebilder* [Travel Sketches]. And Heine must have actually meant it when he supposed that his poems "would now sail into the sea of oblivion,"[8] for he was willing to forego any honorarium or royalties (Campe, in fact, paid him fifty Louis d'or by canceling a debt). He lived to experience his world fame as the poet of the **Buch der Lieder,** with translations into many languages. It was the first German book to be translated into Japanese—comparable to *Werther*'s translation into Chinese, a parallel which did not escape Heine's notice. But at the time of its publication, he believed that he had done with lyrical poetry and that his strength and his mission lay elsewhere. He had established himself as a successful, albeit controversial, author of brilliant, scintillating, challenging prose.

Notes

[1] In the context of *Buch der Lieder,* this poem is a love plaint. But it was originally written to commiserate with Heine's Düsseldorf school friend Gustav Friedrich von Unzer, who had been badly wounded at Waterloo and returned to the Lycée while still on crutches. See *Düsseldorfer Heine Ausgabe,* vol. 1, pt. 2, p. 686.

[2] "Und was soll werden dein Weib und Kind? Edward, Edward . . . Die Welt ist gross, lass sie betteln drin, Mutter, Mutter!" Johann Gottfried Herder, *Stimmen der Völker in Liedern* (Leipzig: Reclam, 1968).

[3] This is the only instance of such "irregularity" in "Lyrisches Intermezzo," where tetrametric lines usually alternate with trimetric ones.

[4] *Düsseldorfer Heine Ausgabe,* vol. 1, pt. 2, pp. 812-14.

[5] Gerhard Storz, *Heinrich Heines Lyrische Dichtung,* (Stuttgart: Klett, 1971), pp. 40, 48.

[6] Manfred Windfuhr, "Heine und der Petrarkismus," in *Heinrich Heine,* ed. Helmut Koopmann (Darmstadt 1975), pp. 207-31.

[7] Transl. by Howard Mumford Jones, in *Heine's Poem "The North Sea"* (Chicago, 1916).

[8] Hirth, 1:329, October 30, 1827.

Jeffrey L. Sammons (essay date 1985)

SOURCE: "Mortification of the Emancipated Flesh: The Case of Heine," in *Hypatia: Essays in Classics, Comparative Literature, and Philosophy,* edited by William M. Calder III, Ulrich K. Goldsmith, and Phyllis B. Kenevan, Colorado Associated University Press, 1985, pp. 187-98.

[*In the following essay, Sammons studies the link between Heine's illness and his literary creativity.*]

The medical report on nineteenth-century German literature is quite varied and therefore probably statistically insignificant; no specific theme seems to run through it. There is, of course, the litany of early deaths: Wilhelm Heinrich Wackenroder, dead of typhus at twenty-five in 1798; Novalis of tuberculosis at twenty-nine in 1801; Schiller of acute pneumonia, his system weakened by a long list of internal disorders, including peritonitis, strangulation of the colon, chronic bronchitis, nephritis, and myocarditis, at forty-five in 1805.[1] The young genius Georg Büchner was lamentably cut off by meningitis at twenty-three in 1837, just at the point at which his beleaguered life had taken a decided turn for the better; and Karl Immermann, who had struggled many years to find his own voice, died unexpectedly at the age of forty-four in 1840 just as he had discovered his true métier, the satirical, social-critical novel. But there were long lives also. Best known, of course, is that of Goethe, who retained his extraordinarily resourceful creativity until his death at eighty-three. Ludwig Tieck died at eighty; it is not always remembered that Tieck, one of the first of the late eighteenth-century Romantics, lived long enough to become one of the first mid-nineteenth-century realists. Eduard Mörike, flaccid, listless, and neurotic, lived to be seventy-one. Most of the Young Germans, usually associated with the episode of literary dissidence in the 1830s, were actually around for quite a while: Ludolf Wienbarg died at seventy in 1872; Karl Gutzkow at sixty-seven in 1878; Heinrich Laube at seventy-eight in 1884. Both of the major novelists of the second half of the century, Wilhelm Raabe and Theodor Fontane, lived to be seventy-nine, dying in 1910 and 1898, respectively.

Pathological cases, physical and mental, are also found. The patriotic novelist and talented critic Willibald Alexis suffered a stroke in 1856 at the age of fifty-eight that prevented him from speaking or writing, a condition in which he survived for another fifteen years—a gruesome fate for a writer. Hölderlin became insane in midlife, and Clemens Brentano was thought to be nearly so by those who knew him, who sometimes referred to him as "Demens" Brentano. Gutzkow's eccentricities gradually verged on madness as he developed a manic persecution complex; his odd death—he suffocated from the smoke of a lamp he knocked over at his bedside—has been thought by some to have been a suicide, but I believe it was probably an accident. There were actual suicides, however. The most famous was Heinrich von Kleist, who said of himself that he was a man who could not be helped and who in 1811, at thirty-four, shot himself and his lady friend. The sixty-three-year-old Adalbert Stifter, a hypochondriac who came to experience real suffering from liver cancer, is now believed to have cut his throat in 1868. The Swiss poet Conrad Ferdinand Meyer (1825-98), genetically burdened, as he believed, by a tendency to pathology and suicide, conquered it with psychiatric aid. This is one of the success stories of nineteenth-century medicine, though it may have been owing as much to his determination not to succumb as to the science of the time, and indeed symptoms of mental illness reappeared in his last years.

The most spectacular medical case of the century, however, was that of Heinrich Heine (1797-1856). There are several reasons for this. For one thing, by the 1840s Heine was doubtless the most famous living writer in the German language and an eminent figure on the international literary scene, a star by the standards of those times and an object of public scrutiny. He was something of a tourist attraction in Paris, and a good many of the tourists who sought him out were hoping to publish something about him. This irritated Heine, who liked to keep his public relations under firm personal control. When he became paralyzed and bed-ridden in 1848, this development, too, became a theme for reportage. But it soon became more than that, for the visitors were amazed by the magnitude and, in time, the endurance of his suffering. I have the notion that nineteenth-century people were more inured to the sight of intractable pain and suffering than we outside the medical professions are today; nevertheless, Heine's condition, in its severity and protractedness, made a stunning impression on observers at the time. They were aroused to pity and, while Heine fought off sentimental

exploitation of his condition, he nevertheless benefited from the mood of sympathy, for he had offended large segments of his public over the years and the recognition of his suffering substantially relieved the hostility toward him. But there was more to it yet; for Heine's spectacular physical collapse appeared to challenge the whole intellectual and ideological strategy of his life. He had become an actor in the oldest morality play known to the human race: the tragedy of the fragility and transitoriness of the physical and sensory being.

At no time in his life does Heine give the impression of being particularly robust. He was a high-strung, neurasthenic person who hated tobacco smoke, did not like to drink very much, and was very sensitive to noise. On the whole he was sedentary and not very athletic, though on his famous Harz journey of 1824 he hiked some 280 miles of mildly mountainous terrain in about three weeks, a not inconsiderable achievement, and he regularly traveled from home to his universities on foot. During a North Sea vacation in 1827 he learned how to swim, but he seems to have made no further use of this skill. He had no sports, could not dance, and, as far as I can discover, never rode a horse. While up to midlife we rarely find him actually *sick,* he was often indisposed and complained particularly of debilitating headaches. Since he was in general much given to grumbling and to attracting attention to himself, and was notoriously disinclined to do anything he did not want to do, his acquaintances tended to ascribe these complaints to malingering, but I believe he often genuinely felt unwell.

The onset of his serious illness began in his late thirties, although there were flickers of symptoms earlier. In 1837 he began to complain of signs of paralysis in his left hand. Then he experienced eye troubles that at times made him fear he was going blind; from time to time his doctor forbade him to read and write. These symptoms, which began in the summer of 1837, recurred in the following spring, again in the summer of 1838, when he complained that everything he looked at shimmered and took on a partly grayish, partly silver color, and returned again in March 1841. Reports of recurrent eye trouble, migraine headaches, and facial paralysis now become thematic in his correspondence. To his brother Maximilian, a physician, he wrote in 1843 of numbness on the left side of his body and pressure in his forehead. He consulted various physicians, whose best advice was to send him to spas. These "cures" seem always to have made him worse. The symptoms grew increasingly dangerous through 1845, 1846, and 1847; in the late summer of 1847 he wrote that his feet, legs, and lower torso were paralyzed and that he was unable to walk. The paralysis would shift from one part of his body to another, go intermittently into remission, then return. He got his locomotion back for a while, but in early 1848 he lived in a hospital. The definitive collapse occurred in May 1848. Thereafter he was never to walk again; his legs felt like cotton. The paralysis attacked his eyelids, so that he had to hold his eye open while reading. He suffered great pain from spinal contractions that rolled him into a ball for days on end. His physicians quarreled with one another and with Heine's wife, and he had no real confidence in most of them. Wounds were kept open on his spine in order to drip morphine into them. He was barely able to write, except in a large scrawl with pencil on cardboard; most of his works and letters of his last years were dictated to secretaries. In this manner Heine lived for nearly eight years in his "mattress-grave."

The diagnosis of Heine's disease has presented considerable difficulties. At the time, everyone, including Heine himself, believed it was venereal. This has also been the majority judgment of subsequent observers, the most modern conclusion being that he suffered from a syphilitic infection of the spinal cord.[2] But the diagnosticians have always remained uneasy, partly because of the deliberate, halting progress of the disease but mainly because it clearly never affected Heine's mind, which remained remarkably clear and active until almost his last hour, despite the large quantities of opiates he was obliged to take.[3] Not long ago an effort was made to identify his disease as acute intermittent porphyria, but the argument is grounded in such serious biographical and psychological misapprehensions that I cannot find it persuasive.[4] A physician in London wrote to me that it looked to him like multiple sclerosis.[5] I understand that there is an effort under way in Germany to argue for "Lou Gehrig's Disease," amyotrophic lateral sclerosis.[6]

Such inquiries, though doubtless interesting in their own right, have little bearing on Heine's own situation. It is clear that he presumed his affliction was venereal. In a letter a few months after his collapse he spoke of "cette maladie des hommes heureux"; in the manuscript he has crossed out the word "amoureux."[7] In one of his late poems we read:

> It was the dark woman who pressed my head
> Against her heart one day.
> Ah, where her poisoned tears were shed
> My hair has turned to gray.
>
> She kissed me sick, she kissed me lame
> And blind in these eyes of mine;
> She wildly drank, in passion's name,
> The strength from out my spine.[8]

In what is believed to be his last poem, usually titled **"For the Mouche,"** in a stanza that was suppressed in the nineteenth century, he gives a vivid image of the ruin of his life's allegiances:

> And here lie many female forms in stone,
> Covered with grass and in the weeds' embrace;
> And time, worst kind of syphilis yet known,
> Has robbed a piece of a nymph's majestic face.[9]

To have been struck down by the disease of lovers struck down at the same time a whole strategy of Heine's life. Virtually from the beginning of his career he had built his aesthetic, political, and historical views around the dichotomy of what he variously called sensualism and spiritualism, or Hellenism and Nazarenism. He saw all oppression,

past and present, in terms of the repression of sensual pleasure, of the gratification of the flesh and the material needs of man. Wherever he detected traces of asceticism and puritanism, he attacked; on these grounds he was hostile to religious institutions, especially Christianity in its alliance with despotic government, and it was also on these grounds that he opposed the radicals and republicans of his time, whom he suspected of an intrinsically reactionary puritanism. Thus he wrote in a famous passage:

> We are fighting not for the human rights of the people, but for the divine rights of humans. In this, and in many other things, we differ from the men of the revolution. We do not want to be sansculottes, frugal burghers, cheap presidents; we are founding a democracy of equally magnificent, equally holy, equally blissful gods. You demand simple dress, abstemious habits, and unseasoned pleasures; we, on the other hand, demand nectar and ambrosia, purple cloaks, sumptuous aromas, voluptuousness and luxury, laughing nymph-dance, music and comedies—be not annoyed, you virtuous republicans! We reply to your censorious reproaches with what one of Shakespeare's fools has already said: Dost thou think, because thou art virtuous, there shall be no more cakes and ale?[10]

And now?

> I am no longer a divine biped; I am no longer the "freest German after Goethe," as Ruge called me in healthier days; I am no longer the great pagan no. 2 who was compared to the vine-wreathed Dionysus, while my colleague no. 1 was given the title of a Grandducal Weimarian Jupiter; I am no longer a zestful, somewhat corpulent Hellene smiling down on gloomy Nazarenes—I am now only a mortally ill Jew, an emaciated image of misery, an unhappy man![11]

Heine astonished the public by confessing his return to a personal God. His aggressive anticlericalism and pantheism, which he sometimes allowed to skirt the edge of atheism, was notorious in Europe. But now?

> The God of the pantheists I could not use. This poor dreamy being is woven and grown together with the world, imprisoned in it, as it were, and yawns at you, without will or power. . . . When one requires a God who is able to help—and that is the main thing—then one must assume His personality, His transcendence, and His sacred attributes, perfect goodness, perfect wisdom, perfect justice, etc.[12]

Perhaps the reader has already been struck by the tone of these few representative examples of Heine's late utterances. The matter is serious, even grim, but the manner is anything but lugubrious. That his wit, his rationality, his stylistic resourcefulness did not flag in these circumstances is remarkable, especially as Heine had never been notable for facing life's adversities with stoic equanimity. I have suggested in the past that Heine may have had a psychological dividend from his suffering.[13] He had, perhaps, a streak of masochism; he had always been inclined to see himself as ill-used; now he really was ill-used, and the world at large must now acknowledge it, as indeed it did. His surprising courage in the "mattress-grave"—Heine himself was surprised by it—may be partly explicable in this way.

But one might also look upon him as engaged in an effort to rescue the coherence and integrity of his views and his public image in this new situation. Given his commitment to his sensualist doctrine, this was no easy task. He had, after all, written in the previous decade: "So many free-thinkers are converted on their deathbeds—but make no fuss about it! These conversion stories belong at best to pathology and would yield poor witness for your cause. In the end they prove only that it was not possible for you to convert those freethinkers so long as they went about with healthy senses under God's open sky and were completely in command of their reason."[14] It was important to Heine that he should not appear disloyal to his progressive convictions, and he tried by various stratagems to retain as much continuity as he could plausibly assert. He was particularly concerned that his return to a personal God should not appear to be a conversion to organized religion or—horror of horrors—an example for edifying homilies. Thus in his dialogue with God he maintained a flippant, uppity tone that sometimes can disconcert the reader but was necessary to his purposes. He needed God, the great persecutor, to accuse of unjust governance of the world, best exemplified by his inconsistency:

> Permit me, Lord, I'm shocked at this,
> I think you've made a bloomer:
> You formed the merriest poet and now
> You rob him of his good humor.[15]

"Yes," he wrote,

> the lye of scorn that the Master pours over me is horrible, and grimly cruel is His jest. Humbly I confess His superiority, and I bow down to Him in the dust. But even if I lack such creative power in the highest degree, still eternal reason flashes in my spirit, and I may even call God's jest before reason's forum and subject it to a respectful criticism. And there I take the liberty of uttering the submissive hint: methinks that cruel jest with which the Master afflicts his poor pupil is being dragged out somewhat too long; it has lasted now more than six years, which is becoming downright boring.[16]

Thus poet and God, creator and Creator, confront one another on at least a pretense of even terms. The sovereign dignity of the poet is insisted upon:

> Any poet who possesses
> This, God's grace, we call a genius:
> Monarch in the realm of thought, he
> Is responsible to no man.[17]

But in that same poem, **"Jehuda ben Halevy,"** we learn that all poets are descendants of the original Schlemihl, accidentally killed by the zealous Phinehas, who, we will remember from the Bible, is the ancestor of all the high

priests.[18] Thus Heine, as had always been his habit, extrapolates and universalizes from his own self and situation. The destruction of his body and his aspirations symbolizes the poet's vulnerability before a cruder but invincible power; in turn, the vulnerability of the poet as the anointed but unacknowledged and frustrated legislator of mankind is extended to a pervasive theme of the late poetry: the inevitable victory of the worse man over the better.

With this thematic chain Heine endeavors to close the circle to his political radicalism. The collapse of his physical being occurred virtually simultaneously with the Revolution of 1848. The uproar of the Revolution caused him serious personal inconvenience, exacerbating the desperateness of his condition. On the whole, Heine took a sour view of the Revolution, regarding it as a victory of the sort of petty and mean-spirited fools he had scorned all his life. As the Revolution retreated in one country after another before the counterattacks of reactionary might, he settled back into his customary posture of implacable satire, now shaded by a bitterness that verged on pessimism. He portrayed himself rather theatrically as a freedom fighter fallen, broken but unvanquished, at the front.[19] Thus Heine strives for coherence of pattern: the shattered poet before the acknowledged but questioned power of God is in a sense a metonymy for the shattered cause of freedom before the at least temporarily invincible power of traditional authority. Furthermore, Heine was able to involve in the pattern, along with tyranny, his other great enemy: capitalism. For he *also* ascribed the breakdown of his health to the malevolent cruelties of his rich relatives in a long, bitter feud over his uncle's inheritance that began in 1845.[20]

Defeat, however, is not total. For the poet retains his voice, his reason, and his superior power over the word. He retains the ability to employ his eloquence to call God to the bar of justice, to protest oppression and expose tyrants as dunces, and to immortalize his hated relatives in a Dantean inferno of a sort that only the poet can ignite. Out of his anguish he cries out his freedom; out of his prostration, his superiority. Here, too, intractable illness seems, almost perversely, to have served him. He had long associated creativity and refined sensibility with sickness. Long before his own collapse he wrote that "sick people are truly always more refined than healthy ones; for only the sick human being is a human being; his limbs have a history of suffering, they are spiritually permeated," and later: "I myself belong to this sick old world, and the poet rightly says: scoffing at one's crutches does not enable one to walk any better. I am the sickest of you all and the more pitiable, since I know what health is."[21] He has another writer complain that he is growing too healthy, which weakens his intellectual gifts.[22] In earlier years he had asked whether poesy is not the product of sickness, as the pearl is the product of the oyster, and defined the components of the imagination as "dreams and death and madness."[23] In a poem that parodistically sees God's creativity as parallel to the poet's, sickness is said to be the cause of God's own creation, and creation its cure.[24]

The association of illness with sensitivity and creativity probably requires a sociological translation. The healthy person is the adapted civilian, comfortable in the status quo despite its injustice and human incompleteness, a person of uncircumcised ears and heart, as the Bible has it. It is not the commonplace person who is alienated or, if he is, his alienation is hidden from him by false consciousness; it is the person thrown out of the groove of health who is alienated or more aware of the alienation around him. Illness thrusts the self out of the commonplace, expands the attention to alternative possibilities, both tragic and utopian. Thus, in a fallen world, imagination and poesy itself are born in suffering, and there accrues to suffering the aristocratic otherness that for Heine was always the mark of the true poet despite his claims to spokesmanship for the people. Whatever one may think of all this, there seems to have been some subjective truth to it in Heine's case. For illness undoubtedly did deepen his creativity. Modern critics are almost unanimous that the late poetry, composed in the "mattress-grave," is the finest of Heine's career, a body of sophisticated mid-nineteenth-century verse with premonitions of the modern. Mortality having been thrust upon him in so brutal a way, the tragic dimension of his imagination deepened, as did his sense of the might and inertia of the enemies of the good and the beautiful; yet courage and hope, though challenged and badly battered, were never wholly abandoned as long as the poet could wring out of his interminable dying works of the resistant imagination.

Heine was concerned to stress that he did not undergo a polar conversion with the collapse of his health, and it is true that he did not. There are thematic continuities throughout his whole career. But the emphases shift, in some cases rather radically. The disaster represented a defeat, physically and morally. But Heine had never been a good loser. If he was not to repudiate himself altogether, he needed to find a way to integrate the experience of extreme illness into his imagination and into the role he had shaped for himself as poet, revolutionary, and visionary. To this end he wove a complex fabric that is certainly not without tangled threads and clashing colors. But the ambiguities and contradictions are the consequence of Heine's sometimes oblique but nevertheless real honesty; what seemed to him unresolvable remained unresolved. There was no victory to be snatched from the jaws of defeat, but there was reflective analysis and, above all, there was protest. Few poets, I should think, have managed to cope with severe physical suffering and the constant imminence of death so resourcefully without denying their reality or submitting passively to a transcendental realm.

Notes

1 There has been much controversy over the diagnosis of Schiller's illnesses, complicated in part by the sectarian right-wing theory thriving among some of the Nazis that Schiller had been poisoned by Goethe as an agent of Jews and Freemasons. The diagnosis generally accepted today is that given by Wolfgang H. Veil, *Schillers Krankheit: Eine Studie über das Krankheitsgeschehen in Schillers Leben und über den natürlichen Todesausgang* (Naumburg-Saale, 1945). The study was first published in 1936 but was suppressed by the Nazis.

2 Arthur Stern, "Heinrich Heines Krankheit und seine Ärzte," *Heine-Jahrbuch 1964*, pp. 63-79. The study, however, is not all that recent; it was originally published in the *Schweizer Rundschau für Medizin* 45 (1956): 357-64.

3 It is not without interest that the same kind of discussion with the same kind of problems has emerged about the ultimately fatal disease of E. T. A. Hoffmann. See James M. McGlathery, *Mysticism and Sexuality: E. T. A. Hoffmann*, pt. 1, *Hoffmann and His Sources* (Las Vegas, Berne, Francfort/Main, 1981), pp. 74-75.

4 Nathan Roth, M.D., "The Porphyria of Heinrich Heine," *Comprehensive Psychiatry* 10, no. 2 (March 1969): 90-106; reprinted without reference notes as "The Porphyria of Heinrich Heine," *Elmcrest Classic of the Month*, vol. 3, no. 3 (Portland, Conn., 1978).

5 Dr. Max Mayer to JLS, personal communication, September 2, 1984.

6 Mentioned in passing in *Heine in Paris 1831*-1856, ed. Joseph A. Kruse et al. (Düsseldorf, 1981), p. 81. I have heard privately that a study is in progress. Stern, p. 76, already denied both of these possibilities, claiming that the cardinal symptoms are absent. Needless to say, I can have no competent judgment on these matters.

7 Heine to Louis-Désiré Véron, September 15, 1848, *Heinrich Heine Säkularausgabe*, ed. Nationale Forschungs- und Gedenkstätten der klassischen deutschen Literatur in Weimar and Centre National de la Recherche Scientifique in Paris (Berlin and Paris, 1970-), 22:295; 22K:200.

8 *Gedichte 1853 und 1854*, "Zum Lazarus" 2, in Heinrich Heine, *Sämtliche Schriften*, ed. Klaus Briegleb et al. (Munich, 1968-76), 6/1:202. All quotations from Heine's literary texts will be referred to this edition by volume and page number. English translation from Hal Draper, *The Complete Poems of Heinrich Heine: A Modern English Version* (Boston, 1982), p. 710. All verse translations will be taken from this outstanding work.

9 Heine, 6/1:345; Draper, p. 822.

10 *Zur Geschichte der Religion und Philosophie in Deutschland*, Heine, 3:570.

11 "Berichtigung" (April 15, 1849), Heine, 5:109.

12 "Nachwort zum *Romanzero*," Heine, 6/1:182-83.

13 In *Heinrich Heine: The Elusive Poet* (New Haven, Conn., and London, 1969), p. 350 and, perhaps more cautiously, in *Heinrich Heine: A Modern Biography* (Princeton, N.J., 1979), p. 297.

14 *Zur Geschichte der Religion und Philosophie in Deutschland*, Heine, 3:364.

15 "Miserere," Heine 6/1:332; Draper, p. 813.

16 *Geständnisse*, Heine 6/1:499.

17 Heine, 6/1:135; Draper, p. 659.

18 Heine, 6/1:155-56; Draper, pp. 675-76.

19 "Enfant perdu"; Heine, 6/1:120-21; Draper, pp. 649-50. "Enfant perdu"

is a French term for a soldier on the front line who is expected to die there.

[20] On this see Sammons, *Heinrich Heine: A Modern Biography,* pp. 278-85.

[21] *Reise von München nach Genua,* chap. 27, Heine, 2:371; *Zur Geschichte der Religion und Philosophie in Deutschland,* Heine, 3:593-94. The "poet" is doubtless Lessing, in *Nathan the Wise,* 4:4, where it is chains rather than crutches.

[22] *Ludwig Börne: Eine Denkschrift,* Heine, 4:21. The remark is ascribed to Börne, but like others in that book, it is probably an attitude of Heine's put in Börne's mouth.

[23] *Die Romantische Schule,* Heine, 3:441; *Atta Troll,* Caput 20, Heine 5:545; Draper, p. 460.

[24] *Neue Gedichte,* "Schöpfungslieder" 7, Heine, 4:358-59; Draper, p. 356.

Heinz R. Kuehn (essay date 1989)

SOURCE: "Rediscovering Heinrich Heine," in *The Sewanee Review,* Vol. XCVII, No. 1, Winter, 1989, pp. 123-38.

[*In the following essay, Kuehn offers his impressions of Heine and his poetry.*]

As with most of the German poems I still know by heart, nearly forty years after I had left Germany, it was my father's voice that first conjured up in my young and receptive soul the images of Heine's poetry, the bewitching images of a world in which joy and sadness, scorn and trust, hope and despair, candor and irony, dream and reality seem, incredibly, to fuse into an awesome and irresistibly attractive symphony. It was not a wholesome world for a child whose inner vision should have been formed by images inspiring love and trust. I never found out whether my mother, being Jewish, was secretly pleased with my early exposure to a Jewish poet, or whether she was troubled when she heard her ten-year-old recite, for example, verses such as these:

There was an agèd monarch;
   His heart and head were gray with strife,
This poor old monarch wedded
   A young and lovely wife.

There was a pretty page-boy;
   His hair was light, his heart was clean,
He carried the long and silken
   Train of the fair young queen.

You know the old, old story
   So sweet to hear, so sad to tell.
Both of them had to perish;
   They loved each other too well.[1]

(Untermeyer)

When I became of school age the Third Reich had begun and Heine was stricken from the textbooks. Those of his poems that had become folk songs not even the Nazis could suppress were by-lined "Author unknown." Heine thus remained a childhood impression until, several years ago, one of my daughters gave me for Christmas a German paperback edition of his selected works. As soon as I had read the first few poems, I realized, to my amazement, that Heine attracted me as powerfully in my sixties as he had fascinated me in my childhood. I set about to study him and his time systematically, in the typically German professorial manner. Books by and about him, in various editions, are taking up more and more shelf space in my study. The poet, himself a serious student of everything that pricked his curiosity, be it medieval folklore or Kantian idealism, would have approved—with slightly raised eyebrows and his usual ironic smile, I am sure. "Zu fragmentarisch ist Welt und Leben . . ." he might have thought—

Life in this world is a muddled existence—
Our German professor will give me assistance.
He knows how to whip the whole thing into order;
He'll make a neat System and keep it in line.
With scraps from his nightcap and dressing-gown's
   border
He'd fill all the gaps in Creation's design.

(Untermeyer)

There has been more to my rediscovery of Heine than the mere acquisition and study of books. The man is far from being dead and forgotten, a subject for academicians or poetry enthusiasts at best. The Heine Jahrbuch, published in Düsseldorf where the poet was born in 1797, lists for the years 1984/85 alone more than 200 new contributions to the Heine literature from Germany, France, Russia, Japan, the United States of America, and other countries, along with countless lectures and recitals. Heine's very spirit is roaming among us, and one may recognize him unexpectedly by—well, a bunch of fresh flowers on a grave in Paris, for example. Heine went to Paris in 1831, when he was thirty-four. Already one of Europe's most famous writers (and certainly the most notorious), he chose exile from his own country because of his liberal views inspired by the ideals of the French Revolution. From here, the political, cultural, and social center of Europe, he continued his fight for political liberty and social justice in Germany. He also reported in trenchant essays what he saw and heard on the streets, in dance halls and museums, and in the government offices of the tumultuous French capital. This would have been a difficult task for any writer at a time when Germany consisted of a loose federation of thirty-seven sovereign states whose autocratic rulers sought protection against liberal ideas behind a shield of strict censorship. For Heine, who never learned how to mince words, these constraints on his pen were a source of constant frustration, anger, and bitterness, and forced him into ambiguities, evasions, and distortions. This was also a time when Jews in Germany, after enjoying a brief period of civil liberties under the rule of Napoleon, were again deprived of the rights and privileges of citizenship. Still, as bitingly as he would assail much of what was held sacrosanct in German history, art, music, and literature, Heine never lost his deep love for his fatherland. Besides struggling to penetrate the tight web of censorship with his writings for his compatriots (he never wanted to become a French citizen), he also devoted himself to explaining to his French hosts what he considered admirable and of enduring value in German life and German history, a mission that produced works unexcelled in brilliance of style, depth of perception, and richness of ideas. The French admired and feted him, and the French editions of his works were widely read and discussed. He enjoyed the friendship and admiration of Balzac, Gautier, Ferdinand Lassalle, Alexandre Dumas, Victor Hugo, George Sand, and Karl Marx. He married a Parisian "grisette" who for many years had been his mistress, a seemingly preposterous alliance but one that held together purely on the strength of Heine's "love beyond reason" for this illiterate shopgirl. According to his last will, he was buried in a Parisian cemetery, and his wife, who survived him by twenty-seven years, was buried at his side.

I visited Heine's grave in the Cimetière de Montmartre on a cool cloudy morning in May several years ago. Within a stone's throw of the cemetery, the little squares and narrow streets surrounding the Basilica of the Sacré Cœur had been thronged with tourists and gigantic tourist buses in spite of the early hour, but the vast burial grounds, shrouded in mist, were deserted and silent. A map was posted near the entrance but was so badly weatherworn as to be indecipherable. Mustering my best French, I asked a young gendarme at the guardhouse for directions. "Ah oui, le tombeau de Monsieur Einé," was the immediate reply, followed by an explosion of words that I guessed described markers on the way. Nodding politely I left him, none the wiser. I found the grave eventually, but even before I could take in the details of the monument, I was startled by the exuberance of spring flowers that covered the slab of white marble at the base of a slender column crowned with Heine's bust and inscribed "Heinrich Heine and Frau Heine." Plants and flowers had adorned many of the grave sites I had passed, but they had been formally arranged in bowls and urns in the manner in which a cemetery gardener would be apt to do such things. Here, on Heine's grave, spring, the season that always lifted his heavy spirit and made his heart ring out joyfully in verse or prose, had erupted in jubilant colors. Lilies of the valley and sweetheart roses, daisies and tulips, violets and iris, cyclamen and impatiens, roses and carnations—some were in vases, others in pots, but most of them had been gathered loosely in a small bunch and placed haphazardly on the white stone. All of them were fresh, as if picked that very morning. They were the offerings of pilgrims, of worshipers at a shrine. The center of the slab was sculptured in the form of a laurel wreath and two books placed one upon the other, and encircling the sculpture on three sides were the words of Heine's poem that begins "Where will I, the wander-wearied, find a haven and a shrine?" and that ends with the verse to which these flowers attested so eloquently:

> Well, what matter! God has given
> Wider spaces there than here.

And the stars that swing in Heaven
Will be lamps above my bier.

(Untermeyer)

While I busied myself at some distance from the monument with finding a good spot for taking a photograph, a young woman approached and stopped at the grave. She carried a shopping bag, and as was the custom among young people that year in Paris, she was dressed in expensive leather. Her face, framed by long dark curls, was serene and extraordinarily attractive. For two or three minutes she stood motionless as if in meditation or prayer, while I did not dare to interrupt her homage with the click of my camera. When she made to leave, I walked up to her and asked if she would stay long enough for me to include her in my photographs. She obliged with a friendly smile, and when I was finished, she walked away briskly. On my return to the cemetery gate, a group of German students stopped me to ask if I knew where Heine was buried. They had just about abandoned their search and were delighted that I could show them the way. Only much later, when I noted the visit to the cemetery in my diary, did it occur to me that, as far as I could observe, the only people on the vast grounds of the Montmartre cemetery that Saturday morning in May had been a group of German boys and girls, a young French woman, and myself, an American tourist, all paying homage to a German poet who had been dead for 125 years.

Once I was attuned to Heine, he never left me without a sign of his presence for very long. In Paris, again, a bookstore on the Boulevard St. Germain displays in its window a large poster showing a book sinking into a rough sea. The book is Heine's verse epic ***Germany: A Winter's Tale***, and the inscription, a quotation from that poem, reads: "Die Freiheit Stirbt Zentimeterweise—" "Liberty Dies Centimeter by Centimeter." In Berlin I discover a "Heinrich Heine Buchhandlung"—a discovery because the store is built into the viaduct of the notorious Zoo railroad station, a hangout for drug pushers, prostitutes, and similar urban wildlife. A sympathetic clerk takes me into a stockroom and lets me climb a ladder to a shelf directly below the ceiling, where I find an extensive collection of Heine literature. I return from the expedition coughing, half-blinded from dust, and blackened with soot, but with a dozen precious volumes on my favorite subject. In a side street in one of the city's suburbs, I come upon a little used-books store, enter, and ask my usual question, not expecting to find anything. I walk out with a little-known twelve-volume nineteenth-century edition of Heine's complete works, purchased at the incredible bargain price of less than fifty dollars. Back in America, on a visit to a Benedictine monastery, I discover in its library Adolph Strodtmann's 1876 edition of Heine's works, the edition that Heine scholars use as a principal reference. I have no difficulty persuading an understanding Father librarian that a loan of the volumes to me makes more sense than keeping them, unused, in dusty stacks, and they now grace my shelves. Such are the precious trophies and delectable triumphs of the amateur.

1981, the year I visited Paris and Berlin, was the 125th anniversary of Heine's death. Düsseldorf, Heine's native town, staged a Heine exhibition, as did Paris, the poet's beloved "Lutezia," the name the Romans gave to the city, and the title of one of Heine's books. That anniversary also saw a reenactment of an old but never dormant tragicomedy about an issue that erupted the moment French soil had covered the poet's coffin: whether Heine deserved a monument, and if he did, where it should be placed. Düsseldorf occupied center stage, but occasionally the scene also shifted to Hamburg, which had played an important role in his and his family's life, and to other European cities. The controversy pitted German nationalists (who branded him a turncoat), purists of the "moral majority" stripe (who could not stomach his bawdiness and effulgent sensuality), and, of course, anti-Semites against an alliance of Heine devotees that included not only Germans of such different character as the statesman Otto von Bismarck, the philosopher Friedrich Wilhelm Nietzsche, the historian Leopold von Ranke, and the poet Rainer Maria Rilke, but also a galaxy of writers such as John Galsworthy, Theodore Dreiser, Upton Sinclair, H. L. Mencken, Emile Zola, and Rabindranath Tagore. Liberal residents of Vienna had donated the splendid monument that now stands in the Montmartre cemetery, and even New York in 1889 erected a "Loreley" fountain in his memory, but in Germany the quarrel continued with unabated passion until the Nazis put an end to all talk about a monument for "one of the biggest Jewish swine of the past century." A statue given to Hamburg by the Empress Elizabeth of Austria was used by the Nazis for target practice, and Heine's grave in Paris was ruthlessly destroyed on Hitler's personal orders when the Germans occupied the city. When, in 1981, Düsseldorf finally unveiled a monument to its most famous native son (with the French secretary of state attending the ceremonies), the design immediately became a matter of heated and ugly debate in the German press—a debate coupled with the revival of another old controversial issue: whether the University of Düsseldorf should be renamed "Heinrich Heine Universität." "Comfort yourself," Heine would have said,

> Comfort yourself. No use pretending
>   This doesn't happen everywhere.
> Whatever's good, and great, and fair,
>   Always will have a shabby ending.

(Untermeyer)

Heine can still, more than one and a quarter centuries after death liberated him from the agonies of a paralyzing illness that chained him for his last eight years to his "mattress grave," stir the German spirit—some German spirits. Yet although there are signs of a "Heine renaissance," he seems to be condemned to remain, as one of his biographers put it in typically Heinesque melancholy, "a classic who missed the connection to canonization," a "short chapter in the histories of literature." What is it then that still makes men and women reach for his writings in preference to those of other giants of world literature; makes them place flowers on his grave, design posters in his spirit, quote him on matters of life, love, and death; form clubs devoted to a study of his life and work, and occasionally write a book about him? What accounts for my own fascination with a man whose views

and whose life were in so many important ways radically different from my own life and my own convictions? I was mistaken when I thought I could find the answer to these questions in the testimonials of his contemporaries, or in the books by his biographers. Few disagree that Heine was a great poet. "Let Heine stop being a street urchin, and he is the greatest poet in Germany," Goethe said of the young Heine. For Nietzsche he was "the highest concept of the lyric poet," and he added, "Once it will be said that Heine and I were by far the greatest masters of the German language." But whatever agreement exists about "the case Heine," it stops with the writer of songs and the stylist. After that there is only sharp disagreement; I pick up six books about Heine, and I get six different, often conflicting, views on the man's works and on his life. Just look at the subtitles of some Heine biographies: "The Artist in Revolt" (Max Brod); "The Elusive Poet" (Jeffrey L. Simmons); "Melancholic, Fighter in Marx, Epicurean" (Ludwig Marcuse); "Humanity's Soldier" (Frederic Ewen). Or read the quotations from Heine with which different biographers preface their work: "He who does not go as far as his heart urges, and reason permits, is a poltroon; he who goes farther than he wanted to go is a slave" (Max Brod); "Magis amica veritas" (Max J. Wolff); "Nothing turned out well for me in this world" (Fritz J. Raddatz); "On this gigantic world stage everything happens exactly as it does on our shabby boards" (Barker Farley); "Because the poet's heart is the center of the world, it must in our time be miserably torn apart" (Lew Kopelew). Trying to discover Heine turns into something like trying to discover the source of the Nile.

To most of his admirers in Germany or elsewhere, Heine is known only as a poet, principally as the author of the **Book of Songs**, although many who hum or whistle one or another of the more than three thousand compositions in which his lyrics have been used never realize that Heine was the writer of those poignant syllables. Yet all of his poetry comprises less than one-fourth of his work; the rest is prose. It was when I began to read his prose that my interest in Heine became intense. Here, and in the poems of his last years, the lovelorn flippant street urchin shows himself to be a man whose tourtured genius, whose *daimon,* wrestles with the large issues of the human condition: liberty, justice, beauty, truth, power, God, death. Others in his age wrestled with these issues too, and many of their utterances, unlike Heine's, had truly earth-shaking consequences. This was after all the age of Kant, Hegel, Marx, Fichte, and Kierkegaard. It was an age in which views about the meaning and purpose of life, about the ideal order of society, about the nature and destiny of man and his creations were still matters of passionate public debate and found expression in literature, music, art, and architecture. Classicists saw their model in the disciplined rational harmony of Greek antiquity. Romanticists turned to the dark, highly individualistic and emotional mysticism of the Middle Ages. Realists sought to find answers and guidance in the palpable practical realities of the day. The industrial age had begun, socialism was nascent, and the revolutions of 1830 and 1848 foreboded the collapse of a feudal system by which Europeans had been governed for one thousand years. Heine, disdaining systems, assigning logic to the works of the devil, and incapable of abstractions, embraced these issues and ideas as only a poet can embrace them: by living them, by suffering them. He was at all times "engagé—meshed and interlocked—with what he saw and heard and felt, but without ever permitting himself to be possessed. He wrote beautifully and with flashes of brilliant insights about Luther, Kant, and communism, about Paganini, Berlioz, and Napoleon, about art and politics, and he is at his best (for me, at any rate) when the sight of a shopgirl in the streets of Paris, the sound of a nightingale or the smell of a rose, or the arrangement of forms and colors in a painting lift him from immediate feelings and impressions into the world of ideas.

Heine witnessed only the first half of that century, but his observations and reflections make me see its brilliance and turmoil with the eyes of a genius who lived it with every fiber of his being, and they make me understand why the shockwaves sent out by the exploding ideologies of his era are still rocking the world in which I live. Heaven knows, his writings are full of inconsistencies, superficial generalizations, and deeply rooted biases, but these flaws, as substantial and irritating as they often are, weigh light against the unerring accuracy of his visions. At a time when virtually nobody paid any attention to the communists (or, for that matter, had heard that name), he warned "with the greatest anxiety and sorrow" that the future belonged to them, that they would destroy the old world order and with it his "***Book of Songs*** and all the marble statues of my beloved art world." He saw "as one who expected in the realm of reality the same revolution that has taken place in the realm of the intellect" that the thought systems of Kant, Fichte, Hegel, and the nature philosophers would "unleash that brutal Germanic lust for battle" and "a play will be performed in Germany compared with which the French Revolution might seem merely an innocent idyll." He saw the rise of mass democracy under the leadership of America, and while he welcomed the dawning realization of his lifelong dream of liberty and justice for all, he shuddered at the thought that "the great unwashed" would govern the western world. He praised in a poem the marvelous and as yet unheard-of things that the railroad would initiate for mankind, but with typical Heinesque irony collapsed the whole poem at the end with one line expressing his fervent hope that he would be dead by the time these marvels came to pass.

Heine makes me see . . . With him, it is rarely a matter of rational discernment. Reading him strikes me like the midnight stroke of a cathedral bell that vivifies the statuary in a park: queens, kings, generals, philosophers, and artists begin to dance and frolic with nymphs, mermaids, fairies, witches, and courtesans in that particular garden-plot of my mind marked "nineteenth century." Does the dance tell me something about the convictions of the man whose pen evokes that tumultuous scene? Was he a bourgeois, a royalist, or a revolutionary? It depends on which of his works you are reading. Was he a classicist, romanticist, naturalist, idealist, or socialist? It depends on whether you listen to the young or the old, the healthy or the sick writer. For most of his life he was, or believed himself to be, an epicurean, a materialist who divided mankind into Hellenes and Nazarenes, into sensualists freely indulging the pleasures of life, and spiritualists walking the barren footpaths of the "religions of pain," Christianity and Judaism. I read him as a visionary and natural mystic who never left the world of romanticism, those "old ruins" among which he had roamed in his youth and on which he heaped bitter scorn in his later years. His heart moved in dream and miracle, in faith and fable and legend. At the end he ruefully confessed that the Greek gods have "no arms and cannot help," and one of his last and finest poems is a hymn to that "faith in marvels," that

> . . . old blue flower
> Now forgotten—how resplendent
> Was its blooming in our spirit
> In the days of which we sing.
>
> (Draper)

But what about the question that still, as it did in his time, divides more readers of Heine into friends and foes than anything else he has written, the ages-old question with which Goethe has Gretchen confront Faust, "Nun sag', wie hast du's mit der Religion?" ("How do you feel about religion? Tell me, pray.") Was Heine an atheist? An agnostic? A mystic? A believer? Heine's biographers to this day differ sharply on the answer, as they differ on almost everything about their man. My own persuasion is that, just as he was a romanticist of the purest species in spite of his avowals to the contrary, so he was keenly and reverently aware of a superhuman power governing his life, no matter how mercilessly at times he mocked believers or how viciously he could lash out against the defined and structured religions of Judaism and Christianity. For him "everything has its beginning and its end in God," and I believe he was entirely truthful when he said "God has always been the beginning and the end of all my thoughts." And six years before his death, lying in agony in his "mattress grave," in utter loneliness, he confesses: "Yes, I have returned to God like the Prodigal Son. . . . When one longs for a God who has the power to help—and this is the main point, after all—then one must also accept his persona, his otherworldliness, and his holy attributes as the all-beautiful, all-wise, all-just and so on." And what his mind confesses, his heart sings out:

> The Lord God's glory I proclaim:
>   Here as in Heaven, great is He.
>   To Him I sing a kyrie,
> A hallelujah to His name.
>
> He wrought so fair, he wrought so fine
> The human heart. With breath divine
>   He blew therein from Heaven above
>   The spirit's soul, whose name is love.
>
> Away with the wanton lyre of Greece,
> And let the libertine Muses cease
>   Their dancing! With more pious lays
>   I'll sing the great Creator's praise.
>
> Hence, pagan music, hence! I vow
>   That David's pious harp shall ring

Through all the songs of praise I sing!
My psalm cries *Hallelujah* now!

(Draper)

Heine was no doubt in dead earnest when he wrote this hymn. But Heine being Heine, there were still to come, from the dying poet's lips, songs that are reminiscent more of Ovid than of David.

Heine is no guide for minds seeking meaning and order in human life and the affairs of men and nations, no comfort for souls searching for light in dark and troubled times. Yet the unreliability of his views, the inconsistencies and self-contradictions of his most persuasively rendered confessions, are pardonable for a man who caught pneumonia where ordinary mortals felt only a gentle breeze, even though they test the generosity and elasticity of one's mind severely. His writings on religion, philosophy, politics, and the arts are masterpieces. Unlike similar works that are classics of nineteenth-century German literature, they have the sharpness and urgency of modern reportage, a flavor that has made their author the first modern essayist and journalist. "Heine," says Golo Mann, the German historian, "spoke for a century. . . . Because he stood above that which was before his eyes, his work remained much more alive than that of his more self-assured contemporaries. . . . He was the herald of the crisis of the Western world."

Much has been made by Heine's contemporaries and biographers of the looseness of his sexual mores and his frequent long periods of plain debauchery. My own persuasion is that his reputed lechery was made up for the most part of mere bragging by Heine himself, spiteful slander by his enemies, and the usual gossip in literary circles. Aside from the fact that his chronic severe headaches would have made a life of dissipation impossible for men more robust than Heine, I read him as naturally shy and even prudish, and as self-destructive when he was truly in love. For the rest—what does it matter? Where others try to hide their clay feet, Heine put his on the table and pointed at them. When he was close to death and no longer had any need or desire to brag or lie or cover up, he wrote:

I never robbed a maiden's[2] honor
With lies and amorous dallying;
I never laid a hand upon her
If *her* hand bore a wedding ring.

Upon my word, if that's a story
My name does not deserve to grace
The Book of Honor in all its glory—
You should instead spit in my face.

(Draper)

I consider this historical truth. It is more than most of us will be able to say when our hour comes.

There are sides to Heine that are more troublesome than his sexual mores. The trait that flawed his character most severely, that alienated many of his most loyal friends, and that still today causes many to reject the man and all

his works out of hand was his viciousness in his literary battles. Heine was a polemicist of formidable influence in Europe; he did not exaggerate when he called his pen a sword. He was a dirty fighter who respected no rules, who knew neither generosity nor mercy, and who became enraged by the slightest criticism of his work or person. When he was provoked, his sole aim was to destroy his supposed adversary, an aim he often achieved but that as often caused him immeasurable harm.

It is not surprising, therefore, that many of Heine's biographers preface their studies with a disclaimer that typically runs like this:

> The genius of Heinrich Heine (1797-1856) has influenced German cultural life immensely, and yet an objective study of his life cannot be done without ineradicable prejudices. Still today Heine's life appears to many as shallow and offensive, his poetry as sick and worm-eaten. Many venomous things have been written about him, and yet scarcely another German poet has been as widely translated, admired, and also imitated as he whose *Lieder* have found such an immense dispersion throughout the world of German song. Of course, the circumstances of Heine's life were sometimes embarrassing and the weaknesses of his character unpleasant. But this biography . . . [3]

I read such *apologiae,* and I can see Heine's smile and hear his voice (a charming smile that made his brown eyes sparkle, and a soft pleasing voice, according to those who knew him):

They have told you many stories
    And made a great to-do;
But why my spirit worries
    Has not been told to you.

They made such a stir and pother,
    Complained of the life I led;
"A devil!" they said to each other;
    And you believed all they said.

And yet the very worst thing
    They never have even guessed;
For the worst and most accurst thing
    I carry hid in my breast.

(Untermeyer)

He who talks incessantly about himself and his world always stops just short of handing us the key to his innermost self, of letting us in on the things that really mattered to him. Was he incapable of unlocking both the worst and the best thing? Did he so distrust, so fear his sentiments that he had to destroy his own and his readers' belief in the authenticity of what he saw and felt? Is this the reason why, with the last verse or the last line of so many of his finest poems, he mercilessly startles us out of the enchanting reverie, the grandiose vision, the lovely dream, the bewitching scene with a shrill whistle blast?

When the spring comes in and the sun is bright,
Then every small blossom beckons and blows.

When the moon on her shining journey goes,
Then stars swim after her through the night.
When the singer looks into two clear eyes,
Then something is stirred and lyrics arise . . .
But flowers and stars and songs just begun,
And moonbeams and eyes and the light of the sun,
No matter how much such stuff may please,
One can't keep living on things like these.

(Untermeyer)

Conceivably he was simply influenced by the prevailing doctrine of "Romantic irony" which held that art is its own purpose and justification, and that the poet, any artist, should stand aloof from his own creation, free to destroy it, as a child with one sweeping motion of his hand laughingly destroys the sand castle on which he has looked only a moment before with satisfaction and pride. Perhaps he merely wanted to expose the insincerity, the cloying sentimentality, that tarred a truly romantic perception of life. Yet in Heine's case it seems much more likely that his oversensitive, overwrought, deeply vulnerable nature that twisted and turned with every sight, every sound, every smell used irony as the only defense, the only barrier, he had against a reality which, if he had had to face it head-on, would have driven him to despair, insanity, or suicide. His metaphysical terror shows plainly through the cracks in the veneer of flippancy. He knew, after all, that "because the poet's heart is the center of the world, it must in our time be miserably torn apart."

Heine might have remained for me a marginal, even though enjoyable and stimulating, pastime, were it not for his last years when his life painfully fused into that of Everyman, and the writer and his work became one without pretense, dissimulation, or evasion. Heine was fifty-one when, one day in May, he left his apartment to pay a visit to his beloved Venus of Milo in the Louvre. This was his last unaided walk. From then on until his death eight years later, in 1856, he was chained to his "mattress grave," a layer of mattresses piled up on the floor, paralyzed, almost blind, shrunk to the size of an emaciated child, and most of the time tortured by abdominal cramps that could be relieved only occasionally with morphine. His illness, a gradual disintegration of the body and its functions that may or may not have been the consequence of syphilis, did not, however, affect his mental clarity and acuity. He continued writing to his last breath: letters, essays, and poems. Especially poems. Gone were the days when he could toss off with seeming nonchalance those verses that excited and inspired a whole people and almost overnight became immortal songs. What he created now in the agony of his mind and body came from deeper darker regions of his soul. These poems did not lend themselves to easy dreamy song. They are the outcries of a creature who, in the embrace of death, conjures up in images of heart-wrenching beauty the eternal eschatological questions of life and suffering, of God and immortality. Tones such as these had never before been heard in all of German poetry:

How slowly Time, the frightful snail,
    Crawls to the corner that I lie in;

While I, who cannot move at all,
    Watch from the place that I must die in.

Here in my darkened cell no hope
    Enters and breaks the gloom asunder;
I know I shall not leave this room
    Except for one that's six feet under.

Perhaps I have been dead some time;
    Perhaps my bright and whirling fancies
Are only ghosts that, in my head,
    Keep up their wild, nocturnal dances.

They well might be a pack of ghosts,
    Some sort of pagan gods or devils;
And a dead poet's skull is just
    The place they'd choose to have their revels.

Those orgies, furious and sweet,
    Come suddenly, without a warning . . .
And then the poet's cold, dead hand
    Attempts to write them down next morning.

(Untermeyer)

When I read these "bright and whirling fancies," these "orgies, furious and sweet," for the first time, I knew that I had to stay with Heine. I would have enjoyed the poems he wrote in his prouder, happier days; I would have been animated, amused, and entertainingly instructed by his prose writings, and I would have admired him for both—and left him. But when I read the poems of his last years—grouped under such headings as "Lazarus," "Lamentations," and "Hebrew Melodies"—I took possession of him or, better, he took possession of me. I was drawn to him as I am drawn to the Old Testament. I recognized in his voice and images the voices and images of the prophets and the psalmists: lamenting, imploring, arguing, mocking, raging, and, ultimately, adoring. Not that Heine in his "mattress grave" turned into a servant of the Lord. Here, in his last and greatest—and least known—creation, there are the same poignant eroticism, the same occasional lapses into tastelessness, and the same vacillation between lighthearted sarcasm and anguished seriousness that to this day have made him unpalatable to those for whom the poet's laurel wreath is the secular version of the saint's halo. He could write:

. . . O God, cut short my agony,
Hasten the muffled drum!
You know I have no talent for
The art of martyrdom.

Permit me, Lord, I'm shocked at this,
I think you've made a bloomer:
You formed the merriest poet and now
You rob him of his good humor.

The pain has dulled my sense of fun,
I'm melancholy when sick;
If there's no end to this sorry jest,
I'll end up a Catholic.

Like other good Christians, I fill your ears
With wails—if I persist,
O Miserere! You will lose
Your very best humorist!

(Draper)

Yet a moment later he would cry out:

How sweet it is, yet full of pain:
Of fire and beauty blended
Is this our fevered dream of love—
God, let it soon be ended.

Open your land of shades to me:
My lips I would be wetting
In your cool waters, whose gift is
Eternally forgetting.

All is forgot—it's love alone
that's not forgot after death!
The Lethe myth was born upon
A loveless Greek bard's breath.

(Draper)

Heine returned to God, the God of Moses, but to his last breath he remained unmistakably, provocatively, and enigmatically Heinrich Heine.

After I finish reading a Heine biography, I almost invariably put the book aside with sometimes a slight, sometimes a profound, sense of letdown. I have learned many interesting details and absorbed illuminating explanations and conclusions, but somehow the portrait seems to lack those hues, those contours, those contrasts that would make it glow from within and help me understand why I am drawn to it more irresistibly than to other portraits in the crowded gallery of nineteenth-century writers. So it is I, isn't it, who am ultimately the answer to Why Heine? I suppose that is true of everything we like, whether books, or music, or people, or things. Our preferences define and sometimes redefine us. They are a measure of our height and our depth. They show up our genes, our character, and our inner world, and they determine our relationship to others. If I said that I like Dante, for example, or Thomas Mann, I would be acceptable to literate people of any taste, be they heathen or Christian. To say that I like Heine, the whole Heine, would raise eyebrows; to confess that he fascinates me would make me persona non grata in many circles.

What, then, do we have in common, where do I find—where do I discover—myself in this man whom his countrymen have called everything, from "the highest concept of the lyric poet" to "the biggest Jewish swine"? Is it my Jewishness, my mother's precious legacy? Yes. There is much, too much, in Heine that must elude anyone who does not share at least in some part of his innermost being in the burden and the glory of Abraham's children. Is it my experience as an immigrant? Yes. Immigrants and political exiles are displaced persons who are permanently scarred by transplantation. If they have taken root in their new country, yet still love the old, as did Heine, they

speak a language unique to those who support the weights and absorb the stresses of a life bridging the border between two cultures. Is it God? That is the most difficult question, but the answer is Yes. I am a convert to Roman Catholicism, and as I have an ear for the language of immigrants (which of course has nothing to do with "accents"), so I can discern the tonality and cadence of the language of converts. The young Heine's opportunistic conversion to Protestantism is meaningless: he hoped—in vain, as it turned out—that baptism would buy him a professorship at a German university, or, as he himself put it, "a ticket to European culture." The real Heine appears to me always poised on the brink of conversion to either orthodox Judaism or Roman Catholicism. His ranting against organized religions was not merely a largely justified bitterness over their moral and political support of entrenched autocratic governments, but also a revelation of the intensity of his fear of the abyss of faith. God was at the stillpoint of this seething soul, and that stillpoint is discernible only by those who themselves believe in God.

Heine the Jew, Heine the immigrant (or political exile, if you will), and Heine the God-centered soul—they are keys that are unique and essential to an understanding of the total Heine, but by no means do they unlock all the doors to this enigmatic figure.

Notes

[1] The translations of Heine's prose are my own. They derive from *Heinrich Heine Werke* (Insel Verlag, 1968). The names of the translators of Heine's poems appear in parentheses at the end of each poem and are taken from: *Poems of Heinrich Heine*, selected and translated by Louis Untermeyer (Heritage Press, 1957) and *The Complete Poems of Heinrich Heine: A Modern English Version*, translated by Hal Draper (Suhrkamp/Insel, 1982).

[2] "Jungfrau," that is "virgin," in the German original.

[3] This appears as a publisher's notice on the back cover of *Heinrich Heine: Sein Leben, Seine Werke*, by Walter Wadepuhl (Wilhelm Heyne Verlag, 1974). The translation is my own.

Michael Perraudin (essay date 1989)

SOURCE: *Heinrich Heine Poetry in Context: A Study of 'Buch der Lieder,'* Berg Publishers Ltd., 1989, 292 p.

[*In the following excerpt, Perraudin discusses imagery, theme, and style in two chronologically distinct poems of Buch der Lieder.*]

Two of the most complex, important and, given their importance, also most neglected poems of Heine's **Buch der Lieder** period are the principal objects of attention of this chapter. It is evident that in a simply chronological sense **'Die Weihe'** of 1816 and **'Im Hafen'** of 1826 represent the 'Anfang und Ende meines lyrischen Jugendlebens'—the phrase is Heine's own epistolary characterisation of the **Buch der Lieder** collection[1]—for the one is his first published work, and the other is one of his last compositions for **"Die Nordsee"** II, the final cycle of his anthology. But they are so in a more momentous sense too, and it is this which is my concern here. Heine was a poet much given to public reflection on his work, a tendency observable even in the conception of **Buch der Lieder** indicated by the above phrase, but seen perhaps at its most familiar in the poetic prologues and epilogues which he habitually appended to his cycles when he assembled them. We are not always quite happy with the results of such reflection. **Buch der Lieder** itself is a falsified account, for many poems from the early portion of his career which in 1827 he relativised as his 'Young Sufferings' were suppressed (as unfashionable and therefore discreditable). Likewise his prologues and epilogues have a way of misrepresenting the content of the cycle they enclose, or claiming a resolution or progress which has not been achieved. Thus (to mention a couple of familiar examples), the last poem of **"Die Heimkehr"** (No.88) suggests that cycle to be *merely* a monument to the death of love; or 'Wahrhaftig' (**Romanzen** 20) asserts the superseding of a form of poetic expression which is in fact anything but superseded in his work by that stage.[2] Yet it is clear at the same time that precisely this tendency is among the most interesting and valuable facets of Heine's creativity. 'Wahrhaftig' may be a dubious epilogue, but it is also a memorable document of the consciousness of the age; and generally we find that his autodialectical habit is the source of much of the tension of mood and complexity of idea which are his poetry's qualities. **'Die Weihe'** and **'Im Hafen'** are very much in the tradition of his self-reflective verse, and indeed are among its most elaborate examples, but they are unusual in that they are also prologue/epilogue poems which markedly enlighten us about the processes and intentions of the other work they refer to. If **Buch der Lieder** was a falsifying 'Anfang und Ende', and if the *post factum* prologues and epilogues to its cycles misrepresent the cycles themselves, we find in these two poems true reflections on, and a true beginning and end to, the whole of Heine's early lyricism. For **'Die Weihe'**, early as it is, is a detailed prediction of his creative life to come, and **'Im Hafen'** a replique to the other poem and both a review and a conscious culmination of his poetic progress to date.

'Die Weihe' and **'Im Hafen'** are also, it should be said, quite obscure poems. I have already demonstrated in some detail the young Heine's practice of basing his verses on other people's poetic utterances, which are echoed or alluded to specifically, a procedure which he shares in considerable measure with others of his epoch. This he does in these two poems also, indeed perhaps in greater detail than anywhere else, and their meanings can only be elicited when we investigate the objects of allusion thoroughly. However, whereas usually such allusiveness is a public matter, assumed to be accessible to the normal reader, here the allusions become so very complicated and varied, that some of the final thoughts these poems contain are esoteric, and in intention maybe even wholly private, as the poet talks really only to himself. The two poems are still, in the main, public reflections and self-assertions, as

we shall see, but they have a residue of pure privacy which we are less accustomed to in Heine's lyrical production. Here—and these are arguably the only such examples among the poems discussed in this monograph—Heine's technique of quotation begins to take on a kind of twentieth-century arcaneness.

. . . . .

'Die Weihe' was published in early February 1817 in Hamburg, where Heine was then living, in the anti-Semitic journal *Hamburgs Wächter,* as one of 'Zwei Lieder der Minne'.[3] It was signed with the preposterously Germanic *nom be plume* 'Sy. Freudhold Riesenharf', an anagram of the rather less Germanic-sounding 'Harry Heine. Düsseldorff'. The text, which falls into three metrically heterogeneous sections, is as follows:

> Einsam in der Waldkapelle,
> Vor dem Bild der Himmelsjungfrau,
> Lag ein frommer, bleicher Knabe,
> Demutsvoll dahingesunken.
>
> O Madonna! laß mich ewig
> Hier auf dieser Schwelle knieen,
> Wollest nimmer mich verstoßen
> In die Welt so kalt und sündig.
>
> O Madonna! sonnig wallen
> Deines Hauptes Strahlenlocken;
> Süßes Lächeln mild umspielet
> Deines Mundes heilge Rosen.
>
> O Madonna! deine Augen
> Leuchten mir wie Sternenlichter;
> Lebensschifflein treibet irre,
> Sternlein leiten ewig sicher.
>
> O Madonna! sonder Wanken
> Trug ich deine Schmerzenprüfung,
> Frommer Minne blind vertrauend,
> Nur in deinen Gluten glühend.
>
> O Madonna! hör mich heute,
> Gnadenvolle, wunderreiche,
> Spende mir ein Huldeszeichen,
> Nur ein leises Huldeszeichen!
>
> Da tät sich ein schauerlich Wunder bekunden,
> Wald und Kapell sind auf einmal verschwunden;
> Knabe nicht wuße, wie ihm geschehn,
> Hat alles auf einmal umwandelt gesehn.
>
> Und staunend stand er im schmucken Saale,
> Da saß Madonna, doch ohne Strahlen;
> Sie hat sich verwandelt in liebliche Maid,
> Und grüßet und lächelt mit kindlicher Freud.
>
> Und sieh! vom blonden Lockenhaupte
> Sie selber sich eine Locke raubte,
> Und sprach zum Knaben mit himmlischem Ton:
> Nimm hin deinen besten Erdenlohn!

Sprich nun, wer bezeugt die Weihe?
Sahst du nicht die Farben wogen
Flammig an der Himmelsbläue?
Menschen nennens Regenbogen.

Englein steigen auf und nieder,
Schlagen rauschend mit den Schwingen,
Flüstern wundersame Lieder,
Süßer Harmonieen Klingen.

Knabe hat es wohl verstanden,
Was mit Sehnsuchtglut ihn ziehet
Fort und fort nach jenen Landen,
Wo wie Myrte ewig blühet.[4]

We may deal first with the poem's background in Heine's experience, which is not unimportant. **'Die Weihe'** was written at what was undoubtedly a high point of anguish in the poet's famous unrequited adolescent infatuation for his cousin Amalie (Molly), the daughter of his rich uncle and patron in Hamburg, Salomon Heine. His personal intentions and overwrought emotional state at the time find their prime expression in a well-known letter of 27 October 1816 to his friend Christian Sethe, where he laments his rejection ('Sie liebt mich *nicht*—[. . .]'), thinks of a compensatory conversion to Catholicism ('Aber ich *muß* ja eine Madonna haben. Wird mir die Himlische die Irdische ersetzen?'), and contemplates the likelihood of enforced departure from Hamburg ('Onkel will mich hier weg haben [. . .]').[5] The poem has a number of elements which link it strongly with that letter, notably the notion of a departure, the association of beloved and Madonna, and the reference to a lock of her hair which he carries agonisingly around with him ('Gerade wo das arme Herz schlägt, hängt ein [. . .] Kreutz, darin liegt M-.s Locke. Hu! das brennt!').[6] Though **'Die Weihe'** does not articulate his mood and experience of the time with what might be called Goethean immediacy, they underlie the poem and are part of its motivation.

At the same time, however, **'Die Weihe'** has strong—indeed rather stronger—roots in literature, and these we must try to trace in detail. To begin with, the early parts of the poem clearly are largely an effect of Heine's youthful espousal of aspects of Catholic Romanticism (the same *literary* experience which led him in his letter to contemplate conversion), namely the fashion for poetic Mariolatry, and Fouqué's pseudo-medieval *Minnedichtung.* The initial scene of the poem, it has been indicated persuasively,[7] is based in fact on a *Marienlied* from Volume I of *Des Knaben Wunderhorn* called 'Abschied von Maria', in which a (female) supplicant enters the 'Waldkapelle' to prostrate herself in front of the Virgin and take leave before an unwelcome journey:

[. . .]'O Maria, jezt ist Zeit,
     Daß ich wieder von dir scheid,
     Fort ich muß, auf lange fort,
     Ach Ade du Gnadenort![. . .]

O du gnadenreiches Bild!
O Maria, Mutter mild!

O wie hart scheid ich von dir,
Wie so gern blieb ich allhier.[. . .]

O Maria, noch die Bitt,
Mich im Tod verlasse nit,
Sey gegrüßet tausendmal,
Ach Ade viel tausendmal!'[etc.][8]

From 'Abschied von Maria' Heine has in fact retained not only the *Waldkapelle* scene. Also the motif of the journey, though muted in **'Die Weihe',** is still present, in 'Wollest nimmer mich verstoßen/In die Welt so kalt und sündig' (as well as in the idea of departure, 'Fort und fort nach jenen Landen', on which the poem ends). And the wish which concludes his first section ('O Madonna! hör mich heute', str. 6) is likewise reminiscent of 'Abschied'. In other respects, however, the encounter in that first section suggests Fouqué. The idea of 'fromme Minne' is certainly *intended* to evoke Fouqué; the 'Petrarchistic' hyperboles which Heine employs for his Madonna's appearance probably have their immediate origins in verse by Fouqué; and the character herself bears a marked resemblance to his *Minnesang*-based quasi-love goddess 'Frau Minnetrost'.[9] Finally, even the form of those first six strophes suggests Fouqué, but not his *Minnedichtung,* for they are in the 'Spanish' pattern of assonantal trochaic tetrameters (note the final assonances in the second and fourth lines of each strophe), used by Heine for the contemporaneous ballad **'Die Romanze vom Rodrigo'** (later **'Don Ramiro'**: *Romanzen* 9), which he demonstrably based on Fouqué's 'Donna Clara und Don Gayferos' from *Der Zauberring.*[10] I shall suggest below a reason why this form should figure in **'Die Weihe'** too.

In the second section of Heine's poem, the 'bleicher Knabe' has his prayer answered, the scene changes and he is transported into the kind of *Festsaal* setting which in other poems by Heine (including **'Rodrigo'**) is a symbol of his alienation, and which generally we associate with the *Schauerballade.* The metre changes too, to a striking pattern of anapaestic and iambic, but mainly anapaestic, tetrameters, in rhyming couplets with alternating masculine and feminine line endings, in fact a variety of *Knittelvers* which was identified at the epoch as a modern balladesque metre. The poem which used anapaestic tetrameters in rhyming couplets in the least adulterated way, and with which the form was then above all associated, was Bürger's 'Lenardo und Blandine' of 1776. Heine's familiarity with this work is elsewhere attested,[11] and in his theme of tragic *Standesliebe* it is also thoroughly germane to his own customary thematic preoccupations (and recent experience). That a recollection of Bürger's poem underlies this part of **'Die Weihe'** is further suggested by the shared motif of the beloved's festal gift-giving, introduced in both by 'Nimm hin'. However, the form of 'Lenardo und Blandine', which Heine comes very close to in **'Die Weihe'** (and uses precisely in *Traumbild* 7), is also quite similar to that of various ballads by Goethe, like 'Der getreue Eckart', 'Hochzeitlied', 'Der Totentanz' and 'Ballade' (which Heine likewise demonstrably knew[12]). Although **'Die Weihe'** is metrically closer to Bürger, the alliteration and assonance in Heine's strophes 7 to 9 must be linked to Goethe's use in those ballads of the same devices, which have no correspondence in Bürger's piece. Finally, we note in Heine's strophes the archaic diction (not a feature of the other two sections), seen especially in the elisions and omitted articles, and also the 'Knabe' character. Both are strongly suggestive of others of Goethe's balladesque poems, 'Heidenröslein' ('Knabe sprach: Ich breche dich', etc.) and 'Der untreue Knabe' (aspects of the scene of which—'Auf einmal steht er hoch im Saal, [. . .]/Er sieht sein Schätzel untenan'—Heine's poem also repeats).[13] We can see powerful thematic causes of the young Heine's attraction to many of these poems—as wish-fulfilling re-arrangements of his own emotional situation—but we must give him credit too for a conscious purpose in using them. The central strophes of **'Die Weihe'** are his own assertive essay in modern Germanic balladry; he is exploring the mode through the work of its principal exponents, and introducing variations—an alternation of masculine and feminine rhymes, and especially a metre which balances anapaestic and iambic feet and exploits the distinction between them—which is to be his own characteristic manner.

There is a further important literary source to this middle section, one, indeed, which draws a connection with the first part and arguably gives coherence to the whole poem. This is Heine's model for the actual transformation of Madonna into beloved, namely the *Märchen von Hyazinth und Rosenblütchen* in *Die Lehrlinge zu Sais* of Novalis, the original exponent in the Romantic movement of an identity of the two figures. August Fischer points to detailed parallels between the *Märchen* and **'Die Weihe'**.[14] In the *Märchen,* Hyazinth, upon receiving the instructions of 'die alte Frau im Walde', leaves Rosenblütchen to follow his *Sehnsucht* and journey in search of the figure called variously 'die Mutter der Dinge', 'die verschleierte Jungfrau', 'die heilige Göttin Isis' and, finally, 'die heilige Jungfrau'. When at last he finds her, in a distant yet familiar tropical paradise, and unveils her, she is revealed as Rosenblütchen herself; the love that was previously transient has now become eternal. Certainly much of Novalis's Romantic scheme underlies, and is invoked by, Heine's poem. Here the 'Knabe' comes to perceive his compulsory departure as in fact desirable ('Knabe hat es wohl verstanden/Was mit Sehnsuchtglut ihn ziehet'), for it will entail a new awareness, an awareness which is likewise associated (we shall see) with love made eternal.

The second part of **'Die Weihe'** ends with the Madonna/beloved's curious 'divine' benediction, 'mit himmlischem Ton'. This anticipates or introduces the biblical reminiscence in the third section, the allusion—'Englein steigen auf und nieder'—to the story of Jacob's Ladder in *Genesis* 28: '[. . .] Die Engel Gottes stiegen dran auf und nieder'.[15] This image of the path to heaven (which Heine uses again in **'Im Hafen'**, among other places)[16] is the content of the dream in which God promises Jacob, on his way to marry his cousin, that he, Jacob, is the chosen one and will return to the site of the dream, Beth-El, to found the Tribe of Israel. An analogy is certainly possible here with Heine's own personal situation: may we discern a private joke, according to which he does win his cousin,

and in which he, not his uncle, is the father of the dynasty? At any rate, an identification with Jacob the Jewish *Erzvater* is inherent in this allusion—the kind of identification to which he returned explicitly a few years later in the poem **'An Edom!'**, where the poetic *Ich* is the Jewish race itself[17]—and thus the poet's longing in **'Die Weihe'** ('Knabe hat es wohl! verstanden [. . .]') is at least in part for Israel and Beth-El, his racial home (a longing which is incidentally also the exact message of the companion piece to **'An Edom!'**, 'Brich aus in lauten Klagen').[18] Clearly this allusion *is* a cryptic one, indeed quite a good private joke. Like his anagrammatic signature, his lyrical contribution to an organ of Hamburg anti-Semitism conceals behind its Germanness a Jewish confession.[19]

This by no means exhausts Part Three of **'Die Weihe'**, however. The work ends, as Manfred Windfuhr notes, with an echo of Goethe's 'Mignon'-poem, 'Kennst du das Land, wo die Zitronen blün?' ('[. . .] Die Myrte still und hoch der Lorbeer steht,/Kennst du es wohl?/Dahin! Dahin [. . .]'),[20] the poem which for the epoch was the archetypal expression of *Sehnsucht*—Heine in fact used it thus on several occasions subsequently. Whatever the myrtle means in 'Mignon', in the slightly crude symbolism of the young Heine, who moves it to the centre of attention in his poem, it signifies love—as also in the sixth *Fresko-Sonett*.[21] The longing with which **'Die Weihe'** emphatically concludes is thus also for a realm where love is everlasting.

In 'Mignon' itself the distant, longed-for land was of course Italy. In his various subsequent echoings of Goethe's poem, Heine not only uses it himself to refer to Italy (in *Reise von München nach Genua,* Chapters 26 to 27, and in the discarded **"Nordsee"** poem 'Sonnenaufgang': '[. . .] Vom alten, blauen Wunderlande,/ Von Zitronenwäldern und Banditen [. . .]'), but also transfers it to his Rhenish homeland (in the sonnets **'An J.B.R.'**: **'O, könnt ich hin zu dir, zu dir, Getreuer'**, and **'An Fritz von Beughem'**: **'Im Zauberland, wo Schweinebohnen blühen [. . .]'**), to Spain (in the poem **'Almansor'**: 'Auf dem Weg nach Alkolea, / Dem Guadalquivir entlange, / Wo die weissen Mandeln blüchen, / Und die duftgen Goldorangen', and in the *Almansor* tragedy: 'So sogen wir begierig ein den Duft / Der spanschen Myrten- und Zitronenwälder'), and to the Orient (with the 'Zitronenwälder' of **'Im Hafen'**, to be discussed below, which become in turn the 'Banianenwälder Hindostans' in **"Nordsee"** III and *Buch le Grand!*[22]). A general clarification of the meaning for him of 'Mignon' is provided much later, by the *Matratzengruft* poem **'Citronia'**, where the poet tells of his fantasies of youth:

Citronia hab ich genannt
Das wunderbare Zauberland,
Das ich einst [. . .]
Erblickt im goldnen Sonnenglanz—
Es war so zärtlich ideal,
Zitronenfarbig und oval,
So anmutvoll und freundlich mild
Und stolz empört zugleich—dein Bild,
Du erste Blüte meiner Minne!
Es kam mir niemals aus dem Sinne.[23]

and ends by associating this explicitly with the delusions of 'jene Blume [. . .] mit dem blauen Kelche [. . .] in des Ofterdingen Lied'; thus the young poet's imagination had fused the longing for a Romantic *Wunderland* based on 'Mignon' and Novalis with the image of and longing for the lost beloved. In **'Citronia'** we clearly have several of the ingredients of **'Die Weihe'**—note also the ironic allusion to his *Minnesang* period. But those various specific 'Mignon'-esque *Wunderländer* can also be related back to the earlier poem. As the letter to Sethe indicated, Heine was contemplating the prospect of an enforced physical migration from Hamburg to his Rhenish home.[24] The odd Spanish mode of the first part of the poem (the assonating trochaic tetrameters described above) alludes to the distant land to which he migrates poetically in order to produce **'Rodrigo'**. And in the final section, strophes 10 to 12, a further journey of the imagination is undertaken, to the poetic Orient.

This is the most extraordinary of the literary allusions in **'Die Weihe'**. The distinctive mode of these strophes, regular trochaic tetrameters with alternating rhyme and consistent feminine line-endings, is rare in Heine, occurring in only one other of the **Gedichte**,[25] not at all in *Lyrisches Intermezzo,* and in a small number of poems in **"Die Heimkehr"**—notably Nos. 42 and 77—which are intended to suggest Goethe's *West-östlicher Divan.*[26] This is in fact one of the predominant forms, and with its feminine line-endings certainly the most distinctive form, of the *Divan,* the first poems of which had begun to appear in 1816 (pieces like 'Hegire', 'Beiname' and 'Selige Sehnsucht'), following the collection's premature but prominent 'Ankündigung' early that year.[27] With remarkable alacrity the young Heine, already late in 1816, had taken note of the *Divan* project and announced his intention and ability to emulate it. And his poem follows Goethe's orientalism not only formally. Various quite striking affinities of image and expression present themselves.[28] But patently the most important connection of all is the way **'Die Weihe'** actually manages to accomplish Goethe's *Divan* journey itself, not only in its migration eastwards, but also in its culmination in an ascent to paradise—the conception which Goethe himself stated most clearly in 'Hegire':

> Wolltet ihr ihm dies beneiden,
> Oder etwa gar verleiden,
> Wisset nur, daß Dichterworte
> Um des Paradieses Pforte
> Immer leise klopfend schweben,
> Sich erbittend ewges Leben.[29]

To give coherence to the tremendous amalgam of 'literarische Reminiszenzen' which makes up **'Die Weihe'** (the phrase is that used by Windfuhr, the only critic who even pauses at the work—and he very soon dismisses it),[30] we must consider what the poem as a whole attempts to say. Its message appears to be that, equipped with his tragic experience of love,[31] the poet's destiny is not only physical departure, but to follow his poetic longing to an imaginative—*west-östlich*—journey across the world—from Germany to Spain, to the Jewish *and* Persian Orient, and

eventually to a poet's paradise where love is eternal. And the 'Weihe' of the poem's title is his consecration or initiation to the priestly calling of poet, which this entails. I should not wish to deny that there is an element of incoherence in all this—under any circumstances it is a mishmash; some details, notably the confession to a Jewish *Sehnsucht,* accord dubiously with the rest; and a number of other aspects of it seem imperfectly worked out. But none the less, **'Die Weihe'** remains an impressive *tour de force,* as Heine exercises his prowess in the modes he will use in his career to come (*Minnelied,* Germanic ballad, Hispanic romance, oriental lyric). It is an extraordinary assertion of the force of his poetic imagination from the nineteen- or twenty-year-old poet. And it reveals how crucial facets of his thought which one had believed to be products of the mid-1820s—his sense of his poetic *exploitation* of the love experience, his concealed Jewish theme, his preoccupation with the sovereign power of the imagination—were in fact established in his mind from the very beginning of his creative life.

. . . . .

We may say that a number of strands lead from **'Die Weihe'** through the following ten years of Heine's poetry to the end of **"Nordsee II"** and **'Im Hafen'**, as the poet pursues the various aspects of his 'calling'. But certainly the most important is the Goethean-oriental strand, some of the details of which it is useful to take account of before we pass on to **'Im Hafen'** itself (especially since they represent a connection which Heine criticism has never very thoroughly come to terms with).[32] In the two central cycles of **Buch der Lieder, Lyrisches Intermezzo** and **"Die Heimkehr,"** there are something over half a dozen poems intended specifically to echo Goethe's *Divan.* The **'Teuer Freund'** poems, **"Heimkehr"** 32, 42, 54 and 88,[33] adopt the distinctive dialogical manner, readily identifiable to the contemporary reader, of the *Schenkenbuch,* exchanges between the poet and the solicitous and affectionate young 'Schenke' who watches over his intoxication. The 'Schenke' character then appears more explicitly in **"Heimkehr 65"** ('Diesen liebenswürdgen Jüngling'),[34] but interestingly Germanised ('Oft traktiert er mich mit Austern,/Und mit Rheinwein und Likören'), and also made clearly into one of Heine's *Doppelgänger* figures (the **'Teurer Freund'** poems having been only implicitly auto-dialogical). Meanwhile, **"Heimkehr 64"** ('Gaben mir Rat und gute Lehren') and two earlier lyrics from *Lyrisches Intermezzo,* 24 ('Sie haben dir viel erzählet,/Und haben viel geklagt') and 47 ('Sie haben mich gequälet,/Geärgert blau und blaß'), expressions of the poet's social alienation, echo unmistakably two related poems in similar mood from the *Divan*: 'Haben sie von deinen Fehlen/Immer viel erzählt', from *Buch der Betrachtungen,* and 'Sie haben wegen der Trunkenheit/Vielfältig uns verklagt', from the *Schenkenbuch.*[35] For our purposes the poems by Heine which are involved here are not especially notable in themselves (although the 'Schenke' character will reappear prominently in **'Im Hafen'**), but they are distinctly important for the aspects of the *Divan* to which they show Heine being drawn—not just his predictable attraction to Goethe's expressions of social disaffection, but above all his interest in the idea of the poet's intoxication representing a heightened consciousness and inspiration (we note how the *Divan* poetry Heine uses here all concerns the poet's drunken elevation). As one of the first poems of the *Schenkenbuch* itself had put it: 'Der Trinkende, wie es auch immer sei, / Blickt Gott frischer ins Angesicht'.[36]

The mood of the *Divan,* of course, is not only alcoholic inebriation. The consciousness through which the poet attains Paradise (as at the end of 'Hegire') is achieved in *various* forms of intoxication—wine, poetry and love. As the ending of **'Sie haben wegen der Trunkenheit'** explains:

> Es ist die Liebestrunkenheit,
> Die mich erbärmlich plagt,
> Von Tag zu Nacht, von Nacht zu Tag
> In meinem Herzen zagt.
> Dem Herzen, das in Trunkenheit
> Der Lieder schwillt und ragt,
> Daß keine nüchterne Trunkenheit
> Sich gleich zu heben wagt.
> Lieb-, Lied- und Weines Trunkenheit,
> Ob's nachtet oder tagt,
> Die göttlichste Betrunkenheit,
> Die mich entzückt und plagt.[37]
>
> (Vv. 9-20)

And the access of the lover to a consciousness denied to others is likewise an idea of which the young Heine is fond. That love is a key the end of *Die Harzreise* tells us, also Chapter 7 of *Die Bäder von Lucca,* and various of the poems, like **'Erklärung'** and **'Epilog'** in **"Die Nordsee,"**[38] and the notable *Lyrisches Intermezzo* **8:**

> Es stehen unbeweglich
> Die Sterne in der Höh,
> Viel tausend Jahr, und schauen
> Sich an mit Liebesweh.
>
> Sie sprechen eine Sprache,
> Die ist so reich, so schön;
> Doch keiner der Philologen
> Kann diese Sprache verstehn.
>
> Ich aber hab sie gelernet,
> Und ich vergesse sie nicht;
> Mir diente als Grammatik
> Der Herzallerliebsten Gesicht.[39]

The parallels between this last lyric and both Goethe's 'Höheres und Höchstes' ('Doch man horcht nun Dialekten/Wie sich Mensch und Engel kosen,/Der Grammatik, der versteckten,/Deklinierend Mohn und Rosen') and a poem from Hafis's own *Diwan* (in the Hammer-Purgstall translation: 'Lies einen Vers vom Buch/Des Angesichts des Liebchens,/Er hellt und kläret auf/Der dunkeln Stellen [i.e. des Korans] Zweifel') have been pointed out.[40] And Heine's use of these motifs here is no less serious than it is in Goethe. They concern precisely what he had found and valued in Goethe's orientalism, namely the transcendent, irrational consciousness, far beyond normal understanding, which is the intoxicated poet-lover's power.

This, then, is an important part of the background to **'Im Hafen',** the poem Heine composed—with no little difficulty[41]—in mid-October 1826, as a conscious culmination of his early verse:

> Glücklich der Mann, der den Hafen erreicht hat,
> Und hinter sich ließ das Meer und die Stürme,
> Und jetzo warm und ruhig sitzt
> Im guten Ratskeller zu Bremen.
>
> Wie doch die Welt so traulich und lieblich
> Im Römerglas sich wiederspiegelt,
> Und wie der wogende Mikrokosmos
> Sonnig hinabfließt ins durstige Herz!
> Alles erblick ich im Glas,
> Alte und neue Völkergeschichte,
> Türken und Griechen, Hegel und Gans,
> Zitronenwälder und Wachtparaden,
> Berlin und Schilda und Tunis und Hamburg,
> Vor allem aber das Bild der Geliebten,
> Das Engelköpfchen auf Rheinweingoldgrund.
>
> O, wie schön! wie schön bist du, Geliebte!
> Du bist wie eine Rose!
> Nicht wie die Rose von Schiras,
> Die hafisbesungene Nachtigallbraut;
> Nicht wie die Rose von Saron,
> Die heiligrote, prophetengefeierte; –
> Du bist wie die Ros im Ratskeller zu Bremen!
> Das ist die Rose der Rosen,
> Je älter sie wird, je lieblicher blüht sie,
> Und ihr himmlischer Duft, er hat mich beseligt,
> Er hat mich begeistert, er hat mich berauscht,
> Und hielt mich nicht fest, am Schopfe fest,
> Der Ratskellermeister von Bremen,
> Ich wäre gepurzelt!
>
> Der brave Mann! wir saßen beisammen
> Und tranken wie Brüder,
> Wir sprachen von hohen, heimlichen Dingen,
> Wir seufzten und sanken uns in die Arme,
> Und er hat mich bekehrt zum Glauben der Liebe—
> Ich trank auf das Wohl meiner bittersten Feinde,
> Und allen schlechten Poeten vergab ich,
> Wie einst mir selber vergeben soll werden—
> Ich weinte vor Andacht, und endlich
> Erschlossen sich mir die Pforten des Heils,
> Wo die zwölf Apostel, die heilgen Stückfässer,
> Schweigend predgen, und doch so verständlich
> Für alle Völker.
>
> Das sind Männer!
> Unscheinbar von außen, in hölzernen Röcklein,
> Sind sie von innen schöner und leuchtender
> Denn all die stolzen Leviten des Tempels
> Und des Herodes Trabanten und Höflinge,
> Die goldgeschmückten, die purpurgekleideten—
> Hab ich doch immer gesagt,
> Nicht unter ganz gemeinen Leuten,
> Nein, in der allerbesten Gesellschaft,
> Lebte beständig der König des Himmels!

Hallelujah! Wie lieblich umwehen mich
Die Palmen von Beth El!
Wie duften die Myrrhen von Hebron!
Wie rauscht der Jordan und taumelt vor Freude!—
Auch meine unsterbliche Seele taumelt,
Und ich taumle mit ihr, und taumelnd
Bringt mich die Treppe hinauf, ans Tagslicht,
Der brave Ratskellermeister von Bremen.
Du braver Ratskellermeister von Bremen!
Siehst du, auf den Dächern der Häuser sitzen
Die Engel und sind betrunken und singen;
Die glühende Sonne dort oben
Ist nur eine rote, betrunkene Nase,
Die Nase des Weltgeists;
Und um die rote Weltgeistnase
Dreht sich die ganze, betrunkene Welt.[42]

The poem, like **'Die Weihe'**, has a certain basis in personal experience, referring to Heine's brief stay in Bremen late in September 1826 after his second summer on Norderney, and recording in particular a visit to the *Bremer Ratskeller,* several details of which are used. However, the experience is of much less inherent relevance than in the earlier poem. Whereas **'Die Weihe'** concerned a physical departure—albeit a prospective one—to which a mythical dimension was added, the arrival which **'Im Hafen'** records is wholly mythical. The poem presents the conclusion of an epic journey: the initial classical-heroic phrase reiterates the Odyssean identification of the poet used repeatedly through the **'Nordsee'** cycles[43]—thus **'Im Hafen'** is the end of his Odyssey. And the arrival is in Bremen because this entails a reminiscence of the famous *Wunderhorn* lyric 'Abschied von Bremen', with which Heine had mythicised his real departure from Hamburg in 1819.[44]

The haven the poet has found in **'Im Hafen'** is obviously one of alcoholic bliss, but it is more, for in his inebriation he is completing (again after the pattern of the *Divan*) a journey to Paradise. Klaus Briegleb goes into some interesting detail about the features of the real *Ratskeller zu Bremen* which Heine builds in to his poem[45]—the rose as a ceiling motif in one of the wine cellars with a motto associating wine and love, the 'Twelve Apostles' as the name of twelve wine-barrels in another cellar—but he misses an important part of Heine's meaning. As Wilhelm Hauff's *Phantasien im Bremer Ratskeller* indicate (Hauff visited the premises shortly before Heine, but his work, published in mid-1827, must itself have been suggested by Heine's),[46] the principal features of the *Ratskeller* in Heine's day were a set of twelve largish barrels called 'die zwölf Aposteln', and two huge ones, 'die Rose' and 'Bacchus', the last-named having a grotesque picture of the wine-god painted on it. Bacchus is the god to whose religion the poet of **'Im Hafen'** is blasphemously converted, the 'König des Himmels' whose paradise he attains. The burlesque of a Judaeo-Christian entry into Paradise culminates in the final two strophes with a return to the 'Jacob's Ladder' image used in **'Die Weihe'**, alluding to Jacob's dream at Beth-El of a ladder between Heaven and Earth with angels passing up and down it, a vision—in Jacob's own phrase—of 'die Pforte des Himmels';[47] **'Im Hafen'** speaks of 'die Pforten des Heils'. Thus, as the poet ascends the stair out of the *Ratskeller* (the metaphor operates with a certain intoxicated imprecision), his immortal soul—'meine unsterbliche Seele'—ascends into a Bacchanalian heaven.

'Im Hafen' is also a poem extolling the virtues of wine, and in doing so it has specific recourse to *various* prefigurations of the idea. Elements of the fifth strophe (v.43f.) are drawn from folk-song *Weinlieder* which Heine found in *Wunderhorn,* notably the 'hölzerne Röcklein', and, beyond that, the poet's amorous interest in a barrel of wine:

Die liebste Buhle, die ich han,
Die liegt beim Wirt im Keller,
Sie hat ein hölzern Röcklein an,
Und heißt der Muskateller.[48]

Indeed, despite the un-folk-song-like manner of **'Im Hafen'**, the very notion of a poem on the *Bremer Ratskeller* suggests German folk-song, and is intended to do so.[49] However, the poem's German milieu and connotations are balanced by allusion to the other, oriental, tradition of wine-worship, as communicated by Hafis and Goethe's *Divan*, and indeed it is clear that the association in Heine's poem of intoxication through wine with the attainment of paradise is intended to invoke the *Divan*. Further, the 'Ratskellermeister', philosopher and priest of the religion of wine and love, is cast very evidently in the role of a Persian 'Schenke' (note, for instance, the homoerotic suggestion in Heine's 'Und sanken uns in die Arme'), for all his equally German-*volkstümlich* qualities (and we remember the Germanised 'Schenke' of **'Heimkehr' 65**); Briegleb quotes ghazels from Hafis's *Buch der Schenken* which may have established the character for Heine in 'Im Hafen' (he is perhaps closer here to Hafis's than to Goethe's figure).[50] In addition, Briegleb quotes, likewise from the *Buch der Schenken,* a quatrain:

Schöner Vogel, süße Seele,
Schwing die Flügel, brich den Käfig,
Sitz aufs Dach der sieben Dome,
Wo die Seelen Ruhe halten.—

which he suggests to have engendered the image in Heine's last strophe (v.62).[51] Yet Heine's scene of the drunken angels on the roof-tops is certainly also designed to evoke German *Schlaraffenland* folk-song, of the kind he had used earlier for **'Heimkehr 66'** ('[. . .] Und Englein sitzen um mich her', etc.).[52] Altogether the *west-östlich* construction and purpose of Heine's poem of paradisal inebriation can be seen.

The central image of **'Im Hafen'** also follows this pattern, a Rhenish 'Römerglas' which is at the same time the Cup of Giamshid, the wine-goblet which in Persian myth granted whomsoever gazed into it a vision of the whole world, and of all past and future time. Of this image Hafis's translator Hammer had observed: 'In der mystischen Sprache der Scheiche und Sofis ist das Glas Dschems das Herz des Betrachtenden, dem sich die Geheimnisse der inneren Welt auftun'.[53] For Heine, both in '**Im Hafen**' and in the contemporaneous *Buch le Grand* (where it is the focal image in a very similar wine-cellar scene),[54] it grants and represents an awareness of the world, transcending time and space, which is at the same time an awareness of self. This goblet is the source and symbol of the poet's own *west-östlich* consciousness,[55] of races old and new, oriental-exotic (the 'Zitronenwälder'—Heine's extension of the image from 'Mignon') and occidental-familiar ('Wachtparaden'—the Prussian reality which concluded his earlier fantasy, '**Heimkehr 66**'). Grappin quotes Hessel's remark that the poet's vision represents 'all die Gedanken [. . .], die durch seine Meerlieder sich hindurchranken'.[56] So it does, and more, for it is the full content and power of his poetic imagination. This, akin to inebriation in its capacity to escape reason and the restrictions of empirical reality, enables him to leap across the ages, and seize the world in an instant.

Here too, most interestingly, is the point of the barb in the poem's last strophe against Hegel, which emerges as not just a fleeting pastiche, but a purposeful critique. For the endlessly, laboriously rational system by which Hegel (in his *Philosophie der Weltgeschichte*) strove to comprehend the ages of the world—he and his fellow rationalist 'Systematiker', like Eduard Gans, whom the poem also names (v.11)[57]—is equalled and outdone by one leap of the free fantasy of the poet, who is his own intoxicated *Weltgeist*, around which the world revolves.

What principally occupies the poet's imagination in '**Im Hafen**', as throughout *Buch der Lieder,* is the picture of the beloved. As in Goethe's *Divan,* 'Lied- und Weines Trunkenheit'[58] are accompanied in '**Im Hafen**' by the intoxication of love, and we are reminded in particular of poems of the *Buch Suleika*:

> Bist du von deiner Geliebten getrennt
> Wie Orient vom Okzident,
> Das Herz durch alle Wüsten rennt;
> Es gibt sich überall selbst das Geleit,
> Für Liebende ist Bagdad nicht weit.[59]

What '**Im Hafen**' in fact says explicitly is that the beloved is *not* 'wie die Rose von Schiras,/Die hafisbesungene Nachtigallbraut', or 'wie die Rose von Saron', but is 'wie die Ros im Ratskeller zu Bremen'. But in these several similes, behind the burlesque, there lies a crucial multiplication of the figure of the beloved, precisely the kind of multiplication which was the cumulative effect of the *Buch der Lieder* poetry as a whole. '**Im Hafen**' (like *Buch le Grand,* which operates an equivalent, though much more elaborate, system of multiplied beloved-figures) thus offers a summary account of the early love poetry itself.

There is more to the beloveds of '**Im Hafen**', however, for they also conceal what amounts to a philosophical and cultural confession. The three similes represent German, Persian and Jew (for 'die Rose von Saron' echoes the *Song of Solomon*).[60] We have here something very like the three symbolic 'holde Frauenbilder' of *Atta Troll,* Diana, Abunde and Herodias, indeed this is the seed of the scheme which that later epic offers.[61] Bremen and Schiras represent obviously his *west-östlich* spirit.[62] But the Jewish beloved is no irrelevance either (and we remember how in *Atta Troll* it is Herodias to whom the poet finally gives preference). In the penultimate strophe of '**Im Hafen**', where the allusion to Jacob's Ladder begins, the poet himself imaginatively *becomes* Jacob: 'Hallelujah! Wie lieblich umwehen mich/Die Palmen von Beth El!', as he had earlier in '**An Edom!**'—Jacob who founded the Tribe of Israel at Beth-El—and he *perceives* also the Jordan and Hebron ('Wie duften [. . .],/Wie rauscht [. . .]'), other historic sites of the origin of the Jewish people. For all the blasphemous creed '**Im Hafen**' presents, the poet, just as in the earlier '**Die Weihe**', has access in his transcendent imagination to the race memory of the Jews.[63]

'**Im Hafen**', it is quite clear, is a perfectly conscious return to the material and reflections of '**Die Weihe**'—and thereby conclusive evidence of the earlier poem's personal importance for Heine. With '**Die Weihe**' he had embarked on a journey towards creative self-realisation. With unrequited love as his initial inspiration he would embrace poetically a full range of genres (in accordance with the contemporary fashion for such eclecticism),[64] moods and facets of his own being. '**Im Hafen**' is the conclusion of his Odyssey, as he both reaches Paradise and yet also returns home. Here too love is the inspiration, his Jewish identity is a cryptic theme, the Germanic-Oriental juxtaposition provides an underlying structure, and the self-assertive poetic philosophy which already in 1816 he had begun to link with or derive from Goethe's *Divan* has reached fruition, still in close (indeed, closer) association with Goethe's collection and its models. This poem is also, again like '**Die Weihe**', not thoroughly coherent, but, in contrast to the earlier work, it now offers its own inbuilt justification of the incoherence, articulating an irrationalist view irrationally.

'**Die Weihe**' was a very surprising poem (or at any rate became so when properly investigated), above all for its revelation of the sense of purpose in Heine's lyricising from the earliest stages. '**Im Hafen**' perhaps disturbs our preconceptions less, but it reveals itself as all the more remarkable and impressive a work. The emotional immaturity and stylistic vulgarity are gone, and what remains is a poem possessing a rare suggestive variety and complexity—rare not only in Heine's work—which make it indeed a fitting realisation of the imaginative power it extolls. Genuinely it is Heine's epilogue, as '**Die Weihe**' was his prologue, to *Buch der Lieder,* to the styles, processes, inspiration and philosophy of the collection. Where others of his epilogic poems attempted to diminish or reject what they encompassed, reducing it to the status of agonised juvenilia, in '**Im Hafen**' he takes the opposite path, or shows the courage of his convictions, as he returns emphatically to, expounds and exults in the creative achievement of his 'lyrical youth'.

Notes

[1] 24.10.1826. Heine, *Briefe,* 6 vols., ed. Friedrich Hirth, Mainz, 1950-1, I, p. 295.

[2] B I, pp. 149, 64.

[3] See DHA I, p. 1074. The poem reappeared in *Gedichte,* 1822, but was evidently deemed wrong for the poet's presentation of his 'junge Leiden' in 1827 and did not figure in editions of *Buch der Lieder* in Heine's lifetime.

[4] B I, pp. 219-21.

[5] *Briefe,* I, pp. 5-9.

[6] Ibid., p. 9.

[7] August Fischer, *Ueber die volksthümlichen Elemente in den Gedichten Heines,* Berlin, 1905, p. 73; Eduard Thorn, *Heinrich Heines Beziehungen zu Clemens Brentano,* Berlin, 1913, p. 78.

[8] *Des Knaben Wunderhorn. Alte deutsche Leider,* ed. L. Achim von Arnim and Clemens Brentano, Heidelberg, 1806-8, I, p. 178.

[9] Cf. for example Friedrich de la Motte Fouqué, *Gedichte,* Vienna, 1816-19, I, p. 136, 'Minnelied'; II, p. 72, 'Fromme Minne'; II, p. 53, 'Verloren'. Cf. also Heine's letter to Fouqué of 10.6.1823: *Briefe,* I, p. 81.

[10] B I, pp. 50-4. See Paul Beyer, *Der junge Heine,* Berlin, 1911, pp. 24-8; DHA I, pp. 702-10 (Grappin), esp. pp. 708-9.

[11] Bürger, *Gedichte,* ed. Arnold Berger, Leipzig, n.d., pp. 92-102. Cf. *Traumbild* 8, vv.115f., B I, p. 34: see Fischer, *Volksthümliche Elemente,* p. 94; DHA I, p. 673 (Grappin).

[12] Goethe, GA I, pp. 143, 123, 144, 465. Cf. especially *Traumbild* 8, vv.1-30, B I, pp. 30-1. See Rudolf Greinz, *Heinrich Heine und das deutsche Volkslied,* Neuwied, 1894, p. 26; E(2) I, p. 434 (Elster); DHA I, p. 672 (Grappin).

[13] GA I, p. 18 (cf. Manfred Windfuhr, *Heinrich Heine. Revolution und Reflexion,* Stuttgart, 1969, p. 23); GA I, pp. 114-15.

[14] Novalis, *Schriften,* ed. Paul Kluckhohn, Stuttgart, 1977, I, pp. 91-5. Fischer, *Volksthümliche Elemente,* pp. 73-4.

[15] Quoted from Luther's Bible. 1. *Mose,* 28, v. 12.

[16] 'Im Hafen', see below. See also, *inter alia,* B VI/I, p. 657, one of Heine's posthumously published *brouillons.*

[17] B I, p. 271.

[18] Ibid.: 'Und all die Tränen fliessen/Nach Süden, im stillen Verein,/Sie fliessen und ergiessen/Sich all in den Jordan hinein' (final str. of 4).

[19] Cf. the letter to Sethe, *Briefe,* I, p. 8: 'Bey so bewandten Umständen [namely racial hatred in Hamburg] lässt sich leicht voraussehen dass Christliche Liebe die Liebeslieder eines Juden nicht ungehudelt lassen wird'.

[20] GA I, p. 111. Windfuhr, *Revolution und Reflexion,* p. 23.

[21] B I, p. 70.

[22] Respectively B II, pp. 367, 369; I, pp. 264-5; I, pp. 223-4, 261 (both ca. 1820); I, pp. 160 (1825), 285-6 (1821); I, p. 210, II, pp. 236, 251.

[23] B VI/I, pp. 314-17.

[24] *Briefe,* I, p. 9.

[25] B I, p. 62.

[26] Ibid., pp. 129, 145. See the discussion below.

[27] The 'Ankündigung', with the heading 'West-östlicher Divan oder Versammlung deutscher Gedichte in stetem Bezug auf den Orient', was published in Cotta's *Morgenblatt,* 24.2.1816 (GA III, pp. 764f.), these poems (GA III, pp. 287, 300, 299) and others in the *Taschenbuch für Damen* 1817. The latter will have appeared, as the annual belletristic *Taschenbücher* customarily did, in the autumn preceding its nominal date, hence autumn 1816. See Waltraud Hagen, *Die Drucke von Goethes Werken,* Berlin (East), 1971, pp. 319-23.

[28] Firstly, the rainbow image which introduces Heine's strophes noticeably repeats the central image of 'Phänomen', one of the *Divan* poems published in the *Taschenbuch für Damen* (GA III, p. 293: see Hagen, *Die Drucke von Goethes Werken,* p. 322). And secondly, it becomes a little hard in the context to accept that the line 'Menschen nennens Regenbogen' is merely a chance echo of the famous phrase from the (metrically identical) *Schenkenbuch* poem 'Welch ein Zustand', 'Perser nennen's Bidamag buden' (a line for which Heine also showed marked fondness on subsequent occasions—GA III, p. 375: see for instance his letter of 4.9.1824, *Briefe,* I, p. 180), even though this poem of Goethe's, written in 1814, had not formally been issued. It is quite possible that Heine somehow got wind of it in Hamburg prior to its publication, for example through some of the prominent partisans of Goethe whom he is thought to have encountered there in his uncle's circle, like Elise von Hohenhausen (who was not only a Byronist!).

[29] GA III, p. 288.

[30] Windfuhr, *Revolution und Reflexion,* p. 23: '[. . .] ein glattes, in die Breite gehendes Lied'.

[31] On this, cf. also his quotation in the letter of 27.10.1816 of the familiar passage from *Tasso* ending 'Gab mir ein Gott, zu sagen, wie ich leide' ('Die Muse ist mir [. . .] jetzt noch weit lieber als je. [. . .] Wie tief treffen mich jetzt die Worte Goethes im Tasso', etc.): *Briefe,* I, p. 7.

3

[2] Michael Birkenbihl, 'Die orientalischen Elemente in der Poesie Heinrich Heines', in *Analecta Germanica für Hermann Paul,* Amberg, 1906, pp. 261-322, discusses briefly contemporary orientalism in general, and then catalogues orientalistic elements in early Heine, but all with little reference to the *Divan.* Barker Fairley's short article with the promising title 'Heine, Goethe and the *Divan*', *German Life and Letters* 9 (1955), pp. 166-70, proves to be rather a slight comparison. Its beginning sets the tone: 'This paper is prompted by [. . .] a suspicion that the *Divan* offers points of comparison with the poetry of Heine. [. . .] Whether Heine was aware of the connection is another matter. Probably not'. Mounir Fendri's recent long monograph, *Halbmond, Kreuz und Schibboleth. Heinrich Heine und der islamische Orient,* Hamburg, 1980, certainly contributes significantly to study of Heine's sources, but gives remarkably short shrift to the *Divan,* and never really elicits what it was that Goethean orientalism meant to Heine. The two recent annotated editions of *Buch der Lieder* by Grappin (DHA I) and Briegleb (B I) show a stronger sense that the *Divan* itself is important, especially Briegleb, who points out a number of links with poems from

it, as well as some from Hafis; but even in his remarks no real clarity about Heine's purposes emerges. The first chapter of Karl-Heinz Fingerhut's interesting *Standortbestimmungen. Vier Untersuchungen zu Heinrich Heine,* Heidenheim, 1971, makes occasional reference to the *Divan* (pp. 15, 31, 33); he points to a general affinity between one *Buch der Lieder* poem and one from Goethe's *Buch der Liebe,* and he quotes Heine's later praise (in *Die romantische Schule* of the early 1830s, and from the ideological position of those years) of the *Divan*'s emancipatory 'Sensualismus' (B III, p. 403), but he does not argue for significant application by Heine of material from the *Divan* to his own collection. George Peters, 'Heines Beurteilung des *Westöstlichen Divan*', *Heine-Jahrbuch* 22 (1983), pp. 30-46, is concerned almost wholly with the *Romantische Schule* remarks and period, and scarcely refers to specific poems by Heine. Finally, Norbert Altenhofer, in an article called 'Ästhetik des Arrangements. Zu Heines "Buch der Lieder"' (*Text und Kritik* 18/19 (1982): *Heinrich Heine,* pp. 16-32), argues quite instructively that Heine's cyclical organisation of poems in *Buch der Lieder* and the poetological approach which underlay this ('literarisch-reflektiv', 'historisierend', 'dialektisch') must have found a 'maßgebendes [. . .] Vorbild' in the *Divan;* but Altenhofer too does not propose or concern himself with close textual parallels.

³³ B I, pp. 124, 129, 134, 149.

³⁴ Ibid., p. 138. Cf. B I, p. 733 (Briegleb).

³⁵ Ibid., pp. 138, 84, 94; GA III, pp. 318, 374.

³⁶ GA III, p. 372.

³⁷ Ibid., p. 374.

³⁸ B II, pp. 164-6, 420-2; I, pp. 187-8, 211-12. This is a conception, moreover, which shows Heine very much as the child of his epoch. Cf. F.Sengle, *Biedermeierzeit,* 3 vols., Stuttgart, 1971f., II, p. 521.

³⁹ B I; p. 77.

⁴⁰ GA III, p. 397: see Barker Fairley, 'Heine, Goethe and the Divan', p. 168. Hafis: see Birkenbihl, 'Die orientalischen Elemente', p. 296, and B I, p. 707 (Briegleb).

⁴¹ See *Briefe,* I, pp. 283, 291; 13.10.1826, 17.10.1826. Cf. DHA I, p. 1000.

⁴² B I, pp. 209-11. The form of this poem is difficult: rhymeless, edging towards free verse, but with a strong tetrameter predominance, the standard mode of *Nordsee* II. One is tempted to discern a cultural synthesis, as in other aspects of 'Im Hafen': rhymeless tetrameters with largely feminine line-endings, as in Hammer's Hafis, a general pseudo-Homeric *hoher Ton,* and a German balladesque quality in the verse's rhythmic vigour, single and double *Senkung* forcefully intermingled. But I am not at all sure about this.

⁴³ Cf. Lydia Baer, 'Anklaenge an Homer nach Voss in der *Nordsee* Heinrich Heines', *Journal of English and Germanic Philology* 29 (1930), pp. 1-17. In fact, Heine's phrase, 'Glücklich der Mann, der den Hafen erreicht hat', seems not to be directly from Homer. If it refers specifically to anything, it is probably to Ovid's sea-voyage descriptions, in *Tristia ex Ponto* and *Metamorphoses.*

⁴⁴ In *Lieder* 5 and 6 and *Romanzen* 14; see Chap. 3. He also used 'Abschied von Bremen', as we saw in Chap. 2, as a basis for his earlier 'homecoming' poems (recording an actual return to Hamburg) in 1823/4, *Heimkehr* 16, 17, 18 and 20.

⁴⁵ B I, pp. 762-3.

⁴⁶ Hauff, *Werke,* ed. Max Drescher, Berlin, n.d., VI, pp. 18-22, also pp. 7-8.

⁴⁷ Luther's Bible, 1. *Mose,* 28, v.17.

⁴⁸ *Wunderhorn,* II, p. 423. Cf. E(2) I, p. 470 (Elster), and DHA I, p. 1057 (Grappin).

⁴⁹ Cf. *Wunderhorn,* II, p. 430, 'Evoe'.

⁵⁰ B I, p. 762.

⁵¹ Ibid., p. 763.

⁵² Ibid., p. 139. Cf. *Wunderhorn,* I, p. 304, 'Der Himmel hängt voll Geigen'.

⁵³ Quoted from B I, p. 760 (Briegleb).

⁵⁴ B II, p. 251.

⁵⁵ Cf. Goethe, *Divan,* GA III, pp. 350, 356-7.

⁵⁶ DHA I, p. 1056.

⁵⁷ Gans, a Jewish friend of Heine's in Berlin, was a pupil of Hegel's and author of a Hegelian history of law, *Das Erbrecht in weltgeschichtlicher Entwickelung,* Berlin, 1824f.

'Systematik' is the term Heine himself uses in this connection. See *Buch le Grand,* Chap. 13, B II, p. 287.

⁵⁸ GA III, p. 374.

⁵⁹ Ibid., p. 357.

⁶⁰ *Song of Solomon,* 2, v.1. Cf. E(2) I, p. 470 (Elster).

⁶¹ B IV, pp. 540-8.

⁶² Cf. the interesting letter of 21.1.1824 to Moser. *Briefe,* I, p. 136: 'Ich bin stolz darauf, ein Perser zu seyn.[. . .] Ach, es ist ein schreckliches Schicksal für einen persischen Dichter, daß er sich abmühen muß in Eurer niederträchtig holprigen deutschen Sprache.[. . .] Ach! wie sehne ich mich nach den Rosen von Schiras!' Cf. also the Persian fantasy in *Die Harzreise,* B II, p. 155.

⁶³ A context for this is provided by a passage in Heine's exactly contemporaneous *Die Nordsee* III, where he talks of Scott's novels and the theme in them which 'alle Herzen Europas bewegt [hat]': 'Dieses Thema ist aber nicht bloß eine elegische Klage über Schottlands volkstümliche Herrlichkeit, die allmählig verdrängt wurde von fremder Sitte, Herrschaft und Denkweise; sondern es ist der große Schmerz über den Verlust der National-Besonderheiten die in der Allgemeinheit neuerer Kultur verloren gehen, ein Schmerz, der jetzt in den Herzen aller Völker zuckt. Denn Nationalerinner-ungen liegen tiefer in der Menschen Brust, als man gewöhnlich glaubt. Man wage es nur, die alten Bilder wieder auszugraben, und über Nacht blüht hervor auch die alte Liebe mit ihren

Blumen' (B II, p. 236). The 'Nationaler-innerung' in Heine's own breast, so he is telling us—if rather discreetly—in 'Im Hafen' and elsewhere, is a Jewish as well as a German one.

I should add that the manifestations of the Jewish theme which I describe in this chapter go unnoticed, to my knowledge, in all the literature, even the most recent, on Heine's Jewishness. See Prawer, *Heine's Jewish Comedy. A Study of His Portraits of Jews and Judaism,* Oxford, 1983.

[64] Cf. Sengle, *Biedermeierzeit*, II, pp. 549f., I, pp. 93-4. In the light of Sengle's discussion, remarked on in my Introduction, 'Die Weihe' becomes in effect Heine's youthful *Bekenntnis* to this aspect of prevailing aesthetics.

John Carson Pettey (essay date 1993)

SOURCE: "Anticolonialism in Heine's 'Vitzliputzli'," in *Colloquia Germanica*, Vol. 26, No. 1, 1993, pp. 37-47.

[*In the following essay, Pettey investigates Heine's representation of the Spanish conquest of Mexico in his poem "Vitzliputzli" as primarily a violent clash of religions.*]

In **"Vitzliputzli"**,[1] the longest of the "Historien" in *Romanzero* (1851), Heine avoided sentimentalizing the Aztecs vis-à-vis their Spanish conquerors and colonizers. He was chiefly concerned with presenting his historical vision in a disturbingly vivid, nightmarish account of the clash between two diverse cultures. Following a major theme found in the "Historien," **"Vitzliputzli"** illustrates the dominance of barbarity attended by a baffling lack of transcendent benevolence in human history.[2] As was always his wont, Heine sided overtly with the underdog, and yet he pulled no punches about the cruelty in Aztec rituals. Indeed, the historical problem addressed deals primarily with a conflict between religions. His poetic rendering of the Conquest of Mexico would seem to corroborate the assertion of that country's Nobel laureate, Octavio Paz, who believes, "[i]f Mexico was born in the sixteenth century, we must agree that it was the child of a double violence, imperial and unifying: that of the Aztecs and that of the Spaniards."[3] Thus, if we are to consider this poem as an expression of Heine's anticolonialism, we need to examine both its revision of historical fact and its reservations about historical progress as evidenced in his rendering of the Conquest. For **"Vitzliputzli"** reveals Heine's contempt for two forces underlying colonialism—gold-lust and, more important, the desire for new souls.

The poem attacks these forces in each of its four parts: a prelude describing the poet's visit to the pristine paradise of pre-Conquest America; and the three separate of the poem proper, dealing with 1) the death of Montezuma and the ensuing battle in Tenochtitlan, 2) the sacrifice of captured Conquistadores before the Aztec war-god, and 3)Vitzliputzli's revenge. By combining his poetic imagination and history, Heine achieves a structural coherence—namely, the fanciful monologues in the prelude and in Part III (the poet's voice and that of the Aztec war-god,

respectively) that bracket the history grounding Parts I and II. Also apparent is the narrative's continual telescoping downward from the panoramic view in the "Präludium" through battle scenes in Tenochtitlan to the human sacrifices atop that city's holiest pyramid. And in this process we are led to some disquieting realizations about the ramifications of Spain's desire for hegemony in the New World. The "Präludium" praises the New World as a continent not yet contaminated by the moribund mores of Europe. A sampling of the adjectives used to describe the Old and New Worlds illustrates Heine's prejudices: America's natural attributes are "neu," "gesund," "wild," and "farbensprühend"; in stark contrast Europe remains but "alt," "verschimmelt," "versteinert," and "blasirt" (P, 5-20). Again, this America is not the one of Heine's day, but rather the healthy wilderness devoid of civilization's corruption. Here the poet meets no other human beings; instead he communes happily at first with brightly colored birds whose languages he can decipher, and in the end with a monkey that (ironically and anachronistically) crosses itself before this specter from the Old World. The poet must explain to this terrified simian that he is not a ghostly apparition, but "des Lebens treuster Sohn" (P, 64). The poet remains conscious of present time despite his imagined journey into the past. That Heine did not want to romanticize the New World in obscurantist fashion can be seen in the attacks on romantic icons, as well as humorous coloration of the monkey's backside, "Schwarz-roth-gold-gelb" (P, 77). These were not just the colors of Barbarossa's banner, but also those of an ineptly executed attempt at democracy in 1848, whose nationalism Heine both misunderstood and despised.[4] In a later poem directly connected with the European discovery of the New World, **"Bimini"** (published posthumously in 1869), allusions to Romanticism and nationalism also continued. In that lyrical account of Ponce de Léon's search for eternal youth, Heine's reference to the legendary crusading emperor moves beyond the political considerations surrounding the *Paulskirche,* since the mention of Barbarossa's banner inaugurates "the reluctant and somewhat melancholy confession that poetic endeavor is impossible for him without recourse to a creativity he associates with Romanticism."[5] In a manner reminiscent of the "Loreley," that confessional attitude towards the Romantic imagination can also be found already in the prelude's closing lines, though the vitriolic neologism "Affensteißcouleuren" must temper our reading of the source for the poetic voice's melancholy (P, 78-80). But more important than any aesthetic commentary remains, then, the poetic principle that future events determine impressions of the historic past. Thus, **"Vitzliputzli"** will delineate facts only to promote a specific historical consciousness; it will describe a specific historical event only to remind the reader of its consequences.[6]

Out of the prelude's placid paradise we are transported, quite literally with the speed of Pegasus (P, 49), to its antithesis: Part I opens with the coming of Cortez, an intruder with opposite intentions to the poet's own in the "Präludium." The first stanza describes the Conquistador as wearing both laurels on his head and golden spurs on his boots. Here Heine begins no panegyric, since the characterization continues thus: "Nicht ein Held und auch kein Ritter, / Nur ein Räuberhauptmann war er" (I, 4-5). In the New World's pantheon his name would come immediately after that of Columbus, but Heine destroys any glorification in contrasting these two adventurers. Heine does not find their close connection in the history of the New World a felicitous one, since for him Columbus's daring foresight would be lost in historical memory to Cortez's marauding actions. Critics have been quick to point out that here Heine's subjectivity overrides any objective view; also, in seeing only the evil in Cortez, Heine unjustly characterized the Conquistador.[7] With a reference to the condemned criminals at the Crucifixion in Luke 23:39-42, Cortez becomes a "Schächer" (I, 19), whose name links the present with the past in historical memory as the direct result of "Helden-schicksals letzte Tücke" (I, 17); whereas Columbus deserves comparison with Moses in his importance for European civilization (I, 47). Nonetheless, Heine was not blinded by the magnitude of Columbus's feats, since he summarizes those deeds in such skeptical and portentous words:

> Nicht befreien konnt' er uns
> Aus dem öden Erdenkerker,
> Doch er wußt' ihn zu erweitern
> Und die Ketten zu verlängern.
>
> (I, 33-36)

If Columbus was not the scoundrel that Cortez was in Heine's eyes, his discovery was still not an emancipation. Just how taut the chain of colonialism would become would be revealed in the final section.

In fairness to Heine, at least part of his description of the Conquistador was correct: Hernàn Cortez was not of noble birth, and in 1519, as he ventured with his fleet from Cuba to Mexico, he was indeed a thief, since he had absconded with these vessels against the wishes of the island's viceroy Velasquez.[8] That Cortez was not heroic must, indeed, be doubted. Despite his brutal dealings with indigenous peoples, in all acounts of the Conquest of Mexico, Cortez is rightly shown to be as courageous in battle as he was covetous of gold. Indeed, he was perhaps one of the most cunning military leaders in history whose adherence to alliances and promises was never firm. But above all, and this fact is completely absent in Heine's acount, Cortez was inordinately lucky. Though not the first European to land in Mexico, Cortez came in exactly the right year for subduing the Aztecs. 1519 was a year of "One Reed" according to Aztec cosmological reckoning. "One Reed" was a by-name of the exiled god Quetzacoatl, whose return from the East marked the close of an old world-cycle (that of Huitzilopochtli), the advent of a new one, and the end of Aztec domination.[9] Cortez's appearance on the mainland paralleled that supreme deity's epiphany, but it also reinforced the spiritual resignation of the Aztecs, a people whose deepest belief lay in their own fated demise.

But these facts could not have been known to Heine, since the *Florentine Codex,* the history of the Aztecs compiled by Father Sahagùn in Nahuatl, had not been translated in his day. As a consequence, his depiction of the encounter between Montezuma and Cortez remained consistent with traditional sources[10]: the Aztec's generosity countered by the Spaniard's treachery. At a feast held in his honor, Montezuma is taken hostage and eventually dies. This feast bears the ironic title "Span'sche Treue," whose author is none other than Cortez (I, 83). Once Montezuma dies, the dam is broken, and a raging sea of Aztec warriors rushes in upon the Spanish troops. With this obvious pathetic fallacy, Heine sets the stage for the danger-fraught retreat of Cortez's men along the causeways leading out of Tenochtitlan. Overladen with gold— "das teuflische Metall" or "die gelbe Südenlast" (I, 172-174), many Spaniards drown as they fall from the causeway into the surrounding lake. Not only are these Spaniards physically defeated, but their spiritual banner bearing the Virgin Mary's image must suffer Aztec arrows. In sum, the toll of Spanish perfidy: 160 dead, many wounded, and 80 captured soldiers (I, 205-208).

Symbolically, the fighting ceases with the setting sun, and after the day comes the horrific "Spuknacht des Triumphes" (II, 218). Up to now Heine has remained faithful to the chronology of *La Noche Triste,* but in the second section he anachronistically mixes two historical incidents. We know from the chroniclers of Cortez's weeping after his defeat in Tenochtitlan. That the Aztecs sacrificed any captured Spaniards then is not known from those records, nor that Cortez and his men watched the terrifying spectacle. We do, however, find such an instance of sacrificing Spanish captives a year later during the retaking of Tenochtitlan, though it was observed not by Cortez but by Alvarado.[11] One can excuse the inaccuracy because of Heine's motivation—namely, to focus our attention on the Aztec rites and on Vitzliputzli, who has seemingly vanquished the Virgin and her adherents. Further contrasting the colonizer's religion with that of the soon to be colonized, Heine compares Vitzliputzli's temple with colossal, Old Testament structures, bringing to mind Nebuchadnezzar's fiery furnace (Daniel 3:17).[12] But Heine must add a touch of irony: "Mexikos blutdürst'ger Kriegsgott" is described as so "putzig, / So verschnörkelt und so kindisch" that he "dennoch unsre Lachlust kitzelt" (II, 249-252). Heine then compares the temple to two unlikely monuments: Basel's "Pale Death" and Brussels's "Mannke-Piß" (II, 255-256). Thus, with one curiously intuitive stroke Heine can evoke the underlying meaning of the sacrificial ritual—death's horror combined with the innocence of regained youth. The Aztecs believed both ideas were contained in rites to Vitzliputzli, whose life, as incarnation of the Sun, was rejuvenated by a constant infusion of red and precious liquid—blood.[13]

Unlike the tragedy derived from "Span'sche Treue," the new drama of "Menschenopfer" is neither tragic nor comic; rather it is "ein Mysterium," a religious drama quite different from Christianity's eucharistic ceremonies:

> "Menschenofer" heißt das Stück.
> Uralt ist der Stoff, die Fabel;
> In der christlichen Behandlung
> Ist das Schauspiel nicht so gräßlich.

Denn dem Blute wurde Rotwein,
Und dem Leichnam, welcher vorkam,
Wurde eine harmlos dünne
Mehlbreispeis transsubstituiret—

(II, 301-308)

Here the cultural clash takes on an appropriate solemnity: Aztec cruelty answers Spanish brutality with cannibalism; the body and "das Vollblut von Altchristen" will be offered up. The blood of these victims was never tainted by that of Moors or Jews (II, 313-116). Of course, Heine is referring here to the Fall of Granada and the expulsion of the Jews from Spain, both of which occurred five hundred years ago. Typically, just when our sympathies are about to take a new course and we begin to align ourselves with these victims, Heine complicates those feelings, since he does not want us to forget the consequences of the Spaniards' religious prejudice. As Susanne Zantop has so convincingly argued, the use of cannibalism here functions mutually for both the parties involved, since "[c]olonial appropriation is answered by the incorporation of the colonizers, and both colonizers and colonized are transformed in the process."[14] We as readers are also transformed by the sensory imagery provided. As the Spanish soldiers and noblemen are tortured before the visage of Vitzliputzli, the uproarious "Kannibalen-Charivari" drowns out their screams, while the stench of their spilt blood reaches our nostrils. Across the lake in counterpoint to this "Mexikanisches Tedeum," Cortez's men sing "De profundis," as fiery images blind our eyes (II, 341-356). Perhaps nowhere in Heine's works does a literal synaesthesia assume such dramatic intensity. In accordance with chronicled tradition, Heine concludes this emotionally disturbing section with stout Cortez reduced to tears, and thereafter the curtain goes down on the blood-smeared mystery play.

When it rises again in the final section, the "Spuknacht" has ended, and a new day breaks on the great pyramid. Heine mingles the horrible with the mundane: we see both priests and laity denched in blood and snoring after their nocturnal debauch (III, 373-376). Reintroduced is Rotjacke, the one-hundred-year-old high priest, who has come to speak with his god. With all due reverence he promises Vitzliputzli that the Spanish horses will be sacrifices on the morrow, and that, if need be, he will personally offer up his own grandsons to gain victory over the colonizing army (III, 393-396). At this point Heine has moved again from the historical into the fanciful, to that realm evinced earlier in the prelude. We know today from anthropological studies that Aztecs never willfully sacrificed kinsmen to Vitzliputzli, nor were rituals ever performed for individual desires, such as Rotjacke's. Yet what the high priest finds most curious, if not inexplicable, is the lack of piety in the Spaniards, men who are so "moralisch häßlich" that they can eat their gods— "daß sie sogar / Ihre eigenen Götter fräßen" (III, 429-432). Again, Heine did not have access to scholarly materials on Aztec rituals. Otherwise, he would have understood that the *ixiptlas,* or those sacrificed, paid for "an involutary debt to the earth deities, contracted through the ingestion of the fruits of the earth," and "[t]hat debt could be acknowledged by the payment

of a regular token levy—namely, offerings of one's own blood—but it could be extinguished only by death, when the earth lords would feed upon the bodies of men, as men had perforce fed upon them."[15] Regardless of these facts, Heine's was not trying to provide a treatise on Aztec religious rites, but rather to underscore the religiously based, mutual misunderstanding between colonizing and colonized cultures.

Up to now the title figure has remained silent. But his priest's questions awaken in him a desire to communicate. In a wrathful display Vitzliputzli corrects Rotjacke's misguided notions, since as a god he can interpret the signs of things to come. The war-god utters an eschatological pronouncement on the fate of the Aztecs:

In Erfüllung geht die böse,
Uralt böse Prophezeiung
Von des Reiches Untergang
Durch die furchtbar bärt'gen Männer

. . . . .

wir müssen untergehen,
Ich, der ärmste aller Götter,
Und mein armes Mexiko.

(III, 467-484)

It is the power of the Virgin Mary that has fired the war-god's wrath. Through her the Spaniards will be victorious, and Mexico will thereafter lie in smoke and ruins. Vitzliputzli may fall, but he will not die; for gods live as long as parrots. Paronomastically using the verb "mausern," in both senses of "to moult" and "to transform for one's own benefit" (III, 495), Vitzliputzli closes the poem with the tale of his revenge through his metamorphosis. His will be a diabolical one, and he will flee destruction by going to Europe and joining the historically regressive ranks of Satan, Belzebub, and Lilith (III, 515-518). Going into exile, the newly transformed god will walk the colonizing chain linking the two continents back to Europe, where he will play havoc with both the foolish and the wise by tempting them through his mastery of the "Kunst der Lüge" (III, 520).

The exact nature of Vitzliputzli's revenge has generated much critical speculation. For Susanne Zantop the economic and political evils of colonialism and its later development as imperialism seem by implication probable answers[16]; the text would seem to support this through a reversed alchemy taking gold and turning it into sulphur (III, 507). For Horst Rüdiger lust for gold and missionary zeal are not evil enough for Heine, who "läßt sich etwas Teuflischeres einfallen"[17]—namely, the epidemic spread of syphilis in early modern Europe. Speculating further on the nature of Heine's own illness—that is, on the possibility of it having been *leus cerebrospinalis,* Rüdiger sees Heine's grotesque ballad as directly relating to the poet's own fate.[18] And if one wishes to make the connection between Vitzliputzli's revenge and the epigraph to the "Lamentationen"— "Das Glück ist eine leichte Dirne," as well as the "Lazarus" cycle, then such an assumption may indeed have textual justification.

Nonetheless, the narrative's substantive concern revolves around religious differences between the two sides of colonialism, while the impetus behind Vitzliputzli's exile and his revenge lies not with the Spaniards *per se,* but with their symbol, the Virgin Mary (III, 473-480). Though the hellish company Vitzliputzli will keep can clearly be associated with sexual licence, his new career has a decidedly different slant:

> Ich verteufle mich, der Gott
> Wird jetzund ein Gott-sei-bei-uns;
> Als der Feinde böser Feind
> Kann ich dorten wirken, schaffen.
>
> Quälen will ich dort die Feinde,
> Mit Phantomen sie erschrecken—
> Vorgeschmack der Hölle, Schwefel
> Sollen sie beständig riechen.
>
> (III, 501-508)

If we are to read these lines with the idea of an omnipresent sense of hell, then venereal disease and economics cannot be the only important consequences. Another likelihood could also be the sixteenth-century obsession with the Devil as brutally demonstrated in the Inquisition. Though it began before the Conquest of Mexico, its influence increased dramatically after the 1520s. The Conquest did not cause the Inquisition, but its holy mission and the experiences garnered from it did help pave the way to formalizing Spanish intolerance for others.[19] Also, the source for the modern German usage of Huitzilopochtli's garbled name as some sort of bogyman (*Teufel* or *Kinderschreck*) may have originated along the road taken to visit the holy shrines of Santiago de Compostela. That pilgrimage route grew in importance after the fall of Constantinople (1453) and later after the Wars of Religion in the latter part of sixteenth century (1562-1598). Peregrine Christians from German-speaking lands, travelling either the southern path that originated in Zürich and Einsiedeln or the northern one beginning in Aachen, would have necessarily passed through the homeland of many Conquistadors and encountered two inquisitional tribunals at Logroño (1512) and their goal Santiago (1574).[20] The combination of Conquest and Inquisition would have most assuredly helped to stengthen the Vitzliputzli's demonization in the European imagination. Just when and whence the Aztec war-god's name entered German popular consciousness has remained a matter of speculation. His first literary appearance, as "Vitzliputzli," with an obviously devilish connotation occurred in Lindenborn's *Diogenes* (1742) as part of a common curse of milkmaids ("nach ihrer gewöhnlichen groben redensart").[21] This vernacular usage would seem to illustrate that German popular culture had already absorbed his new incarnation, even if Vitzliputzli would not have become enshired in a *Sprichwort.*[22]

The exact nature of Vitzliputzli's revenge remains ostensibly ambiguous at the poem's conclusion, and thereby invites a variety of possible interpretations from the textual evidence. What is, however, beyond any doubt is the fact that, despite Heine's return to a personal God in his last years, an aggressive pessimism still dominated much of his thoughts on institutionalized religion, as discussed in his *Geständnisse* (1853-1854). Indeed, his **"Vitzliputzli"** could then serve as a historical counterpart to **"Disputation,"** which concludes the *Romanzero's* **"Hebräische Melodien"** and underscores his cynical view of religious disputes.[23] Finally, the Aztec war-god's threat of revenge complements our own transformation as readers, since our historical understanding has changed as our emotions have been buffetted between those affected. We have come to realize not only that the Conquest meant brutal subjugation of indigenous peoples and wanton destruction of their cultural achievements including religion, but also that it had ominous ramifications for future generations of Europeans. Our sympathies as readers must then lie with both groups. With this particular move back in time, Heine confirmed his strong pessimism regarding human progress, especially in any spiritual sense. As an anticolonial statement, **"Vitzliputzli"** ultimately reveals to us just how vainglorious sublime ideals can become once they are taken up in the brutish hands of men.

Notes

This essay constitutes the revised version of a talk delivered at the American Association of Teachers of German Annual Meeting in Baden-Baden in July 1992.

[1] All quotes from "Vitzliputzli" are taken from Heinrich Heine, *Werke, Briefwechsel, Lebenszeugnisse: Säkularausgabe,* ed. Nationale Forschungs- und Gedenkstätte der klassischen Literatur in Weimar and the Centre National de la Recherche Scientifique in Paris, vol. 3: *Gedichte 1845-1856,* rev. Helmut Brandt and Renate Francke (Berlin: Akademie-Verlag; Paris: Editions du CNRS, 1986) 48 65. All future references will be given parenthetically by the respective part and lines.

[2] This critical commonplace for the "Historien" is perhaps most succinctly formulated as "daß Macht nicht nach Moral fragt." See Joachim Bark, "'Versifizirtes Herzblut'. Zur Entstehung und Gehalt von Heines 'Romanzero,'" *Wirkendes Wort* 36.2 (March-April 1986): 91.

[3] Octavio Paz, "The Conquest and Colonialism," trans. Lysander Kemp, *The Labyrinth of Solitude* (New York: Grove Press, 1985,[1]1961) 100.

[4] On Heine's disdain for the Frankfurt nationalists, see Walter Hinck, "Exil als Zuflucht der Resignation. Der Herrscher-Dichter-Konflikt der Firdusi-Romanze und die Ästhetik des späten Heines," *Von Heine zu Brecht. Lyrik im Geschichtsprozeß* (Frankfurt a.M.: Suhrkamp, 1978) 48-51; and Jeffrey L. Sammons, *Heinrich Heine: A Modern Biography* (Princeton: Princeton University Press, 1979) 301-302.

[5] Robert C. Holub, "Heine and the New World," *Colloquia Germanica* 22 (1989): The pertinent lines of "Bimini" (157-164) are taken from an alternative version of the poem in Heine, *Säkularausgabe,* vol. 3, 258:

Fantasie sitzt an dem Steuer,
Gute Laune bläht die Segel
Schiffsjung ist der Witz, der flinke,
Ob Verstand an Bord? Ich weiß nicht!

Meine Raen sind Metapfern
Meine Hyperbel ist mein Mastbaum

Schwarz roth Gold ist meine Flagge,
Farbelfarben der Romantik—

Thereafter the poetic voice utters his mixed feelings, both alienated and sympathetic, about his earlier connection to Romantic ideals.

[6] Hans-Peter Bayerdörfer, "'Politische Ballade'. Zu den 'Historien' in Heine's 'Romanzero,'" *Deutsche Vierteljahrsschrift* 46 (July 1972): 441. I have taken this concept out of context for Bayerdörfer's argument, since it readily encompasses more than just Heine's use of traditional motifs and elements.

[7] Hella Gebhard, "Interpretation der 'Historien' aus Heine's 'Romanzero,'" Diss., Friedrich-August-Universität zu Erlange, 1956, 108-109.

[8] Caesar C. Cantu, *Cortes and the Fall of the Aztec Empire* (Los Angeles: Modern World, 1966) 11-13 and 38-44.

[9] Charles E. Dibble, *The Conquest through Aztec Eyes. The 41st Annual Frederick William Reynolds Lecture* (Salt lake City: University of Utah Press, 1978) 16-17.

[10] One source for Heine was Michel Chevalier's article, "Du Mexique avant et pendant la conquête," which appeared in the Parisian *Revue des deux mondes* (1845), the same periodical in which Heine would first publish "Vitzliputzli" and other "Historien" in 1851. See Gebhard, 108-109.

[11] Dibble, 26-27; Cantu, 356.

[12] Here Heine refers incorrectly to the paintings of "Henri Martin" instead of the John Martin, whose fantastically colored renderings of Old Testament scenes reflect a vogue in nineteenth-century tastes. The image evoked seems to be a synthesis of two of Martin's enormous works, *Fall of Babylon* and *Belshazzar's Feast.* On this point, see S. S. Prawer, *Frankenstein's Island: England and the English in the Writings of Heinrich Heine* (Cambridge: Cambridge University Press, 1986) 293-294.

[13] Miguel Léon-Portilla, *Aztec Thought and Culture: A Study of the Ancient Mind of Mexico,* trans. Jack Emory David (Norman: University of Oklahoma Press, 1963) 162.

[14] Susanne Zantop, "Colonialism, Cannibalism, and Literary Incorporation: Heine in Mexico," *Heinrich Heine and the Occident: Multiple Identities, Multiple Receptions,* ed. Peter Uwe Hohendahl and Sander L. Gilman (Lincoln / London: University of Nebraska Press, 1991) 111. One ought to consider the earlier and similar arguments by Zantop in "Lateinamerika in Heine—Heine in Lateinamerika: 'das gesamte Kannibalencharivri,'" *Heine-Jahrbuch* 28 (1989): 72-87.

[15] Inga Clendinnen, *Aztecs: An Interpretation* (Cambridge/New York: Cambridge University Press, 1991) 74-75.

[16] Zantop, "Colonialism, Cannibalism, and Literary Incorporation: Heine in Mexico," 128-129. Admittedly, the interpretation presented here of this convincing article is based on my inferences of Zantop's continual references to economic and political aspects of colonialism. In support of her major assertions, see Eric R. Wolf, *Europe and the People without History* (Berleley / Los Angeles / London: University of California Press, 1982) 133-134 and 145-147.

[17] Horst Rüdiger, "Vitzliputzli im Exil," *Untersuchungen zur Literatur als Geschichte. Festschrift für Benno von Wiese,* ed. Vincent J. Günther, et al. (Berlin: Schmidt, 1973) 313.

[18] Rüdiger, 318-319. Interestingly, Heine's name remains conspicuously absent in a recent history of the disease. See Claude Quétel, *Le Mal de Naples: histoire de la syphilis* (Paris: Editions Seghers, 1986).

[19] Henry Kamen, *Inquistion and Society in Spain in the Sixteenth and Seventeenth Centuries* (Bloomington: Indiana University Press, 1985) 67ff. See also Jeffrey Burton Russell, *The Prince of Darkness: Radical Evil and the Power of Good in History* (Ithaca: Cornell University Press, 1988) 168-170.

[20] For the phases of popularity of and access to the Road of St. James, see Sir Thomas Kendrick, "Introduction," Vera and Hellmut Hell, *The Great Pilgrimage of the Middle Ages: The Road of St. James of Compostela* (New York: Potter, 1966) 26-28.

[21] Jacob and Wilhelm Grimm, *Deutsches Wörterbuch,* vol. XII, part II, rev. Rudolf Mieszner (Leipzig: Hirzel, 1951) 386-387. Rüdiger finds the earliest literary source as Christian Weise's dramatic *speculum stultitiae, Drey ärgsten Ertz-Narren in der ganzen Welt* (1672), but he fails to mention the satanic image found in Lindenborn in connection with Vitzliputzli's appearance in later works of German literature up to Heine. Moreover, he does not think the search for Heine's source is especially relevant to the issue at hand—namely, the spread of syphilis; see Rüdiger, 308.

[22] There is no mention of Vitzliputzli as part of a German adage in Karl Simrock, *Die deutschen Sprichwörter,* ed. Wolfgang Mieder (Stuttgart: Relam, 1988).

[23] For an early connection between these two poems, see Richard M. Meyer, "Der Dichter des 'Romanzero,'" *Die Nation* 17.11 (1899): 148-151. The cynicism of "Disputation" culminates in the final comment given by Donna Blanka (437-440); see Heine, *Sakularausgabe,* vol. 3, 148:

Welcher Recht hat, weiß ich nicht—
Doch es will mich schier bedünken,
Daß der Rabbi und der Mönch,
Daß sie alle beide stinken.

Roger F. Cook (essay date 1996)

SOURCE: "'Citronia'—'Kennst du das Land . . . ?': A Riddle of Sexuality and Desire," in *Heine-Jahrbuch 1996,* Verlag J. B. Metzler, 1996, pp. 81-112.

[*In the following excerpt, Cook evaluates Heine's portrayal of sexual desire in his poem "Citronia."*]

Of all of Heine's posthumously published poems perhaps none has such a checkered past as **"Citronia".** First mention of it came in June 1856 when Mathilda's lawyer, Henri Julia, placed it first in the list of 35 poems he sent to Christian Schad for publication in *Der Deutsche Musenalmanach.* But when the final agreement with Schad was reached, **"Citronia"** was one of the poems Schad decided not to publish because he anticipated difficulties with the German censors. Schad had copies of these poems made before sending them back to Julia, but this copy of "Citronia" has been lost. The title also appeared in the table of contents of a packet with 54 poems Julia sent to Campe for inclusion in the first collected works. In this collection, that was copied by the same writer who prepared the texts for the *Musenalmanach,* "Citronia" was listed together with "Fragment", an entry that probably referred to the "Nachwort" as a separate poem. However, due to inconsistencies in the manuscripts Campe decided not to use them. The copy of "Citronia" and the separately listed "Nachwort" is one of only eight poems from this packet that are missing from the collection at the Houghton Library today. Nor was "Citronia" one of a group of 25 posthumously published poems in the handwriting of Heine's private secretary Richard Reinhardt that are preserved as part of the Gottschalk collection at the Heine-Institut. But a single copy of "Citronia" in Reinhardt's handwriting has been preserved. While not in a final, clean form, it does present a finished version and, on the basis of Jules Legras' 1894 description of a working manuscript in Heine's handwriting (since lost), we know that it is a complete and accurate rendition of Heine's work.[1]

Thus despite its precarious and seemingly ill-fated history the poem has survived. But its history of publication and recognition by scholars has been as checkered and difficult as its path to survival. After Schad determined it was too controversial to appear in the *Musenalmanach* in 1857, Adolf Strodtmann decided against including it in *Letzte Gedichte und Gedanken,* the first edition of collected posthumous poems published in 1869 as a supplementary volume to the 1863 collected works. In the foreword he justifies his decision to omit "Citronia" and other poems that display a "weltverachtende[n] Nihilismus" and, in some cases, even "skurrile Obscönität" with the claim that they are "Krankheitsphantasien".[2] He then quotes verses 85-98 of the "Nachwort" as an example of nihilistic outbursts "nicht gegen die romantischen Auswüchse allein, sondern gegen die Poesie selber."[3] Strodtmann included "Citronia" in the second edition of the collected works (1876), as did Eduard Engel in his 1884 edition of the *Memoiren,* but in both cases "in kastrierter Gestalt"[4], with verses 19-24 and 77-78 omitted, apparently because they exceeded the limits of decency. Jonas Fränkel published the complete poem for the first time in the third volume (1913) of the *Sämtliche Werke* (W III, 412-414). He reconstructed it on the basis of the discussion of Strodtmann's emendations in journal articles by Anton Englert (1892) and Jules Legras (1894).[5]

Yet even 80 years after it finally appeared in complete form the early pre-judices against "Citronia" still seem to hinder scholars from reading it with a clear critical eye. Although the objections to its freedom with sexual issues are no longer a problem, the preoccupation with those objections is. No one has even attempted a comprehensive interpretation of the poem, even though in 1894 Legras commented on the extensive and detailed revisions on Heine's working copy of the poem: "Dieses Gedicht [. . .] hat seine Aufmerksamkeit ebenso lange gefesselt, als es die höchste

seiner poetischen Inspirationen nur immer vermocht hätte. Die ausgestrichenen Stellen sind nicht zu zählen, und jedesmal gibt eine neue Korrektur dem Satze mehr Einfachheit oder einen schärferen Ausdruck."[6] The fragment of an earlier working manuscript (that contains a preliminary version of verses 45-58) indicates that Heine spent even more time shaping the poem than was evident from the manuscript studied by Legras. Nevertheless, the notion that the poem is frivolous and scurrilous in its treatment of its sexual themes continues to influence readings of it and to inhibit further analysis. Alberto Destro begins his DHA commentary (1992) on "Citronia" with the cautious assertion: "Ein in seinen Intentionen vielleicht unterschätztes Gedicht." He attributes the extensive formal reworking of the poem to Heine's efforts to make the poem seem playfully light even though it deals with highly provocative subjects: "Diese sorgfältige formale Ausarbeitung (die bekanntlich bei Heine die Regel ist) läuft der provokatorisch *skurrilen* Themenstellung zuwider [emphasis added]" (DHA III/II, 1747). The choice of Strodtmann's word here is not merely coincidental, for the commentary concludes that Heine's intentions were perhaps none other than producing a poem that would counter those, such as Strodtmann, who consider its provocative and scurrile treatment of such sexual themes inappropriate for serious poetry:

> "Citronia" mag als der Versuch angesehen werden, ein wertvolles Gedicht über ein nicht nur ungewöhnliches, sondern sogar skandalöses und verpöntes Thema zu schreiben. "Citronia" ist demnach nicht nur Heines Hang zur Herausforderung, besonders auf erotischem Gebiet, zuzuordnen, sondern soll auch als poetologisches Dokument gelesen werden, das die potentielle Eignung eines jeden beliebigen, somit auch nach traditionellen Maßstäben unpassenden Sujets für die Lyrik zu verkünden. (DHA III/II, 1748)

Thus, the DHA ascribes a rather meager purpose to a text that, according to its own commentary, went through painstaking reworkings and revisions before reaching its final form.

1. "Was Citronia gewesen"

Destro's commentary does offer the right first step to a detailed reading when it points to the "Nachwort" as the key to the poem. There are a couple of obvious reasons for this. This is the only time Heine furnished a single poem with an afterword. And if there were any question whether the lines in the "Nachwort" were actually intended to be a separate poem (as Henri Julia apparently treated them), the Reinhardt manuscript puts this matter to rest.[7] Also, as one might expect from an afterword, the speaker there seems to be much closer to the author of the text as a whole than the speaker in the poem proper. Particularly from the last part of the second stanza to the end of the fourth the poetic persona is much less reflective, venting his anger at the moral codes that prohibit him from satisfying his erotic urges. The "Nachwort", on the other hand, returns to the thematic point introduced in the second stanza. The tone is not that of the wronged and suffering poet, but rather one of recollection and reassessment, one similar to the voice of the poetic persona in the first two stanzas before he became caught up in the frustrated desire to experience Citronia.

The "**Nachwort**" breaks off the poet's ranting and raving in order to reflect once more on this mysterious object of his desire. The account of Citronia in the first four stanzas is obscure and confusing, and seemingly self-contradictory. At times it appears to represent an actual physical female presence, a thinly veiled bottom whose powers of arousal go back to that innocent event in Frau Hindermans' classroom. The golden dream remains latent in the poet throughout his youth and into manhood, when it suddenly resurfaces in the flesh and fuels the young man's sexual desires. The naked bottoms, now belonging to sexually mature women, reappear in close physical vicinity and reawaken the desire:

> Ich hauche ein der holden Nähe
> Gewürzten Odem—
>
> (B VI/I, 315).

The poet has become sexually active, as indicated by "Bin ich ein Mann sogar—", and yet the fulfillment of the youthful dream remains impossible. And when the poet curses the moral standards of his day and age at the end of the fourth stanza it seems clear that Citronia spurs a sexual lust frustrated by social injunctions.

At other times, however, it stands for an ideal form of love—"Du erste Blüte meiner Minne!"—one associates with Romanticism and, in particular, with the symbol of the blue flower addressed in the "**Nachwort**". While the first stanza describes the poet's actual experiences as a young child in his first school, the second concerns the memory and visions that derive from those events. The poet calls the naked bottoms of his young schoolgirl classmates a "magical land" which he later named Citronia. His interest shifts from what he saw in Frau Hindermans' classroom to his later vision of them. Those bottoms he gazed upon in the golden sunlight became a mysterious, alluring land that then dominated his imagination:

> Es war so zärtlich ideal,
> Zitronenfarbig und oval,
> So anmutvoll und freundlich mild
> Und stolz empört zugleich—dein Bild,
>
> (B VI/I, 315).

The name he gives his fantasy stems not from the actual visual perceptions of his youth, but rather from the color he ascribes to this ideal vision. The sight of the girls' bottoms reminded him sometimes of roses, and other times of lilies or yellow violets. But the lemon color of his magical fantasy seems to have its own source, one which remains a mystery until the "**Nachwort**".

But the "**Nachwort**" also offers no clear answer to this mystery. There is the promise that we will read in another place, in clear and direct words, what Citronia is, yet he gives no clue as to where we will find the answer and whether it will come from his own pen or possibly from some future writer. He cites a maxim that, ostensibly, is supposed to help explain his secrecy:

> Unterdes—wer ihn versteht,
> Einen Meister nie verrät—
>
> (B VI/I, 316).

But the following verses divert the reader intentionally from the right path. The remaining fourteen verses of the "**Nachwort**" all allude openly to Novalis, giving rise to the notion that he is the "Meister" and holds the key to "**Citronia**". If Novalis is indeed the master to whom he is referring, then he has turned around and immediately betrayed his own stated resolve. Although Heine is capable of capricious play in poems on almost any subject, such an open contradiction of a clearly stated motto would be uncharacteristic of the consistent ethical relationship he establishes in his works between his poetic persona and the reader. If, on the other hand, his intention is to lead astray the critic who fails to take his direct word at face value, as a kind of sly and sweet revenge more typical of Heine, then this ploy remains successful even today. For the only attempt to give a possible explanation of the poem (in the DHA commentary) centers around the references to Novalis in the "**Nachwort**". One could also read the adage about the "Meister" as a self-reference, particularly since the mystery in question concerns the poet's own "Zauberland" of erotic desire. But the account of an event in Frau Hindermans' elementary school, which Heine did in fact attend, indicates that he is not the unnamed master. With the addition of the "**Nachwort**", I believe Heine not only intentionally delayed a successful reading of the poem, but even created a type of Sphinxian riddle for future critics.

If the last part of the "**Nachwort**" intentionally diverts attention away from the real master, then the question remains how the verses alluding to Novalis relate to this magical realm of Citronia. Destro's explanation of the importance of the "**Nachwort**" focuses solely on the reference to Novalis and the juxtaposition of lofty poetic themes with direct sexual content. However, the references to Novalis cite specific passages in *Heinrich von Ofterdingen* and have a closer connection to the thematic issues addressed in the poem. The blue flower, from Heinrich's dream in the opening chapter, had become the archetypal symbol of German Romanticism early in the nineteenth century and was well known. The claim that all art is, in the end, "ein blauer Dunst" is also a specific reference, one less familiar to most readers. This specific formulation appears twice in Klingsohr's *Märchen* in chapter 9 of *Heinrich von Ofterdingen,* but the blue mist also plays a similar role in Heinrich's dream in chapter I. In both cases, it stands for a state of poetic inspiration that leads to a heightened, Romanticized form of experience. In the cave scene in his dream Heinrich discovers a large basin that collects the waters of a spring and is enveloped in "ein mattes, bläuliches Licht"[8] cast off by the cave's moist walls. When he climbs into the basin he is carried away by the spring's current to the clearing with the blue flower. In the *Märchen* the basin is replaced by a bowl, whose waters dissolve into "ein blauer Dunst"[9] when they come into contact with the highly eroticized figures of Eros or his wetnurse Ginnistan.

The second appearance of "ein blauer Dunst"[10] is more directly significant for **"Citronia"**. It occurs in the lyrical insert that heralds Eros and Ginnistan on their journey. There the blue mist envelopes them and together with fantasy carries "Love" across the lands. This section of Klingsohr's *Märchen* is probably the most openly erotic passage in Novalis' writings. First, Eros' father, seeing Eros and his mother in a motionless embrace, sneaked away into his chamber with Ginnistan in order to recover in her arms from the day's toils. The verses that accompany Eros and Ginnistan like a blue mist serve as a lyrical prelude to their lovemaking. Before they consummate their physical desires, a vision appears to Eros and portrays their sexual intercourse in Romantic symbolism:

> Eine wunderschöne Blume schwamm glänzend auf den sanften Wogen. [. . .] Ein Lilienblatt bog sich über den Kelch der schwimmenden Blume; die kleine Fabel sass auf demselben, und sang zur Harfe die süssesten Lieder. In dem Kelch lag Eros selbst, über ein schönes schlummerndes Mädchen hergebeugt, die ihn fest umschlungen hielt. Eine kleinere Blüte schloss sich um beide her, so dass sie von Hüften an in *eine* Blume verwandelt zu sein schienen.[11]

The direct question Heine poses in the **"Nachwort"** refers not just to the more general symbol of the blue flower, but to this particular scene:

> Was war jene Blume, welche
> Weiland mit dem blauen Kelche
> So romantisch süss geblüht
> In des Ofterdingen Lied?
>
> (B VI/I, 317)

And the answer is given in the *Märchen* itself in no uncertain terms when immediately after the vision Eros and Ginnistan retire to a secluded bath where she leads him into manhood: "Sie führte ihn zu einem abgelegenen Bade, zog ihm die Rüstung aus, und zog selbst ein Nachtkleid an, in welchem sie fremd und verführerisch aussah. Eros tauchte sich in die gefährlichen Wellen, und stieg berauscht wieder heraus. Ginnistan trocknete ihn, und rieb seine starken von Jugendkraft gespannten Glieder".[12]

There is obviously a correspondence between the sexual desires described in **"Citronia"** and the erotic episodes in *Heinrich von Ofterdingen.* But it remains unclear what more specific connections would cause Heine to allude to these passages in Novalis' works. One could argue that he added the **"Nachwort"** as an afterthought, concerned that he was too daring or provocative in his treatment of sexual themes. However, his concern about possible objections seems to go beyond just the open discussion of sexuality. His poem not only associates the ideal realm of poetic vision with carnal desires, but even suggests that the etheral poetic (Romantic) imagination has its roots in primary sexual instincts. It contends that Novalis' blue

flower, like his own Citronia must have had its origins in some formative sexual event. The most sublime symbol that inspired an entire generation of German Romantics owes its favored status to an erotic fixation on some incidental blue object! Such a notion, although now commonplace for those familiar at all with Freudian psychology, would have given many cause to doubt the sanity of its author in the middle of the nineteenth century. Thus Heine closes the **"Nachwort"** with an ambiguous flourish that one could interpret as a disavowal of the strange claim he has just made—"Firlefanz!" Is this intended as a disclaimer for the wild notions he presents in the poem and the **"Nachwort"**? Or does it mean that, in the end, all art is indeed nothing more than "ein blauer Dunst"? Or, in the opposite vein, that this revelation, even though true, should not affect the worth and importance of art?

While Heine alludes openly to Novalis and suggests, even if cautiously and ambiguously, that all Romantic poetry has origins similar to those of Citronia, he guards actively against disclosing exactly what Citronia is. The lemon-like color seems, as I have argued above, to be arbitrary. Or rather, it would be arbitrary if it referred to the colors the poet associated with the actual naked bottoms of Frau Hindermans' young girls. But in actuality it refers to the ideal image that replaced those original physical objects of desire. The color betrays that the actual point of reference is not the *blue* flower of Novalis' Romantic novel. The name Citronia refers not to the color, but to the object that in German literature came to symbolize an idealized *Zauberland* beyond the Alps: "Kennst du des Land, wo die Zitronen blühen?" It stands here first of all for that ideal vision which inspires every artist or poet, but more specifically as well for the particular form of "blauer Dunst" created by the master poet of German idealism whose persona had always been integral in Heine's attempts to forge his own art and poetic identity. The unnamed master of the **"Nachwort"**, the same literary figure who lurked behind every attempt of Heine's generation to create its own artistic vision, is of course Goethe. In his usual slyly provocative manner, Heine provides another clue to the master of Citronia even as he swears its secrecy:

> Unterdes—wer ihn versteht,
> Einen [Wilhelm] Meister nie verrät—.

Who else is this master than the author of *Wilhelm Meisters Lehrjahre,* the master German poet whose vision of "das Land, wo die Zitronen blühen" (Citronia) represents for Heine the very essence of the "Kunstperiode"?. . .

. . . . .

3. Sexuality, Desire, and Self-Deception

[Heine's] ambivalence toward Goethe remained unresolved as it gradually took a backseat to more pressing concerns after [he] left Germany in 1831. As his reputation grew and censorship became a persistent problem after 1835 there were more immediate and ominous foes at hand than the artistic autonomy of the "Kunstperiode". When he takes up this theme again in **"Citronia"** it is within a whole new context. After the failed revolution of 1848 and the dramatic turn for the worse with his health he began to question his own political involvement which had formed the backdrop for his criticism of Goethe. In fact, the motto poem to **"Hebräische Melodien"** in *Romanzero* recommends a practical approach to life similar to the one he had criticized so strongly in Goethe:

> O lass nicht ohne Lebensgenuss
> Dein Leben verfliessen!
> Und bist du sicher vor dem Schuss,
> So lass sie nur schiessen.
>
> Fliegt dir das Glück vorbei einmal
> So fass es am Zipfel.
> Auch rat ich dir, baue dein Hüttchen im Tal
> Und nicht auf dem Gipfel.
>
> (B VI/I, 124)

When he addresses Goethe's idealized view of Italy once more in **"Citronia"**, his enthusiasm for revolutionary change gives way to a reflective, retrospective analysis of the poetic psyche, one that includes the classical (Goethe) and Romantic (Novalis) genius, as well as, of course, his own ambivalent nature that oscillated between the two poles. Even where his late poetry inquires more directly into the universal nature of human desire, it still features the poetic persona that had been omnipresent in his writings as the starting point for its psycho-analysis. And if he remained true to his formula for revealing the "Signatura" of his existence, then it is only logical that this late poetry would take into account the physical side of erotic desire. For after 1848 not only did his physical condition overshadow his preoccupation with his psychic wounds, but he was convinced as well that his illness had been caused by a veneral infection and was thus a direct result of his romantic passion.[18]

Indeed, as I have already suggested, **"Citronia"** is informed throughout by the dual nature of desire, by the unavoidable conflict between sexual urges and ideal representations of the desired object. The poet's expression of his frustration reveals the impossibility of gaining satisfaction on either level. The tension between social taboo and feverous desire in the first six verses of the fourth stanza hits a sensitive point familiar in some way to every reader. The poet's bold resistance to the injunctions against the satisfaction of sexual urges,

> Es treibt mich dann, mit kecker Hand
> Die seidne Hülle abzustreifen,
> Nach meinem nackten Glück zu greifen
>
> (B VI/I, 116),

gives the sense that a basic right is being denied. In the second half of the stanza he shows contempt for the unreasonable self-denial demanded of the individual in what is ostensibly a higher form of culture. The indeterminate "aus allerlei Rücksichten" implies *ex negativo* that there is *no good reason* for such self-denial. The word "Auch" at the beginning of line 75 has no logical semantic meaning following "allerlei Rücksichten", rather serves to reinforce the tone of contempt. The ending to his protest,

> Es heilight jetzt der Sitte Codex
> Die Unantastbarkeit des Podex
>
> (B VI/I, 116),

expresses the accumulated frustration of centuries in which civilization, despite its advances, has made what seems like only half-hearted attempts to compensate for the renunciation of instincts it demands.

However, throughout his railing against the restrictions placed on him by society there is the lurking realization that the repression of instinct is a prerequisite for every form of civilization. To rail absolutely against it would be pure anarchy that soon results in gross contradictions or holds out for rights that only a privileged few could exercise. Thus, as often is the case with Heine, the poem ends with an ironic and humorous twist that trivializes the poet's own laments. However, as is also usually the case in poems with such endings, the trivilization does not debunk the poet's demands, but rather validates them as justifiable discontent with a world that ignores the individual's fundamental rights to happiness.

While the poetic persona's charges against the excessive repression of sexual desires are granted validity, the poet also reveals the deeper historical roots to the problem. The very nature of Citronia clearly distinguishes the poetic persona's desire from basic, instinctual wants. The object of his desire is several times removed from the flesh. The silken veil hides from his view[1] the glory[2] of his wonderland[3] named[4] Citronia, which itself was only an image[5] ("dein Bild") that derived from an idealized past perception[6] ("so zärtlich ideal, / Zitronenfarbig und oval") and became an aesthetic object of sublimated desire[7] ("Du erste Blüte meiner Minne!"). The author-poet has taken extensive measures to set the poetic persona's grievances off against a much clearer awareness of the real nature of (his) desire. His raging against those powers that inhibit him from fulfilling his sexual urges acts rhetorically as a foil to shed light on the real source of discontent. Even before the author-poet restores a more level-headed, reflective tone to the poem with the **"Nachwort"**, the poetic persona knows subconsciously that his more injurious complaint is not with the moral laws enforced by society. This is ultimately the soruce of his deepest frustration and the reason that he slips (at the end of the fourth stanza) into a tone of sardonic resignation. As the poet works himself up into a lather in his bitter contempt for a civilization that represses basic instincts, he blames his own age ("Nicht mehr im Geiste unsrer Zeit—"). All the while, he knows fully well that this repression has not only been internalized, but it has also changed fundamentally the nature of desire so that the immediate satisfaction of instincts no longer brings full gratification. When he compares himself to King Tantalus his frustrations are aimed at society's moral codes, but the ancient myth tells of the alienation inherent in desire itself. And when he laments that the fruit which he desires eludes him just like the drink Tantalus thirsts after, there is another, possibly intentional, allusion to Goethe:

> Der Trunk, wonach die Lippen dürsten,
> Entgleitet mir wie jenem Fürsten;

Die Frucht, die ich genösse gern,
Sie ist mir nah und doch so fern!

(B VI/I, 116)

Who is this "prince"? On one hand a simple correlative to "King" Tantalus that completes the rhyme, it also alludes to "Prince" Faust, who, in spite of the worldly power and pleasure Mephisto could grant him, remained tied to those structures of desiring that deny fulfillment. The fruit dangling above Tantalus symbolizes "the Faustian restlessness of man in history [that] shows that men are not satisfied by the satisfaction of their conscious desires".[19] Rather, those desires that propel history are unconscious and their real objects are unattainable: "Zeig mir die Frucht, die fault, eh' man sie bricht."[20]

The poetic persona's recall and discussion of his Citronia fantasy reveals a quite sophisticated analysis into the psychic system that structures desire. In some ways it functions very similarly to an analytical session, with, of course, an extra layer of conscious reworking *(Nachträglichkeit)* factored into the elaboration of the imaginary. As a poet the narrator has worked it into a literary text that is in part detached from the real psychic history of the individual's sexual development. In this respect, it functions more as a metapsychological text that examines the structural relations between real events, unconscious fantasy, and secondary reworkings of the two into coherent scenarios of desire. On the other hand, the poetic formulation of individual desire can never be totally divorced from the poet's psychic history, particularly when the central focus of the analysis is a real event in the author's life. This individual history is, however, formed to a large degree within the poetic texts that have reworked this desire into an expanded and more formally structured network of fantasy. Such poetic elaboration of desire mirrors in itself the secondary structuring that takes place within the imaginary of every individual. But it is more than just a mimetic representation in a separate realm of discourse. The poetic text is integrally interconnected with the whole complex of sexual history, dreams, daydreams, unconscious desire, etc. that constitutes the poet's life as subject. The degree to which this is true varies of course greatly among poets, but it is particularly true of a poet like Heine whose work had focused so heavily on love, sensuality and erotic desire, and whose literary texts had almost without fail inscribed his own individual subject of desire, either as an extant fictional figure or a narrative voice, or as both.

In **"Citronia"** Heine indicates how the desire incited by what he saw in Frau Hindermans' classroom became structured by his poetic reworking of it. The comparison of the small globes with different flowers derives not only from later experience, but it also invokes the meaning Heine gave to that experience in his poetry. Often in his writing these flowers are associated with particular types of women who serve as the object of the poet's desire and structure the poetic subject as other according to their particular symbolic order. The rose generally represented fiery, passionate woman, the lily woman pure and chaste, and the yellow violet the otherworldly, melancholic woman.[21] Heine describes the evolution of his Citronia fantasy, show-

ing how early sexual events determine the psychic organization of the individual in general, and in particular, how they feed into literary imagination. It is in both these senses that one is to understand the claim with which Heine begins the account of his youth in the *Memoiren*: "Aus den frühesten Anfängen erklären sich die spätesten Erscheinungen" (B VI/I, 557). In his psychic life as poet the Citronia fantasy gained particular significance as a recurring vision that structures desire. It became an ideal image that dominated his visions of happiness, much like the early Loreley legend: there, "Das kommt mir nicht aus dem Sinn" (B I, 107), and here, "Es kam mir niemals aus dem Sinne" (B VI/I, 315). Only here, to the poet's great surprise ("o Wunder"), this golden dream of youth even intercedes in his adult sexual life. The dream image takes on the corporal sensuality of the female image

Es wandelt leiblich vor mir her,
Ich hauche ein der holden Nähe
Gewürzten Odem—

(B VI/I, 315)

and still fulfillment remains out of sight

Raubt mir die süße Augenweide!

(B VI/I, 315)

and out of reach

Nach meinem nackten Glück zu greifen!

(B VI/I, 316)

It remains an ideal image ("so zärtlich ideal") that excludes its own realization even as it structures the mature adult's sexual urges.

The description of this fantasy and its significance for all forms of desire in the adult anticipates some specific aspects of Freud's theories on sexuality and psychic organization. In his structural analysis of the path libidinal energy takes through the parts of the psyche Freud describes the inner workings of sublimation: "All that we know about [the libido] relates to the ego, in which at first the whole available quota of libido is stored up. We call this state absolute, primary *narcissism.* It lasts till the ego begins to cathect the *ideas of objects* [emphasis added] with libido, to transform narcissistic libido into object-libido."[22] Heine's account of his path to the ideal object Citronia offers a poetic version of this process. That is not to say, of course, that the event in Frau Hindermans' elementary classroom constituted this psychic stage in Heine's life. Rather, **"Citronia"** gives a metaphorical scenario of this early stage of psychic development. This scenario illustrates as well how the shift from primary narcissism to the "ideas of objects" restructures desire in a fundamental way. The poet's initial fascination with the "small globes" of his classmates is playful and open-ended, unaffected by the feverish desire for the end-pleasure that drives and frustrates the mature man. The description of how their appearance shifted from that of one flower to the next mirrors the free sexual life of the infant that knows no restrictions and makes no distinctions, giving free rein to the child to explore all areas of pleasure. Again, the poet's description of this event is not, of course, an actual account of polymorphous play from his own childhood. The period of such free play is limited to only a short period during infancy when the child explores diverse pleasures on the various erogenous zones of its own body. Still, the poet's account of the early event is a memory that has obviously transposed objects or images onto its early visual perceptions. In this memory of the schoolroom experience the still undifferentiated erotic meaning of the sighting is freely interchangeable with the three flowers. In later life they appear separately, in different poems fixed as individuated objects of the poet's directed desire. These two different positions they assume in his poetic imagery represent the free erotic play of infantile sexuality on the one hand, versus the later genitally organized sexuality of the adult. The changes in his vision in the second stanza are a result of the resurfacing of the strong infantile sexuality after its long period of latency. But now it appears in reality:

> Der goldne Traum der Kinderzeit
> Taucht wieder auf in Wirklichkeit!
>
> (B VI/I, 315).

In Freudian terms, the reality principle has taken over and suppressed the pleasure principle dominant in early childhood, supplanting the polymorphous perversity of infancy with a genitally organized sexuality.

Now there is a, if not single, at least predominant object of the sex *drive,* one that intensifies the desire because it is for the most part a forbidden object:

> Ein Vorhang von schwarzbrauner Seide
> Raubt mir die süße Augenweide!
>
> (B VI/I, 315).

But in the context of the poem the thin veil of silk represents much more than just the social injunction against free sexual intercourse. It is that form of sexual organization in civilization that relegates the free polymorphous play experienced in early childhood to a golden dream of past pleasure. Thus, when at the end of the fourth stanza the poet curses the moral codes that restrict sexual activity, the tone of sardonic resignation reveals an underlying awareness that the "free love" he demands can not alleviate the frustration caused by the repression of sexual instincts.[23] But by setting off the frustrations of the sexually mature adult against the true nature of (erotic) desire, the third and fourth stanzas also reflect on the universal change this psychic process has brought to bear on human kind. When the "ideas of objects" replace the actual objects of instinctual (primarily sexual) wants the prohibitions enacted by civilization have become internalized and the instincts are superseded by the exclusively human form of desire. The thin weblike veil that covers, but also intimates the availability of the poet's glorious object of desire represents the firmly entrenched network of displacement that relegates our instinctual needs to (and alienates them in) a cultural realm of pleasure.[24] It, like the myth of Tantalus in the next stanza, signifies how the immediate

satisfaction of our sexual wants is no longer possible, regardless of how permissive a society may be.

The oscillation in the poem between this understanding of desire and the conviction that the easing of sexual renunciation would reduce mankind's psychic frustrations seems to indicate conceptual equivocation on Heine's part. But I would argue rather that he pursues his analysis exhaustively to the point where he had to accept this apparent contradiction. When the poem oscillates between desire (over)determined by ideal representations and the demands for sexual gratification it touches on a central problem area in psychoanalytical theory. Both Freud and his various successors have struggled to account for the development of both psychical re-presentation (fantasy) and biological function (sexual urges) in a manner consonant with these very different forms of experience. Freud employed the still incompletely defined notion of anaclictic object choice *(Anlehnung)* to describe the decisive moment when the primal condition is disturbed and human psychic life begins to take shape. In its genesis, the sexual urge to form a union with objects in the world follows the pattern of ("leans up against") the basic self-preservation instincts—feeding, dependence, protection. Freud's early conceptual picture of this early, anaclictic development of object-choice is complicated by its dual nature, by the distinction between a "pure" anaclictic object-choice, where the erotic aim is to possess the object, and a narcissistic object-choice, where it is to identify with the object.[25]

The difficulty in mapping the development of the ego in this transitional realm where sexual function and fantasy overlap has consequences not only for the analysis of the origins of human sexuality, but also for the therapy that might abate the discontent it creates. Again, **"Citronia"** speaks to both these aspects. In the first two stanzas it points to a common origin for the psychical and biological realms of sexuality. And the third and fourth stanzas suggest that this dualism complicates the satisfaction of such wants in both realms. Still, the poem clearly indicates that this does not in any way lessen the need to emancipate mankind from the overzealous prohibitions against sensual and sexual pleasures. However, it also implies that an enlightened understanding of the role fantasy and ideal representations play in the fulfillment of desire is equally important for treating mankind's neurotic compulsion. Indeed, the **"Nachwort"** ultimately concludes that desire, even where it is almost totally alienated from the physical object, also demands "fulfillment" and that this fulfillment is to be found in the ideal representation of the wish fantasy. This is the sense of the final line that warns the reader not to take the revelations about Citronia as a condemnation of the poetic visions of Goethe or the Romantics—nor to dismiss out of hand the idealist art of his/her own age.

"Citronia" has, I believe, even more to say about this dualistic nature of desire. While Freud was able to show the integral role that a previously denied, yet rampant infantile sexuality plays in our psychic organization, the question of its origin remained a thorny one in his metapsychological theories until the end. He seems to waver between the belief in a biological reality behind the elaborations of fantasy, and the idea that the primal fantasies in the unconscious are autonomous from any ontogenetic event in the infantile sexual life and responsible for the structuring of the psyche. Ultimately, he posited the existence of primal fantasies in the unconscious that often could not be traced back to either an individual's sexual or psychical history. The only explanation he could offer was phylogenesis. From *Totem and Taboo* in 1913 to *Moses and Monotheism* near the end of his life, Freud hypothesized that our fantasies derive from real events that occurred in a primeval past. It is this perceived need "to postulate an organization made of signifiers anteceding the effect of the event and the signified as a whole"[26] which has caught the fancy of a whole line of neo-structuralist thinkers ready and willing to appropriate the results of Freud's psychoanalytical investigations for their own systems of belief. This is not the place to become embroiled in what has become an enormously complicated debate spanning a growing number of academic fields. However, before asking what Heine may have to say about these questions, it would be wise to heed a warning Jean Laplanche and Jean-Bertrand Pontalis offered in the context of their own more confined and also more cautiously formulated revision of Freud's views on "Fantasy and the Origins of Sexuality":

> It is tempting to accept the 'reality' which inspires the work of imagination according to its own laws, as a prefiguration of the 'symbolic order' defined by Lévi-Strauss and Lacan in the ethnological and psychoanalytical fields respectively. [. . .] However we should not be in a hurry to replace the phylogenic explanation by a structural type of explanation. The original fantasy is first and foremost fantasy—it lies beyond the history of the subject but nevertheless in history—a kind of language and a symbolic sequence, but loaded with elements of imagination; a structure, but activated by contingent elements.[27]

While to this point the emphasis here has been on the ontogenetic investigations in "**Citronia**", there is another level to the metaphor of "der dumme Lappen" that conceals our nakedness. The poet curses first the worm that spun the silk and the weaver, man, who wove the taffeta that conceals both mankind's nature and its self-deception. In his late writing Heine frequently uses clothes as a metaphor for this self-deception that alienates mankind from the rest of nature, including its own human nature. At times the clothes metaphor either appears in conjunction with other figures of speech that represent language or stands itself for language. As a writer whose life and identity was informed in a conscious manner by that metaphorical language which retells and in part structures fantasy, Heine was always concerned with the ability of language to state the truth (or better, history) of our psychic condition. The self-reflective references to such language use in the late writings almost invariably characterize it as a practice in self-deception. Possibly the most dramatic such characterization of his own literary work with language comes at the end of "**Der Scheidende**", a verse fragment closely related to both "**Sie erlischt**" in *Romanzero* and the "**Epilog**" poem of *Gedichte. 1853 und 1854.*[28] As in "**Sie**

erlischt**", the poet takes leave of his "liebes deutsches Publikum", paraphrasing—as he does in "**Epilog**"—Homer's Achilles:

> Der kleinste lebendige Philister
> Zu Stukkert am Neckar, viel glücklicher ist er
> Als ich, der Pelide, der tote Held,
> Der Schattenfürst in der Unterwelt.
>
> (B VI/I, 350)

In "**Der Scheidende**" the allusion to the poet's life in the world of language is more obvious than in either of the published poems on the same theme. The underworld refers here to that realm of language in which he sought his fame and fortune, carved out his very identity, and gained his happiness or suffered his demise. But, as one would expect from Heine, these parting words contain an irony which counteracts his express regret that he had missed the boat in life. The unspoken, but everpresent truth about human existence is that revealed in "**Citronia**"—the desire that (pre)determines our fulfillments and our failures is relegated to this underworld of language, and our life "as we know it" exists only in this realm. All human existence is prefigured by the fall from paradise into the self-deceptive structures of language and dialectical thought,

> den Taft,
> Woraus der dunkle schauderhaft
> Infame Vorhang ward gemacht,
>
> (B VI/I, 316)

4. "Unterdes—wer ihn versteht,

Einen Meister nie verrät"

In the end, we return again to the question why Heine left the reference to Goethe shrouded in mystery. In some ways, it seems as if the analysis into desire exhibited in "**Citronia**" might have helped resolve the ambivalence Heine had always shown toward him. The concept of sublimation laid out in blueprint form in "**Citronia**" reveals a basic antagonism between the human animal and its culture, one that might justify withdrawal from the world stage. If mankind can neither find complete gratification through sublimation nor revert from this sublimation back to an adequate satisfaction of instinctual urges, then this leaves serious doubts about human nature that threaten the very existence of civilization. For an answer the poem defers to a future point in time when scientific analysis will have explained the structures of the psyche and their historical development. In his late treatises on civilization, Freud too left open the question of mankind's ability to deal with the tension created by the repression of instincts. At the beginning of *Future of an Illusion* he points to this central question for the future of humanity: "The decisive question is whether and to what extent it is possible to lessen the burden of the instinctual sacrifices imposed on men, to reconcile men to those which must necessarily remain and to provide a compensation for them."[29] One finds in "**Citronia**" the same conviction that a combination of these two approaches is necessary. The poet must accept the irreversible fact of alienated desire, but maintains as well the importance of progressing toward a more liberal moral order that would "lessen the burden of the instinctual sacrifices."

In this regard, Goethe's artistic re-presentation of the world as whole and intact provides one form of compensation that reconciles the individual to the sacrifices he/she must make on behalf of civilization. Novalis' blue flower that heightens the longing for the object of desire (but also consigns gratification to a utopian realm of the imaginary) offers similar compensation, and is defended in the **"Nachwort"**. But Heine accords a special status to the unnamed master for the same reasons that he had sworn unfailing allegiance "zum Goetheschen Freykorps" in the 1820s. In its health and wholeness Goethe's "Blume, die, im Miste unserer Zeit, immer blühender gedeihen wird" (B I, 455) constituted an anachronistic way of thinking, one free of the sickness that, in Heine's view, afflicted his age: "Dieser würdevolle Leib war nie gekrümmt von christlicher Wurmdemut" (B III, 405). In **"Citronia"**, however, he seems to associate Goethe less with an age that predated the pathogenic split between body and spirit, and to see him rather as an embodiment of those emotional and intellectual advances which civilization has yet to make. This, too, Heine had already suggested indirectly in the early *Reisebilder,* when he maintained that a later generation would be able to see "wie gesund, einheitlich und plastisch sich Goethe in seinen Werken zeigt" (B II, 221). In this sense, Goethe's works function for Heine as more than just compensation for instinctual renunciation, they present the constructed visions of an intact and resourceful psyche that is able to enjoy physical pleasures *and* compensate itself for the lack experienced in the structured fantasies of its own imaginary.

This final positive view of Goethe also raises the question of how Heine assessed his own work at the end. While he had praised Goethe's ability to set aside his subjective impulses and to represent the world as it is, he himself had always adhered to another aesthetic principle, "wo der Autor so treu sein eignes Bild abspiegelt" (B VI/I, 488). Not only was this approach true to his own desires and frustrations, but it was also part of an oppositional aesthetic strategy that incriminates the social order for its failure to deal justly with the instinctual sacrifices it requires. When he was accused after 1848 of betraying his liberal beliefs, Heine responded that politically "verharrte [ich] bei denselben demokratischen Prinzipien, denen meine früheste Jugend huldigte und für die ich seitdem immer flammender erglühte" (B VI/I, 184). The claims of betrayal were to a large degree an extension of a misunderstanding that had followed him since his earliest political engagement. Both his allies and his opponents had continually tried to connect him with political ideas and goals he had consistently and adamantly rejected. His primary political concern had always been mankind's emancipation from the oppressive and unnecessary renunciation of sensuality. His focus in **"Citronia"** is consistent with that cause which he had represented steadfastly in his writing—the rehabilitation of the flesh in a rational social organization liberated from the chains of privilege.[30]

While **"Citronia"** offers no utopian hope of reconciling instinctual urges with desire, the **"Nachwort"** does display a guarded optimism in scientific inquiry. It does seem to suggest that through increased knowledge of the human psyche and the history of repression the libido will gain its legitimate place in a highly civilized society, one that offers gratification in the here and now rather than demanding surplus repression in exchange for promises of gratification in a utopian future or an imaginary paradise beyond life. If this is true, then it expresses a faith and a goal very similar to those expressed by Freud in his polemic against the religious opponents of psychoanalysis: "We [those who believe in *logos*] believe that it is possible for scientific work to gain some knowledge about the reality of the world, by means of which we can increase our power and in accordance with which we can arrange our life."[31] One can even read the opening lines of the **"Nachwort"** as a prophecy that correctly anticipates Freud:

> Unverblümt, an andern Orten,
> Werdet Ihr in klaren Worten
> Später ganz ausführlich lesen,
> Was Citronia gewesen.
>
> (B VI/I, 116)

Thus, in its own less revolutionary manner **"Citronia"** too calls for the end of "das alte Entsagungslied" (B IV, 577). But his late poetry no longer evokes images of the cloaked executioner who accompanies his words with an axe and turns the poet's thoughts into bloody deeds (*Deutschland, Ein Wintermärchen,* Caput VI-VII). Rather here the poet-author looks ahead to a gradual and inevitable change that will occur as the individual demands the liberation of the sexual instincts from an excess repression which only serves to solidify the unjust privileges of those who reap its benefits. In this respect, it reflects the same revolutionary spirit expressed in *Deutschland, Ein Wintermärchen*:

> Wir wollen hier auf Erden schon
> Das Himmelreich errichten.
>
> Wir wollen auf Erden glücklich sein,
> Und wollen nicht mehr darben;
>
> (B IV, 578)

Even those late poems that depict mankind's alienation in a system of representation (re-presented desire) most pessimistically hold out hope for betterment. When the departing poet (**"Der Scheidende"**) calls himself a "Schattenfürst" and questions his lifelong engagement in the underworld of language, it happens only as he is severing all his ties to this life. Only when his words remain behind without any individual investment in the economy of pain and pleasure does he become the "Schattenfürst der Unterwelt", in whom only death lives—"Und in mir lebt nur noch der Tod!" (B VI/I, 349). But that which dies last in him reveals that his poetry does not exert its force only in a shadow world:

> Erstorben ist in meiner Brust
> Jedwede weltlich eitle Lust,

Schier ist mir auch erstorben drin
Der Haß des Schlechten, sogar der Sinn
Für eigne wie für fremde Not—

(B VI/I, 349).

What had motivated the poet Heine to the end was the power of words not only to compensate for human distress, but also to lessen it.

Thus the poet ("der tote Held") departs knowing that his battles were fought for those least heroic Philistines who know to avoid such strife and enjoy what life has to offer. It is, I believe, this final reservation that always kept him from betraying the master poet who chose practical reason over the delayed gratification promised for heroic devotion to a cause. This is the same ambivalence Heine had always felt both in his own make-up and in his earlier criticism of Goethe. It was because of "angeborene Neigung zur Schwärmerey" (HSA XX, 200) that, against his own better judgment, he continually engaged in the struggle for "die Emanzipation der ganzen Welt [. . .] von dem eisernen Gängelbande der Bevorrechteten" (B II, 376). But in this same passage, where he declared this emancipation to be the great task of his age, he also points out the paradox involved in any such activism. As he looks out over the battlefield at Marengo in *Reise von München nach Genua,* he asks:

> Aber ach! jeder Zoll, den die Menschheit weiter rückt, kostet Ströme Blutes; und ist das nicht etwas zu teuer? Ist das Leben des Individuums nicht vielleicht eben so viel wert wie das des ganzen Geschlechtes? Denn jeder einzelne Mensch ist schon eine Welt, die mit ihm geboren wird und mit ihm stirbt, unter jedem Grabstein liegt eine Weltgeschichte—Still davon, so würden die Toten sprechen, die hier gefallen sind, wir aber leben und wollen weiter kämpfen im heiligen Befreiungskriege der Menschheit. (B II, 378)

In the end, from Heine's personal point of view, it remains the prerogative of the dead (**"Der Scheidende"**) to raise this objection. But he was also willing to accept this dictate to fight against unjust privilege as an aspect of his own personal psychic need and not a universal imperative. Ultimately the individual right to choose to participate in this struggle for more freedom, or not, is the very principle for which he had fought. True to his lifelong commitment to democratic principles, he gave high priority to individual desire even in the political arena. For this reason, he refuses in **"Citronia"** to betray the unnamed master whose literary vision and life choices remained in accordance with his desire and were consistent with the belief that each individual life is its own world history.

Notes

1 The only existing manuscript in Heine's handwriting is an earlier working version of lines 45-58.

2 Adolf Strodtmann: "Vorwort des Herausgebers". In: Heinrich Heine: *Letzte Gedichte und Gedanken* (Hamburg: Hoffmann and Campe, 1869), XV.

3 Strodtmann [Anm. 2], XVI.

4 Jonas Fränkel: "Anmerkungen". In: W III, 531.

5 Anton Englert: "Heines Beiträge zu Schads Almanach". In: *Vierteljahrsschrift für Litteraturgeschichte* 5.2 (1892): 315-328; and Jules Legras: "Heinrich Heine in Paris". In: *Deutsche Rundschau* 79 (1894): 348-371; cp. the commentary in the DHA III/II, 1744.

6 Legras [Anm. 5], 353.

7 Legras' article based on the working copy of the poem in Heine's handwriting indicates that the "Nachwort" was a part of the poem at an early stage of its development; see Legras [Anm. 5], 353-354.

8 Novalis: *Heinrich von Ofterdingen.* In: *Schriften. Das Werk Friedrich von Hardenbergs.* Ed. Paul Kluckhohn and Richard Samuel. Vol. I (Stuttgart: Kohlhammer 1960), 196.

9 Novalis [Anm. 8], 294.

10 Novalis [Anm. 8], 297.

11 Novalis [Anm. 8], 300.

12 Novalis [Anm. 8], 300.

18 See Gerhard Höhn: *Heine Handbuch: Zeit, Person, Werk* (Stuttgart, Metzler, 1987), 114; and Joseph A. Kruse: "Heinrich Heine—urologisch gelesen". *NBP* 1 (1994), 18-19.

19 Norman O. Brown: *Life Against Death: The Psychoanalytical Meaning of History* (Hanover, NH: Wesleyan University Press, 1959), 18.

20 Johann Wolfgang Goethe: *Faust. Eine Tragödie.* In: *Goethes Werke.* Ed. Erich Trunz. Vol. III, 10th ed. (München: C. H. Beck, 1976), 56.

21 Heine employs each of these flowers in other ways as well, but in connection with women the typology I offer seems to hold consistently. In poems VI-XXXVI in *Neuer Frühling* the rose and the lily appear a number of times representing the love relations I mention (B IV, 301-315). As one would expect from Heine, the rose symbolizing passionate love is more common by far both in this group of poems and throughout his writing. The lily also occurs frequently; two additional passages which show clearly the connection to pure and chaste love can be found in *Schnabelewopski* (BI, 611-612) and in the poem "Wechsel" in *Neue Gedichte* (BIV, 388-389). Violets, usually assumed to be blue unless specifically designated as yellow, also appear as the third main flower in this section of *Neuer Frühling,* but as blue violets they connote blue eyes and loyalty. The much less common yellow violet is usually associated with death, and in the case of a specific woman or type of woman it seems to indicate an otherworldy aura. One such occurrence is in the bedroom where the narrator views the corpse of the mysterious Maria in *Reise von München nach Genua* (B II, 367). In another, I believe unique, case that is possibly most closely associated to the use in "Citronia", Heine refers to a fire-yellow violet. This is in the Lazarus cycle of *Gedichte. 1853 und 1854* where the poet regrets that he arrogantly ignored many women ("Blumen") in his life with whom he could have enjoyed a relation, and in particular one fire-yellow violet—apparently a young woman whose melancholic nature gave her a sultry appeal (B VI/I, 203).

22 Sigmund Freud: *An Outline of Psycho-Analysis.* In: *The Standard Edition of the Complete Psychological Works.* Vol. XXIII, trans. James

Strachey (London: Hogarth Press, 1964), 150. [Hereafter cited as SE.]

[23] Freud argued this same point in response to those followers (most notably Wilhelm Reich, but also Karl Abraham and Otto Fenichel) who used psychoanalysis to advocate that the freer pursuit of genital intercourse and sexual orgasm were crucial to the solution of mankind's physical and social problems. See Norman O. Brown [Anm. 19], 29.

[24] Cp. Max Horkheimer and Theodor W. Adorno: "Natur kennt nicht eigentlich Genuß: sie bringt es nicht weiter als zur Stillung des Bedürfnisses. Alle Lust ist gesellschaftlich in den unsublimierten Affekten nicht weniger als in den sublimierten." In: *Dialektik der Aufklärung* (Frankfurt a.M.: Fischer, 1969), 112.

[25] See Freud's [Anm. 22] discussion of these concepts in "On Narcissism" (SE XIV, 87-88) and part III of "The Ego and the Id" (SE XIX, 28-39).

[26] Jean Laplanche and Jean-Bertrand Pontalis, "Fantasy and the Origins of Sexuality". In: *Formations of Fantasy*. Ed. Victor Burgin, et. al., (New York: Metheun, 1986), 17.

[27] Laplanche and Pontalis [Anm. 26], 17-18.

[28] Apparently Heine worked on this text first at the same time he was preparing the "Lazarus" cycle of *Romanzero*, and then again while putting together the collection *Gedichte. 1853 und 1854*. In each case it seems he abandoned work on it because it contained lines that coincided closely with first "Sie erlischt" and then with "Epilog". Strodtmann restored two sections of the text that Heine had marked out (B VI/I, 349, ll. 1-6, and 350, ll. 13-18), apparently in an attempt to reform the poem using formulations distinct from those already published. In doing so, Strodtmann followed Heine's corrections in the manuscripts, except for those in the latest version where Heine began a rewriting of the fragment which he then gave up. Thus the characterization of Strodtmann's version (which was taken up by the later editions, including Brieglebʼs, to which I am referring here) as "eine Kontamination aus verschiedenen Arbeitsstufen" (DHA III/II, 1504) is justified with respect to Heine's intentions for a finished, publishable poem. But it is also clear that the three sections of the poem in Strodtmann's version (ll. 1-6, ll. 7-12, and ll. 13-18) belonged together as a complete, although unfinished poem at the time Heine was compiling *Gedichte. 1853 und 1854*. For this reason, I feel justified in reading the poem as a whole.

[29] Freud [Anm. 22], SE XXI, 7.

[30] See here the famous passage in chapter 29 of *Reise von München nach Genua* (B VI/I, 376-378).

[31] Freud [Anm. 22], *The Future of an Illusion*, SE XXI, 55.

FURTHER READING

Biography

Brod, Max. *Heinrich Heine: The Artist in Revolt*. Translated by Joseph Witriol. New York: New York University Press, 1957, 355 p.

A comprehensive biography that approaches Heine's life and work through an awareness of his German-Jewish background.

Hofrichter, Laura. *Heinrich Heine*. Translated by Barker Fairley. Oxford: Oxford at the Clarendon Press, 1963, 174 p.

Critical biography that emphasizes the importance of Heine's later poetry.

Kossoff, Philip. *Valiant Heart: A Biography of Heinrich Heine*. New York: Cornwall Books, 1983, 217 p.

Offers extensive biographical background concerning the composition of Heine's works.

Pawel, Ernst. *The Poet Dying: Heinrich Heine's Last Years in Paris*. New York: Farrar, Straus and Giroux, 1995, 277 p.

Biography primarily focused on Heine's place in the historical upheavals of nineteenth-century Germany and on the literary output of his final, ailing years.

Spann, Memo. *Heine*. London: Bowes and Bowes, 1966, 111 p.

Studies Heine as a German and a Jew. Concludes with an evaluation of Heine's place in literary criticism.

Winegarten, Renee. "Revolutionary Desires and Fears: Heine." In her *Writers and Revolution: The Fatal Lure of Action*, pp. 113-26. New York: New Viewpoints, 1974.

A sympathetic portrait of Heine as a prominent figure in an era of great social unrest.

Zantop, Susanne. "1844: After a Self-Imposed Exile in Paris, Heinrich Heine writes *Deutschland: Ein Wintermärchen*." In *Yale Companion to Jewish Writing and Thought in German Culture 1096-1996*, edited by Sander L. Gilman and Jack Zipes, pp. 178-85. New Haven, Conn.: Yale University Press, 1997.

Views *Deutschland: Ein Wintermärchen* as demonstrating a turning point in Heine's perception of the German government.

Criticism

Block, Haskell M. "Heine and the French Symbolists." In *Creative Encounter: Festschrift for Herman Salinger*, edited by Leland R. Phelps, pp. 25-39. Chapel Hill: The University of North Carolina Press, 1978.

Discusses Heine's profound influence on the French Symbolist poets of the mid and late nineteenth century.

Bodi, Leslie. "Heinrich Heine: The Poet as *Frondeur*," in *Intellectuals and Revolution: Socialism and the Experience of 1848*, edited by Eugene Kamenka and F. B. Smith, pp. 43-60. London: Edward Arnold, 1979.

Explores the relationship of Heine's writings to the revolutionary atmosphere of mid nineteenth-century Germany.

Chase, Jefferson S. "Lying in Swift's *Gulliver's Travels* and Heine's *Atta Troll*." *Comparative Literature* 45, No. 4 (Fall

1993): 330-45.

Argues that the complex satire of Heine's poem *Atta Troll* extends beyond its ostensible subjects to additionally ridicule its readers and the notion of reading for edification.

Fairley, Barker. *Heinrich Heine: An Interpretation.* Oxford: Oxford at the Clarendon Press, 1954, 176 p.

An important study of Heine's imagery.

Hueppe, Frederick E. *Unity and Synthesis in the Work of Heinrich Heine.* Bern: Peter Lang, 1979, 68 p.

Reevaluation of Heine's poetry that emphasizes "the harmony of integration and consistency of thought" revealed in his works.

Holub, Robert C. "Heinrich Heine and the Slave Trade: Cultural Repression and the Persistence of History." *The German Quarterly* 65, Nos. 3-4 (Summer-Fall 1992): 328-39.

Probes Heine's skilled and incisive critique of the dehumanizing and hypocritical New World slave trade in his poem "Das Sklavenschiff."

Justis, Diana Lynn. *The Feminine in Heine's Life and Oeuvre: Self and Other.* New York: Peter Lang, 1997, 247 p.

Analyzes the marginalized feminine in Heine's writings.

Peters, Paul. "*Ergriffenheit* and *Kritik:* or, Decolonizing Heine." *Monatshefte für deutschen Unterricht, deutsche Sprache und Literatur* 89, No. 3 (Fall 1997): 285-306.

Examines the legacy of anti-Semitism in criticism of Heine's poetry.

Prawer, S. S. *Heine: 'Buch der Lieder.'* London: Edward Arnold, 1960, 64 p.

Attempts to assess Heine's poetic achievement in *Book of Songs,* considering themes such as escape and return, nature, and the divided self.

———. *Heine the Tragic Satirist: A Study of the Later Poetry 1827-1856.* Cambridge: Cambridge at the University Press,

1961, 315 p.

Focuses on theme, style, and irony in Heine's poetic work after *Book of Songs.*

Preisendanz, Wolfgang. "Bridging the Gap Between Heine the Poet and Heine the Journalist." In *New Perspectives in German Literary Criticism: A Collection of Essays,* edited by Richard E. Amacher and Victor Lange, pp. 225-59. Princeton, N. J.: Princeton University Press, 1979.

Traces the revolutionary element in Heine's prose to his blending of poetry and journalism.

Sachs, H. B. *Heine in America.* Philadelphia: Publications of the University of Pennsylvania, 1916, 193 p.

Studies early American assessments of Heine's work and considers his influence on American literature.

Salinger, Herman. "Helping Heinrich Heine Explain His Archetypal 'Night Journey' Poem." *Literature and Psychology* XIII, No. 1 (Winter 1963): 30-36.

Observes the mythical and psychological resonances of Heine's poem "Nächtliche Fahrt."

Sammons, Jeffrey L. "Hunting Bears and Trapping Wolves: *Atta Troll* and *Deutschland. Ein Wintermärchen.*" In *Heinrich Heine: Artistik und Engagement,* edited by Wolfgang Kuttenkeuler, pp. 105-17. Stuttgart: J. B. Metzler, 1977.

Compares Heine's political satires *Atta Troll* and *Deutschland: Ein Wintermärchen,* finding *Atta Troll* to be the more complex and aesthetically coherent poem.

Veit, Philipp F. "Heine's Imperfect Muses in *Atta Troll:* Biographical Romance or Literary Symbolism?" *The Germanic Review* XXXIX (1964): 262-80.

Evaluates evidence of autobiographical reference and mythological allusion in the Witches' Sabbath portion of Heine's *Atta Troll.*

Wikoff, Jerold. *Heinrich Heine: A Study of 'Neue Gedichte.'* Bern: Herbert Lang, 1975, 90 p.

Contends that *New Poems* is a "varied yet single and cohesive poetic cycle."

N. Scott Momaday
1934-

(Full name Navarre Scott Momaday; also rendered as Navarro and Novarro) American novelist, poet, autobiographer, nonfiction writer, editor, artist, and children's writer.

INTRODUCTION

Of Kiowa descent, Momaday is widely recognized as a seminal figure in both Native American and mainstream American literature. Considered a major influence by numerous native writers, he has garnered critical acclaim for his focus on Kiowa traditions, customs, beliefs, and the role of Native Americans in contemporary society. Although highly regarded for the novel *House Made of Dawn* (1968), winner of the 1969 Pulitzer Prize for fiction, Momaday considers himself primarily a poet and notes that his writings are greatly influenced by the oral tradition and typically concern man's relationship to the earth, the importance of heritage and dreams, the elusive nature of reality, and the nature and origins of Native American myths.

Biographical Information

Born in Lawton, Oklahoma, to Alfred Morris and Mayme Natachee Scott, Momaday is of Kiowa, white, and Cherokee ancestry. His father was a Kiowa artist and educator whose work has often been featured in Momaday's books. Although primarily of white descent, Momaday's mother, who was also an educator, strongly identified with her Cherokee roots—even dressing in native clothes and adopting the name "Little Moon." Her advocacy of "self-imagining" as a means of achieving native identity is considered a basic premise of Momaday's writings. During his early years, Momaday moved about the American Southwest with his parents, who eventually settled on the Jemez Pueblo reservation in New Mexico. He attended a military school in Virginia, the University of New Mexico, and Stanford University where he worked under the guidance of American critic and poet Yvor Winters, (who strongly influenced his early poetry.) Momaday published his first poem, "Earth and I Give You Turquoise," in 1959 in the *New Mexico Quarterly*. He later gained widespread critical attention after winning the Pulitzer Prize for *House Made of Dawn*. A member of the Gourd Dance Society and an accomplished artist, Momaday has taught at numerous schools, including Stanford, the University of Arizona-Tucson, and the University of California-Berkeley where he was instrumental in instituting a Native American literature program.

Major Works of Poetry

Momaday's verse is collected in *Angle of Geese* (1974), *The Gourd Dancer* (1976), and *In the Presence of the Sun* (1993). In *Angle of Geese,* which contains eighteen poems, Momaday utilizes iambic verse, short-line free verse, and prose poems to explore such themes as identity, death, native customs, survival, and philosophical issues regarding nature. One of the best-known poems in the volume, "The Bear," is written in syllabic verse and is influenced by American writer William Faulkner's short story of the same name. In this poem, Momaday uses abstract language to describe an old, maimed bear. Another descriptive poem written in syllabic verse, "Buteo Regalis" utilizes rhythmic language to reflect a hawk's movements as it attacks its prey. "Before an Old Painting of the Crucifixion," a poem that describes a person contemplating a mural of Christ's crucifixion located in an old mission by the sea, is filled with post-symbolist imagery and explores the ways people react to death. "Angle of Geese," a difficult and obscure poem, is considered a masterpiece of syllabic rhythm. In this work, Momaday relates the death of a friend's first-born child to the killing of a goose by a hunter in order to address the inadequacy of language, its relationship to identity, and mysteries of time and nature. *Angle of Geese* also contains Momaday's four "Plainview" poems: "Plainview 1" is a modified sonnet and describes the approach of a storm in Oklahoma; "Plainview 2" utilizes Native American oral tradition and is an elegy for the lost horse culture of the plains; "Plainview 3" is a celebration of the sun, which is venerated among plains tribes; and "Plainview 4" relates the story of Milly Durgan, who was captured by the Kiowas in 1864 when she was eighteen months old. It is a pessimistic view of the death of plains Indian culture. Momaday's next collection, *The Gourd Dancer,* consists of three parts—"Angle of Geese," "The Gourd Dancer," and "Anywhere Is a Street into the Night"—with each section dedicated to one of Momaday's three daughters. Each represents different aspects of Momaday's poetic philosophy and development. The first section addresses the themes of death and mutability, and contains all of "Angle of Geese" as well as two additional poems. "The Gourd Dancer" focuses on Native American culture and includes all of the "Plainview" poems and "The Gourd Dancer," a poem in four sections written as a tribute to Momaday's grandfather Mammedaty. This section also contains the poem "The Delight Song of Tsoai-Talee," which celebrates the land and native culture. Tsoai-Talee is a Kiowa name given to Momaday by a paternal relative. The name, which means "rock-tree boy," refers to the two-hundred foot volcanic butte in Wyoming which is sacred to the Kiowas and is known to Anglo-Americans as Devil's Tower. Many of the poems in part three of *The Gourd Dancer* were written when Momaday was in the Soviet Union in 1974 and evince his poetic mastery. The poems in this section focus on the American Southwest as well as Momaday's experiences in Russia. *In the Presence of the Sun* (1993) is a collection of Momaday's short stories and poems. In addition to including early poetic works, the volume contains numerous new poems and a poetic sequence concerning the legendary outlaw Billy the Kid, a prominent figure in Momaday's artwork and his novel *The Ancient Child.*

Critical Reception

Critical reaction to Momaday's poetry has been enthusiastic, with commentators praising both his early syllabic verse and his later prose poems and free verse. Yvor Winters first brought critical attention to Momaday's poetry in his 1967 study *Forms of Discovery,* in which he placed Momaday within the post-symbolist tradition. Since then, critics have both agreed with and refuted Winters' conclusions. Although Momaday's early poetry has been hailed as among the most significant of the century, with some critics calling such poems as "The Bear" and "Before an Old Painting of the Crucifixion" masterpieces of syllabic verse in English, more recent critics have stated that they prefer Momaday's prose poems for their exploration of Kiowa concerns and incorporation of native oral traditions. They also note that these works are less abstract and more personal and celebratory than Momaday's earlier, more formal works. Momaday himself has stated

that after composing his syllabic poems, "I worked myself into such a confinement of form that I started to write fiction and didn't get back to poetry until much later." Despite the tendency to divide Momaday's poetry into two distinct types or periods, scholars have consistently praised Momaday for his ability to work with various poetic forms, his talent for exploring different cultures from diverse perspectives, and his imaginative interweaving of myth, history, and contemporary Native American experience.

PRINCIPAL WORKS

Poetry

Angle of Geese, and Other Poems 1974
The Gourd Dancer 1976
In the Presence of the Sun: Stories and Poems, 1961-1991 1993

Other Major Works

The Complete Poems of Frederick Goddard Tuckerman [editor] (poetry) 1965
The Journey of Tai-me (folktales) 1967
House Made of Dawn (novel) 1968
The Way to Rainy Mountain (autobiography) 1969
Colorado: Summer, Fall, Winter, Spring (nonfiction) 1973
The Names: A Memoir (autobiography) 1976
The Ancient Child (novel) 1989
Circle of Wonder: A Native American Christmas Story (juvenilia) 1994
The Man Made of Words: Essays, Stories, Passages (essays, short stories, sketches) 1997

CRITICISM

Yvor Winters (essay date 1967)

SOURCE: "The Post-Symbolist Methods," in *Forms of Discovery: Critical and Historical Essays on the Forms of the Short Poem in English,* Alan Swallow, 1967, pp. 251-97.

[*Winters was an American critic, poet, short story writer, and editor who emphasized that all good literature serves a conscious moral purpose. Momaday, who studied under Winters at Stanford University, has noted that Winters greatly influenced his writing. In the excerpt below, Winters offers an analysis of "The Bear," "Buteo Regalis," and "Before an Old Painting of the Crucifixion," placing Momaday's work within the Post-Symbolist tradition.*]

I use the term "post-Symbolist" to describe a kind of poetry which develops most commonly and most clearly after the French Symbolists but which sometimes appears before them or independently of them. Logically, it should follow them and should follow from them, but these things happen as they will.

The associationistic doctrines taught that all ideas arise from sensory perceptions, and gradually it came to be thought that all ideas could be expressed in terms of sensory perceptions, but this effort, as in Pound's *Cantos* or in much of Williams ("no ideas but in things"), was doomed to failure. The result is very often a situation in which the poet offers us, or seems to offer us, sense-perceptions for their own sake, and for the sake of whatever vague feelings they may evoke. This dissociation of sense-perception and feeling on the one hand from conceptual understanding on the other finds its chief theorist in Mallarmé, although Rimbaud and Verlaine are also such theorists. These three men are the most distinguished apologists for, and practitioners of, deliberate obscurity. The reader may examine Rimbaud's "Larme" as a remarkably brilliant example of the practice.

The Romantic poets, both English and French, were interested in sensory perception, natural detail, but the interest was for the greater part theoretic; they talk about sensory details, they refer to them, but in stereotyped language . . . they do not see them or even try to see them. My three Frenchmen see them, hear them, feel them, and sometimes smell them, and with clarity and intensity which is often startling; and they try to isolate them from meaning, and they are surprisingly successful at it. There is nothing like this in British poetry. There is comparable visual imagery in Hardy, but it is not so employed. This clarity of perception, usually of visual perception, is characteristic of the post-Symbolist poets, but the clear perception is employed in ways different from the Symbolist way and different from Hardy's.

Valéry, in his two great poems, "Ebauche d'un Serpent" and "Le Cimetière Marin," is the heir to this sensory perception—but these two poems are not poems of hallucination; they are philosophical poems. Both poems contain a good deal of abstract statement, so that there can be no real doubt as to their themes. The sensory details are a part of this statement—they are not ornament or background. The language is often sensory and conceptual at the same time, for example in this line describing the sea: "Masse de calme et visible réserve." The line should be considered carefully. *Calme* and *réserve* are both nouns indicating potency; but both suggest the possibility of immediate act. They are metaphysical abstractions; or to be more precise, they are clearly substitutes for the metaphysical abstraction *potency,* substitutes brought closer to the visual, very close indeed when we remember that the line describes the sea, and substitutes which suggest the abstraction *act,* or *actuality,* but *act* in visible form. *Masse* and *visible* render the perception clearly visible, make it clearly the sea. That is, the sea is rendered as visibly the embodiment of potency on the verge of becoming actual. As a visual image, the line is brilliant; as an intellectual perception it is profound; the visual and the intellectual are simultaneous—they cannot be separated in fact.

There is nothing resembling this line, in the totality of its qualities, in any of the Symbolist predecessors. Nor is there anything comparable in British poetry save, perhaps, for a few lines in Bridges and T. Sturge Moore. The two poems by Valéry are what one might call classical examples of the method, but I have discussed them elsewhere and will not discuss them here. Equally clear examples are "The Cricket," by F. G. Tuckerman, a poem written about 1870 or shortly before, and without benefit of the French, and "Sunday Morning," by Wallace Stevens, which was written and the early version of which was published a year or two before the first of the two poems by Valéry (Stevens, of course, knew the French Symbolists quite as well as did Valéry). . . . The poem of the kind which I shall describe is usually but not always put together from beginning to end on the principle of carefully controlled association. We have seen controlled association without imagery in Churchill's "Dedication." In some of the poems which I shall discuss we have controlled association in conjunction with post-Symbolist imagery; in some we have post-Symbolist imagery with the rational structure of the Renaissance. The controlled association offers the possibility, at least, of greater flexibility and greater inclusiveness of matter (and without confusion) than we can find in the Renaissance structures; the post-Symbolist imagery provides a greater range of thinking and perceiving than we have ever had before. The method, I believe, is potentially the richest method to appear. In fact, I will go farther: I believe that the greatest poems employing this method are the greatest poems that we have. . . .

N. Scott Momaday (1934-) may seem too young for inclusion in a discussion of this kind, but I would remind the reader of my definition of a great poet: a poet who has written at least one great poem. In my opinion Momaday has written the poem, as well as a few fine lesser poems, and his work is very much to my purpose.

I will quote a poem called **"The Bear."** The poem owes something to Faulkner, but it is essentially Momaday's. It is written in syllabic verse. The first and third lines of each stanza contain five syllables apiece, the second and fourth contain seven; as in all syllabic verse, the accented syllables must vary sufficiently in number and position that they do not form a pattern (a pattern would give us standard meter) but must still contribute to the rhythm:

> What ruse of vision,
> escarping the wall of leaves,
> rending incision
> into countless surfaces,
>
> would cull and color
> his somnolence, whose old age
> has outworn valor,
> all but the fact of courage?
>
> Seen, he does not come,
> move, but seems forever there,
> dimensionless, dumb,
> in the windless noon's hot glare.
>
> More scarred than others
> these years since the trap maimed him,
> pain slants his withers,

drawing up the crooked limb.

> Then he is gone, whole,
> without urgency, from sight,
>   as buzzards control,
> imperceptibly, their flight.

The poem is more descriptive than anything else, yet in the third and last stanzas the details are more than physical and indicate something of the essential wilderness. The sensory perception is very acute, very quiet, as if the observer himself were almost as much at home in the wilderness as the bear. The language is at every point very quiet and could as well be the language of distinguished prose. The poem is poetry by virtue of the careful selection of details and the careful juxtaposition of these details, selection and juxtaposition which result in concentration of meaning, and by virtue of its rhythm, which is the rhythm of verse, but very subtle. Of all the poets of the past decade or so who have experimented with syllabic verse, Momaday is the only one to use it with real success.

My next poem, **"Buteo Regalis,"** describes a hawk at the moment of attack. The lines of this poem are of ten syllables each; lines two, four, five, and six are in iambic pentameter, and the others are syllabic—Momaday controls this change of movement with perfect success:

> His frailty discrete, the rodent turns, looks.
> What sense first warns? The winging is unheard,
> Unseen but as distant motion made whole,
> Singular, slow, unbroken in its glide.
> It veers, and veering, tilts broad-surfaced wings.
> Aligned, the span bends to begin the dive
> And falls, alternately white and russet,
> Angle and curve, gathering momentum.

This seems to be more purely descriptive than **"The Bear."** The language could be that of prose, except for the rhythm, but of absolutely distinguished prose, free of all cliché, not of journalistic prose. Yet the language deserves more attention. We are given a *rodent,* not a rabbit, or a prairie dog, or a kangaroo rat. His frailty is *discrete,* that is, considered separately, just as his purely rodent nature is considered separately, in the defensive turn. It is the abstract movement of the abstract rodent, which we might get in a line-drawing of two or three strokes. The first and third lines, in their syllabic rhythm suggest the sudden hesitation; the four pentameter lines suggest the smooth motion of the soaring hawk; the last two lines in their syllabic rhythm and fragmented phrasing, suggest the rapid and confusing descent. This is done with absolute economy, quietly, yet with uncanny perception. Perception of what, however? Is it only the perception of physical objects observed? It seems rather perception of the "discrete" wilderness, the essential wilderness. It is this quality in both of these poems which brings them within the limits of my present subject.

Both of the poems just quoted, though remarkably fine, are minor poems. The next poem is Momaday's most impressive achievement. It is in standard meter throughout;

the general method is that of controlled association:

"Before an Old Painting of the Crucifixion"
The Mission Carmel
June 1960

> I ponder how He died, despairing once.
> I've heard the cry subside in vacant skies,
> In clearings where no other was. Despair,
> Which, in the vibrant wake of utterance,
> Resides in desolate calm, preoccupies,
> Though it is still. There is no solace there.
>
> That calm inhabits wilderness, the sea,
> And where no peace inheres but solitude;
> Near death it most impends. It was for Him,
> Absurd and public in His agony,
> Inscrutably itself, nor misconstrued,
> Nor metaphrased in art or pseudonym:
>
> A vague contagion. Old, the mural fades . . .
> Reminded of the fainter sea I scanned,
> I recollect: How mute in constancy!
> I could not leave the wall of palisades
> Till cormorants returned my eyes on land.
> The mural but implies eternity:
>
> Not death, but silence after death is change.
> Judean hills, the endless afternoon,
> The farther groves and arbors seasonless
> But fix the mind within the moment's range.
> Where evening would obscure our sorrow soon,
> There shines too much a sterile loveliness.
>
> No imprecisions of commingled shade,
> No shimmering deceptions of the sun,
> Herein no semblances remark the cold
> Unhindered swell of time, for time is stayed.
> The Passion wanes into oblivion,
> And time and timelessness confuse, I'm told.
> These centuries removed from either fact
>
> Have lain upon the critical expanse
> And been of little consequence. The void
> Is calendared in stone; the human act,
> Outrageous, is in vain. The hours advance
> Like flecks of foam borne landward and destroyed.

The first two stanzas deal with the experience of the Crucified, as it was suggested in the mural. They bring up the idea which will recur in the fourth stanza, the desolate calm following any tragic event, a calm the nature of which we may sense in the wilderness, near the sea, especially near death; and in the latter part of the second stanza we have a statement of the uniqueness of this experience for the Crucified. These lines are worth our attention: to say that the experience was unique and then try to describe it would be a contradiction, a falsification; Momaday does not try to render the unique experience but instead gives us a statement of the nature of uniqueness, in relation to the inner experience of Christ, after the line on his outer and public appearance. These lines are as powerful as any I know; they illustrate a way in which abstract statement can be utilized effectively. In the third stanza he recollects that this is, after all, a mural, old and disintegrating; the scene of the mural, mute in constancy, is not real. The sea is real, but in the distance it also is mute in constancy; he remembers how the view of the sea had held him till his eyes had drifted back after the cormorants. And then the mural comes back to mind. The third stanza may seem obscure on first reading if we do not keep in mind the position of the observer, in the old mission near the ocean, his mind moving back and forth between the two objects.

"The mural *but implies* eternity." I have italicized two important words. The mural does not render eternity, nor explain it; Momaday is too cautious an observer of his experience to suspect anything so foolish. It merely implies eternity but it does imply it, and it implies nothing else. The line ends with a colon, which indicates that the implication will be explored. The first line of the fourth stanza may bother the reader for a moment, for, in the usual sense, death, like any other occurrence, is change; but this is not what Momaday is talking about. Death itself is a process, a part of life; but in the silence after death we have a different state entirely, an essentially inscrutable state, which is implied by the immobile mural. The remainder of the fourth stanza describes the mural, with reference to the details which imply eternity, details which resemble our experience but suggest a state removed from it, details which are neither the one thing nor the other, which are sterile though beautiful.

The fifth stanza is a commentary on the fourth but refers back to the third as well: it tells us that in the mural there are none of the movements which indicate the presence of time, nothing to

> remark the cold
> Unhindered swell of time,

a phrase in which we are reminded of the ocean swell outside, now as if it were at hand and powerful, but in which the swell appears to be stayed even before the fact is stated in the next few words. Time is stayed; we are in eternity in the mural; but for the moment we are in eternity this side of the mural as well. On this side of the mural the Passion wanes into oblivion; time and timelessness seem to become one. The phrase "I'm told" is not something inserted for a final foot and a rime, as one of my young friends once suggested; it is there for a clear purpose. It is a weary confession that we are dealing with a mystery, about which we cannot know as much as some people claim.

In the first two lines of the fifth stanza we have a quick light rhythm as we see the little movements which indicate life in time; this is slowed somewhat in the third line, which summarizes and begins to move into the magnificent image of time; this sentence is compact but complex in syntax and rhythm alike. The rhythm of the fifth line is slow and pensive, and that of the sixth is similar. The command of rhythm, whether linear, syntactic, or in some other way stanzaic, is that of a master; but the reader who has learned to read poetry aloud can find this command throughout.

The last stanza is a commentary on what has preceded, a summing up and a final judgment. The phrase *either fact* indicates two facts: the real crucifixion and the crucifixion depicted in the mural. The *expanse* has been *critical* in two senses: it has been a test of the centuries following the Crucifixion; it should have been a period of crisis, of great change. But nothing really to the purpose has occurred; there was a moral void; time was geological, not human; the extreme sacrifice was in vain. The indications of time before us are as trivial as flecks of foam moving in to disappear in the beachsand.

I have tried to explain this poem in great detail, because the poem, although not obscure, is difficult and requires careful reading. I myself did not understand it for a long time, and I know other readers, and very intelligent readers, who do not understand it yet. The poem is worth understanding. Every word, every mark of punctuation, every cadence, every detail of grammar and syntax is a precise and essential part of an act of profound understanding.

The poem displays both of the post-Symbolist methods which I have been discussing. First we have controlled association: this is seen most clearly in the third stanza and in the movement back and forth thereafter between the mural and the ocean, but it occurs throughout the poem. Second, we have post-Symbolist imagery, imagery weighted with intellectual content; the fifth stanza is the most obvious example, in "the cold unhindered swell of time," but we can find it elsewhere. And there is purely abstract statement on occasion, and very powerful abstract statement.

John Finlay (review date 1975)

SOURCE: "N. Scott Momaday's *Angle of Geese*," in *The Southern Review,* Louisiana State University, Vol. XI, No. 3, Summer, 1975, pp. 658-61.

[*In the following review, Finlay offers a stylistic and thematic description of* Angle of Geese, *praising the volume as Momaday's best work.*]

N. Scott Momaday's reputation, before **Angle of Geese,** rested upon two works of prose, *House Made of Dawn,* a novel concerned with the dislocation and eventual disintegration of an Indian youth in urban America (parts of which were first published in *The Southern Review*), and *The Way to Rainy Mountain,* a half-mythical, half-historical account of Momaday's Kiowa ancestors, beautifully illustrated by the poet's father. These two books are considerable achievements, especially *The Way to Rainy Mountain,* which contains some of the most powerful prose written in recent years, or any year, for that matter. Yet **Angle of Geese,** made up of eighteen poems, three of which are in prose, is by far the greatest thing Momaday has done and should, by itself, earn for him a permanent place in our literature. Considering, though, the general insistence upon the loose and the anecdotal in contemporary poetry, I should realistically add that Momaday's poetic reputation will probably be quiet and underground.

Nearly all of his poems are concerned with what Yvor Winters, in his discussion of Momaday in *Forms of Discovery,* calls "the essential wilderness," the post-Romantic landscape of modern, secular thought, inscrutable and divested of ethical values, against which the human act takes place. More often than not, this act is personified by an animal, but one that has become, in the poem, emblematic and applicable to human terms. Because Momaday realizes the ultimately philosophical implications of this wilderness, his poems end up as serious meditations on the absolute distinction between what he calls in the title poem "the pale angle of time," the informed world of identity and purpose, and the state of death and non-being, "the essential wilderness" that finally destroys that world. Like Bowers and the other post-Symbolist poets, his approach is through description permeated with philosophic awareness:

>   . . . this
> cold, bright body
> of the fish
> upon the planks,
> the coil and
> crescent of flesh
> extending
> just into death.

This theme is most perfectly realized in his greatest poem, **"Before an Old Painting of the Crucifixion."** On the one hand, there is the "critical expanse," operating in time and motivated by the human desire for "utterance" in art and religious thought; on the other, the nonhuman vacancy of a universe that completely frustrates that desire:

> These centuries removed from either fact
> Have lain upon the critical expanse
> And been of little consequence. The void
> Is calendared in stone; the human act,
> Outrageous, is in vain. The hours advance
> Like flecks of foam borne landward and de-
>   stroyed.

The emotional control he is able to maintain in the face of this tragic perception, and with no religious belief to support him, is a measure of his greatness. The quietness and the concentration of the style reveal a mind that is as humanly fortified as it can be against the despair necessarily inherent in the subject.

In other poems this perception is less extreme. They are more concerned with the conditions of survival than with the inevitability of extinction. **"The Bear,"** along with **"Pit Viper,"** is an excellent example. The identity of the creature, worn down to the mere "fact of courage," holds itself together in the wilderness through an attitude of self-sufficient stoicism, a sort of expert indifference to the dangers

always lurking behind the "countless surfaces" of the leaves. And in **"Walk on the Moon,"** an epigram inspired by the Apollo mission, the emphasis is on the tentative human extension into and appropriation of the essentially nonhuman:

> Extend, there where you venture and come back,
> The edge of time. Be it your furthest track.
> Time in that distance wanes. What is *to be.*
> That present verb, there in Tranquility?

And other times he is capable, after the fact of annihilation, of a beautiful evocation of what he most loved in the past, the laughter and the old stories of his race, which is the subject of **"Earth and I Gave You Turquoise,"** one of the most moving elegies in modern poetry:

> Tonight they dance near Chinle
>   by the seven elms
> There your loom whispered beauty
>   They will eat mutton
> and drink coffee till morning
> You and I will not be there

Finally, to give one an idea of the stylistic achievement evident throughout all of *Angle of Geese*, I should like to quote entire a poem entitled **"Buteo Regalis":**

> His frailty discrete, the rodent turns, looks.
> What sense first warns? The winging is unheard,
> Unseen but as distant motion made whole,
> Singular, slow, unbroken in its glide.
> It veers, and veering, tilts board-surfaced wings.
> Aligned, the span bends to begin the dive
> And falls, alternately white and russet,
> Angle and curve, gathering momentum.

What we have in this brief poem is a concise descriptive statement of a creature that knows its aim and lets nothing interfere with itself as it goes straight to the object. The intense concentration and power of the bird as it swoops down, "gathering momentum," upon the unprotected rodent, is unforgettable. The style also has the same concentration and singleness of purpose. The meter is syllabic, with no rhyme or rhetorical embellishments to enliven its "dryness," as J. V. Cunningham characterizes syllabic verse; the diction and word order as close to prose as is possible; and the tone of the poem is objective and matter-of-fact, each word quietly insistent upon its denotative value. Nothing stands out of the evenly controlled context. And the movement of the poem is lean and muscular. If for no other reason than for its style, *Angle of Geese* would be an important book for anyone seriously interested in what modern American poetry is still capable of.

Roger Dickinson-Brown   **(essay date 1978)**

SOURCE: "The Art and Importance of N. Scott Momaday," in *The Southern Review,* Lousiana State University, Vol. XIV, No. 1, January, 1978, pp. 30-45.

[In the excerpt below, Dickinson-Brown offers a stylistic analysis of several poems in Angle of Geese.]

It is surprising that Momaday has published so few poems. *Angle of Geese* contains only eighteen—the considered work of a great poet around the age of forty. But the poems are there, astonishing in their depth and range. **"Simile," "Four Notions of Love and Marriage," "The Fear of Bo-talee," "The Story of a Well-Made Shield,"** and **"The Horse that Died of Shame"** are variously free verse (the first two, which are slight and sentimental) or prose poems. They partake of the same discrete intensity that characterizes the storytelling in *The Way to Rainy Mountain,* and which makes them some of the few real prose poems in English.

The poems written in grammatical parallels are much better: **"The Delight Song of Tsoai-talee"** and **"Plainview:2."** In the latter, Momaday has used a form and created emotions without precedent in English:

I saw an old Indian
At Saddle Mountain.
He drank and dreamed of drinking
And a blue-black horse.
Remember my horse running.
Remember my horse.
Remember my horse running.
Remember my horse.

Remember my horse wheeling.
Remember my horse.
Remember my horse wheeling.
Remember my horse.

Remember my horse blowing.
Remember my horse.
Remember my horse blowing.
Remember my horse.

Remember my horse standing.
Remember my horse.
Remember my horse standing.
Remember my horse.

Remember my horse hurting.
Remember my horse.
Remember my horse hurting.
Remember my horse.

Remember my horse falling.
Remember my horse.
Remember my horse falling.
Remember my horse.

Remember my horse dying.
Remember my horse.
Remember my horse dying.
Remember my horse.

A horse is one thing,
An Indian another;

An old horse is old;
An old Indian is sad.

I saw an old Indian
At Saddle Mountain.
He drank and dreamed of drinking
And a blue-black horse.

Remember my horse running.
Remember my horse.
Remember my horse wheeling.
Remember my horse.
Remember my horse blowing.
Remember my horse.
Remember my horse standing.
Remember my horse.
Remember my horse falling.
Remember my horse.
Remember my horse dying.
Remember my horse.
Remember my blue-black horse.
Remember my blue-black horse.
Remember my horse.
Remember my horse.
Remember.
Remember.

A chant or a parallel poem is necessarily bulky and especially oral. I have often recited this poem to individuals and groups, in part to test its effect upon an English-language audience. My own voice is consciously based upon the oral readings of Pound, Winters, and Native American chant, with a dash of childhood Latin Mass. I read the lines without musical intonation but with emphatic regularity and little rhetorical variation. The results are extreme: about half the listeners are bored, the other half moved, sometimes to tears. The poem is obviously derived from Momaday's experience of Indian chant, in which, as in most other cultures, small distinction is made between music and poetry. In this respect **"Plainview:2"** is a part of the abandoned traditions of Homer, *The Song of Roland,* oral formulas, the Christian, Muslim, and Jewish chant, and even certain Renaissance poems. The various forms of repetition in these works are still common in the Islamic and black African and certain other worlds, but they survive in the West (where individual originality has destroyed community), only through such traditional popular genres as commercial song (which, unlike "modern intellectual" poetry and "classical" music, preserves the fusion), nursery rhymes, and among the non-white minorities. These are our surviving traditions of form, which is by nature repetitive.

In addition to the obvious repetitions in **"Plainview:2,"** the repetition of stanza 1 at stanza 10, and the two-line rehearsal of the four-line stanzas turn the poem. The whole poem is, in fact, simply a subtle variation, development, and restatement of the first stanza, with the extended, reiterated illustration of both the beauty of the horse's actions and its death. The ninth stanza occupies the poem like a kernel of gloss, but even its third and fourth lines are simply restatements of its first and second.

The form of this poem distinguishes with rare clarity what we call denotative and connotative. In a literate age of recorded language, where memory and repetition—sides of a coin—have each faded from our experience, we are inclined to regard such hammering as a waste of time—but it can, instead, be an intensification and a kind of experience we have lost. That is precisely the division of modern response to the poem.

Momaday on being labeled a post-Symbolist poet:

Post-symbolist is a term I heard a great deal as a graduate student, and I fail even now to understand it. I see my poetry as being also cross-cultural in a sense. When I was exercising my earliest knowledge of traditional English forms, I was doing a lot of very closely controlled writing, and I came to understand the value of such control. But at the same time I was concerned to develop my voice as a projection of the oral tradition. So I keep the two things going, and I think probably that it's good for me to work across those boundaries.

N. Scott Momaday, in an interview with Louis Owens, in This Is About Vision: Interviews with Southwestern Writers, *edited by William Balassi, John F. Crawford, and Annie O. Eysturoy, 1990.*

The rest of Momaday's poetry is traditionally iambic or experimentally syllabic. Winters has called the iambic pentameter **"Before an Old Painting of the Crucifixion"** a great poem, and perhaps it is, in spite of a certain stiltedness and melodrama, reminiscent of the worst aspects of *House Made of Dawn*. Yet the iambic poems are certainly among the best of their kind in Momaday's generation, and it is only the exigency of space that limits me to a few lines from **"Rainy Mountain Cemetery"**:

> Most is your name the name of this dark stone.
> Deranged in death, the mind to be inheres
> Forever in the nominal unknown. . . .

Momaday's theme here is an inheritance from Winters, though it is as old as our civilization: the tension, the gorgeous hostility between the human and the wild—a tension always finally relaxed in death. Winters did a great deal to restore and articulate that consciousness, after and in the light of Romanticism. And it was Winters too who taught Momaday one of his greatest virtues, the power and humanity of abstraction—heresy in the cant of our time: *deranged* is a pure and perfect abstraction.

And there is more Winters:

> . . . silence is the long approach of noon
> Upon the shadow that your name defines—
> And death this cold, black density of stone.

We have already seen this in *House Made of Dawn*. Winters called it post-symbolist method. The physical images carry the full force, often through double sense, of

abstraction: the shadow *defines;* and death is the impenetrability, the incomprehensibility, of black *density*. Yet the images are not metaphors, for they are not subservient to the abstractions they communicate, nor are they synecdochical. They persist in the very mortal obstinacy which they mean. This style is everywhere in Momaday, but it is something which Winters could not have duplicated, for it is also profoundly Kiowa.

Momaday's syllabic verse is best introduced with a brief general introduction to the nature and current state of syllabic verse in English. Syllabic verse—a patterning of the number of syllables per line, with no other competing patterns—has been written occasionally in English at least since the Renaissance in England. There it reached a kind of peak at the turn of the century in major syllabic poems by Robert Bridges. His daughter Elizabeth Daryush, who continued her father's tradition in her own way, was (during her lifetime) England's most underestimated poet.

So many American poets—J. V. Cunningham, Lewis Turco, John Hollander, for examples—have recently turned to syllabic verse that, in statistical quantity at least, the prosody offers to become something other than the minor experimental form it has been. Syllabic verse in English could solve a major problem for contemporary poets: the malady of the iamb, which poets as different as Turco and Cunningham have sometimes perceived as overweighted with historical emotions and meanings unavailable to a contemporary poet—a kind of verse cathedral. And of course most contemporary poets, all over the Western world, have simply dropped tradition and form altogether, as if the latter were fused to the former. In English, syllabic verse is a form without tradition.

The arguments against syllabic meter in English are weak. Syllabic prosody has been perhaps the world's most important prosody, not only in unaccented languages like French but also in Spanish and Italian, which are certainly not accented as English is, but which are close enough to establish a strong theoretical possibility of success for the prosody in English, and to eliminate the usual argument that syllabic poetry in accented English is "finger-counting." And then, we have by now an important body of successful syllabic poems in English—easily enough for an intelligent and interesting anthology.

Yet most syllabic poetry in English *is* finger-counting— I am sure that the poets themselves have had to count, for there is no meter, nothing to feel. All of the world's syllabic poetries, be they Japanese or Italian or French, have created modes of distinguishing the lines as entities, usually by end-stop or rhyme, so that the lines (which, with the syllables, are the only units), may be felt rhythmically, may distinguish themselves, and may thereby, through an individuality played against the intensity of pattern, create and control meaning and, especially, feeling. English- language syllabic poets have sometimes, like Cunningham, also thought it wise to avoid even numbers of syllables, because of potential confusion with iambic measure; sometimes, like Daryush, they have argued for an incomplete departure from iambic movement (some of Daryush's syllabic poems are in fact iambic)—in any case the irregularized "sprung" accent will be the most important variant in the line; sometimes, like Momaday, they have marked the line-end with off-rhyme, that major aspect of modern prosody first mastered by Dickinson. In general, Daryush's own intense statement of the subject is the best I know:

> . . . a strict syllable-count, although of course essential, is, in my view, merely the lifeless shell of its more vital requirements.

> Accepting that not only a work of art but every aspect of its medium is intrinsically a contrived relation between the known and the uncomprehended, the fixed and the unpredictable, recalling, too, that in accentual verse, as in barred music, the fixed element is that of time, and the unfixed that of number (of syllables or notes) we can assess what part should be played by these factors in a truly syllabic system. Here the position is reversed: the fixed element is no longer time but number; the integrity of line and syllable is challenged by the stress-demands of sense or syntax. The aim of the artist will be so to balance these incommensurables as to reflect his own predicament of thought or feeling, thereby enhancing his consciousness of an imagined relation with the unattainable. The rules for achieving this are by their very nature unwritten ones, but a few guidelines can be laid down.

> In general, meaning should make the greatest possible use of time-variety without losing sight of the number-pattern. First, therefore, the line-ending, the highest point of emphasis and tension, being no longer led up to by steps of regular stress, must be established and maintained by other means. The first few lines of a syllabic poem should when possible be complete sentences or phrases. Rhyme is almost indispensable, but since it can be unaccented need be neither over-obvious nor monotonous. The integrity of the syllable must be ensured by the avoidance of all dubious elisions. Stress-variations are more effective in fairly short lines, and more easily obtained from those with an odd syllable-count, since here there is a choice of two equally accessible stress-counts. Full advantage should of course be taken of the release from stress-restrictions, with their often unavoidable distortions of the natural speech-rhythm. Inversions should now be used only for meaningful emphasis.

> With these main principles in mind, the writer replaces the usual regular stress-waves by such other currents and cross-currents, such expectations and disappointments, as may further his purpose. He may, for instance, introduce the same irregularities into the corresponding lines of a lyric's every stanza; or he may repeat, often with great effect, in the last line of a poem, some startling upheaval in the first; or, again, he may use a similar break in a previously established pattern to express some violent change of mood or thought. These and many similar devices will with practice become the instinctively chosen instruments of the poet whose ear is attuned to their possibilities.

> Without them, there will be no poem.

> (Elizabeth Daryush, *Collected Poems* [Carcanet New Press, 1976]).

Momaday's syllabic poetry is his best and experimentally most exciting work. Even deprived of the rest of the poem, the middle stanza of **"The Bear"** seems to me among the perfect stanzas in English, rhythmically exquisite in its poise between iamb and an excess of syllabic looseness, utterly comprehensive in its presentation of the motionless wild bear and its relationship to time:

> Seen, he does not come,
> move, but seems forever there,
> dimensionless, dumb,
> in the windless noon's hot glare.

"Comparatives" is a tour-de-force of alternating unrhymed three- and four-syllable lines, again with Momaday's abstract and physical fusion. Momaday succeeds in presenting such unrhymed, short lines rhythmically, in spite of a necessarily high incidence of enjambment; the faint lines convey a melancholy appropriate to the antiquity and death which are the consequence of his juxtaposition of the dead and the fossil fish:

> . . . cold, bright body
> of the fish
> upon the planks,
> the coil and
> crescent of flesh
> extending
> just into death.

> Even so,
> in the distant,
> inland sea,
> a shadow runs,
> radiant,
> rude in the rock:

> fossil fish,
> fissure of bone
> forever.
> It is perhaps
> the same thing,
> an agony
> twice perceived.

Momaday's greatest poem is certainly **"Angle of Geese,"** a masterpiece of syllabic rhythm, of modulated rhyme, of post-symbolic images, and of the meaning of language in human experience. Although perhaps none of its stanzas is equal to the best stanza of **"The Bear,"** each functions in a similar way, shifting from perfect to imperfect to no rhyme with the same supple responsiveness Dryden mastered, but with more range. Nevertheless the largest importance of this poem, even beyond its extraordinary form, is its theme, which is probably the greatest of our century: the extended understanding of the significance of language and its relation to identity—an understanding increased not only by the important work done by the linguists of our century but also by the increased mixture of languages which has continued to accelerate over the last hundred years or so: French or English among Asians and Africans, often as first or only languages among nonetheless profoundly non-European people; Spanish established on an Indian continent; and, of course, English in America. These are non-native native speakers of English, as it were, further distinguishing literature in English from English literature. Their potential has much to do with their relative freedom from the disaster and degeneracy which Romantic ideas have created among their European-American counterparts: many of these new English writers still have deep connections with their communities, instead of the individualistic elitism which characterizes contemporary European-American art, music, and poetry. They are more like Shakespeare, Rembrandt, and Homer. And they often have fewer neuroses about the evils of form. Momaday, as a Kiowa, a university scholar, and a poet of major talent, is in an excellent position to take advantage of these multi-cultural possibilities. The result is **"Angle of Geese"**:

How shall we adorn
Recognition with our speech?—
    Now the dead firstborn
Will lag in the wake of words.

    Custom intervenes;
We are civil, something more:
    More than language means,
The mute presence mulls and marks.

    Almost of a mind,
We take measure of the loss;
    I am slow to find
The mere margin of repose.

    And one November
It was longer in the watch,
    As if forever,
Of the huge ancestral goose.

    So much symmetry!
Like the pale angle of time
    And eternity.
The great shape labored and fell.

    Quit of hope and hurt,
It held a motionless gaze,
    Wide of time, alert,
On the dark distant flurry.

The poem is difficult and a little obscure, mostly because the subject is—but also because Momaday has indulged a little in the obscurantism that makes modern poetry what it is—and an explication of the poem is therefore necessary.

The first stanza presents the subject and observes that the Darwinian animal which we were, who is our ancestor, cannot be rediscovered in our language, which is what moved us away and distinguished us from the animal.

The second stanza explains the divorce: we have become civilized, but not wholly. "The mute presence" may, by syntax, seem to be the presence of language, but it is not. It is the presence of wilderness which is mute. We live in connotation, which is wild response. "Mulls" and "civil" are odd diction.

The third stanza contemplates this ambivalence, this incompleteness, and moves from the general to the particular. We are almost whole, or wholly civilized and conscious, and to precisely this extent we have lost our own wilderness. The speaker, introduced at this point, is slow to realize, outside language, what is wild in him. The language is typical of Momaday in its outright and exact abstraction: "mere" in the old sense of pure or unadulterated—here, by language and civilization; "margin" because this is where humans, with their names and mortality, overlap with wilderness, which has neither; "repose" because what is wild is forever and at every moment perfect and complete, without urgency, going nowhere, perpetuating itself beautifully for no sake at all. It is useful to remember wilderness here primarily in terms of immortal molecules and galaxies, without number or name—except those collective names imposed upon them by men who have to that extent simply perceived and thought about that which is unaltered by thought, which does not know the thinker, and which is, finally, a kind of god—not a god, as Stevens said, "but as a god might be." It is a kind of altered Romantic god, but one supported rather more by the pure sciences than by Deism and Benevolism: a nature pure and perfect, composed of sub-atomic particles and framed in an unimaginable universe with no edge. Language contradicts itself with this god, who is its enemy. It is the wilderness of our century, deprived of Romantic benevolence but retaining its old terrifying innocence and immense and nameless beauty, which ignores us and must destroy us, one by one. It is a god of mere repose. The goose, which the hunter waits for one November, is almost perfectly a part of the god (Momaday only implies the word), although a goose shares with men certain forms of individual consciousness of itself and others. Some animals have some language, and to this extent the goose knows the same clear and lonely condition we do, and is an imperfect symbol of the wilderness. The long watch, in any case, implies the eternity which is the whole of which the goose is an indiscriminate part: *as if forever.* The goose is huge because it is inseparable from the wild deity: what Emerson called the "not I," which neither names nor knows itself, which cannot die—whatever is, like the grasshopper of the ancient Greeks, immortal because the individuals have no name. That is our ancestor who does not know us, whom we hardly know.

So, in the fifth stanza, the symmetry of the angle or V of the flock of geese implies the perfection for which geometry and symmetry have always served as imaginary means. A goose is shot, and falls out of the angle, into the speaker's world.

Momaday's greatest poem is certainly "Angle of Geese," a masterpiece of syllabic rhythm, of modulated rhyme, of post-symbolic images, and of the meaning of language in human experience.

—Roger Dickinson-Brown

The last stanza gives the goose a little of that hope and hurt which grants this sophisticated animal a part of what will kill the speaker: a conscious identity. But the goose is essentially wild, and it holds, like an immortal cockatrice, an inhuman gaze—motionless, outside the time in which we live and die, wildly, purely alert—fixed on the receding flurry of the flock out of which it fell, growing as dark and distant physically as it is in truth to the dying speaker who watches it too and for whom, alone, something has changed. The word "flurry" fuses with the flock all the huge vagueness which is our blind source.

"Angle of Geese" seems to me the best example both of Momaday's greatness and his importance to contemporary literature: it profoundly realizes its subject, both denotatively and connotatively, with greater art in an important new prosodic form than anyone except Bridges and Daryush. It also presents, better than any other work I know—especially in the light of what has only recently been so developed and understood—perhaps the most important subject of our age: the tragic conflict between what we have felt in wilderness and what our language means.

Kenneth C. Mason   (essay date 1980)

SOURCE: "Beautyway: The Poetry of N. Scott Momaday," in *South Dakota Review,* Vol. 18, No. 2, Summer, 1980, pp. 61-83.

[*In the following essay, Mason provides an in-depth analysis of* The Gourd Dancer, *examining the major themes of each section and the volume as a whole.*]

N. Scott Momaday's first full-length collection of poems was finally published in 1976. Previously he had published some eighteen poems in the chapbook, *Angle of Geese and Other Poems.* These poems plus two others make up part 1 of *The Gourd Dancer,* a book which is the summation in poetry of that evolution of ideas and verbal skill we have observed in prose in *House Made of Dawn, The Way to Rainy Mountain,* and *The Names.*

The Gourd Dancer clearly establishes Momaday as a poet of some stature and demands that the close attention given his prose be given to his poetry as well. The book presents a distinct and distinguished music in post-modern poetry and a fresh and compelling vision. Momaday has brought the same intense concision, the same scrupulous craftsmanship to his poems that he brought to his prose. More important perhaps, he has treated the themes of his prose with a poetic rhetoric of marked originality.

The Gourd Dancer is divided into three parts, each of which is dedicated to one of Momaday's three daughters. This tripartite structure is a departure from his prose works, which make use of a four-part division as a thematic device. Here, however, the structure is not so much thematically as chronologically determined. Each successive part investigates a different facet of Momaday's poetic con-

sciousness, and each notes a progression in the development of a broad artistic sensibility. This does not mean that each new part leaves behind the concerns of past parts, but that the themes and subjects of each successive part are leavened with vital new elements to create a richer, stronger poetic voice.

Part I, "Angle of Geese," includes those poems we have often seen in anthologies: **"The Bear," "Bueto Regalis," "Pit Viper," "Earth and I Give You Turquoise,"** etc. It is one of the best-known of these poems, **"Angle of Geese,"** that we can turn to for an indication of the themes Momaday will be examining in this part. **"Angle of Geese"** evinces the qualities of precision and cervine grace that are the hallmarks of all Momaday's poetry. This poem (like most of Momaday's poems) is in syllabic verse: each quatrain is composed of alternating lines of five and seven syllables. Lines so short place great demands on the poet for exactness and compression of statement, and lend a certain tautness to the rhetoric of each quatrain (each of which is end-stopped). There is also the conscious use of alliteration: "Will lag in the wake of words," "The mute presence of mulls and marks;" and assonance: "The great shape labored and fell."

But more importantly we find the dense complexity and penetration of utterance—nearly, but never wholly obscure. The poem is highly serious: it charts the poet's reaction to death. The death is that of a friend's first-born child, and the occasion of the poem is the first meeting of the friends in grief. The first three stanzas are a subtle evocation of the psychology of that meeting: before the hard, ineluctable datum of death, they are initially chary of speech, but "custom" leads them to speak. Real communication though, is subverted by the stark consciousness of death—the force of its recognition is beyond the power of words to comprehend or express: "More than language means, / The mute presence mulls and marks." The friends are left to "take measure of the loss," to try to live with it. We are assured that, painful as this is, the poet does "find / The mere margin of repose," the least edge of acceptance.

How the poet finds it is revealed in the final three stanzas. The death of the child is related to the death of the "huge ancestral goose." The shooting of the goose is a reenactment of an ancient pattern from the poet's heritage. Appropriately, the poet is filled with wonder at the beauty and mystery of the geese. Their "symmetry" in flight suggests a transcendent order and harmony—a meeting of "time / And eternity." The dead goose is delivered from the accidents of time, it is "quit of hope and hurt." Its "gaze" is "wide of time" and "held" "On the dark distant flurry"—the symbolic angle. It is in this transfiguration of death that the poet finds solace for the loss of the child. Both deaths become part of the greater order of time's conjunction with eternity in nature.

A similar poetic structure is used in **"Comparatives,"** another meditative poem on the meaning of death. In this poem death is seen as an ever-recurring process in the larger action of nature. First there is the death of the caught fish, which is the one startling circumstance on "the seaside / of any day." This reminds the poet of the fossil fish once seen far inland. The poet concludes that the dying of the present moment and the timeless, ancient death preserved in the rock are "the same thing, / an agony / twice perceived." Momaday's craft adds greatly to the impression of the identity of the two deaths by making the fossil fish seem vital and alive. This is conveyed by alliteration, which gives the lines describing the fossil a sense of urgency and immediacy: "a shadow runs, / radiant, / rude in the rock. . . ." The succeeding lines (again, noticeably alliterative) in effect cancel this perception of animation in the fossil and leaves the reader with the objective perception of death written in rock: "fossil fish, / fissure of bone / forever." Momaday has allowed the reader himself to experience these two events as "the same thing," to see the present "agony" in the silence and hard stillness of the fossil in the rock.

The result of this imaginative perception of the ubiquitous presence of death is offered in the final stanza, in which this "agony" is viewed as "mere commotion," part of the ceaseless agitation and flux of material being. And this is all we can know or conclude about it; the naked fact of death is "perceptible—but that is all."

The two poems, **"Angle of Geese"** and **"Comparatives,"** show that Momaday is primarily a meditative poet—working directly in the American tradition of meditative poetry. The predominant mood is quiet reflection; the tone is sober and serious. We can also say that Momaday is a metaphysical poet, since he seeks to explore the difficult and elusive nature of reality: not only the facts of death and mortality, but also those of life and the immortality of the moment. This last brings us to the second major intention of the poems in part I of *The Gourd Dancer*: to reveal something of the secret core of existence through the intense presentation of a single moment—through an act of imagination that magnifies and imbues this moment with a profundity of meaning and import.

"Pit Viper" is an especially effective poem of this sort. The poem captures in an instant of vision the beauty and dangerous power in nature's renewal of itself, the viper's sloughing of the old skin and the shining emergence of the new. The change is rendered in keenly descriptive lines, charged with the excitement of the reactivation of the creative process in nature. An indication of the adeptness with which Momaday suits form to subject is the first sentence: "The cordate head meanders through himself: / Metamorphosis." The meter places an end-stop after the first line, giving the word "Metamorphosis" in the second line a suddenness and impact that creates the very impression of quick transformation that the lines describe.

But with an intellectual subtlety that is a distinctive feature in Momaday's art, the poet turns from the viper, an instrument of death, to the poet's ability to concentrate force in language, giving his words the imaginative potency of the viper's bite: "Blurred eyes . . . have seen death— / Or simile—come nigh and overcome." Actually, the whole poem can be read as an elaborate "simile," a conceit about

the poetic process and the latent power inherent in the poet's shaping of words. **"Pit Viper"** is an example of the complexity of thought and the suggestiveness of image that Momaday can achieve in the fewest possible lines.

"Pit Viper" succeeds well in presenting a dynamic moment of closely-rendered vision. Momaday offers even greater intensity in his treatment of Isaac McCaslin's first encounter with Old Ben in **"The Bear."** More than just the title suggests the identification of the scene in the poem with the scene in Faulkner's short story. The physical details of the bear's maimed foot and of his ghost-like coming and going are taken from the story. Further, Momaday's superb line drawing of a boy rapt in wonderment that faces the poem supports this identification. But just how much has Momaday borrowed from Faulkner? The encounter in the story is in actuality shorter than the poem:

> He only heard the drumming of the woodpecker stop short off, and knew that the bear was looking at him. He never saw it. He did not know whether it was facing him from the cane or behind him. He did not move, holding facing useless gun which he knew now he would never fire at it, now or never, tasting in his saliva that taint of brass which he had smelled in the huddled dogs when he peered under the kitchen.

> Then it was gone. As abruptly as it had stopped the woodpecker's dry hammering set up again. . . .

This passage from the story is particularly helpful in explaining the question with which the poem begins. The "ruse of vision" refers to the fact that the bear is not really seen, but only apprehended intuitively. Yet that initial question is open to another interpretation, which can exist independent of any connection with the story. The "ruse of vision" is the image created in words by the poet, and the answer to the question, "What ruse of vision . . . / would cull and color / his somnolence," is the moment of epiphanic vision that is the poem.

Yvor Winters notes this about **"The Bear"** [in his 1967 *Forms of Discovery: Critical and Historical Essays on the Forms of the Short Poem in English*]: "The poem is more descriptive than anything else, yet in the third and last stanzas the details are more physical and indicate something of the essential wilderness." The bear in the poem, then, like the bear in Faulkner's story, represents the potent, primordial force of nature, and the poem offers a moment of insight, in which we understand something of the age and mystery of the land.

"The Bear" is distinguished for the strength and solidarity of its lines and the grace with which it carries its syllabic rhythm and rhyme. We might single out for comment two examples of Momaday's poetic command of his subject. The first stanza is notable for the sibilance of its lines, which creates verbally a dazzling sensation of wonder. Secondly, stanzas number three and five enlarge on the sudden coming and going of the bear given in Faulkner, with marvelous effect. These stanzas give the poem greater dramatic moment, and infuse it with a sense of the mystery and ineffability of nature. The final simile is not only rather ingenious, but also singularly effective in generalizing the mystery of the bear to include all of nature: "Then he is gone, whole, / without urgency, from sight, / as buzzards control, / imperceptibly, their flight." This lends the poem's suggestiveness far greater impact. **"The Bear"** is certainly one of the very finest of Momaday's early poems.

"Bueto Regalis" is a brief but startlingly vivid insight into a totally different aspect of nature. It is meant, like **"The Bear,"** to present an epiphanic moment. But unlike **"The Bear,"** its object is to give a potent sense of the raw wild strength in nature.

"Bueto Regalis" is wholly descriptive. As such, it meets Momaday's own requirement for descriptive writing [as outlined in an interview with Momaday appearing in the March 1973 issue of *Puerto del Sol*]:

> I'm interested in description and when I describe something in writing I always ask myself if I have described what it is I set out to describe; of course, you can write beautiful description which is inaccurate but still beautiful. But my idea of writing good description is writing something accurately.

It is just its accuracy in description which is so impressive in this poem. Lines two and three—"What sense first warns? / The winging is unheard, / Unseen but as distant motion made whole . . ."—are remarkable for their realism and their apparent ease in handling a very difficult perception. Lines five through eight recall Hopkins' "The Windhover" in their sound effects and imagery, and not altogether to their disadvantage. Indeed, when we remember that Hopkins' poem is also wholly descriptive, we can see a similarity, in the intentions of the two poems. Hopkins makes his falcon a symbol of the glory of Christ, while Momaday makes his hawk an emblem of the physical glory of nature.

We can see, then, that Momaday has two principle concerns in Part I of **The Gourd Dancer**: to present meditations on death and mutability, and to offer instants of vision that penetrate to the very essence of nature. Both of these concerns are evident in what may be the strongest poems in this part, the four "Plainview" poems.

"Plainview: 1" is perhaps Momaday's most lyrically beautiful, yet also poignant, poem. In form the poem is a modified sonnet, written in seven heroic couplets. It is Momaday's only published attempt in this traditional form, but its success shows that he has fully mastered its difficulties. The poem's purpose is to offer an almost mystical insight into nature—a "plainview." Essentially, the poem is a description of the slow advance of a storm, and as such, it is telling in its realism. Yet the grave tone, the meditative mood, and the haunting, evanescent imagery suggest something far deeper.

The key is the magpies. They appear three times, and are seemingly a clear, distinct perception: there are eleven of them. When the storm breaks, however, we find that they are "illusion." So, the magpies come to symbolize the limited nature of human percipience, as well as the fundamentally illusory nature of material reality: i.e., material things have no reality per se, but only as they symbolize spiritual or ideal reality. Momaday makes much this same point in the third of his *Santa Fe New Mexico Viva* columns, where we see his attraction to a rather Berkleyan idealism: "A thing is realized by means of perception, and not otherwise. Existence itself is illusory; we inhabit a dream in the mind of God" [30 April 1972]. This idea is supported by the shimmering caducity of the images in the poem: "a wind informs / This distance with a gathering of storms / And drifts in silver crescents on the grass, / Configurations that appear, and pass." "Plainview: 1" allows us to see the whole panorama of the plains in an intensified moment of flux and change. Still, there is permanency too. Behind the transitoriness of the moment, there is the initially tentative, but later forcibly manifest, presence of the storm—the greater pattern of reality behind the ephemeral impressions.

"Plainview: 1" amply evinces the sureness of Momaday's poetic control, as well as the difficulty and depth of his perceptions. It is one of the finest of post-modern sonnets. In fact, stanzas two, three, and seven are reminiscent of Shakespeare's own sonnets in their measured music and grace.

"Plainview: 2" takes its form from the Native American oral tradition (which should not disguise its syllabic rhythm). It is a powerfully sustained elegy for the horse culture of the American Indian. It is a commentary on the death of a culture, of a way of life. The old Indian in the poem now lives solaced by drinking and the dream of drinking. But he challenges the reader (and we must assume, particularly the Indian reader) to preserve and hold the old life in memory. The exhortation, "Remember my horse," is repeated again and again like a drumbeat in the poem.

We can only realize the importance of this idea when we understand the significance of the horse to the Plains Indians. Momaday explains this significance in an early essay:

> . . . the horse brought a new and material way of life. The Kiowa pulled up the roots which had always held him to the ground. He was given the means to prevail against distance. For the first time he could move beyond the limits of his human strength, of his vision, even of his former dreams. . . . But the greatest change was psychological. Seated behind the withers of a horse elevated to a height from which the far world was made a possession of the eye, sensually conscious of an immense fund of living power under him and nearly part of him the Kiowa was greater than he was.

["The Morality of Indian Hating," *Ramparts 3,* No. 1 (Summer 1969)]

The psychological destruction necessarily inherent in the destruction of the horse culture then, is staggering. This gives the overwhelming sense of sorrow and loss to the poem. The middle stanza is especially expressive of this loss: "A horse is one thing / An Indian another / An old horse is old / An old Indian sad."

This elegiac treatment of cultural death is reinforced by the movement of the imagery, very evident in the last stanza: first the horse is seen as vigorous and healthy: "running," "wheeling," "blowing," "standing"; then the horse is seen in images of death: "hurting," "falling," and "dying." The joining of the first two lines from stanzas two through eight creates a very swift, intense finale to the poem. The closing lines, moving from "Remember my blue-black horse" to "Remember my horse" to "Remember / Remember" is forceful and potent in evoking the theme. The drumbeats become more rapid, and suddenly stop. "Plainview: 2" as a whole is incredibly moving. It places the human experience in the plains. This experience is tragic. "Plainview: 3" returns to the impersonal view of the land of "Plainview: 1," which suggests an affirmation of the eternality of nature behind the human pathos. The poem is a brief, incisive succession of metaphors for dawn. It carries us quickly beyond the mere fact of sunrise to a joyous celebration of the spirit of the renewal, beautiful and harmonious, of the day. It is a poem of spiritual regeneration through the land.

"Plainview: 3" can also be read as prayer of praise to the sun. For, as James Mooney tells us in *Calendar History of the Kiowa Indians,* the Kiowas were a sun-worshipping people: "The greatest of the Kiowa gods is the Sun; by him they swear, to him they make sacrifice of their own flesh, and in his honour they hold the great annual *kado* or sun dance." The note of praise is evident in the increasing vibrancy in the images of the poem. "Plainview: 3" is doubtless a minor effort; but it plays an important role in the development of the sequence.

"Plainview: 4" turns again to the darker vision of human experience. Indeed, the movement from "Plainview: 3" to "Plainview: 4" is a movement from the golden age of the Plains Indian culture to its death. The predominant tone here is one of remorse, of sad regret. Poor Buffalo's house is empty now. Yet the poet had known a time when it was filled with life, when the Kiowa captive, Millie Durgan, had lived there. The mood in the first part of the poem is wistful reflection. The mention of Millie Durgan leads to the jauntier ballad stanza on the captive. The tone now is light and happy: the time recalled is the heroic age of the Kiowas, when they commanded the prairies, stole captives, and relished the freedom of distance. Millie Durgan was stolen in 1864 at the age of 18 months. Mildred P. Mayhall mentions her in her book, *The Kiowas:* "Millie (Sain-toh-oodie) grew up a Kiowa, married a chief, Goombi, had children, and only learned late in life of her true origin." So, Millie Durgan was wholly a Kiowa in culture.

The last part of the poem is heavily ironic in its statement. The poet hears "a music" "about the house"—the folksong, "Shoot the Buffalo." Though this song gives a superficially lively ending to the poem, it lends a profoundly pathetic note to the poem's subject. The killing of the buffalo effectively marked the extinction of the old,

nomadic life of the plains. Momaday says this about the destruction of the buffalo in "The Morality of Indian Hating": "Perhaps the most immoral act ever committed against the land was the senseless killing of the buffalo. The loss of the Sun Dance was the blow that killed the Kiowa culture. The Kiowas might have endured every privation but that, the destruction of their faith. Without their religion there was nothing to sustain them." The sequence closes then on a note of deep sadness. Together with "Plainview: 2" this poem offers a tragic meditation on the death of a great culture, a loss that transcends the personal and becomes a moral failure for all Americans.

This sequence of "Plainview" poems not only contains two of Momaday's finest poems, it also marks as a whole the most powerful single moment in part I of *The Gourd Dancer*. It also prefigures the dominant theme of part II: Momaday's Native American heritage.

"The Delight Song of Tsoai-Talee" is Momaday's own song of joy, and it is particularly expressive of his Plains Indian heritage. In form the poem makes a playful glance at Whitman's catalogues, but it really reflects the oral tradition. The poem is about the imaginative integration of the self into the land. Momaday has identified his spirit with the land, and shown the beauty and psychic sanity that identification promises. That this integration is peculiarly an act of the imagination is shown in the last line of the first stanza: "I am the whole dream of these things."

Momaday has emphasized many times in his *Viva* columns his feeling of unity with and fulfillment in the land:

> I came to know the land by going out upon it in all seasons, getting into it until it became the very element in which I lived my daily life. [25 June 1972]

> And I too, happen to take place, each day of my life, in my environment. I exist in a landscape and my existence is indivisible with the land. [30 July 1972]

What really emerges from the poem's first stanza is Momaday's perception of the beauty of the land, and of its vitality. Momaday asks in his essay, "A First American Views His Land," [which appeared in *National Geographic* 150, No. 1 (July 1976),] where the Native American concept of the land derives from: "Perhaps it begins with the recognition of beauty, the realization that the physical world *is* beautiful." This appreciation of beauty has its moral aspects, too. Momaday explains the Indian view of the land and how it is achieved in that same essay:

> Very old in the Native American view is the conviction that the earth is vital, that there is a spiritual dimension to it, a dimension in which man rightly exists. It follows logically that there are ethical imperatives in this matter. I think: Inasmuch as I am in the land, it is appropriate that I should affirm myself in the spirit of the land. I shall celebrate my life in the world and the world in my life. In the natural order man invests himself in the landscape and at the same time incorporates the landscape into his own most fundamental experience. The trust is sacred.

The process of investment and appropriation is, I believe, preeminently a function of the imagination. It is accomplished by means of an act of the imagination that is especially ethical in kind.

It is this very "investment" in the land, this celebratory affirmation of the spirit of the land that is the purpose and subject of this poem. The repeated line, "You see, I am alive, I am alive," emphasizes the fact that it is in making this imaginative investment in the land that man fully realizes himself as a living creature. The poem is truly a "delight song," a singing of the beauty of the union of man and land. It is a meditative poem, but unlike the other meditations in part I, it is a meditation on the meaning of life, not death. In part I of *The Gourd Dancer,* "Angle of Geese," we see the whole nature of human existence examined, both life and death. It is just these two themes that we find in the sister poems from *The Way to Rainy Mountain,* "Headwaters" and "Rainy Mountain Cemetery."

"Headwaters" is about the Kiowa emergence myth narrated in *The Way to Rainy Mountain.* The poem revisits— just as Momaday does in prose in the conclusion of *The Names*—the log in the intermontane marsh from which the Kiowas emerged one at a time into this world. The log is described in the poem, but the real theme of the poem comes in the final four lines.

The last lines evince the focus of the poem as the power that made the myth, which related conscious man to his universe, endowing him with identity and a place in the land. This power of the mind, the imagination, is awe-engendering in the endless fertility of its resources. Momaday surveys the physical scene in a finely drawn still-life and asks, "What moves?" His answer is a recognition and affirmation of the myth-making power: "What moves on this archaic force / Was wild and welling at the source." These lines are filled with the resonance of the spiritual health and strength of the Kiowa people. There is a suggestion of unbounded energy in the creations of the cultural mind.

Still, the poem is not merely nostalgic. For in the very imaginative act that is the poem, there is a recrudescence of the primeval power that shaped the original myths. And in the waters that "Stand brimming to the stalks," there is a hint that this power is still a dynamic force, a spiritual resource.

"Rainy Mountain Cemetery" is a searching meditation on death; in this case, that of Momaday's grandmother, Aho. The name of the poet's grandmother no longer stands as a symbol of herself, but of "this dark stone." Death "deranges" the possibilities of a life, precludes them ("the mind to be"), and they remain "Forever in the nominal unknown." The last lines of the first stanza reveal the pathetic position of the living, who, in trying to confront and understand the personal significance of a death, hear only "The wake of nothing audible."

In stanza two the eternal presence of the land is contrasted with the personal loss of death. The mood is one of resigned grief, of acceptance of the irrefragable obscurity of death. One instance of the subtlety of Momaday's craft

is how the half-rhyme at the end of each stanza (the poem's only irregular rhymes) serves to create the feeling of painful and inescapable loss. This may show the influence of Emily Dickinson, one of Momaday's favorite poets.

We come nearly full circle in **"Before an Old Painting of the Crucifixion"** to the themes we discussed in **"Angle of Geese."** Yvor Winters is certainly right in thinking this poem "Momaday's most impressive achievement" among his early poems; and Winters' remarks on the poem show great sensitivity. The poem's first two stanzas reveal the attitude of Christ toward his self-sacrifice. The first stanza enlarges upon the last moment of critical despair. In the "vibrant wake of utterance," Christ's outcry, despair is overweening; it "preoccupies, / Though it is still." It "preoccupies," that is, the poet, who is compelled by its power: it is a despair for which "There is no solace there," in the silence after the cry. There is no possibility of amelioration or assuagement.

The second stanza makes another comment on the silence after the cry. It is the "calm" of nature, a stillness in which the human mind can find no assurance or "peace" but in the face of silence or "solitude" itself. The poet turns to consider the sacrifice itself.

Christ, though to the onlookers who are excluded from his knowledge and despair, "Absurd and public in his agony," himself owns a moment of crystal lucidity: his despair at his imminent death is for Him, "Inscrutably itself, nor misconstrued, / Nor metaphrased in art or pseudonym: / / A vague contagion." This is the inner understanding that has nothing to do, really, with the outer spectacle. This is the moment of clairvoyant consciousness that so "preoccupies" the poet.

The Gourd Dancer **is an organically unified body of poems tracing the evolution of a new and accomplished voice in American poetry. . . . Through his skill and the power of his rhetoric Momaday is able to make the themes that emerge distinctly his own: death and time, the beauty of the land, and his Indian heritage.**

—Kenneth C. Mason

In the third stanza we turn from the mural and the thoughts it inspires to the poet's memory of the sea, the sea in which the poet has told us (in stanza two) that this same "calm" of despair is perceived. The sea, so "mute in constancy," represents the eternity that "The mural but implies." In meditating on the muteness of the sea, the poet comes to understand the reality of death: "Not death, but silence after death is change." In the "calm" then, of Christ's despair, and in the muteness of the sea, we have an apprehension of death—the reality that is in its stark fact, a "change" from life.

The fourth and fifth stanzas take us back into the scene described by the mural. In the meditative entrance into the painting, the poet knows for a moment the "eternity" implied by the scene depicted.

The final stanza reflects a moral dimension not hitherto evident in the poem. The concern with time in the preceding stanzas reminds the poet that "These centuries removed from either fact / Have lain upon the critical expanse / And been of little consequence." Man, perhaps because he has perceived only the "Absurd and public" aspect of the crucifixion, has learned little from the great act of suffering and sacrifice: "The void / Is calendared in stone; the human act, / Outrageous, is in vain." There is genuine pathos in the realization that not only have these twenty centuries been a moral "void," but that time continues, without abatement, with no moral transformation evident: "the hours advance / Like flecks of foam borne landwards and destroyed." The metaphoric return to the sea, here so utterly opposite, in its association, the serene sea of stanza three, creates a depth of suggestion and a structural unity in the poem.

"Before an Old Painting of the Crucifixion" is a brilliant achievement in meditative poetry, begging comparison with the best poems of Theodore Roethke's "North American Sequence" or the finest of Robert Lowell's meditations in *Lord Weary's Castle*.

Part II, **"The Gourd Dancer,"** departs from the metaphysical themes of part I and engages in a consideration of the subject Momaday is best known for: his Kiowa heritage. The first poem in this part is the title poem, **"The Gourd Dancer."** This is one of Momaday's two or three strongest poems, and certainly the outstanding poem in part II. It enunciates the themes of this second part, just as **"Angle of Geese"** enunciates those of the first part.

"The Gourd Dancer" is divided into four sections; section 1 is called, "The Omen." It is written in blank verse, and is very much akin to those poems of part I which describe an epiphanic appreciation of nature. The first line—"Another season centers on this place"—tells us that time has passed, and that the poem's subject, the poet's grandfather, Mammedaty remains only in memory. The next lines show the poet's identification with the land, which is said to be "like memory," an act of the mind.

The final two lines of the first stanza and the whole of the second stanza are descriptive. The appearance of the owl is the omen, though its meaning is obscure. In speaking of the Kiowas' religious beliefs, James Mooney makes a comment on owls that may be helpful here: "There is an indistinct idea of transmigration, owls and other night birds being supposed to be animated by the souls of the dead. . . ." Thus the owl can function for the poet as a symbolic reminder of Mammedaty. The omen provides an occasion for the rest of the poem, which is three separate but related memories of Mammedaty.

Section 2 is called "The Dream." It is told in prose, and is in its narrative manner reminiscent of the stories in *The*

Way to Rainy Mountain. The first lines are lyrically descriptive, telling of Mammedaty's building of his house—a house we come to know well in *The Names*. But the truly important lines deal with his "dreaming," which should remind us that dreaming for the Plains Indian cultures is equivalent to having a religious vision. Mooney explains that "dreams and visions are supernatural revelations, to be trusted and obeyed implicitly." Mammedaty dreams while dancing in the Gourd Dance: "He dreamed of dreaming and of the summer breaking upon his spirit, as drums break upon the intervals of the dance, and of the gleaming gourds." This dance leads to the dream and to union with the earth ("summer"). This brings us to the third section of the poem, titled "The Dance," written in free verse lines of increasing length in each stanza—which may be a reflection of the physical progress of the dance.

Momaday has devoted [his 23 July 1972 *Viva* column] to the Gourd Dance, relating the legend of the dance's origin, and telling of his own initiation in 1969 into the Taimpe (Gourd Dance) Society. He also offers a description of the dance, which should be of help in looking at "The Dance":

> It is an ineffable music, low like thunder, and hypnotic. You become caught up in it, dancing, and it carries you away to the center of the world. For a time there is no reality but that, the pure celebration of your being in relation to the singing and the drums and the dance. It is the most profound experience of music that I have ever known.

Likewise, Mammedaty "dreams" as he dances, and becomes one with the center of reality; there is a pure identity of the land and the spirit: "The long-wind glances, moves / Forever as a music to the mind; / The gourds are flashes of the sun." The Gourd Dance unites the dancer, too, with the ancient, enduring traditions of his people: "He takes the inward, mincing steps / That conjure old processions and returns." The dance is the living evidence as well as the symbol of the strength and vitality of the culture.

The second stanza evinces how the accoutrements of the dance, the moccasins, sash, and bandolier, "Contain him [the dancer] in insignia"—symbolize the essence of the man who has given himself up to the dancing. Mammedaty's eagle-feather fan "holds upon the deep, ancestral air," again revealing the union in the dance with his heritage.

"The Giveaway," the final, prose section of the poem, may require some cultural background to be fully appreciated. Momaday explains in the same *Viva* column: "After each song there is a 'giveaway' ceremony, an ancient custom of the Plains whereby various people are honored through the giving of gifts." Momaday's whole poem first appeared in his column for November 4, 1973. But in an earlier column, he had described Mammedaty's dancing and the giveaway afterwards. The details are essentially the same as those of the poem, but the poem gives some a greater emphasis. For example, the earlier column reads: "Mammedaty's name was called out, and he arose and stepped forward." This moment in the poem is highly intensified. The cultural significance of the name is explained, and the calling of Mammedaty's name is given special importance: "Someone spoke his name, Mammedaty, in which his essence was and is. It was a serious matter that his name should be spoken there in the circle, among the many people, and he was thoughtful, full of wonder, and aware of himself and of his name." This enlargement upon the bare journalistic fact of the column not only serves to create a finer dramatic moment, it also reveals something of the man, Mammedaty. In similar fashion, the description of the black horse is lyrically intensified in the poem.

We must remember the absolute preeminence of the horse in Plains Indian cultures if we are to fully comprehend the meaning and force of the gift of the horse in the giveaway. Mooney's comments on the acquisition of the horse by the Plains tribes add to what we have learned from Momaday:

> It is unnecessary to dilate on the revolution made in the life of the Indian by this possession of the horse. Without it he was a half-starved skulker in the timber, creeping up on foot toward the unwary deer or building a brush corral with infinite labor to surround a herd of antelope, and seldom venturing more than a few days' journey from home. With the horse he was transformed into the daring buffalo hunter, able to procure in a single day enough food to supply his family for a year, leaving him free to sweep the plains with his war parties along a range of a thousand miles.

Hence, the gift of a horse is the greatest possible gift; it is an event of the highest magnitude. The last sentence of the poem tells us that the gift "was for Mammedaty, in his honor," and that the poem is, too. **"The Gourd Dancer"** is a superb tribute to the man, Mammedaty, and it is a remarkable example of imagined recollection.

"New World" leaves the personal and historical for the mythical past, telling of primal man's first view of his pristine new world on earth. **"New World"** opens with the command, "First Man, / Behold," and the rest of the poem is an evocation of the world he beholds. The four sections of the poem are spliced into Momaday's essay, "A First American Views His Land," and Momaday's comments on the Indian's aesthetic, moral, and religious perceptions of the land illustrate well the values implicit in this poem. **"New World"** illustrates particularly well what Momaday says in the "first truth" of the Indian: "The first truth is that I *love* the land; I see that it is beautiful; I delight in it; I am alive in it." The poem, with its crisp formalism (two beat syllabic rhythm), shows in a succession of quickly drawn but poignant images the beauty of the wild land, and the delight one can take in it. For one example we might take the almost Virgilian simplicity and lyricism of section 3: "At noon / turtles / enter / slowly / into / the warm / dark loam / Bees hold / the swarm. / Meadows / recede / through places / of heat / and pure / distance." There is no sense at all here of man. There is only untamed natural beauty.

The first section of **"New World"** presents a broad first vision of the new land. Sections 2-4 seek to capture the essential spirit of the land at three representative moments: dawn, noon, and dusk. The imagery for each section is appropriate, and there is no lapse in the purity of Momaday's vision in any section. Together, these three moments stand for a whole day and the day presented offers an integral vision of a sacred natural richness before the advent of the course of empire. **"New World"** is a poem of imaginative celebration of the earth. It resembles, earlier poems like **"Pit Viper"** and **"Bueto Regalis"** in that its form is based on what might be called a series of epiphanic perceptions of nature.

"Carriers of the Dream Wheel" defines better than any poem I know the spirit of the oral tradition. William Stafford, in his poem, "A Stared Story," addresses the Indian "survivors" of the twentieth century, who are "slung here in our cynical constellation." These people must now "live by imagination." Momaday's poem shows that it is the imagination that has always given life to Indian cultures. It is the "Wheel of Dreams," their "sacred songs" and "old stories," living orally, ever one generation from extinction, that expresses their reality, and enables them to find and feel a wholeness and meaning in existence: "This is the Wheel of Dreams / Which is carried on their voices, / By means of which their voices turn / And center upon being." The Wheel of Dreams, which is both the body of the songs and stories and the dynamic imagination that calls them into being, defines the reality of the First World: men "shape their songs upon the wheel / And spin the names of the earth and sky, / The aboriginal names." In *The Names* Momaday explains his belief that the real essences of things are inherent in their names. Thus, the great power of the Wheel that enables men to name things, and, in a manner of speaking, create or reveal the nature of the world.

The most evocative lines in the poems are the final four. They express just how the oral tradition sustained and renewed itself and gave life to the people. The contemporary relevance of these lines and of the poem is that it states how the old traditions can be preserved and regenerated today. Contemporary Indian poets are the current "Carriers of the Dream Wheel," and it is through their poems that contemporary Indians can define their reality and "center upon being." This is obviously what Duane Niatum had in mind when he used this poem as the title poem of his anthology of contemporary Indian poetry.

If **"Carriers of the Dream Wheel"** reveals the essence of the oral tradition, **"The Colors of Night"** presents it directly in eight brief prose stories. Each of these stories reveals a different aspect of the Indian world view, Section 1, "White," is based on a historical incident recorded by Mooney, and it is an excellent example of how the poetic imagination can shape historical fact to its own purposes. Here is Mooney's account:

> In the spring of 1870, before the last sun dance, the son of the noted chief Set-angya ("Sitting Bear") . . . had made a raid with a few followers into Texas, where, while making an attack upon a house, he had been shot and killed. After the dance, his father with some friends went to Texas, found his bones and

wrapped them in several line blankets, put the bundle upon the back of a led horse and brought them home. . . . While on a march the remains were always put upon the saddle of a led horse, as when first brought home. . . .

What Momaday has added to this bare narrative is the father's emotional response to his son's death. The death is seen, not as a tragic event, but rather, as a transcendence. The boy has become part of the beautiful pattern of nature, beyond loss or pain; his bones now "gleam like glass in the light of the sun and moon," and the boy has become "very beautiful."

Section 2, "Yellow," also treats the theme of death's transcendence. A boy drowns, but he does so fulfilling a vision that is beyond place and time: "His vision ran along the path of light and reached across the wide night and took hold of the moon." Perhaps because of the power of the vision, a grace is found beyond death; the boy is transformed and a black dog emerges on the other shore. The dog howls all night at the moon, showing the continuing truth of the vision. As in all stories of transformation, there is a distinct air of mystery here, a mystery that excites the imagination, even as it precludes certitude.

Section 3, "Brown," is a somewhat humorous parable on the pursuit of knowledge. Quite simply the story shows how mere empiricism, minute knowledge of external detail, cannot reveal the essence of a thing. The boy looks hard at the terrapin and memorizes its face, yet "he [fails] to see how it was that the terrapin knew anything at all." This knowledge requires a spiritual insight, an intuitive rapport with nature and a humility before its mysteries.

Section 4, "Red," however, shows how knowledge can be misused and what the consequences are. The man has the "powerful medicine," and he is able to fashion the woman out of leaves. But when the man abuses the woman, the result is destruction and death. She is "blown apart" by a whirlwind and scattered as leaves across the plain. The whirlwind represents the power and potency of the sacred, a force that is always removed from man's complete comprehension.

Section 5, "Green," is the shortest and most enigmatic of the stories. But like section 2, it testifies to the truth of visionary perception. Though the vision of the tree and the shape made of smoke are objectively qualified by the statement that they are "only an appearance," the last words of the sentence affirm the strength of the vision: "there was a tree." This section of the poem is a glimpse into the nature of extra-visual knowledge, and it is imbued with a sense of mysterious potency.

Section 6, "Blue," also treats an instance of visionary perception. Here, however, the reality of the perception is denied. If the tribe is right in denying the vision, the story illustrates that a requisite of visions is that they not be too obscure to be of any use: "'After all,' said an old man, 'how can we believe in the child? It gave us not one word of sense to hold onto.'"

The irrational nature of human evil is examined in section 7, "Purple." The man kills a buffalo for no reason but to see it die. The tribe is ashamed of and grief-stricken at the deed. But the blood of the buffalo runs into the sky and is transformed into the stars. In its etiology the story reaffirms the power of the sacred even over the most heinous human crime.

That the mystery of the sacred is real and that it interpenetrates the affairs of man seems to be the point of section 8, "Black." The long black hair, the "shadow which the firelight cannot cleave," is a good emblem for this mystery. This section of the poem enunciates a theme of the whole poem: there is a mystery in the nature of things which can be partially penetrated or intuitively comprehended—as through stories—but never fully dispelled; and it should not be. The eight stories or myths of this poem are each colors of the night, explorations of this mystery, and each has something unique to reveal about the Indian's world view.

The last four poems in part II, "The Gourd Dancer," are more contemporary in their subjects. But they are nonetheless related to the themes of the preceding poems in this part. Each of the poems presents an insight into nature or place that is particularly Indian. Part II, as we have seen, basically tries to present the philosophy and world view of the Native American. The poems are a rich and valuable extension of the themes Momaday treated in *The Way to Rainy Mountain.*

Part III of *The Gourd Dancer*, "Anywhere Is a Street into the Night," represents a final maturity in Momaday's poetic development. Now the poet is the master of his craft and all his circumstances. Anything can provide a subject for a poem—"anywhere is a street into the night." The poet can write about the intrusion of crows in a winter solitude, an old woman sitting in a room, two women who differ radically in personality, an observance of an acting class, the danger of praise to the artist, or the social isolation of the tourist visiting the Soviet Union. Anything that appeals to the poet's imagination can provide an entrance into a poem. This is the theme of the poem that gives its title to this section. In this poem the poet waits at the window (the symbol of poetic observation of life), and of itself the desire for creation comes. The poet feels the "old urgency," and "anywhere / Is a street into the night, / Deliverance and delight. . . ." The mastery of the poet is not only seen in this imaginative ability, but also in his recognition that each poem, each street into the night of the imagination, "will pass"—that for the poet there can be no standing on the achievements of any one poem; he must return another time to the window and wait.

Given this new poetic assurance, it is not surprising that Momaday can treat his Native American themes with a new freshness and intensity. **"The Burning,"** like **"Plainview: 2,"** is an elegy for the heroic age of the Indian cultures. The poem is a conceit: the apocalyptic destructiveness of the fire is a very apt metaphor for the ravaging advent of the white man ("always alien and alike"). The poem catches with great success the tragic innocence of the Indians as they learn of the approaching disaster, watch for its arrival, and finally succumb to the inexorable will of its drive. What is most striking about the poem is the ease and naturalness with which Momaday sustains the conceit. The imagery is stark and suggestive, and the detail precise and telling. The final lines are extremely moving in their desperate inevitability: "And in the foreground the fields were fixed in fire / And the flames flowered in our flesh." **"The Burning"** is a new and significant direction for Momaday in his treatment of native materials. It is also a fine attempt at a mature summation of the themes he has treated before.

"Forms of the Earth at Abiquiu" is a major poem, summing up Momaday's ideas about the land. It is a joyful meditation on the beauty of the earth. The real subject of the poem, though, is the special bond and communion between two artists; it is fitting that Momaday should find Georgia O'Keeffe a kindred spirit. In his [10 December 1972] *Viva* column he has spoken of her with admiration: "In her the sense of place is definitive of her great, artistic spirit. She perceives in the landscape of New Mexico an essence and quality of life that enables her to express her genius, and she, too, is a native in her soul." Like Momaday, Georgia O'Keeffe finds her inspiration and her spiritual sustenance in the land, and she is identified with it.

Because they are open to the beauty of the earth the poet and the artist stand in good relation to it. They share an appreciation of the dried snake bones, the cow and sheep skulls, and most of all, the small stones (which are the very emblem of the land). The poet wishes "to feel the sun in the stones," the life source and principle. He gives a stone to the artist and she "[knows] at once that it [is] beautiful," just as she knows the greater forms of the earth at Abiquiu. The final lines evoke the timeless impersonality and grandeur of grandeur of the land forms in winter.

As the first lines of **"Forms of the Earth . . ."** tell us, the poem is an act of imagination. It is in the imagined recreation of experience that the poet can find and reveal the meaning of experience. And it is in the making of the poem, that the experience is given a timeless form. Momaday has achieved this timelessness in **"Forms of the Earth at Abiquiu."**

Momaday closes *The Gourd Dancer* with the short poem, **"Two Figures."** Brief as this poem is, it is singularly poignant. The poet faces his own mortality, faces it with a stoic acceptance of its inevitability. Though his poems have an independent life of their own, the poet is inescapably involved in death and time. **"Two Figures"** rounds the collection very nicely back to the themes of part I, making the structural circle that is the hallmark of all Momaday's books, the circle of wholeness and completion.

The Gourd Dancer is an organically unified body of poems tracing the evolution of a new and accomplished voice in American poetry. It is a summation of nearly twenty years of writing. Through his skill and the power of his rhetoric Momaday is able to make the themes that emerge distinctly his own: death and time, the beauty of the land, and his Indian heritage. *The Gourd Dancer* will surely bring the attention to Momaday's poetry that has already been awarded his prose. One only hopes that we will not have to wait another twenty years for his next book of poems.

N. Scott Momaday with Joseph Bruchac (interview date 1982)

SOURCE: An interview with N. Scott Momaday, in *American Poetry Review,* Vol. 13, No. 4, July/August, 1984, pp. 13-18.

[*In the following excerpt from an interview conducted in December 1982, Momaday discusses such subjects as Yvor Winters' influence on his works, the difference between poetry and prose, the major themes in his poetry, and Native American literature.*]

[*Joseph Bruchac*]: *In a recent book entitled* Four American Indian Literary Masters, *Alan R. Velie links your poetry strongly with those whom he calls "the post-symbolists" and your former teacher, Yvor Winters. Do you think that really was correct?*

[N. Scott Momaday]: Well, to an extent, yes. I don't remember what Velie had to say, exactly. "Post-symbolist," by the way is Yvor Winters's term, not Velie's. It is an important concept in Winters's critical canon, and I would not presume to say what it is or what it has to do with my work. Anyone interested in it ought to go directly to Winters's last work, *Forms of Discovery.* I didn't know much about the traditional aspects of poetry until I went to Stanford and studied under Winters. Winters was a very fine teacher, and no doubt he had a significant influence upon a good many of his students over the years. In 1959, when I went to Stanford, I was just ready to be educated in terms of prosody, and I owe a good deal of what I know about poetry to Yvor Winters. I think that my early poems, especially those that are structured according to traditional English forms, are in some respects the immediate result of his encouragement and of his teaching.

Poems such as "Angle of Geese" or "The Bear". . . .

"Angle of Geese" and **"The Bear"** are written in syllabics; that is, the number of syllables in each line is predetermined and invariable; it is therefore the number of syllables to the line, rather than the number of "feet," which constitutes the measure. I was just playing around a lot with syllabics at Stanford—I wasn't even aware of the term "syllabics" until I went to Winters's class in the writing of poetry. So, yes, those would be two examples. But I got tired of the traditional forms. When I left Stanford I had worked myself into such a confinement of form that I started writing fiction and didn't get back to poetry until much later—three years, perhaps—and when I did, I started writing a very different kind of poetry.

I notice, before we talk about that different kind of poetry, that you chose the poem, "The Bear." What is it that made you choose that poem to read [before our interview]? What is important to you about that particular poem?

It was pretty much a random choice, but I like the poem because it is early and it is one of my first really successful poems, as I think of it. It deals with nature, as much of my work does, and it is rhymed in syllabics, and so there are good, solid controlling devices at work in the poem, and that, that aspect of control, is important to me. I wanted to see how closely I could control the statement, and it seems to me that I controlled it about as well as I could. "The Bear" won some sort of prize at Stanford—a prize awarded by the Academy of American Poets, I think. I was ecstatic.

What forms do you think you're working in now in your poetry? I've heard them described as prose poems by Velie and other people. In some cases, I know some aren't.

No. I continue working in syllabics. I have written what is called "free verse," though to my mind that is a contradiction in terms. I'm greatly interested in the so-called "prose poem," another contradiction in terms, but what I mean is, I like writing what is essentially a lyrical prose in which I'm not concerned with meter, but with rhythms and fluencies of sound, primarily. I wrote a piece, which no doubt you've seen in *The Gourd Dancer,* called **"The Colors of Night,"** which is really a collection of quintessential novels, I suppose—very short, lyrical stories. I would like to continue working in that free form.

As a matter of fact that particular poem is one of my favorites in **The Gourd Dancer.** *I thought it interesting that in that book you combine both the earlier poems and the later poems, and they didn't seem to be combined in a chronological order but rather in terms of subject matter. When you put the book together what was your structuring theory or device?*

I wanted, as you say, to group the several poems in certain ways. There is a chronological progression to it. The early poems, recognizably traditional forms, I think, are contained in the first section, then the second section is of a very different character, informed by a native voice, and the third section is, or was then, quite recent work. Much of it was written in the Soviet Union.

Did it affect your writing when you worked in another country?

I think it did. I'm not sure that I can say how, exactly. There was a great compulsion there to write, and that surprised me; I could not have anticipated that. But when I got there and had been there a while and had begun to understand a little bit about my isolation and my distance from my native land, this somehow became a creative impulse for me, and so I wrote much more than I thought I would. And I wrote about things I saw and felt in the Soviet Union. **"Krasnopresnenskaya Station"** is an exam-

ple. The little poem called **"Anywhere is a Street into the Night"** is a comment upon my understanding of that distance that I mentioned a moment ago. But I also found myself writing about my homeland, the Southwest—perhaps as a kind of therapy. I wrote the poem that I dedicated to Georgia O'Keeffe (**"Forms of the Earth at Abiquiu"**) there, for example, and it is very much an evocation of the Southwest, isn't it?

This Southwestern landscape which turns up in your poems throughout your writing . . . how do you define that landscape? What are the important qualities of it for you? The qualities of life in the Southwest which are important. . . .

Well, I think it's a much more spiritual landscape than any other that I know personally. And it is beautiful, simply in physical terms. The colors in that landscape are very vivid, as you know, and I've always been greatly moved by the quality of light upon the colored landscape of New Mexico and Arizona.

Yes, that's evident in your work.

And I think of it as being inhabited by a people who are truly involved in it. The Indians of the Southwest, and the Pueblo people, for example, and the Navajos with whom I grew up, they don't live on the land; they live *in* it, in a real sense. And that is very important to me, and I like to evoke as best I can that sense of belonging to the earth.

I think that idea of belonging is also of central importance. In The Names *or even in some of your poems, you present us with situations where there is a possibility for distance, or a possibility for alienation. But I don't see that alienation coming about. I see, rather, a motion in a different direction—towards a kind of resolution. Am I correct in seeing this?*

I think that's a fair statement.

> I have written what is called "free verse," though to my mind that is a contradiction in terms. I'm greatly interested in the so-called "prose poem," another contradiction in terms, but what I mean is, I like writing what is essentially a lyrical prose in which I'm not concerned with meter, but with rhythms and fluencies of sound, primarily.
>
> —*N. Scott Momaday*

Why is that so? Why are you not an existentialist, for example, a "modern" man looking at the world as separate from the person?

Well, I'm a product of my experience, surely, of what I have seen and known of the world. I've had, by the way, what I think of as a very fortunate growing up. On the basis of my experience, trusting my own perceptions, I don't see any validity in the separation of man and the landscape. Oh, I know that the notion of alienation is very widespread, in a sense very popular. But I think it's an unfortunate point of view and a false one, where the relationship between man and the earth is concerned. Certainly it is one of the great afflictions of our time, this conviction of alienation, separation, isolation. And it is certainly an affliction in the Indian world. But there it has the least chance of taking hold, I believe, for there it is opposed by very strong forces. The whole world view of the Indian is predicated upon the principle of harmony in the universe. You can't tinker much with that; it has the look of an absolute.

Do you differentiate between prose and poetry in a strict sense?

When I talk about definitions, yes. Prose and poetry are opposed in a certain way. It's hard to define poetry. Poetry is a statement concerning the human condition, composed in verse. (I did not invent this definition, skeletal as it is. I think I may be repeating something I heard in class years ago.) In that refinement, in that reservation, "composed in verse," is really, finally, the matter that establishes the idea of poetry and sets it apart.

I wonder, because I see in the work of a number of American Indian writers, for example Leslie Silko, places where prose suddenly breaks into what appears to be verse in parts of Ceremony. *There the stories that are told are in a form I would describe as verse. I see, also, in a number of other writers who are American Indians, if not a blurring of that distinction, a passing back and forth, rather freely, between verse and prose. I see it, also, in your work . . . your prose in such books as* House Made of Dawn, *and especially* The Way to Rainy Mountain. *There are sections which one could read as poems. Is this observation a good one? Why do you think it's like this, with yourself and other American Indian prose writers?*

That's a large question, and I've thought about it before. The prose pieces in *The Way to Rainy Mountain* are illustrations of the very thing that I was talking about before, the lyrical prose, the thing that is called the prose poem. The oral tradition of the American Indian is intrinsically poetic in certain, obvious ways. I believe that a good many Indian writers rely upon a kind of poetic expression out of necessity, a necessary homage to the native tradition, and they have every right and reason to do so. It is much harder, I suspect, for an Indian to write a novel than to write a poem. The novel, as a form, is more unfamiliar to him in his native context. (That he does it at all is a kind of tour de force. I am thinking of Jim Welche's *Winter in the Blood,* for example, a fine novel, to my mind.) Again, I have to quibble with the word "verse." Verse, after all, strictly speaking, is a very precise meter of measure. My **"Plainview: 1,"** for example, is composed in verse. If you look at it closely you see that it is a sonnet, composed in heroic couplets, rhymed iambic pentameter. **"The Colors of Night,"** on the other hand, is not verse.

Meter, as such, is simply not a consideration in that piece. You can make the same distinction between, say, **"Abstract: Old Woman in a Room"** and **"Forms of the Earth at Abiquiu."** I will indeed quibble over terms here, for they are important. Verse greatly matters, though too few contemporary poets take it seriously, I'm afraid. Verse enables you to sharpen your expression considerably, to explore and realize more closely the possibilities of language. A given prose poem, so-called, may be superior to a given Shakespearean sonnet, but we are talking about an exception; the odds are against it. Sometimes, of course, it is worthwhile to go against the odds.

Vine Deloria complained, in an interview in 1977 in Sun Tracks that so many young American Indian writers turned to verse rather than writing in what he thought was a more useful form to communicate with the Anglo world, fiction or prose. Yet you're saying that really isn't so much of a choice, as a natural step.

I think so. At least, that's how I think of it.

I have noticed that certain themes appear to turn up again and again in your work. What are those themes? Do you think about them or are they there subconsciously?

I would say that much of my writing has been concerned with the question of man's relationship to the earth, for one thing. Another theme that has interested me is man's relationship to himself, to his past, his heritage. When I was growing up on the reservations of the Southwest, I saw people who were deeply involved in their traditional life, in the memories of their blood. They had, as far as I could see, a certain strength and beauty that I find missing in the modern world at large. I like to celebrate that involvement in my writing.

You don't think of yourself though as a person who is sort of conserving something that's disappearing, do you? I've heard that description of their work given by many non-Indian writers who have written about Indian ways. And I'm not just talking about anthropologists, but also some of the novelists of the early part of the century who thought of themselves as both celebrating and preserving—almost like an artifact—something which was vanishing. Yet I don't think that is characteristic of your approach.

No, I wouldn't say so. There is an aspect of this matter that has to do with preservation, of course—with a realization that things are passing. I feel this very keenly. But I'm not concerned to preserve relics and artifacts. Only superfically have things changed in the world I knew as a child. I can enumerate them. When I was growing up at Jemez Pueblo—I lived there for several years from the time I was twelve—I saw things that are not to be seen now. I wrote about some of them in *The Names*. I remember one day looking out upon a dirt road and seeing a caravan of covered wagons that reached as far as the eye could see. These were the Navajos coming in from Torreon to the annual Jemez feast on November 12, 1946. It was simply an unforgettable sight. But the next year it had changed considerably; there were fewer wagons, and there were some pickups, and the year after that there were still fewer wagons and more pickups, and the year after that there were no wagons. And I had later the sense that I had been in the right place at the right time, that I had seen something that will not be seen again, and I thank God for that. But the loss is less important to me than the spirit which informs the remembrance, the spirit that informs that pageantry across all ages and which persists in the imagination of every man everywhere.

Yes, that's a great example. Are words magical?

Oh, yes.

How so?

Well, words are powerful beyond our knowledge, certainly. And they are beautiful. Words are intrinsically powerful, I believe. And there is magic in that. Words come from nothing into being. They are created in the imagination and given life on the human voice. You know, we used to believe—and I'm talking now about all of us, regardless of our ethnic backgrounds—in the magic of words. The Anglo-Saxon who uttered spells over his fields so that the seeds would come out of the ground on the sheer strength of his voice, knew a good deal about language, and he believed absolutely in the efficacy of language. That man's faith—and may I say, wisdom—has been lost upon modern man, by and large. It survives in the poets of the world, I suppose, the singers. We do not now know what we can do with words. But as long as there are those among us who try to find out, literature will be secure; literature will remain a thing worthy of our highest level of human being.

You mention poets and singers. Are they related or are they different?

I think they are the same thing. You might make this sort of superficial distinction. The poet is concerned to construct his expression according to traditional and prescribed forms. The singer, too, composes his expression according to strict rules, but he is a more religious being, on the whole, less concerned with form than with the most fundamental and creative possibilities of language. The American Indian would be in the second of these categories. This distinction, of course, requires elucidation, but, for the time being, I shall spare you that.

And do you think there are some Indian poets who are still singers or vice versa?

Yes.

Could I ask you to read this one? I think it goes well with what we were just talking about.

Yes.

"The Delight Song of Tsoai-talee"

I am a feather on the bright sky
I am the blue horse that runs in the plain

I am the fish that rolls, shining, in the water
I am the shadow that follows a child
I am the evening light, the lustre of meadows
I am an eagle playing with the wind
I am a cluster of bright beads
I am the farthest star
I am the cold of the dawn
I am the roaring of the rain
I am the glitter on the crust of the snow
I am the long track of the moon in a lake
I am a flame of four colors
I am a deer standing away in the dusk
I am a field of sumac and the pomme blanche
I am an angle of geese in the winter sky
I am the hunger of a young wolf
I am the whole dream of these things
You see, I am alive, I am alive
I stand in good relation to the earth
I stand in good relation to the gods
I stand in good relation to all that is beautiful
I stand in good relation to the daughter of Tsen-
    tainte
You see, I am alive, I am alive

I've always liked this poem of yours very much. As you may know I chose it for translation into some European languages. This is your own song, isn't it?

Yes.

This is the name which you were given by an older relative?

The name was given to me by an old man, a paternal relative, actually. His name was Pohd-lohk, and he gave me the name when I was very young, less than a year old. Tsoai-talee means "rock-tree boy." It commemorates my having been taken, at the age of six months or so, to Devils Tower, Wyoming, which is a sacred place in Kiowa tradition. And the Kiowas call it "rock-tree." Therefore, Pohd-lohk gave me the name. All of this is set down in detail in *The Names*.

This poem or song makes me think of some very traditional poems or songs. I feel as though I can see, for example, that Southwestern influence, the traditional songs of the Navajos and Pueblo people. Especially the Navajo people. I also feel I see something which comes out of Plains Indians structures, a statement of who you are. Not so much a boasting song as a definition of being alive. Do you see all those things coming together in this? Is this part of what you did consciously or did the form of the poem come in and of itself?

I see those things in it, but I'm not sure that I set out to reflect them consciously in the poem. As I recall, the writing of it came quickly, without effort . . . it's not a poem that I crafted over a long period of time. It is more spontaneous than most of my poems.

Yes, you mention the word "dream" in here. Again it seems to me like the poem that comes out of a dream . . . the poem that traditionally would come as an inspiration from another voice.

Dreams, I suppose, are also a constant theme in my work. I'm very much aware of the visionary aspect of the Plains culture, especially the vision quest, so-called. I have more to say about that, I think, in another context. I'm writing a piece now, based upon a vision quest. It will be a novel, I think.

The idea of dreams, then . . . what are dreams?

Yeah, what are dreams? Has there ever been an answer to that? There is so much we have yet to know about dreams and dreaming. Dreams are prophetic, meaningful, revealing of inmost life. But no one knows how they work, as far as I know. I have powerful dreams, and I believe they determine who I am and what I do. But how, I'm not sure. Maybe that is how it ought to be. Mystery is, perhaps, the necessary condition of dreams.

The term, "the great mystery," is often used by some of the plains people to describe the Creator or that life force which is beyond and above all human, in other life. That's not a mystery that, I sense, native people wish to pierce. It's a mystery which they live in the knowledge of, without wanting to know "what" it is. It seems rather counter to the Western approach to things. The Anglo approach is to always know.

Yes, yes. I don't know.

I was talking about the contrast between the Western, Anglo, view and the American Indian view. I'd like to take that back directly to literature and ask what you think the difference is between, let's say, an Indian view of what literature is, and I don't mean just a traditional Indian person, but, let's say someone who has been raised in the twentieth century and who is writing still as an Indian, as opposed to that writer who is non-Indian.

I think there is only one real difference between the two, and that is that the Indian has the advantage of a very rich spiritual experience. As much can be said, certainly, of some non-Indian writers. But the non-Indian writers of today are culturally deprived, I think, in the sense that they don't have the same sense of heritage that the Indian has. I'm told this time and time again by my students, who say, "Oh, I wish I knew more about my grandparents; I wish I knew more about my ancestors and where they came from and what they did." I've come to believe them. It seems to me that the Indian writer ought to make use of that advantage. One of his subjects ought certainly to be his cultural investment in the world. It is a unique and complete experience, and it is a great subject in itself.

One thing which I'm concerned with is a sense of the continuance and the survival of various things which seem to be central to a number of American Indian writers. Do you see your work as continuing some tradition?

Yes. I think that my work proceeds from the American Indian oral tradition, and I think it sustains that tradition and carries it along. And vice versa. And my writing is also of a piece. I've written several books, but to me they are all parts of the same story. And I like to repeat myself, if you will, from book to book, in the way that Faulkner did—in an even more obvious way, perhaps. My purpose is to carry on what was begun a long time ago; there's no end to it that I can see.

That's a question that I was going to ask. I'm glad you led into it. In House Made of Dawn *there is a sermon which is given by a Kiowa character. He's not terribly likeable in some ways. Yet those words turn up again in* The Way to Rainy Mountain *out of, I assume, your own lips. The things that happen in* **The Gourd Dancer** *also seem to be a continuance of that same voice and, of course, in* The Names *you have that repetition. I've heard some people say, "Momaday's repeating himself. Dosen't he have any new material?" But I've suspected this repetition was a conscious thing.*

Oh, yes. In a sense I'm not concerned to change my subject from book to book. Rather, I'm concerned to keep the story going. I mean to keep the same subject, to carry it farther with each telling.

Some traditional songs and stories begin each new movement by repeating. They repeat and then go a bit further. That's the structure in your work?

Yes, indeed, and I believe that is a good way in which to proceed. It establishes a continuity that is important to me.

What are the links in your everyday life to American Indian traditions?

Well, I have the conviction that I am an Indian. I have an idea of myself as an Indian, and that idea is quite secure. My father was Huan-toa; my grandfather was Mammedaty; my great-grandfather was Guipagho. How can I not be an Indian? I'm a member of the Gourd Dance society in the Kiowa tribe, and when I can, I go to the annual meeting of that society, and it is a great thing for me, full of excitement and restoration, the deepest meaning. Since I've returned to the Southwest I feel new and stronger links with the Indian world than I felt in California, where I was for twenty years in exile. Then, too, I have children. And my children are, much to my delight, greatly interested in their stake in the Indian world. So that's another link for me as well as for them. Of course I have Indian relatives. I lost my father, who was my closest tie with the Kiowa world; he died last year. But there are others who sustain me. I keep in touch.

You could say then, perhaps, of "The Gourd Dancer," of your poem (although it's dedicated to your grandfather) that Gourd Dancer is also you.

Oh, yes, yes. Again the continuity. That part of the poem which refers to the giving away of a horse: I wasn't there, of course. But it really did happen; my father was only eight years old, but it remained in his memory as long as he lived. And I absorbed it when I was the same age, so that it became my memory as well. This is a profound continuity, something at the very center of the Indian perception of the world. We are talking about immortality, or something very close to it, though the American Indian would not have that name for it. He would say, perhaps, if he were Kiowa, *Akeah-de,* "they were camping." In that word is the seed of the same idea.

The American writer some people might link you most closely to who is non-Indian is Walt Whitman. Whitman's life was a single work. Leaves of Grass, which went through different stages of development. Vine Deloria and Geary Hobson have both pointed out, (Geary in an article in New America Magazine and Vine in that Sun Tracks interview), that there have been cycles of interest in American Indians and in the publication of American Indian literary work. As you know D'arcy McNickle more or less stopped being published after a certain point in the late thirties and only was published just before his death in the current resurgence in the late seventies. In the thirties, it was Luther Standing Bear, twenty years before that Charles Eastman. Do you think that this kind of cycle will happen again with American Indian literature or is there something different about the current surge of writing by American Indians and interest in their writing?

I really don't know the answer to that. Oh, I suppose there will be cycles; the popularity of books by and about American Indians will pass, and then there will be regenerations of interest, ad infinitum. That's the nature of the publishing world, isn't it? I'm not worried about it. The American Indian is indispensable to the soil and the dream and the destiny of America. That's the important thing. He always was and always will be a central figure in the American imagination, a central figure in American literature. We can't very well do without him.

I also wonder if, too, it might not be different this time because we now have more Indian people who are literate, who do read. We now have also our own audience as opposed to an audience of people who are non-Indian.

> **Prose and poetry are opposed in a certain way. It's hard to define poetry. Poetry is a statement concerning the human condition, composed in verse. In that refinement, in that reservation, "composed in verse," is really, finally, the matter that establishes the idea of poetry and sets it apart.**
>
> —*N. Scott Momaday*

I'm sure that's true.

What is it that contemporary American Indian poetry has to offer to the world of literature or to the world as a whole?

Well, I think it's a legitimate and artistic expression in itself, first of all. Here is my voice, and my voice proceeds out of an intelligence that touches upon the inexorable motions of the world. There is design and symmetry in the pattern of my speech, my words. That in itself is a noteworthy thing. Another such thing is the perception that we were talking about a moment ago. I believe that the Indian has an understanding of the physical world and of the earth as a spiritual entity that is his, very much his own. The non-Indian can benefit a good deal by having that perception revealed to him.

I've been interested in the place that women seem to be taking in American Indian literature. There seems to be a good deal of strong writing coming from American Indian women, perhaps more so than any other ethnic minority, if you want to call it that, in America. Why is that so? Do you have any ideas on that subject?

No. It's not something that I have thought much about. But it doesn't surprise me, what you say. Women in the Indian world have always had strong, sometimes supernatural, voices. In Plains culture those voices were often understated for obvious reasons—it was a warrior society, after all—but even in that culture women have always had a prominent position. And it is appropriate that we see Indian women writing now. You're right, there are many, and more to come. And some are doing remarkably fine work. I spoke at the Institute of American Indian Arts in Santa Fe a few months ago. I was speaking particularly to the creative writing students there, and I met several young women, in particular, whose work was very impressive. I met very good young men who were writing well, too, but the women won the day.

In a recent interview, as a part of a National Public Radio program that focused on American Indian women poets called "The Key is in Remembering," Paula Gunn Allen said that reading House Made of Dawn *was one of the major turning points in her life. It made things possible for her that were never possible before. And it is certainly true that you've been a very important inspiration for many American Indian writers. Just the fact that the two best anthologies of American Indian writing, Carriers of the Dream Wheel and The Remembered Earth, both draw their titles from your work, is a very clear indication of how important people think you are to them. What do you feel about your place as a sort of, to use an academic term, dean of American Indian writers?*

It's something that I don't often think about. I don't know what that's worth, really. I do very much appreciate people who say the sorts of things that Paula Gunn Allen said on that occasion. But I'm not conscious of my place in that whole scheme of things as yet. And I'm rather reluctant to think in those terms, really, because I want to get on with my work. I'm afraid that if I started thinking of myself as the dean of American Indian writers I might not work so well. I might be tempted to slow down and accept the deanship when I really want to be out there among the subordinates doing my thing.

Deans tend to be administrators, right.

Exactly.

Well, I would like, if you would, for you to read one more poem just to finish things off. I'd like you to choose one that perhaps continues those central concerns in your work, those strong images.

This one, let me read **"Plainview: 1"**:

There in the hollow of the hills I see,
Eleven magpies stand away from me.

Low light upon the rim; a wind informs
This distance with a gathering of storms

And drifts in silver crescents on the grass,
Configurations that appear, and pass.

There falls a final shadow on the glare,
A stillness on the dark, erratic air.

I do not hear the longer wind that lows
Among the magpies. Silences disclose,

Until no rhythms of unrest remain,
Eleven magpies standing in the plain

They are illusion—wind and rain revolve—
And they recede in darkness, and dissolve.

Alan R. Velie   (essay date 1982)

SOURCE: "The Search for Identity: N. Scott Momaday's Autobiographical Works," in his *Four American Indian Literary Masters: N. Scott Momaday, James Welch, Leslie Marmon Silko, and Gerald Vizenor,* University of Oklahoma Press, 1982, pp. 34-49.

[*In the essay below, Velie provides background information on Momaday's life and career and discusses how Yvor Winters and Frederick Goddard Tuckerman influenced his early poetry. Velie concludes that although Momaday is a good poet overall, he is at his best in his prose poems.*]

After he had exhausted reservation schools, Momaday spent his last year of high school at a military school in Virginia and then enrolled in the University of New Mexico. It was there that he began writing poetry, and in 1959 published his first poem, **"Earth and I Give You Turquoise,"** in the *New Mexico Quarterly.* After college Momaday tried a year of law school in the University of Virginia but decided that he did not like it.

When Momaday submitted some poems to a creative writing contest sponsored by Stanford University, Yvor Winters, who judged the poetry entries, awarded Momaday a graduate scholarship to Stanford and took him under his wing. Winters was a distinguished poet, famous for his powerful personality as well as for his scholarship and criticism, and he exercised an enormous influence on Momaday's verse. Winters died in 1968, and Momaday is now experimenting with new forms that Winters probably would have taken a dim view of, but his influence is still evident in much of Momaday's work.

Winters was a great whale of a man, imposing both intellectually and physically, with very marked ideas and a decidedly contentious disposition. His major scholarship was the championing of poets whose work, though excellent, had fallen into obscurity. Among his favorites were Barnabe Googe, Fulke Greville, Jones Very, and Frederick Goddard Tuckerman. None of these names are household words today, of course, but their poetry is worth reading, and, thanks to Winters's attentions, it has been republished recently. In fact, Momaday put together an edition of Tuckerman's works [*The Complete Poems of Frederick Goddard Tuckerman,* 1965] for his dissertation at Stanford.

Along with his habit of heralding the obscure, Winters had a way of dismissing the famous. He viewed the works of Wordsworth, Keats, Poe, and Whitman with contempt. All this may make Winters sound like a crank, but he was a very sound scholar and a brilliant teacher, and those who knew him never ignored or slighted his opinions. Momaday was very fond of Winters, although, as he admits now, his affection was mixed with awe. Winters, for his part, was endlessly impressed with Momaday. Winters was not one to understate, and after Momaday left Stanford, Winters used to tell students that not only was Scott a great poet and scholar, but he was also powerful enough to pull down the pillars of the building in which they were sitting.

Momaday earned his Ph.D. in English at Stanford and has taught English and comparative literature in the University of California (both Santa Barbara and Berkeley) and at Stanford, and is now teaching at the University of Arizona.

Winters meticulously taught Momaday the poet's craft. He introduced Momaday to a kind of poetry that Winters called post-symbolist, and under Winters's tutelage Momaday adopted post-symbolist methods.

The poets Winters identifies as post-symbolists are a diverse lot, starting with Frederick Goddard Tuckerman and Emily Dickinson, and including Wallace Stevens, Louise Bogan, Edgar Bowers, and Winters himself. As Winters was well aware, the post-symbolists were in no sense a group. He makes clear that Tuckerman and Dickinson, who lived only a few miles apart in Massachusetts, neither knew, nor were influenced by, each other and certainly never thought of themselves as part of a movement. In fact, Winters makes no case for the influence of any of the post-symbolists on any of the others.

What the post-symbolists have in common is the use of imagery in such a way that descriptions of sensory details are charged with abstract meaning. Winters argues that in traditional European poetry, before the symbolists, imagery was primarily ornamental. Donne, for instance, used metaphor to illustrate a clearly stated theme. "The vehicles are more interesting than the tenor," Winters wrote, "therefore they are ornaments, and the tenor—the essential theme—suffers." With the symbolists, image and sensory description largely replace abstract meaning. Symbolist poetry cannot be paraphrased or reduced to rational meaning; meaning, such as it is, resides in the feeling and tone of the poem. Mallarmé, Rimbaud, and Verlaine are among the writers whose poems disassociate sense perception and feeling from conceptual understanding. In post-symbolist poetry, according to Winters, "the sharp sensory detail contained in a poem or passage is of such a nature that the detail is charged with meaning without our being told of the meaning explicitly, or is described in language indicating such meaning indirectly but clearly." Let us consider Momaday's **"Angle of Geese"** to see how a post-symbolist merges abstract meaning and sensory detail:

> How shall we adorn
> Recognition with our speech?—
> Now the dead firstborn
> Will lag in the wake of words.
>
> Custom intervenes;
> We are civil, something more:
> More than language means,
> The mute presence mulls and marks.
>
> Almost of a mind,
> We take measure of the loss;
> I am slow to find
> The mere margin of repose.
>
> And one November
> It was longer in the watch,
>   as if forever,
> Of the huge ancestral goose.
>
> So much symmetry!
> Like the pale angle of time
>   And eternity.
> The great shape labored and fell.
>
> Quit of hope and hurt,
> It held a motionless gaze,
>   Wide of time, alert,
> On the dark distant flurry.

The poem is difficult to understand until we know more about the circumstances Momaday is describing. The first three stanzas are his reflections on the death of a friend's child, and describe the inadequacy of language to encompass such grief. The last three stanzas turn to an incident that happened on a hunting trip Momaday took as a teenager: he had retrieved a goose that one of the hunters had shot and was holding it as it died. In the lines "How shall we adorn / Recognition with our speech?" Momaday indicates, by his choice of the verb *adorn,* that language functions in this painful situation merely as decoration. He is alluding to the poverty of words that one always feels in our culture at such times. Very few Americans say, "I'm sorry your little boy is dead"; it sounds so pitifully inad-

equate. They usually use some periphrasis—"I'm sorry to hear the news"—hoping by vagueness to imply something more meaningful. But the idea here is that, whatever is said, the "Dead first-born / Will lag in the wake of words."

It is important to remember Momaday's roots in Indian culture in reading the poem. When he says "We are civil," one should be aware of the connotation of *civilized* and should contrast the traditional Indian custom of keening the tremolo, cutting off one's hair, and even occasionally a finger, in wild lamentation, with the "civilized" Anglo's custom of repressing grief. Indian mourning is a violent release and purgation of grief. Accompanied by the passionate emotions of the Indian mourning ceremonies, words would have more force. "I am sorry that your child is dead," would not have a hollow ring in an Indian context. The context of **"Angle of Geese,"** however, is Anglo-Saxon America, and in taking "measure of the loss," Momaday is "slow to find / The mere margin of repose," the way to come to grips with the event emotionally. He cannot even find the margin, the edge, or beginning, of repose.

In the second half of the poem Momaday shifts without transition from the dead child to the dying goose. The link between the two is associational, to use one of Winters's favorite terms. The doctrine of association can be traced to Hobbes and Locke, who argued that ideas arise from association of sensory perceptions. The literary application of this idea affected poetic structure by replacing the traditional logical construction of poems with what Winters called "the structure of revery," and it brought about the post-symbolist practice of expressing ideas through images, which are a verbal record of sensory impressions.

In **"Angle of Geese"** Momaday moves in memory from the dead child of the present to the dying goose of his childhood. Momaday has described the incident at length in a column he wrote in the *Santa Fe New Mexican* [September 23, 1973]. His account is beautifully written, and seems worth reprinting in total, both for its own sake and for its help in explaining the poem. It also shows the work of compression that Momaday has done in turning the childhood incident into poetry.

One of the Wild Beautiful Creatures

That day the sun never did come out. It was a strange, indefinite illumination, almost obscure, set very deep in the sky,—a heavy, humid cold without wind. Flurries of snow moved down from the mountains, one after another, and clouds of swirling mist spilled slowly down the slopes splashing in slow, slow motion on the plain.

For days I had seen migrating birds. They moved down the long corridor of the valley, keeping to the river. The day before I had seen a flock of twenty or thirty geese descend into the willows a mile or more downstream. They were still there, as far as I knew.

I was thirteen or fourteen years old, I suppose. I had a different view of hunting in those days, an exalted view, which was natural enough, given my situation.

I had grown up in mountain and desert country, always in touch with the wilderness, and I took it all for granted. The men of my acquaintance were hunters. Indeed they were deeply committed to a hunting tradition. And I admired them in precisely those terms.

We drew near the river and began to creep, the way a cat creeps upon a sparrow. I remember that I placed my feet very carefully, one after the other, in the snow without sound. I felt an excitement welling up within me. Before us was a rise which now we were using as a blind. Beyond and below it was the river, which we could not yet see, except where it reached away at either end of our view, curving away into the pale, winter landscape. We advanced up the shallow slope, crouching, leaned into the snow and raised ourselves up on our toes in order to see. The geese were there, motionless on the water, riding like decoys. But though they were still they were not calm. I could sense their wariness, the tension that was holding them in that stiff, tentative attitude of alert.

And suddenly they exploded from the water. They became a terrible, clamorous swarm, struggling to gain their element. Their great bodies, trailing water, seemed to heave under the wild, beating wings. They disintegrated into a blur of commotion, panic. There was a deafening roar; my heart was beating like the wings of the geese.

And just as suddenly out of this apparent chaos there emerged a perfect fluent symmetry. The geese assembled on the cold air, even as the river was still crumpled with their going, and formed a bright angle on the distance. Nothing could have been more beautiful, more wonderfully realized upon the vision of a single moment. Such beauty is inspirational in itself; for it exists for its own sake.

One of the wild, beautiful creatures remained in the river, mortally wounded, its side perforated with buckshot. I waded out into the hard, icy undercurrent and took it up in my arm. The living weight of it was very great, and with its life's blood it warmed my frozen hands. I carried it for a long time. There was no longer any fear in its eyes, only something like sadness and yearning, until at last the eyes curdled in death. The great shape seemed perceptibly lighter, diminished in my hold, as if the ghost given up had gone at last to take its place in that pale angle in the long distance.

These words, like the poem, were written long after the event, after Momaday had undergone a change from an unquestioning, romantic acceptance of hunting to a viewpoint which, the reader can infer, is more critical. What remains in his mind as an adult is a memory of the pathos of the dying goose, yearning to take its place in the "bright angle" with the rest of the flock.

The poem is post-symbolist in technique because Momaday imbues his childhood experience with an abstract significance. The goose becomes the "huge ancestral goose," a prototype of geese, rather than one bird. Momaday compares the formation of the flock in flight to the angle of time and eternity, imbuing their flight with a metaphysical or transcendental dimension. The wounded goose, between life and death, is still alive and alert, and yet it is "wide of time"; that is, its impending death has released it from the bondage of time.

Using post-symbolist technique, Momaday implies a meaning in his description of the scene, though never implicitly stating it. Put baldly, the meaning is that death is not something to be dreaded but a means of escaping the trammels of time. This formulation is oversimple, only a portion of the statement that the description makes, but it does inhere in and is at the center of it. Post-symbolist images cannot be very satisfactorily reduced to prose, yet the prose element, the tenor, is definitely a crucial part of them.

"Angle of Geese" is written in syllabic verse, rather than in the accentual syllabic verse of most traditional poetry. In a syllabic line the "accented syllables must vary sufficiently in number and position that they do not follow a pattern (a pattern would give us standard meter) but must still contribute to the rhythm," whereas accentual syllabic verse contains a regular alternation of stressed and unstressed syllables. In **"Angle of Geese"** the first and third lines of each stanza contain five syllables and the second and fourth lines contain seven. The rhythm of the poem is very subtle, and its effect not markedly different from that of prose, even though the first and third lines of each stanza rhyme. Since the rhymed lines are not usually heavily endstopped, they are not at all obtrusive and, indeed, might even escape the notice of a casual reader.

The poem recalls Winters in its solemn tone and stately rhythm, in its curiously formal and abstract diction, and in its fondness for polysyllabic, latinate words. "How shall we adorn / Recognition with our speech?" is reminiscent of some of Winters's verse, for instance ["To William Dinsmore Briggs Conducting His Seminar"]:

> Amid the walls' insensate white, some crime
> Is redefined above the sunken mass
> Of crumbled years; logic reclaims the crass,
> Frees from historic dross the invidious mime.

The rhyme is heavier, the meter iambic pentameter, but, as in Momaday's poem, the diction is formal, the language abstract and latinate.

Winters was considered an academic poet, and in Momaday's early verse we can sometimes get a faint whiff of the lamp. Consider, for instance, **"The Bear."**

> What ruse of vision,
> escarping the wall of leaves,
> rending incision
> into countless surfaces,
>
> would cull and color
> his somnolence, whose old age
> has outworn valor,
> all but the fact of courage?

Seen, he does not come,
move, but seems forever there,
dimensionless, dumb,
in the windless noon's hot glare.

More scarred than others
these years since the trap maimed him,
pain slants his withers,
drawing up the crooked limb.

Then he is gone, whole,
without urgency, from sight,
as buzzards control,
imperceptibly, their flight.

The reader might naturally suppose that a poem by an Indian about a bear has been inspired by a hunting incident, but, as it happens, the model for this bear is Old Ben in Faulkner's "The Bear." Momaday not only depicts the same scene as Faulkner—the confrontation of the hunter and the huge, old bear—but he borrows from Faulkner's diction as well:

Then he saw the bear. It did not emerge, appear: it was just there, immobile, fixed in the green and windless noon's hot dappling, not as big as he had dreamed it but as big as he had expected, bigger, dimensionless against the dappled obscurity, looking at him.

Momaday uses Faulkner's passage the way Shakespeare uses Plutarch's description of Cleopatra's barge, borrowing the most vivid phrases, preserving the essence of the description, and transmuting prose into poetry. Like **"Angle of Geese,"** **"The Bear"** is syllabic verse, lines one and three of each stanza having five syllables, and lines two and four having seven. Momaday makes greater use of rhyme here than in **"Angle of Geese,"** with alternating lines rhyming. Still, there is not much endstopping or heavy stress on final syllables, so the rhyme is unobtrusive.

Winters had commented that the language of the poem is very quiet, and "could well be the language of distinguished prose." He concludes that it is poetry "by virtue of the careful selection of details and the careful juxtaposition of these details, selection and juxtaposition which result in concentration of meaning, and by virtue of its rhythm, which is the rhythm of verse, but very subtle." This is exaggerated, since the language of prose never includes rhyme, but it is worth noting because it indicates that, even at its most formal, Momaday's poetry was not that far from his recent prose poetry, although at first the new poems seem a dramatic departure.

The importance of noting that Faulkner's Ben and not some real bear provided the model for Momaday's poem is that it reminds the reader that Momaday is a man of letters, not a noble savage, and that his poetry is in the same literary tradition as that of any American writing today. But **"The Bear"** is not only literary; like most of Momaday's verse, it is vividly descriptive. More than anything else Winters detested vagueness, and inveighed against it to Momaday and all his other students. Winter's

argument with the romantics was that they seldom described poetic subjects in visual terms.

Shelley was one of Winters' favorite examples of this romantic tendency, because his famous poem "The Skylark" is a series of similes, none of which serve to describe the bird in its avian manifestation. In the poem Shelley compares the lark to a "cloud of fire," a "poet hidden," a "high-born maiden," and an "unbodied joy." In contrast, Momaday presents the bear, not in full detail, but in a few descriptive strokes, as in a line drawing that suggests as much as it depicts, but nonetheless presents a fully realized creature. We see, or sense, the bear—massive, old, still, and maimed.

Momaday's bear, however, is no less a symbol than Shelley's lark. To Faulkner, Old Ben was not only a bear, but also a symbol of the vanishing wilderness. Momaday incorporates a sense of this into his poem. As Winters describes it, "The poem is more descriptive than anything else, yet in the third and last stanzas the details are more than physical and indicate something of the essential wilderness." Momaday is careful to soften the effect by the use of "seems," but the bear, "dimensionless, . . . forever there," is clearly more than one particular animal; he is also the incarnation of some primeval, fundamental truth about the wilderness.

Another poem in which Momaday combines symbols with minute and keen description is **"Buteo Regalis"**:

His frailty discrete, the rodent turns, looks.
What sense first warns? The winging is unheard,
Unseen but as distant motion made whole,
Singular, slow, unbroken in its glide.
It veers, and veering, tilts broad-surfaced wings.
Aligned, the span bends to begin the dive
And falls, alternately white and russet,
Angle and curve, gathering momentum.

Here is a brief sketch of a hawk swooping to its kill. The prey is an unspecified rodent; we are not told whether it is a rat, mouse, or prairie dog. Momaday alternates the use of syllabic verse with iambic pentameter (lines 2, 4, 5, and 6 are iambic), and Winters suggests, persuasively, that "the first and third lines, in their syllabic rhythm suggest the sudden hesitation; the four pentameter lines suggest the smooth motion of the soaring hawk; the last two lines in their syllabic rhythm and fragmented phrasing, suggest the rapid and confusing descent."

Notice Momaday's description of the rodent: its frailty is "discrete"—separate—a reference to its isolation in its last moments of life. Momaday depicts the hawk impressionistically. The rodent senses it more than sees it— "Unseen but as a distant motion made whole." The vignette is not completed—Momaday does not tell us whether the hawk gets his prey or not. Somehow the outcome seems less important than the iconic glimpse we get: hawk stooping, rodent turning. It is a glimpse into the wild heart of nature. As Winters puts it, "It seems rather a perception of the 'discrete' wilderness, the essential wilderness."

After Winters, the most important influence on Momaday's early poetry was the work of Frederick Goddard Tuckerman, the nineteenth-century New Englander whose poems were the subject of Momaday's Ph.D. dissertation at Stanford. Momaday's interest in Tuckerman persisted beyond his dissertation. He wrote an article on Tuckermans' "The Cricket," published an edition of Tuckerman's poems, and still includes Tuckerman in his course on the antiromantic movement in nineteenth-century American literature.

There are some notable parallels between Momaday and Tuckerman. Tuckerman, the earliest of the post-symbolists, wrote poetry that combined subtle and detailed descriptions of nature with symbolism, a practice Momaday has emulated. Momaday, like Tuckerman before him, is an amateur naturalist. Furthermore, both men studied but never practiced the law, preferring to become poets.

Tuckerman influenced Momaday both stylistically and philosophically. Stylistically, Momaday admired and adopted Tuckerman's naturalist's eye for detail. Tuckerman's poems are full of references to flowers like bloodroot, king orchis, pearlwort, and jacinth, and herbs like wastebalm and feverfew. Sometimes Tuckerman just names the plants; sometimes, in his best verse, he describes them, briefly but vividly. Momaday describes Tuckerman's poems as "remarkable, point-blank descriptions of nature; they are filled with small, precise, and whole things: purring bees and varvain spikes, shives and amaryllis, wind flowers and stramony." The impression one has to Tuckerman is of a man who sees the world of nature clearly and distinctly, rather than through a romantic blur.

But Tuckerman is just as capable as Shelley of making a creature into a symbol. In "The Cricket," which in Momaday's opinion is Tuckerman's greatest poem, the cricket is a complex figure symbolizing the forces of nature. Tuckerman asserts that to understand the cricket's song is to understand the universe, an idea akin to Tennyson's statement in "Flower in the Crannied Wall." Tuckerman concludes that it is an immoral act to pry into nature's secrets, what Chaucer called "Goddes pryvetee." Although Tuckerman does not make the comparison, he apparently sees the invasion of the natural world by the probing mind as similar to the original sin of eating of the tree of knowledge. Tuckerman's conclusion is existential; the universe is impenetrable, and the important question, as Momaday put it in his article on "The Cricket," ["The Heretical Cricket," *Southern Review* 3, Nos. 1-2 (1967)] is "how to live in the certainty of death."

Philosphically, although it would be too simplistic to attribute Momaday's existential views solely to Tuckerman's influence, it is worth noting that the men share a similar outlook. Momaday's poem **"Before an Old Painting of the Crucifixion"** is informed by ideas very similar to those of "The Cricket":

I ponder how He died, despairing once.
I've heard the cry subside in vacant skies,
In clearings where no other was. Despair,

Which, in the vibrant wake of utterance,
Resides in desolate calm, preoccupies,
Though it is still. There is no solace there.

That calm inhabits wilderness, the sea,
And where no peace inheres but solitude;
Near death it most impends. It was for Him,
Absurd and public in His agony,
Inscrutably itself, nor misconstrued,
Nor metaphrased in art or pseudonym:

A vague contagion. Old, the mural fades . . .
Reminded of the fainter sea I scanned,
I recollect: How mute in constancy!
I could not leave the wall of palisades
Till cormorants returned my eyes on land.
The mural but implies eternity:

Not death, but silence after death is change.
Judean hills, the endless afternoon,
The farther groves and arbors seasonless
But fix the mind within the moment's range.
Where evening would obscure our sorrow soon,
There shines too much a sterile loveliness.

No imprecisions of commingled shade,
No shimmering deceptions of the sun,
Herein no semblances remark the cold
Unhindered swell of time, for time is stayed
The Passion wanes into oblivion,
And time and timelessness confuse, I'm told.

These centuries removed from either fact
Have lain upon the critical expanse
And been of little consequence. The void
Is calendared in stone; the human act,
Outrageous, is in vain. The hours advance
Like flecks of foam borne landward and destroyed.

Like W. H. Auden's "Musée des Beaux Arts," this poem is about a poet's reaction to a painting, and his consequent reflections about life. From the outset it is apparent that Momaday takes an existential view of the crucifixion: God is dead. Christ dies in despair, his cry subsiding in "vacant skies"—skies empty of God. Man is alone on earth, "where no peace inheres but solitude." To Momaday, Christ's agony is absurd and inscrutable, or it has meaning only as a singular gesture; it did not, as Christianity teaches, bring redemption to man. Christ's death is often misconstrued, Momaday says, or translated into art, into pictures like the mural. The mural implies eternity, but there is none. The change after death is not to eternal life, but to silence, nothingness. During one's lifetime there is little comfort because time is relentless. Momaday's great image is taken from the sea he watches in the poem. "The cold / Unhindered swell of time" is a prototypical example of a post-symbolist image. Momaday expands on the image in the last stanza: "The hours advance / Like flecks of foam borne landward and destroyed."

The idea that time is passing ceaselessly is of course one of the most familiar themes in poetry, the basis of *ubi sunt* and *carpe diem* poems, for example, but Momaday's lines are particularly reminiscent of the best lines in "The Cricket":

> Behold the autumn goes,
> The Shadow grows,
> The moments take hold of eternity;
> Even while we stop to wrangle or repine
> Our lives are gone
> Like thinnest mist,
> Like yon escaping colour in the trees.

Momaday continues to write poems in his conservative, Wintersian mode—poems, for instance, like **"Anywhere Is a Street into the Night,"** the title poem from the collection that he published after a trip to Russia. But he has also begun to experiment with a more fluid form, the prose poem. These are usually about Indian subjects, and although, as Winters pointed out, even his most traditional poems approached the "rhythm of stately prose," these prose poems seem a radical departure. They most resemble the oral tradition of the Indian tale, and, indeed, most of them are short narratives.

"The Fear of Bo-Talee"

> Bo-talee rode easily among his enemies, once, twice, three—
> and four times. And all who saw him were amazed, for he
> was utterly without fear; so it seemed. But afterwards he said:
> Certainly I was afraid. I was afraid of the fear in the eyes of
> my enemies.

"The Stalker"

> Sampt'e drew the string back and back until he felt the bow
> wobble in his hand, and he let the arrow go. It shot across
> the long light of the morning and struck the black face of a
> stone in the meadow; it glanced then away towards the west,
> limping along in the air; and then it settled down in the grass
> and lay still. Sampt'e approached; he looked at it with wonder
> and was wary; honestly he believed that the arrow might take
> flight again; so much of his life did he give into it.

These two short recitatives might have appeared as chapters in *The Way to Rainy Mountain.* They have the stately oral cadence of the Indian teller of tales and, although strongly rhythmical, have shed the last formal regular strictures of verse.

Momaday is a fine poet, but in my opinion he is at his best in prose. His prose is masterful in *House Made of Dawn,* but it is at its best in the lyrical short passages of *The Way*

to Rainy Mountain and *The Names.* These new poems, like **"The Fear of Bo-talee,"** seem to indicate that Momaday's verse and prose, once so different, are conjoining to create a single and powerful voice. Momaday's prose, both fiction and nonfiction, had been written solely from an Indian point of view; his verse, academic and formal, showed more trace of his literary than of his ethnic beginnings. These new prose poems are Indian in tone and subject.

Momaday on the oral tradition and the American literary canon:

That whole oral tradition which goes back probably to beyond the invention of the alphabet; the storyteller was the man who was standing with a piece of charcoal in his hand making, placing, the wonderful images in his mind's eye on the wall of the cave, that's probably one of the origins of American literature. He has begun to tell a story, and he develops in the course of time that storytelling capacity in himself to such a wonderful degree that we have to recognize it as being somewhere in the line, in the evolution of what we think of American literature. I have an idea that American literature really begins with the first human expression of man in the American landscape, and who knows how far back that goes; but it certainly antedates writing, and it probably goes back a thousand years or more. So we have to admit it now, and always think in terms of it. We cannot think of Melville without thinking of American Indian antecedents in the oral tradition, because the two things are not to be separated logically at all.

N. Scott Momaday, in an interview with Laura Coltelli in her Winged Words: American Indian Writers Speak, *1990.*

Matthias Schubnell (essay date 1985)

SOURCE: "Momaday's Poetry," in his *N. Scott Momaday: The Cultural and Literary Background,* University of Oklahoma Press, 1985, pp. 189-254.

[*In the following excerpt, Schubnell discusses Momaday's poems that center on his Native American heritage, focusing in particular on part two of* The Gourd Dancer.]

This [essay] is devoted to Momaday's poetic statements on his American Indian heritage and his particular treatment of the American earth. Most of the poems I will discuss belong to part two of Momaday's **_The Gourd Dancer_** collection. While many of them are written in a loose style approaching prose, there are also examples of syllabic and free verse as well as one sonnet. This variety of styles suggests a greater ease of expression compared with the rigid and formalized work of Momaday's Stanford period.

In three short pieces of prose poetry, similar in style to those in *The Way to Rainy Mountain,* Momaday evokes different stages in the evolution of Kiowa life. **"The Stalker"** shows the fragility of Kiowa existence before the acquisition of the horse; **"The Fear of Bo-talee"** is a salute to the heroism and humanity of a Kiowa warrior at the height of the horse culture; **"The Horse that Died of Shame"** combines a story of an act of cowardice, signifying the decline of the Kiowa spirit, with a description of the way in which this traditional tale prevails in Momaday's imagination and dreams and affects his vision of the world around him. In a fourth poem of similar character, **"The Story of a Well-Made Shield,"** Momaday tries to approximate the inexpressible potency he senses in nature.

"The Delight Song of Tsoai-talee" reflects an aboriginal ethic which holds that man is an integral, but not dominant part of creation. It is a prayer of thanks for having existence in a world of endless wonder and beauty. Momaday, one of whose Kiowa names is Tsoai-talee, introduced an early version of this poem with the following words: "It is a day to sing a song, or to run deep into a sunlit field, or to sit easily with someone who is old and alone. It is a day to rejoice. On such a day as this I would tell a story to a child, I would deal in delight. I would say, and the child would say after me: 'I am a feather in the bright sky.'"

The lines which follow illuminate a particularly native attitude toward the natural world, and its form is a deliberate emulation of Navajo song patterns. Mary Austin, whose life and work in the Southwest and study of aboriginal American verse gave her a deep insight into the Indian's sense of the land, described [in her *The Land of Journeys' Ending*] the embeddedness of Indian life in the natural environment which is at the heart of Momaday's poem, in these paragraphs:

> Man is not himself only, not solely a variation of his racial type in the pattern of his immediate experience. He is all that he sees; all that flows to him from a thousand sources, half noted, or noted not at all except by some sense that lies too deep for naming. He is the land, the lift of its mountain lines, the reach of its valleys; his is the rhythm of its seasonal processions, the involution and variation of its vegetable patterns. . . .

> . . . By land, I mean all those things common to a given region . . . : the flow of prevailing winds, the succession of vegetal cover, the legend of ancient life; and the scene, above everything the magnificently shaped and colored scene.

The use of parallel structures, repetition, and accretion is a common feature in Navajo songs. The final six lines of the poem, which are separated from the main body, correspond to the traditional evocation of personal harmony which concludes many Navajo chants. Such evocations are designed to place the singer into the center of the universe, surrounded by the four cardinal directions, the spirit world above, and the underworld below. The following example is a case in point:

> May it be beautiful before me
> May it be beautiful behind me

> May it be beautiful below me
> May it be beautiful above me
> May it be beautiful all around me
> In beauty it is finished.

"The Delight Song of Tsoai-talee" is a contemporary appropriation of the individual to the universe, based on native tradition and resulting in harmony and delight.

The four poems of the "Plainview" sequence are, as the title suggests, reflections on the world of the Kiowas in the southern plains. **"Plainview: 1"** and **"Plainview: 3"** are evocations of the Oklahoma landscape at Rainy Mountain, near Mountain View, the home of Momaday's father. **"Plainview: 2"** and **"Plainview: 4"** deal with Kiowa history; the first poem delineates the glory and decline of a Plains culture, the second relates the extraordinary captivity story of Milly Durgan among the Kiowas. The widely differing forms of the four poems indicate Momaday's technical virtuosity and scope.

Momaday introduced the first publication of **"Plainview: 1"** by saying: "I remember having been at Rainy Mountain in a stormy season, and I write a commemorative poem, a sonnet." The poem is one of the clearest examples of Momaday's kinship with Wallace Stevens. The landscape Momaday creates is more than the sum of carefully selected and precisely observed details. Momaday renders the scene in terms of its impact not only on the senses but also on the imagination. It is this poetic strategy, the creation of a landscape of the mind, which is also the hallmark of Steven's work. Steven's poems fuse reality and imagination to create a fiction, a constructed world particular to the poet alone. One critic has summarized the relevance of this theory to geography: "The idea that place is made of an integration of human concept and external reality and that man's familiar scenes are dependent on his imagination—this idea is basic to an understanding of the supreme fiction" [Frank Doggett, in "This Invented World," in *The Act of the Mind,* edited by Roy Harvey Pearce and J. Hillis Miller].

In **"Plainview: 1"** Momaday composes a fiction out of sense perceptions—light and shadow, sound and motion, shapes and color—combined with the result of his imaginative response to the ominous mood which informs a landscape under the threat of an approaching storm. The eleven magpies the person sees are figments of the imagination, "illusions," as the last stanza makes clear. But at the same time they are an integral part of the poet's reality; the poem proceeds in relating the imaginative magpies to the physical world. The resulting reality is a synthesis of sense perceptions and imagination.

"Plainview: 2" is an emulation of indigenous poetic patterns: as with **"The Delight Song of Tsoai-talee,"** its parallel structures, repetition, and accretion are characteristic of American Indian chants. The poem is an elegy on the decline of the Plains Indian world. The peoples of the plains—among them the Kiowas, Comanches, Cheyennes, Arapahos, and Dakotas—reached their golden age after acquiring horses from the Spaniards. Horses gave them mobility and power, both as buffalo hunters and warriors. It is therefore appropriate to render the disintegration of these cultures in terms of the demise of a horse. Deprived of the animal around which his culture flourished, the old Indian is left with memories and dreams of a better time. His flight into alcoholism is an expression of his inability to adapt to new circumstances as well as a way of easing the pain of his nostalgia.

"Plainview: 3" is a celebration of the sun, the central object of veneration among the Plains tribes. Momaday renders the spectacle of sunrise impressionistically, using concrete language and images. Three metaphors are compounded in this depiction of the rising sun: "a pendant / of clear cutbeads, flashing; / a drift of pollen and glitter / lapping, and overlapping night; / a prairie fire."

"Plainview: 4" deals with the extraordinary story of Milly Durgan, whose experience epitomizes the drama of frontier life in Texas and Oklahoma at a time when white settlers were still at the mercy of powerful Kiowa raiders. When she was eighteen months old, Milly Durgan was kidnapped in a raid led by the Kiowa warrior Little Buffalo at Elm Creek, Young County, Texas, on 13 October 1864. While the other captives were later ransomed, Milly was adopted by the famous Kiowa warrior, Au-soant-sai-mah, and given her Indian name, Sain-toh-oodie. Most Kiowa captives were treated as slaves, but Milly was raised by kind foster parents and enjoyed the wealth, status, and protection of a respected family. She worshiped the Kiowa idols, Tai-me and the Ten Grandmother bundles, and when the first Baptist missionaries arrived at Rainy Mountain, she fiercely resisted their demand that she adopt the new religion. It was only in old age that she converted to Christianity. She married the Kiowa chief, Goombi, and never regretted her Indian existence when, late in life, she learned about her true origin. After a brief visit to her relations in Texas she returned to the Kiowas in Oklahoma.

In a manuscript version of "Plainview: 4," Momaday described this remarkable woman: "She was made much of in her time, for she had come over an unimaginable distance and crossed the native strain with a hard, exotic blood—a frontier intercession." The two worlds of Milly Durgan are reflected in Momaday's use of excerpts from American folksongs and his emulation of Kiowa oral tradition. The introduction of the first prose section, "Once upon a time I saw the people there," indicates that Momaday is creating an oral tradition out of his direct knowledge of the Kiowa captive and his imaginative recreation of her life.

The middle section takes the form of a folksong. In the manuscript version the two final lines of this passage read: 'Aye, Milly Durgan, you've gone from your home / Away to the prairie with red men to roam." While this version refers to the kidnap only, the two lines in their published form are ambiguous: they suggest not only Milly's forceful removal from her home in Texas by the Kiowas but her departure in death from her house at Rainy Mountain. It is now her spirit which roams the prairie.

The excerpt from "Shoot the Buffalo" that concludes "Plainview: 4" is a reminder of the tragic consequences for the Kiowas of the encroachment of the settlers and buffalo hunters. It must have been particularly traumatic for Milly Durgan to see her adopted culture destroyed by people of her own blood. The four poems of the "Plainview" cycle are celebrations of a place in which Momaday is rooted by birth and of a time which prevails in the poet's mind.

"The Gourd Dancer" is a tribute in four sections to Momaday's grandfather Mammedaty, whom he never knew in person but came to know in his racial memory and the verbal dimension of Kiowa lore. Momaday is a successor to his grandfather in the Gourd Dance Society. Thus, the poem makes a statement about the relation between generations in the larger context of Kiowa history and, on a metaphysical level, about the notion of immortality and individual human life in an oral tradition.

In a number of prose works Momaday has directed his energy at salvaging the memory of his ancestor, most notably in *The Names* and in two of his *Viva* columns. In [the column] "A Memory that Persists in the Blood" he deals with the giveaway in honor of Mammedaty which is the subject of the fourth section of "The Gourd Dancer." He points out that the event took place ". . . some years ago, before I was born. And yet it is an important event in my mind, important to me and to my understanding of an Indian heritage. I remember it, as it were, in the way that we human beings seem at times to remember Genesis—across evolutionary distances. It is a memory that persists in the blood, and there only."

The first section of "The Gourd Dancer" is entitled "The Omen." Consisting of two quatrains in blank verse, it establishes in its opening line the centrality of the Kiowa homeland. "This place" is the repository of tribal myth and history, the focal point of Momaday's personal and racial heritage. Through the use of grammatical inversion in lines two and three, Momaday stresses the dependence of blood memory and the passage of time—the receding sun and the seasonal rhythm stand as images of change—on the changeless, everlasting land. Memory and time have existence only in relation to place.

Lines five and six describe the physical landscape, but they also suggest its effect on the human imagination. "A vagrant heat" intimates the flux and intensity of memories, while "shadows turning like smoke" evoke the elusive and indistinct imaginative responses to the physical environment. The omen refers to the owl, a bird which symbolizes transmigration in Kiowa thought. The owl, a creature animated by the souls of the dead, functions as a catalyst for Momaday's epiphany of his grandfather. "Remote within its motion, intricate with age," the bird signifies the world of the past. In its distant and aloof nature, it is a challenge to the human imagination.

In this context the owl carries a second meaning. It refers to Mammedaty, who was an owl prophet. According to a newspaper description of the Gourd Dance, he "received the medicine of the owl when he was cooling off at a creek and a screech owl spoke to him. At a later time, he went into a cataleptic state, visiting the land of the dead. He became knowledgeable about the spirit world." In the light of this biographical detail it becomes apparent that Momaday is presenting a landscape twice perceived: once by Mammedaty, whose encounter with the owl made him a medicine man, and then by the poet himself, who conceives of the bird as a carrier of an ancestral spirit. Momaday and Mammedaty are linked by memory and the imagination, which in turn are moored to the land. Change within constancy finds expression not only in the cycle of seasons but in the chain of generations passing through the Kiowa world.

The poem's second section, "The Dream," reinforces the notion of ancestral interrelatedness established in "The Omen." It consists of Momaday's dream of his grandfather's dreaming about dreaming, a deliberate construction of a chain of imaginative experiences, dreams, and recollections which constitute the oral tradition. Again, the opening line establishes the fixed point as "this house," to which everything else is related. This first sentence, "Mammedaty saw to the building of this house," suggests more than just a physical activity. The verb points beyond its primary meaning of "attending to" the construction of the building; Mammedaty is involved in a spiritual activity, having envisioned the house and pursued this vision as a matter of course. Momaday establishes a link between the sound of the hammers, implied in the silence after the day of work, and the sounds of nature, which take over when human activity rests. The blows of hammers find an echo in the drumbeats of Mammedaty's imaginative dance. The magnificent image, "a low, hectic wind upon the pale, slanting plane of the moon's light," owes something perhaps to the opening line of Emily Dickinson's "There's a certain Slant of light."

Mammedaty's dreaming of the imaginative in the last three lines of this second section is described in terms of the physical. The dream of "the summer breaking upon the spirit" is likened to the drumbeats and gleaming gourds of the Gourd Dance. Implicit in this poetic strategy is the notion that the worlds of dream and reality are the same, an idea corroborated by Momaday's beliefs in the illusory nature of existence and the reality of dreams.

Section three, "The Dance," of **"The Gourd Dancer"** opens with an inversion: at the end of "The Dream" Mammedaty was dreaming of the Gourd Dance; now he is actually dancing, dreaming of the mythical past which gave rise to the Gourd Dance ceremony. This inversion is designed to dissolve even further the separation between the real and the ideal dominant in Anglocentric thought but alien to American Indian philosophy.

In the third line Momaday again takes up the images of wind and "the pale slanting plane of the moon's light." Momaday's use of the verb "glance" is an example of the richness and economy of his language. In its first meaning, "to strike a surface obliquely so as to go off at an angle," "glance" refers to the wind being deflected by the

slanting plane of the moonlight. In a second meaning, "to flash or gleam with quick intermittent rays of light," the image is linked to the flashing and gleaming of the gourd rattles. In its third meaning, "to make sudden quick movements," it is related to the "mincing steps" of the dancer. While the first meaning establishes a connection within the poem, the second and third meanings point beyond its immediate context to the story about the beginning of the Gourd Dance.

The three lines "The long wind glances, moves / Forever as a music to the mind; / The gourds are flashes of the sun," suggest that Mammedaty, in his dream, is drawn toward the mythical origin of his dance. The story of the origin of the Gourd Dance tells of a young man who, on a solitary quest, encounters an enemy in the shape of a wolf. He kills the wolf-like man. "Then," the story continues, "the young man took up the enemy's arrows in his right hand and held them high and shook them. They rattled loudly like dry leaves in a hard wind, and to the music the young man danced around the dead enemy."

The sound and motion of the wind in Mammedaty's dream evoke the music to which the hero in the story is dancing. As the landscape in "The Omen" is a landscape twice perceived, so the wind is a music twice heard. It is "a music in the tribal mind," where it prevails. The motion of the wind relates to the movement of the dance, suggesting a kinship between ritual and nature. The same expression of ritual in terms of nature informs the line "The gourds are flashes of the sun." While the stress here is on the visual impression, the image also evokes the sound and motion of the rattling arrows, again a reminder of the Gourd Dance's origin. In taking the "inward, mincing steps," both in the dance and in the imagination, the past becomes alive for Mammedaty in "old processions and returns." The ritual creates a realm in which time is suspended and the accumulated experience of the race is accessible to the participant.

The second stanza of "The Dance" elaborates on Mammedaty's place within Kiowa tradition. His being is contained in his ritual garb as well as in his name and the story of the giveaway. His part in the Gourd Dance ensures cultural survival. By simulating an eagle's flight, the eagle-feather fan effects Mammedaty's extension not only into the natural world but, more important, into the tribal past and future. His hold upon "the deep ancestral air" constitutes a privilege as well as a responsibility. Momaday's careful use of the word "air," with its double meaning of song and life, implies that through a scrupulous adherence to ritual and song the Gourd Dance will keep Kiowa tradition alive and breathing. The adjective "concise" in the description of Mammedaty's handling of the fan suggests language in being "marked by brevity of expression or statement; free from elaboration and superfluous detail." Momaday appears to draw a deliberate parallel between the motion of the fan and the style of his writing about it, indicating his personal investment in the perpetuation of Kiowa tradition both as a Gourd Dancer and as an artist.

The final section of **"The Gourd Dancer,"** "The Giveaway," amplifies the significance of language in Kiowa

culture. Momaday's imaginative reenactment of the ceremony in Mammedaty's honor is framed by two statements
on the physical and verbal dimension of human existence.
According to Kiowa thought a name is "as much part of
the owner as his hand or his foot." It is never dealt with
lightly. A name contains the essence of its bearer, not
only during his lifetime but beyond it. This attitude toward
names is typical of oral cultures. Mammedaty, on hearing
his name spoken in public, is aware of the seriousness of
the impending event. He is "thoughtful, full of wonder,
and aware of himself and of his name." Momaday draws
attention to this dual existence in body and language
which constitutes the central premise of the oral tradition.
It is in the verbal dimension that life becomes timeless.
Existence in place is temporary; in language it is eternal,
as long as the old stories continue and the names prevail
in the memory of the people.

Momaday conjures up the giveaway ceremony in all its
dignity and excitement. The black horse, Mammedaty's
gift of honor, is a symbol of the life force, of "the wild
way." Its excitement is analogous to Mammedaty's in view
of the seriousness of the occasion. For the ceremony is
not only a matter of honor; it represents the making of a
tradition. In that his name is attached to the ceremony,
which is perpetuated as a story in Kiowa oral tradition, he
is being immortalized. The giveaway is thus something of
an initiation ceremony in which Mammedaty enters the
verbal dimension of existence which goes on forever in
the tribal mind.

In **"New World"** Momaday combines syllabic verse and
imagistic expression with the ambiguity and creativity of
sound typical of the oral tradition to generate a sense of
the aboriginal perception of the universe. The poem was
published simultaneously in *The Gourd Dancer* and as
part of an essay entitled "A First American Views His
Land" [*National Geographic Magazine* 150, No. 1 (July
1996)], in which Momaday adumbrates the moral implications of the relationship between Indians and their land.
Some statements from this article are useful for putting the
poem into perspective. Momaday noted that "Native
American oral tradition is rich with songs and tales that
celebrate natural beauty, the beauty of the natural world."
"New World" exemplifies the oral-aural quality of some of
Momaday's poetry because of not only its subject matter
but also its subtle use of imitative sound and phonic
effects. These effects come alive when the poem is read
aloud or, better still, when one listens to Momaday's own
reading of it.

"New World" is a hymn to the beauty of nature. If the
language, at times, has a biblical ring to it, the implication
is clearly that the scene generates a religious experience
in the beholder, a sense of communion between man and
earth. Momaday expressed this communion: "The first
truth is that I *love* the land; I see that it is beautiful; I
delight in it; I am alive in it." It would be wrong to see the
poem merely as an attempt to reconstruct the scene as it
presented itself, in the beginning, to "First Man." As in
"The Gourd Dancer," the landscape is mythical, but it is
also contemporary. If the perceiving eye can take hold of

the mystery of the natural world, its field of vision extends
across time to the moment of creation. Momaday describes
the experience [in "So Crisply Summer," *Viva*, October 8,
1972]: "It was simply exciting to be overtaken by the
dawn, to see the world emerge from the darkness. There
is something like Genesis, like Creation at that hour of the
day; and outside, breathing deeply of it, you feel intensely
alive." **"New World"** is more than a poem; it is a prayer
for communion with the universe and for the strength
which emanates from the beginning of the world.

Momaday's poetic construction of the natural world rests
on the use of juxtapositions and the careful selection of
minute details. The main oppositions are earth and sky,
sun and moon, light and shadow, heat and cold, motion
and motion suspended. The poem's structure is cyclical:
after setting the scene in the first stanza, Momaday follows the course of a day from dawn to noon in stanzas
two and three to dusk and night in the last stanza.

The three opening words, "First Man / behold," are characteristic of American Indian creation myths, in which a
creator lines up the people to view, for the first time, their
new world. The notions of creation and procreation are
sustained by the images of rain and pollen, two fundamental elements in the chain of life. The sun, implicit in the
glittering of leaves and the glistening of the sky, and the
wind as carrier of pollen and seed are other life-giving
agents. Momaday indicates that what he selects for description is beautiful not only in its appearance but in its
interrelatedness and function within nature. Sky and wind
attain a distinct concreteness: the sky is conceived of as a
surface reflecting the sunlight; the "winds that low and lean
upon the mountains" have almost a personal character.
"Low" suggests not only sound, a voice, but also movement, as the winds lower themselves on the mountains for
support. Apart from alliteration, which occurs frequently
throughout the poem, the choice of words with phonic
effects is the most striking device Momaday employs and
the one most closely related to the oral tradition.

Another example of such ambiguity of sound is the word
"borne" in "Pollen / is borne / on winds." In print the
distinction of "borne" and "born" is obvious, but it is
much less so in the poem's true medium of sound, where
the verb's suggestiveness of birth connects with the explicit theme of creation in the first stanza. The unusual
choice of the archaic word "hie" in the second stanza is
justified by the homophonous character of the word, suggesting at the same time the rapid motion and height of
the eagles at dawn. Similarly, "plain" in "eagles / hie and
/ hover / above / the plain" resonates with the additional
meaning of "plane," evokes an image of light as in "The
Dream" section of **"The Gourd Dancer,"** and anticipates
the "planes / of heat" in the third stanza. The verb "lie"
in "shadows / withdraw / and lie / away / like smoke" is
another case in point. Not only does it suggest the retreat
and eventual disappearance of shadows, it simultaneously
connotes the deceptiveness of the phenomenon.

In this second stanza Momaday also succeeds in creating
a sense of the space and height of his world. He uses a

double perspective, one angle of vision from below, focusing on the eagles in the sky, and one from the eagles' vantage point above, centering on the pools of light on the plain. Finally, the image of the moving shadows is a powerful evocation of the passage of time as the sun approaches its pivotal point at noon.

The opening of the third stanza suggests a slowing down of life in the heat of noon. Through the use of long vowels Momaday achieves an effect of phonic mimesis. The second sentence, "Bees hold / the swarm," is of twofold interest. On the level of sound "Bees hold" is a play on "behold" in the first stanza, a deliberate repetition with a variation, another call to be mindful of the natural world. On the conceptual level this sentence raises the question of the relation between the parts and the whole; inasmuch as the bees hold the swarm, the swarm unites the bees. It is a small example of the mystery of nature: the interrelatedness of individual parts which form an organic whole.

The final stanza opens with a stark silhouette. Momaday's images of animal life immobilized in the cold of the approaching night have the quality of abstract line drawings. In the atmospheric cold motion is suspended, "foxes / stiffen" and "blackbirds / are fixed / in the / branches." The latter image is reminiscent of Wallace Stevens's solitary blackbirds sitting "in the cedar-limbs" on a snowy and dark winter afternoon.

The final image of moonlight over the river is rendered by one of Momaday's typical poetic devices, inversion: "Rivers / follow / the moon, / the long / white track / of the / full moon." It is, of course, the moonlight which follows the track of the river; but in ignoring logical order, Momaday creates a sense of wonder and mystery. He points to a dimension of reality which is closed to the analytical mind. The vision of the river following the moon is an imaginative transformation, a mode of reality based on belief rather than knowledge, and therefore mythical in character.

In **"The Eagle-Feather Fan,"** Momaday turns his attention to ritual. The poem reflects his participation in the annual Kiowa Gourd Dance ceremonials at Carnegie, Oklahoma. It captures some typically indigenous assumptions about human existence: the belief in magic, the belief in the value of tradition, the belief in the unity of creation, and the belief in the relationship of reality and the imagination.

Central to the magical world view is the idea of power, or medicine. It is conceived of as an intrinsic element of the natural order, a force which the individual can appropriate through ritual and utilize in his dealings with the world. The opening lines, "The eagle is my power, / And my fan is an eagle," indicate the connection between the dancer and his power through the ritual implement of the eagle-feather fan. The fan "is real," not a symbol of power but power itself. No distinction is made between the physical and spiritual, the "real" and the imaginative; such a separation would be alien to the American Indian view of the universe. The equation of the fan's beaded handle with "the twist of bristlecone" suggests the ancient nature of

the ritual and its potential for tapping the life force. Bristlecones are among the oldest known living trees, and Momaday has noted "the impulse of life" in these "thorns of the ancient earth."

The next lines express man's ritual extension into and identification with the natural world: "The bones of my hand are fine / and hollow; the fan bears them. / My hand veers in the thin air / of the summit." The bones are fine and hollow like those of an eagle's wing; moreover, Momaday makes the point that the fan bears the hand rather than the other way around, as one might expect. This inversion implies first and foremost that ritual sustains human existence and, second, that man's ritual activity sustains the ceremony.

Through his adherence to tradition, his capacity for belief, and the power of his imagination, the Gourd Dancer can transcend the individual boundaries of human existence and unite himself with the cosmos. The association of power with the eagle, eagle with the fan, fan with the bristlecone, and the Gourd Dancer with all of them suggests the infinite chain of creation of which man is one small link.

If ritual is one form of human expression which ensures man's link to tradition and the web of life, the oral tradition is another. In **"Carriers of the Dream Wheel,"** Momaday explores the verbal dimension of American Indian cultures. An individual inherits his tribe's accumulated wealth of orally transmitted stories and songs, "the dream wheel," which shapes his existence and his perception of the world around him.

The first four lines of the poem establish the reciprocal relation between the dream wheel and its carriers. The imaginary realm of histories and myths, visions and songs, survives in their voices, and the keepers of the oral tradition have existence in and through it. It is a fundamental tenet of American Indian thought that the world came into existence through language, that nothing truly exists unless it has existence in language. This theory of creation is intimated in the lines "It [the Dream Wheel] encircles the First World, / This powerful wheel. / They shape their songs upon the wheel / And spin the names of the earth and sky, / The aboriginal names." The concluding six lines combine the ancient and contemporary aspects of the oral tradition: as long as this heritage is kept alive in the communal experience of American Indians, they will continue to know who they are and what their destiny is.

The sequence of eight prose poems which constitutes **"The Colors of Night"** is a product of Momaday's stay in Moscow in 1974. He has described the poems as "quintessential novels, concentrated stories of time, place, and presence." In attributing a color to each of the sections Momaday creates a spectrum, a dark prism which makes up night. He explained that he "was not thinking of traditional Indian colors," but "of times of day, and trying to associate all the colors of night into one thing." Traditionally, of course, night is the time of Indian storytelling; the poetic sequence manifests a slice of the oral tradition, revealing a number of characteristic ethical and epistemological issues. The stories are imbued with a sense of wonder and mystery which accounts for their peculiar charm.

The first story, about a man who retrieves and cherishes the bones of his dead son, is a moving example of the respect for the deceased which is common among Indian peoples. Moreover, the old man's proclamation "that now his son consists in his bones" powerfully attests to his belief in the indestructibility of a man's essence or, to use the Christian term, his soul. The color white refers to the polished bones which "gleam like glass in the light of the sun and the moon." The story is a poetic treatment of a historical incident recorded by James Mooney [in *Calendar History of the Kiowa Indians*.]:

> In the spring of 1870, before the last sun dance, the son of the noted chief Set-ängya ("Sitting-bear"), . . . had made a raid with a few followers into Texas, where . . . he had been shot and killed. After the dance his father with some friends went to Texas, found his bones and wrapped them in several fine blankets, put the bundle upon the back of a led horse and brought them home. . . . While on the march the remains were always put upon the saddle of a led horse, as when first brought home, the [funeral] tipi and the horse thus burdened being a matter of personal knowledge to all middle-age people of the tribe now living. He continued to care for his son's bones in this manner until he himself was killed at Fort Sill about a year later, when the Kiowa buried them.

The second section, "Yellow," is an etiologic myth about how it came about that dogs howl at the moon. Enchanted by the yellow brilliance of moonlight on a river, and inspired to sing what is to be his death song, a boy follows the mystery of sound and vision and drowns in the swirling waters. The story is, however, primarily concerned not with death but with metamorphosis: the boy emerges from the river as a dog, howling at the moon, presumably reproaching the moon for its deceit. As in the first poem, death is presented as a matter of transformation rather than annihilation.

In the third section, "Brown," Momaday makes a humorous claim against empiricism. The secret of how terrapins evade a flood by climbing to higher ground defies the most scrupulous observation. The implication here seems to be that although nature has been stripped of many of its wonders by analytical, scientific investigation, there still remain mysteries which frustrate reason and feed the imagination.

Section four, "Red," deals with the moral implications of magic. A man has used his "powerful medicine" to create a woman out of sumac leaves, and he lives with her for a while. The title of the poem refers to the woman's skin color, which resembles that of pipestone. When the man mistreats her, he loses both his magic power and the woman, who disintegrates and becomes part of nature again, "leaves scattered in the plain." Once more, the story bears witness to the belief in the infinite possibilities of creation, transformation, and deconstruction.

The fifth section, "Green," is a puzzling statement on the nature of reality: "A young girl awoke one night and looked out into the moonlit meadow. There appeared to be a tree; but it was only an appearance; there was a shape made of smoke; but it was only an appearance; there was a tree." Momaday's oral reading of this passage shows a declining stress from the first "there," which carries great weight and functions as a demonstrative and prepositional referent, putting the existence of the tree beyond doubt, to the third "there," which is no more than an unstressed reference to an indefinite object.

Despite this variance of stress and the repetition of "it was only an appearance," Momaday's intention is obvious: he is trying to eliminate the distinction between appearance and reality. Human reality goes beyond what is verifiable by reason; it is constituted as well by dreams, visions, and illusions. Momaday had noted that "there are modes and modes of existence." The reality of a tree, he seems to say, is valid, whether it is a product of sense perception or of the imagination.

In the following section, "Blue," Momaday qualifies the nature of reality in an important way: reality, he suggests, is ultimately a function of language; only what has existence in language can be said to be real. The parable of the child who appears in a camp and talks to the people in an unintelligible language is the account of a vision the reality of which is denied because it cannot be transformed into language: "After all . . . how can we believe in the child? It gave us not one word of sense to hold on to." Had the child given his name, he would have acquired an identity and a sense of reality.

Section seven, "Purple," relates the transgression of the sacred rules which regulate the relation between man and the animal world. A man has slaughtered a buffalo, the animal representation of the sun, for no reason other than sport. His fellow people witness the sacrilege with shame and grief. The moral implications of the story are amplified by its etiologic character. The buffalo's hump and spine are transformed into a mountain on the western horizon, and its blood, bright and purple, colors the setting sun, darkens, and creates the night sky. The results of these metamorphoses are permanent reminders of the sacrilegious act in the people's physical environment.

The final section, "Black," is another illustration of the existence of mysterious forces in the universe which cannot be accounted for but have to be believed. What the woman who "steals into the men's societies and fits her voice into their holiest songs" represents remains in doubt. However, what is important is not what she is but *that* she is, timeless, ever-present, inexplicable. At the end of a sequence of poems which centers on a world of magic and mystery, she stands as the embodiment of mystery itself.

"Colors of Night" is an attempt to give some clues to the way in which American Indians view the world. Theirs is a mythical world view, a fact which accounts for the difficulties a non-Indian reader may have with this poetic cycle. Momaday once quoted Isak Dinesen's remark that "it is not necessarily bad that a story should only be half understood." If the eight poems generate a sense of wonder and delight, they have fulfilled their purpose. If they set in motion the reader's imagination and motivate him to expand and retell them, they indeed acquire the status of "quintessential novels" which Momaday intended for them.

The concluding five poems of part two of *The Ground Dancer* are evocations of different landscapes, delineating various human reactions to the natural world. **"The Monoliths"** seems to refer to the three awesome stone columns which tower over Monument Valley. The four-line poem suggests that the poetic persona experiences simultaneously a communion with and separation from his environment. While the wind upon him makes him part of the scene, the monoliths are of an order which defies his approach. Defined by the contrast of stone against light, they appear as pillars of eternity, generating the sense of awe and wonder which enters the human mind when man is obliged to relate his existence to the grandeur of the world around him.

"North Dakota, North Light" is a reflection on the terrible powers of winter. Man and animals seem frozen in a dazzling, brilliant winter landscape. After an opening statement on the encroaching presence of cold, Momaday frames the remainder of the poem by references to "the sheer, lucent plane," repeated with slight modification in the final line, ". . . the sheer, shining plane." The only motion in this scene of extraordinary beauty is the wind which is deflected from the hunter's weapon: "A glassy wind glances / from the ball of bone in my wrist."

Life has come to a total halt. The rabbits in the foreground rest under the force of the sky which is "clenched upon them" like the claws of a bird of prey. The hunter, too, seems motionless, arrested by the deadening cold. Significantly, its effect is both physical and mental: ". . . and I cannot conceive / of summer, / and another man in me / stands for it, / wills even to remain, / figurative, fixed, / among the hard, hunchbacked rabbits." The cold is so overwhelming that it halts even the imagination; the pronoun "it" in line eleven refers back to "summer," suggesting that there are two separate manifestations of the persona, one for winter, another for summer. This distinction may indicate man's spiritual and physical subordination to the cyclical, seasonal rhythms of nature. Since the summer manifestation is powerless in the face of wintry forces, it wills to remain "figurative, fixed," submitting itself to their reign as do the "hard, hunchbacked rabbits."

"Winter Holding off the Coast of North America" addresses itself to man's instinctual fear when he confronts irresistible natural forces. Momaday captures this abstract idea in the word "dread" in the opening line. The simile and images which follow evoke this notion through clear sensory details and communicate tightly controlled emotions in response to the facts of human vulnerability and insignificance.

The simile "like a calm" and the adjective "colorless" simultaneously describe and explain the sense of dread. The powerful forces at work are beyond visual and auditory perception, but they are nevertheless real and make

themselves felt. They are defined in terms of cold and suspension of motion and represent a kind of anti-life. This theme is suggested by Momaday's use of the adjective "dead" to describe the approaching cold. The poem is related to **"Before an Old Painting of the Crucifixion,"** in which the latent presence of death also informs the calm of the sea. The only reference to human presence in **"Winter Holding off the Coast of North America"** is "the stricken palm," an image of man's exposure and fragility which evokes the crucifixion.

The last stanza, in its depiction of the natural world charged with an irresistible and inexorable destiny, belongs to Momaday's most powerful poetic statements: "Out there, beyond the floes, / On the thin pewter plane, / The polar currents close, / And stiffen, and remain."

While the previous two poems dealt with hostile, life-denying winter landscapes, **"To a Child Running with Outstretched Arms in Canyon de Chelly"** communicates the exhilaration and joy derived from the spectacular scenery near Chinle, New Mexico, where Momaday spent a brief part of his childhood. The poem can therefore be seen as a projection of Momaday's own wonder and delight into the figure of the child. The idea of "spirit of place" is related to aesthetic and historical considerations in this poem. The play of light and shadow as well as the natural stone sculptures which abound in the canyon appeal to the aesthetic sense.

But it is not only in geographical terms that "the backdrop is immense." Rock paintings and ruins of cliff dwellings are silent witnesses to the culture of the Anazasi, the Ancient Ones, who lived in Canyon de Chelly centuries before the Navajos made it their home. Here also the Navajos made their brave if futile stand against Kit Carson's military expedition in 1864, which led to the enforced relocation of the tribe known as the Long Walk, perhaps the darkest chapter in Navajo history. But the Navajos returned, and their sense of belonging to a homeland of majestic beauty is ample reason for excitement and joy.

"Long Shadows at Dulce" is written in syllabic verse of six syllables to the line and consists of four individually numbered stanzas, each of which represents a miniature poem in its own right. These four stanzas capture in a highly personal, imagistic manner the mood and activities of autumn at Dulce, a small town on the Jicarilla Apache Reservation in northern New Mexico. Although only two months are referred to by name, the four stanzas form a sequence from September to December. In its progression through the season, its compressed imagistic form, and perhaps even in the title the poem shows parallels to Yvor Winters's poetic cycle "The Magpie's Shadow." Winters's one-line poems are reflections on a year at Madrid, a coal mining camp twenty miles south of Santa Fe where he taught grade school in 1922 after recovering from tuberculosis. Momaday's poem is a commemoration of impressions during a brief stay at Dulce where he worked as a schoolteacher in 1958.

In the first stanza Momaday addresses the ambiguous nature of September. His characterization of the month as "a long illusion of itself" presumably refers to the transition from summer to fall which lies in the air but is nothing more than a vague presence defying sensory perception. The third line, "the elders bide their time," is ambiguous: it may refer to old people who await the approach of winter, perhaps of death; simultaneously it alludes to the elderberry trees which seem to defer the change of color, the sign of the arrival of autumn.

Stanza two captures the joy and excitement among the children when, at the end of summer, the sheep are rounded up in the camps and the community gathers for social activities. Stanza three communicates the atmosphere of November by way of an extended metaphor. It is the time of the bear hunt: "November is the flesh / And blood of the black bear, / Dusk its bone and marrow." The sense of melancholy and the slowing down of life which announces the coming of winter are brilliantly reflected in the image of the final stanza: "In the huddled horses / That know of perfect cold / There is a calm, like sorrow."

These five poems which conclude part two of *The Gourd Dancer* reflect not only a greater freedom and flexibility in poetic expression compared to the Stanford period but also a shift from the largely abstract, philosophical themes explored under Winters's supervision to more immediate, personal concerns. The self-exploration in terms of his American Indian background, which Momaday pursued in prose in *The Way to Rainy Mountain,* is the central theme in the second part of *The Gourd Dancer.*

Momaday on the oral tradition

The works of Indian poets proceed from the oral tradition, I believe. That tradition is there in the background, and it can scarcely be ignored. We are talking about a sensitivity to language, a faith in the efficacy of the word. That is an important legacy for the Indian writer. Beyond that, there are certain themes, certain attitudes and perceptions that demand expression. Among these are the relationships between Man and the other creatures of the earth, between Man and the landscape, between Man and supernatural beings.

N. Scott Momaday, in MELUS, *Vol. 10, No. 4, Winter, 1983.*

Scott Edward Anderson (review date 1993)

SOURCE: A review of *In the Presence of the Sun: Stories and Poems, 1961-1991,* in *The Bloomsbury Review,* Vol. 13, No. 4, July-August, 1993, pp. 14, 22.

[*Below, Anderson provides a thematic and stylistic review of* In the Presence of the Sun.]

There have been a number of notable collected and selected volumes of poetry over the past few years, including award-winning books by Mary Oliver and Hayden Car-

ruth, as well as important editions from Gary Snyder, Donald Hall, Derek Mahon, Cynthia Macdonald, Adrienne Rich, and others. The significance of this is not lost: As we approach the end of the millennium, many of our poets are at the top of their form. These collections allow us to assess their accomplishments as well as gauge the state of the art over the past several decades.

We are fortunate to add to the growing list of retrospective collections this new book from N. Scott Momaday. *In the Presence of the Sun* offers "stories," poems, and drawings from over 30 years. Many of us first became aware of Momaday through his Pulitzer Prize-winning novel, *House Made of Dawn,* but it was as a poet that he first appeared on the literary scene.

Momaday's early work, still some of his best, bears the influence of his teacher at Stanford, Yvor Winters. These are, nonetheless, poems of grace and resonance. Winters encouraged the young Momaday to work in a variety of traditional forms, including syllabic verse, in which the number of syllables in a line determines the rhythmic structure. Momaday used this method to great effect in such early poems as **"Buteo Regalis,"** and again in **"The Bear"**:

> What ruse of vision,
> escarping on the wall of leaves,
>   rending incision
> into countless surfaces,
>
>   would cull and color
> his somnolence, whose old age
>   has outworn valor,
> all but the fact of courage?

In **"Angle of Geese,"** from the same period, the poet examines the differences between the human concept of death and death in wild nature:

> Almost of a mind,
> We take measure of the loss;
>   I am slow to find
> The mere margin of repose.
>
>   . . . . .
>
>   So much symmetry!—
> Like the pale angle of time
>   And eternity.
> The great shape labored and fell.

This is perhaps the first of Momaday's poems to reject, philosophically if not technically, Winters' influence. In the wake of this poem, Momaday turned increasingly to nature and to his Kiowa heritage, exploring native themes and the old ways and employing forms that more accurately present these concerns. This change is further exemplified by the incantatory style of his **"The Delight Song of Tsoai-talee"**:

> I am a flame of four colors
> I am a deer standing away in the dusk
> I am a field of sumac and the pomme blanche

I am an angle of geese in the winter sky
I am the hunger of a young wolf
I am the whole dream of these things
You see, I am alive, I am alive

Momaday participates annually in the Gourd Dance Society, where he is the successor to his grandfather, Mammedaty. His poem **"The Gourd Dancer"** is at once an homage to his grandfather and an expression of respect for the tradition:

Someone spoke his name, Mammedaty, in which
his essence was and is. It was a serious matter
that his name should be spoken there in the circle, among the many people, and he was
thoughtful, full of wonder, and aware of himself
and of his name.

Here magic and tradition, reality and the dreamland come together for the poet and, through his storytelling, for the reader.

Myth, too, plays an important part in his work. Included in this volume is a long sequence of poems titled **"The Strange and True Story of My Life with Billy the Kid."** The mythic figure of Billy the Kid represents a significant influence on the imagination of Scott Momaday. While Momaday's choice of the legendary outlaw as a subject for a sustained sequence might at first seem odd, it illustrates the unique bicultural nature of both his outlook and his work. "The Kid" died in Momaday's home territory of New Mexico; we can imagine the young poet heard of his legend alongside the stories of his native culture, and the sequence has all the earmarks of the oral tradition in its form and function. Composed of songs, epigraphs, and prose poems as well as narrative poems, this sustained imaginative meditation captures the essence of the myth and its effect on the psyche of the author. For Momaday, Billy is not only an outlaw hero (and hence, like the poet's own people, both outcast and venerated presence), he is also a sensitive individual, a youth with a sense of valor if not a conscience:

Billy fetched a plug of tobacco from his coat pocket,
cut it in two with a jackknife, and gave the old man
half. We said goodbye . . . Later, on the way to Santa
Fe, I said to Billy: "Say, amigo, I have never seen you
chew tobacco." "No, and it isn't likely that you ever
will," he said. "I have no use for the weed. . . . I
bought the tobacco at La Junta because I knew that we
were coming this way . . . to see the old man . . . He
has a taste for it. And I offered him half instead of the
whole because he should prefer that I did not give him
something outright; it pleased him that I should share
something of my own with him. . . . I have thrown
away my share . . . But that is an unimportant matter
. . . this the old man understands and appreciates more
even than the tobacco itself."

When Billy (né Henry McCarty) witnesses the marriage of his mother, we see another side of the outlaw, one the tall tales never revealed:

She is pale, lovely, and lithe.
Her sons are stiff and homely,

And they make hard witnesses.
Joe is careless, distant, dumb;
Henry imagines marriage,
The remorse and agonies
Of age. He looks upon her,
His mother, and his mind turns
Upon him; the beautiful
His example of despair.

Yet Billy can also instill terror in an individual: He is "the only man I have ever known in whose eyes there was no expression whatsoever."

In the "Gathering of Shields," which gives *In the Presence of the Sun* its title, Momaday turns to a further exploration of myth and legend. Each shield, carefully executed in ink, is rendered on the facing page in a brief prose translation. "The Sun Dance Shield," "The Shield That Died," "The Floating Feathers Shield," and "The Shield That Was Touched by Pretty Mouth" are all brought to life by the poetry. Take, for example, the tragic story of "The Shield of Which the Less Said the Better":

A man—his name is of no importance—owned a shield.
The shield came down in the man's family. The man's
grandson carried the shield into a fight at Stinking
Creek, and he was killed. Soldiers took away the shield.
Some years ago old man Red Horn bought the shield
in a white man's store at Clinton, Oklahoma, for
seventeen dollars. The shield was worth seventeen
dollars, more or less.

The shield drawings are powerful, in part because the form is such an intriguing one: circles, objects of protection, ornament, and deep spiritual value. Each shield tells a story, but its decoration only provides the skeleton of a narra-tive—the trick, Momaday implies, is to *listen* to the shield.

In "The Shield of Two Dreams," a woman named Dark Water inherits her father's shield through the simple act of dream-ing. This, we imagine, is a fairly radical event, for nothing else like it appears in this gathering of shields; no other woman receives this power. Momaday has, rather appropriately, placed this shield at the end of the section, as if to under-score its adaptation of the old ways to new times.

Of the "New Poems" in this collection, only a few seem to live up to the promise of Momaday's earlier work: **"The Great Fillmore Street Buffalo Drive," "Carnegie, Okla-homa, 1919," "Mogollon Morning,"** and **"Wreckage"**:

Had my bones, like the sun,
been splintered on this canyon wall
and burned among these buckled plates,
this bright debris; had it been so,
I should not have lingered so long
among my losses. I should have come
loudly, like a warrior, to my time.

The other poems in this section seem vague and affected, and their weakness stands out in the face of the strong earlier work of the collection.

The drawings throughout the volume are evocative, especially the various bears, which in many ways resemble the author. (Momaday's biography proclaims: "He is a bear.") They are robust creatures, well rounded yet full of energy. It is a contradiction that serves well this bear of an artist—poet, painter, and storyteller, and in all these things a "man made of words." *In the Presence of the Sun* gives us the unique opportunity to witness this bear as he articulates "the appropriate expression of his spirit."

FURTHER READING

Bibliography

Trimble, Martha Scott. "N. Scott Momaday (1934-)." In *Fifty Western Writers: A Bio-Bibliographical Sourcebook,* edited by Fred Erisman and Richard W. Etulain, pp. 313-24. Westport, Conn.: Greenwood Press, 1982.

> Provides an overview of Momaday's life, a discussion of the major themes of his works, critical reception of his writings, and a listing of primary and secondary sources.

Criticism

Bode, Barbara. "Imagination Man." *The New York Times Book Review* (March 14, 1993): 15.

> Praises Momaday's descriptions of Kiowa culture and history as well as his use of voice and language in *In the Presence of the Sun.*

World Literature Today 67, No. 3 (Summer 1993): 680.

> Argues that *In the Presence of the Sun* achieves Momaday's purpose, which is to "express my spirit fairly."

Reynolds, Susan Salter. Review of *In the Presence of the Sun: Stories and Poems, 1961-1991,* by N. Scott Momaday. *Los Angeles Times Book Review* (27 December 1992): 6.

> Praises Momaday's focus on identity, nature, native chants, artifacts, and traditions in *In the Presence of the Sun.*

Roemer, Kenneth M. "Bear and Elk: The Nature(s) of Contemporary American Indian Poetry." In *Studies in American Indian Literature: Critical Essays and Course Designs,* edited by Paula Gunn Allen, pp. 178-91. New York: The Modern Language Association of America, 1983.

> Comparative analysis of Momaday's "The Bear" and Leslie Marmon Silko's poem "Snow Elk."

Additional coverage of Momaday's life and career is contained in the following sources published by The Gale Group: *Authors & Artists for Young Adults,* Vol. 11; *Contemporary Authors,* Vols. 25-28 (rev. ed.); *Contemporary Authors New Revision Series,* Vols. 14, 34; *Contemporary Literary Criticism,* Vols. 2, 19, 85; *Discovering Authors; Native North American Literature;* and *Something About the Author,* Vols. 30, 48.

Léopold Sédar Senghor
1906-

(Has also written under pseudonyms of Silmang Diamano and Patrice Maguilene Kaymor) Senegalese poet, essayist, nonfiction writer, critic, and editor.

INTRODUCTION

An influential statesman who served as President of the Republic of Senegal for twenty years following its independence from France in 1960, Senghor is also considered an important poet and essayist whose work affirms the rich traditions of his African heritage. He is perhaps best known as one of the most outspoken proponents of *négritude,* a literary ideology that urges black people worldwide to resist the cultural manifestations of European colonialism and to reclaim and embellish their African past. A recipient of many honors and literary prizes, Senghor became the first black member of the Académie Française upon his election in 1983.

Biographical Information

Senghor was born in the predominantly Islamic province of Joal, French West Africa. Raised as a Roman Catholic, he attended French missionary schools in preparation for the priesthood but abandoned his religious studies in favor of the classics and modern literature. Upon graduation from the Lycée of Dakar in 1928, Senghor earned a scholarship to study at the Sorbonne. While in Paris, he met the West Indian writers Aimé Césaire and Léon Gontran Damas, who introduced him to the works of such Harlem Renaissance authors as Claude McKay, Countee Cullen, and Langston Hughes. In 1934, with Césaire and Damas, Senghor founded the literary and cultural journal *L'etudiant noir,* which helped delineate the principles of négritude and published the works of other francophone writers.

After serving in the French Colonial Army during World War II, Senghor became active in politics. In 1946 he began serving his first term as Senegale député in the French National Assembly in Paris, and in 1948, he formed the socialist party Bloc Démocratique Sénégalais in his own country. During the early 1950s, Senghor served as French delegate to the United Nations General Assembly. He was elected the first president of the new republic of Senegal on September 5, 1960. During his long rule, he continued to publish poetry and political essays, and won several international awards for his work. He resigned from the presidency in 1979 and four years later, he was the first black African elected to the Académie Française.

Major Works

The poems in Senghor's first major collection, *Chants d'ombre,* were written during the 1930s. Although largely

traditional in structure and meter, these pieces also evoke the intricate rhythmic patterns of compositions by musicians in Senghor's native village. Published in 1948, *Hosties noires* reflects Senghor's growing interest in Pan-Africanism and contains some of his strongest attacks on French colonialism. The majority of the poems in this collection relate his experiences as a soldier and prisoner of war while serving in the French Colonial Army during World War II. *Nocturnes* contains a series of elegies discussing the nature of poetry and the role of the poet in contemporary society. During the 1970s, Senghor published *Elégie des eaux* and *Lettres d'hivernage,* which expanded on his earlier themes. In recent years, he has revised several early volumes of verse, including *Poèmes,* which features a cycle of elegies dedicated to his deceased son as well as other meditations on life and death.

Critical Reception

Many commentators have noted elements of both European and African culture in Senghor's poetry, attributing this synthesis to his French education and his long service in the French government. He is often praised for his deft imagery, symbolism, and the rhythm of his language, which is often compared to the sounds of African drums. While some critics notice a lack of tension in his work, some appreciate its lush sensuality and positive message that attempts to celebrate African heritage and culture. In fact, critics agree that Senghor's poetry often serves to bridge the chasm between African and European literature.

PRINCIPAL WORKS

Poetry

Chants d' ombre [*Songs of Shadow*] 1945
Hosties noires [*Black Sacrifices*] 1948
Chants pour Naeett [*Songs for Naeett*] 1949
Ethiopiques 1956
Nocturnes 1961
Lettres d'hivernage 1973
Paroles 1975

CRITICISM

Jonathan Peters (essay date 1973)

SOURCE: "L. S. Senghor: The Mask Poems of *Chants d'Ombre*," in *African Literature Today*, edited by Eldred Durosimi Jones, Africana Publishing Co., 1973, pp. 76-92.

[*In the following essay, Peters explores the way in which African aesthetic sensibility influences Senghor's work.*]

Critical judgement of Léopold Senghor's poetry is fraught with a number of problems, not all of them literary. As the poet-President of Senegal there is a distinct temptation for admirers of his versatility to be overwhelming in their praise by eulogising the politician instead of judging the poet. In addition, as the most eloquent champion of Négritude there is the tendency for novitiates as well as loyal adherents of long standing to extol the leader's poetry because he is a good and faithful leader rather than because he is a good poet.

On the other hand, those who criticise Négritude as a strait-jacket in so far as it tries to impose a form and style of Negro-African writing instead of allowing the artist's imagination free rein are apt to see in Senghor's poetry nothing but propaganda and racism, or what Sartre in his celebrated essay, *Orphée noir,* written as a preface to Senghor's black poetry *Anthologie* of 1948 [referred] to as '*racisme anti-raciste*'.

These two kinds of problems—adulation and scorn—cast a shadow over assessments of the real value of Senghor's poetry but our major concern here is with the question of vehicle and tradition. Senghor writes in an adopted language, French, and has the French literary heritage as a frame of reference and as an influence on his work—witness the echoes and correspondences of other writers that critics have detected.[1] He has also studied the language and poetry of traditional African languages (notably those of Senegal) and claims these as his models as well as the work of Negro-American poets of the Negro Renaissance of the '20s. Questions of judgement thus arise, in view of these differing if not conflicting allegiances. For example, when Senghor—and Césaire, too—is criticised for being monotonous by French critics, is it because these critics have failed to appreciate the African rhythm of the poem which is monotonous only to the untrained ear that cannot distinguish subtle variations and that is denied the benefit of the percussion instruments which should accompany the chanting of the poem?[2] When English-speaking Africans reject his poetry and his philosophy is it because they cannot read and speak French fluently and have to rely on imperfect translations?[3] And when Senghor sings the praise of black woman or black culture is it racism, racial pride or simply an imitation of the troubadour of his native Joal? No systematic answer to these broad questions is attempted in this limited study; rather, it is hoped that a close examination of the mask-poems of *Chants d'Ombre*—'**Femme noire**', '**Masque nègre**', '**Prière aux Masques**', and '**Totem**'—will point up the ambivalence in Senghor's aesthetic sensibility as a basis for judging his strengths and weaknesses.

The first of these—'**Black Woman**'—addresses an unnamed woman, passive and gentle, with whom the speaker in the poem is in communion. Unlike the woman in an earlier poem, '**Nuit de Sine**', the portrait of this woman fills the whole canvas as first her classic attributes followed by her particular features and finally her enduring universal traits are etched out. The poem opens into a sun-baked noon in summer, and the sight of this classic black woman whose form is remembered from childhood prompts the praise song that Senghor chants:

> Naked woman, black woman
> Clothed with your colour which is life, with your
>   form which is beauty!
> In your shadow I have grown up; the gentleness of
>   your hands was laid over my eyes.
> And now, high up on the sun-baked pass, at the
>   heart of summer, at the heart of noon, I come
>   upon you, my Promised Land,
> And your beauty strikes me to the heart like the
>   flash of an eagle.[4]

The first detail about this woman is that she is naked. In all Western poetry, even in the most sensual, it is unusual to find a poem praising a woman's beauty that introduces her simple nakedness as her first attribute.[5] This detail is followed by the revelation of her black colour which indicates her race and the reader realises that he is not reading a conventional poem written in the Western tradition. This realisation is quickly confirmed by the line following which celebrates her 'colour which is life', her 'form which is beauty'. Thus, without trepidation or fanfare, but rather with a quiet assurance, the first two lines of **'Black Woman'** have asserted that the subject is nude and black, black the colour of life, and her figure the form of beauty. These critical standards established, less striking and more specific details follow. Always responsive to the tender, soothing hands on his brow, Senghor uses the recall of such a moment to introduce the sudden impact of the beauty of the black woman.

With the exception of the change from 'black' to 'dark' in the two middle sections, the first line of the poem becomes the opening refrain in all subsequent verse paragraphs. The surrealist imagery is sensual and daring in turn. From 'firm-fleshed ripe fruit', 'somebre raptures of black wine' and 'mouth making lyrical my mouth', the associations dilate into the 'savannah shuddering beneath the East Wind's eager caresses' and then contract to the 'carved tom-tom, taut tom-tom' muttering in a 'solemn contralto voice'. In the third verse paragraph the descriptive images are less bold. The woman is

> Naked woman, dark woman
> Oil that no breath ruffles, calm oil on the athlete's
>   flanks, on the flanks of the Princes of Mali
> Gazelle limbed in Paradise,

as Senghor prepares, at the end, to

> . . . sing your beauty that passes, the form that I fix
>   in the Eternal,
> Before jealous Fate turn you to ashes to feed the
>   roots of life.

As a rule, Senghor's most successful poems thrive on correspondences and contradictions, on ambiguity and paradox. **'Black Woman'** is no exception to this rule. The provocative refrain would seem to indicate that the emotion is mere eroticism, with the celebrant poised, in Eliot's phrase, 'between the desire and the spasm'; yet in its development, even allowing for the apparent flights of fancy and fortuitousness of surrealist imagery, very little (if any) physical passion for the woman is manifested. In the second section of the poem where the images are the most sensual, no attempt is made to exploit the woman's nudity, for, excepting the reference to her mouth in 'mouth making lyrical my mouth' and 'Your solemn contralto voice' her beauty is not in any way inventoried. In the third section, only her skin, hair and eyes are mentioned, and with these, the promise of a sensually stimulating experience has been abrogated, as the poem reverts to generalities.

Does Senghor therefore fail in his attempt to sing the beauty of his black woman? If his aim is to celebrate the alluring charms of a beloved black woman, then, perhaps, he would do well to follow the example of the West Indian poet, Guy Tirolien, who utilises a similar order of imagery in 'Black Beauty' to achieve a far more erotic effect:

> your breast of black satin
> trembling to the gallop of your blood
> leaping

> your arms supple and long rippling in their
>   sleekness
> that white smile
> eyes
> set in a night-sky face
> waken in me
> this night
>
>   . . . . .
>
> dark-skinned twilights heavy with passion
>
>   . . . . .
>
> in the sweep of restless strength along your loins . . . [6]

Or else he must wait till *Chants pour Naëtt* (*Songs for Naëtt*, 1949) and the twin lyrics 'For two horns and a balafong':

> She flies through the white flat lands, and patiently
>   I take my aim
> Giddy with desire. She takes her chances to the
>   bush
> Passion of thorns and thickets. Then I will bring her
>   to bay in the chain of hours
> Snuffing the soft panting of her flanks, mottled with
>   shadow
> And under the foolish Great Noon, I will twist her
>   arms of glass.
> The antelope's jubilant death rattle will intoxicate
>   me, new palm wine
> And I will drink long long the wild blood that rises
>   to her heart
> The milk blood that flows to her mouth, odours of
>   damp earth.
>
> Am I not the son of Dyogoye? Dyogoye the
>   famished Lion

And again,

> I will go leaping over the hills, defying the fear of
>   the winds of the steppes
> Defying the rivers, where virgin bodies drown in
>   the lowest depths of their grief.
> I will climb the sweet belly of the dunes and the
>   ruddy thighs of day
> To the shadowy gorges where with a sharp blow I
>   will slay the dappled fawn of my dream.

The central hunting metaphor exploited in these lines to represent the high-voltage charge of desire in the lover is far removed from the unimpassioned worship of the figure in **'Black Woman'**.

It would however be premature to dismiss **'Black Woman'** as uninspired without ascertaining what Senghor's purpose is, especially as the rejection of European standards of beauty and the life-source in favour of African models evinced in the opening lines of the poem is not accidental. Since he has deliberately chosen an African ideal of beauty, an African aesthetic is no doubt a valid frame of reference in judging the aim and, to a large extent, the achievement of the poem.

Comparing the function of imagery in European and African art in his essay 'L'esprit de la civilisation ou les lois de la culture' which was read at the First International Conference of Black Writers and Artists Senghor wrote:

> The African image is . . . not image-equation, but image-analogy—a surrealist image. . . . The object does not mean what it represents, but what it suggests, what it creates. . . . Every representation is an image, and the image, I repeat, is not an equation but a *symbol,* an ideogramme. Not only the image-figuration but also the substance—stone, earth, copper, gold, fibre—and even its line and colour. . . . I spoke of the surrealist image. But, as you no doubt suppose, African surrealism is different from European surrealism. European surrealism is empiric whilst African surrealism is mystical and metaphysical. Negro analogy presupposes and manifests the universe as a hierarchy of life-forces.[8]

This basis of interpretation renders the evocation of the African woman in **'Black Woman'** an 'image-analogy' which is not simply the equivalent of an individual African woman but rather a symbol of whatever the figure suggests or creates in the mind of both artist and audience. The line and colour of the descriptive portrait are an ideogrammatic figuration of a mystical and metaphysical being which is projected but not named. But the question remains. What being is behind this projection that, in identifying with 'Negro analogy presupposes and manifests the universe as a hierarchy of life-forces'?

In **'Black Woman'** Senghor invokes the universal black woman who has many guises in black poetry. She has been featured as a beautiful virgin of royal stock in pastoral poetry, as a suffering but steadfast Mother Africa in typically anti-slavery and anti-oppression poetry, as a voluptuous woman linked to the fertility principle in some modern poetry (including poetry of Négritude) that utilises traditional African concepts. Sometimes two or more roles are combined in a single poem. In this regard, the poet who readily comes to mind is David Diop who, in two poems—'Afrique, à ma mère' and 'A une danseuse noire'—depicts the black woman as having many of these functions. In Senghor's poem, the images are subtly suggestive of a variety of roles, but ultimately it is the portrait of the universal woman that stands out, invested with the many attributes of various manifestations. The origin of these mythical conceptions of African woman Senghor ascribes to the transformation of a *fait économico-social* in the essay 'Eléments constitutifs d'une civilisation d'inspiration négro-africaine' presented at the Second Congress of Black Artists and Writers:

> In Black Africa, woman holds, or rather used to hold, first place, since Arabo-Berber and European influence and the influence of nomadic civilisations have continually reduced her role. This role is explained by the agrarian character of the black world. The explanation is correct but it goes beyond that. As always, consciousness has translated socio-economic

fact into myth. Because the woman is 'permanent' in the family and life-giver (*donneuse de vie*) she has been elevated as source of the life-force (*source de force vitale*) and guardian of the home, that is, repository of the past and guarantor of the clan's future.[9]

The idealisation of the black woman in traditional Africa is seen by Senghor as a parallel to that by the Negro American poets of the 'New Negro' movement. The philosophy of these poets who precede and influence poets of Négritude is outlined in another essay, 'La poésie négro-africaine'. Senghor cites Claude Mackay, Countee Cullen, Langston Hughes and Gwendolyn Bennett among the contemporary poets (1950) who embrace this concept which he summarises as follows:

> These [poets] are convinced that they contribute, with the new values, a fresh sap which will make American Civilisation blossom once again. And they possess their own special cult consisting of respect and love, of desire and adoration for *Black Woman* as symbol of Négritude. This is because Woman is, more so than Man, sensitive to the mysterious currents of life and of the cosmos and more susceptible to joy and sorrow. . . . Woman is indeed symbol, as in Africa the aim is, beyond her plastic beauty (none of whose features escapes the poet) to express her spiritual wealth.[10]

Whatever spiritual wealth the woman of Senghor's poem has is expressed in images relating to the world of nature and thus to the life principle, since, in African ontology, the physical and spiritual unite in a common hierarchy. Consequently, the elemental imagery in the two middle verse paragraphs of **'Black Woman'** is full of suggestions of ripeness and maturity, desire and embrace amid drumming and spiritual song, and of cosmic forces at work:

> Naked woman, dark woman
> Firm-fleshed ripe fruit, sombre raptures of black
>   wine, mouth making lyrical my mouth
> Savannah stretching to clear horizons, savannah
>   shuddering beneath the East Wind's eager caresses
> Carved tom-tom, taut tom-tom, muttering under the
>   Conqueror's fingers
> Your solemn contralto voice is the spiritual song of
>   the Beloved.
>
> Naked woman, dark woman
> Oil that no breath ruffles, calm oil on the athlete's
>   flanks, on the flanks of the Princes of Mali
> Gazelle limbed in Paradise, pearls are stars on the
>   night of your skin
> Under the shadow of your hair, my care is lightened
>   by the neighbouring suns of your eyes.

At the beginning of *Orphée noir* (*Black Orpheus*) Sartre makes the following remark about Senghor's **'Black Woman'**:

> A black poet—unconcerned with us—whispers to
> the woman he loves:
>
> Naked woman, black woman
> Dressed in your color which is life . . .

Naked woman, dark woman,
Firm fleshed ripe fruit, somber ecstasies of black
    wine.

and our whiteness seems to us to be a strange livid
    varnish that keeps
our skin from breathing—white tights, worn out at
    the elbows and
knees, under which we would find real human flesh
    the color of black
wine if we could remove them.[11]

A recent critic, S. O. Mezu, in his penetrating study on Senghor entitled *Leopold Senghor et la defense et illustration de la civilisation noire* has remarked that the poem is 'too often quoted and as badly commented upon since the majority of critics see nothing in this poem but the "special cult consisting of respect and love, of desire and adoration for *Black Woman*" '.[12] Mezu adds that Sartre's interpretation goes beyond the meaning of the superficial lines of the poem in which elements of racism are present with or without the poet's awareness. He further points out that European writers like Dante, Petrarch and Spenser, since they did not think of race in their exaltation of White Woman are not guilty of racism, concluding with a statement about the failure of the poem as an inspired work of art that celebrates Black Woman as symbol of Négritude:

> The poem expresses a disincarnated emotion, an
> adoration without real love, a contemplation without
> the desire for possession, a simple eroticism. This dry
> desire for a generic woman indicates the lack of
> spontaneity and personal attachment. The writing is
> far from spontaneous let alone automatic. . . . This
> poem is neither very personal nor very inspired. It is
> a beautiful painting which is a trifle cold, marvellously
> vivid, but in which the disengaged artist has put little
> of himself.[13]

The problem with Mezu's critique is that it is not so much an independent analysis of the poem as an acceptance (with some reservations) of Sartre's claim of 'anti-racist racism' without allowing that the poem is inspired. It is his reluctance to credit a work that is racist-oriented with serious artistic quality that leads him to conclude that the poem is lacking in warmth and the product of a disengaged artist, while he concedes that it is a "beautiful painting' and 'marvellously vivid'. And since Senghor's claim that African art is *engagé* is well known, the assertion that he is disengaged from the poem is as much as to say that it is not an African poem in the best tradition. The fact remains, however, that on internal evidence this is one of the least racially inspired poems of *Chants d'Ombre* if the reader makes a willing suspension of belief based on such poems as **'Snow Upon Paris'** and **'Prayer to Masks'**, which have racist undertones, and considers **'Black Woman'** on its own merits. Then he would find the poem so richly connotative that the label of racist or disengaged or uninspired becomes hasty and narrow. Indeed, a careful reading of the poem reveals that the woman being sung is, beyond the immediate profile, an exquisitely sculptured

African statue carved in the 'verbal alchemy of African poems'.[14]

Apart from the parenthetic remark by Senghor in a passage already cited that in Africa Woman is a symbol whose plastic beauty is noticed in all its facets by the poet and the verbal echo in 'Carved tom-tom' within the poem itself, Senghor has a penchant for casting the black woman in many of his poems in the *immobilité mobile* of the African mask—a tendency that is particularly evident in *Chants pour Naëtt* (*Songs for Naëtt*). These songs were almost certainly inspired by an actual black woman and the following lines represent the most striking example:

> Your brows have taken that Eternal stance found on
>   the faces of statues
> But there flutters about your mask the bright wing
>   of the seamew.
> It is that haunting smile, like the leitmotiv of your
>   melodic face.

Further evidence that he identifies the living flesh of the black woman with the solid statue comes from a comparison of some of the images in the poem with a prose passage from the essay, 'L'esprit de la civilisation'. In it, Senghor, appraising a feminine statuette of the Baoulé, comments on the 'two themes of sweetness [which] sing alternately', namely, 'the ripe fruits of the breasts' as well as the fruits of the neck, knees, crest and calves; and the columns of black honey. Other particulars from a *Fang* statuette and a *Bambara* mask-antelope include fruits of breasts, navel and knees, curved cylinders of bust, legs and thighs, strophe of horns and ears and antistrophe of 'the hair of a mane arising from the imagination of the sculptor'.[15] The two alternating themes are reminiscent of the 'firm-fleshed ripe fruit' and 'sombre raptures of black wine' in **'Black Woman'** and they delineate the contours of the body that are adumbrated in the poem. For their part, the images of the mask-antelope associate with the 'Gazelle limbed in Paradise', thus sanctifying the woman in her role as totem-ancestor. The apparently fortuitous imagery of the poem is in fact carefully ordered to project an archetypal being whom Senghor decides to 'fix in the Eternal, / Before jealous Fate turn you to ashes to feed the roots of life'. As a poem rooted in the African poetic tradition, therefore, this comment by Senghor concerning the African aesthetic is applicable to it:

> It is first of all sensual, profoundly rooted in subjectivity;
> it however transcends 'the world of feelings' *(le cadre
> sensible),* to discover its sense and finality in the Beyond.[16]

A detailed study of **'Black Woman'** in terms of Senghor's African aesthetics is of value in approaching the kindred poem **'Negro Mask'**. In this poem, the identity of the figure as a mask is one of the *données* supplied in the very title. In contrast to the expectation of a frigid, immobile and lifeless piece of sculpture the poem introduces the black mask as a sleeping woman, individualised as Koumba Tam. The ambience is somewhat reminiscent of the peacefulness that informs the atmosphere of **'Night of Sine'** which is placed earlier in *Songs of Shadow:*

She sleeps peacefully in sombre purity.
Koumba Tam sleeps. A green palm veils the fever
 of the hair, coppers the curved forehead.
The closed eyelids, double cups and sealed sources.
This subtle crescent, this lip just a little blacker and
 thicker—from which comes the smile of the privy
 woman?
The patens of the cheeks and the design of the chin
 sing in silent accord.
Mask's face closed to the ephemeral, without eyes,
 without substance
Perfect bronze head and its patina of time
Untainted by varnish, blush, wrinkle trace of tears
 or kisses
O face as God created you even before the memory
 of ages
Face of the world's dawn, do not lay yourself open
 like a tender pass to move my flesh
I adore you, O Beauty, with my monochord eye!

Once again we have a carefully ordered setting, for Koumba Tam is none other than the goddess of beauty among the Serers, Senghor's own people. The tone of this poem is one of quiet adoration from which the sensuality of **'Black Woman'** is virtually excluded. The preoccupation rests, instead, in the etching of the lineaments of the face of the goddess which achieve a perfect symmetry: 'the patens of the cheeks, the design of the chin sing in silent accord'.

Since the poem is dedicated to Picasso who early recognised and was influenced by black art forms, the first half of the poem emphasises the lines, curves and accents of the face of the sleeping goddess, Koumba Tam, whose features are the ultimate in perfection and grace. The transition comes when both the sleeping goddess and the human form she takes crystallise into the bronze head of the mask in the form and style of God's original model created 'even before the memory of ages'. Because the mask is made of bronze that ages it is not without its 'patina of time', but it is not subject to human caresses and emotions; nevertheless the original vision of the sleeping human form has been so appealing that at the end Senghor implores the mask-goddess not to come alive and move his flesh to a purely lustful contemplation.

In his *Léopold Sédar Senghor, l'Homme et l'Oeuvre* Armant Guibert perceptively comments on the poem's architecture as it combines the social and the sacred in a 'double current'. 'Since this poem of youth', he writes,

> Senghor revealed the double current which animates the African genius: on the one hand the influence of the flesh perceptible in the play of colours and forms, and, on the other, the cult of the sacred whose images are only a lining and a semblance. Starting with a sensual evocation which still throbs with a residue of life ('the fever of the hair', 'the curved forehead'), he then suggests the silence ('silent accord') and the intemporal character of the form he contemplates ('closed to the ephemeral . . . without eyes, without substance').[17]

We have already seen the 'double current' at work in **'Black Woman'**, where sensual images predominate. In **'Negro Mask'** the emphasis is on the religious, as the poet pays humble tribute to the goddess who, reflecting the image of the original model, is 'Face of the world's dawn', and therefore already fixed in the eternal. Much of the imagery adorns the mask-goddess with an aura of divinity or with a sense of permanence as well as peace. 'Double cups' and 'the patens of the cheeks', for example, in their association with the chalice and the silver platter recall the celebration of the Eucharist, a ritualistic and symbolic re-enactment of the act of sacrifice. And sacrifice is a fundamentally integral part of African religious worship.

The paradoxes and contradistinctions of **'Negro Mask'** stem from the symbiosis of three entities—woman, ancestral mask and deity—so that the figure is both human and divine, dead and alive, form and essence, bronze mask and human flesh. Woman as symbol of life-giving forces and the statue as symbol of the ancestors are here combined with a third principle, the goddess, constituting three closely associated entities in the African sensibility.

As a rule, Senghor's most successful poems thrive on correspondences and contradictions, on ambiguity and paradox.

—*Jonathan Peters*

According to the ontology of animism, the whole universe is composed of vital forces forming a hierarchy in which God, the Supreme Force, is at the apex and the grain of sand or the pebble at the base. Man is the centre of this physical and spiritual universe which he bridges through the help of his ancestors who have been translated into another plane of existence. In an early essay, 'Ce que l'homme noir apporte', Senghor points to the fact that African man invests the whole cosmos with a 'human presence' which includes the tree and the pebble as well as natural phenomena and the animal world.[18]

This phenomenon explains the mutual dependence of descendant and ancestor. The ancestors occupying a higher sphere in the hierarchy may become deified as a result of a fusion—or confusion—of myth and legend. They are intercessors on behalf of the living who keep them from becoming 'perfectly dead' by proffering them libations and other forms of earthly nourishment. The gods, to the extent that they are distinguished from the ancestors, are found still higher up in the hierarchy and it is to them that sacrifice is made and not directly to God who is the source of the life-force. The gods or spirits are themselves subordinate to male Sky or Sun and female Earth whose union, symbolised in the rain and sun fertilising the earth, gave birth to the spirit-gods who are, after all, natural phenomena, animals and plants.[19]

The sculptured masks and statues are representations of the dead ancestors who are not dead, and of the spirit-gods. They are 'at the same time symbol and dwelling. They capture and make the personal felt as effective will and give rise to the *surreal.*'[20] When the wearer of the mask performs the dance of the deity whom the mask represents he takes on the power of the god, becomes the living presence of the god, thus emphasising the importance of rhythm and dance in the psychology of the African. 'Negro Mask' is thus richly connotative of the African *Weltanschauung,* of an African *Da-sein* or *Negersein,* to use Senghor's own phrase.[21]

In 'Prayer to Masks' Senghor, as poet of Négritude, shows his concern for the white world. The title suggests that the poem is a prayer made to the gods and spirits who watch over his race. It is more than just a prayer, however, for it contains a basic statement of Senghor's poetic credo.

An obvious distinction of 'Prayer to Masks' is that unlike 'Black Woman' and 'Negro Mask' not one but several masks are involved and their summons from the four cardinal points stresses the importance of the occasion:

> Black mask, red mask, you black-and-white masks
> Masks of the four points from which the Spirit
>   breathes
> I greet you in silence!

Senghor scrupulously follows the alphabetic order in his salutation to the masks—'masque *n*oir, masque *r*ouge, vous masques *b*lanc-et-noir'—as he paints them in black, red and white, the colours of traditional Africa. His greeting is a silent one of reverence in a place whose very air smacks of eternity in its isolation from all contact with the profane.

Although the primary intent of the invocation is a plea to the masks, something of their character is revealed in the last lines of the preliminary address which takes up half the poem:

> You distill this air of eternity in which I breathe the
>   air of my Fathers.
> Masks with faces without mask, free from all
>   dimples and wrinkles
> You who have composed this portrait, this face of
>   mine bent over the altar of white paper
> In your own image, hear me!

In these lines is something of the paradox inherent in the African mystique, at least from a Western standpoint. In African social art the mask is a symbolic representation of the human face, which is, in Senghor's words, 'the most faithful reflection of the soul'.[22] Far from hiding or disguising the identity beyond it, the African mask reveals in its form and texture the character of the deity it represents. The sacred masks in this poem are therefore 'without mask' because they illumine the presence of the very founders of the race. There is on the one hand an image-analogy between the face of the suppliant and the sacred mask-Fathers that have modelled his face and on the other a contrast between his own face and the 'altar of white

paper', which is consecrated because it is used to record the prayer to the masks.

Following the appeal for the masks' kindly audience Senghor proceeds to the prayer proper. The subsequent six lines of the poem feature Black Africa and White Europe as objective correlatives:

> See the Africa of empires dying—it is the agony of
>   a pitiful princess
> And Europe too to whom we are linked by the
>   navel.
> Fix your immobile eyes on your children who
>   receive orders
> Who give away their lives like the poor man his
>   last garment.
> Let us answer 'Present!' at the rebirth of the world
> As the leaven that the white flour needs.

The futures of the two continents are inextricably linked because they have the same life-line. Thus the death of Africa, the proud and pitiful princess also spells doom for Europe. The African empires which held sway up to the nineteenth century have been disintegrating under European influence and the Second World War threatens the life of Europe torn by an inward struggle, a struggle in which the black man has been called upon to sacrifice his life for peace. But after this physical death, a new world will be born in which Africa will again have a key function, 'As the leaven that the white flour needs'.

This last phrase suggests that the black man will be charged with the task of infusing a spiritual essence into a world that is for all practical purposes white—and sterile. There follows an elaboration of the black man's role in a question and answer situation followed by an affirmation of that role:

> For who will teach rhythm to the word laid low by
>   machines and cannons
> Who will shout with joy to wake up the dead and
>   the orphans at the
>   dawn?
> Say, who will give back the memory of life to the
>   man with eviscerated hopes?
> They call us cotton men, coffee men oily men
> They call us men of death.
> We are the men of the dance, whose feet regain
>   force by drumming on the hard earth.

The implication here is that only the black man who has maintained a constant connection with the world of nature and the world of spirits can fulfil this vital task, for the white man, in his preoccupation with a machine civilisation, has brought the world to ruin by this very machine. The Negro, who has up till the present been the downtrodden of the earth will then become the hero and the apostle of the dawn of tomorrow's world, making it rise, phoenix-like, from its own ashes.

The assertion of the black man's contribution is made with full awareness of his current existential position. He has many stereotypes, all of them revealing a bias against his colour, above all, through which is forced on him a myth of inferiority. Ironically Senghor reverts to a European myth, that of the Greek Antaeus, to make his final postulate of the black man's identity as well as his role: 'We are the men of the dance, whose feet regain force by pounding on the hard earth.'

Senghor views rhythm as the corner-stone of the Negro mystique, as the essential quality that distinguishes the Negro-African culture from that of other races. The import of this is not that the Negro has a monopoly of rhythm, but that his dependence on rhythm is unique. This dependence is particularly evident when it is compared with European art which, Senghor suggests, lapsed into decadence towards the end of the nineteenth century on account of the strictures imposed by narrow and conventional rules; the Negro's contribution in the twentieth century has been to provide the young sap needed to nourish the ailing organs of European sensibility. But rhythm for Senghor not only represents forces in art but also and more significantly forces in life, since African art is a symbol of more profound realities beyond the perceived object. Not surprisingly, therefore, in one of many definitions Senghor avers that rhythm is 'flux and reflux, night and day, inspiration and expiration, death and birth. Rhythm is spirituality expressed by the most material means: volume, surfaces and lines in sculpture and architecture, stresses in poetry and music, movements in the dance.'[23]

The messianic note of much Négritude poetry is present in the questions that are posed in **'Prayer to Masks'**. The apocalyptic day of destruction caused by the machines of white culture is to be followed by a day of resurrection achieved through the rhythmic flow of sap from the black aesthetic. Inasmuch as rhythm is the correlative principle of death and life and similar dualities, only beings endowed with it can infuse the vital sap into the asphyxiated nerve centre of occidental civilisation. According to Senghor, the Negro reigns supreme in the domain of rhythm; consequently, it will be his duty to teach the resuscitated world the rhythm of life and to announce the Good News in the impending dawn—an honour he has by virtue of his retention of the vital link with the cosmic forces ruling the universe as he dances the dance of the world.

What Senghor seems to have done in **'Prayer to Masks'** is to accept part of the Negro stereotype which he then modifies at the same time as he tacitly rejects the other half. The physical characteristics of the Negro ('cotton men coffee men oily men') which also refer to his humble or peasant status have been sublimated in **'Black Woman'** and **'Negro Mask'**. What cannot be accepted here is that the Negro is black, the colour of death, for in Senghor's ontology the colour, black, during this phase, symbolises life. In any event death and life are twin aspects of the same reality. In particular, in Africa 'there is no irreducible opposition between life and death'.[24] As 'men of the dance' therefore the black race engages in a dance celebrating the renewing cycle of life and death.

The tone and attitude of **'Totem'** differ from those at work in the other mask-poems. From the sensuality of **'Black Woman'**, the worship of **'Negro Mask'** and the homily of **'Prayer to Masks'** all of which have a serious outlook Senghor's mood alters in **'Totem'** as he speaks in a detached, ironic vein. Hitherto he has captured imaginatively the presence of the masks which disclose a reality that goes beyond the surface to the essence. Here he must hide this very presence because of his self-conscious attempt to ward off charges of barbarism by the 'civilised' races:

> I must hide in the intimate depths of my veins
> The Ancestor, storm-dark skinned, shot with
>   lightning and thunder
> And my guardian animal, I must hide him
> Lest I smash through the boom of scandal.
> He is my faithful blood and demands fidelity
> Protecting my naked pride against
> Myself and all the insolence of lucky races.

In the first two mask-poems of *Songs of Shadow* Senghor crystallises the living human flesh into the statue, the mask and the mask-antelope or totem. In them he celebrates the marriage of African archetypes, creating a composite view of African thought. **'Prayer to Masks'** shows him emerging as the doyen of Négritude; it is not the much altered Négritude of later years which Senghor was to define as 'the sum total of the values of the black world' but in fact 'a weapon of defence and attack and inspiration rather than an instrument of construction'.[25] The function of the totem-ancestor in African thought is well illustrated in the opening pages of Laye Camara's *L'Enfant noir* (*The Dark Child*). Senghor's **'Totem'** deploys a stance of dissimulation in order to avoid scandalous gossip by uncomprehending Europeans. It is this reaction of shame that leads (in part at least) to an opposing assertion of pride in their race and its values by Césaire, Senghor, Damas and others when their self-awareness is stirred. With the exception of this mock concealment of totem and ancestor in this poem Senghor continually lays claim to the presence of the royal blood of the ancestors in his veins and throughout his poetry emphasises their influence in his changing roles of spokesman, ambassador, politician and leader. As defender of the peasant black people of royal ancestry he dwells on their nobility and courage, their purity and innocence, their wisdom and pride, thus sounding the keynote of Négritude in its unreserved glorification of the African past. In conformity with his role as peasant, however, he displays, from time to time, his barbarous accent, his pagan desires and his bewilderment in Paris where he is among people of 'lucky races'.

The paradoxes of royal peasant and naive wisdom arise out of an acceptance-rejection syndrome of Negro stereotypes which is again typical of the school of Négritude. Thus Aimé Césaire in his *Cahier* accepts, among other things, the Negro's uninventiveness in an oft-quoted passage, for although this means that he cannot lay claim to the architectural splendour of Europe, for example, he can no more be held responsible for the lethal weapons of war. Another Négritude poet, Leon Damas demands

Give me back my black dolls
That I may play with them
The naive games of my instinct

    . . . . .

I am again myself
a new self
from what I was Yesterday
yesterday
      without complexity
            yesterday[.][26]

Senghor, after an intense and sustained personal conflict returns in *Nocturnes* to the Kingdom of Childhood which he has in a sense never really left, singing his own lullaby:

I shall sleep at dawn, my pink doll in my arms
My doll with green eyes and golden, and so
    wonderful a tongue
Being the tongue of the poem.

The very year, 1945, that Senghor published *Chants d'Ombre* was the year that he entered fully into politics. Although the themes in his poetry remain more or less the same, there is a trend towards a more accommodating stance with reference to Europe and France, especially in his poetry which comes increasingly under the influence of his politics. Consequently, the ambivalence towards France which in effect begins in '**For Koras and Balafong**' of *Chants d'Ombre* is carried through '**The Prayer for Peace**' of *Hosties noires,* the epistles of *Ethiopiques* and the elegies of *Nocturnes.* All the same, in judging his poetry we should keep his politics as far as possible at a distance so as to produce valid appraisals of his work. And when we look for masters and influences in the poetic tradition, in addition to searches for imitations of a Gobineau, a Claudel or a St Jean Perse and traces of surrealism, racism or Négritude, we should not neglect to look to see if there are any on the black side of the self-admitted *métis culturel.*

Notes

[1] The most comprehensive account of these influences is chapter 10 of S. O. Mezu's excellent critique on Senghor entitled *Léopold Sédar Senghor et la défense et illustration de la civilisation noire* (Paris, Didier, 1968).

[2] Senghor often indicated instrumental accompaniment for the reading of his poems, e.g., 'For Koras and Balafong'.

[3] This claim is made in Senghor's 'De la négritude', *Diogène,* No. 37, 1962, p. 22.

[4] Senghor, *Poèmes* (abbreviated PO in this text), (Paris, Editions du Seuil, 1964). Citations are from the English translation by Reed and Wake in *Prose and Poetry* (London, O.U.P.), referred to as PP in this article, except for 'Prayer to Masks' and 'Black Mask' which are the present writer's own rendition.

[5] Cp. C. S. Lewis, *The Four Loves* (London, Fontana Books, 1963), p. 96.

[6] From the translation by Norman Shapiro in *Négritude: Black Poetry from Africa and the Caribbean* (New York, October House, 1970), p. 65.

[7] *Chants pour Naëtt* was included in the last volume of Senghor's poetry, *Nocturnes,* published in 1961. Quotations are from *Nocturnes* translated by Reed and Wake (London, Heinemann, 1969), pp. 34-5.

[8] *Liberté I: Négritude et Humanisme* (Paris, Editions du Seuil, 1964), p. 210. The article is slightly modified and retitled 'l'esthétique négro-africaine'.

[9] ibid., p. 269.

[10] ibid., p. 117.

[11] Quoted from *Black American Writer, Volume 2: Poetry and Drama,* edited by C. W. E. Bigsby (London, Penguin, 1969).

[12] op. cit., p. 72.

[13] ibid., pp. 73-4.

[14] Senghor, op. cit., p. 167.

[15] ibid., p. 214. For discussions of the importance of masks and statues in African society, see *inter alia* B. Holas, 'L'Imagerie rituelle on Afrique noire' and L. Marfurt, 'Les Masques africains', both in *African Arts/Arts d'Afrique,* Spring 1968, pp. 48-53 and 54-61; H. Himmelheber, 'Sculptors and Sculptures of the Dan' in *Proceedings of the First International Congress of Africanists* (Northwestern University Press, 1964), pp. 243-55 and G. Moore's 'The Theme of the Ancestors in Senghor's Poetry', *Black Orpheus,* May 1959, pp. 15-17.

[16] Senghor, op. cit., p. 164.

[17] In *Léopold Sédar Senghor: l'Homme et l'Oeuvre* (Présence Africaine, 1962).

[18] Senghor, op. cit., pp. 24-5.

[19] ibid., p. 267.

[20] ibid., p. 34.

[21] *De la négritude,* loc. cit., p. 23.

[22] *Liberté I,* p. 34.

[23] ibid., 211.

[24] ibid., p. 114.

[25] Quoted from *Prose and Poetry,* ed. Reed and Wake, p. 97.

[26] Leon Damas, *Pigments.* Quoted from Senghor's *Anthologie de la nouvelle poésie nègre et malgache, Présence Africaine,* 1948, p. 8 (my translation). There is a double meaning to 'black dolls' suggesting a preference for black women as well as a return to childhood.

John Reed (essay date 1975)

SOURCE: "Léopold Sédar Senghor's Poetry," in *A Celebration of Black and African Writing,* edited by Bruce

King and Kolawole Ogungbesan, Oxford University Press, 1975, pp. 102-11.

[In the following essay, Reed offers a positive assessment of Lettres d'Hivernage *and suggests a literary context for Senghor's poetry.]*

Towards the end of a long essay which is still the best introduction to Senghor's poetry, Armand Guibert reflects that Senghor, who had recently become the President of his country, was perhaps already at the end of his career as a poet.

> As this problem of the coexistence of political leader with poet has been posed it is worth noting that circumstances have already slowed down the career of the poetry which has been the subject of this essay. In the last five years, only five elegies have been added. Will the demands of public life in the end have the better of the inward man? Strictly every poet carries the rank of prince, whether he is a cut-purse like Villon or a ploughman like Burns. But if the Prince also holds real temporal power, he will envy cut-purse and ploughman the obscurity that guarantees their freedom.[1]

Guibert was writing in 1961. Senghor's last new volume of poetry was *Ethiopiques*, published in 1956. The recent *Nocturnes* (1961) was really a revised version of *Chants pour Naëtt* (1949) with the addition of the five elegies. In the years that followed, the slowing down became very nearly a standstill. There was one more elegy published in *Présence Africaine.* Then nothing. The Editions du Seuil hard-back collected *Poèmes* of 1961 included a small additional section, *Poèmes Divers,* but these are evidently juvenilia or at least poems earlier than *Chants d'Ombre.* Thus it had all the appearance of finality.

As the years passed, the incompatibility of poetry and political power seemed demonstrated. Then the tide of intellectual opinion in Africa began to turn against the cultural theory of Négritude which Senghor had assiduously elaborated in speeches and essays. Through the sixties as the political spectrum formed by the new states in Africa grew clear, Senghor appeared rather to the right. His interest and influence hardly seemed to reach English-speaking Africa, and the poet of *Chaka* had little to say about the south. At the Second International Conference of Africanists in Dakar in the late 60s he spoke of the political problems of Africa as having been solved, leaving only social and cultural problems to be tackled. Later in 1972 he was advocating dialogue with South Africa, long before this became politically respectable. Senghor's poetry was, in some parts of Africa at least, as suspect as his politics: but not therefore neglected, for the meteoric rise of African literature as an academic subject and the expansion of French studies in English-speaking Africa were bound to make much of an *oeuvre* which had the advantages of being substantial and evidently complete.

Then in 1973 appeared, simultaneously under the imprint of Seuil in Paris and Nouvelles Editions Africaines in Dakar, Senghor's first volume of new poems since *Ethiopiques,* seventeen years before. The title, *Lettres d'Hivernage* (Letters of the Rainy Season).[2] It has now been incorporated into, and is most easily accessible in a second, paper-back edition of the complete *Poèmes.* Asked in an interview the same year how he was able to reconcile his two roles, Senghor replied:

> One complements the other. I've always liked to have several projects on the go at once, and everything interpenetrating. It's a matter of organizing one's time practically.

> I work on poems during my holidays—that's about six weeks a year—especially in the summer when I take off a whole month. During the rest of the year I draft out poems, make notes, write *versets*—and, more important, I live my poems. At the moment I'm living an *Elegy for the Queen of Sheba.* Then when I have a bit of time to myself, I get down to it. Living my poems, that means imagining them. Then the poem inside me grows richer and richer in images. It feeds on my ideas and feelings.[3]

The practical man of affairs can make arrangements to accommodate the composer of *versets.* But has the poet survived the long reign of the secular prince? I think on the evidence of *Lettres d'Hivernage* that he has. The years have not transformed Senghor's poetry. There is no radical difference in technique, in subject matter or mood. But these new poems are not vapid self-imitations—even if they seem full of specific reference to the earlier poems, as though for Senghor himself these now have a kind of classical status. These poems add to and enrich although they do not transform or compel a complete reassessment of Senghor's poetic achievement.

Lettres d'Hivernage is a sequence of thirty poems. In length, and in the relation of the separate poems to the sequence, it resembles the *Chants pour Naëtt*, poems which Senghor wrote to his first wife. But in theme and also in imagery, especially in the contrasted images of Africa and Northern—or at least non-Mediterranean—Europe, they are much closer to the set of six poems in *Ethiopiques* entitled *Epîtres à la Princesse.* In these poems the poet addresses a European princess from whom he is separated by his responsibilities in Africa. These *Epîtres* have usually been interpreted as a celebration in poetry of Senghor's love for the woman who was to become his second wife. Yet the circumstances are not directly presented. Senghor gives himself the persona of a traditional, tribal, almost patriarchal ruler, owing more probably to Saint-John Perse's *Anabase,* than to his own earliest memories of Africa and a far cry from the incisive leader of a mass party which at the time he was; and his lady is some snow princess from a Nordic fairy-tale. The sequence ends with a poem entitled **"The Death of the Princess."** These longer, mythologically elaborate *Epîtres* or epistles have become simple letters, much concerned in content with waiting for, receiving, and sending letters. They are thus tender poems of an aging man to his wife, written during periods of separation. The background, though other resounding landscapes also occur, is often simply Dakar itself with its view of the Ile de Gorée lying just off shore and the poet seems to see his scenery not from camelback as once but through the windows of descending aircraft or helicopters.

An example of one of the briefest of these poems will give the quality.

Ta Lettre sur le Drap

Ta lettre sur le drap, sous la lampe odorante
Bleue comme la chemise neuve que lisse le jeune
    homme
En chantonnant, comme le ciel et la mer et mon
    rêve
Ta lettre. Et la mer a son sel, et l'air le lait le pain
    le riz, je dis son sel
La vie contient sa sève, et la terre son sens
Le sens de Dieu et son mouvement.
Ta lettre sans quoi la vie ne serait pas vie
Tes lèvres mon sel mon soleil, mon air frais et ma
    neige.
(Your letter on the sheet, beneath the sweet-
    smelling lamp,
Blue as a new shirt a young man smooths,
Humming to himself; as the sky and the sea and my
    dream
Your letter. And the sea has its salt, and the air
    milk, bread, rice, I say its salt
Life holds its sap and earth its meaning
The meaning of God and his movement.
Your letter life would not be life without
Your lips my salt my sun, my fresh air and my snow.)

There is much in the *Lettres d'Hivernage* that is pitched more eloquently and elaborately than this, and passages which could be taken as coming from the earlier volumes. Yet the comparative simplification of manner found in *"Ta Lettre sur le Drap"* is characteristic of *Lettres d'Hivernage* as a whole. The difference does not amount to a change of poetic manner. Senghor is writing in a less dense and overgrown area of his familiar wood, but he has certainly not gone seeking fresh woods. From the immediate experience in sensation—in this poem not an emotion but something seen, a still life, the blue notepaper lying on the white sheet under the lamp—the poet moves with a directness that might seem self-assured or merely facile, to the stark lists of nouns which are like a basic inventory of the cosmos. The poet, to affirm his love, affirms succinctly because urgently the whole human and natural universe in which he lives and breathes and is. Some of the words he uses—for example, sun and snow—have a special, as well as the more general, significance from the theme of the whole poetic sequence. But still, the elements are named, invoked, or as it were implicated (as when a person is named in a legal enquiry), not merely referred to. Here the process is so abrupt that it is unmistakable but it is the same process—the transition from the immediate and personal to the cosmic by way of a naming and implication, which on a larger scale and to the accompaniment of a more decorative rhetoric is found throughout Senghor's work.

It is not difficult to relate this structure in Senghor's poetry to the French poetry of his time. French critics see Senghor's poetry as deeply influenced by Paul Claudel whose most important single poetic collection, the *Cinq Grandes Odes* appeared in 1910. Senghor has never denied this debt. Signs of his familiarity not only with Claudel's poetry but his thought about the nature of poetry are evident everywhere in Senghor's work. The other major influence is Saint-John Perse. Here Senghor insists that he had read no work of this poet until 1945 when all the poems that were to appear in *Chants d'Ombre* and *Hosties Noires* were already written, but that on his reading of Saint-John Perse's poem *"Exil"* in that year, he was 'struck blind like Paul on the road to Damascus'.[4]

Senghor himself stresses the variety of his sources. 'I have read a great deal from the troubadors to Paul Claudel—and imitated a great deal.'[5] Senghor reads English and knew the work of the black American poets of the 1920s and 30s. In 1948 he edited the important *Anthologie de la nouvelle poésie nègre et malgache.* This anthology of work by black poets writing in French was mainly Caribbean. Most of Senghor's critical writing is an attempt to characterize this black poetry rather than to examine the nature of his own poetic inspiration. There are throughout Senghor's poems allusions to and imitations of other black poets. In one of the poems in *Lettres d'Hivernage* there is the following scrap of dialogue:

  —Fais que toujours tu me sois joie, mon Prince
        mon Athlète et mon ébène.
  —Point n'ai pris habitude des promesses; je sais
        oui mon amour de toi

  —(See that forever you may be joy to me, my
        Prince, my Athlete, my Ebony.
  —Never have I caught the habit of promises: I
        know Yes my love of thee.)[6]

This catches the flavour of the *Vieilles Chansons* of the Madagascan poet Rabéarivelo, themselves adaptations into French of the Madagascan folk poetry of the Hain-teny. Senghor had already made a similar imitation in his **"Elégie des Saudades"** in *Nocturnes.*

Yet these are hommages to other poets. They do not affect the texture of Senghor's own poetry. It is natural to be led, in the critical examination of Senghor's poetry, by what he says in his own criticism about the nature of 'black poetry'. Yet Senghor's thought about his poetry, as distinct from his practice as a poet, has found its literary associations not in the tradition of Claudel, but, in what in the 1920s and 30s when Senghor lived in Paris was the most *avant garde* and revolutionary movement of poetry, with surrealism. In Senghor's exposition of black poetry it is Aimé Césaire's and not Senghor's own poetry which is the central model. Even when he is writing about traditional poetry in African languages Senghor seems to interpret its qualities through the critical vocabulary of surrealism: These qualities which he finds in traditional African poetry and in the new black poets (who, he asserts, have only been enabled to express Négritude in the French language because of the surrealist revolution[7]), the violent image, the disintegration of the phrase, the destruction of syntax, elimination of tool-words or connectives, are none of them characteristic of Senghor's own verse. Here and there in Senghor there may occur a passage of pastiche surrealism but Senghor's violence to language characteristically goes no further than

> sous les cris blancs des mouettes
> (beneath the white cries of the gulls).[8]

And in Senghor the omission of tool-words amounts to no more than a fondness for omitting *and* between nouns. Sometimes there are syntactical ambiguities in Senghor, as in all poetry and indeed all speech. In *"Ta Lettre sur le Drap"* the fourth line might seem to be devoid of all syntax, permitting us to arrange the words together, to allow them to interact with each other as we wish. But a closer look reveals that there is nothing more extreme here than the omission of commas between the items of a list and having the verb *have* understood and not repeated in the second clause. This is as natural in French as it would be in English.

Significantly it is in an article on Saint-John Perse that Senghor seems to clarify the distinctness of his own kind of poetry from that of surrealism. The article appeared in *La Table Ronde* in 1962—after the publication of Senghor's main volumes. In this article he notes that Saint-John Perse's poetry is a tissue of images or symbols. Symbols, uttered by speech, are an elucidation, an order. Through them, the poet, who is 'Ordinateur et Ordonnateur'—one who both sets in order and ordains—maintains or restores the order of the world, the ordered world without which man cannot have full existence, since he is, as Teilhard de Chardin says, 'a cosmic being'. But if it can create order, the symbol can also by perversion of its true function sow confusion. The contrast between the images of Saint-John Perse and the surrealists is made:

> The images of Saint-John Perse are as new as those of the surrealists. They are more beautiful. Why? Because they are clothed in the grace of language. Because they are more taking, gripping you at the very root of *being*. Because they are not gratuitous. They share in the truth of the *archetypal images* laid down in the depths of Man's Collective Soul.[9]

The surrealists were without the grace of language because language was one of the objects of their destructive rage, a social institution to be swept away with the rest of an oppressive social order for the total liberation of the individual. The link between surrealism and black poetry is a common interest in revolution—but a revolution which swept away civilization and technology would be as self-contradictory as a poetry which succeeded in destroying language. Those who do not find with Teilhard de Chardin that man is a cosmic being but for whom 'this is not our place', will not in any case be blessed by 'the grace of language'.

In the same article Senghor identifies poets like Saint-John Perse with the Priests and Magicians of African and traditional civilizations, and the world of his poetry with the articulated symbolic worlds of Africa. This seems to me a mistake, the mistake of using the myth of the poem as the guide to the critical understanding of its true nature. The urge to create a poetry in which the poet himself appears centrally as the Mage, Demiurge or Logos of the poetically summoned cosmos can only arise when the poet has in the social reality of his day no magic powers and there are no more Priest-Kings or Mages whose powers of ordering and maintaining the universe are accepted. The need to make the evocation of the world and the acceptance of it central to poetry only arises when the sense of cosmos has been lost and when rejection instead of acceptance is conceivable.

During the nineteenth century it became possible—and so necessary—for poetry to move beyond the expression of personal experience and personal vision through a shared literary tradition which reflected and ultimately implied a whole, diverse, developing but still shared civilization. Poetry itself would have to assert its own cultural cosmos—the alternatives were to keep traditional poetry going as a kind of folklore, or to be resigned to côterie verse and hermeticism. Of course this cosmos was not a clean creation of the poet's. Just as socially shared cultures depend on the inescapable realities of the natural world and shape the raw material of human psychology, so the poet has to draw and select and shape from the conflicting and incoherent diversity around him. Hence the main poets of this tradition are men like Senghor whose life has been shaped by diversity of cultural experience. Claudel's *Cinq Grandes Odes* were written mostly in China where he had a diplomatic posting. Saint-John Perse was born and spent his earliest years in Guadeloupe. His mature poetry was written in exile in the United States where he was driven after the fall of France in 1940. The cosmos of the poem depends on the assertion of the poet. He is at its centre and he has to create for himself a persona of a kind that does not appear in earlier poetry. The cosmos of the poem is also the world of the poet's own experience, is indeed the medium through which his own experience can find coherence, meaning and hence expression. Thus he cannot abandon his real self in the poem and adopt a purely formal or mythic role. At the same time he has to assume inside the cosmos of the poem the central, princely, demiurgic role.

The kind of poetry we have been describing was first created by Walt Whitman, working in the cultural diversity and unrooted quality of American life, and with only a trivial poetic tradition to break free of. The strange quality of the 'I' figure in Whitman's poetry, firmly identified by name and experience with the real man, yet also functioning in the poems as a kind of Son of Man, has engaged much attention from the critics. The poems, out of widely varied sources in Whitman's reading and experience, by listing, naming, evocation, assert a universe. The poetry created great interest in Europe, especially in France where the American experience was more likely to be understood than in England with its traditional continuities unbroken by recent revolutionary change. Whitman's breakthrough made a new, more powerful poetry available but only where individual genius and a certain set of conditions occurred. What is common to all is that the poet asserts his own universe. We should not expect the universes to look alike. Whitman's is democratic, libertarian, ordered by opportunity not hierarchy; both Claudel's and Saint-John Perse's are aristocratic and exclusive. Senghor's cosmos shows great similarities to the two French poets who are not only direct influences but created their poetic worlds out of material that overlaps directly with his own. Senghor observes that Saint-John Perse like Senghor himself spent his childhood in the black world. Yet in some ways Senghor comes closer to Whitman's inclusiveness than either of his French predecessors. I think we should see his poetry as much in its place within this modern supranational tradition belonging to the times of the melting pot, of interacting and conflicting cultures, as belonging to French poetry or to African poetry.

Senghor's poetry asserts a universe on the poet's authority, a universe which is an ordering and an ordination of African, Mediterranean, Gallic, Catholic, Islamic elements. At the centre of these is the 'I' of Senghor himself, a figure both mythic and actual. Senghor has never confused the princely role he plays in his own poetry with his own political position and nor should his readers. Yet his own personal experience is central to the cosmos of his poems. The two guiding experiences of Senghor's poetry are imprisonment—the poems in **"Camp 1940"** and in a sense the whole of the collection *Hosties Noires* of which this forms a part—and love. In the *Lettres d'Hivernage* we can see how personal poetry of a direct kind can rest within the cosmos of the poet's creation and yet through each new occasional poem succeed in articulating it further and in maintaining the rhythm of its connections and correspondences.

Auden said that time would pardon Paul Claudel and his views—'for writing well'. It would certainly be sad if we rejected all the poetry which did not reflect our own views. It would after all cut us off from almost all the poetry of earlier generations. But the point I think is not to go to this kind of poetry looking for views to overlook. Certainly there are in Senghor's work poems which are direct reactions on a public level to political events, poems of protest. **"Tyaroye"** in *Hosties Noires* is one of these, though no one I think is likely to raise objections to the views it expresses. But my suggestion is that poetry like Whitman's, Claudel's, Senghor's does not, except incidentally, express views. It asserts not opinions or doctrines but a cosmos. Among the elements of that cosmos there may be doctrines and opinions. With the advent of Whitman the poet surrenders the role of teacher—or becomes as Whitman says, the teacher of 'no lesson'. We can only teach within the settled conventions of a stable and accepted culture.

I have tried to suggest a description of the kind of poetry to which I think Senghor's belongs. I have no theory of the way this poetry works on the reader, of the nature of the delight that comes from reading Whitman or Claudel or Senghor except that taking them together, the soothing of our political opinions cannot be any part of it. Some lines from Whitman do not provide that missing theory but may perhaps illustrate the delight.

The words of the true poems give you more than poems,
They give you to form for yourself poems, religions, politics, war, peace, behavior, histories, essays, daily life and everything else,

They balance ranks, colors, races, creeds, and the sexes

     . . . . .

Whom they take they take into space to behold the birth of stars, to learn one of the meanings,

To launch off with absolute faith, to sweep through the ceaseless rings and never be quiet again.[10]

Notes

[1] Armand Guibert. *Léopold Sédar Senghor* (Poètes d'aujourd'hui, Paris: Pierre Seghers, 1961), p. 96.

[2] *Lettres d'Hivernage* (illustrations originales de Marc Chagall, Paris: Seuil, 1973 and Dakar: Nouvelles Editions Africaines, 1973).

[3] Interview with René Minguet, published in *Les Nouvelles Littéraires,* 17-23 December 1973.

[4] *Comme les lamantins vont boire à la source,* Postface to *Ethiopiques* (Paris: Seuil, 1956), p. 106.

[5] *Ibid,* p. 106.

[6] *Ta Lettre Trémulation.*

[7] 'L'Apport de la Poésie Nègre au Demi-Siècle', in *Liberté* 1: *Négritude et Humanisme* (Paris: Seuil, 1964), p. 143.

[8] *Je Repasse, Lettres d'Hivernage.*

[9] 'Saint-John Perse ou Poésie du Royaume d' Enfance', in *Liberté* 1: *Négritude et Humanisme,* p. 343.

[10] From 'Song of the Answerer' in *Calamus.*

Vladimir Klima (essay date 1976)

SOURCE: "Politics and Poetry—The Subjects of Senghor," in *African Culture and Integration,* Oriental Institute in Academia, 1976, pp. 46-81.

[In the following excerpt, Klima examines how Senghor's poetry is informed by his politics and the political situation in West Africa.]

Léopold Sédar Senghor's activities have been examined from various points of view. For the last thirty years he has kept his reputation of one of the major poets in Black Africa. As a leading representative of Négritude, whose evaluation has not yet been completed he has affected the political and ideological life of West Africa. Outside Africa, he has been widely recognized as a champion of African cultural values. His Négritude has become a kind of official doctrine in Senegalese culture. Dakar, the capital of the country, was often a meeting place of black artists; the World Festival of Negro Art and Culture was organized there in 1966.

Senghor has studied contemporary ideological trends and his variant of African Socialism has represented chiefly his reaction to Marxism. Those who are interested in modern ideologies of Africa should pay attention to his criticism of Marx's opinions, which reflects in a symptomatic manner the obvious retardment of class differentiation south of the Sahara and the survival of idealistic thought in those regions. Senghor's philosophical views are, of course, hardly separable from his personal experiences gained during his long career in practical political life. In the period when the French colonial system was being destroyed by the national liberation movement of colonial peoples, Senghor attempted to preserve the unity of French West Africa, hoping that large multi-national wholes could be turned into federations. He has been strongly opposed to the so-called Balkanization but he has been aware of the existing tribal and national differences which complicate the unifying and integration efforts.

Senghor's aesthetic thinking—as we can judge it on the basis of his essays, speeches, papers and poems—has been inspired by African, European (mainly French) and American sources. The significance of Senghorian aesthetics consists in the fact that it has affected numerous authors of French-writing Africa. Senghor's ideas have been accepted or refused but they have invariably proved to be stimulating. Moreover, Senghor's works have frequently been discussed by overseas critics, while his creative principles have been commented upon by his translators. Few African collections of poetry have become so widespread in translations as Senghor's. His first book of poems—**Chants d'ombre**—was first translated into Czech (in 1947) but the most detailed methodical discussions concerned the translations into English, which, owing to its tendency to monosyllabism, presents certain difficulties in looking for equivalents of Senghor's long verse.

The present study aims to characterize Senghor's main subjects—politics and poetry—corresponding to the two poles of his personality. Here we do not deal with his psychological motivation as this has been explained by his biographers. The case of the Senegalese intellectual, who is the President of the Republic and a gifted poet and critic at the same time, is rather special. The present study follows, however, mainly what is not restricted to Senghor's personal fate, what possesses a broader social relevance. Due to the limited extent of this study, Senghor's literary criticism and recent political activities (in the 1960's and in the early 1970's) have been left out.

Senghor was born on September 9, 1906. His birthplace, Joal - la - Portugaise, was a small town, where his father was a dealer in ground-nuts. Senegal, inhabited by the Wolof, the Serere (to whom Senghor belongs) and other

nationalities, was then ruled by the French colonial administration trying to assimilate the Africans. These policies could best be seen in large towns, where educated and wealthy circles were partly Frenchified. The "evolués" living in four privileged towns (Dakar, St. Louis, Gorée and Rufisque) became French citizens and enjoyed political rights, while the rest of the population was treated as primitive "subjects". Christianity, or more precisely Roman Catholicism, was an attribute of "civilization".

Senghor started learning French at the age of seven and as a young gifted man intended to become a priest. Catholic influences can be well traced both in his philosophy and in his poetry. As a student he became interested in French culture. In Dakar he got a secular education and never studied theology. Instead, he continued his educational career at *École Normale Supérieure* in Paris (from 1928). The capital of France appeared to him as an immense museum, or as a shop-window where different cultures meet. Senghor met there Césaire of Martinique, Léon Damas of French Guiana and other students coming from French overseas colonies. Senghor was very successful in Paris and took his *agrégé* degree at the Sorbonne. Then he taught French literature at French secondary schools. At that time he already started his own literary activities, producing his first poems. He also took interest in ideological and political problems, principally in the emancipation of colonial peoples

The Paris cultural life in the 1930's was very dynamic. Black intellectuals were absorbing the recent ideological and artistic impulses from the Negro milieu: Pan-Africanist congresses, Garvey's Negro Zionism, the *negrismo* movement of Cuba, the activities of Haitian writers, etc. The Haitians were searching for some links with African cultural traditions, the *negrismo* movement emphasized mainly authenticity of artistic expression. The aesthetic influences of French symbolism, surrealism and existentialism also proved to be inspiring. The original front of black students in Paris was formed on their common racial basis, which later, after World War Two, lost its justification. All coloured intellectuals shared also aversion to capitalism, colonial exploitation, some of them even to Christianity and European rationalism.

The journal *Légitime Défense* (1932) was inspired by Marxism and expressed some programme of anti-colonialist struggle. The editors believed that a political revolution should precede a cultural one. But apart from the revolutionary doctrine, there were also other sources of inspiration, e.g. Freud and Breton. Communist (or left-wing) ideology was thus combined with surrealist methodology. After this short-lived journal there was *L'étudiant noir* (1934) in whose activities Senghor took part. This group was less radical, stressing the primary importance of cultural problems, namely of traditional African values. For this reason, the members of this group refused to join any political party and to respect any western, no-Negro values. They continued their protest against the French colonial policies of assimilation. Their Black Messianism resulted from idealizations of the African past and of the traditional way of life. The increasing interest in African history, sociology, folklore and ethnography corresponded to the development of African nationalism. The spiritual life of black intellectuals was influenced by the success of the socialist revolution in the Soviet Union, and in particular by the Soviet doctrines of racial equality and the right to self-determination, which was applied to national problems in the first socialist country.

On the other hand, the Negro thinkers and artists realized the general decline of western morality quickened by the bloodsheds of World War One. The white man's prestige, formerly connected with his "civilizing mission" in the backward parts of the world, was partly lost. The increased awareness of the existence of specific cultural values among the black peoples led to the formation of African revivalist concepts. While some black intellectuals strengthened that Africa experienced its glory in the past and that one of the highest civilizations of Antiquity originated in Egypt, others held the white man's technological civilization in contempt. This latter approach is characteristic of Aimé Césaire's *Cahier d'un retour au pays natal* (1939), where the expression Négritude was coined to denote a fresh ideological concept.

Négritude has already been analyzed in detail. It expresses the black man's self-assertive contribution to world civilization, his own search for African cultural roots. It has been treated both as an intellectual notion and as a French-African concept, which was mostly refused outside French-speaking Africa. English-speaking Africans did not need it because they did not have to react to assimilationist policies.[1]

Senghor has presented many detailed comments on his conception of Négritude. It is rather ironical that the world-wide recognition of Negro civilization should be ensured through the romantic "noble savage" idea. Senghor's book *Liberté I: Négritude and Humanisme* was reviewed by Renato Berger[2], who observed the author's vague terms. He quoted Senghor's characteristics of Négritude: ". . . the presence in the world, the participation of the human being in the cosmical forces, the communion of the individuals between themselves and moreover with everything that exists, from stone to God."[3]

Senghor's formulations have not made Négritude clearer but have shown it as a complicated notion. They have also betrayed the paradoxical circumstance that the sophisticated, partly Frenchified intellectuals started their re-discovery of specific African values in a distant and foreign milieu. Some critics tended, therefore, to consider Négritude to be a kind of cultural manifesto, a confession of a new literary movement. In consequence of this approach, Négritude was sometimes reduced to a branch of African surrealism.

One of the frequently discussed questions was whether Négritude would be only temporary, suitable for the transition period only. Those who believed so usually failed to see it as something positive, something which might represent a long-lasting contribution in the general context of world culture. The opposite views was taken by the

Belgian scholar Lilyan Kesteloot who refused the idea of Négritude self-destruction as "Négritude is not only due to racial conflict and colonial problems but stands on a common civilization of all black Africans."[4]

Négritude is obviously a temporary notion suitable for the revivalist period of Africa's struggle for emancipation. Its retarding, conservative aspect resulting from the emphasis laid on its racial basis has become constantly more apparent and Black Africa has had to find new, fresh concepts for its era of independence. Négritude has been preserved and celebrated mainly in the meaning in which Kesteloot referred to it: as a popular and fairly widespread current involving masses of African population with the black colour of the skin. But the awareness of being black is not identical with the intellectual notion, which is rather remote from the African man-in-the-street.

The disagreement of Kesteloot and Sartre cannot take us very far as each of them used Négritude in a different meaning. Moreover, Kestellot does not answer to the idea, which seems to be exceedingly relevant, of the insufficiency of Négritude for the purposes of class war in African countries.

Another difficulty in interpreting Négritude arises from the fact that Senghor and his coleagues have defined it primarily in the negative sense, as a reaction to "white" culture. Senghor himself wrote that Négritude was "a weapon of refuge, of struggle and of hope rather than an instrument of construction" and that "we retained only those values that were opposed to Europe".[5] Négritude, like Senghor himself, has borne the basic contradiction since its origin and that is why it has been considered as a French-African concept. "Senghor, in particular, convinced as he is of the need to return to Negro roots, is all the same a keen advocate of a mixture of cultures."[6]

Also Soviet specialists have seen the excessive emphasizing of racial basis, the "inverse racism" of Négritude as one of its main weaknesses. F. M. Breskina wrote: "Fanon has discovered the historical roots and role of Négritude in the first stage of overcoming cultural assimilation, but also the historical limitation of this doctrine, its dependence on the influence of European theories and examples of exoticism, the danger of conserving traditions, of forming rigid canons of the 'black' culture as opposed to the 'white' culture."[7]

One of the most often criticized ideas relates to the distribution of domains according to races: the white man is supposed to dominate the rational, while the black the emotional. Senghor later revised and modified this opinion but the fate of Négritude has been connected with him. The distorted pictures of Négritude are partly due to the twists in the political development of its representatives. Clive Wake[8] and Yambo Ouologuem[9] of Mali believe that the decline of Négritude has been brought about and strengthened by the growing opposition to Senghor - politician. And such attitudes concern also Césaire and others. Césaire was criticized chiefly after 1956 when he left the French Communist Party. Césaire failed to respect the most urgent tasks of the Party and the needs of the proletarian movement of the world. His departure from the revolutionary line took place in the period of the Hungarian crisis in 1956. Négritude must be examined not only on the basis of the statements of its adherents and opponents but mainly according to the behaviour of its representatives. Let us follow, for some time, Senghor's further experiences. At the beginning of World War Two, he was a soldier of the 23rd and then of the 3rd regiment of colonial infantry. On June 20, 1940 he was taken prisoner by the Germans at La Carité-sur-Loire. He was released for illness in 1942 and taught again at the Marcelin Berthelot lyceum. During the War, he participated in the National University Front. One of his inspiring experiences was the liberation of France by the American troops among whom he saw also black American soldiers. He celebrated them in his well known poem **"To the American Negro Troops."**

After *Chants d'ombre* (*Songs of Shadow*, 1945), containing his earlier poetry he published two different collections of poems: *Hosties Noires* (*Black Victims*, 1948), still fairly radical in spirit, and *Chants pour Naëtt* (*Songs for Naëtt*, 1949), containing love poems dedicated to his first wife. The following collection—*Ethiopiques* (1956)—is remarkable for its lyrical tones and philosophical depth. Religious elements increase and more care is devoted to the form of his verse. This is true particularly about his fifth book of verses *Nocturnes* (1961), where *Chants pour Naëtt* are included too. The English translation of Senghor's *Selected Poems* appeared in London (1964).

Literary criticism and political speeches and articles can be found in his *Liberté I: Négritude et humanisme* (Paris 1964). For Senghor's ideological opinions the most essential source is *Nation et voie africaine du socialisme* (Paris 1961), which appeared also in the English translation: *Nationhood and the African Road to Socialism* (Paris 1962). It is useful, however, to follow Senghor's political career in the post-World War Two period. . . .

Senghor's philosophical idealism has dominated his aesthetic views, expressed in a number of theoretical essays and realized in his own poetry. Senghor soon became aware of the danger of imitativeness as he had inevitably absorbed numerous influences. It is necessary to take into account that he started his literary career already in the period when imaginative writing of French West Africa was almost negligible. Nobody could speculate about any independent, national literatures written in French, let alone in vernacular languages. But precisely the heavily imposed policies of assimilation provoked a revivalist tendency to rehabilitate the traditional cultural values of Black Africa. Against the triumphant argument of colonial propaganda that the Negro is unable to develop written prose, poetry and drama, the first patriotic intellectuals of Black Africa emphasized the relatively high standard of oral traditions and the widespread and socially relevant art of the word.

Collections of folklore creations have been published with increasing frequency and the African compilers have found

it advisable to explain that no celebration of primitivism is intended. Rather recently Taban lo Liyong, the editor of oral texts, wrote as follows:

> "This is not a 'return to the caves' war cry. It is rather the transmission of the old spirit; the old fire; the reenshrining of our inner vitality, it is the request for the blessing saliva of our ancestors to help us face the future like men, sons of men."[26]

Again, we come across the sincere desire of the African intellectual not to dwell upon the problem of the past but to utilize the so-called cultural heritage for the purposes of the contemporary renasce nce. In Senghor's poetry, there is a clear intention to exploit imagery for an authentically African synthesis despite the incontestable fact that his sophisticated verse reaches the best-trained audience in France and its neighbours. Senghor knew that already his first collection—*Chants d'ombre*—contained some "difficult" African expressions, which the overseas readers could hardly understand. He decided to add a brief glossary to his collection *Chants pour Naëtt* (Paris, 1949) in order to explain at least some "exotic" meanings. But his comment stresses that his verses are intended mainly for his own people. Moreover, he does not believe that the reader's understanding is based solely on the knowledge of foreign words and realities. He seems to suggest that his own poetry should be understood on a higher than verbal level though the exact meanings are indispensable for a correct interpretation and analysis of all his poems. He feels that his reader must show his understanding through com-prehending (in French com-prendre), which is, in his opinion, sur-real rather than real. This approach of his probably results from the aesthetic thinking of the French surrealists, who were convinced that dictates of thought ought to be recorded by a "pure" psychic automatism.

> **Senghor may appear to have represented a compromise between indigenous and foreign poetical traditions but his conception of rhythm in poetry is definitely African.**
>
> —*Vladimir Klima*

Senghor's biographer Armand Guibert praises the poet for having remained "faithful to a mode of expression which implies the participation of the audience in the dynamics of the song"[27] but remarks that Senghor joined André Breton's principle that "tous les grands poètes ont été des auditifs". It is clear, of course, that the knowledge of meanings is essential both for listeners and readers. Most critics share the opinion that Senghor should not be accused of an intentional hunt for exoticism or "cheap hermetism" as he calls it himself.[28]

In reality, African elements have increased in his poetry since the 1940's. This is confirmed also by John Reed and

Clive Wake, who wrote in their Introduction to their own translation of *Nocturnes* (London, Heinemann 1969) as follows:

> "There is a tendency, for example, to substitute a specific African term for the more general French word: a 'channel' becomes a 'bolong', 'flowers' become 'aderas'. Surprisingly perhaps, this does not make the poems more obscure—the poet supplies a glossary—nor more exotic; instead, the imagery becomes more precise and more evocative, as well as more authentic, for these are the poems of an African poet who, by the time he had come to revise the Songs, had moved from the uncomfortable hesitation between Africa and France to a more definite personal and cultural position."[29]

This opinion was based on the comparison of the collection *Chants pour Naëtt*, mentioned above, with the first part of *Nocturnes* (1961), where this collection re-appears under the new name *Chants pour Signare*; the translators find this new name more suitable because *Chants pour Naëtt* was originally dedicated to Ginette Eboué, the poet's first wife, while *Nocturnes*, including this older collection of love poems, is dedicated to Senghor's second (French) wife.[30]

Senghor has often touched on the existing differences between Europe and Africa as far as literary taste is concerned. He realizes the role of various fashions and snobishness in accepting or refusing the so-called exotic elements. Europe and Africa appear to him as spheres of the world culture, which, being mutually enriched, should contribute to the common treasury of all nations. Senghor never means any contribution but invariably a specific one. There have been long discussions concerning African speciality. Janheinz Jahn (Federal Republic of Germany) thought that in the field of poetry it resulted from the order of words and images, which is allegedly reverse than in the tradition of European poetry.

Without going into details, we may pay here some attention to this interpretation. According to it, European poetry is essentially based on the meaning of ideas as it was explained by Plato, the old Greek philosopher. While in this idealistic conception an image is supposed to precede a word, the African Word (nommo) is viewed as a magical force capable of changing an object into an image.[31] This later appearance of an image may be, however, explained also by the practical experience of a man surrounded by nature and inevitably respecting the priority of material existence.

Like many African poets, Senghor is inclined to suppose that the poet can use his extraordinary gift in giving names to objects. The question remains, however, whether this automatically creates poetic imagery. This approach somehow overestimates the psychological assumption that images arise from conflicts between neighbouring expressions. Senghor's interesting comments on imagery can be found in his preface to Antoine-Roger Bolamba's collection *Esanzo: chants pour mon pays* (1956), where he suggested how to explain Bolamba's style.[32] In Bolamba's "syntax of juxtaposition", chains of images allegedly originate from the tension arising between expressions even though these expressions might have been recalled in a purely accidental manner. This reminds us, again, of the role of subconscious elements as ascribed to them by surrealists. The case of Bolamba, the well-known poet of Zaire, is not exceptional. Some noteworthy experiments have occurred also in English African writing. The Nigerian poet Kay Epelle used Whitman—like long enumerations in order to make his poetry more persuasive, Lenrie Peters (Gambia) showed remarkable feeling for modern experiments, etc.

It seems that certain surrealist techniques (borrowed from France) are in Senghor's poetry intricately combined with incantations in the style of traditional African medicine-men, trying to affect reality in a supernatural way. It is evident that the poet's inspiration cannot be looked for only in Africa. Senghor developed his aesthetic exploration on the basis of French symbolism. Hence follows his anti-rationalism and his sense of secret meanings in verses. Senghor has never admired rationalist trends and methods of European literature (e.g. critical realism, Parnassianism etc.). He has never paid much attention to purely formal aspects of poetry in the line of Art for Art's sake. Among his poetical forefathers may have been Gérald de Nerval (1808-1855), the author of *Les Chimères,* his artistic expression was perhaps influenced by *Art poétique* (1907), written by Paul Claudel.

There have been numerous considerations relating to the symbolical validity of colours (chiefly white and black) in Senghor's poetry. Guibert mentions that Nerval's black Sun is melancholic, while in Senghor blackness accompanies only the idea of aesthetic perfection and glorification.[33] Senghor's **"Femme noire"** (in *Chants d'ombre*) is praised for her blackness, representing an essence of positive qualities, and for her nakedness, i.e. for being free from all useless "jewels" of a foreign civilization. This is Senghor's conception of Négritude in its purest form, and the idea of blackness and darkness is echoed also in the titles of his volumes of verse: ombre - shadow, Hosties noires - Black Victims, Nocturnes-Night, darkness and shadow are celebrated as symbols of life and contrasted with the negative whiteness. During the Spanish Civil War he produced his poem **"Neige sur Paris,"** in which the white colour is associated with the coldness of snow covering the roofs of the city. Also death and the colonialists' hands are white. He exploits also other colours (e.g. in *Nocturnes* dark melody, purple voice, burning voice, green odour etc.) but the white and the black colours occupy a central position in his picturesque pallet.

Senghor shares the French symbolists's affiliation to music, his verses are long and melodious, suitable for recitation and for musical accompaniment. The poet even feels that poetry is incomplete if music and singing are absent. Similar approaches to recitation existed already in ancient Oriental civilizations and in classical Antiquity (Egypt, Greece, etc.). Senghor's verse is comparatively rich in sound effects due to the vowel structure, alliteration, assonance, rhythmic repetition of consonants, onomatopoeia, rare rhymes, etc. The accompaniment of African musical instruments is sometimes prescribed by the poet: kora and sorong resemble our harp, khalam our violin with three strings, riti has only one string, balafong is a sort of xylophone and there are, of course, many different kinds of tomtoms and drums: talmbatt, sabar, tabala, tama, ndeundeu, gorong, dyoung-dyoung, etc.

Senghor believes that poetry must become a combination of music, singing and words, which will enable it to return to its original condition. His most successful poems reveal the virtue of his symbolical imagery: it can be enjoyed in itself but also the meanings hidden behind it can be disclosed. Thus we learn what the poet has to say about the reality to which his symbolical imagery refers. Senghor sometimes uses his symbols in their usual, fixed meanings but he also tries to attack this conventional perception by giving his symbols a second, unusual meaning, which is purely personal. One is tempted to denote this second meaning as non-traditional but the poet would probably object to this, saying that this second meaning may seem non-traditional from the viewpoint of European poetics though it is in fact traditional enough in the cultural milieu of West Africa. His principle of "mixing cultures" makes him derive his imagery both from French sources and from African systems of symbols as they have been set up by griots, African popular bards.

Senghor may appear to have represented a compromise between indigenous and foreign poetical traditions but his conception of rhythm in poetry is definitely African. He distinguishes between the French manner of poems organized as "drames" and the African composition of verbal symphonies, containing words instead of tones. "But the monotony of tone does distinguish poetry from prose; this is the seal of Négritude, the incantation which makes the essential things—the cosmic forces—accede to the truth".[34] Here as well as in other essays he stresses the significance of the rhythmic pattern of the verse as, for him, rhythm in an architecture of being. The so-called pure images in Senghor's poetry occur rarely, whenever the poet intentionally avoids symptoms of his own intellectual interpretation, thus demonstrating the effect of "subconscious automatism". Senghor usually manages to make "expression" subordinated to content, in other words, "expression" is seldom a purpose in itself; it is functional in most cases. Under these circumstances, the poet's individuality does not make itself felt in a straightforward manner (as of a political commentator, a lover, etc.) but through the expected relevance of his quasi-impartial "message". This does not mean that his poems could be thought of as sequences of unbiassed descriptive statements because logical lines of argumentation are practically missing, the artistic impression resulting mainly from the fascinating novelty of his "ideography", as we have characterized it above.

To this approach also the syntactical structure and punctuation correspond. Thanks to the comparison of *Chants pour Naëtt* with *Nocturnes*, Reed and Wake succeeded in discovering Senghor's revisions showing characteristic tendencies in his mature development. They say that "effective concentration, precision and evocativeness of im-

agery is achieved by omission of secondary words, such as articles, simple conjuctions and the verb 'to be'. Thus:

> "'Les arbres sont de feuilles d'or et leurs fleurs sont de flamboyant becomes Arbres de feuilles d'or, leurs fleurs de flamboyant.'"[35]

Then they mention the poet's increased use of commas and continue:

> "The limited use of punctuation, which is a common feature of modern poetry, was intended to enable the poet to exploit ambiguities of syntax and to allow the verse to find its own rhythms, independent of the rhythms of speech or logic imposed by conventional punctuation. This was particularly relevant to Senghor because of his belief that African poetry, even if written in French or English, must reflect African, not French or English rhythms. Why Senghor abandons his earlier practice is hard to say."[36]

Three years later, the same translators have already suggested an answer to his complicated question in the following lines:

> "Protagonists of Négritude have insisted that African poetry contains the rhythms of traditional oral African poetry and of the African languages. The freedom of vers libre makes this possible. But poetry which is written in French can only become rhythmical through those patterns of rhythm which are inherent in the language, though these may be deployed in ways which are original and answer to the rhythms of other languages. But to say, as has been said, that to grasp the rhythm of a poem by Senghor we must break away from the French way of accentuating words is to say that poet has failed to realise his rhythm through the medium of the language he is using."[37]

Another difficulty for translators results from the fact that—according to the poet—the poem is not realized completely through a visual perception of the text. For Senghor, poems are like jazz and the actual performance of the reciter is important. He is rather critical about the "French" manner of underlining the accent of each group of words and despite his excellent knowledge of the French language, he stresses that it is not his own. In order to master it, he had to look for examples and this brings us to a crowd of French poets, who are supposed to have exerted influence on him.

Senghor himself mentions many names "from troubadours up to Paul Claudel"[38] but it seems that especially Victor Hugo and Saint-John Perse were most brilliant examples, It is well known that Birago Diop, another major poet of Senegal, started by reading and imitating Alfred de Musset and Paul Verlaine. We must make distinction between the real influences, including those that were not reflected in Senghor's poems but only in his aesthetic thinking, and the authors, whose works the poet likes to read. The latter category comprises his poetical geography consisting mainly of Africa, America and Western Europe. But while he has always felt some affinity with the Caribbean poets, he has never been interested in North African Arabic poetry. Apart from Aimé Césaire and Léon G. Damas, he certainly recognizes James Weldon Johnson, Langston Hughes, Sterling Brown and Richard Wright, whom Mercer Cook mentions as having exerted some influence on the tone of his earlier verses.[39] But it is not easy to discover precisely these American influences, while he appears to stand very close to one generation of French poets. The Czech translator Jirí Navrátil mentions particularly Valéry's diction, Claudel's rhythms and Saint-John Perse's inner features of imagination.[40] Senghor wrote that he had loved Barrès, Proust, Gide, Baudelaire and Rimbaud,[41] but they all belong to the second category exerting no direct influences on his works.

In connection with Senghor's inspiration, it is perhaps useful to mention the widespread assumption that the poet is an "innovator in an African poetic context but not in the European."[42] Reed and Wake suggest this in their Introduction to **Selected Poems** and they look for Senghor's "equivalents" in English. It is interesting that they find them in Whitman and his followers in the next passage:

> Indeed Whitman is an indirect source of Senghor's style, for his work had important influence around the turn of the century on the whole school of free-verse writing in France from which Senghor derives. Like Senghor, Whitman is a poet of reconciliation or at least of all-acceptance. He, too, takes it upon himself to speak on behalf of others. He celebrates a nation coming into being. Even the slightly off-hand way in which Whitman uses the English language, his adoption of French and Spanish words to suggest a mixture of cultures and peoples, has its parallel in Senghor. Some passages in Senghor sound very like Whitman. Others sound like Robinson Jeffers".[43]

But one need not go so far as to find out what Ulli Beier stated at the end of his study *The Theme of the Ancestors in Senghor's Poetry:* "Senghor, then, is not merely a Frenchified African who tries to give exotic interest to his French poems; he is an African who uses the French language to express his African soul."[44] Gerald Moore calls him not a Black Frenchman but a French African,[45] while Barend van Niekerk speaks about "dualism in the poet's soul".[46] One the most sharply criticized verses by Senghor runs as follows:

Seigneur, parmi les nations blanches, place la
　France
à la droite du Père
Lord, amid the white nations, place France on the
right hand of the Father

Moore comments on it as follows: "Here the dignity and compassion of **'Paris in the Snow'** are replaced by something perilously close to the paper dagger and the ingratiating smile"[47] and adds that "Senghor's poetry is often at its best when he abandons the search for reconciliation and is content to register a single emotion without too much care for the consequences."[48] The more Senghor rose in the political arena, the less he could afford detached criticism of colonialism. Simultaneously with the decrease

of his political radicalism, his inner conflict became increasingly reflected in his poetry by his transition from dynamic to more static imagery. It is sufficient to recall his poem **"Joal"** from his first collection **Chants d'ombre**, where he celebrated his birthplace by means of powerful images and sounds. "Les choeurs de lutte" and "le pur cri d'amour" of Joal was contrasted with Europe, where he finds "un jazz orphelin qui sanglote, sanglote, sanglote." The Soviet scholar G.I. Potekhina remarks that this first collection fully embodied the themes of Négritude "from praising great African civilizations up to a sharp contraposition of the West and Africa and the conviction that the black race has the mission to pour fresh blood into the veins of the perishing European civilization."[49] But already in the 1950's Senghor emphasizes the idea of reconciliation, developed from the basic idea of the poem **"Prière aux Masques"** that Africa will be "le levain qui est nécessaire à la farine blanche—the leaven that is necessary for the white flour". At the same time, Senghor tries to solve his inner interrelation of a poet and a politician. It is rather paradoxical that Senghor practically stopped writing political verses when he was becoming constantly more active in political life. In his later collections, lyrical love poems prevailed.

In *Ethiopiques*, for instance, the most committed piece is **"Chaka,"** a long dramatic poem, appreciating the ruler who united Zulu tribes. Judith Illsley Gleason wrote about the poem as follows:

> Senghor, like the English romantics who later made Satan the hero of the piece, has temporarily abrogated the moral framework in which Mofolo wrote."[50]

The famous Basuto writer Thomas Mofolo treated this subject in terms of Christian doctrine and consequently condemned the Zulu king for his atrocities. Senghor was much more concerned with the hero's double function and wrote the following words of **"Chaka"**:

> "Je devins une tête, un bras sans tremblement, ni guerrier ni boucher. Un politique tu l'as dit—je tuai le poète—un homme d'action seul. Un homme seul et déjà mort avant les autres, comme ceux que tu plains. Qui saura ma passion? . . .

> I became a head, a steady arm, neither warrior nor butcher. A politician you have said—I killed the poet—man of action alone, a man alone and already dead before the others, like those you pity. Who can know my passion?[51]

Clive Wake comments on this poem in the following passage:

> His poetry expresses the deeply-felt dilemma of many African intellectuals and writers of the time: can creative writing be reconciled with the need to become politically involved? . . . The historical situation recalled in the poem is thoroughly distorted to make it fit the dilemma it is meant to illustrate. The answer: the poet must destroy his muse in order to concentrate on the task of freeing his people . . . The politically committed,

like Senghor, Nkrumah and even Sekou Touré, have, through their political writings, exerted a definite influence on creative writing and have initiated the endless discussions about the nature of the African personality which has been the chief red-herring of the period.[52]

Senghor's political and artistic evolution shows very clearly how politics and poetry have been interlaced in the post-war Black Africa, and in particular in its French-writing zone. No complex evaluation of Senghor's activities is possible if only one aspect (political or artistic) is taken into consideration. The two spheres have not been separated; on the contrary, any detailed analysis of the post-war literary and artistic development in Black Africa must pay attention to the profound political and socio-economic changes which have taken place there. But also those who deal with the complicated twists of the political situation in Sub-Saharan countries may derive some profit from the knowledge of that part of African creative writing that has reacted to the topical events in political, social, economic and cultural life.

Notes

[1] Gerald Moore, *Seven African Writers*, Introduction, Oxford University Press, London 1962, pp. XVI-XIX.

[2] In *Nigeria Magazine*, December 1967, No. 95, pp. 338-341; the translated quotation from Senghor p. 339.

[3] Senghor, *Négritude et humanisme*, Paris 1964.

[4] Lilyan Kestellot, *Anthologie négro-africaine*, Marabout Université, Verviers 1967, p. 134.

[5] Senghor, *Négritude et marxisme;* quoted in *Procès à la négritude, Afrique littéraire et artistique*, 1969, No. 7, p. 16; cf. Senghor, Pierre Teilhard de Chardin et la politique africaine, Paris 1962, p. 20.

[6] Claude Wauthier, *The Literature and Thought of Modern Africa*, Pall Mall Press, London 1966, p. 105.

[7] F. M. Breskina, *O samobytnosti sovremennykh afrikanskikh literatur na evropejskikh jazykakh, Aktualnye problemy literatur Afriki*, Nauka, Moskva 1969, p. 73.

[8] In *The Political and Cultural Revolution in Protest and Conflict in African Literature*, Heinemann, London 1969, p. 48.

[9] An interview with *Yambo Ouologuem in Alger*, Afrique littéraire et artistique, 1969, No. 7, p. 21. . . . .

[26] *Popular Culture of East Africa*, edited by Taban lo Liyong, Longmans, Nairobi 1972, Introduction, p. XII.

[27] Armand Guibert, *Léopold Sédar Senghor*, Editions Pierre Seghers, Paris 1961, p. 81.

[28] In *Chants pour Naëtt*, Paris 1949.

[29] Senghor, *Nocturnes*, Heinemann, London 1969 - Introduction pp. VII-VIII; the French original appeared in Paris 1961 (Editions du Seuil).

[30] Ibid., p. VII.

[31] Janheinz Jahn, Muntu, London 1961.

[32] Antoine-Roger Bolamba, *Esanzo:chants pour mon pays*, Paris 1956.

[33] Armand Guibert, *Léopold Sédar Senghor*, Editions Pierre Seghers, Paris 1961, p. 79.

[34] Senghor, "Comme les Lamantins vont boire à la source" (Postface to *Ethiopiques*) in *Poèmes*, Editions du Seuil, Paris 1964, p. 166.

[35] John Reed, Clive Wake, Introduction to *Nocturnes*, Heinemann, London 1969, p. VIII.

[36] Ibid., pp. VIII-IX.

[37] *French African Verse*, Introduction by John Reed and Clive Wake, Heinemann, London 1972, p. X.

[38] Senghor, "Comme les Lamantins vont boire à la source," (Postface to *Ethiopiques*) in *Poèmes*, Editions du Seuil, Paris 1964, p. 157.

[39] Mercer Cook in his review in *African Forum*, vol. 1, No. 4, 1966, p. 136.

[40] Jiuí Navrátil, *ivotopisná poznámka k Nokturnum* (Biographical Comment on *Nocturnes*), Praha 1965, p. 58.

[41] In *Figaro Littéraire* on May 12, 1962.

[42] Discussed in some detail in Senghor, *Selected Poems*, Introduction by John Reed and Clive Wake, Oxford University Press, London 1964, pp. XVII-XVIII.

[43] Ibid., p. XIX.

[44] Ulli Beier, "The Theme of the Ancestors in Senghor's Poetry" in *Introduction to African Literature*, edited by Ulli Beier, Longmans, London 1967, p. 98.

[45] Gerald Moore, *Seven African Writers*, Oxford University Press, London 1962, p. 2.

[46] Barend van Niekerk, *The African Image in the Work of Senghor*, Cape Town 1970, p. 45.

[47] Gerald Moore, *Seven African Writers*, Oxford University Press, London 1962, p. 11.

[48] Ibid., p. 12.

[49] G. I. Potekhina, *Ocherki sovremennoy literatury zapadnoy Afriki*, Nauka, Moskva 1968, p. 40.

[50] Judith Illsley Gleason, *This Africa*, Northwestern University Press, Evanston 1965, p. 65.

[51] Quoted with the English translation in Claude Wauthier, *The Literature and Thought of Modern Africa*, Pall Mall Press, London 1966, p. 98.

⁵² Clive Wake, *The Political and Cultural Revolution in Protest and Conflict in African Literature,* Heinemann, London 1969, pp. 45-40.

Charles O'Keefe (essay date 1984)

SOURCE: "Recall in Léopold Sédar Senghor's 'Joal'," in *The French Review,* Vol. LVII, No. 5, April, 1984, pp. 625-33.

[In the following essay, O'Keefe discusses the influence of Senghor's early environment on his work, maintaining that "if the eponymous subject of this poem lies at the heart of Senghor's artistic material, what is true for 'Joal' will be informative about all his poetry."]

As both thinker and doer, Léopold Sédar Senghor has been an influential presence globally. The prominent roles that he has played include theoretician of *négritude,* member of the French *Assemblée Constituante* (in 1945) and *Chambre des Députés,* a delegate to the Council of Europe, to the UN, and to UNESCO, and the first president of the Republic of Senegal. One might think that the poet in him would derive much inspiration from all that the intellectual and the statesman have achieved and seen. Yet Senghor has made the striking statement that almost all his poetic material comes from the small area where he spent his childhood: "Et puisqu'il faut m'expliquer sur mes poèmes, je confesserai encore que presque tous les êtres et choses qu'ils évoquent sont de mon canton: quelques villages *sérères* perdus parmi les *tanns,* les bois, les *bolongs* et les champs."¹ For those interested in Senghor's art, this imposing restriction invites thought.

A consideration of the poem **"Joal,"**² which appeared in 1945 in Senghor's first collection of poetry ***Chants d'ombre***, is a good way to approach the matter because for our poet one of the focal points of his childhood environment has been Joal, the coastal Senegalese village where he was born.³ If the eponymous subject of this poem lies at the heart of Senghor's artistic material, what is true for **"Joal"** will be informative about all his poetry.

The use of *je me rappelle* stands as one of the most salient features of **"Joal,"** clearly justifying critical attention from the outset, because the poem in its entirety has only that one main verb and repeats it eight times:

Joal!
Je me rappelle.

Je me rappelle les signares à l'ombre verte des
    vérandas
Les signares aux yeux surréels comme un clair de
    lune sur la grève.

Je me rappelle les fastes du Couchant
Où Koumba N'Dofène voulait faire tailler son
    manteau royal.
Je me rappelle les festins funèbres fumant du sang

des troupeaux égorgés
Du bruit des querelles, des rhapsodies des griots.

Je me rappelle les voix païennes rythmant le
    Tantum Ergo
Et les processions et les palmes et les arcs de
    triomphe.
Je me rappelle la danse des filles nubiles
Les chœurs de lutte—oh! la danse finale des jeunes
    hommes, buste
Penché élancé, et le pur cri d'amour des femmes—
    Kor Siga!

Je me rappelle, je me rappelle . . .
Ma tête rythmant
Quelle marche lasse le long des jours d'Europe où
    parfois
Apparaît un jazz orphelin qui sanglote sanglote
    sanglote.

Since poetry for Senghor is nothing if not sound ("Je le confesse, je suis un *auditif,*" Senghor, *Liberté I,* emphasis his), let us listen to the first example of *je me rappelle* in its auditory context and allow what we hear to start and guide our analysis: "Joal! / Je me rappelle." It can be noticed that the opening and closing consonants of the word *Joal,* the constrictives [ʒ] and [l], also open and close the sentence *Je me rappelle,* discretely inclining the message of each line to assimilate phonetically with the other's. We listen as Joal and the poet in the act of recall seem to be matching and merging with each other on the level of sound and thus of poetic sense: Joal recalled immediately starts to become the poet recalling.

We should note that this process of identification and absorption becomes heightened through syntax. While the *me* of *je me rappelle* ordinarily functions as an indirect object, here it operates without any other complement and so, in poetic multivalence, it can be understood as a direct object. ("C'est lorsqu'il bascule la grammaire que le poète se révèle artiste," *Libertè I*) By recalling Joal in the first verse, by recalling its women in the second, its past in the third, and its customs in the fourth and fifth verses, the poet seeks to recall himself: "Joal! / Je me rappelle."

Now let us approach from another angle the auditory context of this first example of *je me rappelle,* considering this time not so much the elements as the character of the word *Joal.* The line in which *Joal* appears, the opening one, is a truly arresting overture. Since the whole line consists only of that one word, we have its obvious and isolating brevity, the impact of which is intensified by an exclamation point (which is even more emphatic than it would ordinarily be, for Senghor tends to be sparing of punctuation in poetry). But what is most important in a work by a self-confessed *auditif,* attention is aroused by the line's peculiar sound and it is at least partially in order to emphasize that peculiarity that the poem singles out the word so forcefully. For francophones or speakers of a native African tongue, the place-name Joal cannot be easily situated because *Joal* has a Portuguese origin, as its complete form *Joal-la-Portugaise* indicates. What is essential is the foreign, mixed ring of the word *Joal,* for, while we can be sure that the hurt black voice singing **Chants d'ombre** from the inhospitable white Paris of the 1930's is nostalgically evoking here idealized memories of Africa, they are not memories of an exclusively African Africa, as one might expect. Rather, to counteract better the outrage of racism, the poet recalls and seeks union with a vision of Joal that is half-breed instead of purely African, as half-breed as the word *Joal* itself.

Other unusual-sounding words that occur later in the poem reinforce and refine this important distinction, one that comes as no surprise to those familiar with Senghor's views on *métissage* (see, for example, his "Le Problème de la culture" in *Liberté I*). The repeated use of the word *signares* in the second verse, for instance, strengthens the impression that *métissage* is one of the values, perhaps the principal value, found in this vision of Joal. Portuguese in origin like the word *Joal, signares* (from *senhora,* 'lady') can be viewed as referring to prestigious black or mulatto women of West Africa who entered into quasi-legal marriages with European men.[4] In remembering Joal, the poet calls up images first of women prominently associated with *métissage.* It is among them that he wishes to be, in a community that blends and softens racial differences instead of isolating and highlighting them. Out of that *métissage* something new and superior arises, as is suggested by the fact that the *signares* can see a higher plane of things, i.e., they have "yeux surréels." (For a longer, more explicit illustration of the sense in which Senghor tends to use *surréel,* see *Liberté I*).

The poem goes on to tease the ear with certain words whose sounds intimate a cultural as well as racial *métissage* at work in the poet's Joal. One hears mixed in with the French some straightforward foreign words, such as the African *Koumba N'Dofène* (the name of the last king of Sine, the former domain where Joal is found) on line 6, and *Kor Siga* (a Serer cry of admiration) on line 13.[5] Moreover, other foreign words in the poem, although long ago absorbed completely into French, can still betray origins that cut across geography and history. (Senghor has often shown himself to be highly conscious of word origins. See for example his "L'Esthétique négro-africaine" in *Liberté I.*) We find the partly Hindi, partly Portuguese *vérandas* on line 3, words of classical Greek origin such as *triomphe* and *chœurs* on lines 10 and 12 respectively, and *jazz* on line 17, a word of uncertain origin but with a clearly black American linkage. This emphasis on Joal's cultural *métissage* is even more noticeable in the bold yoking of words spanning enormous cultural distances: the Greek and African "rhapsodies des griots" on line 8, the pagan and Christian "les voix païennes rythmant le *Tantum Ergo*" on line 9 (*Tantum Ergo* being the title of the Catholic hymn glorifying the Eucharist).

Line 9 communicates still another dimension of Joal's *métissage,* the religious. While Senghor's Joal (like the actual one) accepts Christianity, it is not a strictly Western Christianity that we see, but rather one grafted onto African tellurism.[6] For the etymology-conscious poet, this can be felt in the Latin source of *païen,* i.e., *paganus,*

which means both 'peasant,' one living off the earth, and 'pagan,' one with animistic views about the earth. As was the case on the racial and cultural level, *métissage,* now on a religious level, offers Senghor experiences richer than those of the exclusionary West of the 1930s. For example, "les voix païennes rythmant le *Tantum Ergo*" could readily appreciate the appropriateness of the blood sacrifice at the center of the significance of the Eucharist—and indeed of Christianity itself—precisely because of fidelity to pagan practices (v. "les festins funèbres fumant du sang des troupeaux égorgés," line 7). In this half-breed context, moreover, rhythmic sounds and blood sacrifices involved life-enhancing rites and customs. But in the Europe that Senghor experienced, the dominant rhythms were becoming more and more those of marching armies and blood sacrifice too easily carried connotations of military holocaust.

Once we appreciate the different ways *métissage* works in **"Joal,"** we find additional appropriateness in the phonetic affinities between the words *Joal* and *je me rappelle,* the basis for the opening of this analysis. Now that we know that the Joal recalled by the poet is half-breed racially, culturally, and religiously, it becomes even more apparent that the poet actually recalls himself, for Senghor incarnates the three sorts of *métissage* that he posits in Joal. Racially, his ancestors represent Africa—and different peoples of Africa, at that—as well as Europe (as do his names, *Sédar* being Serer, and *Senghor* probably Portuguese).[7] Moreover, as a brilliant intellectual trained in France but still faithful to and proud of Africa, and as a devout Catholic continuing to live the insights of animism, he straddles the two continents culturally and religiously.

One would think, then, that his attempts at union with Joal through identification based on recall could readily reach a satisfactory conclusion. But at the end the poem records failure. To understand the cause and meaning of that failure, we must return to the syntax of *je me rappelle.* In it we can discover a verbal impasse that subtly forebodes the emotional impasse that builds as the poem continues. For all their semantic and physical proximity, the *je* and the *me* are not identical, whereas the impetus for the poem comes from the need for identification through assimilation. The two French pronouns remain distinct, respectively subject and object both grammatically and psychologically. Their irreducible distance in spite of paradoxical closeness encapsulates the doomed quest upon which the poet embarks in this poem. If we regard the poem in terms of the myth of Orpheus (as Jean-Paul Sartre did for much of the poetry written by francophone blacks of the contemporary world),[8] the *je* of adulthood—the voice of the poem—having suffered solitude and rejection in Europe, appears to be seeking Orpheus-like to resurrect and join an idealized *me,* his Eurydice, the privileged inhabitant-vessel of his *royaume d'enfance.* But although the poet yearns to assimilate and to be assimilated completely by that aspect of himself that he sees as having been at one with a perfect Joal, he cannot. He cannot recall fully (i.e., become) himself as he imagines he once was, in harmony with a utopian vision; indeed, he cannot reach even a modest approximation of such a condition, because he cannot forget himself fully as he is now, still closely attached to Joal but changed and diminished by what he endures in Europe.

The effects of the short but insuperable distance between the *je* and the *me* first begin to make themselves felt toward the middle of the poem, when the poet recalls the ceremonies surrounding Serer wrestling matches (wrestling being the national sport of Senegal—see Irele, *Selected Poems of Senghor*): "Je me rappelle la danse des filles nubiles / Les chœurs de lutte—oh! la danse finale des jeunes hommes buste / Penché élancé, et le pur cri d'amour des femmes—*Kor Siga!*" One of the most noteworthy features of these lines is the sudden interjection "—oh!" which leaps out at us, starting a breakdown of regularity in the pace of the poem. The preceding verses all flow within a controlled twofold structure in which the second line completes or complements the first in a very straightforward way. But starting with "—oh!" the previously contained cadences falter under imperious feelings that cannot confine themselves to a regular, stately rhythm. There is on the contrary an emotional spillover into a third line that brings further attention to itself through the potent enjambment "buste / Penché élancé." In keeping with the outburst, the strophe ends on a note of excitement with the isolated exclamation: "—*Kor Siga!*"

> **If the eponymous subject of this poem lies at the heart of Senghor's artistic material, what is true for "Joal" will be informative about all his poetry.**
>
> —*Charles O'Keefe*

But why does a breakdown begin at this particular point? If we consider it as the poet's reaction to what he recalls here, an explanation will become apparent. Behind the two subjects of lines 11-14 there is the promise of intense physical coupling. First, it is clear that wrestling will take place among the "chœurs de lutte." Second, it seems probable that sexual contact is imminent among the dancing men and women. The adjective "nubiles", in stressed position at the end of line 11, guides thought in that direction, as does the men's phallic stance, which the enjambment "buste / Penché élancé" boldly captures and which receives a vocal response in "le pur cri d'amour des femmes." Recalling this scene so suggestive of physical union can only underscore for the poet his feelings of personal solitude, increasing intolerably the yearning of the *je* for union with the *me.* Frustration then leads to emotional and rhythmic disorder.

The breakdown becomes complete in the sixth and final strophe, doubtless because of the sting of self-reproach that carries over from the very end of the fifth strophe where the poet recalled the cry of admiration *Kor Siga.* That cry is traditionally raised for Serer champions who

"are defending their honour before their women" (Irele, *Selected Poems of Senghor*), whereas for our black poet so sensitive to honor (see *Liberté I*), feelings of humiliation have not been rare in Paris (see "Neige sur Paris," *Poèmes*). In the first line of this strophe, the poet nonetheless tries to revive the act of recall and with it his Joal-Eurydice, by twice repeating his incantation: "Je me rappelle, je me rappelle . . .". But emptiness is the only result, with his voice trailing off into the void that follows the three ellipsis points. The note of failure continues in the second line, a listless sentence fragment: "Ma tête rythmant." If we keep in mind Senghor's longstanding reservations about uncomplemented rationality, we can see how painfully suitable for him "tête rythmant" is at this particular point. The words suggest that his poetry, an *acte rythmant,* now comes only from his head—his will and his intellect—instead of from the wholeness to which he aspires and which he recalled in earlier lines. There, unlike here, the griots at the feasts, along with the young people at the ceremonies and dances, developed their rhapsodies and rhythms in a full context, spiritual and physical as well as mental. But the humiliated Orpheus, having lost to emotion and shame his hold on Eurydice, cannot sustain his resurrecting song of recall by using his head alone.

Following the fragmentary sigh of failure, there occurs a line with elements of meter which, while rare in French poetry, are not uncommon in Senghor's verse.[9] Starting off with three words ending in mute *e,* the line sets up a trochee-like beat ("Quelle / marche / lasse") that then slips into a different two-count pattern, i.e., iambs ("le long / des jours / d' Europe"). The stumbling transition between the contrary two-count beats imparts a sense of the poet's *via dolorosa,* that life imposed on him in Europe, a life wearisome almost to the point of pain ("marche lasse"). That he describes it as a *marche* adds a further, chilling dimension. For the word, spawned almost necessarily by the two-count beats, summons up one of the truly feared rhythms of Europe of the 1930s, that of the monotonous tramping of warrior states bent on creating national, political, and even racial uniformity. For an *auditif* like Senghor, the ruthlessly regular cadence of marching would perversely suit a culture that he viewed as obsessed by the rigidities of logic. That cadence also becomes an almost demonic counterpoint both to the wholesome synesthetic confusion of his Joal that smokes with noise and rhapsodies ("les festins funèbres fumant . . . / Du bruit des querelles, des rhapsodies des griots") and to the phonetic irregularities produced by Joal's verbal *métissage.*

The concluding line, however, holds out the possibility of solace and reaffirms the value of recall even in failure. In what is only the poem's second run-on ("où parfois / Apparaît un jazz orphelin"), the verb form *Apparaît* stands out with the special prominence befitting an infrequent apparition that relieves the *marche lasse.* (That the apparition turns out, synesthetically, to be sound should in no way surprise us, of course.) But the solace stems not only from having the beat of the *marche lasse* interrupted by jazz, but also from solidarity. While the suffering poet-Orpheus may have failed to resurrect and unite with an idealized Joal-Eurydice, his very isolation paradoxically promotes union, but of another sort. Through parallels it links him to black people in America—and by implication to all black people—who, as the words "jazz orphelin qui sanglote" suggest, create out of a painful sense of isolation similar to his. Furthermore, insofar as a combination of black African and white American music produced jazz, the latter's sobbing song represents still another form of half-breed recall that creates sounds and rhythms which, in communicating with new beauty about isolation, transcend it. To the extent that recall so communicates, it is redemptive.

We are now in a position to discover that the word *rappeler* has several applications in the poem, all of them tied up in the wordplay *rappeler / re-appeler*. Initially, a recall involved a nostalgic looking back on one's past. But in looking back on the past, one can not only recall (*rappeler*) but also re-call (*re-appeler*) in the sense of 'redefine,' just as Senghor in recalling/remembering Joal re-called/redefined both it and himself, first by idealizing Joal and second by identifying himself with that idealized memory. To rephrase our earlier formulation, Joal recalled/re-called becomes the poet recalling/re-calling himself. The motive behind his nostalgic recall/remembrance was dissatisfaction with a racist present that caused him pain and humiliation. Not unexpectedly, he felt a need to re-call/redefine himself (and so that preponderant part of himself, his past) in a way that would do away with his torment.

What was, however, unexpected was that the re-calling/redefining did not completely repudiate Western civilization, but rather aspired to a *métissage* of African and Western elements. In effect, by recalling/remembering directly and indirectly the blending of various factors from Africa and Europe in an attractive, idealized vision of Joal-self, he was asserting that the mix of both traditions had qualities superior to either one alone. Thus, *métissage* too becomes a recall/re-call: a recall/remembrance of different heritages, as well as a re-call/redefinition of them in new racial, cultural, and religious terms.

The use of language itself in this poem can now be seen as an act of recall/re-call: recall/remembrance, since the poem brings into play historical and cultural recollections implicit in the origins of several of its words; re-call/redefinition, in that Senghor gives the poem's words new meaning by altering their cultural frame of reference. The words in his poem assume a half-breed redefinition, that is, they work in a way that brings his own African and European influences to bear simultaneously on them, thus making them become something unique.

Furthermore, for Senghor who once prepared for the Catholic priesthood and who has a taste for Baudelaire and Claudel, poets sensitive to Roman ritual, recall easily took on sacramental overtones when he recollected the "Tantum Ergo" in a black African setting. He re-called/redefined in terms of Joal's past the symbols of blood-sacrifice behind the Eucharist, the rite of recall par excellence for Catholics. The frame of archetypal reference was no longer the culture of the Biblical Jews but that of animistic Africa. At that point the poem itself, like the sacrament

evoked in the *"Tantum Ergo,"* became an act of sanctifying recall, in that the customs and rituals of Joal, set in a pagan-Catholic vision, were re-called/redefined into new, vivifying symbols rich in spiritual resonance.

As was indicated on the opening page of this discussion, **"Joal"** carries implications for all of Senghor's poetry, insofar as that poem's subject lies at the heart of his source material. It appears warranted therefore to hypothesize that the process of *rappeler/re-appeler* comprises one of the mainsprings of his poetry, and that **"Joal"** is a veiled *ars poetica*. According to the hypothesis, the poet would tend to find his material in an act of recall of his homeland that turns out to be more a re-call of an idealized self. That act, moreover, taking the verbal form of a *rappel métis* cutting across African and European cultures, turns out to be a *re-appel métis* that is the novel, highly personal product of a unique voice. A religious inspiration would impart a sacramental dimension to his poems by recalling animistic and Catholic elements in a re-call that integrates the spiritual archetypes and insights of both traditions.

There is no evidence, however, to indicate that Senghor intended **"Joal"** as an *ars poetica,* and in opposition to the above hypothesis it could be argued that an *ars poetica* is by tradition explicit and overt. But the objection itself highlights a feature of **"Joal"** that constitutes an indispensable aspect of any Senghorian statement of poetic principles: equivocation. Every level of recall/re-call in **"Joal"** depends on equivocation, for it is verbal duplicity that makes *rappeler* function within this poem now in one sense, now in another. In brief, a poetic process hinging on duplicity can appropriately generate a statement of principles that is equivocal in its indirection.

But an even more important kind of duplicity—an emotional ne—offers a better argument for an equivocal *ars poetica*. Equivocation attaches to what stands as the primary emotional drive behind the whole effort of recall/re-call in **"Joal,"** the question of responding to racism. For, on the one hand, Senghor led a relentless fight against racism by passionately expounding *négritude* in the face of claims of black insignificance and by messianically advocating *métissage* as the path to a humane civilization of the future. But on the other hand, he collaborated in racist moments. As a boy in Africa, he had enough reservations about his being *métis* to keep it hidden from his playmates and, as an adult, he senses enough significance in the incident to remember it clearly. Furthermore, as a young man in Europe he made an effort to adapt to, and to become a part of, white culture, and so to repudiate to a certain extent his blackness. In fact, to become the first black African *agrégé* in France, he was obliged to take French citizenship and so to redefine officially his nationality. Finally, many have charged that even Senghor's version of *négritude* stands on white-racist views of blacks.[10]

The majestic leader and would-be prophet whose life's work militates against racism may have found himself incapable of exploring explicitly or even consciously the implications of such moments that, while all too human and very scattered, remain charged with powerful symbolism. The implication of interest here is what appears to be his deep-seated equivocation about self-identity ("Ah! ne suis-je pas assez divisé, **"Poème liminaire,"** *Poèmes*) and about the relative value of blackness and whiteness, of African culture and European culture. The focus of his personality being subject to equivocation, it stands to reason that one of the dynamics of his poetry, in reflecting its creator, would have a slippery core of equivocation, to the point of allowing itself only a cryptic self-definition.

Notes

[1] Léopold Sédar Senghor, *Liberté I: Négritude et humanisme* (Paris: Seuil, 1964), p. 221.

[2] Senghor, *Poèmes* (Paris: Seuil, 1964 and 1973), pp. 13-14. All quotations of his poetry will come from this edition and the page numbers will be incorporated in the text.

[3] For a general treatment of the role of childhood in Senghor's poetry, see Geneviève Lebaud, *Léopold Sédar Senghor ou la poésie du royaume d'enfance* (Dakar: Nouvelles Editions Africaines, 1976)

[4] Michael Crowder, *Senegal, A Study of French Assimilation Policy* (London: Methuen and Co., 1967), p. 10; and Andrea Benton Rushing, "A Note on Senghor's *Signare*," *Umoja*, 3 (Spring 1979), 54-56. For a different interpretation, see Barend van Nierkerk, *The African Image in the Work of Senghor* (Cape Town: A.A. Balkema, 1970), p. 116, n. 63.

[5] For very helpful factual information on references in Senghor's more important poems, see Abiola Irele, ed., *Selected Poems of Léopold Sédar Senghor* (Cambridge: Cambridge University Press, 1977).

[6] Armand Guibert, *Léopold Sédar Senghor*, Collection Poètes d'aujourd'hui, (Paris: Editions Seghers, 1969), p. 6.

[7] Senghor, *Elégies majeures*, suivi de *Dialogue sur la poésie francophone* (Paris: Editions du Seuil, 1979), p. 86; and Senghor, *La Poésie de l'action: Conversation avec Mohamed Aziza* (Paris: Stock, 1980), pp. 91-92.

[8] Jean-Paul Sartre, "Orphée noir," in *Anthologie de la nouvelle poésie nègre et malgache de langue française*, ed. Léopold Sédar Senghor (Paris: Presses Universitaires de France, 1969), pp. ix-xliv.

[9] Janheinz Jahn, *Neo-African Literature: A History of Black Writing*, trans. Oliver Coburn and Ursula Lehrburger (New York: Grove Press, 1969), pp. 244-45.

[10] See, for example, Marcien Towa, *Léopold Sédar Senghor: Négritude ou servitude?* (Yaoundé, Cameroun: Editions Clé, 1971).

Janice Spleth (essay date 1985)

SOURCE: "The Language of Flowers in Senghor's *Lettres d'Hivernage*," in *French Studies in Honor of Philip A. Wadsworth*, edited by Donald W. Tappan and William A. Mould, Summa Publications, 1985, pp. 29-39.

[*In the following essay, Spleth delineates the function of the flower imagery found in Senghor's poetry collection.*]

Published in 1973, **Lettres d'Hivernage** constituted a new phase in Senghor's poetic career which had hitherto been dominated by works that, on some level at least, carried a strong political or cultural message. Every previous collection illustrated various facets of the writer's theory of Negritude or recounted one of the stages in Africa's postwar identity crisis. In **Lettres**, however, the dominant inspiration is the poet's love for a woman, and, while not entirely abandoning the familiar dichotomies of black and white or African and European, he relegates the social issues to the background and concentrates instead on the expression of emotions which are common to us all. R. J. Sherrington describes the new orientation of these poems as ". . . une véritable rénovation, d'une poésie plus personnelle quoique moins ouvertement autobiographique, plus intériorisée et partant plus authentique; ce qui ne l'empêche pas, bien au contraire, d'être aussi plus universelle."[1] Not only does this collection differ from its predecessors in its subject matter, but, perhaps as a consequence of its unusual perspective, it also speaks in its own personal idiom, an immediately obvious characteristic of which is the poet's consistent use of floral imagery.[2]

Certainly, an abundance of nature images is a distinguishing feature of Senghor's style in all of his works, but in **Lettres d'Hivernage**, his references to specific flowers, flowering shrubs, and fruit- and flower-bearing trees are both more frequent and more varied. An actual count has been made which shows that from Senghor's first collection of poems through **Lettres d'Hivernage** there are allusions to thirty-three such plants (including wild jasmine as a flowering shrub), twenty of which appear in **Lettres** and eleven of which, an exact third, appear only in **Lettres**. Furthermore, more total references to flowering plants occur in **Lettres** than in any previous collection.[3] The use of flowers in poetry dedicated to love and feminine beauty is a standard literary device, but Senghor's images rarely serve only as decoration. He repeatedly affirms his concept of the function of images in his discussions of the African esthetic: "L'image dépasse naturellement les apparences pour pénétrer les idées. C'est, du moins, ce que fait, presque toujours, l'image négro-africaine, qui est analogie, *symbole,* expression du monde moral, du sens par le signe."[4] Thus, we should expect a more complex use of images in **Lettres**, one which requires a reading on a deeper level. Although no serious criticism of this work has missed the point that nature images figure importantly in the collection and some have even noted the profusion of flower images, neither has any previous study sought to examine in depth the reasons behind this peculiar feature or to establish its consequences for the work as a whole.[5] It is therefore my purpose here to demonstrate the function of these images, to show, in effect, that, far from simply ornamenting the poems, they play a key role, the understanding of which is essential to an appreciation of the literary strength of **Lettres d'Hivernage**.

The thirty poems which comprise the collection take the form of letters written by the poet to the beloved during a period of separation which coincides with the West African rainy season or "hivernage." The woman, while never named directly by the writer and normally left politely in anonymity by the critics, must surely be Senghor's second wife, Colette Hubert, who regularly chose the humid months of late summer and early autumn to return for a visit to her native Normandy. Her physical description, age, nationality, and relationship to the narrator in the poems leave little doubt as to her identity, but, like the poet, I shall refer to her only in impersonal terms or as Sopé, an African term of endearment by which he identifies her. The major themes of the collection are the poet's love for the woman, their relationship, her absence, his longing. Such simple, intimate concerns stand in marked contrast to Senghor's usual preoccupation with the problems of racism and nation-building. The cycle begins with the woman's departure and the onslaught of the rains; the closing poem announces the arrival of the gentle tradewinds which coincide with the end of the tempests and the promised return of the beloved.

The limited subject and the strictly delineated period of time in which the "drama" unfolds work together to give the poems the extraordinary unity commented on by Hubert de Leusse: "Senghor a mis un soin particulier à la composition des ***Lettres d'Hivernage***. Nul de ses ouvrages antérieurs—sauf peut-être ***Hosties Noires***—ne possède une telle unité dans la variété."[6] To keep us reminded of the seasonal framework which contributes so much to this unified organization, Senghor regularly refers to the way in which the changing weather affects the flora and fauna. The use of floral imagery, at least in this context, cannot be construed as gratuitous but must be considered as a necessary, underlying structural device. In the fourth poem of the collection, for example, the rains have only just begun as the poet observes the changes in nature which parallel their arrival:

> Les roses altières les lauriers roses délacent leurs
>   derniers parfums
> Signares à la fin du bal
> Les fleurs fanent délicates des bauhinias tigrées
> Quand les tamariniers aux senteurs de citron
>   allument leurs étoiles d'or.
> Du ravin monte, assaillant mes narines, l'odeur des
>   serpents noirs
> Qui intronise l'hivernage.[7]

The roses and the bauhinias in decline confirm the poet's mood as established in the preceding poems, for, from the beginning, the woman's absence is a source of anguish tempered chiefly by his thoughts of her. The rose, too, is particularly significant, since, in the course of the collection, it becomes the woman's emblem, and thus it is appropriate that the fading of its flower should occur during the early stages of her absence.

Toward the end of the collection, the first indication that the woman will soon be returning also comes with the poet's noticing yet a further change in nature: "Mais déjà tu t'es annoncée aux marées de Septembre / Forte houle d'odeurs du côté des menthes sauvages." Here, the writer associates the scent of wild mint and advancing of the season which it implies with the time when his separation from the beloved will be ended. In contrast with the earlier passages, however, those images which parallel the arrival of the tradewinds are of a joyous nature:

> Et s'en vinrent les Alizés, et sur leurs ailes lent
>   rythmées
> Comme des pétales de neige et de grâce
> Des papillons blancs axés de noir . . .

Instead of the falling blossoms and threatening serpents in the fourth poem, we have a cloud of graceful butterflies. There are no flowers here, of course, but the poet describes the butterflies as petals and therefore as flower-like.

In the final poem of the cycle, light images, bird song, and the flight of bees herald the return of Sopé, and, along with a repeated reference to the odor of wild mint, there is one last floral image: "Ton parfum toujours ton parfum, de la brousse bordonnant des buissons / Plus exaltant que l'odeur du lys dans sa surrection." The surrection of the lily here in the final lines of the concluding poem mirrors the trope of the dying rose at the beginning of the letters and again reflects the new mood of the poet, elated this time at the prospect of the woman's return. In terms of the season, however, the image of the lily is out of place, and unlike the references to the roses or the wild mint which are real and present, this allusion seems to exist exclusively for its symbolic value. Like the rose, the lily, too, is a plant which denotes Europe rather than Africa; additionally, it is one by which poets traditionally describe fair-complected mistresses. A suitable symbol, then, for the poet's Norman wife, the lily also bears significant association with spring and especially with Easter, and this association has been amply foreshadowed by Senghor in spite of the fact that the actual season here is early fall. He has, indeed, already said that the end of the rainy season reminds him of spring in Europe, and in several instances, he has linked the woman's absence and the time of year with thoughts of death. In **"Et Le Sursaut Soudain,"** for example, he cries out with anguish that he is torn between his fear of death and the horror of living; only the woman's presence can save him: "Toi seule peux me sauver mon espoir . . .". Elsewhere, her eyes are depicted as "forteresses contre la mort," and in yet another poem, he calls her his very being: "Lumière musique senteurs, sens sans qui je ne serais pas." That the poet's imagination should cause him to equate the woman's return with spring, the season of rebirth, and the paschal symbol of the lily provides a fitting finale for the previously developed configuration which linked death, absence, and the season together.

Carrying this analogy a little further, we have little difficulty in seeing in the ***Lettres*** a variation on the archetypal myth of the dying and reviving god or goddess. In Europe, such myths explained the barren seasons of the year as periods of mourning or sorrow for a dead or absent deity who governed fertility and the crops. Frazer's *The Golden Bough* abounds with examples, but the story of Demeter and Persephone is one of the most familiar. The myth cannot be derived from Senghor's poems with complete satisfaction, however, because of the differences in climatic conditions. In spite of the poet's obvious sadness, the tropical foliage remains lush and green as indicated by his frequent references to the heavy perfumes of exotic plants, feminine scents which trouble him by their association with the absent woman. The notion of sterility necessary for the archetypal reading is conveyed only by the poet's attitude toward the season—in the midst of this tropical paradise, he chooses to emphasize the dying roses—or in metaphorical terms when he describes his spirit as "plus dèsert que le Sahara" or his heart as "une fleur séchée" due to the beloved's absence. Obviously, the floral images are essential here to support the depiction of even a figuratively dormant landscape.

In a similar vein, another myth (or type of myth) seems also to have served as Senghor's inspiration for at least one of the pieces in the collection: the myth of Adonis. Tradition has it that when Venus mourned the death of the beautiful young man, either her tears or drops of his blood—depending on the version of the story—were transformed into a new flower, the anemone. (Interestingly, Adonis was also the object of an extensive fertility cult, and Frazer devotes considerable space to his rites.[8]) The reference which recalls the story of Adonis appears in the initial letter where, in the poet's lamenting of the woman's departure, his tears have caused the flowering of the wild jasmine whose scent reminds him of her:

> Et montaient alentour, jaillissant de la lumière de
>   l'ombre
> Blanches et roses, tes odeurs de jasmin sauvage: la
>   *Feretia apodanthera*
> Que dans la nuit mes larmes avaient arrosée.

The implication that the lover's distress might have some creative potential provides a means for understanding the inspiration of the collection as a whole where each poem is, in a sense, a flower born from the writer's longing for the beloved. Here, at least, the floral motif takes on a dimension somewhat beyond its association with the woman and becomes a metaphor for the poetry she inspires.

In addition to the careful meshing of the writer's drama with the arrival and departure of the rainy season, a second unifying feature of the *Lettres* arises, on yet another axis, from the imagery of place. The locus for the writer is Dakar and for the woman, France. To convey these two opposing poles of the world as it is viewed from the standpoint of the poet's personal concerns, Senghor again relies heavily on nature imagery. The previously cited references to the use of non-tropical flowers such as the rose and the lily to denote the woman are indicative. In other instances, the European flora and the African flora are placed in contrast with each other as in **"Ton Soir Mon Soir"** whose very title (and opening line) pave the way for the parallel images: "De la haute terrasse, le parc à mes pieds flamboyant et la mer et Gorée / Et devant toi, les vagues bruissantes des blés sur le versant des terres hautes." In the first verse, the flowering tree, the flamboyant, situates the poet in Dakar, probably in the presidential pal-

ace overlooking the sea which, in the second verse, becomes the sea of grain, the French farmland, which meets the gaze of the woman as he imagines her, too, enjoying the evening but on another continent, in another climate. The juxtaposition of the two landscapes only serves, however, to emphasize the distance between the separated lovers and sets a tone in keeping with the rest of the poem where the man turns to contemplating—with a sense of longing—the lights of the ships in the harbor.

Occasionally, references to the landscape provide the signposts for following the meanderings of the poet's mind. In this sense, they again serve as a structural device. In **"Ta Lettre,"** we are at one moment with the poet in Senegal as he is reading a letter from the woman, but, in the next instant the scene shifts, and he is imagining Europe:

> Je sens le parc en fleurs, les promenades lentes et le
>   sous-bois
> Et les douces fleurs d'ombre, la lumière des
>   cyclamens.
> Je vois l'odeur des roses, l'arôme des vins vieux
>   qui montent
> Et de la plage monte le parfum de ta peau de pain
>   brûlé
> Ta peau d'or rouge. Sourdent les senteurs des
>   jujubiers. . . .

The transition from one continent to another depends chiefly here on the flora, the mentioning of the cyclamen and the rose. Each is native only to the temperate zone, and each has varieties which bloom in France during the period in question—late summer and early autumn. The writer thus indicates to the woman that the intensity of his thoughts of her are so strong that for a brief time they seem to transport him to other regions, but soon the odor of the jujube, a tropical fruit tree which could not grow in Normandy, reminds him that he is separated from her, and the reader realizes that the poet's thoughts have once again returned to Africa.

A final example of nature images used to depict the Europe/Africa dichotomy is to be found in the poem **"Tu Te Languis."** The poet opens this letter by reaffirming the obvious: she misses him and he misses her. He then tells how he anticipates her return at the end of the summer:

> A la fin de l'été, pour chanter tes yeux tes senteurs
>   beauté
> Dieu! que je vête la chape d'or des marronniers,
>   non! pourpre des érables sur les Laurentides
> Ou sous la lune, le long pagne d'opale des
>   peupliers au bord de l'eau.
> Tu viendras, et je t'attendrai à la fin de l'hivernage.
> Sous la rosée qui s'irise, tu seras comme le filao
>   sous une neige de grâce.

Whereas in the previous examples the contrast between tropical and temperate helped to reinforce the theme of separation and the awareness of the distance between the lovers, in this poem, the opposing images have the effect of symbolizing the reunited couple, for the African has taken as his colors the blazing hues of autumn in a cooler climate, while the beauty of his blond mate is described, not by delicate French flowers, but in terms of the tall West African filao tree. Beyond their pictorial effectiveness, these lines in which both the man and the woman are each enriched by being depicted in figures normally associated with the flora typical of the other's country of origin, have a characteristically Senghorian message to impart. On one level, they aptly express the writer's philosophy of "métissage culturel," the synthesizing principle with which the proponent of Negritude early in his career replaced the notion of assimilation and which he used as a powerful defense against the Frenchman's assumption of his own cultural superiority. On another level, however, they reveal as well Senghor's idea of what love should be. In an interview which took place at about the same time as the publication of **Lettres d'Hivernage**, he spoke at length on the subject:

> Je vous renvoie aux pages admirables que le père Teilhard de Chardin a écrites sur le couple et l'amour. Dans l'amour, nous dit-il, il s'agit, pour chacun des deux êtres, de répondre à l'appel de l'Autre, d'aller sur les ondes de l'Autre, de s'identifier à l'Autre, de se perdre dans l'Autre, et, ce faisant, d'assimiler l'*être* de l'Autre. C'est ainsi que les deux êtres se complètent, en s'enrichissant, se dèveloppant réciproquement.[9]

The stress which the writer places on mutuality and reciprocity between lovers makes it necessary to consider the passage quoted from **"Tu Te Languis"** as a great deal more than a circumstantially striking image and to read in it a poetic translation of Senghor's concept of love.

As witnessed by several of the poems previously cited, imagery related to the woman often involves flowers and especially the rose. In one poem, he dreams of her thinking of him as she stands "parmi les rosiers." Elsewhere, a mention of Tinchebray roses evokes an image of her as "une fille au coeur odorant." (Sherrington suggests that the youth of the woman in the image indicates someone else in the poet's life besides his wife, but there seems no reason why it shouldn't be merely a memory of her in days gone by, an idea which makes as much sense as the introduction of a new female interest in the middle of a cycle of poems dedicated to connubial love.[10]) Her hands are described as "pétales de laurier rose," and her letter is "floraison de roses." In conventional French poetry, the appearance of flower metaphors or references to flowers, including roses, in poems praising feminine charms—take Ronsard as a classic example—often operates as a means of calling attention to the ephemeral nature of those charms. In **Lettres**, however, Senghor explicitly announces in his "Argument" that one of his subjects is the figurative interpretation of *hivernage* to mean the woman in the summer or autumn of her beauty. This viewpoint provides yet another possible motive for linking the beloved with the rose, a flower which has a long blooming season and which can blossom even in the autumn. The poem **"Tu Parles"** reassures the woman, who is concerned about her age, that the poet continues to admire her beauty: "J'aime tes jeunes rides, ces ombres que colore d'un vieux rose / Ton

sourire de Septembre, ces fleurs commissures de tes yeux de ta bouche." There is an awareness in these lines that time is passing but, unlike Ronsard, the African poet chooses not to make the woman its victim, and, through the use of floral images, he likens her beauty to that of the autumn gardens of France. Age, in fact, seems to add to her allure in the following passage: "Dans l'arrière-saison, avant que ne soient les vendanges / Jamais mais jamais tu ne seras plus pathétiquement belle." The reference to the harvest, the time which Senghor often associates with death, is unusual in this collection where autumn generally is not used to remind us figuratively of our mortality—as it might be in French Romantic poetry—but rather as a season which, like the woman in her maturity, has a special glory all its own. With respect to Europe, autumn is usually referred to against a floral background; the month of September, for example, is often mentioned in conjunction with the word "floraison" or with roses. Similarly, the end of the rainy season in Senegal has a positive connotation and even reminds the poet, as we have seen, of springtime. Thus, we have nature imagery functioning again in a way which is more than strictly ornamental, this time in a thematic role to convey the poet's admiration for the beauty of a woman who is no longer in her youth.

In *Letters*, the dominant inspiration is the poet's love for a woman, and, while not entirely abandoning the familiar dichotomies of black and white or African and European, he relegates the social issues to the background and concentrates instead on the expression of emotions which are common to us all.

—*Janice Spleth*

Over and above its relevance to the unity of the collection or these particular themes, the depiction of woman as flower or in a setting of flowers is predetermined by at least two other factors peculiar to Senghorian poetics. The first of these derives from the poet's tendency to build his verses around a series of associations normally linked by sensory images. From the first through the last poem of **Lettres**, a triad of sensations—light, music, and perfume—helps to conjure up memories of the beloved. In the case of perfume, the scents of flowers and fruit-bearing trees become the triggering mechanism for inspiring the poem and are instrumental in guiding the poet's thoughts. As a consequence, the allusions to flowers are often olfactory rather than visual, as in the following examples: "les odeurs de jasmin sauvage," "la fragrance des mangues," "les tamariniers aux senteurs de citron," "des jujubiers, ton parfum," "l'odeur des roses," "des orchidées odorantes," "l'odeur du lys." In contrast with the traditional device where the beauty of the woman demands to be depicted in floral similes, in **Lettres**, it is frequently the fragrance of the flower which reminds the poet of the woman and thereby brings the poem into being.

Not only do the flower references emerge naturally out of Senghor's penchant for the use of sensory images, they also result logically from his agrarian background and upbringing and the view of the world they imply:

> The constant recourse to organic and especially vegetal imagery is an indication of a consciousness formed by an agricultural society, and shows the same kind of preoccupation with growth, with an immediate sense of the surge of life in the natural world, characteristic of an animist outlook, to which Senghor's deepest poetic inclinations approximate.[11]

The perspective which Irele describes in the above passage suggests a further function for the nature imagery used to depict the woman in the poem; it also provides a basis for understanding the many other references to flowers and plants throughout the collection, references which do indeed appear to transform the universe into a green and growing thing. Other women besides the beloved are also described as flowers. In his reveries, the man dreams of faraway places which might give him a change of scenery, of Brazil where "les mulâtresses sont des orchidées odorantes." A memory of spring processions during his childhood depicts the women as "froufroutant dans la floraison de leurs rubans." Elsewhere, he imagines sunbathers on French beaches: "le premier soleil sur les corolles des corps blonds." The poet even speaks of himself as if he, too, had affinities with the plant kingdom; he mentions "la sève de mon sang." and tells us that his heart, in the absence of the loved one, bleeds "sur la vigne vierge," that it is like "une fleur séchée" or is the "couleur d'ampélopsis." Flower tropes are not limited, however, to human beings but are liberally scattered throughout the cosmos. He describes the sky as "les espaces noirs fleuris d'étoiles" and the sea as "la mer prodigieuse, où fleurissent tous les poissons." Birds and butterflies are both likened to flowers, and Senghor longs for a child who might draw him pictures of flower-birds ("oiseaux-fleurs"). A relationship seems to exist in the poet's mind between happiness and flowers: Sundays are "une guirlande de bonheurs mêlés," and the promise which the woman asks the poet to make that their life together would be a happy one is depicted as a request for, among other things, "des après-midis en fleurs." Not only does the poet picture the world as a vast garden, but he also describes himself, on occasion, as a simple tiller of the soil. It is only in this humble guise that he allows himself in **"Toujours 'Miroirs'"** to brag a little about his own achievements: ". . . des mots inouïs j'ai fait germer ainsi que des céréales nouvelles, et des timbres jamais subodorés / Une nouvelle manière de danser les formes, de rythmer les rythmes." Maintaining the analogy between himself and a farmer or peasant which is suggested by the verb "germer," the father of Negritude, architect of African independence, and first president of the Republic of Senegal figuratively sums up his contribution: ". . . je fais mûrir les rêves."

The many references to flowers and other plants which occur in *Lettres d'Hivernage* do indeed have the effect of rendering the poems suitably feminine and decorative. As I have shown, however, their function in this particular collection is considerably more sophisticated. In addition to serving as an appropriate emblem for the woman on several levels, floral images help to convey the necessary notions of time and place against which the letters are exchanged and which help to give the poems their remarkable unity. They further provide the writer with a mechanism by which he can give full play to his preference for sensory images, especially olfactory images, and pursue his creative technique of constructing the individual poems by means of a series of associations. Finally, the prominence of botanical terms gives us a glimpse of the way in which Senghor's formation in an agrarian society influences his perception of the world. The special focus of this study has required that some aspects of the collection be neglected or ignored, and, certainly, its beauty and effectiveness depend on a variety of techniques and images. Nevertheless, this analysis clearly proves that an understanding of the role of floral imagery in *Lettres d'Hivernage* contributes substantially to an appreciation of the poems and constitutes an interesting direction from which to approach the collection.

Notes

[1] R. J. Sherrington, "La Femme ambiguë des 'Lettres d'hivernage,'" in *Hommage à Léopold Sédar Senghor: Homme de Culture* (Paris: Presence Africaine, 1976), p. 278.

[2] See Hubert de Leusse, *Des "Poèmes" aux "Lettres d'Hivernage" Senghor, Profil d'une oeuvre,* No. 50 (Paris: Hatier, 1975) for a discussion of other stylistic elements which distinguish this collection, i.e., its vocabulary, pp. 83-84, and its strophic structure, p. 88.

[3] See tables in Gusine Gawdat Osman, *L'Afrique dans l'univers poétique de Léopold Sédar Senghor* (Dakar. Les Nouvelles Editions Africaines, 1978), pp. 117-120.

[4] Léopold Sédar Senghor, "Langage et poësie nëgro-africaine," in *Liberté I: Négritude et Humanisme* (Paris: Seuil, 1964), p. 161.

[5] In addition to the article by Sherrington and the book by Leusse cited above, another work which deals in a major way with *Lettres d'Hivernage* is Lamine Diakhaté, *Lecture libre de Lettres d'Hivernage et d'Hosties Noires de Léopold Sédar Senghor* (Dakar: Les Nouvelles Editions Africaines, 1976).

[6] Leusse, p. 86.

[7] Léopold Sédar Senghor, *Poèmes,* Collection "Points" (Paris: Seuil, 1973), p. 222. Although *Lettres d'Hivernage* also appeared separately in 1973 through Editions de Seuil, I have chosen to cite from the edition which includes most of Senghor's previous works as well because it is more widely available. All further references to *Lettres d'Hivernage* will be taken from this edition and page numbers indicated in parentheses in the text.

[8] See James George Frazer, *The Golden Bough: A Study in Magic and*

Religion (1922; rpt. New York: Macmillan, 1958), pp. 376-403.

[9] Léopold Sédar Senghor quoted in Mohamed Aziza, *Léopold Sédar Senghor: La Poésie de l'action. Conversations avec Mohamed Aziza* (Paris: Stock, 1980), p. 152.

[10] Sherrington, pp. 287-288.

[11] Abiola Irele, ed., *Selected Poems of Léopold Sédar Senghor* (Cambridge: Cambridge UP, 1977), p. 26.

Marin Sorescu with Léopold Sédar Senghor (essay date 1986)

SOURCE: "Thoughts about Poetry," in *Romanian Review*, No. 6, 1986, pp. 72-6.

[*In the following interview, Senghor discusses his creative process, stylistic aspects of his poetry, and the role of politics in his life.*]

Léopold Sédar Senghor: Before writing them, I live my poems. This lasts for a couple of days or weeks and sometimes even for whole years. There are poems I have lived for a long time now but which I have not written yet. When I experience a strong emotion, I am sure I'll write something . . .

Marin Sorescu: *And you begin courting that emotion, that experience.*

Yes, that's right. I seek to preserve it carefully, to capture its vibration . . . I am rather a musical than visual person.

We have arrived at the thorny question of inspiration. All your poems are characterized by musicality, by a particular rhythm. Your pen relies on a generous resonator: Africa. The whole of Africa. It has bequeathed to you ancestral echoes.

Not long ago, I wrote a paper on inspiration. I never make notes on a poem. Let me give you an example. When my friend Pompidou died, I suffered a lot. I would have liked to write a poem. I hesitated, perhaps it was a matter of inhibition, too, thinking that it would be something too political. But, one morning, I suddenly started to write the elegy on Pompidou which I finished at Madras in India, among the blacks of India. This is an example of the strange way inspiration works. Another example. I was on a presidential electoral campaign. In Senegal, poetry and song mean a lot on such occasions. In a locality, several girls welcomed me with an improvised song. To thank them I wrote a poem. Therefore, intimate thoughts get richer with suggestions from outside.

In my opinion, you are a typical case of representative poet. As I have stated before, your poetry feels responsible, in the noblest acceptation of the word, for the destiny of a generous community. A poetry which is permeated by Africa. It is born in Africa and receives nourishment from it. To black people, art is spiritual food par excellence. It is

neither philosophy nor science but poetry that holds the major place. In order to get accomplished, to attain the ideal of beauty, a young girl should also be a poet capable to sing the beauty of her lover. Poets are known all over the country. Poetry confers on one nobility and fame. On the other hand, in my kin, a man is also remarked if he engages in fight, in wrestling, in the village square by a great log fire. But, this is not enough for a young man to be complete. He must also be able to sing and make poems.

This reminds me of the Greeks' rhetoric battles in the agora.

Right. I once told my Senegalese people: we should be black Greece. I have almost a mystical reverence for ancient Greece.

Which is your daily schedule?

I have remained a peasant, I wake up at five a.m. and go to bed early, at ten p.m. From time to time during the day I have a cup of coffee to get refreshed. I write in the morning from about 8:30 to 12:30. In the afternoon, I dictate letters or read. (laughing) I really am a peasant.

An African peasant, of course.

Yes, I am very African, too. After breakfast, I take a quarter-of-an-hour nap. It is a Mediterranean and African manner of dividing the day by a little rest.

Let us pass from the Greeks to the Romans in order to get to the Romanians. I know you visited Romania.

Yes, when I was president. I was very delighted by your country. I do not state this out of courtesy. The Romanians are very close to the Romans not only by their name but also by the customs I could note there and, of course, by their language. As a former professor of Greek and Latin, I state this in full knowledge of the case.

Besides the vocabulary, the Romanian language has preserved from the Latin language from which it evolved also virtues of logic and clarity.

There is in Senegal a classic department where students have to choose between Latin-Greek and classic Arabian. Thirty-five per cent choose Latin and Greek. In the Greek department, all teachers are Muslim women. But we also learn other languages, as well, among which Russian. We learn all neo-Latin languages, English, German, Russian. I am the president of the Asturias society where Latin-American and African cultures are studied. I intend to include in our curriculum the neo-Latin countries in the Mediterranean.

Do not forget Romanian. We are Mediterranean through Pontus Euxinus and the Latin of Ovid whom I regard as the first Romanian poet.

That's what I wanted to say: I shall not forget neo-Greek and Romanian which actually deserve to be included in this circuit to a greater extent. Think of me as of a good friend of Romania.

Returning to poetry. I am in an African country for the first time. It is a fascinating world which I would like to know better. Here, on African soil, I think I understand better certain aspects in your poetry. I understand better the importance you attach to rhythm, to polyphony. Then, there is in your poetry a certain energy: an energy both mysterious and transparent. Mysterious because it is poetry, transparent because through it one can see a deep, highly-humanistic message. I consider Senghor's work as a praise brought to everyday Africa. To the humble Africa of ordinary people. The right to art and life of all tribes. In a way your poetry is Whitmanian: it is the poetry of a continent. How do reverie, contemplation coexist with this earthy, vitalizing energy? Both these aspects are visible, in my opinion, in everything you write. A contemplation that is self-delighted but that also generously turns into a stream for others. How do you do it?

I shall answer by first telling you something from the biography of my writing. As it usually happens, I began to write while in high-school imitating the poets I was reading. Romantics and symbolists.

I think it was a good school.

Exactly. At thirty-five, I was a teacher of French, Latin and Greek. Then I burnt all my poems.

Why?

Because they were very French! I realized that in order to be myself I had to take another road. I returned to the school of the African popular poets and analysed their style. This really was in harmony with myself. I embraced to an ever greater extent a new aesthetics, that of African blacks, based on image, melody and rhythm. When I write a poem, melody, alliteration and assonance come naturally. (Smiling) When I write a speech I have to delete a lot of words because they are poetic imagery.

Yes, rhythm is almost everything in my case. It comes much like imagery, quite spontaneously. When I read a completed poem once, twice I realize that sounds, alliterations, everything got organized under the impact of a rhythm which I should call inner. An instinctive, inborn rhythm. Perhaps Senegalese is a descendant of the language of the old Egyptians. Anyhow it is related to it. In old times, blacks lived all over Africa. Ancient conquests, especially Germanic ones—Vandals, Ostrogoths—pushed the blacks to the interior. They "whitened" the Mediterranean coast. There is a kinship between the languages of southern India and those in Africa. Agglutinated languages. In Africa there are two races. From the Mediterranean to the jungle-one. From there throughout the jungle another one. Pygmies. I have had a passion for sociological anthropology. By profession I am a professor not a politician.

Our talk is occasioned by the Seventh World Congress of Poetry which has brought here representatives of all continents.

Morocco was a deliberate choice because it is a bridge between Arabians and Blacks. Moroccans are metis.

When reading Aristophanes, I had the impression that I was in my village. In the beginning I didn't know why, Then I realized that the chorus was accountable for it. The chorus danced and spoke rhythmically, A kind of local Aristophanes is still played in our villages. The roots of this art are very old. Physicians, too, have understood the importance of rhythm. One means of healing a person with a nervous problem was to make him dance. Rhythm is to be found in prayers, too. That is why I attach so much importance to rhythm in poetry as well. For this reason I endeavour to write a polyphonic poetry.

As a student at the Paris Institute of Ethnology, I learned there was no poetry in African oral literatures but only 'rhythmic prose' (as if poetry were not defined exactly like that). One day, studying Senegalese poems, as I told you, I started setting them in mathematical formulae. Their metrics is perfect. Reality is more complex than that. There may be counterpoints and syncopes in verses, that is silent moments. Silence is part of poetry, too.

In your opening paper you referred to polyphony.

In Black Africa, folk song always means song in several voices; André Gide was one of the first to note this. It is a feature of the whole continent. As regards poetry, it can be in turn sung or psalmodized. When it is psalmodized, what counts for the rhythm is not the number of syllables but the number of stressed syllables. This also happened in the old Egyptian poetry or in the old Semitic or Germanic poetry.

You referred to the 'revolution of 1889'. What do you mean by that?

It is the date when Bergson's *Essai sur les données immediates de la Conscience* was published. I think it is an important date because it changed the angle wherefrom literature and art were regarded. Intuitive reason prevailed over discursive reason again. I say again because the Greeks, Plato and Aristotle knew that. Thanks to this 1889 revolution, Africa could enter the concert of nations with its aesthetic values influencing, as it is known, plastic arts—cubism and expressionism. In poetry, it influenced—surrealism. Not to mention music, the Negro spiritual, jazz, blues. Spreading all over the world, this melos, accompanied by the new techniques, brought about a new spiritual life.

You mentioned a beautiful Senegalese definition of poetry: words that enchant the heart and ear. Therefore, the heart is touched via the ear. Poetry must possess a great musical loading . . . A rhythmic spell. Do you consider African rhythm as repetitions which are not repeated?

Indeed, the same word, the same syntagma, the same expression is repeated but not in the same manner. Something is permanently added. The word is placed in another part of the line or is slightly altered. I exemplified this by a hymnic poem from Senegal. The same can be remarked about the Egyptians.

In folk literature, curses and charms follow the same principle, having cores of words, that recur, striking the ear. Your poetry draws on this archaic layer, lost long ago in the too polished literatures, that orchestrates the wealth of artistic means oferred by tradition into a polyphony that truly delights the ear and heart.

. . . . .

Obviously, Mr. Léopold Sédar Senghor is an uncommon collocutor, an ideal partner for a talk about poetry. He is an experienced writer, a connoisseur of African poetic tradition from the interior of the magic circle and of European tradition also from the interior of the circle, we may call it magic, too, but of a more "rationalist" magic, seeking, as already remarked, a synthesis of the two; he also has a keen theoretical appetite for suchlike matters. He feels at home in theory. He is fully entitled to favour, in the positive acceptation of the word, the experience of his continent which is said to have been the first cradle of mankind, the place where man rose to his bipedal condition. A continent of bamboo and ivory, preserving a living antiquity and a genuine oral classicism which disappeared in other parts two thousand years ago. Through the tradition he defends like a gladiator using a flower, present-day artistic Africa is contemporary with Hesiod, the Greek tragics, Vergil and Ovid. The primordial word floating above waters, caught into the enchanted branch of a palm tree after the waters withdrew or fell and hid in the empty space of a tom-tom. It is sufficient for a well-stretched goatskin, a well-tanned snakeskin or God knows what other skin of a genius or elf stretched on a riddle frame or drum to be touched by the fingers of the trance-fallen singer that the wonder, pinched into its face, should revive and rise to the sky. But not before passing through the souls of the listeners. The wonder of creation which is equally music, dance and poetry.

The man who is Senghor, with his prominent forehead and thick, slightly greyish hair is discreet, modest and punctual like a solar clock or a sand glass. A famous man capable to laugh and to be moved, like any other man, by a show.

A few days afterwards, I attended a homage-paying afternoon and could listen to his poems recited in several languages. Whereas the voice of their author is somewhat neutral, blank, intellectual, the voice of his poems bursts forth filling you with instinct and temperament. The words seem to be augmented by an unseen amplifier, to mark the rhythm and seize you, attracting you into the dance. A dance in which the lips also take part, whispering and the nerves discharge their electricity, producing a sweet pleasure. "I have come into the world to bring joy" stated our Brancusi. The essence of true art is to produce joy. Senghor's poetry has rehabilitated the tom-tom. In it, things regain their hollows, asperities and angles and become creators of echoes. Wind and string instruments have their share in this vast poetry. But, it is chiefly created for the most polyphonic instrument: the human heart.

Janice Spleth (essay date 1993)

SOURCE: "The Political Context of Senghor's 'Elégie pour Georges Pompidou'," in *Critical Perspectives on Léopold Sédar Senghor*, edited by Janice Spleth, Three Continents Press, 1993, pp. 217-28.

[In the following essay, Spleth contends that Senghor's poem denotes his expanding political horizons.]

Senghor's early poems are united in their political vision by the challenges and dreams characteristic of the end of the colonial period. They focus on the injustices of a specific political system and look forward to the creation of a new egalitarian society. With the coming of independence to Senegal in 1960 and the restructuring of the global political reality, many of the constraints that shaped the old visions had weakened or disappeared entirely, and it is only to be expected that in his later poetry, the poet-president, reacting to this transition, would reflect new political perspectives and begin to develop a new vision of the future. The volume of poetry entitled *Elégies majeures* and published in 1979 shortly before Senghor's retirement as president of Senegal contains six fairly long poems written during the period since independence, including the **"Elégie pour Georges Pompidou."**[1] This eulogy for France's leader contains some moving and memorable lines on the subjects of friendship, courage, and death, but woven into the text—sometimes incongruously and even a bit awkwardly—are numerous allusions to the writer's own expanding political horizons and to the kaleidoscope of changing patterns in international politics as they relate to an emerging Third World country.

Written in 1974 after the French president's death in office from Waldenström syndrome, this elegy is considerably more than the official poetry that could logically be expected given the circumstances. The friendship between Senghor and Pompidou was personal and longstanding, dating from their years together as students at the Lycée Louis-le-Grand. In his article, "Lycée Louis-le-Grand, haut lieu de culture française," Senghor describes his memories of that period:

> "Pourquoi ne pas le dire? l'influence de Georges Pompidou sur moi a été, ici, prépondérante. C'est lui qui m'a converti au Socialisme, qui m'a fait aimer Barrès, Proust, Gide, Baudelaire, Rimbaud, qui m'a donné le goût du théâtre et des musées. Et aussi le goût de Paris. Je me rappelle nos longues promenades. . . ."[2]

Before the war, Senghor had vacationed at Château-Gontier, the family home of Pompidou's wife, and the poem is dedicated to her. During World War II when Senghor was a prisoner-of-war in France, it was to Pompidou that he managed, via a sympathetic prison guard, to send the manuscript of his war poems, the future *Hosties noires* (1948), and **"Prière de paix,"** the final poem in that collection, is dedicated to Georges and Claude Pompidou. Despite political differences, the friendship endured, as Pompidou attests in his introduction to a biography of Senghor: "La suite assez extraordinaire de nos vies n'a rien changé aux sentiments qui nous unissaient. Nos lettres quand j'étais chef de Gouvernement et lui chef d'Etat, nous aurions pu les écrire au temps des copains . . ."[3]

Later, with each serving as president of his country, they continued to enjoy a special relationship. In his interview with Mohamed Aziza, published in 1980, Senghor had commented frankly on his relationship with Pompidou: "Il a été, de son vivant, mon meilleur ami français vous le savez. Jamais pendant sa vie et sur le plan individuel, je n'ai surpris son amitié en défaut."[4]

Divided into seven parts, the elegy begins with an introductory section relating the circumstances surrounding the composition of the poem—a presidential trip to Asia—and Senghor's own intense grief on the death of his friend. He poignantly recalls his last meeting with Pompidou shortly before his death, describes his courageous battle with his fatal illness, and asks him, in the name of a love for all humanity, to intercede with Heaven on behalf of the world's suffering. Finally, Senghor reflects on a visit to Pompidou's grave before closing the poem with lines that return to the present. Above and beyond the writer's honest intention to pay his last respects to an old friend, however, there are elements here that are politically revealing, and Senghor has placed this memorial to the French statesman against a background of global change which suggests that Senghor's own long association with France is being challenged by other interests and new priorities.

Politics, especially the politics of the relationship between France and Africa, frame most of Senghor's work. The self-affirming poetry of *Chants d'ombre* (1945) had been formulated in reaction to the failure of France's assimilation policy which, among its other consequences, characteristically devalued African culture. As Crowder puts it, "Africans were considered to be a people without history, without any civilization worthy of the name, constantly at war with one another and fortunate to have been put in touch with the fruits of French civilization."[5] In poems like **"Nuit de Sine"** and **"Que m'accompagne kôras et balafong,"** Senghor effectively refuted those assumptions. In *Hosties noires*, published in 1948 after Senghor's election to the French National Assembly in 1946, his response to colonialism had evolved to reflect a more active political commitment as he sought to exact a fairer treatment of the African colonies in recognition of the sacrifices they had made in support of France during the war. The rapport with France is thematically less important in *Ethiopiques* (1956) where poems such as **"Messages," "Teddungal"** and **"L'Absente"** were inspired by Senegalese elections as Senghor worked to build a new political base at home, but the simplified notion of the world as confrontation largely between African and Western values continued to be dramatized in **"A New York," "Chaka,"** and **"Epîtres à la Princesse."** Virtually all of the elegies in *Nocturnes* (1961) betray the writer's political concerns: in **"Elégie de minuit,"** the poet considers the burden of leadership, and in **"Elégie des circoncis,"** he anticipates the coming of independence. **"Elégie des saudades,"** celebrates the Portuguese role in Africa, and **"Elégie des eaux"** is a prayer for pardon that includes France only as one of several troubled lands in need of the rain that, in the poem, symbolized God's blessing: "Il pleut sur Moscou et sur Pompidou, sur Paris et banlieue, sur Melbourne sur Messine sur Morzine / Il pleut sur l'Inde et sur la Chine—quatre cent mille Chinois sont noyés, douze millions de Chinois sont sauvés, les bons et méchants." These lines demonstrate Senghor's expanding geographical focus; they also anticipate the juxtaposition of Pompidou with China and India in **"Elégie pour Georges Pompidou."**

The decreasing visibility of France in *Ethiopiques* and *Nocturnes* testifies to the growing tendency on the part of French-speaking Africans—with independence imminent—to see their continent in a broader international framework, although France's actual political role vis-à-vis most of her former colonies obviously continues to be tremendously important after 1960. Both the positive and negative nuances of that relationship are subtly defined in the poems of *Elégies majeures*. Within this 1979 collection, Senghor reveals a great deal about Senegal's dealings with France in two poems eulogizing French citizens. In addition to the poem for Pompidou, **"Elégie pour Jean-Marie"** (1968), the second poem in the collection, also mourns the death of a Frenchman, a young participant in France's development program in Africa. While most of the poem is of a highly personal nature, it is preceded by a more general dedication to the French volunteers, **"Coopérants du contingent,"** and at one point, the poet acknowledges the positive value of their efforts. He begins by addressing Jean-Marie:

> Tu nous as partagé ton savoir louis d'or, ne laissant rien pour toi
> Pour nous moquer et dominer.
> Je te bénis toi Jean-Marie, je bénis les bataillons de tes compagnons
> Dans la communion des hommes des âmes, des nations et des confessions
> Et il n'y a plus, sur toute la surface de la terre, une seule terre ignorée.
> Béni soit ton pays et ta patrie. . . . [6]

The prayer offered in these lines is not only for Jean-Marie, as an individual, but for the organization he had represented and for the country that had sponsored him. The official nature of the dedication and the poet's tendency to turn this particular occasion for gratitude into a general recognition of the contribution of the *Coopération* enthusiastically affirms the political and economic ties that Senegal retains with France. The poem is dated only eight years after independence.

The inclusion in *Elégies majeures* of a poem dedicated to the *Coopération* reflects the economic importance of Senegal's relationship with France during the early years of nationhood. We are told that "Senegal's special relationship with France has probably been closer than that between any other metropolitan authority and its former colonial state in Africa."[7] Cooperation agreements with France had been signed in 1960 shortly after independence, and between 1960 and 1966, France contributed 85% of the total bilateral foreign aid to Senegal where foreign aid constituted 40% of the annual national budget.[8] French development personnel in Africa included servicemen who had opted to work in the cooperation program during their obligatory period of military service; the number of these volunteers in Senegal had increased from 65 in 1964 to 169 in 1967.[9] But aid agreements with France were not without strings: the French maintained an important military presence in Senegal and continued to wield influence over various aspects of the society, including the direction of the University of Dakar. The close relationship which France maintained with its former colony during the De Gaulle presidency was, in fact, the source of a good deal of resentment. When strikes and riots broke out in 1968, "the agitation and unrest in Dakar during this period was in large part triggered by popular resentment over French political, economic, and cultural domination."[10]

The next decade of independence would consequently bring some changes in the tenor of the relationship between Senegal and France. The year 1968, in fact, can be considered an important political turning point. It marks the end of what Sheldon Gellar describes as the first phase of Senegal's foreign policy, the era of De Gaulle. Under his successor, Georges Pompidou (1969-1974):

> France showed more flexibility and less paternalism in dealing with the francophone African states . . . The 1974 revisions of postindependence Franco-Senegalese cooperation agreements reduced the size of the French military contingent in Senegal, transferred French military bases to Senegalese sovereignty, and stepped up the Africanization of the University of Dakar. These were all measures long demanded by Senegaleses nationalists, and their implementation provided tangible signs of the evolution away from the paternalism of the past.[11]

The period between the writing of **"Elégie pour Jean-Marie"** and the death of Pompidou had thus been characterized by the development of a certain political distance between France and Senegal, and Senghor's eulogy for the statesman bears witness to this reservation concerning things French.

It is interesting, first of all, to note the penultimate position of the poem in the collection. Diplomatic protocol could hardly call for the placing of the President of France at the end of a line that includes a young cooperant, Martin Luther King, and Habib Bourguiba—alphabetically France would be seated before Tunisia. Neither is the position of the poem, dated 1974, justified by chronology in as much as it was apparently written before the **"Elégie de Carthage,"** dated 1975, which it follows. Perturbing, too are the poem's opening lines: "Et j'ai dit non! je ne chanterai pas César / Je ne chanterai pas le foie de l'Arverne, ni sa queue ruisselante d'alezan" (313). The identification here of Pompidou with Caesar is especially significant in the light of the rivalry created in the previous poem **"Elégie de Carthage"** between the Berbers on one hand and Rome, as the symbol of the West, on the other; in glowing terms, Senghor had, in that poem, sung the praises of the heroes of Carthage—Dido, Hannibal, and Jugurtha, all of whom had met tragedy at the hands of Rome. Senghor elaborates on this refusal to sing about Caesar by telling us that he would prefer to praise Amilcar Cabral, the leader of the

forces opposing the Portuguese colonial government in Guinea-Bissau; but the poet is obsessed with the death of his friend, and it is as a friend and not as a head of state or Caesar that Pompidou is remembered.

After the initial prefatory stanza, the first word of the second stanza, where Pompidou is first characterized, is *ami* and the last word is *amitié*. Senghor's early outline of *Elégies majeures*, had summarized this poem as follows: "C'est l'amitié et l'amour pour les deux races c'est aussi la réconciliation."[12] The extent to which he succeeded in his objective is indicated by a review of the collection in which Raymond Darricau went as far as to rank this poem among the great texts on friendship that have appeared throughout the ages.[13] Thus, in the placement of the poem, in the reservations expressed in the opening lines, and in the clearly established emphasis on the personal, not official, inspiration of the poem, Senghor appears to recognize that this is a politically inauspicious poem to write, that an expression of sympathy on the occasion of the death of a French leader will be interpreted in certain quarters as evidence that he continues to remain within the French sphere of influence. This reservation is explicitly articulated by Senghor, discussing Pompidou in his interview with Aziza: "Sa mort a été, pour moi, un traumatisme . . . Au lendemain de sa mort, j'avais pensé écrire une élégie pour lui, mais je me suis dit que ce serait mauvais: un poème politique!"[14] Stylistically, he appears to be trying to avoid certain political implications. Whereas **"Elégie pour Jean-Marie"** had sought to extend the praise for the individual to his sponsoring nation, "Elégie pour Georges Pompidou," dated six years later, makes a visible effort not to allow this tribute to Pompidou, based on friendship, to be mistaken for a tribute to the government he headed.

Politics, especially the politics of the relationship between France and Africa, frame most of Senghor's work.

—Janice Spleth

At the same time that the writer resists being associated with the French, the very circumstances of the poem draw him inevitably into association with the countries of the Third World, especially with China and India. The poem is in fact composed during an official state visit to the Orient, and the places of composition identified at the end of the text are Peking and Madras (1974). That an African leader would undertake such a pilgrimage to the capitals of two important Third World powers points to the increasing importance of practical nonalignment in Senegal's foreign policy. The circumstances of composition undoubtedly account for the unusual preponderance of Oriental motifs in a poem dedicated to a man who could have been presented as a function of French civilization, a focus which the poet studiously avoids. France had of course supported the People's Republic in its bid for entrance to the United Nations, and early recognized the legitimacy of the government. Pompidou had actually been in office in 1971 when the PRC was finally admitted to the world community of nations, and his efforts to cultivate favorable relations with China legitimize the Oriental references to some extent, but the poet's insistence on the Eastern background must also be regarded as a logical consequence of Africa's own new-found kinship with other developing regions throughout the world.

During the same period when Senegal was seeking to reduce French domination of its affairs, Senghor was thus discovering the need for solidarity with other Third World nations as illustrated in this excerpt from a 1961 speech in which he addresses the issue of disparity between North and South:

> Faced with this situation, how must we react, we of the Third World, we the proletarian nations? We must admit that, until now, we have not reacted: we were content to vituperate singly, "imperialism, colonialism, and neocolonialism." As if words, even words of vengeance, could kill this three-headed hydra. As for me, I see only one strategy which is efficient in resolving the problem: let the entire Third World, all proletarian nations, unite. Not to insult but to talk; at first among themselves and then, united in a common front, with the rich nations. To enter into dialogue, of course, but also to act in concert.[15]

Subsequently Senegal cosponsored the 1968 UN Conference on Trade and Development held in New Delhi which was preceded by a preparatory meeting of poor nations the year before in Algiers, again at the instigation of Senegal. This group, comprising most of the nations of Asia, Africa, and Latin America, was united behind economic priorities that became the basis for the New International Economic Order requested by the Third World in 1974. In the meetings of unaligned countries, Senegal emerged as a powerful moderate voice.

Senghor's decision to place the elegy against the background of his Asian travels comes at the time of his own shifting cultural horizons. He had long commended the value of sharing between cultures. In the face of France's notorious claims to cultural superiority and the Nazi pretensions of racial superiority, Senghor has affirmed an alternative view of humankind in his concept of *métissge* 'cultural crossbreeding':

> Il n'est pas question de détruire la civilisation l'une de l'autre; il est question en effet d'intégration, d'assimilation active et réciproque: de symbiose. Il ne s'agit pas de corrompre, comme le dit Mauriac, ni la civilisation européenne, ni les civilisations exotiques . . . Mais de faire une greffe pour obtenir des fruits succulents parce que métis, d'aboutir selon l'expression de Frobenius, à un "accord conciliant" entre l'Homme et la nature, et entre tous les hommes.[16]

Drawing from a model similar to Teilhard's notion of the future of humanity as a Universal Banquet to which all cultures would contribute,[17] his elaboration of an African personality represented an attempt to define what Black peoples would contribute to such an amalgam. In the earliest writing, however, the "Universal" Banquet consisted rather narrowly of France on one side of the table and Africa on the other with little reference to any other peoples. In the period after independence in his new capacity as statesman, Senghor's view of the world expands considerably; the inclusion in this collection of a poem that celebrates however obliquely two great civilizations of Asia reflects this new perspective and the new political tendencies associated with it. The suggestion for musical accompaniment that precedes the poem, itself an example of the symbiosis advocated by the philosopher of Negritude, indentifies the four cultures that are brought together to provide the poet with his imagery and reads: "pour orchestre symphonique, dont un orgue et des instruments négro-africain, chinois et indien." Among the various oriental allusions, several are especially successful poetically. A visit to the Great Wall of China in the first stanza anticipates a reference in the second stanza to racial and ideological barriers when the poet affirms: "Ami, si je te chante par-delà les haines de race et delà les murs idéologies / C'est pour bercer l'enfant blanc." Later, the poet blends two cultures when he represents his friend's suffering as a dragon, a conventional motif from Chinese mythology and a suitable metaphor with which to identify the antagonist of a man whose patron saint is the Saint George of Celtic legends. Finally, he compares his poem as a memorial to friendship with the Taj Mahal, a monument that he finds disappointing, "si froid pour un amour si grand." These references pay homage to Eastern culture and demonstrate concretely that the West is not alone in making important contributions to the Universal Banquet of nations.

When asked by Aziza about the most pressing demands of the Third World, Senghor responded that the first priority was in fact cultural: "Il est nécessaire, pour bâtir la civilisation panhumaine du XXIᵉ siècle, que les cultures du Tiers-Monde soient reconnues par l'Euramérique, comme des cultures différentes, mais complémentaires, qui doivent participer au Dialogue, commencé, en rélité, depuis les découvertes de la Renaissance."[18] The second priority he mentions in the same interview is economic, the creation of a new economic order that corrects the imbalances between rich and poor nations.[19] In addition to exemplifying the cultural values of the Third World—its music, its engineering and architectural achievements, its mythology, and elsewhere its religion, the elegy also touches on the economic imperative and the necessity of dealing with existing disparities.

For Senghor, a poem is not merely a literary work; in the spirit of the African tradition that attributes magic power to the spoken word, Senghor's poetry seeks to effect changes in the real world. The poet therefore becomes an alchemist, the Master of the Word. Senghor's poetic opus is replete with poems that are also prayers, that are a ritual act of naming, or that reiterate imperative verbs in order to command the very forces of the cosmos. In **"Elégie pour Georges Pompidou,"** the fifth stanza contains such a prayer, an invocation which seeks to effect a change in the state of things. The poet calls upon his friend, who has surely been admitted to Paradise, to intercede in the name of the love he had for humanity, with Saint George, the slayer of dragons, on behalf of the suffering people of the world:

Donc bénissez mon peuple noir, tous les peuples à
   peau brune à peau beige
Souffrant de par le monde, tous ceux que tu relevas
   fraternel, ceux que tu honoras
Qui étaient à genoux, qui avaient trop longtemps
   mangé le pain amer, le mil le riz de honte les
   haricots:
Les Nègres pour sûr les Arabes, les Juifs avec, les
   Indo-Chinois les Chinois que tu as que j'ai visités
—Pour les Grands blancs aussi pendant que nous y
   sommes, priez, avec leurs super-bombes et leur
   vide, et ils ont besoin d'amour.

At this point in the poem the syntax changes from the imperative characteristic of a prayer to the language of a vision:

Et je vois les Indiens, qui préfigurent l'homme
   trinitaire, dans l'aurore nouvelle d'iridium
Je vois les Latino-Américains, leurs frères sur
   l'autre face du monde
J'entends les appels des trompettes de toutes les
   angoisses
De toutes les souffrances pour qui tu offris tes
   souffrances.

This benediction for those who suffer places the nonwhite races of the world first, those peoples who have known oppression or the yoke of colonialism. Through the magic of words and images, Senghor has transformed this poem on the death of his French friend into a plea to alleviate the suffering of the peoples of the Third World, a rite of expiation in which the suffering of the one is offered in exchange for reducing that of the other, a form of sacrifice that could emerge either from Senghor's Catholicism or from traditional African religions. In spite of the poet's avowed intentions to commemorate his friend, the urgency of global concerns rises to the surface.

Without specifically designating responsibility for the situation—without pointing an accusing finger at the haves, Senghor makes himself the advocate for the have-nots of the world as he bemoans the human misery inflicted by want and exploitation. While the platform of the world's poorer nations has increasingly been an economic one, the original unifying element of the nonaligned had been the common fear of the newly independent states in the face of the nuclear arsenals of the world's two opposing ideologies.[20] Thus the white races, included only parenthetically in the poet's prayer, are represented exclusively in their role as the potential purveyors of nuclear disaster. The attitude here echoes Senghor's warnings against nuclear war in other poems, such as **"Epîtres à la Princesse"** and **"Elégie des Eaux."** The **"Elégie pour Martin Luther King,"** also included in *Elégies majeures*, expresses similar reservations concerning the super powers, who tremble at night "sur leurs silos profonds de bombes et de tomb-

es". The incantatory power of the poet thus crystallizes the statesman's vision and reflects the importance of both economic issues and world peace among his political priorities. This prayer, which overlays the poet's expression of sympathy for the suffering of one courageous individual with a request for divine intervention on behalf of the world, is not, incidently, an original part of the **"Elégie pour Georges Pompidou"**; according to Renée Tillot, it appears only in the fourth version of the poem supplied by the poet.[21]

Any irony that might first be perceived in Senghor's emphasis on the Third World in a poem commemorating Pompidou evaporates quickly when we remember that, to a very large extent, the development of the Third World as a balancing factor in global politics was itself a French concept promoted by De Gaulle and then by his successors and that criticism of America's nuclear arsenal was also a standard component of French political rhetoric during the period.[22] Senghor's new inclinations toward the Orient must therefore be regarded, at least in part, as a legitimate outgrowth of his affiliation with De Gaulle and Pompidou. This political background helps justify the virtually organic relationship established in the elegy between Pompidou's passing and Senghor's new awareness of other cultures. Framed within the familiar pattern of death and rebirth that appears so frequently in Senghor's poems, this cyclical notion is supported by the insistant and reoccuring references to spring. It is a spring wind that ruffles the red flags of China in the first stanza, an indication of the season in which the poem is written but also an appropriate image for celebrating the inauguration of new bonds of friendship. The account of the visit to the French president's grave is dominated by signs of spring that accompany the awakening of new life. The relationship between spring and death derives logically from the emphasis on life after death as depicted in the fourth stanza of the poem or from viewing death as a relief from a winter of suffering, but spring has often served Senghor, too, as a metaphor for a future political reality. In contrast with earlier poems such as **"Chant de Printemps,"** where the poet can only look forward to the dawn of a new era after the sacrifices of war, or **"L'Absente,"** in which future political victory is evoked through images of the coming of spring, the poet describes spring in the elegy as being physically present, suggesting that even personal grief cannot mar the poet's joy in being alive and in participating in the period which has been so long awaited and for which the sacrifices were made. The actual date of Pompidou's death, April 2, prompts an explicit juxtaposition of life and death as the poet laments that it is sad to die "par un jour de printemps, où la lumière est d'or blanc / Et que les jambes vous fourmillent de danses et de chansons". Another reference to dance, one with implicit death/rebirth connotations, concludes the elegy, which is offered to Pompidou as a poem against death, "une libation . . . que danse élancé le Seigneur Shiva". The Dancing Shiva of Hinduism depicts the god who, acording to some sects, created the world by dancing and destroys it in the same way at the end of time. The poem thus ends with yet another tribute to Asian culture and on a reference to the eternal process of renewal that invites interpretation on several levels: an apt device for evoking the creative potential of the poem, a reference to Senghor's own belief in an afterlife, and, at the same time, an image emphasizing the pattern of changes characteristic both of individual lives and of relations between states.

At the beginning of the elegy, Senghor, motivated by friendship and loyalty, demonstrates a need to come to grips with the subject of Pompidou's death, but the situation becomes increasingly infused with personal and political implications for the poet, and as he confronts his work, he also confronts the changes taking place in his own environment. Most of the poem is written in the second person with the narrator addressing his friend with the familiar *tu,* this use of apostrophe serving—as it does characteristically in Senghor's work—to allow the narrator to explore his own feelings.[23] Once divided between French and African cultures—between Isabelle and Soukeïna— the great advocate of *métissage* had over the years reconciled the validity of both cultures in his own life, but this more recent poem demonstrates his increasing openness to other cultures as well, and in the first stanza, he even speaks of taking refuge in his *siniguitude.* The memory of an old friendship is subtly linked to new ones: when the poet describes himself as Pompidou's "comrade" in the second stanza, he is reiterating his use of the term in the initial stanza where he recalls speaking with one of the heroes of China's cultural revolution: ". . . je causais avec le camarade Tchen Yong-kouei, sa pureté bien nouée sur la tête / Debout sur les collines de la brigade de Tatchai". This broadening of the poet's personal horizons mirrors changes in his political focus and reflects the increasing sense of solidarity between new African nations and the other developing countries of the Third World. The decades of opposition to colonialism had, to a very large extent, limited Senghor's political activity to issues engaging only Africa and France; with independence, he was beginning to view his country's role in terms of the larger struggle between North and South and to seek allies for mutual concerns. Themes that appear in the poem—the economic welfare of the world's poor and exploited and the dangers posed by the Cold War and the threat of nuclear disaster—are by 1974 important priorities on the president's political agenda. While the prayer in **"Elégie pour Jean-Marie"** that blesses the French for their aid to underdeveloped countries is in no way incompatible with the prayer in **"Elégie pour Georges Pompidou"** that asks a blessing on the world's poor, it might even be possible to infer a pattern of change within the collection itself parallel to changes in Senghor's political philosophy from 1968 to 1974 as Senegal sought greater autonomy with respect to France. This later poem makes it clear that if the poet-president has past allegiances to France of a personal nature, as a leader of an independent African state, he also has new loyalties—to the struggles for independence by those like Amilcar Cabral, to Third World countries like China and India which share his interests, and to all of the underprivileged of the world.

Notes

[1] When *Elégies majeures* was republished in the new version of *Poèmes* (Paris: Seuil, 1984), it included a seventh poem, the "Elégie pour Phil-ippe-Maguilen Senghor."

[2] *Liberté I: Négritude et humanisme* (Paris: Seuil, 1964) 405.

[3] "Préface," *Léopold Sédar Senghor et la naissance de l'Afrique moderne* by Ernest Milcent and Monique Sordet (Paris: Seghers, 1969) 8.

[4] Senghor quoted in Mohamed Aziza, *Léopold Sédar Senghor: La Poésie de l'action* (Paris: Stock, 1980) 330.

[5] Michael Crowder, *Senegal: A Study of French Assimilation Policy* (London: Methuen, 1967) 2.

[6] *Poèmes* (Paris: Seuil, 1984) 277-78.

[7] Harold D. Nelson et al., *Area Handbook for Senegal,* 2nd ed. (Washington, D.C.: FAS of the American University, 1974) 217.

[8] W.A.E. Skurnik, *The Foreign Policy of Senegal* (Evanston: Northwestern UP, 1972) 125.

[9] Ibid. 129.

[10] Sheldon Gellar, *Senegal: An African Nation Between Islam and the West* (Boulder, Colo.: Westview, 1982) 69.

[11] Ibid. 69.

[12] Senghor quoted in Renée Tillot, *Le Rythme dans la poésie de Léopold Sédar Senghor* (Dakar: Nouvelles Editions Africaines, 1979) 103.

[13] Raymond Darricau, "Les *Elégies majeures* du Président Léopold Sédar Senghor *Revue française d'histoire du livre,* n.s. 25 (1979): 859.

[14] Senghor quoted in Aziza 65.

[15] Skurnik 154-55.

[16] Senghor quoted in Milcent et Sordet 242.

[17] For futher verification of links between Senghor and Teilhard de Chardin, see Léopold Sédar Senghor, *Pierre Teilhard de Chardin et la politique africaine,* Cahiers Pierre Teillard de Chardin 3 (Paris: Seuil, 1962).

[18] Senghor quoted in Aziza 303.

[19] See Aziza 303-4.

[20] For a discussion of the origins of nonalignment, see George W. Shepherd Jr., *Nonaligned Black Africa* (Lexington, MA.: D.C. Heath, 1970) 6-7. He asserts that "three basic interests of the new states form the practical ground for nonalignment. They are 1) self-preservation, 2) cultural and ideological autonomy, and 3) economic growth and modernization" (6).

[21] Tillot 74.

[22] See the chapter on "French International Policy in the Third World: North Africa and the Middle East" in Edward A. Koloziej, *French International Policy Under De Gaulle and Pompidou: The Politics of Grandeur* (Ithaca: Cornell UP, 1974) 447-88.

[23] See Claire Vander Veken, "Analyse de l'axe 'je-tu' dans 'Que m'accompagnent kôras et balafong,'" *Revue Belge de Philologie et d'Histoire* 61-3 (1983): 578-90. Also republished in this collection.

FURTHER READING

Criticism

Pappageorge, Julia Di Stefano. "Senghor Re-evaluated." In *African Literature Today,* edited by Eldred Durosimi Jones, pp. 54-67. New York: Africana Publishing Company, 1973.
    Lists the weaknesses of English translations of Senghor's verse.

Senghor, Léopold Sédar. "Poetic Inspiration, Its Sources and Caprices." *Hermathena,* No. CXXXVI (Summer 1984): 8-20.
    Discusses various sources—historical, literary, and autobiographical—of poetic inspiration.

Additional coverage of Senghor's life and career is contained in the following sources published by The Gale Group: *Contemporary Literature Criticism,* Vol. 54; *Black Literature Criticism,* Vol. 3; *DISCovering Authors: Most Studied Authors Module; DISCovering Authors: Poets Module.*

Karl Shapiro
1913-

(Full name Karl Jay Shapiro) American poet, critic, essayist, editor, novelist, and autobiographer.

INTRODUCTION

Recognized as an iconoclastic and innovative poet, Shapiro composes verse that defies classification because of his varied and unpredictable approach to theme and presentation. Over several decades he has demonstrated a mastery of both traditional and contemporary poetic technique. In his verse, Shapiro explores love, war, religion, and, most notably, the relationship between poetry and prose—a topic that he often addresses by combining the two genres in his works.

Biographical Information

Born in Baltimore, Maryland, on November 10, 1913, Shapiro grew up in Baltimore, Chicago, and Norfolk, Virginia. His Jewish background imbued him with a sense of isolation during his brief time studying at the University of Virginia; this self-consciousness about his heritage and the exploration of other religions are recurring themes in his work. In 1935 *Poems* was published, and secured him a scholarship to Johns Hopkins University; his next collection, *Person, Place, and Thing* attracted favorable critical attention. The poems were composed while Shapiro was stationed in New Guinea during World War II and the collection garnered praise for his adroit use of dramatic monologue. In 1944, Shapiro was awarded the Pulitzer Prize in poetry for *V-Letter and Other Poems.* He continues writing poetry and criticism, and teaching at universities, the most recent being the University of California at Davis.

Major Works

Shapiro burst onto the literary scene with the publication of *V-Letter,* which contains what many critics lauded as the finest war poems ever written by an American. Several selections in his next book, *Trial of a Poet,* were written on Shapiro's homeward journey immediately after the war and eloquently communicate the sense of humanity's irrevocable loss during that turbulent era. *Poems of a Jew* concerns the doctrines of Judaism and Christianity, rebuking and defending both religions while discussing his brief conversion to Catholicism. Shapiro experimented with free verse to great critical success in such works as *The Bourgeois Poet.* In his succeeding volume, *The White-Haired Lover,* which consists of twenty-nine love poems dedicated to his second wife, Shapiro returns to traditional verse forms. *Love & War, Art & God* combines early poetry with new verse in which Shapiro contemplates the eclectic concepts of the volume's title. In the pieces collected in *New and Selected Poems, 1940-1986* and his latest volume *The Old Horsefly,* Shapiro confronts both contemporary social issues and personal concerns.

Critical Reception

Shapiro is praised for his creative mix of prose and poetry, and his poetic style of a stream-of-consciousness narrative reminiscent of the verse of such Beat poets as Allen Ginsberg and Lawrence Ferlinghetti. Such works, in particular *Essay on Rime,* are noted not only for their poetic style but their passionate and controversial commentary on modern poetry; yet some have deemed Shapiro's analysis of twentieth-century poetry as unfocused and tenuous. While some critics maintain that his exploration of such diverse forms as the sonnet, blank verse, and lyric poetry yields erratic results, many regard his extensive output as impressive. Whatever the opinion on his recent verse, most commentators agree that in the 1940s Shapiro produced some of the best war poetry ever written by an American poet.

PRINCIPAL WORKS

Poetry

Poems 1935
Person, Place, and Thing 1942
V-Letter and Other Poems 1944
Essay on Rime 1945
Trial of a Poet 1947
Poems: 1940-1953 1953
Poems of a Jew 1958
The Bourgeois Poet 1964
White-Haired Lover 1968
Love and War, Art and God 1984
New and Selected Poems, 1940-1986 1987
The Old Horsefly 1994
The Wild Card: Selected Poems, Early and Late 1998

Delmore Schwartz (essay date 1943)

SOURCE: "The Poet's Progress," in *The Nation,* Vol. 156, No. 2, January 9, 1943, pp. 63-4.

[*In the following favorable review of* Person, Place, and Thing, *Schwartz determines the influence of W. H. Auden on Shapiro's poetry.*]

Karl Jay Shapiro is a poet of remarkable and original gifts. Yet it is possible that the topicality of his poetry—one of its strongest virtues—and the fact that the poet is now a soldier in Australia may distract attention from the literary feat performed in this book [***Person, Place, and Thing***]. The feat is that of taking the style of Auden and transforming it with an American subject matter, by writing of drugstores, lunch wagons, a conscription camp, a midnight show, a Buick, and many other things equally indigenous.

Most poets begin by taking fire from other poets, and most poets end, sadly enough, in self-imitation. But between the time when the poet is an echoing novice and the time when he is a self-infatuated and tired master, there occurs, if the poet has genuine gifts, a period during which the borrowed or imitated style is gradually altered into something new and strange—as the glove is shaped by the hand, day by day—through the constant pressure of the poet's own and unique subject matter, his own experience. Even in the best poets this wonderful process tends to be broken and uneven. But it proceeds powerfully and serenely in Mr. Shapiro's verse, and the interesting thing is that one can see so clearly several stages of it in this book.

The manner, and especially the diction of Shapiro's writing, is all from Auden. Words such as luck, love, the hostile parents, wound, failure and usages like the personification of places and things occur throughout the book. A stanza such as this one:

> What do you care, dear total stranger,
> For the successful failure of my safest danger,
> My pig in the poke or dog in the manger?
> The dead cry *life* and stagger up the hill;
>
> . . . . .
>
> But is there still the incorrigible city where
> The well enjoy their poverty and the young
> Worship the gutter? Is Wednesday still alive
> And Tuesday wanting terribly to sin?

or, for a briefer example, a line like "It baffles the foreigner like an idiom" is purely Audenesque in style. And yet the matter is wholly Shapiro's, and the latter line is the beginning of a fine poem about a drugstore, in which Shapiro manages to make baseball scores, coca-cola bottles, lipstick, and lending-library books relevant and operative parts of the poem. In most of the other young American poets who have been subjected to Auden's strong influence, Auden's perceptions as well as his words are echoed; in the course of a poem we can sometimes even see Auden's perceptions displacing those native to the poet. In Shapiro, on the contrary, the borrowed style is an aid and not an obstacle; the result is a growing originality.

The source of this originality is undoubtedly Shapiro's inexhaustible power of observation. He can see a great deal, he has taken a long, cunning, and intelligent look at the important objects of modern life, and he has serious and important feelings about what he sees. Yet this strength has, like most virtues, its danger and its weakness. There is not only a sameness of tone and feeling in a good many of these poems but also a tendency to rely too much on dramatic observation, organized merely as a succession of items, to solve all problems and provide the insight which the subject requires.

Observation is not insight, although there is little insight without observation. And this makes one thing of the title of Shapiro's book, which I take to be the declaration of a worthy and humble joy in observation, and of Shapiro's prose Note on Poetry in last year's *Five Young American Poets,* where the title was first used and where Shapiro

expressed a strange hatred of "the dictatorship of criticism" and of general ideas. The statement reached its peak in the extraordinary phrase, "America, the word that is the chief enemy of modern poetry." This is not only in direct contradiction to the excellent use of abstractions, like America and Europe, in Shapiro's verse, but it suggests a serious immaturity in Shapiro's attitude as a poet. The poet can no more afford to hate abstractions or general ideas than he can afford to hate the concrete and the particular. He needs them both, and he needs them at the same time if his verse is to be both vivid and significant. Perhaps Shapiro hates abstractions like America for the same reason that the hero of *A Farewell to Arms* hated words like Democracy, Justice, Liberty, Self-Sacrifice, and Courage; they have been used by politicians and by bad poets. But Democracy, Justice, Self-Sacrifice, Courage, Europe, and America are the abstract and often abused terms for the deep-seated values which inspire Shapiro, at his best, both to rage and to sympathy.

Other abstractions, often capitalized by Shapiro, are necessary parts of Shapiro's best poems. But more than that, it is the abstraction, America, and another concrete abstraction—if the reader will forgive me this true paradox—Europe, which are just as responsible for Shapiro's being in Australia as the troopship which took him there.

The chief enemy of modern poetry is not a word, certainly not a word like America, or a use of abstract terms. Two of the many enemies of all poetry are the inability to see things clearly and exactly, a defect from which Shapiro will never suffer, and, on the other hand, the inability to generalize and make universal one's experience by means of abstractions. The poet has to keep many activities going, but one activity as necessary as any other is *to keep thinking all the time.* It is not easy, but it is necessary. Fortunately Mr. Shapiro's practice is far superior to his theory, so that what we have here is a book which everyone interested in modern poetry ought to read.

F. W. Dupee (essay date 1944)

SOURCE: "Karl Shapiro and the Great Ordeal," in *The Nation,* Vol. 159, No. 12, September 16, 1944, pp. 327-28.

[*In the following review, Dupee offers a mixed assessment of* V-Letter and Other Poems.]

By now most readers are probably tired of war literature and would like to get back to literature. Not only is much of the writing inferior; but we are kept from saying so by reason of the censorship inflicted on us by our war-time piety. Yet in the case of Karl Shapiro, whose new poems were written during the more than two years that he has been on active duty in the Southwest Pacific, it seems impossible not to invoke the war. By what drama of adjustment has he continued writing? The question would be irrelevant, I admit, if his adjustment had resulted in a book which was continuous in thought and quality with his earlier one, **Person, Place, and Thing**. But although *V-Letter* is a remarkable performance, it is still in many ways weaker than the former book—anxious and uneven where the other one was strong and consistent.

The notable thing about *Person, Place, and Thing* was a firmness of mood and singleness of purpose. Its well-written satires on industrial society were not great poetry or even on their way to being that; they were in the best sense "minor." And Shapiro was able to be a successful minor poet in our time because, while renouncing the larger myth-making pretensions of modern poetry, he nevertheless maintained the modernist defiance of middle-class civilization. This ground of self-assurance is now giving way, it is clear, under pressure of the war and prolonged soldiering. His old conviction of identity is gone, and he is experimenting with new roles.

This is apparent in the introduction to *V-Letter*, where he tries to define his relation to the great ordeal. It must be admitted that his ideas seem contradictory. On the one hand he seems anxious to diminish the war to a mere visitation of nature and thus to conjure away its terrors considered as a political or human portent. So he says that "war is an affection of the human spirit, without any particular reference to 'values,'" and that its effect on oneself is to reduce one "in size but not in meaning, like a V-letter." But this relatively complacent view is belied by what Shapiro says of the "suffering" and "private psychological tragedy" of soldiers and even more by the drastic moral effects which he ascribes to war. It "can teach us humility," he says; and by virtue of it "contemporary man should feel divested of the stock attitudes of the last generation, the stance of the political intellectual, the proletarian, the expert, the salesman, the world-traveler, the pundit-poet [and] like the youngster in the crowd make the marvelous discovery that our majesty is naked." Those "stock attitudes," or many of them, were of course at the root of his earlier poems; and in trying to cut them away he is, knowingly, risking the extinction of his old powers. And what, one wonders, is really wrong with those attitudes? They were by-products of the same civilization that produced the war; and if, as seems more and more likely, the war fails to solve the problems that begot it, then why are not the old postures still viable? Where, moreover, are the sources of this Blake-like freshness of vision, this mystical simplicity, of which Shapiro speaks and to which he aspires? Are they to be found in battle, in the pursuit of what he calls in a poem "the rat-toothed enemy"? To accept this war as a hard political necessity is one thing; to completely de-politicalize it in the interests of a confused and supine metaphysics is to leave it a mere meaningless horror. Shapiro may be right in fleeing the old attitudes; but surely he is in danger of demonstrating that a bad civilization can finally compel acceptance of itself, or at least suspension of judgment, by the simple device of becoming worse.

These arguments apply primarily to Shapiro's introduction and not to his poetry. *V-Letter* is so various and so full of excellent verse that it would resist any attempt to sacrifice it to a thesis even if I wanted so to sacrifice it. The poet's peculiar negative-positive adjustment to the war has had the advantage, apparently, of leaving him relatively free to observe, read, reflect, and labor at his poetry as

before. He retains his old wry pleasure in the sights of a country—in this case Australia, not America—and his characteristic interest in religion and history. Whether he is writing poetry or merely versifying—if the distinction is clear—he is as eloquent, as fertile in apt imagery, as wedded to the concrete, as he ever was. And his verse still has its clear metrical line, even though it tends toward excessive regularity and occasionally romps off into conventional dactylics.

Yet only a few of the poems in *V-Letter* seem to me equal to the average of his earlier work. The best single production in the book is probably **"The Synagogue,"** one of a series of satiric-prophetic pieces on Judaism. The subject is the spiritual limitations and historical guilts of the Jewish religion as Shapiro conceives them; and although his point of view is Christian, his temper is that of a Jewish prophet censuring the Jews. To readers not similarly concerned, Shapiro's ideas in these poems may seem atavistic; but they clearly exercised to the utmost his faculties as a poet. In **"The Synagogue"** passion and intellect converge to form one of the great contemporary poems. There is, however, seldom such concentration of forces in the rest of *V-Letter*. For the most part the great ironies and paradoxes of the war escape the satiric comment which other and lesser aspects of modern society received in *Person, Place, and Thing*. Shapiro now reserves his thunder for Judaists and intellectuals. When he writes of military life, as in **"Troop Train"** or **"Elegy for a Dead Soldier,"** he is easy, reportorial, readable; hardly any other poet today could have produced so colloquially-spirited, so tragically-gay a departure scene as he depicts in the first stanza of **"Birthday Poem."** Nevertheless it is curious how often these poems drop into commonplace or even mere folksy sentiment. ("I see you woman-size And this looms larger and more goddess-like Than silver goddesses on screens"—I love you just the way you are, dear.) And it appears that Shapiro's former satirical defiance is being displaced by new and vaguely disturbing attitudes. There is in his work a growing contempt for conscious artistry and intellect, an eagerness to present himself as passionately immersed in the folk life of the soldier, a pride in his acquired toughness.

> I smoke and read my bible and chew gum . . .
> I'd rather be a barber and cut hair
> Than walk with you in gilt museum halls . . .
>
> And on through crummy continents and days,
> Deliberate, grimy, slightly drunk, we crawl,
> The good-bad boys of circumstance and chance . . .

Nor are these new feelings frankly examined in the poet's conscience in such a way that the conversion process becomes itself the subject of his poetry: they are merely taken for granted. It would certainly be an irony of the war if it turned a complex and specialized poet like Shapiro into only another exponent of hard-boiled sentimentality.

F. O. Matthiessen (essay date 1945)

SOURCE: "On the Confusions in Poetry," in *The New York Times Book Review*, October 28, 1945, pp. 1, 18, 20, 22.

[*In the following laudable review of* Essays on Rime, *Matthiessen contends that the "book may very well be the most remarkable contribution to American art yet to have come out of the war."*]

This book may very well be the most remarkable contribution to American art yet to have come out of the war. Its title may suggest to the general reader a bookish piece by a young man growing up in a library and steeped in the period of Boileau and Pope. It happens to have been written by a sergeant in the Medical Corps who was just completing his third year of active duty in the Pacific. When Karl Shapiro was drafted in the spring before Pearl Harbor, his name was probably known only to readers of "New Directions" and the serious little magazines. He was already in New Guinea before his first book, ***Person, Place and Thing***, was published. He was finishing this ***Essay*** in the Netherlands East Indies a year ago, before he had had any chance to realize that his ***V-Letter*** had placed him, among younger readers particularly, at the forefront of the poets of his decade.

Composed without access to books, this verse Essay of over 2,000 lines discusses "rime" in its widest connotation as synonymous with "the art of poetry," and gives a detailed assessment of that art in our time. It is the kind of production one would hardly have believed possible in the special circumstances of soldiering, and yet without the enforced isolation from everything he cared most about and without the equally enforced inwardness of his thoughts Shapiro might never have felt the necessity to take stock of where we now stand "in the mid-century of our art." What makes the result such exciting reading is that here we have no formal estimate, with measured dependence upon authority. We have rather the direct statement of what a poet really knows and believes, what he has absorbed from thirty years of living and ten of learning his craft.

Shapiro is no eclectic, and makes no attempt to include all the leading names in modern poetry. In a closing passage he regrets that he had to leave out certain figures, notably Wallace Stevens and Frost, since he lacked "a whole opinion of their work." Yet he gives a representative picture of the prevailing influences of his particular period, of the state of poetry as it has been experienced by someone who began to practice it in the early Nineteen Thirties. He has written thereby a chapter of cultural and moral history. But he has also written a poem. He has not availed himself of the technical virtuosity displayed in his previous books. In deliberately roughening his blank verse to the "flux and reflux of conversation," he may have produced some needlessly flat lines. But his language is vivid with the eloquence of conviction, and he enlivens his effect with an occasional tightening rhyme. He does not engage in abstract analysis. He knows the difference between a poet and a semanticist, and, as he says, his wish

> is but to call a rose a rose
> And not a trope.

The poets of his time who have made the most impression upon him are Eliot, Hart Crane and Auden. Shapiro followed the Nineteen Twenties in recognizing Eliot to be the master craftsman of American poetry. In 1933 Hart Crane, who had responded deeply to Eliot's technical innovations but had attempted to refute the disillusion of *The Waste Land* by a new affirmation of Whitman's America, had recently killed himself in despair. Auden, who had also learned much from Eliot, was just starting to express political and social concerns very different from anything articulated in *Ash Wednesday*. With the depression had come a marked break in the sequence of American poets. Between 1910 and 1930 this country had witnessed the emergence of a greater abundance and variety of poetic talents than in any previous period in our history. But during the Thirties most of our new writers turned to prose, particularly to the novel of social protest. The new signatures in poetry, with an occasional exception like Delmore Schwartz at the end of the period, were predominantly English.

Shapiro does not agree with Yeats' opinion that since 1900 there have been "more poets of worth" in the English language than in any generation since 1630. He indicates his persistent view by arranging his ***Essay*** under three headings, "The Confusion in Prosody," "The Confusion in Language," "The Confusion in Belief." He writes with modesty, as one involved with his own age, but also with great firmness. His opening section is the most technical in its references, the most unusual to have been created entirely from memory. Living in the period of the breakdown of formal metric, he takes stock of how and when that came about. He discusses what he has learned of the resources of the past from three monuments of scholarship, Bridges' study of Milton, Lanier's *Science of English Verse* and Saintsbury's account of prose rhythms.

From his own immersion in the poets Shapiro has found the "discipline" of Milton's prosody to be the practitioner's "purest guide" to mastery. Only those aware of the acrid academic debates of recent years will recognize Shapiro's catholicity in being able to admire Milton's supremacy, and yet to assert that "by far the two great prosodists of our age" are Joyce and Eliot. Academic critics have usually lined up on one edge of that divide, current readers on the other. Shapiro does not argue. He knows as a poet, through the evidence of his ears, that in Eliot "the triumph of a new form is certain." He has many fresh things to say about that triumph. He is a judicious appraiser of the artesian interflow that Eliot struck anew between French and English verse; but he values Eliot even more for the way his "clean conversational voice" cut through "the late-Victorian lilt." Measuring his words carefully, Shapiro remarks of the metric of *Ash Wednesday* that

> in a hundred years no poem
> Has sung itself so exquisitely well.

He is even more penetrating in his treatment of Joyce. He reckons with *Ulysses* as "a thing of rime entirely," since he believes that it established "a new rhythmical idiom" through the mating of the possibilities of verse and of prose, such as Lanier and Saintsbury foresaw. But Shapiro is by no means easy in his mind about the influence of Joyce's intricacy. He is aware that the master has fallen into the hands of cultists and has fathered many aberrations. But in summation of the vagaries of our time Shapiro recognizes that it has also been marked by much "serious invention," as poets have struggled to find possible verse forms to fit the "tensile strains" in modern speech.

Confusion in language is of even graver import, since language is the living record of our moral history. Shapiro believes that excessive style is an undeniable sign of disequilibrium, and he is disturbed by the violently diverse phases through which so many of our artists have gone in the age of Picasso and Stravinsky. Auden's is the case history of multiple personality in verse, and Shapiro notes Auden's pursuit through the whole "lexicon of forms" after "the lost Eurydice of character." But he is by no means forgetful of the immense stimulus to his own development from Auden's mastery of rhetoric. His passage on the advent of Auden's group recaptures the excitement of that moment when

> *a set*
> *Of more or less Oxford radicals unloaded*
> *Their gear of games and books and politics*
> *Blazers and alcohol and hockeysticks*
> *Into the lap of middle age.*

He has high praise for the concrete vocabulary of immediate things that was thereby inaugurated, but is equally critical of Auden's subsequent deflection into loose abstraction.

An especially perceptive passage probes farther the effects of abstract rhetoric induced by our poets' adoption of an international style. Shapiro cites Pound's "polyglot" *Cantos* as one symptom, and as another the curious influence of such translations as Spender's *Rilke* and the various versions of Lorca, which were then imitated as new idioms. The result was to make much current verse read like a translation "where no original exists," and the end-product, in a characteristic writer like MacLeish, has the unreality of "a linguistic dream."

The confusion, or rather the failure in belief, is introduced by an estimate of the poet whose talent, in Shapiro's view, was greater "than any, excepting the expatriates," since Whitman's:

> *Crane died for modern rime, a wasted death;*
> *I make the accusation with the right*
> *Of one who loved his book; died without cause,*
> *Leaped from the deck-rail of his disbelief*
> *To senseless strangulation. When we shall damn*
> *The artist who interprets all sensation,*
> *All activity, all experience, all*
> *Belief through art, then this chief suicide*
> *May be redeemed.*

Crane is the symbol of the most dangerous fallacy in recent art, the substitution, as traditional faith collapsed, of a frenzied and catastrophic belief in art itself as "the supreme criterion of experience." Other substitute beliefs have been rife in our age, and Shapiro traces their progression from the Darwinian poet of progress to the Marxist poet of revolution. He understands why the political faith of so many of the young radicals of the past decade collapsed so quickly. They staked everything upon the immediate fulfillment of their utopian dream, and when that failed them, their belief failed too. Shapiro reminds us of what our professional patrioteers would now like us to forget, that most of our young writers faced the beginning of the war with little positive conviction. He holds, with quiet discernment, that

> *The rime produced by soldiers of our war*
> *Is the most sterile of the century.*

Shapiro is possessed by a very different mood from those prevailing at the close of the last war. He feels neither liberated nor disillusioned. He is inescapably conscious of the consequences of our trying to live in a "structural universe" which

> *Has neither good nor evil but only true*
> *And false.*

He holds that man is by nature "a believing being," and, in a period of excessive and distracted intellectualism, he also holds that the writer is responsible for putting his own emotions in order. He does not indicate his own particular position, but it is evident here, as it was in *V-Letter,* that Shapiro is increasingly preoccupied with religious values. The only recent poet who has impressed him by the integrity of his concern with faith is Eliot.

The recurrent and concluding aim of the *Essay* is to solidify "the layman's confidence in a plainer art." Shapiro maintains that our complex styles, however brilliant, have brought upon us an unprecedented cleavage between poet and audience. He thereby raises again the familiar complaint, but he gives to it no conventional answer. He is fully aware of the difficulties confronting a true popular art in a period so equipped with all the instruments of vulgarization. His respect for his craft alone would make him realize that the pseudofolksy verse carried by the slick picture magazines, whether called "Corn" or "My Country," is no poetry at all. Shapiro would also stand with Farrell in warning against the incalculable corruption already wrought upon public taste by Hollywood.

But the sure fashion in which he threads his way through such a maze of horrors is a token of his belief in a continuing American tradition. His treatment of Whitman is significant, since he returns to him in all three sections. He declares that the metric of "Leaves of Grass" is,

> *at its best, the strongest*
> *Link in American prosody,*

since it freed us from what was "fake and effeminate" in our imitation of the forms of Europe. But Shapiro also recognizes how flaccid Whitman's free verse can be, and thinks that most of his descendants in our day reflect "but poorly on the prototype." So too with Whitman's language and belief.

Vital as it is in its concrete notations, "the wide style of the dry Americana" is a very misleading model when it falls to mere generalizations about Democracy, Ma Femme. The poet of "person, place and thing" had already pronounced "the word 'America'" to be "the chief enemy of modern poetry." He reinforces what he meant by showing how one of Whitman's abstractions, that of the Perfect State, has become the "optic illusion of our time." It has begotten many swollen epics filled, not with the dramatic tensions of living men and women, but with the bloodless abstractions of "the synthetic myth." Thus Shapiro affirms his central conviction that a poem is not the same kind of construction as a philosopher's system or a political theorist's dialectic:

> Ideas are no more words
> Than phoenixes are birds. The metaphysician
> Deals with ideas as words, the poet with things,
> For in the poet's mind the phoenix sings.

Therefore, despite his response to Whitman's continuing greatness, Shapiro remarks that Poe was

> the last poet
> In the classic signification of the word.

He might have made his meaning less mistakable if he had said Baudelaire, since his concern is to point up the opposition between poetry as craftsmanship and poetry as *Weltanschauung*. Shapiro finds his clearest clue out of the maze by following another substitute belief, that of the Freudian poet, to its dead end. He cites Freud's own final disavowal of psychoanalysis as a *Weltanschauung* and his description of the arts as "beneficent and harmless forms." Instead of being dismayed at the reduction of the arts to such a humble status, Shapiro declares:

> This is the sane perspective, one that brings
> The beloved creative function back to scale.

In denying I. A. Richards' claim that "poetry can save us," in affirming that all great art must have its tap-root in adequately human moral values, Shapiro would seem to have established a solider "hope for poetry" than that expressed a decade ago by Day Lewis. The best of Shapiro's own poems so far, ranging with gusto from tenderness to irony to stinging satire, would already augur his important share in bridging the gap between the poet and the democratic audience of the Nineteen Fifties.

Dayton Kohler (essay date 1946)

SOURCE: "Karl Shapiro: Poet in Uniform," in *College English,* Vol. 7, No. 5, February, 1946, pp. 243-49.

[*In the following essay, Kohler challenges Shapiro's reputation as a war poet, maintaining his work has a larger appeal.*]

The poet in uniform is at a disadvantage today. There is, first, the common reader's conception of the singing soldier, a romantic figure in the image of Rupert Brooke,

whose traditional accents can glorify a cause. But, as Gertrude Stein has pointed out, there is little poetry in the mechanical destruction of modern warfare. So your poet echoes too often the noble sentiments of other men in older wars. If, on the other hand, he is interested in more than literary exploitation of the cruelties and heroism of battle, he must maintain, at all cost, his own integrity as an artist while conforming outwardly to a military ritual that is always against the privacy of the individual.

Karl Shapiro is a case in point. Although he has been called a "war poet," it is clear that he is not the poet of this war in the sense that Mauldin is its best cartoonist and Ernie Pyle its reporter. The poems he wrote while serving with the Army in the Southwest Pacific reflect the topicality of the war; but he manages to relate its horrors and boredom to his picture of the larger world, which he had appraised at something considerably less than its face value before he put on a uniform. Consequently, he was not likely to be aroused to the sentimental optimism of a Rupert Brooke or shocked into the equally sentimental disgust of a Siegfried Sassoon. He belongs to the generation which grew up under the shadow of one war to fight in another, even more disastrous. As a poet facing the spectacle of war, he learned that anger was useless, idealism impossible. There remained only the task of reporting honestly things seen and heard. Aware of the spiritual and emotional climate of his generation, Shapiro can be "as anonymous as the other guy" in recording with sharp, dry imagery his observations of the everyday world, down to the "wonderful nonsense of lotions of Lucky Tiger," and in dramatizing the spirit of an age marked by violence and suspense. The bitterness and crisp irony of his work spring from the temper of his generation, not from his private experience as a soldier.

There is a generation made anonymous by the war, men from schools and shops and farms whose lives were reduced to a military pattern as unvarying as their khakis and dungarees. Their names are as commonplace as a page of any telephone directory, and you have seen their faces in quick newsreel glimpses: soldiers crouching in the shadows of a hedge outside a ruined town in Normandy, a marine coughing in the smoke below Bloody Nose Ridge on Peleliu, a pharmacist's mate running with his kit across the flaming deck of the "Franklin," a black boy from Alabama at his battle station when the kamikaze came over. On blistering coral atolls or in Anzio mud they talked of women, food, and home; and in their fatigue and boredom they forgot that the war was the most common and moving experience of their generation. They are also the picturesque or sentimental figures of most of the journalistic writing of the war. Shapiro has attempted no such reportage about the homesick, wry-humored men with whom he served for three years in Australia and New Guinea. Knowing the difficulties that confront the poet in wartime, he has avoided poetry of action in which the imagination has little part. In his introduction to *V-Letter* he wrote:

> Since the war began, I have tried to be on guard against becoming a "war poet". . . . . It is not the commonplace of suffering or the platitudinous comparison with the

peace, or the focus on the future that should occupy us; but the spiritual progress or retrogression of the man in war, the increase or decrease in his knowledge of beauty, government and religion.

We know very well that the most resounding slogans ring dead after a few years, and that it is not for poetry to keep pace with public speeches and the strategy of events. We learn that war is an affection of the human spirit, without any particular reference to "values." In the totality of striving and suffering we come to see the great configuration abstractly, with oneself at the center reduced in size but not in meaning, like a V-letter. We learn that distance and new spatial arrangements cannot disturb the primordial equation of man equals man and nation nation. We learn finally that if war can teach anything it can teach humility; if it can test anything it can test externality against the soul.

This statement is important in the light of his own development as a poet, for most of the poems which have made him an outstanding figure in his generation were written during the war years. When he was inducted into the Army in March, 1942, his name was known only to readers of a few little magazines and the "New Directions" anthology *Five Young American Poets.* He was already in the Southwest Pacific when his first book, **Person, Place and Thing** appeared in 1942. These poems had a critical success because their concrete substance and variety of subject brought to America the same jolting impact that Auden and his group had given English poetry in the early thirties. In 1944 he received a Guggenheim fellowship and in the same year a special award from the American Academy of Arts and Letters. *V-Letter* was awarded the Pulitzer Poetry Prize for 1944. **Essay on Rime** was published October 30, 1945, after Shapiro's release from service in July. A fourth volume, **The Place of Love**, was printed for limited distribution in Australia in 1942; it will be re-written, however, before publication in this country. It is safe to say that these four books make Karl Shapiro, at thirty-two, the challenging figure among our younger writers, the type of poet who can hold among disturbing circumstances to the difficult discipline of his craft.

This is the chief impression gained from reading **Essay on Rime**, probably his most remarkable book to date. Even more remarkable is the fact that it was written in the jungles of the Dutch East Indies, without recourse to libraries, and that its wide framework of cultural and moral reference was drawn almost entirely from memory. In his poetic essay of more than two thousand lines he takes stock both of modern poetry "in the mid-century of our art" and of his own resources as a writer. There are few abstractions here; his examples and opinions are as crisp and precise as his lyric poems, for, as he states, his wish

     is but to call a rose a rose
and not a trope.

Specifically he is concerned with the confusion in literature which has resulted from the demoralization of Western culture. To this end he examines the critics and poets, who, he feels, are still significant voices in our time; and

he presents his own findings from the readings of these men under three headings: "The Confusion in Prosody," "The Confusion in Language," and "The Confusion in Belief." Faced by the breakdown of traditional forms, he believes that the best resources of the past come to us through Bridges' work on Milton, Lanier's *Science of English Verse,* and Saintsbury's study of prose rhythms. The modern masters, he feels, are Eliot and Joyce, and he speaks as a poet concerned with problems of craftmanship when he says that in Eliot "the triumph of a new form is certain" and of "Ash Wednesday" that

     in a hundred years no poem
has sung itself so exquisitely well.

In Joyce he sees the possibilities of "a new rhythmical idiom" through a fusion of poetry and prose. Many of his conclusions are not new, of course. Only his way of looking at these writers who have put a deep imprint upon the literature of our time and his way of expressing his ideas are new and seasoned by reflection.

He is equally concerned with the confusion of language and diversity of styles that mark the breakdown of a cultural tradition. He acknowledges his debt to Auden, who taught him much about poetry as direct perception and sees an important moment in modern poetry when

       a set
of more or less Oxford radicals unloaded
their gear of games and books and politics
Blazers and alcohol and hockey-sticks
Into the lap of middle age.

But he also sees Auden pursuing "the lost Eurydice of Character" through a confusion of factual statement and private imagery that often results in wilful cleverness with words, rather than language, as experience. Eliot in *The Waste Land* showed the modern world as wreckage. Auden took the material of Eliot but showed other poets how they could laugh, as well as weep, among the ruin. And Shapiro takes much of his liveliness from Auden's example. In **Essay on Rime** he is as nimble and direct as a good boxer.

He is best, however, in his discussion of failure in belief among modern poets. As the traditional faith declined, poets have tried to find a substitute in evolution or politics or art itself. He makes Hart Crane a symbol of the artist's despair when belief has failed:

     Crane died for modern rime, a wasted death;
     I make the accusation with the right
     Of one who loved his book; died without cause
     Leaped from the deck-rail of his disbelief
     To senseless strangulation, When we shall damn
     The artist who interprets all sensation,
     All activity, all experience, all
     Belief through art, then this chief suicide
     May be redeemed.

And he feels that the resigned skepticism over moral values among our younger poets accounts for the fact that

The rime produced by soldiers of our war
Is the most sterile of the century.

This reaffirmation of belief is one of the distinctive qualities of Shapiro's verse. In *Person, Place and Thing* and *V-Letter* there is a growing conviction of the necessity to believe that finds its best expression in "**The Saint**" and in the concluding stanza of "**The Leg**":

The body, what is it, Father, but a sign
To love the force that grows us, to give back
What in Thy palm is senselessness and mud?
Knead, Knead the substance of our understanding
Which must be beautiful in flesh to walk,
That if Thou take me angrily in hand
And hurl me to the shark, I shall not die!

Essay on Rime would be an important book in any period. As the work of a young man soldiering in the Southwest Pacific, it is all the more eloquent in its plea for a poetry based on humanly moral values. Karl Shapiro states with urgent voice the need for poetry that communicates in the direct language of experience what men see and sense, precise with precision of the emotions, not of mind. He comes close to stating his own literary creed when he writes:

Ideas are no more words
Than phoenixes are birds. The metaphysician
Deals with ideas as words, the poet with things,
For in the poet's mind the phoenix sings.

His poetry, like Auden's, is an act within the living world. This he demonstrated in *Five Young American Poets,* where his poems were grouped simply under the title "Noun." *Person, Place and Thing,* one year later, made even more explicit his recognition that poetry can be concrete substance, not tricks of rhetoric. To the discerning reader it was plain that he took much of his manner from Auden, but the material was unmistakably his own. One of the greatest of his gifts was a controlled balance between observation and insight, the ability to look long and steadily at the scattered details of modern life and then to arrange them in a pattern which gave them meaning as well as form. Thus, in "**Drug Store**" he puts down, side by side, his notations of baseball scores, Coca-Cola, juke boxes, lipsticks, cheap fiction, and manages, at the same time, to tell us something relevant about a younger generation lounging wasted hours. This is poetry which seems to move, as one critic has said, from outside in, depending less upon the writer than upon itself. It exists within a larger frame of reference than the private experience of the poet. This is a quality rare in poetry today, when so many poets seem to find their imagery only within private worlds which they inhabit. He uses the same method in one of the best of his war poems, "**Troop Train**":

And on through crummy continents and days,
Deliberate, grimy, slightly drunk we crawl
The good-bad boys of circumstance and chance,
Whose bucket-helmets bang the empty wall
Where twist the murdered bodies of our packs

Next to the guns that only seem themselves.
And distance like a strap adjusted shrinks,
Tightens across the shoulder and holds firm.

Here is a deck of cards, out of this hand,
Dealer, deal me my luck, a pair of bulls,
The right draw to a flush, the one-eyed jack.
Diamonds and hearts are red but spades are
   black,
And spades are spades and clubs are clovers—
   black.
But deal me winners, souvenirs of peace.
This stands to reason and arithmetic,
Luck also travels and not all come back.

Trains lead to ships and ships to death or
   trains,
And trains to death or trucks, and trucks to
   death,
Or trucks lead to the march, the march to death,
Or that survival which is all our hope;
And death leads back to trucks and trains and
   ships,
But life leads to the march, O flag! at last
The place of life found after trains and death
—Nightfall of nations brilliant after war.

In this earlier volume he demonstrated an ironic humor as well. "**Scyros**" set the modern catastrophe into jogging rhythm:

No island singly lay
   But lost its name that day
The Ainu dived across the plunging sands
   From dawn to dawn to dawn
   King George's birds came on
Strafing the tulips from his children's hands

   Thus in the classic sea
   Southeast from Thessaly
The dynamited mermen washed ashore
   And tritons dressed in steel
   Trolled heads with rod and reel
And dredged potatoes from the Aegean floor

   Hot is the sky and green
   Where Germans have been seen
The moon leaks metal on the Atlantic fields
   Pink boys in birthday shrouds
   Loop lightly through the clouds
Or coast the peaks of Finland on their shields

   That prophet year by year
   Lay still but could not hear
Where scholars tapped to find his new remains
   Gog and Magog ate pork
   In vertical New York
And war began next Wednesday on the Danes.

Through his bright visual impressions of persons, places, and things, caught as if with a camera eye "taking at odd angles the bitter scene," one can trace the experiences which have shaped the wry, objective irony of his protest against an industrial middle-class society, with its moral stagnation, unemployment, and poverty of pre-war years. His native Baltimore he describes as row after row of featureless houses drowsing in Sunday afternoon boredom and an artificial park for suburban despair. The University of Virginia, where he spent one year, taught him that

> To hurt the Negro and avoid the Jew
> Is the curriculum.

Johns Hopkins is "the Oxford of all sickness." He was by turn bitter, ironic, chastely sentimental in his indictment of modern society for its affront to the human spirit. These poems were written with firmness of mood and singleness of purpose. Their topicality barred them from the myth-making intentions of much modern poetry, but they revealed a poet who had looked carefully at the important objects of modern life and reflected intelligently upon all that he had seen.

The style which framed his early poems ranged from the traditional rhythms to involved subtleties and loose improvisations. He could turn from an Audenesque jingle like **"To a Guinea Pig"**—

> What do you care, dear total stranger,
> For the successful failure of my safest danger,
> My pig in the poke or dog in the manger,
>
> Or who does what in the where of his chamber
> Probing for his gallstones and the rods of amber
> When the succubae sing and the accusers clamber?—

to a lyric as poised and graceful as **"Travelogue for Exiles"** or a stanza as casual and effective as the ending of **"Nostalgia,"** written in the Indian Ocean in March, 1942:

> Laughter and grief join hands. Always the heart
> Clumps in the breast with heavy stride
> The face grows lined and wrinkled like a chart,
> The eyes bloodshot with tears and tide.
> Let the wind blow, for many a man shall die.

The final impression of *Person, Place and Thing* was one of sensual immediacy of a kind that had been lacking from poetry for several generations. The poet's delight in purely physical phenomena, a sense of man alive in bone and blood and sinew, recalled an Elizabethan richness and cut sharply across what he has called "the Late Victorian lilt." It was masculine poetry in the true sense of the word; and even the rank imagery of **"The Fly"** conveyed, without offense, its mood of horror and disgust. *The Place of Love,* which followed, continues in the strain of physical awareness. Many of these poems have an Old Testament frankness which Shapiro has acknowledged; the fact that they were written in an isolated Army camp in northern Australia will explain, I think, the daring but never crude play of the poet's imagination.

V-Letter is in certain respects a more uneven collection than its predecessors. *Person, Place and Thing* was satiric and passionate at the same time, because he was writing about a middle-class society that he had studied at close range and in careful detail. There was a realistic bite to his presentation of the familiar scene; we recognize the quality of wit which enlivens his verse. But in many of the poems written in the Southwest Pacific he was dealing with a new and different culture which he could view only from the outside. Being involved in the grim business of fighting gave him little time to digest his impressions of a land where war had imposed its mechanical pattern upon the beach and the jungle. He is consistent, however, in his use of concrete details to create an impression or a mood. Some of his poems of "Place," like **"Melbourne"** and **"New Guinea,"** are little more than travelogues in verse. Others, like **"Hill at Parramatta"** and **"Sydney Bridge,"** convey the authentic quality of a landscape and its meaning to a stranger from America. In the anapestic rhythm of **"Sydney Bridge"** he captures not only the appearance of the bridge but also its utilitarian function:

> You are marxist and sweaty! You grind for the
>   labor of days;
> And O sphinx of our harbor of beauty, your
>   banner is red
> And outflung on the street of the world like a
>   silvery phrase!

"Sunday: New Guinea" also captures a human scene in its complexity of foreign scene and mood of homesickness.

Among the "Things" he presents are **"The Gun," "Fireworks," "Piano," "Christmas Tree,"** and **"The Synagogue."** The last is one of the best poems he has written, a study of the Jewish race as reflected by the racial texture of his own mind and imagination:

> We live by virtue of philosophy,
> Past love, and have our devious reward.
> For faith he gave us land and took the land,
> Thinking us exiles of all humankind.
> Our name is yet the identity of God
> That storms the falling altar of the world.

But he is best in his poems of "Persons." **"Elegy for a Dead Soldier"** is quietly reflective in its tribute to a victim of the needless waste of war. It is the epitaph of the common man:

> No history deceived him, for he knew
> Little of times and armies not his own;
> He never felt that peace was but a loan,
> Had never questioned the idea of gain.
> Beyond the headlines once or twice he saw
> The gathering of a power by a few
> But could not tell their names.

There is complete revelation of the poet's own social convictions in his careful recital of the qualities of his unnamed soldier. It is conviction and protest that reaches its ultimate irony when he writes:

More than an accident and less than willed
Is every fall, and this one like the rest.
However others calculated the cost,
To us the final aggregate is *one.*

"Jefferson" acknowledges our debt to the past but points also to the gulf between tradition and the confused present. "Geographers" has its lesson for the political "medicine men":

I have had, I had, I had had, and I hold;
The line protrudes, folds over, now indents;
Yet seen from Jupiter things are as of old;
Wars cannot change the shape of continents.

"Nigger" deals boldly with the race problem, building up through many brief notations a composite study from the lives and fates of different black men. "The Intellectual" repudiates the sterility of a class, with its ironic variation on Wordsworth:

I'd rather be
A milkman walking in his sleep at dawn
Bearing fat quarts of cream, and so be free.

"The Puritan" he presents as one who

sees the hypocrisy of nature mock
His steadfastness, and in old age his fear
Of beauty strikes him dead, becomes a rock
Fixed like a gargoyle on a cathedral wall.

This is not "war poetry." But these poems and the *Essay on Rime* show, it seems to me, that Karl Shapiro has the chance to become the spokesman of his war generation. His social awareness and the sharpness of his wit will undoubtedly keep him from the acquired tough sentimentality of the postwar writers of an earlier generation, just as his common sense will save him from the stock attitudes of the political dreamer, the proletarian, the mystic. He has not yet written major poetry, and he has not yet shed the influences that belong peculiarly to the literature of our time. There are signs in *Essay on Rime*, however, that he is freeing himself from his apprenticeship in language and form. He is still young enough to learn that imagination, experience, and a trained sense of language are equipment enough for a poet in his artistic maturity.

Robert Richman (essay date 1946)

SOURCE: "Alchemy or Poet," in *The Sewanee Review*, Vol. LIV, No. 4, October-December, 1946, pp. 684-90.

[*In the following essay, Richman deems* Essay on Rime *confused, unconvincing, and ultimately unsuccessful.*]

The danger in Karl Shapiro's *Essay On Rime* is that the three arguments seem convincing. It seems that modern poetry does not exist; yet after reading this rule-making,

one realizes that the poetry of Joyce, Yeats, Eliot, Stevens, Auden, Crane and Pound still exists large and strong even though Mr. Shapiro renounces it. The blame he laid on modern poetry, I am convinced, was not its but man's.

The *Essay* seems convincing because many of the observations, and particularly much of the appreciations, are good and significant. But Mr. Shapiro has made pretensions for this work which go beyond the organic need and seed of the type of essay he has written. And, though this is a difficult statement to phrase, the *Essay On Rime* is a poetics in the communication of which critics themselves have helped almost as much as if they had had a hand in the creation. Certain books fall fate to such rewriting and worthless praise: as a result the reading publics are convinced before they begin. For a book such as this one, which by its approach can be taken as canon law in criticism by the uncritical, its fate is the more vicious.

The *Essay* fails to be a significant evaluation of modern poetry because, after one discounts the sensitivity and knowledge and love Mr. Shapiro brings to his work, the three basic principles of criticism he uses are as false as the modern text on military science which deals only with Maginot Line warfare. Poetry has fought a different war in the twentieth century; in fact it came out of the fortress when Blake rushed out of the iron gates of the eighteenth century and sang. Thus, the simplicity with which Mr. Shapiro has reduced his analysis of the three confusions is the source of danger; it is a simplicity that has ignored, rather than explained away, the multiple complications in poetry today.

Mr. Shapiro is somewhat the neo-classic rule maker in his simplifications. In a language and in a literature that is truly classical, such an approach has much the more validity than that of the organic critic who tries to measure achievement with intention. Yet even Aristotle and Horace, within the formal limitations of their great classical languages, have the distinct disadvantage of saying, in total effect, that the principles of literature which the classics are written in are the only orthodox patterns for future writing. Since Aristotle's principle of the tragic flaw, written in his golden age, does not really apply to the *Antigone* or *Oedipus* of Sophocles, which Aristotle used as models for his rules, in effect, I am saying that each age must have in the grain of its literary principles, a creative criticism that exists contemporaneously with its creation and seeks to serve the poet in his working.

The modern critic, then, is most likely to succeed in giving a usable theory if he is in sympathy with the flow of poetry in his own day, and if he seeks to speculate on the perfect poetry that arises in that stream. Otherwise he makes two errors: he does not say that poetry has been sown with these seeds; that this flowering is limited organically by the elements and the seeds. Rather he is saying, in contradiction to a certain botany in poetry, that the seeds *ought* to have been thus and the flower *ought* to have been so.

And Mr. Shapiro writes on how modern poetry has not grown.

The first of the three confusions which he mentions is that in prosody: he says quite arbitrarily that only two types of measure can be applied to English verse—the count of eye and the count of ear. What kind of rule-making is this? The poetry of Skelton, Shakespeare, Donne, Milton, Blake, Hopkins and Eliot proves that there is obviously a third type which is a simple combination of ear and eye count: it is everywhere in the middle comedies and the late tragedies of Shakespeare, in the *Songs of Innocence* and the *Songs of Experience* of Blake, *Ash Wednesday,* or the *Cantos*. Mr. Shapiro surmises this but passes on. Perhaps the modern poet from Hopkins on is becoming so accustomed to both the count of eye and the count of ear that he subconsciously fuses one into the other in his writings of poetry.

Since the English language is the youngest, it absorbs more and copies more than any other. Thus a chance for alliteration and a chance for accent-count happens often in the age of Skelton or of Auden; and I do not think it is by ignorance or accident. In well over half of Milton's blank verse, speech accents fall in variations to the metric pattern for greater music alone. Or the influence of the French syllabic count has not confused the prosody of Marianne Moore's English. Or the word-making of Joyce: surely *Finnegan's Wake* does not fail in its "prosody." Nor does Stevens in *Notes Toward A Supreme Fiction.*

Mr. Shapiro wondered why no great system of English prosody has been made. It seems entirely valid to say that there can be no such formal set of rules as the ear system or the eye system created, for these reasons: English is not a static language, English is not a classic language, (it passed through its "classical" period), and English has been affected either consciously by poets who have brought other prosodies to heel, such as Wyatt and Surrey copying Italians; or by Milton playing on his Latin organ, or by a poet's subconscious fusion of the ear and eye count; or by the slow process of the change in linguistics from its ancient womb to its present youth; or by alliteration, qualitative count, quantitative count, syllabic count and the variation of prose accents against metric stresses. And since rhythm has the poet's personal muscle as well as his adaptation of a pattern of vibrations (largely limited to combinations of two or three beats) in it, the range of prosody is extraordinarily extensive.

Thus there are two possible answers to Mr. Shapiro. All English prosody is confused and the periods of greatest confusion are the sixteenth, eighteenth and twentieth centuries. Or if one tries to set down formal laws and finds modern poets outside the canon, he may call this a confusion. I believe it is sounder to approach prosody from other principles: specifically, the biology of the English line evolves from *Beowulf* and all indigenous rhythms of descending poets are set into counterpoint to the biological form; in poetry, new liberties must be taken in prosody and in language to make a new order; and forms have to be broken and remade. At last, craftsmen such as Yeats, Joyce, Eliot, Pound, Auden and Tate need not be accused of confusion in prosody. I would guess so far as to say

that English can never have formal laws written that will cover all the possibilities of prosody, because our language has great diversity. Shakespeare would have had to retire long before *The Tempest* if he had obeyed the rules of Sidney or Rymer. Or put it another way: the seventeenth century rewrote Shakespeare according to its laws and decorum, but we've lost those copies. My point is that.

For the confusion in language, Mr. Shapiro also desires the definitive set of rules, and he blames the poet today for not observing grammarian's rules. Although Mr. Shapiro does not make the careless error of saying that there is a special language for poetry, he comes near implying it. Charged language and language that has been beaten into submission by the poet's understanding and by his craft seem to me [to] be the raw materials of poetic language. As I fail to see how imagery can be legislated or language divorced from it, so I fail to see how language can be legislated or imagery divorced from it.

But for the explicit: the English language since it is not a classical language cannot be expected to fall into static or formalized idiom, rhetoric or syntax. On the contrary, as Otto Jespersen and other modern linguistic scientists have shown, the pattern of growth in the English language is toward greater diversity. This, I believe, is for the good of poetry; and since any language has its richness and its boundaries or limitations, the poet is ultimately freer in English than in any other language. Thus Joyce chose English rather than Gaelic or French from which to depart, as it were, giving the glands of the English language many injections to enlarge its growth, to speed up its growing diversity, and to expand it into the gesture of idea.

Finally, Mr. Shapiro feels that the modern poet tends too much and too unwisely to merge poetry with the language of common speech, thereby committing more confusions. This which Shapiro calls confusion is actually the highest and best personal use of language: it distinguished Shakespeare's poetry from *Richard II* on; it is the secret of Blake, of Eliot, Joyce, or Auden. Only Milton ignored the social idiom, using music instead. Their use of language is best, for it brings emotion and understanding to the closest idiom or diction for any man, contemporary to the poems, and to those who come afterwards. Archaism reverses this, and sends a reader backwards out of emotion into quaintness and into the archives. If any activity distinguishes modern poetry from its ancestors, it is the emphasis placed on what Eliot calls the "search for a proper modern colloquial idiom." Since language is a growing organism, this search is endless and will not be chained or changed by rules.

One word on Shapiro's analysis of rhetoric: he sees great discipline in the rhetoric of *Ulysses*. I would say that the same in Crane, Auden, Pound, Yeats and Eliot is responsible for their putting music into the common speech—an elaboration that requires a mastery of rhetoric, grammar, and a vocabulary of images and words, before the poet can order them into the tense and sensuous, lyric and dramatic music which poetry ultimately must become. Again rules cannot tell one how to achieve this order.

If Mr. Shapiro were to reduce his hypothesis to its lowest denominator, he would probably say that the confusions in prosody and language are overshadowed by the confusions in belief, which probably even cause the former two confusions. It would seem that he mistakes the lack of belief which modern man can use, for the confused belief in the poets. Before the Industrial Revolution and scientific determinism destroyed what I perhaps dangerously call the popular belief of Western man in the myth of Christianity, such poets as Dante, Shakespeare, or Milton could set their work against the backdrop of the Christian Myth. None of these poets had to do what the modern poet had been forced to do. Once that belief became destroyed, the poet had to take on a new function: he had not only to make the poem; he had to make a myth which would reveal all of the anagogical and psychological counterpoints of the poem too. Spread throughout the creativity of their work, this function was accepted by Yeats, (Hardy before him), Joyce, Crane and Pound. It is still part of the writing of Eliot, Stevens, Auden, Lewis, Thomas, or any good poet.

This occupation does not reveal a confusion in the poets' beliefs. It is more sinister. In this Age man is confronted with resolving the duality between Love and Power. The maelstrom of systems and beliefs, that modern man has invented to dispel the evil and release the good, ranges in its turmoil from tired political mythology to revised Anglo-Catholic mythology. To be sure, there is great confusion in this Maelstrom. But the confusion is not one of bad poetry, futile metaphysics, or loose logic; rather it is a confusion in the yearning and searching of many men who have tried diverse ways to save mankind from incessant turmoil. That all—the poet, the philosopher, the divine, the statesman and the scientist—try to save and give us something in which to believe is some proof of the necessity and the seriousness in our time.

It is one of the simplest essences of art that there be a valid myth used. Further, the poet must believe it intensely and vigorously; and as a maker, he must master the craft to set down the belief and the intensity in a perfect order. Surely then, if there is no myth, the fault is not with the poet. Surely, if art needs a myth today, the poet will try to take on another burden and either seek an old myth not common in the elbow-rubbing with the men in his age; or like Joyce, who in *Ulysses* and *Finnegan's Wake* made a myth out of common man, the procreative principle and the dark primordial unconsciousness of the race, the poet may state his purpose: "to forge in the smithy of my soul the uncreated conscience of my race." Or like Pound, whose great newsreel of culture, history, economy, and polity is mythmaking, the poet may seek to make a socio-economic myth. Or like Stevens, whose ideas prove an order and whose poetry is knowledge, the poet may make of his supreme fiction a usable myth. If the myth and the poem are made in the same creation by the same maker, the poetry matters most. And it must be evaluated first. The myth which suits him might find no universal acceptance; but each of the works I mentioned above is right for many people. Then, it can be said that even though there is no one belief created and no one myth available, there is not confusion in the poets, but diversity. Or it can be said that the confusion is the Age of Love and Power. And the fault is not poetry's, but man's.

I would set against the *Essay on Rime* these principles for poetry:

> *"Whales, branded in the Arctic, are often found cruising in the Antarctic"*—Palinurus.

> *"We are a part of all that went before"*—Marx.

> *"The poet is a maker"*—Aristotle.

> *"All true creation is a thing born out of nothing"*—Paul Klee.

> *"Why not try to understand the singing of the birds"*—Picasso.

> *"A poem is a new compound . . . it may tend to realise itself first as a particular rhythm and this rhythm may bring to birth the idea and the image"*—Eliot.

> *"The liquid letters of speech, symbols of the element of mystery, flowed forth over his brain"*—Joyce.

> *"Art is a habit of the mind"*—an anonymous Medieval poet.

Stephen Spender (essay date 1948)

SOURCE: "The Power and the Hazard," in *Poetry,* Vol. LXXI, No. VI, March, 1948, pp. 314-18.

[*In the following essay, Spender provides a mixed review of* Trial of a Poet.]

This is Mr. Shapiro's fourth volume of published poetry, and in common with his previous volume, **Essay on Rime**, it shows him intensely preoccupied with the problem of how and what the poet should write. Considering that this problem is for him as yet unsolved, it seems a little tiresome that he should be so insistent that the solution should lie in writing like Karl Shapiro. Probably Shapiro would gain by dealing with his own problem as really his own and not every other poet's more than he gains by trying to make literary maps just at the time when his own difficulties are most obvious. Another danger for him lies in his own considerable mental power and energy which enable him to versify very effectively too many situations which are outside the one which is central to him in his present state of crisis.

Nevertheless, it is excellent that he should be in a critical and self-critical position: excellent not only for himself, but also for other poets, if and when he succeeds in getting out of the wood. In this review I shall try to indicate what I believe to be Mr. Shapiro's main strengths, weaknesses, true aims and false aims.

It is obvious that Mr. Shapiro has a considerable gift for projecting himself into dramatic situations, usually conceived in rather abstract terms. The first long poem in this volume, **"Recapitulations,"** is autobiographical self-dramatization. The Conscientious Objector, the Southerner, the Jew, the poet who is on trial in *Trial of a Poet*, with his entourage of the Priest, the Doctor, the Chorus who is the Public, indicate sufficiently Mr. Shapiro's capacity for inventing Masks.

However, Mr. Shapiro seems to have imposed on himself other disciplines which often rob these figures in their dramatic situations of those sensitive and personal turns of thought which are convincing. He is in full reaction against the personal, the sensitive, the peculiar, the idiosyncratic. He is determined to be metrically and intellectually respectable, as against the shoddiness of other contemporary poets whom he compares to crabs walking backwards in their retreat from our scientific hygienic age into superstition, magic and vicious eccentricity. The combination of these aims with self-dramatization results at times in the peculiar effect of a poetry written from a very personal point of view, which has been emptied of all personality. Thus in **"Recapitulations,"** which is an autobiographical confession, he succeeds in turning himself into a public situation, emptied of any emotion which would convince us that here we are confronted by a flesh and blood person:

> I raved like a scarlet banner,
>   Brave cloth of a single piece,
> I learned to despise all uncles,
>   All Congressmen, all police.
>
> I hated the coin of kindness,
>   Good deeds of the Octopus;
> It was evil to give to beggars
>   What beggars could give to us.
>
> O comrade of distant Russia,
>   How difficult for your kind
> To live in that even climate
>   Where no one may change his mind.

This is an intellectual predicament pretending to be a person, it bears no distinguishing note to strike the eye or ear with which one can really sympathize as with another human being.

A writer who passionately identifies himself with Faust, with the Jew, the Poet, etc., must have a personality somewhere, but reading some of these poems reminds one curiously of some work by Pirandello which might be called *Twenty Poems in Search of an Author*. The predicament of Mr. Shapiro seems to be that whilst he has a personality which violently wants to realize itself in poetry, he also has a set of rules, largely based on a critical reaction to his contemporaries, which prevents him from doing so. One searches for this real person and suddenly finds it in occasional lines such as:

>   Within this square
> I am somewhere but difficult to find,
> As in a photograph of graduation
> Where youth predominates and looks alive.

or again, in the same poem, **"Demobilization"**:

> Dimly it comes to me that this is home,
> This is my Maryland, these pines I know,
> This camp itself when budding green and raw
> I watched in agony of shame.

Indeed, I do not wish to give the impression that Mr. Shapiro does not succeed. At times he succeeds very finely as in **"Demobilization."** **"Homecoming"** is at least a partial success, although it suffers from overstatement which is not entirely convincing:

> My smile that would light up all darkness
> And ask forgiveness of the things that thrust
> Shame and all death on millions and on me.

Problems of overstatement such as the one that arises in these lines are important. For the problem here is one of truth. It is the problem not of the stanza and the metrical line but of the word. Not of the *mot juste* even but of the word which is faithful to the emotion felt which, in turn, is betrayed by any exaggeration. The fact is that smiles don't light up all darkness. However, if as well may be, the situation seems to require that the poet should invent such a smile, then he has to invent himself, he has to create his own poetic personality, he has to have the courage to be a monstrous egoist in his poetry, as Heine or D. H. Lawrence or Yeats were in theirs. You cannot eat your cake and have it even in poetry. You cannot substitute a violent, public and mechanical attitude for a vivid, convincing individual personality, through fear of lapsing into poetical incorrectitude. I could wish that Mr. Shapiro were a hundred times more the unabashed egoist in his poems. In a poem such as **"In the Waxworks"** where he gives us a glimpse of something monstrous in his own personality he is magnificent. In the *Trial of a Poet* he shows a power of organizing dramatic material and of expressing intellectual positions, but here again I find the situations mechanical.

Mr. Shapiro is a difficult poet to estimate, because whilst there are elements of technical accomplishment in his poetry which obviously command admiration, there are also elements of crudeness and insensitivity which make him vulnerable to a purist approach, and his very violence makes one uncertain of his power. Nevertheless he is a poet of rare intellectual strength, he has an exceptional power of being able to think of a poem as a single idea, and he has an interesting and perhaps passionate personality which his poetry at present partly conceals. If he were as preoccupied with the single word as he is with the stanza, he would gain enormously. At present he is too inclined to throw his words away on the wings of his stanzas. He is certainly one of the very few poets writing today whose development is an exciting subject for speculation.

Edwin Fussell (essay date 1954)

SOURCE: "Karl Shapiro: The Paradox of Prose and Poetry," in *The Western Review,* Vol. 18, No. 3, Spring, 1954, pp. 225-44.

[In the following essay, Fussell examines Shapiro's poetic development.]

It is now ten years since the publication of Karl Shapiro's first important book of poems, a period long enough for the poet to have produced at least a minor corpus, a group of poems whose homogeneity and range may be taken together as representing qualities that define, in the literary historians' provocative phrase, an "early career"; a period long enough, too, for the reader to have lived with some of these poems in mind for several years, and to have been generally aware of Shapiro as a writer to be reckoned with in his thinking about the poetry immediately contemporaneous with himself. It is now as good a time as any, briefly, for a fairly thorough-going description of Shapiro's poetry and, perhaps, for some tentative evaluations of it.

Discussion of Shapiro's work may start just about any place, but might, in view of the theme of this essay, begin with the title poem in his latest collection, **Trial of a Poet, 1947**. This may not be Shapiro's "best" poem (though I am inclined to maintain against general opinion that it is very near his best), but it is probably the most helpful to those who wish some initial perspectives on where Shapiro has been, where he is now, and where he may go in the next few years.

The poem's context is about equally social and aesthetic, historically concerned with the poet's position in society today, and philosophically concerned with the nature and purposes of poetry and poets eternally. The volume is appropriately dedicated to F. O. Matthiessen, of all American scholars perhaps the most anxious to work out practical and fructifying relations between the aesthetic and social perspectives that Shapiro must equally insist on. The stimulus for the poem, its immediate social cause, or at any rate its historical reason for being, would seem to be the case of Ezra Pound, though its composition antedates the infamous Bollingen controversy by at least two years. Appalled by the violence and dishonesty of the assaults then made on modern poetry, criticism, and thought, Shapiro was evidently already swinging away from the incipient anti-intellectualism which had tempted him in **Essay on Rime** (1945). He has himself always been ready to attack what he conceives to be the weaknesses of contemporary poetry (chiefly, I think, its self-conscious intellectuality; it would be hard, though, to find a more self-conscious and intellectual poet than Shapiro), but only if he is allowed to share the blame. But he is also extraordinarily sensitive to derogation of contemporary art when it comes from those who apparently do not love the arts at all. However irritated Shapiro can sometimes become with "critics" and "intellectuals" (as in **Essay on Rime** and "Farewell to Criticism," *Poetry*, LXXI, January 1948), he is a little of each himself, and it is certain that his art fruitfully participates in the values articulated by their disciplines. It is plain, I think, that during the mid-forties, Shapiro was having a Frost-like lover's quarrel with his world.

The "Poet" in this poem, then, has something to do with Pound. The trial is of an "insane" poet accused of "treason" (this word is used in the poem as a loose charge for all that the Philistine has found to object to in the arts for half a century or more). But beyond a few suggestive details, he is not significantly Pound as much as he is the modern poet generally, or indeed the poet at any time and place. In these respects, he is Shapiro and represents Shapiro's own struggle between self-approval and self-doubt, especially as this struggle is reflected in the social world. The Chorus of Poets are Shapiro, too, as they and the Poet are all of us, poets and readers of poetry alike. Part of the Shapiro signature has always been a strongly developed "communal conscience."

Such identification is enforced by the structure of the poem, which, for the first half, allows the reader an easy and pleasant identification with the Poet who is alternatively abused and defended by three Philistine accusers (Public Officer, Doctor, Priest) and the Chorus of Poets, and then, midway through the poem, compels a sudden disorganization of this relation and the assumption of a wholly new point of view. It is a brilliant satiric technique for the purposes of the poem, which include the engendering of some soul-searching on the part of those who too readily assume fashionable doctrines in the arts; this poem, it must be remembered, is more likely to be read by poets than by Philistines.

At the moment of crisis, the Poet awakes from his trance and speaks for the first time, at first in a melange of quotation that the Public Officer calls "the tag-ends of a demented criticism." Then there is a hint of an important turning, as the Public Officer goes on to characterize the Chorus as

> You Poets who stand aside
> In mutual sympathy, admiring yourselves
> In the fall of one of your numbers

Finally, "the Poet takes the Judge's bench" (at about this time, probably, the reader notices that there is neither judge nor jury nor court in this somewhat Kafka-like trial), and in prose examines the speeches of all the persons, concluding with the Chorus and himself. This kind of technique makes the poem exciting and fresh; its dialectic of attitudes, nearly all of which are more properly read as relevant to each other than to any absolute scheme of things, is exhilarating intellectually and rich in figurative vitality. The technique, of course, also makes for difficulty of interpretation, and for precisely the kind of difficulty that Shapiro intends: the reader zealous for dogma, revelation, the easy answer, will be baffled and misled. The method is thematically and satirically appropriate to the poem's purpose of discomfiting all kinds of oversimplifiers.

The Poet easily disposes of the three Philistines and then takes up the Chorus, whose emotional involvement with him is called, first, "nothing more than the sentimental ruminations of old soldiers," and then, more precisely, "a mixture of sincere good intention and insincere pity." Finally, according to the accused, "in the last analysis they ask to share his guilt." Clearly we do not have here the conventional chorus whose point of view is the author's but that other kind, ironically representative of median capacity, stereotyped opinion. Shapiro's wit has worked well by allowing us, readers who are sympathetic (sentimental?) towards poetry, to identify ourselves, out of self-esteem, with the Chorus, just as the Chorus has, for the same wrong reasons, taken up the cause of the Poet. At this point we may be very near to contemporary realities.

But if so we are soon propelled to the outer regions of aesthetic discourse. The Poet briefly evaluates himself— "in prose and the indirect defense rather than poetry and the frontal attack"—and identifies his quotations, summed up as meaning: "Those who apprehend the uses of poetry as knowledge are afraid of the poet (he thus infers the truth of the charges against him); all ages have deliberated his case and found him guilty; and finally, exile is preferable to local fame." The first clause clearly separates Shapiro from what is perhaps the main line of twentieth century criticism. By "he thus infers the truth of the charges against him," I think that Shapiro refers to the charge which to him sums up the poet's eternal temptation to hubris: the sin of taking oneself too seriously, of being overly concerned with poetry as knowledge, effect, action. A few lines later, the "crime" is defined as "acting upon the sense of poetry as upon the sense of prose." The third statement will do as well as any to show how Shapiro's prose has come into its own, moving away from the Eliot norm near where it began, and how it is now closer to the witty generalization of his verse. What the argument of the poem adds up to so far is the perpetual untenability of the poet's position as soon as his properly high valuation of his calling is transferred from the realm of essence (poetry) to the realm of action (prose). There is a discontinuity between the two worlds and so there will always be an alienation of the poet from the ordinary world. This dualism, insofar as it bears on the poet's *social* relations, appears to be accepted by Shapiro with good humor, as a natural fact that can be adjusted to without self-pity or pride or despair or belligerence.

But this radical discontinuity might be taken as a denial that poetry may legitimately aspire to any human function whatever. So we are immediately reminded that the poem has an epigraph taken from *Samson Agonistes:*

> In seeking just occasion to provoke
> The *Philistine,* thy Countries Enemy,
> Thou never wast remiss, I bear thee witness:
> Yet *Israel* still serves with all his Sons.

And Shapiro explicates: "Israel is poetry. Thy country is America. The Philistine is the enemy within. In destroying the works of the Philistine, the prisoner blindly destroyed himself." Now this may be (I think it is) a rather good description of Pound's poetic tragedy, but what needs underlining is not its possible reference to Pound so much as its certain tragic quality. Whatever Shapiro may mean by "the enemy within," it is surely neither social reform nor normal regeneration that he is asking the poet to undertake. It may be that "the enemy within" is an anti-poetic feeling that exists naturally in a world of prose. And it may also be that Shapiro is admitting that in the realm

of essence there *is* a kind of evil toward which the poet's attitude is necessarily hostile. The evil would be, probably, negation, apathy, accidia, and in his counteraction of this evil the poet would find his socially therapeutic function. But there is always the danger of confusing the essential with the merely social, and in such an event the poet's energies might easily pass over from his proper work to the destruction of an extrinsic evil. Should he do so, he would cease to be poet and thus destroy himself. One recalls the modest, balanced, moderate point of view with which *Essay on Rime* concludes; Shapiro is speaking of Freud on the arts:

> he briefly says that in the main
> They are beneficent and harmless forms.
> This is the sane perspective, one that brings
> The beloved creative function back to scale.

And so finally, for his "crime" of megalomania ("acting upon the sense of poetry as upon the sense of prose"), the prisoner is condemned "to be known hereafter as a dull poet and the lapdog of his age."
This is the obvious climax of the poem. But there is more to this ambiguous drama, and the additional commentary affords further clarification of Shapiro's views of his art. The concluding verse paragraph has the Chorus of Poets addressing the Philistine inquisitors in Shapiro's most effectively winning argumentative manner:

> Ours is the miracle of water and wine,
> Stones to fishes, leaves to loaves,
> And common clay to prayer and pleasure domes.
> Yours is the miracle of the transubstantiation
> Of sculpture to gravel, bread to dirt,
> Fishes to chemicals, wine to vinegar.
> —The crime? There was no crime. Prose is no crime.
> There was, however, a failure of the word;
> The failure was to fall into your hands.

This is rather typical Shapiro. In the first place, there is marked out an area of intellectual discourse and potentially imaginative relationship (the idea of metamorphosis) to which the various figures of speech, in themselves interrelated, are ultimately to be referred. In the second place, there is the dynamic paradox of a double and contradictory process, a deeply structural irony. A metamorphosis may, in Shapiro's witty view, work variously, and from this ambiguty the other ironies are generated. The poet, for example, performs as a natural function the miracle of redeeming the ordinary, the concrete, the mundane experience, and transforming it by his art from common matter to spiritual vision. This, essentially, is the movement from prose to poetry, from material to essence, from experience to vision. The Philistine, on the other hand, practices an opposite "miracle" (I suppose it is a "miracle" to the romantic poet that any one should willingly behave so contrary to nature): the destruction of experience, either formed ("sculpture to gravel): or natural ("fishes to chemicals"). Even religious experience is soiled and soured by this process, wine becoming vinegar, bread dirt, fishes chemicals. But there is no suggestion whatever in Shapiro that art do the work of religion, even though the poet's creative miracle is likened to religious ritual: the implications are simply that art and religion are in some ways analogous, and that at certain times and places the poet may do his job better than the priest does his. But the destructive movement is the main point here: it is from poetry to prose.

Now Shapiro is explicit that it is the *direction contrary to nature* that offends him, and not the materials of experience in themselves. "There was no crime. Prose is no crime." "Prose" lines up here with such neutral terms (taken in and for themselves) as stones, leaves, common clay. These are the materials that man shapes into form, into art, into "prayer and pleasure domes." But the artistic process is directional, and not two-way, and the reverse direction is a blasphemy, a sin against the human spirit. If one wishes any understanding of Shapiro as a poet devoted to formal structures in poetry it is necessary to grasp this point. "Gravel" here is not the neutral word that "stones" is, because "gravel" is the destroyed idea of "sculpture." And the same pejorative quality, for the same reasons, is of course associated with "dirt," "chemicals," and "vinegar."

What seems to lie behind this passage is an assumption that man's spirit moves from experience (prose) to form (art), that this motion is inevitable in the nature of things, and that its distortion or reversal is an act against what appears to be conceived as a quasi-evolutionary development. If there was, then, in the poem no "crime" (acts against society), there was indeed a "failure of the word" (act against nature). According to Shapiro's view, poetry has somehow failed its function, initiative has passed to those who would destroy, and the poet must now fight to recover, not only his place in the contemporary world, but also his true and perpetual quality as poet. Explanation of the failure will turn up later, in terms of Shapiro's thinking in more prosodic terms on the prose-poetry antithesis.

Shapiro might be called a witty Wordsworth, a Romantic poet who is also an intellectual with a sense of humor. But such a description ought to mean a great deal more than that Shapiro is predominantly a party to the later Romantic movement: one needs, more positively, to keep in mind how Shapiro's program for poetry, the problems with which his art is concerned, the techniques through which his poetry is articulated, are all significantly related to the momentous year 1798.

Shapiro's debt to Auden is a commonplace, and a just enough observation, if one goes on to remark how Auden, too, has joined wit to the tradition of Wordsworth (Eliot, it might be submitted, is a somewhat ironic Coleridge. Indeed, it often seems that Eliot's famous remarks about the dissociation of sensibility make just as good sense applied to Wordsworth and Coleridge, Auden and Eliot, as to Dryden and Milton). In *Essay on Rime* Shapiro has a pleasant account of the impact of Auden's early work on contemporary poetic expectations:

> Few thought of now as pertinent
> To the immediate speech, until a set
> Of more or less Oxford radicals unloaded
> Their gear of games and books and politics,
> Blazers and alcohol and hockey-sticks
> Into the lap of middle age. The effect
> We know; but when the confusion was decoded
> Auden stood out the clearest of the young
> Spokesmen. For the first the radio
> The car, the sofa and the new highway
> Came into focus in a poem as things,
> Not symbols of the things. The scenery changed
> To absolute present and the curtain rose
> On the actual place, not Crane's demonic city
> Nor Eliot's weird unreal metropolis,
> But that pedestrian London with which prose
> Alone had previously dealt.

Auden stands, in other words, in direct relation to the tradition of Wordsworth, an essentially realistic poet whose function is to translate larger and larger areas of contemporary experience ("absolute present") into poetry. And the more pedestrian the materials, the greater triumph for the new "things" in art (the miracle is of common clay to pleasure domes). The direction, one notices, is again from prose to poetry. Shapiro consistently affirms that this is the true and natural direction of expression, in spite of an age that likes to pile up evidence on the other side (for example, Edmund Wilson, "Is Verse a Dying Technique?").

Surely it is not difficult to relate Shapiro, by way of his immediate predecessor Auden, to this realistic tradition of accurate observation and predominate *thinginess* (two of Shapiro's early titles were **Noun** and **Person, Place and Thing**, characterized also by its occasional theoretical predilection for simple personal feeling and amateur homiletics, all operating through a relatively simple diction and tight metric. Paradoxically, though, it is when Shapiro is most closely following this tradition of simplicity that he is least effective ("Recapitulations," for instance, in his last book): he is best when he is Wordsworth with a difference, Shapiro's difference being chiefly his wit, his highly developed sense of aesthetic distance.

In a more reactionary mood he asks, at the end of *Essay on Rime*, where is our

> literature
> Of nature, where the love poem and the plain
> Statement of feeling?

And then wants to know, as Wordsworth had a century and a half earlier:

> How and when and why
> Did we conceive our horror for emotion,
> Our fear of beauty?

Finally he suggests, though he does not work out, a possible reading of recent poetic history as a fall from Poe's work ("perhaps it is that Poe was the last poet in the classic signification of the word"), as "the vision of the soul" *through* "poetry of sensation" *to* "poetry of ideas." The movement is the same: from poetry to prose.

But the program for poetry, as Wordsworth saw it, and as Shapiro evidently agrees, requires an opposite development, a constant transformation of pedestrian, natural experience from prosaic to poetic, from diurnal, to essential: "to choose incidents and situations from common life, and to relate or describe them, throughout, as far as was possible in a selection of language really used by men, and, at the same time, to throw over them a certain colouring of imagination, whereby ordinary things should be presented to the mind in an unusual aspect . . ." Thus Wordsworth: and it would be difficult to improve this statement as a general critical description of the intentions of a typical Shapiro poem, say, **"Elegy for a Dead Soldier."**

As a part of his poetic past, Shapiro has thus inherited a concern with the vexing and ambiguous question of the relations between poetry and prose, a question on which Wordsworth and Coleridge, it will be recalled, ultimately disagreed. But their recognition of the problems as of the first importance is one way of distinguishing them as the first "modern" poets. The issue is still very lively: how does the essence of poetry derive from the prose of common experience, and how does it in turn affect that experience? Put another way, the question is this: how can poetry, no longer assumed to be a "delightful teaching," maintain its force as an efficacious social vehicle for the creative vision?

The relations of poetry and prose—in all their bewildering complication of similarity and difference, cause and effect, origin and end—are Shapiro's most pervasive critical interest. This difficult subject must now be examined in some detail. Unfortunately Shapiro's own contributions are sometimes an additional barrier to understanding. For one thing, because of the kind of extension that Shapiro gives to the antithesis, "prose" and "poetry" become terms more or less analogous to the "discursive" or "symbolical" ways of apprehending experience. Characteristically Shapiro's sense of the *difference* between the two modes is controlling, but not, it seems, entirely convincing. For he seems unable to rest satisfied with the *poetic* expression of his vision, and insists upon crossing over into the realm of rational discourse in order to explain and defend and justify values which, by his own definition, are inexplicable and indefensible on the level of linguistic meaning alone.

So far Shapiro's career shows more homogeneity than change, nor does it yet seem time for the reader to demand development of him.

—Edwin Fussell

It is this sharp sense of difference that ought to concern us first, since it is in this respect that the words "prose"

and "poetry" appear to take on for Shapiro their most inclusive significances, sometimes, as in *Trial of a Poet*, to the point of supporting an antithetical relationship as broad as that between "experience" and "art." Throughout Shapiro's writing one is aware of a strongly felt dualism and a constant reaching after its resolution. I do not in any way mean to impair the dignity and seriousness of Shapiro's concern with this problem by pointing out that the antithesis is essentially between "beauty" and "truth," a problem which Keats did *not,* contrary to popular opinion, forever dispose of, and a problem which, contrary to the party line of second-generation "new criticism," contemporary aesthetics has not solved either. Shapiro's inheritance of this Romantic puzzler is focused by his dissatisfaction with the influences upon contemporary criticism of I. A. Richards, which Shapiro seems to regard as mainly dangerous intrusions of "science" into "art." Part of Shapiro's habitual stance is an irritation with contemporary emphasis on "meaning" and on theories of poetry as a "special kind of knowledge." These concerns are all immediately apparent in *Essay on Rime*:

> insofar as Meaning
> Has tried to adopt Poetics, the plot thickens.
> But can the science of definition relate to
> Poetry, even obliquely? To science belongs
> The isolation of knowledge, to art belongs
> The isolation of beauty;

A few lines later Shapiro tells us flatly "that dialectic is the foe of poetry," and in the next verse paragraph he adds:

> criticism
> Has charted poetry into dangerous narrows
> And dashed its own brains out upon the rocks
> Of absolute meaning;

And he says that his whole essay is a protest "to the semantic muse."

Just how ambivalent Shapiro is can be seen when, only a few lines further on, he assures us:

> My wish is but to call a rose a rose
> And not a trope;

managing to sound like any other semantic positivist! This failure fully to resolve the prose-poetry dilemma accounts, I think, for such phenomena as Shapiro's alternate attacks and defenses of contemporary poetry and criticism, for his dislike of semantics, for his interest in prosody (which he persistently wishes to regard as a "science," following the terminology, I suppose, of his favorite Lanier), for his uneasy attitudes about the *effect of art.*

Fairly continuous in *Essay on Rime* is the argument that prose and poetry (with all the extended oppositions they imply) are discrete, their differences a matter of primary essence. Perhaps this is the best summary:

> When ordinary men reverse their collars
> They are not priests; neither can prose and rime
> Interchange natures by a shift of dress.

Another passage seeks to explain the difference in terms of techniques, which Shapiro sees as mainly two, rhythm and figure. In order to get the full sense of the following lines, it is desirable to let "rhythm" stand for a variety of meanings such as form, order, harmony, and to read "trope" as suggestive of a very wide range of fluid and generative symbolic mental activities:

> Rhythm belongs to rhetoric; it is forbidden
> In prose, for instance, to prepare the cadence
> Or to exact the prosody as in rime;
> Similarly in prose the tropes are hidden
> From the eye. But poetry obtrudes these forms
> In full upon the senses and with full care.
> The mind recoils from the poetical
> In every art but poetry.

That last sentence reveals again Shapiro's discomfort with the position he must elsewhere profess: the superior human value of poetry. He appears to hesitate before the consequences of his belief that poetry and prose are radically different modes of knowledge and value and that poetry is "higher." A characteristic, but unsatisfactory, procedure in *Essay on Rime* is to preserve the value of poetry by unduly narrowing its effective scope, thus leaving much of the world unredeemed in prose.

A later essay, "Prosody as the Meaning," (*Poetry*, LXXIII, March 1949), returns to the technical ways of discrimination. Shapiro's position is basically the same, even though here he has a little approached the semanticist and speaks of "multiple meaning" where earlier he spoke of "trope":

> Prose moves toward single meaning and away
> from rhythm; poetry toward rhythm and away
> from single meaning . . . however closely poetry
> may resemble prose or prose poetry, during those
> times when one or the other draws nourishment
> from its opposite, the two forms are nonetheless
> absolutes.

Because they are ultimately divergent principles, Shapiro is uncomfortable when they remain too long in too intimate a relation. This is a fair way of summing up his attitude toward the history of twentieth century poetry: what has chiefly bothered him has been the breakdown of demarcation between two worlds. Shapiro would, of course, qualify this statement by adding that (1) such a breakdown is occasionally inevitable and even desirable and (2) there should be some discernible relation between poetry and prose at all times. For in Shapiro's view a poetry depends, for very definition, upon a prose, much as salvation implies a fall from grace. And finally, all the jacket blurbs and book reviews about Shapiro's conservative return to traditional prosody must be interpreted, if they are to make sense, with just as much reference to Shapiro's sense of his own precise historical position with relation to the alternative approaches and retreats of poetry to and from prose as to any innate preferences and speculations about how absolutely formal poetry ought to be.

But antithesis is not the only conceivable connection between poetry and prose. There is another relation in which the two terms are part of a directional continuum (this I referred to in discussing **"Trial of a Poet"** as a "quasi-evolutionary development"). This view is also found in *Essay on Rime,* and is not inconsistent with the other, since the absolute difference between prose and poetry is, in that view, seen rather as a radical discrimination in tendency and degree and not as a difference in absolute kind.

> In the mathematical sense, rime is a power,
> Prose raised to the numerical exponent
> Of three or six or even *n,* depending
> Upon the propensity of the literature
> At a particular time and on the bent
> Of the particular poet. It is therefore
> A heightening and a measure of intensity.

The act of poetry, then, is to isolate and exalt functions inherent in language, such as rhythm and trope (or, in experience, "form" and "significance"), which the language of prose and the everyday world are always in process of seeking to minimize or deny. Another way of putting the same relation is to take it "in the physical sense": thus, poetry appears rather as origin than end, "the nuclear and vital element of speech and prose" (it is only in *appearance,* though, and not in essence, that poetry may be so conceived). Or one may shift to another of these "approximate metaphors" and find "in the theological sense" poetry as "the ghost and prose the flesh of language."

Poetry as process, then, has something radically different from prose. And so, "paraphrasing, according to my view of poetry, is a total impossibility. Poetry is the only sense of poetry" ("Prosody as the Meaning"). This is merely a firmer statement of what Shapiro said earlier in the same piece: "The so-called prose sense of poetry is relatively insignificant to the experience of poetry." But another statement is perhaps most representative as well as most personal (Shapiro refers here to his earlier essay, "A Farewell to Criticism").

> I hoped somehow to detach the poetry reader from the belief, so thoroughly a part of our literary consciousness, that the feast of the text is all. And I felt myself peculiarly qualified for this job because of my own disinterest in the meaning of poems, a disinterest which had never come into conflict with my own love of poetry or my vocation for it.

Poetry is not all "meaning," but consists instead of four elements that Shapiro calls "figures": they are of "speech meaning," "meter," "sound," and "image." Of these elements it is probably "meter" that is most important and "speech meaning" (or "linguistic sense") that is least. Almost alone among contemporary poets Shapiro has maintained a persistent irritation with *explication de texte* and a steady scholarly interest in prosody.

These two elements, furthermore, as essential elements in poetry and prose, are basically though not totally repugnant. "The sense of poetry," Shapiro explains, "is achieved by suppressing the functional value of the word and by liberating all those non-functional and accidental qualities of which words are capable" ("A Farewell to Criticism"). And the agent of liberation is, chiefly, meter. Finally, although a certain residue of "meaning" remains to the poem, it is so little important to the whole harmony that it is not even desirable to speak of "words" in poetry. "It is my contention that the 'same' word used in a prose line and in a line of poetry are two entirely different words, not even similar, except to the eye. The word in the line of poetry . . . should perhaps be designated otherwise . . . I am content to refer to this other entity as a 'not-word'.

Shapiro would seem to follow Patmore, Bridges, and Hopkins in what he calls " the most idealistic view of metre, as that which in itself was capable of as much poetic expression as words" ("English Prosody and Modern Poetry," *ELH*, XIV, June 1947). And Shapiro has also suggested that when a "new prosody" appears it ought to look into the "causes" and "meanings" (and not merely the description) of meters. Prosody is thus clearly of the essence: and yet, paradoxically, this most vital element of poetry is also derived from prose. I think most readers will agree that the first section of *Essay on Rime* ("The Confusion in Prosody") comes to life only when Shapiro turns to Lanier and his

> prophecy that rime
> Will mate with prose and probably create
> A yet-undreamed-of measure for our verse.

And Shapiro's interest continues to mount as he works over some of the implications of one of his favorite books, Saintsbury's *History of English Prose Rhythm* (1912). But the full significance of Saintsbury appears only at the climax and conclusion of this section (italics are mine):

> I venture this hypothesis; *that rhythm*
> *Flows but in one direction, and that from prose*
> *To rime. The opposite is upstream, against*
> *The grain of language and the course of change.*
> The measure of prosody is the current speech
> The cadences inherent in the voice
> Of one particular generation. Each
> Has its own standard, and no choice exists
> Between the past and present. Before he sang,
> Man spoke, and wrote his deeds before his songs.
> *The fountain of rime wells from a central source,*
> *The language of understanding; all else proceeds*
> *From this,* from the time of David to our day,
> And whether in epic, psalm, or roundelay.

But there seems to be a specter of doubt which refuses to be finally exorcised. In *Essay on Rime,* it is the ghost of James Joyce, still wandering to disturb Shapiro's resolutions. The following pair of lines are plain and simple but eloquent of Shapiro's problem:

> To him we put the question: Do you proceed
> From rime to prose or prose to rime or both?

Shapiro's typical achievement and limitation can be considered in terms of this question. There are many poems

to choose from, three collections so far, but time of composition does not seem to matter much. So far Shapiro's career shows more homogeneity than change, nor does it yet seem time for the reader to demand development of him.

What is obvious is that his first major book set a high level and that that level has been generally maintained. There are few poems that are clearly and wholly failures. There is a great body of work—the bulk of Shapiro's production—of consistently high, though not the highest, poetic quality: poems like **"Auto Wreck," "University," "Necropolis," "Waitress," "Boy-Man,"** that elevate statement to the level of poetry by means of the "sanctifying" agencies of metric and figure.

Then there are those poems that detach themselves from the general run of a poet's work, and which seem to the reader most clearly indicative of Shapiro's qualities of vision. A list of these poems would include, at the least, **"Trial of a Poet," "The Dome of Sunday," "Scyros," "Travelogue for Exiles," "Christmas Eve: Australia," "Elegy for a Dead Soldier,"** and perhaps half a dozen others of each reader's personal choice. I want to take two of these poems now, and show why I think one of them, **"Elegy for a Dead Soldier,"** is not so good as it first appeared, and why another, **"The Dome of Sunday,"** represents Shapiro at his best.

"Elegy for a Dead Soldier" begins with a stanza of Shapiro's best writing, a magnificent example of his ability to make poetry out of commonplace materials, raising them to a level of intensity capable of supporting universal significance. Stanzaic structure, sound pattern, dramatic movement, prosody, figurative language, all unite to produce a unified vision of considerable loveliness and power:

> A white sheet on the tail-gate of a truck
> Becomes an altar; two small candlesticks
> Sputter at each side of the crucifix
> Laid round with flowers brighter than the blood,
> Red as the red of our apocalypse,
> Hibiscus that a marching man will pluck
> To stick into his rifle or his hat,
> And great blue morning-glories pale as lips
> That shall no longer taste or kiss or swear.
> The wind begins a low magnificat,
> The chaplain chats, the palmtrees swirl their hair,
> The columns come together through the mud.

Unfortunately, the poem declines quickly from this initial success. The second stanza is almost all unredeemed prose (i.e.) ("the sorrow, and the simple praise / Of one whose promised thought of other days / Were such as ours, but now wholly destroyed"), only once lit up with the mild wit of: "the service record of his youth wiped out." Shapiro's schema of the various "figures" might be applied here: the stanza is nearly all "speech meaning"; of the other, more important figures, one finds that the sound structure is thin, the rhythms flat, the figurative language sparse and stereotyped.

Then there is a partial recovery, though not to the level of the first stanza, Shapiro finally settling down to a fairly routine, middle-level style that blends gentle satire and restrained pathos in a not unpleasant fashion. But with stanza X, there is another letdown:

> No man can ever prophecy until
> Out of our death some undiscovered germ,
> Whole toleration or pure peace is born.

This, it may be submitted, is prose, and bad prose: what is communicated is entirely intellectual and, judged on that basis, dull and vague. The whole course of the poem is downhill—it begins in poetry, wanders through wit to prose, and ends in banality. It is difficult to see why any critic who has followed the progress of the poem at all closely needs to be surprised at the conclusion:

> Remember that this stranger died in pain;
> And passing here, if you can lift your eyes
> Upon a peace kept by a human creed,
> Know that one soldier has not died in vain.

"Elegy for a Dead Soldier" is an important poem for Shapiro, though, even if it is not a good one. Here one may see the characteristic danger to which his kind of poetry is always subject: failing inspiration.

Shapiro's happier moments are when the current flows in the other direction, the way it should, from prose to poetry. For observation of this process, **"The Dome of Sunday"** is a good poem. The opening lines, with their irregular lengths and hard metric, their expressive rhetorical repetitions, their complex figures of sight, their brilliantly distorted central personification, insist (in the most poetic way!) upon a realism of the most prosaic kind:

> With focus sharp as Flemish-painted face
> In film of varnish brightly fixed
> And through a polished hand-lens deeply seen,
> Sunday at noon through hyaline thin air
> Sees down the street,
> And in the camera of my eye depicts
> Row-houses and row-lives:
> Glass after glass, door after door the same,
> Face after face the same, the same,
> The brutal visibility the same;

What most invites attention is the main figure whose grammar structures the passage ("Sunday at noon . . . sees down the street and in the camera of my eye depicts row-houses and row-lives"). But the figure can be read only in context of the poem's title: the dome of Sunday (one thinks, and it may be relevantly, of Shelley's quite different dome), round, smooth, transparent, brittle, though apparently impervious—these are attributes of the day, a generalized particular or specific abstract, one of the seven days but any Sunday. Within this external figurative landscape, the personification takes its double life. "Sunday at noon" is, first of all, a transference of the qualities of "Sun-day" to the sun whose day it is: the poetic insight is that these qualities (light, glare) are eminently transferable to the day and scene. Thus the sun shines down from or through the dome, through the hyaline thin air, giving

light to the objects of the street, and making them visibly available to the poet's eye ("in the camera of my eye depicts"). "Hyaline," appropriately, has, in addition to its general sense of "transparent, crystalline," biological reference to a horny substance found in certain cysts.

The second complication of the figure seems to be as follows: after the attributes of Sunday are transferred to the sun, the sun is then personified. There is, moreover, additional complication to be found in the introducing subordinate clause where the sun, in its personification, is implicated in the likeness of a person looking through a polished hand-lens (or dome). The passage, on the whole, is adding up to a radical re-vision of the root implications of the word *superficial,* Shapiro's social judgment on the scene. But the sun's focus is also held to be as sharp as that of a face in a Flemish painting, fixed in a film of varnish. In this view the scene is a painting, the sun an eye: but the personification finally transfers the act of vision from sun to poet.

One notices, also, the rich and assured handling of the phonetic medium, the daring but successful reliance on sibilants (voiced, unvoiced, and palatalized), extremely important in the repetitive rhetoric: "glass after glass . . . face after face the same, the same." The sibilant dominance, in most cases, is resolved through a subordinate but valuable emphasis on liquids. Then there are (in addition to such obvious structures as alliteration) such binders and progressions as "Flemish-film" or "focus-face-fix," or (again, variety of vowel sound within a consonantal pattern) "seen, Sunday . . . noon . . . hyaline, thin . . . down."

Prosodically the poem is iambic pentameter with emphatic truncations; as in the second line, unimportant in grammatical position but so powerful in the implicational values of its words for the whole poem that one might easily fail to notice its length; as in the dimeter, "Sees down the street," an isolation of half of Shapiro's fantastic insight, opening with a spondee following the terminal spondee of the proceding enjambed line; as in "Row-houses and row-lives," which completes the insight with another example of Shapiro's prosodic pyrotechnics: a line of three feet and four beats, spondee, pyrrhic, spondee.

The poem proceeds through a series of similarly complicated satiric figures (the reader will have to take on faith the integrity of the poem's middle, on the basis of evidence in its beginning and end) to its ironic conclusion where, although the poem tells us that "nothing happens," we as readers are happily aware that this is not so. What happens is the full poetic vision, richly and substantially built on all that has gone before. It is a thoroughly contemporary climax of precise and sustained elevation; the meter becomes more regular; sound and figure patterns gather together all the poem's ideas; lines, angles, surfaces, and lights converge in the key words "brightness" and "transfixed" (a transcendence of the "fixity" of the opening: the concentrated dialectic gives us a new kind of inaction, contemplation):

> But nothing happens; no diagonal
> With melting shadow falls across the curb:

Neither the blinded negress lurching through fatigue,
Nor exiles bleeding from their pores,
Nor that bright bomb slipped lightly from its rack
To splinter every silvered glass and crystal prism,
Witch-bowl and perfume bottle
And billion candle-power dressing-bulb,
No direct hit to smash the shatter-proof
And lodge at last the quivering needle
Clean in the eye of one who stands transfixed
In fascination of her brightness.

This seems to me such a direct hit as compels criticism, analysis, evaluation, to recognize their limits and retire before they become pompous and justly incur the somewhat exaggerated irritation with too much exegesis that Shapiro speaks for in his **"Ballade of the Critic"**:

I mean just this. Your fingers are all thumbs,
Your thumbs are all in everybody's pies,
Your pies all full of everybody's plums.
All other men sometimes apostrophize
Some things, somehow. You merely analyze
The distant droppings of the higher mind,
The critic sees no farther than behind.

William Carlos Williams (essay date 1946)

SOURCE: "Shapiro is All Right," in *William Carlos Williams,* Random House, 1955, pp. 258-62.

[*In the following essay, originally published in 1946, Williams offers a positive assessment of* Essay on Rime.]

(*Editor's Note: William Carlos Williams is treated by Shapiro as an "objectivist" poet, in part as follows:*

And (if this is not irrelevant) I for one
Have stared long hours at his discoveries
That seem at times the germs of serious science,
At times the baubles of the kaleidoscope.
A red wheelbarrow, a stone, a purple plum,
Things of a fixed world, metaphysics strange
As camera perception, in which no change
Occurs in any image. And prosody yields
To visible invariables; motion fails,
And metric, a fallacy in a static mold
Freezes itself to dazzling shapes, grows cold.)

Kenyon Review, 1946

Suppose all women were delightful, the ugly, the short, the fat, the intellectual, the stupid, even the old—and making a virtue of their qualities, each for each, made themselves available to men, some man, any man—without greed. What a world it could be—for women! In the same figure take all the forms of rime. Take for instance the fat: If she were not too self-conscious, did not regret that she were not lissome and quick afoot but gave herself, full-belly, to the sport! What a game it would make! All would then be, in the best sense, beautiful—entertaining

to the mind as to the eye but especially to that part of a man which we call so mistakenly the intellect. It is rather the whole man, the man himself, alert. He would be analyzed by their deportment and enriched in the very libraries of his conscience. He would be free, freed to the full completion of his desires.

Shapiro speaks lovingly of his "rime," which he defines here and there in his poem—variously, as it should (not) be defined. It is the whole body of the management of words to the formal purposes of expression. We express ourselves there (men) as we might on the whole body of the various female could we ever gain access to her (which we cannot and never shall). Do we have to feel inferior or thwarted because of that? Of course not. We do the best we can—as much as the females of our souls permit. Which isn't much generally. Each man writes as he is able under the circumstances under which he exists.

The trouble with this exercise of Shapiro's is that it is so damned easy to read, so interesting, such a pleasure. One can sympathize with a man sitting down in a "camp" somewhere, bored stiff by removal from his usual environment and playing (*in vacuo,* so to speak) with the problems he must someday face in practical work. He doesn't solve much, he doesn't expect to solve much, he wants only to clarify, to make a definite distinction between the parts of the great body that presents itself to him for his enjoyment. He attacks it bravely. She lies back and smiles—not with any intent to intimidate. She is very definitely sure of herself and—friendly. Whether she will be stirred to passion by his attack is a question. But he is young and that's a lot.

Well, you don't get far with women by quoting Eliot to them. Maybe the Sacred Hind means something to them—and wistfulness is dear to the female heart but I don't believe it beyond a certain point. She gets tired of being tickled merely.

However, we're talking of the art of writing well in a modern world and women haven't much to do with that, I guess. Not directly. America is still too crude for that. I don't think any place is much better. Not France. Not England—so far as I know. And not Russia. Of course it's ridiculous to think of any land, as a land, in this respect. Women are as various (and as rare) as men.

What Shapiro does point out however is that—

No conception
Too far removed from literal position
Can keep its body.

I imagine that will put a quietus on the "abstractionists" so far as writing (with words) is concerned. It's all right to make Maltese crosses of poems and use words as pigments—but, well . . . Women want men to come to the point. Writing, too, is like that. At least I think that is what Shapiro means, relative to the prosody. If so I agree with him.

I admire his respect for Milton (page Winters) especially with reference to the amazing transition Milton effects between the dialogue and the chorus in *Samson*. But I am especially interested in the view he takes of Milton the craftsman, to whom he calls strongest attention—though I must say it would have been better if he had a little stressed the necessity Milton was under in achieving his effects to distort the language in ways we may not descend to. He however ignores, as what craftsman must not, the mere subject of Milton's major poem. Lesser critics do not get beyond that.

Shapiro intimates the *formal* importance of Whitman—another thing nobody notices. Nobody notices enough, that is.

Oh, well, I've only read halfway through his poem as yet. I think it is illuminating in its summations of the field, the large expanse of what we must approach to be masterful.

I came at the book with positive aversion. What the hell! But he has won me. I think Shapiro may very well—at least I permit him to go on writing. He isn't a liar, he isn't an ape, he isn't just sad over the state of the world and the stars, he doesn't even bother to concern himself with humanity, or economics, or sociology or any other trio.

He's almost painfully interested in writing as it has been, masterfully, in the world and as it may be (under changed and changing conditions) in the world again. He keeps on the subject. And that's rare. More power to him. I hope he finds her rarest treasures—I am not jealous.

Beginning toward the last thousand lines I find—

> But grammar
> like prosody is a methodical afterthought,
> A winter flower of language.

There are many such successful aphorisms among the two thousand lines, not the worst part of the poem—good summations of fumbled concepts we all play at remembering.

Then he goes off on A. It may be a personal matter with him but I don't know one man writing in America today who ever reads A. or so much as thinks of him or his work when writing. I may be uninformed, I merely mention what to me is a commonplace. Vazakas once went to see A. at Swarthmore and found him a nice boy, still, and very kind—but I didn't discover that he came away with any broader impression—and with the next sentence we were talking of other matters. This infatuation I think reveals Shapiro's faulty objective in some of his work. A. seems frankly to be desperately fumbling with a complicated apparatus—to find, to find—could it possibly be something not discoverable here? That would really be too bad.

We haven't half enough translations. How can Shapiro say historians will discover we've had too many? I am sure Ezra Pound will be known principally for his translations, the most exquisite in our language. Of bad translations, yes, we've had too many—and of translations of bad poetry, popular at the moment, far, far too many. Rilke

and Rimbaud *ad nauseam*. Why don't we read *them* at least in the originals? Every translation I have ever read of either painfully stinks.

Yop. "And less verse of the mind."

I can't agree on Hart Crane. He had got to the end of his method, it never was more than an excrescence—no matter what the man himself may have been. He had written it right and left, front and back, up and down and round in a circle both ways, crisscross and at varying speeds. He couldn't do it any longer. He was on his way back from Mexico to—work. And couldn't work. He was returning to create and had finished creating. Peggy said that in the last three hours he beat on her cabin door—after being deceived and thrashed. He didn't know where to turn—that was the end of it.

That he had the guts to go over the rail in his pyjamas, unable to sleep or even rest, was, to me (though what do I know—more than another?) a failure to find anywhere *in his "rime"* an outlet. He had tried in Mexico merely to write—to write anything. He couldn't.

Yes, love might have saved him—but if one is to bathe to satiation in others' blood for love's sake . . . ?

Belief would be marvelous if it were not belief but scientific certainty. But you can't go back and believe what you know to be false and no belief has ever existed without holes in stones that emit smoke—to this day. Belief must always for us today signify nothing but the incomplete, the not yet realized, the hypothetical. The unknown.

Where then will you find the only true belief in our day? Only in science. That is the realm of the incomplete, the convinced hypothesis—the frightening embodiment of mysteries, of transmutations from force to body and from body to—nothingness. Light.

The anthropomorphic imaginatives that baffle us by their absence today had better look to Joyce if they want a pope and endless time.
Anyone who has seen two thousand infants born as I have and pulled them one way or another into the world must know that man, as such, is doomed to disappear in not too many thousand years. He just can't go on. No woman will stand for it. Why should she?

We'll have to look to something else. Who are we anyhow? Just man? What the hell's that? Rime is more.

M. L. Rosenthal (essay date 1958)

SOURCE: "The Shapiro Question," in *The Nation,* Vol. 187, No. 1, July 5, 1958, pp. 14-15.

[*In the following review, Rosenthal calls* Poems of a Jew *uneven and desultory.*]

Poems of a Jew, work mainly taken from earlier volumes, has Karl Shapiro's usual unevenness. Look hard at some of the pieces and their interest flies away like the white fluff of aged dandelions in the wind. The best ones, poems of an intense and brooding introvert, glow and crackle and burst into flame—unless the poet tries (as usually he does try) to fan them with his intellect. For it is matter of great sorrow that Shapiro, though his best work is that of an emotionalist sicklied o'er with the pale cast of thought, can't really think. When he makes the attempt he seems an inferior Auden, a decapitated Hamlet, or a flunked-out Talmudist.

I call to witness the mass of ill-fated assertions introducing these pieces on "the theme of the Jew." Example:

> The Jewish Question, whatever that might be, is not my concern. Nor is Judaism. Nor is Jewry. Nor is Israel. The religious question is not my concern. I am one of those who views with disgust and disappointment the evangelism and the backsliding of artists and intellectuals towards religion. . . .

I do not quarrel with these assertions in themselves. But they bear little relation to the actual experience of a Jew who, unless we are all mistaken, was for some time—and not too long ago—a Catholic convert (an experience to which a number of his poems seem to allude). Nor can they be said to describe the sentiments represented in this very book by poems like **"The Synagogue,"** which quite explicitly exalts the unique "factual holiness" of Judaism and everything in it which "marks a separate race," and like **"Israel"**:

> When I see the name of Israel high
>   in print
> The fences crumble in my flesh. . . .

As for "the Jewish Question, whatever that might be"—it must, insofar as it exists, have to do with the relations and attitudes toward each other of the Gentile majority and the Jews within a given nation or culture. Shapiro's poems certainly go at this Question in many ways; titles like **"Shylock"** and **"The Jew at Christmas Eve"** do not misled us, and scattered all through the poems there are enough such passages as the three that follow to make us cough discreetly at the disclaimer:

> The letters of the Jews are black and
>   clean
> And lie in chain-line over Christian
>   pages. . . .
>
>   **("Alphabet")**

> Grandpa, the saintly Jew, keeping his beard
> In difficult Virginia, yet endeared
> Of blacks and farmers, although orthodox
>
>   **("The Southerner")**

> To hurt the Negro and avoid the Jew
> Is the curriculum. . . .
>
>   **("University")**

The many such confrontations, often combined with other motifs in brilliant and moving fashion, show how obsessed this writer is with just the Question he has shrugged away. In fact, he himself uses the word "obsession" in his introduction, though he tries there to generalize it out of all recognition. The poems, he says, are "documents of an obsession" that is "universal and timeless"—"the Jew is at its center, but everyone else partakes of it." Mr. Shapiro wants to resolve the Question by making the particulars of his own life into an ultimate symbol of essential Jewishness, which he can then equate with the naked modern sensibility:

> The Jew is absolutely committed to the world. . . . This people beyond philosophy, beyond art, virtually beyond religion, a stranger even to mysticism, finds itself at the very center of the divine manifestation— man. The Jew represents the primitive ego of the human race. . . . The free modern Jew, celebrated so perfectly in the character of Leopold Bloom, is neither hero nor victim. He is man left over, after everything that can happen has happened.

It may throw some light on this for the most part pretentious nonsense to note that Leopold Bloom is, after all, a figment of the *Irish* imagination. What Mr. Shapiro is really talking about is the way he sees himself at this moment. "Poet" and "Jew" are terms almost interchangeable in his lexicon; in a piece not in this volume he has written that the poet

> . . . is the business man, on beauty trades,
> Dealer in arts and thought who, like the Jew,
> Shall rise from slums and hated dialects
> A tower of bitterness. . . .
>
>   **("Poet")**

Another omitted poem, **"The Dome of Sunday,"** is a brutal criticism of bourgeois Jewish life in Shapiro's native Baltimore; the social type there pictured does not fit his present thesis. Modern Jewish life is actually, and naturally, extremely varied, but one would never guess from this book that many of Saul Bellow's characters could exist, or the working people of our big cities, or the "solid" doctors and lawyers and other professional people whose ego is neither more nor less "primitive" than that of the next member of the American Dental Association.

"Obsession" remains an intriguing word, however. Perhaps the real clue to what the poet feels can be glimpsed in **"The First Time."** Here a boy is about to be initiated into sex by a prostitute. Absorbed in his self-consciousness, he does not notice that she has been scrutinizing his body in her mirror as he has entered her room after undressing outside it. Suddenly

> . . . . she turns around, as one turns at a desk,
> And looks at him, too naked and too soon,
> And almost gently asks: *Are you a Jew?*

"Obsession" is surely the right word! In a note to another poem, Shapiro writes that "in Freud's view, as in that of every Jew, mutilation, circumcision, and 'the fear of being eaten' are all one." The generalization may be dubious, but it does indicate the sexual and traumatic aspects of the poet's conception of Jewishness.

Sometimes the horror of this conception is conveyed without specific sexual allusion. One of Shapiro's best poems, **"Messias,"** recalls his shocked recoil as a child from an old religious Jew who came to the door seeking a "donation for the Holy Land" in the "hieratic language of the heart." The boy fled "in terror from the nameless hurt." More characteristic is the **"Adam and Eve"** sequence, which represents the Fall as essentially the discovery of sex. Fascinated by his phallic and vaginal imagery, which emphatically suggests at times "the fear of being eaten," and which is developed with a prurient, guilty, almost voyeuristic curiosity, the poet follows—as he says—his own interpretation, though influenced by cabalic symbolism and by Reich's ideas. A footnote justifies the inclusion of this sequence on the ground that its viewpoint "that man is for the world, not for the afterworld, is Jewish." It seems clear, however, that its connotations of sexually oriented violence and fear provide the truer reason. (See also the first of the *Five Self-Portraits,* in which the poet tells, fairly humorously but with great sympathy for his own infant wounds, the story of his birth and circumcision amid all the echoes and symbols of American and Christian tradition.)

Fortunately, the Good Lord made Karl Shapiro a genuine poet even though He skimped somewhat on the logical and critical endowment. Despite the traumatic basis of their movement into compassion, a number of these poems reach beautiful resolution. Others explore ponderous themes—the ease with which we forget history's most dreadful lessons, the incommunicability of certain essential differences of tradition and life-principle, and so on—without losing their buoyancy and independent character as works of feeling with a design independent of doctrinal interests. Indeed, when Shapiro succeeds it is through his vibrant language and rhythm, his unabashed candor, and his irresistible emotional force that *will* bring out his true meanings even when he himself is not quite sure of them.

Leslie Fiedler (essay date 1960)

SOURCE: "On the Road; or the Adventures of Karl Shapiro," in *Poetry,* Vol. XCVI, No. 3, June, 1960, pp. 171-78.

[*In the following essay, Fiedler explores the treatment of Jewish themes in Shapiro's poetry.*]

We live in a time when everywhere in the realm of prose Jewish writers have discovered their Jewishness to be an eminently marketable commodity, their much vaunted alienation to be their passport into the heart of Gentile culture. It is, indeed, their quite justified claim to have been *first* to occupy the Lost Desert at the center of the Great American Oasis (toward which every one now races, Coca-Cola in one hand, Martin Buber in the other) which has made certain Jewish authors into representative Americans, even in the eyes of State Department officials plan-

ning cultural interchanges. The autobiography of the urban Jew, whose adolescence coincided with the Depression and who walked the banks of some contaminated river with tags of Lenin ringing in his head, who went forth (or managed not to) to a World War in which he could not quite believe—has come to seem part of the mythical life history of a nation. That the youngster who was Tom Sawyer or Huck Finn become in adolescence (depending on whether you read *The New Yorker* or the *Partisan Review*) Holden Caulfield or Augie March, which is to say, J. D. Salinger or Saul Bellow Revisited surprises no one, though it leaves the best Jewish American writers amused, the second-best embarrassed, and the worst atrociously pleased!

Yet Jewish poets have not prospered in a time of cultural philosemitism as have their opposite numbers in prose. Indeed, no American poets, Jewish or Gentile, had succeeded up to the verge of the forties in projecting images of the Jew capable of possessing the American mind. To be sure, the twenties had produced the anti-semitic caricatures of Pound, Eliot, and E. E. Cummings, but these remain peripheral in their work, even Bleistein or Rachel *née* Rabinovich failing to achieve the authority of Sweeney or Doris. On the other hand, those pre-forties versifiers who bore Jewish names and possessed, doubtless, Jewish parents divided into two essentially inconsequential groups: the popular entertainers and upper-middlebrow Bohemians, like Dorothy Parker or F.P.A., who neither made memorable poetry nor thought of themselves as Jews; and the exponents of a joyous squalor and terror, like Maxwell Bodenheim, who seemed to the imagination of the twenties not only non-Jews but non-participants in anything except non-participation and certain hopeful counterfeits of love.

The "proletarian" literature of the thirties attracted poets from Jewish families, as Marxism in general attracted them, but their political doctrines discouraged the exploitation of Jewishness; so that the poetry section of *Proletarian Literature in the United States* contains the verse of a group of authors most of whom Hitler would have considered Jews but whom he had not yet persuaded that they must speak as Jews. Yet it is from a group of young men touched by Marxism, too, from a generation whose beginnings were in the dying thirties and whose consummation lay ahead in the shadow of World War II (rather than the generation able to think of itself as having fought its hard way out of the twenties, like Isadore Schneider) that the first group of poets emerged who were simultaneously committed to their Jewishness and at the center of American poetry. Needless to say, their Jewishness was for them not a piety but a problem, and they wrote for such magazines as the *Partisan Review* rather than for parochial publications like the *Menorah Journal.*

By the mid-forties, two of these had been recognized generally as among the most talented poets of the decade: Delmore Schwartz and Karl Shapiro. In two long poems, **"Shenendoah"** and **"Genesis,"** Schwartz attempted to mythicize his own life into a paradigm of the times, worked patiently at his Portrait of the Artist as a Young Urban

Jew, pursuing those alternate Messiahs, Marx and Freud, and hearing in his ear his own comic name and the grey lifeless speech of those dispossessed of one language before they had real control of another. Neither poem quite worked, although there are local successes in each; and more recently, Schwartz has abandoned along with the narrative form his first image of himself—substituting that of the assimilated Jew as Comedian, proffering himself as the Danny Kaye of verse. In his latest poetry, Christian ceremonials rather than Jewish ones become the occasions for meditation, Christmas rather than the *brith*. The development of Karl Shapiro is almost precisely the opposite.

Though he assures us in the introduction to *Poems of a Jew* that "the undercurrent of most of my poems is the theme of the Jew", he has only lately begun to make that theme explicit. The road he has traveled is indicated by the shifts in the titles of his books: *Person, Place and Thing* (poetry as the evocation of object and event), *V-Letter* (poetry as communication from a War to a scarcely imaginable place of peace), *Essay on Rime* (poetry as a commentary on itself, itself its own subject), *Trial of a Poet* (poetry as the poet's apology for his strange and treasonable vocation.) Even in the last of these volumes, whose dates are 1942, 1944, 1945 and 1947, Shapiro is still insisting "that poetry instructs language only and that its function stops there." Yet in that very volume, he includes the first and longest version of a then twenty-page poem called "Recapitulations," which is autobiographical and typical, a *document* rather than an exercise in linguistic purification; which is to say, it is Mr. Shapiro's "Shenandoah," a verse analogue to *The Adventures of Augie March*.

In *Poems of a Jew* which appeared in 1959 (between it and *Trial of a Poet*, Mr. Shapiro had published *Poems 1940-1953,* containing less than a dozen uncollected poems), he is quite candid about his change of heart or shift of emphasis, telling us that "It is good to read poems for their own sake, but it is also good to read them as documents. These poems are the documents of an obsession . . . the Jew is at its center." Oddly enough, they are for the most part the same old poems we have seen before, some of them twice over (fewer than a quarter of the poems in the latest collection had been unpublished in earlier volumes); what is new is the context established by the title, a title unparalleled in its specific declaration of allegiance since 1882 when Emma Lazarus's *Songs of a Semite* appeared.

What is Shapiro up to in his new grouping of old poems? Do they represent an attempt to ride beside Wouk and Salinger, Bellow and Malamud, Philip Roth and Uris—the bandwagon which travels our streets, its calliope playing *Hatikvah?* Or is this simply another attempt (the first was *Poems 1940-1953*) to keep in the public eye on the part of a poet who in the past ten or twelve years has not produced enough considerable new poetry to justify a really new volume? It pays to be frank on this score; Karl Shapiro's productivity *has* dwindled since the middle of the forties, perhaps because so much of his energy has been invested in his activities as editor and consultant and teacher; and the quality of his verse has tended to fall along with its quantity.

Among the comparatively few poems he has written over the last decade or decade and a half, some are merely occasional, like "Israel" or "The 151st Psalm," versifying by an established Jewish American poet called upon by his fellow Jews, who consider they have special rights in his creativity; and even the very best of his latest work (so ambitious, complex, and elegantly sensual a poem as "Adam and Eve") does not have the directness, the surety, the absolutely unique idiom, the unpretentiousness of such early poems as "Haircut," "October 1," "The Fly," or "The Twins." These will remain, with the terrible justness that baffles poets not lucky enough to grow in depth and strength, the anthology pieces by which Shapiro is remembered. None of these is included in his latest book, though the voice which says them, the eye which saw them first are the voice and the eye of that Jewish boy whose sentimental education in a Gentile world is defined by "Recapitulations," for instance, and "University," both of which *are* republished here.

It is the intent of *Poems of a Jew* to isolate the documents which illuminate that sentimental education and thus make clear what—to Mr. Shapiro—a Jew is; but to do this means in our time to cast light on a mystery in which we are all involved: "the Jew is at its center, but everyone else partakes of it." His introduction prepares us for his definition negatively only, informing us that "the Jewish question" is not Shapiro's concern, "Nor is Judaism. Nor is Jewry. Nor is Israel. The religious questions is not my concern." As a matter of fact, Mr. Shapiro wants us to believe (perhaps *has* to believe himself) that he not only now "views with disgust and disappointment" the "evangelism" and "the backsliding toward religion", but that he has always done so.

Yet Mr. Shapiro is essentially a religious poet, a part of whose central, even archetypal experience (along with his exposure to Marxism, his Freudian indoctrination and his war service) is an unconsummated adulterous affair with the Catholic Church. It is a final irony that in a recent special issue of the *Times Literary Supplement,* Mr. Shapiro was mistakenly described as an actual Catholic convert—despite a kind of self-expurgation of his earlier writing which has suppressed, for instance, the original section *X* of "Recapitulations" that begins "I lost my father in a dire divorce . . ." and goes on to describe how "I craved the beads and chains of paradise / And counted it a blessing to be blind . . .". In *Poems of a Jew,* "Recapitulations" has been retitled *Five Self-Portraits I, II, III, IV, V* to indicate its final shrinkage (even in *Poems 1940-1953,* it still had eight parts); and, indeed, it appears in what purports to be Mr. Shapiro's most Jewish collection with two of its most specifically Jewish sections excised.

Not only is **X** missing but also the former **XVI**, which is a genre picture of the kind of "Jewish" wedding imposed on non-believers by parents who cling still to traditional conformity if not orthodox faith.

> The atheist bride is dressed in blue,
> The heretic groom in olive drab;
> The rabbi of more sombre hue
> Arrives upon the scene by cab.

Since the model for this poem is Eliot's *Sweeney Among the Nightingales,* and since Mr. Shapiro is insisting these days first that *nobody* among contemporary poets has been influenced by Eliot's example, and second that Eliot's "pedantic and ironic quatrains" are both anti-semitic and bad verse—the evident affiliation must embarrass him profoundly. Yet there is no poem by Shapiro, perhaps no poem by any American poet which renders with so little sentimentality and so much just perception the sense of a Jewish religious occasion participated in by lapsed Jews. And Shapiro's ironic reversal of Eliot's ironic anti-semitism lends to the poem a special savour. One hopes that as good a piece of verse will eventually come out of Shapiro's second "dire divorce" from a father, this time a literary one!

Shapiro is, indeed, as he declares, a "heretic"—not, to be sure, a *meshummed,* an apostate from Israel, but one who remaining still a Jew ("God's book was in my blood") is also a Christian heretic, not unlike Baudelaire, whom he translates and who is, with Eliot, a chief influence on his earlier verse, his earlier view of himself. It would be possible to compile out of Shapiro's total body of verse a collection, quite as convincing as this one, called *Poems of a Christian,* which would include not only his Christmas poems (**"Christmas Eve: Australia," "Christmas Tree," "To Evalyn for Christmas," "The Jew at Christmas Time"**) and his Sunday ones (**"Sunday: New Guinea," "The Dome of Sunday"**), but also **"The Saint," "The Puritan," "The Convert," "Washington Cathedral," "The Confirmation,"** etc., etc.

It is in part the War which confirmed Shapiro's break with his home and his memories of orthodox grandparents, leaving him—as he read the Bible and chewed gum— "thinking of Christ and Christmas". But even out of the War, his year is the Christian year, his week the Christian week; he writes no poems of the Jewish Sabbath, none of *Chanukah* or Passover, since these festivals do not exist for his imagination. It is the Christian day of rest and the Christian holidays which move him to meditation and to verse, leaving him sometimes lulled to peace (dreaming of his children beneath their Christmas tree "like the infant Nazarene") but more often baffled and irked at the mystery of his exclusion, the exclusion of the Jew. Indeed Shapiro's very conception of the Jew is a Christian one once removed, his reaction to the reflection in the Gentile's eye which he yet accepts as a fact.

In poems in which he is not addressing himself directly to the more problematical aspects of his Jewishness and the word "Jew" occurs in casual metaphor, it carries with it the pejorative connotations of the Gentile stereotype: "He trained his joys to be obsequious Jews", "and her dreams are as black as the Jews. . . ." Even in a much more deliberate passage (part of *Poet,* the final word of his first collection), Shapiro links his origins and his vocation, identifies poet and Jew in the following terms:

> He is the business man, on beauty trades,
> Dealer in arts and thoughts who, like the Jew,
> Shall rise from slums and hated dialects
> A tower of bitterness. Shall be always strange . . .

The image is that of Shylock, out of Shakespeare via Pound and Eliot, the image of the merchant whose real merchandise is hate. And finally in the poem called **"Jew"**, his directest confrontation of the difficulties of defining himself, he makes it clear why in his deepest sensibility the name of his people and his fate remains a "dirty word" (he has actually written on the subject a rather unsuccessful prose poem with this title). "And the word for the murder of Christ will cry out on the air / Though the race is no more . . .". The verdict rendered in **"Jew"** is guilty as charged, and the charge the vulgarest anti-semitic accusation: "They killed our Christ!" In his latest revision, Shapiro has changed his own line to "And the word for the murder of God . . .", attempting to translate Christian slander to a Nietzschean boast; but this is a kind of retrospective falsification. He is misleading himself as well as his reader when he asserts in his present introduction that the "shock" of the word "Jew" ("ever a blow on our heart like a fist") has for him "nothing to do with Christ or the Crucifixion". The poems say something quite different; and even emendations will not make them lie.

I am not, of course, interested in catching Shapiro out, or in trying to prove him a worse Jew than anyone else. We are all spiritual Stalinists engaged in a continual falsification of our own histories, and we must pray for critics capable of pointing this out. It seems important to me however, to try to say (quite independently of Shapiro's own *post facto* interpretations) what his poems mean, since they tell a truth relevant not to his plight alone. The self-consciousness of modern Jewish Americans is typically reflexive; the Jewishness which they cannot locate finally in themselves or in Israel or in their grandfathers they discover improbably in the vestigial hostility of those who know they are *not* Jews with a certainty no Jew can feel these days about his identity. It is said often enough (wryly or bitterly or triumphantly) that Hitler made more Jews than God; less melodramatically, it can be added that more Jews have been made by the petty malice of some Gentile neighbor than have ever been made by the urgings of parents or rabbis or Zionist orators. All of which is a way of saying that for most moderns, Jewishness is an awareness not of belonging but of *galuth,* of exile or alienation. It is Shapiro's special triumph as a Jew and a poet to have defined *galuth* in its mid-twentieth century American form: the moment of awareness in which Bleistein realizes that he is still Shylock after all, and the second- or third-generation American that he is as alien as his remotest ancestor. The best of Shapiro's recent poems seem to me the quietest ones, in which he depicts the flowering of Jewish self-conscious not where hate confronts hate but where baffled goodwill comes up against the fact of alienation, as in **"Teasing the Nuns"** or **"The Crucifix in the Filing Cabinet."**

Yet Shapiro has apparently been searching for some more positive content with which to endow Jewishness, something beyond the wince of recognition; and this he seems to have found in the notion of Judaism as anti-asceticism. Shapiro can no more write about a *Bar Mitzvah* than he can about *shabbes* or the *chanukah* lights; but in his poem, **"The Confirmation,"** he contrasts with the orthodox Christian ceremony inducting a boy to spiritual manhood ("girls in white like angels . . . the preacher bound in black . . ."), a heterodox *rite de passage* in which that boy masturbates "to confirm his sex . . . / And unction smooth as holy-oil / Fell from the vessel's level lip / Upon the altar-cloth . . .". The metaphors on both sides of the comparison come from Christian sources, and the divine figure which presides over the second or sexual confirmation is the Great Goddess herself in the form of a movie-star's pin-up picture; but apparently Shapiro thinks of that latter celebration of the "body self-released" as somehow intrinsically Jewish, a secular Judaism, a this-worldliness for which he pretends to find sanctions in the Old Testament. Surely he could have included the poem in the present collection on no other grounds.

This notion is carried further in the *midrash,* the lush poem of exegesis which he calls **"Adam and Eve"** and makes the conclusion of **Poems of a Jew.** A note tells us that the underlying images in his interpretation (which portrays the Fall as a deliberate turning from paradisal blandness through sex to the "present world" and which stars Woman) are derived from "the *Zohar* or central work of the cabala" and "from the renegade Freudian, Wilhelm Reich." But this means, of course, that Shapiro is attempting the kind of synthesis of a traditional mysticism (at least this time not Zen!) and a post-Freudian Fertility Cult that has attracted other Jewish American writers, beat, hip and square, from Saul Bellow and Norman Mailer to Paul Goodman and Allen Ginsberg. He is writing, that is to say, one more chapter of his long autobiographical poem, in which the latest improbable though typical conversions (from Marx to Whitman, from Eliot to Dylan Thomas, from Freud to Reich, from Christian to "Jewish" heresy) are translated into moving and sometimes subtle verse.

Louis D. Rubin, Jr. (essay date 1964)

SOURCE: "The Search for Lost Innocence: Karl Shapiro's *The Bourgeois Poet,*" in *The Hollins Critic,* Vol. I, No. 5, December, 1964, pp. 1-16.

[*In the following stylistic analysis of* The Bourgeois Poet, *Rubin derides the design of* The Bourgeois Poet, *maintaining that the only unifying element is the force of the poet's personality, which fails to add coherence to the poems comprising the volume.*]

1.

In Baltimore, walking in Victorian-movie snow it occurred to me: seek for the opposite. I'm for the Faustian supermarket. The opposite enthralls me.

The Bourgeois Poet

It has been instructive, and certainly very amusing, to watch the reaction to Karl Shapiro's new book of verse, **The Bourgeois Poet.** A few optimistic souls have pronounced it a significant breakthrough, a beacon light by which young poets may henceforth proceed through the foggy seas of contemporary verse. Many others have termed it notes toward a poem, raw material not given meaning, a kind of unmasticated poetic prose striving toward but not achieving form. Even the magazine editors who published portions of it didn't quite know what to do with it; some artfully contrived a middle position, halfway between the legitimate poetry in the front and the admitted and declared prose in the back.

The Bourgeois Poet is odd stuff; there is no escaping that. It consists of ninety-six parts divided into three sections, the first discursive, the second autobiographical, and the third epigrammatic. In the way it appears on the printed page it doesn't much resemble poetry, though sometimes it sounds very much like what we usually expect when we read a Shapiro poem:

> Wood for the fireplace, wood for the floor, what is
> the life span? Sometimes before I lay the log on
> the fire I think: it's sculpture wood, it's walnut.
> Maybe someone would find a figure in it, as
> children find faces in the open fire (I never
> have). Then I lay it on the flames like a heretic,
> where it pauses a moment, then joins in the
> singing. . . .

Remove the parenthesis, give or take a few syllables here and there, and one could without too much difficulty read that as verse which scans and otherwise behaves properly. But sometimes the condition is much more akin to the conventional notion of prose than of poetry:

> In gold I also use my middle initial but spelled out
> JAY. J is for Jacob. My father dropped his first
> name Israel. My son is named Jacob. Upper-class
> Jews call him Jack. My father-in-law's name was
> Jack, probably Jacob.

One might be able to figure out a way to present that in regular lines, but that would be the least of it. The tone is conversational, but the conversation is hardly interesting. If, to quote Shapiro, poetry is how ideas feel, then that is surely prose.

The model is at times obviously Whitman, even to the point of conscious parody. More often it is not parody but genuine use of Whitman:

> Quintana lay in the shallow grave of coral. The
> guns boomed stupidly fifty yards away. The
> plasma trickled into his arm. Naked and filthy,
> covered with mosquitoes, he looked at me as I
> read his white cloth tag. How do you feel,
> Quintana? He looks away from my gaze. I lie:
> we'll get you out of here sometime today.

At other times Carl Sandburg seems to be the model, with a little E. E. Cummings thrown in for good savor:

> Now both are dead, Dylan and Uncle Saul. Dylan was
> taken by the pickling of his beautiful brain. The sacred
> oxygen could not reach the convolutions. Uncle Saul
> was taken thrice by the heart, thrice by the broken

personality. Uncle Saul joked in the lobby of the plush nuthouse, wearing a brilliant sportcoat and shined elegant shoes. The black hair dye had vanished; his hair was snowy white. They gave him the shock treatment until his heart exploded. Dylan lay inert with the Moses bumps on his forehead amidst the screaming of wives and the groans of lovers and drinkers. And the Beat said—iambic killed him.

Then at times Ezra Pound gets in a good lick or two:
To the poor (aux pauvres) crime alone (le crime seul) opens (ouvre) les portes de la vie (the doors of life). Entire libraries of music are hurled in the gutters: the G. I.'s are looking for bottles. The Bavarian Venus is snatched baldheaded.

All we need there is a Chinese ideograph borrowed from Fenollosa. More importantly the book as a whole seems to take its cues from Pound's *Cantos*. Shapiro has always contended that the whole principle of the *Cantos* was discord, and that only Pound thought otherwise. *The Bourgeois Poet* often appears to be constructed on such a principle.

One could go on in this vein, pointing out this and that resemblance, but it would not be an especially profitable thing to do, because *The Bourgeois Poet* is not important for its borrowings or its adaptations of known style. Shapiro has long since proved himself a craftsman of language of the first order, and it is no surprise to know that he can appropriate the distinctive rhythm and style of a number of poets. He always handles what he does very well. There is only one—and I fear major—criticism of the whole thing, so far as the style goes. Granted that the language is varied and not the customary language of poetry, granted that Shapiro can and does modulate, parody and otherwise utilize Whitman, Sandburg, Pound, Crane, Baudelaire, Joyce, Cummings and other stylists, the question remains, Where is Shapiro? If after reading 113 pages of *The Bourgeois Poet* one were to put it down, pick up a copy of a magazine, and come upon ten similar pages, would there be any way to be able to say with any assurance that they were written by Karl Shapiro and not by someone else? I wish I thought so. Only an occasional metaphor seems distinctive. And that is what is wrong with *The Bourgeois Poet.* Not its language as such, not its use of prose rhythms, not even its subject matter, but its form. It doesn't have a recognizable form, which is another way of saying that it doesn't add up to anything, the language and content don't fuse together to do something, and the reader has no feeling of its having set things right. One is willing to accept almost any convention that a poet wishes to adopt, including that of saying "to hell with convention," but he needs to justify some convention. Shapiro hasn't.

The question I wish to propound in this essay is, Why? Why has Shapiro done this? Why has he written *The Bourgeois Poet* at all, and what does the fact that he did write it mean about poetry today? Karl Shapiro is no fool; and he has written entirely too much good poetry to be accused of not knowing what a good poem is. When a man of his reputation and character produces a book like this, we had better ask ourselves why he did it and what made him do so.

2.

The best book has a bad finality. The best book closes too many *rooms. The best poem clicks like a box: you have made yourself a neat little trap, a hideaway with wall-to-wall rhyme. . . .*

The Bourgeois Poet

Some fifteen years ago, in a lecture he gave at the Johns Hopkins University, Shapiro discussed the work of several British poets of the first world war. He quoted from a review he had written of their work some years before, in which he had said something to the effect that the experience of these poets stopped with the war, and he went on to remark that when he had written that statement he had not quite understood what it meant, but that now he had a much better idea. Shapiro was of course referring to his own work and his own career. For like those poets, he was a "war poet." It was while he was in uniform during the years from 1941 to 1945, when the United States was at war with the Axis Powers, that Shapiro first began to attract attention. Actually his first book was published privately some time before that, but it was youthful work and he has properly collected none of it. Several more years were to elapse before the work on which his reputation depends began appearing in literary magazines. In 1941 New Directions collected some of it in *Five Young American Poets,* and the following year there appeared **Person, Place and Thing**, published when Shapiro was already on military service in the South Pacific. This book attracted attention everywhere; it contained many of his most characteristic poems, such as **"Nostalgia," "Haircut," "Buick,"** and **"Auto Wreck."** It was followed, in 1944, by **V-Letter and Other Poems**, which won him the Pulitzer Prize the following year and included such work as **"The Leg,"** and **"Troop Train,"** and what is probably the finest poem written about the second world war, **"Elegy for a Dead Soldier."** The year after that, Shapiro brought out **Essay on Rime**, a non-scholarly scholarly study of the art of verse, composed in a loose blank-verse form, which was so fresh and so original that it attracted widespread notice and sold an astonishing number of copies.

Whatever the personal discomforts of serving in the Pacific, it should be noted that so far as his status and reputation as a poet were concerned, Shapiro's military service conferred at least two distinct advantages. For one thing, it isolated him from the American literary establishment, allowing his reputation to grow and flourish without his getting involved in whatever politics, personalities, and the like go along with making one's professional way in the hierarchy. More importantly, at a time when in technique and status both he was moving from strength to strength, it kept him in a situation whereby he remained an "amateur" rather than a "professional" poet. By this I mean that in the army his experience was of necessity primarily non-intellectual and non-literary, was shared by millions of others who were in no way intellectuals and literary men, and thus did not cut him off from what as a poet was peculiarly the source of his strength—his ability to give form and meaning to common, everyday experience. Very few poets have been able to articulate such experience for us. But when Shapiro describes the red light of an ambulance arriving at the scene of an automobile accident as

> one ruby flare
> Pulsing out red light like an artery

he takes a visual image of something mechanical and inanimate, unites it with the human life and death with which it is connected, and creates a metaphor of the associations of terror and fear that overwhelm us at such a moment. When he refers to "the ambulance with its terrible cargo" leaving the scene, the sense of the cold helplessness of our utter dependence on the physical body is recreated; mangled, the human being at that moment is flesh, "cargo". The whole scene is explored in the images of shock, disbelief and awareness that accompany us at such times. One policeman "with a bucket douches ponds of blood / Into the street and gutter," while another "hangs lanterns on the wrecks that cling, / Empty husks of locusts, to iron poles." Then, after reminding us of the way in which we seek desperately to accommodate the vision of the horror of death on such an occasion to the everyday routine of our own lives ("The grim joke and the banal resolution"), he proceeds to do what we cannot ourselves do at such a time: isolate what our reactions really signify:

> For death in war is done by hands;
> Suicide has cause and stillbirth, logic
> And cancer, simple as a flower, blooms.
> But this invites the occult mind,
> Cancels our physics with a sneer,
> And spatters all we know of denouement
> Across the expedient and wicked stones.

We cannot, in other words, accommodate the violence of sudden death into our cherished systems of cause and effect, meaning and justice, and so the auto wreck is terrible because it reminds us of our helplessness, our inability to understand what life and death really are, and our human and social condition of being at the mercy of blind chances.

Another important quality of his poetry is that not only the experience but the *attitudes* toward it, however heightened and intensified, are true to everyday life. There is not that dissociation from everyday experience and attitudes that marks so much twentieth century poetry. There are no housemaids with damp souls, as in Eliot. Consider, for instance, the vast difference between, say, Eliot's sarcastic reference to "the sound of horns and motors which shall bring / Sweeney to Mrs. Porter in the spring," in which the use of an automobile is portrayed as a sign of modern degeneracy and middle-class crudeness, and Shapiro's (I almost wrote "the American poet's," which I suppose is part of what I am getting at) **"Buick"**:

> And not as the ignorant beast do you squat and
>   watch me depart,

> But with exquisite breathing you smile, with
>   satisfaction of love,
> And I touch you again as you tick in the silence
>   and settle in sleep.

The same holds true for the poet in the emporium, the barber shop, the drug store, and so on; and in wartime the troop train, the induction camp, the troop ship, and other such experiences. Again, the poet's attitude is not one of sophisticated detachment; it is not that of an intellectual looking down self-consciously at the artifacts of a middle-class civilization. The poet does not need to make a distinction between his experience as a citizen or a soldier and his attitude as a poet. In this sense Shapiro isn't really a "soldier"; he is a civilian in the army, who doesn't like it very much but who makes the best of it. It is this ability to articulate the common experience of his generation that made possible his fine **"Elegy for a Dead Soldier."** There is not the slightest bit of ironic qualification of the subject, and no self-consciousness at voicing the ideals for which Americans generally went to war in 1941-1945. They are the poet's as well, and he differs from others who hold them primarily in his ability to articulate them. Again, thoroughly "bourgeois" poetry, by a member of a throughly middle-class society.

I want to make one more observation about Shapiro's earlier work, which is that though essentially social, it is a very personal, autobiographical kind of poetry. This I think is not always realized about Shapiro. The fact is that almost all of Shapiro's earlier poems are drawn directly out of his own experience; they are not conceptual in their thought, which is to say that they do not attempt to impose a philosophical or social system on experience. They consist of the poet's keen and unashamed exploration of the social meaning of his own attitudes; ideas are important, but not ideological systems. The limitation of such work, scarcely apparent at this stage, lies precisely there: it begins with the poet's own experience, it ends with it, and it explores what the experience means, not as tested against a larger system of value judgment but with a pragmatic, no-holds-barred, subjective strategy that can change with each experience and each poem. Everything, in short, depends on the poet's state of mind.

3.

The bourgeois poet closes the door of his study and lights his pipe. Why am I in this box, he says to himself (although it is exactly as he planned). . . .
                                                       —*The Bourgeois Poet*

What happens, though, to the "war poet" who comes out of uniform and back into civilian life? No longer is he a soldier who writes poetry; he is a Man of Letters. In Shapiro's case he was appointed Consultant in Poetry of the Library of Congress, where he served for two years, following which he became Associate Professor of English Writing at the Johns Hopkins University. He became, that is, a member of what some like to call the Establishment. He served on prize committees, was a Fellow in Poetry of the Library of Congress, gave the Phi Beta Kappa poem at Harvard, and in 1950 accepted the editorship of that most influential and important of all American magazines of verse, *Poetry* of Chicago.

In 1947 Shapiro brought out a third collection of his poems, *Trial of a Poet*. This time the hosannas were few; the new book was roundly panned. Save for a few poems, it had much less of the excitement and distinction that had characterized the two earlier collections.

The explanation, I think, was simply that Shapiro had, by the very nature of his intelligence and craft, lost that "innocence" of perception, that familiar and sympathetic identification with the artifacts and attitudes of ordinary middle-class life, that had been the mainstay of his art. The Bourgeois Poet now "knew too much." The intense exploration of immediate impressions, the pragmatic strategy of expanding the social meaning of the everyday occurence, no longer sufficed. He had said all he could say about Buicks and barber shops and auto wrecks, and the common experience of the civilian soldier far from home no longer existed for him. He had become an Intellectual. When he thought of terror now, for example, he thought, not of an automobile wreck, so much as of Hieronymus Bosch. And to make poetry out of that kind of experience required a very different strategy. It is interesting that the chief poem he wrote during this period of not too much poetry was at first entitled **"Eden Retold,"** though later changed to **"Adam and Eve."** For the territory he was now working was no longer largely unexplored and virgin; it was material that was all too familiar to the modern poet, one largely dissociated in language and attitude from that of ordinary middle-class American society. Few good poets before Shapiro had thought to make a poem out of a barber shop, but writers from earliest times down through Milton, Blake, Wordsworth and Mark Twain to the present have been dealing with the Garden of Eden.

What does a good poet such as Shapiro do in such a case? He looks around for an absolute. It is in this light that I see the strategy, in 1958, of collecting some of his best poems, including many of the older ones and a few recent pieces, under the title **Poems of a Jew**. He asks himself, that is, what he is that he can be sure of, and he decides that whatever else he is, he is a Jew, and that this means, in his own words, "a certain state of consciousness which is inescapable." The Jew, whatever else he may or may not be, is someone absolutely committed to this world, who "represents the primitive ego of the human race," and the Jews as a people are "beyond philosophy, beyond art, virtually beyond religion, a stranger even to mysticism . . . at the very center of the divine manifestation—man." Which is another way of saying, I think, that if one thinks of himself in this way he can put aside the search for a cultural system and trust to the concrete cultural identity thus afforded him.

Alas, it doesn't work. Whatever being a Jew might have meant in times past, nowadays it doesn't provide one with a readymade identity that can answer any cultural problem and evaluate any experience—any more so than

Roman Catholicism could for Allen Tate or Zen Buddhism (Shapiro has flirted with that a little, too) for Allen Ginsberg. Shapiro's Jewish identity has served from time to time to give him material and meaning for several good poems (I like especially **"University," "Travelogue for Exiles,"** and **"The Crucifix in the Filing Cabinet,"** though I am not convinced that either of the first two is indebted more to Judaism than to several other aspects of Shapiro's identity.)

4.

The molasses of lecturing is sweet and the rum of
  polemic is good for the stomach. I write prose to
  find out what I think. Then it is printed. The
  whole business is irresponsible. . . .

              —The Bourgeois Poet

Another thing that a poet does, if he has got the kind of fine analytical intelligence that Karl Shapiro has, is to write criticism. Now Shapiro in recent years has become very much a professional anti-critic; his book of essays, *In Defense of Ignorance,* was an attack on all literary criticism and all critics, and all poets who like to write criticism. "It has taken me twenty years," he wrote then, "to break away completely from modern poetry and modern criticism, which I consider to be one and the same thing. Being a teacher has helped me immeasurably to know how pernicious this poetry and criticism really are and how destructive they have been to poetry and the faculty of judging poetry." He even accuses criticism of creating made-to-order poetry.

But the truth is that good poets write criticism not to "capture poetry," as Shapiro has accused Eliot and Pound of doing, but to find out what they think, as he himself admits elsewhere. And Shapiro has always written criticism; the *Essay on Rime* was criticism, even though it was written in free verse. Shapiro wrote criticism all during the 1940s and 1950s, first on the side of the "Culture Poetry" (his own term) and then against it. When he was Consultant in Poetry at the Library of Congress, he even wrote an essay on prosody and threw in a bibliography to boot. He wrote a dialogue on dramatic poetry and a number of pronouncements about the state of poetry in the years when he first took over the editorship of *Poetry*. When he decided to break loose from the Establishment, about the time he gave up the editorship of *Poetry,* he published a series of lectures entitled *Beyond Criticism*. His 1960 collection, *In Defense of Ignorance,* contained only a small portion of his critical prose; he declared in it that "the present essays are intended to be the last criticism I shall ever write." But here it is four years later and the summer 1964 number of *The Carleton Miscellany* turns up with "A Malebolge of 1400 Books," being six lectures by Shapiro amounting to some 50,000 additional words of criticism. So it is highly unlikely that he really intends to stop writing criticism, and one hopes he will not.

Shapiro wrote and writes criticism in order to write poetry; it is as simple as that. If poetry is the mansion, then criticism is entrusted with clearing out the woods and the fields so that the foundations can be laid. If we look at Shapiro's criticism from the *Essay on Rime* up through "A

Malebolge of 1400 Books," we will see that it has at all times really been intended not as an effort to dictate taste or to reform the literary world, but as a way of working out the principles by which he can write his verse. In this respect the *Essay on Rime* is interesting. On the one hand it is a statement of the need for a poetry which does not depend on conceptual systems, upon involvement in and close familiarity with the intellectual life, and which is drawn not out of books but out of everyday experience. Yet at the same time and by its very nature the *Essay on Rime* is an ingenious way of providing just such interpretation, analysis and criticism without actually writing it in prose—as if the poet were getting himself ready for his entry into the intellectual world as Man of Letters, but by doing the book in verse he was avoiding taking the final step just yet (and the verse is at most points very, very close to straightforward prose).

It may be recalled that in 1948 the Fellows in Poetry of the Library of Congress, who constituted many of our most distinguished poets, voted to award the Bollingen Prize for Poetry to Ezra Pound, then a patient at a Washington mental hospital and under indictment for treason because of his pro-Axis broadcasts from Italy during the war. Shapiro was, I believe, the lone dissenter from the vote. In the furore that followed, the *Saturday Review of Literature* asked Shapiro to write an essay attacking the decision. He refused, whereupon Robert Hillyer was commissioned to do it, and he produced a series of articles which all but accused the Fellows of a Fascist plot against American democracy and linked the so-called obscurity of Modern Poetry (which the fuss was really about, when one comes down to it) to an anti-democratic plot. Public outcry was such that the Library of Congress dissociated itself from the Bollingen Prize, and the incident soon became a kind of Dreyfus Case, in which all members of the profession of poetry had to choose sides. If you were for the award to Pound, you were for the practice of poetry as promulgated by its leading poets, and you were also in favor of the New Criticism in particular and the practice of criticism of poetry in general. If you were against the award, you were against modern poetry, and you objected to the New Criticism and generally to "culture poetry" and the primacy of the intellect in modern letters. Either you were on one side or the other. The only poet of reputation I can recall who genuinely attempted to play it down the middle was Peter Viereck, who only succeeded in angering both sides.

As for Shapiro, he felt he had to choose, and he did. He wrote an essay, entitled "What is Anti-Criticism," in which he reversed his decision, and while he was at it he went all the way: he defended the New Criticism, he defended Culture Poetry, and he attacked all those who were against it. Why did Shapiro do this? Again I think the answer is to be found not in his cultural or literary convictions, but in his poetry. The kind of poetry Shapiro defended (and in so doing, explained) was the kind of poetry he was attempting to write at the time. It was "Culture Poetry," to use his term again, the poetry of **"Adam and Eve,"** and of **"A Calder,"** and **"Going to School,"** and **"The Alphabet."** Whatever the merits of this poetry, it was not a poetry based on the discovery and analysis of the meaning of everyday middle-class experience. It is meditative, reflective poetry, which, as in **"Going to School,"** seeks to resolve the physical world of science and the occult imagination of the poet in a metaphor, or as in **"The Alphabet"** would sum up moral history in the authority of the Old Testament.

Shapiro's editorship of *Poetry,* his new-found legitimate critical status, his willingness to accept his role as Man of Letters in the Cultural Establishment, were all very nice, but they involved one drawback: he wrote very little poetry in these years, and what he did write was not conspicuously outstanding. As a poet he wore his new identity very uneasily. And if, as I believe, a poet's critical position, his place in the hierarchy, his livelihood itself are ultimately subservient, in his own scale of values, to his success in writing the verse he wishes to write, then Karl Shapiro's next mutation was entirely predictable.

5.

What interests me is that Sandburg, a long time ago, made an intellectual decision to abdicate from intellectualism . . .

—"A Malebolge of 1400 Books"

He resigned. He quit. He left *Poetry* and he went to California, and finally he wound up in the state of Nebraska, editing a literary magazine and teaching at the university, and he decided to have a try at pulling down the pillars on which the whole edifice of modern poetry rested. His strident assertion of his identity as a Jew, through his choice of title for his 1958 collection of verse, was one way of asserting his independence. Eliot the Anglican, Pound the anti-Semite, Auden the Anglo-Catholic "convert" became the villains who had ensnared all of modern poetry in a conspiracy designed to make it intellectual, effete, highbrow, anti-scientific, sexless, ivory-towerish, and so on. The New Criticism was part of the plot; by removing moral and social judgment from the act of criticism it allowed Eliot and Pound to introduce all manner of un-American doctrines into modern poetry. Even his one-time idol William Butler Yeats was no longer safe; a good poet, Yeats had been spoiled by being seduced into composing "Culture Poetry."

Having gone this far, Shapiro next began to extend the logic of his position, and he began doing, I fear, what he criticizes Eliot and Pound for doing. When Pound decried the poetry of Shakespeare because it did not fit into his system, and Eliot did the same with Milton and others, Shapiro said that both knew perfectly well how good the poetry was that they were thus castigating, but they criticized it anyway. "It is my contention," Shapiro wrote in *In Defense of Ignorance,* "that modern criticism is not honest, though it may be sincere. Its dishonesty results from its undying loyalty to generalities. . . . Pound knows as well as you do that Shakespeare is the finest of all English poets, but he must remain sincere to the system he has blocked out. He thus engages in a fantastic act of dishonesty. . . . Sincerity to the idea always takes precedence in the mental life of the intellectual, whether the idea comprises a total system or is some offshoot of one of the *isms.*"

But Shapiro, I think, proceeded to do precisely the same thing. Eliot was now "a poet of religion, hence a poet of the second or third rank." Pound's *Mauberly* is "a very bad poem." Yeats "will always remain pretty much of a poet of his time, because of his commitment to the historical role" (a qualification worthy of Eliot at his best!). A poem entitled "Hot Afternoons Have Been In Montana" by Eli Siegel is "One of the last authentically American poems . . . before the final triumph of Eliot's culture poetry." William Carlos Williams is, along with D. H. Lawrence, "the leader of what authentic American poetry is being written today." Wallace Stevens is "a beautiful poet who is really devoid of imagination." Henry Miller is "the greatest living author." James Joyce is "that master manufacturer of literary cuckoo clocks." Wilhelm Reich is one of our "true leaders and visionaries." "John Bunyan knew more about the uses of literature than [John] Donne." Robert W. Service is "a superlative poet on the lowest possible level." And so on. Now no more than Pound on Shakespeare or Eliot on Milton, I surmise, did Shapiro really believe all that, but it fitted his own current posture, and so he said it. He knows that as poetry the work of Robert W. Service isn't worth the paper it is printed on, and that by contending that Service's doggerel is "as much poetry as *Hamlet* or the *Rape of the Lock* or the *Ballad of Reading Gaol*" he is guilty of the most blatant kind of casuistry. Shapiro said all that because he thought it "needed to be said," whether or not it happened to be true.

6.

*I seek the entrance of the rabbit hole. Maybe it's
the door that has no name.*
—*The Bourgeois Poet*

I write this not in dispraise of Shapiro, but with a kind of genuine admiration, however much I disagree with him. For to repeat, Shapiro is a *poet,* and an honest poet, and in order to deal honestly with himself as a poet he is quite willing to adopt any posture or critical position he finds useful, and to burn every other book of poetry or criticism ever written.

Now manifestly he could not go back to writing poems about Buicks and haircuts; he had left that kind of poetry for good. On the other hand, there was the distinct feeling that in trying to write Culture Poetry he was trying to be what he wasn't, to falsify, through over-inhibiting, his own experience. The old kind of direct statement, the pleasure of showing things as they are without having to take account of various kinds of cultural cross references, literary, social, and cultural associations, the comfort of not having to be aware of his own consciousness in the act of expressing himself, were being denied him. Very well. What he must do was to find a method of recovering that immediacy and freshness, that "lost innocence."

> Shapiro has long since proved himself a craftsman of language of the first order, and it is no surprise to know that he can appropriate the distinctive rhythm and style of a number of poets.
>
> —*Louis D. Rubin, Jr.*

If he could create poetry free of the kind of formal patterning that conventional rhyme and meter demanded, sufficiently pliable in structure to permit him to work into the poem what he knew about things without having to fit them into the artificial unity of a rigid structure, flexible enough in language and diction to let him qualify his thoughts without falsifying them by making them too ponderous and clumsy, unified by no more severe a logic than that of casual association, a poetry which in its pattern of imagery and its rhetorical structure led the reader ahead toward the next thought without encouraging him to examine each new image in relation to what had preceded it—if he could do this, it would again be possible for him to do what almost since *V-Letter* he had found it so very difficult to do: *get himself down on paper,* in words. For with Shapiro that was the all-important thing; he didn't want to erect a system of culture and belief, he wanted to say what he knew. And what he knew was Karl Shapiro.

The obvious model was Whitman, the poet of *Song of Myself.* The equation, the paradox if one will, whereby Whitman had constructed *song of Myself* was the dual existence of the individual as a solitary being, and as the perceiver and therefore possessor of his society and his culture. Whitman set forth the duality in the first two lines:

> I celebrate myself, and sing myself,
> And what I assume you shall assume,

The resulting consequence Whitman pursued through a division of body and spirit, society and self, pitting one against the other to show how each contained the other, so that one human being constituted within himself history, biology, politics, science, the arts, commerce, geography, and so on, while at the same time he was *not* any of these things, but a private, solitary soul with its own consciousness and integrity. In many, one—in one, many.

Whitman made this believable in two ways. One was through a mystic identification of flesh and spirit, form and substance, in a transcendental unity. The other was through a cumulative rhetoric which brought together rather than set apart, which dealt with a various and numerous experience and made it one by alliteration, repetition, restatement, and copula. Thus Whitman's long lines, his catalogues, his repetition; they were a structure designed to make the reader move along with him, not stand back and examine everything separately. The unifying factor, to repeat, was the individual, the person, to whom all things related and came back, and this person was, through an act of mystical poetic transcendence, the poet himself.

If, therefore, Shapiro could like Whitman write a poem of this kind, in many parts, structured primarily by association of ideas and by rhetoric, in format loose enough and flexible enough to permit anything and everything to be expressed that seemed appropriate, he might at last achieve what he had been looking for: a way to get himself and what he knew into a poem. He needed a way that would enable him to show, without on every occasion having to link up, what he saw. What way would this be? The answer was *The Bourgeois Poet.*
It was a very good idea. The only drawback was that it didn't work.

7.

O pickpock moon, subject of all lost poems,
   birthplace of tides et cetera, true bottom of the
   sea et cetera, O wallsocket.

   —The Bourgeois Poet

The Bourgeois Poet doesn't work because the basic metaphor, the principle of structural oneness by which Whitman was able to make *Song of Myself* a cohesive and unified work of art, and thus control and direct the role of all the parts, is impossible to Shapiro. I am many, Whitman said, therefore I am one; in place of Whitman's mystical transcendental assertion of oneness with the universe, Shapiro attempts to use the principle of solipsism, the notion that one creates the world in the act of comprehending it:

   The world is my dream, says the wild child, ever
      so wise, not stepping on lines. I am the world,
      says the wise-eyed child. I made you, mother. I
      made you, sky. Take care or I'll put you back in
      my dream.

But at once irony must be trained on such an assertion, or else it will collapse into fragments:

   If I look at the sun the sun will explode, says the
      wicked boy. If I look at the moon I'll drain
      away. Where I stay I hold them in their places.
      Don't ask me what I am doing.

And when the first section ends it is with a reminder of the peril involved in being one with nature, and of the potentially disastrous relationship of disembodied, pure thought to the blood-reality of people and events:

   De Sade looks down through the bars of the
      Bastille. They have stepped up the slaughter of
      nobles.

De Sade, the "Divine Marquis," who in another context is said by Shapiro to have known only two varieties of relationship of men to men, "abstract morality and crime," was like Whitman and Emerson willing to look at man

purely as a creature of nature, but unlike them De Sade saw nature as evil instead of good. Shapiro's one-in-many, many-in-one world will thus contain what Walt Whitman's didn't in *Song of Myself*—the possibility that the world within one man's consciousness is an evil world.

But to acknowledge this possibility, to look at the negative side of the metaphor, undercuts the principle of structural unity, because if the fact that one contains the world in one's perceptions may equally mean that one contains everything or nothing, then nothing is no-unity, no-oneness, no-coherence. The whole scheme flies apart. The resultant training of irony onto the confident assertions throws the reader, as Whitman's verse does not, into an awareness of separateness, of dis-unity, which instead of making the poem develop as a unit splits it apart.

Tactically it also works the wrong way. The success in *Song of Myself* of the loose, flowing construction of cumulative detail and succeeding emotions depends rhetorically on the reader's being always propelled forward, without stopping to speculate critically on the appropriateness and conviction of the similes and metaphors. Shapiro, by postulating disunity as well as oneness, draws attention to just such separation, and when the reader sees that things don't go together, the poem becomes a disjointed collection of images and ideas.

The real difficulty is that Shapiro isn't a mystic, however much he tries to be one by dabbling in Zen Buddhism, Wilhelm Reich, Jung, Ouspensky, and "cosmic consciousness." He is essentially a rationalist, and whenever his imagination begins wandering away from the logical his sense of irony comes charging in to rectify the situation. However much Shapiro denounces "Culture Poetry" and intellectual systems, however much he complains that from Dante through Eliot a poem which is philosophical is to that extent weakened as a poem, he can't help putting things together himself. It is amusing, in *In Defense of Ignorance*, after watching him complain because Pound and Eliot try to make everything into a rational system, to see him turn right around and declare that Yeats's preoccupation with magic "weakened his whole structure of thought."

We have in *The Bourgeois Poet*, therefore, the example of a poem which, written by a poet whose art consists in perceiving the relationship between things and social ideas, is structured nevertheless according to the theory that at least half the time things do *not* add up. The result is that often they don't—in his poem, and yet every instinct in the poet, which means every metaphor and every simile, continually works toward making the reader look for relationships. In the end the only unifying principle of *The Bourgeois Poet*, which is another way of saying the only principle designed to keep us reading on, is the personality of the poet. And that isn't nearly enough, because that personality itself isn't naturally unified and whole. So what we get are random thoughts, this idea of that, this memory and that judgment, this reference to an event and that comparison, and so on, for 113 pages, some of them brilliant and intense, some indifferent and flat.

Why does the book end on page 120, at the end of part No. 96? I have read it three times, and I don't know. Shapiro has modelled his final section on that of Whitman's *Song of Myself*. But the irony undercuts it. It is left hanging. Life may be like that, but poetry can't be; the way for a poet to show that nothing adds up is to make a poem add up to a statement of that. Otherwise there is chaos. And chaos itself is a very different matter from the depiction of chaos.

8.

The antithesis of the closed poem is not necessarily the open poem, the freedom of Whitman or surrealism or just plain spillover of feeling, anger or illumination.

—A Malebolge of 1400 Books

The Bourgeois Poet is, I think, a brave attempt by an honest poet, and to the extent that it can give order and coherence to that poet's personality, it is a successful work. But its design is such that nothing in the structure or presentation can help very much to give it that coherence; it is deliberately constructed not to help. The poet's personality, not the poem, must do the job. And it won't do it. All of which goes to show that the traditional machinery of poetry—rhyme, rhythm, metrics, verse forms—are not arbitrary restrictions, however much their overly rigid application may sometimes give that impression. Rather, they are methods of ordering experience through intensifying and controlling language. And if for Karl Shapiro all traditional and known forms are too confining and artificial to allow him to discover such order, then given his uncompromising intelligence there would seem to be but one alternative: to find the form. It will not be enough to pretend that one is not needed. No-form is not the answer, and however attractive it might be to do so, Shapiro no more than anyone else can will himself back to a condition of ignorance and innocence.

Meanwhile there are straws in the wind. In "A Malebolge of 1400 Books" Shapiro shows signs of backtracking in his attitude toward Eliot and Pound. He is "beginning after a decade of swatting the Tse-tse and subverting Pound to appreciate their gift to us," and also "to give in to the *Four Quartets* as a model from which to go into production." He hedges the bet by prefacing it with the statement that the principle of both Eliot's and Pounds' work is disorganization, "a new definition of the organization of life." But Shapiro knows better than that; whatever else may be true of Eliot, the *Four Quartets* are no one's disorganized poem. So it may be that Karl Shapiro is once again ready to move in another direction.

However much he may fence himself in with this or that system, he always manages at the proper moment to leap over the railing and get on with the business of writing new poems. He says of Pound, in "A Malebolge of 1400 Books," that "I am not concerned about making these remarks consistent with any I have made in the past—in the event that anyone should go to the trouble of comparing them." No one is finally going to worry how much or how often Shapiro contradicts himself in his critical writ-

ings, providing that in his poetry he uses his discoveries and his insights to good advantage. I suggest that we view *The Bourgeois Poet* as an attempt to do that, and if as I think he has failed to do it, let us hope that it in its turn will help him on the next try. That Karl Shapiro will keep trying there is not the slightest doubt.

Stephen Stepanchev (essay date 1965)

SOURCE: "Karl Shapiro," in *American Poetry Since 1945*, Harper & Row, 1965, pp. 53-68.

[*In the following essay, Stepanchev discusses the major themes of Shapiro's verse.*]

Karl Shapiro is another "social poet" who found impetus and subject matter in the public crises of the 1940's, when his private predicament as a soldier in the war against Germany and Japan merged with the predicament of American society as a whole, fighting for its survival. But, although a slow, subdued anger is the permanent emotional climate of an army, Shapiro's tone is rarely angry, even in the poems in which he points out the shortcomings of society—the racial, religious, and economic injustices that he sees about him. And, as a relatively "new" American of Jewish ancestry, he sees these very clearly. In one poem he speaks of a university where "To hurt the Negro and avoid the Jew / Is the curriculum"; in another he describes the inequalities of the graveyard, where the rich lie under ornate tombs and the poor under "machined crosses." He is bitter and ironic, but possesses enough spiritual equilibrium to be "at rest in the blast," as Marianne Moore would say. He achieves the sort of cosmic consciousness that makes possible an objectification and dramatization of inner tensions and polarities. All of his best work was done during the years 1940-1948.

Shapiro published his first book of poems in Baltimore, in 1935. It is entitled, simply, *Poems* and contains exercises in such forms as the sonnet, rondeau, triolet, and villanelle, phrased in an archaic diction heavily in debt to nineteenth-century Romantic poetry. The themes are, for the most part, traditional—love and the seasonal changes of nature—but there is an occasional reference to war and revolution in Vienna, Cuba, and China, showing that Shapiro had been "listening to the Communists." There is talk of struggle, pickets, marching; the beauty of the world "is to come," is to be built. And in the best poem in the volume, **"There Are Birds,"** a war poem, Shapiro reveals his awareness of the coexistence of opposites in the world; he describes buzzards hanging over a battlefield and remarks, "There are also/ ever-singing / larks not hawks."

But his first really strong work appeared in a collection of poems published by New Directions in 1941, *Five Young American Poets,* Second Series. At the time of this publication Shapiro had already been inducted into the United States Army and was stationed at Camp Lee, Virginia, where he made this pronouncement: "Today American poetry suffers from the dictatorship of criticism, that branch of literature which is more devoted to dialectics than to the joyful activity of experience. Our poetry has the task of destroying the government of critics and of making a wholesale return to the anarchy of experience." This statement is the first shot in a twenty-year private war against critics, old and new, but it bears little relationship to what Shapiro actually does in his poems. Of all contemporary poets, he is the least interested in projecting "the anarchy of experience." His poems always have a point of view, often so strongly stated that it amounts to an "ideology."

For example, in **"The Dome of Sunday"** he expresses an almost Eliotic dislike of the modern city with its "Row-houses and row-lives." In the poem **"Alexandria"** his social criticism is explicitly anti-Southern and pro-Negro:

> Then let the Negroes creep out of their scars
>   And enter Alexandria
>   To burn the clapboard and the straw
> And cast a vote for whiteness and for trees.

In such poems as **"Elegy Written on a Frontporch"** and **"Midnight Show"** he comments on what he regards as the horrors and obscenities of contemporary social life, and in others, like **"Drug Store"** and **"Buick,"** he tries to "fix" features of the social scene in the fashion of a reporter or sociologist.

Social criticism can also be found in Shapiro's next volume, *Person, Place, and Thing*, which was issued in 1942. In a poem entitled **"Property"** he speaks of a familiar urban process, the devolvement of real estate from the rich to the poor as neighborhoods decay:

> Now nowhere are those tenants to be found
> Who bestowed on later citizens their oldest
>   sections,
> But north of the city in their English valleys
> Their sons and daughters
> Continue the management of a large inheritance
> Of joy and fashion.

A note of envy seems to be present in this poem; one can almost see the stereotype of the poor boy pressing his nose against a mansion window. In another poem, **"Construction,"** Shapiro rejects the heartless city environment of steel and concrete. In a poem entitled **"& Co."** he describes a man who dies spiritually in his job. In **"Emporium"** he shows distaste for an important feature of the business scene, the department store; in **"The Snob"** he attacks a "Greek-letter boy" who despises Negroes and Methodists; and in **"Hollywood"** he is critical of an industry that markets beauty "like a basic food."

In his next book, *V-Letter and Other Poems* (1944), Shapiro's social context expands to include the whole United States Army in the South Pacific, where the "Puritan" with his "fear / Of beauty" moves him to mockery and where the "intellectual" appears ridiculous. Shapiro says he would rather be a milkman or a barber than an intellectual, making the curious assumption that they are mutually exclusive. (One of Shapiro's weaknesses as a poet is his predilection

for categorizing people.) Among the better war poems is **"The Gun,"** in which the weapon is seen as "the means of the practical humor of death / Which is savage to punish the dead for the sake of my sin!" Another is **"Troop Train,"** in which the death-haunted present of the soldier is compared with a fabulous future: "Nightfall of nations brilliant after war." One of the least successful of the war poems is **"Elegy for a Dead Soldier,"** in which the poet's ambivalent attitude toward the man he is presumably mourning is embarrassingly evident in lines like these:

> Of all men poverty pursued him least;
> He was ashamed of all the down and out,
> And saw the unemployed as a vague mass
> Incapable of hunger or revolt.
> He hated other races, south or east,
> And shoved them to the margin of his mind.
> He could recall the justice of the Colt,
> Take interest in gang-war like a game.
> His ancestry was somewhere far behind
> And left him only his peculiar name.
> Doors opened, and he recognized no class.

This astonishing list of the dead man's prejudices ends with an epitaph:

> Underneath this wooden cross there lies
> A Christian killed in battle. You who read,
> Remember that this stranger died in pain;
> And passing here, if you can lift your eyes
> Upon a peace kept by a human creed,
> Know that one soldier has not died in vain.

One tends to doubt the sincerity of these lines—and yet mockery is clearly out of place in the poem. The poet is either unsure of his attitude or unwilling to be frank.

The social theme connects with the religious theme in these poems, for, as the poet remarks in his preface, "It is not the commonplace of suffering or the platitudinous comparison with the peace, or the focus on the future that should occupy us; but the spiritual progress or retrogression of the man in war, the increase or decrease in his knowledge of beauty, government and religion." Actually, some of the poems *are* built around a contrast between the past and the present or between the present and the future; such a contrast makes for a strong poetic structure. For example, in **"Sunday: New Guinea"** the poet describes soldiers going to church on a Sunday morning and then flashes back to intimate details of Sundays at home, where love's "presence" is "snowy, beautiful, and kind." As for "spiritual progress," it is difficult to assess movements of the spirit; but, if acceptance of death represents spiritual progress, one can point to the mail-call rumination in a poem entitled **"Aside,"** in the course of which Shapiro says: "When and where we arrive / Is no matter, but *how* is the question we urgently need, / How to love and to hate, how to die, how to write and to read." And there is the title poem, **"V-Letter,"** one of the best in the book, in which the poet makes this resounding declaration of love:

> I love you first because your years
> Lead to my matter-of-fact and simple death

Or to our open marriage,
And I pray nothing for my safety back,
Not even luck, because our love is whole
Whether I live or fail.

In many poems the religious theme is given a social emphasis through the poet's preoccupation with his identity as a Jew. Like most Americans under the pressure of influences tending toward "democratic" conformity, Shapiro responds either with a proud assertion of separateness and individuality or with a yearning for submergence, a desire to shed the difficult burden of difference. In the poem **"Moses"** he is proud of his heritage; addressing Moses, he says, "Converse with God made you a thinker, / Taught us all early justice, made us a race." And in **"The Synagogue"** he declares, "Our name is yet the identity of God." But in the poem entitled **"Jew"** he speaks of the terror and bondage of history and sees the Jewish identity in this way:

But the name is a language itself that is whispered
    and hissed
Through the house of ages, and ever a language the
    same,
And ever and ever a blow on our heart like a fist.

In an effort to transcend this history and to assume a comradely inclusiveness, Shapiro writes a number of poems from the Christian point of view, almost as though he were a convert. As he says in the preface, "I try to write freely, one day as a Christian, the next as a Jew, the next as a soldier who sees the slapstick of modern war." In **"Christmas Eve: Australia"** one finds lines like these:

I smoke and read my Bible and chew gum,
Thinking of Christ and Christmas of last year,
And what those quizzical soldiers standing near
Ask of the war and Christmases to come,
And sick of causes and the tremendous blame
Curse lightly and pronounce your serious name.

In 1945 the poet published a little book entitled ***Essay on Rime*** in which he maintains that poetry "Is in decline" and attempts to find reasons for the decline in "confusions" in prosody, language, and belief. He argues for a revitalization of poetry through accessions from the storehouses of prose, opposes the poetry of ideas, and lines up with the common man in his suspicion of modern poetry, aiming to "solidify / The layman's confidence in a plainer art." Written for the author's own amusement while he was on a tour of duty in New Guinea, the book is, nevertheless, full of affectations, such as the archaic title, which refers not to rhyme, as one would suppose, but to poetry in general. The margins of the text are spotted with topic titles, as though the author were afraid that the reader would be unable to follow the close reasoning of the argument without their aid. Actually, the book is banal and very badly argued. The quality of the verse can be judged by these lines on the meter of the poem:

The metric of this book is made upon
The classic English decasyllable

Adapted to the cadence of prose speech;
Ten units to the verse by count of eye
Is the ground rhythm, over which is set
The rougher flux and reflux of conversation.

In his next book, ***Trial of a Poet*** (1947), Shapiro returns to his exploration of the social context of religious experience. Here, in **"The Convert,"** he describes sympathetically a man's conversion to Catholicism despite "The groan of positive science, hiss of friends"; the convert knows how heavy "the hand that hates" is and "How light and secret is the sign of love." But a very different view of conversion is presented in **"Recapitulations,"** a seemingly autobiographical poem which traces the poet's development and contains these bitter lines:

Two priests advised me on my rise to grace,
The one among the sacred bric-a-brac
Questioning my devotion to my face,
The other frankly dubious of my race.

Another aspect of the social scene that interests Shapiro in this, his first postwar, volume is the adjustment of the soldier to civilian life, as in the poem **"Demobilization,"** where, speaking for all returned soldiers, he says:

Saviors and spies, we seek the road we lost
When kidnapped from indifference. As before,
Back where I started from, I stare, touch wood.

And, now that the war is over, he takes a generous view of conscientious objectors; they are equal in heroism with the men who died in combat:

Well might the soldier kissing the hot beach
Erupting in his face damn all your kind.
Yet you who save neither yourselves nor us
Are equally with those who shed the blood
The heroes of our cause. Your conscience is
What we come back to in the armistice.

In other poems he is less generous. In **"Boy-Man,"** for example, he describes a male type that he dislikes, and in **"The Southerner"** he pictures a man who knows how to conform and to compel and who still denies "the fall / Of Richmond and man." In some poems he touches on the social meaning of technological advance, as in **"Air Liner"** and **"The Progress of Faust."** In the latter poem the age-old Faustian lust for knowledge spends itself in the orgasm of an atomic explosion in the desert.

Clearly, all these poems of the 1940's have their social meaning. Ideologically, they seem to be liberal, and the formulations of political and social attitude, the abstractions of an intellect at work in categories, owe a great deal to W. H. Auden, who, ironically enough, had already abandoned his liberalism by 1941. Shapiro owes a great deal to Auden in matters of technique also, in his handling of stanza and line, for, like Auden, he works in traditional measures, knowing that a relatively prosaic content requires meter. Within traditional limits he enjoys experiments, particularly in anapaestic measure. This return to formalism was characteristic of American poetry during the late 1940's and early 1950's; as Shapiro remarks in *English Prosody and Modern Poetry* (1947), "Many of our best poets have led a return to verse structures which twenty years ago were held to be dead and gone." For the most part, Shapiro does well with these structures, but now and then he produces incredible verses like this stanza from **"Recapitulations"**:

> Doctors and cousins paid their call,
>   The rabbi and my father helped.
> A crucifix burned on the wall
>   Of the bright room where I was whelped.

Reading these lines, one despairs of meter, rhyme, and poetry in general. One feels like joining Marianne Moore when she confesses that she, too, dislikes poetry.

In 1953, as though to signal the end of an epoch, Shapiro published his **Poems, 1940-1953**. Only five of the poems in the collection were new, and of these the best poem, **"Israel,"** had been written in 1948 to celebrate the founding of the state of Israel and was read at a political meeting in Baltimore in the same year. This "occasional" poem, inspired by a political development in the Near East, marks a turning point in Shapiro's attitude toward his Jewish heritage. Whatever ambivalence may have been present in earlier years is now gone; he is clearly proud of his people and the new state of Israel. He says, "When I see the name of Israel high in print / The fences crumble in my flesh." And he adds, "I say my name / Aloud for the first time unconsciously." This is a remarkable change when one considers that, as a beginning writer, Shapiro once wrote to a fellow poet to ask him "what obstacles one had to overcome to publish poems under a Jewish name." The poem ends on a very positive note:

> Speak of the tillage of a million heads
> No more. Speak of the evil myths no more
> Of one who harried Jesus on his way
> Saying, *Go faster.* Speak no more
> Of the yellow badge, *secta nefaria.*
> Speak the name only of the living land.

The most ambitious poem in the book is a retelling of the story of Adam and Eve in rhymed iambic pentameter. The poem belongs to the new trend in the immediate postwar years toward psychological explorations with a mythological emphasis and relies for its imagery on the Bible, the *Zohar,* and the writings of Wilhelm Reich. Its thesis, according to Shapiro himself, is that "man is for the world, not for the afterworld," but this thesis is so muted—and, indeed, it is contradicted by Eve, who prays to God, "Guide us to Paradise," in the hour of the pair's expulsion from Eden—that it seems like an afterthought. And the verse is easy, facile, and without the precise imagery that makes for visual immediacy.

In 1958, Shapiro published another book, **Poems of a Jew**, which contains twenty-seven poems that had appeared in earlier collections and six new poems, all of them on the familiar social-religious theme that is dominant in the poet's work. The importance of the collection lies in the poet's proud assertion of his identity as a Jew. The nature of this identity is clear enough from the poems themselves, with their vivid social, historical, and religious imagery, but the poet further clarifies it in the introduction to the book: "As everyone knows, a Jew who becomes an atheist remains a Jew. A Jew who becomes a Catholic remains a Jew. Being a Jew is the consciousness of being a Jew, and the Jewish identity, with or without religion, with or without history, is the significant fact." This identity involves an "intimacy" with God, according to Shapiro, but not necessarily with Judaism; it represents worldliness; and it can be equated with "the primitive ego of the human race."

A look through his books reveals that Shapiro published only eleven new poems between 1948 and 1958, either because of the uncongeniality of the period or because of the pressure of his teaching duties and editorial chores. (He was editor of *Poetry* for five years.) He did manage to publish a book of prose, however; this was *Beyond Criticism* (1953), in which he fulminates against all literary dogmas because they are "ruinous to poetry" and attacks "slavery to doctrines of culture under the guise of history and myth" because they lead to the destruction of personality in art. In practice, of course, his own poems frequently invoke social, literary, and historical contexts.

In 1960, Shapiro published a collection of critical essays, *In Defense of Ignorance,* which he says is his last: "The present essays are intended to be the last criticism I shall ever write." In this book Shapiro takes up his lifelong war against critics, intellectuals, and all members of what he calls the "Modernist School," which includes William Butler Yeats, Ezra Pound, and T. S. Eliot. Dismissing all poetry that betrays the impress of ideas or the control of a mind, he declares that "poetry has lost its significance, its relevance, and even its meaning in our time. To begin again it must repair to the wilderness, outside society, outside the city gates, a million miles from books and their keepers." It is clear that he favors the cosmic individualism of such writers as Walt Whitman and Henry Miller and the spontaneity and immediacy of William Carlos Williams. The secret of form, according to Shapiro, is "the eradication of the line between poetry and prose, between life and art."

These pronouncements suggest the poet's awareness of the new spontaneous poetry of the late 1950's and betray his uneasiness over his own carefully measured poetry of the 1940's. A study of the poems in **The Bourgeois Poet** (1964) shows that Shapiro is now writing a very prosaic free verse but that his subject matter is unchanged: he still writes social commentaries, as the very title of his book indicates. His poems have, in the past, been saved from prose by an underpinning of meter; now he has the problem of creating a strong substitute rhythm that can organize his essentially prosaic subject matter.

There is no doubt that Shapiro's best work belongs to the years 1940-1948, when he wrote **"Necropolis," "Buick," "University," "Waitress," "Auto Wreck," "Troop Train," "The Gun," "Jew," "The Leg," "V-Letter," "The Con-**

scientious Objector," "The Convert," and **"Israel."** But these poems are in traditional measures, on which the poet has now turned his back.

Karl Malkoff (essay date 1973)

SOURCE: "The Self in the Modern World: Karl Shapiro's Jewish Poems," in *Contemporary American-Jewish Literature: Critical Essays,* edited by Irving Malin, Indiana University Press, 1973, pp. 213-28.

[*In the following essay, Malkoff places* Poems of a Jew *within the context of Shapiro's other poetic works.*]

"These poems are not for poets," Karl Shapiro begins his Introduction to *Poems of a Jew.*[1] But perhaps they are. Certainly, Jewishness for Shapiro is less a matter of cultural, religious, or historical tradition than a mode of apprehending reality. Shapiro's Jew, obviously a symbol of the human condition in general, may be specifically the archetypal poet. "Poetry is everywhere at its goal, a wise critic once said. And one might add in paraphrase: the Jew is everywhere at his goal."

Later in the brief essay, Jewishness is defined as "a certain state of consciousness which is inescapable. . . . Being a Jew is the consciousness of being a Jew. . . ." A metaphor begins to emerge in which Jew comes to represent a particular quality of mind, one that is intimately related to the creative process. We are dealing with that aspect of consciousness that is conscious of itself, that is, in fact, obsessed with itself; it is "the primitive ego of the human race," attempting to survive against a "background of Nothing." We may begin to suspect that we are dealing with those powers of imagination by which the individual gives shape to his reality, with which he comes to terms with the emptiness that threatens to engulf him.

The discovery of order in apparent chaos, of form in flux, was, of course, a theme that preoccupied the generation preceding Shapiro's, that of Pound, Eliot, Stevens. But important distinctions must be drawn. The older poets were products of the First World War, which called into final question the standards and systems of the civilization that gave rise to it. With all in disarray, structure seemed absolutely crucial. The Second World War, however, was shattering in a different way. Order became the enemy, the concentration camp, the totalitarian state. The nothingness persisted, but now almost as an ally rather than an antagonist; meaninglessness had to serve as the source of meaning. The Jew, then, is appropriate for Shapiro's metaphor not simply because the poet is himself a Jew, but because the Jew has become the terrible symbol of the holocaust, of man brought face to face with annihilation. He is, in short, the symbol of a new way of coming to terms with chaos; no longer wishing to set the universe in order, he must learn to settle for absurd victories or no victory at all.

Poems of a Jew tests the capacity of the Self to survive the chaos it must embrace. If the Self seems to triumph, however uneasily, in this particular volume, we must recognize that the triumph is not necessarily permanent. *Poems of a Jew,* the culmination of a specific phase of Shapiro's career, must finally be understood not only in terms of its own poems, but in the context of the poet's subsequent work as well. This is Shapiro's last book as a relatively formal poet; and there may in fact be some connection between his original commitment to traditional verse and his early faith in the ability of the Self to exist, both of which beliefs are seriously questioned in his later poetry.

Poems of a Jew is divided into three sections: the first seems largely concerned with symbols of the Jewish experience, frequently with art and language; the second specifically places Judaism within the context of a Christian world, a theme that is never far from the surface throughout the entire book; and the final section deals with archetypal figures, most of them Jewish, all in some way relevant to a consideration of Jewishness.

"The Alphabet" begins the first section; emphasizing the power of the word, the poem supports the suggestion that for Shapiro the Jew is above all a creator of form, a namer of things, in short, a poet. But he is a poet of disaster. The letters of the Jewish alphabet are "as strict as flames / Or little terrible flowers . . . ," they "bristle like barbed wire. . . ." There is appropriate irony in the fact that the letters themselves are cruel, at least intimating that the tradition from which they emerge contains an element of self-destructiveness. But the barbed, burning symbols look backward to biblical origins as well as to the contemporary nightmare. "Singing through solid stone," they are man's link with God; a "burning bush," they illuminate the human condition. Finally, combining the sinister movement of the flames with the cutting edges of the barbed wire, these letters "are dancing knives / That carve the heart of darkness seven ways." Evidence of the "almost natural crime," genocide, the letters underline a universal guilt; they are signposts of atrocity.

However, the negative vision does not contract into a deepening gloom. The flickering pyre begins to symbolize the death that precedes resurrection; from "the still speaking embers of ghettos, / There rise the tinder flowers of the Jews." There is logic to Shapiro's introduction of a Christian frame of reference, with its promise of rebirth. The Jewish alphabet lies "in chain-line over Christian pages." The image of the little terrible flowers itself suggests Saint Francis, recalling the configurations of Bernard Malamud's *The Assistant.* Not surprisingly, the total relationship between the two traditions must be finally expressed in paradox: the letters' fire "Unsacrifices the bled son of man / Yet plaits his crown of thorns."

"University" is not a better poem than **"The Alphabet,"** which, even if its suggestion of resurrection is not fully earned, is a remarkably moving performance. But the earlier poem is far more typical of Shapiro's poetic powers in that phase of his career that is culminated by *Poems of a Jew.* He begins with the characteristic flat, prosaic statement: "To hurt the Negro and avoid the Jew / Is the curriculum." The rest of the poem is simply the development of this phrase. Its clarity—not its content—is almost shocking; it reminds us that in order to write satire, what is most required is a distinct point of view, a place of detachment from which to observe what is being satirized, and a coherent self to inhabit that place.

Not that there is a complete lack of complexity or density in the verse. The entering boys are "identified by hats." Presumably, they are entering freshman. But quite naturally, the Jews, singled out by their skullcaps, are brought to mind as well. The imperious columns of the college buildings explicitly become antebellum girls, contemptuous of the "outlanders," whose desire is a potent threat. This, however, seems largely visual dexterity; it lacks the ambiguity of perspective that transformed Hebrew letters into dancing knives.

In **"University,"** the lines of irony are clearly drawn. In fact, it is only Shapiro's wit that prevents the irony from becoming heavy-handed. The university, and the establishment associated with it, condescend to or exclude everything alien to their own traditions; "Like manor houses," the colleges represent that which is aristocratic, high-minded, culturally sound. Intellectual and social acuteness become interdependent: "Within the precincts of this world / Poise is a club." But in the hills, cut off by choice or accident from the movements of American civilization, live the real descendants of the tradition of which the university claims to be heir; there, in their inbred, obsolete world, "The past is absolute." The school "shows us, rotted and endowed, / Its senile pleasure."

The university embodies for Shapiro not all of American society, but a specific and especially powerful aspect of it; the "Curriculum" is the pattern of behavior that has long excluded Jews and Blacks from the "club," but pays lip service to selected egalitarian ideals. Hypocritical and corrupt, betraying its own past, it is a part of the establishment for which Shapiro has little sympathy. Here, the poem shows signs of being dated; the singling out of Wasp society as the enemy, the implicit wish to first violate and then occupy the old manor houses, seem nearly naive and subservient in the light of all that has happened since Shapiro wrote the poem. But certain touches survive. Recalling Pound's "old bitch gone in the teeth," that "botched civilization," Shapiro's suggestion that the vicious snobbery of the aristocrats is a kind of spiritual syphillis thoroughly deflates the nobility of mannered brick and magnolia.

"University" is a very different poem from **"The Alphabet."** But the poems share at least one significant characteristic. In each case, the Jew is important not only in his own right, but as a defining attribute of the world in which he exists, or from which he is excluded. In fact, if we move beyond the evident social implications of the poems, the Jew becomes a metaphysical touchstone, one that reveals both the limitations and possibilities of human experience. The Jew is, in short, something that mankind must sooner or later come up against. He is presented in precisely that light in **"The Synagogue."** The synagogue itself is "the adumbration of the Wall." Literally, of course, Shapiro

refers to *the* Wall in Jerusalem; but it is also symbolic of any enforcer of boundaries. The separateness of the Jew is also suggested by the Wall, and reinforced in the reference to the "calendar that marks a separate race." The poem makes an attempt to define what lies on the Jewish side of the Wall, using the synagogue as emblem in the mode of the seventeenth century metaphysical poets.

While cathedrals draw the soul upward, connecting man with the heavenly spheres, the synagogue is very much of this world: "No relic but a place. . . . Not holy ground but factual holiness. . . ." It is a special kind of worldliness, not to be confused with the antiseptic materialism of glossy American society; it is rather the sense that the things of this world are holy in their own right and not because of any transcendent relation to the spiritual.

> Our wine is wine, our bread is harvest bread
> That feeds the body and is not the body.

Here as elsewhere, Shapiro's province seems located in the terrain between Jewish commitment to this world and the Kierkegaardian Knight of Faith, whose ultimate commitment is paradoxically to the finite.

Of special interest in the first section of *Poems of a Jew* is **"The Dirty World."** It is one of Shapiro's earliest attempts at the free verse (or prose poems) that later comprise *The Bourgeois Poet*. The word, represented in the poem by a frightening black bird, a vulture perhaps, is, within the context of the book, an offensive term for Jew. But as is usually the case, it does service as a more generalized symbol of fear, shame, and self-hatred, a malignancy forced upon the young boy by the society in which he lives, but finally nurtured and even, in a perverse way, loved by the boy.

Although it is probably far more accurate to say that the poem is written in prose than free verse, it has a definite formal structure. Three paragraphs (the first, second, and fourth) of approximately the same length, and a short, sentence-long third paragraph: "And the bird outlives the man, being freed at the man's death-funeral by a word from the rabbi." In spite of this prophecy of longevity, Shapiro, or the *persona,* claims to have outlived the bird, to have murdered it. And here is what is most effective in the poem. The bird is clearly evil and filthy; yet it is taken in by the boy and cherished, its destruction is described as a murder. There is an ambiguity about the poet's attitude toward this aspect of his experience, a suggestion that he is touching upon complexities difficult to unravel. The word, the ostracism, that so terrifies the small child becomes a source of comfort, a protector, so that stepping out from behind the obscenity and asserting one's own self becomes an act of high courage. And while there is no way of convincingly establishing causal relationships, it seems more than coincidence that Shapiro abandons strict meter (present in the other poems even when rhyme is not) just at the moment the perceiving self experiences ambivalence, just at the moment the ego is forced to share its triumphs with forces from beneath the surface of consciousness.

The wall between Jew and non-Jew, or rather the notion of Jew as boundary of the human condition, is touched on in the first section of *Poems of a Jew*. But the contact between Jewish and Gentile worlds forms the explicit subject matter for most of section two, as the very titles of poems in that section indicate: **"The Confirmation," "The Jew at Christmas Eve," "Christmas Eve: Australia," "The Ham-Bone of a Saint," "Teasing the Nuns," "The Crucifix in the Filing Cabinet."** Some of the more interesting poems, however, do not explicitly announce this theme, although they do in fact explore it.

"The First Time" describes a seventeen-year-old boy's visit to a prostitute; in it, the suppressed sexual side of the Jewish question, latent in such poems as **"University,"** becomes the focus of attention. Increasingly detached from the reality of his experience, which begins with clinical imagery "in shadowy quarantine" and ends with the boy transfixed "in space like some grotesque, / Far, far from her where he is still alone . . . ," his otherness is brought into focus by the girl's question: *"Are you a Jew?"* Here the alienation of the Jew and the alienation of the adolescent converge. Sex becomes a pit of darkness threatening to swallow the boy's manhood, as the bed "Spreads its carnivorous flower-mouth for all." Insecurity, tinged with terror, culminate in an attack not only on the boy's masculinity but on his humanness as well: he becomes a Jew, an abstraction, a violation of his own personal identity.

What is most remarkable about the poem is its tone. Shapiro walks the thin line between comedy—the poem's subject is, after all, the butt of the conventional joke—and pathos. The boy is bumbling rather than inept; he is so thoroughly anesthetized he can, if not overcome, at least survive his fear and shame. The girl is ironically younger than he is. The cruel question is asked "almost gently." The image that summarizes the entire poem is that of "A candle swimming down to nothingness / Put out by its own wetted gusts of flame. . . ." A clear reference to the boy's detumescence in the face of his anxieties, it is also the symbol for ultimate annihilation, which is none the less final for its gentleness.

Formally, the poem stands with Shapiro's early work, metrically regular (though with interesting variations), a fixed stanzaic pattern (abcabc), with enjambment and tough, flat, prosaic statement as antidote to ceremonious shape. Shapiro has learned much from Yeats, and is not totally unsuccessful in playing off rigid pattern against a rich, sometimes surreal body of imagery, although one senses it might have gone either way.

One of Shapiro's finest poems, and one of his earliest, is **"The Leg."** With no specific reference at all to Jewishness, a note at the book's end is helpful, if not essential, in understanding the poem's place in the book.

> Freud speaks (it may be all too often) of "violent defloration" and "the fear of being eaten by the Father." In Freud's view, as in that of every other Jew, mutilation, circumcision, and "the fear of being eaten"

are all one. **"The Leg"** is a poem written during war and its subject is the wholeness even of the mutilated. The poem **"Mongolian Idiot"** has the same theme.

The poem and note together offer a fine opportunity to examine concretely the uses to which Shapiro puts Jewishness in his poetry.

The amputation of the leg is not in itself a specifically Jewish experience. But Shapiro's note makes clear what can actually be deduced from the poem: the missing leg becomes the prototype of all loss. And whether, as in the Freudian view, the anxiety of mutilation is the source of all anxiety, or, in a more existential reading, the anxiety of mutilation is the specific symbol of the dread of nonbeing, the lost leg, and the Jew, are placed at the very limits of human consciousness; they become the means of defining those limits.

Some important questions are raised, not least the entire problem of relations between mind and body. The soldier slowly becomes aware of what he has lost; his hands must explore the stump. Is the loss real, is the body anything but an extension of the mind? If the mind persists after the loss of the leg, is the body anything more than a conventional, an artificial, limit to one's existence? Or is the reverse true? Is the centrality of the mind an illusion, does each part of the body have its own connection with reality?

> For the leg is wondering where he is. . . .
> He is its injury, the leg is his orphan,
> He must cultivate the mind of the leg. . . .

I would not suggest that there is in any definite sense an answer to these questions in the poem, but if Shapiro leans in either direction, it is toward the primacy of the body; he is not a thoroughgoing materialist, but he demonstrates that same commitment to the physical world as in **"The Synagogue."** The chief interest of **"The Leg"** lies precisely in that—for Shapiro—characteristically Jewish commitment.

It is a poem about a soldier coming to terms with a terrible fact: the mutilation of his body. The expected means of reconciliation would, for most readers, involve a rejection of the primacy of the body; but Shapiro frustrates this expectation by insisting all the more upon the body's importance, and finding his consolation therein. Again, the commitment to the finite transcends the infinite. The limitation is itself the means of transcending all limits: Now he smiles to the wall: "/ The amputation becomes an acquisition." These lines place Shapiro within the tradition that runs from Donne, who beseeches God to ravish him that he may be chaste, to Hopkins, whose God's descending darkness is His mercy; it is that tradition which views man's relation to God as being most closely approximated in paradox. ". . . If Thou take me angrily in hand," Shapiro concludes, "And hurl me to the shark, I shall not die." What is especially interesting here is Shapiro's locating of the Jew at the precise center of the paradox. For just as circumcision makes the Jew the quintessential mutilated man, so the horrors of the Second World War make him the living emblem of loss. It is all very well to suggest that without the note cited above, and without **"The Leg"**'s inclusion in this particular volume of poetry, there would be no necessity to connect the loss with Jewishness. The correct response to this is not that the original subject of the poem was probably Jewish, but that the very fact that the soldier has experienced a terrifying loss and, having been thoroughly crushed by it, explores it and comes to find salvation through it, makes him a Jew.

It is loss, it is the encounter with the "background of Nothing," that defines the Jew; it is these things that define the boundaries of the human condition; and it is these things that help create the special relation to reality held by the artist. Edmund Wilson's metaphor of the Wound and the Bow is itself a kind of gloss on **"The Leg."** The wound, the artist's inability to function effectively in the world, leads to his estrangement. But it also is the source of his creative powers. Making the amputation an acquisition: Shapiro's own image of the creative imagination, revealing with equal clarity both the limitations and possibilities of that process.

Of the seven poems of **"Adam and Eve,"** which forms a substantial part of the last section of *Poems of a Jew*, Shapiro wrote: "The viewpoint of the sequence, that man is for the world, not for the afterworld, is Jewish." And the viewpoint, from Adam's initial longing, to the final expulsion from the garden, is also specifically sexual. The significant variation on the traditional story lies in Shapiro's unspoken suggestion that banishment from the garden is the cure for the disease rather than the onset of the disease; Shapiro's special contribution to this variation is the notion that sexual consummation is not the prize that must be paid for in banishment, but is itself simply a means of asserting man's rightful place in the scheme of things—that is, in the world, not in the garden. Further, this worldliness is not ultimately rebellion against God, although it may superficially and temporarily take that form, but a cornerstone of God's plan:

> "Needing us greatly, even in our disgrace,
> Guide us, for gladly do we leave this place
> For our own land and wished-for banishment."

The paradox that tempts man to escape the garden is closely related to the paradoxes at the heart of love, and of art. Originally in tune with nature, operating exclusively by instinct, Adam, for no apparent reason except the very quality of his being, enters the world of thought and self-consciousness: "Thinking became a garden of its own." Thought makes a creator of man himself, but the price of this power is the sense of aloneness and separateness from all of the rest of God's creation. Man longs to reestablish unity, and the longing is made concrete in sexual desire. The eating of the apple is transformed into sexual eating.

> So wide
> Their mouths, they drank each other from inside.
> A gland of honey burst within their throats.

The note to **"The Leg"** comes immediately to mind: "In Freud's view, as in that of every Jew, mutilation, circumcision, and 'the fear of being eaten' are all one." But we would not need the note to be aware of the anxiety that accompanies sexual desire throughout the sequence. The sexual world is also the world of time and change, the world of death; but it is because rather than in spite of this that it is welcomed, even as it is feared, by Adam and Eve. "Death is the mother of beauty," Wallace Stevens wrote. And Shapiro echoes this as the angel calls out joyously to the banished pair, who turn to see "Eden ablaze with fires of red and gold, / The garden dressed for dying in cold flame." It is precisely in its consumption (in its being eaten up) by flames that the garden is revealed as most beautiful.

The sequence of poems begins with Adam instinctively praising the nature of things; it ends with Adam and Eve staring in "dark amazement" at the beauty of a dying world. The movement is from union with nature and harmony with the totality of being to consciousness of the self as separate from the rest of creation: in short, a forging of the human ego. The sequence is an appropriate conclusion to *Poems of a Jew*, affirming as it does the value of "autumn and the present world," asserting the power of the self to remain whole in the face of chaos. From instinct, to consciousness, to guilt, to wonder—that is the growth of the individual, that is the development of the artist.

It is probably no accident, then, that **"Adam and Eve"** spans most of the range of Shapiro's mastery of traditional meter and pattern; the triumph of form is the triumph of the integrated self. The meter of each poem is iambic pentameter. The first poem consists of quatrains (abab), the second a favorite seven-line stanza (ababcbc), the third a sonnet, the fourth (xabcbac) and fifth (abbccca) variations on the seven-liner, the sixth six-line stanzas composed of rhymed couplets, and the seventh quatrains with a difference (abba). Off-rhymes, run-on lines, and rough, prosaic rhythms permit a significant degree of variation within the relatively rigid structure. But a powerful sense of regularity and agreement dominates. And the movement from quatrain to more intricate patterns, back to a slightly different quatrain, is surely meant to embody the emotional development of the poem: it is cyclical with crucial changes taking place within the cycle, it is the transformation of praise into wonder.

Many of the pieces in *The Bourgeois Poet* are, from the point of view of subject, parts of *Poems of a Jew* writen too late to be included. Many others would seem to have at least as much right as, say, **"The Leg,"** to be included in any oblique attempt to define the Jewish consciousness. But whether or not the original book could survive these additions without being burnt to cinders is certainly open to question. What has happened, chiefly, is that the poet has been dislocated from the center of his poems; and, ironically enough, it is by adopting a more personal poetic mode that Shapiro achieves this dislocation.

Poems of a jew is Shapiro's last book as a relatively formal poet, and there may in fact be some connection between his original commitment to traditional verse and his early faith in the ability of the Self to exist, both of which beliefs are seriously questioned in his later poetry.

—Karl Malkoff

"Always the character who yells, I insist, I insist on being a Jew!" Shapiro begins poem 61, "(Can't you forget it? Isn't it obsolete? Isn't it faking the evidence?)"[2] Among many possible references, specific and general, the description of the character insisting on being a Jew could well apply to Shapiro himself, in *Poems of a Jew*. But somehow this insistence is now perceived as at best no longer applicable, at worst a fraud. Why? It is possible, of course, that Shapiro's lines are a commentary on the possibilities of being a Jew in the modern world; poets do, after all, occasionally mean what they say. But it seems much more likely that the difficulties of being a Jew are simply local manifestations of the more inclusive difficulty of possessing coherent being in any form whatsoever.

Poem 74 is probably the clearest statement of this in *The Bourgeois Poet*: "The prophets say to Know Thyself: I say it can't be done. . . . Man is mostly involuntary. Consciousness is only a tiny part of us. . . . Those poets who study their own consciousness are their own monsters. Each look in the mirror shows you a different self. . . . Creation renewing itself forever does not look back. . . . The lost ones return to the same old self and sit there in the corner, laughing or crying." Poetry, then, is the expression of a totality of which consciousness is only a tiny part: there can be no clear image of personality, only a series of shifting mirrors. By implication, there can be no single shaping intelligence, no clear-cut perspective from which one can accost reality.

Formal pattern is an immediate casualty: the agreement of rhyme, the regularity of meter, may well depend upon a strong faith in the existence of the self as a possible arbiter of experience. This is a problem that most contemporary poets have had to come to terms with: those of mystical bent define the poem as an expression of that universal self of which the individual self is but a specific manifestation; others have rooted the form and rhythm of the poem in the order and pulse of the human body, in bone and blood, flesh and breath; others still have grounded the particular self in the general myth. Very few other than Shapiro have been content to perceive the disintegration of the self and not attempt instantly to reestablish wholeness; he is again almost Kierkegaardian in his insistence on the finiteness of prose as opposed to the universals of pattern and meter.

The second casualty is the poet's ability to use the Jew as a definer of human boundaries, although the Jew still appears frequently throughout the book. The difference can be clearly seen in a comparison between the concluding words of **"The First Time,"** *"Are you a Jew?"* and the opening line of Poem 87 of *The Bourgeois Poet*, "Cat called me a Jewish pig." In the earlier poem, the question, although gently asked, draws all attention to the vulnerability, the nakedness of the young man, which may in itself be thought of as a kind of essential Jewishness. But the second phrase, although uttered in anger, has not a similar power to wound, nor to define. The relationship between the young man and the prostitute is sharply enough drawn to be a cliché; the relationship between the poet and Cat is mired in ambiguity. Who is victim, who the tormentor? What is the basis of their relationship, the nature of their love? Where in the surreal imagery of the poem does the description of Cat's overt action end and the evocation of her inner world begin? What marks the boundaries between suggestions of sexual intercourse and visions of the slaughterhouse? As was always the case in Shapiro's poetry, there is a great deal of irony involved. But whereas, before, the irony even if double-edged was perceived from a single vantage point, perspective may now shift from line to line. And in many passages throughout the book, tone is for all practical purposes impossible to determine.

Shapiro has not necessarily abandoned all formal poetry; nor is it reasonable to suppose that he utterly disbelieves in the possibility of the integrated self giving shape to experience. Subsequent poems have certainly marked an inevitable retreat from the extremes of *The Bourgeois Poet*. But even within that volume, Shapiro has not totally ceased to proclaim the humanistic values dependent upon the existence of a coherent self; he has continued to affirm even when affirmation is by definition absurd.

Notes

[1] New York, 1958, p. ix. Subsequent references to this book will be followed by page numbers in parentheses.

[2] *The Bourgeois Poet,* New York, 1964, p. 74. Subsequent references to this book will be followed by page numbers in parentheses.

Richard Jackson (essay date 1981)

SOURCE: "Signing the Syllables: The Poetry of Karl Shapiro," in *The South Carolina Review,* Vol. 14, No. 1, Fall, 1981, pp. 109-20.

[*In the following essay, Jackson analyzes Shapiro's stylistic approach to his work and contends that his most successful poems balances both visceral and metaphorical language.*]

I

"Life is the nonrepresentable origin of representation"

—Jacques Derrida, "The Theater of Cruelty and the Closure of Representation"

"The non-translatability of poetic language is not just a pretension of romanticism, but an essential tract of the poetic."

—Paul Ricoeur, *The Rule of Metaphor*

"Real art has the capacity to make us nervous. By reducing the work of art to its context and then interpreting *that,* one tames the work of art. Interpretation makes art manageable, comfortable."[1] So writes Susan Sontag in "Against Interpretation," an essay quite sympathetic to Karl Shapiro's perennial combat against the increasing "encroachment of meaning" and "content" into poetry. Shapiro's strategy for thirty years now has been to expose our critical emphasis on the representationality of poetry. This exposé focuses on the failure to risk transgressing the rehearsed meanings and traditional valuations imposed by our culture on an accepted canon of texts, and in fact questions the validity of the canon itself. Poetry, for him, should follow the lead of non-representational painters such as de Kooning, Rothko and Pollock: "the death of allegory (though it survives in surrealism), of representation of things or figures for the sake of representing, but especially the abandonment of symbols and symbolic objects—all these were moves away from the secure world" ("The True Artificer," *PW*). Ideally, then, the poet should be like Shapiro's blind piano tuner, "Building bridges from both sides of the void, / Coasting the chasms of the harmonies," a man who moves as dangerously between jobs led by his wife, a man who, when his tuning is complete, "plays his comprehensive keyboard song, / The loud paradigm, / The one work of art without content" (**"The Piano Tuner's Wife"**).[2]

Now, this questioning of the representationality of poetry has become, of course, an increasingly important gesture in contemporary thought. Jacques Derrida, for example, suggests that representation is a slavish form of repetition, a re-presencing or re-presentation of a metaphysical content that is assumed to remain constant, timeless, unquestioned, and thus ideal. In fact, suggests Derrida, such content is always an absence, an evasive "trace" that can never really be represented in language.[3] By its very nature, then, the theory of representation is reductive; in itself it represents an attempt to bracket off an authorized meaning or set of meanings from the free play of language. Henry Miller, in Shapiro's estimation, accomplishes this freedom in his naturalistic prose. The response that Shapiro would have poetry make is to deploy a subversive language at the very level of the word:

> The fallacy is that of meaning, the treatment of poetry as language. One might, in the jargon of the age, call it "the understanding fallacy" or "the semantic fallacy." Poetry is not language; its raw material is language, but from this point on the poet goes in one direction, while the critic goes in the opposite direction. The *word* in poetry is not a word in any already existing sense; and I call it a "not-word."[4]

This "not-word" suggests a sense of constant emergence from language, a sense of what Derrida calls a decenter-

ing, a movement away from any logical presuppositions that were thought to control the meaning of language but which are in fact determined by language. It is a movement away from the closed hermeneutic circle of so much contemporary thought. But the actual definition of what constitutes a "not-word," as a negative concept, can never be given (and hence Shapiro's continuous repositionings and revaluations of his stance)—it is always the mark of an absence, what ordinary language cannot give over, the ghostlier demarcation, the trace, that gives poetry its power. The central problem of Shapiro's "poetics," then (an anti-poetics really, in its being against canonized poetry and against itself as any systematic program), emerges in the function of the "not-word." What force does it have? What violence can it do to traditional poetry? What status does it have in Shapiro's poetry?

II

"the formless, mute, unsignifying region where language can find its freedom."

—Foucault, "The Order of Things"

At one level the "not-word" makes a kind of silence, "a quiet like a cathedral close / At the soul's center where substance cannot dwell / And life flowers like music from a bell" (**"The Interlude"**). It makes a use of language that withholds itself in order to reveal itself more fully, the way the cathedral's quiet is revealed as something *like* the bell's music. In a similar way, Shapiro's poem **"The Child Who Is Silent"** uses a language more remarkable for its absences, its silence, than its discursive content:

> The child who is silent stands against his father, lovingly looking up at him as if to say without a trace of defiance: I will speak when I have decided. He marches around the table smiling intelligently, now and then deigning to say something, perhaps "locomotive." It is somewhat frightening, a kind of rebuff to grownups. The doctors smile and shrug. If the parents are worried they don't display it. It's only like living in the last house at the edge of the subdivision. There's a bit of farm left and a highway beyond: if someone should rattle the back door in the night . . . There is a child of two minds who says nothing and who is drinking it all in. Obviously happy, very much loved, handsome and straight, laughing and playing, withholding that gift we all abuse. In that room is a tower of books with their backs to us, eloquently quiet too. Man is a torrent of language, even in death. But visitors use longer words. The little philosopher goes about his business.

> This is the town where the railroads ended, the wagon trains formed in the dry gray grass. It's this frontier of speech we are always crossing. The locomotive is ridiculously dying, lumbering off to the deep clay pits to settle among the mastodon bones. The piano is thinking of Mozart. On the very top, legs crossed, at ease, sits the blue-eyed boy who holds his peace.

The word "locomotive," withheld and uttered almost by chance, crosses the boy's frontiers of speech and establishes a world in the poem through the poet's response. What is crucial here is the way the second paragraph refuses to analyze any symbolic associations evoked by the word, but rather develops the image, the signifier itself. There is a suggestion implicit in the development of the poem that the world the boy draws around the word and the world the poet draws around it are analogous, and that these worlds are supplements to the sterility of the "grownup" world, are at once a "frontier" and "ridiculously dying," are always in need of new beginnings. But there is no sense of closure in these suggestions; they are available, but not pressed, and their "meanings" are very much muted by the physical pictures, the nearly impenetrable, enigmatic signifiers of the second paragraph. "Locomotive," then, becomes a prototype of the "not-word" in its movement beyond the typical meanings it has in speech; it initiates a whole world, opens up an always unexhausted set of relationships.

It is this peculiar ability of the "not-word" to go beyond language, beyond the mere meaning of the word, that is the source of poetry's ability to supplement actuality and to create a history beyond its changes and its shifts in meaning. Thus Shapiro, in his poem **"The Old Poet,"** describes the power of the poet's writing, the profound silence of his inscription:

> In his own city he renames the streets, the ships, the bars. History comes to his hand like a tame pigeon. One of his sentences hangs in the square like the plume of a volcano. Real speech, real life are unwritten. Only these lines have a tendency to remain forever.

It is in this context that, in **"Words for a Wall-Painting,"** he exclaims: "This is the place to sign my syllables / Of deep relief on tiny tiles of sound, / And may my words still stand when the wall falls." What is curious here is the emphasis on "syllables," the "tiles of sound" (actually, the clause "I love you"), rather than on words, on the "thingness" of the inscription—what it does for the love as a gesture more than as a meaning. On this level the poet feels "the physical reality of words," the "sensory quality" of his own locutions, the "not-word" as thing.[5] The poet's words thus become entities that the imagination delights in, not simply vehicles through which the intellect arrives at certain conceptions about the world.

Such a sense of delight in the "thingness" of words is the underlying motivation in **"The Bathers."** The poem describes a man and woman who enter the surf as if into a primitive world of origins where they are "willed by water,/ Weightless and far gone in forgetfulness," where they are "blissful in primeval tears, / Forgotten even by the sea itself, / That rocks them absently." Forgetfulness here suggests something like the Nietzschean casting off in order to begin, to originate.[6] What is cast off here is language, words, the "power of speech" so that a new "physical reality" of the word, the "not-word," can emerge:

> They lose even the power of speech;
> They must go back to learn;
> They make the difficult return

> Where nets of water hold them, feel their legs,
> Cast ropes of coldness round their bellies,
> Trip them, throw gravel at their ankles,
> Until, unpredictably, the entire sea
> Makes them a path and gives them a push to the beach.
> And they lie down between the yellow boats
> Where the sun comes and picks them out
> And rubs its fire into their sea-pale flesh,
> Rubbing their blood, licking their heavy hair,
> Breathing upon their words with drying fire.

The force of the lovers' words here is primitive, sexual, cosmic—not simply reflective of but participating in the entire movement of the sea, their blood, their breath. The poem's movement becomes an incarnation of the bond between the two lovers. The poem itself becomes what W. K. Wimsatt once called a "verbal icon," a term that stresses this material aspect of the poem's medium as much as its connotative power. The truth of the poem, then, lies in the force of the "not-word" to disperse, to initiate new worlds, new perspectives, to continually add its own "physical reality" to the actuality of the world and thus to be always changing it. "Poems, flowers of language, if that's what you are, grow up in the air where books come true. And you, thin packet, let your seed fly, if you have any."

III

> ". . . the interest which the mind attaches to words not only as symbols of the passion, but as things, active and efficient, which are of themselves part of the passion."
> —Wordsworth, "Note" to "The Thorn"

At this point a number of serious questions present themselves. In some essays, and Shapiro makes no pretense at consistency, he emphasizes the symbolic and the metaphoric—the referential quality of language: "A good image is a good picture, a proper likeness, a physical truth, and a symbolic truth," he exclaims in "The True Artificer," an essay in which he emphasizes the metaphoric and metamorphic power of language.[7] Of course, we can understand with Louis Rubin that the basis for Shapiro's varying stances rests on very pragmatic ground: "The kind of poetry Shapiro defended (and in doing so, explained) was the kind of poetry he was attempting to write at the time."[8] But we must ask ourselves if there is one larger, gradually evolving concern of Shapiro's that could reconcile these differences. Is there any way the proclamation "Metaphor has to go, the symbol has to go" can be productively related to the emphasis on symbol and metaphor described just above?

We can begin by considering Shapiro's careful qualification to the proclamation I just cited from "In Defense of Bad Poetry." Shapiro goes on to say, "myth has to go, except, as Camus says, myth 'with no other depth than that of human suffering, and like it, inexhaustible.'"[9] How is this sense of depth achieved and how does it differ from the kinds of "meaning" Shapiro combats? It is helpful in answering this question to refer to Paul Ricoeur's discussion of poetic referentiality. Using Roman Jakobson's notion of "split reference," of the priority of the "poetic function" over any "referential function," Ricoeur suggests that "the meaning of a metaphorical statement rises up from the blockage of any literal interpretation of the statement. . . . The entire strategy of poetic discourse plays upon this point: It seeks the abolition of reference by means of self-destruction of the meaning of metaphorical statements, the self-destruction being made manifest by an impossible literal interpretation."[10] But what this blockage or self-destruction of the "referential" in favor of the "poetic" accomplishes is "the negative condition of the appearance of a more fundamental mode of reference."[11] This mode of reference is broader than the word or even the sentence; it involves a "suspension" of a primary "meaning" in order to allow the physical, *iconic* nature of the "not-words" to form the basis of a "reality" that is difficult to penetrate:

> Language takes on the thickness of a material or a *medium.* The sensible, sensual plenitude of the poem is like that of painted or sculptured forms. The combination of sensual and logical ensures that expression and impression coalesce within the poetic thing. Poetic signification fused thus with its sensible vehicle becomes that particular and "thingy" reality we call a poem.[12]

Now for Ricoeur, as for Jakobson, the poetic "meaning" is ambiguous—and there is always a hermeneutics that can uncover it, but for Shapiro it is unnameable. For all three, though, "poetic" referentiality is not a mimetic but a creative enterprise, as we have seen in Shapiro's sense of the way the poem establishes a new world by adding itself to the old.

Now if we return to his essay "The True Artificer" we find Shapiro's sense of the "knowledge" or "meaning" in poetry fairly in line with Ricoeur's: "Poetic knowledge is at its best profound and manifold, but poetic artifice demands that this knowledge be made to transform the poem into an immediate perceptible whole."[13] A few paragraphs later he distinguishes between the closed referential system of philosophy and the open referential work of the poem: "Poetry creates a total scene only by implication. The scene within the work is whole but it does not signify a system. This kind of knowledge is the opposite of philosophical knowledge, which seeks a whole order of a different kind . . . Poetry lies eternally outside any order of things which seeks or finds a self-contained system of ideas or beliefs."[14] It is this notion of the "whole" which yet contains Camus's "inexhaustible" depth, that provides a balance between a confusing proliferation of ineffable impressions and a rigid "meaning." On the one hand the poet risks being like the man who comes out of his standardized house in **"The Dome of Sunday"** only to see endlessly indistinguishable images—

> As if one life emerging from one house
> Would pause, a single image caught between
> Two facing mirrors where vision multiplies

> Beyond perspective,
> A silent clatter in the high speed eye
> Spinning out photo-circulars of sight.

On the other hand, he risks the rigid "patterns which our feelings make." The result, in either case though, is nearly the same.

The solution to avoid either of these two extremes, as Shapiro does in his best work, is to balance a limiting, plain style that uses numerous colloquial expressions against an event or observation of tremendous metaphoric or symbolic potential. The result is a tension between the referential and the poetic, the named and the unnameable. The poem **"My Father's Funeral"** is an excellent example. Like most of his poems stretching back to the day of the much-anthologized **"Car Wreck,"** the poem moves from a droll reporter's tone towards a slightly incantatory ending. Here is the opening paragraph:

> Lurching from gloomy limousines we slip
> On the warm baby-blanket of Baltimore snow,
> Wet flakes smacking our faces like distraught
> Kisses on cheeks, and step upon the green
> Carpet of artificial grass which crunches
> Underfoot, as if it were eating, and come
> To the canopy, a half-shelter which provides
> A kind of room to enclose us all, and the hole,
> And the camp chairs, and following after,
> The scrolly walnut coffin
> That has my father in it.

Some of the details in the poem are irrelevant or random in that they have marginal or no function in creating "meaning" (say, the "flakes" like "kisses" or the grass crunching "as if it were eating"), and are often dropped for other images in producing a kind of catalogue effect. But they provide a sense of physical reality, of Camus's "depth," the sense of a world, an attitude, that in the context of the gradually intensifying diction, seems to emerge within the confines of the poem itself. There is a sense, then, of an epiphany that evolves in the poem which the meaning of the words in the poem cannot adequately refer to; they embody it. Here are the last two stanzas:

> My father in black knee-socks and high shoes
> Holding a whip to whip a top upstreet;
> My father the court stenographer,
> My father in slouch hat in the Rockies,
> My father kissing my mother,
> My father kissing his secretary,
> In the high-school yearbook captioned Yid,
> In synagogue at six in the morning praying
> Three hundred and sixty-five days for his mother's
>   rest,
> My father at my elbow on the bimah
> And presiding over the Sabbath.
> In the old forgotten purlieus of the city
> A Jewish ghetto in its day, there lie
> My father's father, mother and the rest,
> Now only a ghetto lost to time,
> Ungreen, unwhite, unterraced like the new

Cemetery to which my father goes.
Abbaddon, the old place of destruction;
Sheol, a new-made garden of the dead
Under the snow. Shalom be to his life,
Shalom be to his death.

For a while Shapiro searches an album, real or imagined, for pictures that will re-presence his father, that will bring the sense of emerging detail to a fully created poetic world. But if this catalogue technique proves inadequate, the confrontation of these absences "lost to time" prompts the incantatory and powerful ending that balances old and new, grave and garden, calling upon the evocative and phonetic power of key Jewish words, upon the way the poet's tone and sense of discovery "sign their syllables." The "poetic" as opposed to the "referential" meaning, then, is here constituted mainly by these larger gestures, by the force of language.

Such larger gestures or contexts for "poetic" meaning are evident in most of Shapiro's poems, providing many, in fact, with a typological quality. His well known **"Adult Bookstore,"** for example, is about a specific *type* of man who achieves singularity only through the specific images catalogued within the poem. This dual aspect makes him the object of both satire and compassion, who needs "Awakeners of the tired heart's desire / When love goes wrong." His poem **"Girls Working in Banks"** depicts tellers who spend drab days that end "Out of revolving doors into the glorious anonymous streets." Most of these poems that satirically point out human weakness are thus founded upon a Bergsonian sense of comedy, upon a sense of the rigidity, the predictability of the characters' typical lives that is itself undercut by a sense of their particular, very human condition. In terms of language, the general context of "referential" meaning is always undercut by a "depth" of character revealed in the "physical language" of images that define Shapiro's feelings.

This double focus certainly explains the proportionally large number and the unique quality of Shapiro's descriptive poems. A poem like **"Tornado Warning,"** for example, gradually gathers responses that appeal to physical and mental senses and sensations ("The April freshness seems to rot, a curious smell. / Above the wool pack clouds a rumour stains the sky, / A fallow color deadening atmosphere and mind"), then describes the clouds as a collage of grotesque body parts and diseases ("Downward-projecting bosses of brown cloud grow / Lumps on lymphatic sky, blains, tumors, and dugs"), to finally construct the picture of a mammoth funnel cloud—

We cannot see the mouth,
We cannot see the mammoth's neck hanging from
    cloud
Snout open, lumbering down ancient Nebraska
Where dinosaur lay down in deeps of clay and
    died,
And towering elephant fell and billion buffalo.
We cannot see the horror-movie of the funnel-cloud
Snuffing up cows, crazing the cringing villages,
Exploding homes and barns, bursting the level lakes. . .

The final effect occurs in a dimension, as Shapiro might say, that moves away from the "raw material" of language, a dimension defined more by what is absent, what "We cannot see," than it is by a presence, by a referential meaning. Of course, the "meaning" that nature's power is ancient, like a mammoth, and as unthinkingly threatening, is available here, but it is not pressed. The emphasis remains not on any such abstracted meaning; in fact the complete lack of any abstract thematic statement works against such meaning, but rather the emphasis lies on the experience of the "warning" as it evolves within the poem, upon the experience as it is carried by the "poetic" as opposed to "referential" resources of the text, upon, that is, the "not-word" quality of the language. "In poetic language," says Ricoeur, "the sign is looked at, not through."[15]

IV

"Yes, words really do dream."
　　　　　　—Bachelard, *The Poetics of Reverie*

In the course of watching, as we did in the previous section, how there is a "blockage," even a "self-destruction" of the "referential" aspect of language in favor of the "poetic" aspect, how there is a suspension or repression of one level of language for the opening up of another, a question arises as to the motivation, the psychology of the poet. According to Ricoeur, the three basic traits of poetic language—the fusion of sense and mind, the density of a language that becomes "thingy," and the priority of the experience of language itself as what has been traditionally called an "illusion"—are a source of enormous psychic activity.[16] Our questions, then, involve the relation between what has been suspended and what is opened up. Or, to paraphrase the ending of **"Tornado Warning,"** what is not said, what we cannot see, what the poet cannot see, seems to be itself a major force within the poem.

In order to arrive at a clearer view of this, though, we need first to re-examine what the moment of the poem contains. In an early essay, "Poets of Cosmic Consciousness," Shapiro praises a certain poetic habit of mind—what he calls "cosmic consciousness" as he sees it practiced by thinkers such as Ouspensky and Reich, and by the poet Hart Crane. Of crucial importance to the method is a kind of fullness of consciousness based upon Jungian synchronicity which becomes translated, for Shapiro, into a theory of how poetry can "arrange and even reverse our sense of time."[17] Later, in "The True Artificer," he says, "It may be that it is the time element of poetry which, in fact, takes the poem out of flowing chronological time and puts it into a time-world all its own."[18] Shapiro's poems themselves tend to concentrate large contexts of time, the typological contexts, into the event of the particular poem. This, in fact, is precisely the theme of the grotesque, **"The Minute"**—

The new born minute on the bureau lies,
Scratching the glass with infant kick, cutting
With diamond cry the crystal and expanse

Of timelessness. This pretty tick of death
Etches its name upon the air.

Soon, though, "The loathsome minute grows in length and
length." The movement of the poem is outward as the
minute expands, as the poet becomes more conscious of
what lies beyond, even, paradoxically, within himself: "I
with my distant heart lie wide awake / Smiling at that
Swiss-perfect engine room." The poem then ends "spinning threads of fear" that are never presenced within the
poem. What becomes important, even as the poet becomes more aware of the physical "tick / like a strange
dirt" that constitutes the physicality of the moment, are
the unnamed possibilities beyond the moment. As he says
in **"Absences"**: "Time is mostly absences, oceans generally at peace, and lives we love most often out of reach."

Now, in the light of these "absences," we can say that the
"consciousness discipline" that reveals, for the poet, a
synchronic world of expanded consciousness, also reveals "discipline" as a principle of "suspension" or "blockage." The time of the poem is thus a time of traces,
absences, the physical "not-words" *beyond* the writing in
the poem's text:

> I love you first because you wait, because
> > For your own sake, I cannot write
> Beyond these words. I love you for these words
> That sting and creep like insects and leave filth.
> I love you for the poverty you cry
> > And I bend down with tears of steel
> That melt you hand like wax, not for this war
> > The droplets shattering
> Those candle-glowing fingers of my joy,
> But for your name of agony, my love,
> > That cakes my mouth with salt.
>
> > > > ("V-Letter")

What the poem marks, then, is a play of presence and
absence, the referential and the poetic, consciousness and
unconsciousness, the word and the "not-word"—"all this
love explained and unexplained / Is just a breath," he says
later in this poem. But it is precisely the fact of breath, that
physical quality that comprises the "not-word," the whole
that is the poem however open-ended and extending to
whatever "depth," that controls, "disciplines" the poem,
the moment, the poet.

In terms of the psychology of the poet, this poetic strategy allows a complex tone to emerge in **"V-Letter."** The
poet allows neither the extreme bitterness that war can
produce nor the hope of victory and peace to dominate.
The "hours" that "stand in solid rows" will "Lead to my
matter-of-fact and simple death / Or to our open marriage."
What is primarily left out of the poetic moments, what that
plain style of Shapiro represses, what the silence of the
"not-word" mutes, is perhaps the bitter, extreme, caustic
self that emerges in the prose whose referential aspect is
never suspended and often becomes tyrannical and dicta-
torial—for example, in such essays as "To Abolish Children," where Shapiro takes an obviously one-sided view
about the "flower child" mentality of a decade ago; or in

the decimations, from an emotional and often irrational
point of view, of literary establishment figures such as
Eliot. Such an excess, of course, would wreck a poem like
"Adult Bookstore."

Precisely such a strategy of suspension and repression
governs what is perhaps Shapiro's finest poem, **"The Heili-
genstadt Testament,"** a stream-of-consciousness dramatic
monologue conceived of as spoken by Beethoven on his
death bed. Here the bitterness of the composer ("trust
nobody"—"I did my best to make you hate your mother")
is punctuated, even negated, by the accumulating power of
the rhetoric, and by the temporal sequence which alternates
malevolent and optimistic images. And there is a sense in
the poem that the very ability to go on talking defers death,
that poetic language itself provides something tangible, his
own breath, that the dying man can clutch. Given his dead
infant brother's name at his own birth and with it a problem
of self-identity, now gone deaf ("if you are deaf / and you
are Beethoven / what do you do"), he achieves the discipline of self-creation through his ability to transform silent
sound ("I keep time by the motion of their bows / that way
can almost hear my music"), including his own speech that
is the poem, into his own poetic world:

> I altered the birdsong slightly
> > and made it the eagle of my pen
> the same I did with the singing of peasants
> > my Battle Symphony my birds
> where are my multiplication tables
> is it true that any child can understand them
> 40,000 florins for Karl
> > let nobody say Beethoven was a fool
> > > too late too late
> > > the fire draws the wind
> > > the wine has not arrived

What the "thingness," the physicality of the "not-word"
does for the poet, and this is parallel to Beethoven's
tactile "hearing" of his own music, is provide a sense of
what Roland Barthes has called *Jouissance,* a poetic whose
"depth" subsumes the simple referential meanings of things
for a more complex response. Shapiro could very well be
addressing himself when he speaks of Poe in **"Israel"**—

> What else were his codes
> But diagrams and hideouts of the mind
> Plugged up with corpses and expensive junk,
> Prosopopoeia to keep himself at bay?

Notes

[1] Susan Sontag, *Against Interpretation* (1961; rpt. New York: Dell,
1969), p. 17.

[2] Karl Shapiro, *Collected Poems: 1940-1978* (New York: Random
House, 1978), p. 322. Further references to the poems use this
edition and are included in the text.

[3] Jacques Derrida, *Of Grammatology,* trans. G. C. Spivak (Baltimore: Johns Hopkins University Press, 1976), p. 66ff. (Originally

published in France, 1967.)

[4] Karl Shapiro, *In Defense of Ignorance* (New York: Random House, 1960), p. 270 ("What Is Not Poetry").

[5] Karl Shapiro, *The Poetry Wreck* (New York: Random House, 1975), p. 250 ("The True Artificer").

[6] See *Will To Power,* Sect. 55, also 479, 616; *Gay Science,* 310.

[7] *The Poetry Wreck,* p. 251.

[8] Louis Rubin, *The Curious Death of the Novel* (Baton Rouge: LSU Press, 1967), p. 37.

[9] Karl Shapiro, *To Abolish Children* (Chicago: Quadrangle Books, 1968), p. 72 ("In Defense of Bad Poetry").

[10] Paul Ricoeur, *The Rule of Metaphor,* trans. Robert Czerny (Toronto: University of Toronto Press, 1977), p. 230.

[11] Ricoeur, p. 229.

[12] Ricoeur, p. 225.

[13] *The Poetry Wreck,* p. 261 ("The True Artificer").

[14] *The Poetry Wreck,* p. 263.

[15] Ricoeur, p. 209.

[16] Ricoeur, p. 209.

[17] *In Defense of Ignorance,* pp. 302-303.

[18] *The Poetry Wreck,* p. 251.

Joseph Reino (essay date 1981)

SOURCE: "Low Road Leading Nowhere," in *Karl Shapiro,* Twayne Publishers, 1981, pp. 133-56.

[*In the following essay, Reino provides a stylistic and thematic analysis of* The Bourgeois Poet.]

Several years prior to the appearance of **"Dome of Sunday"** in the generally well-received *Person, Place and Thing*, the son of a European dictator visited the United States (October 1937) and expressed sentiments not unlike those poeticized in the final stanza of that poem. Anti-Fascist committees denounced the visit, warned President Roosevelt not to receive the dictator's son into the White House, and complained that he "bombed defenseless Ethiopians and afterwards stated that he enjoyed it very much." He was widely quoted in the media as having said that the sight of bombs bursting was "beautiful." Even Hollywood, which he briefly visited, could not "breathe freely" until the "rotund little enfant terrible" was gone.[1]

The inexplicable moods of the final stanza of Shapiro's **"Dome of Sunday"**—it now appears first in all selected

and collected editions—are dangerously close to those attributed to the son of a despised dictator. It would be comforting indeed if one could attribute the source of the smashed glass imagery, in particular the bombing of every "silvered glass," "crystal prism," "witch-bowl," and "perfume bottle," to a sense of protest and outrage against the destruction of the Jewish business communities of Nazi Germany during the infamous *Kristalnacht* of 9-10 November 1938, usually considered the official beginning of the Holocaust. So interpreted, the poem would be raising a clenched ethnic fist of righteous indignation—returning, as it were, verbal blows for physical blows. But unfortunately, the wording of the middle-class and obviously Baltimore-based poem does not admit of idealistic interpretations. The intentions of a poet who, in **"Waxworks,"** fell upon his knees before the "Ripper," are much closer to those of the much-denounced pomposities of a dictator's son. The soldier-poet, elsewhere "sick of causes," is "hot as a voyeur" for the sight of the "blinded negress lurching" and "exiles bleeding from their pores." These surrealist yearnings are solely for the purpose of bombing out some Hollywood-like "glare" and "glaze" of an attractive woman's "sheen." (Hollywood was, incidentally, the glamorous topic of several of his own poems.) In a final wished-for but never-achieved blindness, he desires to "stand transfixed in fascination" of an atomic devastation. For readers not similarly oriented, this may be difficult to appreciate; but, for good or ill, much of *Bourgeois Poet* is based on this "humiliation of itch- and scratch-lust, tearing of pleasure into pain, revenge of self and desecration of love."

It is not unusual for Shapiro to blot up these "malformations of the evil mind" from the news media and serenely "seem to fall in love." Such uncontrollable inclinations, coupled with an almost total lack of sympathy and/or idealism, often evoke similar extremes of hostile reactions in critics. Theodore Roethke once called him a "bourgeois poet"—a drunken epithet that Shapiro has rather casually accepted as the title of the literary autobiography and apologia of 1964.[2] Here he quite properly asks himself, "Do I give a damn?" acknowledges that the "cancer" of his poetry is always "blooming," openly confesses himself the "Babbitt metal of the future" taking his "place beside the Philistine," candidly theorizes that the "wrong reason is good enough for me," and realizes how frequently he has set the "ugliest theme" in the "most exquisite stanzas." In his mind's eye, or perhaps only in a Movietone newsreel, the bourgeois poet sees the "Germans enter the Forum" and with the voyeuristic eye of **"Dome of Sunday,"** "proudly gazes at the fine destruction." Intuitively, and not entirely incorrectly, poets are conceived as "conductors of the senses," who "think along electric currents"—sometimes "feel the wrong thing and are thrown through a wall by a million-volt shock." Shapiro wants to break out of the "poetry trap" of his previous life. But like the unfortunate Jewish lad who almost electrocutes himself in Henry Roth's widely acclaimed novel, *Call it Sleep,* only succeeds in shedding the "husks" at each step of the death-deepening consciousness, "tapering always downward / in the funnel of the night" to become ultimately a "seed of nothing."[3] Or to put it another way, the bourgeois poet is here trying to prove in prose what Fugitive poet Laura Riding laments in "Mask" that earlier admired and acclaimed poems were little more than "patches that transformed / The more previous corruptions."[4]

In **Bourgeios Poet** #59, Shapiro remembers collecting his poems for the 1953 edition and uses the analogy of an album of photographs lying lazily on the grass—his selection symbolized by the casual wind moving across the pages. This is hardly an accurate "trope" for the arrangement of the poems in the 1953 edition, since Shapiro there made a deliberate alphabetical arrangement of the titles even though, admittedly, his purpose was to scramble the chronology; but the wind-image does serve as a significant clue to the random arrangements of the ninety-six prose poems of **Bourgeois Poet.** The "wind" that "reads you lazily" and "thumbs my episodes" is the haphazard moods, the idiosyncratic free associations, that cause him to link episode with casual episode. Shapiro admits that "at one point, I literally did the Jackson Pollock *I Ching* trick: I dropped the pages from the top of a ladder and picked them up at random."[5] Anyone reading through **Bourgeois Poet** for the first time, without knowing some of the earlier poetry and certain intriguing aspects of biography and temperament, is likely to suppose the arrangement of the autobiographical prose poems utterly irrational and irresponsible. This contrasts sharply with the intention in the earlier **Place of Love**, the preface of which points out that: "The isolated sentences and paragraphs are extracted from letters written during the progress of the book. I have endeavoured to bind the prose poems to the lyrics by means of these clues, and through them and the general arrangement to provide some sequence of narrative." However, when it came time to submit **Bourgeois Poet** to the editor, Shapiro admits that he "chickened out," providing some sequence of psychological, symbolic, and autobiographical interconnections among the various sections.[6] The motivating aesthetic theory had been articulated as early as **"Magician"** in *V-Letter*, i.e., to show the "result without a trace / Of the cause, end without means, what without why."

The first prose poem catalogs a series of romantic, but not immediately intelligible, comments by a "wise child," a "wicked boy," a "simple son," and "one who says nothing"—slight variants of that part of the Passover service, where four questions are posed by a "wise son," who is eager to learn; a "wicked son," who inquires in a mocking spirit; a "simple son," who is indifferent; and finally, a "son who is unable to inquire." Being completely Shapirical, their reactions are scrambled. The simple son turns technician. The wicked one is deeply embedded in the imagination of the wise one, who like the poem-children of Randall Jarrell, dreams and sickens.[7] More than a hundred pages later, all four are metamorphosed into the girl-child of **"Death of a Student,"** the sleeping and uncomprehending "Nihilo," who "evades" the metaphysical questions raised by the "curt sadistic sermon."

Not yet ready for the psychological disrobings that occur later, the second poem brings together a pair of old friends after years of not meeting, each shocked at their mutual grayness. The "make-up of the years" conceals the seven

Shakespearean stages of man: infant, schoolboy, lover, soldier, judge of others, patriarch, and ultimate old child. Satirizing the grail procession of various Perceval legends, a "pageant . . . passes down the street," while unquestioning children sit on the curb to watch. A "generation moves in stateliness" comprising dignitaries, clowns, cross-carriers, businessmen, dictators, theologians, sickly popes, technologists, "nine of the greatest novelists," etc. Grimly modernizing the exploding chariot that touched the Adamic tree to climax the procession in Dante's *Purgatory* (canto XXXII), the unidentified hero of the "coming generation"—actually, the young movie actor James Dean— "drives a hundred miles an hour into a tree."[8] The identity is less important than the transparency that he is none other than the bourgeois poet, whose writings are always smashing into somebody's favorite symbolic tree.

The unexplained allusion to "two modern saints on letters" evokes suggestions of such spiritual leaders as Mohandas K. Gandhi and the "intelligent Pacelli" [Pope Pius XII], for whom Shapiro once wrote poems—one lost, the other (though part of a prize-winning series), carefully excised from all selected editions.[9] Thus, 3 and 4 toy and tinker with problems of religion. In 3, the oriental mystic who gives and gives (i.e., "pearls," "books and scrolls," "bronze cowbells," "hand-painted poetry") is contrasted with the antimystical poet of practical affairs who also "gives" (e.g., a "power plant for Christmas"). Playing the role of anti-poet, Shapiro smashes into his own predilection for "silk cloths" and "mother-of-pearl chopsticks" with crude interrupting references to "rottern meat for English queens," "vomit," etc.

Poem 4 specifies India as the locale. In language that parodies the injunctions of the Sermon on the Mount, the "rice around the lingam stone will be distributed . . . to the unblessed poor." In the "dying sun" of the East, dualisms abound: love and loathing, peace and terror, sneers and smiles. Though "with the beautiful Hindu woman, I drink in the phallus," nevertheless Ramakrishna's darling Kali, another of Shapiro's "sweet saints," "drank her smile till all was blue" and "joined the hands of all the gods." In her dual aspect Kali holds symbols of both death and immortality, and is worshipped and strangely loved in India as a beautiful, horrible, wonderful, life-giving, life-taking mother. The "nine domes of the temple," associated with this "Divine Mother"—her neck surrounded with a garland of skulls, and her triple eyes bringing peace or terror—subtly parallel the earlier "nine greatest novelists" of the second poem.

Poem 5 opens with a parody of the traditional heroics of major poets: "Of love and death in the Garrison State I sing"—Garrison here referring to the famous abolitionist William Lloyd Garrison (1805-1879). Unlike the more serious singing of Virgil, Milton, and Whitman, these two paragraphs slap together scraps of pseudoscientific advances ("chemical control of behavior by radio waves") and pseudomystical regressions ("waves of asceticisms sweep the automobile industry")—nothing, of course, taken seriously. Repeatedly, the sacred number "two" dominates, and the poem concludes with a half-serious "Anti-

Sky Association" that meets "naked at high noon and prays for color blindness." Placed in quotation marks, a final statement proclaims that "Color is a biological luxury"—a neat development of the grayness theme, given implications both racial and national in the following poem, and thereby linking up with the earlier allusion to the abolitionist Garrison.

In a near-panic of pity, 6 mourns the death of a certain Quintana in a shallow grave of South Pacific coral, hesitantly identified as a "truck driver from Dallas probably." "Naked and filthy," he is "covered with mosquitoes." He tends to remind the reader of the soldier-victim in **"Elegy for a Dead Soldier."** But with "eyes . . . as soft as soot, neck long as a thigh, a cross on his breastbone not far from the dogtags," Quintana here reminds the poet of the Spanish painter El Greco and the banzai attacks of the yellow-colored Japanese upon white American soldiers, and forces him to conclude—not exactly reluctantly—that "soldiers fall in love with the enemy all too easily. It's the allies they hate."

In a single box-shaped paragraph, 7 finds the author inside his study, wondering why he is in this "box," even though "it is exactly as he planned." Here he refers to himself as "bourgeois poet" for the first time. Like so much of this cube-obsessed poetry, his presence here is without purpose: he sits, he stands, he looks for a match, he smokes, he looks out his window, etc. The "Veterans Hospital" (haunted with the dying Quintana) "fronted with a shimmering Indian Summer tree" (recalling the Eastern lignam stone) continues the Orientalisms of the preceding poems, and is typical of the often insubstantial innuendoes, suggestions, and repetitions by which one prose poem is made to connect with something preceding or following. Box-themes continue in 8, when "the Beep" recalls the occasion during his unsuccessful twenties when he worked in his father's office as a file clerk—detailed again in 48—the intensity of his sexual instincts such that he almost exploded: "telephones are hard and kissable," "gold simmers to a boil in braceleted and sunburned cheeks"—this latter another modulation on the color theme. Youth and age again contrast when, in 7, an older and graying poet in his confining study parallels, in 8, the eros-oriented poet of the "elegant windowless world of soft pressures and efficiency joys . . . civilized mishaps."

"Lower the standard" is the repetitive cry of 9, a cry which has humorous connotations considered as an afterthought to the office girls of 8, but more intriguing psychological implications as a bit of foreplay to what follows. For in 10, the "Beep" is waiting to pick up his daughter in front of the columnar high school. "A moment of panic" transfixes him as she approaches and, like Alice in Wonderland, "grows taller." He remembers dropping her off at a football game one night where a "bowl of light lit up" his old female obsession from the University of Virginia, "the creamy Corinthian columns," and where, in a fitful moment of truth, a "cheer went up" like a "massacre of child-brides in a clearing." Surely, he is not the "Intellectual" who, twenty years earlier, had a "private thought" in an "indecent room / Where one might kiss his daughter before

bed," but nevertheless the gray-haired bourgeois poet feels "ashamed and grave." "The horror of their years," and the massive impact of their shouting "stoned me to death."

This moment of desperation, the cause of which is not explained, though suggested in the cry "Lower the standards," is followed in 11 by the hilarious antics of a cat, and in 12 by a "mother of grown children" with a rare skin illness caused by her inability to "consent to herself that the marriage was ended." "The skin has wiles," he shrewdly observes, "undreamed of by bacteria." The relationships between 11 and 12 is the unrevealed pun on the names "Kathy," "Kitty" and "Katz" (German for "cat")—names that have deeply personal associations. All references to "cats" therefore (of which there is an especially savage one later on, 87) are variations of the same female cat-theme. Oddly enough, the cat in 11 turns out to be mostly masculine and Shapirical; e.g., "At bird-watching he is superbly criminal"—or, "after eons of observation, or it may be minutes, he kneads his forepaws, waggles his butt and has what he wants." In one of the canceled passages, two voyeuristic cats watch birds "from behind . . . bright glass doors."[10] Had this been kept in the final published version, the analogy with Shapiro's numerous woman-watching window-experiences would have been more pointed. In the canceled passage, he observes that "their watching pleasures my watching." In the later 96, **"Vacation,"** the last two cats to be mentioned are vaguely identified as "woman" and "homo normalis." They balance precariously on "long thin ropes."

Poem 13 explains how California and Italy, two uncomfortable places far from the poet's midwestern Nebraska residence at the time of the composition of ***Bourgeois Poet***—where he feels equally uncomfortable—have canceled out one another. The trouble with Italy is "Heat of Florence on a Sunday Afternoon." The difficulty with California is "Floods at Christmas in the Sacramento Valley." These mutually annihilating irritations, moody and whimsical, are based on an earlier "Phenomenon"-like discovery: "In Baltimore, walking in the Victorian-movie snow, it occurred to me: seek for the opposite." Opposite-seeking like that of the disastrous ***Essay on Rime*** often leads to a cipher, a zero, a Zen-like nowhere: e.g., "large soft Californians sideswiping the future" or "small burning Italians endlessly plotting nothing." Sometimes it leads to an innocuous joke: like refusing the wine of the locale, listening to a Minnesota accent as if it were music, or calling a farm a "ranch." It also leads to the subject of the next poem, 14, which elaborates upon the "password of the twentieth century: Communications."

Like the "visit to themselves" made by the window figures of **"Dome of Sunday,"** and the "single image caught between / Two facing mirrors where vision multiplies / Beyond perspectives," these "communications" are an *un*-communicating repetition of Shapiro selves. "The Romans had the best roads in the world, but had nothing to communicate over them except other Romans." Similarly, "Americans have conquered world-time and world-space and chat with the four corners of the earth at breakfast," but "have nothing to communicate except other Americans." *Lack* of communication is "sitting in the kitchen in Nebraska and watching a shrouded woman amble down the market in Karachi," desire subsisting only in memory and imagination. He complains of these Indian women that "It's cold and mental love they want . . . the mystic sexuality of Communications." Such thoughts of Oriental eroticism, or rather the lack of it, come while looking out the glass window of a kitchen in Nebraska, and develop at the end of 14 into an imaginative blending of communications and Christianity with familiar Dome-of-Sunday motifs. "Moon in the bottom of the Steuben glass, sun nesting in New Mexican deserts—the primitive Christian communicated with a dirty big toe," drawing a "fish in the dust."

Poem 15 further develops this quasi-religious motif, at first satirically, with emphasis upon such transgressing members of religious communities as alcoholic Jesuits and bald-headed machine-gun Buddhists. Though some of this is hilarious (e.g., "the rabbi is laying the Ladies Aid Society"), 15 concludes somewhat more seriously with: "In the long run the only hope is for more human error on the part of the holy. Their sin is our salvation."

The bourgeois poet then skips to a consideration of clothing in 16. A relationship with the preceding 15 is implied, since certain religions have made a special grace out of clothing the naked—this, though he once blindly thrust himself toward Christianity, Shapiro now rejects. "Nightgowns are nonsense," he smirks, and tosses contemptuous glances at the biblical "lilies of the field" clothed more beautifully than Solomon in all his glory. The passing thought that "Children in uniform insult Jesus in heaven" is yet another variation, among other things, of the child-motif with which the ego-epic began; and leads neatly into 17, about an unidentified child who stands against his father, determined to speak only when he has decided. Like Shapiro, the child is of "two minds" and "is drinking it all in," but unlike voluble and outspoken Shapiro, "says nothing." Furthermore, certain allusions to the technique of the child's speech, and his methods of meaning, reinforce the aesthetic antics of *Bourgeois Poet*: "It's this frontier of speech we are always crossing." Oriental-mysticism surfaces again when the same child sits, Buddha-like, with "legs crossed" and "at ease," on the very top of a piano that is "thinking of Mozart."

As in the conclusions to Poems 1 and 2, the child elicits memories of death in 18—in this instance an older neighbor, an unidentified aunt who pacifies the "young" in the presence of a neighborhood death, only to lose her husband ("a man of reputation, in excellent health") a week later; only to have her paralyzed face twisted into a "grief that parodies a smile." This paradox, among others, between an ability to comfort and an inability to be comforted, evokes the appropriate aphorism in 19, that there is "Always another proverb that contradicts the first one."

By way of specific illustration in 20, a library is exposed as a place of conflicting things: though the director has magnificent quarters, and "dines with names of unknown fame," library lavatories are "rendezvous of desperate homosexuals." The obsessive "room" appears several times ("room . . . of the secret catalogue, room of unlisted books . . . manuscript room with the door of black steel"); and like 7, poem 20 is a single, square-shaped paragraph that concludes with a Shapirical destruction ("tons of trash. . . burning in time with the slow cool . . . fires of poems that gut libraries"). The fragmented paragraphs of 21 stress different aspects of the theme. "Time is mostly absences." One paragraph concerns a two-year-old who has a "motherless week"; a second, a father's trip to the other side of the world; a third, soldiers sitting in an "innocuous bar," afraid after three year's absence to go home; a fourth details a brother's house, shopworn after a thousand days of married words have taken place.

The "thousand days of words" links the scattered absences of 21, to the libraries of 20—a library being a place where fiery words are stored in gutted rooms. Twenty's incidental smell of books in libraries, and 21's carpets in a brother's house ("soft beige carpets smelt like new-mown hay") interweave to create the subject matter of 22—the theme of "smells." It begins with the mold smell of a "letter from Karachi" and a "book I had in New Guinea twenty years ago" (i.e., *Place of Love*), and proceeds to the mold-and-dung odors of the cities in India: "Winter smells of wood smoke and fruit," "castle smells of snow and peat," "acrid smell of copra," "electric smell of hair in rut." Also, Hollandia is "rotting water," and Rome, the intoxicating "armpit of the universe." Each of these fragrances is associated with one of the author's many trips: Karachi, Paris, Salzburg, Dublin, Siena, and Portsmouth. These travel memories meander into 23, and the top floor of a Tulsa hotel, where he is looking out a window at the "night beauty of the cracking-plant." A variation on the Dome-of-Sunday pattern, it develops the following 24 into yet another trip—this time a sight-seeing tour of the Parthenon-reproduction in Nashville, Tennessee.

The historical and literary associations of the Athenian and Nashville Parthenons (the latter readily associated with the Fugitive poetry magazine) are followed in 25 with a contrast between the *Times* and *Partisan*, the "Sestos and Abydos of aspiring poets." The two are painted in conflicting colors: one has the "itch for popularity" and the other a "refined thirst for the avant-garde." The contrasting and not always complimentary evaluations link with the paradoxical proverbs of 19, or the mutually destroying Italy and California of 13; and are important anticipations of the concluding philosophical long poem of the first third of the work, 34, based on similar ambivalences, ambiguities, and contradictions. *Partisan Review* saw the first major publication of Shapiro's literary career (the Fugitive-influenced **"Death of Emma Goldman"**), and is presented so as to associate it with the Nashville literary movement and Shapiro's brief stay at the University of Virginia: "*Partisan* remains with its crew of Southern girls, slicing the fat from literature with hairline knives."

As already noted, this kind of wrist-slapping is not exactly uncommon. In **"University,"** the deans are "dry spinsters over family plate." The subject of **"Poet"** is "epicene."

"Intellectual" has a body that "is an open house / Inviting every passerby to stay." What these inversions are suggesting is that, even though some of the literary journals are among the first to accept his poetry (in fact, one might say that precisely *because* they were the first), their role as critic is unnatural. He even goes so far as to draw a parody parallel between the editors of poetry in 25 and a striptease in 26: Shylock-like, the editors "slice the fat from literature," while a stripteaser in a cheap Kansas City burlesque house drops the "silk muffler that hangs between her buttocks," and "she is all but hairless." The bridge between 25 and 26 is a favorite poet, the sexually "handicapped" Hart Crane, who "did well with the burlesque" stripper ("all but her belly buried in the floor. Magdalene? Perhaps").

Poem 27 concerns a "skinny little book," one of the early unidentified volumes, restrained in some places as if superficially female ("why the cosmetology of font and rule, meters laid on like fingernail enamel"); but goaded in others, as if more actively male ("and you, thin packet, let your seed fly, if you have any"). An "old convent" follows irreverently in 28, with walls of "broken bottles hard-set in cement." The Kansas City "Magdalene" of 26 (a deathlike "cold flows from her steady limbs"), and the lovely convent "Héloises" of 28 (like virgin Athenas who have "no single worshiper left on the face of the earth," 24) are parallels that claw one another with the "long fingernails" of long-since-rejected "theological grief."

> **Anyone reading the *Bourgeois Poet* for the first time, without knowing some of the earlier poetry and certain intriguing aspects of biography and temperament, is likely to suppose the arrangement of the autobiographical prose poems utterly irrational and irresponsible.**
>
> **—Joseph Reino**

A Calder of "broken bottles strung in an empty frame in a fine Connecticut home"—an arty little crack at occupants of convents—has yet another development in 29: the glossy elegance of the living rooms, kitchens, and bathrooms of Nebraska neighbors. "Toilets" are "so highly bred they fill and fall without a sigh." But the bourgeois poet himself—is he really so different? He too, does he not arrange books in his study, as neighbors do Kleenex, towels, and toilets with a view to their appearance, and sometime sit at his window, like the Amsterdam whores of the later 73, so as to be seen by neighbors? This follow-up explains why he self-questions his long obsession with the facades of his own poetry in the preceding 27, where he asks "Why the attractive packaging of stanza?" "Why the un-American-activity of the sonnet?"

His literary career always harks him back to his raw beginnings as a war poet in 1941. Poem 30, therefore, concluding with a "room in the history books," dovetails into the topic of 31, the direct, although unwilling, participation in the history of World War II. Seven paragraphs of ironically related events parallel: boys playing soldier with real weapons after the wars; draftees using dummy rifles in the early days of the American selective service; poet-soldier Shapiro feeling his rough and shallow helmet; soldiers playing war games on a gray wooden battleship built on the grass at a Naval Base; a shell-shocked newsman shouting commands and thumping his truncheon-stick on the ground; ocean-weary soldiers hacking at walls and gouging lounge-room ornamentation at the end of their forty-day journey to Australia; the supreme commander of the Pacific Campaign ("We hated him") being fired by President Truman during the Korean War.

These fritterings of history arrow into a "history of Philosophy Professor" in 32, "elegant as . . . the Budapest String Quartet," "a minor prince who made off with the money" (like "Uncle Saul" and "The Bros" of 89 and 96). Shapiro twists his reminiscences of the "One" who is "never superior to the questioner" and for whom he writes a paper on Jefferson, into carping observations on philosophy, teaching techniques, and final examinations: "Spring comes with Schopenhauer" and "Exams flush everything out of our mind." Unfortunately, a pre-ecology insensitivity betrays itself when philosophic theory is viewed as "always defeating itself . . . chasing after chemistry with 'Wait, Wait!'" Poem 33 proceeds to the "nature of belief"—the poet now bothered by matters to which elsewhere (as in, say, **"Gun," "Waxworks,"** and **"Robbery"**) he was either indifferent or fascinated: sufferings, corruptions, battles, martyrdoms, theologies, praying generals, and children in prison. The neoclassical little creed of the much-anthologized **"Auto Wreck"** ("Suicide has cause, and stillbirth, logic") has now clouded into a "belief" that "makes blood flow," "infects the dead with more belief," and "flows in our veins."

. . . . .

Divided into ten unnumbered parts, 34 offers a kind of Whitmanesque "Song of Myself."[11] It opens with a series of mutually conflicting statements of beliefs and practices, and expands upon the philosophy of 19: "Always another proverb that contradicts the first one." Although Shapiro is an "atheist," yet he says his "prayers." Though he is a "deviate" who likes to "fondle and contribute," yet he is the responsible "father of three." Though he stands "high in the community," yet he "drinks my share and yours" and never has enough. Though he is a "physical coward," yet he antagonizes intellectuals, established poets, rabbis, and popes. He fancies himself "upholding the image of America" as the cliché land of the free and the brave, but nevertheless attacks the insane and acknowledges that—in one of several such offhand remarks—his muscles soften "while the homosexual lectures me brilliantly in the beer booth." Pursuing nowhere, his "tree of nerves electrocutes itself," and "I write my own ticket to oblivion." In short, a middle-class poet is trying to identify himself with everything that middle-class America tended in the 1950s to regard as intellectually, morally, socially, and sexually unacceptable. In a later comment, Shapiro attempts to explain all this as the "paradox of being a poet and a bourgeois American at the same time. I guess some of my essays, like the one on Henry Miller, are attempts to throw over that bourgeois side of me, but I can't do it. I could never be like Bukowski, and I wouldn't want to be. That has something to do with being a Jew."[12]

The remaining nine sections of 34 are scattered free-verse comments, much like the preceding thirty-three only more diffused and—were it possible—more disconnected. Occasionally, as in the unnumbered third section, there appear some rhetorical devices, such as alternating descriptions of New York and Chicago. But most are biographical scraps and moody tidbits, likely to be of little interest to the general reading public. However, the philosophy of a Nowhere-Nebraska is cataloged in Whitman-Sandburg fashion in a portion that Shapiro chose to isolate as an entirely separate **"Nebraska"** in *Collected Poems*:

> I love Nowhere where the factories die of
>   malnutrition,
> I love Nowhere where there are no roads, no rivers,
>   no interesting Indians,
> Where history is invented in the History Department
>   and there are no centennials of anything,
> Where every tree is planted by hand and has a
>   private tutor,
> Where the "parts" have to be ordered and the sky
>   settles all questions,
> Where travelers from California bitch at the
>   backwardness and New Yorkers step on the gas
>   in a panic,
> Where the grass in winter is gray not brown,
> Where the population diminishes. . . .
> I love Nowhere where the human brag is a brag of
>   neither time nor place,
> But an elephant house of Smithsonian bones and
>   white cathedrals of grain,
> The feeding-lots in the snow with the steers
>   huddled in symmetrical misery, backs to the
>   sleet,
> To beef us up in the Beef State plains, something
>   to look at.

. . . . .

This passion for "nowhereness," a place not unlike Hart Crane's "North Labrador," where there are no roads, no rivers, no factories, no history, no time, and no place; where everything, including bourgeois poets, diminishes in stature—continues into the second main division. Curiously called "Doctor Poet," it consists of thirty prose poems based on autobiographical subjects of a similar scattered and disconnected kind: oriental trips, 36; movies of the second World War 37; playing chess games with the children, 40; pushing his left hand through a door glass, 42; being bitten by an oversexed nurse, 45; being aroused by a near-conversion to Catholicism, 46; decorating drug-store windows, 51; turning grey with age, 52; learning Bach partitas while recuperating from an operation, 53; visiting the operator of a switch tower over rail-road tracks, 54; etc. The poems of "Doctor Poet" are arranged with the same disregard for chronology that dominates the first section, once again employing the same seemingly, incidental but nevertheless almost deterministic, connecting devices. A drug store in 50, "where whiskey is sold and every blandishment of skin," reminds him in 51 that he once decorated drug-store windows "selling perfume or soap," and always receiving a "jocular free beer." Traveling on the trans-Atlantic liner *Queen Mary*, in 44, reminds him of his sexual-religious problems in 46, especially that a "serpent" always snares him in the privates when he tries to pray the "Hail Mary." Sexual static interfering with, or perhaps itensifying, his religious practices in 46 recalls how similar sexual yearnings ("one eye peeled for the models") interfered with a job as poetry editor in 47; and how, even earlier, too much staring at secretaries, especially the "one with curves in every direction and deep chiaroscuro make-up," disrupted his youthful job as file clerk in his father's office, 48. When the bourgeois poet learns how to edit poems in 49, especially how to "drive out of the bushes of language their naked shame of thought," he follows it in 50 by expostulating on the naked shame of "Jim Crow gaiety," the "jump and scream of the jazz," the "war of pleasure," the "teeming Negress" who "dumps the entire load of perfume between her breasts."

A goodly number of pieces are devoted to functions as poet-critic. Just as the sequence from the Nashville Parthenon in 24 through the neighborhood bathrooms in 30, are meant to characterize the creative process; so also much of the sequence from 47 to 63 underscores his literary and editorial career. Everything, however, diminishes his literary stature. When he edits poems, it is to be the "click of sharp high heels," 47, and is "shy with the thick blue pencil in my hand," 49. When he remembers his first publication, the privately printed *Poems* of 1935, he shudders at that "bludgeoning and recompense of uncles," 55. When he attacks Virginia in **"University," "Conscription Camp,"** and **"Southerner,"** it is because he "has nothing better to do," 56. When he becomes a prize poet of contacts with significant figures of the literary world, he has "private dreams of murdering the king of the wood," 57. When he ponders his first 1953 edition of selected poems, stained with accidental wine, he understands that they are merely "dirty-dog poems baying at the moon-mother," 59. When he writes prose, it is to "find out what I think," but when the thoughts are published, the "whole business is irresponsible," 60. When he receives an honorary doctorate, he imagines falling through the platform, going down in operatic flames, like another Don Giovanni in Da Ponte's libretto for Mozart's opera, 63.

. . . . .

"Doctor Poet" concludes with forty-eight brief, autobiographical fragments, arbitrarily identified with Roman numerals that appear to have no special significance except their Roman continuity. A goodly number of these autobiographical scraps are quite revealing, so intimate as to be sometimes in bad taste—as if the poet wanted to wash his family's and his own psychiatric dirty linen in public. The poet's father warns him about another young boy who masturbates (i); the young Shapiro refuses to disassociate himself from his "friend" (ii); as a son, finds "filthy pamphlets with real photographs" in his father's top drawer (iii); as a father, cowardly allows his own son to be circumsized (iv); "accidentally" places his hand on his mother's breasts on the occasion of his return from the war (vi); dreams of the enormous privates of his father's second wife (vii); teaches his sister to smoke and fondles the breasts of his sister's girl friend (ix); defecates on railroad tracks (x); remembers stealing candy when he was only five (xi); changes the bad grades on a poor report card (xii); has an affair with the wife of an Air Force officer who is shot down, but cannot feel guilty about it (xiii); and remembers the "beautiful uncircumcised penis" of a soldier he once saw in the showers—"I recall it for years" (xvii). These intimate family and personal sexual recollections stop abruptly at xviii when a soldier, conflicting with the obvious implications of xvii, accuses him of "not being queer." From that point on, though the numbered fragments still consist of things better consigned to the trash-heap, the inconsequentialities amuse rather than embarrass: e.g., insisting on the Christmas tree (xx); hiding a glass of bourbon behind a bookcase (xvi); deliberately losing all his salary at poker (xxiii); never correcting the misprints in his early books (xxvii); consciously deceiving himself when he meets Mies van der Rohe (xxxii); playing tricks on the avant-garde (xxx-iv); and wanting a power saw for Christmas (xxxv).

Despite the sensitive revelations of i through xvii, the most important passages are not so much the racy ones, but rather the realizations that he could "honestly" be "an Arab or an Ultra, a Communist or a Republican" (xxviii); that he has a "longing for the Primitive" and barely "survives as a Modern" (xxix); and that he had "no fear of nonrecognition, no instinct for survival, no regrets for the future, no plans for the present" (xxx). One of the longest of the prose jottings is xxxix, a half-successful attempt to counteract opposite-seeking parts of **Bourgeois Poet,** wherein he suddenly realizes he cannot have "rhyme or reason," "fiction or truth," "vapors of the heart or logic of the case," "poetry and civilization," "involuntary action or a matter of principle." In xlii, "Poetry of the ill" occurs "when the rage of the poem is oned with the fine forms," "bad feeling . . . oned with conscience," and "we flow back into life." In xliii, "Poetry of the hale and hearty" (not really so radically different from "poetry of the ill," except for elimination of form), is the necessity to "feel the natural streamings of life," "pride myself on the general pleasure," and "hate with joy." By such definitions, of course, the ejaculated "unction . . . from the vessel's lip" in "Confirmation," is marred by rhymes, rhythms, and symbols in "Poetry of the ill"; whereas 87's "Cat called me a Jewish pig" and 89's "Uncle Saul was a dandy," without dark myths and strange symbols to conceal the audacity of the revelations, are "poetry of the hale and hearty." It is by such poetic unreason that this middle-aged poem fits together. In fact, these forty-eight prose-snatches are the author's poetic development of a quotation-theme by an otherwise unidentified Dr. Harry B. Lee with which the second long poem is prefaced. *"The creativeness of the artist is a most efficient technique for liquidating guilt*

and re-establishing the function of pity . . . This mental organization is a fortunate one for the artist in the man; but it is an unfortunate one for the man in the artist since it afflicts him with his emotional immaturity, exquisitely narcissistic character, maladjustment to life, and recurrent neurotic depressions. . . ."[13]

. . . . .

By contrast with a Shakespearean parody written twenty years earlier ("Ballade of the Second-Best Bed," *VL,* 54), this third and last canto, "End Paper," is Shapiro's middle-aged last will and testament: a final literary *nihilo* of thirty-two prose poems (65-96), followed by a mishmash antipoem of seven queerly titled segments. "End Paper" begins with a piece of free verse, 65, employing a Whitmanesque cataloging technique on "French Poetry," much of which summarizes his very own poetic dispositions: "drawn with the fist on the pale nuance," "tastes of women and children, spatulas and rubber plants," "utmost gravity and indestructible balance," "upsets the stomach of the future," and "ropey veins of the feet of matrons and whores. . . ."

As expected, 66 to 95 are biographical vignettes, philosophical scraps, Freudian open-confessions, and masochistic self-lacerations. Denunciations abound! Poem 70, excoriates prayer: "In Siena they bring the race horse to the altar; if he empties himself on the floor that is good luck." Poem 71 berates teachers of culture who hate science: "arts carry the sickness of mind past." Poem 72 is dissatisfied with the traditional methods of raising children: "When the child hates the parent or the parent hates the child, both produce soldiers . . . dressed for the kill of 'barbarians.'" Poem 74 fears Socratic self-knowledge: "The coral animal turns to jagged stone after it dies; the dead selves build into an underwater cathedral, housing for brilliant and deadly jaws: 'Know not Thyself.'" Poem 79 looks askance at posterity—a "monstrous grave to swallow the grandchildren, dug by the lean-jawed voices of ideals." Poem 80 gives rabbis their Shapirical comeuppance when one of them entangles a simple-minded bourgeois poet in Jewish concepts of original sin: "The Talmud of his mind flew open like a gate. I followed him through twisting streets, lost him in shadow and dropped into a tavern."

Of the assortment of mysterious biographical whodunits in "End Paper," 75 is most intriguing. The bourgeois poet drives "three thousand miles to ask a question," wanting a firsthand account of *"him."* "Him" turns out to be another heroic lawbreaker, a "mad scientist" and "good German," who was driven "insane" and "murdered," whose disciples are scattered, his equipment smashed by the police, his books "against the law to post." This unidentified Shapiro hero dovetails perfectly with the evaluation of Wilhelm Reich in the essay "Poets of the Cosmic Consciousness"—Reich being the inventor of a useless "orgone-box" in which Shapiro naturally professes belief; and who, along with P. D. Ouspensky and the Robert Graves of *White Goddess,* is one of his grammarians of poetic myth (310). According to *Defense of Ignorance,* Reich "broke with official psychoanalysis and founded a school of his own based upon the concept . . . of a universal cosmic-energy which he named orgone energy." From 1942 to 1954, in an establishment known as the Orgone Institute, "Reich and his workers experimented with the effects of radioactive fissionable matter on orgone-active material"; but "the clash of the two energies produced its own kind of radiation sickness with such dangerous consequences that the experiments were abandoned and the AEC withdrew its support." Reich is identified as the subject of *Bourgeois Poet* #75 in *Collected Poems*, but the essay, happily enough, has been deleted from *Poetry Wreck.*

In *Bourgeois Poet* #75, one of the "beep's" questions was: "Did you visit him in the sunset of his mind?" In addition to cashing a prosaic check, the only answer against the background of a poetic San Diego sunset, was: "I don't want to talk about that." Key motifs of **"Dome of Sunday"** (camera, bulbs, sun, brightness, magnifying glass), appearances of which are often trigger signals of deep interior involvement, show up in the last sentence of 75: "Pictures that he took when the bulbs popped, each brighter than a thousand suns; the spiral poems he wrote under the electronic microscope." The possibility always exists, however, that the bourgeois author is merely committing himself to a fake; hence, the next poem, 76, begins with the shocking discovery that a favorite poet whose writings seem so woman oriented is a homosexual. Shapiro senses "an impersonal sorrow as nagging as envy"; and having been frightened in an imaginary Eden when Eve touched Adam with her first word "thou," he warns the reader to "Beware of the poison of pronouns."

Skeletons are rattled out of the closets with the usual insensitivity to personal reputations or family feelings. With Baudelairean brilliance, 87 unveils a "good Saint Cat" who once called him a "Jewish pig": "She seethed with worms," "she stroked the oxygen tank like a bomb," "Hell flowed from her mouth like streams of horse," "She groaned in the screaming of pork," "Five miles in the air you could hear her scream of love."[14] In 89, a much-misbehaving "Uncle Saul" is contrasted to the Welsh Poet, Dylan Thomas. Like Wilhelm Reich, who violated a court order and landed in jail, this unidentified uncle "used checking accounts that didn't belong to him," "charged at the best shops under others' names," hired women "and kept them in love nests," was discharged from the army "for juggling money records," "kept the table choking with laughter . . . and clowned in a lavender dressing gown." All this, of course, by comparison with Dylan Thomas—nothing more than the other side of the coin—who "stole and borrowed," "wore motley," "was a civilian" whose "look was straight and far into your eyes," "toured America like a favorite nephew, sprinkling dynamite on the nipples of female professors." Along with William Carlos Williams, D. H. Lawrence, and Henry Miller, the Welshman is subject to analysis and dissection in an essay of *Defense of Ignorance.* Among the things for which Thomas is eulogized in the latter work is his Reichian-Freudian belief that sex is the "instrument of belief and knowledge" that will make the sick world "healthy and whole again." However, as Dylan Thomas more and more emphasizes the physical mechanics of love, "love recedes and sex becomes a nightmare," and growing older becomes merely "a Black Mass."

Only in this context of expressionist contradiction may one understand poem 69, an apparent condemnation of the French symbolist Charles Baudelaire, two of whose sonnets Shapiro once translated: "Giantess" and "Blindmen." Matters mentioned with such apparent scorn are echoed in his own most private poetic parts: Poe, the cross, cats, jewels, giant nipples, Christian book, pus, cheap perfume, Black Mass, etc. Indeed, if "Charles" is changed to "Karl," "Iowa" into "Nebraska," "classical alexandrines" into "ballets mécaniques," and *Flowers of Evil* into **Place of Love**, the whole of 69 becomes an almost psychopathic self-laceration, the self-emasculation of an Hegelian synthesizer who dreamed of writing "one day a Christian, the next a Jew"; but who is now a midwestern, middle-aged, middle-class Baudelairean prose poet.

Poem 69 bears a remarkable resemblance to the much-praised Dylan Thomas of *Defense of Ignorance* and *Poetry Wreck.* Dylan moves between "sexual revulsion and sexual ecstasy," "between puritanism and mysticism," between "formalistic ritual . . . and vagueness," between the "telescope and the microscope." Like the bourgeois picture of Baudelaire, Dylan "believed in God and Christ; the Fall and death, the end of all things and the day of eternity"; and, according to this seemingly objective analysis, "what we find is something that fits Thomas into the age: the satanism, the vomitous horror, the self-elected crucifixion of the artist." The Shapirical formula upon which poems 69 and 89 is based is simply this: "Uncle Saul" equals Dylan Thomas, who equals Charles Baudelaire, who equals that "most Victorian Jew," Karl Shapiro. This epithet, "a most Victorian Jew," from a Shapiro girl friend during the war, anticipates the "bourgeois poet" that later came from Theodore Roethke at a drunken party. While a soldier in the South Pacific, Shapiro had pressed a bougainvillaea into a copy of Baudelaire's *Les Fleurs du Mal.* In 69, this romantic bougainvillaea ("the purplest kiss I knew") is metamorphosed into a futuristic flower of "Mexican tin and black nail polish."

. . . . .

"End Paper" concludes with seven separately titled autobiographical scraps, given a covering title "Big Sonnet" when reprinted in *Selected Poems.* Only four of these are reprinted in somewhat abbreviated form and rearranged in *Collected Poems.* Like enigma variations, the connecting links of this mad hebdomad are well hidden, but each seems part of a Salvador Dali version of Shakespeare's "seven ages of man," first mentioned in 2. Thus, *Bourgeois Poet* ends on a theme with which it began, the Shakespearean sequence now scrambled into seven Shapirical stages almost beyond all recognition: lover, bridegroom, survivor, mourner, drunk, American Dreamer, and businessman. Everything seems rather pointless, and in the manner of the much scorned *Waste Land* of Eliot and *Cantos* of Pound, Shapiro has peppered his poetic hash with words from Greek, Latin, French, Spanish, German, Yiddish, and advertising slogans: "freulein," "allumeuse," "nihilo," "trafe," "wholicity," "duende," "Byzant," "Stutz Bearcat," *"hymen hymenaee,"* "verset," "to kalon to kalon."

"Balcony Scene," the lover-stage, brutalizes the Petrarchanisms of *Romeo and Juliet*. The story line suggests that, on some "Memorial Day," a white widow-woman with children, whose husband-pilot was killed at Christmas time during the war, is wearing a black bathing suit. The unmourned death of the husband ("Grief I never heard") associates this passage with the "handsome flyer" of the R.A.F., "down in his first operation," who "knows I cuckold him," but for whom "I try to feel sorry but can't." The widow-woman blends into, or is contrasted with, a "fatlady" (perhaps black) in a white bathing suit, whose grotesques are "slapped together." This one, like the pathetic paralytic of **"Figurehead,"** waddles as she walks. Much in **"Balcony Scene"** matches the obsessives of **"Dome of Sunday"**: box, sun, plane, window, billion, voyeurism, the identifying day, the Christian associations, etc., but nothing is more bizarre than the description of the two women in black-white. The attractive imperatives ("shellacked with silk" "dressed in black" "cheeks . . . soft as muslin") of the earlier poem ("blinded negress lurching through fatigue") pass through the distorted mirrors of middle-age eroticism to emerge "as if one hip . . . were going out of joint"—a "throwing motion." These are the things that "Big Sonnet" loves: the bending down that offers a sodomitic "wall socket" of "pickpock moon." **"Balcony Scene"** is therefore pitiless. Only the willow tree can lament.

"Vacation," the bridegroom stage, gathers together memories and attitudes associated with a honeymoon, an Eliotic version of the earlier and more merry **"Second Best Bed."** The reception was "six cases of bourbon returned to the caterer"; the location, something like Grand Rapids; the consummated "flowers divided" a disappointment, like "ending a sentence with a preposition." "Love," he queries, is it nothing but this—"paper of brides," "vellum of hand," and "skin . . . soft as kid"? These facades and fragilities are broken by the rigid bluntness of "junkyard," "Battle of Waterloo" and "hands of ferroconcrete." Through a series of boredoms and disillusionments the "goldness and whiteness of woman" darkens into the basic Baudelairean biology of "their brown blood," "their stenches," out of which he claims, like the more compassionate William Carlos Williams in an episode of *Paterson*, that the "greatest sonnet cycles" emerge.[15] The poem **"V-Letter"** was a prize-winning prelude to **"Vacation";** and though this particular "hymen hymenaee" may be on its "deathbed," the "single snake" will awaken again, and "burgeon" romantically into an aubade, a ballade, an epithalamium, and a series of love sonnets in his next volume of poetry, ***White-Haired Lover.***

"Anti-poem" attempts to survive, amid the futility of being a famous poet—married, middle-class, middle-aged, and midwestern. Hart Crane's "flashing scene" of interior satisfaction or lyrical exultation, in the proem to his "Bridge" is here "never disclosed"—nothing to look forward to but (as in the subsequent **"Witches are Flying"**) the "third ejaculation of the hanged man." Judaism is reduced to the "Jews next door" who are "less noisy"; and Christianity, about which he once crowed and scratched, is merely "Christ . . . in voice." Only disappointments flourish amid wheatfields, bland satisfactions of mayors, cruel comments of children, love-sensations of "seeing you walk away," and nagging pro- and anti-feminisms. The final paragraph targets a "woman" with "handsome hands" who takes things, handles, and magnetizes them, and then throws them away. Even such bleaknesses, however, cannot completely suppress some powerful one-liners: "hammers of prosperity practice against the too-green corn," and "the secret stairway, passage to the room of Poe, chapel without a god."

Otherwise, everything is coldly dissected, like the viewing that follows in **"Death of a Student,"** the brief fifth segment of "Big Sonnet". Courtesies and externalities of mourners are duly noted in an utterly griefless poem (cf. "Grief I never heard"). But attention zeroes into the "suit without lint," and the three-year-old girl ("Nihilo"), "her golden pony tail flopping," and evading the questions of the curt sermon, "as if tossing her hair." One recalls that, similarly, in the earlier, **"Elegy for a Dead Soldier,"** the "palmtrees swirl their hair," as though in a paroxym of pleasure, as the "chaplain chats."

Drunkenness dominates the fifth section, **"Basement Apartment";** and an exaggerated triumph and an extended tragedy divide the sixth, **"Witches are Flying,"** into equal halves. In the fifth, marriage has descended from heights it never had. Amid drunken insults, the hymen has chilled, the accidental baby aborted, and "trafe" (the Yiddish word for "unclean") has become the "color of my true love's hair." In the sixth, the triumph of an inventor of a car a "hundred feet long" (so useless that it "can't turn corners") degenerates into the pseudo pathos of a "prisoner in Iowa" who gives up the ghost, like an autumn "generation of trees." With indifference and "in bad faith," Shapiro pretends to "hear the creaking of his rope in the sole moment before his neck cracks." As though implying some literary connection, "sixty-five poets cower in the poetry shack expecting advancement."

In **"Teamsters Union,"** the final section of "Big Sonnet," "sorrow moved away like happiness." Shapiro is here vaguely alluding to some family misfortune involving business dealings. Repeated almost litanylike are the phrases "The Bros. depart," "The Bros. are here," "The Bros. pass by," etc. The closest he comes to revealing the actual nature of this misfortune occurs when the "pride of ownership" is "dismantled," and the "pieces to be salvaged in a distant state." The "checkbook with its pink tongue hanging out" reminds one of "Uncle Saul" in 89 who "used checking accounts that didn't belong to him."

Like so much of ***Bourgeois Poet***, this final section has the effect of "angry showers / of arrows upon my back," or "electric needles" of meaninglessness running amok between "my flesh and shirt." In "Canto CXX," Ezra Pound apologizes for the failures and confusions of his difficult *Cantos*, asking friends "to try to forgive / What I have made." Without apology or requests for forgiveness,

Shapiro recognized as early as the above-quoted **"Tingling Back"** in *Poems 1940-1953* that there are occasions when

> . . . I have touched the pain
> of amour-propre, of something yesterday
>   I said and I should not have said,
>   I did and I must not do.
> These needles wing their insights from my brain
>   and through and through my flesh they play
>   to prick my skin with red
> letters of shame and blue blurs of tatoo.

All of the ninety-six prose poems of *Bourgeois Poet*, to say nothing of so much else, seem to fit this peculiar needlelike pain for which the poet (like so many a reader) must take his "medicine" and "study one's sincerity like a crime." The "hurt," constantly hinted at, is never actually named; but like the poetry-reading boy of **"Messias"** mentioned in connection with the mutually repelling dual elements in chapter 6, the Shapiro-readers, too, sometimes want to flee in terror . . ."Down the red ringing of the fire escape / . . . to the green grass" that is "sickeningly green." Thus, the same all-seeing "sun" that functions so violently in **"Dome of Sunday,"** here "goes to the end of the road with immense self-pity," merely to rise on the next day "on the opposite side."

Notes

1 The brief visit of Vittorio Mussolini is covered by the *New York Times* from 8 through 17 October, 1937. For typical editorial opinion, consult "And so, Vittorio," *Nation,* 16 October 1937, p. 393.

2 Bartlett, pp. 33-34.

3 *Call It Sleep* (New York: Avon Books, 1970), p. 429.

4 *Selected Poems in Five Sets* (New York: W. W. Norton, 1973), p. 32.

5 Anthony Ostroff, *The Contemporary Poet as Artist and Critic: Eight Symposia* (Boston: Little, Brown and Company, 1964), p. 214. *BP* #14-16 are therein reprinted along with evaluations by Adrienne Rich, Donald Justice, and William Dickey, along with counterevaluations by Karl Shapiro.

6 Bartlett, p. 340.

7 *BP* #1 is a simplistic but nonetheless attractive imitation of the poeticisms of the six children in the first chapter of Virginia Woolf's 1931 novel, *The Waves.*

8 James Dean was killed in an auto accident in Paso Robles, California, on 30 September 1955. Shapiro identified the high school hero in response to an inquiry.

9 Shapiro won the Eunice Tietjens Memorial Prize for six poems in the April 1961 issue of *Poetry Magazine:* "Garden in Chicago," "Emily Dickinson and Katherine Anne Porter," "Americans are Afraid of Lizards," "Surrounded," "Modest Funeral," and "Waiting

for the Pope." The reference to the "intelligent Pacelli" occurs in the last poem. Only three of these poems (1, 2, and 5) are reprinted in *CP.*

10 For this and other canceled passages, see *College English,* May 1962, pp. 609-17. For the bird-and-cat passage referred to here, see section 12, p. 615. Additional canceled passages may be found in *Poetry: The Fiftieth Anniversary Issue,* October-November 1962, pp. 115-21, and also under the titles "Old Poet," "Bellow," "Winery at Napa," "Sacramental Winos," "Tobacconists," "No Mask," "Mozart's Jew," and "Evangelist" among the "New and Uncollected Poems" in *CP.*

11 The subtitle of this section, "Credo quia Absurdum" ("I believe because it is absurd"), is usually attributed to Tertullian, the second century apologist of the early Christian church, who was for a while the leader of a sect called the Montanists. Shapiro uses the phrase in *BP* #33 as a prelude to catalog of credal paradoxes in #34. The passage is reprinted in *CP* under the title "Nature of Belief" and rather whimsically placed between "Seed Catalogue" (*BP* #27) and "Libraries" (*BP* #20).

12 Bartlett, p. 34.

13 Harry B. Lee is the author of numerous articles on the mental and emotional states of creative artists. In response to an inquiry addressed to him by the present writer, he observed that the Shapiro "quotation" at the beginning of *BP* #64 is "largely a misconstruction placed by the author on what I had written." As indicated by the italicized portions of the following passage, Dr. Lee recomposed almost the entire paragraph:

> The creativeness of the artist is *for the appreciator as well as the creator* a most *salutary means* for liquidating guilt and re-establishing a function of pity. *He achieves this through a shaping of formal contents which express for creator and appreciator the universal pre-conscious significance of "a normative exercise,"* one that atones *for guilt by making reparation and restitution for unconscious repressed impulses to hurt or destroy another person.*

With respect to so much of Shapiro's poetry discussed in this volume, Dr. Lee's reference to "repressed impulses to hurt or destroy" is particularly telling. Significantly, Shapiro's original "quotation" is not reprinted in *SP* or *CP.*

14 Caitlin Thomas was the tempestuous wife of Dylan Thomas. Without explanation, Shapiro uses her name as the title of *BP* #87 in the *CP* reprint, followed immediately by "Clowning," the first line of which is, "Dylan wasn't dapper." That an association is intended is obvious, but not so in *BP* and *SP,* where another poem intervenes and readers would have no way of suspecting a connection. Caitlin Thomas was the author of a candid autobiography, *Leftover Life to Kill* (Boston: Little, Brown and Company, 1957) on which Sidney Michael's 1964 drama *Dylan* is partly based.

15 See "Paterson: Episode from Book III," in W. C. Williams' *Selected Poems* (New York: New Directions, 1949), p. 105—sometimes printed under the title "Paterson: Episode 17." In Williams' poem, the "beat of famous lines / in the few excellent poems / woven to make you / gracious" are "contrapuntal" to the flogging, drunkenness, and ultimately the gangrape of a nurse

prostitute who, repeatedly and with considerable irony, is called "beautiful thing." Without acknowledgment in *CP*, Shapiro cribs this phrase as the title of *BP #45*.

Robert Richman (essay date 1988)

SOURCE: "The Trials of a Poet," in *The New Criterion*, Vol. 6, No. 8, April, 1988, pp. 74-81.

[*In the following mixed review of* New & Selected Poems, 1940-1986, *Richman notes the mediocre level of Shapiro's recent verse and discusses the influence of W. H. Auden on his career.*]

The first thing one notices about Karl Shapiro's *New & Selected Poems, 1940-1986* is the slimness of the volume. Shapiro, who is seventy-four years old, has written some fourteen books of verse—beginning with *Person, Place and Thing*, published in 1942 when the author was a sergeant in the U.S. Army Medical Corps, up through *Love & War Art & God,* which came out four years ago. This substantial body of work, most of which is unavailable, has been reduced by Shapiro to 103 pages. It is therefore no surprise that *New & Selected Poems, 1940-1986* gives no sense of the scale of Shapiro's oeuvre. What it offers instead is only an outline of the twists and turns of the poet's interesting career. Indeed, *New & Selected Poems, 1940-1986* seems to suggest that Shapiro believes the thing of fundamental interest in his career is the contours of its development.

Not that these contours are wholly without interest. Shapiro's early poetry, written during the war, is indebted to W. H. Auden, whose influence in the United States was then at its highest point. (The early poetry of John Berryman and Delmore Schwartz, two of Shapiro's contemporaries, also owes something to Auden's work.) The Auden that Shapiro drew from, however, isn't the Eliot-inspired one of *Poems* (1930), but rather the Auden who by the mid-Thirties had abandoned the deliberate difficulty of modernism for a more accessible style and subject matter. Auden sought, through his use of the language of journalism, advertising, and psychology, to give the raw data of the contemporary world a pre-eminent place in his poetry. This went against Eliot, who incorporated the objects of reality only insofar as they could be given a symbolic meaning or emotion.

It was the abandonment of the symbol- and metaphor-making impulse that the young Karl Shapiro found appealing in Auden's poetry. Later on in his career, in the essays of *In Defense of Ignorance* (1960) and *To Abolish Children* (1968), Shapiro would refine and elaborate Auden's anti-modernist position. He would later maintain, for instance, that symbols are hazardous because they make the poet feel all-powerful. He would insist that the step from transforming reality in a poem to trying to alter the world itself is a dangerously short one. (For proof of this, Shapiro declared, one need only look at Yeats, Eliot, and Pound.) "[T]he world of symbols and its attendant dreams of transcendental knowledge," writes Shapiro in an essay called "The Career of the Poem," from *To Abolish Children,* often delude the poet into thinking he can "speak for the race."

What Shapiro gleaned from Auden, even early in his career, was the necessity of placing oneself and one's poetic powers in the service of reality, not the reverse; of being willing to be mastered *by* reality rather than master it. For Shapiro, this meant the virtual elimination of the poetic ego that transmutes objects into a network of symbolic meaning and emotion. What he appropriated from Auden was a more modest conception of the poet than that suggested by the modernists. Shapiro's remark in "The Career of the Poem"—about how the poet is "neither messiah nor explorer but only a man fully alive in spirit and in body to existence itself"—is really nothing more than an embellishment of Auden's well-known remarks in his essay "Writing" (from *The Dyer's Hand*):

> Poetry is not magic [wrote Auden]. In so far as poetry, or any other of the arts, can be said to have an ulterior purpose, it is, by telling the truth, to disenchant and disintoxicate.

"To disenchant and disintoxicate" is certainly the "ulterior purpose" of all of Shapiro's early poetry. In **"University,"** for example, from *Person, Place and Thing*, the poet seeks to expose the prejudices of this particular institution. The poem begins: "To hurt the Negro and avoid the Jew / Is the curriculum." In **"Necropolis,"** also from Shapiro's first book, the poet challenges the idea of death as the great equalizer. The third stanza reads:

> And even in death the poor are thickly herded In intimate congestion under streets and alleys. Look at the standard sculpture, the cheap Synonymous slabs, the machined crosses.

In **"Washington Cathedral,"** also from *Person, Place and Thing*, the poet points out the "fake magnificence" of the nation's capital. Only here, says Shapiro, would Lincoln be "whittled to a fool's colossus."

Shapiro's commitment to the objective world does not always translate into satire or the shedding of illusions. One of Shapiro's best early poems, **"Haircut"** (from *Person, Place and Thing*), deals with the "wonderful nonsense"

> . . . of lotions of Lucky Tiger,
> Of savory soaps and oils of bottle-bright green,
> The gold of liqueurs, the unguents of Newark
> and Niger,
> Powders and balms and waters washing me
> clean . . .
>
> Scissors and comb are mowing my hair into
> neatness,
> Now pruning my ears, now smoothing my
> neck like a plain;
> In the harvest of hair and the chaff of powdery

sweetness
My snow-covered slopes grow dark with the
    wooly rain.

Here, the poet "tells the truth" about what he sees, as Auden advised; this time, however, he musters a considerable amount of linguistic invention for a seemingly trivial facet of modern life that most poets would not be attracted to.

We see the same loving attention to the details of the everyday world in other poems of this period as well— **"Buick," "Drug Store,"** and **"Waitress,"** to name just a few. In **"Auto Wreck"** from ***Person, Place and Thing***, Shapiro handles a grim detail of contemporary life with delicacy and artistry:

Its quick soft silver bell beating, beating,
And down the dark one ruby flare
Pulsing out red light like an artery,
The ambulance at top speed floating down
Past beacons and illuminated clocks
Wings in a heavy curve, dips down,
And brakes speed, entering the crowd.
The doors leap open, emptying light;
Stretchers are laid out, the mangled lifted
And stowed into the little hospital.
Then the bell, breaking the hush, tolls once,
And the ambulance with its terrible cargo
Rocking, slightly rocking, moves away,
As the doors, an afterthought, are closed. . . .

To focus on the mundane without making it "mean" through the use of a symbolic structure is not a recipe for poetic profundity. But then, Shapiro doesn't appear to want to be profound. Insofar as he aspires only to be "fully alive . . . to existence itself," these early poems are eminently successful.

Nonetheless, as the Forties advanced, Shapiro was evidently becoming unhappy with his work. He was beginning to believe that he wasn't letting *enough* reality into his poems. And he was right: there's more to the world, after all, than automobiles, drugstores, and waitresses. There is, for example, the poet himself. Weren't the poet's ordinary thoughts and feelings a part of reality, too, and therefore worthy of being included in poetry that was truly open to "existence itself"? What Shapiro was contemplating didn't involve violating Auden's golden rule and altering the world for the sake of a private meaning. All he wished to do was make the poet's more unexceptional thoughts and perceptions a part of the procession of reality in his verse. How to present these perceptions raised another problem—the limitations of formal metrics. Didn't rhyme and meter alter reality, too? Didn't the things of the world need to be expressed as honestly as possible, without the poet's resorting to any artifice whatsoever?

Shapiro didn't act on these new thoughts right away. But ***Essay on Rime***, the seventy-two-page poem that was published as a book a year after his second book, ***V-Letter*** (1944), contains evidence that he was beginning to explore them. Ostensibly, the book is not so different from ***V-Letter*** or ***Person, Place and Thing***. Though written in the first person, ***Essay on Rime*** is spoken by Shapiro the poet—not Shapiro the man—and is therefore about as impersonal as his earlier verse. And it is composed in the most punctilious blank verse. All the same, Shapiro later called ***Essay on Rime*** his "first anti-intellectual essay," and for good reason. The poem contained warm words for the poetry of Walt Whitman, D. H. Lawrence, and William Carlos Williams—all poets distinctly unlike both Shapiro and Auden in their celebration of feeling (Whitman and Lawrence) and the unobstructed representation of reality (Williams). In the section on Williams, Shapiro writes respectfully of the New Jersey poet's world, in which "vision reigns, [and] nothing is right / Except the visible. The object is the thing, / The means of understanding is eyesight." In a passage near the end of ***Essay on Rime,*** Shapiro wonders where in contemporary literature one can find "the plain / Statement of feeling."

The chief aim of ***Essay on Rime***, however, is to demonstrate how possible it is for a young poet to come to terms with poetry on his own, without recourse to tradition or the academy. (That Shapiro wrote ***Essay on Rime*** while on duty in the Pacific "proved" this hypothesis.) Although his attack on literary tradition—in the form of an appreciation of Lawrence, Whitman, and Williams—makes ***Essay on Rime*** a significant book, Shapiro's ***New & Selected Poems, 1940-1986*** makes no reference to it.

Interestingly, ***Essay on Rime*** was honored by F. O. Matthiessen in a front-page review in *The New York Times Book Review*. Matthiessen, a Marxist who paradoxically championed Eliot and Henry James, addressed himself primarily to Shapiro's mastery of simple language. Concentrating on lines like—

At what point in the history of art
Has such a cleavage between audience
And poet existed? Where before has rime
Relied so heavily on the interpreter,
The analyst and the critic?

—Matthiessen commended Shapiro for "bridging the gap between the poet and the democratic audience of the Nineteen Fifties."

"Recapitulations," the sequence leading off Shapiro's next book, ***Trial of a Poet*** (1947)—dedicated to Matthiessen— exhibits the first significant change in Shapiro's poetry. The sequence of sixteen formal poems is entirely autobiographical. Unfortunately, **"Recapitulations"** seldom rises above the banal. The first poem begins:

I was born downtown on a wintry day
    And under the roof where Poe expired;
Tended by nuns my mother lay
    Dark-haired and beautiful and tired.

Doctors and cousins paid their call,
    The rabbi and my father helped.
A crucifix burned on the wall
    Of the bright room where I was whelped.

Shapiro has omitted **"Recapitulations"** from *New & Selected Poems, 1940-1986*, and for good reason.

The new work in Shapiro's next book, ***Poems 1940-1953*** (1953), contains more changes. In these poems, Shapiro, much in the custom of Lawrence, transcribes his inner thoughts, no matter how dull they may be. **"Going to School,"** for example, begins: "What shall I teach in the vivid afternoon / With the sun warming the blackboard and a slip / Of cloud catching my eye?" In many poems, Shapiro's thoughts focus on failure. "Ego can fail," he asserts in **"Ego,"** while in **"The Tingling Back,"** he frets over "something . . . I said and I should not have said, / I did and must not do."

Other poems in ***Poems 1940-1953*** deal with the guilt that is in Shapiro's case apparently the consequence of this preoccupation with failure. **"Adam and Eve"** is a long, unsuccessful attempt to explore the origins of this guilt. In **"F.O. Matthiessen: An Anniversary,"** Shapiro asks if he is to blame for Matthiessen's suicide leap from a hotel window:

> . . . What mob did Matthiessen
> Hear chanting in rhythm, and what uniforms
> Tried to retrieve him to the world of men?
> What was he saying in his heavy fall
> Through space, so broken by the hand of stone?
> What word was that stopped like a telephone
> Torn with its nervous wire from the wall?
> Does not the condemned man raise his voice
>   to call
> His phrase of justice down the empty hall?
>
> And who betrayed him finally? Was it I?
> Some poet who turned his praises to blame,
> Some historian of the parlor game
> Of war? Or the easy capture of the schloss
> By Slavs? The Americanization of the spy?
> The death of a friend? Was there no further
>   loss? . . .

Shapiro rises to the occasion with some memorable language which redeems the arbitrary personal intrusion. Regrettably, **"F. O. Matthiessen"** has been excluded from *New & Selected Poems, 1940-1986*.

"Adam and Eve," along with **"Israel"** and **"Six Religious Lyrics"**—all from ***Poems 1940-1953***—offer us a clue to the next phase of Shapiro's poetic career: the discovery of his Jewish identity. This is a strange juncture in Karl Shapiro's career. For religious affiliation would appear to be the last thing a poet like Shapiro, who has been struggling to establish some sense of individuality in his poetry, would want. Actually, **"Israel"** depicts the pitfalls of uniting dogma and individuality. Like most of the poems he was writing during this period, **"Israel"** is a showcase for Shapiro's personal feelings. But in the poem the emotions he presents are the fruit of his new identification with Judaism. He writes, for example, about how "When I think of the liberation of Palestine . . . My heart leaps forward like a hungry dog," and "When I think of the battle of Zion . . . My blood beats like a bird against a wall," and so on. The "personal" feelings Shapiro indulges in here are therefore hardly the expression of his individuality. They are rather the result of the poet's immersing himself—which is to say, losing himself—in an external cause.

Perhaps Shapiro comprehends the contradiction between the pursuit of individuality and the capitulation to religion. In what appears to be an attempt to counterbalance the religious element in **"Israel,"** Shapiro injects himself everywhere in the poem. In the first eighteen lines of **"Israel,"** for example, the words "I" and "my" appear nineteen times.

But for Shapiro there is another obstacle to accommodating the Jewish outlook. For the student of Auden who has made a career lending credence only to what impinges on his senses, the belief in a transcendent reality would appear to be problematic indeed. In the Introduction to ***Poems of a Jew*** (1958), Shapiro's next book, the poet tries to resolve this difficulty by suggesting how similar are his poetic perspective and the perspective of the Jew. He proclaims that the Jew is "absolutely committed to the world."

The truth is, Shapiro's Jewish poems really have little to do with a deity. Most deal with Shapiro's secular experiences as a Jew in America. They are about, that is, feeling shut out, special, and, above all, guilty. To the extent that **"The First Time"**—a poem about a seventeen-year-old's encounter with a prostitute—succeeds, it is because it deals with prejudices and stereotypes, not religious belief. The last two stanzas read:

> The girl is sitting with her back to him;
> She wears a black thing and she rakes her hair,
> Hauling her round face upward like moonrise;
> She is younger than he, her angled arms are
>   slim
> And like a country girl her feet are bare.
> She watches him behind her with old eyes,
>
> Transfixing him in space like some grotesque,
> Far, far from her where he is still alone
> And being here is more and more untrue.
> Then she turns round, as one turns at a desk,
> And looks at him, too naked and too soon,
> And almost gently asks: *Are you a Jew?*

The confusion evident in ***Poems of a Jew*** may have contributed to the frustrated, angry tone of Shapiro's next book. *In Defense of Ignorance* (1960) is a collection of literary essays that do not so much present the poet's beliefs as ram them down the reader's throat. The book, the epigraph of which is *"everything we are taught is false"* (Shapiro's emphasis), seeks, as the author writes in the preface, to break the

> dictatorship of intellectual "modernism," the sanctimonious ministry of "the Tradition," the ugly programmatic quality of twentieth-century criticism

[which] have maimed our poetry and turned it into a monstrosity of literature.

Actually, there is little sustained argument in the book. (Argument, after all, is something taught in school.) What we are offered instead is a flood of opinions that may have been vaguely heretical at the time. Lawrence and Whitman, Shapiro informs us, exhibit the "deepest concern for mankind" in their poetry. Dylan Thomas is admired, meanwhile, for his *"unintellectualism"* (again, Shapiro's emphasis). Henry Miller is declared, in the title of the piece on him, "Our Greatest Living Author." (Wisely, Shapiro changed the title of the Miller article to "The Greatest Living Patagonian" when he reprinted it in the 1975 book *The Poetry Wreck: Selected Essays 1950-1970*. Unwisely, he did not remove the large chunks of Miller's execrable prose from the reprinted essay.) And Lawrence, we are told, "committed the horrible sin of expressing his own feelings in poetry."

As promised in the preface, the modernists are criticized at length. Little of this criticism, however, deals with the innate qualities of the poetry. What Shapiro focuses on instead is the *effect* modern poetry has had on twentieth-century society. Thus we are told how modern poetry, as Shapiro writes in the Yeats essay, has become, through its use of myth and the cultural past, *"a surrogate for religion."* Shapiro's real bête noire here is the historical, political, and cultural pronouncements that many of the modernists made. Yeats, Shapiro tells us, made a "sociological ass" of himself in his historical writings. Eliot and Pound became purveyors of "sociological opinion," not to mention anti-Semites and fascist apologists to boot. (One wonders why there isn't a word about Williams's anti-Semitism in the essay on him in *In Defense of Ignorance*.) The truth is, Shapiro doesn't systematically criticize the poetry of Yeats and Eliot very much at all in *In Defense of Ignorance*. He's so busy discussing their prose and politics, and the professors who've made them into an industry (as well as into a *"surrogate for religion"*), that he never has time to come to terms with the poetry.

The essay on Auden in *In Defense of Ignorance* is surprisingly positive, given how removed Shapiro was by now from Auden's impersonal aesthetic. But there is still one Audenesque idea that Shapiro follows in *In Defense of Ignorance*, and will continue to follow. This is the belief, expressed in Shapiro's essay entitled "The Great Artificer," that "[e]very artist by instinct should fight against the principle of multiplicity of meaning."

In every way but this, then, Shapiro's next book, *The Bourgeois Poet* (1964), was a repudiation of his master. Gone are rhyme and meter and the loving attention to the world. The prose "poems" that make up the book have room for everything under the sun. (As Shapiro admitted later, their "form" was governed by the typewriter's margins.) *The Bourgeois Poet*, which owes much to Allen Ginsberg and the Beats, is the realization of Shapiro's desire to include in his poetry every raw detail he sees, hears, or feels. We can be thankful that the following section, appropriately entitled **"Anti-Poem,"** has not been included in **New & Selected Poems, 1940-1986**:

Orchards hang in the newspaper of sky. It's snowing names and addresses over the world, O lovely splash!

In dry percussion, hammers of prosperity practice against the too-green corn. The wheat field narrows, then disappears, leaving a memory of dry wind-waves. Who eats dry wheat but boys, wheat the hue of the backs of eighteen-century books. Children spring from the doors where there are no trees. Roofer up there, it's been a good day.

In another section, also omitted from the new book, the aspect of "reality" granted unconditional admission into the "poem" is Shapiro's internal musings on one of his new aesthetic beliefs:

Lower the standard: that's my motto. Somebody is always putting the food out of reach. We're tired of falling off ladders. Who says a child can't paint? A pro is somebody who does it for money. Lower the standards. Let's all play poetry. Down with ideals, flags, convention buttons, morals, the scrambled eggs on the admiral's hat. I'm talking sense. Lower the standards. Sabotage the stylistic approach. Let weeds grow in the subdivision. Putty up the incisions in the library facade, those names that frighten grade-school teachers, those names whose U's are cut like V's. Burn the *Synopticon* and *The Harvard Classics*. Lower the standard on classics, battleships, Russian ballet, national anthems (but they're low enough). Break through to the bottom. . . .

If Shapiro is attempting to be ironic here, his irony is lost on me, since in every conceivable way ***The Bourgeois Poet*** tries, and succeeds, in "lower[ing] the standard" in poetry. No doubt the book would have perplexed Auden. But Shapiro's relinquishment of his intellect to the thrust of reality (be it the reality of the world or the reality of his passing thoughts) is arguably the logical fulfillment of Auden's aesthetic of a poetry open to the world.

To Abolish Children (1968), the book of essays that followed ***The Bourgeois Poet***, was primarily Shapiro's attempt to distance himself from the new counterculture. Nothing, of course, could have been more ironic, since Shapiro was responsible for providing the Movement with two of its major literary ornaments. Yet in the title essay of this book Shapiro condemns the "intellectual infantilism" of the radicals, the "patent absurdity" of the open university, and the "largely hypocritical" dissent on the Vietnam War. "The Underground,'" Shapiro asserts, "did not raise its voice against the Russian suppression of Hungary." These sensible observations precede by about fifty pages the utterly nonsensical essay—entitled "A Defense of Bad Poetry"—in which Shapiro argues for a poetry that will "subvert the standards" and "will not please."

Shapiro's last few books of poetry are as debilitated as *To Abolish Children* is confused. In **White-Haired Lover**

(1968), Shapiro returns to rhyme and meter for a series of rather cloying sonnets addressed to his lover. (None is in *New & Selected Poems, 1940-1986*.) In **"I Swore to Stab the Sonnet,"** the poet writes about how his lover helped him gain his formal—and psychological—equilibrium after he had temporarily lost his bearings. If only the poetic result was better:

> I swore to stab the sonnet with my pen,
> Squash the black widow in a grandstand play
> By gunning down the sonnet form—and then
> I heard you quote my schoolboy love Millay.
> I went to find out what she used to say
> About her tribulations and her men
> And loved her poetry though I now am gray
> And found out love of love poems once again.
> Now I'm the one that's stabbed—son of a bitch!
> With my own poisoned ballpoint pen of love
> And write in *sonnet* form to make my *pitch,*
> Words I no longer know the meaning of
> If I could write one honest sentence now
> I'd say I love you but I don't know how.

Adult Bookstore (1976), Shapiro's most recent collection of all new poems, is even more of a repudiation of *The Bourgeois Poet*. *Adult Bookstore* is the least "personal" of all of Shapiro's post-Fifties books. It is therefore very reminiscent of *Person, Place and Thing* and *V-Letter*. The titles alone indicate that Shapiro is once again intent on ferreting out the representative features of the postwar American landscape: **"Garage Sale," "Girls Working in Banks," "The Humanities Building,"** and, of course, the title poem. In **"The Humanities Building,"** Shapiro "tells the truth" about one of the more lamentable aspects of our country. The result is a poem that Auden himself probably would have liked:

> All the bad Bauhaus comes to a head
> In this gray slab, this domino, this plinth
> Standing among the olives or the old oak
>   trees,
> As the case may be, and whatever the
>   clime.
> No bells, no murals, no gargoyles,
> But rearing like a fort with slits of eyes
> Suspicious in the aggregate, its tons
> Of concrete, glaciers of no known color,
> Gaze down upon us. Saint Thomas More,
> Behold the Humanities Building! . . .

But nothing offers solider proof that Shapiro has come full circle poetically than one of the four new poems in *New & Selected Poems, 1940-1986*. **"At Auden's Grave"** relates the poet's journey to the place where his master, as Shapiro writes, "lies sleeping in a vale. . . ." Near the end of the poem, the poet, addressing Auden, says that he has come "to bless this plot where you are lain, / Poet who made poetry whole again."

As moving as Shapiro's return to his master is, however, **"At Auden's Grave"** has none of the sheer dazzle of **"Buick," "Drug Store,"** or **"Haircut."** Shapiro himself seems to be aware of the diminishment of his poetic powers. In **"Grant's Tomb Revisited,"** one of the handful of new poems in *Love & War*, a new-and-selected that came out in 1984, he writes: "We've all seen better days, / Hiram Ulysses."

It would be easy to attribute the mediocre level of Shapiro's recent work to the declining powers of an aging poet. But I doubt that age has much to do with this. What has stymied Shapiro in the last decade of his life is precisely what has stymied him, to one degree or another, throughout his career: the legacy of W.H. Auden. Early on, Shapiro was well-versed in the dangers of the modernist aesthetic, namely, its tendency to make the poet think he can change the world. But Shapiro all but closed his eyes to the equally real dangers of Auden's poetic beliefs. For there is a price to be paid for the exclusive concentration on the world of reality, and for the suppression of the transforming poetic ego. It is a price that is paid in the quality of one's work. Shapiro's poetry is simply too dependent on the more transient aspects of the world. Placing himself at the mercy of reality may have helped Shapiro avoid trying to "speak for the race." But in refusing to make the world *mean* for *him*, he permitted himself to be subsumed constantly by his material. As a result, we have no strong sense of Shapiro's poetic identity running through his oeuvre.

Is Shapiro aware of this? Perhaps. The massive cuts he has made in compiling *New & Selected Poems, 1940-1986* would seem to indicate that all he wishes to preserve is the briefest sketch of his long career. But if this is the reason for the slightness of the new book, Shapiro may have gone too far. Although one can agree with his radical reduction of *The Bourgeois Poet* and the total rejection of *White-Haired Lover*, it is hard to agree with all of Shapiro's exclusions. The truth is, there is still a *Collected Poems* of Karl Shapiro to be done. Such a book would include **"F.O. Matthiessen: An Anniversary,"** part of *Essay on Rime*, and more generous selections from *V-Letter* and *Trial of a Poet*.

In leaving the task of putting together an authentic *Collected Poems* to posterity, Shapiro again mimics his master Auden, whose own *Collected Poems* was scarred by numerous changes and omissions. But then it was to be expected that Karl Shapiro would near the end of his career be as riddled by doubt as Auden was at the end of his.

Ralph Saverse (review date April-May 1994)

SOURCE: "The Loam of the Poem," in *American Book Review*, Vol. 16, No. 1, April-May 1994, p. 20.

[*In the following review, Saverse provides a negative assessment of the poems comprising* The Old Horsefly.]

In an essay on Wordsworth, Matthew Arnold writes, "Wordsworth was a homely man, and himself would certainly never have thought of talking of glory as that which, after all, has the best chance of not being altogether vanity. Yet we may well allow that few things are less vain than *real* glory." Karl Shapiro's latest book of poems [*The Old Horsefly*] is marred by the established poet's confusion of ego and work. What is missing is the "real glory" of excellent poems; what is present, the spectacle of an old artist too strongly affirming—and therefore doubting—his own poetic significance. The book is replete with self-conscious diatribes against his competitors, diatribes whose humor, if they have any humor at all, cannot mask the poet's caballing. The more explicit they are, the more desperate they seem. Take, for example, this one against Lowell, entitled simply **"Robert Lowell"**:

> One should not stink of poetry, said Auden.
> Lowell stank of it.
> Lowell wrote two respectable poems,
> The skunk and (two) the parking lot.
> That's all, folks. But when he was crucified
> On the front of *Time* (the magazine I mean)
> The professoriat drooled in his footsteps
> Behind his jackboots. Just what the academy
>   ordered,
> A bona-fide, non-Jew, New England name,
> Preppy-Harvard, all the kosher credentials. . . .

Coming shortly after a poem entitled **"On Being Yanked from a Favorite Anthology"** and another entitled **"The Jewish Problem,"** this poem—and, by extension, the book—must be read finally as an explanation of Shapiro's own falling out of favor. In short, as a defense of himself. Shapiro offers, and offers too insistently, an alternative to the idea that over the years his poems have simply gotten worse—or, what is just as plausible, that literary favor is bestowed not so much conspiratorily as capriciously and thus should not be something the genuine artist cares very much about.

Admittedly, Shapiro is in a strange position. Having won the Pulitzer Prize for poetry in 1945 at the age of thirty-two, he has lived long enough to witness his own literary demise: his books are no longer being published by major houses; he's being yanked from poetry anthologies; and people—readers and poets alike—actually believe he's dead (his most recent book of prose is entitled *Reports of My Death,* in obvious allusion to Twain's famous remark). This demise clearly bothers him. What begins wittily, even self-deprecatingly in **"On Being Yanked from a Favorite Anthology"** ends quite scathingly:

> Fame gave me a wrench and I cried *Ouch!*
> *That hurt!* who used to use a silky touch,
> Called me illustrious, caressed my name,
> Made me an indispensable. Erato,
> Patroness, how you fawned on me,
> (Gave me the creeps sometimes) held me so high,
> Incised me in the canon. I was fixed,
> Part of the permanent collection, brightest star
> In my constellation of five. Until
> Some text-louse, pilpulistic Joycean cockroach,
> Some antisemitic Jew reached for his rag
> And zilched me out. Bitch-goddess!
> Is this what we deserve
> Who put you on the American map, you whore!

The "we" in the penultimate line is particularly disturbing. It is meant to signify the liberal (often Jewish) left, which consistently lobbied for a literary world that was more inclusive of women and minorities, but it comes across as signifying the conservative (largely male) poetic establishment, which cannot possibly accept its loss of power and privilege. The idea that he has been betrayed is either ludicrous or self-serving (or both). That Robert Lowell and the other white males of Shapiro's generation have retained their places in the canon seems to have more to do with their work than with their not being Jewish. Understandably, though quite unfortunately, Shapiro comprehends these difficult canonical issues in exclusively personal and embittered terms.

Poetry is an odd place to write criticism—explicit criticism. Matthew Arnold talks of poetry as "a criticism of life." The contemporary poet and critic F. D. Reeve suggests much the same thing in *The White Monk* but is at once more specific and more general than Arnold: "The imagination," he writes, "wants a system made by words, colors, sounds or mathematical symbols within which to confront the alternatives behind experience." In *The Hazard of Modern Poetry* Eric Heller puts it still another way: poetry "renders *actual* ever new sectors of the apparently inexhaustible field of *potential* experience." In this way the excellent poem not only points to but *is* the dreamed-of "alternative." Its strength—in fact, its *life*—derives from its indirection, its implicit maneuvering. On at least one level Shapiro would seem to agree with this conception of poetry. In a very odd interview at the end of the book, he responds to a question on this subject by William Packard (the interview is presented as verse, and as such it represents not even half the already limited accomplishment of the much earlier *Essay on Rhyme*):

> Q:
> Your poems are full of social assessment,
> Value judgements [sic]. Don't Ovid poets
> Perform a social function?
>
> A:
> One hopes opinion won't intrude
> Or at least not dominate. At least I pray
> Stupid opinion won't steal the show.
> Let valuation bury itself
> Deep in the loam of the poem.

Turned against him, Shapiro's own words offer the most devastating critique of his most recent work. Again and again "stupid opinion" steals the show. Valuation abounds; there is little if any "loam" for it to bury itself in. A little later in the interview Shapiro remarks, "Poetry of politics is the lowest form, / Lower than doggerel." And yet Shapiro explicitly engages in perhaps the worst kind of politics: literary politics. If poets cannot be above such a thing, then at the very least their poems ought to be.

Even Shapiro's more traditional, apolitical poems are largely unsuccessful. **"The Smokers,"** whose opening lines are "We are the smokers, we are diminishing. / Everywhere there are warnings and death-threats, / Signs with red sickles glaring down on us" verges on the insipid. The poem **"Kleenex"** is really no better than an average MFA "object" exercise. **"The Old Horsefly,"** the book's title poem, comes off as a parody of a much earlier poem entitled **"The Fly,"** which appeared in Shapiro's first book. Like many readers, I prefer the Shapiro of the early books. Poems such as **"Terminal," "Conscription Camp," "Troop Train,"** and **"F.O. Matthiessen: An Anniversary"** are deeply satisfying. The closest he comes to this level of achievement in the volume under consideration is in a small poem entitled **"Future Present."** Reminiscing about "the luxury liners in Manhattan," which "appeared piecemeal in segments at the end of east-west streets" and which "would take a full hour to go past, / as if in no hurry to pass into history," the poet concludes,

> But look there at the top pane of the
>   window!
> A burnished skyliner elegantly
>   moving north,
> as proud as leviathan above the
>   suffering Hudson,
> past the unfinished cathedral, over
> Grant's tomb,
> into the blue-gray morning of the
> future-present.

The "future-present" is upon us. All a poet can do is hope (and work) to write good poems. What will happen to them is the critic's guess.

M. L. Rosenthal (essay date 1998)

SOURCE: An introduction to *The Wild Card: Selected Poems, Early and Late,* by Karl Shapiro, edited by Stanley Kunitz and David Ignatow, University of Illinois Press, 1988, pp. xix-xxiii.

[*In the following essay, Rosenthal surveys the defining characteristics of Shapiro's poetry.*]

"Shapiro Is All Right!" Thus exclaimed the title of a review, years ago, of one of Karl Shapiro's books in the *New York Times Book Review.* The reviewer was William Carlos Williams, Shapiro's senior by three decades and our best-loved avant-garde model since the late 1920s. It was a bit of a surprise. The inventor of the "variable foot," experimenter *par excellence* in search of a poetry rooted in American idiom and speech-rhythms, was praising Shapiro, who had gained his early fame working in conventional forms, with debts to Auden and other British figures. The present collection shows why the younger poet won the Old Master's shout of approval.

Shapiro's rapid leap into recognition, marked by a Pulitzer award, the poetry consultantship at the Library of Congress, the editorship of *Poetry: A Magazine of Verse,* and university professorships, had seemed to take him far from Williams's embattled world. But if we look back at the pieces in his early collection ***Person, Place, and Thing***

(1942), we can see implicit affinities—continuities of attitude and sensibility from the two preceding decades—after all.

The particular American historical moment, in the immediate wake of the relatively Left-tending, socially critical Depression era, was also one of mobilization against the Axis powers and their ideology. Shapiro himself, serving with the army in the South Pacific when his book came out, was hardly a gung-ho flagwaver. His poem **"Conscription Camp,"** set in Virginia, swings a double saber-slash of disgust against both the South's history and any sort of glib patriotism:

> You manufacture history like jute—
> Labor is cheap, Virginia, for high deeds,
> But in your British dream of reputation
> The black man is your conscience and your cost.
> The sunrise gun rasps in the throat of heaven;
> The lungs of dawn are heavy and corrupt;
> We hawk and spit; our flag walks through the air
> Breathing hysteria thickly in each face.

Other pieces in ***Person, Place, and Thing*** reveal an anarcho-bohemian edge akin to Williams's but more emphatic in their antiracist and radical sympathies: attitudes that many young American Jews of Shapiro's generation shared with him. (The amusing, self-ironic sixth poem of his autobiographical sequence **"Recapitulations,"** in his 1947 volume ***Trial of a Poet***, describes his younger days when, as he has written, he "raved like a scarlet banner.") He had attended the University of Virginia, and his poem **"University"** begins, memorably: "To hurt the Negro and avoid the Jew / Is the curriculum."

Another early poem, **"Death of Emma Goldman,"** described that passionate anarchist, "dark conscience of the family" (her own and humanity's), with gentle appreciation. At the same time, it reviled the people who, after her death, called her immoral because she never married her lover, Alexander Berkman:

> Triumphant at the final breath,
>   Their senile God, their cops,
> All the authorities and friends pro tem
> Passing her pillow, keeping her concerned.
> But the cowardly obit was already written:
> Morning would know she was a common slut.

Given the general ignorance, including that of most intellectuals, about Emma Goldman or anarchism, such poetry was hardly what won Shapiro his first success. Other reasons were far more compelling. For one thing, he was our first young American to emerge as a serious poet of World War II. For another, he had the splendid knack of being able to project a heightened vision of commonplace objects and circumstances. Many of his "civilian" poems are brilliant closeups of this sort. One example is **"The Dome of Sunday,"** which points its lens—perhaps unfairly but "with focus sharp as Flemish-painted face / In film of varnish brightly fixed"—on the poet's prosperous Baltimore neighbors as hopelessly vulgar and self-centered.

Others include **"Buick,"** a witty, sexy, very American love song to a car, and the swift-moving, terrified **"Auto Wreck."** In the military context, the candidly gloomy picture of young, newly enlisted soldiers (including the poet) in **"Conscription Camp"** is similarly precise and evocative:

> Through the long school of day, absent in heart,
> Distant in every thought but self we tread,
> Wheeling in blocks like large expensive toys
> That never understand except through fun.
>
>
> To steal aside as aimlessly as curs
> Is our desire; to stare at corporals
> As sceptically as boys; not to believe
> The misty-eyed letter and the cheap snapshot.

Shapiro's first volume showed he could also write lyrical pieces whose feeling, despite their subtleties, had the direct appeal of folksongs. This gift has been a winning wild card for him, from the beginning to the more recent poems at the close of this collection. One moving early instance, expressing the pang of separation from home and from one's beloved in wartime, is his poem **"Nostalgia."** It begins:

> My soul stands at the window of my room,
>   And I ten thousand miles away;
> My days are filled with Ocean's sound of doom,
>   Salt and cloud and the bitter spray.
> *Let the wind blow, for many a man shall die.*
>
> My selfish youth, my books with gilded edge,
>   Knowledge and all gaze down the street;
> The potted plants along the window ledge
>   Gaze down with selfish lives and sweet.
> *Let the wind blow, for many a man shall die.*
>
> My night is now her day, my day her night,
>   So I lie down, and so I rise;
> The sun burns close, the star is losing height,
>   The clock is hunted down the skies.
> *Let the wind blow, for many a man shall die.*

Not to labor the point, the music of pure lyricism makes a number of Shapiro's poems unforgettable, whether in a psychologically demanding piece like **"The Figurehead"** (about coping with a paralytic friend's "cold torture" as he lies imprisoned "on the treacherous shoals of his bed"); or in a piercing war poem like **"Full Moon: New Guinea"** (a Shakespearean sonnet about waiting in fear for the bombers to strike on a beautiful moonlit night); or in a tender, troubled gesture of understanding like **"Mongolian Idiot."**

Shapiro's celebration of the inevitable contradictions in our moral natures, his cultivation of what we might call a principled ambivalence, reaches its climax in his 1964 sequence *The Bourgeois Poet*. It is there, too, that Shapiro, a genuine virtuoso of conventional metrics, repudiates

what he calls "the cosmetology of font and rule, meters laid on like fingernail enamel." "Why," he asks—

> Why the attractive packaging of stanza? Those cartons so pretty, shall I open them up? Why the un-American activity of the sonnet? Why must grown people listen to rhyme? How much longer the polite applause, the tickle in the throat?

The Bourgeois Poet, made up mainly of prose poems, provides the fullest example of Shapiro's shifted poetic values. To some extent it is a series of notebook entries whose essential rhythm is a kind of oracular musing that can rise to a lyrical pitch. Baudelaire may well be the major model for Shapiro in this form. But at times we hear reminiscences of a whole range of free inventors from Whitman through Williams, Fearing, and the Beats. The sound-patterns—shorter units, many single lines, and chantlike parallelism—echo them, and so does the recurrent mockery of fixed attitudes. But Shapiro's idiosyncratic humor and phrasing—and, even more, his introspective obsession with the ambivalence and unresolvable terror life forces upon us—keep the ultimate effect underivatively his own. Thus, section 34 in the original text begins in a series of laughingly depreciative and paradoxical self-definitions:

> I am an atheist who says his prayers.
>
> I am an anarchist, and a full professor at that. I
>   take the loyalty oath.
>
> I am a deviate. I fondle and contribute, backscuttle
>   and brown, father of three.

But later it opens itself to more mordant, fear-ridden utterances:

> My century, take savagery to your heart. Take
>   wooden idols, walk them through the streets.
>   Bow down to Science.
>
> My century that boils history to a pulp for
>   newspaper, my century of the million-dollar
>   portrait, century of the decipherment of
>   Linear B and the old scrolls, century of the
>   dream of penultimate man (he wanders among the
>   abandoned skyscrapers of Kansas; he has already
>   forgotten language), century of the turning-point
>   of time, the human wolf pack and the killing
>   light.

To re-read Shapiro's work in the unfolding, expanding scroll of his entire career is to see its manysidedness as never before. His is the essential, relentlessly self-scrutinizing modern Jewish sensibility. He was hard on his own people in **"The Dome of Sunday"** and yet expressed in **"Israel"** his giddy joy at the founding of the Jewish state—*and yet,* for the most part, shares the secular, antidogmatic mentality that permeates the leading thought of our era, when, indeed, "The best lack all conviction, while the worst / Are full of passionate intensity." (The lines are of course Yeats's, whom Shapiro once parodied, cleverly and affectionately, in his poem **"Going to School."** What they imply is very much what Shapiro meant in the passage about "my century" quoted in the preceding paragraph.)

And more intimately, he is also a poet who deals with desolation as well as joy in love and marriage, and who would be as toughminded as he often claims to be if only his humanity did not stand in the way. He may have begun his exuberantly ugly poem **"The Fly"** with the apostrophe "O hideous little bat, the size of snot." But that masterpiece of revulsion is at least counterbalanced by the concluding sonnet of a little group called **"The Interlude,"** which in its way sums up the pathetic contradictions poets must confront and perhaps, if possible, even resolve:

> Writing, I crushed an insect with my nail
> And thought nothing at all. A bit of wing
> Caught my eye then, a gossamer so frail
>
> And exquisite, I saw in it a thing
> That scorned the grossness of the thing I wrote.
> It hung upon my finger like a sting.
>
> A leg I noticed next, fine as a mote,
> "And on this frail eyelash he walked," I said,
> "And climbed and walked like any mountain-goat."
>
> And in this mood I sought the little head,
> But it was lost; then in my heart a fear
> Cried out, "A life—why beautiful, why dead!"
>
> It was a mite that held itself most dear,
> So small I could have drowned it with a tear.

FURTHER READING

Criticism

Engles, Tim. "Shapiro's 'The Fly.'" The Explicator 55, No. 1 (Fall 1996): 41-3.
Engles maintains: "Although a casual reader of the poem might consider it little more than a humorously inflated portrayal of the battles between flies and

humans, a closer look reveals an intricate example of the steps Shapiro lays out in his conception of poetic vision."

Gerber, Philip L., ed. "Trying to Present America: A Conversation with Karl Shapiro." Southern Humanities Review XV, No. 3 (Summer 1981): 193-208.
Discusses Shapiro's role as poet, influences on his work, and his poetic development.

O'Connor, William Van. "Karl Shapiro: The Development of a Talent." College English 10, No. 1 (October 1948): 71-77
Asserts that "in Shapiro one might see a poet who had quickly diagnosed the stylistic excesses and aberrations, consequences of the neuroticism of certain of the "exiles"; and yet he had recognized the shift in sensibility and attitudes reflected in the new style to be prerequisite to looking at the world through modern eyes."

Reino, Joseph. Karl Shapiro. Boston: Twayne Publishers, 1981, 194 p.
Full-length critical study of Shapiro's work.

Schott, Webster. "Leaves of Glass." The Nation 199, No. 4 (August 1964): 74-6.
Positive assessment of The Bourgeois Poet.

Shapiro, Karl. "Creative Glut." Poetry CXXXV, No. 1 (October 1979):36-50.
Elucidates the poet's views on modern poetry.

Southworth, James G. "The Poetry of Karl Shapiro." The English Journal LI, No. 3 (March 1962): 159-66.
Contends that too much critical attention has been paid to Shapiros early work, and urges a reassessment of the poet's entire oeuvre.

Spencer, Theodore. "The Craft of Poetry." The Saturday Review of Literature 28, No. 47 (24 November 1945): 8-9, 34-5.
Negative review of An Essay on Rime.

Slotkin, Richard. "The Contextual Symbol: Karl Shapiro's Image of 'The Jew.'" American Quarterly XVIII, No. 2 (Summer 1966): 220-26.
Explores Shapiro's treatment of Jewish themes and imagery in his poetry.

Additional coverage of Shapiro's life and career is contained in the following sources published by The Gale Group:*Contemporary Literary Criticism*, Vols. 4, 8, 15, 53; *Contemporary Authors*, Vol. 1-4R; *Contemporary Authors Autobiography Series*, Vol. 6; *Contemporary Authors New Revision Series*, Vols. 1, 33, 36, 66; *Dictionary of Literary Biography*, Vol. 4; *Major 20th-Century Authors*, Vol. 1.

John Skelton
1463-1529

English poet, dramatist, and translator.

INTRODUCTION

Skelton is considered the one of the most important English poets of his time. An idiosyncratic, influential figure, he was a prolific translator and the author of political satire and controversial, bawdy poems. Today he is best known for his use of innovative metric style called "Skeltonic;" this meter has been utilized by a number of twentieth century poets, including Robert Graves, John Crowe Ransom, W. H. Auden, and Edith Sitwell.

Biographical Information

Little is known for certain about Skelton's life. Suppositions about his biography, when not disputed by scholars, are often supported with caution. Some scholars believe the poet was born in Yorkshire, in the north of England; others contend that he was born in East Anglia, in the town of Diss, where he would later serve as a parish priest. A poetic allusion to his own horoscope may date his birth in 1463. He studied at Cambridge and then served as poet and resident scholar for the Howards, a powerful Catholic family in the north of England. In the 1490s he was one of a few poets chosen to serve King Henry VII. Discharged from these duties in 1502, Skelton secured a position as parish priest in the town of Diss.

King Henry VIII ascended to the throne in 1509, and by 1513 Skelton had become his court poet and rhetorician. During this period, Skelton began a long battle with Thomas Cardinal Wolsey—a prelate who amassed a considerable amount of political power both within the Catholic Church and inside the court of Henry VIII. In 1516, fearing reprisal from Wolsey and his faction, Skelton sought sanctuary from the Abbot of Westminster Abbey. Protected by the church, he continued to attack Wolsey, writing *Speke, Parrot; Collyn Clout;* and *Why Come Ye Not to Court?* In 1523 he published an overview of his poetic career, called *The Garlande of Laurell,* with verses that some scholars interpret as an attempt to make peace with Wolsey. If these verses did represent a peace overture, it was not a successful one; Skelton remained in Westminster until his death on June 21, 1529. Records indicate that he was buried in Saint Margaret's Church in Westminster, though no grave markings survive.

Major Works

Skelton wrote several political, satirical poems that have garnered attention by critics and historians, in particular his thinly-veiled attacks on Cardinal Wolsey. *Ware the Hauke* concerns a rogue priest who locks himself in a church to train his hawk. The predatory bird kills two pigeons, drips blood on the Host and the chalice, and defecates on the altar. *Speke, Parrot* is another satire that also involves a bird. In this case, the bird is a demonic, polyglot parrot that compares Wolsey with several biblical embodiments of evil. The central character of *Collyn Clout* attacks the government of the English Catholic Church under Wolsey. Besides his political verse, Skelton is best known for *Phyllyp Sparowe,* a poem about a girl commemorating the death of her pet bird. She is joined by the rector of her church, and the verses combine traditional liturgical language and images with an undertone that some commentators have found erotic.

Critical Reception

In the seventeenth century, Skelton's verse was dismissed by many well-known scholars of the day as scurrilous and superficial. This opinion prevailed, and as a result, he was largely neglected by critics throughout the eighteenth and nineteenth centuries. In the twentieth century, commentators began to reassess his influence and place in the English poetic tradition. Many commentators debate his relationship to medieval traditions represented by Chaucer and the English Renaissance. Others discuss his influential poetic style, now called "Skeltonic," which features a short meter of two or three stresses. Most critics note his idiosyncrasies, his place in English literary history, and his innovations to the poetic form.

PRINCIPAL WORKS

Poetry

The Bouge of Court circa 1499
Ware the Hauke circa 1504-12
Phyllyp Sparowe 1508
A Ballade of the Scottisshe Kynge 1513
The Tunning of Elinor Rumming circa 1521
Speke, Parrot 1521
Collyn Clout 1522
Why Come Ye Nat to Courte? 1522
The Garlande of Laurell 1523
Divers Balettys and Dyties Solacyous 1528

Other Major Works

Magnificence (drama) 1516

CRITICISM

W. H. Auden (essay date 1935)

SOURCE: "John Skelton," in *Prose and Travel Books in Prose and Verse, Volume I: 1926-1938*, edited by Edward Mendelson, Princeton University Press, 1996, pp. 82-93.

[*In the following influential essay, originally published in 1935, Auden provides a reassessment of Skelton's poetic accomplishments.*]

To write an essay on a poet who has no biography, no message, philosophical or moral, who has neither created characters, nor expressed critical ideas about the literary art, who was comparatively uninfluenced by his predecessors, and who exerted no influence upon his successors, is not easy. Skelton's work offers no convenient critical pegs. Until Mr Robert Graves drew attention to his work some years ago, he was virtually unknown outside University-honour students, and even now, though there have been two editions, in the last ten years, those of Mr Hughes and Mr Henderson, it is doubtful whether the number of his readers has very substantially increased. One has only to compare him with another modern discovery, Hopkins, to realise that he has remained a stock literary event rather than a vital influence.

My own interest dates from the day I heard a friend at Oxford, who had just bought the first Hughes edition, make two quotations:

> Also the mad coot
> With bald face to toot;

and

> Till Euphrates that flood driveth me into Ind,

and though I should not claim my own case as typical, yet I doubt if those to whom these lines make no appeal are likely to admire Skelton.

Though little that is authentic is known of Skelton's life, a fairly definite portrait emerges from his work: a conservative cleric with a stray sense of humour, devoted to the organisation to which he belonged and to the cultural tradition it represented, but critical of its abuses, possibly a scholar, but certainly neither an academic-dried boy or a fastidious highbrow; no more unprejudiced or well-informed about affairs outside his own province than the average modern reader of the newspapers, but shrewd enough within it, well read in the conventional good authors of his time, but by temperament more attracted to more popular and less respectable literature, a countryman in sensibility, not particularly vain, but liking to hold the floor, fond of feminine society, and with a quick and hostile eye for *pompositas* in all its forms.

Born in 1460, he probably took his degree at Cambridge in 1484, and was awarded a laureate degree by Cambridge, Oxford, and Louvain, which I suppose did not mean much more then than winning an essay prize or the Newdigate would to-day, became tutor to the future Henry VIII, was sufficiently well known socially to be mentioned by Erasmus and Caxton; took orders at the age of thirty-eight, became Rector of Diss, his probable birthplace, about 1500; began an open attack on Wolsey in 1519, and died in sanctuary at Westminster in 1529. Thus he was born just before Edward IV's accession, grew up during the Wars of the Roses, and died in the year of Wolsey's fall and the Reformation Parliament. In attempting to trace the relations between a poet's work and the age in which he lived, it is well to remember how arbitrary such deductions are. One is presented with a certain number of facts like a heap of pebbles, and the number of possible patterns which one can make from them are almost infinite. To prove the validity of the pattern one chooses, it would be necessary first to predict that if there were a poet in such and such a period he would have such and such poetical qualities, and then for the works of that poet to be discovered with just those qualities. The literary historian can do no more than suggest one out of many possible views.

Politically Skelton's period is one of important change. The Plantagenet line had split into two hostile branches, ending one in a lunatic and the other in a criminal. The barons turned their weapons upon each other and destroyed themselves; all the English Empire in France except Calais was gone; the feudal kind of representative government was discredited and the Church corrupt. The wealth of the country was beginning to accumulate in the hands of the trading classes, such as wool merchants, and to be concentrated in the cities of the traders. Traders want peace which gives them liberty to trade rather than political liberty, secular authority rather than a religious authority which challenges their right to usury and profit. They tend therefore to support an absolute monarchy, and unlike a feudal aristocracy with its international family loyalties, to be nationalist in sentiment. Absolute monarchies adopt *realpolitik* and though Machiavelli's *Prince* was not published till 1513, his principles were already European practice.

Skelton's political views are those of the average man of his time and class. A commoner, he had nothing to lose by the destruction of the old nobility; like the majority of his countrymen, he rejoices at royal weddings and national victories, and weeps at royal funerals and national defeats. With them also he criticises Henry VII's avarice.

> Immensas sibi divitias cumulasse quid horres?

Like a good bourgeois he is horrified at the new fashions and worldliness at Henry VIII's court, but cannot attribute it to the monarch himself, only to his companions; and hates the arrogance and extravagance of Wolsey, who by social origin was no better than himself.

In religious matters he is naturally more intelligent and better informed. Though Wyclif died in 1384, his doctrines were not forgotten among the common people, and though Skelton did not live to see the English Reformation, before he was fifty Luther had pinned his protest to the church door at Wittenberg, and he lived through the period of criticism by the Intelligentsia (*The Praise of Folly* was written in 1503) which always precedes a mass political movement.

The society of Colet, Grocyn, Linacre, and More was an intellectual and international one, a society of scholars who, like all scholars, overestimated their capacity to control or direct events. Skelton's feelings towards them were mixed. Too honest not to see and indeed in **Colin Clout** unsparingly to attack the faults of the Church, he was like them and like the intelligent orthodox at any time, a reformer not a revolutionary, that is to say, he thought that the corruptions of the Church and its dogmatic system were in no way related; that you could by a "change of heart" cure the one without impairing the other; while the revolutionary, on the other hand, attributes the corruption directly to the dogmas, for which he proposes to substitute another set which he imagines to be fool-proof and devil-proof. Towards the extremists he was frightened and hostile.

> And some have a smack
> Of Luther's sack . . .
> And some of them bark
> Clatter and carp
> Of that heresiarch
> Called Wickleuista
> The devilish dogmatista.

His difference from the early reformers was mainly temperamental. He was not in the least donnish and, moving perhaps in less rarefied circles, saw that the effect of their researches on the man in the street, like the effect on our own time, for example of Freud, was different from what they intended.

He has been unjustly accused of opposing the study of Greek; what he actually attacked was the effect produced by the impact of new ideas upon the average man, never in any age an edifying spectacle.

> Let Parrot, I pray you, have liberty to prate
> For aurea lingua greca ought to be magnified
> If it were cond perfitely and after the rate
> As lingua Latina, in school matter occupied
> But our Grekis, their Greek so well have applied
> That they cannot say in Greek, riding by the way,
> "Ho, ostler, fetch my horse a bottle of hay."

As a literary artist, it is difficult to escape the conclusion that Skelton is an oddity, like Blake, who cannot be really fitted into literary history as an inevitable product of the late fifteenth century. There is every reason for the existence of Hawes or even Barclay as the moribund end of the Chaucerian tradition; it is comparatively easy to understand Elizabethan poetry as a fusion of the Italian Renaissance and native folk elements; but the vigour and character of Skelton's work remains unpredictable.

One may point out that the *Narrenschiff* influenced the **Bouge of Court,** that Skeltonics may be found in early literature like the Proverbs of Alfred,

> Ac if þu him lest welde
> 　Werende on worlde.
> Lude and stille
> 　His owene wille,

or that the style of his Latin verses occurs in Goliardic poetry or Abelard.

> Est in Rama
> Vox audita
> Rachel fluentes
> Eiolantes
> Super natos
> Interfectos.

But that a writer should be found at that particular date who would not succumb to aureate diction, and without being a folk writer, should make this kind of rhythm the basis of work, would seem, if it had not occurred, exceedingly improbable.

Excluding *Magnificence,* Skelton's poetry falls naturally into four divisions: the imitations of the "aureate" poetry of Lydgate and similar fifteenth-century verses, such as the elegy on the duke of Northumberland and the prayers to the Trinity; the lyrics; the poems in rhyme royal such as the **Bouge of Court** and **Speke Parrot**; and those like

Elinor Rumming, Philip Sparrow, and *Colin Clout,* written in skeltonics.

Of the first class we may be thankful that it is so small. The attempt to gain for English verse the sonority of Latin by the use of a Latinised vocabulary was a failure in any hands except Milton's, and Skelton was no Milton. It was dull and smelt of the study, and Skelton seems to have realised this, and in his typically ironical way expressed his opinion.

> For, as I tofore have said
> I am but a young maid
> And cannot in effect
> My style as yet direct
> With English words elect. . . .
> Chaucer that famous clerk
> His terms were not dark
> But pleasant, easy and plain
> No word he wrote in vain.
>
> Also John Lydgate
> Writeth after a higher rate
> It is diffuse to find
> The sentence of his mind
> Some men find a fault
> And say he writeth too haut

(Philip Sparrow);

and in the *Duke of Albany* he rags the aureate vocabulary by giving the long words a line a piece:

> Of his nobility
> His magnaminity
> His animosity
> His frugality
> His liberality
> His affability, *etc. etc.*

As a writer of lyrics, on the other hand, had he chosen he could have ranked high enough. He can range from the barrack room "'Twas Xmas day in the workhouse" style of thing, to conventional religious poetry like the poem **"Woefully arrayed"** and the quite unfaked tenderness of the poem to Mistress Isabel Pennell, and always with an unfailing intuition of the right metrical form to employ in each case. Here is an example of his middle manner, Fancy's song about his hawk in *Magnificence.*

> Lo this is
> My fancy ywis
> Now Christ it blesse!
> It is, by Jesse.
>
> A bird full sweet
> For me full meet
> She is furred for the heat
> All to the feet:
>
> Her browès bent
> Her eyen glent
> From Tyne to Trent

> From Stroud to Kent. . . .
> Barbed like a nun
> For burning of the sun
> Her feathers dun
> Well favoured, bonne!

Skelton's use of Rhyme Royal is in some ways the best proof of his originality, because though employing a form used by all his predecessors and contemporaries and at a time when originality of expression was not demanded by the reading public, few stanzas of Skelton's could be confused with those of anyone else.

The most noticeable difference, attained partly by a greater number of patter or unaccented syllables (which relate it more to a teutonic accentual or sprung rhythm for verse) lies in the tempo of his poetry. Compare a stanza of Skelton's with one of Chaucer's:

> Suddenly as he departed me fro
>   Came pressing in one in a wonder array
> Ere I was ware, behind me he said "BO"
>   Then I, astonied of that sudden fray
> Start all at once, I liked nothing his play
>   For, if I had not quickly fled the touch
> He had plucked out the nobles of my pouch.
>
> (Skelton.)

> But o word, lordlings, herkeneth ere I go:
> It were full hard to finde now a dayes
> In all a town Griseldes three or two
> For, if that they were put to such assayes,
> The gold of hem hath no so bad aloyes
> With brass, that though the coyne be fair at ye,
> It would rather breste a-two than plye.
>
> (Chaucer.)

In Chaucer there is a far greater number of iambic feet, and the prevailing number of accents per line is five; in the Skelton it is four.

Indeed, the tempo of Skelton's verse is consistently quicker than that of any other English poet; only the author of *Hudibras,* and in recent times Vachel Lindsay, come anywhere near him in this respect.

It seems to be a rough-and-ready generalisation that the more poetry concerns itself with subjective states, with the inner world of feeling, the slower it becomes, or in other words, that the verse of extrovert poets like Dryden is swift and that of introvert poets like Milton is slow, and that in those masters like Shakespeare who transcend these classifications, in the emotional crises which precede and follow the tragic act, the pace of the verse is retarded.

Thus the average pace of mediæval verse compared with that of later more self-conscious ages is greater, and no poetry is more "outer" than Skelton's.

His best poems, with the exception of **Speke Parrot,** are like triumphantly successful prize poems. The themes— the death of a girl's sparrow, a pub, Wolsey, have all the air of set subjects. They may be lucky choices, but one feels that others would have done almost equally well, not, as with Milton, that his themes were the only ones to which his genius would respond at that particular moment in his life; that, had they not occurred to him, he would have written nothing. They never read as personal experience, brooded upon, and transfigured.

Considering his date, this is largely to the good. Pre-Elizabethan verse, even Chaucer, when it deserts the outer world, and attempts the subjective, except in very simple emotional situations, as in the mystery plays, tends to sentiment and prosy moralising. Skelton avoids that, but at the same time his emotional range is limited. The world of "The soldier's pole is fallen" is not for him:

> We are but dust
> For die we must
> It is general
> To be mortal

is as near as he gets to the terrific. This is moralising, but the metre saves it from sententiousness.

The skeltonic is such a simple metre that it is surprising that more poets have not used it. The natural unit of speech rhythm seems to be one of four accents, dividing into two half verses of two accents. If one tries to write ordinary conversation in verse, it will fall more naturally into this scheme than into any other. Most dramatic blank verse, for example, has four accents rather than five, and it is possible that our habit of prefacing nouns and adjectives by quite pointless adjectives and adverbs as in "the *perfect-ly* priceless" is dictated by our ear, by our need to group accents in pairs. Skelton is said to have spoken as he wrote, and his skeltonics have the natural ease of speech rhythm. It is the metre of many nursery rhymes.

> Little Jack Horner
> Sat in a corner;

or extemporised verse like the *Clerihew*:

> Alfred de Musset
> Used to call his cat pusset;

and study of the Woolworth song books will show its attraction to writers of jazz lyrics:

> For life's a farce
> Sitting on the grass.

No other English poet to my knowledge has this extempore quality, is less "would-be," to use a happy phrase of D. H. Lawrence.

It makes much of his work, of course, quite unmemorable—it slips in at one ear and out at the other; but it is never false, and the lucky shots seem unique, of a kind which a more deliberate and self-conscious poet would never have thought of, or considered worthy of his singing robes:

> Your head would have ached
> To see her naked.

Though much of Skelton's work consists of attacks on people and things, he can scarcely be called a satirist. Satire is an art which can only flourish within a highly sophisticated culture. It aims at creating a new attitude towards the persons or institutions satirised, or at least at crystallising one previously vague and unconscious. It presupposes a society whose prejudices and loyalties are sufficiently diffuse to be destroyed by intellectual assault, or sufficiently economically and politically secure to laugh at its own follies, and to admit that there is something to be said on both sides.

In less secure epochs, such as Skelton's, when friend and foe are more clearly defined, the place of satire is taken by abuse, as it always is taken in personal contact. (If censorship prevents abuse, allegorical symbolism is employed, e.g. **Speke Parrot.**) If two people are having a quarrel, they do not stop to assess who is at fault or to convince the other of his error: they express their feelings of anger by calling each other names. Similarly, among friends, when we express our opinion of an enemy by saying "so and so is a closet" we assume that the reasons are known:

> The Midwife put her hand on his thick skull
> With the prophetic blessing, "Be thou dull,"

is too much emotion recollected in tranquillity to be the language of a quarrel. Abuse in general avoids intellectual tropes other than those of exaggeration which intensify the expression of one's feelings such as, "You're so narrow-minded your ears meet," or the genealogical trees which bargees assign to one another.

Further, the effect on the victim is different. Abuse is an attack on the victim's personal honour, satire on his social self-esteem; it affects him not directly, but through his friends.

Skelton's work is abuse or flyting, not satire, and he is a master at it. Much flyting poetry, like Dunbar's and Skelton's own poems against Garnesche, suffer from the alliterative metre in which they were written, which makes them too verbal; the effect is lost on later generations, to whom the vocabulary is unfamiliar. The freedom and simplicity of the skeltonic was an ideal medium.

> Dundas, drunken and drowsy
> Scabbed, scurvy and lousy
> Of unhappy generation
> And most ungracious nation!
> Dundas
> That drunk ass
> That rates and ranks
> That prates and pranks
> Of Huntly banks
> Take this our thanks:—
> Dundee, Dunbar
> Walk, Scot,
> Walk, sott
> Rail not too far!

Later literary attempts at abuse, such as Browning's lines on Fitzgerald or Belloc's on a don, are too self-conscious and hearty. Blake is the only other poet known to me who has been equally successful.

> You think Fuseli is not a great painter; I'm glad
> This is one of the best compliments he ever had.

With his capacity for abuse Skelton combines a capacity for caricature. His age appears to have been one which has a penchant for the exaggerated and macabre, and he is no exception. His description of a character is as accurate in detail as one of Chaucer's, but as exaggerated as one of Dickens's. Compared with Chaucer he is more violent and dramatic; a favourite device of his is to interpolate the description with remarks by the character itself.

> With that came Riot, rushing all at once
> A rusty gallant, to-ragged and to-rent
> As on the board he whirled a pair of bones
> Quater trey dews he clattered as he went
> Now have at all, by Saint Thomas of Kent!
> And ever he threw and cast I wote n'ere what
> His hair was growen through out his hat. . . .
>
> Counter he could O lux upon a pot,
> An ostrich feather of a capon's tail
> He set up freshly upon his hat aloft:
> "What revel rout!" quod he, and gan to rail
> How oft he had hit Jenet on the tail,
> Of Phillis featuous, and little pretty Kate
> How oft he had knocked at her clicket gate.

This has much more in common with the Gothic gargoyle than with the classicism of Chaucer; *Elinor Rumming* is one of the few poems comparable to Breughel or Rowlandson in painting. The effect is like looking at the human skin through a magnifying glass.

> Then Margery Milkduck
> Her kirtle she did uptuck
> An inch above her knee
> Her legs that ye might see
> But they were sturdy and stubbed
> Mighty pestles and clubbed
> As fair and as white
> As the foot of a kite
> She was somewhat foul
> Crooked-necked like an owl;
> And yet she brought her fees,
> A cantel of Essex cheese,
> Was well a foot thick
> Full of maggots quick:
> It was huge and great
> And mighty strong meat
> For the devil to eat
> It was tart and pungate.

All Skelton's work has this physical appeal. Other poets, such as Spenser and Swinburne, have been no more dependent upon ideas, but they have touched only one sense, the auditory. The Catherine-wheel motion of Skelton's verse is exciting in itself, but his language is never vaguely emotive. Indeed, it is deficient in overtones, but is always precise, both visually and tactually. He uses place-names, not scientifically like Dante, or musically like Milton, but as country proverbs use them, with natural vividness:

> And Syllogisari was drowned at Sturbridge Fair.

Naturally enough the figures of classical mythology which appear in all mediæval work (just as the Sahara or Ohio appears in modern popular verses) occur in Skelton also, but he is never sorry to leave Lycaon or Etna for the Tilbury Ferry and the Plains of Salisbury. The same applies to the Latin quotations in *Philip Sparrow*; not only have they dramatic point, but being mainly quotations from the Psalter, they make no demands upon the erudition of his audience, any more than would "Abide with me" upon a modern reader.

Of Skelton's one excursion into dramatic form, *Magnificence*, not much need be said. It is interesting, because he is one of the few dramatists who have attempted, and with success, to differentiate his characters by making them speak in different metres, thus escaping the tendency of blank verse to make all the characters speak like the author; which obliged the Elizabethans to make their comic characters speak in prose; for the future of poetic comedy it may prove important. Its fault, a fatal one in drama, is its prolixity, but cut by at least two-thirds it might act very much better than one imagines.

Skelton's reputation has suffered in the past from his supposed indecency. This charge is no longer maintained, but there are other misunderstandings of poetry which still prevent appreciation of his work. On the one hand, there are those who read poetry for its message, for great thoughts which can be inscribed on Christmas calendars; on the other, there are admirers of "pure" poetry, which generally means emotive poetry with a minimum of objective reference. Skelton satisfies neither of these: he is too carefree for the one, and too interested in the outer world for the second.

If we accept, and I think we must, a distinction between the visionary and the entertainer, the first being one who extends our knowledge of, insight into, and power of control over human conduct and emotion, without whom our understanding would be so much the poorer, Skelton is definitely among the entertainers. He is not one of the indispensables, but among entertainers—and how few are the indispensables—he takes a high place. Nor is entertainment an unworthy art: it demands a higher standard of technique and a greater lack of self-regard than the average man is prepared to attempt. There have been, and are, many writers of excellent sensibility whose work is spoilt by a bogus vision which deprives it of the entertainment value which it would otherwise have had; in that kind of pride Skelton is entirely lacking.

E. M. Forster (essay date 1950)

SOURCE: "John Skelton," in *Two Cheers for Democracy,* Harcourt, Brace, and Company, 1951, pp. 135-53.

[*In the following lecture given at the Aldeburgh Festival of 1950, Forster offers an introduction to the pleasures of reading Skelton's poetry.*]

John Skelton was an East Anglian; he was a poet, also a clergyman, and he was extremely strange. Partly strange because the age in which he flourished—that of the early Tudors—is remote from us, and difficult to interpret. But he was also a strange creature personally, and whatever you think of him when we've finished—and you will possibly think badly of him—you will agree that we have been in contact with someone unusual.

Let us begin with solidity—with the church where he was rector. That still stands, that can be seen and touched, though its incumbent left it over four hundred years ago. He was rector of Diss, a market town which lies just in Norfolk, just across the river Waveney, here quite a small stream, and Diss church is somewhat of a landmark, for it stands upon a hill. A winding High Street leads up to it, and the High Street, once very narrow, passed through an arch in its tower which still remains. The church is not grand, it is not a great architectural triumph like Blyborough or Framlingham. But it is adequate, it is dignified and commodious, and it successfully asserts its pre-eminence over its surroundings. Here our poet-clergyman functioned for a time, and I may add carried on.

Not much is known about him, though he was the leading literary figure of his age. He was born about 1460, probably in Norfolk, was educated at Cambridge, mastered the voluble inelegant Latin of his day, entered the church, got in touch with the court of Henry VII, and became tutor to the future Henry VIII. He was appointed "Poet Laureate," and this was confirmed by the universities of Cambridge, Oxford and Louvain. In the early years of Henry VIII he voiced official policy—for instance, in his poems against the Scots after Flodden. But, unfortunately for himself, he attacked another and a greater East Anglian, Cardinal Wolsey of Ipswich, and after that his influence declined. He was appointed rector of Diss in 1503, and held the post till his death in 1529. But he only seems to have been in residence during the earlier years. Life couldn't have been congenial for him there. He got across the Bishop of Norwich, perhaps about his marriage or semi-marriage, and he evidently liked London and the court, being a busy contentious fellow, and found plenty to occupy him there. A few bills and documents, a few references in the works of others, a little post-humous gossip, and his own poems, are all that we have when we try to reconstruct him. Beyond doubt he is an extraordinary character, but not one which it is easy to focus. Let us turn to his poems.

I will begin with the East Anglian poems, and with *Philip Sparrow.* This is an unusually charming piece of work. It was written while Skelton was at Diss, and revolves round a young lady called Jane, who was at school at a nunnery close to Norwich. Jane had a pet sparrow—a bird which is far from fashionable today, but which once possessed great social prestige. In ancient Rome, Catullus sang of the sparrow of Lesbia, the dingy little things were housed in gilt cages, and tempted with delicious scraps all through the middle ages, and they only went out when the canary came in. Jane had a sparrow, round which all her maidenly soul was wrapped. Tragedy followed. There was a cat in the nunnery by name Gib, who lay in wait for Philip Sparrow, pounced, killed him and ate him. The poor girl was in tears, and her tragedy was taken up and raised into poetry by her sympathetic admirer, the rector of Diss.

He produced a lengthy poem—it seemed difficult at that time to produce a poem that was not long. *Philip Sparrow* swings along easily enough, and can still be read with pleasure by those who will overlook its volubility, its desultoriness, and its joky Latin.

It begins, believe it or not, with a parody of the office for the dead; Jane herself is supposed to be speaking, and she slings her Latin about well if quaintly. Soon tiring of the church service, she turns to English, and to classical allusions:

> When I remember again
> How my Philip was slain
> Never half the pain
> Was between you twain,
> Pyramus and Thisbe,
> As then befell to me;
> I wept and I wailéd
> The teares down hailéd,
> But nothing it availéd
> To call Philip again
> Whom Gib our cat has slain.
> Gib I say our cat
> Worrowed him on that
> Which I loved best. . . .
> I fell down to the ground[1]

Then—in a jumble of Christian and antique allusions, most typical of that age—she thinks of Hell and Pluto and Cerberus—whom she calls Cerebus—and Medusa and the Furies, and alternately prays Jupiter and Jesus to save her sparrow from the infernal powers.

> It was so pretty a fool
> It would sit upon a stool
> And learned after my school. . . .
> It had a velvet cap
> And would sit upon my lap
> And would seek after small wormés
> And sometimes white bread crumbés
> And many times and oft
> Between my breastés soft
>
> It would lie and rest
> It was proper and prest!
> Sometimes he would gasp
> When he saw a wasp;

A fly or a gnat
He would fly at that
And prettily he would pant
When he saw an ant
Lord how he would pry
After a butterfly
Lord how he would hop
After the grasshop
And when I said "Phip Phip"
Then he would leap and skip
And take me by the lip.
Alas it will me slo
That Philip is gone me fro!

Jane proceeds to record his other merits, which include picking fleas off her person—this was a sixteenth-century girls' school, not a twentieth, vermin were no disgrace, not even a surprise, and Skelton always manages to introduce the coarseness and discomfort of his age. She turns upon the cat again, and hopes the greedy grypes will tear out his tripes.

Those villainous false cats
Were made for mice and rats
And not for birdés small.
Alas, my face waxeth pale . . .

She goes back to the sparrow and to the Church Service, and draws up an enormous catalogue of birds who shall celebrate his obsequies:

Our chanters shall be the cuckoo,
The culver, the stockdoo,
The "peewit," the lapwing,
The Versicles shall sing.

—together with other songsters, unknown in these marshes and even elsewhere. She now wants to write an epitaph, but is held up by her diffidence and ignorance; she has read so few books, though the list of those she has read is formidable; moreover, she has little enthusiasm for the English language—

Our natural tongue is rude,
And hard to be ennewed
With polished termes lusty
Our language is so rusty
So cankered, and so full
Of froward, and so dull,
That if I would apply
To write ornately
I wot not where to find
Terms to serve my mind.

Shall she try Latin? Yes, but she will hand over the job to the Poet Laureate of Britain, Skelton, and, with this neat compliment to himself, Skelton ends the first part of Philip Sparrow.

He occupies the second part with praising Jane,

This most goodly flower,
This blossom of fresh colour

So Jupiter me succour
She flourishes new and new
In beauty and virtue,

by-passes the sparrow, and enters upon a love poem:

But wherefore should I note
How often did I toot
Upon her pretty foot
It bruised mine heart-root
To see her tread the ground
With heeles short and round.

The rector is in fact losing his head over a schoolgirl, and has to pull himself up. No impropriety is intended, he assures us,

There was no vice
Nor yet no villainy,
But only fantasy.". . .
It were no gentle guise
This treatise to despise
Because I have written and said
Honour of this fair maide,
Wherefore shall I be blamed
That I Jane have named
And famously proclaimed?
She is worthy to be enrolled
In letters of gold.

Then he too slides into Latin and back into the office of the dead: *requiem aeternam dona eis Domine,* he chants.

This poem of Philip Sparrow—the pleasantest Skelton ever wrote—helps to emphasise the difference in taste and in style between the sixteenth century and our own. His world is infinitely remote; not only is it coarse and rough, but there is an uncertainty of touch about it which we find hard to discount. Is he being humorous? Undoubtedly, but where are we supposed to laugh? Is he being serious? If so, where and how much? We don't find the same uncertainty when we read his predecessor Chaucer, or his successor Shakespeare. We know where they stand, even when we cannot reach them. Skelton belongs to an age of break-up, which had just been displayed politically in the Wars of the Roses. He belongs to a period when England was trying to find herself—as indeed do we today, though we have to make a different sort of discovery after a different type of war. He is very much the product of his times—a generalisation that can be made of all writers, but not always so aptly. The solidity of the middle ages was giving away beneath his feet, and he did not know that the Elizabethan age was coming—any more than we know what is coming. We have not the least idea, whatever the politicians prophesy. It is appropriate, at this point, to quote the wisest and most impressive lines he ever wrote—they are not well known, and probably they are only a fragment. They have a weight and a thoughtfulness which are unusual in him.

Though ye suppose all jeopardies are passed
  And all is done that ye lookéd for before,
Ware yet, I warn you, of Fortune's double cast,

For one false point she is wont to keep in store,
And under the skin oft festeréd is the sore;
That when ye think all danger for to pass
Ware of the lizard lieth lurking in the grass.

It was a curious experience, with these ominous verses in my mind, to go to Diss and to find, carved on the buttress of the church, a lizard. The carving was there in Skelton's day; that he noticed it, that it entered into his mind when he wrote, there is no reason to suppose. But its appearance, combined with the long grass in the churchyard, helped me to connect the present with the past, helped them to establish that common denominator without which neither has any validity.

That when ye think all danger for to pass
Ware of the lizard lieth lurking in the grass.

So true of the sixteenth century, so true of today! There are two main answers to the eternal menace of the lizard. One of them is caution, the other courage. Skelton was a brave fellow—his opposition to Cardinal Wolsey proves that—but I don't know which answer he recommends.

But let us leave these serious considerations, and enter Diss church itself, where we shall be met by a fantastic scene and by the oddest poem even Skelton ever wrote; the poem of *Ware the Hawk.* Like *Philip Sparrow*, it is about a bird, but a bird of prey, and its owner is not the charming Jane, but an ill-behaved curate, who took his hawk into the church, locked all the doors, and proceeded to train it with the help of two live pigeons and a cushion stuffed with feathers to imitate another pigeon. The noise, the mess, the scandal, was terrific. In vain did the rector thump on the door and command the curate to open. The young man—one assumes he was young—took no notice, but continued his unseemly antics. Diss church is well suited to a sporting purpose, since its nave and choir are unusually lofty, and the rood-loft was convenient for the birds to perch on between the statues of the Virgin and St. John. Up and down he rushed, uttering the cries of his craft, and even clambering on to the communion table. Feathers flew in all directions and the hawk was sick. At last Skelton found "a privy way" in, and managed to stop him. But he remained impenitent, and threatened that another day he would go fox-hunting there, and bring in a whole pack of hounds.

Now is this an exaggeration, or a joke? And why did Skelton delay making a poem out of it until many years had passed? He does not—which is strange—even mention the name of the curate.

He shall be as now nameless,
But he shall not be blameless
Nor he shall not be shameless.
For sure he wrought amiss
To hawk in my church at Diss.

That is moderately put. It was amiss. Winding himself up into a rage, he then calls him a peckish parson and a Domine Dawcock and a frantic falconer and a smeary smith, and scans history in vain for so insolent a parallel; not even the Emperor Julian the Apostate or the Nestorian heretics flew hawks in a church. Nero himself would have hesitated. And the poem ends in a jumble and a splutter, heaps of silly Latin, a cryptogram and a curious impression of gaiety; a good time, one can't help feeling, has been had by all.

How, though, did Skelton get into the church and stop the scandal? Perhaps through the tower. You remember my mentioning that the tower of Diss church has a broad passageway running through it, once part of the High Street. Today the passage only contains a notice saying "No bicycles to be left here," together with a number of bicycles. Formerly, there was a little door leading up from it into the tower. That (conjectures an American scholar) may have been Skelton's privy entrance. He may have climbed up by it, climbed down the belfry into the nave, and spoiled, at long last, the curate's sport.

Skelton was a strange creature personally, and whatever you think of him when we've finished—and you will possibly think badly of him—you will agree that we have been in contact with someone unusual.
—E. M. Forster

There is another poem which comes into this part of Skelton's life. It is entitled **"Two Knaves Sometimes of Diss,"** and attacks two of his parishioners who had displeased him and were now safely dead; John Clerk and Adam Uddersall were their names. Clerk, according to the poet, had raged "like a camel" and now lies "starke dead, Never a tooth in his head, Adieu, Jayberd, adieu," while as for Uddersall, "Belsabub his soule save, who lies here like a knave." The poem is not gentlemanly. Little that Skelton wrote was. Not hit a man when he is down or dead? That's just the moment to wait for. He can't hit back.

The last East Anglian poem to be mentioned, is a touching one: to his wife. As a priest, he was not and could not be married, but he regarded his mistress as his legal consort, and the poem deals with a moment when they were parting and she was about to bear a child:

'Petually
Constrained am I
With weeping eye
   To mourn and plain
That we so nigh
Of progeny
So suddenly
   Should part in twain.

When ye are gone
Comfort is none,

But all alone
　Endure must I
With grievely groan
Making my moan
As it were one
　That should needs die.

There is a story about the birth of this child which was written down after Skelton's death, in a collection called *The Merry Tales of Skelton*. According to it, there were complaints to the bishop from the parish, which Skelton determined to quell. So he preached in Diss church on the text *Vos estis,* you are, and suddenly called out "Wife! bring my child." Which the lady did. And he held the naked baby out to the congregation saying "Is not this child as fair as any of yours? It is not like a pig or a calf, is it? What have you got to complain about to the bishop? The fact is, as I said in my text, *Vos estis,* you be, and have be and will and shall be knaves, to complayne of me without reasonable cause." Historians think that this jest-book story enshrines a tradition. It certainly fits in with what we know of the poet's fearless and abusive character.

Tenderness also entered into that character, though it did not often show itself. Tenderness inspires that poem I have quoted, and is to be found elsewhere in his gentle references to women; for instance, in the charming **"Merry Margaret,"** which often appears in anthologies.

　Merry Margaret
　　As midsummer flower,
　Gentle as falcon
　Or hawk of the tower:
　With solace and gladness
　Much mirth and no madness
　All good and no badness.

And in the less known but still more charming poem **"To Mistress Isabel Pennell"** which I will quote in full. Isabel was a little girl of eight—even younger than Jane of the sparrow. ("Reflaring," near the beginning of the poem, is "redolent." "Nept" means catmint.)

　By Saint Mary, my Lady,
　Your mammy and your daddy
　Brought forth a goodly baby.
　　My maiden Isabel,
　Reflaring rosabel,
　The fragrant camomel:
　　The ruddy rosary,
　The sovereign rosemary
　The pretty strawberry
　　The columbine, the nept,
　The jelofer well set,
　The proper violet:
　　Ennewed your colour
　Is like the daisy flower
　After the April shower;
　　Star of the morrow gray,
　The blossom on the spray
　The freshest flower of May:
　　Maidenly demure,

Of womanhood the lure;
Wherefore I make you sure
　It were an heavenly health,
It were an endless wealth,
A life for God himself
　To hear this nightingale
Among the birdés small
Warbelling in the vale:
Dug dug,
Jug jug,
　Good year and good luck,
　With chuck, chuck, chuck, chuck!

Women could touch his violent and rugged heart and make it gentle and smooth for a little time. It is not the dying tradition of chivalry, it is something personal.

But we must leave these personal and local matters, and turn to London and to the political satires. The main group is directed against Cardinal Wolsey. The allusions are often obscure, for though Skelton sometimes attacks his great adversary openly, at other times he is covering his tracks, and at other times complimentary and even fulsome. The ups and downs of which have furnished many problems for scholars. Two points should be remembered. Firstly, Skelton is not a precursor of the Reformation; he has sometimes been claimed as one by Protestant historians. He attacked the abuses of his church—as exemplified in Wolsey's luxury, immorality and business. He has nothing to say against its doctrines or organisation and was active in the suppression of heresy. He was its loyal if scandalous son.

Secondly, Wolsey appears to have behaved well. When he triumphed, he exacted no vengeance. Perhaps he had too much to think about. The story that Skelton died in sanctuary in St. Margaret's, Westminster, fleeing from the Cardinal's wrath, is not true. He did live for the last years of his life in London, but freely and comfortably; bills for his supper parties have been unearthed. And though he was buried in St. Margaret's it was honourably, under an alabaster inscription. Bells were pealed, candles were burned. Here again we have the bills.

The chief anti-Wolsey poems are *Speke Parrot, Colin Clout, Why come ye not to Court?* and the cumbrous Morality play *Magnificence*.

Speke Parrot—yet another bird; had Skelton a bird complex? ornithologists must decide—*Speke Parrot* is one of those convenient devices where Polly is made to say what Polly's master hesitates to say openly. Poor Polly! Still master is fond of Polly, and introduces him prettily enough.

　Parrot is no churlish chough nor no fleckéd pie,
　　Parrot is no penguin that men call a carling,
　Parrot is no woodcock, nor no butterfly,
　　Parrot is no stammering stare that men call a
　　starling,
　　But Parrot is my own dear heart and my dear
　　darling,
　Melpomene, that fair maid, she burnished his beak:

I pray you, let Parrot have liberty to speak.

Skelton's genuine if intermittent charm continues into the next stanza:

> Parrot is a fair bird for a lady
>   God of his goodness him framéd and wrought:
> When parrot is dead, he doth not putrify.
>   Yet all things mortal shall turn unto nought,
>   Except man's soul, that Christ so dearly bought:
> That never may die, nor never die shall—
> Make much of Parrot, the popinjay royal.

The "popinjay royal"—that is to say the bird of King Henry VIII, whose goodness and generosity Wolsey abuses. And parrot, given his beak, says many sharp things against the Cardinal, who "carrieth a king in his sleeve" and plays the Pope's game rather than his liege's. Subtly and obscurely, with detailed attention to his comings and goings, the great man is attacked. It is a London poem, which could not have been written in a Norfolk rectory.

Much more violent is *Why come ye not to Court?* where the son of the Ipswich butcher gets brutally put in his place.

> Why come ye not to court?
> To which court?
> To the king's court
> Or to Hampton Court?
> The king's court should have the excellence
> But Hampton Court hath the pre-eminence.

And at Hampton Court Wolsey rules, with

>   his base progeny
> And his greasy genealogy,
> He came of the sang royall
> That was cast out from a butcher's stall. . . .
> With lewd conditions coated
> As hereafter be noted—
> Presumption and vainglory,
> Envy, wrath and lechery,
> Covertise and gluttony,
> Slothful to do good,
> Now frantic, now stark mad.

As for *Colin Clout.* The title is the equivalent of Hodge or the Man in the Street, from whose point of view the poem is supposed to be written. It is a long rambling attack on bishops, friars, monks, and the clergy generally, and Wolsey comes in for his share of criticism. I will quote from it not the abusive passages, of which you are getting plenty, but the dignified and devout passage with which it closes. Skelton was after all inside the church he criticised, and held its faith, and now and then he reminds us of this.

>   Now to withdraw my pen
>   And now a while to rest
> Meseemeth it for the best.
>   The forecastle of my ship

> Shall glide and smoothly slip
> Out of the waves wild
> Of the stormy flood
> Shoot anchor and lie at road
> And sail not far abroad
> Till the coast be clear
> And the lode-star appear
> My ship now will I steer
> Towards the port salu
> Of our Saviour Jesu
> Such grace that he us send
> To rectify and amend
> Things that are amiss
> Where that his pleasure is.
>   Amen!

It is a conventional ending, but a sincere one, and reminds us that he had a serious side; his **"Prayer to the Father of Heaven"** was sung in the church here, to the setting of Vaughan Williams. He can show genuine emotion at moments, both about this world and the next. Here are two verses from **"The Manner of the World Nowadays,"** in which he laments the decay of society.

> Sometimes we sang of mirth and play
> But now our joy is gone away
> For so many fall in decay
>   Saw I never:
> Whither is the wealth of England gone?
> The spiritual saith they have none,
> And so many wrongfully undone
>   Saw I never.

Magnificence, the last of the anti-Wolsey group, is a symbol for Henry VIII, who is seduced by wicked flatterers from his old counsellor (i.e. from Skelton himself). Largess, Counterfeit-Countenance, Crafty-Conveyance, Cloaked-Collusion and Courtly-Abusion are some of the names, and all are aspects of Wolsey. At enormous length and with little dramatic skill they ensnare Magnificence and bring him low. By the time Stage 5, Scene 35 is reached he repents, and recalls his former adviser, and all is well.

Well, so much for the quarrel between Skelton and Wolsey—between the parson from Norfolk and the Cardinal from Suffolk, and Suffolk got the best of it. Skelton may have had right on his side and he had courage and sincerity, but there is no doubt that jealousy came in too. At the beginning of Henry VIII's reign he was a very important person. He had been the King's tutor, he went on a semi-diplomatic mission, and as Poet Laureate he was a mouthpiece for official lampoons. With the advent of Wolsey, who tempted the king with pleasure, his importance declined, and he did not live to see the days when Henry preferred power to pleasure, and Wolsey fell.

The satires against the Scots, next to be mentioned, belong to the more influential period of Skelton's life. They centre round the Battle of Flodden (1513). King Henry's brother-in-law, James IV of Scotland, had challenged him, had invaded England, and been killed at Flodden, with most of his nobility. Skelton celebrates the English victory with caddish joy. In quoting a few lines, I do not desire to ruffle any sensitive friends from over the Border. I can anyhow assure them that our Poet Laureate appears to have got as good as he gave:

> King Jamie, Jemsy, Jocky my jo,
> Ye summoned our king—why did ye so
> To you nothing it did accord
> To summon our king your sovereign lord? . . .
> Thus for your guerdon quit are ye,
> Thanked be God in Trinitie
> And sweet Saint George, our Lady's knight
> Your eye is out: adew, good-night.

And still more abusively does he attack an enemy poet called Dundas who wrote Latin verses against him.

> Gup, Scot,
> Ye blot
> Set in better
> Thy pentameter
> This Dundas
> This Scottish ass,
> He rhymes and rails
> That Englishmen have tails. . . .
> Shake thy tail, Scot, like a cur
> For thou beggest at every man's door
> Tut, Scot, I say
> Go shake thee dog, hey. . . .
> Dundas,
> That drunk ass. . . .
> Dundee, Dunbar
> Walk Scot,
> Walk sot,
> Rail not so far.

The accusation that Englishmen have tails is still sometimes made, and is no doubt as true as it ever was. I have not been able to find out how Dundas made it, since his poem has vanished. We can assume he was forcible. Nor have I quoted Skelton in full, out of deference to the twentieth century. He is said to have written it in his Diss rectory. That is unlikely—not because of its tone, but because it implies a close contact with affairs which he could only have maintained at Court.

Our short Skeltonic scamper is nearing its end, but I must refer to the *Tunning of Elinor Rumming,* one of the most famous of Skelton's poems. Elinor Rumming kept a pub—not in East Anglia, but down in Surrey, near Leatherhead. The poem is about her and her clients, who likewise belonged to the fair sex.

> Tell you I will
> If that you will
> A while be still
> Of a comely Jill
> That dwelt on a hill:
> She is somewhat sage
> And well worn in age
> For her visage
> It would assuage

> A man's courage . . .
> Comely crinkled
> Wondrously wrinkled
> Like a roast pig's ear
> Bristled with hair.

You catch the tone. You taste the quality of the brew. It is strong and rumbustious and not too clean. Skelton is going to enjoy himself thoroughly. Under the guise of a satirist and a corrector of morals, he is out for a booze. Now the ladies come tumbling in:

> Early and late
> Thither cometh Kate
> Cisly and Sare
> With their legs bare
> And also their feet
> Fully unsweet
> Their kirtles all to-jagged
> Their smocks all to-ragged,
> With titters and tatters
> Bring dishes and platters
> With all their might running
> To Elinor Rumming
> To have of her tunning.

They get drunk, they tumble down in inelegant attitudes, they trip over the doorstep, they fight—Margery Milkduck, halting Joan, Maud Ruggy, drunken Alice, Bely and Sybil, in they come. Many of them are penniless and are obliged to pay in kind and they bring with them gifts often as unsavoury as the drink they hope to swallow—a rancid side of bacon for example—and they pawn anything they can lay their hands on, from their husband's clothes to the baby's cradle, from a frying pan to a side saddle. Elinor accepts all. It is a most lively and all-embracing poem, which gets wilder and lewder as it proceeds. Then Skelton pulls himself up in characteristic fashion.

> My fingers itch
> I have written too mich
> Of this mad mumming
> Of Elinor Rumming.

And remembering that he is a clergyman and a Poet Laureate he appends some Latin verses saying that he has denounced drunken, dirty and loquacious women, and trusts they will take his warning to heart. I wonder. To my mind he has been thoroughly happy, as he was in the church at Diss when the naughty curate hawked. I often suspect satirists of happiness—and I oftener suspect them of envy. Satire is not a straight trade. Skelton's satires on Wolsey are of the envious type. In *Elinor Rumming* and *Ware the Hawk* I detect a coarse merry character enjoying itself under the guise of censoriousness.

> Thought is frank and free:
> To think a merry thought
> It cost me little nor nought.

One question that may have occurred to you is this: was Skelton typical of the educated parish priest of his age?

My own impression is that he was, and that the men of Henry VIII's reign, parsons and others, were much more unlike ourselves than we suppose, or if you prefer it, much odder. We cannot unlock their hearts. In the reign of his daughter Elizabeth a key begins to be forged. Shakespeare puts it into our hands, and we recover, on a deeper level, the intimacy promised by Chaucer. Skelton belongs to an age of transition: the silly Wars of the Roses were behind him; he appears even to regret them, and he could not see the profounder struggles ahead. This makes him "difficult," though he did not seem so to himself. His coarseness and irreverence will pain some people and must puzzle everyone. It may help us if we remember that religion is older than decorum.

Of his poetry I have given some typical samples, and you will agree that he is entertaining and not quite like anyone else, that he has a feeling for rhythm, and a copious vocabulary. Sometimes—but not often—he is tender and charming, occasionally he is devout and very occasionally he is wise. On the whole he's a comic—a proper comic, with a love for improper fun, and a talent for abuse. He says of himself in one of his Latin verses, that he sings the material of laughter in a harsh voice, and the description is apt; the harshness is often more obvious than the laughter, and leaves us with a buzzing in the ears rather than with a smile on the face. Such a row! Such a lot of complaints! He has indeed our national fondness for grumbling—the government, the country, agriculture, the world, the beer, they are none of them what they ought to be or have been. And although we must not affix our dry little political labels to the fluidity of the past (there is nothing to tie them on to), it is nevertheless safe to say that temperamentally the Rector of Diss was a conservative.

On what note shall we leave him? A musical note commends itself. Let me quote three stanzas from a satire called **"Against a comely Coistroun"**—that is to say, against a good-looking kitchen-boy. The boy has been conjectured to be Lambert Simnel, the pretender to the crown of England. He was silly as well as seditious, and he fancied himself as a musician and "curiously chanted and currishly countered and madly in his musicks mockishly made against the Nine Muses of politic poems and poets matriculate"—the matriculate being Skelton, the Poet Laureate. Listen how he gets basted for his incompetence: you may not follow all the words, but you can hear the blows fall, and that's what matters:

> He cannot find it in rule nor in space,
> He solfas too haute, his treble is too high
> He braggeth of his birth, that born was full base,
> His music without measure, too sharp is his *Mi,*
> He trimmeth in his tenor to counter pirdewy,
> His descant is busy, it is without a mean
> Too fat is his fancy, his wit is too lean.

> He rumbleth on a lewd lute "Roty bully joys"
> Rumble down, tumble down, hey go now now!
> He fumbleth in his fingering an ugly good noise,
> It seemeth the sobbing of an old sow!
> He would be made much of, an he wist how;

> Well sped in spindles and turning of tavells;
> A bungler, a brawler, a picker of quarrels.

> Comely he clappeth a pair of clavichords
> He whistleth so sweetly, he maketh me to sweat;
> His descant is dashed full of dischords
> A red angry man, but easy to entreat:
> An usher of the hall fain would I get
> To point this proud page a place and a room
> For Jack would be a gentleman, that late was a
> 　groom.

Kitchen-boy Simnel, if it be he, was evidently no more a performer than he was a prince. Yet I would have liked to have him here now, red, angry, good-looking, and making a hideous noise, and to have heard Skelton cursing him as he screeched. The pair of them might have revived for us that past which is always too dim, always too muffled, always too refined. With their raucous cries in your ears, with the cries of the falconer in Diss Church, with the squawkings of Speke Parrot, and the belchings of Elinor Rumming, I leave you.

Notes

[1] The quotations are not verbally accurate. The text has been simplified for the purpose of reading aloud.

Alan Swallow　(essay date 1953)

SOURCE: "John Skelton: The Structure of the Poem," in *Philological Quarterly,* Vol. XXXII, No. 1, January, 1953, pp. 29-42.

[In the following essay, Swallow examines Skelton's unique poetic structure and determines how it differs from medieval literary traditions.]

In the work of John Skelton appears the first important Renaissance break with the medieval tradition in poetry. His work covers almost every type of verse practiced in his day, including the morality play; but he proceeded from acceptance of the medieval tradition, through varying stages of revolt against that tradition, to a new form which he devised. This type was highly individualistic, however, in the sense that it did not have much "carryover value." Though he finally broke with the medieval method, Skelton's experiment did not, as did Wyatt's, discover the method which was used so effectively by the great Elizabethan and Jacobean poets.

Skelton's two elegies—**"On the Death of the Noble Prince, King Edward the Fourth,"** and **"Upon the Dolorous Death and Much Lamentable Chance of the Most Honourable Earl of Northumberland"**—and his three prayers—**"To the Father of Heaven," "To the Second Person,"** and **"To the Holy Ghost"**—are clearly in the fifteenth-century literary manner, the manner of Lydgate. They belong to what Nelson calls "the tradition which conceived of literature to be a means of propagating virtue."[1] The theme of the first elegy is that of the Fall-of-Princes:

> Where is now my conquest and my victory?
>> Where is my riches and my royal array?
> Where be my coursers and my horses high?
>> Where is my mirth, my solace, and my play?
>> As vanity, to nought all is withered away.[2]

The theme is old and is not at all re-vitalized in this poem. It has the same lack of imagery as in Lydgate and Hawes. Though the second elegy has a different theme, an argument against the commons who killed Northumberland and a recital of the earl's virtues, it may be characterized in the same fashion. Only a touch of the later Skelton is present, as in the word play of

> Yet shamefully they slew him: that shame may them befall!

and the confused image

>> the commoners under a cloak,
> Which kindled the wild fire that made all this smoke.

The prayers have a characteristic medieval rhetoric of abstractions:

> O Radiant Luminary of light interminable,
>> Celestial Father, potential God of might,
> Of heaven and earth O Lord incomparable,
>> Of all perfections the Essential most perfite!
>> O Maker of mankind, that forméd day and night,
> Whose power imperial comprehendeth every place!

Skelton's first major attempt marks his first unmistakable move away from the medieval tradition. In the large, **The Bouge of Court** is a typical fifteenth-century allegory. It has the

> same astrological introduction, the insistence upon the necessity of "covert Terms," and the usual assumption of modesty: the poet then falls asleep and his dream becomes the substance of the poem: he wakes up at a critical moment in the action and writes his "little book," for which he makes a conventional apology.[3]

In addition, the characters of the poem, with the exception of one, are personifications such as might be found in late medieval allegory. They include Drede (the dreamer himself), Dame Saucepere, Danger, Bon Aventure, Favell, Suspect, Disdain, Riot, Dissimuler, and Deceit.

But the poem is not completely abstract in its conception. It is first of all definitely localized:

> At Harwich port slumb'ring as I lay
> In mine hostes house, called Powers Key.

More important yet, the descriptions of the personified characters are a mixture of medieval abstraction and of

touches of reality. For example, in this description of Disdain,

> He bit his lip, he lookéd passing coy;
>> His face was belimmed as bees had him stung:
> It was no time with him to jape nor toy!
>> Envy had wasted his liver and his lung,
>> Hatred by the heart so had him wrung
> That he looked pale as ashes to my sight:
> Disdain, I ween, this comerous crab is hight.

only the fourth and fifth lines seem to belong to medieval description; such expressions as "His face was belimmed as bees had him stung," "pale as ashes," and "comerous crab" set before us a distinct and physical person. This quality of the poem has its climax, moreover, in the description of Harvey Hafter, a real person with a real name among abstractions:

> Upon his breast he bear a versing-box,
>> His throat was clear, and lustily could fain.
> Methought his gown was all furred with fox,
>> And ever he sang, *"Sith I Am Nothing Plain . . ."*
>> To keep him from picking it was a greate pain:
> He gazed on me with his goatish beard,
> When I looked at him my purse was half-afeard.

John M. Berdan speaks of this last line as a "triumph of suggestiveness."[4] The characterization of Harvey Hafter does not stop here, however; it continues through the medium of his own speech to Drede, one stanza of which is:

> *Princes of youth* can ye sing by rote?
>> *Or shall I sail with you?* afellowship assay?
> For on the book I cannot sing a note.
>> Would to God it would please you some day
>> A ballad book before me for to lay,
> And learn me to sing *re mi fa sol!*
> And, when I fail, bob me on the noll.

It is evident from this poem, then, that at the time he wrote it Skelton was not yet prepared to break completely with the medieval tradition. He had not yet, we may suppose, invented a structure for the poem which would be compatible with the direct way in which he approached experience and to the realistic materials which he wished to place in his poem. His answer to the problem at this time was to borrow an old shell and fill it with new drink.

The same method is also evident in Skelton's morality play, *Magnificence.* He borrowed the structure of a literary type well-known in his day but used for ecclesiastical and moral purposes. His characters all have abstract names. There is the typical abstract argument:

> Liberty. What, Liberty to Measure then would ye bind?
> Measure. What else? for otherwise it were against kind:
>> If Liberty should leap and run where he list

It were no virtue, it were a thing
unbless'd.

But the play is filled with much specific material. Occasionally an image, instead of abstract terms, is used to describe the characters, as in this comment upon the taking of the assumed name, Sure Surveyance, by the character Counterfeit Countenance:

Surveyance! where ye survey
Thrift has lost her coffer-key!

or this comment upon Cloaked Collusion:

By Cock's heart, he looketh high!
He hawketh, methink, for a butterfly.

There is a specific reference to King Louis XII. As Henderson comments, although Skelton's purpose "is distinctly moral, . . . he is chiefly concerned with showing that the wages of imprudent spending, through certain unnamed evil advisers, will be, for a certain unnamed rich prince, adversity and poverty. The case at issue is not so much universal as particular—although, of course, it can be interpreted universally—and the play contains much indirect satire of Wolsey's influence on the young Henry VIII."[5]

A further step from the medieval method is apparent in the first of Skelton's major satires, **Speak, Parrot**. At first thought it would seem that the poem is similar to the medieval type of the bestiary, since a bird is the main character. But in this poem the parrot is not at all approached as were the beasts in the *Physiologi,* with an attempt to find some allegorical significance to the animal's habits or physical character. Rather, here the parrot is realized as the brightly-colored bird who is captured in distant places and brought off in a cage to be a plaything for idle women:

My name is Parrot, a bird of Paradise,
    By nature devised of a wondrous kind,
Daintily dieted with divers delicate spice
    Till Euphrates, that flood, driveth me into Ind,
    Where men of that countrie by fortune me find
And send me to great ladyes of estate:
Then Parrot must have an almond or a date.

A cage curiously carven, with a silver pin,
    Properly painted, to be my coverture;
A mirror of glass, that I may toot therein:
    These, maidens full meekly with many a divers
    flower,
    Freshly they dress, and make sweet my bower,
With "Speak, Parrot, I pray you." Full curtesly they say
"Parrot is a goodly bird, a pretty popinjay!"

With my beake bent, my little wanton eye,
    My feathers fresh as is the emerald green, . . .
    I am a minion to wait upon a queen:
    "My proper Parrot, my little pretty fool!"
With ladies I learn, and go with them to school.

Also, this parrot can speak Latin, Hebrew, Arabic, Chaldean, Greek, Spanish, French, Dutch, English, and Portugese; and like the parrot Skelton garbles his smatterings of words and phrases from these languages. It is this near-confusion of language which has attracted the most attention from scholars, though the purpose of the indirection of statement is frankly admitted:

For in this process Parrot nothing hath surmised,
    No matter pretended, nor nothing enterprised,
But that *metaphora, allegoria* with all,
Shall be his protection, his paves, and his wall.

Underneath the confusion of language two principal attacks are readily apparent, one against the study of Greek, and the other, more violent, against Wolsey.

What is more interesting for our purposes here is the method involved. It certainly is not medieval, for no indirect preparation, no dream setting or allegorical structure, is provided. The poem starts with the description of the parrot, quoted above, continues the description for a number of stanzas, and then proceeds to the statements by the parrot. The parrot provides, then, the single structural element of the poem: about the facts that the parrot lives in places of court intrigue and that he can speak are gathered the satirical matters of the poem. And the principle by which the satirical matters are gathered is simply one of accumulation: the parrot speaks of matters which the author wishes to satirize, and at the time he wishes to satirize them. This is attested not only by the fact that there are two principal objects of satire, as noted above, but also by the fact that the poem has several envoys, each of them dated and "constituting a series of fortnightly reports on the current activities of Cardinal Wolsey."[6] And the parrot remains the only connecting link among these accretions, whether in terms of time or of matter.

The complete break with the medieval manner is apparent in **Colin Clout**. "Here the dream-structure is abandoned in favor of a single dramatic ego; personification and allegory change to direct statement; and the rime-royal is abandoned in favor of the Skeltonical verse."[7] There is no attempt at narrative to link together the various satirical matters of the poem. The structural element, bringing together into one poem such various matters, is provided by the figure of Colin Clout:

Thus I, Colin Clout,
As I go about,
And wand'ring as I walk
I hear the people talk.

Take me as I intend,
For loth I am to offend
In this that I have penn'd:
I tell you as men say.

As the parrot is used in **Speak, Parrot,** so here also the structural element, the "single dramatic ego" of Colin Clout, is used to link not only various materials—which include attacks upon church corruption, the confusion of temporal and spiritual powers of the Church, the lack of learning and the laziness of many priests, and Wolsey's attempt at advancement—but also parts composed at different times.[8] This is apparent also in the third major satire, **Why Come Ye not to Court?** In that poem, only a little more than a quarter of the way through the complete work, appear the lines:

> Thus will I conclude my style,
> And fall to rest a while,
> And so to rest a while.

Thus the poem must have ended at this point once, to be taken up again as new instances of corruption came to Skelton's attention.

The structural relationship among these matters within the poem can be only slight. This is particularly true of **Why Come Ye not to Court?** which does not have a parrot or a Colin Clout to provide some semblance of unity. Combining such various matters at various times in the same poem, Skelton returned often to the same attack, securing intensification and a well-rounded picture by repetition and by the addition of many new examples. As Berdan comments of **Why Come Ye not to Court?,** "The natural result is that the poem is powerful only in detail. As a whole it has the incoherence of anger."[9]

This use of repetition, or parallelism, as it might be called, appears not only in the large units of these poems but also in smaller units. It is a striking characteristic of those poems by Skelton which are out of the medieval tradition; and the same structure, as Nelson notes,[10] is just as strikingly absent from the poems composed in rime-royal. An example is this from **Colin Clout:**

> Farewell benignitie,
> Farewell simplicitie,
> Farewell humilitie,
> Farewell good charitie!

Another is from **The Tunning of Elinor Rumming:**

> Another set of sluts:
> Some brought walnuts,
> Some apples, some pears,
> Some brought their clipping shears,
> Some brought this and that,
> Some brought I wot n'ere what;
> Some brought their husband's hat,
> Some puddings and links,
> Some tripes that stinks.

In these poems, then, Skelton has arrived at a method which is definitely not medieval. The writing is direct, not indirect; there is no allegorical covering, but instead an attempt to provide structure through the dramatic figure of a bird or a man who repeats what he hears. Above all, Skelton has thrown over the psychological and philosophical principles which underlie the medieval method. He does not approach experiences with preconceptions; experience is not intellectualized into categorical compartments. Instead he seems to be trying "to get the facts." His own program for church and civil reform is only slightly empha-

sized compared with his insistence upon the evils which exist. He is gathering data for a program, for a philosophy of action. The poems exhibit a sort of inductive thinking.

In terms of verse structure, we may, for the sake of convenience, term his method "accumulative." He gathers data not once but time after time to cover the same point again and again. "Over and over again he repeats the same things, devoid of all logical form and construction—although these pieces may be said to have certain concentric[11] movement of their own—round and round the same point he goes, always coming back to where he started from."[12] And this accumulative method is apparent not only in terms of materials but also in terms of the structure of the verse from line to line, as has been pointed out.

Skelton's work covers almost every type of verse practiced in his day, including the morality play; but he proceeded from acceptance of the medieval tradition, through varying stages of revolt against that tradition, to a new form which he devised.

—Alan Swallow

The same method of accumulation is characteristic of Skelton's best non-satirical work. It is especially evident in **The Tunning of Elinor Rumming,** an extreme example of a direct, non-intellectualized approach to sordid elements of experience. The poem is composed of scenes and portraits—almost photographic in their fidelity to fact—of women found at a tavern. And the scenes and portraits are left at the level of description: at the end the poet has merely written enough:

> For my fingers itch,
> I have written too mich
> Of this mad mumming
> Of Elinor Rumming!
> Thus endeth the geste
> Of this worthy feast.

At the same time, repetition and accumulation form the dominant verse-structure throughout the poem. One example has already been quoted. Of the same sort, but here used in conversation, is:

> He calleth me his whiting,
> His mulling and his miting,
> His nobbes and his coney,
> His sweeting and his honey,
> With "Bass, my pretty bonny,
> Thou are worth goods and money!"

Broad, indefinite metaphors and similes are often used in the portraits. They cannot be put together, as images, to make a clear picture, for the analogies are drawn from so many realms of experience. They function, then, as momentary impressions of detail, the complete portrait being achieved through the accumulation of many such images. The following, to give an example, are less than a fourth of the lines devoted to the portrait of Elinor Rumming:

> With clothes upon her head
> That weigh a sow of lead,
> Writhen in wondrous wise
> After the Saracen's guise,
> With a whim-wham
> Knit with a trim-tram
> Upon her brain-pan;
> Like an Egyptian
> Cappéd about.
>   When she goeth out
> Herself for to shew,
> She driveth down the dew
> With a pair of heeles
> As broad as two wheeles;
> She hobbles as a gose
> With her blanket hose,
>   Her shoon smeared with tallow,
> Greaséd upon dirt
>   That bawdeth her skirt.

Philip Sparrow is something of a special case, because for the first of its two parts Skelton has again gone to a convention to secure a structure for his poem. In this case, the convention, as Ian Gordon has pointed out, is the Services for the Dead of the Roman Church.[13] Gordon lists all the forms of the Services for the Dead and comments:

> Skelton uses all these forms except that of Matins, and **Philip Sparow** is remarkable in the way it uses first the Vespers in the Office for the Dead, then without indication or warning becomes the medieval Mass of the Birds . . . ; again without warning shifts into the Absolution over the Tomb; and then with a few lines on the coming on of night returns to the close of Vespers in the Office. After a section on the composition of a Latin epitaph . . . we find ourselves at the *Commendatio*—commendations, not of the soul of Philip Sparow, but, with an obvious play on the double meaning of the word, on the beauty of the girl who was supposed to have recited part one.[14]

Within this structure Skelton's method of accumulation of detail and perception is apparent, particularly in the second part, where he proceeds from one aspect of Joanna's beauty to another. The following is his comment upon her wart (perhaps a mole) upon her cheek:

> And when I perceived
> Her wart and conceived,
> It cannot be denay'd
> But it was well conveyed
> And set so womanly,
> And nothing wantonly,
> But right conveniently,
> And full congruently,

> As Nature could devise,
> In most goodly wise!
> Who so list behold,
> It maketh lovers bold
> To her to sue for grace,
> Her favour to purchase;
> The scar upon her chin,
> Enhached on her fair skin,
> Whiter than the swan,
> It would make any man
> To forget deadly sin
> Her favour to win!

Within the first part, also, the same verse-structure is used. A Latin phrase from the Services for the Dead introduces each new movement, and within each appear such passages as:

> Sometime he would gasp
> When he saw a wasp;
> A fly, or a gnat,
> He would fly at that;
> And prettily he would pant
> When he saw an ant!
> Lord, how he would pry
> After a butterfly!
> Lord, how he would hop
> After the gressop!
> And when I said, "Phip, Phip!"
> Then he would leap and skip,
> And take me by the lip.

And:

> O cat of churlish kind,
> The fiend was in thy mind
> When thou my bird untwined!
> I would thou hadst been blind!
> The léopards savage,
> The lions in their rage
> Might catch thee in their paws,
> And gnaw thee in their jaws!
> The serpents of Libany
> Might sting thee venomously!
> The dragons with their tongues
> Might poison thy liver and lungs!
> The manticors of the mountains
> Might feed them on thy brains!

But it is to be noted that in addition to his accumulative method Skelton in this poem makes use of his convention in a way not characteristic of his other poems in which a convention is found. Here the Services for the Dead are not merely framework, as is the dream-framework of **The Bouge of Court.** The Services are integrated into the poem and act as an undercurrent of commentary on Joanna's sorrow and lamentation. Commenting on this usage, Gordon says, "The formulae of the various Services are introduced, but they are unchanged and perhaps not always even ridiculed. Instead they give a mock-serious background to the lament for Philip that is at any time liable to lose its mockery."[15] It is this management of tone between humor and pathos, between burlesque and sentimentality, which is one of the important achievements of ***Philip Sparrow***; and the use of the convention as a functional device in managing the tone represents a further step in Skelton's handling of structural elements in his poetry.

And just as in this poem there is a functional use of the framework, so also is there a functional modification of his characteristic accumulation. In one of her first laments, Joanna says:

> When I remember again
> How my Philip was slain,
> Never half the pain
> Was between you twain,
> Pyramus and Thisbe,
> As then befell to me:
> I wept and I wailed,
> The teares down hailed,
> But nothing it availed
> To call Philip again,
> Whom Gib, our cat, hath slain.

Here the repetitive pattern for the verses is familiar. But it is not so straightforward as before; there is a balance of tone which we found extended throughout the poem by means of the undercurrent of commentary through the parody of the Services for the Dead. The first seven lines quoted seem all of one attitude, a genuine lamentation for the death of the sparrow. But the object of the lamentation is merely a pet bird; a single attitude of such pathos toward such an object would seem sentimental. So against the attitude is balanced one of mockery of the lamentation itself, expressed in this passage by the exaggeration of the metaphor *hailed* in the eighth line and by the near-humor involved in the name of the cat, in the implied situation, and in the exaggerated heroism of the words *hath slain* of the last line. Similar balancings of attitudes are found throughout Joanna's part of the poem. There is straightforward grief in some of the descriptions, as that of the bird crawling beneath the girl's night clothes:

> And on me it would leap
> When I was asleep
> And his feathers shake,
> Wherewith he would make
> Me often for to wake,
> And for to take him in
> Upon my naked skin.
> God wot, we thought no sin:
> What though he crept so low?
> It was no hurt, I trow,
> He did nothing, perde,
> But sit upon my knee!
> Philip, though he were nice,
> In him it was no vice!
> Philip might be bold
> And do what he wold:
> Philip would seek and take
> All the fleas black
> That he could there espy
> With his wanton eye.

Or, after a recollection that with a knowledge of magic she might be able to bring Philip alive again, Joanna thinks of the time she tried to stitch Philip's likeness in a sampler:

> But when I was sewing his beak,
> Methought my sparrow did speak,
> And opened his pretty bill,
> Saying, "Maid, ye are in will
> Again me for to kill!
> Ye prick me in the head! . . .
> My needle and thread
> I threw away for dread.

Finally, this accumulative method is the foundation of Skelton's best lyrics. Occasionally, there is a certain reverse process, a general statement followed by the realistic image; the organization is apparent in this quotation from ***Upon a Dead Man's Head***:

> It is general
> To be mortal:
> I have well espied
> No man may him hide
> From Death hollow-eyed,
> With sinews witheréd,
> With bones shiveréd,
> With his worm-eaten maw,
> And his ghastly jaw
> Gasping aside,
> Naked of hide,
> Neither flesh nor fell.

Obviously even here the interest is not primarily upon the general statement but upon the actual effect of mortality.

At times appears the accumulation of detail towards a general statement, as in the last three stanzas of ***Knowledge, Acquaintance, Resort, Favour with Grace***:

> Remorse have I of your most goodlihood,
>   Of your behavior courteous and benign,
> Of your bounty and of your womanhood,
>   Which maketh my heart oft to leap and spring,
>   And to remember many a pretty thing:
> But absence, alas, with trembling fear and dread
> Abasheth me, albeit I have no need.
>
> You I assure, absence is my foe,
>   My deadly woe, my painful heaviness;
> And if ye list to know the cause why so
>   Open mine heart, behold my mind express:
>   I would ye could! then should ye see, mistress,
> How there nis thing that I covet so fain
> As to embrace you in mine armes twain.
>
> Nothing earthly to me more desirous
>   Than to behold your beauteous countenance:
> But, hateful Absence, to me so envious,
>   Though thou withdraw me from her by long
> distance,
>   Yet shall she never out of my remembrance:

For I have gravéd her within the secret wall
Of my true heart, to love her best of all!

These two poems are also basically "occasional." The former is addressed to a woman who sent the poet a death's head "for a token," and the letter is addressed by the lover to the loved-one. In each case the realistic, accumulative method is at times confused, in the first poem by moralizings upon mortality, and in the second by the intrusion of a medieval personification of Absence. In Skelton's best lyrics, however, there is not this confusion. In a number of them, such as *Lullay, Lullay, like a Child*; *The Ancient Acquaintance, Madam, between Us Twain*; and *Mannerly Margery Milk and Ale*, the poem has a narrative basis. But the interest is not merely in the narrative. The first-named poem is a song, and the music for it has come down to us; it has the quality of statement and the repeated refrain common to the song tradition. In the others appears a greater attempt to get at the details of the narrative situation and of the characterization, with Skelton's favorite method of providing detail:

> What dream'st thou, drunkard, drowsy pate?
>   Thy lust and liking is from thee gone;
> Thou blinkard blowboll, thou wakest too late,
>   Behold thou liest, luggard, alone!
> Well may thou sigh, well may thou groan,
>   To deal with her so cowardly:
> Ywis, pole hatchet, she bleared thin eye.

At their best, then, Skelton's lyrics have dropped the generalization from a place of prime importance. In its place appears an interest in getting the details of characterization and of the experience. These details are expressed, not through a close analysis of the elements or through means of an extended metaphor, but through almost a riot of images which seem to have little connection or coordination but each of which expresses some facet of the experience; and by the accumulation of such facets a rounded, full communication of the experience is occasionally attained. Skelton's method produces at its best, in the lyric, such a poem as **"To Mistress Margaret Hussey"** from *The Garland of Laurel*:

> Merry Margaret,
>   As midsummer flower,
> Gentle as falcon
> Or hawk of the tower:
> With solace and gladness,
> With mirth and no madness,
> All good and no badness;
>   So joyously,
>   So maidenly,
>   So womanly
>   Her demeaning
>   In everything,
>   Far, far passing
>   That I can indite,
>   Or suffice to write
> Of Merry Margaret
>   As midsummer flower,
> Gentle as falcon

> Or hawk of the tower.
>   As patient and still
> And as full of good will
> As fair Isaphill,
> Coliander,
> Sweet pomander,
> Good Cassander,
> Steadfast of thought,
> Well made, well wrought,
> Far may be sought
> Ere that he can find
> So courteous, so kind
> As Merry Margaret,
>   This midsummer flower,
> Gentle as falcon
> Or hawk of the tower.

Notes

[1] William Nelson, *John Skelton, Laureate* (New York, 1939), p. 142.

[2] *The Complete Poems of John Skelton, Laureate*, edited by Philip Henderson (London, 1931), pp. 2-3. All quotations from Skelton are from this edition.

[3] *Ibid*, p. XXVIII.

[4] John M. Berdan, *Early Tudor Poetry, 1485-1547* (New York, 1931), p. 97.

[5] Henderson, p. XXVII.

[6] Nelson, p. 135.

[7] Berdan, p. 179.

[8] *Ibid.*, pp. 195-198, gives indications that Colin Clout was circulated in fragments and thus must have been composed piecemeal.

[9] *Ibid.*, p. 193.

[10] Nelson, p. 87.

[11] Ten Brink, as Arthur Koelbing points out ("Barclay and Skelton," *The Cambridge History of English Literature* [Cambridge, 1909], III, 84) called Skelton's method "concentric."

[12] Henderson, p. XXIX.

[13] Ian A. Gordon, "Skelton's Philip Sparow' and the Roman Service-Book," *Modern Language Review*, XXIX (1934), 389-396.

[14] *Ibid.*, p. 390.

[15] *Ibid.*, p. 396.

John Holloway (essay date 1960)

SOURCE: "Skelton," in *The Charted Mirror: Literary and Critical Essays*, Routledge & Kegan Paul, 1960, pp. 3-24.

[In the following excerpt, Holloway praises Skelton's vernacular poetry as well as his careful attention to common experience.]

To discuss Skelton effectively is to do more than elucidate the past on its own terms, and for its own sake. There is no constraint on anyone to do more than this, and to think that there is, is to think like a barbarian. But if a critic finds that his subject empowers him to do more, he ought to say so. Although Skelton was writing more than 450 years ago, there are certain respects in which his poetry offers us enlightenment and guidance in the literary and cultural problems which confront us today. To seize on the essence of his poetry is to be wiser for our own time. Were that not so, I should perhaps have left the subject of Skelton to others, because I find it congenial but do not find it reassuringly easy.

The problems of today upon which this poet casts light may be indicated by two quotations: one from Mr Robert Graves and one from Bernard Berenson. Mr Graves, writing in 1943 on the development of modern prose, referred to the 'eccentrically individual styles' of Meredith, Doughty, James, and others, and added, 'many more styles were invented as the twentieth century advanced and since there was keen competition among writers as to who should be "great" and since it was admitted that "greatness" was achieved only by a highly individual style, new tricks and new devices multiplied'.[1] Forty years before this, Berenson in his essay on the decline of art pointed out how modern European culture, 'mad for newness' as he put it, has committed itself to a ritual of unremitting dynamism. 'We are thus perpetually changing: and our art cycles, compared to those of Egypt or China, are of short duration, not three centuries at the longest; and our genius is as frequently destructive as constructive.'[1]

Modern English literature surely illustrates what Berenson referred to. The unremitting search for a new way with words, a new kind of hero, a new device for carrying matters a stage further, a new model from some past writer or some foreign literature—these features of the scene are familiar. The search for newness is not itself new, and probably no age has been quite without it. Naturalizing foreign models was an integral part of Chaucer's achievement (though very far of course from the whole of it). But the question is not one merely of innovation; it is of a growing need for constant innovation, and a sense that however often the game of change is played, we are always soon back with what is played out and old-fashioned.

This attitude to writing seems to have become established in England in the course of the sixteenth century. There is a well-known passage in Bacon's *De Augmentis Scientiarum,* written towards the close of his life, in which he adverts to the playing-out first of the vogue for Cicero, then of the vogue for Seneca, shortly before, and shortly after, 1600. More to our immediate purpose is a passage from Puttenham's *Art of English Poetry* of 1589. Puttenham was himself the author of the best and best known manual of a new poetry, which was learning amply from ancient and from foreign models, and which had for many years been coming to dominate the English literary scene. The following passage not only illustrates how Puttenham saw Skelton as the last of the bad old days, and Skelton's immediate successors as those who laid the foundations for the new and stylish; it also points unconsciously forward, in several turns of phrase, to the derivativeness, the vacuous grandiosity, the empty ingenuity, which have plagued us intermittently ever since:

> Skelton (was) a sharp satirist, but with more rayling and scoffery than became a Poet Lawreat, such among the Greeks were called Pantomimi, with us Buffons, altogether applying their wits to scurrilities and other ridiculous matters. *Henry* Earle of Surrey and Sir *Thomas Wyat,* betweene whom I find very littel difference, I repute them. . . for the two chief lanterns of light to all others that have since employed their pennes upon English Poesie, their conceits were loftie, their stiles stately, their conveyance cleanly, their termes proper, their meetre sweete and well proportioned, in all imitating very naturally and studiously their Maister *Francis Petrarcha.*[1]

Ever since the time of these two indistinguishable lanterns of light, imitating one's master naturally and studiously, or finding a new master, or going one better than the old master, have figured prominently, in English verse; and whether the end sought has been stateliness and loftiness, or cleanness and propriety, or sweetness and naturalness, the underlying ideas of a regulation of poetry or a reform of poetry have seldom been far distant.

To take Skelton as representative of something different from this tradition, and as instructive on account of the difference, is not to see him merely as an illiterate extemporising buffoon. He has been seen in these terms in the past, but modern scholarship has made the view quite untenable. Skelton was one of a group of Latinists—the proto-humanists we might call them—whom Henry VII drew into his service, and of whom Polydore Vergil is perhaps the best known.[2] He was an accomplished rhetorician, and his employment of the figures of rhetoric is as deliberate (if somewhat more intelligent) as that of his contemporary Stephen Hawes.[3] His best known poem, *Phyllyp Sparowe,* is a kind of reverent burlesque of the ritual of the Mass in accordance with established medieval convention;[4] and in the description of his heroine in this poem, we can recognize the two places, and no more, where Skelton the poet abandoned the literary model, for the sake one supposes of the real girl.[5] That model was the first specimen *descriptio* in Geoffrey de Vinsauf's *Poetria Nova,* and this work was as much the medieval poetic handbook as Puttenham's work was the Elizabethan one. Skelton's own disclaimer 'though my rhyme be ragged',[1] is itself something of a literary convention: his first modern editor, in 1843, pointed out that Sir David Lindsay and Spenser say the same of their own verse. William Caxton notices that in his translation of Diodorus Siculus Skelton wrote 'not in rude and old language but in polished and ornate terms craftily', and it is essentially the same kind of compliment as Caxton pays elsewhere, justly, to Chaucer ('crafty and sugared eloquence'), and as Spenser's spokesman E. K. was later to pay to the 'well trussed up' verse of Spenser. Skelton was a learned, a professional writer, conversant with his craft and art, an aureate poet as well as a laureate one.

There is always a danger, however, that in registering the qualities of a poem which have been laboriously and scrupulously brought into focus by scholarship, we become blind to the qualities which were never in need of such focusing, because they sprang off the page at us. This is a vital point for Skelton. One of his shorter poems, which begins: *Knolege, aquayntance, resort, fauour with grace,* has been described as 'an ecphrasis in the aureate manner of Lydgate'[2] so it is: we can easily see that it conforms to a literary recipe, and there is little to see in it besides. A companion piece is in part very similar. Also an address to a woman, it closes with an appeal to her to observe the conventional courtly code. It opens with the literary convention at its limpest and most stilted:

> The auncient acquaintance, madam, betwen vs
> twayn,
>   The famylyaryte, the formar dalyaunce,
> Causyth me that I can not myself refrayne
>   But that I must wryte for my plesaunt pastaunce

But Skelton's tongue is in his cheek; this poem is rapidly transformed; its subject—a wife who has been playing fast and loose with her husband—turns into a hectic stable-yard scene, and a horseman struggling with a mare that has the devil in her, 'ware, ware, the mare wynsyth wyth her wanton hele!', 'Haue in sergeaunt ferrour (farrier)'. The violence and confusion veritably explode what was only a mock-decorous poem. It is not, of course, the first English poem to explode the convention in which it is ostensibly written; but to explode a literary convention it is necessary to obtain a powerful charge drawn from outside convention.

What this is may be seen, perhaps, by turning to the most misjudged of all Skelton's poems, *The Tunnying of Elynour Rummyng.* To say that the tradition of this rough, vernacular poetry has been lost, is not to say everything about it; but is certainly to point towards the difficulty which this poem has created for one critic after another. Henry Morley saw it as 'a very humble rendering to simple wits of the repulsive aspects of intemperance in women';[1] Miss E. P. Hammond refers to its wallowing coarseness;[2] even Professor Lewis seems to see the problem as one of tolerating ugliness for the sake of the liveliness, and expresses his preference for the Scottish poem *Christis Kirk on the Grene,* which he praises for melody, gaiety, and orderliness, and which attracts him through its occasional underlying lyricism.[3]

To experience these feelings about *Elynour Rummyng* is to wish that it were different in kind from what it is, rather than better in quality. This picture of a morning in a low country ale-house is if anything less coarse than Langland's superb account of Gluttony in the ale-house, in *Piers Plowman,*[4] and melody and gaiety are as far from Skelton's purpose as they were from Langland's. Indeed, to mention Langland is at once to become aware that Skel-

ton's piece is no thoughtless extemporisation, but has its literary antecedents. Its subject, and its attitude to that subject, were both recurrent in medieval writing;[5] and it is possible that Skelton's poem, with its old and ugly ale-wife whose customers are all old and ugly women, is even a kind of calculated counterpart to a poem by Lydgate, the *Ballade on an Ale-Seller,* in which (to express oneself in modern terms) a bold and handsome barmaid attracts an exclusively male clientele. In Lydgate's poem, we certainly have orderliness, the order of the ballade; and we have a literary, even sometimes a lofty diction. But they are quite out of key with the subject; and

> With your kissyng thouh that ye do plesaunce
>   It shall be derrer, er thei do ther way
> Than al ther ale, to them I dar wel say

—that is perhaps the best that Lydgate's poem can do: a hasty glimpse of fact, a trite moral, a reader nonplussed with tedium.

The ugly side of *Elynour Rummyng* is simply an honest reflection of the poverty and primitiveness which were the staple of life for a rural peasantry in England at that time, as they doubtless are still for rural peasants over most of the planet. If we find coarseness, it is not through identifying what Skelton is trying to make of his material, but through plain unfamiliarity with the material itself. In a now almost unknown poem of just after Skelton's time (happily almost unknown, for in the main it is very bad), we can glimpse those same conditions, but they peer through despite the poet's almost admitted inability to render them. The poem is Copland's *Hie Waie to the Spitale Hous,* and the passage is that which describes the beggars and vagrants as the Watch sees them at night:

> But surely, every night here is found
>   One or other lying by the pound
> In the sheep cotes or in the hay loft
> And at Saint Bartholomew's church door full oft
> And even here alway by this brick wall
>   We do them find, that do both chide and brawl
> And like as beasts together they be throng
>   Both lame and sick and whole them among,
> And in many corners where that we go,
>   Whereof I greatly wonder that they do so.[1]

Copland virtually confesses, with that disastrous last line, how his facts defeat him. Skelton's poem is in another world; or rather, his ale-wife with her skin that is 'grained lyke a sacke', her customers who tie their hair up in a shoe-rag when they come to pawn their crocks for ale, her pigs that wander in and out of the bar and scratch themselves on the furniture, take us back with exuberant vitality into the real world.

This extraordinary vividness, where many find vividness an embarrassment, has prevented readers from grasping the full range of the poem, as a record of fact. *Elynour Rummyng* is not, as it has been called, a 'purely objective' record of peasant reality.[1] It is not a moralizing poem, but it is full of an awareness of the essential humanity of the scene it depicts, and of a such comprehension of this (a comprehension neither harsh nor slack and casual) as is the only foundation for significant moralizing. It is easy to miss this subtler side to the poem; but it is there, in the customers who

> lothe to be espyde,
> Start in at the backe syde,
> Ouer the hedge and pale,
> And all for the good ale.

It is there in those who sit glumly because they have nothing to barter for ale, and can only drink as much as they can chalk up on the beam. It shows in the differences among what customers bring to barter: some the reasonable merchandise of the prosperous peasant, some the last thing in the house or the last thing that they ought to part with. Once we are conscious of these aspects of the poem, even the character of Elynour herself takes on a new light. Her shocked indignation when one of the customers falls over and lets her skirts fly up is a genuine and convincing turn of peasant character. Some of the customers ask for drink and have no money. Skelton writes:

> Elynour swered, Nay,
> Ye shall not beare away
> My ale for nought,
> *By hym that me bought!*

This does not merely contrast the bargains which men and women strike, with that which Christ struck: it brings them disquietingly, revealingly together. With these things in mind, one can see that the opening description of Elynour herself has a somewhat similar deeper significance. It clearly resembles one of the most humane and moving passages in the whole of Chaucer's writings, the *Reve's Prologe*:

> For sikerly, whan I was bore, anon
> Deeth drough the tappe of lyf and leet it gon;
> And ever sithe hath so the tappe yronne
> Til that almoost al empty is the tonne.

Incidentally, the elderly Reeve's 'grene tayl' may have its connexion with 'Parot hath a blacke beard and a fayre grene tale' in Skelton's **Speke, Parot,** a poem which I shall discuss later. But there is a clear detailed link with **Elynour Rummyng** too. Chaucer's Reeve says:

> But ik am oold, me list not for pley for age;
> Gras tyme is doon, my fodder is now forage
> This white top writeth myne old yeris.

Skelton uses just this idea of fresh plants and dead forage, and when he does so, it is difficult not to see both Chaucer's direct influence, and the general quality of his insight into human transience:

> Her eyen. . .
> . . . are blered
> And she gray hered . . .
> Her youth is farre past:

> Foted lyke a plane
> Leged lyke a crane;
> And yet she wyll iet,
> Lyke a jolly fet . . .
> Her huke of Lyncole grene,
> It had been hers, I wene,
> More then fourty yere;
> And so doth it apere,
> For the grene bare thredes
> Loke lyke sere *wedes,*
> Wyddered lyke *hay* . . .

As against this poem, *Christis Kirk on the Grene* is gay boisterous comedy with something even of slapstick; and to compare it with Skelton's poem is to bring out not the defects, but the distinctiveness, and the depth of the latter.

Miss M. M. Gray has pointed out that the spirit of poems like *Christis Kirk on the Grene* is not typical of the Scottish poetry of its period.[1] If **The Tunnyng of Elynour Rummyng** is related instead to such poems as *Tydingis fra the Sessioun,* which is by Dunbar, or *The Devillis Inquest,* which is almost certainly not so, a quite new kind of difference emerges. In *The Devillis Inquest* we find:

> 'Be Goddis blud,' quod the taverneir,
> 'Thair is sic wyine in my selleir
> Hes never come in this cuntrie.'
> 'Yit,' quod the Devill, 'thou sellis our deir,
> With thy fals met cum downe to me.'

This is not a Chaucerian movement of thought; it is a vision which concentrates on the evil in the fact, sees it intensely, and is directed by uncompromising though sternly controlled indignation. One side of reality is brought into a clear focus by a cold and masterly economy of language. This is still a link with Chaucer, but it is not Skelton's kind of link. With rare exceptions, Chaucer's firm linguistic line, his masterly economy, do not serve purposes like these, but less severe ones. Dr Edwards, discussing Skelton's lyrics, wrote: 'He possessed none of Chaucer's smiling acceptance of men and women as they are.'[2] Even as an account of Chaucer, that might need a little amendment; but what is relevant for the moment is that it distinguishes too sharply between Chaucer and Skelton.

In my view **Elynour Rummyng** is the most significant of the poems which Skelton wrote in the short metre which has been named after him. **Philip Sparow** has great grace and charm, but its chief character is to be an endearing poem, and one which deserves a rather higher place in our affections than it does in our minds as a whole. What may be found in it is not far from what may readily be found elsewhere, and its principle of organization lacks the vitality and distinctiveness of what integrates **Elynour Rummyng,** the single scene of the poem itself as that is brought progressively into focus. . . .

Colyn Cloute and **Why Come Ye Nat to Courte** can by no means be passed over altogether, and if I pass them over for the moment, it is in order to give emphasis to a more general point. The poems which Skelton wrote in short lines, rhyming consecutively—in 'Skeltonics'—are usually thought of as his most distinctive and most interesting ones. Long ago, this idea supplied Isaac D'Israeli with a cumbrous joke and a mixed metaphor: 'Whenever (Skelton's) muse plunges into the long measure of heroic verse, she is drowned in no Heliconian stream.'[1] The idea reappears implicitly in what has surely been the most influential of recent pronouncements on Skelton, Mr Graves' poem *John Skelton*,[2] which is itself written in a kind of Skeltonics, and which catalogues most of 'helter-skelter John's' short-line poems, without any reference to his other works. And when Professor Lewis writes[3] 'the things that Mr Graves gets out of Skelton's work are much better than anything Skelton put in', he is clearly not taking issue with this conception of Skelton, even if it is not entirely clear that he is endorsing it.

Although Skelton was writing more than 450 years ago, there are certain respects in which his poetry offers us enlightenment and guidance in the literary and cultural problems which confront us today.

—John Holloway

This notion of what most distinguishes Skelton is erroneous; the Skeltonics are what stand out if we survey only the externals of his work, if our findings are a little too much like what a computer could find if Skelton's poems were fed into it. Some of the most remarkable qualities of Skelton's work are obscured and concealed by his short line. It is in what D'Israeli misleadingly called 'the long measure of his heroic verse' that these qualities are most abundantly manifested; and when this is realized, Mr Graves's

> What could be *dafter*
> Than John Skelton's laughter?
> What sound more *tenderly*
> Than his *pretty* poetry?

falls short of adequacy.

Skelton's **The Bouge of Court** is widely recognized as a poem which gives a new individuality to a conventional form, that of the dream-poem; but this is perhaps to praise that work on too easy terms. References to Skelton's avoidance of 'the conventional arbor'[1] or statements like 'for the first time the medieval vision is given a strictly local habitat'[2] ignore such things as the opening of the *Kingis Quair*: King James of Scotland's sleepless night, with his book at his bedside and the matins bell to disturb him. With this, one might perhaps take Henryson in his study mending the fire and taking strong drink to keep out the cold before he settles down to write *The Testament of Cresseid*. The distinction of Skelton's poem lies less in

any simple change in its mechanical organization, than in something which is woven intimately into its texture. Among the various allegorical figures whom Skelton meets as passengers when he boards the ship, from which the poem takes its title, that of *Riot* is perhaps the best known.

> Wyth that came Ryotte, russhynge all at onces,
>   A rusty gallande, to-ragged and to-rente;
> And on the borde he whyrled a payre of bones,
>   Quater treye dews he clatered as he wente;
> Now haue at all, by saynte Thomas of Kente!
> And euer he threwe and kyst I wote nere what:
> His here was growen thorowe oute his hat.
>
> Thenne I behelde how he dysgysed was:
>   His hede was heuy for watchynge ouer nyghte;
> His eyen blered, his face shone lyke a glas;
>   His gowne so shorte that it ne couer myghte
>   His rumpe, he wente so all for somer lyghte;
> His hose was garded wyth a lyste of grene,
> Yet at the knee they were broken, I wene.

This account, as a whole, is more than 'a brilliant sketch of the seedy, jazz-humming early Tudor roué' as it has been called;[3] and it displays more than 'a genius for satirical portraiture'[4] *tout court*. The affinity with Chaucer's *Pardoner's Tale* may be partial, but it is unmistakable. The note of pathos, of tragedy in Riot's high spirits and gay tatters is not, surely, the mere interpolation of a modern mind. 'Counter he coude *O lux* vpon a potte,' Skelton writes: it is the medieval hymn *O lux beata trinitas* that Riot counters. We are never—even if only through the oaths that come incessantly throughout this poem—allowed to forget the religious dimension in which all these essentially human and mortal figures have their being. '. . . by that Lorde that bought dere all mankynde, I can not flater, I muste be playne to thë; 'by that Lorde that is one, two, and thre, I haue an errande to rounde in your ere' (an echo of Chaucer echoing Dante). This note might not be clear as irony, were it not for the constantly scriptural note, also sounding ironically, of the rest:

> Loo, what it is a man to haue connynge!
> All erthly tresoure it is surmountynge.

and

> Nay, naye, be sure, whyles I am on your syde,
> Ye may not fall, truste me, ye may not fayle

and

> Maystress, quod I, I haue none aquentaunce,
> That wyll for me be medyatoure and mene

—all these illustrate something which is sustained so much without intermission through the poem, that in the end it is quite inescapable. Skelton is leading us to see these figures—figures 'for whome Tybourne groneth both daye and nyghte'—as erring mortal creatures in the fullest sense; in fact his compassionate comprehension is if anything more in evidence here, and more sombrely and solemnly in evidence, than it was in **Elynour Rummyng.**

Something else is in evidence also. Skelton's insight into men's behaviour, exact and humane as it was, could not but equip him with real power for dramatization. English literature seems to have reached fully dramatic writing only with difficulty: perhaps because this demands a sense of realistic detail, a power of comprehension and selection which is more than realism, and also (if it is to be in verse) an appropriately developed metrical vehicle. Chaucer mastered it even as early as the *Hous of Fame*; most English medieval plays only strive towards it. In **The Bouge of Court** it is otherwise. Dyssymulation, for example, tells the poet that the people in the court are all malicious gossips. Then he makes an exception of himself:

> For all be it that this longe not to me,
>   Yet on my backe I bere suche lewde delynge:
> Ryghte now I spake with one, I trowe, I see;
>   But, what, a strawe! I maye not tell all thynge.
> By God, I saye there is grete herte brennynge
> Betwene the persone ye wote of, (and) you.

These lines are typical, and to read them is to find oneself in almost total contact with the movement of a living mind as it works its way from word to word.

Contrast that moment in Stephen Hawes' *Example of Vertue* when the poet meets Dame Sensuality riding on a goat. If we have any hopes that her arrival will infuse a little vitality into the poem, the poet extinguishes those hopes with stunning celerity:

> 'Nay,' said Discretion, 'that may nat be'
> 'No,' said I, 'in no maner of wise
> To her request will I now agree
> But evermore her foul Lust despise . . .

'So forth I went . . . Hawes' next stanza baldly opens. That is a phrase which recurs throughout his poem: each time it marks an evasion of reality, a giving up by the poet before material he cannot handle.

By contrast, the personifications of **The Bouge of Court** have a vivid vernacular life. . . .

I have not seen any explicit recognition of how much Skelton's work owes to proverbial language, and in doing so, to the whole way of life and cast of mind which finds its expression in proverbial language; although the first modern edition of his work is full of information on this very subject. Here the short line poems are relevant once again. 'Such apple-tree, such fruit'; 'loth to hang the bell / About the cattes neck'; 'hearted like an hen'; 'not worth a leek'; 'as wise as Waltham's calfe'; 'all is fish that cometh to net'; 'we may blow at the coal'; 'Mock hath lost her shoe'; '. . . . it is a wily mouse / That can build hys dwellyng house / Within the cat's ear'—it is not a matter merely of Skelton's using proverbial wise sayings. His verse draws on the proverbial kind of expression for a good deal of its vivid metaphorical wealth, and for something of its whole attitude to its subject—bold yet unassuming, essentially down-to-earth. It uses the clichés of ordinary people (which are not clichés at all, because instead of making the mind gloss over the plain facts, they bring it abruptly up against them) but it is using these in

order to assimilate the whole idea which ordinary people form of reality. To notice Skelton's reliance on the proverbial expression is not to notice a literary trick or a literary routine, but to notice, at its most easily recognizable point, the essential quality of what was creative in his mind. It is the same quality which shows, if we consider the use that he made of the authors on whose work he draws. Juvenal in his eighth satire, for example, had written:

> quo, si nocturnus adulter
> Tempora Santonico velas adoperta cucullo

Skelton almost certainly has this passage in mind when he attacks Wolsey in **Why Come Ye Nat to Courte.** But what he writes is:

> Ye may weare a cockes come;
> Your fonde hed in your furred hood,
> Holde ye your tong, ye can no goode:

Juvenal's line embodies penetrating diagnosis of a fact, and an attitude of angry superiority to it; Skelton replaces this by the common sense, and the impudence towards the great, of the plain man.[1] In the **Garlande of Laurell** there is an account of how the Phoenix consumes itself in the fire. Skelton probably had a passage from Ovid's *Metamorphoses*, Book XV, in mind. But he adds something of his own about this Phoenix:

> her wynges betwene
> She *bet up a fyre* with the sparkis full kene.

Perhaps it is not fanciful to suggest that this comes nearer to an early morning scene in Skelton's own Norfolk parsonage, than it does to Ovid. Again, when Skelton in the same poem describes the bard Iopas singing his song in the garden of the Muses, he follows the closing lines of the first book of the Aeneid; but there is nothing in Virgil which corresponds to the lively turn of thought, humorous rather than witty, whereby Skelton's Iopas, in his songs about the constellations, includes

> that pole artike which doth remayne
> *Behynde the taile* of Vrsa so clere

and there is nothing in Virgil, beyond a plain 'rainy Hyades', which could produce the vividness in Skelton's homely touch of the Hyades' 'misling eye'.

Thus, Skelton's manner of drawing on proverbial language and of drawing away from literary models both show the essential quality of his mind. So, more important perhaps, do his rhythms. Dr Nelson argues that of all the various progenitors which have been suggested for Skelton's short-line verse, the brief chiming cadences of Latin rhyming prose are the most likely.[2] In this he seems clearly right. It is much more open to question, though, whether he is right in suggesting that the transition from prose to verse was, in Skelton's case, one towards smoothness and regularity. Across Skelton's short lines there seems often to be an irregular longer rhythm; one which is essentially a long spoken rhythm, the angry accelerating tirade brought to a halt by an emphatic rallentando and pause. ***Why Come Ye Nat to Courte,*** ll. 65-81, seem to be a good illustration of this. If this is so, it is yet another example of how Skelton adapts what is literary in origin to vehement speech and to the cast of mind which lies behind that kind of speech.

However this may be, a parallel trend is quite indisputable in the case of Skelton's longer metre. His long lines, it is true, can sometimes be seen almost as two short 'Skeltonic' lines combined into one: but that is by no means the whole of the story. The convention that the poet should disparage his own work may have been why Skelton makes one of the characters in *Magnyfycence* say that his big speech—really a dramatic chorus—will be 'In bastarde ryme after the dogrell gyse'. But again, that is not the whole story. Ramsay, in his admirable Introduction to *Magnyfycence,* made it clear that Skelton's long line, even in the rhyme-royal sections of this poem, is not the regular five-stress line of Chaucer at all, but a four-stress line, which never carries the sense on from line to line; which is marked by constant alliteration; which may vary in length from seven to fourteen syllables; and which (in its ampler forms) centres round a very emphatic central pause. The result is a loose and exceedingly flexible verse form, which can vary from almost naïve spareness to great amplitude and copiousness, which has as its metrical unit not the foot at all, but the self-dependent phrase, and which is such as we might expect, in fact, if the *sense* of rhythm which we have in Langland were to be forced into expression through a Chaucerian rhythmic *form.* It is essentially a metre dominated by the speaking voice, as against a metre which dominates the voice. Here is one part of its connexion with proverbial utterance, and the cast of mind which goes with that. Another part is how it resists enjambement—each line makes a separate statement—and how it naturally falls into two parts around its central pause, for this is also common in proverbs. (Many hands, light work; if wishes were horses, beggars would ride.)

Skelton may be the master of this metre, but he did not invent it. A fifteenth-century poem like 'Lex is layde and lethyrly lukys'[1] falls not only into the metre, but also into the gnomic quality, the macaronics, and the general attitudes, which are common in Skelton:

> Veritas is demytt to hange one the ruyde,
> Verecundia was drownytt at the laste fluyde,
> So that few freyndes may a man fynde,
> ffor rectum iudicium commys so farre be-hynde.
> ffraus is fykyll as a fox, and reuys in this lande
> ffuror is hys freynde, as I vnderstande . . .

Another poem of this general period is especially interesting, because it shows the attitude of mind which tended to force a poet into using the stress metre. Like Skelton's ***Ancient Aqueyntaunce,*** it begins as a deceptively decorous compliment to a lady, and turns into a ribald and telling palinode against her. As it makes this transition in attitude, its rhythm changes from smooth, regular rhythm by feet, to an abrupt Skeltonic rhythm of the half-line and the independent phrase.[2] The poem opens:

> O mosy Quince hangyng by your stalke
> The whyche no man may pluk away ner take

but by the time it is speaking out, as it were, we find lines like:

> My louely lewde masterasse take consideracion
> I am so sorrowfull there as yet be absent
> The flowre of the barkfate[3] the fowlyst of all the
>   nacion
> To loue you but a lytyll hit myne entent.

Counterfeit Countenaunce's chorus speech, to which I referred just now, is essentially in this stress-rhythm also; and it is this which enables it to move, with great freedom and ease, out of abrupt and lively dialogue into what is almost a rhetoric of moral denunciation. It opens with a light rhythm like

> Fansy hath cachyd in a flye net
> This noble man Magnyfycence

and little by little, in a kind of flux and reflux, it is amplified into lines like

> Counterfet preaching and byleue the contrary
> Counterfet conscyence, peuysshe pope holy:
> Counterfet sadness, with delynge full madly;
> Counterfet holyness is called ypocrysy;
> Counterfet reason is not worth a flye;
> Counterfet wysdome, and workes of foly;
> Counterfet countenaunce every man doth occupy:

In fact, the general recurrent movement of this play is to modulate from dialogue to this kind of moralistic verse, solemn yet essentially popular and traditional in both its style and its attitudes.

This same kind of poetry is constantly breaking through the 'literary' tedium of ***The Garlande of Laurell***:

> He is not wyse ageyne the streme that stryvith;
>   Dun is in the myre, dame, reche me my spur;
> Nedes must he rin that the deuyll dryuith;
>   When the stede is stolyn, spar the stable dur;
> A ientyll hownde shulde neuer play the kur;
> It is sone aspyed where the thorne prikketh;
> And wele wotith the cat whose berde she likketh.

But it is in ***Speke, Parot*** that these qualities of Skelton's work are most important, for that extraordinary poem is surely his masterpiece. Historically, this poem marks not only Skelton's hostility to Wolsey, and those policies of Wolsey which were inescapably bringing the whole traditional order to an end, but also Skelton's general hostility to the growing Erastianism of the time,[1] and his now final abandonment of London and the Court, for the great conservative family of the Earl of Surrey. Indeed, everything which shows Skelton's place in the culture of his time seems to converge in this poem. Morality based upon the Bible and the people's proverbial wisdom goes here with an essentially vernacular use of language throughout, with a distinctive development of the polyglot macaronic kind of writing (a popular and goliardic mode rather than a literary one), and with a structure, perhaps, somewhat like those commonplace books which passed from hand to hand in the country houses of the time and contained, as Dr Person writes, 'poetry and prose, English, Latin, or French, long poems and scraps, religion and science, devotional and satiric works, riddles and proverbs'.[1] Yet out of this gallimaufry, Skelton has made a poem which (though a chaos from a mechanical standpoint) is imaginatively perhaps the most unified of his works. It is unified in the persistent vivid presence and exceedingly distinctive tone—the tone of one who threatens and is himself in danger—of the parrot itself. Above all it is unified in the gathering power and directness of the attack as this gradually breaks through the speaker's prudence, and at last converts his glancing blows into the finale: a fierce and solemn denunciation of Wolsey himself:

> So braynles caluys hedes, so many shepis taylys;
>   So bolde a braggyng bocher, and flesshe sold so
>   dere;
> So many plucte partryches, and so fat quaylles;
>   So mangye a mastyfe curre, the grete grey
>   houndes pere;
>   So bygge a bulke of brow antlers cabagyd that
>   yere;
> So many swannes dede, and so small revell;—
> Syns Dewcalyons flodde, I trow, no man can tell.

We scarcely need to trace Wolsey's father the butcher in these lines, nor the Tudor greyhound, nor the swan of the Duke of Buckingham. The passionate, unflinching, comprehensive grasp of reality, and embodiment of it in an idiom wholly the writer's own, are unmistakable. If we think that we are not in the presence here of poetic greatness, it is because there is a kind of poetic greatness which we have not learnt to know.

To make this claim is not to make every claim. Nothing in Skelton has the poignancy, strangeness, and deep compassion of the scene in Henryson's poem where Cressid the leper begs an alms of Prince Troilus, and his memory of her swims half way to the light, but then goes back into darkness. Skelton has nothing of the imaginative brilliance of Sir David Lindsay's *Ane Satire of the Thrie Estatis,* in the opening words of Sensualitie:

> Luifers awalk, behald the fyrie spheir,
> Behauld the naturall dochter of Venus.

This is not going far afield. But what we do see in Skelton is one quite distinctive kind of excellence. A variety of vernacular traditions, a vernacular kind of insight, a metre and a rhythm which had for long had contact with vernacular expression—all these are things that come together in Skelton's verse. Once again George Puttenham, cicerone of the new and more literary poetic which succeeded Skelton and put him out of favour, settles that matter for us (though he settles less than he thinks) when he ridicules

> small and popular musickes song . . . upon benches
> and barrels heads where they have none other audience

then boys or countrey fellowes that passe them in the streete, or else by blind harpers or such like taverne minstrels that give a fit of mirth for a groat, and their matters being for the most part stories of old time". . . . also they be used in Carols and rounds and such light or lascivious Poemes, which are commonly more commodiously uttered by these buffons or vices in plays then by any other person. Such were the rimes of Skelton . . . in our courtly maker we banish them utterly.[1]

To accept this view of Skelton as essentially in contact with the apprehension of life of the ordinary man is not to accept what Puttenham thought it meant: that his work was crude and artless. I hope I have shown how he drew upon, or sometimes transformed, the work of his precedessors or models. His rhythmic spontaneity and flexibility is in fact a high technical achievement, towards which we can see him working from *The Bouge of Court* on to *Speke, Parot.* But when we open our minds to what is most distinctive of the truly literary quality of his verse, what we find is amplitude, immediacy, rhythmic vitality, a suggestion of embodied power for growth. What Henry James called 'felt life' seems to operate in the texture of his language with a quite special freedom and directness; and when that language moves, as it often does, beyond plain speech, it moves in a different direction from that which is conspicuous in Donne, say, and the poets who followed Donne: it moves less towards wit and argumentation through figurative language, than towards the proverbial gnomic solemnity of the traditional and popular mind. The result is no mere mirror of life, no mere Skeltonic realism, but something of an embodiment of life's permanent contours and essential vitality. Much may be absent from Skelton, but this, with the deep refreshment which it brings, is not absent.

When a literature—like our own—is old, and has been forming and re-forming for centuries, and has been reacting with other literatures for centuries also, there is a strong tendency for your courtly maker or his counterpart to predominate, and for writers generally to seek and expect success through naturally and studiously imitating their master Francis Petrarch or whoever may be the Francis Petrarch of the hour. We cannot but recall at this point the views of Graves and Berenson, which I quoted earlier, about multiplying tricks and devices, achieving a highly individual style, perpetually changing, displaying genius which is as frequently destructive and constructive. 'What has not been done? What is left to do?' seems more and more insistently to become the cry. Perhaps this cannot but tend to happen, as the centuries go by, and the past tends to weigh down, more and more, upon the present. But in Skelton, although he had the interests of a serious poet, and although his civilization was old rather than young, something else has happened. In his work, the dominance of artistry by reality is peculiarly thorough-going, peculiarly intimate and genuine. This may or may not be the balance which we find at the very pinnacle of artistic achievement; but I think it is one which we greatly need to contemplate, and to learn from, today.

Notes

[1] *The Reader over Your Shoulder* (1943), p. 120.

[1] *Italian Painters of the Renaissance* (1938 edition), p. 331.

[1] *op. cit.*, I. xxxi; ed. G. D. Willcock and A. Walker, 1936, p. 62.
[2] W. Nelson, *John Skelton* (1939), pp. 4-59.

[3] V. L. Rubel, *Poetic Diction in the English Renaissance* (1941), pp. 37-9.

[4] See, e.g., Ian A. Gordon, *John Skelton* (1943), pp. 122 *et seq.*

[5] See the introduction to Skelton's translation of the *Bibliotheca Historica* of Diodorus Siculus (ed. F. M. Salter and H. H. L. Edwards, 1956; E.E.T.S. original series 229, p. xxxix).

[1] *Colyn Cloute*, I. 83.

[2] Salter and Edwards, *ed. cit.* p. xxxvii.

[1] *English Writers*, Vol. 7 (1891), p. 190.

[2] *English Verse between Chaucer and Surrey* (1927), p. 337.

[3] C. S. Lewis, *English Literature in the Sixteenth Century* (1954), p. 138; p. 106.

[4] C Text, Passus VII, II. 349-441.

[5] Cf. R. L. Greene, *Early English Carols* (1935), No. 419 ('The Gossips' Meeting'); Greene compares this with the 'Good Gossippes Songe' in the Chester play of the Deluge, but this is too short and slight to have much in common with Skelton's poem.

[1] Quoted from A. V. Judges, *The Elizabethan Underworld* (1930), pp. 4-5.

[1] W. L. Renwick and H. Orton, *The Beginnings of English Literature to Skelton* (second ed., 1952), p. 114.

[1] M. M. Gray, *Scottish Poetry from Barbour to James VI,* Introduction (1935 edition, p. xvii); these remarks relate specifically to another similar work, *Peblis to the Play,* but also generally to the humourous poems in the Bannatyne and Maitland MSS. which stand out (like *Christis Kirke on the Grene*) for their 'boisterous merriment and rough-and-tumble'.

[2] H. L. R. Edwards, *Skelton* (1949), p. 53.

[1] *Amenities of Literature* (1841), Vol. II, p. 69.

[2] *Poems (1914-26)*, pp. 6-8.

[3] *op. cit.*, p. 143.

[1] Nelson, *op. cit.*, p. 78.

[2] Edwards, *op. cit.*, p. 62.

[3] Edwards, *op. cit.*, p. 63.

[4] Nelson, *op. cit.*, p. 82.

[1] Juvenal, *Satires*, VIII, 144-5; *Why Come Ye Nat to Courte*, II. 1232-4. It should be noticed that at I. 1224 Skelton has quoted *verbatim* part of I. 140 of the Eighth Satire.

[2] *op. cit.*, pp. 90 *et seq.*
[1] Carleton Brown, *Religious Lyrics of the Fifteenth Century* (1959), No. 176, p. 269.

[2] Henry A. Person (ed.), *Cambridge Middle English Lyrics* (1953), No. 49, p. 40.

[1] See J. M. Berdan, 'Speke, Parrot'; *MLN*, Vol. 30 (1915), p. 140.

[1] Person, *op. cit.*, p. iv.

[1] *op. cit.*, ed. Willcock and Walker, pp. 83-4.

Stanley Eugene Fish (essay date 1965)

SOURCE: "Some Graver Fish," in *John Skelton's Poetry*, Yale University Press, 1965, pp. 82-123.

[*In the following essay, Fish determines how Skelton utilizes the medieval rhetorical tradition in* Philip Sparrow.]

Philip Sparrow is perhaps Skelton's best-known poem. Countless readers have been enchanted by what C. S. Lewis calls "the lightest—the most like a bubble—of all the poems I know."[8] Yet it is one of the ironies of literary history that a good third of the poem is consistently ignored and sometimes deplored. Of its 1382 lines, only the first 833 (Jane Scrope's lament for her slain sparrow) are generally admired, while lines 834-1267 (the poet's extended commendation of Jane's beauty) and lines 1268-1382 (his reply to those who have objected on moral grounds to sections one and two) receive only passing attention. Ian Gordon remarks of the "Commendations," "It is a charming tribute, but of little importance beside the first part of the poem." "The structure of the 'Commendacions' is completely different from that of the lament and there is actually no great connection between the two parts."[9]

It seems to me that the critical silence on the third section is justified. Skelton had the disconcerting habit of attaching afterthoughts to his poems, and in this case the "adicyon made by maister Skelton" (which also appears in the ***Garland of Laurel***) was probably written in 1523, some fifteen years after the composition of the main body of the poem. But with the dismissal of the middle section as "charming" (and, as Gordon implies, irrelevant), I cannot concur; for the very differences which separate it from the preceding 833 lines and lead Gordon, among others, to question its relevancy seem to me to provide the key to the poem's total meaning. Briefly, I see ***Philip Sparrow*** as a comparative study of innocence and experience, built around the contrasting reactions of its two personae to a single event, the death of the title figure.

If we read only for the Skelton "whimsicality" celebrated by Robert Graves ("What could be dafter / Than John Skelton's laughter"), C. S. Lewis' partial encomium will seem wholly adequate; but the lightness which captivates Lewis is a single strain in a poem so complex that the resources of several disciplines are necessary for its interpretation.[1]

Once again Skelton builds his poem on the conventions of rhetoric. In **Ware the Hawk** the dramatic and the rhetorical are obviously incongruous, and a reader with no formal rhetorical training can respond fully to the humor. In **Philip Sparrow** Skelton makes more delicate discriminations, which can only be articulated against the background of a finely graduated formal system, and the reader must bring the system to the poem.

As Skelton comes to see a relationship between the difficulty of making moral distinctions and the inadequacy of language, the index of innocence becomes verbal. Conveniently, the rhetoric of his day provides him with formulae to measure that index. The dissociation of rhetorical method from the organic theory which gave it relevance engendered many curiosities. In the *De inventione,* Cicero lists the personal attributes (characteristics) which could legitimately be cited either to support or discredit testimony: "Omnes res argumentando confirmantur aut ex eo quod personis aut ex eo quod negotiis est attributum. Ac personis has res attributas putamus: nomen, naturam, victum, fortunam, habitum, affectionem, studia consilia, facta, casus, orationes."[2] What is to Cicero one more area for legal argument becomes in medieval poetics a hard and fast rule of characterization. Both Marbodus in his *De ornamentis verbis*[3] and Matthew de Vendôme in his *Ars versificatoria*[4] advise aspiring authors to keep before them the natural characteristics of Cicero; John of Garland in the sixth chapter of his *Poetria*[5] provides a list of the same—with illustrations; and Geoffrey de Vinsauf's descriptio's became authoritative models.

The doctrine of the three styles (high, middle, plain) underwent a similar transformation. Where Cicero had seen them in relation to the efforts of the orator (the "plain" for presenting evidence, the "middle" for gaining the ear of the audience, and the "high" for swaying the audience),[6] they became in the poetry manuals of the twelfth and thirteenth centuries a means of indicating social norms. Atkins writes, "Classical doctrine had distinguished three main styles . . . which were differentiated . . . by their degrees of ornamentation.". . . By this date [the twelfth century] a new and strange meaning was often given to these terms. The distinctions were said to rest on the social dignity of the personages or subject matter concerned";[7] and goes on to note that of the sixty-four figures described in the *Ad herennium,* the ten tropes or "difficult ornaments" (*ornatus difficilis*) were allowed only to the high style, while poets were forced in the middle and plain registers to limp along with the fifty-four figures of speech (*verborum*) and thought (*sententiarum*). In short, by the thirteenth century, a hardening of the rhetorical arteries had combined with an imperfect understanding of Horace's doctrine of "decorum" to produce a highly stylized art of characterization. Tropes,

not clothes, made the man (or woman) in the world of medieval poetic.[8] Through the manipulation of this poetic Skelton will create in a context of artificiality and innuendo, a personality whose innocence and artlessness are overwhelming. In many ways, it will be his finest effort.

In the first section, Skelton's strategy is largely negative. From the opening interrogatio,

> *Place bo*
> Who is there who?
> *Di le xi.*
> Dame Margery;
> Fa, re, my, my,
> Wherefore and why, why?
> For the sowle of Philip Sparowe
> That was late slayn at Carowe,

the fifteenth-century reader would expect (1) a parody of the Mass in the Goliardic tradition, (2) a play on the phallic possibilities of the sparrow in the tradition of Catullus and Ovid. As Skelton presents her, however, Jane is dramatically ignorant of either tradition, and the power of her monologue will depend on the disparity between the reader's (potential) sophistication and her naïveté. The possibility of blasphemy never occurs to her, nor, after the first hundred lines, to us. Although Jane does chant a Mass for Philip, she does not parody the service. Gordon, who has examined the services she draws upon—*Officium Defunctorum* (Breviary), 1-386, *Missa pro Defunctis* (Missal), 387-512, *Absolutio Super Tomulum* (Missal), 513-70, *Officium Defunctorum* (Breviary), 571-602[9]—notes the fidelity of her borrowings and the absence of parody:

> The borrowed passages run in pairs—in every case an antiphon followed by the first lines of the following psalm, the whole rigidly keeping to the order in the Office—and never, strange though it appears, once parodying it, though the temptation to parody . . . was obvious enough.[1]

From the opening lines the only departure from orthodoxy is the service itself, and if this assumes a belief in the immortality of the animal soul, her youth and sincerity (it is *in*sincerity that characterizes the parodies) would seem to absolve her from the charge of heresy.

Although Skelton never allows us to question the reality of Jane's sorrow, he does undercut its significance. Lewis calls **Philip Sparrow** "our first great poem of childhood."[2] Jane *is* a child, and her perspective is childlike (but not childish); if Skelton is to succeed, he must allow his reader to be simultaneously condescending and sympathetic; for like the persona of **Ware the Hawk** she will bring the entire universe to bear on her problem, and where he offends, she must charm.

She begins in the best elegiac style with a demonstratio, "When I remembre agayn / How mi Philyp was slayn" (17-18), which leads to a characteristically hyperbolic exclamatio: "I syghed and I sobbed, / For that I was robbed / Of my sparowes lyfe, / O mayden, wydow, and wyfe / Of what estate ye be, / Of hye or lowe degre, / Great sorowe than ye myght se, / And lerne to wepe at me!" (50-57). In these early lines the relationship between the figures is logical, even natural; recollection triggers reaction and the sense of formality is minimal. We hear echoes from medieval romance and even Marian lament;[3] but we feel that the allusiveness of her complaint is accidental or unconscious or somehow not her own, and it is the hyperbole of it all rather than the erudition that captivates even as it amuses.

But at line 67 the comfortable pattern of demonstratio-exclamatio is broken by the first of a series of Skeltonic lists that are, in effect, formal digressio's: Jane prays that Philip's soul may be saved from

> the marees deepe
> Of Acherontes well,
> That is a flode of hell;
> And from the great Pluto,
> The prynce of endles wo;
> And from foule Alecto,

and from a score of other horrors that fill the next fifteen lines. What begins as a petition to Jesus becomes an encyclopedic recital of the mythology of the underworld, and it is difficult (for both speaker and reader) to return at line 114 to tearful reminiscence. For some 150 lines, the alternation of demonstratio-exclamatio is once again regular; but at line 273 a cry for vengeance "on all the hole nacyon / Of cattes" grows into a wonderfully imaginative catalogue of tortures:

> Of Inde the gredy grypes
> Myght tere out all thy trypes!
> Of Arcady the beares
> Might plucke away thynes eares!
> The wylde wolfe Lyacon
> Byte asondre thy backe bone!
>
> [307-12]

and it is with a distinct shock that we come back at line 323 to the inspiration of this impressive performance:

> Was never byrde in cage
> More gentle of corage.

What is happening is clear. Skelton is using a rhetorical pattern to point up the central paradox of this section—a genuine sorrow which cannot, however, be sustained. Although Jane's affection for Philip can hardly be questioned, the natural recuperative powers of childhood will not allow her an extended period of mourning. She is still very much alive, very much enchanted with the wonders of the vital world she lives in, and, as the poem develops, it becomes more and more difficult for her to return from her excursions (or digressions) into life to her self-imposed preoccupation with the dead.[4] Her difficulty is also the reader's difficulty. Trained to read "figuratively," he will recognize the demonstratio-exclamatio pattern and fall into its comfortable rhythm. The catalogues will break that rhythm and force him to construct a new pattern. In order to retain control of the reading experience, he must *place* this additional rhetorical component; and the name of the figure in question (digressio) will help him to see in its appearance and gradual ascendancy a comment on the figures it supersedes. The very demonstratio's she evokes to feed her sorrow defeat her, for sorrow can hardly be sustained in the face of such scenes as this:

> Sometyme he wolde gaspe
> Whan he sawe a waspe;
> A fly or a gnat,
> He wolde flye at that
> And prytely he wold pant
> Whan he saw an ant;
> Lord, how he wolde pry
> After the butterfly!
> Lorde, how he wolde hop
> After the gressop!
>
> [128-37]

The fact that Jane is now the natural rhetorician whose verbal gestures are the inadequate signs of an emotional reality, and now the sophist who offers to her audience endless exercises in amplificatio, tells us more about her than do her own statements and explanations. It is in the effort to understand the rhetorical movement of the poem that the reader comes to understand its heroine.

As her dirge continues, Jane returns to Philip only as a pretext for another digression. At line 387 she calls upon "all manner of byrdes in your kynd" to "wepe with me" and presides, for one hundred lines, over a Bird-Mass in which the solemnity of the occasion is lost in the vivacity of a virtuoso performance. This one large digressio contains a host of smaller ones as the girl enlivens her assignments to the feathered clerics with a little unnatural natural history:

> Chaunteclere, our coke,
> Must tell what is of the clocke
> By the astrology
> That he hath naturally
> Conceyved and cought
> And was never tought
> By Albumazar
> The astronomer,
> Nor by Ptholemy
> Prince of astronomy,
> Nor yet by Haly.
>
> [740-44]

And at line 614 the necessity of an epitaph and Jane's admitted ignorance of "Elyconys well / Where the Muses dwell" lead to a 150-line recital of the literature she *does* know, a delightful collection of myth and folk tales:

> of the Wyfe of Bath
> That worketh moch scath
> When her tale is tolde
> Among huswyves bolde.
>
> [618-21]

> of the love so hote
> That made Troylus to dote

Upon fayre Cressyde,
And what they wrote and sayd.

[677-80]

the fable
Of Penelope most stable.

[724-25]

of great Assuerus,
And of Vesca his queene,
Whom he forsoke with teene
And of Hester his other wyfe,
With whom he ledd a plesaunt life.

[740-44]

These are an especially attractive illustration of what
Skelton can do with the Skeltonic. By eschewing the feminine rhymes which go with the verse form in his flytings,
Skelton draws attention to the couplets. In this way the
Wife of Bath is delineated by the four rhyme words, "Bath,"
"scath," "tolde," "bolde," and Troilus and Cresseid by "hote"
and "dote." At the same time the unusual pattern of run-on
lines makes the basic unit of the passage (what the reader
takes in between visual breaths) the capsule narrative itself
rather than the line as in **Colin Clout** and **Why Come Ye
Not to Court?**; and the closing line of each unit is somewhat fuller than its antecedents, forcing the reader to pause
and consider what he has read. The end result of these
effects is the characterization of the speaker who becomes
identified with the Ogden Nash-like jingle of the rhymes
(Bath, scath) and the charmingly simplistic reduction of
complex emotional and narrative conflicts (hote, dote). In
order to provide a rhyme for her couplet at line 744, Jane
obviously seizes on the first filler line that comes to mind
("With whom he ledd a plesaunt life"), producing the kind
of emphatic doggerel Skelton so easily avoids. In any other
context "a plesaunt life" would be anticlimactic or bathet-
ic or even suggestive; here we smile as literary and social
sophistication fall before the naïveté of an innocent mind.

To appreciate **Philip Sparrow** one must recognize the effort of will Skelton exercises in making the first 833 lines
Jane's. (Imagine, if you will, Marlowe writing both parts of
Hero and Leander.) The poem has been misread because
the girl has been denied her own opinions. When she comments critically on Gower, Chaucer, and Lydgate, literary
historians assume that it is Skelton who speaks with all the
authority of his profession; when she reflects on that medieval commonplace, mutability ("Of fortune this the chaunce
/ Standeth on varyaunce / . . . No man can be sure / Allway
to have pleasure," 366-67, 370-71), we are to assume that the
poet thus indicates his philosophical position. Skelton may or
may not share Jane's opinion of the English poets (lines 393-
448 of the **Garland of Laurel** suggest that he does), and he
certainly is concerned with mutability; but as these passages
appear in the poem, they flow naturally from the character of
his persona as he has created it. Jane obviously delivers her
critical clichés by rote, as a child might, and when she supports her musings on mutability by citing her own "tragedy"
as an example, it is not difficult to see the poet at work,
skillfully (though not maliciously) pointing up a childlike
lack of proportion. Each block of digressive material is longer

than the preceding block; the connection between them and
the lament for Philip Sparrow becomes more and more tenuous, and when Jane reaches the "turn" in her elegy and commends Philip's soul to God, we know that sorrow has passed:

But whereto shuld I
Longer morne or crye?
To Jupyter I call
Of heven emperyall,
That Phyllyp may fly
Above the starry sky.

In the final two hundred lines of her monologue, it is the
technical problem of fashioning an epitaph that concerns
Jane; and the rhetoric is, as might be expected, external to
her as a thinking and feeling being. The entire section is a
complex *expolitio*, the most elaborate of the amplificatory
figures in which variations on a single theme are supported
by *exempla*, reasons, illustrations, and framed by a formal
introduction and conclusion. Here the theme is the inexpressibility *topos*, introduced by Jane at line 605:

An epytaphe I wold have
For Phyllyppes grave:
But for I am a mayde,
Tymerous, halfe afrayde,
That never yet asayde
Of Elyconys well,
Where the Muses dwell.

This simple admission of ignorance is followed by the
lengthy *digressio* noted above in which each myth or tale
she refers to is, in a negative way, an example of the kind
of literature to which she *cannot* refer. At line 754 the
original declaration is rephrased,

Yet I am nothing sped,
And can but lytell skyll,

and supported by an amazing catalogue of the authors
unknown to her:

Of Ovyd or Virgyll,
Or of Plutharke,
Or Frauncys Petrarke,
Alcheus or Sapho,
Or such other poetes mo,
As Linus and Homerus,
Euphorion and Theocritus,
Anacreon and Arion,
Sophocles and Philemon,
Pyndarus and Symonides,
Philistion and Phorocides;
These poetes of auncyente,
They ar to diffuse for me.

A third statement of self-disparagement,

For, as I tofore have sayd,
I am but a yong mayd,
And cannot in effect
My style as yet direct,

precedes an indictment of the English language as the source (or in terms of the expolitio, the reason) for her difficulty:

> Our natural tong is rude,
> And hard to be enneude
> With pullysshed termes lusty . . .
>
> I wot not where to fynd
> Termes to serve my mynde.

This, in turn, suggests a survey of English poetry and a recital of the critical clichés of the day—"Gowers Englysh is olde," "Chaucer, that famus clerke, / His termes were not darke," "Johnn Lydgate / Wryteth after an hyer rate" (784, 800-01, 804-05). With the word "Wherefore" in line 813, Jane formally concludes the expolitio and offers a final variation of the basic assertion:

> Wherefore hold me excused
> If I have not well perused
> Myne Englyssh halfe abused;
> Though it be refused,
> In worth I shall it take,
> And fewer wordes make.

For the reader, Jane's expolitio is simultaneously an indication of her recovery from the shock of Philip's death, and a true statement of her intellectual limitations as they are mirrored in, indeed *proven by,* her stylistic limitations; it seals his attitude toward her. That attitude is, I think, compounded, in equal parts, of affection and condescension. As her exclamations lose contact with their supposed inspiration (the death of Philip), we fasten on them as relevant to what becomes the poem's real inspiration, the girl herself. We accept her stories, her judgments, her reflections, not because they tell us anything about birds, or myths, or poets or language, but because they are hers. In other words, while we reject her view of the situation as limited, we believe in her completely. At the same time, our understanding of her allows us to patronize her. We are so much wiser, so much more mature; unlike her, we *do* have terms to serve our mind; our English is aureate rather than rude; and we are aware, as she is not, of the sexual implications of her demonstratio's:

> And many tymes and ofte
> Betwene my brestes softe
> It wolde lye and rest.
>
> [124-26]
>
> Wherwith he wolde make
> Me often for to wake,
> And for to take him in
> Upon my naked skyn.
>
> [164-67]
>
> my byrde so fayre,
> That was wont to repayre
> And go in at my spayre,
> And crepe in at my gore
> Of my gowne before,
> Flyckerynge with his wynges!
>
> [343-48]

It is perhaps difficult to read these lines without questioning her innocence, but we make the necessary effort and accept her demurral:

> What though he crept so lowe?
> It was no hurt, I trowe,
> He dyd nothynge perde
> But syt upon my kne:
> Phyllyp, though he were nyse,
> In him it was no vyse.

It is, however, a conscious effort, and Skelton insists that we make it. If his poem is to succeed, we must be continually aware of the distance between what Jane in her innocence would intend and what we would interpolate. As its first section ends, *Philip Sparrow* may seem little more than an invitation to the luxury of condescension: we smile gently at a grief which is disproportionate and at protests which are at least naive. But if we have forgotten Catullus' sparrow and the Venus masses of the Goliardic tradition, Skelton has not; and at line 834 he enters his own poem to disturb our self-satisfaction, to suggest that the wonderful directness of a girl who can wrap her being about a sparrow and believe momentarily in the immutability of her affections is infinitely superior to the triumphs of sophistication.

I see *Philip Sparrow* as a comparative study of innocence and experience, built around the contrasting reactions of its two personae to a single event, the death of the title figure.

—Stanley Eugene Fish

It would not be exaggeration to say that every man who reads Jane's lament falls in love with her. Skelton takes great care to establish a relationship between his heroine and her audience, but in the second half of the poem the focus is narrowed as her creator becomes our surrogate. C. S. Lewis writes, "The lady who is lamenting her bird may not really have been a child. . . . But it is as a child she is imagined in the poem—a little girl to whom the bird's death is a tragedy and who though well read in romances, finds Lydgate beyond her, and has `little skill in Ovid or Virgil.'. . . Skelton is not. . . ridiculing. He is at once tender and mocking—like an affectionate bachelor uncle or even a grandfather."[5] He is far too conservative; the poet's affection is anything but grandfatherly. His entrance into the poem is unheralded; he merely continues the Latin hexameters of Jane's final farewell:

> *Semper erunt nitido*
> *Radiantia sidera coelo;*
> *Impressusque meo*
> *Pectore semper eris.*

(There will always be gleaming stars in the brilliant sky and you will always be engraven in my heart.)

Per me laurigerum
Britonum Skeltonida vatem
Haec cecinesse licet
Ficta sub imagine texta. . .
Candida Nais erat,
Formosior ista Joanna est;
Docta Corinna fuit,
Sed magis ista sapit.

(I Skelton, laureated, Poet of Britain, have been permitted to sing this under an imaginary likeness. . . Nais was dazzling, but this Jane is more beautiful, Corinna was learned but this Jane knows more.)

Trumpets, however, are unnecessary. One realizes immediately that the style and tone of lines 826-33 and 834-43 are antithetical; from the moment he announces at line 872 "my pen hath enbybed / With the aureat droppes," artificiality and innuendo replace the ingenuousness of the first section, and in Skelton's characteristic fashion, the drama of **Philip Sparrow** is a drama of style.

Jane describes her epitaph for Philip as "Latyne playne and lyght," and in fact her entire monologue is conspicuously free of the studied stylization of aureate rhetoric. W. G. Crane divides rhetorical figures into three groups:

> The first consists of the figures of thought, which are based upon the process of dialectical investigation. . . . The second group consists of a number of varieties of exclamation, interrogation, and description, all of which direct their appeal to the emotions. The third class comprises about one hundred and fifty figures of a somewhat mechanical nature, produced by alteration from normal spelling, diction or syntax.[6]

If we retain Crane's classification but shift our focus from the figures themselves to the audience which responds to them, we shall be able almost to graph Skelton's method in **Philip Sparrow.** All rhetoric, like all art, is studied; artlessness is an illusory and hard-won effect. It is to Crane's second group that the poet who would create this illusion must turn; for "the exclamations, interrogations, and descriptions which appeal to the emotion" will seduce the reader into an intellectual languor, while the process of dialectic and the precision of syntactical configurations will make him very conscious of the effort behind the effect. In other words, one kind of rhetoric calls attention to itself, the other is in hiding.

Jane's monologue is a triumph of emotional rhetoric. Although the educated reader is aware of its formality (the service itself is a formal situation), he would attribute the familiar apostrophes and the echoes of other, more stylized laments to the poet who stands behind his heroine and who speaks through her, but not with her, to his audience. (Skelton admits himself that it is he who writes this first section "under a feigned likeness." This is more than an admission of literary "unreality," for it complicates the relationship between the two voices in the poem which are now in some ways one.) Indeed, she seems uncomfortable with the literary machinery her situation requires (note her repeated declarations of incompetence, conventional, but in this case "sincere"), and is certainly unaware of either the suggestiveness of her exclamatio's or her own very real appeal. The poet, on the other hand, parades his rhetoric almost flamboyantly. When he announces that Nais is dazzling but Jane is more beautiful, Corinna learned, but Jane wiser still, he deliberately calls up the traditional body of love poetry in which such comparisons are made again and again. While in Jane's monologue the frequency and occurrence of the various figures exist in a describable relationship with her emotional development, the rhetorical pattern in the "Commendations" is static. The poet, as the master rhetorician, is always in control as he declares, "Now will I enterprise / Thorow the grace dyvyne / Of the Muses nyne / Her beauty to commende" (856-59). Exclamatio's in the form of tag lines from the *Ordo Commendationis Animae* follow a set refrain at regular intervals and call attention to themselves rather than springing (or seeming to spring) naturally from the poem:

> For this most goodly floure,
> This blossome of fresshe coulour,
> So Jupiter me socour.
> She floryssheth new and new
>
> In bewte and vertew:
> *Hac claritate gemina*
> *O gloriosa foemina*
> *Retribue servo tuo, vivifica me!*

This passage, with variations in the Latin, is repeated eleven times in less than two hundred lines and establishes *pronominatio* (*antonomasia*) as the dominant figure of the section. Except for an extended attack on Envy (which, I shall argue, is not digressive), the poet proceeds in an orderly fashion with his markedly conventional descriptio, carefully noting the lips as red as cherries, the skin as white as a swan, the hands soft as silk, the hair golden as the sun. It is the self-consciousness of his art which impresses, as we involuntarily contrast him with his creation. In other words, the poet presents himself as everything Jane is not, cultivated, learned, mature, aureate; and since we have come to understand the distance between ourselves and the girl in exactly these terms, we feel a kinship with him. But as the poem proceeds, our identification with this aureate voice will make us increasingly uncomfortable.

The distance between them is obvious, even to the reader who knows nothing of tropes and schemes, although the social and intellectual codifications of tropes and schemes will give that distance meaning. Characterization through style is possible in any literature; one needs only the idiom of conversation and a formal (in this case, aureate) vocabulary that can be parodied. Skelton is able, in addition, to call on the resources of a system that measures style almost mathematically. Of the 126 instances of twenty-two figures in the first 833 lines, forty-five of these (or nearly forty per cent) involve what de Vinsauf lists as methods of amplification—*circuitio, conformatio, correctio, digressio, exclamatio, expolitio,* and *interpretatio.* Ten more instances (*conduplicatio* and *repetitio*) involve purely mechanical repetitions; and a majority of the thirty-nine *exempla* are found in the catalogue-like *digressio*'s of the last 300 lines. Over 75 per cent of the figures in this first section are either repetitious or amplificatory. There are only seven instances (less than six per cent) of the "difficult figures." The statistics reverse themselves in the commendations: of 110 instances of twenty-two figures, there are fifty-two (nearly 50 per cent) of the "difficult" ornaments (*denominatio, intellectio, pronominatio, simile, superlatio*); conspicuously absent are the figures of repetition (*conduplicatio, repetitio*) and amplification (*conformatio, digressio, interpretatio*) which dominate the earlier section. The comparison, however, is more than statistical; it becomes moral. When Jane repeatedly proclaims her ignorance of rhetoric ("I wot not where to fynd / Termes to serve my mynde"), a stale verbal formula (what Curtius calls the modesty topos) seems fresh and disarmingly sincere, because her speech *is* demonstrably free of syntactical inversion, simile, word play; but when the poet writes, "My pen it is unable, / My hand it is unstable, / My reson rude and dull," the humility is a pose, and in the context of her simplicity, offensive.[7]

The "Commendations" is one long essay on contrasting sensibilities, as the reader is offered Jane's monologue from a new perspective which is in comparison unattractive. While Skelton pointedly avoids parodying the service in his first section, he risks blasphemy in this one. The *Ordo Commendationis Animae,* the commendation of the soul to God, becomes a courtly lyric in which the poet is the soul, "Now wyll I enterpryse, / Thorow the grace dyvyne / Of the Muses nyne, / Her beautye to commende," and Jane his God, "O gloriosa foemina, / Quomodo dilexi legem tuam, domina!" Every line is a potential double entendre. Lines from Psalm 118, which examines the relationship between the law of God and man, are placed to suggest a quite different relationship. "Deficit in salutatione tua anima mea," the psalmist cries, acknowledging his dependence on the Grace of God. In *Philip Sparrow,* this same petition (1090) is addressed to another deity who offers a grace that is hardly spiritual:

Who so lyst beholde,
It maketh lovers bolde
To her to sewe for *grace,*
Her favoure to purchase;
The sker upon her chyn,
Enhached on her fayre skyn,
Whyter than the swan,
It wold make any man
To forget *deadly syn*
Her favour to wyn.

[emphasis mine]

The liturgical framework which, in the first section, underlines Jane's virtual humanization of her sparrow is here the vehicle for a passion that can only be expressed through innuendo.[8]

In the same way, the girl's *demonstratio*'s are echoed and even parodied; in his fantasy the poet replaces the sparrow, vicariously enjoying the no longer innocent delights of their play. Jane's artless

my byrde so fayre,
. . . was wont to repayre,
And go in at my spayre,
And crepe in at my gore,
Of my gowne before,
Flyckerynge with his wynges,

is here a studied compliment:

Her kyrtell so goodly lased,
And under that is brased
Such plasures that I may
Neyther wryte nor say.

The "modest hiatus" is, of course, conventional, but with Jane's childishly frank outbursts ringing in our ears, it is not only trite, but faintly prurient.[1] The finality with which the girl's innocence has been established in Part One makes it difficult for us to accept her as even the passive object of a passion that is not at all innocent; and the careful patterning of detail forces us to do just that: if Jane recalls a daily scene,

With his byll betwene my lippes;
It was my pretty Phyppes!
Many a pretty Kusse
Had I of his sweet musse,

the poet imagines an assignation:

Her lyppes soft and mery
Emblomed lyke the chery,
It were an hevenly blysse
Her sugred mouth to kysse.

Her disclaimers are natural:

Phyllyp, though he were nyse,
In him it was no vyse;
Phyllyp had leve to go
To pyke my lytell too;
Phyllip myght be bolde
And do what he wolde;

His are forced and coy:

To tell you what conceyte
I had than in a tryce,
The matter were to nyse
And yet there was no vyce,
Nor yet no villany
But only fantasy.

The parallels are innumerable, and their effect is always the same, to force upon the reader an even greater awareness of the distance that separates them. He can never again capture the simplicity she brings to her every day. He can never express himself with the assurance and singlemindedness she commands. Experience has bound him to fetters of flesh, and sophistication has left him with only irony and innuendo. In the end it is almost obscene when Jane's plaintive cry, "Alas, my heart it stynges / Remembrynge prety thynges!" is absorbed into the sexual fantasies of a literary lover: "Yet though I wryte not with ynke / No man can let me thynke, / For thought hath lyberte, / Thought is franke and fre."

When all is said and done, however, his affection is as real as hers, and perhaps even more poignant. From time to time the elaborate screen of convention the poet builds around him falls away and reveals a shrillness which belies his characteristic composure. His response to a suggestion that his interest in the girl is less than impersonal is so overlong and overwrought that it becomes an admission of "guilt." And as his section of the poem closes, a final attempt at self-justification, a *subiectio,* is surprisingly nonaureate, a trifle desperate, and, I think, sincere:

> I have not offended, I trust,
> If it be sadly dyscust
>
> [1249-50]

> Because I have wrytten and sayd
> Honour of this fayre mayd;
> Wherefore shulde I be blamed,
> That I Jane have named,
> And famously proclamed?
> She is worthy to be enrolde
> With letters of golde.
>
> [1253-59]

Curiously enough, it is in the most artificial of contexts that an undercurrent of real emotion is most clearly heard. When the poet exclaims, "Clamavi in toto corde, exaudi me," the anguish rings true, despite the Chinese box-like structure of a parody (of the liturgy) within a parody (of Jane). "Servus tuus sum ego," I am your servant, he admits, and we believe him. In terms of the dramatic crux of the poem, this is still another indication of the inverse relationship between maturity and the possibility of direct self-expression; but when we recall that Jane's "artless" lament is no less the result of complex rhetorical configurations, and is itself the product of this convention-bound mind, it becomes impossible to continue, since the terms of our comparison shift, Chaucer-like, before our eyes. The poet's admission that both parts of the poem are his (*Ficta sub imagine texta*) becomes a problem for the reader who is continually invited to distinguish between them. What is innocence, and can only the disillusioned recognize it? What is simplicity, and can only the artful produce its similitude? In **Philip Sparrow** Skelton is busily exploring the limits of his art, extending the intuition of "Knolege, aquayntance, resort"; language itself is incapable of mirroring reality; it is only through the juxtaposition of contrasting degrees of artificiality that man can suggest what *is,* or hint at what *may* be.

And the poet himself is aware of all this, even as he spins out his interminable compliment. It is Jane who has always fascinated, but to understand the poem is to realize that the truly complex personality is her (fictional) cre-

ator. For since it is he who has so painstakingly constructed the first section, he surely recognizes the hopelessness of his love. While Jane is capable of firing his passion, her monologue reveals her incapable of responding to it. When she presses his hand and his heart leaps ("Wher wyth my hand she strayned, / Lorde, how I was payned! / Unneth I me refrayned"), her heart no doubt beats on with a crushing regularity, and he is left to imagine a scene that will never take place:

> Unneth I me refrayned
>
> [1124]

> Enbrasynge therwithall
> Her goodly myddell small
> With sydes longe and streyte;
> To tell you what conceyte
> I had than in a tryce,
> The matter were to nyse,
>
> [1127-32]

There is no resolution as the poem ends, because, as the poet knows only too well, no resolution is possible. Amidst the hyperbole of the mock curses in the third section, Skelton re-establishes momentarily the poignancy of the first two; the poem, laments its author, is so complex and so delicate that even the girl herself misunderstands, or understands too well:

> Alas, that goodly mayd,
> Why shuld she be afrayde?
> Why shuld she take shame
> That her goodly name,
> Honorably reported,
> Sholde be set and sorted,
> To be matriculate
> With ladyes of estate?

Alas, indeed, for all fallings away from innocence, for all impossible loves, for all misunderstandings and failures of communication.

Notes

[8] *English Literature in the Sixteenth Century,* p. 138.

[9] *John Skelton, Poet Laureate,* pp. 74, 131-32.

[1] This section has appeared in another form in *Studia Neophilologica, 34,* No. 2 (1962), 216-38. In *Philip Sparrow* the evidence that Skelton not only knew rhetoric but wrote with the rhetorical vocabulary in the forefront of his consciousness is overwhelming. As Edwards and Salter note (*Bibliotheca Historica,* p. xxxix), the leisurely examination of Jane's anatomy in lines 998-1193 is a direct imitation of de Vinsauf's first descriptio; and when the girl turns to curse Gib the Cat, she prefaces her outburst with a citation of the proper figure, exclamatio: "vengeaunce I aske and crye, / By way of *exclamacyon*" (273-74). Again, when she concludes her recital of the Troilus and Cresseide legend by summarizing the consequences of their actions, she points to the rhetorical ploy involved, conclusio: "Thus in *conclusyon* / She brought him in abusyon." (Italics are mine.) The most obvious instance of Skelton's conscious use of rhetoric is Jane's capsule recapitulation of the Punic War at line 668: "How Scipion dyd wake / The cytye of

Cartage, / Which by his unmerciful rage / He bete down to the grounde." These four lines translate the very *circuitio* offered as an example in the *Ad herennium* (4.32.43): "Circumitio est oratio rem simplicem adsumpta circumscribens elocutione, hoc pacto: `Scipionis providentia Kartaginis opes fregit'" (ed. Harry Caplan, Cambridge, Mass., 1954, p. 336). Since the unknown author of this most popular of rhetorical manuals makes a point of the originality of his examples (as opposed to other rhetoricians who plundered the poets), it seems clear that Skelton either wrote with the document by his side or had committed it to memory.

[2] 1.24.34 (p. 70). "All propositions are supported in argument by attributes of persons or of actions. We hold the following to be the attributes of persons: name, nature, manner of life, fortune, habit, feeling, interests, purposes, achievements, accidents, speeches made."

[3] Migne, *Patrologia Latina,* CLXXI, cols. 1687-92.

[4] Edmond Faral, *Les Arts poétiques du XIIième et du XIIIième siècle* (Paris, 1924), pp. 118-19.

[5] For text see *Romanische Forschungen, 13* (1902), 893-965.

[6] *Orator,* XXI, 69.

[7] *English Literary History: The Medieval Phase,* p. 107.

[8] Thus de Vinsauf writes: "Et tales recipiunt appellationes ratione personarum vel rerum de quibus fit tractatus. Quando enim de generalibus personis vel rebus tractatur, tunc es stylus grandiloquus; quando de humilibus, humilis; quando de mediocribus, mediocris." "The styles receive such names from a consideration of the persons and things with which the style is associated. When the style is associated with universal things or persons, then the style is lofty; when it is associated with low persons or things, then the style is low; when the style is associated with middle persons or things, the style is the middle style." (Faral, *Les Arts poétiques,* p. 312). He goes on to stress the importance of consistency: "consideratum est ut stylum materiae non variemus, id est ut de grandiloquo stylo non descendamus ad humilem." "We must be careful not to vary the style of our matter lest from the lofty style we descend to the low." (Faral, *Les Arts poétiques,* p. 315). The initial section then is a *notatio* (character portrayal) and behind the girl's every word stands the poet, bound by the twin laws of decorum and consistency to put into her mouth a certain kind of rhetoric.

[9] *John Skelton, Poet Laureate,* p. 132. Gordon also cites the *Ordo Commendationis Animae,* or "Commendations," as the basis of the second section; but this service presents a special problem to be considered later.

[1] Ibid., p. 125.

[2] *English Literature in the Sixteenth Century,* p. 138.

[3] "`So my soon is bobbid / & of his lif robbid' / forsooth than I sobbid, / Veryfying the wordis she seid to me. / Who cannot wepe may lerne at thee." From *Religious Lyrics of the XVth Century,* ed. Carleton Brown (Oxford, 1938), p. 18.

[4] Edwards' (*Skelton,* p. 108) comment on this tension is especially fine: "while the vespers are murmured around her, Jane's attention flickers back over her memories . . . with all the vivid inconsequences of her girlish mind until, mysteriously, the elegy becomes transmitted into its opposite—a paean to life, its inexplicable loveliness."

[5] *English Literature in the Sixteenth Century,* p. 138.

[6] *Wit and Rhetoric in the Renaissance* (New York, 1937), pp. 59-60.

[7] For a more detailed statistical analysis see my "Aspects of Rhetorical Analysis: Skelton's *Philip Sparrow,*" *Studia Neophilologica, 34,* No. 2 (1962), 216-38.

[8] Edwards (*Skelton,* p. 110) was the first to note that "nothing could disguise the fact that the whole of the *Commendations* were a supreme blasphemy. It was not only that Jane replaced the soul of the defunct; more than that, she was quite literally deified."

[1] This passage is also a form of *praecisio* or *aposiopesis,* the technique of significant omission, i.e., insinuation, a figure of which the poet seems especially fond.

Norma Phillips (essay date 1966)

SOURCE: "Observations on the Derivative Method of Skelton's Realism," in *JEGP: Journal of English and Germanic Philology,* Vol. LXV, No. 1, January, 1966, pp. 19-35.

[In the following essay, Phillips discusses the influence of poets Geoffrey Chaucer and William Langland on Skelton's poetry.]

John Skelton has been fortunate in his critics during our century, and perhaps notably so during the last decade. Following closely upon the large number of books and articles which appeared in the 1930's, '40's, and early '50's, recent work on Skelton has attempted to answer rather more special questions and, in doing so, has shed considerable light on the nature of his literary relationships, an area of inquiry long neglected. My purpose here is to explore this vein a little further and to try to consider what relevance such evidence may have for our reading of Skelton's poetry and for our estimates of his particular talents as a poet. If I dissent from the highly flattering conclusions reached by some other critics, it is in the hope that such dissension may prove useful as a clarification of problems, if not as answers to them, for Skelton seems to me to illustrate singularly well some of the difficulties encountered in the criticism of a certain kind of poetry, poetry that is at once both undeniably original and undeniably derivative.

I shall isolate for comment three of Skelton's longer works which offer a substantial unity of material and which also represent fairly separated periods of the poet's career, *The Bowge of Court, Magnificence,* and *The Tunning of Elinor Rumming.*[1] Of the three, the early dream allegory the *Bowge of Court* offers the best point of departure. The poem seems to me in significant ways the most impressive item in the Skelton canon, the one poem which, through a subtly wrought structure of poetic implication, creates a convincing world. Its distingushing quality is a pervasive tonality, a controlled and muted emotional environment of quiet intensity made possible chiefly by Skelton's complex use of the traditional *persona* of the narrator-poet; Dread, the poetic "I" who, like so much else in Skelton, traces his origin to a combination of influences from Chaucer and Langland,[2] functions dramatically in this world, and the novelty and interest of the ***Bowge of Court*** lie far less in its application of the form of the dream-vision to the purposes of satire than in this skillful use of a wholly negative dreamer who functions as the integrating and harmonizing factor for the entire poem.

An argument which makes of Dread a kind of Tudor anti-hero, wistfully attracted to and excited by the Establishment he both loathes and envies, would not be difficult to construct. It is, for example, noteworthy that the one positive choice which he makes in the entire poem is the decision to follow the advice of Desire and to implicate himself in the struggle for favor, and that, having done so, he becomes helpless and passive, unable to cope with the real conditions into which he is thrust. During his brief sojourn on the Bowge of Court he oscillates between his desire for participation in the things to be got from Lady Fortune in this world which she whimsically governs and his increasingly fearful perception of the moral and rational aberrations which such participation entails. Skelton's means of dramatizing this state of mind are simple but very effective. From Dread's opening remarks in which, as the still aloof narrator, he comments, in an admittedly very conventional medieval formula,

> Whan Luna, full of mutabylyte,
>   As emperes the dyademe hath worne
>   Of our pole artyke, symlynge halfe in scorne
> At our foly and our vnstedfastnesse,[3]

it is the uncertainty and instability of things which he sadly but resignedly sees reflected everywhere. And throughout the nightmare which becomes his poem his remarks on what he sees or on what happens to him, as well as his decisions, are intoned in a similar key; they are made tentatively, almost always with a qualifying "me thoughte," or similar phrase revealing hesitation and unwillingness to commit himself as to the truth and reliability of his own vision. Even at the end, when he sees his enemies approaching to slay him, his quality of thinking remains tentative:

> Me thoughte, I see lewde felawes here and there
>   Came for to slee me of mortall entente;
>   And, as they came, the shypborde faste I hente,
> And thoughte to lepe. . . .

> (ll. 528-31)

Significant, too, in creating the special environment of this poem, is the poet's strategic interweaving of monologue, description, and gesture with carefully spaced, graduated scenes of revelation. Events move to and away from Dread, the seven courtiers play scenes in front of him which he must creep forward, as on a stage, to overhear, and all of the characters gesticulate and speak as if in a theater. These scenes, however, which operate chiefly to delineate the seven rogues by showing their representative sins at work, never for a moment remove the real focus of the poem from the narrator-poet, for it is he who interprets them, filters them through his own sensibility, gives them the stamp of his terror and timidity, and their cumulative effect, both for him and for us, is increasingly to isolate him in the awareness of his dilemma.

Dread exists, in fact, like the Bowge of Court itself, in a kind of suspension between reality and sheer illusion; throughout the narration he seems to be hesitating, hanging between his initial decision to play the game with these people and his increasingly horrified recognition of the kind of world which they inhabit. This indecisiveness, coupled with his muffled fear, accounts for the peculiar floating quality of the poem: events, images, characters rise as if from a vacuum and pass as if unattached to anything, even to an unequivocal point of view. The apprehension and uncertainty of Dread's divided and confused mind act as a kind of stained glass through which the reality it both faces and avoids is reflected, and give to the poem its distinct and cumulative atmosphere of muted and sinister intensity.

Dread seems to me, then—and largely through him the poem—a striking instance of Skelton's imaginative development and renewing of medieval formulas. Other elements in the poem, however, lead to other and to more characteristic and recurrent Skeltonic problems. Most obtrusive and thorniest of these is the question of Skelton's technique of literary realism, projected in this poem and in the others we are considering chiefly, though not entirely, through the satirical portraits. I take it we need not argue the old, standard biographical snares, whether or not the people and situations were drawn from life, whether or not he really met an historical Alianora Romyng, and similar questions, and that we may concentrate only on the relevant textual ones. Almost every critic praises Skelton for just this realistic dimension in his work, for the freshness, vigor, and density of realistic detail with which he invests his low life characters and scenes in all three poems, the ability with which, for example, he revivifies the old tradition of ale-wife poems in ***Elinor Rumming*** and carries the courtiers and vices of the ***Bowge of Court*** and *Magnificence* out of the traditional context of the Deadly Sins and applies conventional terminology to secular purposes. If I am dissatisfied with this judgment, it is mainly because it bypasses questions raised by the method intrinsic to these portraits and situations, questions which are not answered by invoking vague concepts like tradition or even by speaking generally of a pervasive influence from Chaucer and Langland.

The phenomenon which the realistic materials of these poems seem to me to reveal is nothing less than an immense and scarcely to be exaggerated reliance on very limited and definite portions of the work of the two great fourteenth-century English poets. This reliance may take the form of direct and circumstantial borrowing of descriptive details; it may involve taking the name, moral cast, or psychological structure of a character from them; it may be a question of a revealing phrase in Skelton suggesting that certain lines of association recalled for him parts of their poetry so vividly that he echoed it almost automatically; or it may even be a question of the ordonnance of a poem being directly dependent on structural motifs in their work.

I take as instances first several of the rogues of the ***Bowge of Court*** and the corresponding vices of *Magnificence*. The most obvious of these is Favell, a figure coming directly of course from Langland's field full of folk and, in Skelton as in Langland, flattering through his "faire speche."[4] Again, from the same poem, the two allegorical figures, Suspect and Disdain, derive their details of symbolic realism directly from Langland's Invidia, whose various disfigurements are set forth in the confession scene:

> Enuye with heuy herte asked after schrifte,
> And carefullich *mea culpa* he comsed to shewe.
> He was pale as a pelet in the palsye he semed,
> . . . .
> His body was to-bolle for wratthe that he bote his
> lippes,
> And wryngynge he zede with the fiste to wreke
> hymself
> he thouzte
> With werkes or with wordes whan he seighe his
> tyme,
> Eche a worde that he warpe was of an addres tonge,
> Of chydynge and of chalangynge was his chief
> lyflode,
> With bakbitynge and bismer and beryng of fals
> witnesse;
>
> . . . . .
>
> "I myzte nouzte eet many zeres as a man ouzte,
> For enuye and yuel wille is yuel is defye;
> May no sugre ne swete thinge asswage my
> swellynge,
> Ne no *diapenidion* dryue it fro myne herte."
>   (B, V, 76-78, 84-89, 120-23)

These details, the paleness, palsy, the biting of the lips, the body corroded with envy, have given to Skelton's vignettes virtually all of their circumstantial realistic life. The initial description of Suspect,

> And whan he came walkynge soberly,
>   Wyth whom and ha, and with a croked loke,
> Me thoughte, his hede was full of gelousy,
>   His eyen rollynge, his hondes faste they quoke;
> And to me warde the strayte wayc he toke,

and Dread's first glimpse of him,

> The seconde was Suspecte, whiche that dayly
>   Mysdempte eche man, with face deedly and pale,

as well as his description of Disdain,

> He bote the lyppe, he loked passynge coye;
>   His face was belymmed, as byes had him stounge:
> It was no tyme with him to jape nor toye;
>   Enuye hathe wasted his lyuer and his lounge,
>   Hatred by the herte so had hym wrounge,
> That he loked pale as asshes to my syghte,

provide their own obvious documentation.

Invidia's confession does service again and again in Skelton, though perhaps not elsewhere so successfully as here.

The long monologue of Cloaked Collusion in *Magnificence* represents the virtual wholesale importation of the psychology of envy as it had been conceived by Langland. Here the influence is so all-pervasive that only fairly extensive quotation of the two relevant passages can effectively illustrate Skelton's procedure. Langland's lines are as follows:

> Eche a worde that he warpe was of an addres tonge,
> Of chydynge and of chalangynge was his chief
> lyflode,
> With bakbitynge and bismer and beryng of fals
> witnesse;
> This was al his curteisye where that euere he
> shewed hym.
>
> . . . . .
>
> I haue a neighbore neyze me I haue ennuyed hym
> ofte,
> And lowen on hym to lordes to don hym lese his
> siluer,
> And made his frendes ben his foon thorw my false
> tonge;
> His grace and his good happes greueth me ful sore.
> Bitwene many and many I make debate ofte,
> That bothe lyf and lyme is lost thorw my speche.
> And whan I mete him in market that I moste hate,
> I hailse hym hendeliche as I his frende were;
>
> . . . . .
>
> And of mennes lesynge I laughe that liketh myn
> herte;
> And for her wynnynge I wepe and waille the tyme,
> And deme that hij don ille there I do wel worse;
>
> . . . . .
>
> "I am sori," quod that segge "I am but selde other,
> And that maketh me thus megre for I ne may me
> venge.
> Amonges burgeyses haue I be dwellynge at Londoun,
> And gert bakbitinge be a brocoure to blame mennes
> ware.
> Whan he solde and I nouzte thanne was I redy
> To lye and to loure on my neighbore and to lakke
> his chaffre."

The monologue of Cloaked Collusion retains the confessional attitude (it is perhaps worth noting that both characters are wearing clerical garments), though certainly Skelton's context is not an explicitly religious one. But the monologue clearly follows the model provided by Langland:

> And though I be so odyous a geste,
> And euery man gladly my company wolde refuse,
> In faythe, yet am I occupyed with the best;
>
> Ful fewe that can themselfe of me excuse.
> Whan other men laughe, than study I and muse,
> Deuysynge the meanes and wayes that I can,
> Howe I may hurte and hynder euery man.

. . . . .

Comberaunce and trouble in Englande fyrst I began;
From that lorde to that lorde I rode and I ran,
And flatered them with fables fayre before theyr
    face,
And tolde all the Myschyef I coude behynde theyr
    backe,
And made as I had known nothynge of the case,—
I wolde begyn all Myschyef, but I wolde bere no
    lacke.
Thus can I lerne you, Syrs, to bere the deuyls
    sacke;
And yet, I trowe, some of you be better sped than I
Frendshyp to fayne and thynke full lytherly.
Paynte to a purpose Good Countenaunce I can,
And craftely can I grope howe euery man is
    mynded;
My purpose is to spy and to poynte euery man;
My tonge is with Fauell forked and tyned.
By Cloked Colusyon thus many one is begyled.
Eche man to hynder I gape and I gaspe;
My speche is all Pleasure, but I stynge lyke a
    waspe.
I am neuer glad but whan I may do yll,
And neuer am I sory but whan that I se
I can not myne appetyte accomplysshe and fulfyll
In hynderaunce of Welthe and Prosperyte.
I laughe at all Shrewdenes, and lye at Lyberte.
I muster, I medle amonge these grete estates;
I sowe sedycyous sedes of Dyscorde and debates.[5]

Comparison of the two passages reveals that the accents in Skelton are, as in Langland, on envy not only as an internal state but as an active way of life, though predictably Skelton prunes away a good deal of the earlier poet's proliferation of rich, evocative detail, and the effect is thinner, more abstract, and more naïvely didactic.

A final note on Skelton's use of Invidia in these poems should point out his rather incongruous brief reappearance, quaking hands and all, in the portrait of the unfortunate Maude Ruggy in *The Tunning of Elinor Rumming*:

Maude Ruggy thyther skypped:
She was vgly hypped,
And vgly thycke lypped,
Lyke an onyon syded,
Lyke tan ledder hyded:
She had her so guyded
Betwene the cup and the wall,
That she was there wythall
Into a palsey fall;
Wyth that her hed shaked,
And her handes quaked:

Ones hed wold haue aked
To se her naked:
She dranke so of the dregges,
The dropsy was in her legges;
Her face glystryng lyke glas;
All foggy fat she was;

She had also the gout
In all her ioyntes about.[6]

Here, though, it should be noted that Invidia is given the thick lips and tanned, leathery skin of Langland's Avaricia, a casual, loose, and seemingly haphazard jumbling of items appropriate to Skeltonics, with their affinity for the irresponsible accumulation of physical details.

Another example revealing roughly the same process of derivation will perhaps suffice. Skelton's portrait of Riot, the seedy, impoverished, lecherous court hanger-on in the *Bowge of Court,* is one of his most complex and interesting. Here the primary source for the details of the physical description is the confession scene of Avaricia in the *Visio.* The borrowing is so close and so precise that parallel quotations are instructive:

Avaricia.
    And thanne cam Coueytise can I hym nouzte
    descryue
    So hungriliche and holwe sire Heruy hym loked.
    He was bitelbrowed and baberlipped also,
    With two blered eyghen as a blynde hagge;
    And as a letheren purs lolled his chekes,
    Wel sydder than his chyn thei chiueled for elde;
    And as a bondman of his bacoun his berde was
    bidraueled.
    With an hode on his hed a lousi hatte aboue,
    And in a tauny tabarde of twelue wynter age,
    Al totorne and baudy and ful of lys crepynge;
    But if that a lous couthe have lopen the bettre,
    She sholde nouzte have walked on that welche so
    was it thredeba re.[7]
                                        (B, V, 188-99)

Riot.
        His here was growen thorowe oute his hat.
        Thenne I behelde how he dysgysed was:
            His hede was heuy for watchynge ouer
    nyghte,
            His eyen blereed, his face shone lyke a glas;
            His gowne so shorte that it ne couer
    myghte
            His rumpe, he wente so all for somer
    lyghte;
            His hose was garded wyth a lyste of grene,
            Yet at the knee they were broken, I wene.

            His cote was checked with patches rede and
    blewe;
            Of Kyrkeby Kendall was his shorte demye;
            And ay he sange, In fayth, decon thou
    crewe;
            His elbowe bare, he ware his gere so nye;
            His nose a droppynge, his lyppes were full
    drye;
            And by his syde his whynarde and his
    pouche,
            The deuyll myghte daunce therin for ony
    crowche.

                                        (ll. 350-64)

But although Langland's Avaricia has given him his clothes and his ill health, I am in complete agreement with John Holloway that Chaucer's Pardoner is his real spiritual ancestor. The headlong, spasmodic rhythm of the monologue, the disorderly, nonsequential gestures and almost hysterical ejaculations impart a total effect very much like that of the Pardoner's self-revelation.[8]

This monologue offers another curious and revealing Chaucerian motif. Riot's advice to Dread includes the admonition,

Plucke vp thyne herte vpon a mery pyne,

in which one hears the echo of Placebo's flattery of January in the *Merchant's Tale,*

Youre herte hangeth on a joly pyn.[9]

This is precisely similar to an instance noted long ago by F. P. Magoun,[10] who observed that the remark made by the prince Magnificence to Courtly Abusion in their discussion of women,

A, I haue spyed ye can moche broken sorowe,[11]

might well have derived from January's remarks on the widows whom he did not wish to marry,

They conne so muche craft on Wades boot,
So muchel broken harm, whan that hem leste.[12]

There seems to me no doubt whatsoever about the influence, but again it is the mode of operation of that influence which is most interesting. Such echoes, occurring with so little change and in such parallel contexts, indicate the way Skelton's poetic mentality worked when it approached these recurrent problems of realistic representation: it employed static models—certain situations and lines—taken from his reading, and it made constant, perhaps even automatic, associations of such problems with analogous problems and solutions in Chaucer and Langland. Moreover, and equally important for our understanding of Skelton, the same models—especially Invidia, Avaricia, the *Merchant's Tale,* and the Wife of Bath[13]—which served him in 1499 were still serving him, and in the same way, some twenty years later, just as his vocabulary of denunciation reveals, as a valuable essay on *Magnificence* has recently put it, that "the whole system of psychological, ethical, and political ideas conveyed by the terms underlies not the play and the satires alone but the whole career of Skelton."[14]

Perhaps Skelton thought that many areas of experience and the world had been interpreted and definitively glossed by the giants who had gone before; what remained for him was something else.

—Norma Phillips

We can watch the operation of this derivative technique in another dimension of Skelton's work also; in the structure of these poems, in their disposition of materials, we find again diligently applied the lessons Skelton learned from his medieval masters. Before the turn of our century, Albert Rey commented in passing that the "hypothesis that Langland's *Piers Plowman* furnished the original idea of the *Bowge of Court* might well be produced," and he noted the similar societies of the poems, grouped respectively around Lady Meed and Lady Fortune.[15] Since then other critics have also observed the probable influence of the *House of Fame* on this and on other Skelton poems,[16] and it has become almost a commonplace to link Glutton's tavern in the *Visio* with Elinor's in Leatherhead, for Skelton's whole conception of the tavern scene, the women's names, the analogous activities, especially the single most distinctive piece of realism,[17] in short, almost everything "realistic" reveals a direct adaptation from Langland.[18]

The case of *Magnificence* is subtler but discloses the same pattern of borrowed structural motifs, even of ideological scaffolding. The fundamental thematic opposition of the morality, that of Measure to Liberty, is established in the debate which opens it, and what follows is little more than an *exemplum* of the abuse of the conclusions of the debate. Ramsay, whose edition of *Magnificence* held for so long an oracular position in Skelton studies, could do no better than to attribute the source of this opposition to Aristotle, and he hoped that the then lost *Speculum Principis* of Skelton would hold the answer to the "introduction of the quite new conception of Liberty to put over against Felicity,"[19] but although his edition has recently come in for some long-overdue criticism, no one has yet observed, I believe, that the mysterious source is again simply *Piers Plowman* in another of its myriad appearances. The triumvirate of the earlier poem, Reason, Conscience, and Lady Meed, and their relationship with the nameless king, have their counterparts in Skelton's Measure, Felicity, and Liberty in their ideal relationship to the prince, Magnificence. The philosophical, political, and ethical status given Reason are not only paralleled in Measure, but each is called upon to settle the debate, in the one case between Conscience and Meed, in the other between Felicity and Liberty; each is made the first counselor of the king-prince, each is given dominion over the others. In adapting Conscience to his more secular situation, Skelton reduced Felicity to an almost purely materialistic symbol, and, unlike Conscience, he functions in the debate largely as a yes-man.

But perhaps the most interesting contribution of *Piers Plowman* to the aligning of relationships, and incidentally the answer to Ramsay's puzzle, is that of the inconstant and wayward Lady Meed to the inconstant and wayward Liberty. The two characters occupy the same neutral position, neither essentially good nor bad, but only potentially so according to the uses to which they are put. As defined by their contexts, however, they show a natural affinity for evil and incline inevitably toward manipulation by its agents. Hence, the necessity, emphasized throughout both poems, of keeping them under careful observation and stern control.[20]

The deliberate parallelism in the two debate situations is so sustained throughout and is made so apparent by their resolutions that again quotation is useful. In each case the king or prince has been awakened to the perilous qualities natural to Meed or to Liberty, and in each case he has selected the two advisers who are to reign with him. The closing lines of this episode in *Piers Plowman* are as follows:

> The kynge called Conscience and afterwardes Resoun,
> And recorded that Resoun had riztfullich schewed,
> And modilich vppon Mede with myzte the kynge loked,
> And gan wax wrothe with lawe for Mede almoste had shent it,
> And seide, "thorw zowre lawe, as I leue I lese many chetes;
> Mede ouer-maistrieth lawe and moche treuthe letteth.
> Ac Resoun shal rekene with zow zif I regne any while,
> And deme zow, bi this day as ze han deserued.
> Mede shal nouzte meynprise zow bi the Marie of heuene!
> I will haue leute in lawe and lete be al zowre Ianglyng,
> And as moste folke witnesseth wel wronge shal be demed."
> Quod Conscience to the kynge "but the comune will assent,
> It is ful hard, bi myn hed here-to to brynge it,
> Alle zowre lige leodes to lede thus euene."
> "By hym that rauzte on the rode" quod Resoun to the kynge,
> "But if I reule thus zowre rewme rende out my guttes!
> zif ze bidden buxomnes be of myne assente."
> "And I assent," seith the kynge "by seynt Marie my lady,
> Be my conseille comen of clerkis and of erlis.
> Ac redili, Resoun thou shalt nouzte ride fro me,
> For as longe as I lyue lete the I nelle."
> "I am aredy," quod Resoun "to reste with zow euere,
> So Conscience be of owre conseille I kepe no bettere."
> "And I graunt," quod the kynge "goddes forbode it faile,
> Als longe as owre lyf lasteth lyue we togideres."
> (B, IV, 171-95)

Skelton's lines are much more repetitive, but a specimen will suffice to reveal the resemblance:

> MAGN. Conuenyent persons for any prynce ryall.
> Welthe with Lyberte, with me bothe dwell ye shall,
> To the gydynge of my Measure you bothe commyttynge;
> That Measure be mayster, vs semeth it is syttynge.
>
> MEAS. Where as ye haue, Syr, to me them assygned,
> Suche order I trust with them for to take,

> So that Welthe with Measure shalbe conbyned,
> And Lyberte his large with Measure shall make.
>
> FEL. Your ordenaunce, Syr, I wyll not forsake.
>
> LYB. And I my selfe hooly to you wyll inclyne.
>
> MAGN. Then may I say that ye be seruauntys myne.
> For by Measure I warne you we thynke to be gydyd;
> Wherin it is necessary my pleasure you knowe:
> Measure and I wyll neuer be deuydyd,
> For no dyscorde that any man can sawe;
> For Measure is a meane, nother to hy nor to lawe,
> In whose attemperaunce I haue suche delyght,
> That Measure shall neuer departe from my syght.
>
> FEL. Laudable your Consayte is to be acountyd,
> For Welthe without Measure sodenly wyll slyde.
>
> LYB. As your grace full nobly hath recountyd,
> Measure with Noblenesse sholde be alyde.
>
> MAGN. Then Lyberte, se that Measure be your gyde,
> For I wyll vse you by his aduertysment.
>
> FEL. Then shall you haue with you Prosperyte resydent.
>
> MEAS. I trowe Good Fortune hath annexyd vs together,
> To se howe greable we are of one mynde.[21]

As striking as the imitation, of course, is the difference in poetic effect; the mechanical, automatic quality of the debate in *Magnificence* contrasts strangely with the passion and even the humor of Langland's poem where, in spite of the not infrequent conceptual ambiguity, the movement of the Meed-Conscience debate is urgent and real; that of Liberty-Felicity is a monotonous shuttling back and forth from one speaker to another, a continual rhetorical amplification of initially simple points. Moreover, all the arguments in Skelton are intellectually one-dimensional and static. The devices so carefully manipulated, repetition, metrical patterning, rhyme variations and similar stylistic ornaments,[22] reveal that quality which W. H. Auden probably had in mind or at least suggested when he spoke of Skelton's "best poems, with the exception of *Speke Parrot*," being "like triumphantly successful prize poems."[23] Their subtlety is extrinsic; in the movement of the language itself we feel little urgency, intellectual or otherwise.

Similarly, one notes the prominence of proverbs in this play and elsewhere in Skelton's work. John Holloway, in commenting on this phenomenon, has remarked that "To notice Skelton's reliance on the proverbial expression is not to notice a literary trick or a literary routine, but to notice, at its most easily point, the essential quality of what was creative in his mind."[24] With this I should agree, and if I find the element less impressive than he does, that is of no consequence. Still, it is at least worth distinguishing Skelton's use of it a little more carefully, for he clearly does not use the proverb, as Chaucer so frequently does, for example, as a manipulated literary device within the texture of the poem, capable of making a nexus for a complex of meanings. Nor does he, like Langland, employ the proverb critically and tentatively, as one of the many roads by which truth may be approached and tried, but never asserted. In Skelton the proverb or maxim is most likely to appear, with startling insistence and aggressive simplicity, at a climactic point in a poem. The self-styled "argument" of Measure, for example, is simply a catalogue of rhetorical parallelisms, a hypnotically repetitious string of proverbs and maxims:

> Where Measure is mayster, Plenty dothe none
>   offence;
> Where Measure lackyth, all thynge desorderyd is:
> Where Measure is absent, Ryot kepeth resydence;
> Where Measure is ruler, there is nothynge amysse.
> Measure is treasure; howe say ye, is it not this?[25]

(It is perhaps not irrelevant to remark here that Felicity's brief responses to Measure's long speeches, often linked to them by rhyme, are so pat as to be almost antiphonal, thereby intensifying the atmosphere of make-believe which prevails throughout the debate.) In short, the proverbial element in *Magnificence,* and not infrequently in Skelton's other work, acts as an assimilated part of the very ideology on which the poem rests, and one sees in its functioning a characteristic strategy: it provides, like his other derivative materials, a field of easy and immediate judgment, with again the tendency to make a simple and direct connection between a problem and a pre-established solution.

A brief summary is now perhaps in order. I have tried to demonstrate that in three of Skelton's major poems, those in which he was most concerned with building fictional frameworks that demanded low-life scenes and figures, he relied in precise, deliberate, and extensive ways on the poems of his two great English predecessors, Chaucer and Langland. It should perhaps be stressed again that this reliance was not simply a matter of "tradition," the inevitable process of literary continuity, but involved a direct, concrete, and specific influence upon his poems by their poems. The area in which this influence operated was primarily that of realistic representation, and the method was that of relevant association. When confronted with the need to represent envy or some similar quality, either in its psychological state or in its symbolic physical manifestions, as in the varying cases of Suspect and Disdain in the **Bowge of Court,** Cloaked Collusion in *Magnificence,* or just the abstract "odyous Enui" in *Philip Sparrow,*[26] Skelton turned to the confession of Invidia in the *Visio of Piers Plowman.* When lechery in a seedy court sycophant had to be depicted, whether in Riot's advice to Dread or in the conversation about women between Courtly Abusion and Magnificence, Skelton was reminded of the quintessential moral degeneracy and callousness of the *Merchant's Tale,* and particularly of the analogous conversation of January and Placebo. Both the lady in the monologue of Counterfeit Countenance and Elinor Rumming had, by the same logic, to draw upon the inspiration of the Wife of Bath, and the events in Elinor's tavern had to be patterned on those of Glutton. Sometimes, of course, the connection was not especially predictable, as in the case of Maude Ruggy, who borrows from Invidia and Avaricia. Again, the derivations are sometimes rather complex; in Riot, for example, Avaricia, the Pardoner, and January-Placebo meet in one.

Skelton's debts, however, were not confined solely to problems of characterization and to the activities of the tavern; in all three poems they also involved structural and even ideological borrowings. In the **Bowge of Court** the poetic structure was determined at least in part by the *House of Fame,* by the whole Chaucerian use of the *persona,* and by the tableau of Lady Meed and her corrupters in the field full of folk. In *Magnificence* the entire scaffolding of ideas which underlies the most important figures and their interrelationships is derived from the Meed-Conscience-Reason debate in the *Visio;* the monologues of the vices, in addition to their circumstantial debts to Chaucer and Langland, may well represent an attempt at a pattern somewhat like that of the confessions of the Deadly Sins in *Piers Plowman,* just as the surface organization of **The Tunning of Elinor Rumming** into *passus* may similarly represent another result of Langland's influence.

It is more than probable that much additional documentation of this kind is to be found throughout Skelton's work, but we have enough, I believe, to permit us to draw a few tentative conclusions. I wish at all costs to avoid incurring the suspicion that I have assembled this material as a kind of exposure of Skelton's plagiaristic sins, for whatever inferences may be deduced from such evidence are clearly not so simple. That Skelton is an "original" poet, whatever that may mean to different critics, is hardly a point to prove or refute. His adaptation of traditional forms and formulas to his own purposes, his innovations in language and experiments in prosody, the stirrings and murmurings we do sense in him of changes to come in ideas and perspectives, the passion of his denunciation, which was perhaps the most directly personal quality in him, all of these are certainly there. Still, whatever final values we may assign to Skelton's work, we should at least be sure that those values are founded on accurate reading. We cannot really go on asserting his lack of "real predecessors,"[27] his refusal to "approach experience with preconceptions,"[28] and praising his fresh, unacademic delight in the real world, when it is frequently the very academic, cautious skill in filling out his own defects through borrowing and adapting the work of his predecessors which is his most impressive attribute. Such evidence as we have, it seems to me, points to a glaring disparity between Skelton's, medieval immersion and his own secularized, non-introspective, antisymbolic, abstract sensibility. At the heart of his retreat into extremes of rhetorical rigidity, on the one hand, and Skeltonics, which have their own kind of rigidity, on the other, and of his willingness to surrender so much to the eyes and language of others, lay a peculiar impersonality, just as behind all of his overt ebullience and nervous energy was a profound intellectual inertia. Perhaps he thought that many areas of experience and the world had been interpreted and definitively glossed by the giants who had gone before; what remained for Skelton was something else. Fortunately, literature has many worlds and there are many ways of writing interesting poems, but if part of the vexing problem of Skelton is, as I remarked at the beginning of this essay, the problem of approaching a poetic imagination which is both original and supinely imitative, we shall approach it better if we know something of the way that imagination worked.

Notes

1 *The Poetical Works of John Skelton,* ed. Alexander Dyce, 2 vols. (London, 1843), is still the standard edition for most of Skelton's work and will be the source for all quotations from or references to these poems in this essay, unless otherwise noted.

2 For Langland I have in mind those lines from *Piers Plowman* where the corrupt attendants of Lady Meed are on the point of being dispersed and Dread stands at the door eavesdropping; see William Langland, *The Vision of William Concerning Piers the Plowman in Three Parallel Texts, Together with Richard the Redeless,* ed. W. W. Skeat, 2 vols. (Oxford, 1886), I, B, II, 205-209. All citations of Langland in my text are from the first volume of this edition. For Chaucer it is principally the situation in the *House of Fame* with the rout surrounding Lady Fame crying for largesse which influenced the beginning of the *Bowge of Court* and the crowds surrounding Lady Fortune begging favor; see especially, in *The Poetical Works of Chaucer,* ed. F. N. Robinson (Cambridge, Mass., 1933)—hereafter cited as *Works*—ll. 1282-87, 1307-15, 1356-67 of the *House of Fame.* There are also a number of parallels between the role of Dread in Skelton's poem and Chaucer's manipulation of the poet-dreamer in the *House of Fame.* There is a much fuller discussion of these matters in my unpublished dissertation, "John Skelton and the Tradition of English Realism" (Yale, 1957), pp. 51 ff. I have not thought it necessary to reproduce here the arguments and evidence concerning Dread and his origins because A. R. Heiserman's *Skelton and Satire* (Chicago, 1961; pp. 42-51) has produced roughly the same evidence, thereby rendering further documentation of this particular point superfluous. Judith Larson, in her recent article, "What Is *The Bowge of Court?*" (*JEGP,* LXI [1962], 288-95), has suggested other possible items of Chaucerian influence, chiefly from his translation of the *Roman de la Rose* and from the *Book of the Duchess.*

3 Ll. 3-6. See Dyce, 1, 30-50, for the text of *The Bowge of Court.*

4 See especially ll. 134-35 and 147; for Langland note especially B, II, 41, and B, II, 64.

5 Ramsay, ll. 703-709, 715-37; Dyce, ll. 713-19, 725-47. Since R. L. Ramsay's celebrated edition of this morality, *Magnyfycence, A Moral Play by John Skelton,* EETS, extra ser., XCVIII (London, 1908 [1906]), is in general the more available text, I shall base my quotations and line references on it rather than on Dyce. For the possible convenience of some readers, however, I shall give the line numbers of both.

6 For the text of *The Tunning of Elinor Rumming* see Dyce, I, 95-115.

7 Albert Rey (*Skelton's Satirical Poems in Their Relation to Lydgate's "Order of Fools," "Cock Lorell's Bote," and Barclay's "Ship of Fools"* [Bern, 1899], p. 28) comments, "Langland's Auaricia is likely to have lent him some features, at least covetousness also has two bleared eyes and a lousy hat."

8 This point is discussed more fully in my Yale dissertation of 1957 (see above, n. 2) and in John Holloway's valuable essay, "Skelton," Chatterton Lecture on an English Poet, read 26 February 1958 and published in the *Proceedings of the British Academy: 1958* (London, 1959), p. 92.

9 Chaucer, *Works,* E 1516. I owe the discovery of this item, and very much more not so easily documented, to Professor E. Talbot Donaldson, of Yale, who first perceived the immense debt of Skelton to Chaucer and Langland and set me working on it some time ago.

10 F. P. Magoun, "'Muchel *Broken* Harm,' C.-T., E 1425," *Anglia,* LIII (1929), 223-24.

11 Ramsay, l. 1587; Dyce, l. 1606.

12 *Works,* E 1424-25.

13 Skelton's description of Elinor Rumming, ll. 64-79, is fairly clearly based on Chaucer's description of the Wife in the General Prologue, *Works,* A 449-458. And the monologue of Counterfeit Countenance in *Magnificence,* when it touches on the subject of pride and hypocrisy in women (Ramsay, 452-65; Dyce, 458-70), reverts to the language originally intended for the Wife at the beginning of the *Shipman's Tale—Works,* B 1201-1209.

14 William O. Harris, "Wolsey and Skelton's *Magnyfycence:* A Re-evaluation," *SP,* LVII (1960), 111-12.

15 *Skelton's Satirical Poems,* p. 58.

16 See above, n. 2. That Skelton knew the *House of Fame* very well indeed is hardly a recent discovery, however; see, for example, for its detailed influence on the *Garland of Laurel* Albert S. Cook, "Skelton's 'Garland of Laurel' and Chaucer's 'House of Fame,'" *MLR,* XI (1916), 9-14.

17 Compare B, V, 346-51, with *Elinor Rumming,* ll. 565-79.

18 One wonders if *Elinor Rumming* was not also influenced by the confession of Avaricia in those lines where he speaks of setting up his wife in the brewery trade; see B, V, 219-27. But for the most part the materials of *Elinor Rumming* are drawn from Glutton's confession, especially B, V, 310-26, 344-51. Ian A. Gordon, in *John Skelton, Poet Laureate* (Melbourne and London, 1943; p. 76), was the first, I believe, to note that Langland's "picture of the ale-house in the sketch of gluttony gave Skelton the form of the poem."

19 Ramsay, p. lxxiii. See F. M. Salter, "Skelton's 'Speculum Principis,'" *Speculum,* IX (1934), 25-37, for a reprint of the text of this treatise.

20 T. P. Dunning's *Piers Plowman: An Interpretation of the A-Text* (Dublin, 1937; pp. 69-112) gives a long and interesting analysis of the theological significance of Meed and of her episodes with the king, Conscience, and Reason.

21 Ramsay, ll. 173-99; Dyce, ll. 175-201.

22 Ramsay, pp. li-lxxi, gives an exhaustive account of the versification of *Magnificence,* of the types of poetic lines employed, and of its use of metrical variations. His enthusiasm over the mechanical complexity of these variations, however, led him to rather simple value judgments; see pp. lxv-lxvi: "The possession of so rich a scale of metrical variations, far richer than any other morality can boast, gave Skelton the opportunity of making subtle and effective distinctions in characterizing the tone of different scenes and characters; and the studied care with which this is done is perhaps the play's best title to be considered a work of conscious art." A rather different point of view is suggested by J. E. Bernard, Jr., *The Prosody of the Tudor Interlude,* Yale Studies in English, XC (New Haven, 1939), pp. 35-39; see especially p. 39:

"The most striking feature of John Skelton's dramatic prosody is the disregard of all the Latin he learned. He follows the English tradition alone in his tetrameter couplets and in his rime royal. . . . Quite unlike the original methods of prosodic treatment, the varying of verse in *Magnificence* is extrinsic. There is no connexion between character and verse or between theme and verse. . . . On the whole, the use of couplets and rime royal seems to be owing only to the dramatist's desire to talk to his audience with more or less concentrated zeal. It betrays a lack of interest in character as such, and even in morality as such, morality play though this is."

[23] W. H. Auden, "John Skelton," *The Great Tudors,* ed. Katherine Garvin (London, 1935), p. 62.

[24] "Skelton," p. 96.

[25] Ramsay, ll. 121-25; Dyce, ll. 122-26.

[26] Dyce, 1, 78, ll. 902-49.

[27] C. S. Lewis, *English Literature in the Sixteenth Century* (Oxford, 1954), p. 143.

[28] Alan Swallow, "John Skelton: The Structure of the Poem," *PQ,* XXXII (1953), 35.

John Scattergood   (essay date 1990)

SOURCE: "Skelton's *Garlande of Laurell* and the Chaucerian Tradition," in *Chaucer Traditions: Studies in Honour of Derek Brewer,* edited by Ruth Morse and Barry Windeatt, Cambridge University Press, 1990, pp. 122-38.

[*In the following essay, Scattergood compares Skelton's* The Garlande of Laurell *to Geoffrey Chaucer's* House of Fame *and discusses Skelton's belief in the "all-embracing relevance of poetry."*]

Of all the English Chaucerians nobody wrote more about poetry, about the nature of the poetic tradition, and his own role in it than Skelton, and *The Garlande of Laurell* is in many ways his most considered statement. Usually his comments appear in the context of some other subject, but this poem is about poetry and nothing else. For all that, it is not a particularly unified or cohesive performance, partly due to the circumstances of its composition. From the astrological opening[1] it would seem that Skelton began the poem in 1495 on the occasion of a celebration at Sheriff Hutton Castle (Yorkshire) organized by Elizabeth Tylney Howard, Countess of Surrey, and her circle, to mark Skelton's laureations by three universities—Oxford in 1490, Louvain in 1492, and Cambridge in 1493. But the revised version published by Richard Fakes on 3 October 1523 included a defence of *Phyllyp Sparowe* (lines 1261-1366) which must post-date 1509 and a list of works including some which date from the early 1520s. In a sense, this is not unusual: Skelton's poems frequently grow by addition and augmentation. What is important in relation to *The Garlande of Laurell,* however, is that by 1523 its original celebratory purpose had waned somewhat, and

it had become rather a retrospective review of a lengthy career spent on poetry, and an attempt at justifying that career.

In view of its subject matter, it is a less complacent poem than it might have been. Skelton's dream of fame is set in a forbiddingly unfavourable context. The traditional enemies of fame are chance, time and death, and Skelton contextualizes his examination of the subject as he meditates, at the beginning of his poem, on the mutability of things:

In place alone then musynge in my thought
How all thynge passyth as doth the somer flower,
On every halfe my reasons forth I sought,
How oftyn fortune varyth in an howre,
Now clere wether, forthwith a stormy showre;
All thynge compassyd, no perpetuyte,
But now in welthe, now in adversyte.

In his despair he leans for rest on the stump of an oak tree in Galtres Forest, but it provides no comfort and merely reinforces those fears that are troubling his mind, for the once mighty and noble tree is now no more than an emblem of the ravages of time: its 'bewte blastyd was with the boystors wynde', its leaves were gone and the sap had left its bark. He aspires instead to the everlasting laurel, 'Enverdurid with leves contynually grene', the symbol of poetic fame, and this is granted him, though with reservations. Pallas, goddess of wisdom and the deity controlling the academic curriculum ('Madame regent of the scyence sevyn'), vouches for Skelton's excellence and the Quene of Fame allows his name to be registered 'With laureate tryumphe in the courte of Fame' because he has spent his time 'studyously', but this is only after a rigorous examination of his case and the raising of a number of serious objections. For Skelton, fame is not easily acquired. And even after he is acclaimed and accepted, once out of his dream the poem ends with another figure of transience— the double-faced Janus, Roman god of beginnings and endings, who is making calculations about time with his 'tirikkis' and his 'volvell'. In order to come to terms with what constitutes everlasting fame for the poet Skelton meditates profoundly on the past and the future.

Everlasting fame, glory, and honour are frequent subjects in poetry and in *The Garlande of Laurell,* Skelton uses many traditional ideas. There is no agreement, however, about whether he used closely any specific source. It has been argued, by Edvige Schulte, that his inspiration came from Italian, from Dante's *Purgatorio* and from Petrarch's *Africa,* the *Triumph of Fame* Chapter III and from *Canzone* CCXXIII.[2] On the other hand, Gordon Kipling has seen the French *rhétoriquer* tradition, as developed in the courts of Flanders, as providing Skelton with models for this and other poems.[3] Again, Gregory Kratzmann proposes Gavin Douglas's *Palice of Honour* as a significant influence.[4] It may be that Skelton derived something from all these sources; it is clear that in *The Garlande of Laurell* he identifies himself with a tradition of poetry which he takes back to its mythic origins and which incorporates many languages and many periods both ancient and modern. But predominantly, this concern is with England and the English tradition. The poem is infused with a sort of literary nationalism: Skelton pays particular attention to the gate of the palace of Fame which is called 'Anglea' and which bears the English heraldic beast, 'a lybbard, crownyd with golde and stones'; and it is Gower, Chaucer, and Lydgate 'Theis Englysshe poetis thre' who escort him to the Quene of Fame. The most substantial earlier treatment of the subject of *The Garlande of Laurell* in English poetry was Chaucer's *House of Fame,* and this is the poem, as was long ago proposed, which seems to me most important to Skelton here.

It is perhaps unfortunate that A. S. Cook chose to make the case for the 'dependence' of *The Garlande of Laurell* on Chaucer by citing parallel passages.[5] His evidence shows that the same general ideas and literary strategies occur, but that there is no specific verbal correspondence. Though both poems are dream-visions in which the narrator confronts allegorical figures of authority, Skelton's poem is much simpler than the *House of Fame*: it is less inventive (there is no Dantean eagle to act as guide, and no aerial flight through the cosmos as there is in Chaucer's lines 496-1053); it is philosophically less enquiring (there is no disquisition on the way sound travels as in lines 765-852, or on the relation of rumour to fame in lines 1916-2120); and crucially it is much narrower in its conception of fame (there is no comparable equivalent to the various companies who put their cases to Chaucer's goddess in lines 1520-1867). Skelton is concerned, almost exclusively, with literary fame.

Yet something of Chaucer's poem is recalled by Skelton, though transmuted so as to be almost unrecognizable. In the *House of Fame* Eolus blows 'bad fame' or 'shame' out of his black trumpet to one company of petitioners:

> . . . thrughout every regioun
> Wente this foule trumpes soun,
> As swifte as pelet out of gonne
> When fyr is in the poudre ronne.
> And such a smoke gan out wende
> Out of his foule trumpes ende,
> Blak, bloo, grenyssh, swartish red,
> As doth where that men melte led,
> Loo, al on high fro the tuel.
> And therto oo thing saugh I well,
> That the ferther that hit ran,
> The gretter wexen hit began,
> As dooth the ryver from a welle,
> And hyt stank as the pit of helle.

Chaucer is concerned to show how bad fame spreads, and uses, amongst other comparisons, some of the traditional images associated with vainglory—smoke and stench.[6] Though Eolus appears also in Skelton he is not an agent for the distribution of fame, being now no more than someone who performs ceremonial duties, calling for attention and such like. Yet Skelton remembers and responds to Chaucer's passage, though not by direct imitation. He takes Chaucer's simile, 'as pelet out of gonne', and literalizes it. He causes the presumptuously clamouring, unworthy

figures who are besieging the palace of Fame to be scattered by gunfire from the walls:

> With a pellit of pevisshenes they had suche a
>   stroke,
> That all the dayes of ther lyfe shall styck by ther
>   rybbis.
> Foo, foisty bawdias, sum smellid of the smoke . . .

—retaining the two traditional images. Similarly, in Chaucer 'good fame' from Eolus' golden trumpet is spread like a fragrance:

> And, certes, al the breth that wente
> Out of his trumpes mouth it smelde
> As men a pot of bawme helde
> Among a basket ful of roses.

This reappears in Skelton as the fragrance from the olive-wood fire kindled by the phoenix in the top of the laurel tree in Fame's garden: 'It passid al bawmys that ever were namyd'. Though he steals odd lines here and there, Skelton rarely makes extensive use of literary sources: the relationship between these poems is not one of direct borrowing. Rather, Skelton engages with some of the ideas in the *House of Fame,* and in some of Chaucer's other poems, in order to define his own position.

Even a cursory examination of the two poems, however, is enough to indicate that Skelton makes claims for his own importance as a poet—claims about the status of the poet writing in English, about his relation to the literary tradition, about his role as a perpetuator of noble subjects, and about fame acquired through labour and the multiplication of readers—which are more substantial than Chaucer ever felt able to make. This, as I shall seek to argue, is not simply to be attributed to Skelton's vanity,[7] but is rather a reflection of a substantially different way of thinking about literature which had emerged in England in the hundred and fifty years separating the two poems, and of a new confidence which English poets were beginning to feel.

Chaucer sought to invest poetry with more dignity and significance than his predecessors in English. In a mode of high clowning, he frequently presents himself as a minstrel or a court entertainer and little more, but as A. C. Spearing rightly points out, the three invocations or apostrophes in Proem II of the *House of Fame,* imitated from Dante, are important in that Chaucer envisages, for the first time in English, the idea of poetry as a vocation, the idea of the poet as prophet, and the idea that sublime poetry was possible in the vernacular.[8] Chaucer is also the first poet in English to use the evocative image of the laurel, symbolic of the everlasting fame of poets: the Muse Polyhymnia sings 'with vois memorial in the shade / Under the laurer which that may not fade' (*Anelida and Arcite*). And in Proem III to the *House of Fame* Chaucer asks Apollo, the god of poetry, for his help and promises, if he receives it:

> Thou shalt se me go as blyve
> Unto the nexte laure y see,

And kysse yt, for hyt is thy tree.
Now entre in my brest anoon!

But he also knew about Petrarch's laureation in Rome in 1341, a ceremony which formed the model for similar Renaissance occasions, for he refers to 'Fraunceys Petrak, the lauriat poete' whose sweet rhetoric had spread the idea of poetry over all Italy. But Chaucer never claims the laurel, and expresses no pretensions to fame through laureation.

This modesty clearly disappointed his fifteenth-century followers, for they repeatedly suggest that he ought to have been invested with the honour. Lydgate praises Chaucer for 'the golde dewe dropes of speche and eloquence' in English and says that he 'worthy was the laurer too have / of poetry',[9] and elsewhere suggests that he has an equal right to 'be registred in þe house of fame' with Petrarch.[10] Caxton, in the Prohemye to the second edition of the *Canterbury Tales,* commends Chaucer 'the whiche for his ornate wrytyng in our tongue maye wel have the name of a laureate poete'.[11] And in the final stanza of *The Kingis Quair,* James I of Scotland extends the claim to include Gower as well as Chaucer, who were together 'Superlative as poetis laureate / In moralitee and eloquence ornate'.[12]

When Skelton confronts Gower, Chaucer and Lydgate in **The Garlande of Laurell,** he honours them as the establishers and enrichers of the English language as a medium for poetry: one of them 'first garnisshed our Englysshe rude', and another 'nobly enterprysed/How that our Englysshe myght fresshely be ennewed'. He remarks, however, that 'Thei wantid nothynge but the laurell'—an enigmatic line which has been read off as a not very subtle attempt on Skelton's part to enhance his own reputation, because he had been laureated, at the expense of theirs.[13] The implication of it, however, may be the same as when Lydgate, Caxton and James I had treated the subject earlier, that becaus: of the nature and importance of their achievements in poetry these English poets ought to have been awarded the laurel, but had not been. In the *House of Fame,* Chaucer approaches Apollo's laurel but does not claim it, just as he approaches the palace of Fame, but not to get fame. Skelton hesitates ('I made it straunge, and drew bak ones or twyse') but not for long; fame and the laurel are his due, he feels, not necessarily because he is a better poet than his English predecessors, but because English poetry itself and its representatives, including Skelton, deserve more honour and in more formal terms than had been accorded to them previously. Skelton appreciated the importance for English poets of claiming fame through status: he insists on his titles of 'laureate' and, after 1512-13, of *orator regius.* He may be following the example of the *rhétoriquers* in this: Octavien de Saint-Gelays refers to himself as 'simple orateur du roi'.[14] But Skelton is the first English poet to feel able to do this.

In the second place, Skelton appears to have believed that fame consisted, in part, of belonging to a tradition of notable writers, of being able to set oneself in the context of illustrious predecessors. Norman Blake has pointed out the lack of a sense of tradition in much Middle English literature, and that 'texts often seem to appear quite fortuitously without past or future',[15] though they are sometimes used as sources or quarried for ideas. With Chaucer this altered. He habitually seeks to define his own position by referring to authors of the classical and medieval past, usually with a sense of uneasiness and anxious deference: at the end of *Troilus and Criseyde* he urges his 'litel bok' to 'kis the steppes' of 'Virgile, Ovide, Omer, Lucan and Stace' (v, 1786-92). Chaucerian poets of the fifteenth century follow his example and, in addition, defer to him: he is referred to by Hoccleve as 'maister deere' or 'fadir reverent', and others echo this.[16]

Chaucer's method of definition by reference to other poets was taken over by Skelton's admirers (of whom in his lifetime there were many) and later by Skelton himself, who was doubtless encouraged by what he read about himself. The earliest praise of Skelton, by Caxton in 1490, sets him in a context of classical authors: 'he hath late translated the *Epystlys* of Tulle, and the *Boke of Dyodorus Syculus* and diverse other werkes out of Latyn into Englysshe . . . as he that hath redde Vyrgyle, Ovyde, Tullye and all the other noble poetes and oratours . . . '[17] In 1499 Erasmus goes further. Skelton has not only read classical authors, but is their equal: What Greece owes to Homer, and what Mantua owes to Virgil, by so much is Britain in debt to Skelton:

> . . . Te principe Skelton
> Anglia nil metuat
> Vel cum Romanis versu certare poetis.[18]

> [While you are its principal poet, O Skelton,
>   England need fear nothing, for you are worthy to
>   vie in versifying with Roman poets.]

This is elaborated by Roberet Whittinton in 1519 in his *In Clarissimi Scheltonis Louaniensis Poeti: Laudes Epigramma.* On Parnassus Apollo praises the 'monumenta suorum vatum' mentioning Homer, Orpheus, Musaeus, Aristophanes, Aeschylus and others among the Greeks, and Virgil, Ovid, Horace, Statius and others among the Romans. Then he turns to Britain, a land which nourishes poets, and at considerable length he praises Skelton for his rhetorical speech, his eloquence and his power to move. He is in no doubt about Skelton's claim to fame: 'Ecce virum de quo splendida fama volat', and he calls upon the Muses to make his glory eternal:

> Aeterno vireat quo vos celebravit honore
>   Illius ac astris fama perennis eat.[19]
> [Let him flourish in the eternal honour with which
>   he celebrated you, and let his fame be perennial
>   in the stars.]

Similarly, Skelton's contemporaries testify to his fame by setting him in a tradition of English poetry and among English poets. In 1510 the author of *The Great Chronicle of London,* perhaps Robert Fabyan, links him with William Cornish, Sir Thomas More, and Chaucer 'if he were now in lyffe'.[20] And a little later Henry Bradshaw twice defers to the authority of Skelton in association with Chaucer, Lydgate and Barclay.[21]

In *The Garlande of Laurell,* Skelton sets himself in a comprehensive tradition of poetry incorporating Greek and Latin authors, poets from the Middle Ages such as Petrarch and Boccaccio, Renaissance figures such as Poggio 'that famous Florentine' and contemporaries such as Robert Gaguin; the list is closed by his three eminent English predecessors. In the fiction of his poem, the poets of this tradition approve his claim to fame: *'Triumpha, triumpha!* they cryid all aboute'. His vanity has provoked criticism from modern scholars, in part justifiably: 'For him, the poetic tradition which he evokes so fully seems to exist for his sake, rather than he for its . . . the tradition of poetry exists in order that Skelton may be its latest and most glorious representative'.[22] But it has to be remembered that Skelton is here not claiming for himself anything more than his contemporaries thought he deserved.

When one turns, thirdly, to the subject of fame and poetry as perpetuation one finds on Skelton's part the same engagement with traditional ideas, with Chaucer and his followers, and the same desire to equal or outdo. The idea appears early that poets bestowed eternal fame on those whom they celebrated in their verses, and by doing so acquired fame for themselves.[23] Chaucer takes the idea up in the *House of Fame* where the notable poets of antiquity, whose durability is indicated by their positions on pillars of metal like caryatids, 'bar. . . up the fame' of men, events and peoples of the past, like Aeneas, Caesar, Pompey, the Jews, the Greeks, the Trojans, or the fame of mythical personages, like the 'god of love' or Pluto and Proserpina. So far as is known, Chaucer never wrote for patrons, but his followers—Hoccleve, Lydgate, Ashby, and the like—appear to have sought readily the favour of the great and powerful, and in return provided the kind of verses which were asked for: apart from any material benefits which may have been forthcoming, to have a famous patron provided some assurance of acceptability and eminence for the poet. Frontispieces to presentation copies of poems which show the poet kneeling before the patron become common. So too do headings like the following to the copy of Lydgate's *Guy of Warwick* from BL MS Harley 7333 fol. 33r: 'Here now begynneþe an abstracte out of the Cronicles in Latyn made by Gyrarde Cornubyence the worþy Croniculer of Westsexse, and translated in to Englishe by Lydegate daun Iohan at þe requeste of Margarite Countas of Shrowesbury Lady Talbot fournyval and Lisle of the lyf of the most worþy knyght Guy of Warwike, of whos blood she is lyneally descended'.[24] The fame of one's ancestors and hence the fame of one's family and one's own fame may be procured and perpetuated in poetry.

Skelton's earliest datable poem is written firmly within this tradition. In *Upon the Dolorus Dethe . . . of the . . . Erle of Northumberlande* he seeks to 'make memoryall' for Henry Percy, the Fourth Earl, murdered by tax rebels at Topcliffe, near Thirsk, in 1489. He appeals to Clio, the muse of history, to help his 'elect uteraunce' by refreshing his 'homely rudnes' and adverts to the idea that poetry of this sort preserves fame:

> Of noble actes auncyently enrolde
> Of famous princis and lordes of astate,

By thy report ar wonte to be extolde
Regestringe trewly every formare date . . .

Whether Skelton was commissioned to write this poem is difficult to tell, but he offers his services to the son of the dead earl in a prefatory Latin verse: 'Ad libitum cuius ipse paratus ero'. And an elaborately written and rubricated copy of the poem is preserved in BL MS Royal 18. D. ii, a sumptuous Percy manuscript.[25] Thereafter, from time to time, but especially after 1512-13 in his capacity as *orator regius,* Skelton writes in praise of Henry VIII to memorialize his achievements and those of England. So when Skelton thinks of his own fame in *The Garlande of Laurell* it is partly in these terms: it depends on the mutual interest of those celebrated in poetry and the poet who celebrates them. The Countess of Surrey and her companions feel bound to 'rewarde' Skelton with an embroidered garland of laurel (779) to signal his pre-eminence as a poet because he has in the past celebrated the fame of ladies:

> . . . of all ladyes he hath the library,
> Ther names recountyng in the court of Fame;
> Of all gentylwomen he hath the scruteny,
> In Fames court reportyng the same". . .

In his turn he has to thank them, at the prompting of Occupacyon, with a series of lyrics 'In goodly wordes plesauntly comprysid'. The whole process is then perpetuated 'in pycture, by his industrious wit' by 'maister Newton', presumably a painter or illuminator. Skelton's frequent allusion to those who appear to be his patrons—the Percy family, Henry VIII, the Howards, and latterly Wolsey—was no doubt in part a recognition of kindnesses received or expected, but it may well also have had the function in his mind of establishing his fame by associating him with the famous.

However, the fourth aspect of the poet's claim to fame as treated in *The Garlande of Laurell*—the expenditure of labour over a long time to produce a body of work which will be read—is probably the most important to Skelton. The formula 'Idleness is to be shunned' is a favourite topic of the exordium among classical authors. Seneca's warning, 'Otium sine litteris mors est et hominis vivi sepulta' (Idleness without studies is death and a sepulture for a living man), was often quoted, and the practice of poetry came to be seen as a virtuous cure for sloth.[26] On one occasion Chaucer uses the idleness topic in a prefatory position: the Second Nun sees the telling of the life of St Cecilia as a way to avoid 'ydelnesse' by means of 'leveful bisyness'.[27] But the idea also occurs in the *House of Fame*: the seventh company ask for Fame but the goddess instructs Eolus to blow 'a sory grace' for them from his black trumpet because they are 'ydel wrechches' who will 'do noskynnes labour. Fame without labour is impossible, and for a poet labour consists of producing poems which will be read by posterity and recognized.

Chaucer worries about the stability of his texts at the end of *Troilus and Criseyde*: the 'gret diversite / In Englissh and in writyng of oure tonge' may cause the metre of his book to be ruined or its sense misunderstood (v, 1793-8).

He curses his scribe Adam for his incorrect copying and complains that he has to 'rubbe and scrape' the parchment in correction of Adam's versions of his texts. These complaints may to some extent be traditional[28] and the second is deliberately amusing, but behind the comedy lies a deep concern for the lastingness of his works. And doubtless it was this same motive—the wish to establish his fame by ensuring his identification with certain works which he hoped would last—that caused Chaucer to include lists of his works in his writings. None of the lists is very formal or complete and all are contextualized by disparaging reservations about the poet's achievement. In the F Prologue to the *Legend of Good Women* it is said that 'he kan nat wel endite' though he has written a great deal about love. According to the Man of Law, 'thogh he kan but lewedly / On metres and on rymyng craftily', Chaucer has told, in one place or another, all the seemly stories there are to tell—and he lists some of Chaucer's works about women. And in the Retractions to the *Canterbury Tales* Chaucer, in his own person, asks that God 'foryeve me the synne' of his secular writings which, nevertheless, he names along with those works which he feels are morally sound and need no apology. In his habitual, self-deprecating way Chaucer talks himself down, but at the same time seeks to establish his fame, for the first time in English, by associating his name with a defined body of work.

Of all the English Chaucerians nobody wrote more about poetry, about the nature of poetic tradition, and his own role in it than Skelton, and *The Garlande of Laurell* is in many ways his most considered statement.

—*John Scattergood*

Chaucer's followers pick up and develop these ideas, too. The idleness topic is frequently used—poignantly by George Ashby, who wrote while in the Fleet Prison, 'Thus occupying me'.[29] Yet one of its most assiduous users was Caxton, than whom there can have been few more active men of letters. In his Prologue to the 1483 edition of the *Game of Chesse* he mentions that he undertook the translation 'in eschewyng of ydlenes',[30] and in the Prologue to *Charles the Great* (1485) he asks God for grace so that he may 'laboure and occupye myself vertuously that I may come oute of dette and dedely synne'.[31] Most interesting, however, in his Prologue to the *Golden Legend* (c. 1481) which begins with a quotation from Jerome, 'Do alweye somme good werke to th'ende that the devyl fynde the not ydle', and in a lengthy passage he adds quotations from a number of other authorities to the same effect.[32] Most of the Prologue is based on the introduction to the French version of the work which Caxton was using, but he adds a certain amount—notably an extensive but incomplete list of translations made before 1482 which justify the way he has spent his time. Though he worries, like Chau-

cer, about 'dyversite and chaunge in language'[33] and though he worries about his own literary capacities, he has faith in the virtues of hard work and productivity.

And so too does Skelton. The Quene of Fame makes the point to Dame Pallas that Skelton will have to be banished from her court 'As he that aquentyth him with ydilnes' unless he can give a convincing account of his productivity. In response, Occupacyon reads off an enormous list of his works which, nevertheless, is said to be merely a selection 'in as moche as it were to longe a process to reherse all by name that he hath compylyd'. It is in many ways an odd list. Not all the descriptions of extant works are very accurate, and a great many of the works are evidently lost.[34] Perhaps some never existed at all, and it may be that the list is partly parodic. Chaucer's lists included items which, to a sixteenth-century reader such as Skelton as to a twentieth-century reader, must have appeared lost: 'Origenes upon the Maudeleyne', 'the book of the Leoun', and so on. It may be that Skelton invented his own 'lost' works in emulation of Chaucer. Yet he shows no uneasiness about the lastingness of his achievement: the stability of print was, no doubt, reassuring to him. Indeed, this very stability imposed its own pressures and responsibilities: 'Beware, for wrytyng remayneth of recorde' warns Dame Pallas. On one occasion, in the person of Jane Scrope, Skelton complains that the English language is 'rude', 'cankered', and 'rusty', and that it is difficult to find the terms in which to write 'ornatly' (VII, 774-83). But this doubt about the capacity of the language for eloquence did not extend to fears about durability. At the end of *The Garlande of Laurell*, Skelton reassures his 'littill quaire' that though it is written in English and not Latin that does not mean that people will not read it:

> That so indede
> Your fame may sprede
> In length and brede.

His fame is assured through the multiplication of readers of his works—a point he makes in other places.[35]

It seems clear, therefore, that Skelton saw himself, in much the same way as his contemporaries saw him, as a poet whose lasting fame was secure: he had status because of his laureation, poetic identity because he belonged to a definable historical tradition which embraced classical authors and his illustrious English predecessors, a role as perpetuator and memorialist of the famous, and a body of work to his credit that was likely to be read down the ages. Yet, for all this, he is sufficiently self-aware and self-critical to realize that there were aspects of his poetry that might cause his fame to be questioned, and in *The Garlande of Laurell* he expresses these doubts.

They principally concern his satires and polemical verses. When questions are raised, Dame Pallas interprets the Quene of Fame's reservations about accepting Skelton into her court as having to do with the fact that he does not always write in the style of courtly compliment and that he is therefore 'sum what to dull'. In order to defend him she seeks to broaden the notion of what are acceptable forms of poetry, and to justify his use of more demotic styles. The lines:

> And if so hym fortune to wryte true and plaine,
> As sumtyme he must vyces remorde,
> Then sum wyll say he hath but lyttil brayne . . .

express similar misgivings to lines in the opening of *Collyn Clout*:

> Or yf he speke playne
> Than he lacketh brayne.

What is being referred to here is the low style of direct invective used by Skelton in his later satires, which, he affirms in *Collyn Clout,* may be 'tattered and jagged', but, nevertheless, is of some substance: 'it hath in it some pyth'.[36] A few lines later Dame Pallas refers to the indirect Galfridian manner of political prophecy:

> A pocte somtyme may for his pleasure taunt
> Spekyng in paroblis, how the fox, the grey,
> The gander, the gose, and the hudge oliphaunt,
> Went with the pecok ageyne the fesaunt . . .

This is the mode of some lines of *Why Come Ye Nat to Courte?* (XX, 118-22), which he may have in mind here, and for most of *Speke Parott,* where Skelton defends himself by saying that metaphor and allegory shall be 'his protectyon, his pavys and his wall', presumably against charges that he has defamed and slandered those he writes about. The disadvantage of this style is its obscurity and difficulty. At the end of *Speke Parott,* Galathea asks in desperation for a change of style of the poem: 'Sette asyde all sophysms, and speke now trew and playne', and this and other remarks indicate that Skelton had some sense that his readers found it hard to understand. In *The Garlande of Laurell* Dame Pallas defends this manner by affirming that those who are 'industryous of reason' will find in 'suche an endarkid chapiter sum season', but even she admits it is 'harde'.[37]

Skelton is also concerned about the fate of satirists: Dame Pallas recalls the banishment of Ovid by Augustus Caesar and the threats to Juvenal, perhaps by Domitian, because he 'rubbid sum on the gall'. She defends Juvenal by saying, 'Yet wrote he none ill', but she later admits that in this sort of writing it is difficult to satisfy everybody: " '. . . harde is to make but sum fawt be founde'. These examples are adduced to help defend Skelton, 'to furnisshe better his excuse'. And, indeed, throughout his work he is conscious of his role as a controversialist, and aware that there are those who disagree with what he writes. The traditional prayer of the medieval poet:

> I aske no more but God, of his mercy,
> My book conserve from sklaundre and envy . . . [38]

takes on an added force in Skelton's writings. Though it is not always possible to identify them, his enemies are not vague figures, for he often feels it necessary to answer specific charges. He writes a reply to the 'dyvers people' who thought his verses on the death of James IV at Flodden tasteless (XII 'Unto Dyvers People . . .'). Similarly, he appends to *Why Come Ye Nat to Courte?* some lines 'Contra quendam doctorem/Suam calumpniatorem'—a doctor of canon law evidently, who has not been further identified. Some of his enemies are, however, known by name. In 1509 Barclay attacked *Phyllyp Sparowe* for its 'wantones'[39] and Skelton wrote a 115-line reply which is appended to the poem in the printed editions: he notes in the account of *Phyllyp Sparowe* in *The Garlande of Laurell* that some 'grudge' at his poem 'with frownyng countenaunce' and includes the reply, closing with the line 'Est tamen invidia mors tibi continua'. And among the writers who are called upon to approve his laureation there is at least one former opponent who appears not to have entirely forgiven him:

> . . . a frere of Fraunce men call Sir Gagwyne,
> That frowned on me full angerly and pale

—Robert Gaguin, with whom Skelton had earlier engaged in polemical exchange.[40] For a controversial writer fame does not imply universal approval, and it is Skelton's consciousness of this which, no doubt, caused him to ponder at length the case of Aeschines, defeated in controversy by Demosthenes in 330 BC. He is allowed a place in her court, according to the Quene of Fame, because he provoked Demosthenes to great works, because he was overcome by no one but Demosthenes, and because of his subsequent acknowledgement of Demosthenes' superior ability: 'though he were venquesshid, yet was he not shamyd'. There is generous inclusiveness in Skelton's conception of fame, particularly in relation to satirists and polemicists.

But Skelton's view of poetry was also an extremely inclusive one, and one which conferred a dignity and an importance on poetry and poets which was far greater than Chaucer or most of his followers ever felt able to give it. Poetry embraced everything and the poet's realm was everywhere. In the paradisal garden of the Quene of Fame performs no courtly entertainer and no love poet, but the Carthaginian bard Iopas who sang before Aeneas in Dido's palace, and, as in *Aeneid,* 1, 740 ff., he sings of the whole cosmic order, 'Of Atlas astrology, and many noble thyngis . . . Of men and bestis, and whereof they begone . . .', to which, as A. C. Spearing has acutely pointed out,[41] Skelton adds a line of his own which suggests that his subjects include the whole moral order also: 'How wronge was no ryght, and ryght was no wronge'. The poet is privileged to speak of all things.

It is a large claim but Skelton develops and goes beyond it in *'A Replycacion',* his last extant poem. Here he undertakes to defend the Christian faith against heresy by means of satirical verse and in the course of his poem he also finds himself defending the right of poets to deal with theological matters,[42] for which he uses the impeccable authority of Jerome who, in his letter to Paulinus prefacing the Vulgate, had praised the poetry of the psalms of David:

> Than, if this noble kyng,
> Thus can harpe and syng

With his harpe of prophecy
And spyrituall poetry,
And saynt Jerome saythe,
To whom we must give faythe,
Warblynge with his strynges
Of suche theologicall thynges,
Why have ye than disdayne
At poetes, and complayne
Howe poetes do but fayne?

What is more, says Skelton, those who disparage the 'fame matryculate/Of poetes laureate' do wrong, because poetic inspiration comes from God, and it is this which causes poets to write:

. . . there is a spyrituall,
And a mysteriall,
And a mysticall
Effecte energiall,
As Grekes do it call,
Of suche an industry
And suche a pregnacy,
Of hevenly inspyracion
In laureate creacyon,
Of poetes commendacion,
That of divyne myseracion
God maketh his habitacion
In poetes whiche excelles,
And sojourns with them and dwelles.

By whose inflammacion
Of spyrituall instygacion
And divyne inspyracion
We are kyndled in suche facyon
With hete of the Holy Gost,
Which is God of myghtes most,
That he our penne dothe lede,
And maketh in us suche spede
That forthwith we must nede
With penne and ynke procede . . .

Skelton fuses classical and Christian ideas about poetic inspiration in this comprehensive defence. It rests on a well-defined tradition but probably takes its immediate origin from Boccaccio's *De Genealogia Deorum Gentilium* XIV, 7: 'Thus poetry, which ignorant triflers cast aside, is a sort of fervid and exquisite expression, in speech or writing, of that which the mind has invented. It proceeds from the bosom of God, and few, I find, are the souls in whom this gift is born, indeed, so wonderful a gift it is that true poets have always been the rarest of men. This fervor of poetry is sublime in its effects: it impels the soul to a longing for utterance . . . [43] And this inspiration, given to the few, rare poets, operates whether they write for 'affection', 'sadde dyrection', or 'correction'—that is to say, it encompasses satire. It is hard to imagine how a Christian poet could make a more complete vindication of his practice: the poet partakes of the divine, and this validates all aspects of his art.

In ***The Garlande of Laurell*** Skelton tries to come to terms with his poetic lineage, particularly with Chaucer, and to establish a claim to fame by justifying a career spent in the service of poetry. Skelton is not unaware of possible criticisms of past writers: according to Jane Scrope, Gower's English is 'old / And of no value told'; Lydgate is difficult and 'some men fynde a faute / And say he wryteth to haute'. Skelton's references to Chaucer, however, are always admiring, though it is equally clear that he recognizes how different he is. In Seneca's terms Skelton resembles him 'as a child resembles his father, and not as a picture resembles its original'.[44] And that he should be more assertive than Chaucer is perhaps not surprising. In the *House of Fame,* if the Egle is to be believed, poetry is for Chaucer something to be indulged in 'when thy labour doon al ys', a bookish, essentially solitary, pastime which keeps him in ignorance of 'tydynges' from far and near in the world at large. And though this may not be the whole truth, it is at least part of it: Chaucer recognizes the marginal nature of poetry and the poet in his society, though he is uneasy about it and takes some, albeit hesitant, steps to change things. Skelton, in a way that was becoming common, confident of the all-embracing relevance of poetry and confident also of his capacities and status as a poet, seeks to put himself at the centre of things, whether the sphere is social, political or spiritual. Part of Skelton's self-respect, indeed, derived from his status as a poet. When he defends himself in verse against Sir Christopher Garneshe[45] he says on one occasion: 'I am laureat, I am no lorell' and, no doubt pleased with the pun, elaborates on it later:

A kynge too me myn habyte gave
At Oxforth, the universyte,
Avaunsid I was to that degre;
By hole consent of theyr senate,
I was made poete lawreate.
To cal me lorell ye ar to lewde . . .

Skelton had acquired a way of thinking in which it was inconceivable for a 'laureate' to be a 'lorell' (= worthless person, wretch). The dignity of the poet's calling enhances and validates the dignity of the individual. The essentially modest claims for their status and art characteristic of most Chaucerian poets are insufficient to contain this.

Notes

[1] *John Skelton: The Complete English Poems,* ed. John Scattergood (New Haven and London, 1983). References and quotations are from this edition.

[2] 'Skelton, Petrarca e l'amore della gloria nel *The Garland of Laurel',* *Annali Istituto Universitario Orientale Napoli, Sexione Germanica* 5 (1962), 135-63, repr. in *La Poesia di John Skelton* (Napoli, 1963).

[3] 'John Skelton and Burgundian Letters', in *Ten Studies in Anglo-Dutch Relations,* ed. Jan van Dorsten (Leiden and London, 1974), pp. 1-29.

[4] *Anglo-Scottish Literary Relations 1430-1550* (Cambridge, 1980), p. 165.

[5] 'Skelton's *Garland of Laurel* and Chaucer's *House of Fame*', *Modern Language Review,* 11 (1916), 9-14.

[6] See Piero Boitani, *Chaucer and the Imaginary World of Fame* (Cambridge, 1984), pp. 161-3. Many of the ideas on fame and poetry which

I use were suggested by this comprehensive survey.

[7] See, for example, the remarks in *The Poetical Works of John Skelton*, ed. Rev. Alexander Dyce, 2 vols. (London, 1843), vol. 1, p. xlix. See also H. L. R. Edwards, *Skelton: The Life and Times of an Early Tudor Poet* (London, 1949), pp. 22-3 for a similar judgement.

[8] *Medieval to Renaissance in English Poetry* (Cambridge, 1985), pp. 22-30. I am much indebted to this fine account of the poem. See also the interesting article by Vincent Gillespie, 'Justification by Good Works: Skelton's *The Garland of Laurel*', *Reading Medieval Studies*, 7 (1981), 19-31.

[9] See *The Lyfe of Our Lady*, ed. J. Lauritis, R. Klinefelter and V. Gallagher (Pittsburg, 1961), lines 1628-34. See also *Chaucer: The Critical Heritage*, ed. Derek Brewer, vol. 1, 1385-1837 (London, 1978), p. 46.

[10] See *Troy Book*, ed. H. Bergen, 4 vols., *EETS*, e.s. 97, 103, 106, 126 (London, 1906-20) III, 4534-59. See also *Chaucer: The Critical Heritage* vol. 1, p. 48.

[11] *Caxton's Own Prose*, ed. N. F. Blake (London, 1973), p. 61. See also *Chaucer: The Critical Heritage*, vol. 1, p. 76.

[12] ed. John Norton-Smith (Oxford, 1970).

[13] A. C. Spearing, *Medieval Dream Poetry* (Cambridge, 1976), p. 214 says he deals 'patronisingly' with them. See also Stanley Eugene Fish, *John Skelton's Poetry* (New Haven and London, 1965), pp. 231-2. Compare the interesting account of Richard Firth Green, 'the lavish praise which fifteenth-century writers heaped on Chaucer, Gower, and, later, Lydgate was rarely completely disinterested; living poets were manifestly raising their own stock by venerating their predecessors' (*Poets and Princepleasers: Literature and the English Court in the Late Middle Ages* (Toronto, 1980) p. 208.

[14] See H-J. Molinier, *Essai Biographique et Littéraire sur Octavien de Saint-Gelays: Évêque d'Angoulême 1468-1502* (Rodez, 1910), pp. 58-9. See also Pierre Jodogne, 'Les Rhétoriquers et l'Humanisme' in A. H. T. Levi (ed.), *Humanism in France at the End of the Middle Ages and in the Early Renaissance* (Manchester, 1970), pp. 160-1.

[15] *The English Language in Medieval Literature* (London, 1977), p. 14. See also pp. 21-7 for other relevant comments on this problem.

[16] *Hoccleve's Works*, ed. F. J. Furnivall, *EETS*, e.s. 61, 72 (London 1892-7), III, ll. 1961-2. See also *Chaucer: The Critical Heritage*, vol. 1, p. 62.

[17] *Caxton's Own Prose*, p. 80.

[18] See *Skelton: The Critical Heritage*, ed. A. S. G. Edwards (London, 1981), pp. 44-5.

[19] *Ibid*, pp. 49-53.

[20] *Ibid*, pp. 46-7.

[21] *Ibid*, pp. 47-8.

[22] See A. C. Spearing, *Medieval to Renaissance in English Poetry*, p. 243.

[23] For the background to the idea of poetry as perpetuation, see E. R. Curtius, *European Literature and the Latin Middle Ages*, trans. W. R. Trask (London, 1953), pp. 476-7.

[24] See *The Minor Poems of John Lydgate*, ed. H. N. MacCracken, 2 vols. *EETS*, o.s. 107, 192 (London, 1911-34), vol. 2, p. 516.

[25] On this poem see my essay 'Skelton and the Elegy', *Proceedings of the Royal Irish Academy*, 84 C10 (1984), 333-47; and for some interesting comments on the manuscript see Mervyn James, *Society, Politics and Culture: Studies in Early Modern England* (Cambridge, 1986), pp. 83-90.

[26] On this topic see Curtius, *European Literature*, pp. 88-9, whence I derive the example from Seneca.

[27] On the background to this Prologue, see Richard Hazleton, 'Chaucer and Cato', *Speculum*, 35 (1960), 357-80.

[28] See R. K. Root, 'Publication before Printing', *PMLA*, 28 (1913), 417-31. For a famous instance see Petrarch's complaint in *Epistolae de Rebus Senilium*, v, i, in Franciscus Petrarcha, *Opera* (Basel, 1581), pp. 790-2.

[29] *George Ashby's Poems*, ed. Mary Bateson, *EETS*, e.s. 76 (London, 1899), p. 12.

[30] *Caxton's Own Prose*, p. 88.

[31] *Ibid*, p. 68.

[32] *Ibid*, pp. 88-9.

[33] *Ibid*, p. 80.

[34] For a comprehensive survey, see R. S. Kinsman and Theodore Yonge, *John Skelton: Canon and Census*, Renaissance Society of America: Bibliographies and Indexes No. 4 (New York, 1967).

[35] See, for example, the epigraphs to *Speke Parott*: 'Lectoribus auctor recepit opusculy huius auxesim. / Crescet in immensem me vivo pagina presens / Hinc mea dicetur Skeltonidis aurea fama.' [By his readers an author receives an amplification of his short poem. The present book will grow greatly while I am alive; thence will the golden reputation of Skelton be proclaimed]. See also *Why Come Ye Nat to Courte?* 29-30: 'Hec vates ille / De quo loquntur mille' [About these things the famous bard of whom a thousand speak]. This is repeated at the end of the poem.

[36] For the deliberately rustic nature of *Collyn Clout* see R. S. Kinsman, 'Skelton's *Colyn Cloute*: The Mask of Vox Populi', in *Essays Critical and Historical dedicated to Lily B. Campbell* (Berkeley and Los Angeles, 1950), pp. 17-23. For the literary antecedents for this style see A. R. Heiserman, *Skelton and Satire* (Chicago, 1961), 208-43.

[37] For the stylistic affinities of *Speke Parott* see Heiserman, *Skelton and Satire*, pp. 126-89.

[38] *The Court of Sapience*, ed. E. Ruth Harvey (Toronto, 1984), lines 69-70.

[39] This comes in 'A brefe addicion to the syngularyte of some new Folys' added to his *Shyp of Foles*; see *Skelton: The Critical Heritage*

p. 46. In 1519 the grammarian William Lyly attacked Skelton as 'neither learned nor a poet' (see *ibid.* p. 48).

[40] See also *Why Come Ye Nat to Courte?* 718-41. For Skelton's dispute with this man see H. L. R. Edwards, 'Robert Gaguin and the English Poets 1489-1490', *Modern Language Review,* 32 (1937), 430-4. Another enemy appears to have been Rogerus Stathum, referred to by means of a number code in *The Garlande of Laurel* 742-65; he is also called Envyous Rancour, but so far as is known was not a poet.

[41] *Medieval to Renaissance in English Poetry,* p. 246.

[42] For the background to this problem see Curtius, *European Literature,* pp. 214-27, and for the sixteenth-century development of some of these ideas John N. King, *English Reformation Literature: The Tudor Origins of the Protestant Tradition* (Princeton, 1982), pp. 14-19, 209-31.

[43] Quoted in the translation of Charles G. Osgood, *Boccaccio on Poetry* (Princeton, 1930), pp. 39-42.

[44] *Ad Lucilium Epistulae Morales* LXXXIV, 7-8 '". . . quomodo filium, non quomodo imaginem". . . ' from *Seneca* ed. and trans. by Richard R. Gummere, 10 vols. (Loeb Classical Library: Cambridge: Mass., 1970), vol. 5, pp. 280-1.

[45] For the background to these poems see Helen Stearns Sale, 'John Skelton and Christopher Garnesche', *Modern Language Notes,* 43 (1928), 518-32.

Richard Halpern   (essay date 1991)

SOURCE: "The Twittering Machine: Skelton's Ornithology of the Early Tudor State," in *The Poetics of Primitive Accumulation: English Renaissance Culture and the Genealogy of Capital,* Cornell University Press, 1991, pp. 103-35.

[*In the following excerpt, Halpern relates Skelton's poetry to political and cultural changes in Tudor England, particularly the transition from a feudal society to an absolute monarchy.*]

If he was nothing else, John Skelton was certainly one of the most obstreperous English poets; his literary gifts were inseparable from a bottomless and apparently free-floating aggression. Henry VIII employed him briefly as a writer of vituperative verses against the French and Scots and then to entertain the court in a display of "flytyng," a crude form of poetical name-calling. Yet the self-styled *orator regius* remained a marginal figure at court, and in his resentment he composed a series of vicious and ill-considered satires against the powerful Cardinal Wolsey, even taking a few swipes at Henry himself. Just as abruptly he then changed face and put himself in Wolsey's employ to write attacks on Protestant heretics and a rebellious Scots duke. Yet Wolsey witheld the promised reward of an ecclesiastical living, and the poet never succeeded in making nastiness anything more than an intermittently profitable vocation. Even after his death Skelton was re-

garded largely as a bundle of quirky and unassimilable energies. Despite his priestly calling, his name soon became attached to a collection of "merry tales," according to which he kept a woman in his church at Diss, fathered a bastard, defecated on a sleeping friar, and otherwise distinguished himself for piety and devotion.[1] Wordsworth complimented him as "a demon in point of genius,"[2] but Pope simply dismissed him as "beastly Skelton."

In matters of poetic influence he was no less difficult. Skelton portrayed his own genius as both autogenerated and prodigious; he describes himself as England's incomparable "phoenix" in **Ware the Hawk,** and he seems largely to have arrogated to himself the titles of poet laureate and king's orator. Indeed, as C. S. Lewis correctly observed, he had "no real predecessors and no important disciples."[3] His turbulent verse owed little to the polish of Chaucer and even less to the dullness of fifteenth-century predecessors such as Hoccleve or Lydgate.[4] His influence on English verse was just as small as its influence on him. It is true that he enjoyed brief fame as a prophet of the Reformation and that Spenser borrowed the name of Skelton's Colin Clout for his Protestant pastorals. Yet no important successors took up Skelton's distinctive verse form, doubtless finding it too colloquial, too jarring, and too deeply imprinted with his personality. Skelton also developed a bitter hatred for the Erasmian humanism that began to take hold in the early sixteenth century. He was a vigorous participant in the so-called Grammarians' War of 1519, during which he and his fellow "Trojans" defended the old scholastic method of learning Latin against the humanist innovations of the "Greeks."[5] Skelton deemed it absurd that

> Platus with his comedies a chyld shall now reherse,
> And medyll with Quintylyan in his *Declemacyons,*
> That *Pety Caton* can scantly construe a verse,
> With, *"Aveto"* in *Greco,* and such solempne
>   salutacyons,
> Can skantly the tensis of his conjugacyons;
> Settyng theyr myndys so moch of eloquens,
> That of theyr scole maters lost is the hole sentens.
>
> (***Speke Parott***)[6]

Skelton even exchanged insulting Latin verses with the humanist grammarian William Lily. Here, as elsewhere, his conservative instincts put him on the losing side, and in rejecting humanism he cut himself off from the future of Renaissance verse. Skelton's relative uninterest in "eloquens" also probably impeded his career as a court poet.[7] It sometimes seems as if Skelton tried to write himself out of literary history by sheer force of will. His career testifies to the fact that a poet can indeed be too original.

Skelton's idiosyncracies have caused problems for critics trying to fit him into the scheme of cultural periodization which characterizes traditional literary history. Ian Gordon delineated the problem in 1943 when he wrote that "Skelton fell between two periods, the receding Middle Ages and the advancing Renaissance, without being a part of either." Reverting, Pope-like, to the vocabulary of the monstrous, Gordon calls Skelton "a Mr. Facing-Both-Ways" and adds, "Seldom has a poet borne the marks of a transition age so clearly as Skelton."[8] In *John Skelton's Poetry* (1965), Stanley Fish nuances Gordon's formulation but does not fundamentally alter it. "Skelton's poetry," he writes, "gives us neither the old made new nor the new made old, but a statement of the potentiality for disturbance of the unassimilated. It is a poetry which could only have been written between 1498 and 1530, when the intrusive could no longer be ignored as Lydgate had ignored it and before it would become part of a new and difficult stability as it would after 1536."[9] Fish's formulation suggests that Skelton's poetry is historically determined, or at least bounded; yet the agent of this determination is, paradoxically, a gap or hiatus between periods. It is as if Skelton sailed his lyrical boat by the force of a vacuum. A. C. Spearing conveys a similar sense of paradox, arguing that "Skelton's attitude is more, not less medieval than Chaucer's," yet finding that the difficulty and poetic manner of *Speke Parott* strongly anticipate *The Waste Land*.[10] The problem here is Skelton's seemingly perverse refusal to act like a "transitional" figure. He was the only poet of really considerable talents writing at the beginning of the sixteenth century and was therefore in a perfect position to bridge the gap between medieval and Renaissance poetics. Yet he seems somehow to have sensed his literary-historical mission and then mischievously to have dodged it. Or perhaps his mission *was* to dodge it, to occupy the transitional space in such a way as to reveal a dramatic gap or break between periods, and even to scramble the linear model that underlies this history.

One way around this problem is to look for influences outside of the literary canon and thus to situate Skelton's poetics in a larger cultural field. Some scholarly work has elucidated Skelton's poetry by demonstrating both the formal and thematic influence of church liturgy and by considering Skelton's vocation as poet-priest.[11] A very different approach has traced Skelton's career as failed or frustrated courtier and read his work in relation to the political events of the 1520s. These two paths intersect, of course, especially when Skelton begins his series of satires against Cardinal Wolsey. Yet they have not so much resolved the problems of Skelton's difficult transitional status as they have displaced and enlarged them. For the Christian interpreters have produced a conservative and strongly "medieval" Skelton, the orthodox and devoted priest who fights for traditional church and aristocratic privileges and against the encroachments of the early Tudor state. But the courtly Skelton is a more recognizably modern figure—self-promoting, dissatisfied with his duties in a rural parish, lacking strong convictions or social allegiances, willing to use his literary talents in any way that will serve his own ambitions.[12] Skelton's alleged social role thus splits as well into irreconcilably "medieval" and "Renaissance" components.

This is, clearly, the moment to wheel a Marxist theoretical apparatus onstage and triumphantly announce its ability to sublate these contradictions within a larger totalizing movement. I will not do so, however, because Skelton's poetical career signifies in its most interesting way when it remains fissured. It is these Skeltonic gaps and discontinuities that I want to articulate more precisely, by posing

them in relation to the rise of the absolutist state and its role in reorganizing the late feudal polity.

Cultural Territoriality in *Ware the Hawk*

It has long been recognized that the absolutist state played a decisive part in the transition to capitalism, though precisely what this part was has been the subject of extended debate. Marx and Engels held that absolutism represented a balance of political power between the feudal ruling class and the emergent bourgeoisie and that it prepared the way for capitalist production by carrying out many of the functions of primitive accumulation.[13] Nicos Poulantzas rejects the first half of this thesis and develops the second in order to argue for the relative autonomy of the absolutist state, as I discuss in the Introduction. Perry Anderson takes a somewhat different (though not irreconcilable) approach, contending that absolutism reorganized the rule of the nobility in response to certain mutations in the late feudal economy:

> Feudalism as a mode of production was originally defined by an organic *unity* of economy and polity, paradoxically distributed in a chain of parcellized sovereignties throughout the social formation. The institution of serfdom as a mechanism of surplus extraction fused economic exploitation and politico-legal coercion at the molecular level of the village. The lord in his turn typically owed liege—loyalty and knight—service to the seigneurial overlord, who claimed the land as his ultimate domain. With the generalized commutation of dues into money rents, the cellular unity of political and economic oppression of the peasantry was gravely weakened, and threatened to become dissociated (the end of this road was "free labor" and the "wage contract"). The class power of the feudal lords was thus directly at stake with the gradual disappearance of serfdom. The result was a *displacement* of politico-legal coercion upwards towards a centralized, militarized summit—the Absolutist State. Diluted at village level, it became concentrated at "national" level.[14]

Yet while Anderson argues that the absolutist state reorganized the conditions of feudal class rule, he does not hold that it was in any simple sense the instrument of the landowning classes. For one thing, the whole process was overdetermined by the interests of the mercantile bourgeoisie.[15] For another, political centralization was achieved at the expense of baronial power, beginning with Henry VII's "primitive accumulation" of state power after the Wars of the Roses.[16] The emergence of absolutism thus dislocated the structural conditions of feudal rule; insofar as it protected the economic interests of the landlord class, it did so by drastically reducing their independent political authority. By de- and reterritorializing the parcelized sovereignty of feudalism, the absolutist state dissolved its own concrete implication in a structure of pyramidized dependency in order to *represent* the ruling groups. "The sovereign commanded authority not as the person residing at the apex of the hierarchy," John E. Martin notes, "but as the detached symbolic representative of the unity of the landlord class."[17] The state thereby achieved a relative autonomy with respect to the class it represented and could claim to act in the interests of the nation as a whole.

The relations between state and church in the early Tudor period—of central importance to Skelton's career—were largely determined by absolutism's rearticulation of class rule, for the church represented a significant fraction of the landlord class. It owned about one-third of the land in England, enjoyed a jurisdiction at least partially independent of the king's law, and exercised an especially rigorous, conservative, and tenacious form of feudal land-ownership.[18] The crown viewed the church as at once a desired source of wealth, an impediment to political centralization, and even a potential source of sedition (aristocratic families often furnished monastic leaders). The Dissolution was therefore prompted by political as well as economic considerations.[19] Even before the Dissolution, however, the Tudors made significant efforts to restrict the independent jurisdiction of the church, for the most part by attacking sanctuary rights. The privilege of sanctuary was "purely secular and jurisdictional," according to Isabel Thornley, that is to say, purely an effect of the church's political authority as feudal landowner, "but long before the Tudor period had opened, circumstances had given it a false ecclesiastical cover," and this enabled the church to retain its protective jurisdiction after similar rights had already been taken from lay persons.[20] Sanctuary was both a symbolic and a real affront to royal jurisdiction, and one that could be exploited for seditious purposes.

Significantly, Henry VII's first major assault on the sanctuary privilege was designed to suppress a threat of political revolt. In 1486 when the Yorkist Thomas Stafford was dragged from sanctuary and taken to the Tower, the King's Bench ruled that "sanctuary was a common-law matter in which the Pope could not interfere . . . and that the privilege did not cover treasonable offenses."[21] As Henry VIII's lord chancellor, Cardinal Wolsey continued this assault on church privilege by dissolving some monasteries and further restricting rights of sanctuary.

> For all privileged places
> He brekes and defaces,
> All placis of relygion
> He hathe them in derisyon.

So wrote Skelton in *Why Come Ye Nat to Courte?* (1522). If the jurisdictional privilege represented by sanctuary was, in one sense, indistinguishable from secular forms of parcelized sovereignty, its "false ecclesiastical covering" nevertheless imparted a significant ideological difference, for sanctuary was not perceived as just another expression of feudal landownership. It was, rather, invested with a sacred character, and its inviolability was thus hedged about with the massive ideological resources of the medieval church. It is largely for this reason that sanctuary outlived secular forms of independent jurisdiction. Indeed, I think it is fair to view sanctuary as the ideological *paradigm* for such jurisdiction, and thus to say that the distinction between "sacred" and "profane" ground provided an ideological undergirding for the entire feudal system of parcelized sovereignties. This is why attacks on sanctuary were of political as well as cultural or religious significance, and why the early Tudor state directed such considerable energies toward incorporating the church in its jurisdiction.

The traditional account of Skelton's life and career places him in a simple and unitary relation to this process: as a vigorous, life-long opponent. According to this account, Skelton was for most of his career a client of the Howard family. They in turn belonged to a group of conservative lords opposed to Wolsey, whom they blamed for the execution in 1521 of Edward Stafford, third duke of Buckingham and a relative by marriage of the Howards.[22] The anti-Wolsey satires, in this view, grew in part from the patronage of a group of powerful northern lords frustrated by the loss of influence over the king and angered by the death of an ally on possibly trumped-up charges of treason. If this version is correct, Skelton would be in the employ of powerful victims of Tudor centralization. At the same time, he was a priest, whose work was deeply influenced by Christian liturgy and belief, and he therefore felt a more purely personal and religious objection to Wolsey's attacks on church privilege.[23] The anti-Wolsey satires were all prompted in part by Wolsey's dissolution of some monasteries in 1521. They were, moreover, written from the confines of the Abbey at Westminster, where Skelton had lived since 1518 and where he enjoyed the relative protection of sanctuary.[24] By combining political loyalty to a group of aggrieved feudal lords with personal dependence on and fervent religious belief in the church's rights of sanctuary, Skelton allied himself in every conceivable fashion with the conservative forces fighting the consolidation of absolutist rule.

Recently, however, this portrait of Skelton has been subjected to a devastating revisionist critique by Greg Walker. He finds no evidence for a Howard-Wolsey feud in the 1520s; on the contrary, the Howards seem to have been loyal and happy supporters of Wolsey's handling of crown policy. Further, the theory that they were patrons of Skelton is based on spurious suppositions and misdatings of poems.[25] There is reason to doubt the sincerity of Skelton's religious convictions as well, for he clearly viewed his move to a rectory at Diss in Norfolk as a calamitous falling off from his earlier position at court, where he had served as a Latin tutor to the young Prince Henry. When Henry ascended the throne, Skelton sent his former pupil a desperate letter describing himself as "a man utterly doomed to oblivion and, so to say, dead in his heart" and then compared his exile to Ovid's.[26] In any case, he abandoned Diss forever at his earliest opportunity and never resumed his priestly duties.[27] The notion that the anti-Wolsey satires were prompted by sincere outrage is challenged by the reversal in 1523, when Skelton turned around and wrote not only on behalf of Wolsey but in apparent collaboration with him.[28] "He seems to have swiftly considered the advantages to be gained from aligning himself with his erstwhile target," writes Walker, "compared them with the less certain gains to be won by continuing his wooing of patronage from the city [of London], and promptly thrown in his lot with Wolsey."[29]

In place of the conservative and somewhat romantic image of Skelton as defender of church and nobility Walker offers a rather less flattering image of the poet as a self-serving mercenary whose rise was inhibited by misjudgments and ineptitude. He makes a largely compelling case for viewing the satires not as expressions of prophetic wrath but as a search for patronage and advancement, first from the king and then, failing that, from among the prosperous and disaffected citizens of London. This Skelton is neither a sworn enemy of absolutism nor a reliable defender of it but someone who is ready to profit from it if given the chance.

Walker successfully destroys many of the historical assumptions that underlie the traditional view of Skelton, but his own version isn't quite coherent either. He argues, for instance, that **Speke Parott** attempts to profit from apparent tensions between Henry and Wolsey in order to secure royal patronage.[30] Yet if this is the case, how does one explain lines such as "Bo-ho [Henry] doth bark wel, Hough-ho [Wolsey] he rulyth the ring" (130)? Even someone as eccentric as Skelton couldn't possibly expect to please the king with language like this. It also seems likely that Skelton's ultimate reconciliation (or cooperation) with Wolsey was at least partly determined by ideological commitments as well as by considerations of personal gain, for his poetic assignments on Wolsey's behalf involved writing satires against foreign invasion (Skelton was, if nothing else, a sincere xenophobe) and religious heresy. A residue of the "old" Skelton thus persists despite attempts to banish him. The fact is that no fully coherent or unified account of his career is possible. Skelton is neither the conservative prophet nor the self-serving courtier, neither the consistent opponent nor the consistent parasite of the Tudor court, but someone who oscillates erratically between these positions, and whose career is therefore full of strange folds and detours. His poetry is obsessed with the changes in the late feudal polity wrought by absolutism, but his reactions to them are shifting and contradictory. Skelton's historical significance can be read primarily through his internal divisions and fissures if he is understood as a kind of relay or switching station through which conflicting social energies are routed.

Ware the Hawk was composed while Skelton was rector at Diss, presumably around the time he wrote **Phyllyp Sparowe** (1505?). This period witnessed Skelton's peculiar and somewhat inexplicable "break" with the conventional formulas of late medieval lyric. The poem, which exemplifies the beginnings of Skelton's distinctive poetics, describes and denounces the actions of a neighboring priest who becomes so involved in his hawking that he pursues his prey right into Skelton's church. There the hawks tear a pigeon apart on the holy altar and defecate on the communion cloth, while the priest himself overturns the offering box, cross, and lectern. The poem vents its rage at the desecration of holy places, flinging both crude and pedantic insults at the offending priest.

Ware the Hawk directs its anger at an act of profanation which it understands primarily as the violation of a boundary or territory; it condemns those who

> playe the daw
> To hawke, or els to hunt
> From the auter to the funt,
> Wyth cry unreverent,

> Before the sacrament,
> Wythin the holy church bowndis,
> That of our fayth the grownd is.

Skelton's church is, of course, the literal as well as the metaphorical "ground" of faith; the hawking priest offends not only because he has intruded on divine territory but because he has intruded on Skelton's territory. "For sure he wrought amys / To hawke in *my* church of Dys" (41-42, my emphasis). I do not wish to suggest that the concept of the holy place merely expresses property rights, either for Skelton or in general. But the sanctity of the medieval church, which was articulated within the feudal structure of parceled sovereignty, represents Skelton's primary experience of this structure. Certainly the violation of the church's boundaries in **Ware the Hawk** seems to threaten its sovereignty:

> Or els is thys Goddis law,
>
> . . . . .
>
> Thus within the wals
> Of holy church to deale,
> Thus to ryng a peale
> Wyth his hawkys bels?
> Dowtles such losels
> Make the churche to be
> In smale auctoryte.

For Skelton, the whole hierarchical taxonomy of late medieval culture is interwritten with the church's territorial sanctity. When this is broken, all other structures collapse like a house of cards.[31]

These objections are not particularly novel in themselves. The interest of Skelton's poem arises from its formal reaction to the trespass, for **Ware the Hawk** responds to the violation of a politico-religious territory by subjecting itself to a strict rhetorical territoriality. The poem is meticulously constructed according to what Stanley Fish aptly calls the "machinery of the artes praedicandi." After a formal exordium (*prologus*), "the text is punctuated by eight hortatory exclamations (*Observate, Deliberate, Vigilate, Deplorate, Divinitate*—probably for *Divinate—Reformate,* and *Pensitate*) which correspond to the development of the *thema* as taught in the manuals."[32] The conspicuous rhetorical formalism of the poem clearly represents a kind of reaction formation to the disturbance of the church's boundaries; the anarchic trajectory of the hawk finds its answering principle in an exaggerated reterritorialization by the poet, thus producing a striking—and, for Skelton, characteristic—cohesion between political and rhetorical topographies. This coincidence of spaces produces brilliant formal effects in **Phyllyp Sparowe** and offers the privileged means by which Skelton transcodes history into literature.

But an additional element transforms the nature of the poem's process. Stanley Fish describes **Ware the Hawk** as "a burlesque in the Chaucerian tradition." Both the incident itself and Skelton's indignation, Fish argues, are ironized; despite its obsessive formalism, the poem's rhetoric constantly undercuts itself, thereby dissolving the seriousness of the priest's offense.[33] *Ware the Hawk* may not be as thoroughly ironic as that, but a festive excess of rhetoric certainly renders the poem and its defensive reterritorialization highly ambivalent. A gay destructiveness delights in the violation of boundaries and in the consequent evaporation of the authority constituted by them. At least part of Skelton's imagination both enjoys and extends the profanities committed by the neighboring priest, who, the poet claims,

> wysshed withall
> That the dowves donge downe myght fall
> Into my chalys at mas,
> When consecratyd was
> The blessyd sacrament.

The pleasurable onomatopoeia of "dowves donge downe" exemplifies the festive counterlogic of *Ware the Hawk,* which can enjoy polluting even that final cultural territory, the space of the blessed sacrament. The poem's very title, which seems at first to mean "beware the hawk" and thus to make a defensive or warning gesture, was actually "a proverbial cry used to encourage the hawk to obtain its prey."[34] It is as if Skelton had marshaled the forces of rhetorical territoriality in a mock-defensive gesture, the better to overthrow *all* boundaries in one totalizing motion. . . .

Skelton's idiosyncracies have caused problems for critics trying to fit him into the scheme of cultural periodization which characterizes traditional literary history.

—Richard Halpern

Speke Parott and the Delegation of Speech

Speke Parott, the first of Skelton's anti-Wolsey satires, does go considerably farther than *Phyllyp Sparowe* in maintaining a quarrel with state authority. Written in 1521, when Skelton was already residing in sanctuary at Westminster, *Speke Parott* both develops and dramatically revises the poetics of *Phyllyp Sparowe.* A bird is once again the center of attention, but this bird is very much alive—immortal, in fact—and is no longer merely the subject but the speaker of the poem:

> My name ys Parott, a byrde of Paradyse,
> By Nature devysed of a wonderowus kynde,
> Deyntely dyetyd with dyvers delycate spyce,
> Tyll Eufrates, that flodde, dryvythe me into Ynde,
> Where men of that contre by fortune me fynde,
> And send me to greate ladyes of estate;
> Then Parot moste have an almon or a date.

> A cage curyowsly carven, with sylver pynne,
> Properly payntyd to be my coverture;
> A myrrour of glasse, that I may tote therin;
> These maydens full meryly with many a dyvers
>   flowur
> Fresshely they dresse and make swete my bowur,
> With "Speke, Parott, I pray yow," full curteslye they
>   sey,
> "Parott ys a goodlye byrde and a pratye popagay."

> Wythe my beke bente, and my lytell wanton iye,
> My fethyrs fresshe as ys the emerawde grene,
> Abowte my necke a cerculett lyke the ryche rubye,
> My lytell legges, my fete both fete and clene,
> I am a mynyon to wayte apon a quene;
> "My propyr Parott, my lytell pratye fole."
> With ladyes I lerne and goe with them to scole.

With his "lytell wanton iye," Parott is clearly a ladies' bird, just as Phyllyp Sparowe was.[53] One of the literary models for *Speke Parott* is the *Epistres de l'amant verd* by Jean Lemaire de Belges, a series of despairingly erotic letters from a pet parrot to his departing mistress. Yet even from these opening lines it is clear that Skelton's Parott, unlike Lemaire's, is primarily autoerotic. He lovingly enumerates his *own* body parts, "totes" in his mirror, and seems to value the ladies of the court mostly because they make much of him. Parott thus appropriates not only speech but sexuality as well; in his disturbing autonomy he is like a strange hybrid of Phyllyp and Jane.[54] Parott's sexuality is not entirely innocent, however, and his is given to knowing, phallic innuendo.[55]

Not only sexually but more generally, *Speke Parott* may be said to rewrite *Phyllyp Sparowe* into a song of experience. Parott has fallen from Paradise, "that place of pleasure perdurable" (186), which may in part be identified with *Phyllyp Sparowe*'s realm of "rien que playsere." Parott is a polyglot who both embodies and masters the curse of Babel. "Yn Latyn, in Ebrue, and in Caldee, /In Greke tong Parott can bothe speke and sey" (25-26)—as well as in French, Spanish, Dutch, and several English dialects. And he employs this multilingualism together with dense layers of figure to protect himself in the dangerous world of court:

> But of that supposicyon that callyd is arte,
> *Confuse distrybutyve,* as Parrot hath devysed,
> Let every man after his merit take his parte;
> For in this processe, Parrot nothing hath surmysed,
> No matter pretendyd, nor nothyng enterprysed,
> But that *metaphora, alegoria* withall,
> Shall be his protectyon, his pavys [shield] and his
>   wall.

But allegory is not the only means of defense on which the poem relies. A. C. Spearing has suggested that Parott's cage may represent the confinement and relative safety of the sanctuary of Westminster.[56] I say "relative safety" because one of the poem's satirical targets is Wolsey's assaults on sanctuary rights: "So myche sayntuary brekyng, and prevylegidde barryd—/ Syns Dewcalyons flodde was nevyr sene nor lyerd."[57] In every way, the world of *Speke Parott* is therefore more dangerous, covert, and sinister than that of *Phyllyp Sparowe,* and accordingly, Parott is a cannier type of bird.

In its rambling course, *Speke Parott* criticizes numerous evils in the early Tudor polity, for almost all of which it blames Thomas Cardinal Wolsey. As Greg Walker has observed, Skelton's satires almost entirely abjure social analysis in favor of ad hominem attacks[58] against a man who seemed to embody in his person the entire machinery of the Tudor state. Nor was Skelton alone in this perception. The Venetian ambassador Sebastian Giustiani described Wolsey as a man "of vast ability and indefatigable. He alone transacts the same business as that which occupies all the magistracies, offices and councils of Venice, both civil and criminal, and all state affairs are likewise handled by him let their nature be what it may."[59] Even more than Henry VIII, Wolsey represented the concentration of administrative and jurisdictional power carried out by early absolutism. Not only did he run most of the governmental apparatus as lord chancellor, but in 1518 he was granted vast ecclesiastical powers when he was named papal legate *a latere.* Wolsey used his new authority to reorganize and interfere with the government of every diocese, "appointing his own protégés, regardless of the rights of patrons, and set[ting] up legatine courts to which he summoned men from all over England,"[60] in addition to dissolving monasteries and attempting to curtail rights of sanctuary. By centralizing diocesan government and subjecting it to the interests of the crown, Wolsey helped prepare the way for the Tudor state's more formal rule of the church. It is Wolsey, far more than Henry, who embodies for Skelton the centralizing force of early Tudor absolutism.

Superficially, *Speke Parott* seems to react to Wolsey as *Phyllyp Sparowe* reacted to its own despotic signifiers: by de- and reterritorializing into autonomous parcels. Parott even devises a name for this poetic mode—*"confuse distrybutyve"* (198)—and describes the recombinatory method that produces it:

> Suche shredis of sentence, strowed in the shop
> Of auncyent Aristippus and such other mo,
> I gader togyther and close in my crop,
> Of my wanton conseyt, *unde depromo*
> *Dilemata docta in pedagogio*
> *Sacro vatum,*[61] whereof to you I breke;
> I pray you, let Parot have lyberte to speke.

Parott's "wanton conseyt" works according to the mechanisms of poetic imagination I described in Chapter 1, atomizing and scrambling received texts so as to decode them ideologically. The poem thus registers a tension between Parott's role as a conscious and unified speaker who is an apparent source of speech and his position as mere relay or switching station in an uncontrolled and seemingly random field of language-flows. The figure of the parrot, a bird who memorizes "scraps of sentence" and repeats them unexpectedly, offers a striking image for the decontextualizing labor of poetic imagination. The more

speech that is fed into Parott, the more uncanny and disconcerting he becomes: "Thus dyvers of language by lernyng I grow." Unlike those of *Phyllyp Sparowe,* the textual fragments shuttled through *Speke Parott* are not even subjected to the constraints of a consistent poetic voice or persona; Parott shifts abruptly between languages and dialects, like a tape recorder gone mad:

> *Ulula,* Esebon, for Jeromy doth wepe!
> Sion is in sadness, Rachell ruly doth loke;
> Midionita Jetro, our Moyses kepyth his shepe;
> Gedeon is gon, that Zalmane undertoke,
> Oreb *et* Zeb, of *Judicum* rede the boke.
> Now Geball, Amon and Amaloch—"Harke, harke,
> Parrot pretendith to be a bybyll clarke!"

Yet the slippery, obscure, and seemingly aleatory surface of the poem conceals a dense allegorical coherence. While "some folys say ye arre furnysshyd with knakkes, / That hang togedyr as fethyrs in the wynde" (292-93), they lack the learning to construe the poem's message—so says the first of the envoys that Skelton attached to *Speke Parott* in an attempt to explain it to an uncomprehending audience.[62] Recent commentators have unveiled most of the poem's linguistic, scriptural, and allegorical mysteries and found a coherent, detailed attack on Cardinal Wolsey. Once interpreted, the poem reveals not incoherence but, if anything, a hypercoherence verging on paranoia that traces almost all of England's social, political, and religious disorders back to this one source. It is around the cardinal as fetishized signifier that all the poem's allegorical codes crystallize and congeal, thus establishing a stark dialectic between de- and reterritorialization. What *Phyllyp Sparowe* distributed between two parts of the poem *Speke Parott* enacts simultaneously, at once flying apart to avoid capture and recomposing itself to direct all its obsessive force at a single target.

The formal and linguistic strategies of *Speke Parott,* though they owe more than a little to some of Skelton's earlier works, are both honed and transformed by the poet's engagement with real political authority. Wolsey, in fact, confronts Skelton with a very specific model for the relation between language and power: that of *delegation,* the transfer of juridical or administrative authority by means of speech or language. Wolsey had recently become the recipient of two different forms of delegated power. Having already been appointed papal legate in 1518, he was then sent by King Henry to Calais for a series of diplomatic negotiations in the fall of 1521. Wolsey's ostensible purpose was to mediate between French and imperial forces in order to avoid a war into which England would be drawn by treaty, but his real purpose was to arrange a secret agreement with the imperial delegates for a combined assault on France. In any case, Wolsey brought the Great Seal of England with him to Calais as a sign of his plenipotentiary powers—an event of some symbolic importance.[63]

Delegation is itself a complex symbolic act in that the delegate becomes an actual bearer of authority but only by representing or standing in for the delegating power.

Paradoxically, the act of delegation can grant a certain autonomy if delegates are asked to exercise their own judgment; yet ultimately their decisions must all serve the interests of another, so that they are at once both actant and symbol. Delegation as speech act, the sending forth of the delegate to act on behalf of another, is a real linguistic transfer or exchange of power but one that is bounded by the relation of representing or signifying. It serves as a linguistic conduit for centralized power, allowing it to extend its operations and jurisdiction over a wide territorial field. Delegation is therefore a characteristic mode of propagating authority within despotic, absolutist, or bureaucratic states.

That Wolsey tended to drive the tensions or complexities of delegation into open contradiction was, I think, part of his fascination for Skelton. Wolsey accumulated enormous jurisdictional and administrative authority in the course of his various duties, and if this allowed him to carry out the will of his superiors more fully, it also threatened to destabilize or overturn the relations of power that bound him to them. England's papal legate was well known to covet the papacy himself and had already engaged in unsuccessful machinations to attain it. "Hyt ys to fere leste he wolde were the garland on hys pate," warns Parott. As to secular power, the Venetian ambassador observed that "the Cardinal, for authority, may in point of fact be styled *ipse rex*,"[64] and *Speke Parott* likewise warns Henry that his indulgence allows Wolsey to "rule the ring." Skelton apparently took advantage of some tensions that developed between king and lord chancellor during the course of the Calais negotiations to launch his satire, though in the end he misread both these and the true nature of Wolsey's mission.[65] *Speke Parott* thus finds an opening for satire in the assumption that Wolsey has arrogated so much power that he betrays his diplomatic tasks.

It is in relation to Wolsey's position as unreliable or usurping delegate, I believe, that the persona of Parott takes on his full satirical force. Parrots, of course, are known for repeating only what their masters teach them. Incapable of independent thought, they can only mimic the words of others, and they thus represent a simple and absolute relation between language and authority. The parrot is pure linguistic instrument, subject to another, without understanding, unable to argue back. "Speke Parott," the phrase that titles Skelton's poem, suggests an absolutist brand of linguistic delegation which determines both the moment and the content of speech. Accordingly, Parott can be a shameless flatterer of authority:

> In Englysshe to God Parott can supple:
> "Cryste save Kyng Herry the viiith, owur royall
>   kyng,
> The red rose in honour to flowrysshe and sprynge!"
>
> "With Kateryne incomporabyll, owur royall quene
>   also,
> That pereles pomegarnat, Cryste save her nobyll
>   grace!"

In one sense, then, Parott's role is to debase or degrade Wolsey's position as delegate. Skelton's satire relies on an implicit parallel between Parott's position as poetic persona, speaking only the words that his creator supplies, and the lord chancellor's role as mere instrument or tool of royal policy: "A narrow unfethered and without an hed, / A bagpype without blowynge standeth in no sted." In one sense the arrow is Wolsey, whose flight has taken him from England to Calais, and Skelton reminds him that without his "head" (Henry) and "feathers" (presumably, diplomatic finery and status), the lord chancellor is useless and impotent.[66] But this image also figures Skelton's poem as satirical arrow, with its feathered persona and guiding poetical author or "head." However much he may plume himself on his borrowed authority, Skelton suggests, Wolsey is just a trained bird, provided with a few phrases to utter on behalf of another. Like Parott, Wolsey is only a vain and lascivious "popagay."

The notion of parroting, incidentally, connects the satire of Wolsey with another, apparently unrelated part of the poem: Skelton's attack on humanist methods of language instruction. Wolsey was known to have sponsored the "Greeks" at Oxford, and this in itself was sufficient provocation for Skelton's attack.[67] But what *Speke Parott* objects to more specifically is humanism's divorce of speech from content or "matter" and hence from understanding. The child who can say "'*Aveto*' in *Greco*, and such solempne salutacyons," yet "Can skantly the tensis of his conjugacyons" seems uncomfortably like a parrot who can repeat phrases without knowing what they mean or how to use them. Skelton regarded humanist education as a degrading form of linguistic delegation producing servile and ignorant speakers, a reflection of its hated patron.

If the parrot symbolized a flattering and obedient form of imitation, however, another and somewhat contradictory tradition viewed it as a wanton, mischievous, or satirical speaker, "roughly comparable to the court jester who offers garbled scraps of wisdom in snatches of foreign tongues, an outspoken revealer of confidences, indulged because he is not responsible for his sometimes telling juxtaposition of random phrases."[68] The seemingly mechanical repetition of speech which makes parrots seem so subservient from one perspective can also make them appear uncanny or disturbing from another. Maybe they really are independent intellects whose phrases aren't random. In mimicking us, do they mock us? Skelton's articulate Parott raises just this doubt; he derives more than a little of his satirical energy from his ability to twist and garble various kinds of speech, thus rendering them either strange or risible. Parott embodies repetition as alienation, where it gives birth to the illusion of a weirdly autonomous mind. Parott is "wanton"; he demands "lyberty to speke" and thus appropriates a power that was seemingly only lent to him. In this, of course, he also represents Wolsey, another mouthpiece or verbal instrument who (Skelton thinks) has gotten out of hand. Like Parott, Wolsey is a delegated speaker who mysteriously becomes a *source* of speech and authority.

Through its feathered persona, *Speke Parott* adopts a complex and contradictory stance toward linguistic delegation. In some respects the poem enacts a kind of latent pun on the word: it "delegalizes" speech, not only by investing it with unofficial or seditious meanings but, more fundamentally, by collapsing the law of speech, by disarticulating or decoding those linguistic structures that make language a reliable conduit for the transmission of authority. Here Parott plays his crucial role as a language machine run amok, switching suddenly from shrewdness to frenzy, from wisdom to foolery, shuttling textual fragments and linguistic flows in unpredictable directions, oscillating unexpectedly between communication and mechanical sound production. Parott dislocates the speaking subject, referring to himself by name and in the third person, as if he were elsewhere, not in this voice that emerges from his body. Parott, in fact, does for language what Jane Scrope does for sexuality, snatching it from the stroke of a despotic signifier.

But *Speke Parott* is not *Phyllyp Sparowe,* and thus while it traces lines of flight from power it also tries to mount a counterattack by harnessing the force of delegation for its own purposes. If Greg Walker's reading of the poem is accepted—and I think it should be, at least in part— then *Speke Parott* is Skelton's attempt to regain royal favor by exploiting what he thought to be Henry's serious dissatisfactions with Wolsey's diplomatic efforts. The poem is thus an unsolicited barb loosed on Henry's "behalf" and a proleptic resumption of Skelton's post as *orator regius,* the title by which he identifies himself at the poem's end. The second envoy, dated three days after Henry sent a letter recalling Wolsey from Calais, rejoices over the apparent failure of the lord chancellor's mission, and contrasts what it takes to be Skelton's new poetic delegation with Wolsey's failed diplomatic one:

> Passe forthe, Parotte, towardes some passengere;
> Require hym to convey yow ovyr the salte fome;
> Addressyng your selfe, lyke a sadde messengere,
> To owur soleyne Seigneour Sadoke, desire hym to
>   cum home,
> Makyng hys pylgrimage by *Nostre Dame de Crome:*
> For Jerico and Jerssey shall mete togethyr as sone
> As he to exployte the man owte of the mone.

Skelton's poetic missive steps in for Henry's letter recalling the failed and wayward ambassador; just as Parott is sent to speak for his author, so Skelton believes himself now to be speaking for the king. The only problem with this royal delegation is that it was entirely fictive, an autodelegation. Relying on gossip and rumor, Skelton was uninformed of Wolsey's real mission at Calais and was apparently taken by surprise when the king welcomed and thanked the returning lord chancellor.[69] Ironically, then, it was Skelton, not Wolsey, who abused the power of delegation by appropriating royal powers of speech while only posing as the representative of authority. If he thought Wolsey capable of almost magical powers of usurpation, mightn't this be in part because his own career was based on the usurpation of titles, those of poet laureate and king's orator?

At the same time that Skelton puts his pretended authority as *orator regius* up against the secular power of the lord

chancellor, however, he also invokes a second, prophetic delegation with which to berate the worldly cardinal. The poem's prophetic voice and vocation emerge most clearly in the final envoy, where a complaint against contemporary abuses is joined to an implicit threat of divine retribution:

> So many thevys hangyd, and thevys neverthelesse;
> So myche presonment, for matyrs not worth a hawe;
> So myche papers weryng for ryghte a smalle
>   exesse;
> So myche pelory pajauntes undyr colowur of good
>   lawe;
> So myche towrnyng on the cooke-stole for every
>   guy-gaw;
> So myche mokkyshe makyng of statutes of array—
> Syns Dewcalyons flodde was nevyr, I dar sey.
>
> . . . . .
>
> So many trusys takyn, and so lytyll perfyte trowthe;
> So myche bely-joye, and so wastefull banketyng;
> So pynchyng and sparyng, and so lytell profyte
>   growth;
> So many howgye howsys byldyng, and so small
>   howse-holdyng;
> Such statutes apon diettes, suche pyllyng and
>   pollyng—
>
> . . . . .
>
> So many vacabondes, so many beggers bolde,
> So myche decay of monesteries and relygious
>   places;
> So hote hatered agaynste the Chyrche, and cheryte
>   so colde;
> So myche of my lordes grace, and in hym no grace
>   ys;
> So many holow hartes, and so dowbyll faces;
> So myche sayntuary brekyng, and prevylegidde
>   barryd—
> Syns Dewcalyons flodde was nevyr sene nor lyerd.
>
>   (477-83, 491-95, 498-504)

Skelton's jeremiad nicely balances a sense of social dissolution with an awareness of the increasing centralization and severity of royal power, so that his depicted polity is at once anarchic and totalitarian. If only empirically, he manages to grasp the dynamic of primitive accumulation. But this contradictory state is also that of his poem and its two delegations. For as *orator regius,* Skelton attempts to recall the aberrant and excessive Wolsey in the name of the king, and thus to restore the political order of the kingdom. From this perspective Henry is viewed as a "mercyfull" ruler, the embodiment of a feudal or limited monarchy, and emergent absolutism is mistakenly regarded as the product of a renegade lord chancellor. As prophet, however, Skelton stands apart from all political authority. Now he seems to promise not the restoration of a lost order but the loss of all order, for "Dewcalyons flodde" suggests a divine punishment that would both complete and literalize the dissolution of the late feudal polity.

The de- and recoding operations of Skelton's later poetics are thus tied to two incompatible concepts of poetic delegation, explaining, I think, the sometimes contradictory stance of **Speke Parott,** which seems on the whole to criticize Wolsey on behalf of the king, yet sometimes inexplicably attacks Henry as well. As papal legate and lord chancellor Wolsey was able to effect a preliminary subordination of church to state, and this double role was reflected in an unacceptably "worldly" manner. Skelton, by contrast, endures an unstable alternation between his delegated roles, and this constitutes his divided experience of early absolutism. Ironically, however, his most fully elaborated statement on the prophetic nature of poetry occurs in his final work, **"A Replycacion"** (1528), written on behalf of the formerly reviled Wolsey, whom it fulsomely praises. This final turn of Skelton's career has proven to be a puzzling one, at least to those who thought that Skelton had fought a principled and even dangerous battle against the lord chancellor. It certainly suggests a mercenary or at least an opportunistic side to his character. This development is foreshadowed, however, by Skelton's own poetical birds, all of whom have undergone some degree of taming. Even the irascible Parott "must have an almon or a date" and probably isn't too choosy about where he gets it. Yet it is also unfair to privilege **"A Replycacion"** just because it was Skelton's last poem. Had he lived, the poet might well have turned wild once more and bitten the hand that fed him.

Notes

[1] *Merrie Tales . . . by Master John Skelton* (1567), in *Shakespeare Jest-Books,* ed. W. Carew Hazlitt (1864; rpt. New York: Burt Franklin, [196?]), 2:1-36.

[2] In a letter to Allan Cunningham, 23 November 1823, quoted by Arthur B. Kinney in *John Skelton, Priest as Poet: Seasons of Discovery* (Chapel Hill: University of North Carolina Press, 1987), p. 206.

[3] C. S. Lewis, *English Literature in the Sixteenth Century* (New York: Oxford University Press, 1954), p. 143.

[4] In a fine discussion of Skelton's place in literary history, A. C. Spearing maintains that "Skelton is the only English poet . . . [of his age who] wants something more than to *be* Chaucer" and that this larger desire paradoxically enables him to develop Chaucer's work. *Medieval to Renaissance in English Poetry* (Cambridge: Cambridge University Press, 1985), p. 234. For an argument that the dullness of fifteenth-century poetry was a consciously adopted literary and political strategy, see David Lawton, "Dulness and the Fifteenth Century," *ELH* 54 (1987), 761-99.

[5] For a description of the Grammarians' War see William Nelson, *John Skelton, Laureate* (New York: Columbia University Press, 1939), pp. 148-58.

[6] All quotations of Skelton's poetry are taken from *John Skelton: The Complete English Poems,* ed. John Scattergood (New Haven: Yale University Press, 1983).

[7] Greg Walker, *John Skelton and the Politics of the 1520s* (Cambridge: Cambridge University Press, 1988), p. 48.

[8] Ian A. Gordon, *John Skelton: Poet Laureate* (Melbourne, Aus.: Melbourne University Press, 1943), pp. 9, 45.

[9] Stanley Fish, *John Skelton's Poetry* (New Haven: Yale University Press, 1965), p. 249.

[10] Spearing, *Medieval to Renaissance,* pp. 229, 265. Spearing's very suggestive reading of the transition from medieval to Renaissance poetics is based on a similar structure of anticipation. Briefly, Spearing argues that Chaucer really became the first "Renaissance" poet as a result of influences he picked up on his travels to Italy. His English successors then re-medievalized what they found in Chaucer, so that the literary history of the fifteenth century progresses, in a sense, backward.

[11] F. L. Brownlow, "*The Boke of Phyllyp Sparowe* and the Liturgy," *English Literary Renaissance* 9 (1979), 5-20; Kinney, *John Skelton.*

[12] Walker, *John Skelton.*

[13] See Perry Anderson, *Lineages of the Absolutist State* (London: New Left Books, 1974), pp. 15-17.

[14] Ibid., p. 19.

[15] Ibid., pp. 20-24.

[16] Ibid., p. 119.

[17] John E. Martin, *Feudalism to Capitalism: Peasant and Landlord in English Agrarian Development* (Atlantic Highlands, N.J.: Humanities Press, 1983), p. 109.

[18] "In England the religious foundations made extensive use of labour-rent and demesne production, they tended to persist with labour-services longer, to manage their estates more carefully and to supervise production more thoroughly, and to defend their rights of labour-service more tenaciously, than any other type of feudal landlord." Barry Hindess and Paul Q. Hirst, *Pre-capitalist Modes of Production* (London: Routledge and Kegan Paul, 1975), p. 253. Also see G. R. Elton, *England under the Tudors* (2d ed.; London: Methuen, 1974), p. 103.

[19] J. Thomas Kelly, *Thorns on the Tudor Rose: Monks, Rogues, Vagabonds, and Sturdy Beggars* (Jackson: University Press of Mississippi, 1977), p. 3.

[20] Isabel D. Thornley, "The Destruction of Sanctuary," in R. W. Seton-Watson, ed., *Tudor Studies* (London: Longmans, 1924), pp. 183-84.

[21] Elton, *England under the Tudors,* pp. 21-22.

[22] Walker, *John Skelton,* p. 5.

[23] Kinney, in particular, argues this line *(John Skelton).*

[24] Walker, *John Skelton,* p. 88.

[25] Ibid., chap. 1.

[26] Ibid., p. 42.

[27] Ibid., p. 151.

[28] Ibid., chap. 6.

[29] Ibid., p. 190.

[30] Ibid., pp. 53-100.

[31]   Evangelia
Concha et conchelia,
Accipiter et sonalia,
Et bruta animalia,
Cetera quoque talia
Tibi sunt equalia
          (311-16)

The Gospels, vessels and vestments, a hawk with its bells and unreasoning animals and other such things are all the same to you. (Scattergood trans.)

[32] Fish, *Skelton's Poetry*, p. 89.

[33] Ibid., pp. 89-98.

[34] Kinney, *John Skelton*, p. 83.

[53] Cf. *Phyllyp Sparowe* 182: "With his wanton eye."

[54] Compare *Phyllyp Sparowe* 175-76—"Phyllyp had leve to go / To pyke my lytell too"—with *Speke Parott* 107—"With my beke I can pyke my lyttel praty too."

[55] See Fish, *Skelton's Poetry*, p. 146; and F. L. Brownlow, "The Boke Compiled by Maister Skelton, Poet Laureate, Called Speake Parrot," *English Literary Renaissance* 1 (1971), 21.

[56] Spearing, *Medieval to Renaissance*, p. 269.

[57] Cf. also 124-25: "And *assilum, whilom refugium miserorum, / Non phanum, sed prophanum*, standyth in lytyll sted [And asylum, formerly the refuge of wretches, is not a sanctuary but is to be made secular]" (Scattergood trans.).

[58] Walker, *John Skelton*, pp. 85-86, 132.

[59] Sebastian Giustiani, quoted ibid., p. 162.

[60] Kinney, *John Skelton*, pp. 133-34.

[61] "Whence I bring forth arguments in a sacred school of poets" (Scattergood trans.).

[62] Walker, *John Skelton*, p. 91, says that the poem's obscurities baffled its original readers.

[63] Ibid., pp. 79-80.

[64] Quoted ibid., p. 173.

[65] Ibid., pp. 73-78, 80-89.

[66] The headless arrow also has another, more specific reference. During the negotiations at Calais the emperor Charles asked Henry to send six thousand English archers in fulfillment of his treaty obligations. Henry and Wolsey disagreed over whether the archers should be sent at all while the negotiations were still proceeding, and they then quarreled bitterly over who should "head" them. See J. J. Scarisbrick, *Henry VIII*

(Berkeley: University of California Press, 1968), p. 86. The issue of the archers marked the first serious breach between Henry and his negotiator and raised the issue of which of the two was the other's "head." Thus I read the image of the arrow as referring both to the specific subject of the quarrel and to Wolsey in his role as delegate.

[67] Nelson, *John Skelton*, p. 182.

[68] Fish, *Skelton's Poetry*, p. 135.

[69] Walker, *John Skelton*, p. 93.

Peter C. Herman (essay date 1994)

SOURCE: "Leaky Ladies and Droopy Dames: The Grotesque Realism of Skelton's *The Tunnynge of Elynour Rummynge*," in *Rethinking the Henrician Era: Essays on Early Tudor Texts and Contexts*, edited by Peter C. Herman, University of Illinois Press, 1994, pp. 145-67.

[*In the following essay, Herman deems Skelton's poem* The Tunning of Elinor Rumming *as grotesque realism and maintains that the action of the poem is best understood as a reversal of power relationships typical of the Tudor era.*]

Despite John Skelton's consistent presence in modern anthologies of sixteenth-century literature, he occupies the margins of the canon rather than a central position.[1] Erasmus's praise for Skelton's abilities notwithstanding, the majority of Skelton's contemporaries considered him more of an embarrassment than an adornment to English letters.[2] Indeed, his antics were so bizarre that they became the subject of a jest book, making Skelton the only major poet, let alone priest, so honored. While he was alive, Skelton enjoyed a modicum of fame as the class clown of English literature, and after his death his already dubious reputation managed to plummet even further. Pope, for example, called the man "beastly," and as we shall see, few have dissented from this opinion. Skelton's ill repute among the elite did not prevent his works from enjoying a certain popularity in the Renaissance or his style (if not his life) from serving as a model for other writers; however, his work endured in spite of the disparagement of such influential tastemakers as George Puttenham, who found both the man and his works "ridiculous," and Sir Philip Sidney, who omits him altogether from the canon set out in his *Apology for Poetry*.[3]

Not insignificantly, critics have singled out Skelton's most popular work, ***The Tunnynge of Elynour Rummynge***, as the prime target for abuse. In *The Plaine Man's Pathway to Heaven* (1590), for example, the Elizabethan divine Arthur Dent linked *"Ellen of Rumming"* with other "vaine and frivolous bookes of Tales, Iestes, and lies," which he dismissed as "so much trashe and rubbish."[4] Nor do modern critics depart all that much from their Renaissance counterparts. John Berdan set the tone by describing ***Elynour Rummynge*** as "a poem rather notorious than known," and evidently most critics concur, which helps explain the rather amazing silence about this text.[5] Susan Staub's "Recent Studies in Skelton (1970-1988)" does not contain even one article devoted to Elynour and her crew,[6] and the rare critic who does grant the poem's existence usually does so only to condemn it. Like Berdan, C. S. Lewis calls the poem a "shapeless volley of rhymes," granting it a legitimate place in the canon but only barely so: "it works, but we cannot forget that art has much better cards in its hand."[7] And Stanley E. Fish, doubtless for the first and last time, agrees with Lewis: *The Tunning of Eleanor Rumming* [*sic*] is a picture, a verbal painting—and designedly nothing more. . . . As one of the few really abstract poems in the language, *Eleanor Rumming* pleases (if it pleases at all) because of its virtuosity. One doesn't think about the poem, one only takes it in."[8]

The distaste, if not outright disgust, of both Renaissance and modern critics originates in the poem's unsparing physicality, especially its treatment of the female body. Lewis sums up the poem thus: "We have noisome details about Elinor's methods of brewing, and there are foul words, foul breath, and foul sights in plenty. The merit of the thing lies in its speed: guests are arriving hotfoot, ordering, quarrelling, succumbing to the liquor, every moment. We get a vivid impression of riotous bustle, chatter, and crazy disorder."[9] The poem is meaningless and gross, meaningless *because* it is gross. Such Christian interpreters as Arthur F. Kinney and Robert D. Newman agree that the poem's treatment of the body is vile, but they try to rescue *Elynour Rummynge* by reading it as an orthodox condemnation of sin.[10] Feminist critics also condemn the poem, but in place of a description of vice, a topers' Mass, or a mindless series of images, Elizabeth Fowler, Gail K. Paster, and Linda Woodbridge interpret *Elynour Rummynge*'s descriptions of the female body as a rehearsal of either clerical antifeminist satire or more generalized masculine fears of women meeting together.[11]

Now, to our sensibilities, Skelton's treatment of women *does* seem repulsive:[12]

> Her lewde lyppes twayne,
> They slaver, men sayne,
> Lyke a ropy rayne,
> A gummy glayre
> She is ugly fayre:
> Her nose somdele hoked
> And camously croked,
> Never stoppynge
> But ever droppynge;
> Her skynne lose and slacke,
> Greuyned lyke a sacke;
> With a croked backe.

Only a mother could love such a face. But how to interpret Elynour's ugliness remains less obvious than critics have assumed. On the one hand, Elynour's looks can be interpreted as sign of evil. Deborah Wyrick, for example, notes that Elynour's features correspond to "the archetype of the *maleficus*." Along these lines, Kinney also suggests that the poem describes a witch's sabbath that burlesques the Resurrection, the Crucifixion, and other church rituals.[13]

However, it is exactly Elynour's physical appearance that provides the key to a more sympathetic, more complex view of this work. Rather than interpreting Elynour's visage using the conventional standards of beauty or orthodox Christianity, I want to argue that Elynour's startling appearance begs to be interpreted through the lens of what Mikhail Bakhtin, in *Rabelais and His World,* terms "grotesque realism."[14] In other words, instead of judging Skelton's representations of the female body as evidence of personal or cultural misogyny, I suggest we consider that he challenges conventional expectations by turning Elynour and her customers into vessels, albeit leaky ones, for the festive values of transgression, contestation, and inversion. The alehouse itself clearly constitutes a festive marketplace writ small, a delimited area where holiday license rules amid the noise and confusion. But at the same time, Skelton's text is far from monological, and just as one strand valorizes Elynour, another draws us away from unqualified sympathy with the denizens of the alehouse, making *Elynour Rummynge* a much more difficult, much more *dialogical,* to invoke another of Bakhtin's terms, work whose thematic range comprehends both gender and the nature of interpretation.[15] However, we first need to locate *Elynour Rummynge* within the discourse of grotesque realism. Although the general outlines of Bakhtin's theories are by now quite familiar, I shall briefly rehearse his morphology, partially for the sake of clarity, but also because in recent years the linguistic Bakhtin has displaced the Bakhtin of *Rabelais and His World.*

Bakhtin defines carnival as "the suspension of all hierarchical rank, privileges, norms and prohibitions." Not only suspension but also inversion of power relationships mark carnival: the woman rules the man, the student whips the teacher, the ass drives the man, the mouse chases the cat, and so on.[16] Festive transgressions include the disruptions of physical as well as political or social boundaries, and the bodily images in Rabelais illustrate what Bakhtin calls "the concept of grotesque realism." Just as carnival challenges the social order, the grotesque body, Bakhtin writes, "is not a closed, completed unit; it is unfinished, outgrows itself, transgresses its own limits."[17] More precisely, if one can be precise about something whose essence lies in mutability: "The grotesque body . . . is a body in the act of becoming. It is never finished, never completed; it is continually built, created, and builds and creates another body. . . . [I]t outgrows its own self, transgressing its won body." The classical body, on the other hand, is constructed in the opposite fashion. Where the grotesque body emphasizes and celebrates its porousness, "[a]ll orifices of the [classical] body are closed"; where perpetual flux marks the grotesque body, "[the classical body] presents an entirely finished, completed, strictly limited body." And where the ideology underlying the classical body privileges the upper body, the mind, the head, to the denigration of the lower strata (i.e., the genitalia and the anus), the grotesque body privileges "the material acts and eliminations of the body—eating, drinking, defecation, sexual life" because the body finds renewal in these activites. The grotesque foregrounds and exaggerates the anus and the phallus because dung is recycled as fertilizer, eating restores life, sex creates life, and so on. Consequently, the activities of the grotesque body center on the areas of "interchange." The classical body, on the other hand, is constructed as "opaque," denying and hiding the seepages that distinguish the grotesque body.

Bakhtin's theories of carnival and the grotesque have not gone unchallenged, and Peter Stallybrass's modifications are particularly relevant to my argument. Stallybrass rightly points out that even though Bakhtin concentrates on class, not gender, he nonetheless leaves himself open to be critiqued for not bothering to "gender" the body described above, for assuming that the ungendered body will of course be a male body.[18] Stallybrass then argues that the distinction between the grotesque and the classical body very much concerns gender because of the widespread assumption that the female body is ipso facto grotesque, that "[i]t must be subjected to constant surveillance precisely because, as Bakhtin says of the grotesque body, it is 'unfinished, outgrows itself, transgresses its own limits.'"[19] Now, both Bakhtin and Stallybrass focus on post-1530 texts, assuming that the cultural discourses they talk about come after the early Henrician era. Stallybrass, for example, cites Norbert Elias, who documents in *The History of Manners* the creations of new kinds of behavior that will go under the rubric of *civilité*. According to Elias, these developments will follow in the wake of Erasmus's *De civilitate morum puerilium* (1530; first published in English, 1531).[20] In other words, critics appear to have assumed that Skelton predates the transformation of the body into a locus of class and gender conflict, thereby ruling out the possibility of analyzing his texts using the same theoretical paradigms. However, even though Bakhtin defeminizes, as it were, the grotesque body through his masculinist assumptions, his analysis contains two salient points. First, the tradition of grotesque realism vastly predates the 1530s, and Bakhtin cites many examples taken from late antiquity and the Middle Ages. Second, the earliest expression of this tradition uses the female body as its vehicle. Bakhtin found the principle of grotesque realism first embodied in the Kerch terracotta figurines of naked, laughing, senile hags. To understand the full complexity of Skelton's treatment of women, we need to recognize the validity of the misogynist traditions brought to bear by Kinney or Wyrick *and* to reinscribe these women back into the discourse of feminine grotesque realism that begins at least as far back as the Kerch terracottas, a discourse that for Skelton had not yet faded into obscurity.

Instead of judging Skelton's representations of the female body as evidence of personal or cultural misogyny, I suggest we consider that he challenges conventional expectations by turning Elynour and her customers into vessels, albeit leaky ones, for the festive values of transgression, contestation, and inversion.

—Peter C. Herman

The Tunnynge of Elynour Rummynge so perfectly fits Bakhtin's descriptions of grotesque realism that it seems as if Skelton magically used *Rabelais and His World* as a blueprint for his poem. The treatment of the body, says Bakhtin, constitutes the most important aspect of grotesque realism, and so let us begin there.

The proprietress of Skelton's imaginary tippling house establishes the standard that her customers will follow. As per Bakhtin's morphology, Elynour's body continuously overflows its limits. Her lips slaver, "lyke a ropy rayne," her nose never stops dripping, and her skin hangs loosely about her like a sack. Even though "her youth is farre past," yet she still "wyll jet, / Lyke a joyly fet" about the town in an ancient, threadbare coat, which is of course green, the color of life. And her brew so rejuvenates her and her mate that:

> Ich am not cast away,
> That can my husband say,
> Whan we kys and play
> In lust and in lyking.
> He calleth me his whytyng,
> His mullyng and his mytyng.

Like the Kerch terracottas that sparked Bakhtin's thinking, Elynour combines physical decrepitude with a sense of life, of renewal, and of joyful sexuality. As we have seen, her body refuses stability, various fluids (sweat, drool, nasal mucous) are perpetually seeping out of it and are reintroduced in the form of ale.

The bodies of Elynour's customers similarly refuse closure. Indeed, it seems that the abandonment of all corporeal boundaries acts as the price of admission into the tavern. The first group enters having thrown off the conventional means of restraining their breasts and their hair:

> Some wenches come unlased,
> Some huswyves come unbrased,
> Wyth theyr naked pappes,
> That flyppes and flappes
> It wygges and it wagges
> Lyke tawny saffron bagges.

Others arrive without "herelace, / Theyr lockes aboute theyr face / Theyr tresses untrust, / All full of unlust" or "Unbrased and unlast." Or if they come suitably reined in, upon entering this restraint quickly disappears:

> There came an old rybybe;
> She halted of a kybe,
> And had broken her shyn
> At the threshold comyng in,
> And fell so wyde open
> That one might see her token.

Nearly all are so ugly that they scarcely seem human. One Maude Ruggy "was ugly hypped, / And ugly thycke-lypped / Lyke an onyon syded, / Lyke tan ledder hyded." Another anonymous patron has a neck "lyke an olyfant; / It was a bullyfant, / A gredy cormerant." Margery Mylkeducke tucks her kirtel about an inch above her knee, so that:

Her legges that ye might se;
But they were sturdy and stubbed,
Myghty pestels and clubbed
As fayre and as whyte
As the fote of a kyte.
She was somwhat foule,
Crokenebbed lyke an oule.

And just as Elynour is always leaking one fluid or another, so do their bodies transgress their limits at every opportunity. Some "renne tyll they swete" to the alehouse; one's "mouth formed / And her bely groned." Another manages to combine nearly every form of physical and verbal seepage into one visit. She arrives "full of tales," which she gladly shares with the accompaniment of "snevelyng in her nose." Then, as Gail K. Paster neatly puts it, "having overflowed at one end, she proceeds to flow at the other."[21] After taking a long swig of ale, "She pyst where she stood. / Than began she to wepe." Like the anonymous tale-teller, the open pores are matched by open mouths. Elymour yells and swears at her customers and her customers yell and swear right back:

Jone sayd she had eten a fyest.
"By Chryst," sayde she, "thou lyest.
I have as swete a breath

As though, wyth shameful deth!"
Then Elynour sayde, "Ye calettes,
I shall breke your palettes,
Wythout ye now cease!"
And so was made the peace.

In his analysis of the Kerch terracottas, Bakhtin isolates how these figures intertwine life and death: "It is pregnant death, a death that gives birth. . . . Life is shown its two-fold contradictory process; it is the epitome of incompleteness." Elynour herself, as we have seen, constantly transgresses the barrier between youth and old age. And the food brought to her establishment also straddles the border between ripeness and rottenness. To pay for her ale, Margery Mylkeducke totes along "A cantell of Essex chese [that] / Was well a fote thycke, / Full of magottes." Skelton depicts the cheese as grotesquely large (one foot thick), but more importantly, it is simultaneously wholesome and decaying, life-giving and poisonous. And Skelton concludes this section with the food singled out by Bakhtin as the most emblematic of grotesque realism: "trypes that stynkes." Tripes are so resonant (or redolent) because they combine the ambivalence of life's processes: intake and elimination, nutrition and excrement. In addition, tripes represents the near erasure of the boundary separating the swallower from the swallowed: "the belly does not only eat and swallow, it is also eaten, as tripe." Finally, tripes represent both death, because the animal had to be disembowelled, and life, because its consumption leads to regeneration: "Thus, in the image of tripe life and death, birth, excrement, and food are all drawn together and tied in one grotesque knot; this is the center of bodily topography in which the upper and lower stratum penetrate each other."

The same applies to the composition of Elynour's ale. On the one hand, Elynour touts her ale as a fountain of youth:

Drinke now whyle it is new;
And ye may it broke,
It shall make you loke
Yonger than ye be
Yeres two or thre,
For ye may prove it by me.

And she proves its virtues by providing scenes from her connubial erotic life. Now, the image of a sexually active Elynour appears grotesque in precisely the same way that the Kerch terracottas are grotesque; what I want to note here is that Skelton depicts Elynour's restorative ale as a carnivalesque food. Like tripes, her ale ties together rebirth and decay in a "grotesque knot" because Elynour's secret ingredient is chicken shit:

But let us turne playne,
There we lefte agayne.
For, as yll a patch as that,
The hennes ron in the mashfat;
For they go to roust,
Streyght over the ale-joust,
And donge, whan it commes,
In the ale tunnes.
Than Elynour taketh
The mashe bolle, and shaketh
The hennes donge awaye,
And skommeth it into a tray
Where as the yeest is,
With her maungy fystis.
And sometyme she blennes
The donge of her hennes
And the tale togyder.

. . . . .

For I may tell you,
I lerned it of a Jewe,
Whan I began to brewe,
And I have found it trew.

If one chooses to interpret this poem solely from the standpoint of orthodoxy, the source of this recipe only further condemns both Jews and Elynour. However, its Jewish origin only increases the complexity, the ambivalence, of the "grotesque knot." Jews were commonly associated with the death of the spirit, but Elynour's brew reinvigorates. Furthermore, the alliance between Elynour and her anonymous teacher is particularly apposite since the dominant powers marginalize and demonize both (the former for religious reasons, the latter because she is an unruly woman), and much of carnival's point lies in the reevaluation of the rigorously opposed and excluded.

Pigs function in this text in much the same way. At every opportunity, Skelton associates Elynour with swine. In his opening description, for example, Skelton compares Elynour's face to "a rost pygges eare, / Brystled with here," and her customers must compete with them for her brew:

With, "Hey, dogge, hay,
Have these hogges away!"

With, "Get me a staffe,
The swyne eat my draffe!
Stryke the hogges with a clubbe,
They have dronke up my swyllyng tubbe!"

If one opts to read the poem through the template of orthodoxy, the pigs, long a symbol of everything low and
bestial, suggest Elynour's own depravity. But as Stallybrass and White pointed out, "the pig". . . occupied a
focal symbolic place at the fair (and in the carnival)."[22]
Simultaneously demonized and praised for their ability to
ingest offal, for their skin's similarity to human skin, for
the closeness of their food to human food, they are both
among the most essential of barnyard animals and the most
hated.[23] Ironically, given the traditional Jewish view of
pigs, the two occupy the same ideological position as both
represent the socially peripheral, if not outrightly demonized, that in a carnivalesque universe becomes symbolically central—the Jew, because he gave Elynour his (or
her) "grotesque" recipe, pigs, because they challenge the
binary opposition between the human and the nonhuman.

It should be clear that all the elements of grotesque realism are not only copiously present in Skelton's text but
that each overlaps and reinforces the other. The drinking
and the physical coarseness suggest the pigs, whose carnivalesque overtones point us back toward the leaky,
droopy female bodies; the ale again brings us back to the
pigs, whose defecations remind us of the hens's, the tripe,
Elynour's Jewish teacher, and so on. In sum, nearly every
detail in this poem joins in the "grotesque knot" that firmly holds *The Tunnynge of Elynour Rummynge* within
the carnivalesque tradition. But when we have ascertained
that Skelton scrupulously inscribes Elynour and her customers within this discourse, the question arises as to what
sort of intervention, what sort of cultural work, this inscription performs.

By situating *Elynour Rummynge* within
the shift from a female-dominated to a
male-dominated beer industry, we can see
that the poem's cultural work goes
beyond mere satire or misogyny.

—Peter C. Herman

Critics and anthropologists have pointed out that carnival
and carnivalesque texts can serve to reinforce rather than
subvert the dominant social structures.[24] Festivity and festive
texts, to simplify the argument greatly, provide a "safety-
valve" for the release of tensions or resentments that might
otherwise build into an effective oppositional social movement, and so carnival preserves and strengthens the culture or the values that it ostensibly opposes. This interpretation has found recent support in the later work of Michel
Foucault, who in such works as *Discipline and Punish*
and *The History of Sexuality* argued that power operates

not so much by repressing opposition as by organizing
and producing it, and in Stephen Greenblatt's earlier model
(much indebted to Foucault) of an authority which produces subversions only to contain them. Thus, using this
mode of analysis, whatever challenges *Elynour Rummynge* delivers are contained by the degradation of women's
bodies, the reader's laughter, and by the reauthorization
of misogyny at the end of the text. But if the relationship
between carnival and contestation is more complicated than
Bakhtin initially allows, to assume that carnival is *always*
contained also oversimplifies the matter. Sometimes the
critiques are contained, sometimes not, and a considerable
body of evidence has been collected illustrating how carnival and carnivalesque texts can function effectively as
social critiques. As Michael D. Bristol writes, "Carnival
misrule is overt and deliberate, but, by accurately mimicking the pretensions of ruling families, the covert and possibly willful misrule of constituted authority is exposed."[25]
Natalie Z. Davis and Emmanuel Le Roy Ladurie have
both shown how carnivals have led to genuine political
upheavals, and Peter Stallybrass has written on the complicated relations between the carnivalesque Robin Hood
ballads and the dominant authorities.[26] I propose that Skelton's *The Tunnynge of Elynour Rummynge* also constitutes a similarly complicated, similarly festive intervention into the gender politics of the Henrician era.

Elynour Rummynge's most obvious target would be the
discourse of the closed, classical body soon to be codified
in such texts as Erasmus's *De civilitate.*[27] The leaky, droopy
bodies of the alehouse women, like their Jonsonian progeny, Ursula the pig-woman, not only destabilize the boundaries separating the body from the outer world, they privilege exactly those aspects of the body that Erasmus *et alii*
wish most to suppress.[28] Furthermore, their carnivalesque
bodies uncover the nexus where the construction of gender roles and the rules of politeness intersect. Thus, the
refusal of breast and hair restraints in the initial description of Elynour's customers suggests that *from the start*
these women are declaring their independence from the
cultural imperative to bind up, hide, and control the em-
blematically feminine parts of their bodies. Similarly, their
crude, loud (impolite) speech defies the patriarchal attempt to silence women.[29]

However, the text's grotesque realism also has a less obvious and more subtle focus: the place of women within a
dominantly male economy. First, Skelton transforms
Elynour's establishment into an exclusively female club.
Although the narrator initially describes the alehouse as
open to all kinds of people, so long as they are "all good
ale-drynkers," all of Elynour's customers are women, a fact
that would have appeared quite remarkable to Skelton's
original audience since there were no alehouses serving only
women.[30] Moreover, the popular ballads and carols that made
up Skelton's sources place at least some men, if only wait-
ers and bartenders, in the tavern.[31] None exclude men altogether, as Skelton does. The first to enter are "Kate, / Cysly
and Sare," then come "wenches" and "huswyves," then a
host of anonymous female patrons, "haltyng Jone," the
sniveling, urinating, tale-teller, Margery Mylkeducke, with
her huge Essex cheese, and Maude Ruggy. Furthermore,

going to the alehouse, according to the women in the poem, constitutes an act of defiance against male domination:

> Some go streyght thyder,
> Be it slaty or slyder;
> They holde the hye waye,
> They care not what men saye!

Elynour's husband remains the only male allowed to enter the poem's narrative, but even he constitutes an "absent presence" since Elynour only *talks* about him: he never actually sets foot in the ale-house. And since the spirit of carnival informs nearly every detail of this poem, Elynour's treatment of her husband suggests that she has become a "woman on top" insofar as she reverses the customary hierarchy by reducing her husband to a sexual object whose purpose is to service his wife and to praise her unstintingly. In other words, she casts him as the ideal wife.

Having created a women-only alehouse, Skelton then proceeds to feminize the alehouse's legal tender. In place of utilizing a money economy, Elynour's customers prefer to barter for their ale:

> In stede of coyne and monny
> Some brynge her a conny,
> And some a pot with honny,
> Some a salt, and some a spone,
> Some their hose, some their shone;
> Some ranne a good trot
> With a skellet or a pot.

The goods brought to the alehouse can be divided into roughly three categories, all of which emblematize the mandated and subservient roles of women within patriarchy. The first group consists of culinary items, foodstuffs and such cooking utensils as pots, frying pans, and cutlery. The next category consists of items that symbolize women's labor in general, but especially weaving and spinning:

> And some went so narrowe
> They layde to pledge theyr wharrowe,
> Theyr rybskyn and theyr spyndell,
> Theyr nedell and theyr thymbell.

Another group brings in a "sylke lace," a pincase, a "pyllowe of downe" and "some of the nappery," while other women enter with "a skeyne of threde, / And . . . skeyne of yarne." Finally, a number of women bring their husbands' property and even the symbols of their marriages for swapping. One women offers "Her hernest gyrdle, her weddynge rynge," while "some bryngeth her husbandis hood". . . / Another brought her his cap / To offer to the ale tap."

True, Elynour's customers appear to take whatever they can lay their hands on to satisfy their dipsomania, but they are also challenging patriarchy in a number of very interesting ways. First, the women are fashioning a precapitalist economy in which goods circulate through bartering rather than money. By deliberately ("In stede of coyne and monny") returning to an older form of economy in which women had more opportunities for empowerment than in the later money-based economy, the text's women seem to be undoing the economic process by which they were increasingly marginalized.[32] In addition, the bartering system itself has contestatory overtones because the women trade in symbols of female labor and subjugation. In an analogous fashion to how the grotesque realism of their bodies challenges women's subservient role, bringing these symbols within the festive confines of the alehouse/marketplace allows these women the freedom to *invert* these emblems of female disempowerment, to first metamorphose them into a currency of their own and then utilize it to buy a product made by a woman for women. In sum, the pins, pans, and wedding rings that Elynour's customers barter for their drinks are more than simple domestic items, they are the constitutive elements of an autonomous, exclusively female economy that challenges the increasing marginalization of women.

Skelton's use of grotesque realism in his depiction of female bodies and his invention of a contestatory female economy takes on further point when one situates them within the history of women's labor. The historicizing of ***Elynour Rummynge*** conventionally begins and ends with the identification of Elynour with one "Alianora Romyng," a "common tippellar of ale" who was fined in 1525 for selling her product at "at excessive price by small measures," the ruling interpretation being that Elynour is as criminal as her real-life counterpart.[33] The identification of Elynour with a dishonest woman remains significant (we shall return to it below), but we need to complicate the easy interpretation by looking at the position of women ale-brewers circa 1520.

From the twelfth to about the end of the fifteenth century, the production of ale was (given a certain amount of regional fluctuation) a predominantly female activity. According to Peter Clark, in the early thirteenth century almost all of Wallingford's fifty or sixty brewers were women, and a century later the proportions had not significantly altered, the records showing only four male brewers as compared to over fifty women. And Wallingford does not represent an atypical example.[34] Judith M. Bennett, in her study of the role of women in medieval Brigstock's industries, confirms that in the fourteenth century women made up the majority of those involved in the brewing and selling of ale.[35] By the end of the 1400s, the alewife had started to become a stock figure in literature, as evidenced by the appearance of the dishonest brewster in the Chester mystery cycle lamenting her lot from hell:[36]

> Of cans I kept no true measure
> My cups I sold at my pleasure
> Deceiving many a creature
> Though my ale was nought

The pronouns employed in the various bylaws regulating the cost and quality of ale testify to the degree to which women dominated the brewing industry. Whereas the laws pertaining to other industries (e.g., textiles or baking) assume that they will apply to men, the laws directed at the brewing industry consistently employ feminine pronouns (i.e., brewster, not brewer).[37]

How much the feminization of brewing contributed to the empowerment of women remains in dispute. Bennett, for example, argues that the preponderance of female brewers did not contribute significantly to the betterment of their situation because the complexity and the expense of this enterprise necessitated marriage and a full household. Single women could not raise the capital to buy the necessary ingredients or do all the work brewing required. Consequently, "Ale-wives were classic female workers: their work changed with shifts in marital status, their work was relatively low-skilled, their work was unpredictable and unsteady, and their work was highly sensitive to male economic priorities (and susceptible to male incursions)."[38] However, others suggest that the female near-monopoly on brewing did contribute materially to female empowerment. Alice Clark asserts that the later exclusion of women from the trade "seriously reduced [the] opportunities [open to women] for earning an independence."[39] And Rodney Hilton argues that marriage notwithstanding, brewing allowed women to enjoy a not insignificant amount of independence, even legal standing. Hilton cites manorial court records indicating that "a considerable body of pleadings . . . seems to have been conducted by women in their own names and only rarely through attorneys." Furthermore, despite the political marginalization of women during the Middle Ages (and the Renaissance), women were allowed to become official ale-tasters.[40]

The crucial event that led to the defeminization of the ale trade was the introduction of hops into the brewing process in the late fourteenth century, which allowed beer (as the drink was now called) to last much longer without souring.[41] The exact relationship between this innovation and the professionalization of the industry remains unclear; nonetheless, the two developments coincide with each other, and it seems likely that the discovery of beer's commercial viability resulted in women's being pushed out of this suddenly more profitable enterprise.[42] Alice Clark has suggested that the seventeenth century witnessed the exclusion of women from brewing, but one can see this movement starting to begin within the late fifteenth century as well. The establishment of guilds and monopoly usually meant the exclusion of women from profitable trades, a process especially evident in the beer industry.[43] In 1464, for example, a group approached the mayor and aldermen of London with a petition asking for more official recognition of their trade; significantly, they refer to themselves as "bruers of Bere," using the masculine term, not the feminine "brewster."[44] On September 24, 1493, the brewers were officially recognized as a guild, and their request assumes that the master brewers would be men, not women (e.g., "That no member take into his service any one who had been proved by the Fellowship to be an 'untrue or a decyvable servaunt in myscarying or mystailling' between his master and his customers").[45]

Even though the brewing industry underwent considerable growth throughout Henry's reign, the independent female producer began to die out.[46] Women were not banned from the industry, but because the guilds allowed

only men to become masters, they tended to be relegated to positions of inferiority. For example, the records of a late-fifteenth-century guild feast record that "2 women [were] engaged to draw the ale in the buttery for 2 days and 2 others . . . were kept busy washing and cleaning dishes." A century earlier, those women might have been paid to produce the ale; now, however, they hold the same position as dishwashers.[47] In sum, the actual position of women within the trade steadily deteriorated as the industry became more formalized, more professionalized, a trend which only accelerated during the later Tudor and Stuart eras.[48]

By situating *Elynour Rummynge* within the shift from a female-dominated to a male-dominated beer industry, we can see that the poem's cultural work goes beyond mere satire or misogyny. Elynour represents a type that by Skelton's time was already an endangered species—the independent female producer of ale and beer. In all probability, the text's first audience would have recognized Skelton's originality because his sources always present women as consumers, never as producers, a convention that will obtain well into the seventeeth century.[49] In sum, notwithstanding the popularity of the literary topos of the alewife, Skelton's poem intervenes in the gradual exclusion of women from this industry by representing activities that sound for all the world like an early modern economic self-help group. By setting up a business run by a woman only for women, a business not dependent upon masculine capital or patronage, Elynour keeps herself in business while the other women of the beer industry were being pushed out.

The text's protofeminism exhibits itself, then, in two complementary ways. Just as the carnivalesque representation of female bodies contests patriarchal attempts at enclosure and control, the precapitalist barter system of the alehouse resists women's economic disempowerment. The combination of the two suggests that Elynour's alehouse performs roughly the same function as the women's clubs described by the anthropologist Ernest Crawley in *The Mystic Rose.* After enumerating several primitive male associations designed to keep women in subjection, Crawley then shows how the opposite side returned the favor: "Women in their turn form such organisations amongst themselves, in which, for instance, they discuss their wrongs and form plans of revenge. Mpongwe women have an institution of this kind which is really feared by the men. Similarly amongst the Bakalais and other African tribes."[50] Like these clubs, Elynour's alehouse forms a kind of society of consolation, but instead of plotting physical retributions for wrongs done, this "club" supports women's business ventures as well as translates symbols of female oppression into a currency supporting female independence.[51]

However, if there are many elements of this text that valorize female autonomy, it contains important qualifying elements as well. Most obviously, Skelton uses the name of a woman who was hauled into court and fined for dishonesty, which strongly suggests that the poem's immediate audience would catch the reference and judge Skelton's

Elynour accordingly. Also, the life-affirming aspects of grotesque realism are balanced, if not subverted, by the narrator's repeated assertions that these women are sexually repulsive. Elynour's face, all "Scurvey and lowsy" would "aswage / A mannes courage." Maude Ruggy is so "ugly hypped, / And ugly thycke-lypped" that "Ones hed wold have aked / To se her naked." And a third anonymous "dant" "was nothynge plesant; / Necked lyke an olyfant; / It was a bullyfant, / A gredy cormerant." Furthermore, the narrator makes his disgust with these ladies apparent at every opportunity. At one point he describes them as a "rabell," frequently calls them foul sluts, and associates them with the devil. For example, the narrator says that "The devyll and she [Elynour] be syb," a customer "could make a charme / To helpe withall a stytch; / She semed to be a wytch," and when another customer stumbles, exposing her "token," the narrator exclaims "The devyll thereon be wroken!" Finally, Skelton's Latin colophon interprets the poem as a tirade against the wicked and invites the guilty to listen and learn: "All women who are either very fond of drinking, or who bear the dirty stain of filth, or who have the sordid blemish of squalor, or who are marked out by garrulous loquacity, the poet invites to listen to this little satire. Drunken, filthy, sordid, gossiping woman, let her run here, let her hasten, let her come; this little satire will willingly record her deeds: Apollo, sounding his lyre, will sing the theme of laughter in a hoarse song" (Scattergood trans.).

The narrative stance of this text, a masculine "I" reporting on an exclusively feminine gathering and then turning to the reader at the end with an antifeminist moralization, is a common motif of this genre. William Dunbar, for example, uses this technique in his roughly contemporary *Tretis of the tua mariit Wemen and the Wedo,* and one also finds it in the late-fifteenth-century ballad, *A Talk of Ten Wives on their Husbands Ware.*[52] As Linda Woodbridge suggests, the eavesdropping motif implies, at the very least, male curiosity about what women do when they are alone, and more probably, considerable anxiety at the thought of autonomous women.[53] Critics have tended to assume that Skelton's text follows this convention to the letter, that the voice of the colophon represents a misogynist authorial intention. In other words, the narrative "I" and the Latinate voice are coterminous and meant to be taken as authoritative. This view, however, needs complicating because Skelton's text repeatedly calls attention to the role gender plays in the formulation of the "I"'s and the audience's views.

Elynour's looks would "aswage / A *Mannes* courage," "A *man* wolde have pytty" to see her gums, "As *men* say," Elynour lives in Surrey (my emphasis). Having established at the start that the "I"'s reactions are not neutral but masculine, Skelton then masculinizes the audience. What women say about Elynour, we may assume, does not count because women do not make up this poem's audience. They are not part of the "one" whose heads would have ached to see Maude Ruggy naked. And the invitation to listen and learn (although the colophon sounds more like an invitation to abuse) would perforce fall on uncomprehending female ears because Elynour and her customers, on account of their relative poverty and their gender, were barred from having an education. In general, only men had access to the "universal" language, Latin.

Now, the gendering of audience and narrator cuts two ways. Certainly, one could argue that the text shows no sign of irony, that Skelton intended his audience to regard Elynour and company with contempt. However, another view also presents itself as equally plausible—by rendering explicit the gender of both audience and narrator, Skelton also renders explicit the conditions of interpretation by forcing us to recognize that both the narrative "I"'s and the implied reader's reactions are grounded in their masculinity, not objective reality. The question implied, then, by the opening emphasis on what men say or think is whether or not *women* might agree. By raising the possibility of difference, Skelton reminds us that interpretations are not universally valid but contingent upon any number of factors, not the least of course being gender. Given that the few critics who have looked seriously at *Elynour Rummynge* all agree on its misogyny, my own interpretation may sound more fanciful than plausible, but this process also occurs in *Elynour Rummynge*'s companion poem.

Susan Schibanoff has cogently argued that in *Phyllyp Sparrowe* Skelton involves us "in the conscious examination of how we are actually reading," and I would argue that the same project informs *Elynour Rummynge.*[54] In *Phyllyp Sparrowe,* Jane illustrates how gender can govern reading through her (re)readings of medieval and liturgical texts.[55]

Rewriting in her own image, an important part of which is her sex, Jane models her grief on that of two female mourners, Thisbe and Mary. As a reading woman, she has, in other words, rewritten the placebo, the psalm subtitled "the prayer of the just man in affliction," to give herself the role of a female mourner. And Skelton has enormously empowered this fictional female reader to make a place for herself in the predominantly male world of textuality. In her text she can even transform Gyb, the familiar tomcat of earlier vernacular literature, into a female.

But having given with one hand, Skelton then takes away with the other by reclaiming ownership of Jane's text "and arrogates to himself the exclusive control of her body."[56] In *The Tunnynge of Elynour Rummynge,* Skelton applies analogous strategies. He first valorizes the alehouse's women by situating them within a contestatory tradition but then condemns them for their trangressiveness.[57] He inscribes numerous testimonials to the women's sexual and moral repulsiveness, but then he brackets these testimonials by ascribing them to the masculine gender, suggesting at least the possibility that a feminine interpretation of Elynour, like Jane's interpretation of the tradition, might be different. Finally, just as *Phyllyp Sparrowe* moves in the end to comment upon reading, *Elynour Rummynge* follows suit by suggesting how the text's use of grotesque realism parallels a concern with the text's interpretations of itself and of narrative in general.

To conclude, then, *The Tunnynge of Elynour Rummynge* moves in two directions simultaneously, and the trick in reading this poem is not to totalize it into either an expression of misogyny *or* a carnivalesque challenge to male hegemony. To claim that the text belongs exclusively to either discourse, the reader would have to repress necessary evidence, and so *Elynour Rummynge* privileges neither reading while insisting upon the partiality of any interpretation. Thus Skelton's text works in a fundamentally different manner than other examples of grotesque realism but rather similarly to *Elynour Rummynge*'s companion poem, *Phyllyp Sparrowe.*[58] The carnivalesque construction of female bodies is undeniably qualified by the disgusting physical details of the poem and the misogyny of both the narrator's asides and the colophon, in which Skelton's "I" re-presents the alehouse's women as objects of ridicule. But at the same time, the "I"'s judgments are not objectively valid either, since they stem from a masculine perspective. Furthermore, the narrator, or even the reader, may not much like or be attracted to the alehouse's women, but the very act of representing independent women, especially, given the conditions of the beer industry circa 1520, an independent producer of ale, grants them a legitimacy that cannot be entirely contained. *The Tunnynge of Elynour Rummynge,* then, should not be considered a purely carnivalesque or a purely antifeminist text but rather an unstable, complex mixture of both.

Notes

[1] Although the editors of the *Norton Anthology* grant that Skelton is a "major" poet, they are among the few who mention him without condescension. For example, Roy Lamson and Hallett Smith cite Skelton's "roughness, his vulgarity, and his mediaeval prolixity" as reasons for his obscurity over the ages (*The Golden Hind* [New York: Norton, 1956], 16). John Williams damns Skelton with faint praise. He is a "primitive" poet, but "within the limits of that primitivism . . . [his poetry is] always skillful and frequently moving" (*English Renaissance Poetry: A Collection of Shorter Poems from Skelton to Jonson* [Garden City: Anchor Books, 1963], 1).

[2] As Greg Walker reminds us, at the time that Erasmus penned his eulogy he could not read English and probably had never heard of Skelton before. Furthermore, in 1519, Erasmus created a list of the distinguished scholars who graced the court of Henry VIII, and Skelton is not among them (*John Skelton and the Politics of the 1520s* [Cambridge: Cambridge University Press, 1988], 40-41).

[3] Quoted in Anthony S. G. Edwards, *Skelton: The Critical Heritage* (London: Routledge and Kegan Paul, 1981), 61.

[4] Quoted in ibid., 16-17.

[5] John M. Berdan, *Early Tudor Poetry: 1485-1547* (New York: Macmillan, 1931), 215.

[6] Susan Staub, "Recent Studies in Skelton (1970-1988)," *English Literary Renaissance* 20 (1990), 505-16. Actually, Staub omits the solitary (albeit very short) publication on *The Tunnynge of Elynour Rummynge:* Robert D. Newman, "The Visual Nature of Skelton's 'The Tunnynge of Elynour Rummyng,'" *College Literature* 12 (1985), 135-40.

[7] C. S. Lewis, *English Literature in the Sixteenth Century, Excluding Drama* (London: Oxford University Press, 1954), 138.

[8] Stanley E. Fish, *John Skelton's Poetry* (New Haven: Yale University Press, 1965), 251 and 255.

[9] Lewis, *English Literature in the Sixteenth Century,* 138.

[10] Arthur F. Kinney, *John Skelton, Priest as Poet: Seasons of Discovery* (Chapel Hill: University of North Carolina Press, 1987), 172.

[11] Elizabeth Fowler, "Elynour Rummynge and Lady Mede: The Sexual Conduct of the Money Economy" (paper presented at the International Congress on Medieval Studies, Kalamazoo, Mich., 1989), 2; Linda Woodbridge, *Women and the English Renaissance: Literature and the Nature of Womankind, 1540-1620* (Urbana: University of Illinois Press, 1984), 225; Gail Kern Paster, "The Incontinent Women of City Comedy," *Renaissance Drama* 18 (1987), 51. I am grateful to Fowler for allowing me to read her paper and to make use of it.

[12] All references to Skelton's poems are to *John Skelton: The Complete English Poems,* ed. John Scattergood (New Haven: Yale University Press, 1983).

[13] Deborah B. Wyrick, "'Within that Develes Temple': An Examination of Skelton's *The Tunnynge of Elynour Rummynge,*" *Journal of Medieval and Renaissance Studies* 10 (1980), 249-50; Kinney, *John Skelton,* 177-79.

[14] Using Bakhtin to analyze Skelton seems anachronistic until one realizes that "grotesque realism" is a tradition that stretches back to antiquity and to which Skelton belongs (Mikhail Bakhtin, *Rabelais and His World,* trans. Michael Holquist [Bloomington: Indiana University Press, 1984]; all further references will be given parenthetically).

[15] By *dialogical,* I mean to apply Bakhtin's sense that each utterance contains within it competing definitions for the same things. In this case, the competing definitions that defy a centralized, unitary meaning would apply to the different interpretations of Elynour and her customers. See Mikhail Bakhtin, *The Dialogic Imagination: Four Essays,* trans. Caryl Emerson and Michael Holquist (Austin: University of Texas Press, 1981), 272, and the editors' definition of *dialogical* in the accompanying glossary (426-27).

[16] I have in mind the illustrations of the *mundus inversus* reproduced and analyzed by David Kunzle in "World Upside Down: The Iconography of a European Broadsheet Type," in *The Reversible World,* ed. Barbara Babcock (Ithaca: Cornell University Press, 1978), 39-94.

[17] I am assuming here that the subversions of licensed misrule are not either necessarily or completely contained by the dominant culture.

[18] Peter Stallybrass, "Patriarchal Territories: The Body Enclosed," in *Rewriting the Renaissance: The Discourses of Sexual Difference in Early Modern Europe,* ed. Margaret W. Ferguson, Maureen Quilligan, and Nancy J. Vickers (Chicago: University of Chicago Press, 1986), 125. For a very different view of the grotesque, see Geoffrey G. Harpham, *On the Grotesque: Strategies in Art and Literature* (Princeton: Princeton University Press, 1982). Harpham understands the grotesque as occupying the margins, neither inside nor outside, neither art nor non-art; it is, as Harpham says, "a species of confusion" (xxi). Although I find Harpham's arguments provocative, he is more concerned with the aesthetics of the grotesque than with their social and political implications.

[19] Stallybrass, "Patriarchal Territories," 126, and Bakhtin, *Rabelais,* 26.

[20] Stallybrass, "Patriarchal Territories," 124-25.

[21] Paster, "Incontinent Women of City Comedy," 51.

[22] Peter Stallybrass and Allon White, *The Politics and Poetics of Transgression* (Ithaca: Cornell University Press, 1986), 44.

[23] Ibid., 46-47.

[24] See, for example, C. L. Barber, *Shakespeare's Festive Comedies: A Study of Dramatic Form* (New York: Meridian Books, 1963); Emile Durkheim, *The Elementary Forms of the Religious Life,* trans. J. Swain (London: George Allen and Unwin, 1982); Victor Turner, *Dramas, Fields, and Metaphors: Symbolic Action in Human Society* (Ithaca: Cornell University Press, 1974) and *The Ritual Process: Structure and Anti-Structure* (Ithaca: Cornell University Press, 1977).

[25] Michael D. Bristol, *Carnival and Theater: Plebeian Culture and the Structure of Authority in Renaissance England* (New York: Routledge, 1985). The same paradigm also applies to the exposure of rule as role in Shakespeare's history plays. See, for example, David Scott Kastan, "Proud Majesty Made a Subject: Shakespeare and the Spectacle of Rule," *Shakespeare Quarterly* 37 (1986), 459-75, and Peter C. Herman, "'O, 'tis a Gallant King': Shakespeare's *Henry V* and the Crisis of the 1590s," in *Tudor Political Culture: Ideas, Images and Action,* ed. Dale Hoak (Cambridge: Cambridge University Press, forthcoming).

[26] Natalie Z. Davis, *Society and Culture in Early Modern France* (1975; reprint, Stanford: Stanford University Press, 1987), 97-151; Emmanuel Le Roy Ladurie, *Carnival in Romans,* trans. Mary Feeney (New York: G. Braziller, 1979); Peter Stallybrass, "'Drunk with the Cup of Liberty': Robin Hood, the Carnivalesque, and the Rhetoric of Violence in Early Modern England," in *The Violence of Representation: Literature and the History of Violence* (London: Routledge, 1989), 45-76.

[27] Stallybrass and White, *Politics and Poetics of Transgression,* 64.

[28] On Ursula as the embodiment of the material bodily principle, see ibid., 64-66, and Jonathan Haynes, "Festivity and the Dramatic Economy of Jonson's *Bartholomew Fair,*" *ELH* 51 (1984), 647.

[29] In this sense, *The Tunnynge of Elynour Rummynge* is a protofeminist text rather than solely an expression of cultural misogyny. On the justifications for calling Renaissance literature feminist (or even protofeminist) long before the term actually existed, see Constance Jordan, *Renaissance Feminism: Literary Texts and Political Models* (Ithaca: Cornell University Press, 1990), 1-10.

[30] Peter Clark, *The English Alehouse: A Social History* (London: Longman, 1983), 131-32.

[31] R. H. Robbins, "John Crophill's Ale-Pots," *Review of English Studies* 20 (1969), 182-89; "How Gossip myne," in *The Early English Carols,* ed. Richard I. Greene (Oxford: Clarendon Press, 1935), 280-84; and "Four Witty Gossips," *The Pepys Ballads,* ed. H. E. Rollins (Cambridge: Harvard University Press, 1929), 174-79. The only critical survey of alewife literature remains Woodbridge, *Women and the English Renaissance,* 224-43.

[32] On the increasing exclusion of women from the European and English work force throughout the 1400s and early 1500s, see David Herlihy, *Opera Mulieria: Women and Work in Medieval Europe* (New York: McGraw-Hill, 1990), 178-80. Although the barter economy dominated the rural areas until much later in the century, the towns (like Leatherhead, Surrey) and cities had a money economy (W. G. Hoskins,

The Age of Plunder: King Henry's England 1500-1547 [London: Longman, 1976], 225).

[33] See Fowler, "Elynour Rummynge and Lady Mede," 4-5, and Kinney, *John Skelton,* 167. The citation is quoted in Edwards, *Critical Heritage,* 115; in Kinney, *John Skelton,* 167; and in Scattergood's notes for this poem.

[34] Peter Clark, *English Alehouse,* 21.

[35] Judith M. Bennett, "The Village Ale-Wife: Women and Brewing in Fourteenth-Century England," in *Women and Work in Preindustrial Europe,* ed. Barbarba A. Hanawalt (Bloomington: Indiana University Press, 1986), 22-23.

[36] Quoted in Peter Clark, *English Alehouse,* 30.

[37] Alice Clark, *The Working Life of Women in the Seventeenth Century* (London: George Routledge, 1919), 221-22.

[38] Bennett, "Village Ale-Wife," 24-25 and 30. See also Herlihy, *Opera Mulieria,* 190.

[39] Alice Clark, *Working Life of Women,* 228.

[40] H. Hilton, *The English Peasantry in the Later Middle Ages* (Oxford: Clarendon Press, 1975), 104-5.

[41] Bennett, "The Village Ale-Wife," 35, n. 32.

[42] On the reduction of the numbers of brewers in the fifteenth century and the gradual professionalization of the industry, see Christopher Dyer, *Lords and Peasants in a Changing Society: The Estates of the Bishopric of Worcester, 680-1540* (Cambridge: Cambridge University Press, 1980), 347.

[43] Herlihy, *Opera Mulieria,* 196-87.

[44] Quoted in Herbert A. Monckton, *A History of English Ale and Beer* (London: Bodley Head, 1966), 68. Cf. Alice Clark, *Working Life of Women,* 225-33.

[45] Quoted in Monckton, *History of English Ale,* 70-71.

[46] Hoskins, *Age of Plunder,* 231.

[47] Monckton, *History of English Ale,* 81.

[48] On the professionalization of the beer industry, see Peter Clark, *English Alehouse,* 14.

[49] E.g., Samuel Rowlands, *'Tis Merry When Gossips Meet* (London, 1602).

[50] Ernest Crawley, *The Mystic Rose: A Study of Primitive Marriage and of Primitive Thought in Its Bearing on Marriage,* ed. Theodore Besterman, 2 vols. (New York: Boni and Liveright, 1927), vol. 1, 55. Woodbridge, citing this passage, thinks that *Elynour Rummynge* and all the other Good Gossip poems suggest "male apprehensiveness that women, intractable enough as individuals, might begin making a habit of banding together to improve their lot" (*Women and the English Renaissance,* 241-42).

[51] Perhaps because he found himself marginalized during his life, in his

poetry Skelton repeatedly and sympathetically deals with liminal characters who trangress boundaries. Susan Schibanoff, for example, persuasively reads *Phyllyp Sparrowe,* which is commonly taken as a companion poem to *Elynour Rummynge* (e.g., H. L. R. Edwards, *Skelton: The Life and Times of an Early Tudor Poet* [London: Cape, 1949], 212), as a text that empowers the female reader by presenting Jane, whose marginality rests in her gender and her age, rewriting the canon so as to privilege the feminine ("Taking Jane's Cue: *Phyllyp Sparrowe* as a Primer for Women Readers," *PMLA* 101 [1986], 835 and 834). The same paradigm functions in the satires as well. Richard Halpern notes that even though *Ware the Hawk* directs its anger at the falconer who violates the Church's boundaries, the poem's "gay destructiveness delights in the violation of boundaries and in the consequent evaporation of the authority constituted by them" (*The Poetics of Primitive Accumulation: English Renaissance Culture and the Genealogy of Capital* [Ithaca: Cornell University Press, 1991], 112). On Skelton's rocky political career, see Walker's important revisionary work, *John Skelton and the Politics of the 1520s,* cited above, n. 2.

[52] *A Talk of Ten Wives on their Husbands' Ware,* in *Jyl of Brentford's Testament,* ed. F. J. Furnivall (London: Taylor, 1871); William Dunbar, *Poems,* ed. James Kinsley (Oxford: Clarendon Press, 1958).

[53] Woodbridge, *Women and the English Renaissance,* 236.

[54] Schibanoff, "Taking Jane's Cue," 835.

[55] Ibid., 834.

[56] Ibid., 841.

[57] Ibid., 841.

[58] One could argue that by setting the "protofeminist" and "misogynist" strands in the text against each other, I have created a false dichotomy because such double-edged treatment is typical of the carnivalesque tradition, that it always degrades while it celebrates. Although this paradigm may accurately describe (and I am not sure that it does) such other examples as Chaucer's Wife of Bath, Rabelais, and Jonson's Ursula, these texts lack *Elynour Rummynge's* overtly misogynist narrator and the most uncarnivalesque Latinate voice in the colophon. In this text, Skelton departs from the tradition by separating the two edges, as it were, and then pitting one against the other.

Celia R. Daileader (essay date 1996)

SOURCE: "When a Sparrow Falls: Woman Readers, Male Critics, and John Skelton's *Phyllyp Sparowe,*" in *Philological Quarterly,* Vol. 75, No. 4, Fall, 1996, pp. 391-409.

[*In the following essay, Daileader provides a stylistic and thematic analysis of Skelton's Phyllyp Sparowe.*]

In the lush, wild terrain of John Skelton's ***Phyllyp Sparowe,*** the few paths laid by critics are fraught with pitfalls. Scholars who have taken up this initially charming but ultimately unsettling poem about a girl, a dead sparrow, and a lascivious poet, have been hampered by two questions. Firstly, how many "voices" does the poem contain? Three decades ago, Stanley Fish laid the groundwork for interpreting the poem in terms of two voices: the voice of "innocence" embodied in the persona of Jane Scrope, and

the voice of "experience" embodied in the persona of "Skelton, Poet Laureate," who breaks into the poem roughly halfway through, reminding us retroactively (and some might add, annoyingly) of his role in creating the child speaker of the sparrow's elegy.[1] Secondly, how are we to reconcile the religious and the erotic elements of the poem? The tension between these elements manifests itself not only in the apparently dichotomous first and second halves of the poem, but also in several corresponding dichotomies: the Catullan, phallic connotation of the "wanton" sparrow versus the biblical connotation of the sparrow whose fall is marked by God; Jane's apparent innocence versus her sensual delight at Phyllyp's provocative flutterings (and her perhaps naive references to sex); and Skelton's Marian language in the Commendacions versus their cupiditous overtones. Which of the foregoing elements should determine our approach to the work?

My answer to these questions is a resounding "all of the above," and I base this answer upon the text's collapsing of the artist/subject or creator/creature binarism. For Jane, like the speaker, is an artist herself: in her lament she re-creates and re-presents Phyllyp, while Skelton as poet simultaneously represents her; the three figures thus reflect one another in endlessly complex, often paradoxical ways. And this triptych, in unhinging one zero sum, brings on the collapse of other binarisms: man/woman; human/animal; sacred/profane; innocence/experience; redemption/sin. Thus the poem's central symbol and namesake, the sparrow, embodies not *either* lust or mortality, but *both*; he is Jane in miniature and hence he is also Skelton in miniature; in short, he is *humanity,* with all the weaknesses that name implies—the frailty which requires protection, the sinfulness which requires forgiving, the death which requires salvation. . . .

In the case of ***Phyllyp Sparowe*** we have, for the umpteenth time, a male poet depicting a female subject, and we have, in this essay, a female reader responding to her. As in any case of this sort, the feminist critic faces a "schizophrenic" task. First, she must take a more sympathetic approach to the female poetic subject, must never assume that we are getting "her side of the story"; that is the easy part, the part that comes, so to speak, naturally to women readers. Yet alongside this reflex, feminist critics must cultivate a counter-response which insists that the poetic "she" we may react to so viscerally, so empathetically, does not exist as such, that "she" is merely a creation of the male poet/poet-speaker, and hence reflects his own fantasies and biases—or rather, those of his culture. This last is particularly obvious in ***Phyllyp Sparowe,*** where the poet-speaker makes explicit his role in creating Jane:

Per me laurigerum
Britanum Skeltonida vatem
Hec cecinisse licet
Ficta sub imagine texta.

[I Skelton laureat, poet of Britain, have been permitted to sing this under an imaginary likeness.]

Although much criticism of the poem gestures toward the import of the above lines, few critics are willing to follow the passage to its fullest implications: that there is, technically, only one voice, that of the poet-speaker; that the poem does not consist of two diametrically opposed halves, one "Jane's" and one "Skelton's"; that questions regarding Jane's characteristics, her age, her maturity, her sexual "innocence" or lack thereof, are only relevant in light of why or why not "Skelton" would have us perceive such qualities in his heroine. And to be aware of these things is not to rule out a careful consideration of "Jane's" own experience, as the text presents it to us, for "Jane"—regardless of the poem's biographical resonances—had in Skelton's world and still has in our own *real relevance to real women* by virtue of the fact that readers want to make her real.

A feminist reading of ***Phyllyp Sparowe*** must therefore eschew the binarism of Fish's reading and look for connections rather than contrasts, elisions rather than interruptions, must look for places where the poet slips into his subject. One such moment occurs in the passage describing Jane's attempt to stitch an image of her lost sparrow, for her own "comfort" and "solace."

> But whan I was sowing his beke,
> Me thought my sparow did spek,
> And opened his prety byll,
> Saynge, 'Mayd, ye are in wyll
> Agayne me for to kyll!
> Ye prycke me in the head!'
> With that my nedle waxed red,
> Me thought, of Phyllyps blode.
> Myne hear ryght upstode,
> And was in suche a fray
> My speche was taken away.
> I kest downe that there was,
> And sayd, 'Alas, alas,
> How commeth this to pas?'
> My fyngers, dead and colde,
> Coude not my sampler holde;
> My nedle and threde
> I threwe away for drede.

Although we know that, in effect, Jane has been re-creating Phyllyp's image throughout her elegy, here we see her pick up a phallic instrument very like Skelton's stylus and attempt to sketch Phyllyp, as Skelton sketches Jane, on a blank text or rather textile (both from *textare,* to weave). The passage is so heavy with gender-play it is almost too good to be true: here Skelton reverses the familiar trope of male stylus and virgin female text, placing the phallic needle in female hands and gendering the text(ile) as male. The blood, of course, suggests some kind of sexual initiation for this "sparow whyte as mylke"; yet the gender reversal becomes muddled when we consider that the virginal blood "really" is Jane's, not Phyllyp's. What does this passage say, then, about the act of "representation" (this is Jane's surprisingly post-modern term)—and how is Skelton as an artist reflected in this crucial scene? Does Jane, in experiencing the frustrations and the (here, literal) pain of creativity parallel Skelton and his poet-persona? Or does her ultimate throwing aside of her needle/pen con-

firm her feminine ineptitude in the phallic act of creation? Do these lines thus reassert the poet/subject dichotomy?

In answering these questions, it may help to look at another moment when we are called upon to think of Jane as an artist—or as an aspiring artist, at least—and this is where she apologizes for her lack of poetic skill:

> For as I tofore have sayd,
> I am but a young mayd,
> And can not in effect
> My style as yet direct
> With Englysh wordes elect. . . .

Richard Halpern is one critic who cannot resist reading Jane's poetic "lack" in a Freudian light:

> What Jane has, then, is matter—enough to 'fyll bougets and males'—but she cannot 'direct' her 'style'. . . . A *bouget* is a pouch, bag, or wallet; the word, related to *bulge,* comes from the Latin *bulga,* a leather bag or a womb. A *male* is also a leather bag or wallet, but the word lends itself to witty associations with the testicles. Jane thus bulges with the necessary matter for a poem but cannot 'direct' her 'style'. . . . She cannot direct her stylus . . . with its all-too-obvious symbolization. . . . [13]

At this point Halpern's Freudian reading seems to reinforce the Skelton/Jane opposition posited above. Here, once again, Jane struggles to direct a phallic implement, to appropriate the male role of creator, with the consequence, however, of hurting herself. At this point Fish's male reader can smile upon Jane with "affection and condescension."[14] To him it is no surprise that Jane slips up in her attempts to represent her beloved, and that when given the patriarchal stylus, she fumbles, *pricks* herself, bleeds. Having read Catullus, he knows that, after all, the sparrow *is* the phallus, and having read Freud, he knows that Jane is castrated, sparrow-less, helpless.

And yet Jane is not the only one who stumbles in the act of phallic creation. Here "Skelton" describes his own artistic impotence:

> My pen it is unable,
> My hand it is unstable,
> My reson rude and dull
> To prayse her at the full. . . .

We may recognize here the "inexpressibility motif" ubiquitous in the genre, but I would argue that the emphasis on the unstable pen takes on a new significance in relation to Jane's artistic struggles. Halpern adds an unexpected twist to his own Freudian reading of the poem: he extends Jane's phallic "lack" to the poet-persona himself. For despite his attempt rhetorically to master his young subject, the poet's tone throughout the Commendacions is one of extreme "erotic submissiveness." Halpern argues:

> 'Skelton' unwittingly illustrates his shortcomings in his very first English phrase, when he promises to devote his 'hole imagination' to praising his mistress. If this persona organizes things into wholes, he also

reduces them to holes. . . . The phallic organizer who pretends to totalize and complete the poem proves to be precisely the space of its 'hole' or lack.[15]

I would only modify Halpern's judgment to say that the poet-speaker is not *the* space of lack in the poem, but rather he demonstrates the lack which imbues the *entire* poem. As Halpern himself points out, "*Phyllyp Sparowe* is, in some sense, founded on the void, specifically that left by the disappearance of its namesake. Elegy is supremely the genre of lack. . . ."[16] What links Skelton and Jane is their mutual experience of lack, of separation from a beloved. Jane lacks Phyllyp, Skelton lacks Jane, and both attempt (with limited success) to fill this void by means of representation. It is the yearning in both "voices"—as Jane relives her time spent with Phyllyp, and as "Skelton" indulges in "fantasy" of the delights Jane will always withhold from him—that unifies the poem. I think it is not unreasonable to assume that many or most readers bring to the poem some experience of this bittersweet play of the imagination against the absence of a beloved. This is the key to the poem's poignancy.

Yet I would like to move away from "lack" in the Freudian sense. For the sparrow whose loss occasions the poem need not exclusively stand for the phallus. Beryl Rowland, in her extensive study of bird symbolism, documents the medieval literary tradition of the lecherous sparrow, but also points out an alternative vein of symbolism.

> In general the Biblical sparrow was a very different breed from the bird which, according to Bartholomew the Englishman, was 'full hot . . . and lecherous.' 'Are not two sparrows sold for a farthing?' said Christ. 'And one of them shall not fall on the ground, without your Father knoweth.' Under mosaic Law two sparrows were a purification offering. . . . St. Ambrose regarded the sparrows as the body and the soul, 'For both are lifted up to God by spiritual wings'. . . . 'Even the sparrow finds a home. . . where she may lay her young, at Thy altars, O Lord of Hosts!' cried the psalmist. (lxxxiv.3)[17]

It seems likely that Skelton, a clergyman, was as conscious of the biblical connotations of the sparrow as of the Catullan tradition: it is possible, in fact, that he intended both symbolic valences to play in the minds of his readers. And why need one choose? The biblical use of the sparrow highlights its delicacy, its humble size, in order to illustrate the pervasiveness of divine providence (a lesson that Jane might find comforting)—but there is no need to consider *this* sparrow "a very different breed" than Catullus' sparrow. Why should a lecherous sparrow, any more than a lecherous person, slip between the fingers of divine providence? Let us not forget that lechery is a sin only in humans, not in animals, who have neither reason with which to combat sin nor souls with which to be damned.[18] When Chaucer describes his Summoner as "lecherous as a sparwe,"[19] undoubtedly he means us to fault, if anyone, the man, not the bird.

Indeed, there is no denying that Phyllyp is (or was) as sexual as any bird. Perhaps the most startling and comic moment in Jane's elegy is her wish

That Phyllyp may fly
Above the starry sky,
To treade the prety wren
That is our Ladyes hen.
Amen, amen, amen!

The beautiful absurdity of this prayer lies in its naive conflation of animal doings with the afterlife of the human spirit. Jane does not seem to realize that, as intimated above, one might find neither wrens nor "treading" in heaven. But more importantly, these lines reveal Jane's delight in Phyllyp's sex-life, a sex-life she imagines she has shared with him by letting him under her clothes. And if some readers find these quasi-sexual references jarring within what otherwise seems a child's prattle, ultimately it is not inconceivable that a young girl coming of age in the isolation of a nunnery would seek entertainment in the mating of birds or in a make-believe romance with a sparrow. I would argue that it is only in retrospect, when we learn of the poet-speaker's presence throughout Jane's elegy, that her delight in Phyllyp's sexuality begins to look less than naive, and that Phyllyp's fluttering contact with her bosom takes on an intense eroticism. But I will come back to these issues. In any case, I feel that our over-riding impression of this bird is of his birdlike rather than his supposedly phallic qualities: like any other bird, he was small and feathered, and he spent his day singing and hunting for females or bugs. Like any other bird, he was prey to cats.

And ultimately, it all comes down to Phyllyp's death. The focus of the poem is Phyllyp's vulnerable and mortal nature—something he of course shares with human beings. I have already pointed out Jane's link to the sparrow as an object of love and a subject of poetry. Both girl and bird are adored, are described as "whyte as mylke"; another common quality is that of smallness, delicacy, vulnerability—something brought to light in the pinpricking scene discussed above. The Commendacions, in fact, foreground these features: the poet's doting eye traces not only Jane's ruby lips and white cheeks, but also a scar on her chin. Despite the poet's attempt to trope the scar into something celestial, this detail works against the overall deifying language of the Commendacions by pointing up the maiden's mortality, her susceptibility to wounding, bleeding, harm. The flower image Skelton reiterates in each refrain was a common symbol for mutability, for the frailty and transience of beautiful things; the poet's use of epithets like "smale" and "quickly veined," however conventional in this type of poetry, reinforce our sense of Jane as a tender little specimen. Thus we are apt to smile in charmed disbelief when the speaker declares:

Ther is no beest savage,
Ne no tyger so wood,
But she wolde chaunge his mood. . . .

Another poetic convention? Certainly—but in light of the Jane-Phyllyp parallel we have been pondering, the reference to the tiger may work on more than one level. Can it be any accident that the speaker chooses a cat as the potential enemy that Jane's beauty (he claims) will vanquish? Were it not for the fact that Phyllyp—Jane's counterpart—has fallen prey to a cat; were it not for the scar on Jane's chin (a cat scratch?); were it not for Jane's smallness and delicacy, we might perhaps dismiss as mere embellishment the speaker's hyperbolic claim. But I read these lines as a subtle hint that Jane is in more peril than she knows—and not from imaginary tigers.

For there is one binarism whose undoing can be far more unsettling on a subliminal level than the collapsing of the erotic and the sacred (something which Kinney argues can be done without profanity): this is the human versus the bestial. For, in my reading-as-a-woman, something about the poem's animal imagery struck me as vaguely troubling. My unease began with Jane's use of the term "treading" to depict Phyllyp's animal love-making. Any Chaucerian, of course, would associate the term with our favorite barnyard Casanova, Chaunteclere. And a glance at the *OED* proves that the term was used to describe birds mating for as long as it was used to mean "to step upon" (both uses occur, in fact, in *Phyllyp Sparowe*: see 1149). Still, I cannot help but feel that the potential violence of the primary meaning is intrinsic to the secondary, as suggested by Jane's off-hand reference to Chaucer's ever-popular rooster:

> Chaunteclere, our coke, . . .
> With Partlot his hen,
> Whom now and then
> He plucketh by the hede
> Whan he doth her trede.

I would hazard to guess that most women readers cannot help but flinch here on poor Partlot's behalf. Even if a male bird literally does "tread" or grab hold of the female's back with his claws during mating, one can hardly forget the sense in which "to tread" means "to step or walk with pressure on (something) esp. so as to crush, beat down, injure, or destroy it; to trample." And perhaps Skelton wishes both senses to play here. Clearly, the "treading" Chaucer depicts in the *Nun's Priest's Tale* functions as a crucial factor in the tale's mock-romantic effect; the "treading" satirically comments on the essentially bestial act that the romance genre prettifies. The word is meant to be somewhat jarring, an unsettling reminder of the animal element in human sexuality.

Yet I would argue that Skelton's version of treading goes farther in its suggestions of violence than Chaucer's depiction of Chaunteclere's barnyard antics, and not only by adding the brutal pluck of the head. Viewing these lines in the context of the poem's other animal references brings to light a disturbing emphasis on the *predatory*. It is, after all, a predatory act which occasions the poem: Phyllyp falls prey to Gyb the cat, just as the fleas on Jane's skin fall prey to him, and just as the female birds fall prey, in a sexual sense, to the male birds in the poem. Placed within this predatory framework, the longing of the poet after Jane's physical person takes on a rather sinister aspect; his ocular absorption of her every bodily feature begins to resemble the mesmerized stare of the poised feline just before the fatal pounce. Perhaps it is this predatory view of sex which underlies Skelton's feminizing of

the traditionally male tomcat Gyb—something critics have remarked upon but not, to my knowledge, accounted for.[20] Perhaps Gyb must be female in order to prey, sexually, on Phyllyp, a male.

This focus on the predatory provides, in part, an explanation for some of the discomfort inspired by the poem's sensuality. Why does it disturb readers when "Jane" describes Phyllyp's contact with her "naked skyn"? According to Fish, "It is perhaps difficult to read these lines without questioning her innocence"—but I protest that there is nothing at all un-childlike or worldly about the sensual thrill attributed to Jane here. Rather, what readers find unsettling is their voyeuristic participation in these scenes. I do agree with Fish's claim that "we must be continually aware of the distance between what Jane in her innocence would contend and what we would interpolate,"[21] but I would add that his sophisticated reader must also contend with a suppressed sense of guilt at making these sexual interpolations in a child's elegy to a dead pet. And when the amorous poet-speaker interrupts Jane's narrative, this discomfort is raised to a pitch. Now we learn that all along there has been an invisible third party, a sophisticated older male, not only witnessing, but in fact orchestrating our less-than-innocent responses to this girl's private moments. As "Skelton" launches into his obsessive musings, and we wonder to what degree the poet has "planted" the sexual innuendo in Jane's narrative, we feel implicated in his moral universe. And it cannot assuage the reader's discomfort to realize that this moral universe equates human sexual urges with barnyard rutting.

Given Skelton's pointed use of animal imagery, there is a delightful irony in Alexander Pope's epithet of "beastly Skelton," as well as in Elizabeth Barret Browning's more laudatory description of the poet as "rabid . . . a wild beast in a forest. . . . In his wonderful dominion over language, he tears it, as with teeth and paws, ravenously, savagely; devastating rather than creating. . . . Mark him as a satyr of poets! fear him as the Juvenal of satyrs!"[22] Yet, I have a hunch that Skelton would not have disputed this description. The three-way linkage of poet, maiden, and sparrow implicates the Skelton persona in base animal impulses. And Skelton the satirist may indeed have intended, in implicating his persona, to implicate all humankind.

Also, Browning's misuse of the term "satyr" strikes me as a fruitful and perhaps deliberate misuse. The *OED* provides a long heritage to the etymological and semantic confusion surrounding the terms "satyr" and "satire"—which in fact are not linguistically related. The satyr, a creature human to the waist and goat below (another reputedly lecherous animal),[23] embodies the human race at its basest, and reifies the philosophical commonplace most succinctly stated by Pope's "Essay on Man," which situates mankind "on this isthmus of a middle state" between God and beasts. It is therefore a happy semantic accident that the term "satyr" so closely resembles "satire," a genre that often deploys animal imagery in order to deflate human presumption. Browning, in dubbing Skelton "a satyr of poets," both lauds the poet's satirical wit, and conflates him with the universal target of satire. The satyr of satire mocks even himself.

Although I do not call **Phyllyp Sparowe** a satiric poem, I find subtly satirical its collapsing of human and animal sexuality. One is reminded of the bizarre landscapes of Hieronymous Bosch, filled with half-bird, half-human monsters and with the orgiastic intermingling of naked human bodies and animal and vegetable life forms. Of course from our post-modern secular perspective these pictorial dream-visions seem more psychedelic than moralistic, but contemporaries of Bosch were inclined to view his work as painterly sermonizing, as "a stern warning against the vice of *Luxuria*."[24] Either way, in light of these bizarre images and their melding of feathers and human flesh, Phyllyp's contact with Jane's virginal skin becomes even more sexually suggestive.

But perhaps this is to over-stress the negative uses of animal iconography. I do not read **Phyllyp Sparowe** as a blanket condemnation of human vice, but as a symbolically complex and a profound statement about human behavior at its most exalted and most base. The medieval bestiaries attested to the belief that since all of God's creation reflected its maker, the "Book of Nature" could be turned to for moral instruction as readily as the book of Scripture.[25] And if, as Augustine holds, God's symbols carry meanings both *in bono* and *in malo*,[26] any beast, including humankind, can be read both ways. Just as human physicality could serve either as a vehicle to God (through, for instance, *imitatio christi*) or as an instrument of sin, nature could either direct the soul to contemplation of its creator, or else distract the soul through sensual pleasure. Likewise, we might say that literary critics, over the years, have presented *in bono* and *in malo* readings both of Skelton's iconographic sparrow and of the poem as a whole. Either: the bird is a phallus; Jane has found sexual fulfillment in his contact with her "naked skyn"; the poet-speaker pines to fill the sexual lack Jane suffers in the wake of Phyllyp's death. Or: Phyllyp is a symbol of divine providence; both bird and girl are innocent playmates; the poet-speaker views Jane in her grief as a *pieta* figure, worships her chastely, and attempts to solace her with his verse.

I present my reading as a means of reconciling these discordant critical voices. By recognizing the poem's complex dynamic of representation, by looking at the points in the text where binary categories collapse—male into female, poet into subject, human into animal—we can see how Skelton's art embraces all the paradoxes of human existence. Is Phyllyp a phallic symbol or a sign of God's all-sheltering love? He is both, and much more. Is Jane a child or a young woman; is she "innocent" or knowing? She is both; as representative of the poet, she is the voice of innocence spoken through the voice of experience; she is poet and poem, stylus and text. And finally, we can answer this question: what is **Phyllyp Sparowe?** an elegy or a love-song? a sexual fantasy or a Marian prayer? Once more, the poem is all of these things. For, however startling and disturbing, however singular we find the text's phantasmagoria, **Phyllyp Sparowe** can yet be understood in terms of those two common literary themes, sex and death. The poem's central figure—as both "wanton" phallus and the frail, mortal body to which it belongs—represents in the end human fleshly existence in its joys and limitations, in its sinfulness and its need for salvation. Like the sparrow, we rise and fall, love and hurt, mate and die. Like the sparrow, Skelton tells us, we are small, so small in the order of things.

Notes

1. Stanley Eugene Fish, *John Skelton's Poetry* (Yale U. Press, 1965), 99.

2. Susan Schibanoff, "Taking Jane's Cue: 'Phyllyp Sparowe' as a Primer for Women Readers," *PMLA* 101 (1986): 832.

3. Fish, *John Skelton's Poetry*, 112.

4. F. W. Brownlow, "'The Boke of Phyllyp Sparowe' and the Liturgy," *English Literary Renaissance* 9 (1979): 5.

5. All references to *Phyllyp Sparowe* are from John Skelton, *The Complete English Poems*, ed., John Scattergood (Yale U. Press, 1983) and will be cited in the text of my essay.

6. Fish, *John Skelton's Poetry*, 105.

7. Ibid., 138.

8. Ibid., 18n16.

9. *John Skelton, Priest as Poet: Seasons of Discovery* (U. of North Carolina Press, 1987), 107.

10. Ibid., 115.

11. Schibanoff, "Taking Jane's Cue," 832.

12. Kinney, *John Skelton*, 116.

13. *The Poetics of Primitive Accumulation: English Renaissance Culture and the Genealogy of Capital* (Cornell U. Press, 1991), 121-22.

14. Fish, *John Skelton's Poetry*, 111.

15. Halpern, *The Poetics of Primitive Accumulation*, 124-25.

16. Ibid., 122.

17. Beryl Rowland, *Birds with Human Souls: A Guide to Bird Symbolism* (U. of Tennessee Press, 1978), 158.

18. Beryl Rowland, *Blind Beasts: Chaucer's Animal World* (Kent State U. Press, 1971), 20.

19. Geoffrey Chaucer, *The General Prologue, in The Canterbury Tales*, ed. Larry D. Benson (Boston: Houghton Miflin, 1987), 1.626.

20. See Schibanoff, "Taking Jane's Cue," 834.

21. Fish, *John Skelton's Poetry*, 112.

22. Anthony S. G. Edwards, ed., *Skelton: The Critical Heritage* (London: Routledge & Kegan Paul, 1987), 75, 99.

[23] Rowland, *Blind Beasts*, 126.

[24] Francis Klingender, *Animals in Art and Thought to the End of the Middle Ages*, ed., Evelyn Antal and John Harthan (The M. I. T. Press, 1971), 488.

[25] Robert P. Miller, ed., *Chaucer: Sources and Backgrounds* (New York U. Press, 1977), 3-5.

[26] St. Augustine, *On Christian Doctrine*, trans. D. W. Robertson (New York: Macmillan Publishing, 1958), 99-101.

FURTHER READING

Bibliography

Kinsman, Robert S. and Yonge, Theodore. *John Skelton: Canon and Census*. New York: Monographic Press, 1967, 88 p.

    Primary and secondary listings of Skelton's work.

Biography

Nelson, William. *John Skelton: Laureate*. New York: Columbia University Press, 1939, 266 p.

    Survey of Skelton's life and the historical circumstances surrounding his poetry.

Criticism

Archibald, Elizabeth. "Tradition and Innovation in the Macaronic Poetry of Dunbar and Skelton." *Modern Language Quarterly* 53, No. 1 (March 1992): 126-49.

    Assesses the tradition of combining both English and Latin or Greek in the same poem.

Carlson, David. "John Skelton and Ancient Authors: Two Notes." *Humanistica Lovaniensia* XXXVIII (1989): 100-09.

    Analyzes Skelton's allusions to Latin poetry and concludes that the poet's classical allusions, though accurate, were not of the same sophistication as Renaissance humanists.

Colley, John Scott. "John Skelton's Ironic *Apologia*: The Medieval Sciences, Wolsey, and the *Garlande of Laurell*." *Tennessee Studies in Literature* XVIII (1973): 19-32.

    Explores the political climate surrounding Skelton's *The Garland of Laurel*.

Doherty, M. J. "The Patristic Humanism of Skelton's *Phyllyp Sparowe*." In *From Cloister to Classroom: Monastic and Scholastic Approaches to Truth*, edited by E. Rozanne Elder, Cistercian Publications, 1986, pp. 202-38.

    Maintains that Skelton's satire promotes intellectual and spiritual values.

Evans, Maurice. "John Skelton." In *English Poetry in the Sixteenth Century*, pp. 47-64. London: Hutchinson & Co., Ltd., 1955.

    Determines Skelton's place in English literary history and suggests that he played an important role in the beginning of the English Renaissance.

Fish, Stanley Eugene. *John Skelton's Poetry*. New Haven: Yale University Press, 1965, 268 p.

    Critical study of Skelton's verse.

Gillespie, Vincent. "Justification by Good Works: Skelton's *The Garland of Laurel*." *Reading Medieval Studies* VII (1981): 19-31.

    Examines Skelton's ideas about the uses of poetry, particularly its role in religious and political debates.

Gingerich, Owen, and Tucker, Melvin J. "The Astronomical Dating of Skelton's *Garland of Laurel*." *Huntington Library Quarterly* XXXII, No. 3 (1969): 207-20.

    Links a descriptive passage in the poem with a known astronomical event to date the writing of the majority of the *Garland of Laure*.

Heiserman, A. R. *Skelton and Satire*. Chicago: University of Chicago Press, 1961, 326 p.

    Explores the relationship between Skelton's satirical works and medieval literary tradition.

Kinney, Arthur F. *John Skelton, Priest as Poet: Seasons of Discovery*. Chapel Hill: University of North Carolina Press, 1987, 236 p.

    Maintains that the primary purpose of Skelton's poetry is religious instruction.

Kinsman, Robert S. "Skelton's 'Uppon a Deedmans Hed': New Light on the Origin of the Skeltonic." *Studies in Philology* L, No. 2 (April 1953): 101-09.

    Traces the roots of the English meter known as the "Skeltonic" to Latin and English poetry from the thirteenth and fourteenth centuries.

——. "Skelton Mocks the Muse: References to Romance Matters in His Poetry." In *Medieval Epic to the "Epic Theater" of Brecht*, edited by Rosario P. Armato and John M. Spalek, pp. 35-46. Los Angeles: University of Southern California Press, 1968.

    Examines Skelton's poetic relationship to chivalric romances such as *Morte Arthur*.

Lawton, David. "Skelton's Use of Persona." *Essays in Criticism* XXX, No. 1 (January 1980): 9-28.

    Explores Skelton's use of *personae*, or characters, to narrate his major poems.

Loewenstein, David A. "Skelton's Triumph: *The Garland of Laurel* and Literary Fame." *Neophilologus* 68, No. 4 (October 1984): 611-22.

    Contends that *Garland of Laurel* "deserves attention because it evaluates, in a lively and imaginative manner, Skelton's poetic career and the meaning of literary fame."

Newman, Robert D. "The Visual Nature of Skelton's 'The

Tunnying of Elynour Rummying.'" *College Literature* XII, No. 2 (1985): pp. 135-40.
    Discusses both the visual details and the social panorama in Skelton's poem.

Scattergood, John. "Skelton and Traditional Satire: *Ware the Hauke.*" *Medium Aevum* LV, No. 2 (1986): 203-16.
    Examines the historical basis of Skelton's poem.

Skelton, Robin. "The Master Poet: John Skelton as Conscious Craftsman." *Mosaic* VI, No. 3 (Spring 1973): 67-92.
    Contends that Skelton identified his own poetic skill with the medieval guild tradition of master craftsman.

Wallace, Nathaniel Owen. "The Responsibilities of Madness: John Skelton, 'Speke, Parrot,' and Homeopathic Satire." *Studies in Philology* LXXXII, No. 1 (Winter 1985): 60-80.
    Considers the role of madness in Skelton's poem and asserts that the poem has a sharply defined moral purpose.

West, Michael. "Skelton and the Renaissance Theme of Folly." *Philological Quarterly* L, No. 1 (January 1971): 23-35.
    Maintains that the fools in Skelton's poetry occupy a transitional position between medieval and Renaissance conceptions of folly.

Poetry Criticism
INDEXES

Literary Criticism Series
Cumulative Author Index

Cumulative Nationality Index

Cumulative Title Index

How to Use This Index

The main references

> **Calvino, Italo**
> 1923–1985 .... **CLC 5, 8, 11, 22, 33, 39,**
> **73; SSC 3**

list all author entries in the following Gale Literary Criticism series:

BLC = *Black Literature Criticism*
CLC = *Contemporary Literary Criticism*
CLR = *Children's Literature Review*
CMLC = *Classical and Medieval Literature Criticism*
DA = *DISCovering Authors*
DAB = *DISCovering Authors: British*
DAC = *DISCovering Authors: Canadian*
DAM = *DISCovering Authors: Modules*
      DRAM: *Dramatists Module;* **MST**: *Most-Studied Authors Module;*
      MULT: *Multicultural Authors Module;* **NOV**: *Novelists Module;*
      POET: *Poets Module;* **POP**: *Popular Fiction and Genre Authors Module*
DC = *Drama Criticism*
HLC = *Hispanic Literature Criticism*
LC = *Literature Criticism from 1400 to 1800*
NCLC = *Nineteenth-Century Literature Criticism*
PC = *Poetry Criticism*
SSC = *Short Story Criticism*
TCLC = *Twentieth-Century Literary Criticism*
WLC = *World Literature Criticism, 1500 to the Present*

The cross-references

> See also CANR 23; CA 85-88;
>   obituary CA116

list all author entries in the following Gale biographical and literary sources:

AAYA = *Authors & Artists for Young Adults*
AITN = *Authors in the News*
BEST = *Bestsellers*
BW = *Black Writers*
CA = *Contemporary Authors*
CAAS = *Contemporary Authors Autobiography Series*
CABS = *Contemporary Authors Bibliographical Series*
CANR = *Contemporary Authors New Revision Series*
CAP = *Contemporary Authors Permanent Series*
CDALB = *Concise Dictionary of American Literary Biography*
CDBLB = *Concise Dictionary of British Literary Biography*
DLB = *Dictionary of Literary Biography*
DLBD = *Dictionary of Literary Biography Documentary Series*
DLBY = *Dictionary of Literary Biography Yearbook*
HW = *Hispanic Writers*
JRDA = *Junior DISCovering Authors*
MAICYA = *Major Authors and Illustrators for Children and Young Adults*
MTCW = *Major 20th-Century Writers*
NNAL = *Native North American Literature*
SAAS = *Something about the Author Autobiography Series*
SATA = *Something about the Author*
YABC = *Yesterday's Authors of Books for Children*

Literary Criticism Series
Cumulative Author Index

Astley, Thea (Beatrice May) 1925- .. **CLC 41**
See also CA 65-68; CANR 11, 43
Aston, James
See White, T(erence) H(anbury)
Asturias, Miguel Angel 1899-1974...**CLC 3, 8, 13; DAM MULT, NOV; HLC**
See also CA 25-28; 49-52; CANR 32; CAP 2; DLB 113; HW; MTCW 1
Atares, Carlos Saura
See Saura (Atares), Carlos
Atheling, William
See Pound, Ezra (Weston Loomis)
Atheling, William, Jr.
See Blish, James (Benjamin)
Atherton, Gertrude (Franklin Horn) 1857-1948 **TCLC 2**
See also CA 104; 155; DLB 9, 78, 186
Atherton, Lucius
See Masters, Edgar Lee
Atkins, Jack
See Harris, Mark
Atkinson, Kate .... **CLC 99**
See also CA 166
Attaway, William (Alexander) 1911-1986 **CLC 92; BLC 1; DAM MULT**
See also BW 2; CA 143; DLB 76
Atticus
See Fleming, Ian (Lancaster); Wilson, (Thomas) Woodrow
Atwood, Margaret (Eleanor) 1939-... **CLC 2, 3, 4, 8, 13, 15, 25, 44, 84; DA; DAB; DAC; DAM MST, NOV, POET; PC 8; SSC 2; WLC**
See also AAYA 12; BEST 89:2; CA 49-52; CANR 3, 24, 33, 59; DLB 53; INT CANR-24; MTCW 1; SATA 50
Aubigny, Pierre d'
See Mencken, H(enry) L(ouis)
Aubin, Penelope 1685-1731(?)............... **LC 9**
See also DLB 39
Auchincloss, Louis (Stanton) 1917-... **CLC 4, 6, 9, 18, 45; DAM NOV; SSC 22**
See also CA 1-4R; CANR 6, 29, 55; DLB 2; DLBY 80; INT CANR-29; MTCW 1
Auden, W(ystan) H(ugh) 1907-1973... **C L C 1, 2, 3, 4, 6, 9, 11, 14, 43; DA; DAB; DAC; DAM DRAM, MST, POET; PC 1; WLC**
See also AAYA 18; CA 9-12R; 45-48; CANR 5, 61; CDBLB 1914-1945; DLB 10, 20; MTCW 1
Audiberti, Jacques 1900-1965 .... **CLC 38; DAM DRAM**
See also CA 25-28R
Audubon, John James 1785-1851...**NCLC 47**
Auel, Jean M(arie) 1936- ..... **CLC 31, 107; DAM POP**
See also AAYA 7; BEST 90:4; CA 103; CANR 21, 64; INT CANR-21; SATA 91
Auerbach, Erich 1892-1957 .... **TCLC 43**
See also CA 118; 155
Augier, Emile 1820-1889 .... **NCLC 31**
See also DLB 192
August, John
See De Voto, Bernard (Augustine)
Augustine, St. 354-430 .... **CMLC 6; DAB**
Aurelius
See Bourne, Randolph S(illiman)
Aurobindo, Sri
See Ghose, Aurabinda
Austen, Jane 1775-1817 **NCLC 1, 13, 19, 33, 51; DA; DAB; DAC; DAM MST, NOV; WLC**
See also AAYA 19; CDBLB 1789-1832; DLB 116

Auster, Paul 1947- ....**CLC 47**
See also CA 69-72; CANR 23, 52, 75
Austin, Frank
See Faust, Frederick (Schiller)
Austin, Mary (Hunter) 1868-1934...**TCLC 25**
See also CA 109; DLB 9, 78, 206
Autran Dourado, Waldomiro
See Dourado, (Waldomiro Freitas) Autran
Averroes 1126-1198 .... **CMLC 7**
See also DLB 115
Avicenna 980-1037 .... **CMLC 16**
See also DLB 115
Avison, Margaret 1918-...**CLC 2, 4, 97; DAC; DAM POET**
See also CA 17-20R; DLB 53; MTCW 1
Axton, David
See Koontz, Dean R(ay)
Ayckbourn, Alan 1939-...**CLC 5, 8, 18, 33, 74; DAB; DAM DRAM**
See also CA 21-24R; CANR 31, 59; DLB 13; MTCW 1
Aydy, Catherine
See Tennant, Emma (Christina)
Ayme, Marcel (Andre) 1902-1967 ..... **CLC 11**
See also CA 89-92; CANR 67; CLR 25; DLB 72; SATA 91
Ayrton, Michael 1921-1975 .... **CLC 7**
See also CA 5-8R; 61-64; CANR 9, 21
Azorin .... **CLC 11**
See also Martinez Ruiz, Jose
Azuela, Mariano 1873-1952 . **TCLC 3; DAM MULT; HLC**
See also CA 104; 131; HW; MTCW 1
Baastad, Babbis Friis
See Friis-Baastad, Babbis Ellinor
Bab
See Gilbert, W(illiam) S(chwenck)
Babbis, Eleanor
See Friis-Baastad, Babbis Ellinor
Babel, Isaac
See Babel, Isaak (Emmanuilovich)
Babel, Isaak (Emmanuilovich) 1894-1941(?) **TCLC 2, 13; SSC 16**
See also CA 104; 155
Babits, Mihaly 1883-1941 .... **TCLC 14**
See also CA 114
Babur 1483-1530 .... **LC 18**
Bacchelli, Riccardo 1891-1985..........**CLC 19**
See also CA 29-32R; 117
Bach, Richard (David) 1936-...**CLC 14; DAM NOV, POP**
See also AITN 1; BEST 89:2; CA 9-12R; CANR 18; MTCW 1; SATA 13
Bachman, Richard
See King, Stephen (Edwin)
Bachmann, Ingeborg 1926-1973 ....**CLC 69**
See also CA 93-96; 45-48; CANR 69; DLB 85
Bacon, Francis 1561-1626 .... **LC 18, 32**
See also CDBLB Before 1660; DLB 151
Bacon, Roger 1214(?)-1292 .... **CMLC 14**
See also DLB 115
Bacovia, George .... **TCLC 24**
See also Vasiliu, Gheorghe
Badanes, Jerome 1937- ....**CLC 59**
Bagehot, Walter 1826-1877 ....**NCLC 10**
See also DLB 55
Bagnold, Enid 1889-1981 ...... **CLC 25; DAM DRAM**
See also CA 5-8R; 103; CANR 5, 40; DLB 13, 160, 191; MAICYA; SATA 1, 25
Bagritsky, Eduard 1895-1934 .... **TCLC 60**
Bagrjana, Elisaveta
See Belcheva, Elisaveta

Bagryana, Elisaveta .... **CLC 10**
See also Belcheva, Elisaveta
See also DLB 147
Bailey, Paul 1937- .... **CLC 45**
See also CA 21-24R; CANR 16, 62; DLB 14
Baillie, Joanna 1762-1851 .... **NCLC 71**
See also DLB 93
Bainbridge, Beryl (Margaret) 1933-**CLC 4, 5, 8, 10, 14, 18, 22, 62; DAM NOV**
See also CA 21-24R; CANR 24, 55, 75; DLB 14; MTCW 1
Baker, Elliott 1922- ....**CLC 8**
See also CA 45-48; CANR 2, 63
Baker, Jean H. ....**TCLC 3, 10**
See also Russell, George William
Baker, Nicholson 1957-...**CLC 61; DAM POP**
See also CA 135; CANR 63
Baker, Ray Stannard 1870-1946 .... **TCLC 47**
See also CA 118
Baker, Russell (Wayne) 1925- .... **CLC 31**
See also BEST 89:4; CA 57-60; CANR 11, 41, 59; MTCW 1
Bakhtin, M.
See Bakhtin, Mikhail Mikhailovich
Bakhtin, M. M.
See Bakhtin, Mikhail Mikhailovich
Bakhtin, Mikhail
See Bakhtin, Mikhail Mikhailovich
Bakhtin, Mikhail Mikhailovich 1895-1975 **CLC 83**
See also CA 128; 113
Bakshi, Ralph 1938(?)- .... **CLC 26**
See also CA 112; 138
Bakunin, Mikhail (Alexandrovich) 1814-1876 **NCLC 25, 58**
Baldwin, James (Arthur) 1924-1987...**CLC 1, 2, 3, 4, 5, 8, 13, 15, 17, 42, 50, 67, 90; BLC 1; DA; DAB; DAC; DAM MST, MULT, NOV, POP; DC 1; SSC 10, 33; WLC**
See also AAYA 4; BW 1; CA 1-4R; 124; CABS 1; CANR 3, 24; CDALB 1941-1968; DLB 2, 7, 33; DLBY 87; MTCW 1; SATA 9; SATA-Obit 54
Ballard, J(ames) G(raham) 1930-...**CLC 3, 6, 14, 36; DAM NOV, POP; SSC 1**
See also AAYA 3; CA 5-8R; CANR 15, 39, 65; DLB 14; MTCW 1; SATA 93
Balmont, Konstantin (Dmitriyevich) 1867-1943 **TCLC 11**
See also CA 109; 155
Baltausis, Vincas
See Mikszath, Kalman
Balzac, Honore de 1799-1850 . **NCLC 5, 35, 53; DA; DAB; DAC; DAM MST, NOV; SSC 5; WLC**
See also DLB 119
Bambara, Toni Cade 1939-1995...**CLC 19, 88; BLC 1; DA; DAC; DAM MST, MULT; WLCS**
See also AAYA 5; BW 2; CA 29-32R; 150; CANR 24, 49; DLB 38; MTCW 1
Bamdad, A.
See Shamlu, Ahmad
Banat, D. R.
See Bradbury, Ray (Douglas)
Bancroft, Laura
See Baum, L(yman) Frank
Banim, John 1798-1842 .... **NCLC 13**
See also DLB 116, 158, 159
Banim, Michael 1796-1874 .... **NCLC 13**
See also DLB 158, 159
Banjo, The
See Paterson, A(ndrew) B(arton)

Banks, Iain
See Banks, Iain M(enzies)
Banks, Iain M(enzies) 1954- .... **CLC 34**
See also CA 123; 128; CANR 61; DLB 194;
INT 128
Banks, Lynne Reid .... **CLC 23**
See also Reid Banks, Lynne
See also AAYA 6
Banks, Russell 1940- .... **CLC 37, 72**
See also CA 65-68; CAAS 15; CANR 19, 52,
73; DLB 130
Banville, John 1945-......................... **CLC 46**
See also CA 117; 128; DLB 14; INT 128
Banville, Theodore (Faullain) de 1832-1891
NCLC 9
Baraka, Amiri 1934-...**CLC 1, 2, 3, 5, 10, 14,
33, 115; BLC 1; DA; DAC; DAM MST,
MULT, POET, POP; DC 6; PC 4; WLCS**
See also Jones, LeRoi
See also BW 2; CA 21-24R; CABS 3; CANR
27, 38, 61; CDALB 1941-1968; DLB 5, 7,
16, 38; DLBD 8; MTCW 1
Barbauld, Anna Laetitia 1743-1825...**NCLC 50**
See also DLB 107, 109, 142, 158
Barbellion, W. N. P. .... **TCLC 24**
See also Cummings, Bruce F(rederick)
Barbera, Jack (Vincent) 1945- .... **CLC 44**
See also CA 110; CANR 45
Barbey d'Aurevilly, Jules Amedee 1808-1889
NCLC 1; SSC 17
See also DLB 119
Barbusse, Henri 1873-1935 .... **TCLC 5**
See also CA 105; 154; DLB 65
Barclay, Bill
See Moorcock, Michael (John)
Barclay, William Ewert
See Moorcock, Michael (John)
Barea, Arturo 1897-1957 .... **TCLC 14**
See also CA 111
Barfoot, Joan 1946-.......................... **CLC 18**
See also CA 105
Baring, Maurice 1874-1945 .... **TCLC 8**
See also CA 105; 168; DLB 34
Baring-Gould, Sabine 1834-1924 .. **TCLC 88**
See also DLB 156, 190
Barker, Clive 1952- .... **CLC 52; DAM POP**
See also AAYA 10; BEST 90:3; CA 121; 129;
CANR 71; INT 129; MTCW 1
Barker, George Granville 1913-1991...**CLC 8,
48; DAM POET**
See also CA 9-12R; 135; CANR 7, 38; DLB
20; MTCW 1
Barker, Harley Granville
See Granville-Barker, Harley
See also DLB 10
Barker, Howard 1946- .... **CLC 37**
See also CA 102; DLB 13
Barker, Jane 1652-1732 .... **LC 42**
Barker, Pat(ricia) 1943- .... **CLC 32, 94**
See also CA 117; 122; CANR 50; INT 122
Barlach, Ernst 1870-1938 .... **TCLC 84**
See also DLB 56, 118
Barlow, Joel 1754-1812 .... **NCLC 23**
See also DLB 37
Barnard, Mary (Ethel) 1909- .... **CLC 48**
See also CA 21-22; CAP 2
Barnes, Djuna 1892-1982...**CLC 3, 4, 8, 11,
29; SSC 3**
See also CA 9-12R; 107; CANR 16, 55; DLB
4, 9, 45; MTCW 1
Barnes, Julian (Patrick) 1946-**CLC 42; DAB**
See also CA 102; CANR 19, 54; DLB 194;
DLBY 93

Barnes, Peter 1931- .... **CLC 5, 56**
See also CA 65-68; CAAS 12; CANR 33, 34,
64; DLB 13; MTCW 1
Baroja (y Nessi), Pio 1872-1956 .... **TCLC 8;
HLC**
See also CA 104
Baron, David
See Pinter, Harold
Baron Corvo
See Rolfe, Frederick (William Serafino Austin
Lewis Mary)
Barondess, Sue K(aufman) 1926-1977...**C L C
8**
See also Kaufman, Sue
See also CA 1-4R; 69-72; CANR 1
Baron de Teive
See Pessoa, Fernando (Antonio Nogueira)
Baroness Von S.
See Zangwill, Israel
Barres, (Auguste-) Maurice 1862-1923
TCLC 47
See also CA 164; DLB 123
Barreto, Afonso Henrique de Lima
See Lima Barreto, Afonso Henrique de
Barrett, (Roger) Syd 1946- ....**CLC 35**
Barrett, William (Christopher) 1913-1992
CLC 27
See also CA 13-16R; 139; CANR 11, 67; INT
CANR-11
Barrie, J(ames) M(atthew) 1860-1937...**TCLC
2; DAB; DAM DRAM**
See also CA 104; 136; CDBLB 1890-1914;
CLR 16; DLB 10, 141, 156; MAICYA; SATA
100; YABC 1
Barrington, Michael
See Moorcock, Michael (John)
Barrol, Grady
See Bograd, Larry
Barry, Mike
See Malzberg, Barry N(athaniel)
Barry, Philip 1896-1949 .... **TCLC 11**
See also CA 109; DLB 7
Bart, Andre Schwarz
See Schwarz-Bart, Andre
Barth, John (Simmons) 1930-...**CLC 1, 2, 3, 5,
7, 9, 10, 14, 27, 51, 89; DAM NOV; SSC 10**
See also AITN 1, 2; CA 1-4R; CABS 1; CANR
5, 23, 49, 64; DLB 2; MTCW 1
Barthelme, Donald 1931-1989...**CLC 1, 2, 3,
5, 6, 8, 13, 23, 46, 59, 115; DAM NOV;
SSC 2**
See also CA 21-24R; 129; CANR 20, 58; DLB
2; DLBY 80, 89; MTCW 1; SATA 7; SATA-
Obit 62
Barthelme, Frederick 1943- ......**CLC 36, 117**
See also CA 114; 122; DLBY 85; INT 122
Barthes, Roland (Gerard) 1915-1980... **C L C
24, 83**
See also CA 130; 97-100; CANR 66; MTCW 1
Barzun, Jacques (Martin) 1907- ....**CLC 51**
See also CA 61-64; CANR 22
Bashevis, Isaac
See Singer, Isaac Bashevis
Bashkirtseff, Marie 1859-1884 ......**NCLC 27**
Basho
See Matsuo Basho
Bass, Kingsley B., Jr.
See Bullins, Ed
Bass, Rick 1958-.................................**CLC 79**
See also CA 126; CANR 53
Bassani, Giorgio 1916-.........................**CLC 9**
See also CA 65-68; CANR 33; DLB 128, 177;
MTCW 1

Bastos, Augusto (Antonio) Roa
See Roa Bastos, Augusto (Antonio)
Bataille, Georges 1897-1962 ....**CLC 29**
See also CA 101; 89-92
Bates, H(erbert) E(rnest) 1905-1974..**CLC 46;
DAB; DAM POP; SSC 10**
See also CA 93-96; 45-48; CANR 34; DLB 162,
191; MTCW 1
Bauchart
See Camus, Albert
Baudelaire, Charles 1821-1867...**NCLC 6, 29,
55; DA; DAB; DAC; DAM MST, POET;
PC 1; SSC 18; WLC**
Baudrillard, Jean 1929-.....................**CLC 60**
Baum, L(yman) Frank 1856-1919 ... **TCLC 7**
See also CA 108; 133; CLR 15; DLB 22; JRDA;
MAICYA; MTCW 1; SATA 18, 100
Baum, Louis F.
See Baum, L(yman) Frank
Baumbach, Jonathan 1933-.......... **CLC 6, 23**
See also CA 13-16R; CAAS 5; CANR 12, 66;
DLBY 80; INT CANR-12; MTCW 1
Bausch, Richard (Carl) 1945- ....**CLC 51**
See also CA 101; CAAS 14; CANR 43, 61; DLB
130
Baxter, Charles (Morley) 1947-...**CLC 45, 78;
DAM POP**
See also CA 57-60; CANR 40, 64; DLB 130
Baxter, George Owen
See Faust, Frederick (Schiller)
Baxter, James K(eir) 1926-1972 ....**CLC 14**
See also CA 77-80
Baxter, John
See Hunt, E(verette) Howard, (Jr.)
Bayer, Sylvia
See Glassco, John
Baynton, Barbara 1857-1929 .... **TCLC 57**
Beagle, Peter S(oyer) 1939- .... **CLC 7, 104**
See also CA 9-12R; CANR 4, 51, 73; DLBY
80; INT CANR-4; SATA 60
Bean, Normal
See Burroughs, Edgar Rice
Beard, Charles A(ustin) 1874-1948...**TCLC
15**
See also CA 115; DLB 17; SATA 18
Beardsley, Aubrey 1872-1898 ....**NCLC 6**
Beattie, Ann 1947- ....**CLC 8, 13, 18, 40, 63;
DAM NOV, POP; SSC 11**
See also BEST 90:2; CA 81-84; CANR 53, 73;
DLBY 82; MTCW 1
Beattie, James 1735-1803 ....**NCLC 25**
See also DLB 109
Beauchamp, Kathleen Mansfield 1888-1923
See Mansfield, Katherine
See also CA 104; 134; DA; DAC; DAM MST
Beaumarchais, Pierre-Augustin Caron de 1732-
1799 .... **DC 4**
See also DAM DRAM
Beaumont, Francis 1584(?)-1616...**LC 33;
DC 6**
See also CDBLB Before 1660; DLB 58, 121
**Beauvoir, Simone (Lucie Ernestine Marie
Bertrand) de** 1908-1986...**CLC 1, 2, 4, 8,
14, 31, 44, 50, 71; DA; DAB; DAC; DAM
MST, NOV; WLC**
See also CA 9-12R; 118; CANR 28, 61; DLB
72; DLBY 86; MTCW 1
Becker, Carl (Lotus) 1873-1945 ..... **TCLC 63**
See also CA 157; DLB 17
Becker, Jurek 1937-1997 .... **CLC 7, 19**
See also CA 85-88; 157; CANR 60; DLB 75

Berger, Thomas (Louis) 1924-... **CLC 3, 5, 8, 11, 18, 38; DAM NOV**
See also CA 1-4R; CANR 5, 28, 51; DLB 2; DLBY 80; INT CANR-28; MTCW 1

Bergman, (Ernst) Ingmar 1918 ...**CLC 16, 72**
See also CA 81-84; CANR 33, 70

Bergson, Henri(-Louis) 1859-1941...**TCLC 32**
See also CA 164

Bergstein, Eleanor 1938- ....**CLC 4**
See also CA 53-56; CANR 5

Berkoff, Steven 1937- ....**CLC 56**
See also CA 104; CANR 72

Bermant, Chaim (Icyk) 1929- ....**CLC 40**
See also CA 57-60; CANR 6, 31, 57

Bern, Victoria
See Fisher, M(ary) F(rances) K(ennedy)

Bernanos, (Paul Louis) Georges 1888-1948
TCLC 3
See also CA 104; 130; DLB 72

Bernard, April 1956-.........................**CLC 59**
See also CA 131

Berne, Victoria
See Fisher, M(ary) F(rances) K(ennedy)

Bernhard, Thomas 1931-1989...**CLC 3, 32, 61**
See also CA 85-88; 127; CANR 32, 57; DLB 85, 124; MTCW 1

Bernhardt, Sarah (Henriette Rosine) 1844-1923
TCLC 75
See also CA 157

Berriault, Gina 1926-...**CLC 54, 109; SSC 30**
See also CA 116; 129; CANR 66; DLB 130

Berrigan, Daniel 1921- ....**CLC 4**
See also CA 33-36R; CAAS 1; CANR 11, 43; DLB 5

Berrigan, Edmund Joseph Michael, Jr. 1934-1983
See Berrigan, Ted
See also CA 61-64; 110; CANR 14

Berrigan, Ted ....**CLC 37**
See also Berrigan, Edmund Joseph Michael, Jr.
See also DLB 5, 169

Berry, Charles Edward Anderson 1931-
See Berry, Chuck
See also CA 115

Berry, Chuck ....**CLC 17**
See also Berry, Charles Edward Anderson

Berry, Jonas
See Ashbery, John (Lawrence)

Berry, Wendell (Erdman) 1934-...**CLC 4, 6, 8, 27, 46; DAM POET**
See also AITN 1; CA 73-76; CANR 50, 73; DLB 5, 6

Berryman, John 1914-1972...**CLC 1, 2, 3, 4, 6, 8, 10, 13, 25, 62; DAM POET**
See also CA 13-16; 33-36R; CABS 2; CANR 35; CAP 1; CDALB 1941-1968; DLB 48; MTCW 1

Bertolucci, Bernardo 1940- ....**CLC 16**
See also CA 106

Berton, Pierre (Francis Demarigny) 1920-
CLC 104
See also CA 1-4R; CANR 2, 56; DLB 68; SATA 99

Bertrand, Aloysius 1807-1841 ....**NCLC 31**

Bertran de Born c. 1140-1215 ....**CMLC 5**

Besant, Annie (Wood) 1847-1933 ....**TCLC 9**
See also CA 105

Bessie, Alvah 1904-1985 ....**CLC 23**
See also CA 5-8R; 116; CANR 2; DLB 26

Bethlen, T. D.
See Silverberg, Robert

Beti, Mongo ... **CLC 27; BLC 1; DAM MULT**
See also Biyidi, Alexandre

Betjeman, John 1906-1984...**CLC 2, 6, 10, 34, 43; DAB; DAM MST, POET**
See also CA 9-12R; 112; CANR 33, 56; CDBLB 1945-1960; DLB 20; DLBY 84; MTCW 1

Bettelheim, Bruno 1903-1990 ....**CLC 79**

Betti, Ugo 1892-1953 ....**TCLC 5**
See also CA 104; 155

Betts, Doris (Waugh) 1932- ......**CLC 3, 6, 28**
See also CA 13-16R; CANR 9, 66; DLBY 82; INT CANR-9

Bevan, Alistair
See Roberts, Keith (John Kingston)

Bey, Pilaff
See Douglas, (George) Norman

Bialik, Chaim Nachman 1873-1934...**TCLC 25**
See also CA 170

Bickerstaff, Isaac
See Swift, Jonathan

Bidart, Frank 1939- ....**CLC 33**
See also CA 140

Bienek, Horst 1930- ....**CLC 7, 11**
See also CA 73-76; DLB 75

Bierce, Ambrose (Gwinett) 1842-1914(?)
TCLC 1, 7, 44; DA; DAC; DAM MST; SSC 9; WLC
See also CA 104; 139; CDALB 1865-1917; DLB 11, 12, 23, 71, 74, 186

Biggers, Earl Derr 1884-1933 ....**TCLC 65**
See also CA 108; 153

Billings, Josh
See Shaw, Henry Wheeler

Billington, (Lady) Rachel (Mary) 1942-
CLC 43
See also AITN 2; CA 33-36R; CANR 44

Binyon, T(imothy) J(ohn) 1936- ....**CLC 34**
See also CA 111; CANR 28

Bioy Casares, Adolfo 1914-1984... **CLC 4, 8, 13, 88; DAM MULT; HLC; SSC 17**
See also CA 29-32R; CANR 19, 43, 66; DLB 113; HW; MTCW 1

Bird, Cordwainer
See Ellison, Harlan (Jay)

Bird, Robert Montgomery 1806-1854...**NCLC 1**
See also DLB 202

Birkerts, Sven 1951- ....**CLC 116**
See also CA 128; 133; CAAS 29; INT 133

Birney, (Alfred) Earle 1904-1995...**CLC 1, 4, 6, 11; DAC; DAM MST, POET**
See also CA 1-4R; CANR 5, 20; DLB 88; MTCW 1

Biruni, al 973-1048(?) ....**CMLC 28**

Bishop, Elizabeth 1911-1979...**CLC 1, 4, 9, 13, 15, 32; DA; DAC; DAM MST, POET; PC 3**
See also CA 5-8R; 89-92; CABS 2; CANR 26, 61; CDALB 1968-1988; DLB 5, 169; MTCW 1; SATA-Obit 24

Bishop, John 1935- ....**CLC 10**
See also CA 105

Bissett, Bill 1939- ....**CLC 18; PC 14**
See also CA 69-72; CAAS 19; CANR 15; DLB 53; MTCW 1

Bitov, Andrei (Georgievich) 1937- ....**CLC 57**
See also CA 142

Biyidi, Alexandre 1932-
See Beti, Mongo
See also BW 1; CA 114; 124; MTCW 1

Bjarme, Brynjolf
See Ibsen, Henrik (Johan)

Bjoernson, Bjoernstjerne (Martinius) 1832-1910 ....**TCLC 7, 37**
See also CA 104

Black, Robert
See Holdstock, Robert P.

Blackburn, Paul 1926-1971 ....**CLC 9, 43**
See also CA 81-84; 33-36R; CANR 34; DLB 16; DLBY 81

Black Elk 1863-1950...**TCLC 33; DAM MULT**
See also CA 144; NNAL

Black Hobart
See Sanders, (James) Ed(ward)

Blacklin, Malcolm
See Chambers, Aidan

Blackmore, R(ichard) D(oddridge) 1825-1900
TCLC 27
See also CA 120; DLB 18

Blackmur, R(ichard) P(almer) 1904-1965
CLC 2, 24
See also CA 11-12; 25-28R; CANR 71; CAP 1; DLB 63

Black Tarantula
See Acker, Kathy

Blackwood, Algernon (Henry) 1869-1951
TCLC 5
See also CA 105; 150; DLB 153, 156, 178

Blackwood, Caroline 1931-1996 ..**CLC 6, 9, 100**
See also CA 85-88; 151; CANR 32, 61, 65; DLB 14; MTCW 1

Blade, Alexander
See Hamilton, Edmond; Silverberg, Robert

Blaga, Lucian 1895-1961 ....**CLC 75**
See also CA 157

Blair, Eric (Arthur) 1903-1950
See Orwell, George
See also CA 104; 132; DA; DAB; DAC; DAM MST, NOV; MTCW 1; SATA 29

Blais, Marie-Claire 1939-...**CLC 2, 4, 6, 13, 22; DAC; DAM MST**
See also CA 21-24R; CAAS 4; CANR 38, 75; DLB 53; MTCW 1

Blaise, Clark 1940- ....**CLC 29**
See also AITN 2; CA 53-56; CAAS 3; CANR 5, 66; DLB 53

Blake, Fairley
See De Voto, Bernard (Augustine)

Blake, Nicholas
See Day Lewis, C(ecil)
See also DLB 77

Blake, William 1757-1827...**NCLC 13, 37, 57; DA; DAB; DAC; DAM MST, POET; PC 12; WLC**
See also CDBLB 1789-1832; CLR 52; DLB 93, 163; MAICYA; SATA 30

Blasco Ibanez, Vicente 1867-1928...**TCLC 12; DAM NOV**
See also CA 110; 131; HW; MTCW 1

Blatty, William Peter 1928-**CLC 2; DAM POP**
See also CA 5-8R; CANR 9

Bleeck, Oliver
See Thomas, Ross (Elmore)

Blessing, Lee 1949- ....**CLC 54**

Blish, James (Benjamin) 1921-1975...**CLC 14**
See also CA 1-4R; 57-60; CANR 3; DLB 8; MTCW 1; SATA 66

Bliss, Reginald
See Wells, H(erbert) G(eorge)

Blixen, Karen (Christentze Dinesen) 1885-1962
See Dinesen, Isak
See also CA 25-28; CANR 22, 50; CAP 2; MTCW 1; SATA 44

Bloch, Robert (Albert) 1917-1994 ....**CLC 33**
See also CA 5-8R; 146; CAAS 20; CANR 5; DLB 44; INT CANR-5; SATA 12; SATA-Obit 82

Blok, Alexander (Alexandrovich) 1880-1921
TCLC 5; PC 21
See also CA 104

Blom, Jan
See Breytenbach, Breyten

Bloom, Harold 1930- .... **CLC 24, 103**
See also CA 13-16R; CANR 39, 75; DLB 67

Bloomfield, Aurelius
See Bourne, Randolph S(illiman)

Blount, Roy (Alton), Jr. 1941- .... **CLC 38**
See also CA 53-56; CANR 10, 28, 61; INT CANR-28; MTCW 1

Bloy, Leon 1846-1917 .... **TCLC 22**
See also CA 121; DLB 123

Blume, Judy (Sussman) 1938- ... **CLC 12, 30; DAM NOV, POP**
See also AAYA 3, 26; CA 29-32R; CANR 13, 37, 66; CLR 2, 15; DLB 52; JRDA; MAICYA; MTCW 1; SATA 2, 31, 79

Blunden, Edmund (Charles) 1896-1974
CLC 2, 56
See also CA 17-18; 45-48; CANR 54; CAP 2; DLB 20, 100, 155; MTCW 1

Bly, Robert (Elwood) 1926-...**CLC 1, 2, 5, 10, 15, 38; DAM POET**
See also CA 5-8R; CANR 41, 73; DLB 5; MTCW 1

Boas, Franz 1858-1942 .... **TCLC 56**
See also CA 115

Bobette
See Simenon, Georges (Jacques Christian)

Boccaccio, Giovanni 1313-1375 .. **CMLC 13; SSC 10**

Bochco, Steven 1943- .... **CLC 35**
See also AAYA 11; CA 124; 138

Bodel, Jean 1167(?)-1210 .... **CMLC 28**

Bodenheim, Maxwell 1892-1954 .... **TCLC 44**
See also CA 110; DLB 9, 45

Bodker, Cecil 1927- .... **CLC 21**
See also CA 73-76; CANR 13, 44; CLR 23; MAICYA; SATA 14

Boell, Heinrich (Theodor) 1917-1985
CLC 2, 3, 6, 9, 11, 15, 27, 32, 72; DA; DAB; DAC; DAM MST, NOV; SSC 23; WLC
See also CA 21-24R; 116; CANR 24; DLB 69; DLBY 85; MTCW 1

Boerne, Alfred
See Doeblin, Alfred

Boethius 480(?)-524(?) .... **CMLC 15**
See also DLB 115

Bogan, Louise 1897-1970...**CLC 4, 39, 46, 93; DAM POET; PC 12**
See also CA 73-76; 25-28R; CANR 33; DLB 45, 169; MTCW 1

Bogarde, Dirk .... **CLC 19**
See also Van Den Bogarde, Derek Jules Gaspard Ulric Niven
See also DLB 14

Bogosian, Eric 1953- .... **CLC 45**
See also CA 138

Bograd, Larry 1953- .... **CLC 35**
See also CA 93-96; CANR 57; SAAS 21; SATA 33, 89

Boiardo, Matteo Maria 1441-1494 .... **LC 6**

Boileau-Despreaux, Nicolas 1636-1711
LC 3

Bojer, Johan 1872-1959............. **TCLC 64**

Boland, Eavan (Aisling) 1944- .**CLC 40, 67, 113; DAM POET**
See also CA 143; CANR 61; DLB 40

Boll, Heinrich
See Boell, Heinrich (Theodor)

Bolt, Lee
See Faust, Frederick (Schiller)

Bolt, Robert (Oxton) 1924-1995 .. **C L C 14; DAM DRAM**
See also CA 17-20R; 147; CANR 35, 67; DLB 13; MTCW 1

Bombet, Louis-Alexandre-Cesar
See Stendhal

Bomkauf
See Kaufman, Bob (Garnell)

Bonaventura .... **NCLC 35**
See also DLB 90

Bond, Edward 1934- ...**CLC 4, 6, 13, 23; DAM DRAM**
See also CA 25-28R; CANR 38, 67; DLB 13; MTCW 1

Bonham, Frank 1914-1989 ....**CLC 12**
See also AAYA 1; CA 9-12R; CANR 4, 36; JRDA; MAICYA; SAAS 3; SATA 1, 49; SATA-Obit 62

Bonnefoy, Yves 1923- .. **CLC 9, 15, 58; DAM MST, POET**
See also CA 85-88; CANR 33, 75; MTCW 1

Bontemps, Arna(ud Wendell) 1902-1973
CLC 1, 18; BLC 1; DAM MULT, NOV, POET
See also BW 1; CA 1-4R; 41-44R; CANR 4, 35; CLR 6; DLB 48, 51; JRDA; MAICYA; MTCW 1; SATA 2, 44; SATA-Obit 24

Booth, Martin 1944- ....**CLC 13**
See also CA 93-96; CAAS 2

Booth, Philip 1925- ....**CLC 23**
See also CA 5-8R; CANR 5; DLBY 82

Booth, Wayne C(layson) 1921- .... **CLC 24**
See also CA 1-4R; CAAS 5; CANR 3, 43; DLB 67

Borchert, Wolfgang 1921-1947 .... **TCLC 5**
See also CA 104; DLB 69, 124

Borel, Petrus 1809-1859 ....**NCLC 41**

Borges, Jorge Luis 1899-1986... **CLC 1, 2, 3, 4, 6, 8, 9, 10, 13, 19, 44, 48, 83; DA; DAB; DAC; DAM MST, MULT; HLC; PC 22; SSC 4; WLC**
See also AAYA 26; CA 21-24R; CANR 19, 33, 75; DLB 113; DLBY 86; HW; MTCW 1

Borowski, Tadeusz 1922-1951 .... **TCLC 9**
See also CA 106; 154

Borrow, George (Henry) 1803-1881
NCLC 9
See also DLB 21, 55, 166

Bosman, Herman Charles 1905-1951
TCLC 49
See also Malan, Herman
See also CA 160

Bosschere, Jean de 1878(?)-1953 ... **TCLC 19**
See also CA 115

Boswell, James 1740-1795 ... **LC 4; DA; DAB; DAC; DAM MST; WLC**
See also CDBLB 1660-1789; DLB 104, 142

Bottoms, David 1949- ....**CLC 53**
See also CA 105; CANR 22; DLB 120; DLBY 83

Boucicault, Dion 1820-1890 ....**NCLC 41**

Boucolon, Maryse 1937(?)-
See Conde, Maryse
See also CA 110; CANR 30, 53

Bourget, Paul (Charles Joseph) 1852-1935
TCLC 12
See also CA 107; DLB 123

Bourjaily, Vance (Nye) 1922- .... **CLC 8, 62**
See also CA 1-4R; CAAS 1; CANR 2, 72; DLB 2, 143

Bourne, Randolph S(illiman) 1886-1918
TCLC 16
See also CA 117; 155; DLB 63

Bova, Ben(jamin William) 1932-.. **C L C 45**
See also AAYA 16; CA 5-8R; CAAS 18; CANR 11, 56; CLR 3; DLBY 81; INT CANR-11; MAICYA; MTCW 1; SATA 6, 68

Bowen, Elizabeth (Dorothea Cole) 1899-1973**CLC 1, 3, 6, 11, 15, 22; DAM NOV; SSC 3, 28**
See also CA 17-18; 41-44R; CANR 35; CAP 2; CDBLB 1945-1960; DLB 15, 162; MTCW 1

Bowering, George 1935- .... **CLC 15, 47**
See also CA 21-24R; CAAS 16; CANR 10; DLB 53

Bowering, Marilyn R(uthe) 1949- ... **CLC 32**
See also CA 101; CANR 49

Bowers, Edgar 1924-...........................**CLC 9**
See also CA 5-8R; CANR 24; DLB 5

Bowie, David .... **CLC 17**
See also Jones, David Robert

Bowles, Jane (Sydney) 1917-1973...**C L C 3, 68**
See also CA 19-20; 41-44R; CAP 2

Bowles, Paul (Frederick) 1910-...**CLC 1, 2, 19, 53; SSC 3**
See also CA 1-4R; CAAS 1; CANR 1, 19, 50, 75; DLB 5, 6; MTCW 1

Box, Edgar
See Vidal, Gore

Boyd, Nancy
See Millay, Edna St. Vincent

Boyd, William 1952-.............. **CLC 28, 53, 70**
See also CA 114; 120; CANR 51, 71

Boyle, Kay 1902-1992...**CLC 1, 5, 19, 58; SSC 5**
See also CA 13-16R; 140; CAAS 1; CANR 29, 61; DLB 4, 9, 48, 86; DLBY 93; MTCW 1

Boyle, Mark
See Kienzle, William X(avier)

Boyle, Patrick 1905-1982 .... **CLC 19**
See also CA 127

Boyle, T. C. 1948-
See Boyle, T(homas) Coraghessan

Boyle, T(homas) Coraghessan 1948-
CLC 36, 55, 90; DAM POP; SSC 16
See also BEST 90:4; CA 120; CANR 44; DLBY 86

Boz
See Dickens, Charles (John Huffam)

Brackenridge, Hugh Henry 1748-1816
NCLC 7
See also DLB 11, 37

Bradbury, Edward P.
See Moorcock, Michael (John)

Bradbury, Malcolm (Stanley) 1932-
CLC 32, 61; DAM NOV
See also CA 1-4R; CANR 1, 33; DLB 14; MTCW 1

Bradbury, Ray (Douglas) 1920-... **C L C 1, 3, 10, 15, 42, 98; DA; DAB; DAC; DAM MST, NOV, POP; SSC 29; WLC**
See also AAYA 15; AITN 1, 2; CA 1-4R; CANR 2, 30, 75; CDALB 1968-1988; DLB 2, 8; MTCW 1; SATA 11, 64

Bradford, Gamaliel 1863-1932 ...... **TCLC 36**
See also CA 160; DLB 17

Bradley, David (Henry, Jr.) 1950-... **C L C 23; BLC 1; DAM MULT**
See also BW 1; CA 104; CANR 26; DLB 33

Bradley, John Ed(mund, Jr.) 1958-
CLC 55
See also CA 139

Bradley, Marion Zimmer 1930-......**C L C 30; DAM POP**
See also AAYA 9; CA 57-60; CAAS 10; CANR 7, 31, 51, 75; DLB 8; MTCW 1; SATA 90

Bradstreet, Anne 1612(?)-1672...**LC 4, 30; DA; DAC; DAM MST, POET; PC 10**
See also CDALB 1640-1865; DLB 24

Brady, Joan 1939- ....**CLC 86**
See also CA 141

Bragg, Melvyn 1939-.........................**CLC 10**
See also BEST 89:3; CA 57-60; CANR 10, 48; DLB 14

Brahe, Tycho 1546-1601 ....**LC 45**

Braine, John (Gerard) 1922-1986...**C L C 1, 3, 41**
See also CA 1-4R; 120; CANR 1, 33; CDBLB 1945-1960; DLB 15; DLBY 86; MTCW 1

Bramah, Ernest 1868-1942 ....**TCLC 72**
See also CA 156; DLB 70

Brammer, William 1930(?)-1978......**CLC 31**
See also CA 77-80

Brancati, Vitaliano 1907-1954 ....**TCLC 12**
See also CA 109

Brancato, Robin F(idler) 1936- ....**CLC 35**
See also AAYA 9; CA 69-72; CANR 11, 45; CLR 32; JRDA; SAAS 9; SATA 97

Brand, Max
See Faust, Frederick (Schiller)

Brand, Millen 1906-1980 ....**CLC 7**
See also CA 21-24R; 97-100; CANR 72

Branden, Barbara .... **CLC 44**
See also CA 148

Brandes, Georg (Morris Cohen) 1842-1927
TCLC 10
See also CA 105

Brandys, Kazimierz 1916- .... **CLC 62**

Branley, Franklyn M(ansfield) 1915-
CLC 21
See also CA 33-36R; CANR 14, 39; CLR 13; MAICYA; SAAS 16; SATA 4, 68

Brathwaite, Edward Kamau 1930-...**C L C 11; BLCS; DAM POET**
See also BW 2; CA 25-28R; CANR 11, 26, 47; DLB 125

Brautigan, Richard (Gary) 1935-1984
CLC 1, 3, 5, 9, 12, 34, 42; DAM NOV
See also CA 53-56; 113; CANR 34; DLB 2, 5, 206; DLBY 80, 84; MTCW 1; SATA 56

Brave Bird, Mary 1953-
See Crow Dog, Mary (Ellen)
See also NNAL

Braverman, Kate 1950- .... **CLC 67**
See also CA 89-92

Brecht, (Eugen) Bertolt (Friedrich) 1898-1956
TCLC 1, 6, 13, 35; DA; DAB; DAC; DAM DRAM, MST; DC 3; WLC
See also CA 104; 133; CANR 62; DLB 56, 124; MTCW 1

Brecht, Eugen Berthold Friedrich
See Brecht, (Eugen) Bertolt (Friedrich)

Bremer, Fredrika 1801-1865 ....**NCLC 11**

Brennan, Christopher John 1870-1932
TCLC 17
See also CA 117

Brennan, Maeve 1917-1993 ....**CLC 5**
See also CA 81-84; CANR 72

Brent, Linda
See Jacobs, Harriet A(nn)

Brentano, Clemens (Maria) 1778-1842
NCLC 1
See also DLB 90

Brent of Bin Bin
See Franklin, (Stella Maria Sarah) Miles (Lampe)

Brenton, Howard 1942-...............**CLC 31**
See also CA 69-72; CANR 33, 67; DLB 13; MTCW 1

Breslin, James 1930-1996
See Breslin, Jimmy
See also CA 73-76; CANR 31, 75; DAM NOV; MTCW 1

Breslin, Jimmy .... **CLC 4, 43**
See also Breslin, James
See also AITN 1; DLB 185

Bresson, Robert 1901-........................**CLC 16**
See also CA 110; CANR 49

Breton, Andre 1896-1966...**CLC 2, 9, 15, 54; PC 15**
See also CA 19-20; 25-28R; CANR 40, 60; CAP 2; DLB 65; MTCW 1

Breytenbach, Breyten 1939(?)-...**CLC 23, 37; DAM POET**
See also CA 113; 129; CANR 61

Bridgers, Sue Ellen 1942- ....**CLC 26**
See also AAYA 8; CA 65-68; CANR 11, 36; CLR 18; DLB 52; JRDA; MAICYA; SAAS 1; SATA 22, 90

Bridges, Robert (Seymour) 1844-1930
TCLC 1; DAM POET
See also CA 104; 152; CDBLB 1890-1914; DLB 19, 98

Bridie, James .... **TCLC 3**
See also Mavor, Osborne Henry
See also DLB 10

Brin, David 1950- ....**CLC 34**
See also AAYA 21; CA 102; CANR 24, 70; INT CANR-24; SATA 65

Brink, Andre (Philippus) 1935-...**CLC 18, 36, 106**
See also CA 104; CANR 39, 62; INT 103; MTCW 1

Brinsmead, H(esba) F(ay) 1922- ....**CLC 21**
See also CA 21-24R; CANR 10; CLR 47; MAICYA; SAAS 5; SATA 18, 78

Brittain, Vera (Mary) 1893(?)-1970
CLC 23
See also CA 13-16; 25-28R; CANR 58; CAP 1; DLB 191; MTCW 1

Broch, Hermann 1886-1951 ....**TCLC 20**
See also CA 117; DLB 85, 124

Brock, Rose
See Hansen, Joseph

Brodkey, Harold (Roy) 1930-1996 ....**CLC 56**
See also CA 111; 151; CANR 71; DLB 130

Brodskii, Iosif
See Brodsky, Joseph

Brodsky, Iosif Alexandrovich 1940-1996
See Brodsky, Joseph
See also AITN 1; CA 41-44R; 151; CANR 37; DAM POET; MTCW 1

Brodsky, Joseph 1940-1996....**CLC 4, 6, 13, 36, 100; PC 9**
See also Brodskii, Iosif; Brodsky, Iosif Alexandrovich

Brodsky, Michael (Mark) 1948-.........**CLC 19**
See also CA 102; CANR 18, 41, 58

Bromell, Henry 1947- ....**CLC 5**
See also CA 53-56; CANR 9

Bromfield, Louis (Brucker) 1896-1956
TCLC 11
See also CA 107; 155; DLB 4, 9, 86

Broner, E(sther) M(asserman) 1930-
CLC 19
See also CA 17-20R; CANR 8, 25, 72; DLB 28

Bronk, William 1918-................**CLC 10**
See also CA 89-92; CANR 23; DLB 165

Bronstein, Lev Davidovich
See Trotsky, Leon

Bronte, Anne 1820-1849 ....**NCLC 71**
See also DLB 21, 199

Bronte, Charlotte 1816-1855...**NCLC 3, 8, 33, 58; DA; DAB; DAC; DAM MST, NOV; WLC**
See also AAYA 17; CDBLB 1832-1890; DLB 21, 159, 199

Bronte, Emily (Jane) 1818-1848...**N C L C 16, 35; DA; DAB; DAC; DAM MST, NOV, POET; PC 8; WLC**
See also AAYA 17; CDBLB 1832-1890; DLB 21, 32, 199

Brooke, Frances 1724-1789 .... **LC 6, 48**
See also DLB 39, 99

Brooke, Henry 1703(?)-1783 .... **LC 1**
See also DLB 39

Brooke, Rupert (Chawner) 1887-1915
TCLC 2, 7; DA; DAB; DAC; DAM MST, POET; PC 24; WLC
See also CA 104; 132; CANR 61; CDBLB 1914-1945; DLB 19; MTCW 1

Brooke-Haven, P.
See Wodehouse, P(elham) G(renville)

Brooke-Rose, Christine 1926(?)- ....**CLC 40**
See also CA 13-16R; CANR 58; DLB 14

Brookner, Anita 1928-...**CLC 32, 34, 51; DAB; DAM POP**
See also CA 114; 120; CANR 37, 56; DLB 194; DLBY 87; MTCW 1

Brooks, Cleanth 1906-1994...**CLC 24, 86, 110**
See also CA 17-20R; 145; CANR 33, 35; DLB 63; DLBY 94; INT CANR-35; MTCW 1

Brooks, George
See Baum, L(yman) Frank

Brooks, Gwendolyn 1917-...**CLC 1, 2, 4, 5, 15, 49; BLC 1; DA; DAC; DAM MST, MULT, POET; PC 7; WLC**
See also AAYA 20; AITN 1; BW 2; CA 1-4R; CANR 1, 27, 52, 75; CDALB 1941-1968; CLR 27; DLB 5, 76, 165; MTCW 1; SATA 6

Brooks, Mel ....**CLC 12**
See also Kaminsky, Melvin
See also AAYA 13; DLB 26

Brooks, Peter 1938- ....**CLC 34**
See also CA 45-48; CANR 1

Brooks, Van Wyck 1886-1963 ....**CLC 29**
See also CA 1-4R; CANR 6; DLB 45, 63, 103

Brophy, Brigid (Antonia) 1929-1995
CLC 6, 11, 29, 105
See also CA 5-8R; 149; CAAS 4; CANR 25, 53; DLB 14; MTCW 1

Brosman, Catharine Savage 1934- .....**CLC 9**
See also CA 61-64; CANR 21, 46

Brossard, Nicole 1943- ....**CLC 115**
See also CA 122; CAAS 16; DLB 53

Brother Antoninus
See Everson, William (Oliver)

The Brothers Quay
See Quay, Stephen; Quay, Timothy

Broughton, T(homas) Alan 1936- .....**CLC 19**
See also CA 45-48; CANR 2, 23, 48

Broumas, Olga 1949- ....**CLC 10, 73**
See also CA 85-88; CANR 20, 69

Busch, Frederick 1941-...**CLC 7, 10, 18, 47**
See also CA 33-36R; CAAS 1; CANR 45, 73;
DLB 6
Bush, Ronald 1946- .... **CLC 34**
See also CA 136
Bustos, F(rancisco)
See Borges, Jorge Luis
Bustos Domecq, H(onorio)
See Bioy Casares, Adolfo; Borges, Jorge Luis
Butler, Octavia E(stelle) 1947-...**CLC 38;
BLCS; DAM MULT, POP**
See also AAYA 18; BW 2; CA 73-76; CANR
12, 24, 38, 73; DLB 33; MTCW 1; SATA 84
Butler, Robert Olen (Jr.) 1945-...**C L C
81; DAM POP**
See also CA 112; CANR 66; DLB 173; INT 112
Butler, Samuel 1612-1680 .... **LC 16, 43**
See also DLB 101, 126
Butler, Samuel 1835-1902...**TCLC 1, 33;
DA; DAB; DAC; DAM MST, NOV;
WLC**
See also CA 143; CDBLB 1890-1914; DLB 18,
57, 174
Butler, Walter C.
See Faust, Frederick (Schiller)
Butor, Michel (Marie Francois) 1926-
CLC 1, 3, 8, 11, 15
See also CA 9-12R; CANR 33, 66; DLB 83;
MTCW 1
Butts, Mary 1892(?)-1937 .... **TCLC 77**
See also CA 148
Buzo, Alexander (John) 1944- .... **CLC 61**
See also CA 97-100; CANR 17, 39, 69
Buzzati, Dino 1906-1972 .... **CLC 36**
See also CA 160; 33-36R; DLB 177
Byars, Betsy (Cromer) 1928-............ **CLC 35**
See also AAYA 19; CA 33-36R; CANR 18, 36,
57; CLR 1, 16; DLB 52; INT CANR-18;
JRDA; MAICYA; MTCW 1; SAAS 1; SATA
4, 46, 80
Byatt, A(ntonia) S(usan Drabble) 1936-
CLC 19, 65; DAM NOV, POP
See also CA 13-16R; CANR 13, 33, 50, 75;
DLB 14, 194; MTCW 1
Byrne, David 1952- .... **CLC 26**
See also CA 127
Byrne, John Keyes 1926-
See Leonard, Hugh
See also CA 102; INT 102
Byron, George Gordon (Noel) 1788-1824
**NCLC 2, 12; DA; DAB; DAC; DAM MST,
POET; PC 16; WLC**
See also CDBLB 1789-1832; DLB 96, 110
Byron, Robert 1905-1941 .... **TCLC 67**
See also CA 160; DLB 195
C. 3. 3.
See Wilde, Oscar (Fingal O'Flahertie Wills)
Caballero, Fernan 1796-1877.........**NCLC 10**
Cabell, Branch
See Cabell, James Branch
Cabell, James Branch 1879-1958 .... **TCLC 6**
See also CA 105; 152; DLB 9, 78
Cable, George Washington 1844-1925
TCLC 4; SSC 4
See also CA 104; 155; DLB 12, 74; DLBD
13
Cabral de Melo Neto, Joao 1920-...**C L C
76; DAM MULT**
See also CA 151
Cabrera Infante, G(uillermo) 1929-
CLC 5, 25, 45; DAM MULT; HLC
See also CA 85-88; CANR 29, 65; DLB 113;
HW; MTCW 1

Cade, Toni
See Bambara, Toni Cade
Cadmus and Harmonia
See Buchan, John
Caedmon fl. 658-680 .... **CMLC 7**
See also DLB 146
Caeiro, Alberto
See Pessoa, Fernando (Antonio Nogueira)
Cage, John (Milton, Jr.) 1912-1992
CLC 41
See also CA 13-16R; 169; CANR 9; DLB
193; INT CANR-9
Cahan, Abraham 1860-1951 .... **TCLC 71**
See also CA 108; 154; DLB 9, 25, 28
Cain, G.
See Cabrera Infante, G(uillermo)
Cain, Guillermo
See Cabrera Infante, G(uillermo)
Cain, James M(allahan) 1892-1977
CLC 3, 11, 28
See also AITN 1; CA 17-20R; 73-76; CANR
8, 34, 61; MTCW 1
Caine, Mark
See Raphael, Frederic (Michael)
Calasso, Roberto 1941- ....**CLC 81**
See also CA 143
Calderon de la Barca, Pedro 1600-1681
LC 23; DC 3
Caldwell, Erskine (Preston) 1903-1987
CLC 1, 8, 14, 50, 60; DAM NOV; SSC 19
See also AITN 1; CA 1-4R; 121; CAAS 1;
CANR 2, 33; DLB 9, 86; MTCW 1
Caldwell, (Janet Miriam) Taylor (Holland)
1900-1985...... **CLC 2, 28, 39; DAM
NOV, POP**
See also CA 5-8R; 116; CANR 5; DLBD 17
Calhoun, John Caldwell 1782-1850**NCLC 15**
See also DLB 3
Calisher, Hortense 1911-...**CLC 2, 4, 8,
38; DAM NOV; SSC 15**
See also CA 1-4R; CANR 1, 22, 67; DLB 2;
INT CANR-22; MTCW 1
Callaghan, Morley Edward 1903-1990
CLC 3, 14, 41, 65; DAC; DAM MST
See also CA 9-12R; 132; CANR 33, 73; DLB
68; MTCW 1
Callimachus c. 305B.C.-c. 240B.C.
CMLC 18
See also DLB 176
Calvin, John 1509-1564 .... **LC 37**
Calvino, Italo 1923-1985...**CLC 5, 8, 11,
22, 33, 39, 73; DAM NOV; SSC 3**
See also CA 85-88; 116; CANR 23, 61; DLB
196; MTCW 1
Cameron, Carey 1952- ....**CLC 59**
See also CA 135
Cameron, Peter 1959- ....**CLC 44**
See also CA 125; CANR 50
Campana, Dino 1885-1932 .... **TCLC 20**
See also CA 117; DLB 114
Campanella, Tommaso 1568-1639 ...... **LC 32**
Campbell, John W(ood, Jr.) 1910-1971
CLC 32
See also CA 21-22; 29-32R; CANR 34; CAP
2; DLB 8; MTCW 1
Campbell, Joseph 1904-1987 ....**CLC 69**
See also AAYA 3; BEST 89:2; CA 1-4R; 124;
CANR 3, 28, 61; MTCW 1
Campbell, Maria 1940- ....**CLC 85; DAC**
See also CA 102; CANR 54; NNAL
Campbell, (John) Ramsey 1946-...**C L C
42; SSC 19**
See also CA 57-60; CANR 7; INT CANR-7

Campbell, (Ignatius) Roy (Dunnachie)
1901-1957 .... **TCLC 5**
See also CA 104; 155; DLB 20
Campbell, Thomas 1777-1844 .... **NCLC 19**
See also DLB 93; 144
Campbell, Wilfred .... **TCLC 9**
See also Campbell, William
Campbell, William 1858(?)-1918
See Campbell, Wilfred
See also CA 106; DLB 92
Campion, Jane ....**CLC 95**
See also CA 138
Campos, Alvaro de
See Pessoa, Fernando (Antonio Nogueira)
Camus, Albert 1913-1960...**CLC 1, 2, 4,
9, 11, 14, 32, 63, 69; DA; DAB; DAC;
DAM DRAM, MST, NOV; DC 2; SSC
9; WLC**
See also CA 89-92; DLB 72; MTCW 1
Canby, Vincent 1924- .... **CLC 13**
See also CA 81-84
Cancale
See Desnos, Robert
Canetti, Elias 1905-1994...**CLC 3, 14, 25,
75, 86**
See also CA 21-24R; 146; CANR 23, 61;
DLB 85, 124; MTCW 1
Canfield, Dorothea F.
See Fisher, Dorothy (Frances) Canfield
Canfield, Dorothea Frances
See Fisher, Dorothy (Frances) Canfield
Canfield, Dorothy
See Fisher, Dorothy (Frances) Canfield
Canin, Ethan 1960- ....**CLC 55**
See also CA 131; 135
Cannon, Curt
See Hunter, Evan
Cao, Lan 1961- .... **CLC 109**
See also CA 165
Cape, Judith
See Page, P(atricia) K(athleen)
Capek, Karel 1890-1938 ... **TCLC 6, 37; DA;
DAB; DAC; DAM DRAM, MST, NOV; DC
1; WLC**
See also CA 104; 140
Capote, Truman 1924-1984...**CLC 1, 3, 8,
13, 19, 34, 38, 58; DA; DAB; DAC;
DAM MST, NOV, POP; SSC 2; WLC**
See also CA 5-8R; 113; CANR 18, 62; CDALB
1941-1968; DLB 2, 185; DLBY 80, 84;
MTCW 1; SATA 91
Capra, Frank 1897-1991 ....**CLC 16**
See also CA 61-64; 135
Caputo, Philip 1941- ....**CLC 32**
See also CA 73-76; CANR 40
Caragiale, Ion Luca 1852-1912 ...... **TCLC 76**
See also CA 157
Card, Orson Scott 1951-... **CLC 44, 47,
50; DAM POP**
See also AAYA 11; CA 102; CANR 27, 47, 73;
INT CANR-27; MTCW 1; SATA 83
Cardenal, Ernesto 1925- ....**CLC 31; DAM
MULT, POET; HLC; PC 22**
See also CA 49-52; CANR 2, 32, 66; HW;
MTCW 1
Cardozo, Benjamin N(athan) 1870-1938
TCLC 65
See also CA 117; 164
Carducci, Giosue (Alessandro Giuseppe)
1835-1907 .... **TCLC 32**
See also CA 163
Carew, Thomas 1595(?)-1640 .... **LC 13**
See also DLB 126

Chambers, Jessie
  See Lawrence, D(avid) H(erbert Richards)
Chambers, Robert W(illiam) 1865-1933
    TCLC 41
  See also CA 165; DLB 202
Chandler, Raymond (Thornton) 1888-1959
    TCLC 1, 7; SSC 23
  See also AAYA 25; CA 104; 129; CANR
    60; CDALB 1929-1941; DLBD 6;
    MTCW 1
Chang, Eileen 1920-1995 ....SSC 28
  See also CA 166
Chang, Jung 1952- ....CLC 71
  See also CA 142
Chang Ai-Ling
  See Chang, Eileen
Channing, William Ellery 1780-1842
    NCLC 17
  See also DLB 1, 59
Chaplin, Charles Spencer 1889-1977
    CLC 16
  See also Chaplin, Charlie
  See also CA 81-84; 73-76
Chaplin, Charlie
  See Chaplin, Charles Spencer
  See also DLB 44
Chapman, George 1559(?)-1634...LC 22;
    DAM DRAM
  See also DLB 62, 121
Chapman, Graham 1941-1989 ....CLC 21
  See also Monty Python
  See also CA 116; 129; CANR 35
Chapman, John Jay 1862-1933 ....TCLC 7
  See also CA 104
Chapman, Lee
  See Bradley, Marion Zimmer
Chapman, Walker
  See Silverberg, Robert
Chappell, Fred (Davis) 1936- .....CLC 40, 78
  See also CA 5-8R; CAAS 4; CANR 8, 33, 67;
    DLB 6, 105
Char, Rene(-Emile) 1907-1988...CLC 9,
    11, 14, 55; DAM POET
  See also CA 13-16R; 124; CANR 32; MTCW 1
Charby, Jay
  See Ellison, Harlan (Jay)
Chardin, Pierre Teilhard de
  See Teilhard de Chardin, (Marie Joseph) Pierre
Charles I 1600-1649 ....LC 13
Charriere, Isabelle de 1740-1805 ..NCLC 66
Charyn, Jerome 1937- .... CLC 5, 8, 18
  See also CA 5-8R; CAAS 1; CANR 7, 61;
    DLBY 83; MTCW 1
Chase, Mary (Coyle) 1907-1981 ....DC 1
  See also CA 77-80; 105; SATA 17; SATA-Obit
    29
Chase, Mary Ellen 1887-1973 ....CLC 2
  See also CA 13-16; 41-44R; CAP 1; SATA 10
Chase, Nicholas
  See Hyde, Anthony
Chateaubriand, Francois Rene de 1768-1848
    NCLC 3
  See also DLB 119
Chatterje, Sarat Chandra 1876-1936(?)
  See Chatterji, Saratchandra
  See also CA 109
Chatterji, Bankim Chandra 1838-1894
    NCLC 19
Chatterji, Saratchandra ....TCLC 13
  See also Chatterje, Sarat Chandra
Chatterton, Thomas 1752-1770 .LC 3; DAM
    POET
  See also DLB 109

Chatwin, (Charles) Bruce 1940-1989
    CLC 28, 57, 59; DAM POP
  See also AAYA 4; BEST 90:1; CA 85-88;
    127; DLB 194
Chaucer, Daniel
  See Ford, Ford Madox
Chaucer, Geoffrey 1340(?)-1400...LC 17;
    DA; DAB; DAC; DAM MST, POET; PC
    19; WLCS
  See also CDBLB Before 1660; DLB 146
Chaviaras, Strates 1935-
  See Haviaras, Stratis
  See also CA 105
Chayefsky, Paddy ....CLC 23
  See also Chayefsky, Sidney
  See also DLB 7, 44; DLBY 81
Chayefsky, Sidney 1923-1981
  See Chayefsky, Paddy
  See also CA 9-12R; 104; CANR 18; DAM
    DRAM
Chedid, Andree 1920- ....CLC 47
  See also CA 145
Cheever, John 1912-1982...CLC 3, 7, 8,
    11, 15, 25, 64; DA; DAB; DAC; DAM
    MST, NOV, POP; SSC 1; WLC
  See also CA 5-8R; 106; CABS 1; CANR 5, 27;
    CDALB 1941-1968; DLB 2, 102; DLBY 80,
    82; INT CANR-5; MTCW 1
Cheever, Susan 1943- .... CLC 18, 48
  See also CA 103; CANR 27, 51; DLBY 82; INT
    CANR-27
Chekhonte, Antosha
  See Chekhov, Anton (Pavlovich)
Chekhov, Anton (Pavlovich) 1860-1904
    TCLC 3, 10, 31, 55; DA; DAB; DAC;
    DAM DRAM, MST; DC 9; SSC 2, 28;
    WLC
  See also CA 104; 124; SATA 90
Chernyshevsky, Nikolay Gavrilovich 1828-1889
    NCLC 1
Cherry, Carolyn Janice 1942-
  See Cherryh, C. J.
  See also CA 65-68; CANR 10
Cherryh, C. J. ....CLC 35
  See also Cherry, Carolyn Janice
  See also AAYA 24; DLBY 80; SATA 93
Chesnutt, Charles W(addell) 1858-1932
    TCLC 5, 39; BLC 1; DAM MULT; SSC 7
  See also BW 1; CA 106; 125; DLB 12, 50, 78;
    MTCW 1
Chester, Alfred 1929(?)-1971 ....CLC 49
  See also CA 33-36R; DLB 130
Chesterton, G(ilbert) K(eith) 1874-1936
    TCLC 1, 6, 64; DAM NOV, POET; SSC 1
  See also CA 104; 132; CANR 73; CDBLB
    1914-1945; DLB 10, 19, 34, 70, 98, 149,
    178; MTCW 1; SATA 27
Chiang, Pin-chin 1904-1986
  See Ding Ling
  See also CA 118
Ch'ien Chung-shu 1910- ....CLC 22
  See also CA 130; CANR 73; MTCW 1
Child, L. Maria
  See Child, Lydia Maria
Child, Lydia Maria 1802-1880 ...NCLC 6, 73
  See also DLB 1, 74; SATA 67
Child, Mrs.
  See Child, Lydia Maria
Child, Philip 1898-1978 .... CLC 19, 68
  See also CA 13-14; CAP 1; SATA 47
Childers, (Robert) Erskine 1870-1922
    TCLC 65
  See also CA 113; 153; DLB 70

Childress, Alice 1920-1994...CLC 12, 15,
    86, 96; BLC 1; DAM DRAM, MULT,
    NOV; DC 4
  See also AAYA 8; BW 2; CA 45-48; 146; CANR
    3, 27, 50, 74; CLR 14; DLB 7, 38; JRDA;
    MAICYA; MTCW 1; SATA 7, 48, 81
Chin, Frank (Chew, Jr.) 1940- .... DC 7
  See also CA 33-36R; CANR 71; DAM MULT
Chislett, (Margaret) Anne 1943-CLC 34
  See also CA 151
Chitty, Thomas Willes 1926- ....CLC 11
  See also Hinde, Thomas
  See also CA 5-8R
Chivers, Thomas Holley 1809-1858
    NCLC 49
  See also DLB 3
Chomette, Rene Lucien 1898-1981
  See Clair, Rene
  See also CA 103
Chopin, Kate ..TCLC 5, 14; DA; DAB;
    SSC 8; WLCS
  See also Chopin, Katherine
  See also CDALB 1865-1917; DLB 12, 78
Chopin, Katherine 1851-1904
  See Chopin, Kate
  See also CA 104; 122; DAC; DAM MST,
    NOV
Chretien de Troyes c. 12th cent.
    CMLC 10
Christie
  See Ichikawa, Kon
Christie, Agatha (Mary Clarissa) 1890-1976
    CLC 1, 6, 8, 12, 39, 48, 110; DAB; DAC;
    DAM NOV
  See also AAYA 9; AITN 1, 2; CA 17-20R; 61-
    64; CANR 10, 37; CDBLB 1914-1945; DLB
    13, 77; MTCW 1; SATA 36
Christie, (Ann) Philippa
  See Pearce, Philippa
  See also CA 5-8R; CANR 4
Christine de Pizan 1365(?)-1431(?) ...... LC 9
Chubb, Elmer
  See Masters, Edgar Lee
Chulkov, Mikhail Dmitrievich 1743-1792
    LC 2
  See also DLB 150
Churchill, Caryl 1938- .....CLC 31, 55; DC 5
  See also CA 102; CANR 22, 46; DLB 13;
    MTCW 1
Churchill, Charles 1731-1764 ....LC 3
  See also DLB 109
Chute, Carolyn 1947- ....CLC 39
  See also CA 123
Ciardi, John (Anthony) 1916-1986...CLC
    10, 40, 44; DAM POET
  See also CA 5-8R; 118; CAAS 2; CANR 5, 33;
    CLR 19; DLB 5; DLBY 86; INT CANR-5;
    MAICYA; MTCW 1; SAAS 26; SATA 1, 65;
    SATA-Obit 46
Cicero, Marcus Tullius 106B.C.-43B.C.
    CMLC 3
Cimino, Michael 1943- ....CLC 16
  See also CA 105
Cioran, E(mil) M. 1911-1995 ....CLC 64
  See also CA 25-28R; 149
Cisneros, Sandra 1954-...CLC 69; DAM
    MULT; HLC; SSC 32
  See also AAYA 9; CA 131; CANR 64; DLB 122,
    152; HW
Cixous, Helene 1937- ....CLC 92
  See also CA 126; CANR 55; DLB 83; MTCW 1
Clair, Rene .... CLC 20
  See also Chomette, Rene Lucien

Clampitt, Amy 1920-1994...**CLC 32; PC 19**
See also CA 110; 146; CANR 29; DLB 105
Clancy, Thomas L., Jr. 1947-
See Clancy, Tom
See also CA 125; 131; CANR 62; INT 131;
MTCW 1
Clancy, Tom...**CLC 45, 112; DAM NOV,
POP**
See also Clancy, Thomas L., Jr.
See also AAYA 9; BEST 89:1, 90:1
Clare, John 1793-1864 .. **NCLC 9; DAB;
DAM POET; PC 23**
See also DLB 55, 96
Clarin
See Alas (y Urena), Leopoldo (Enrique Garcia)
Clark, Al C.
See Goines, Donald
Clark, (Robert) Brian 1932- .... **CLC 29**
See also CA 41-44R; CANR 67
Clark, Curt
See Westlake, Donald E(dwin)
Clark, Eleanor 1913-1996 .... **CLC 5, 19**
See also CA 9-12R; 151; CANR 41; DLB 6
Clark, J. P.
See Clark, John Pepper
See also DLB 117
Clark, John Pepper 1935-......**CLC 38;
BLC 1; DAM DRAM, MULT; DC 5**
See also Clark, J. P.
See also BW 1; CA 65-68; CANR 16, 72
Clark, M. R.
See Clark, Mavis Thorpe
Clark, Mavis Thorpe 1909- .... **CLC 12**
See also CA 57-60; CANR 8, 37; CLR 30;
MAICYA; SAAS 5; SATA 8, 74
Clark, Walter Van Tilburg 1909-1971
CLC 28
See also CA 9-12R; 33-36R; CANR 63; DLB
9; SATA 8
Clark Bekederemo, J(ohnson) P(epper)
See Clark, John Pepper
Clarke, Arthur C(harles) 1917-... **C L C
1, 4, 13, 18, 35; DAM POP; SSC 3**
See also AAYA 4; CA 1-4R; CANR 2, 28, 55, 74;
JRDA; MAICYA; MTCW 1; SATA 13, 70
Clarke, Austin 1896-1974**CLC 6, 9; DAM
POET**
See also CA 29-32; 49-52; CAP 2; DLB 10, 20
Clarke, Austin C(hesterfield) 1934-**CLC 8, 53;
BLC 1; DAC; DAM MULT**
See also BW 1; CA 25-28R; CAAS 16; CANR
14, 32, 68; DLB 53, 125
Clarke, Gillian 1937-........................... **CLC 61**
See also CA 106; DLB 40
Clarke, Marcus (Andrew Hislop) 1846-1881
NCLC 19
Clarke, Shirley 1925- .... **CLC 16**
Clash, The
See Headon, (Nicky) Topper; Jones, Mick;
Simonon, Paul; Strummer, Joe
Claudel, Paul (Louis Charles Marie) 1868-1955
TCLC 2, 10
See also CA 104; 165; DLB 192
Clavell, James (duMaresq) 1925-1994
CLC 6, 25, 87; DAM NOV, POP
See also CA 25-28R; 146; CANR 26, 48;
MTCW 1
Cleaver, (Leroy) Eldridge 1935-1998
CLC 30; BLC 1; DAM MULT
See also BW 1; CA 21-24R; 167; CANR 16, 75
Cleese, John (Marwood) 1939-...**CLC 21**
See also Monty Python
See also CA 112; 116; CANR 35; MTCW 1

Cleishbotham, Jebediah
See Scott, Walter
Cleland, John 1710-1789 .... **LC 2, 48**
See also DLB 39
Clemens, Samuel Langhorne 1835-1910
See Twain, Mark
See also CA 104; 135; CDALB 1865-1917;
DA; DAB; DAC; DAM MST, NOV; DLB
11, 12, 23, 64, 74, 186, 189; JRDA;
MAICYA; SATA 100; YABC 2
Cleophil
See Congreve, William
Clerihew, E.
See Bentley, E(dmund) C(lerihew)
Clerk, N. W.
See Lewis, C(live) S(taples)
Cliff, Jimmy ....**CLC 21**
See also Chambers, James
Clifton, (Thelma) Lucille 1936-.. **C L C
19, 66; BLC 1; DAM MULT, POET; PC 17**
See also BW 2; CA 49-52; CANR 2, 24, 42;
CLR 5; DLB 5, 41; MAICYA; MTCW 1;
SATA 20, 69
Clinton, Dirk
See Silverberg, Robert
Clough, Arthur Hugh 1819-1861...**NCLC
27**
See also DLB 32
Clutha, Janet Paterson Frame 1924-
See Frame, Janet
See also CA 1-4R; CANR 2, 36; MTCW 1
Clyne, Terence
See Blatty, William Peter
Cobalt, Martin
See Mayne, William (James Carter)
Cobb, Irvin S. 1876-1944 .... **TCLC 77**
See also DLB 11, 25, 86
Cobbett, William 1763-1835 .... **NCLC 49**
See also DLB 43, 107, 158
Coburn, D(onald) L(ee) 1938- .... **CLC 10**
See also CA 89-92
Cocteau, Jean (Maurice Eugene Clement)
1889-1963...**CLC 1, 8, 15, 16, 43; DA;
DAB; DAC; DAM DRAM, MST, NOV;
WLC**
See also CA 25-28; CANR 40; CAP 2; DLB
65; MTCW 1
Codrescu, Andrei 1946-...**CLC 46; DAM
POET**
See also CA 33-36R; CAAS 19; CANR 13,
34, 53
Coe, Max
See Bourne, Randolph S(illiman)
Coe, Tucker
See Westlake, Donald E(dwin)
Coen, Ethan 1958- .... **CLC 108**
See also CA 126
Coen, Joel 1955- .... **CLC 108**
See also CA 126
The Coen Brothers
See Coen, Ethan; Coen, Joel
Coetzee, J(ohn) M(ichael) 1940-...**CLC 23,
33, 66, 117; DAM NOV**
See also CA 77-80; CANR 41, 54, 74; MTCW 1
Coffey, Brian
See Koontz, Dean R(ay)
Cohan, George M(ichael) 1878-1942
TCLC 60
See also CA 157
Cohen, Arthur A(llen) 1928-1986...**CLC
7, 31**
See also CA 1-4R; 120; CANR 1, 17, 42;
DLB 28

Cohen, Leonard (Norman) 1934-... **C L C
3, 38; DAC; DAM MST**
See also CA 21-24R; CANR 14, 69; DLB 53;
MTCW 1
Cohen, Matt 1942- .... **CLC 19; DAC**
See also CA 61-64; CAAS 18; CANR 40; DLB
53
Cohen-Solal, Annie 19(?)- .... **CLC 50**
Colegate, Isabel 1931-................. **CLC 36**
See also CA 17-20R; CANR 8, 22, 74; DLB
14; INT CANR-22; MTCW 1
Coleman, Emmett
See Reed, Ishmael
Coleridge, M. E.
See Coleridge, Mary E(lizabeth)
Coleridge, Mary E(lizabeth) 1861-1907
TCLC 73
See also CA 116; 166; DLB 19, 98
Coleridge, Samuel Taylor 1772-1834
**NCLC 9, 54; DA; DAB; DAC; DAM
MST, POET; PC 11; WLC**
See also CDBLB 1789-1832; DLB 93, 107
Coleridge, Sara 1802-1852 .... **NCLC 31**
See also DLB 199
Coles, Don 1928- .... **CLC 46**
See also CA 115; CANR 38
Coles, Robert (Martin) 1929-...**CLC 108**
See also CA 45-48; CANR 3, 32, 66, 70; INT
CANR-32; SATA 23
Colette, (Sidonie-Gabrielle) 1873-1954
TCLC 1, 5, 16; DAM NOV; SSC 10
See also CA 104; 131; DLB 65; MTCW
1
Collett, (Jacobine) Camilla (Wergeland)
1813-1895 .... **NCLC 22**
Collier, Christopher 1930- .... **CLC 30**
See also AAYA 13; CA 33-36R; CANR 13,
33; JRDA; MAICYA; SATA 16, 70
Collier, James L(incoln) 1928-...**CLC 30;
DAM POP**
See also AAYA 13; CA 9-12R; CANR 4, 33,
60; CLR 3; JRDA; MAICYA; SAAS 21;
SATA 8, 70
Collier, Jeremy 1650-1726 .... **LC 6**
Collier, John 1901-1980 .... **SSC 19**
See also CA 65-68; 97-100; CANR 10; DLB
77
Collingwood, R(obin) G(eorge) 1889(?)-
1943 .... **TCLC 67**
See also CA 117; 155
Collins, Hunt
See Hunter, Evan
Collins, Linda 1931- .... **CLC 44**
See also CA 125
Collins, (William) Wilkie 1824-1889
NCLC 1, 18
See also CDBLB 1832-1890; DLB 18, 70,
159
Collins, William 1721-1759 ... **LC 4, 40;
DAM POET**
See also DLB 109
Collodi, Carlo 1826-1890 .... **NCLC 54**
See also Lorenzini, Carlo
See also CLR 5
Colman, George 1732-1794
See Glassco, John
Colt, Winchester Remington
See Hubbard, L(afayette) Ron(ald)
Colter, Cyrus 1910-...................... **CLC 58**
See also BW 1; CA 65-68; CANR 10, 66;
DLB 33
Colton, James
See Hansen, Joseph

Colum, Padraic 1881-1972 .... **CLC 28**
See also CA 73-76; 33-36R; CANR 35; CLR 36; MAICYA; MTCW 1; SATA 15
Colvin, James
See Moorcock, Michael (John)
Colwin, Laurie (E.) 1944 1992... **CLC 5, 13, 23, 84**
See also CA 89-92; 139; CANR 20, 46; DLBY 80; MTCW 1
Comfort, Alex(ander) 1920- .... **CLC 7; DAM POP**
See also CA 1-4R; CANR 1, 45
Comfort, Montgomery
See Campbell, (John) Ramsey
Compton-Burnett, I(vy) 1884(?)-1969 **CLC 1, 3, 10, 15, 34; DAM NOV**
See also CA 1-4R; 25-28R; CANR 4; DLB 36; MTCW 1
Comstock, Anthony 1844-1915 ...... **TCLC 13**
See also CA 110; 169
Comte, Auguste 1798-1857 ..... **NCLC 54**
Conan Doyle, Arthur
See Doyle, Arthur Conan
Conde, Maryse 1937- .... **CLC 52, 92; BLCS; DAM MULT**
See also Boucolon, Maryse
See also BW 2
Condillac, Etienne Bonnot de 1714-1780 **LC 26**
Condon, Richard (Thomas) 1915-1996 **CLC 4, 6, 8, 10, 45, 100; DAM NOV**
See also BEST 90:3; CA 1-4R; 151; CAAS 1; CANR 2, 23; INT CANR-23; MTCW 1
Confucius 551B.C.-479B.C....**CMLC 19; DA; DAB; DAC; DAM MST; WLCS**
Congreve, William 1670-1729...**LC 5, 21; DA; DAB; DAC; DAM DRAM, MST, POET; DC 2; WLC**
See also CDBLB 1660-1789; DLB 39, 84
Connell, Evan S(helby), Jr. 1924- **CLC 4, 6, 45; DAM NOV**
See also AAYA 7; CA 1-4R; CAAS 2; CANR 2, 39; DLB 2; DLBY 81; MTCW 1
Connelly, Marc(us Cook) 1890-1980 ..**CLC 7**
See also CA 85-88; 102; CANR 30; DLB 7; DLBY 80; SATA-Obit 25
Connor, Ralph .... **TCLC 31**
See also Gordon, Charles William
See also DLB 92
Conrad, Joseph 1857-1924...**TCLC 1, 6, 13, 25, 43, 57; DA; DAB; DAC; DAM MST, NOV; SSC 9; WLC**
See also AAYA 26; CA 104; 131; CANR 60; CDBLB 1890-1914; DLB 10, 34, 98, 156; MTCW 1; SATA 27
Conrad, Robert Arnold
See Hart, Moss
Conroy, Pat
See Conroy, (Donald) Pat(rick)
Conroy, (Donald) Pat(rick) 1945-...**C L C 30, 74; DAM NOV, POP**
See also AAYA 8; AITN 1; CA 85-88; CANR 24, 53; DLB 6; MTCW 1
Constant (de Rebecque), (Henri) Benjamin 1767-1830 .... **NCLC 6**
See also DLB 119
Conybeare, Charles Augustus
See Eliot, T(homas) S(tearns)
Cook, Michael 1933- .... **CLC 58**
See also CA 93-96; CANR 68; DLB 53
Cook, Robin 1940-...**CLC 14; DAM POP**
See also BEST 90:2; CA 108; 111; CANR 41; INT 111

Cook, Roy
See Silverberg, Robert
Cooke, Elizabeth 1948- .... **CLC 55**
See also CA 129
Cooke, John Esten 1830-1886 .. **NCLC 5**
See also DLB 3
Cooke, John Estes
See Baum, L(yman) Frank
Cooke, M. E.
See Creasey, John
Cooke, Margaret
See Creasey, John
Cook-Lynn, Elizabeth 1930- .... **CLC 93; DAM MULT**
See also CA 133; DLB 175; NNAL
Cooney, Ray .... **CLC 62**
Cooper, Douglas 1960- .... **CLC 86**
Cooper, Henry St. John
See Creasey, John
Cooper, J(oan) California ...... **CLC 56; DAM MULT**
See also AAYA 12; BW 1; CA 125; CANR 55
Cooper, James Fenimore 1789-1851 **NCLC 1, 27, 54**
See also AAYA 22; CDALB 1640-1865; DLB 3; SATA 19
Coover, Robert (Lowell) 1932-... **CLC 3, 7, 15, 32, 46, 87; DAM NOV; SSC 15**
See also CA 45-48; CANR 3, 37, 58; DLB 2; DLBY 81; MTCW 1
Copeland, Stewart (Armstrong) 1952- **CLC 26**
Copernicus, Nicolaus 1473-1543 ..**LC 45**
Coppard, A(lfred) E(dgar) 1878-1957 **TCLC 5; SSC 21**
See also CA 114; 167; DLB 162; YABC 1
Coppee, Francois 1842-1908 .... **TCLC 25**
See also CA 170
Coppola, Francis Ford 1939- ....**CLC 16**
See also CA 77-80; CANR 40; DLB 44
Corbiere, Tristan 1845-1875 .... **NCLC 43**
Corcoran, Barbara 1911- ....**CLC 17**
See also AAYA 14; CA 21-24R; CAAS 2; CANR 11, 28, 48; CLR 50; DLB 52; JRDA; SAAS 20; SATA 3, 77
Cordelier, Maurice
See Giraudoux, (Hippolyte) Jean
Corelli, Marie 1855-1924 .... **TCLC 51**
See also Mackay, Mary
See also DLB 34, 156
Corman, Cid 1924- .... **CLC 9**
See also Corman, Sidney
See also CAAS 2; DLB 5, 193
Corman, Sidney 1924-
See Corman, Cid
See also CA 85-88; CANR 44; DAM POET
Cormier, Robert (Edmund) 1925-..**C L C 12, 30; DA; DAB; DAC; DAM MST, NOV**
See also AAYA 3, 19; CA 1-4R; CANR 5, 23; CDALB 1968-1988; CLR 12, 55; DLB 52; INT CANR-23; JRDA; MAICYA; MTCW 1; SATA 10, 45, 83
Corn, Alfred (DeWitt III) 1943- ....**CLC 33**
See also CA 104; CAAS 25; CANR 44; DLB 120; DLBY 80
Corneille, Pierre 1606-1684 ......**LC 28; DAB; DAM MST**
Cornwell, David (John Moore) 1931- **CLC 9, 15; DAM POP**
See also le Carre, John
See also CA 5-8R; CANR 13, 33, 59; MTCW 1

Corso, (Nunzio) Gregory 1930-...**CLC 1, 11**
See also CA 5-8R; CANR 41; DLB 5, 16; MTCW 1
Cortazar, Julio 1914-1984...**CLC 2, 3, 5, 10, 13, 15, 33, 34, 92; DAM MULT, NOV; HLC; SSC 7**
See also CA 21-24R; CANR 12, 32; DLB 113; HW; MTCW 1
CORTES, HERNAN 1484-1547 .... **LC 31**
Corvinus, Jakob
See Raabe, Wilhelm (Karl)
Corwin, Cecil
See Kornbluth, C(yril) M.
Cosic, Dobrica 1921- .... **CLC 14**
See also CA 122; 138; DLB 181
Costain, Thomas B(ertram) 1885-1965 **CLC 30**
See also CA 5-8R; 25-28R; DLB 9
Costantini, Humberto 1924(?)-1987 **CLC 49**
See also CA 131; 122; HW
Costello, Elvis 1955- .... **CLC 21**
Cotes, Cecil V.
See Duncan, Sara Jeannette
Cotter, Joseph Seamon Sr. 1861-1949 **TCLC 28; BLC 1; DAM MULT**
See also BW 1; CA 124; DLB 50
Couch, Arthur Thomas Quiller
See Quiller-Couch, SirArthur (Thomas)
Coulton, James
See Hansen, Joseph
Couperus, Louis (Marie Anne) 1863-1923 **TCLC 15**
See also CA 115
Coupland, Douglas 1961- .... **CLC 85; DAC; DAM POP**
See also CA 142; CANR 57
Court, Wesli
See Turco, Lewis (Putnam)
Courtenay, Bryce 1933- .... **CLC 59**
See also CA 138
Courtney, Robert
See Ellison, Harlan (Jay)
Cousteau, Jacques-Yves 1910-1997 ..**CLC 30**
See also CA 65-68; 159; CANR 15, 67; MTCW 1; SATA 38, 98
Coventry, Francis 1725-1754 .... **LC 46**
Cowan, Peter (Walkinshaw) 1914- ....**SSC 28**
See also CA 21-24R; CANR 9, 25, 50
Coward, Noel (Peirce) 1899-1973 **CLC 1, 9, 29, 51; DAM DRAM**
See also AITN 1; CA 17-18; 41-44R; CANR 35; CAP 2; CDBLB 1914-1945; DLB 10; MTCW 1
Cowley, Abraham 1618-1667 ....**LC 43**
See also DLB 131, 151
Cowley, Malcolm 1898-1989 ....**CLC 39**
See also CA 5-8R; 128; CANR 3, 55; DLB 4, 48; DLBY 81, 89; MTCW 1
Cowper, William 1731-1800 ...**NCLC 8; DAM POET**
See also DLB 104, 109
Cox, William Trevor 1928- .... **CLC 9, 14, 71; DAM NOV**
See also Trevor, William
See also CA 9-12R; CANR 4, 37, 55; DLB 14; INT CANR-37; MTCW 1
Coyne, P. J.
See Masters, Hilary
Cozzens, James Gould 1903-1978 **CLC 1, 4, 11, 92**
See also CA 9-12R; 81-84; CANR 19; CDALB 1941-1968; DLB 9; DLBD 2; DLBY 84, 97; MTCW 1

Crabbe, George 1754-1832 ..... NCLC 26
See also DLB 93
Craddock, Charles Egbert
See Murfree, Mary Noailles
Craig, A. A.
See Anderson, Poul (William)
Craik, Dinah Maria (Mulock) 1826-1887
NCLC 38
See also DLB 35, 163; MAICYA; SATA 34
Cram, Ralph Adams 1863-1942 ..... TCLC 45
See also CA 160
Crane, (Harold) Hart 1899-1932...T C L C
2, 5, 80; DA; DAB; DAC; DAM MST,
POET; PC 3; WLC
See also CA 104; 127; CDALB 1917-1929;
DLB 4, 48; MTCW 1
Crane, R(onald) S(almon) 1886-1967
CLC 27
See also CA 85-88; DLB 63
Crane, Stephen (Townley) 1871-1900
TCLC 11, 17, 32; DA; DAB; DAC; DAM
MST, NOV, POET; SSC 7; WLC
See also AAYA 21; CA 109; 140; CDALB
1865-1917; DLB 12, 54, 78; YABC 2
Cranshaw, Stanley
See Fisher, Dorothy (Frances) Canfield
Crase, Douglas 1944- .... CLC 58
See also CA 106
Crashaw, Richard 1612(?)-1649 .... LC 24
See also DLB 126
Craven, Margaret 1901-1980...CLC 17;
DAC
See also CA 103
Crawford, F(rancis) Marion 1854-1909
TCLC 10
See also CA 107; 168; DLB 71
Crawford, Isabella Valancy 1850-1887
NCLC 12
See also DLB 92
Crayon, Geoffrey
See Irving, Washington
Creasey, John 1908-1973 .... CLC 11
See also CA 5-8R; 41-44R; CANR 8, 59; DLB
77; MTCW 1
Crebillon, Claude Prosper Jolyot de (fils) 1707-
1777 .... LC 1, 28
Credo
See Creasey, John
Credo, Alvaro J. de
See Prado (Calvo), Pedro
Creeley, Robert (White) 1926-...CLC 1,
2, 4, 8, 11, 15, 36, 78; DAM POET
See also CA 1-4R; CAAS 10; CANR 23, 43;
DLB 5, 16, 169; DLBD 17; MTCW 1
Crews, Harry (Eugene) 1935-...CLC 6, 23,
49
See also AITN 1; CA 25-28R; CANR 20, 57;
DLB 6, 143, 185; MTCW 1
Crichton, (John) Michael 1942-...CLC 2,
6, 54, 90; DAM NOV, POP
See also AAYA 10; AITN 2; CA 25-28R; CANR
13, 40, 54; DLBY 81; INT CANR-13; JRDA;
MTCW 1; SATA 9, 88
Crispin, Edmund .... CLC 22
See also Montgomery, (Robert) Bruce
See also DLB 87
Cristofer, Michael 1945(?)-.... CLC 28; DAM
DRAM
See also CA 110; 152; DLB 7
Croce, Benedetto 1866-1952 .... TCLC 37
See also CA 120; 155
Crockett, David 1786-1836 .... NCLC 8
See also DLB 3, 11

Crockett, Davy
See Crockett, David
Crofts, Freeman Wills 1879-1957
TCLC 55
See also CA 115; DLB 77
Croker, John Wilson 1780-1857
NCLC 10
See also DLB 110
Crommelynck, Fernand 1885-1970 ..CLC 75
See also CA 89-92
Cromwell, Oliver 1599-1658 .... LC 43
Cronin, A(rchibald) J(oseph) 1896-1981
CLC 32
See also CA 1-4R; 102; CANR 5; DLB 191;
SATA 47; SATA-Obit 25
Cross, Amanda
See Heilbrun, Carolyn G(old)
Crothers, Rachel 1878(?)-1958...TCLC 19
See also CA 113; DLB 7
Croves, Hal
See Traven, B.
Crow Dog, Mary (Ellen) (?)- .... CLC 93
See also Brave Bird, Mary
See also CA 154
Crowfield, Christopher
See Stowe, Harriet (Elizabeth) Beecher
Crowley, Aleister .... TCLC 7
See also Crowley, Edward Alexander
Crowley, Edward Alexander 1875-1947
See Crowley, Aleister
See also CA 104
Crowley, John 1942- .... CLC 57
See also CA 61-64; CANR 43; DLBY 82; SATA
65
Crud
See Crumb, R(obert)
Crumarums
See Crumb, R(obert)
Crumb, R(obert) 1943- .... CLC 17
See also CA 106
Crumbum
See Crumb, R(obert)
Crumski
See Crumb, R(obert)
Crum the Bum
See Crumb, R(obert)
Crunk
See Crumb, R(obert)
Crustt
See Crumb, R(obert)
Cryer, Gretchen (Kiger) 1935-.......... CLC 21
See also CA 114; 123
Csath, Geza 1887-1919 .... TCLC 13
See also CA 111
Cudlip, David 1933- .... CLC 34
Cullen, Countee 1903-1946 . TCLC 4,
37; BLC 1; DA; DAC; DAM MST,
MULT, POET; PC 20; WLCS
See also BW 1; CA 108; 124; CDALB 1917-
1929; DLB 4, 48, 51; MTCW 1; SATA 18
Cum, R.
See Crumb, R(obert)
Cummings, Bruce F(rederick) 1889-1919
See Barbellion, W. N. P.
See also CA 123
Cummings, E(dward) E(stlin) 1894-1962
CLC 1, 3, 8, 12, 15, 68; DA; DAB; DAC;
DAM MST, POET; PC 5; WLC
See also CA 73-76; CANR 31; CDALB 1929-
1941; DLB 4, 48; MTCW 1
Cunha, Euclides (Rodrigues Pimenta) da
1866-1909 .... TCLC 24
See also CA 123

Cunningham, E. V.
See Fast, Howard (Melvin)
Cunningham, J(ames) V(incent) 1911-
1985 .... CLC 3, 31
See also CA 1-4R; 115; CANR 1, 72; DLB 5
Cunningham, Julia (Woolfolk) 1916-
CLC 12
See also CA 9-12R; CANR 4, 19, 36; JRDA;
MAICYA; SAAS 2; SATA 1, 26
Cunningham, Michael 1952- .... CLC 34
See also CA 136
Cunninghame Graham, R(obert)
B(ontine) 1852-1936 .... TCLC 19
See also Graham, R(obert) B(ontine)
Cunninghame
See also CA 119; DLB 98
Currie, Ellen 19(?)- .... CLC 44
Curtin, Philip
See Lowndes, Marie Adelaide (Belloc)
Curtis, Price
See Ellison, Harlan (Jay)
Cutrate, Joe
See Spiegelman, Art
Cynewulf c. 770-c. 840 .... CMLC 23
Czaczkes, Shmuel Yosef
See Agnon, S(hmuel) Y(osef Halevi)
Dabrowska, Maria (Szumska) 1889-1965
CLC 15
See also CA 106
Dabydeen, David 1955- .... CLC 34
See also BW 1; CA 125; CANR 56
Dacey, Philip 1939-........................... CLC 51
See also CA 37-40R; CAAS 17; CANR 14, 32,
64; DLB 105
Dagerman, Stig (Halvard) 1923-1954...TCLC
17
See also CA 117; 155
Dahl, Roald 1916-1990...CLC 1, 6, 18,
79; DAB; DAC; DAM MST, NOV, POP
See also AAYA 15; CA 1-4R; 133; CANR 6,
32, 37, 62; CLR 1, 7, 41; DLB 139; JRDA;
MAICYA; MTCW 1; SATA 1, 26, 73; SATA-
Obit 65
Dahlberg, Edward 1900-1977 .. CLC 1, 7, 14
See also CA 9-12R; 69-72; CANR 31, 62; DLB
48; MTCW 1
Daitch, Susan 1954-......................... CLC 103
See also CA 161
Dale, Colin .... TCLC 18
See also Lawrence, T(homas) E(dward)
Dale, George E.
See Asimov, Isaac
Daly, Elizabeth 1878-1967 .... CLC 52
See also CA 23-24; 25-28R; CANR 60; CAP 2
Daly, Maureen 1921- .... CLC 17
See also AAYA 5; CANR 37; JRDA; MAICYA;
SAAS 1; SATA 2
Damas, Leon-Gontran 1912-1978 .... CLC 84
See also BW 1; CA 125; 73-76
Dana, Richard Henry Sr. 1787-1879
NCLC 53
Daniel, Samuel 1562(?)-1619 ....LC 24
See also DLB 62
Daniels, Brett
See Adler, Renata
Dannay, Frederic 1905-1982...CLC 11;
DAM POP
See also Queen, Ellery
See also CA 1-4R; 107; CANR 1, 39; DLB
137; MTCW 1
D'Annunzio, Gabriele 1863-1938...TCLC
6, 40
See also CA 104; 155

Danois, N. le
See Gourmont, Remy (-Marie-Charles) de
Dante 1265-1321 .... CMLC 3, 18; DA;
DAB; DAC; DAM MST, POET; PC 21;
WLCS
d'Antibes, Germain
See Simenon, Georges (Jacques Christian)
Danticat, Edwidge 1969- .... CLC 94
See also CA 152; CANR 73
Danvers, Dennis 1947- .... CLC 70
Danziger, Paula 1944- .... CLC 21
See also AAYA 4; CA 112; 115; CANR 37; CLR
20; JRDA; MAICYA; SATA 36, 63, 102;
SATA-Brief 30
Da Ponte, Lorenzo 1749-1838 .... NCLC 50
Dario, Ruben 1867-1916 .... TCLC 4; DAM
MULT; HLC; PC 15
See also CA 131; HW; MTCW 1
Darley, George 1795-1846 .... NCLC 2
See also DLB 96
Darrow, Clarence (Seward) 1857-1938
TCLC 81
See also CA 164
Darwin, Charles 1809-1882 .... NCLC 57
See also DLB 57, 166
Daryush, Elizabeth 1887-1977 ... CLC 6,
19
See also CA 49-52; CANR 3; DLB 20
Dasgupta, Surendranath 1887-1952
TCLC 81
See also CA 157
Dashwood, Edmee Elizabeth Monica de la Pas-
ture 1890-1943
See Delafield, E. M.
See also CA 119; 154
Daudet, (Louis Marie) Alphonse 1840-1897
NCLC 1
See also DLB 123
Daumal, Rene 1908-1944 .... TCLC 14
See also CA 114
Davenant, William 1606-1668 .... LC 13
See also DLB 58, 126
Davenport, Guy (Mattison, Jr.) 1927-
CLC 6, 14, 38; SSC 16
See also CA 33-36R; CANR 23, 73; DLB
130
Davidson, Avram 1923-1993
See Queen, Ellery
See also CA 101; 171; CANR 26; DLB 8
Davidson, Donald (Grady) 1893-1968
CLC 2, 13, 19
See also CA 5-8R; 25-28R; CANR 4; DLB
45
Davidson, Hugh
See Hamilton, Edmond
Davidson, John 1857-1909 .... TCLC 24
See also CA 118; DLB 19
Davidson, Sara 1943- .... CLC 9
See also CA 81-84; CANR 44, 68; DLB 185
Davie, Donald (Alfred) 1922-1995 ... CLC
5, 8, 10, 31
See also CA 1-4R; 149; CAAS 3; CANR 1,
44; DLB 27; MTCW 1
Davies, Ray(mond Douglas) 1944- ... CLC 21
See also CA 116; 146
Davies, Rhys 1901-1978 .... CLC 23
See also CA 9-12R; 81-84; CANR 4; DLB 139,
191
Davies, (William) Robertson 1913-1995
CLC 2, 7, 13, 25, 42, 75, 91; DA; DAB;
DAC; DAM MST, NOV, POP; WLC
See also BEST 89:2; CA 33-36R; 150; CANR
17, 42; DLB 68; INT CANR-17; MTCW 1

Davies, W(illiam) H(enry) 1871-1940
TCLC 5
See also CA 104; DLB 19, 174
Davies, Walter C.
See Kornbluth, C(yril) M.
Davis, Angela (Yvonne) 1944- . CLC 77;
DAM MULT
See also BW 2; CA 57-60; CANR 10
Davis, B. Lynch
See Bioy Casares, Adolfo; Borges, Jorge Luis
Davis, Harold Lenoir 1896-1960 ......CLC 49
See also CA 89-92; DLB 9
Davis, Rebecca (Blaine) Harding 1831-
1910 .... TCLC 6
See also CA 104; DLB 74
Davis, Richard Harding 1864-1916
TCLC 24
See also CA 114; DLB 12, 23, 78, 79, 189;
DLBD 13
Davison, Frank Dalby 1893-1970 ..... CLC 15
See also CA 116
Davison, Lawrence H.
See Lawrence, D(avid) H(erbert Richards)
Davison, Peter (Hubert) 1928-...CLC 28
See also CA 9-12R; CAAS 4; CANR 3, 43;
DLB 5
Davys, Mary 1674-1732 .... LC 1, 46
See also DLB 39
Dawson, Fielding 1930- .... CLC 6
See also CA 85-88; DLB 130
Dawson, Peter
See Faust, Frederick (Schiller)
Day, Clarence (Shepard, Jr.) 1874-1935
TCLC 25
See also CA 108; DLB 11
Day, Thomas 1748-1789 .... LC 1
See also DLB 39; YABC 1
Day Lewis, C(ecil) 1904-1972...CLC 1, 6,
10; DAM POET; PC 11
See also Blake, Nicholas
See also CA 13-16; 33-36R; CANR 34; CAP 1;
DLB 15, 20; MTCW 1
Dazai Osamu 1909-1948 .... TCLC 11
See also Tsushima, Shuji
See also CA 164; DLB 182
de Andrade, Carlos Drummond
See Drummond de Andrade, Carlos
Deane, Norman
See Creasey, John
de Beauvoir, Simone (Lucie Ernestine Marie
Bertrand)
See Beauvoir, Simone (Lucie Ernestine Marie
Bertrand) de
de Beer, P.
See Bosman, Herman Charles
de Brissac, Malcolm
See Dickinson, Peter (Malcolm)
de Chardin, Pierre Teilhard
See Teilhard de Chardin, (Marie Joseph) Pierre
Dee, John 1527-1608 .... LC 20
Deer, Sandra 1940- ....CLC 45
De Ferrari, Gabriella 1941- ....CLC 65
See also CA 146
Defoe, Daniel 1660(?)-1731 ..... LC 1, 42; DA;
DAB; DAC; DAM MST, NOV; WLC
See also AAYA 27; CDBLB 1660-1789; DLB
39, 95, 101; JRDA; MAICYA; SATA 22
de Gourmont, Remy(-Marie-Charles)
See Gourmont, Remy (-Marie-Charles) de
de Hartog, Jan 1914- ....CLC 19
See also CA 1-4R; CANR 1
de Hostos, E. M.
See Hostos (y Bonilla), Eugenio Maria de

de Hostos, Eugenio M.
See Hostos (y Bonilla), Eugenio Maria de
Deighton, Len .... CLC 4, 7, 22, 46
See also Deighton, Leonard Cyril
See also AAYA 6; BEST 89:2; CDBLB 1960
to Present; DLB 87
Deighton, Leonard Cyril 1929-
See Deighton, Len
See also CA 9-12R; CANR 19, 33, 68; DAM
NOV, POP; MTCW 1
Dekker, Thomas 1572(?)-1632 ..LC 22; DAM
DRAM
See also CDBLB Before 1660; DLB 62, 172
Delafield, E. M. 1890-1943 .... TCLC 61
See also Dashwood, Edmee Elizabeth Monica
de la Pasture
See also DLB 34
de la Mare, Walter (John) 1873-1956
TCLC 4, 53; DAB; DAC; DAM MST,
POET; SSC 14; WLC
See also CA 163; CDBLB 1914-1945; CLR
23; DLB 162; SATA 16
Delaney, Franey
See O'Hara, John (Henry)
Delaney, Shelagh 1939-...CLC 29; DAM
DRAM
See also CA 17-20R; CANR 30, 67; CDBLB
1960 to Present; DLB 13; MTCW 1
Delany, Mary (Granville Pendarves) 1700-
1788 ....LC 12
Delany, Samuel R(ay, Jr.) 1942-...CLC 8,
14, 38; BLC 1; DAM MULT
See also AAYA 24; BW 2; CA 81-84; CANR
27, 43; DLB 8, 33; MTCW 1
De La Ramee, (Marie) Louise 1839-1908
See Ouida
See also SATA 20
de la Roche, Mazo 1879-1961 .... CLC 14
See also CA 85-88; CANR 30; DLB 68; SATA
64
De La Salle, Innocent
See Hartmann, Sadakichi
Delbanco, Nicholas (Franklin) 1942-
CLC 6, 13
See also CA 17-20R; CAAS 2; CANR 29, 55;
DLB 6
del Castillo, Michel 1933- .... CLC 38
See also CA 109
Deledda, Grazia (Cosima) 1875(?)-1936
TCLC 23
See also CA 123
Delibes, Miguel .... CLC 8, 18
See also Delibes Setien, Miguel
Delibes Setien, Miguel 1920-
See Delibes, Miguel
See also CA 45-48; CANR 1, 32; HW; MTCW 1
DeLillo, Don 1936-...CLC 8, 10, 13, 27, 39,
54, 76; DAM NOV, POP
See also BEST 89:1; CA 81-84; CANR 21;
DLB 6, 173; MTCW 1
de Lisser, H. G.
See De Lisser, H(erbert) G(eorge)
See also DLB 117
De Lisser, H(erbert) G(eorge) 1878-1944
TCLC 12
See also de Lisser, H. G.
See also BW 2; CA 109; 152
Deloney, Thomas 1560(?)-1600 .... LC 41
See also DLB 167
Deloria, Vine (Victor), Jr. 1933-...CLC
21; DAM MULT
See also CA 53-56; CANR 5, 20, 48; DLB
175; MTCW 1; NNAL; SATA 21

Doeblin, Alfred 1878-1957 .... **TCLC 13**
See also Doblin, Alfred
See also CA 110; 141; DLB 66

Doerr, Harriet 1910- .... **CLC 34**
See also CA 117; 122; CANR 47; INT 122

Domecq, H(onorio) Bustos
See Bioy Casares, Adolfo; Borges, Jorge Luis

Domini, Rey
See Lorde, Audre (Geraldine)

Dominique
See Proust, (Valentin-Louis-George-Eugene-) Marcel

Don, A
See Stephen, SirLeslie

Donaldson, Stephen R. 1947-...**CLC 46;**
DAM POP
See also CA 89-92; CANR 13, 55; INT CANR-13

Donleavy, J(ames) P(atrick) 1926-...**CLC 1, 4, 6, 10, 45**
See also AITN 2; CA 9-12R; CANR 24, 49, 62; DLB 6, 173; INT CANR-24; MTCW 1

Donne, John 1572-1631...**LC 10, 24; DA; DAB; DAC; DAM MST, POET; PC 1; WLC**
See also CDBLB Before 1660; DLB 121, 151

Donnell, David 1939(?)- .... **CLC 34**

Donoghue, P. S.
See Hunt, E(verette) Howard, (Jr.)

Donoso (Yanez), Jose 1924-1996...**CLC 4, 8, 11, 32, 99; DAM MULT; HLC**
See also CA 81-84; 155; CANR 32, 73; DLB 113; HW; MTCW 1

Donovan, John 1928-1992 .... **CLC 35**
See also AAYA 20; CA 97-100; 137; CLR 3; MAICYA; SATA 72; SATA-Brief 29

Don Roberto
See Cunninghame Graham, R(obert) B(ontine)

Doolittle, Hilda 1886-1961...**CLC 3, 8, 14, 31, 34, 73; DA; DAC; DAM MST, POET; PC 5; WLC**
See also H. D.
See also CA 97-100; CANR 35; DLB 4, 45; MTCW 1

Dorfman, Ariel 1942-...**CLC 48, 77; DAM MULT; HLC**
See also CA 124; 130; CANR 67, 70; HW; INT 130

Dorn, Edward (Merton) 1929- ... **CLC 10, 18**
See also CA 93-96; CANR 42; DLB 5; INT 93-96

Dorris, Michael (Anthony) 1945-1997...**CLC 109; DAM MULT, NOV**
See also AAYA 20; BEST 90:1; CA 102; 157; CANR 19, 46, 75; DLB 175; NNAL; SATA 75; SATA-Obit 94

Dorris, Michael A.
See Dorris, Michael (Anthony)

Dorsan, Luc
See Simenon, Georges (Jacques Christian)

Dorsange, Jean
See Simenon, Georges (Jacques Christian)

Dos Passos, John (Roderigo) 1896-1970
CLC 1, 4, 8, 11, 15, 25, 34, 82; DA; DAB; DAC; DAM MST, NOV; WLC
See also CA 1-4R; 29-32R; CANR 3; CDALB 1929-1941; DLB 4, 9; DLBD 1, 15; DLBY 96; MTCW 1

Dossage, Jean
See Simenon, Georges (Jacques Christian)

Dostoevsky, Fedor Mikhailovich 1821-1881
NCLC 2, 7, 21, 33, 43; DA; DAB; DAC; DAM MST, NOV; SSC 2, 33; WLC

Doughty, Charles M(ontagu) 1843-1926
TCLC 27
See also CA 115; DLB 19, 57, 174

Douglas, Ellen .... **CLC 73**
See also Haxton, Josephine Ayres; Williamson, Ellen Douglas

Douglas, Gavin 1475(?)-1522 .... **LC 20**
See also DLB 132

Douglas, George
See Brown, George Douglas

Douglas, Keith (Castellain) 1920-1944
TCLC 40
See also CA 160; DLB 27

Douglas, Leonard
See Bradbury, Ray (Douglas)

Douglas, Michael
See Crichton, (John) Michael

Douglas, (George) Norman 1868-1952
TCLC 68
See also CA 119; 157; DLB 34, 195

Douglas, William
See Brown, George Douglas

Douglass, Frederick 1817(?)-1895
NCLC 7, 55; BLC 1; DA; DAC; DAM MST, MULT; WLC
See also CDALB 1640-1865; DLB 1, 43, 50, 79; SATA 29

Dourado, (Waldomiro Freitas) Autran 1926- .... **CLC 23, 60**
See also CA 25-28R; CANR 34

Dourado, Waldomiro Autran
See Dourado, (Waldomiro Freitas) Autran

Dove, Rita (Frances) 1952-...**CLC 50, 81; BLCS; DAM MULT, POET; PC 6**
See also BW 2; CA 109; CAAS 19; CANR 27, 42, 68; DLB 120

Doveglion
See Villa, Jose Garcia

Dowell, Coleman 1925-1985 .... **CLC 60**
See also CA 25-28R; 117; CANR 10; DLB 130

Dowson, Ernest (Christopher) 1867-1900
TCLC 4
See also CA 105; 150; DLB 19, 135

Doyle, A. Conan
See Doyle, Arthur Conan

Doyle, Arthur Conan 1859-1930...**TCLC 7; DA; DAB; DAC; DAM MST, NOV; SSC 12; WLC**
See also AAYA 14; CA 104; 122; CDBLB 1890-1914; DLB 18, 70, 156, 178; MTCW 1; SATA 24

Doyle, Conan
See Doyle, Arthur Conan

Doyle, John
See Graves, Robert (von Ranke)

Doyle, Roddy 1958(?)- .... **CLC 81**
See also AAYA 14; CA 143; CANR 73; DLB 194

Doyle, Sir A. Conan
See Doyle, Arthur Conan

Doyle, Sir Arthur Conan
See Doyle, Arthur Conan

Dr. A
See Asimov, Isaac; Silverstein, Alvin

Drabble, Margaret 1939-...**CLC 2, 3, 5, 8, 10, 22, 53; DAB; DAC; DAM MST, NOV, POP**
See also CA 13-16R; CANR 18, 35, 63; CDBLB 1960 to Present; DLB 14, 155; MTCW 1; SATA 48

Drapier, M. B.
See Swift, Jonathan

Drayham, James
See Mencken, H(enry) L(ouis)

Drayton, Michael 1563-1631.......**LC 8; DAM POET**
See also DLB 121

Dreadstone, Carl
See Campbell, (John) Ramsey

Dreiser, Theodore (Herman Albert) 1871-1945...**TCLC 10, 18, 35, 83; DA; DAC; DAM MST, NOV; SSC 30; WLC**
See also CA 106; 132; CDALB 1865-1917; DLB 9, 12, 102, 137; DLBD 1; MTCW 1

Drexler, Rosalyn 1926- .... **CLC 2, 6**
See also CA 81-84; CANR 68

Dreyer, Carl Theodor 1889-1968 ...... **CLC 16**
See also CA 116

Drieu la Rochelle, Pierre(-Eugene) 1893-1945
TCLC 21
See also CA 117; DLB 72

Drinkwater, John 1882-1937 ... **TCLC 57**
See also CA 109; 149; DLB 10, 19, 149

Drop Shot
See Cable, George Washington

Droste-Hulshoff, Annette Freiin von 1797-1848
NCLC 3
See also DLB 133

Drummond, Walter
See Silverberg, Robert

Drummond, William Henry 1854-1907
TCLC 25
See also CA 160; DLB 92

Drummond de Andrade, Carlos 1902-1987
CLC 18
See also Andrade, Carlos Drummond de
See also CA 132, 123

Drury, Allen (Stuart) 1918-1998 .... **CLC 37**
See also CA 57-60; 170; CANR 18, 52; INT CANR-18

Dryden, John 1631-1700 ..**LC 3, 21; DA; DAB; DAC; DAM DRAM, MST, POET; DC 3; PC 25; WLC**
See also CDBLB 1660-1789; DLB 80, 101, 131

Duberman, Martin (Bauml) 1930- ......**CLC 8**
See also CA 1-4R; CANR 2, 63

Dubie, Norman (Evans) 1945-.... **CLC 36**
See also CA 69-72; CANR 12; DLB 120

Du Bois, W(illiam) E(dward) B(urghardt) 1868-1963 ...**CLC 1, 2, 13, 64, 96; BLC 1; DA; DAC; DAM MST, MULT, NOV; WLC**
See also BW 1; CA 85-88; CANR 34; CDALB 1865-1917; DLB 47, 50, 91; MTCW 1; SATA 42

Dubus, Andre 1936-...**CLC 13, 36, 97; SSC 15**
See also CA 21-24R; CANR 17; DLB 130; INT CANR-17

Duca Minimo
See D'Annunzio, Gabriele

Ducharme, Rejean 1941- .... **CLC 74**
See also CA 165; DLB 60

Duclos, Charles Pinot 1704-1772 .... **LC 1**

Dudek, Louis 1918- .... **CLC 11, 19**
See also CA 45-48; CAAS 14; CANR 1; DLB 88

Duerrenmatt, Friedrich 1921-1990
CLC 1, 4, 8, 11, 15, 43, 102; DAM DRAM
See also CA 17-20R; CANR 33; DLB 69, 124; MTCW 1

Duffy, Bruce (?)- .... **CLC 50**

Duffy, Maureen 1933- .... **CLC 37**
See also CA 25-28R; CANR 33, 68; DLB 14; MTCW 1

Eichendorff, Joseph Freiherr von 1788-1857 .... **NCLC 8**
See also DLB 90
Eigner, Larry .... **CLC 9**
See also Eigner, Laurence (Joel)
See also CAAS 23; DLB 5
Eigner, Laurence (Joel) 1927-1996
See Eigner, Larry
See also CA 9-12R; 151; CANR 6; DLB 193
Einstein, Albert 1879-1955 ..... **TCLC 65**
See also CA 121; 133; MTCW 1
Eiseley, Loren Corey 1907-1977...**CLC 7**
See also AAYA 5; CA 1-4R; 73-76; CANR 6; DLBD 17
Eisenstadt, Jill 1963- .... **CLC 50**
See also CA 140
Eisenstein, Sergei (Mikhailovich) 1898-1948 .... **TCLC 57**
See also CA 114; 149
Eisner, Simon
See Kornbluth, C(yril) M.
Ekeloef, (Bengt) Gunnar 1907-1968
CLC 27; DAM POET; PC 23
See also CA 123; 25-28R
Ekelof, (Bengt) Gunnar
See Ekeloef, (Bengt) Gunnar
Ekelund, Vilhelm 1880-1949.....**TCLC 75**
Ekwensi, C. O. D.
See Ekwensi, Cyprian (Odiatu Duaka)
Ekwensi, Cyprian (Odiatu Duaka) 1921-
CLC 4; BLC 1; DAM MULT
See also BW 2; CA 29-32R; CANR 18, 42, 74; DLB 117; MTCW 1; SATA 66
Elaine .... **TCLC 18**
See also Leverson, Ada
El Crummo
See Crumb, R(obert)
Elder, Lonne III 1931-1996 .... **DC 8**
See also BLC 1; BW 1; CA 81-84; 152; CANR 25; DAM MULT; DLB 7, 38, 44
Elia
See Lamb, Charles
Eliade, Mircea 1907-1986........... **CLC 19**
See also CA 65-68; 119; CANR 30, 62; MTCW 1
Eliot, A. D.
See Jewett, (Theodora) Sarah Orne
Eliot, Alice
See Jewett, (Theodora) Sarah Orne
Eliot, Dan
See Silverberg, Robert
Eliot, George 1819-1880...**NCLC 4, 13, 23, 41, 49; DA; DAB; DAC; DAM MST, NOV; PC 20; WLC**
See also CDBLB 1832-1890; DLB 21, 35, 55
Eliot, John 1604-1690...................... **LC 5**
See also DLB 24
Eliot, T(homas) S(tearns) 1888-1965
CLC 1, 2, 3, 6, 9, 10, 13, 15, 24, 34, 41, 55, 57, 113; DA; DAB; DAC; DAM DRAM, MST, POET; PC 5; WLC
See also CA 5-8R; 25-28R; CANR 41; CDALB 1929-1941; DLB 7, 10, 45, 63; DLBY 88; MTCW 1
Elizabeth 1866-1941 .... **TCLC 41**
Elkin, Stanley L(awrence) 1930-1995
CLC 4, 6, 9, 14, 27, 51, 91; DAM NOV, POP; SSC 12
See also CA 9-12R; 148; CANR 8, 46; DLB 2, 28; DLBY 80; INT CANR-8; MTCW 1
Elledge, Scott .... **CLC 34**

Elliot, Don
See Silverberg, Robert
Elliott, Don
See Silverberg, Robert
Elliott, George P(aul) 1918-1980...**CLC 2**
See also CA 1-4R; 97-100; CANR 2
Elliott, Janice 1931-..................... **CLC 47**
See also CA 13-16R; CANR 8, 29; DLB 14
Elliott, Sumner Locke 1917-1991...**CLC 38**
See also CA 5-8R; 134; CANR 2, 21
Elliott, William
See Bradbury, Ray (Douglas)
Ellis, A. E. .... **CLC 7**
Ellis, Alice Thomas .... **CLC 40**
See also Haycraft, Anna
See also DLB 194
Ellis, Bret Easton 1964-...**CLC 39, 71, 117; DAM POP**
See also AAYA 2; CA 118; 123; CANR 51, 74; INT 123
Ellis, (Henry) Havelock 1859-1939
TCLC 14
See also CA 109; 169; DLB 190
Ellis, Landon
See Ellison, Harlan (Jay)
Ellis, Trey 1962-............................. **CLC 55**
See also CA 146
Ellison, Harlan (Jay) 1934-...**CLC 1, 13, 42; DAM POP; SSC 14**
See also CA 5-8R; CANR 5, 46; DLB 8; INT CANR-5; MTCW 1
Ellison, Ralph (Waldo) 1914-1994...**CLC 1, 3, 11, 54, 86, 114; BLC 1; DA; DAB; DAC; DAM MST, MULT, NOV; SSC 26; WLC**
See also AAYA 19; BW 1; CA 9-12R; 145; CANR 24, 53; CDALB 1941-1968; DLB 2, 76; DLBY 94; MTCW 1
Ellmann, Lucy (Elizabeth) 1956-...**CLC 61**
See also CA 128
Ellmann, Richard (David) 1918-1987
CLC 50
See also BEST 89:2; CA 1-4R; 122; CANR 2, 28, 61; DLB 103; DLBY 87; MTCW 1
Elman, Richard (Martin) 1934-1997**CLC 19**
See also CA 17-20R; 163; CAAS 3; CANR 47
Elron
See Hubbard, L(afayette) Ron(ald)
Eluard, Paul .... **TCLC 7, 41**
See also Grindel, Eugene
Elyot, Sir Thomas 1490(?)-1546...**LC 11**
Elytis, Odysseus 1911-1996...**CLC 15, 49, 100; DAM POET; PC 21**
See also CA 102; 151; MTCW 1
Emecheta, (Florence Onye) Buchi 1944-
CLC 14, 48; BLC 2; DAM MULT
See also BW 2; CA 81-84; CANR 27; DLB 117; MTCW 1; SATA 66
Emerson, Mary Moody 1774-1863
NCLC 66
Emerson, Ralph Waldo 1803-1882
NCLC 1, 38; DA; DAB; DAC; DAM MST, POET; PC 18; WLC
See also CDALB 1640-1865; DLB 1, 59, 73
Eminescu, Mihail 1850-1889.**NCLC 33**
Empson, William 1906-1984.**CLC 3, 8, 19, 33, 34**
See also CA 17-20R; 112; CANR 31, 61; DLB 20; MTCW 1

Enchi, Fumiko (Ueda) 1905-1986...**CLC 31**
See also CA 129; 121
Ende, Michael (Andreas Helmuth) 1929-1995 .... **CLC 31**
See also CA 118, 124; 149; CANR 36; CLR 14; DLB 75; MAICYA; SATA 61; SATA-Brief 42; SATA-Obit 86
Endo, Shusaku 1923-1996...**CLC 7, 14, 19, 54, 99; DAM NOV**
See also CA 29-32R; 153; CANR 21, 54; DLB 182; MTCW 1
Engel, Marian 1933-1985 .... **CLC 36**
See also CA 25-28R; CANR 12; DLB 53; INT CANR-12
Engelhardt, Frederick
See Hubbard, L(afayette) Ron(ald)
Enright, D(ennis) J(oseph) 1920-...**CLC 4, 8, 31**
See also CA 1-4R; CANR 1, 42; DLB 27; SATA 25
Enzensberger, Hans Magnus 1929-...**CLC 43**
See also CA 116; 119
Ephron, Nora 1941-............... **CLC 17, 31**
See also AITN 2; CA 65-68; CANR 12, 39
Epicurus 341B.C.-270B.C........ **CMLC 21**
See also DLB 176
Epsilon
See Betjeman, John
Epstein, Daniel Mark 1948- .... **CLC 7**
See also CA 49-52; CANR 2, 53
Epstein, Jacob 1956- .... **CLC 19**
See also CA 114-
Epstein, Joseph 1937-.................. **CLC 39**
See also CA 112; 119; CANR 50, 65
Epstein, Leslie 1938- .... **CLC 27**
See also CA 73-76; CAAS 12; CANR 23, 69
Equiano, Olaudah 1745(?)-1797...**LC 16; BLC 2; DAM MULT**
See also DLB 37, 50
ER .... **TCLC 33**
See also CA 160; DLB 85
Erasmus, Desiderius 1469(?)-1536**LC 16**
Erdman, Paul E(mil) 1932- .... **CLC 25**
See also AITN 1; CA 61-64; CANR 13, 43
Erdrich, Louise 1954-...**CLC 39, 54; DAM MULT, NOV, POP**
See also AAYA 10; BEST 89:1; CA 114; CANR 41, 62; DLB 152, 175; MTCW 1; NNAL; SATA 94
Erenburg, Ilya (Grigoryevich)
See Ehrenburg, Ilya (Grigoryevich)
Erickson, Stephen Michael 1950-
See Erickson, Steve
See also CA 129
Erickson, Steve 1950- .... **CLC 64**
See also Erickson, Stephen Michael
See also CANR 60, 68
Ericson, Walter
See Fast, Howard (Melvin)
Eriksson, Buntel
See Bergman, (Ernst) Ingmar
Ernaux, Annie 1940- .... **CLC 88**
See also CA 147
Erskine, John 1879-1951 .... **TCLC 84**
See also CA 112; 159; DLB 9, 102
Eschenbach, Wolfram von
See Wolfram von Eschenbach
Eseki, Bruno
See Mphahlele, Ezekiel
Esenin, Sergei (Alexandrovich) 1895-1925
TCLC 4
See also CA 104

Feuillet, Octave 1821-1890 ..... **NCLC 45**
See also DLB 192

Feydeau, Georges (Leon Jules Marie)
1862-1921 ..... **TCLC 22; DAM DRAM**
See also CA 113; 152; DLB 192

Fichte, Johann Gottlieb 1762-1814 ... **NCLC 62**
See also DLB 90

Ficino, Marsilio 1433-1499 .... **LC 12**

Fiedeler, Hans
See Doeblin, Alfred

Fiedler, Leslie A(aron) 1917- ... **CLC 4, 13, 24**
See also CA 9-12R; CANR 7, 63; DLB 28, 67; MTCW 1

Field, Andrew 1938- .... **CLC 44**
See also CA 97-100; CANR 25

Field, Eugene 1850-1895 .... **NCLC 3**
See also DLB 23, 42, 140; DLBD 13; MAICYA; SATA 16

Field, Gans T.
See Wellman, Manly Wade

Field, Michael 1915-1971 .... **TCLC 43**
See also CA 29-32R

Field, Peter
See Hobson, Laura Z(ametkin)

Fielding, Henry 1707-1754 ..... **LC 1, 46; DA; DAB; DAC; DAM DRAM, MST, NOV; WLC**
See also CDBLB 1660-1789; DLB 39, 84, 101

Fielding, Sarah 1710-1768 .... **LC 1, 44**
See also DLB 39

Fields, W. C. 1880-1946 .... **TCLC 80**
See also DLB 44

Fierstein, Harvey (Forbes) 1954- .... **CLC 33; DAM DRAM, POP**
See also CA 123; 129

Figes, Eva 1932- .... **CLC 31**
See also CA 53-56; CANR 4, 44; DLB 14

Finch, Anne 1661-1720 .... **LC 3; PC 21**
See also DLB 95

Finch, Robert (Duer Claydon) 1900- **CLC 18**
See also CA 57-60; CANR 9, 24, 49; DLB 88

Findley, Timothy 1930- ... **CLC 27, 102; DAC; DAM MST**
See also CA 25-28R; CANR 12, 42, 69; DLB 53

Fink, William
See Mencken, H(enry) L(ouis)

Firbank, Louis 1942-
See Reed, Lou
See also CA 117

Firbank, (Arthur Annesley) Ronald 1886-1926 **TCLC 1**
See also CA 104; DLB 36

Fisher, Dorothy (Frances) Canfield 1879-1958 **TCLC 87**
See also CA 114; 136; DLB 9, 102; MAICYA; YABC 1

Fisher, M(ary) F(rances) K(ennedy) 1908-1992 **CLC 76, 87**
See also CA 77-80; 138; CANR 44

Fisher, Roy 1930- .... **CLC 25**
See also CA 81-84; CAAS 10; CANR 16; DLB 40

Fisher, Rudolph 1897-1934 .... **TCLC 11; BLC 2; DAM MULT; SSC 25**
See also BW 1; CA 107; 124; DLB 51, 102

Fisher, Vardis (Alvero) 1895-1968 .. **CLC 7**
See also CA 5-8R; 25-28R; CANR 68; DLB 9

Fiske, Tarleton
See Bloch, Robert (Albert)

Fitch, Clarke
See Sinclair, Upton (Beall)

Fitch, John IV
See Cormier, Robert (Edmund)

Fitzgerald, Captain Hugh
See Baum, L(yman) Frank

FitzGerald, Edward 1809-1883 .... **NCLC 9**
See also DLB 32

Fitzgerald, F(rancis) Scott (Key) 1896-1940 **TCLC 1, 6, 14, 28, 55; DA; DAB; DAC; DAM MST, NOV; SSC 6, 31; WLC**
See also AAYA 24; AITN 1; CA 110; 123; CDALB 1917-1929; DLB 4, 9, 86; DLBD 1, 15, 16; DLBY 81, 96; MTCW 1

Fitzgerald, Penelope 1916- ... **CLC 19, 51, 61**
See also CA 85-88; CAAS 10; CANR 56; DLB 14, 194

Fitzgerald, Robert (Stuart) 1910-1985 **CLC 39**
See also CA 1-4R; 114; CANR 1; DLBY 80

FitzGerald, Robert D(avid) 1902-1987 **CLC 19**
See also CA 17-20R

Fitzgerald, Zelda (Sayre) 1900-1948 **TCLC 52**
See also CA 117; 126; DLBY 84

Flanagan, Thomas (James Bonner) 1923- **CLC 25, 52**
See also CA 108; CANR 55; DLBY 80; INT 108; MTCW 1

Flaubert, Gustave 1821-1880 ... **NCLC 2, 10, 19, 62, 66; DA; DAB; DAC; DAM MST, NOV; SSC 11; WLC**
See also DLB 119

Flecker, Herman Elroy
See Flecker, (Herman) James Elroy

Flecker, (Herman) James Elroy 1884-1915 **TCLC 43**
See also CA 109; 150; DLB 10, 19

Fleming, Ian (Lancaster) 1908-1964 ... **CLC 3, 30; DAM POP**
See also AAYA 26; CA 5-8R; CANR 59; CDBLB 1945-1960; DLB 87, 201; MTCW 1; SATA 9

Fleming, Thomas (James) 1927- ... **CLC 37**
See also CA 5-8R; CANR 10; INT CANR-10; SATA 8

Fletcher, John 1579-1625 .... **LC 33; DC 6**
See also CDBLB Before 1660; DLB 58

Fletcher, John Gould 1886-1950 .... **TCLC 35**
See also CA 107; 167; DLB 4, 45

Fleur, Paul
See Pohl, Frederik

Flooglebuckle, Al
See Spiegelman, Art

Flying Officer X
See Bates, H(erbert) E(rnest)

Fo, Dario 1926- ... **CLC 32, 109; DAM DRAM; DC 10**
See also CA 116; 128; CANR 68; DLBY 97; MTCW 1

Fogarty, Jonathan Titulescu Esq.
See Farrell, James T(homas)

Folke, Will
See Bloch, Robert (Albert)

Follett, Ken(neth Martin) 1949- ..... **CLC 18; DAM NOV, POP**
See also AAYA 6; BEST 89:4; CA 81-84; CANR 13, 33, 54; DLB 87; DLBY 81; INT CANR-33; MTCW 1

Fontane, Theodor 1819-1898 .... **NCLC 26**
See also DLB 129

Foote, Horton 1916- ... **CLC 51, 91; DAM DRAM**
See also CA 73-76; CANR 34, 51; DLB 26; INT CANR-34

Foote, Shelby 1916- ... **CLC 75; DAM NOV, POP**
See also CA 5-8R; CANR 3, 45, 74; DLB 2, 17

Forbes, Esther 1891-1967 .... **CLC 12**
See also AAYA 17; CA 13-14; 25-28R; CAP 1; CLR 27; DLB 22; JRDA; MAICYA; SATA 2, 100

Forche, Carolyn (Louise) 1950- ... **CLC 25, 83, 86; DAM POET; PC 10**
See also CA 109; 117; CANR 50, 74; DLB 5, 193; INT 117

Ford, Elbur
See Hibbert, Eleanor Alice Burford

Ford, Ford Madox 1873-1939 **TCLC 1, 15, 39, 57; DAM NOV**
See also CA 104; 132; CANR 74; CDBLB 1914-1945; DLB 162; MTCW 1

Ford, Henry 1863-1947 .... **TCLC 73**
See also CA 115; 148

Ford, John 1586-(?) .... **DC 8**
See also CDBLB Before 1660; DAM DRAM; DLB 58

Ford, John 1895-1973 .... **CLC 16**
See also CA 45-48

Ford, Richard 1944- .... **CLC 46, 99**
See also CA 69-72; CANR 11, 47

Ford, Webster
See Masters, Edgar Lee

Foreman, Richard 1937- .... **CLC 50**
See also CA 65-68; CANR 32, 63

Forester, C(ecil) S(cott) 1899-1966 ... **CLC 35**
See also CA 73-76; 25-28R; DLB 191; SATA 13

Forez
See Mauriac, Francois (Charles)

Forman, James Douglas 1932- .... **CLC 21**
See also AAYA 17; CA 9-12R; CANR 4, 19, 42; JRDA; MAICYA; SATA 8, 70

Fornes, Maria Irene 1930- **CLC 39, 61; DC 10**
See also CA 25-28R; CANR 28; DLB 7; HW; INT CANR-28; MTCW 1

Forrest, Leon (Richard) 1937-1997 ... **CLC 4; BLCS**
See also BW 2; CA 89-92; 162; CAAS 7; CANR 25, 52; DLB 33

Forster, E(dward) M(organ) 1879-1970 ... **CLC 1, 2, 3, 4, 9, 10, 13, 15, 22, 45, 77; DA; DAB; DAC; DAM MST, NOV; SSC 27; WLC**
See also AAYA 2; CA 13-14; 25-28R; CANR 45; CAP 1; CDBLB 1914-1945; DLB 34, 98, 162, 178, 195; DLBD 10; MTCW 1; SATA 57

Forster, John 1812-1876 .... **NCLC 11**
See also DLB 144, 184

Forsyth, Frederick 1938- ... **CLC 2, 5, 36; DAM NOV, POP**
See also BEST 89:4; CA 85-88; CANR 38, 62; DLB 87; MTCW 1

Forten, Charlotte L. .... **TCLC 16; BLC 2**
See also Grimke, Charlotte L(ottie) Forten
See also DLB 50

Foscolo, Ugo 1778-1827 .... **NCLC 8**

Fosse, Bob .... **CLC 20**
See also Fosse, Robert Louis

Fosse, Robert Louis 1927-1987
See Fosse, Bob
See also CA 110; 123

Foster, Stephen Collins 1826-1864
NCLC 26

Foucault, Michel 1926-1984...CLC 31, 34, 69
See also CA 105; 113; CANR 34; MTCW 1

Fouque, Friedrich (Heinrich Karl) de la
Motte 1777-1843 .... NCLC 2
See also DLB 90

Fourier, Charles 1772-1837 .... NCLC 51

Fournier, Henri Alban 1886-1914
See Alain-Fournier
See also CA 104

Fournier, Pierre 1916- .... CLC 11
See also Gascar, Pierre
See also CA 89-92; CANR 16, 40

Fowles, John (Philip) 1926-...CLC 1, 2, 3,
4, 6, 9, 10, 15, 33, 87; DAB; DAC; DAM
MST; SSC 33
See also CA 5-8R; CANR 25, 71; CDBLB
1960 to Present; DLB 14, 139; MTCW 1;
SATA 22

Fox, Paula 1923- .... CLC 2, 8
See also AAYA 3; CA 73-76; CANR 20, 36,
62; CLR 1, 44; DLB 52; JRDA; MAICYA;
MTCW 1; SATA 17, 60

Fox, William Price (Jr.) 1926- .... CLC 22
See also CA 17-20R; CAAS 19; CANR 11; DLB
2; DLBY 81

Foxe, John 1516(?)-1587 .... LC 14
See also DLB 132

Frame, Janet 1924-...CLC 2, 3, 6, 22, 66,
96; SSC 29
See also Clutha, Janet Paterson Frame

France, Anatole .... TCLC 9
See also Thibault, Jacques Anatole Francois
See also DLB 123

Francis, Claude 19(?)- .... CLC 50

Francis, Dick 1920-...CLC 2, 22, 42, 102;
DAM POP
See also AAYA 5, 21; BEST 89:3; CA 5-8R;
CANR 9, 42, 68; CDBLB 1960 to Present;
DLB 87; INT CANR-9; MTCW 1

Francis, Robert (Churchill) 1901-1987...CLC
15
See also CA 1-4R; 123; CANR 1

Frank, Anne(lies Marie) 1929-1945
TCLC 17; DA; DAB; DAC; DAM MST;
WLC
See also AAYA 12; CA 113; 133; CANR 68;
MTCW 1; SATA 87; SATA-Brief 42

Frank, Bruno 1887-1945 .... TCLC 81
See also DLB 118

Frank, Elizabeth 1945- .... CLC 39
See also CA 121; 126; INT 126

Frankl, Viktor E(mil) 1905-1997 ..... CLC 93
See also CA 65-68; 161

Franklin, Benjamin
See Hasek, Jaroslav (Matej Frantisek)

Franklin, Benjamin 1706-1790 .. LC 25; DA;
DAB; DAC; DAM MST; WLCS
See also CDALB 1640-1865; DLB 24, 43,
73

Franklin, (Stella Maria Sarah) Miles
(Lampe) 1879-1954 .... TCLC 7
See also CA 104; 164

Fraser, (Lady) Antonia (Pakenham) 1932-
CLC 32, 107
See also CA 85-88; CANR 44, 65; MTCW 1;
SATA-Brief 32

Fraser, George MacDonald 1925- ......CLC 7
See also CA 45-48; CANR 2, 48, 74

Fraser, Sylvia 1935- .... CLC 64
See also CA 45-48; CANR 1, 16, 60

Frayn, Michael 1933-..CLC 3, 7, 31, 47;
DAM DRAM, NOV
See also CA 5-8R; CANR 30, 69; DLB 13, 14,
194; MTCW 1

Fraze, Candida (Merrill) 1945- .... CLC 50
See also CA 126

Frazer, J(ames) G(eorge) 1854-1941
TCLC 32
See also CA 118

Frazer, Robert Caine
See Creasey, John

Frazer, Sir James George
See Frazer, J(ames) G(eorge)

Frazier, Charles 1950- .... CLC 109
See also CA 161

Frazier, Ian 1951- ....CLC 46
See also CA 130; CANR 54

Frederic, Harold 1856-1898 .... NCLC 10
See also DLB 12, 23; DLBD 13

Frederick, John
See Faust, Frederick (Schiller)

Frederick the Great 1712-1786 ..... LC 14

Fredro, Aleksander 1793-1876...NCLC 8

Freeling, Nicolas 1927- .... CLC 38
See also CA 49-52; CAAS 12; CANR 1, 17,
50; DLB 87

Freeman, Douglas Southall 1886-1953
TCLC 11
See also CA 109; DLB 17; DLBD 17

Freeman, Judith 1946- .... CLC 55
See also CA 148

Freeman, Mary Eleanor Wilkins 1852-1930
TCLC 9; SSC 1
See also CA 106; DLB 12, 78

Freeman, R(ichard) Austin 1862-1943
TCLC 21
See also CA 113; DLB 70

French, Albert 1943- .... CLC 86
See also CA 167

French, Marilyn 1929-...CLC 10, 18, 60;
DAM DRAM, NOV, POP
See also CA 69-72; CANR 3, 31; INT CANR-
31; MTCW 1

French, Paul
See Asimov, Isaac

Freneau, Philip Morin 1752-1832
NCLC 1
See also DLB 37, 43

Freud, Sigmund 1856-1939 ...... TCLC 52
See also CA 115; 133; CANR 69; MTCW 1

Friedan, Betty (Naomi) 1921- .... CLC 74
See also CA 65-68; CANR 18, 45, 74; MTCW 1

Friedlander, Saul 1932- .... CLC 90
See also CA 117; 130; CANR 72

Friedman, B(ernard) H(arper) 1926-..CLC 7
See also CA 1-4R; CANR 3, 48

Friedman, Bruce Jay 1930-...CLC 3, 5, 56
See also CA 9-12R; CANR 25, 52; DLB 2,
28; INT CANR-25

Friel, Brian 1929-...CLC 5, 42, 59, 115; DC
8
See also CA 21-24R; CANR 33, 69; DLB 13;
MTCW 1

Friis-Baastad, Babbis Ellinor 1921-1970
CLC 12
See also CA 17-20R; 134; SATA 7

Frisch, Max (Rudolf) 1911-1991...CLC 3,
9, 14, 18, 32, 44; DAM DRAM, NOV
See also CA 85-88; 134; CANR 32, 74; DLB
69, 124; MTCW 1

Fromentin, Eugene (Samuel Auguste)
1820-1876 .... NCLC 10
See also DLB 123

Frost, Frederick
See Faust, Frederick (Schiller)

Frost, Robert (Lee) 1874-1963...CLC 1, 3,
4, 9, 10, 13, 15, 26, 34, 44; DA; DAB;
DAC; DAM MST, POET; PC 1; WLC
See also AAYA 21; CA 89-92; CANR 33;
CDALB 1917-1929; DLB 54; DLBD 7;
MTCW 1; SATA 14

Froude, James Anthony 1818-1894
NCLC 43
See also DLB 18, 57, 144

Froy, Herald
See Waterhouse, Keith (Spencer)

Fry, Christopher 1907-... CLC 2, 10, 14;
DAM DRAM
See also CA 17-20R; CAAS 23; CANR 9, 30,
74; DLB 13; MTCW 1; SATA 66

Frye, (Herman) Northrop 1912-1991
CLC 24, 70
See also CA 5-8R; 133; CANR 8, 37; DLB
67, 68; MTCW 1

Fuchs, Daniel 1909-1993 ....CLC 8, 22
See also CA 81-84; 142; CAAS 5; CANR 40;
DLB 9, 26, 28; DLBY 93

Fuchs, Daniel 1934- .... CLC 34
See also CA 37-40R; CANR 14, 48

Fuentes, Carlos 1928-...CLC 3, 8, 10, 13,
22, 41, 60, 113; DA; DAB; DAC; DAM
MST, MULT, NOV; HLC; SSC 24; WLC
See also AAYA 4; AITN 2; CA 69-72; CANR
10, 32, 68; DLB 113; HW; MTCW 1

Fuentes, Gregorio Lopez y
See Lopez y Fuentes, Gregorio

Fugard, (Harold) Athol 1932-...CLC 5, 9,
14, 25, 40, 80; DAM DRAM; DC 3
See also AAYA 17; CA 85-88; CANR 32, 54;
MTCW 1

Fugard, Sheila 1932- .... CLC 48
See also CA 125

Fuller, Charles (H., Jr.) 1939-...CLC 25;
BLC 2; DAM DRAM, MULT; DC 1
See also BW 2; CA 108; 112; DLB 38; INT 112;
MTCW 1

Fuller, John (Leopold) 1937-............ CLC 62
See also CA 21-24R; CANR 9, 44; DLB 40

Fuller, Margaret ....NCLC 5, 50
See also Ossoli, Sarah Margaret (Fuller
marchesa d')

Fuller, Roy (Broadbent) 1912-1991...CLC
4, 28
See also CA 5-8R; 135; CAAS 10; CANR 53;
DLB 15, 20; SATA 87

Fulton, Alice 1952- .... CLC 52
See also CA 116; CANR 57; DLB 193

Furphy, Joseph 1843-1912 .... TCLC 25
See also CA 163

Fussell, Paul 1924-............................ CLC 74
See also BEST 90:1; CA 17-20R; CANR 8, 21,
35, 69; INT CANR-21; MTCW 1

Futabatei, Shimei 1864-1909 ..TCLC 44
See also CA 162; DLB 180

Futrelle, Jacques 1875-1912 .... TCLC 19
See also CA 113; 155

Gaboriau, Emile 1835-1873 ....NCLC 14

Gadda, Carlo Emilio 1893-1973 .... CLC 11
See also CA 89-92; DLB 177

Gaddis, William 1922-...CLC 1, 3, 6, 8, 10,
19, 43, 86
See also CA 17-20R; CANR 21, 48; DLB 2;
MTCW 1

Gage, Walter
See Inge, William (Motter)

Gaines, Ernest J(ames) 1933-...**CLC 3, 11, 18, 86; BLC 2; DAM MULT**
See also AAYA 18; AITN 1; BW 2; CA 9-12R; CANR 6, 24, 42, 75; CDALB 1968-1988; DLB 2, 33, 152; DLBY 80; MTCW 1; SATA 86

Gaitskill, Mary 1954- .... **CLC 69**
See also CA 128; CANR 61

Galdos, Benito Perez
See Perez Galdos, Benito

Gale, Zona 1874-1938 ...... **TCLC 7; DAM DRAM**
See also CA 105; 153; DLB 9, 78

Galeano, Eduardo (Hughes) 1940- .. **CLC 72**
See also CA 29-32R; CANR 13, 32; HW

Galiano, Juan Valera y Alcala
See Valera y Alcala-Galiano, Juan

Galilei, Galileo 1546-1642 .... **LC 45**

Gallagher, Tess 1943- ...... **CLC 18, 63; DAM POET; PC 9**
See also CA 106; DLB 120

Gallant, Mavis 1922-...**CLC 7, 18, 38; DAC; DAM MST; SSC 5**
See also CA 69-72; CANR 29, 69; DLB 53; MTCW 1

Gallant, Roy A(rthur) 1924- .... **CLC 17**
See also CA 5-8R; CANR 4, 29, 54; CLR 30; MAICYA; SATA 4, 68

Gallico, Paul (William) 1897-1976 ..... **CLC 2**
See also AITN 1; CA 5-8R; 69-72; CANR 23; DLB 9, 171; MAICYA; SATA 13

Gallo, Max Louis 1932- .... **CLC 95**
See also CA 85-88

Gallois, Lucien
See Desnos, Robert

Gallup, Ralph
See Whitemore, Hugh (John)

Galsworthy, John 1867-1933...**TCLC 1, 45; DA; DAB; DAC; DAM DRAM, MST, NOV; SSC 22; WLC**
See also CA 104; 141; CANR 75; CDBLB 1890-1914; DLB 10, 34, 98, 162; DLBD 16

Galt, John 1779-1839 .... **NCLC 1**
See also DLB 99, 116, 159

Galvin, James 1951- .... **CLC 38**
See also CA 108; CANR 26

Gamboa, Federico 1864-1939 ..**TCLC 36**
See also CA 167

Gandhi, M. K.
See Gandhi, Mohandas Karamchand

Gandhi, Mahatma
See Gandhi, Mohandas Karamchand

Gandhi, Mohandas Karamchand 1869-1948
TCLC 59; DAM MULT
See also CA 121; 132; MTCW 1

Gann, Ernest Kellogg 1910-1991 ..... **CLC 23**
See also AITN 1; CA 1-4R; 136; CANR 1

Garcia, Cristina 1958- .... **CLC 76**
See also CA 141; CANR 73

Garcia Lorca, Federico 1898-1936
TCLC 1, 7, 49; DA; DAB; DAC; DAM DRAM, MST, MULT, POET; DC 2; HLC; PC 3; WLC
See also CA 104; 131; DLB 108; HW; MTCW 1

Garcia Marquez, Gabriel (Jose) 1928-
CLC 2, 3, 8, 10, 15, 27, 47, 55, 68; DA; DAB; DAC; DAM MST, MULT, NOV, POP; HLC; SSC 8; WLC
See also AAYA 3; BEST 89:1, 90:4; CA 33-36R; CANR 10, 28, 50, 75; DLB 113; HW; MTCW 1

Gard, Janice
See Latham, Jean Lee

Gard, Roger Martin du
See Martin du Gard, Roger

Gardam, Jane 1928- .... **CLC 43**
See also CA 49-52; CANR 2, 18, 33, 54; CLR 12; DLB 14, 161; MAICYA; MTCW 1; SAAS 9; SATA 39, 76; SATA-Brief 28

Gardner, Herb(ert) 1934- .... **CLC 44**
See also CA 149

Gardner, John (Champlin), Jr. 1933-1982
CLC 2, 3, 5, 7, 8, 10, 18, 28, 34; DAM NOV, POP; SSC 7
See also AITN 1; CA 65-68; 107; CANR 33, 73; DLB 2; DLBY 82; MTCW 1; SATA 40; SATA-Obit 31

Gardner, John (Edmund) 1926-...**CLC 30; DAM POP**
See also CA 103; CANR 15, 69; MTCW 1

Gardner, Miriam
See Bradley, Marion Zimmer

Gardner, Noel
See Kuttner, Henry

Gardons, S. S.
See Snodgrass, W(illiam) D(e Witt)

Garfield, Leon 1921-1996 .... **CLC 12**
See also AAYA 8; CA 17-20R; 152; CANR 38, 41; CLR 21; DLB 161; JRDA; MAICYA; SATA 1, 32, 76; SATA-Obit 90

Garland, (Hannibal) Hamlin 1860-1940
TCLC 3; SSC 18
See also CA 104; DLB 12, 71, 78, 186

Garneau, (Hector de) Saint-Denys 1912-1943 .... **TCLC 13**
See also CA 111; DLB 88

Garner, Alan 1934-...**CLC 17; DAB; DAM POP**
See also AAYA 18; CA 73-76; CANR 15, 64; CLR 20; DLB 161; MAICYA; MTCW 1; SATA 18, 69

Garner, Hugh 1913-1979 .... **CLC 13**
See also CA 69-72; CANR 31; DLB 68

Garnett, David 1892-1981 .... **CLC 3**
See also CA 5-8R; 103; CANR 17; DLB 34

Garos, Stephanie
See Katz, Steve

Garrett, George (Palmer) 1929-...**CLC 3, 11, 51; SSC 30**
See also CA 1-4R; CAAS 5; CANR 1, 42, 67; DLB 2, 5, 130, 152; DLBY 83

Garrick, David 1717-1779...**LC 15; DAM DRAM**
See also DLB 84

Garrigue, Jean 1914-1972 .... **CLC 2, 8**
See also CA 5-8R; 37-40R; CANR 20

Garrison, Frederick
See Sinclair, Upton (Beall)

Garth, Will
See Hamilton, Edmond; Kuttner, Henry

Garvey, Marcus (Moziah, Jr.) 1887-1940
TCLC 41; BLC 2; DAM MULT
See also BW 1; CA 120; 124

Gary, Romain .... **CLC 25**
See also Kacew, Romain
See also DLB 83

Gascar, Pierre .... **CLC 11**
See also Fournier, Pierre

Gascoyne, David (Emery) 1916- .... **CLC 45**
See also CA 65-68; CANR 10, 28, 54; DLB 20; MTCW 1

Gaskell, Elizabeth Cleghorn 1810-1865
NCLC 70; DAB; DAM MST; SSC 25
See also CDBLB 1832-1890; DLB 21, 144, 159

Gass, William H(oward) 1924-...**CLC 1, 2, 8, 11, 15, 39; SSC 12**
See also CA 17-20R; CANR 30, 71; DLB 2; MTCW 1

Gasset, Jose Ortega y
See Ortega y Gasset, Jose

Gates, Henry Louis, Jr. 1950-...**CLC 65; BLCS; DAM MULT**
See also BW 2; CA 109; CANR 25, 53, 75; DLB 67

Gautier, Theophile 1811-1872...**NCLC 1, 59; DAM POET; PC 18; SSC 20**
See also DLB 119

Gawsworth, John
See Bates, H(erbert) E(rnest)

Gay, Oliver
See Gogarty, Oliver St. John

Gaye, Marvin (Penze) 1939-1984...**CLC 26**
See also CA 112

Gebler, Carlo (Ernest) 1954- .... **CLC 39**
See also CA 119; 133

Gee, Maggie (Mary) 1948-.......... **CLC 57**
See also CA 130

Gee, Maurice (Gough) 1931-............. **CLC 29**
See also CA 97-100; CANR 67; SATA 46, 101

Gelbart, Larry (Simon) 1923-.... **CLC 21, 61**
See also CA 73-76; CANR 45

Gelber, Jack 1932-............... **CLC 1, 6, 14, 79**
See also CA 1-4R; CANR 2; DLB 7

Gellhorn, Martha (Ellis) 1908-1998...**CLC 14, 60**
See also CA 77-80; 164; CANR 44; DLBY 82

Genet, Jean 1910-1986...**CLC 1, 2, 5, 10, 14, 44, 46; DAM DRAM**
See also CA 13-16R; CANR 18; DLB 72; DLBY 86; MTCW 1

Gent, Peter 1942-...................................**CLC 29**
See also AITN 1; CA 89-92; DLBY 82

Gentlewoman in New England, A
See Bradstreet, Anne

Gentlewoman in Those Parts, A
See Bradstreet, Anne

George, Jean Craighead 1919- ....**CLC 35**
See also AAYA 8; CA 5-8R; CANR 25; CLR 1; DLB 52; JRDA; MAICYA; SATA 2, 68

George, Stefan (Anton) 1868-1933
TCLC 2, 14
See also CA 104

Georges, Georges Martin
See Simenon, Georges (Jacques Christian)

Gerhardi, William Alexander
See Gerhardie, William Alexander

Gerhardie, William Alexander 1895-1977
CLC 5
See also CA 25-28R; 73-76; CANR 18; DLB 36

Gerstler, Amy 1956- ....**CLC 70**
See also CA 146

Gertler, T. ....**CLC 34**
See also CA 116; 121; INT 121

Ghalib .... **NCLC 39**
See also Ghalib, Hsadullah Khan

Ghalib, Hsadullah Khan 1797-1869
See Ghalib
See also DAM POET

Ghelderode, Michel de 1898-1962...**C L C 6, 11; DAM DRAM**
See also CA 85-88; CANR 40

Ghiselin, Brewster 1903- ....**CLC 23**
See also CA 13-16R; CAAS 10; CANR 13

Ghose, Aurabinda 1872-1950 ....**TCLC 63**
See also CA 163

Gombrowicz, Witold 1904-1969...CLC 4, 7, 11, 49; DAM DRAM
See also CA 19-20; 25-28R; CAP 2
Gomez de la Serna, Ramon 1888-1963
CLC 9
See also CA 153; 116; HW
Goncharov, Ivan Alexandrovich 1812-1891
NCLC 1, 63
Goncourt, Edmond (Louis Antoine Huot) de 1822-1896 .... NCLC 7
See also DLB 123
Goncourt, Jules (Alfred Huot) de 1830-1870 .... NCLC 7
See also DLB 123
Gontier, Fernande 19(?)- .... CLC 50
Gonzalez Martinez, Enrique 1871-1952
TCLC 72
See also CA 166; HW
Goodman, Paul 1911-1972 ..... CLC 1, 2, 4, 7
See also CA 19-20; 37-40R; CANR 34; CAP 2; DLB 130; MTCW 1
Gordimer, Nadine 1923-...CLC 3, 5, 7, 10, 18, 33, 51, 70; DA; DAB; DAC; DAM MST, NOV; SSC 17; WLCS
See also CA 5-8R; CANR 3, 28, 56; INT CANR-28; MTCW 1
Gordon, Adam Lindsay 1833-1870
NCLC 21
Gordon, Caroline 1895-1981...CLC 6, 13, 29, 83; SSC 15
See also CA 11-12; 103; CANR 36; CAP 1; DLB 4, 9, 102; DLBD 17; DLBY 81; MTCW 1
Gordon, Charles William 1860-1937
See Connor, Ralph
See also CA 109
Gordon, Mary (Catherine) 1949-...CLC 13, 22
See also CA 102; CANR 44; DLB 6; DLBY 81; INT 102; MTCW 1
Gordon, N. J.
See Bosman, Herman Charles
Gordon, Sol 1923- .... CLC 26
See also CA 53-56; CANR 4; SATA 11
Gordone, Charles 1925-1995...CLC 1, 4; DAM DRAM; DC 8
See also BW 1; CA 93-96; 150; CANR 55; DLB 7; INT 93-96; MTCW 1
Gore, Catherine 1800-1861 .... NCLC 65
See also DLB 116
Gorenko, Anna Andreevna
See Akhmatova, Anna
Gorky, Maxim 1868-1936......TCLC 8; DAB; SSC 28; WLC
See also Peshkov, Alexei Maximovich
Goryan, Sirak
See Saroyan, William
Gosse, Edmund (William) 1849-1928
TCLC 28
See also CA 117; DLB 57, 144, 184
Gotlieb, Phyllis Fay (Bloom) 1926-
CLC 18
See also CA 13-16R; CANR 7; DLB 88
Gottesman, S. D.
See Kornbluth, C(yril) M.; Pohl, Frederik
Gottfried von Strassburg fl. c. 1210.............................CMLC 10
See also DLB 138
Gould, Lois .... CLC 4, 10
See also CA 77-80; CANR 29; MTCW 1
Gourmont, Remy (-Marie-Charles) de 1858-1915 .... TCLC 17
See also CA 109; 150

Govier, Katherine 1948- .... CLC 51
See also CA 101; CANR 18, 40
Goyen, (Charles) William 1915-1983
CLC 5, 8, 14, 40
See also AITN 2; CA 5-8R; 110; CANR 6, 71; DLB 2; DLBY 83; INT CANR-6
Goytisolo, Juan 1931-...CLC 5, 10, 23; DAM MULT; HLC
See also CA 85-88; CANR 32, 61; HW; MTCW 1
Gozzano, Guido 1883-1916 .... PC 10
See also CA 154; DLB 114
Gozzi, (Conte) Carlo 1720-1806
NCLC 23
Grabbe, Christian Dietrich 1801-1836
NCLC 2
See also DLB 133
Grace, Patricia 1937- .... CLC 56
Gracian y Morales, Baltasar 1601-1658
LC 15
Gracq, Julien............................CLC 11, 48
See also Poirier, Louis
See also DLB 83
Grade, Chaim 1910-1982 .... CLC 10
See also CA 93-96; 107
Graduate of Oxford, A
See Ruskin, John
Grafton, Garth
See Duncan, Sara Jeannette
Graham, John
See Phillips, David Graham
Graham, Jorie 1951- .... CLC 48
See also CA 111; CANR 63; DLB 120
Graham, R(obert) B(ontine) Cunninghame
See Cunninghame Graham, R(obert) B(ontine)
See also DLB 98, 135, 174
Graham, Robert
See Haldeman, Joe (William)
Graham, Tom
See Lewis, (Harry) Sinclair
Graham, W(illiam) S(ydney) 1918-1986
CLC 29
See also CA 73-76; 118; DLB 20
Graham, Winston (Mawdsley) 1910-
CLC 23
See also CA 49-52; CANR 2, 22, 45, 66; DLB 77
Grahame, Kenneth 1859-1932 .. T C L C 64; DAB
See also CA 108; 136; CLR 5; DLB 34, 141, 178; MAICYA; SATA 100; YABC 1
Grant, Skeeter
See Spiegelman, Art
Granville-Barker, Harley 1877-1946
TCLC 2; DAM DRAM
See also Barker, Harley Granville
See also CA 104
Grass, Guenter (Wilhelm) 1927-...CLC 1, 2, 4, 6, 11, 15, 22, 32, 49, 88; DA; DAB; DAC; DAM MST, NOV; WLC
See also CA 13-16R; CANR 20, 75; DLB 75, 124; MTCW 1
Gratton, Thomas
See Hulme, T(homas) E(rnest)
Grau, Shirley Ann 1929- ..CLC 4, 9; SSC 15
See also CA 89-92; CANR 22, 69; DLB 2; INT CANR-22; MTCW 1
Gravel, Fern
See Hall, James Norman
Graver, Elizabeth 1964- .... CLC 70
See also CA 135; CANR 71
Graves, Richard Perceval 1945- .... CLC 44
See also CA 65-68; CANR 9, 26, 51

Graves, Robert (von Ranke) 1895-1985
CLC 1, 2, 6, 11, 39, 44, 45; DAB; DAC; DAM MST, POET; PC 6
See also CA 5-8R; 117; CANR 5, 36; CDBLB 1914-1945; DLB 20, 100, 191; DLBD 18; DLBY 85; MTCW 1; SATA 45
Graves, Valerie
See Bradley, Marion Zimmer
Gray, Alasdair (James) 1934- ....CLC 41
See also CA 126; CANR 47, 69; DLB 194; INT 126; MTCW 1
Gray, Amlin 1946- ....CLC 29
See also CA 138
Gray, Francine du Plessix 1930-...CLC 22; DAM NOV
See also BEST 90:3; CA 61-64; CAAS 2; CANR 11, 33, 75; INT CANR-11; MTCW 1
Gray, John (Henry) 1866-1934 ...... TCLC 19
See also CA 119; 162
Gray, Simon (James Holliday) 1936-
CLC 9, 14, 36
See also AITN 1; CA 21-24R; CAAS 3; CANR 32, 69; DLB 13; MTCW 1
Gray, Spalding 1941- ......CLC 49, 112; DAM POP; DC 7
See also CA 128; CANR 74
Gray, Thomas 1716-1771...LC 4, 40; DA; DAB; DAC; DAM MST; PC 2; WLC
See also CDBLB 1660-1789; DLB 109
Grayson, David
See Baker, Ray Stannard
Grayson, Richard (A.) 1951- ...... CLC 38
See also CA 85-88; CANR 14, 31, 57
Greeley, Andrew M(oran) 1928- ..... CLC 28; DAM POP
See also CA 5-8R; CAAS 7; CANR 7, 43, 69; MTCW 1
Green, Anna Katharine 1846-1935...TCLC 63
See also CA 112; 159; DLB 202
Green, Brian
See Card, Orson Scott
Green, Hannah
See Greenberg, Joanne (Goldenberg)
Green, Hannah 1927(?)-1996 .... CLC 3
See also CA 73-76; CANR 59
Green, Henry 1905-1973 .... CLC 2, 13, 97
See also Yorke, Henry Vincent
See also DLB 15
Green, Julian (Hartridge) 1900-1998
See Green, Julien
See also CA 21-24R; 169; CANR 33; DLB 4, 72; MTCW 1
Green, Julien .... CLC 3, 11, 77
See also Green, Julian (Hartridge)
Green, Paul (Eliot) 1894-1981 . CLC 25; DAM DRAM
See also AITN 1; CA 5-8R; 103; CANR 3; DLB 7, 9; DLBY 81
Greenberg, Ivan 1908-1973
See Rahv, Philip
See also CA 85-88
Greenberg, Joanne (Goldenberg) 1932-
CLC 7, 30
See also AAYA 12; CA 5-8R; CANR 14, 32, 69; SATA 25
Greenberg, Richard 1959(?)- .... CLC 57
See also CA 138
Greene, Bette 1934- ....CLC 30
See also AAYA 7; CA 53-56; CANR 4; CLR 2; JRDA; MAICYA; SAAS 16; SATA 8, 102
Greene, Gael ....CLC 8
See also CA 13-16R; CANR 10

Habermas, Jurgen
See Habermas, Juergen
Hacker, Marilyn 1942-...**CLC 5, 9, 23, 72, 91; DAM POET**
See also CA 77-80; CANR 68; DLB 120
Haeckel, Ernst Heinrich (Philipp August) 1834-1919 .... **TCLC 83**
See also CA 157
Haggard, H(enry) Rider 1856-1925 **TCLC 11**
See also CA 108; 148; DLB 70, 156, 174, 178; SATA 16
Hagiosy, L.
See Larbaud, Valery (Nicolas)
Hagiwara Sakutaro 1886-1942...**TCLC 60; PC 18**
Haig, Fenil
See Ford, Ford Madox
Haig-Brown, Roderick (Langmere) 1908-1976 .... **CLC 21**
See also CA 5-8R; 69-72; CANR 4, 38; CLR 31; DLB 88; MAICYA; SATA 12
Hailey, Arthur 1920- ...... **CLC 5; DAM NOV, POP**
See also AITN 2; BEST 90:3; CA 1-4R; CANR 2, 36, 75; DLB 88; DLBY 82; MTCW 1
Hailey, Elizabeth Forsythe 1938- .... **CLC 40**
See also CA 93-96; CAAS 1; CANR 15, 48; INT CANR-15
Haines, John (Meade) 1924-............ **CLC 58**
See also CA 17-20R; CANR 13, 34; DLB 5
Hakluyt, Richard 1552-1616 .... **LC 31**
Haldeman, Joe (William) 1943-...**CLC 61**
See also CA 53-56; CAAS 25; CANR 6, 70, 72; DLB 8; INT CANR-6
Haley, Alex(ander Murray Palmer) 1921-1992 **CLC 8, 12, 76; BLC 2; DA; DAB; DAC; DAM MST, MULT, POP**
See also AAYA 26; BW 2; CA 77-80; 136; CANR 61; DLB 38; MTCW 1
Haliburton, Thomas Chandler 1796-1865 **NCLC 15**
See also DLB 11, 99
Hall, Donald (Andrew, Jr.) 1928-...**CLC 1, 13, 37, 59; DAM POET**
See also CA 5-8R; CAAS 7; CANR 2, 44, 64; DLB 5; SATA 23, 97
Hall, Frederic Sauser
See Sauser-Hall, Frederic
Hall, James
See Kuttner, Henry
Hall, James Norman 1887-1951 ..... **TCLC 23**
See also CA 123; SATA 21
Hall, Radclyffe
See Hall, (Marguerite) Radclyffe
Hall, (Marguerite) Radclyffe 1886-1943 **TCLC 12**
See also CA 110; 150; DLB 191
Hall, Rodney 1935-........................ **CLC 51**
See also CA 109; CANR 69
Halleck, Fitz-Greene 1790-1867 .... **NCLC 47**
See also DLB 3
Halliday, Michael
See Creasey, John
Halpern, Daniel 1945-................. **CLC 14**
See also CA 33-36R
Hamburger, Michael (Peter Leopold) 1924- **CLC 5, 14**
See also CA 5-8R; CAAS 4; CANR 2, 47; DLB 27
Hamill, Pete 1935- .... **CLC 10**
See also CA 25-28R; CANR 18, 71

Hamilton, Alexander 1755(?)-1804 **NCLC 49**
See also DLB 37
Hamilton, Clive
See Lewis, C(live) S(taples)
Hamilton, Edmond 1904-1977 ...... **CLC 1**
See also CA 1-4R; CANR 3; DLB 8
Hamilton, Eugene (Jacob) Lee
See Lee-Hamilton, Eugene (Jacob)
Hamilton, Franklin
See Silverberg, Robert
Hamilton, Gail
See Corcoran, Barbara
Hamilton, Mollie
See Kaye, M(ary) M(argaret)
Hamilton, (Anthony Walter) Patrick 1904-1962 .... **CLC 51**
See also CA 113; DLB 10
Hamilton, Virginia 1936-...**CLC 26; DAM MULT**
See also AAYA 2, 21; BW 2; CA 25-28R; CANR 20, 37, 73; CLR 1, 11, 40; DLB 33, 52; INT CANR-20; JRDA; MAICYA; MTCW 1; SATA 4, 56, 79
Hammett, (Samuel) Dashiell 1894-1961...**CLC 3, 5, 10, 19, 47; SSC 17**
See also AITN 1; CA 81-84; CANR 42; CDALB 1929-1941; DLBD 6; DLBY 96; MTCW 1
Hammon, Jupiter 1711(?)-1800(?)...**NCLC 5; BLC 2; DAM MULT, POET; PC 16**
See also DLB 31, 50
Hammond, Keith
See Kuttner, Henry
Hamner, Earl (Henry), Jr. 1923-...**CLC 12**
See also AITN 2; CA 73-76; DLB 6
Hampton, Christopher (James) 1946- **CLC 4**
See also CA 25-28R; DLB 13; MTCW 1
Hamsun, Knut .... **TCLC 2, 14, 49**
See also Pedersen, Knut
Handke, Peter 1942-...**CLC 5, 8, 10, 15, 38; DAM DRAM, NOV**
See also CA 77-80; CANR 33, 75; DLB 85, 124; MTCW 1
Hanley, James 1901-1985 ..... **CLC 3, 5, 8, 13**
See also CA 73-76; 117; CANR 36; DLB 191; MTCW 1
Hannah, Barry 1942- .... **CLC 23, 38, 90**
See also CA 108; 110; CANR 43, 68; DLB 6; INT 110; MTCW 1
Hannon, Ezra
See Hunter, Evan
Hansberry, Lorraine (Vivian) 1930-1965 **CLC 17, 62; BLC 2; DA; DAB; DAC; DAM DRAM, MST, MULT; DC 2**
See also AAYA 25; BW 1; CA 109; 25-28R; CABS 3; CANR 58; CDALB 1941-1968; DLB 7, 38; MTCW 1
Hansen, Joseph 1923- .... **CLC 38**
See also CA 29-32R; CAAS 17; CANR 16, 44, 66; INT CANR-16
Hansen, Martin A(lfred) 1909-1955 **TCLC 32**
See also CA 167
Hanson, Kenneth O(stlin) 1922- .... **CLC 13**
See also CA 53-56; CANR 7
Hardwick, Elizabeth (Bruce) 1916- **CLC 13; DAM NOV**
See also CA 5-8R; CANR 3, 32, 70; DLB 6; MTCW 1

Hardy, Thomas 1840-1928.....**TCLC 4, 10, 18, 32, 48, 53, 72; DA; DAB; DAC; DAM MST, NOV, POET; PC 8; SSC 2; WLC**
See also CA 104; 123; CDBLB 1890-1914; DLB 18, 19, 135; MTCW 1
Hare, David 1947- .... **CLC 29, 58**
See also CA 97-100; CANR 39; DLB 13; MTCW 1
Harewood, John
See Van Druten, John (William)
Harford, Henry
See Hudson, W(illiam) H(enry)
Hargrave, Leonie
See Disch, Thomas M(ichael)
Harjo, Joy 1951- .... **CLC 83; DAM MULT**
See also CA 114; CANR 35, 67; DLB 120, 175; NNAL
Harlan, Louis R(udolph) 1922-......... **CLC 34**
See also CA 21-24R; CANR 25, 55
Harling, Robert 1951(?)- .... **CLC 53**
See also CA 147
Harmon, William (Ruth) 1938-...**CLC 38**
See also CA 33-36R; CANR 14, 32, 35; SATA 65
Harper, F. E. W.
See Harper, Frances Ellen Watkins
Harper, Frances E. W.
See Harper, Frances Ellen Watkins
Harper, Frances E. Watkins
See Harper, Frances Ellen Watkins
Harper, Frances Ellen
See Harper, Frances Ellen Watkins
Harper, Frances Ellen Watkins 1825-1911 **TCLC 14; BLC 2; DAM MULT, POET; PC 21**
See also BW 1; CA 111; 125; DLB 50
Harper, Michael S(teven) 1938-...**CLC 7, 22**
See also BW 1; CA 33-36R; CANR 24; DLB 41
Harper, Mrs. F. E. W.
See Harper, Frances Ellen Watkins
Harris, Christie (Lucy) Irwin 1907-...**CLC 12**
See also CA 5-8R; CANR 6; CLR 47; DLB 88; JRDA; MAICYA; SAAS 10; SATA 6, 74
Harris, Frank 1856-1931 .... **TCLC 24**
See also CA 109; 150; DLB 156, 197
Harris, George Washington 1814-1869 **NCLC 23**
See also DLB 3, 11
Harris, Joel Chandler 1848-1908 ...**TCLC 2; SSC 19**
See also CA 104; 137; CLR 49; DLB 11, 23, 42, 78, 91; MAICYA; SATA 100; YABC 1
Harris, John (Wyndham Parkes Lucas) Beynon 1903-1969
See Wyndham, John
See also CA 102; 89-92
Harris, MacDonald .... **CLC 9**
See also Heiney, Donald (William)
Harris, Mark 1922- .... **CLC 19**
See also CA 5-8R; CAAS 3; CANR 2, 55; DLB 2; DLBY 80
Harris, (Theodore) Wilson 1921- **CLC 25**
See also BW 2; CA 65-68; CAAS 16; CANR 11, 27, 69; DLB 117; MTCW 1
Harrison, Elizabeth Cavanna 1909-
See Cavanna, Betty
See also CA 9-12R; CANR 6, 27

Howard, Robert E(rvin) 1906-1936
TCLC **8**
See also CA 105; 157
Howard, Warren F.
See Pohl, Frederik
Howe, Fanny (Quincy) 1940- .... CLC **47**
See also CA 117; CAAS 27; CANR 70; SATA-Brief 52
Howe, Irving 1920-1993 .... CLC **85**
See also CA 9-12R; 141; CANR 21, 50; DLB 67; MTCW 1
Howe, Julia Ward 1819-1910 .. TCLC **21**
See also CA 117; DLB 1, 189
Howe, Susan 1937- .... CLC **72**
See also CA 160; DLB 120
Howe, Tina 1937- .... CLC **48**
See also CA 109
Howell, James 1594(?)-1666 .... LC **13**
See also DLB 151
Howells, W. D.
See Howells, William Dean
Howells, William D.
See Howells, William Dean
Howells, William Dean 1837-1920
TCLC **7, 17, 41**
See also CA 104; 134; CDALB 1865-1917; DLB 12, 64, 74, 79, 189
Howes, Barbara 1914-1996 .... CLC **15**
See also CA 9-12R; 151; CAAS 3; CANR 53; SATA 5
Hrabal, Bohumil 1914-1997...CLC **13, 67**
See also CA 106; 156; CAAS 12; CANR 57
Hroswitha of Gandersheim c. 935-c. 1002
CMLC **29**
See also DLB 148
Hsun, Lu
See Lu Hsun
Hubbard, L(afayette) Ron(ald) 1911-1986
CLC **43; DAM POP**
See also CA 77-80; 118; CANR 52
Huch, Ricarda (Octavia) 1864-1947
TCLC **13**
See also CA 111; DLB 66
Huddle, David 1942- .... CLC **49**
See also CA 57-60; CAAS 20; DLB 130
Hudson, Jeffrey
See Crichton, (John) Michael
Hudson, W(illiam) H(enry) 1841-1922
TCLC **29**
See also CA 115; DLB 98, 153, 174; SATA 35
Hueffer, Ford Madox
See Ford, Ford Madox
Hughart, Barry 1934- .... CLC **39**
See also CA 137
Hughes, Colin
See Creasey, John
Hughes, David (John) 1930- ...... CLC **48**
See also CA 116; 129; DLB 14
Hughes, Edward James
See Hughes, Ted
See also DAM MST, POET
Hughes, (James) Langston 1902-1967
CLC **1, 5, 10, 15, 35, 44, 108; BLC 2; DA; DAB; DAC; DAM DRAM, MST, MULT, POET; DC 3; PC 1; SSC 6; WLC**
See also AAYA 12; BW 1; CA 1-4R; 25-28R; CANR 1, 34; CDALB 1929-1941; CLR 17; DLB 4, 7, 48, 51, 86; JRDA; MAICYA; MTCW 1; SATA 4, 33
Hughes, Richard (Arthur Warren) 1900-1976 .... CLC **1, 11; DAM NOV**
See also CA 5-8R; 65-68; CANR 4; DLB 15, 161; MTCW 1; SATA 8; SATA-Obit 25

Hughes, Ted 1930-1998...CLC **2, 4, 9, 14, 37; DAB; DAC; PC 7**
See also Hughes, Edward James
See also CA 1-4R; 171; CANR 1, 33, 66; CLR 3; DLB 40, 161; MAICYA; MTCW 1, SATA 49; SATA-Brief 27
Hugo, Richard F(ranklin) 1923-1982
CLC **6, 18, 32; DAM POET**
See also CA 49-52; 108; CANR 3; DLB 5
Hugo, Victor (Marie) 1802-1885
NCLC **3, 10, 21; DA; DAB; DAC; DAM DRAM, MST, NOV, POET; PC 17; WLC**
See also DLB 119, 192; SATA 47
Huidobro, Vicente
See Huidobro Fernandez, Vicente Garcia
Huidobro Fernandez, Vicente Garcia 1893-1948 .... TCLC **31**
See also CA 131; HW
Hulme, Keri 1947- .... CLC **39**
See also CA 125; CANR 69; INT 125
Hulme, T(homas) E(rnest) 1883-1917
TCLC **21**
See also CA 117; DLB 19
Hume, David 1711-1776 .... LC **7**
See also DLB 104
Humphrey, William 1924-1997 .... CLC **45**
See also CA 77-80; 160; CANR 68; DLB 6
Humphreys, Emyr Owen 1919- .... CLC **47**
See also CA 5-8R; CANR 3, 24; DLB 15
Humphreys, Josephine 1945-...CLC **34, 57**
See also CA 121; 127; INT 127
Huneker, James Gibbons 1857-1921
TCLC **65**
See also DLB 71
Hungerford, Pixie
See Brinsmead, H(esba) F(ay)
Hunt, E(verette) Howard, (Jr.) 1918-
CLC **3**
See also AITN 1; CA 45-48; CANR 2, 47
Hunt, Kyle
See Creasey, John
Hunt, (James Henry) Leigh 1784-1859
NCLC **1, 70; DAM POET**
See also DLB 96, 110, 144
Hunt, Marsha 1946- .... CLC **70**
See also BW 2; CA 143
Hunt, Violet 1866(?)-1942 .... TCLC **53**
See also DLB 162, 197
Hunter, E. Waldo
See Sturgeon, Theodore (Hamilton)
Hunter, Evan 1926-...CLC **11, 31; DAM POP**
See also CA 5-8R; CANR 5, 38, 62; DLBY 82; INT CANR-5; MTCW 1; SATA 25
Hunter, Kristin (Eggleston) 1931- ....CLC **35**
See also AITN 1; BW 1; CA 13-16R; CANR 13; CLR 3; DLB 33; INT CANR-13; MAICYA; SAAS 10; SATA 12
Hunter, Mollie 1922- .... CLC **21**
See also McIlwraith, Maureen Mollie Hunter
See also AAYA 13; CANR 37; CLR 25; DLB 161; JRDA; MAICYA; SAAS 7; SATA 54
Hunter, Robert (?)-1734 .... LC **7**
Hurston, Zora Neale 1903-1960...CLC **7, 30, 61; BLC 2; DA; DAC; DAM MST, MULT, NOV; SSC 4; WLCS**
See also AAYA 15; BW 1; CA 85-88; CANR 61; DLB 51, 86; MTCW 1
Huston, John (Marcellus) 1906-1987...CLC **20**
See also CA 73-76; 123; CANR 34; DLB 26

Hustvedt, Siri 1955- .... CLC **76**
See also CA 137
Hutten, Ulrich von 1488-1523 .... LC **16**
See also DLB 179
Huxley, Aldous (Leonard) 1894-1963
CLC **1, 3, 4, 5, 8, 11, 18, 35, 79; DA; DAB; DAC; DAM MST, NOV; WLC**
See also AAYA 11; CA 85-88; CANR 44; CDBLB 1914-1945; DLB 36, 100, 162, 195; MTCW 1; SATA 63
Huxley, T(homas) H(enry) 1825-1895
NCLC **67**
See also DLB 57
Huysmans, Joris-Karl 1848-1907
TCLC **7, 69**
See also CA 104; 165; DLB 123
Hwang, David Henry 1957- ..... CLC **55; DAM DRAM; DC 4**
See also CA 127; 132; INT 132
Hyde, Anthony 1946- ....CLC **42**
See also CA 136
Hyde, Margaret O(ldroyd) 1917- ..... CLC **21**
See also CA 1-4R; CANR 1, 36; CLR 23; JRDA; MAICYA; SAAS 8; SATA 1, 42, 76
Hynes, James 1956(?)- .... CLC **65**
See also CA 164
Ian, Janis 1951- .... CLC **21**
See also CA 105
Ibanez, Vicente Blasco
See Blasco Ibanez, Vicente
Ibarguengoitia, Jorge 1928-1983 ......CLC **37**
See also CA 124; 113; HW
Ibsen, Henrik (Johan) 1828-1906
TCLC **2, 8, 16, 37, 52; DA; DAB; DAC; DAM DRAM, MST; DC 2; WLC**
See also CA 104; 141
Ibuse, Masuji 1898-1993 .... CLC **22**
See also CA 127; 141; DLB 180
Ichikawa, Kon 1915- .... CLC **20**
See also CA 121
Idle, Eric 1943- .... CLC **21**
See also Monty Python
See also CA 116; CANR 35
Ignatow, David 1914-1997 .. CLC **4, 7, 14, 40**
See also CA 9-12R; 162; CAAS 3; CANR 31, 57; DLB 5
Ihimaera, Witi 1944- .... CLC **46**
See also CA 77-80
Ilf, Ilya ....TCLC **21**
See also Fainzilberg, Ilya Arnoldovich
Illyes, Gyula 1902-1983 .... PC **16**
See also CA 114; 109
Immermann, Karl (Lebrecht) 1796-1840
NCLC **4, 49**
See also DLB 133
Ince, Thomas H. 1882-1924 .... TCLC **89**
Inchbald, Elizabeth 1753-1821 ......NCLC **62**
See also DLB 39, 89
Inclan, Ramon (Maria) del Valle
See Valle-Inclan, Ramon (Maria) del
Infante, G(uillermo) Cabrera
See Cabrera Infante, G(uillermo)
Ingalls, Rachel (Holmes) 1940- CLC **42**
See also CA 123; 127
Ingamells, Reginald Charles
See Ingamells, Rex
Ingamells, Rex 1913-1955 .... TCLC **35**
See also CA 167
Inge, William (Motter) 1913-1973...CLC **1, 8, 19; DAM DRAM**
See also CA 9-12R; CDALB 1941-1968; DLB 7; MTCW 1

Jibran, Kahlil
See Gibran, Kahlil
Jibran, Khalil
See Gibran, Kahlil
Jiles, Paulette 1943-............. **CLC 13, 58**
See also CA 101; CANR 70
Jimenez (Mantecon), Juan Ramon 1881-
1958 ....**TCLC 4; DAM MULT, POET;**
HLC; PC 7
See also CA 104; 131; CANR 74; DLB 134;
HW; MTCW 1
Jimenez, Ramon
See Jimenez (Mantecon), Juan Ramon
Jimenez Mantecon, Juan
See Jimenez (Mantecon), Juan Ramon
Jin, Ha 1956-............................**CLC 109**
See also CA 152
Joel, Billy...**CLC 26**
See also Joel, William Martin
Joel, William Martin 1949-
See Joel, Billy
See also CA 108
John, Saint 7th cent. - .... **CMLC 27**
John of the Cross, St. 1542-1591...**LC 18**
Johnson, B(ryan) S(tanley William) 1933-
1973 ....**CLC 6, 9**
See also CA 9-12R; 53-56; CANR 9; DLB
14, 40
Johnson, Benj. F. of Boo
See Riley, James Whitcomb
Johnson, Benjamin F. of Boo
See Riley, James Whitcomb
Johnson, Charles (Richard) 1948-
CLC 7, 51, 65; BLC 2; DAM MULT
See also BW 2; CA 116; CAAS 18; CANR
42, 66; DLB 33
Johnson, Denis 1949- ....**CLC 52**
See also CA 117; 121; CANR 71; DLB 120
Johnson, Diane 1934-.............. **CLC 5, 13, 48**
See also CA 41-44R; CANR 17, 40, 62; DLBY
80; INT CANR-17; MTCW 1
Johnson, Eyvind (Olof Verner) 1900-1976
CLC 14
See also CA 73-76; 69-72; CANR 34
Johnson, J. R.
See James, C(yril) L(ionel) R(obert)
Johnson, James Weldon 1871-1938
TCLC 3, 19; BLC 2; DAM MULT, POET;
PC 24
See also BW 1; CA 104; 125; CDALB 1917-
1929; CLR 32; DLB 51; MTCW 1; SATA
31
Johnson, Joyce 1935- ....**CLC 58**
See also CA 125; 129
Johnson, Lionel (Pigot) 1867-1902
TCLC 19
See also CA 117; DLB 19
Johnson, Marguerite (Annie)
See Angelou, Maya
Johnson, Mel
See Malzberg, Barry N(athaniel)
Johnson, Pamela Hansford 1912-1981
CLC 1, 7, 27
See also CA 1-4R; 104; CANR 2, 28; DLB
15; MTCW 1
Johnson, Robert 1911(?)-1938 .... **TCLC 69**
Johnson, Samuel 1709-1784**LC 15; DA; DAB;**
DAC; DAM MST; WLC
See also CDBLB 1660-1789; DLB 39, 95, 104,
142
Johnson, Uwe 1934-1984 .. **CLC 5, 10, 15, 40**
See also CA 1-4R; 112; CANR 1, 39; DLB 75;
MTCW 1

Johnston, George (Benson) 1913-
CLC 51
See also CA 1-4R; CANR 5, 20; DLB 88
Johnston, Jennifer 1930-.............**CLC 7**
See also CA 85-88; DLB 14
Jolley, (Monica) Elizabeth 1923-...**CLC 46;**
SSC 19
See also CA 127; CAAS 13; CANR 59
Jones, Arthur Llewellyn 1863-1947
See Machen, Arthur
See also CA 104
Jones, D(ouglas) G(ordon) 1929-......**CLC 10**
See also CA 29-32R; CANR 13; DLB 53
Jones, David (Michael) 1895-1974...**C L C**
2, 4, 7, 13, 42
See also CA 9-12R; 53-56; CANR 28; CDBLB
1945-1960; DLB 20, 100; MTCW 1
Jones, David Robert 1947-
See Bowie, David
See also CA 103
Jones, Diana Wynne 1934-........**CLC 26**
See also AAYA 12; CA 49-52; CANR 4, 26,
56; CLR 23; DLB 161; JRDA; MAICYA;
SAAS 7; SATA 9, 70
Jones, Edward P. 1950- ....**CLC 76**
See also BW 2; CA 142
Jones, Gayl 1949- ... **CLC 6, 9; BLC 2; DAM**
MULT
See also BW 2; CA 77-80; CANR 27, 66; DLB
33; MTCW 1
Jones, James 1921-1977...**CLC 1, 3, 10, 39**
See also AITN 1, 2; CA 1-4R; 69-72; CANR
6; DLB 2, 143; DLBD 17; MTCW 1
Jones, John J.
See Lovecraft, H(oward) P(hillips)
Jones, LeRoi ....**CLC 1, 2, 3, 5, 10, 14**
See also Baraka, Amiri
Jones, Louis B. 1953- ....**CLC 65**
See also CA 141; CANR 73
Jones, Madison (Percy, Jr.) 1925-.......**CLC 4**
See also CA 13-16R; CAAS 11; CANR 7, 54;
DLB 152
Jones, Mervyn 1922- .... **CLC 10, 52**
See also CA 45-48; CAAS 5; CANR 1;
MTCW 1
Jones, Mick 1956(?)- ....**CLC 30**
Jones, Nettie (Pearl) 1941- ....**CLC 34**
See also BW 2; CA 137; CAAS 20
Jones, Preston 1936-1979 ....**CLC 10**
See also CA 73-76; 89-92; DLB 7
Jones, Robert F(rancis) 1934-.........**CLC 7**
See also CA 49-52; CANR 2, 61
Jones, Rod 1953- ....**CLC 50**
See also CA 128
Jones, Terence Graham Parry 1942-
CLC 21
See also Jones, Terry; Monty Python
See also CA 112; 116; CANR 35; INT 116
Jones, Terry
See Jones, Terence Graham Parry
See also SATA 67; SATA-Brief 51
Jones, Thom 1945(?)- ....**CLC 81**
See also CA 157
Jong, Erica 1942-...**CLC 4, 6, 8, 18, 83;**
DAM NOV, POP
See also AITN 1; BEST 90:2; CA 73-76; CANR
26, 52, 75; DLB 2, 5, 28, 152; INT CANR-
26; MTCW 1
Jonson, Ben(jamin) 1572(?)-1637...**LC 6,**
33; DA; DAB; DAC; DAM DRAM, MST,
POET; DC 4; PC 17; WLC
See also CDBLB Before 1660; DLB 62,
121

Jordan, June 1936-...**CLC 5, 11, 23, 114;**
BLCS; DAM MULT, POET
See also AAYA 2; BW 2; CA 33-36R; CANR
25, 70; CLR 10; DLB 38; MAICYA; MTCW
1; SATA 4
Jordan, Neil (Patrick) 1950- .... **CLC 110**
See also CA 124; 130; CANR 54; INT 130
Jordan, Pat(rick M.) 1941- ....**CLC 37**
See also CA 33-36R
Jorgensen, Ivar
See Ellison, Harlan (Jay)
Jorgenson, Ivar
See Silverberg, Robert
Josephus, Flavius c. 37-100 .... **CMLC 13**
Josipovici, Gabriel 1940- ....**CLC 6, 43**
See also CA 37-40R; CAAS 8; CANR 47;
DLB 14
Joubert, Joseph 1754-1824 .... **NCLC 9**
Jouve, Pierre Jean 1887-1976 .... **CLC 47**
See also CA 65-68
Jovine, Francesco 1902-1950 .... **TCLC 79**
Joyce, James (Augustine Aloysius) 1882-
1941...**TCLC 3, 8, 16, 35, 52; DA; DAB;**
DAC; DAM MST, NOV, POET; PC 22;
SSC 3, 26; WLC
See also CA 104; 126; CDBLB 1914-1945;
DLB 10, 19, 36, 162; MTCW 1
Jozsef, Attila 1905-1937 ....**TCLC 22**
See also CA 116
Juana Ines de la Cruz 1651(?)-1695
LC 5; PC 24
Judd, Cyril
See Kornbluth, C(yril) M.; Pohl, Frederik
Julian of Norwich 1342(?)-1416(?) .... **LC 6**
See also DLB 146
Junger, Sebastian 1962- ....**CLC 109**
See also CA 165
Juniper, Alex
See Hospital, Janette Turner
Junius
See Luxemburg, Rosa
Just, Ward (Swift) 1935- ....**CLC 4, 27**
See also CA 25-28R; CANR 32; INT CANR-
32
Justice, Donald (Rodney) 1925- .. **CLC 6, 19,**
102; DAM POET
See also CA 5-8R; CANR 26, 54, 74; DLBY
83; INT CANR-26
Juvenal...**CMLC 8**
See also Juvenalis, Decimus Junius
Juvenalis, Decimus Junius 55(?)-c. 127(?)
See Juvenal
Juvenis
See Bourne, Randolph S(illiman)
Kacew, Romain 1914-1980
See Gary, Romain
See also CA 108; 102
Kadare, Ismail 1936- ....**CLC 52**
See also CA 161
Kadohata, Cynthia ....**CLC 59**
See also CA 140
Kafka, Franz 1883-1924...**TCLC 2, 6, 13,**
29, 47, 53; DA; DAB; DAC; DAM MST,
NOV; SSC 5, 29; WLC
See also CA 105; 126; DLB 81; MTCW 1
Kahanovitsch, Pinkhes
See Der Nister
Kahn, Roger 1927- ....**CLC 30**
See also CA 25-28R; CANR 44, 69; DLB 171;
SATA 37
Kain, Saul
See Sassoon, Siegfried (Lorraine)

Key, Ellen 1849-1926 .... TCLC 65
Keyber, Conny
    See Fielding, Henry
Keyes, Daniel 1927-...CLC 80; DA; DAC;
    DAM MST, NOV
    See also AAYA 23; CA 17-20R; CANR 10, 26,
    54, 74; SATA 37
Keynes, John Maynard 1883-1946
    TCLC 64
    See also CA 114; 162, 163; DLBD 10
Khanshendel, Chiron
    See Rose, Wendy
Khayyam, Omar 1048-1131...CMLC 11;
    DAM POET; PC 8
Kherdian, David 1931- .... CLC 6, 9
    See also CA 21-24R; CAAS 2; CANR 39; CLR
    24; JRDA; MAICYA; SATA 16, 74
Khlebnikov, Velimir .... TCLC 20
    See also Khlebnikov, Viktor Vladimirovich
Khlebnikov, Viktor Vladimirovich 1885-1922
    See Khlebnikov, Velimir
    See also CA 117
Khodasevich, Vladislav (Felitsianovich)
    1886-1939 .... TCLC 15
    See also CA 115
Kielland, Alexander Lange 1849-1906
    TCLC 5
    See also CA 104
Kiely, Benedict 1919- .... CLC 23, 43
    See also CA 1-4R; CANR 2; DLB 15
Kienzle, William X(avier) 1928- ..C L C
    25; DAM POP
    See also CA 93-96; CAAS 1; CANR 9, 31, 59;
    INT CANR-31; MTCW 1
Kierkegaard, Soren 1813-1855
    NCLC 34
Killens, John Oliver 1916-1987...CLC 10
    See also BW 2; CA 77-80; 123; CAAS 2;
    CANR 26; DLB 33
Killigrew, Anne 1660-1685 .... LC 4
    See also DLB 131
Kim
    See Simenon, Georges (Jacques Christian)
Kincaid, Jamaica 1949-...CLC 43, 68; BLC
    2; DAM MULT, NOV
    See also AAYA 13; BW 2; CA 125; CANR 47,
    59; DLB 157
King, Francis (Henry) 1923-...CLC 8, 53;
    DAM NOV
    See also CA 1-4R; CANR 1, 33; DLB 15, 139;
    MTCW 1
King, Kennedy
    See Brown, George Douglas
King, Martin Luther, Jr. 1929-1968
    CLC 83; BLC 2; DA; DAB; DAC;
    DAM MST, MULT; WLCS
    See also BW 2; CA 25-28; CANR 27, 44;
    CAP 2; MTCW 1; SATA 14
King, Stephen (Edwin) 1947-...CLC 12, 26,
    37, 61, 113; DAM NOV, POP; SSC 17
    See also AAYA 1, 17; BEST 90:1; CA 61-64;
    CANR 1, 30, 52; DLB 143; DLBY 80;
    JRDA; MTCW 1; SATA 9, 55
King, Steve
    See King, Stephen (Edwin)
King, Thomas 1943- .... CLC 89; DAC; DAM
    MULT
    See also CA 144; DLB 175; NNAL; SATA 96
Kingman, Lee .... CLC 17
    See also Natti, (Mary) Lee
    See also SAAS 3; SATA 1, 67
Kingsley, Charles 1819-1875 . NCLC 35
    See also DLB 21, 32, 163, 190; YABC 2

Kingsley, Sidney 1906-1995 .... CLC 44
    See also CA 85-88; 147; DLB 7
Kingsolver, Barbara 1955-...CLC 55, 81;
    DAM POP
    See also AAYA 15; CA 129; 134; CANR 60;
    INT 134
Kingston, Maxine (Ting Ting) Hong 1940-
    CLC 12, 19, 58; DAM MULT, NOV;
    WLCS
    See also AAYA 8; CA 69-72; CANR 13, 38,
    74; DLB 173; DLBY 80; INT CANR-13;
    MTCW 1; SATA 53
Kinnell, Galway 1927-...CLC 1, 2, 3, 5,
    13, 29
    See also CA 9-12R; CANR 10, 34, 66; DLB
    5; DLBY 87; INT CANR-34; MTCW 1
Kinsella, Thomas 1928- .... CLC 4, 19
    See also CA 17-20R; CANR 15; DLB 27;
    MTCW 1
Kinsella, W(illiam) P(atrick) 1935-
    CLC 27, 43; DAC; DAM NOV, POP
    See also AAYA 7; CA 97-100; CAAS 7;
    CANR 21, 35, 66, 75; INT CANR-21;
    MTCW 1
Kipling, (Joseph) Rudyard 1865-1936
    TCLC 8, 17; DA; DAB; DAC; DAM
    MST, POET; PC 3; SSC 5; WLC
    See also CA 105; 120; CANR 33; CDBLB
    1890-1914; CLR 39; DLB 19, 34, 141, 156;
    MAICYA; MTCW 1; SATA 100; YABC 2
Kirkup, James 1918- .... CLC 1
    See also CA 1-4R; CAAS 4; CANR 2; DLB
    27; SATA 12
Kirkwood, James 1930(?)-1989 ....CLC 9
    See also AITN 2; CA 1-4R; 128; CANR 6, 40
Kirshner, Sidney
    See Kingsley, Sidney
Kis, Danilo 1935-1989 .... CLC 57
    See also CA 109; 118; 129; CANR 61; DLB
    181; MTCW 1
Kivi, Aleksis 1834-1872 .... NCLC 30
Kizer, Carolyn (Ashley) 1925-...CLC 15,
    39, 80; DAM POET
    See also CA 65-68; CAAS 5; CANR 24, 70;
    DLB 5, 169
Klabund 1890-1928 .... TCLC 44
    See also CA 162; DLB 66
Klappert, Peter 1942- .... CLC 57
    See also CA 33-36R; DLB 5
Klein, A(braham) M(oses) 1909-1972
    CLC 19; DAB; DAC; DAM MST
    See also CA 101; 37-40R; DLB 68
Klein, Norma 1938-1989 .... CLC 30
    See also AAYA 2; CA 41-44R; 128; CANR 15,
    37; CLR 2, 19; INT CANR-15; JRDA;
    MAICYA; SAAS 1; SATA 7, 57
Klein, T(heodore) E(ibon) D(onald) 1947-
    CLC 34
    See also CA 119; CANR 44, 75
Kleist, Heinrich von 1777-1811
    NCLC 2, 37; DAM DRAM; SSC 22
    See also DLB 90
Klima, Ivan 1931- .... CLC 56; DAM NOV
    See also CA 25-28R; CANR 17, 50
Klimentov, Andrei Platonovich 1899-1951
    See Platonov, Andrei
    See also CA 108
Klinger, Friedrich Maximilian von 1752-1831
    NCLC 1
    See also DLB 94
Klingsor the Magician
    See Hartmann, Sadakichi

Klopstock, Friedrich Gottlieb 1724-1803
    NCLC 11
    See also DLB 97
Knapp, Caroline 1959- .... CLC 99
    See also CA 154
Knebel, Fletcher 1911-1993 .... CLC 14
    See also AITN 1; CA 1-4R; 140; CAAS 3;
    CANR 1, 36; SATA 36; SATA-Obit 75
Knickerbocker, Diedrich
    See Irving, Washington
Knight, Etheridge 1931-1991 .. CLC 40;
    BLC 2; DAM POET; PC 14
    See also BW 1; CA 21-24R; 133; CANR 23;
    DLB 41
Knight, Sarah Kemble 1666-1727 .. LC 7
    See also DLB 24, 200
Knister, Raymond 1899-1932 .... TCLC 56
    See also DLB 68
Knowles, John 1926-...CLC 1, 4, 10, 26;
    DA; DAC; DAM MST, NOV
    See also AAYA 10; CA 17-20R; CANR 40, 74;
    CDALB 1968-1988; DLB 6; MTCW 1;
    SATA 8, 89
Knox, Calvin M.
    See Silverberg, Robert
Knox, John c. 1505-1572 .... LC 37
    See also DLB 132
Knye, Cassandra
    See Disch, Thomas M(ichael)
Koch, C(hristopher) J(ohn) 1932- ....CLC 42
    See also CA 127
Koch, Christopher
    See Koch, C(hristopher) J(ohn)
Koch, Kenneth 1925- ..... CLC 5, 8, 44;
    DAM POET
    See also CA 1-4R; CANR 6, 36, 57; DLB 5;
    INT CANR-36; SATA 65
Kochanowski, Jan 1530-1584 .... LC 10
Kock, Charles Paul de 1794-1871 N C L C
    16
Koda Shigeyuki 1867-1947
    See Rohan, Koda
    See also CA 121
Koestler, Arthur 1905-1983... CLC 1, 3,
    6, 8, 15, 33
    See also CA 1-4R; 109; CANR 1, 33; CDBLB
    1945-1960; DLBY 83; MTCW 1
Kogawa, Joy Nozomi 1935- .. CLC 78; DAC;
    DAM MST, MULT
    See also CA 101; CANR 19, 62; SATA 99
Kohout, Pavel 1928- .... CLC 13
    See also CA 45-48; CANR 3
Koizumi, Yakumo
    See Hearn, (Patricio) Lafcadio (Tessima Carlos)
Kolmar, Gertrud 1894-1943 .... TCLC 40
    See also CA 167
Komunyakaa, Yusef 1947-...CLC 86, 94;
    BLCS
    See also CA 147; DLB 120
Konrad, George
    See Konrad, Gyoergy
Konrad, Gyoergy 1933- .... CLC 4, 10, 73
    See also CA 85-88
Konwicki, Tadeusz 1926-...CLC 8, 28, 54,
    117
    See also CA 101; CAAS 9; CANR 39, 59;
    MTCW 1
Koontz, Dean R(ay) 1945- ..... CLC 78; DAM
    NOV, POP
    See also AAYA 9; BEST 89:3, 90:2; CA 108;
    CANR 19, 36, 52; MTCW 1; SATA 92
Kopernik, Mikolaj
    See Copernicus, Nicolaus

Landis, John 1950- .... **CLC 26**
See also CA 112; 122
Landolfi, Tommaso 1908-1979 .... **CLC 11, 49**
See also CA 127; 117; DLB 177
Landon, Letitia Elizabeth 1802-1838
NCLC 15
See also DLB 96
Landor, Walter Savage 1775-1864...**NCLC 14**
See also DLB 93, 107
Landwirth, Heinz 1927-
See Lind, Jakov
See also CA 9-12R; CANR 7
Lane, Patrick 1939- ...... **CLC 25; DAM POET**
See also CA 97-100; CANR 54; DLB 53; INT 97-100
Lang, Andrew 1844-1912 .... **TCLC 16**
See also CA 114; 137; DLB 98, 141, 184; MAICYA; SATA 16
Lang, Fritz 1890-1976 .... **CLC 20, 103**
See also CA 77-80; 69-72; CANR 30
Lange, John
See Crichton, (John) Michael
Langer, Elinor 1939- .... **CLC 34**
See also CA 121
Langland, William 1330(?)-1400(?) ... **LC 19; DA; DAB; DAC; DAM MST, POET**
See also DLB 146
Langstaff, Launcelot
See Irving, Washington
Lanier, Sidney 1842-1881 ..... **NCLC 6; DAM POET**
See also DLB 64; DLBD 13; MAICYA; SATA 18
Lanyer, Aemilia 1569-1645 .... **LC 10, 30**
See also DLB 121
Lao-Tzu
See Lao Tzu
Lao Tzu fl. 6th cent. B.C.- .... **CMLC 7**
Lapine, James (Elliot) 1949- ..... **CLC 39**
See also CA 123; 130; CANR 54; INT 130
Larbaud, Valery (Nicolas) 1881-1957
TCLC 9
See also CA 106; 152
Lardner, Ring
See Lardner, Ring(gold) W(ilmer)
Lardner, Ring W., Jr.
See Lardner, Ring(gold) W(ilmer)
Lardner, Ring(gold) W(ilmer) 1885-1933
TCLC 2, 14; SSC 32
See also CA 104; 131; CDALB 1917-1929; DLB 11, 25, 86; DLBD 16; MTCW 1
Laredo, Betty
See Codrescu, Andrei
Larkin, Maia
See Wojciechowska, Maia (Teresa)
Larkin, Philip (Arthur) 1922-1985
CLC 3, 5, 8, 9, 13, 18, 33, 39, 64; DAB; DAM MST, POET; PC 21
See also CA 5-8R; 117; CANR 24, 62; CDBLB 1960 to Present; DLB 27; MTCW 1
Larra (y Sanchez de Castro), Mariano Jose de 1809-1837 .... **NCLC 17**
Larsen, Eric 1941- .... **CLC 55**
See also CA 132
Larsen, Nella 1891-1964 .... **CLC 37; BLC 2; DAM MULT**
See also BW 1; CA 125; DLB 51
Larson, Charles R(aymond) 1938- .. **CLC 31**
See also CA 53-56; CANR 4
Larson, Jonathan 1961-1996 ..... **CLC 99**
See also CA 156

Las Casas, Bartolome de 1474-1566
LC 31
Lasch, Christopher 1932-1994...**CLC 102**
See also CA 73-76; 144; CANR 25; MTCW 1
Lasker-Schueler, Else 1869-1945...**TCLC 57**
See also DLB 66, 124
Laski, Harold 1893-1950 .... **TCLC 79**
Latham, Jean Lee 1902-1995 .... **CLC 12**
See also AITN 1; CA 5-8R; CANR 7; CLR 50; MAICYA; SATA 2, 68
Latham, Mavis
See Clark, Mavis Thorpe
Lathen, Emma ....**CLC 2**
See also Hennissart, Martha; Latsis, Mary J(ane)
Lathrop, Francis
See Leiber, Fritz (Reuter, Jr.)
Latsis, Mary J(ane) 1927(?)-1997
See Lathen, Emma
See also CA 85-88; 162
Lattimore, Richmond (Alexander) 1906-1984
CLC 3
See also CA 1-4R; 112; CANR 1
Laughlin, James 1914-1997....... **CLC 49**
See also CA 21-24R; 162; CAAS 22; CANR 9, 47; DLB 48; DLBY 96, 97
Laurence, (Jean) Margaret (Wemyss) 1926-1987**CLC 3, 6, 13, 50, 62; DAC; DAM MST; SSC 7**
See also CA 5-8R; 121; CANR 33; DLB 53; MTCW 1; SATA-Obit 50
Laurent, Antoine 1952- .... **CLC 50**
Lauscher, Hermann
See Hesse, Hermann
Lautreamont, Comte de 1846-1870
NCLC 12; SSC 14
Laverty, Donald
See Blish, James (Benjamin)
Lavin, Mary 1912-1996 ..**CLC 4, 18, 99; SSC 4**
See also CA 9-12R; 151; CANR 33; DLB 15; MTCW 1
Lavond, Paul Dennis
See Kornbluth, C(yril) M.; Pohl, Frederik
Lawler, Raymond Evenor 1922- .... **CLC 58**
See also CA 103
Lawrence, D(avid) H(erbert Richards) 1885-1930...**TCLC 2, 9, 16, 33, 48, 61; DA; DAB; DAC; DAM MST, NOV, POET; SSC 4, 19; WLC**
See also CA 104; 121; CDBLB 1914-1945; DLB 10, 19, 36, 98, 162, 195; MTCW 1
Lawrence, T(homas) E(dward) 1888-1935
TCLC 18
See also Dale, Colin
See also CA 115; 167; DLB 195
Lawrence of Arabia
See Lawrence, T(homas) E(dward)
Lawson, Henry (Archibald Hertzberg) 1867-1922 .... **TCLC 27; SSC 18**
· See also CA 120
Lawton, Dennis
See Faust, Frederick (Schiller)
Laxness, Halldor..............................**CLC 25**
See also Gudjonsson, Halldor Kiljan
Layamon fl. c. 1200- .... **CMLC 10**
See also DLB 146
Laye, Camara 1928-1980...**CLC 4, 38; BLC 2; DAM MULT**
See also BW 1; CA 85-88; 97-100; CANR 25; MTCW 1

Layton, Irving (Peter) 1912-...**CLC 2, 15; DAC; DAM MST, POET**
See also CA 1-4R; CANR 2, 33, 43, 66; DLB 88; MTCW 1
Lazarus, Emma 1849-1887 .... **NCLC 8**
Lazarus, Felix
See Cable, George Washington
Lazarus, Henry
See Slavitt, David R(ytman)
Lea, Joan
See Neufeld, John (Arthur)
Leacock, Stephen (Butler) 1869-1944
TCLC 2; DAC; DAM MST
See also CA 104; 141; DLB 92
Lear, Edward 1812-1888 .... **NCLC 3**
See also CLR 1; DLB 32, 163, 166; MAICYA; SATA 18, 100
Lear, Norman (Milton) 1922- .... **CLC 12**
See also CA 73-76
Leautaud, Paul 1872-1956........ **TCLC 83**
See also DLB 65
Leavis, F(rank) R(aymond) 1895-1978
CLC 24
See also CA 21-24R; 77-80; CANR 44; MTCW 1
Leavitt, David 1961-...**CLC 34; DAM POP**
See also CA 116; 122; CANR 50, 62; DLB 130; INT 122
Leblanc, Maurice (Marie Emile) 1864-1941
TCLC 49
See also CA 110
Lebowitz, Fran(ces Ann) 1951(?)-...**C L C 11, 36**
See also CA 81-84; CANR 14, 60, 70; INT CANR-14; MTCW 1
Lebrecht, Peter
See Tieck, (Johann) Ludwig
le Carre, John .... **CLC 3, 5, 9, 15, 28**
See also Cornwell, David (John Moore)
See also BEST 89:4; CDBLB 1960 to Present; DLB 87
Le Clezio, J(ean) M(arie) G(ustave) 1940-
CLC 31
See also CA 116; 128; DLB 83
Leconte de Lisle, Charles-Marie-Rene 1818-1894 .... **NCLC 29**
Le Coq, Monsieur
See Simenon, Georges (Jacques Christian)
Leduc, Violette 1907-1972 .... **CLC 22**
See also CA 13-14; 33-36R; CANR 69; CAP 1
Ledwidge, Francis 1887(?)-1917 .... **TCLC 23**
See also CA 123; DLB 20
Lee, Andrea 1953- .... **CLC 36; BLC 2; DAM MULT**
See also BW 1; CA 125
Lee, Andrew
See Auchincloss, Louis (Stanton)
Lee, Chang-rae 1965- ....**CLC 91**
See also CA 148
Lee, Don L. ....**CLC 2**
See also Madhubuti, Haki R.
Lee, George W(ashington) 1894-1976
CLC 52; BLC 2; DAM MULT
See also BW 1; CA 125; DLB 51
Lee, (Nelle) Harper 1926-..**CLC 12, 60; DA; DAB; DAC; DAM MST, NOV; WLC**
See also AAYA 13; CA 13-16R; CANR 51; CDALB 1941-1968; DLB 6; MTCW 1; SATA 11
Lee, Helen Elaine 1959(?)- .... **CLC 86**
See also CA 148
Lee, Julian
See Latham, Jean Lee

Lewis, (Harry) Sinclair 1885-1951
TCLC 4, 13, 23, 39; DA; DAB; DAC;
DAM MST, NOV; WLC
See also CA 104; 133; CDALB 1917-1929;
DLB 9, 102; DLBD 1; MTCW 1

Lewis, (Percy) Wyndham 1882(?)-1957
TCLC 2, 9
See also CA 104; 157; DLB 15

Lewisohn, Ludwig 1883-1955 .... TCLC 19
See also CA 107; DLB 4, 9, 28, 102

Lewton, Val 1904-1951 .... TCLC 76

Leyner, Mark 1956- .... CLC 92
See also CA 110; CANR 28, 53

Lezama Lima, Jose 1910-1976...CLC 4,
10, 101; DAM MULT
See also CA 77-80; CANR 71; DLB 113; HW

L'Heureux, John (Clarke) 1934-
CLC 52
See also CA 13-16R; CANR 23, 45

Liddell, C. H.
See Kuttner, Henry

Lie, Jonas (Lauritz Idemil) 1833-1908(?)
TCLC 5
See also CA 115

Lieber, Joel 1937-1971 .... CLC 6
See also CA 73-76; 29-32R

Lieber, Stanley Martin
See Lee, Stan

Lieberman, Laurence (James) 1935-...CLC
4, 36
See also CA 17-20R; CANR 8, 36

Lieh Tzu fl. 7th cent. B.C.-5th cent. B.C.
CMLC 27

Lieksman, Anders
See Haavikko, Paavo Juhani

Li Fei-kan 1904-
See Pa Chin
See also CA 105

Lifton, Robert Jay 1926- .... CLC 67
See also CA 17-20R; CANR 27; INT CANR-
27; SATA 66

Lightfoot, Gordon 1938- .... CLC 26
See also CA 109

Lightman, Alan P(aige) 1948- .... CLC 81
See also CA 141; CANR 63

Ligotti, Thomas (Robert) 1953-...CLC 44;
SSC 16
See also CA 123; CANR 49

Li Ho 791-817 .... PC 13

Liliencron, (Friedrich Adolf Axel) Detlev
von 1844-1909 .... TCLC 18
See also CA 117

Lilly, William 1602-1681 .... LC 27

Lima, Jose Lezama
See Lezama Lima, Jose

Lima Barreto, Afonso Henrique de 1881-1922
TCLC 23
See also CA 117

Limonov, Edward 1944- .... CLC 67
See also CA 137

Lin, Frank
See Atherton, Gertrude (Franklin Horn)

Lincoln, Abraham 1809-1865 .... NCLC 18

Lind, Jakov .... CLC 1, 2, 4, 27, 82
See also Landwirth, Heinz
See also CAAS 4

Lindbergh, Anne (Spencer) Morrow 1906-
CLC 82; DAM NOV
See also CA 17-20R; CANR 16, 73; MTCW 1;
SATA 33

Lindsay, David 1878-1945 .... TCLC 15
See also CA 113

Lindsay, (Nicholas) Vachel 1879-1931
TCLC 17; DA; DAC; DAM MST, POET;
PC 23; WLC
See also CA 114; 135; CDALB 1865-1917;
DLB 54; SATA 40

Linke-Poot
See Doeblin, Alfred

Linney, Romulus 1930- .... CLC 51
See also CA 1-4R; CANR 40, 44

Linton, Eliza Lynn 1822-1898 .... NCLC 41
See also DLB 18

Li Po 701-763 .... CMLC 2

Lipsius, Justus 1547-1606 .... LC 16

Lipsyte, Robert (Michael) 1938-...CLC 21;
DA; DAC; DAM MST, NOV
See also AAYA 7; CA 17-20R; CANR 8, 57;
CLR 23; JRDA; MAICYA; SATA 5, 68

Lish, Gordon (Jay) 1934-...CLC 45; SSC
18
See also CA 113; 117; DLB 130; INT 117

Lispector, Clarice 1925(?)-1977 .... CLC 43
See also CA 139; 116; CANR 71; DLB 113

Littell, Robert 1935(?)- ....CLC 42
See also CA 109; 112; CANR 64

Little, Malcolm 1925-1965
See Malcolm X
See also BW 1; CA 125; 111; DA; DAB;
DAC; DAM MST, MULT; MTCW 1

Littlewit, Humphrey Gent.
See Lovecraft, H(oward) P(hillips)

Litwos
See Sienkiewicz, Henryk (Adam Alexander
Pius)

Liu, E 1857-1909 .... TCLC 15
See also CA 115

Lively, Penelope (Margaret) 1933-...CLC
32, 50; DAM NOV
See also CA 41-44R; CANR 29, 67; CLR 7;
DLB 14, 161; JRDA; MAICYA; MTCW 1;
SATA 7, 60, 101

Livesay, Dorothy (Kathleen) 1909-
CLC 4, 15, 79; DAC; DAM MST, POET
See also AITN 2; CA 25-28R; CAAS 8;
CANR 36, 67; DLB 68; MTCW 1

Livy c. 59B.C.-c. 17 .... CMLC 11

Lizardi, Jose Joaquin Fernandez de 1776-
1827 .... NCLC 30

Llewellyn, Richard
See Llewellyn Lloyd, Richard Dafydd Vivian
See also DLB 15

Llewellyn Lloyd, Richard Dafydd Vivian
1906-1983 .... CLC 7, 80
See also Llewellyn, Richard
See also CA 53-56; 111; CANR 7, 71; SATA
11; SATA-Obit 37

Llosa, (Jorge) Mario (Pedro) Vargas
See Vargas Llosa, (Jorge) Mario (Pedro)

Lloyd, Manda
See Mander, (Mary) Jane

Lloyd Webber, Andrew 1948-
See Webber, Andrew Lloyd
See also AAYA 1; CA 116; 149; DAM DRAM;
SATA 56

Llull, Ramon c. 1235-c. 1316 .... CMLC 12

Lobb, Ebenezer
See Upward, Allen

Locke, Alain (Le Roy) 1886-1954...TCLC
43; BLCS
See also BW 1; CA 106; 124; DLB 51

Locke, John 1632-1704 .... LC 7, 35
See also DLB 101

Locke-Elliott, Sumner
See Elliott, Sumner Locke

Lockhart, John Gibson 1794-1854
NCLC 6
See also DLB 110, 116, 144

Lodge, David (John) 1935-...CLC 36; DAM
POP
See also BEST 90:1; CA 17-20R; CANR 19,
53; DLB 14, 194; INT CANR-19;
MTCW 1

Lodge, Thomas 1558-1625 .... LC 41

Lodge, Thomas 1558-1625 .... LC 41
See also DLB 172

Loennbohm, Armas Eino Leopold 1878-1926
See Leino, Eino
See also CA 123

Loewinsohn, Ron(ald William) 1937-
CLC 52
See also CA 25-28R; CANR 71

Logan, Jake
See Smith, Martin Cruz

Logan, John (Burton) 1923-1987...CLC 5
See also CA 77-80; 124; CANR 45; DLB 5

Lo Kuan-chung 1330(?)-1400(?) .... LC 12

Lombard, Nap
See Johnson, Pamela Hansford

London, Jack ...TCLC 9, 15, 39; SSC 4;
WLC
See also London, John Griffith
See also AAYA 13; AITN 2; CDALB 1865-
1917; DLB 8, 12, 78; SATA 18

London, John Griffith 1876-1916
See London, Jack
See also CA 110; 119; CANR 73; DA; DAB;
DAC; DAM MST, NOV; JRDA; MAICYA;
MTCW 1

Long, Emmett
See Leonard, Elmore (John, Jr.)

Longbaugh, Harry
See Goldman, William (W.)

Longfellow, Henry Wadsworth 1807-1882
NCLC 2, 45; DA; DAB; DAC; DAM MST,
POET; WLCS
See also CDALB 1640-1865; DLB 1, 59;
SATA 19

Longinus c. 1st cent. - .... CMLC 27
See also DLB 176

Longley, Michael 1939-...................CLC 29
See also CA 102; DLB 40

Longus fl. c. 2nd cent. - .... CMLC 7

Longway, A. Hugh
See Lang, Andrew

Lonnrot, Elias 1802-1884 .... NCLC 53

Lopate, Phillip 1943- ....CLC 29
See also CA 97-100; DLBY 80; INT 97-100

Lopez Portillo (y Pacheco), Jose 1920-
CLC 46
See also CA 129; HW

Lopez y Fuentes, Gregorio 1897(?)-1966
CLC 32
See also CA 131; HW

Lorca, Federico Garcia
See Garcia Lorca, Federico

Lord, Bette Bao 1938- ....CLC 23
See also BEST 90:3; CA 107; CANR 41; INT
107; SATA 58

Lord Auch
See Bataille, Georges

Lord Byron
See Byron, George Gordon (Noel)

Lorde, Audre (Geraldine) 1934-1992
CLC 18, 71; BLC 2; DAM MULT,
POET; PC 12
See also BW 1; CA 25-28R; 142; CANR 16,
26, 46; DLB 41; MTCW 1

Maclean, Norman (Fitzroy) 1902-1990
CLC 78; DAM POP; SSC 13
See also CA 102; 132; CANR 49
MacLeish, Archibald 1892-1982...CLC 3,
8, 14, 68; DAM POET
See also CA 9-12R; 106; CANR 33, 63; DLB
4, 7, 45; DLBY 82; MTCW 1
MacLennan, (John) Hugh 1907-1990...CLC
2, 14, 92; DAC; DAM MST
See also CA 5-8R; 142; CANR 33; DLB 68;
MTCW 1
MacLeod, Alistair 1936-...CLC 56; DAC;
DAM MST
See also CA 123; DLB 60

Macleod, Fiona
See Sharp, William

MacNeice, (Frederick) Louis 1907-1963
CLC 1, 4, 10, 53; DAB; DAM POET
See also CA 85-88; CANR 61; DLB 10, 20;
MTCW 1
MacNeill, Dand
See Fraser, George MacDonald
Macpherson, James 1736-1796 ..... LC 29
See also Ossian
See also DLB 109
Macpherson, (Jean) Jay 1931- .... CLC 14
See also CA 5-8R; DLB 53
MacShane, Frank 1927- .... CLC 39
See also CA 9-12R; CANR 3, 33; DLB 111
Macumber, Mari
See Sandoz, Mari(e Susette)
Madach, Imre 1823-1864 .... NCLC 19
Madden, (Jerry) David 1933-...CLC 5, 15
See also CA 1-4R; CAAS 3; CANR 4, 45;
DLB 6; MTCW 1

Maddern, Al(an)
See Ellison, Harlan (Jay)

Madhubuti, Haki R. 1942-...CLC 6, 73;
BLC 2; DAM MULT, POET; PC 5
See also Lee, Don L.
See also BW 2; CA 73-76; CANR 24, 51, 73;
DLB 5, 41; DLBD 8
Maepenn, Hugh
See Kuttner, Henry
Maepenn, K. H.
See Kuttner, Henry
Maeterlinck, Maurice 1862-1949....TCLC 3;
DAM DRAM
See also CA 104; 136; DLB 192; SATA 66
Maginn, William 1794-1842 .... NCLC 8
See also DLB 110, 159
Mahapatra, Jayanta 1928-...CLC 33; DAM
MULT
See also CA 73-76; CAAS 9; CANR 15, 33, 66
Mahfuz, Naguib (Abdel Aziz Al-Sabilgi)
1911(?)-
See Mahfuz, Najib
See also BEST 89:2; CA 128; CANR 55; DAM
NOV; MTCW 1
Mahfuz, Najib .... CLC 52, 55
See also Mahfouz, Naguib (Abdel Aziz Al-
Sabilgi)
See also DLBY 88
Mahon, Derek 1941- .... CLC 27
See also CA 113; 128; DLB 40
Mailer, Norman 1923-...CLC 1, 2, 3, 4, 5,
8, 11, 14, 28, 39, 74, 111; DA; DAB;
DAC; DAM MST, NOV, POP
See also AITN 2; CA 9-12R; CABS 1; CANR
28, 74; CDALB 1968-1988; DLB 2, 16, 28,
185; DLBD 3; DLBY 80, 83; MTCW 1

Maillet, Antonine 1929- . CLC 54; DAC
See also CA 115; 120; CANR 46, 74; DLB
60; INT 120
Mais, Roger 1905-1955 .... TCLC 8
See also BW 1; CA 105; 124; DLB 125;
MTCW 1
Maistre, Joseph de 1753-1821 .... NCLC 37
Maitland, Frederic 1850-1906 .... TCLC 65
Maitland, Sara (Louise) 1950- .... CLC 49
See also CA 69-72; CANR 13, 59
Major, Clarence 1936-...CLC 3, 19, 48;
BLC 2; DAM MULT
See also BW 2; CA 21-24R; CAAS 6; CANR
13, 25, 53; DLB 33
Major, Kevin (Gerald) 1949-.... CLC 26;
DAC
See also AAYA 16; CA 97-100; CANR 21,
38; CLR 11; DLB 60; INT CANR-21;
JRDA; MAICYA; SATA 32, 82
Maki, James
See Ozu, Yasujiro
Malabaila, Damiano
See Levi, Primo
Malamud, Bernard 1914-1986...CLC 1, 2,
3, 5, 8, 9, 11, 18, 27, 44, 78, 85; DA;
DAB; DAC; DAM MST, NOV, POP;
SSC 15; WLC
See also AAYA 16; CA 5-8R; 118; CABS 1;
CANR 28, 62; CDALB 1941-1968; DLB 2,
28, 152; DLBY 80, 86; MTCW 1
Malan, Herman
See Bosman, Herman Charles; Bosman, Herman
Charles
Malaparte, Curzio 1898-1957...TCLC 52
Malcolm, Dan
See Silverberg, Robert
Malcolm X .... CLC 82, 117; BLC 2; WLCS
See also Little, Malcolm
Malherbe, Francois de 1555-1628 .... LC 5
Mallarme, Stephane 1842-1898... N C L C
4, 41; DAM POET; PC 4
Mallet-Joris, Françoise 1930- .... CLC 11
See also CA 65-68; CANR 17; DLB 83
Malley, Ern
See McAuley, James Phillip
Mallowan, Agatha Christie
See Christie, Agatha (Mary Clarissa)
Maloff, Saul 1922- .... CLC 5
See also CA 33-36R
Malone, Louis
See MacNeice, (Frederick) Louis
Malone, Michael (Christopher) 1942-
CLC 43
See also CA 77-80; CANR 14, 32, 57
Malory, (Sir) Thomas 1410(?)-1471(?)
LC 11; DA; DAB; DAC; DAM MST;
WLCS
See also CDBLB Before 1660; DLB 146; SATA
59; SATA-Brief 33
Malouf, (George Joseph) David 1934-
CLC 28, 86
See also CA 124; CANR 50
Malraux, (Georges-)Andre 1901-1976
CLC 1, 4, 9, 13, 15, 57; DAM NOV
See also CA 21-22; 69-72; CANR 34, 58;
CAP 2; DLB 72; MTCW 1
Malzberg, Barry N(athaniel) 1939-....CLC 7
See also CA 61-64; CAAS 4; CANR 16; DLB
8
Mamet, David (Alan) 1947-CLC 9, 15, 34, 46,
91; DAM DRAM; DC 4
See also AAYA 3; CA 81-84; CABS 3; CANR
15, 41, 67, 72; DLB 7; MTCW 1

Mamoulian, Rouben (Zachary) 1897-1987
CLC 16
See also CA 25-28R; 124
Mandelstam, Osip (Emilievich) 1891(?)-
1938(?) .... TCLC 2, 6; PC 14
See also CA 104; 150
Mander, (Mary) Jane 1877-1949
TCLC 31
See also CA 162
Mandeville, John fl. 1350- .... CMLC 19
See also DLB 146
Mandiargues, Andre Pieyre de .... CLC 41
See also Pieyre de Mandiargues, Andre
See also DLB 83
Mandrake, Ethel Belle
See Thurman, Wallace (Henry)
Mangan, James Clarence 1803-1849
NCLC 27
Maniere, J.-E.
See Giraudoux, (Hippolyte) Jean
Mankiewicz, Herman (Jacob) 1897-1953
TCLC 85
See also CA 120; 169; DLB 26
Manley, (Mary) Delariviere 1672(?)-1724
LC 1, 42
See also DLB 39, 80
Mann, Abel
See Creasey, John
Mann, Emily 1952- .... DC 7
See also CA 130; CANR 55
Mann, (Luiz) Heinrich 1871-1950
TCLC 9
See also CA 106; 164; DLB 66
Mann, (Paul) Thomas 1875-1955...TCLC
2, 8, 14, 21, 35, 44, 60; DA; DAB; DAC;
DAM MST, NOV; SSC 5; WLC
See also CA 104; 128; DLB 66; MTCW 1
Mannheim, Karl 1893-1947 ..... TCLC 65
Manning, David
See Faust, Frederick (Schiller)
Manning, Frederic 1887(?)-1935 ... TCLC 25
See also CA 124
Manning, Olivia 1915-1980 .... CLC 5, 19
See also CA 5-8R; 101; CANR 29; MTCW 1
Mano, D. Keith 1942- .... CLC 2, 10
See also CA 25-28R; CAAS 6; CANR 26, 57;
DLB 6
Mansfield, Katherine .... TCLC 2, 8, 39;
DAB; SSC 9, 23; WLC
See also Beauchamp, Kathleen Mansfield
See also DLB 162
Manso, Peter 1940- .... CLC 39
See also CA 29-32R; CANR 44
Mantecon, Juan Jimenez
See Jimenez (Mantecon), Juan Ramon
Manton, Peter
See Creasey, John
Man Without a Spleen, A
See Chekhov, Anton (Pavlovich)
Manzoni, Alessandro 1785-1873
NCLC 29
Mapu, Abraham (ben Jekutiel) 1808-1867
NCLC 18
Mara, Sally
See Queneau, Raymond
Marat, Jean Paul 1743-1793 .... LC 10
Marcel, Gabriel Honore 1889-1973
CLC 15
See also CA 102; 45-48; MTCW 1
Marchbanks, Samuel
See Davies, (William) Robertson
Marchi, Giacomo
See Bassani, Giorgio

Margulies, Donald .... CLC 76

Marie de France c. 12th cent....CMLC 8;
PC 22

Marie de l'Incarnation 1599-1672 ...... LC 10

Marier, Captain Victor
See Griffith, D(avid Lewelyn) W(ark)

Mariner, Scott
See Pohl, Frederik

Marinetti, Filippo Tommaso 1876-1944
TCLC 10
See also CA 107; DLB 114

Marivaux, Pierre Carlet de Chamblain de 1688-
1763 .... LC 4; DC 7

Markandaya, Kamala .... CLC 8, 38
See also Taylor, Kamala (Purnaiya)

Markfield, Wallace 1926- ....CLC 8
See also CA 69-72; CAAS 3; DLB 2, 28

Markham, Edwin 1852-1940 .... TCLC 47
See also CA 160; DLB 54, 186

Markham, Robert
See Amis, Kingsley (William)

Marks, J
See Highwater, Jamake (Mamake)

Marks-Highwater, J
See Highwater, Jamake (Mamake)

Markson, David M(errill) 1927-...CLC 67
See also CA 49-52; CANR 1

Marley, Bob .... CLC 17
See also Marley, Robert Nesta

Marley, Robert Nesta 1945-1981
See Marley, Bob
See also CA 107; 103

Marlowe, Christopher 1564-1593
LC 22, 47; DA; DAB; DAC; DAM
DRAM, MST; DC 1; WLC
See also CDBLB Before 1660; DLB 62

Marlowe, Stephen 1928-
See Queen, Ellery
See also CA 13-16R; CANR 6, 55

Marmontel, Jean-Francois 1723-1799
LC 2

Marquand, John P(hillips) 1893-1960
CLC 2, 10
See also CA 85-88; CANR 73; DLB 9, 102

Marques, Rene 1919-1979 ..... CLC 96; DAM
MULT; HLC
See also CA 97-100; 85-88; DLB 113; HW

Marquez, Gabriel (Jose) Garcia
See Garcia Marquez, Gabriel (Jose)

Marquis, Don(ald Robert Perry) 1878-1937
TCLC 7
See also CA 104; 166; DLB 11, 25

Marric, J. J.
See Creasey, John

Marryat, Frederick 1792-1848 .. NCLC 3
See also DLB 21, 163

Marsden, James
See Creasey, John

Marsh, (Edith) Ngaio 1899-1982...CLC 7,
53; DAM POP
See also CA 9-12R; CANR 6, 58; DLB 77;
MTCW 1

Marshall, Garry 1934-................. CLC 17
See also AAYA 3; CA 111; SATA 60

Marshall, Paule 1929-.. CLC 27, 72; BLC 3;
DAM MULT; SSC 3
See also BW 2; CA 77-80; CANR 25, 73; DLB
157; MTCW 1

Marshallik
See Zangwill, Israel

Marsten, Richard
See Hunter, Evan

Marston, John 1576-1634 ...... LC 33;
DAM DRAM
See also DLB 58, 172

Martha, Henry
See Harris, Mark

Marti, Jose 1853-1895 ..... NCLC 63;
DAM MULT; HLC

Martial c. 40-c. 104 .... PC 10

Martin, Ken
See Hubbard, L(afayette) Ron(ald)

Martin, Richard
See Creasey, John

Martin, Steve 1945- .... CLC 30
See also CA 97-100; CANR 30; MTCW 1

Martin, Valerie 1948-........................CLC 89
See also BEST 90:2; CA 85-88; CANR 49

Martin, Violet Florence 1862-1915
TCLC 51

Martin, Webber
See Silverberg, Robert

Martindale, Patrick Victor
See White, Patrick (Victor Martindale)

Martin du Gard, Roger 1881-1958
TCLC 24
See also CA 118; DLB 65

Martineau, Harriet 1802-1876...NCLC 26
See also DLB 21, 55, 159, 163, 166, 190;
YABC 2

Martines, Julia
See O'Faolain, Julia

Martinez, Enrique Gonzalez
See Gonzalez Martinez, Enrique

Martinez, Jacinto Benavente y
See Benavente (y Martinez), Jacinto

Martinez Ruiz, Jose 1873-1967
See Azorin; Ruiz, Jose Martinez
See also CA 93-96; HW

Martinez Sierra, Gregorio 1881-1947
TCLC 6
See also CA 115

Martinez Sierra, Maria (de la
O'LeJarraga) 1874-1974 .... TCLC 6
See also CA 115

Martinsen, Martin
See Follett, Ken(neth Martin)

Martinson, Harry (Edmund) 1904-1978
CLC 14
See also CA 77-80; CANR 34

Marut, Ret
See Traven, B.

Marut, Robert
See Traven, B.

Marvell, Andrew 1621-1678 ... LC 4, 43; DA;
DAB; DAC; DAM MST, POET; PC 10;
WLC
See also CDBLB 1660-1789; DLB 131

Marx, Karl (Heinrich) 1818-1883...NCLC
17
See also DLB 129

Masaoka Shiki .... TCLC 18
See also Masaoka Tsunenori

Masaoka Tsunenori 1867-1902
See Masaoka Shiki
See also CA 117

Masefield, John (Edward) 1878-1967
CLC 11, 47; DAM POET
See also CA 19-20; 25-28R; CANR 33; CAP
2; CDBLB 1890-1914; DLB 10, 19, 153,
160; MTCW 1; SATA 19

Maso, Carole 19(?)- .... CLC 44
See also CA 170

Mason, Bobbie Ann 1940-...CLC 28, 43,
82; SSC 4
See also AAYA 5; CA 53-56; CANR 11, 31,
58; DLB 173; DLBY 87; INT CANR-31;
MTCW 1

Mason, Ernst
See Pohl, Frederik

Mason, Lee W.
See Malzberg, Barry N(athaniel)

Mason, Nick 1945- .... CLC 35

Mason, Tally
See Derleth, August (William)

Mass, William
See Gibson, William

Master Lao
See Lao Tzu

Masters, Edgar Lee 1868-1950...TCLC 2,
25; DA; DAC; DAM MST, POET; PC 1;
WLCS
See also CA 104; 133; CDALB 1865-1917;
DLB 54; MTCW 1

Masters, Hilary 1928- .... CLC 48
See also CA 25-28R; CANR 13, 47

Mastrosimone, William 19(?)- . CLC 36

Mathe, Albert
See Camus, Albert

Mather, Cotton 1663-1728 .... LC 38
See also CDALB 1640-1865; DLB 24, 30, 140

Mather, Increase 1639-1723 .... LC 38
See also DLB 24

Matheson, Richard Burton 1926- .... CLC 37
See also CA 97-100; DLB 8, 44; INT 97-100

Mathews, Harry 1930- .... CLC 6, 52
See also CA 21-24R; CAAS 6; CANR 18, 40

Mathews, John Joseph 1894-1979 .. CLC 84;
DAM MULT
See also CA 19-20; 142; CANR 45; CAP 2;
DLB 175; NNAL

Mathias, Roland (Glyn) 1915-... CLC 45
See also CA 97-100; CANR 19, 41; DLB 27

Matsuo Basho 1644-1694 .... PC 3
See also DAM POET

Mattheson, Rodney
See Creasey, John

Matthews, Greg 1949-...................... CLC 45
See also CA 135

Matthews, William (Procter, III) 1942-1997
CLC 40
See also CA 29-32R; 162; CAAS 18; CANR
12, 57; DLB 5

Matthias, John (Edward) 1941-.......... CLC 9
See also CA 33-36R; CANR 56

Matthiessen, Peter 1927-...CLC 5, 7, 11,
32, 64; DAM NOV
See also AAYA 6; BEST 90:4; CA 9-12R;
CANR 21, 50, 73; DLB 6, 173; MTCW 1;
SATA 27

Maturin, Charles Robert 1780(?)-1824
NCLC 6
See also DLB 178

Matute (Ausejo), Ana Maria 1925-
CLC 11
See also CA 89-92; MTCW 1

Maugham, W. S.
See Maugham, W(illiam) Somerset

Maugham, W(illiam) Somerset 1874-1965
CLC 1, 11, 15, 67, 93; DA; DAB; DAC;
DAM DRAM, MST, NOV; SSC 8; WLC
See also CA 5-8R; 25-28R; CANR 40; CDBLB
1914-1945; DLB 10, 36, 77, 100, 162, 195;
MTCW 1; SATA 54

Maugham, William Somerset
See Maugham, W(illiam) Somerset

Maupassant, (Henri Rene Albert) Guy de
1850-1893 .... **NCLC 1, 42; DA; DAB;
DAC; DAM MST; SSC 1; WLC**
See also DLB 123

Maupin, Armistead 1944- ...... **CLC 95;
DAM POP**
See also CA 125; 130; CANR 58; INT 130

Maurhut, Richard
See Traven, B.

Mauriac, Claude 1914-1996 .... **CLC 9**
See also CA 89-92; 152; DLB 83

Mauriac, Francois (Charles) 1885-1970
CLC 4, 9, 56; SSC 24
See also CA 25-28; CAP 2; DLB 65; MTCW 1

Mavor, Osborne Henry 1888-1951
See Bridie, James
See also CA 104

Maxwell, William (Keepers, Jr.) 1908-
CLC 19
See also CA 93-96; CANR 54; DLBY 80;
INT 93-96

May, Elaine 1932- .... **CLC 16**
See also CA 124; 142; DLB 44

Mayakovski, Vladimir (Vladimirovich)
1893-1930 .... **TCLC 4, 18**
See also CA 104; 158

Mayhew, Henry 1812-1887 .... **NCLC 31**
See also DLB 18, 55, 190

Mayle, Peter 1939(?)- .... **CLC 89**
See also CA 139; CANR 64

Maynard, Joyce 1953- .... **CLC 23**
See also CA 111; 129; CANR 64

Mayne, William (James Carter) 1928-
CLC 12
See also AAYA 20; CA 9-12R; CANR 37;
CLR 25; JRDA; MAICYA; SAAS 11; SATA
6, 68

Mayo, Jim
See L'Amour, Louis (Dearborn)

Maysles, Albert 1926- .... **CLC 16**
See also CA 29-32R

Maysles, David 1932- .... **CLC 16**

Mazer, Norma Fox 1931- .... **CLC 26**
See also AAYA 5; CA 69-72; CANR 12, 32,
66; CLR 23; JRDA; MAICYA; SAAS 1;
SATA 24, 67

Mazzini, Guiseppe 1805-1872 ... **NCLC 34**

McAuley, James Phillip 1917-1976
CLC 45
See also CA 97-100

McBain, Ed
See Hunter, Evan

McBrien, William Augustine 1930- . **CLC 44**
See also CA 107

McCaffrey, Anne (Inez) 1926- ... **CLC 17;
DAM NOV, POP**
See also AAYA 6; AITN 2; BEST 89:2; CA 25-
28R; CANR 15, 35, 55; CLR 49; DLB 8;
JRDA; MAICYA; MTCW 1; SAAS 11; SATA
8, 70

McCall, Nathan 1955(?)- .... **CLC 86**
See also CA 146

McCann, Arthur
See Campbell, John W(ood, Jr.)

McCann, Edson
See Pohl, Frederik

McCarthy, Charles, Jr. 1933-
See McCarthy, Cormac
See also CANR 42, 69; DAM POP

McCarthy, Cormac 1933- ... **CLC 4, 57, 59,
101**
See also McCarthy, Charles, Jr.
See also DLB 6, 143

McCarthy, Mary (Therese) 1912-1989
CLC 1, 3, 5, 14, 24, 39, 59; SSC 24
See also CA 5-8R; 129; CANR 16, 50, 64;
DLB 2; DLBY 81; INT CANR-16; MTCW
1

McCartney, (James) Paul 1942- ... **CLC 12,
35**
See also CA 146

McCauley, Stephen (D.) 1955- .... **CLC 50**
See also CA 141

McClure, Michael (Thomas) 1932- ... **CLC
6, 10**
See also CA 21-24R; CANR 17, 46; DLB 16

McCorkle, Jill (Collins) 1958- .... **CLC 51**
See also CA 121; DLBY 87

McCourt, Frank 1930- .... **CLC 109**
See also CA 157

McCourt, James 1941- .... **CLC 5**
See also CA 57-60

McCoy, Horace (Stanley) 1897-1955
TCLC 28
See also CA 108; 155; DLB 9

McCrae, John 1872-1918 .... **TCLC 12**
See also CA 109; DLB 92

McCreigh, James
See Pohl, Frederik

McCullers, (Lula) Carson (Smith) 1917-
1967 . **CLC 1, 4, 10, 12, 48, 100; DA;
DAB; DAC; DAM MST, NOV; SSC 9,
24; WLC**
See also AAYA 21; CA 5-8R; 25-28R; CABS
1, 3; CANR 18; CDALB 1941-1968; DLB
2, 7, 173; MTCW 1; SATA 27

McCulloch, John Tyler
See Burroughs, Edgar Rice

McCullough, Colleen 1938(?)- ... **CLC 27,
107; DAM NOV, POP**
See also CA 81-84; CANR 17, 46, 67; MTCW
1

McDermott, Alice 1953- .... **CLC 90**
See also CA 109; CANR 40

McElroy, Joseph 1930- .... **CLC 5, 47**
See also CA 17-20R

McEwan, Ian (Russell) 1948- ... **CLC 13, 66;
DAM NOV**
See also BEST 90:4; CA 61-64; CANR 14, 41,
69; DLB 14, 194; MTCW 1

McFadden, David 1940- .... **CLC 48**
See also CA 104; DLB 60; INT 104

McFarland, Dennis 1950- .... **CLC 65**
See also CA 165

McGahern, John 1934- ... **CLC 5, 9, 48;
SSC 17**
See also CA 17-20R; CANR 29, 68; DLB 14;
MTCW 1

McGinley, Patrick (Anthony) 1937- ... **CLC
41**
See also CA 120; 127; CANR 56; INT 127

McGinley, Phyllis 1905-1978 .... **CLC 14**
See also CA 9-12R; 77-80; CANR 19; DLB 11,
48; SATA 2, 44; SATA-Obit 24

McGinniss, Joe 1942- .... **CLC 32**
See also AITN 2; BEST 89:2; CA 25-28R;
CANR 26, 70; DLB 185; INT CANR-26

McGivern, Maureen Daly
See Daly, Maureen

McGrath, Patrick 1950- .... **CLC 55**
See also CA 136; CANR 65

McGrath, Thomas (Matthew) 1916-1990
CLC 28, 59; DAM POET
See also CA 9-12R; 132; CANR 6, 33;
MTCW 1; SATA 41; SATA-Obit 66

McGuane, Thomas (Francis III) 1939-
CLC 3, 7, 18, 45
See also AITN 2; CA 49-52; CANR 5, 24,
49; DLB 2; DLBY 80; INT CANR-24;
MTCW 1

McGuckian, Medbh 1950- ...... **CLC 48;
DAM POET**
See also CA 143; DLB 40

McHale, Tom 1942(?)-1982 .... **CLC 3, 5**
See also AITN 1; CA 77-80; 106

McIlvanney, William 1936- .... **CLC 42**
See also CA 25-28R; CANR 61; DLB 14

McIlwraith, Maureen Mollie Hunter
See Hunter, Mollie
See also SATA 2

McInerney, Jay 1955- ..... **CLC 34, 112;
DAM POP**
See also AAYA 18; CA 116; 123; CANR 45,
68; INT 123

McIntyre, Vonda N(eel) 1948- ... **CLC 18**
See also CA 81-84; CANR 17, 34, 69;
MTCW 1

McKay, Claude .... **TCLC 7, 41; BLC 3;
DAB; PC 2**
See also McKay, Festus Claudius
See also DLB 4, 45, 51, 117

McKay, Festus Claudius 1889-1948
See McKay, Claude
See also BW 1; CA 104; 124; CANR 73; DA;
DAC; DAM MST, MULT, NOV, POET;
MTCW 1; WLC

McKuen, Rod 1933- .... **CLC 1, 3**
See also AITN 1; CA 41-44R; CANR 40

McLoughlin, R. B.
See Mencken, H(enry) L(ouis)

McLuhan, (Herbert) Marshall 1911-1980
CLC 37, 83
See also CA 9-12R; 102; CANR 12, 34, 61;
DLB 88; INT CANR-12; MTCW 1

McMillan, Terry (L.) 1951- ... **CLC 50, 61,
112; BLCS; DAM MULT, NOV, POP**
See also AAYA 21; BW 2; CA 140; CANR 60

McMurtry, Larry (Jeff) 1936- ... **CLC 2, 3,
7, 11, 27, 44; DAM NOV, POP**
See also AAYA 15; AITN 2; BEST 89:2;
CA 5-8R; CANR 19, 43, 64; CDALB
1968-1988; DLB 2, 143; DLBY 80, 87;
MTCW 1

McNally, T. M. 1961- .... **CLC 82**

McNally, Terrence 1939- ... **CLC 4, 7, 41,
91; DAM DRAM**
See also CA 45-48; CANR 2, 56; DLB 7

McNamer, Deirdre 1950- .... **CLC 70**

McNeile, Herman Cyril 1888-1937
See Sapper
See also DLB 77

McNickle, (William) D'Arcy 1904-1977
CLC 89; DAM MULT
See also CA 9-12R; 85-88; CANR 5, 45; DLB
175; NNAL; SATA-Obit 22

McPhee, John (Angus) 1931- .... **CLC 36**
See also BEST 90:1; CA 65-68; CANR 20, 46,
64, 69; DLB 185; MTCW 1

McPherson, James Alan 1943- .. **CLC 19, 77;
BLCS**
See also BW 1; CA 25-28R; CAAS 17; CANR
24, 74; DLB 38; MTCW 1

McPherson, William (Alexander) 1933-
CLC 34
See also CA 69-72; CANR 28; INT CANR-
28

Mead, George Herbert 1873-1958 ... **TCLC
89**

Mead, Margaret 1901-1978 .... **CLC 37**
See also AITN 1; CA 1-4R; 81-84; CANR 4;
MTCW 1; SATA-Obit 20

Meaker, Marijane (Agnes) 1927-
See Kerr, M. E.
See also CA 107; CANR 37, 63; INT 107;
JRDA; MAICYA; MTCW 1; SATA 20, 61,
99

Medoff, Mark (Howard) 1940-...**CLC 6, 23;**
DAM DRAM
See also AITN 1; CA 53-56; CANR 5; DLB 7;
INT CANR-5

Medvedev, P. N.
See Bakhtin, Mikhail Mikhailovich

Meged, Aharon
See Megged, Aharon

Meged, Aron
See Megged, Aharon

Megged, Aharon 1920- ....**CLC 9**
See also CA 49-52; CAAS 13; CANR 1

Mehta, Ved (Parkash) 1934- ...... **CLC 37**
See also CA 1-4R; CANR 2, 23, 69; MTCW
1

Melanter
See Blackmore, R(ichard) D(oddridge)

Melies, Georges 1861-1938 ...... **TCLC 81**

Melikow, Loris
See Hofmannsthal, Hugo von

Melmoth, Sebastian
See Wilde, Oscar (Fingal O'Flahertie Wills)

Meltzer, Milton 1915- ....**CLC 26**
See also AAYA 8; CA 13-16R; CANR 38; CLR
13; DLB 61; JRDA; MAICYA; SAAS 1;
SATA 1, 50, 80

Melville, Herman 1819-1891... **NCLC 3,**
12, 29, 45, 49; DA; DAB; DAC; DAM
MST, NOV; SSC 1, 17; WLC
See also AAYA 25; CDALB 1640-1865; DLB
3, 74; SATA 59

Menander c. 342B.C.-c. 292B.C. .... **CMLC 9;**
DAM DRAM; DC 3
See also DLB 176

Mencken, H(enry) L(ouis) 1880-1956
TCLC 13
See also CA 105; 125; CDALB 1917-1929;
DLB 11, 29, 63, 137; MTCW 1

Mendelsohn, Jane 1965(?)- .... **CLC 99**
See also CA 154

Mercer, David 1928-1980 ... **CLC 5; DAM**
DRAM
See also CA 9-12R; 102; CANR 23; DLB 13;
MTCW 1

Merchant, Paul
See Ellison, Harlan (Jay)

Meredith, George 1828-1909...**TCLC 17,**
43; DAM POET
See also CA 117; 153; CDBLB 1832-1890;
DLB 18, 35, 57, 159

Meredith, William (Morris) 1919-...**CLC**
4, 13, 22, 55; DAM POET
See also CA 9-12R; CAAS 14; CANR 6, 40;
DLB 5

Merezhkovsky, Dmitry Sergeyevich 1865-1941
TCLC 29
See also CA 169

Merimee, Prosper 1803-1870 . **NCLC 6,**
65; SSC 7
See also DLB 119, 192

Merkin, Daphne 1954- .... **CLC 44**
See also CA 123

Merlin, Arthur
See Blish, James (Benjamin)

Merrill, James (Ingram) 1926-1995
CLC 2, 3, 6, 8, 13, 18, 34, 91; DAM
POET
See also CA 13-16R; 147; CANR 10, 49, 63;
DLB 5, 165; DLBY 85; INT CANR-10;
MTCW 1

Merriman, Alex
See Silverberg, Robert

Merriman, Brian 1747-1805 ... **NCLC 70**

Merritt, E. B.
See Waddington, Miriam

Merton, Thomas 1915-1968...**CLC 1, 3, 11,**
34, 83; PC 10
See also CA 5-8R; 25-28R; CANR 22, 53; DLB
48; DLBY 81; MTCW 1

Merwin, W(illiam) S(tanley) 1927-
CLC 1, 2, 3, 5, 8, 13, 18, 45, 88; DAM
POET
See also CA 13-16R; CANR 15, 51; DLB 5,
169; INT CANR-15; MTCW 1

Metcalf, John 1938- ....**CLC 37**
See also CA 113; DLB 60

Metcalf, Suzanne
See Baum, L(yman) Frank

Mew, Charlotte (Mary) 1870-1928
TCLC 8
See also CA 105; DLB 19, 135

Mewshaw, Michael 1943- .... **CLC 9**
See also CA 53-56; CANR 7, 47; DLBY 80

Meyer, June
See Jordan, June

Meyer, Lynn
See Slavitt, David R(ytman)

Meyer-Meyrink, Gustav 1868-1932
See Meyrink, Gustav
See also CA 117

Meyers, Jeffrey 1939- .... **CLC 39**
See also CA 73-76; CANR 54; DLB 111

Meynell, Alice (Christina Gertrude
Thompson) 1847-1922 .... **TCLC 6**
See also CA 104; DLB 19, 98

Meyrink, Gustav .... **TCLC 21**
See also Meyer-Meyrink, Gustav
See also DLB 81

Michaels, Leonard 1933-...**CLC 6, 25; SSC**
16
See also CA 61-64; CANR 21, 62; DLB 130;
MTCW 1

Michaux, Henri 1899-1984 ....**CLC 8, 19**
See also CA 85-88; 114

Micheaux, Oscar 1884-1951 .... **TCLC 76**
See also DLB 50

Michelangelo 1475-1564 .... **LC 12**

Michelet, Jules 1798-1874 ...... **NCLC 31**

Michels, Robert 1876-1936 ...... **TCLC 88**

Michener, James A(lbert) 1907(?)-1997
CLC 1, 5, 11, 29, 60, 109; DAM NOV,
POP
See also AAYA 27; AITN 1; BEST 90:1; CA 5-
8R; 161; CANR 21, 45, 68; DLB 6; MTCW
1

Mickiewicz, Adam 1798-1855 .... **NCLC 3**

Middleton, Christopher 1926- .... **CLC 13**
See also CA 13-16R; CANR 29, 54; DLB 40

Middleton, Richard (Barham) 1882-1911
TCLC 56
See also DLB 156

Middleton, Stanley 1919- .... **CLC 7, 38**
See also CA 25-28R; CAAS 23; CANR 21, 46;
DLB 14

Middleton, Thomas 1580-1627...**LC 33;**
DAM DRAM, MST; DC 5
See also DLB 58

Migueis, Jose Rodrigues 1901-...**CLC 10**

Mikszath, Kalman 1847-1910...**TCLC 31**
See also CA 170

Miles, Jack ....**CLC 100**

Miles, Josephine (Louise) 1911-1985
CLC 1, 2, 14, 34, 39; DAM POET
See also CA 1-4R; 116; CANR 2, 55; DLB 48

Militant
See Sandburg, Carl (August)

Mill, John Stuart 1806-1873...**NCLC 11,**
58
See also CDBLB 1832-1890; DLB 55, 190

Millar, Kenneth 1915-1983 ..... **CLC 14;**
DAM POP
See also Macdonald, Ross
See also CA 9-12R; 110; CANR 16, 63; DLB
2; DLBD 6; DLBY 83; MTCW 1

Millay, E. Vincent
See Millay, Edna St. Vincent

Millay, Edna St. Vincent 1892-1950
TCLC 4, 49; DA; DAB; DAC; DAM
MST, POET; PC 6; WLCS
See also CA 104; 130; CDALB 1917-1929;
DLB 45; MTCW 1

Miller, Arthur 1915-...**CLC 1, 2, 6, 10, 15,**
26, 47, 78; DA; DAB; DAC; DAM
DRAM, MST; DC 1; WLC
See also AAYA 15; AITN 1; CA 1-4R; CABS
3; CANR 2, 30, 54; CDALB 1941-1968;
DLB 7; MTCW 1

Miller, Henry (Valentine) 1891-1980
CLC 1, 2, 4, 9, 14, 43, 84; DA; DAB;
DAC; DAM MST, NOV; WLC
See also CA 9-12R; 97-100; CANR 33, 64;
CDALB 1929-1941; DLB 4, 9; DLBY 80;
MTCW 1

Miller, Jason 1939(?)- ....**CLC 2**
See also AITN 1; CA 73-76; DLB 7

Miller, Sue 1943- ....**CLC 44; DAM POP**
See also BEST 90:3; CA 139; CANR 59; DLB
143

Miller, Walter M(ichael, Jr.) 1923-
CLC 4, 30
See also CA 85-88; DLB 8

Millett, Kate 1934- ....**CLC 67**
See also AITN 1; CA 73-76; CANR 32, 53;
MTCW 1

Millhauser, Steven (Lewis) 1943-...**CLC**
21, 54, 109
See also CA 110; 111; CANR 63; DLB 2; INT
111

Millin, Sarah Gertrude 1889-1968...**CLC**
49
See also CA 102; 93-96

Milne, A(lan) A(lexander) 1882-1956
TCLC 6, 88; DAB; DAC; DAM MST
See also CA 104; 133; CLR 1, 26; DLB 10,
77, 100, 160; MAICYA; MTCW 1; SATA
100; YABC 1

Milner, Ron(ald) 1938-...**CLC 56; BLC 3;**
DAM MULT
See also AITN 1; BW 1; CA 73-76; CANR 24;
DLB 38; MTCW 1

Milnes, Richard Monckton 1809-1885
NCLC 61
See also DLB 32, 184

Milosz, Czeslaw 1911-...**CLC 5, 11, 22, 31,**
56, 82; DAM MST, POET; PC 8; WLCS
See also CA 81-84; CANR 23, 51; MTCW 1

Milton, John 1608-1674 . **LC 9, 43; DA;**
DAB; DAC; DAM MST, POET; PC 19;
WLC
See also CDBLB 1660-1789; DLB 131, 151

Min, Anchee 1957- .... **CLC 86**
See also CA 146
Minehaha, Cornelius
See Wedekind, (Benjamin) Frank(lin)
Miner, Valerie 1947- .... **CLC 40**
See also CA 97-100; CANR 59
Minimo, Duca
See D'Annunzio, Gabriele
Minot, Susan 1956- .... **CLC 44**
See also CA 134
Minus, Ed 1938- .... **CLC 39**
Miranda, Javier
See Bioy Casares, Adolfo
Mirbeau, Octave 1848-1917 ..... **TCLC 55**
See also DLB 123, 192
Miro (Ferrer), Gabriel (Francisco Victor)
1879-1930 .... **TCLC 5**
See also CA 104
Mishima, Yukio 1925-1970...**CLC 2, 4, 6,
9, 27; DC 1; SSC 4**
See also Hiraoka, Kimitake
See also DLB 182
Mistral, Frederic 1830-1914 .... **TCLC 51**
See also CA 122
Mistral, Gabriela .... **TCLC 2; HLC**
See also Godoy Alcayaga, Lucila
Mistry, Rohinton 1952- .... **CLC 71; DAC**
See also CA 141
Mitchell, Clyde
See Ellison, Harlan (Jay); Silverberg, Robert
Mitchell, James Leslie 1901-1935
See Gibbon, Lewis Grassic
See also CA 104; DLB 15
Mitchell, Joni 1943- .... **CLC 12**
See also CA 112
Mitchell, Joseph (Quincy) 1908-1996
CLC 98
See also CA 77-80; 152; CANR 69; DLB
185; DLBY 96
Mitchell, Margaret (Munnerlyn) 1900-
1949 .... **TCLC 11; DAM NOV, POP**
See also AAYA 23; CA 109; 125; CANR 55;
DLB 9; MTCW 1
Mitchell, Peggy
See Mitchell, Margaret (Munnerlyn)
Mitchell, S(ilas) Weir 1829-1914 ... **TCLC 36**
See also CA 165; DLB 202
Mitchell, W(illiam) O(rmond) 1914-1998
CLC 25; DAC; DAM MST
See also CA 77-80; 165; CANR 15, 43; DLB
88
Mitchell, William 1879-1936...**TCLC 81**
Mitford, Mary Russell 1787-1855**NCLC 4**
See also DLB 110, 116
Mitford, Nancy 1904-1973 .... **CLC 44**
See also CA 9-12R; DLB 191
Miyamoto, Yuriko 1899-1951 .... **TCLC 37**
See also CA 170; DLB 180
Miyazawa, Kenji 1896-1933 .... **TCLC 76**
See also CA 157
Mizoguchi, Kenji 1898-1956 ... **TCLC 72**
See also CA 167
Mo, Timothy (Peter) 1950(?)- .... **CLC 46**
See also CA 117; DLB 194; MTCW 1
Modarressi, Taghi (M.) 1931- .... **CLC 44**
See also CA 121; 134; INT 134
Modiano, Patrick (Jean) 1945- .... **CLC 18**
See also CA 85-88; CANR 17, 40; DLB 83
Moerck, Paal
See Roelvaag, O(le) E(dvart)
Mofolo, Thomas (Mokopu) 1875(?)-1948
TCLC 22; BLC 3; DAM MULT
See also CA 121; 153

Mohr, Nicholasa 1938- .... **CLC 12; DAM
MULT; HLC**
See also AAYA 8; CA 49-52; CANR 1, 32, 64;
CLR 22; DLB 145; HW; JRDA; SAAS 8;
SATA 8, 97
Mojtabai, A(nn) G(race) 1938-...**CLC 5, 9,
15, 29**
See also CA 85-88
Moliere 1622-1673...**LC 10, 28; DA; DAB;
DAC; DAM DRAM, MST; WLC**
Molin, Charles
See Mayne, William (James Carter)
Molnar, Ferenc 1878-1952 .... **TCLC 20;
DAM DRAM**
See also CA 109; 153
Momaday, N(avarre) Scott 1934-...**CLC 2,
19, 85, 95; DA; DAB; DAC; DAM MST,
MULT, NOV, POP; PC 25; WLCS**
See also AAYA 11; CA 25-28R; CANR 14, 34,
68; DLB 143, 175; INT CANR-14; MTCW
1; NNAL; SATA 48; SATA-Brief 30
Monette, Paul 1945-1995 .... **CLC 82**
See also CA 139; 147
Monroe, Harriet 1860-1936 .... **TCLC 12**
See also CA 109; DLB 54, 91
Monroe, Lyle
See Heinlein, Robert A(nson)
Montagu, Elizabeth 1720-1800 .... **NCLC 7**
Montagu, Mary (Pierrepont) Wortley 1689-
1762 .... **LC 9; PC 16**
See also DLB 95, 101
Montagu, W. H.
See Coleridge, Samuel Taylor
Montague, John (Patrick) 1929-
CLC 13, 46
See also CA 9-12R; CANR 9, 69; DLB 40;
MTCW 1
Montaigne, Michel (Eyquem) de 1533-1592
**LC 8; DA; DAB; DAC; DAM MST;
WLC**
Montale, Eugenio 1896-1981...**CLC 7, 9,
18; PC 13**
See also CA 17-20R; 104; CANR 30; DLB 114;
MTCW 1
Montesquieu, Charles-Louis de Secondat 1689-
1755 .... **LC 7**
Montgomery, (Robert) Bruce 1921-1978
See Crispin, Edmund
See also CA 104
Montgomery, L(ucy) M(aud) 1874-1942
TCLC 51; DAC; DAM MST
See also AAYA 12; CA 108; 137; CLR 8; DLB
92; DLBD 14; JRDA; MAICYA; SATA 100;
YABC 1
Montgomery, Marion H., Jr. 1925-
CLC 7
See also AITN 1; CA 1-4R; CANR 3, 48;
DLB 6
Montgomery, Max
See Davenport, Guy (Mattison, Jr.)
Montherlant, Henry (Milon) de 1896-1972
CLC 8, 19; DAM DRAM
See also CA 85-88; 37-40R; DLB 72; MTCW
1
Monty Python
See Chapman, Graham; Cleese, John
(Marwood); Gilliam, Terry (Vance); Idle,
Eric; Jones, Terence Graham Parry; Palin,
Michael (Edward)
See also AAYA 7
Moodie, Susanna (Strickland) 1803-1885
NCLC 14
See also DLB 99

Mooney, Edward 1951-
See Mooney, Ted
See also CA 130
Mooney, Ted .... **CLC 25**
See also Mooney, Edward
Moorcock, Michael (John) 1939-...**CLC 5,
27, 58**
See also AAYA 26; CA 45-48; CAAS 5; CANR
2, 17, 38, 64; DLB 14; MTCW 1; SATA 93
Moore, Brian 1921-...**CLC 1, 3, 5, 7, 8, 19,
32, 90; DAB; DAC; DAM MST**
See also CA 1-4R; CANR 1, 25, 42, 63; MTCW
1
Moore, Edward
See Muir, Edwin
Moore, G. E. 1873-1958 .... **TCLC 89**
Moore, George Augustus 1852-1933
TCLC 7; SSC 19
See also CA 104; DLB 10, 18, 57, 135
Moore, Lorrie .... **CLC 39, 45, 68**
See also Moore, Marie Lorena
Moore, Marianne (Craig) 1887-1972
**CLC 1, 2, 4, 8, 10, 13, 19, 47; DA; DAB;
DAC; DAM MST, POET; PC 4; WLCS**
See also CA 1-4R; 33-36R; CANR 3, 61;
CDALB 1929-1941; DLB 45; DLBD 7;
MTCW 1; SATA 20
Moore, Marie Lorena 1957-
See Moore, Lorrie
See also CA 116; CANR 39
Moore, Thomas 1779-1852 .... **NCLC 6**
See also DLB 96, 144
Morand, Paul 1888-1976 .... **CLC 41; SSC 22**
See also CA 69-72; DLB 65
Morante, Elsa 1918-1985 .... **CLC 8, 47**
See also CA 85-88; 117; CANR 35; DLB
177; MTCW 1
Moravia, Alberto 1907-1990...**CLC 2, 7,
11, 27, 46; SSC 26**
See also Pincherle, Alberto
See also DLB 177
More, Hannah 1745-1833 .... **NCLC 27**
See also DLB 107, 109, 116, 158
More, Henry 1614-1687 .... **LC 9**
See also DLB 126
More, Sir Thomas 1478-1535 .... **LC 10, 32**
Moreas, Jean .... **TCLC 18**
See also Papadiamantopoulos, Johannes
Morgan, Berry 1919- .... **CLC 6**
See also CA 49-52; DLB 6
Morgan, Claire
See Highsmith, (Mary) Patricia
Morgan, Edwin (George) 1920- .... **CLC 31**
See also CA 5-8R; CANR 3, 43; DLB 27
Morgan, (George) Frederick 1922-
CLC 23
See also CA 17-20R; CANR 21
Morgan, Harriet
See Mencken, H(enry) L(ouis)
Morgan, Jane
See Cooper, James Fenimore
Morgan, Janet 1945- .... **CLC 39**
See also CA 65-68
Morgan, Lady 1776(?)-1859 .... **NCLC 29**
See also DLB 116, 158
Morgan, Robin (Evonne) 1941- .... **CLC 2**
See also CA 69-72; CANR 29, 68; MTCW 1;
SATA 80
Morgan, Scott
See Kuttner, Henry
Morgan, Seth 1949(?)-1990 .... **CLC 65**
See also CA 132

Morgenstern, Christian 1871-1914
      TCLC 8
   See also CA 105
Morgenstern, S.
   See Goldman, William (W.)
Moricz, Zsigmond 1879-1942 .. TCLC 33
   See also CA 165
Morike, Eduard (Friedrich) 1804-1875
      NCLC 10
   See also DLB 133
Moritz, Karl Philipp 1756-1793 ...... LC 2
   See also DLB 94
Morland, Peter Henry
   See Faust, Frederick (Schiller)
Morley, Christopher (Darlington) 1890-
      1957 .... TCLC 87
   See also CA 112; DLB 9
Morren, Theophil
   See Hofmannsthal, Hugo von
Morris, Bill 1952- .... CLC 76
Morris, Julian
   See West, Morris L(anglo)
Morris, Steveland Judkins 1950(?)-
   See Wonder, Stevie
   See also CA 111
Morris, William 1834-1896 .... NCLC 4
   See also CDBLB 1832-1890; DLB 18, 35, 57,
      156, 178, 184
Morris, Wright 1910-1998...CLC 1, 3, 7,
      18, 37
   See also CA 9-12R; 167; CANR 21; DLB 2;
      DLBY 81; MTCW 1
Morrison, Arthur 1863-1945 .... TCLC 72
   See also CA 120; 157; DLB 70, 135, 197
Morrison, Chloe Anthony Wofford
   See Morrison, Toni
Morrison, James Douglas 1943-1971
   See Morrison, Jim
   See also CA 73-76; CANR 40
Morrison, Jim .... CLC 17
   See also Morrison, James Douglas
Morrison, Toni 1931-...CLC 4, 10, 22, 55,
      81, 87; BLC 3; DA; DAB; DAC; DAM
      MST, MULT, NOV, POP
   See also AAYA 1, 22; BW 2; CA 29-32R;
      CANR 27, 42, 67; CDALB 1968-1988;
      DLB 6, 33, 143; DLBY 81; MTCW 1;
      SATA 57
Morrison, Van 1945- .... CLC 21
   See also CA 116; 168
Morrissy, Mary 1958- .... CLC 99
Mortimer, John (Clifford) 1923-CLC 28,
      43; DAM DRAM, POP
   See also CA 13-16R; CANR 21, 69; CDBLB
      1960 to Present; DLB 13; INT CANR-21;
      MTCW 1
Mortimer, Penelope (Ruth) 1918- .... CLC 5
   See also CA 57-60; CANR 45
Morton, Anthony
   See Creasey, John
Mosca, Gaetano 1858-1941 .... TCLC 75
Mosher, Howard Frank 1943- .... CLC 62
   See also CA 139; CANR 65
Mosley, Nicholas 1923- .... CLC 43, 70
   See also CA 69-72; CANR 41, 60; DLB 14
Mosley, Walter 1952-...CLC 97; BLCS;
      DAM MULT, POP
   See also AAYA 17; BW 2; CA 142; CANR 57
Moss, Howard 1922-1987...CLC 7, 14, 45,
      50; DAM POET
   See also CA 1-4R; 123; CANR 1, 44; DLB 5
Mossgiel, Rab
   See Burns, Robert

Motion, Andrew (Peter) 1952-... CLC 47
   See also CA 146; DLB 40
Motley, Willard (Francis) 1909-1965
      CLC 18
   See also BW 1; CA 117; 106; DLB 76, 143
Motoori, Norinaga 1730-1801...NCLC 45
Mott, Michael (Charles Alston) 1930-
      CLC 15, 34
   See also CA 5-8R; CAAS 7; CANR 7, 29
Mountain Wolf Woman 1884-1960
      CLC 92
   See also CA 144; NNAL
Moure, Erin 1955- ....CLC 88
   See also CA 113; DLB 60
Mowat, Farley (McGill) 1921- . CLC 26;
      DAC; DAM MST
   See also AAYA 1; CA 1-4R; CANR 4, 24, 42,
      68; CLR 20; DLB 68; INT CANR-24; JRDA;
      MAICYA; MTCW 1; SATA 3, 55
Mowatt, Anna Cora 1819-1870...NCLC 74
Moyers, Bill 1934- .... CLC 74
   See also AITN 2; CA 61-64; CANR 31, 52

Mphahlele, Es'kia
   See Mphahlele, Ezekiel
   See also DLB 125
Mphahlele, Ezekiel 1919-1983...CLC 25;
      BLC 3; DAM MULT
   See also Mphahlele, Es'kia
   See also BW 2; CA 81-84; CANR 26
Mqhayi, S(amuel) E(dward) K(rune Loliwe)
      1875-1945 .... TCLC 25; BLC 3; DAM
      MULT
   See also CA 153
Mrozek, Slawomir 1930- .... CLC 3, 13
   See also CA 13-16R; CAAS 10; CANR 29;
      MTCW 1
Mrs. Belloc-Lowndes
   See Lowndes, Marie Adelaide (Belloc)
Mtwa, Percy (?)- ....C L C 47
Mueller, Lisel 1924- .... CLC 13, 51
   See also CA 93-96; DLB 105
Muir, Edwin 1887-1959 .... TCLC 2, 87
   See also CA 104; DLB 20, 100, 191
Muir, John 1838-1914 .... TCLC 28
   See also CA 165; DLB 186
Mujica Lainez, Manuel 1910-1984...C L C
      31
   See also Lainez, Manuel Mujica
   See also CA 81-84; 112; CANR 32; HW
Mukherjee, Bharati 1940-...CLC 53, 115;
      DAM NOV
   See also BEST 89:2; CA 107; CANR 45, 72;
      DLB 60; MTCW 1
Muldoon, Paul 1951-...CLC 32, 72; DAM
      POET
   See also CA 113; 129; CANR 52; DLB 40;
      INT 129
Mulisch, Harry 1927- ....CLC 42
   See also CA 9-12R; CANR 6, 26, 56
Mull, Martin 1943- .... CLC 17
   See also CA 105
Muller, Wilhelm .... NCLC 73
Mulock, Dinah Maria
   See Craik, Dinah Maria (Mulock)
Munford, Robert 1737(?)-1783 .... LC 5
   See also DLB 31
Mungo, Raymond 1946- .... CLC 72
   See also CA 49-52; CANR 2
Munro, Alice 1931-.... CLC 6, 10, 19, 50, 95;
      DAC; DAM MST, NOV; SSC 3; WLCS
   See also AITN 2; CA 33-36R; CANR 33, 53,
      75; DLB 53; MTCW 1; SATA 29

Munro, H(ector) H(ugh) 1870-1916
   See Saki
   See also CA 104; 130; CDBLB 1890-1914;
      DA; DAB; DAC; DAM MST, NOV; DLB
      34, 162; MTCW 1; WLC
Murdoch, (Jean) Iris 1919-...CLC 1, 2, 3,
      4, 6, 8, 11, 15, 22, 31, 51; DAB; DAC;
      DAM MST, NOV
   See also CA 13-16R; CANR 8, 43, 68; CDBLB
      1960 to Present; DLB 14, 194; INT CANR-
      8; MTCW 1
Murfree, Mary Noailles 1850-1922
      SSC 22
   See also CA 122; DLB 12, 74
Murnau, Friedrich Wilhelm
   See Plumpe, Friedrich Wilhelm
Murphy, Richard 1927- .... CLC 41
   See also CA 29-32R; DLB 40
Murphy, Sylvia 1937-.................... CLC 34
   See also CA 121
Murphy, Thomas (Bernard) 1935- .. CLC 51
   See also CA 101
Murray, Albert L. 1916- .... CLC 73
   See also BW 2; CA 49-52; CANR 26, 52;
      DLB 38
Murray, Judith Sargent 1751-1820
      NCLC 63
   See also DLB 37, 200
Murray, Les(lie) A(llan) 1938-...CLC 40;
      DAM POET
   See also CA 21-24R; CANR 11, 27, 56
Murry, J. Middleton
   See Murry, John Middleton
Murry, John Middleton 1889-1957
      TCLC 16
   See also CA 118; DLB 149
Musgrave, Susan 1951- .... CLC 13, 54
   See also CA 69-72; CANR 45
Musil, Robert (Edler von) 1880-1942
      TCLC 12, 68; SSC 18
   See also CA 109; CANR 55; DLB 81, 124
Muske, Carol 1945- .... CLC 90
   See also Muske-Dukes, Carol (Anne)
Muske-Dukes, Carol (Anne) 1945-
   See Muske, Carol
   See also CA 65-68; CANR 32, 70
Musset, (Louis Charles) Alfred de 1810-
      1857 .... NCLC 7
   See also DLB 192
My Brother's Brother
   See Chekhov, Anton (Pavlovich)
Myers, L(eopold) H(amilton) 1881-1944
      TCLC 59
   See also CA 157; DLB 15
Myers, Walter Dean 1937-CLC 35; BLC
      3; DAM MULT, NOV
   See also AAYA 4, 23; BW 2; CA 33-36R;
      CANR 20, 42, 67; CLR 4, 16, 35; DLB 33;
      INT CANR-20; JRDA; MAICYA; SAAS 2;
      SATA 41, 71; SATA-Brief 27
Myers, Walter M.
   See Myers, Walter Dean
Myles, Symon
   See Follett, Ken(neth Martin)
Nabokov, Vladimir (Vladimirovich) 1899-
      1977...CLC 1, 2, 3, 6, 8, 11, 15, 23, 44,
      46, 64; DA; DAB; DAC; DAM MST,
      NOV; SSC 11; WLC
   See also CA 5-8R; 69-72; CANR 20; CDALB
      1941-1968; DLB 2; DLBD 3; DLBY 80, 91;
      MTCW 1

Nagai Kafu 1879-1959 .... **TCLC 51**
See also Nagai Sokichi
See also DLB 180
Nagai Sokichi 1879-1959
See Nagai Kafu
See also CA 117
Nagy, Laszlo 1925-1978 .... **CLC 7**
See also CA 129; 112
Naidu, Sarojini 1879-1943 .... **TCLC 80**
Naipaul, Shiva(dhar Srinivasa) 1945-1985
CLC 32, 39; DAM NOV
See also CA 110; 112; 116; CANR 33; DLB
157; DLBY 85; MTCW 1
Naipaul, V(idiadhar) S(urajprasad) 1932-
**CLC 4, 7, 9, 13, 18, 37, 105; DAB; DAC;
DAM MST, NOV**
See also CA 1-4R; CANR 1, 33, 51; CDBLB
1960 to Present; DLB 125; DLBY 85;
MTCW 1
Nakos, Lilika 1899(?)- .... **CLC 29**
Narayan, R(asipuram) K(rishnaswami)
1906-...**CLC 7, 28, 47; DAM NOV; SSC
25**
See also CA 81-84; CANR 33, 61; MTCW 1;
SATA 62
Nash, (Frediric) Ogden 1902-1971...**C L C
23; DAM POET; PC 21**
See also CA 13-14; 29-32R; CANR 34, 61; CAP
1; DLB 11; MAICYA; MTCW 1; SATA 2, 46
Nashe, Thomas 1567-1601(?) .... **LC 41**
See also DLB 167
Nashe, Thomas 1567-1601 .... **LC 41**
Nathan, Daniel
See Dannay, Frederic
Nathan, George Jean 1882-1958 .... **TCLC 18**
See also Hatteras, Owen
See also CA 114; 169; DLB 137
Natsume, Kinnosuke 1867-1916
See Natsume, Soseki
See also CA 104
Natsume, Soseki 1867-1916 .... **TCLC 2, 10**
See also Natsume, Kinnosuke
See also DLB 180
Natti, (Mary) Lee 1919-
See Kingman, Lee
See also CA 5-8R; CANR 2
Naylor, Gloria 1950-...**CLC 28, 52; BLC
3; DA; DAC; DAM MST, MULT, NOV,
POP; WLCS**
See also AAYA 6; BW 2; CA 107; CANR 27,
51, 74; DLB 173; MTCW 1
Neihardt, John Gneisenau 1881-1973
CLC 32
See also CA 13-14; CANR 65; CAP 1; DLB
9, 54
Nekrasov, Nikolai Alekseevich 1821-1878
NCLC 11
Nelligan, Emile 1879-1941 .... **TCLC 14**
See also CA 114; DLB 92
Nelson, Willie 1933- .... **CLC 17**
See also CA 107
Nemerov, Howard (Stanley) 1920-1991
CLC 2, 6, 9, 36; DAM POET; PC 24
See also CA 1-4R; 134; CABS 2; CANR 1,
27, 53; DLB 5, 6; DLBY 83; INT CANR-
27; MTCW 1
Neruda, Pablo 1904-1973...**CLC 1, 2, 5, 7,
9, 28, 62; DA; DAB; DAC; DAM MST,
MULT, POET; HLC; PC 4; WLC**
See also CA 19-20; 45-48; CAP 2; HW;
MTCW 1
Nerval, Gerard de 1808-1855...**NCLC 1,
67; PC 13; SSC 18**

Nervo, (Jose) Amado (Ruiz de) 1870-1919
TCLC 11
See also CA 109; 131; HW
Nessi, Pio Baroja y
See Baroja (y Nessi), Pio
Nestroy, Johann 1801 1862 ..... **NCLC 42**
See also DLB 133
Netterville, Luke
See O'Grady, Standish (James)
Neufeld, John (Arthur) 1938- ....**CLC 17**
See also AAYA 11; CA 25-28R; CANR 11, 37,
56; CLR 52; MAICYA; SAAS 3; SATA 6,
81
Neville, Emily Cheney 1919- .... **CLC 12**
See also CA 5-8R; CANR 3, 37; JRDA;
MAICYA; SAAS 2; SATA 1
Newbound, Bernard Slade 1930-
See Slade, Bernard
See also CA 81-84; CANR 49; DAM DRAM
Newby, P(ercy) H(oward) 1918-1997
CLC 2, 13; DAM NOV
See also CA 5-8R; 161; CANR 32, 67; DLB
15; MTCW 1
Newlove, Donald 1928- ....**CLC 6**
See also CA 29-32R; CANR 25
Newlove, John (Herbert) 1938-.........**CLC 14**
See also CA 21-24R; CANR 9, 25
Newman, Charles 1938- .... **CLC 2, 8**
See also CA 21-24R
Newman, Edwin (Harold) 1919- ....**CLC 14**
See also AITN 1; CA 69-72; CANR 5
Newman, John Henry 1801-1890
NCLC 38
See also DLB 18, 32, 55
Newton, (Sir)Isaac 1642-1727 .... **LC 35**
Newton, Suzanne 1936-......................**CLC 35**
See also CA 41-44R; CANR 14; JRDA; SATA
5, 77
Nexo, Martin Andersen 1869-1954...**TCLC
43**
Nezval, Vitezslav 1900-1958 .... **TCLC 44**
See also CA 123
Ng, Fae Myenne 1957(?)- ....**CLC 81**
See also CA 146
Ngema, Mbongeni 1955- ....**CLC 57**
See also BW 2; CA 143
Ngugi, James T(hiong'o) ..... **CLC 3, 7, 13**
See also Ngugi wa Thiong'o
Ngugi wa Thiong'o 1938-...**CLC 36; BLC
3; DAM MULT, NOV**
See also Ngugi, James T(hiong'o)
See also BW 2; CA 81-84; CANR 27, 58; DLB
125; MTCW 1
Nichol, B(arrie) P(hillip) 1944-1988
CLC 18
See also CA 53-56; DLB 53; SATA 66
Nichols, John (Treadwell) 1940-...**CLC 38**
See also CA 9-12R; CAAS 2; CANR 6, 70;
DLBY 82
Nichols, Leigh
See Koontz, Dean R(ay)
Nichols, Peter (Richard) 1927-...**CLC 5,
36, 65**
See also CA 104; CANR 33; DLB 13; MTCW
1
Nicolas, F. R. E.
See Freeling, Nicolas
Niedecker, Lorine 1903-1970...**CLC 10, 42;
DAM POET**
See also CA 25-28; CAP 2; DLB 48
Nietzsche, Friedrich (Wilhelm) 1844-1900
TCLC 10, 18, 55
See also CA 107; 121; DLB 129

Nievo, Ippolito 1831-1861 .... **NCLC 22**
Nightingale, Anne Redmon 1943-
See Redmon, Anne
See also CA 103
Nightingale, Florence 1820-1910
TCLC 85
See also DLB 166
Nik. T. O.
See Annensky, Innokenty (Fyodorovich)
Nin, Anais 1903-1977...**CLC 1, 4, 8, 11, 14,
60; DAM NOV, POP; SSC 10**
See also AITN 2; CA 13-16R; 69-72; CANR
22, 53; DLB 2, 4, 152; MTCW 1
Nishida, Kitaro 1870-1945 .... **TCLC 83**
Nishiwaki, Junzaburo 1894-1982 .... **PC 15**
See also CA 107
Nissenson, Hugh 1933- .... **CLC 4, 9**
See also CA 17-20R; CANR 27; DLB 28
Niven, Larry...**CLC 8**
See also Niven, Laurence Van Cott
See also AAYA 27; DLB 8
Niven, Laurence Van Cott 1938-
See Niven, Larry
See also CA 21-24R; CAAS 12; CANR 14,
44, 66; DAM POP; MTCW 1; SATA 95
Nixon, Agnes Eckhardt 1927- ....**CLC 21**
See also CA 110
Nizan, Paul 1905-1940 .... **TCLC 40**
See also CA 161; DLB 72
Nkosi, Lewis 1936-...**CLC 45; BLC 3; DAM
MULT**
See also BW 1; CA 65-68; CANR 27; DLB 157
Nodier, (Jean) Charles (Emmanuel) 1780-
1844 .... **NCLC 19**
See also DLB 119
Noguchi, Yone 1875-1947 .... **TCLC 80**
Nolan, Christopher 1965- .... **CLC 58**
See also CA 111
Noon, Jeff 1957-.................................**CLC 91**
See also CA 148
Norden, Charles
See Durrell, Lawrence (George)
Nordhoff, Charles (Bernard) 1887-1947
TCLC 23
See also CA 108; DLB 9; SATA 23
Norfolk, Lawrence 1963- .... **CLC 76**
See also CA 144
Norman, Marsha 1947- ... **CLC 28; DAM
DRAM; DC 8**
See also CA 105; CABS 3; CANR 41; DLBY
84
Normyx
See Douglas, (George) Norman
Norris, Frank 1870-1902 .... **SSC 28**
See also Norris, (Benjamin) Frank(lin, Jr.)
See also CDALB 1865-1917; DLB 12, 71, 186
Norris, (Benjamin) Frank(lin, Jr.) 1870-
1902 .... **TCLC 24**
See also Norris, Frank
See also CA 110; 160
Norris, Leslie 1921- ....**CLC 14**
See also CA 11-12; CANR 14; CAP 1; DLB
27
North, Andrew
See Norton, Andre
North, Anthony
See Koontz, Dean R(ay)
North, Captain George
See Stevenson, Robert Louis (Balfour)
North, Milou
See Erdrich, Louise
Northrup, B. A.
See Hubbard, L(afayette) Ron(ald)

North Staffs
See Hulme, T(homas) E(rnest)
Norton, Alice Mary
See Norton, Andre
See also MAICYA; SATA 1, 43
Norton, Andre 1912- .... CLC 12
See also Norton, Alice Mary
See also AAYA 14; CA 1-4R; CANR 68; CLR
50; DLB 8, 52; JRDA; MTCW 1; SATA
91
Norton, Caroline 1808-1877 ... NCLC 47
See also DLB 21, 159, 199
Norway, Nevil Shute 1899-1960
See Shute, Nevil
See also CA 102; 93-96
Norwid, Cyprian Kamil 1821-1883
NCLC 17
Nosille, Nabrah
See Ellison, Harlan (Jay)
Nossack, Hans Erich 1901-1978 .. CLC 6
See also CA 93-96; 85-88; DLB 69
Nostradamus 1503-1566 .... LC 27
Nosu, Chuji
See Ozu, Yasujiro
Notenburg, Eleanora (Genrikhovna) von
See Guro, Elena
Nova, Craig 1945- .... CLC 7, 31
See also CA 45-48; CANR 2, 53
Novak, Joseph
See Kosinski, Jerzy (Nikodem)
Novalis 1772-1801 .... NCLC 13
See also DLB 90
Novis, Emile
See Weil, Simone (Adolphine)
Nowlan, Alden (Albert) 1933-1983
CLC 15; DAC; DAM MST
See also CA 9-12R; CANR 5; DLB 53
Noyes, Alfred 1880-1958 .... TCLC 7
See also CA 104; DLB 20
Nunn, Kem .... CLC 34
See also CA 159
Nye, Robert 1939-...CLC 13, 42; DAM NOV
See also CA 33-36R; CANR 29, 67; DLB 14;
MTCW 1; SATA 6
Nyro, Laura 1947- .... CLC 17
Oates, Joyce Carol 1938-...CLC 1, 2, 3, 6,
9, 11, 15, 19, 33, 52, 108; DA; DAB;
DAC; DAM MST, NOV, POP; SSC 6;
WLC
See also AAYA 15; AITN 1; BEST 89:2; CA 5-
8R; CANR 25, 45, 74; CDALB 1968-1988;
DLB 2, 5, 130; DLBY 81; INT CANR-25;
MTCW 1
O'Brien, Darcy 1939-1998 .... CLC 11
See also CA 21-24R; 167; CANR 8, 59
O'Brien, E. G.
See Clarke, Arthur C(harles)
O'Brien, Edna 1936-...CLC 3, 5, 8, 13, 36,
65, 116; DAM NOV; SSC 10
See also CA 1-4R; CANR 6, 41, 65; CDBLB
1960 to Present; DLB 14; MTCW 1
O'Brien, Fitz-James 1828-1862 ..... NCLC 21
See also DLB 74
O'Brien, Flann .... CLC 1, 4, 5, 7, 10, 47
See also O Nuallain, Brian
O'Brien, Richard 1942- .... CLC 17
See also CA 124
O'Brien, (William) Tim(othy) 1946-..CLC
7, 19, 40, 103; DAM POP
See also AAYA 16; CA 85-88; CANR 40, 58;
DLB 152; DLBY 80
Obstfelder, Sigbjoern 1866-1900TCLC 23
See also CA 123

O'Casey, Sean 1880-1964...CLC 1, 5, 9,
11, 15, 88; DAB; DAC; DAM DRAM,
MST; WLCS
See also CA 89-92; CANR 62; CDBLB 1914-
1945; DLB 10; MTCW 1
O'Cathasaigh, Sean
See O'Casey, Sean
Ochs, Phil 1940-1976 ....CLC 17
See also CA 65-68
O'Connor, Edwin (Greene) 1918-1968
CLC 14
See also CA 93-96; 25-28R
O'Connor, (Mary) Flannery 1925-1964
CLC 1, 2, 3, 6, 10, 13, 15, 21, 66, 104;
DA; DAB; DAC; DAM MST, NOV; SSC
1, 23; WLC
See also AAYA 7; CA 1-4R; CANR 3, 41;
CDALB 1941-1968; DLB 2, 152; DLBD 12;
DLBY 80; MTCW 1
O'Connor, Frank ....CLC 23; SSC 5
See also O'Donovan, Michael John
See also DLB 162
O'Dell, Scott 1898-1989 .... CLC 30
See also AAYA 3; CA 61-64; 129; CANR 12,
30; CLR 1, 16; DLB 52; JRDA; MAICYA;
SATA 12, 60
Odets, Clifford 1906-1963...CLC 2, 28, 98;
DAM DRAM; DC 6
See also CA 85-88; CANR 62; DLB 7, 26;
MTCW 1
O'Doherty, Brian 1934- ....CLC 76
See also CA 105
O'Donnell, K. M.
See Malzberg, Barry N(athaniel)
O'Donnell, Lawrence
See Kuttner, Henry
O'Donovan, Michael John 1903-1966
CLC 14
See also O'Connor, Frank
See also CA 93-96
Oe, Kenzaburo 1935-.... CLC 10, 36, 86;
DAM NOV; SSC 20
See also CA 97-100; CANR 36, 50, 74; DLB
182; DLBY 94; MTCW 1
O'Faolain, Julia 1932- .... CLC 6, 19, 47, 108
See also CA 81-84; CAAS 2; CANR 12, 61;
DLB 14; MTCW 1
O'Faolain, Sean 1900-1991...CLC 1, 7, 14,
32, 70; SSC 13
See also CA 61-64; 134; CANR 12, 66; DLB
15, 162; MTCW 1
O'Flaherty, Liam 1896-1984...CLC 5, 34;
SSC 6
See also CA 101; 113; CANR 35; DLB 36,
162; DLBY 84; MTCW 1
Ogilvy, Gavin
See Barrie, J(ames) M(atthew)
O'Grady, Standish (James) 1846-1928
TCLC 5
See also CA 104; 157
O'Grady, Timothy 1951- .... CLC 59
See also CA 138
O'Hara, Frank 1926-1966...CLC 2, 5, 13,
78; DAM POET
See also CA 9-12R; 25-28R; CANR 33; DLB
5, 16, 193; MTCW 1
O'Hara, John (Henry) 1905-1970...CLC
1, 2, 3, 6, 11, 42; DAM NOV; SSC 15
See also CA 5-8R; 25-28R; CANR 31, 60;
CDALB 1929-1941; DLB 9, 86; DLBD 2;
MTCW 1
O Hehir, Diana 1922- ....CLC 41
See also CA 93-96

Okigbo, Christopher (Ifenayichukwu)
1932-1967...CLC 25, 84; BLC 3; DAM
MULT, POET; PC 7
See also BW 1; CA 77-80; CANR 74; DLB 125;
MTCW 1
Okri, Ben 1959- .... CLC 87
See also BW 2; CA 130; 138; CANR 65; DLB
157; INT 138
Olds, Sharon 1942-...CLC 32, 39, 85; DAM
POET; PC 22
See also CA 101; CANR 18, 41, 66; DLB 120
Oldstyle, Jonathan
See Irving, Washington
Olesha, Yuri (Karlovich) 1899-1960C L C
8
See also CA 85-88
Oliphant, Laurence 1829(?)-1888
NCLC 47
See also DLB 18, 166
Oliphant, Margaret (Oliphant Wilson) 1828-
1897 .... NCLC 11, 61; SSC 25
See also DLB 18, 159, 190
Oliver, Mary 1935- .... CLC 19, 34, 98
See also CA 21-24R; CANR 9, 43; DLB 5, 193
Olivier, Laurence (Kerr) 1907-1989
CLC 20
See also CA 111; 150; 129
Olsen, Tillie 1912-...CLC 4, 13, 114; DA;
DAB; DAC; DAM MST; SSC 11
See also CA 1-4R; CANR 1, 43, 74; DLB 28;
DLBY 80; MTCW 1
Olson, Charles (John) 1910-1970CLC 1,
2, 5, 6, 9, 11, 29; DAM POET; PC 19
See also CA 13-16; 25-28R; CABS 2; CANR
35, 61; CAP 1; DLB 5, 16, 193; MTCW 1
Olson, Toby 1937-............................. CLC 28
See also CA 65-68; CANR 9, 31
Olyesha, Yuri
See Olesha, Yuri (Karlovich)
Ondaatje, (Philip) Michael 1943-..C L C
14, 29, 51, 76; DAB; DAC; DAM MST
See also CA 77-80; CANR 42, 74; DLB 60
Oneal, Elizabeth 1934-
See Oneal, Zibby
See also CA 106; CANR 28; MAICYA; SATA
30, 82
Oneal, Zibby .... CLC 30
See also Oneal, Elizabeth
See also AAYA 5; CLR 13; JRDA
O'Neill, Eugene (Gladstone) 1888-1953
TCLC 1, 6, 27, 49; DA; DAB; DAC;
DAM DRAM, MST; WLC
See also AITN 1; CA 110; 132; CDALB
1929-1941; DLB 7; MTCW 1
Onetti, Juan Carlos 1909-1994 ... CLC 7, 10;
DAM MULT, NOV; SSC 23
See also CA 85-88; 145; CANR 32, 63; DLB
113; HW; MTCW 1
O Nuallain, Brian 1911-1966
See O'Brien, Flann
See also CA 21-22; 25-28R; CAP 2
Ophuls, Max 1902-1957 .... TCLC 79
See also CA 113
Opie, Amelia 1769-1853 .... NCLC 65
See also DLB 116, 159
Oppen, George 1908-1984 ...... CLC 7, 13, 34
See also CA 13-16R; 113; CANR 8; DLB 5,
165
Oppenheim, E(dward) Phillips 1866-1946
TCLC 45
See also CA 111; DLB 70
Opuls, Max
See Ophuls, Max

Origen c. 185-c. 254 .... **CMLC 19**

Orlovitz, Gil 1918-1973 .... **CLC 22**
See also CA 77-80; 45-48; DLB 2, 5

Orris
See Ingelow, Jean

Ortega y Gasset, Jose 1883-1955
TCLC 9; DAM MULT; HLC
See also CA 106; 130; HW; MTCW 1

Ortese, Anna Maria 1914- .... **CLC 89**
See also DLB 177

Ortiz, Simon J(oseph) 1941-... **CLC 45;
DAM MULT, POET; PC 17**
See also CA 134; CANR 69; DLB 120, 175;
NNAL

Orton, Joe .... **CLC 4, 13, 43; DC 3**
See also Orton, John Kingsley
See also CDBLB 1960 to Present; DLB 13

Orton, John Kingsley 1933-1967
See Orton, Joe
See also CA 85-88; CANR 35, 66; DAM
DRAM; MTCW 1

Orwell, George ...**TCLC 2, 6, 15, 31, 51;
DAB; WLC**
See also Blair, Eric (Arthur)
See also CDBLB 1945-1960; DLB 15, 98, 195

Osborne, David
See Silverberg, Robert

Osborne, George
See Silverberg, Robert

Osborne, John (James) 1929-1994
**CLC 1, 2, 5, 11, 45; DA; DAB; DAC;
DAM DRAM, MST; WLC**
See also CA 13-16R; 147; CANR 21, 56;
CDBLB 1945-1960; DLB 13; MTCW 1

Osborne, Lawrence 1958- .... **CLC 50**

Oshima, Nagisa 1932- .... **CLC 20**
See also CA 116; 121

Oskison, John Milton 1874-1947
TCLC 35; DAM MULT
See also CA 144; DLB 175; NNAL

Ossian c. 3rd cent. - .... **CMLC 28**
See also Macpherson, James

Ossoli, Sarah Margaret (Fuller marchesa
d') 1810-1850
See Fuller, Margaret
See also SATA 25

Ostrovsky, Alexander 1823-1886
NCLC 30, 57

Otero, Blas de 1916-1979 .... **CLC 11**
See also CA 89-92; DLB 134

Otto, Rudolf 1869-1937 .... **TCLC 85**

Otto, Whitney 1955- .... **CLC 70**
See also CA 140

Ouida .... **TCLC 43**
See also De La Ramee, (Marie) Louise
See also DLB 18, 156

Ousmane, Sembene 1923- .... **CLC 66; BLC 3**
See also BW 1; CA 117; 125; MTCW 1

Ovid 43B.C.-18(?)...**CMLC 7; DAM POET;
PC 2**

Owen, Hugh
See Faust, Frederick (Schiller)

Owen, Wilfred (Edward Salter) 1893-1918
**TCLC 5, 27; DA; DAB; DAC; DAM MST,
POET; PC 19; WLC**
See also CA 104; 141; CDBLB 1914-1945;
DLB 20

Owens, Rochelle 1936- .... **CLC 8**
See also CA 17-20R; CAAS 2; CANR 39

Oz, Amos 1939-...**CLC 5, 8, 11, 27, 33, 54;
DAM NOV**
See also CA 53-56; CANR 27, 47, 65; MTCW
1

Ozick, Cynthia 1928-...**CLC 3, 7, 28, 62;
DAM NOV, POP; SSC 15**
See also BEST 90:1; CA 17-20R; CANR 23,
58; DLB 28, 152; DLBY 82; INT CANR-
23; MTCW 1

Ozu, Yasujiro 1903-1963 .... **CLC 16**
See also CA 112

Pacheco, C.
See Pessoa, Fernando (Antonio Nogueira)

Pa Chin ....**CLC 18**
See also Li Fei-kan

Pack, Robert 1929- .... **CLC 13**
See also CA 1-4R; CANR 3, 44; DLB 5

Padgett, Lewis
See Kuttner, Henry

Padilla (Lorenzo), Heberto 1932-
CLC 38
See also AITN 1; CA 123; 131; HW

Page, Jimmy 1944- ....**CLC 12**

Page, Louise 1955- ....**CLC 40**
See also CA 140

Page, P(atricia) K(athleen) 1916-...**CLC
7, 18; DAC; DAM MST; PC 12**
See also CA 53-56; CANR 4, 22, 65; DLB 68;
MTCW 1

Page, Thomas Nelson 1853-1922 ....**SSC 23**
See also CA 118; DLB 12, 78; DLBD 13

Pagels, Elaine Hiesey 1943- .... **CLC 104**
See also CA 45-48; CANR 2, 24, 51

Paget, Violet 1856-1935
See Lee, Vernon
See also CA 104; 166

Paget-Lowe, Henry
See Lovecraft, H(oward) P(hillips)

Paglia, Camille (Anna) 1947- ... **CLC 68**
See also CA 140; CANR 72

Paige, Richard
See Koontz, Dean R(ay)

Paine, Thomas 1737-1809 .... **NCLC 62**
See also CDALB 1640-1865; DLB 31, 43,
73, 158

Pakenham, Antonia
See Fraser, (Lady) Antonia (Pakenham)

Palamas, Kostes 1859-1943 .... **TCLC 5**
See also CA 105

Palazzeschi, Aldo 1885-1974 .... **CLC 11**
See also CA 89-92; 53-56; DLB 114

Paley, Grace 1922-... **CLC 4, 6, 37; DAM
POP; SSC 8**
See also CA 25-28R; CANR 13, 46, 74; DLB
28; INT CANR-13; MTCW 1

Palin, Michael (Edward) 1943- ....**CLC 21**
See also Monty Python
See also CA 107; CANR 35; SATA 67

Palliser, Charles 1947- .... **CLC 65**
See also CA 136

Palma, Ricardo 1833-1919 .... **TCLC 29**
See also CA 168

Pancake, Breece Dexter 1952-1979
See Pancake, Breece D'J
See also CA 123; 109

Pancake, Breece D'J ....**CLC 29**
See also Pancake, Breece Dexter
See also DLB 130

Panko, Rudy
See Gogol, Nikolai (Vasilyevich)

Papadiamantis, Alexandros 1851-1911
TCLC 29
See also CA 168

Papadiamantopoulos, Johannes 1856-1910
See Moreas, Jean
See also CA 117

Papini, Giovanni 1881-1956 .... **TCLC 22**
See also CA 121

Paracelsus 1493-1541 .... **LC 14**
See also DLB 179

Parasol, Peter
See Stevens, Wallace

Pardo Bazan, Emilia 1851-1921...**SSC 30**

Pareto, Vilfredo 1848-1923 ...... **TCLC 69**

Parfenie, Maria
See Codrescu, Andrei

Parini, Jay (Lee) 1948- ....**CLC 54**
See also CA 97-100; CAAS 16; CANR 32

Park, Jordan
See Kornbluth, C(yril) M.; Pohl, Frederik

Park, Robert E(zra) 1864-1944 ...... **TCLC 73**
See also CA 122; 165

Parker, Bert
See Ellison, Harlan (Jay)

Parker, Dorothy (Rothschild) 1893-1967
CLC 15, 68; DAM POET; SSC 2
See also CA 19-20; 25-28R; CAP 2; DLB 11,
45, 86; MTCW 1

Parker, Robert B(rown) 1932-...**CLC 27;
DAM NOV, POP**
See also BEST 89:4; CA 49-52; CANR 1, 26,
52; INT CANR-26; MTCW 1

Parkin, Frank 1940- ....**CLC 43**
See also CA 147

Parkman, Francis, Jr. 1823-1893 ...**NCLC 12**
See also DLB 1, 30, 186

Parks, Gordon (Alexander Buchanan)
1912-...**CLC 1, 16; BLC 3; DAM MULT**
See also AITN 2; BW 2; CA 41-44R; CANR
26, 66; DLB 33; SATA 8

Parmenides c. 515B.C.-c. 450B.C....**CMLC
22**
See also DLB 176

Parnell, Thomas 1679-1718 .... **LC 3**
See also DLB 94

Parra, Nicanor 1914-...**CLC 2, 102; DAM
MULT; HLC**
See also CA 85-88; CANR 32; HW; MTCW 1

Parrish, Mary Frances
See Fisher, M(ary) F(rances) K(ennedy)

Parson
See Coleridge, Samuel Taylor

Parson Lot
See Kingsley, Charles

Partridge, Anthony
See Oppenheim, E(dward) Phillips

Pascal, Blaise 1623-1662 .... **LC 35**

Pascoli, Giovanni 1855-1912 .... **TCLC 45**
See also CA 170

Pasolini, Pier Paolo 1922-1975 . **CLC 20, 37,
106; PC 17**
See also CA 93-96; 61-64; CANR 63; DLB 128,
177; MTCW 1

Pasquini
See Silone, Ignazio

Pastan, Linda (Olenik) 1932- . **CLC 27;
DAM POET**
See also CA 61-64; CANR 18, 40, 61; DLB 5

Pasternak, Boris (Leonidovich) 1890-1960
**CLC 7, 10, 18, 63; DA; DAB; DAC; DAM
MST, NOV, POET; PC 6; SSC 31; WLC**
See also CA 127; 116; MTCW 1

Patchen, Kenneth 1911-1972...**CLC 1, 2,
18; DAM POET**
See also CA 1-4R; 33-36R; CANR 3, 35; DLB
16, 48; MTCW 1

Pater, Walter (Horatio) 1839-1894
NCLC 7
See also CDBLB 1832-1890; DLB 57, 156

Pincherle, Alberto 1907-1990...**CLC 11, 18; DAM NOV**
See also Moravia, Alberto
See also CA 25-28R; 132; CANR 33, 63; MTCW 1
Pinckney, Darryl 1953- **CLC 76**
See also BW 2; CA 143
Pindar 518B.C.-446B.C. ... **CMLC 12; PC 19**
See also DLB 176
Pineda, Cecile 1942- .... **CLC 39**
See also CA 118
Pinero, Arthur Wing 1855-1934 ..**T C L C 32; DAM DRAM**
See also CA 110; 153; DLB 10
Pinero, Miguel (Antonio Gomez) 1946-1988 **CLC 4, 55**
See also CA 61-64; 125; CANR 29; HW
Pinget, Robert 1919-1997...**CLC 7, 13, 37**
See also CA 85-88; 160; DLB 83
Pink Floyd
See Barrett, (Roger) Syd; Gilmour, David; Mason, Nick; Waters, Roger; Wright, Rick
Pinkney, Edward 1802-1828 .... **NCLC 31**
Pinkwater, Daniel Manus 1941- .... **CLC 35**
See also Pinkwater, Manus
See also AAYA 1; CA 29-32R; CANR 12, 38; CLR 4; JRDA; MAICYA; SAAS 3; SATA 46, 76
Pinkwater, Manus
See Pinkwater, Daniel Manus
See also SATA 8
Pinsky, Robert 1940-...**CLC 9, 19, 38, 94; DAM POET**
See also CA 29-32R; CAAS 4; CANR 58; DLBY 82
Pinta, Harold
See Pinter, Harold
Pinter, Harold 1930-...**CLC 1, 3, 6, 9, 11, 15, 27, 58, 73; DA; DAB; DAC; DAM DRAM, MST; WLC**
See also CA 5-8R; CANR 33, 65; CDBLB 1960 to Present; DLB 13; MTCW 1
Piozzi, Hester Lynch (Thrale) 1741-1821 **NCLC 57**
See also DLB 104, 142
Pirandello, Luigi 1867-1936...**TCLC 4, 29; DA; DAB; DAC; DAM DRAM, MST; DC 5; SSC 22; WLC**
See also CA 104; 153
Pirsig, Robert M(aynard) 1928-...**CLC 4, 6, 73; DAM POP**
See also CA 53-56; CANR 42, 74; MTCW 1; SATA 39
Pisarev, Dmitry Ivanovich 1840-1868 **NCLC 25**
Pix, Mary (Griffith) 1666-1709 .... **LC 8**
See also DLB 80
Pixerecourt, (Rene Charles) Guilbert de 1773-1844 .... **NCLC 39**
See also DLB 192
Plaatje, Sol(omon) T(shekisho) 1876-1932 **TCLC 73; BLCS**
See also BW 2; CA 141
Plaidy, Jean
See Hibbert, Eleanor Alice Burford
Planche, James Robinson 1796-1880 **NCLC 42**
Plant, Robert 1948- .... **CLC 12**
Plante, David (Robert) 1940-...**CLC 7, 23, 38; DAM NOV**
See also CA 37-40R; CANR 12, 36, 58; DLBY 83; INT CANR-12; MTCW 1

Plath, Sylvia 1932-1963...**CLC 1, 2, 3, 5, 9, 11, 14, 17, 50, 51, 62, 111; DA; DAB; DAC; DAM MST, POET; PC 1; WLC**
See also AAYA 13; CA 19-20; CANR 34; CAP 2; CDALB 1941-1968; DLB 5, 6, 152; MTCW 1; SATA 96
Plato 428(?)B.C.-348(?)B.C. .. **CMLC 8; DA; DAB; DAC; DAM MST; WLCS**
See also DLB 176
Platonov, Andrei .... **TCLC 14**
See also Klimentov, Andrei Platonovich
Platt, Kin 1911- .... **CLC 26**
See also AAYA 11; CA 17-20R; CANR 11; JRDA; SAAS 17; SATA 21, 86
Plautus c. 251B.C.-184B.C....**CMLC 24; DC 6**
Plick et Plock
See Simenon, Georges (Jacques Christian)
Plimpton, George (Ames) 1927-...**CLC 36**
See also AITN 1; CA 21-24R; CANR 32, 70; DLB 185; MTCW 1; SATA 10
Pliny the Elder c. 23-79 .... **CMLC 23**
Plomer, William Charles Franklin 1903-1973 **CLC 4, 8**
See also CA 21-22; CANR 34; CAP 2; DLB 20, 162, 191; MTCW 1; SATA 24
Plowman, Piers
See Kavanagh, Patrick (Joseph)
Plum, J.
See Wodehouse, P(elham) G(renville)
Plumly, Stanley (Ross) 1939- .... **CLC 33**
See also CA 108; 110; DLB 5, 193; INT 110
Plumpe, Friedrich Wilhelm 1888-1931 **TCLC 53**
See also CA 112
Po Chu-i 772-846 .... **CMLC 24**
Poe, Edgar Allan 1809-1849...**NCLC 1, 16, 55; DA; DAB; DAC; DAM MST, POET; PC 1; SSC 1, 22; WLC**
See also AAYA 14; CDALB 1640-1865; DLB 3, 59, 73, 74; SATA 23
Poet of Titchfield Street, The
See Pound, Ezra (Weston Loomis)
Pohl, Frederik 1919-... **CLC 18; SSC 25**
See also AAYA 24; CA 61-64; CAAS 1; CANR 11, 37; DLB 8; INT CANR-11; MTCW 1; SATA 24
Poirier, Louis 1910-
See Gracq, Julien
See also CA 122; 126
Poitier, Sidney 1927- .... **CLC 26**
See also BW 1; CA 117
Polanski, Roman 1933- .... **CLC 16**
See also CA 77-80
Poliakoff, Stephen 1952- .... **CLC 38**
See also CA 106; DLB 13
Police, The
See Copeland, Stewart (Armstrong); Summers, Andrew James; Sumner, Gordon Matthew
Polidori, John William 1795-1821 **NCLC 51**
See also DLB 116
Pollitt, Katha 1949- .... **CLC 28**
See also CA 120; 122; CANR 66; MTCW 1
Pollock, (Mary) Sharon 1936-...**CLC 50; DAC; DAM DRAM, MST**
See also CA 141; DLB 60
Polo, Marco 1254-1324 .... **CMLC 15**
Polonsky, Abraham (Lincoln) 1910- **CLC 92**
See also CA 104; DLB 26; INT 104

Polybius c. 200B.C.-c. 118B.C....**CMLC 17**
See also DLB 176
Pomerance, Bernard 1940- ..... **CLC 13; DAM DRAM**
See also CA 101; CANR 49
Ponge, Francis (Jean Gaston Alfred) 1899-1988 .... **CLC 6, 18; DAM POET**
See also CA 85-88; 126; CANR 40
Pontoppidan, Henrik 1857-1943 .... **TCLC 29**
See also CA 170
Poole, Josephine .... **CLC 17**
See also Helyar, Jane Penelope Josephine
See also SAAS 2; SATA 5
Popa, Vasko 1922-1991 .... **CLC 19**
See also CA 112; 148; DLB 181
Pope, Alexander 1688-1744 ...**LC 3; DA; DAB; DAC; DAM MST, POET; WLC**
See also CDBLB 1660-1789; DLB 95, 101
Porter, Connie (Rose) 1959(?)-...**CLC 70**
See also BW 2; CA 142; SATA 81
Porter, Gene(va Grace) Stratton 1863(?)-1924 **TCLC 21**
See also CA 112
Porter, Katherine Anne 1890-1980...**CLC 1, 3, 7, 10, 13, 15, 27, 101; DA; DAB; DAC; DAM MST, NOV; SSC 4, 31**
See also AITN 2; CA 1-4R; 101; CANR 1, 65; DLB 4, 9, 102; DLBD 12; DLBY 80; MTCW 1; SATA 39; SATA-Obit 23
Porter, Peter (Neville Frederick) 1929- **CLC 5, 13, 33**
See also CA 85-88; DLB 40
Porter, William Sydney 1862-1910
See Henry, O.
See also CA 104; 131; CDALB 1865-1917; DA; DAB; DAC; DAM MST; DLB 12, 78, 79; MTCW 1; YABC 2
Portillo (y Pacheco), Jose Lopez
See Lopez Portillo (y Pacheco), Jose
Post, Melville Davisson 1869-1930 **TCLC 39**
See also CA 110
Potok, Chaim 1929- .... **CLC 2, 7, 14, 26, 112; DAM NOV**
See also AAYA 15; AITN 1, 2; CA 17-20R; CANR 19, 35, 64; DLB 28, 152; INT CANR-19; MTCW 1; SATA 33
Potter, (Helen) Beatrix 1866-1943
See Webb, (Martha) Beatrice (Potter)
See also MAICYA
Potter, Dennis (Christopher George) 1935-1994 .... **CLC 58, 86**
See also CA 107; 145; CANR 33, 61; MTCW 1
Pound, Ezra (Weston Loomis) 1885-1972 **CLC 1, 2, 3, 4, 5, 7, 10, 13, 18, 34, 48, 50, 112; DA; DAB; DAC; DAM MST, POET; PC 4; WLC**
See also CA 5-8R; 37-40R; CANR 40; CDALB 1917-1929; DLB 4, 45, 63; DLBD 15; MTCW 1
Povod, Reinaldo 1959-1994 ....**CLC 44**
See also CA 136; 146
Powell, Adam Clayton, Jr. 1908-1972 **CLC 89; BLC 3; DAM MULT**
See also BW 1; CA 102; 33-36R
Powell, Anthony (Dymoke) 1905- **CLC 1, 3, 7, 9, 10, 31**
See also CA 1-4R; CANR 1, 32, 62; CDBLB 1945-1960; DLB 15; MTCW 1
Powell, Dawn 1897-1965 .... **CLC 66**
See also CA 5-8R; DLBY 97
Powell, Padgett 1952- .... **CLC 34**
See also CA 126; CANR 63

Radnoti, Miklos 1909-1944 ...... **TCLC 16**
See also CA 118
Rado, James 1939- .... **CLC 17**
See also CA 105
Radvanyi, Netty 1900-1983
See Seghers, Anna
See also CA 85-88; 110
Rae, Ben
See Griffiths, Trevor
Raeburn, John (Hay) 1941- .... **CLC 34**
See also CA 57-60
Ragni, Gerome 1942-1991 .... **CLC 17**
See also CA 105; 134
Rahv, Philip 1908-1973 .... **CLC 24**
See also Greenberg, Ivan
See also DLB 137
Raimund, Ferdinand Jakob 1790-1836
NCLC 69
See also DLB 90
Raine, Craig 1944- .... **CLC 32, 103**
See also CA 108; CANR 29, 51; DLB 40
Raine, Kathleen (Jessie) 1908-...**CLC 7, 45**
See also CA 85-88; CANR 46; DLB 20;
MTCW 1
Rainis, Janis 1865-1929 .... **TCLC 29**
See also CA 170
Rakosi, Carl 1903- .... **CLC 47**
See also Rawley, Callman
See also CAAS 5; DLB 193
Raleigh, Richard
See Lovecraft, H(oward) P(hillips)
Raleigh, Sir Walter 1554(?)-1618...**LC 31, 39**
See also CDBLB Before 1660; DLB 172
Rallentando, H. P.
See Sayers, Dorothy L(eigh)
Ramal, Walter
See de la Mare, Walter (John)
Ramana Maharshi 1879-1950...**TCLC 84**
Ramon, Juan
See Jimenez (Mantecon), Juan Ramon
Ramos, Graciliano 1892-1953 .... **TCLC 32**
See also CA 167
Rampersad, Arnold 1941- .... **CLC 44**
See also BW 2; CA 127; 133; DLB 111; INT
133
Rampling, Anne
See Rice, Anne
Ramsay, Allan 1684(?)-1758 .... **LC 29**
See also DLB 95
Ramuz, Charles-Ferdinand 1878-1947
TCLC 33
See also CA 165
Rand, Ayn 1905-1982...**CLC 3, 30, 44, 79;
DA; DAC; DAM MST, NOV, POP;
WLC**
See also AAYA 10; CA 13-16R; 105; CANR
27, 73; MTCW 1
Randall, Dudley (Felker) 1914-...**CLC 1;
BLC 3; DAM MULT**
See also BW 1; CA 25-28R; CANR 23; DLB
41
Randall, Robert
See Silverberg, Robert
Ranger, Ken
See Creasey, John
Ransom, John Crowe 1888-1974... **C L C
2, 4, 5, 11, 24; DAM POET**
See also CA 5-8R; 49-52; CANR 6, 34; DLB
45, 63; MTCW 1
Rao, Raja 1909- ...... **CLC 25, 56; DAM NOV**
See also CA 73-76; CANR 51; MTCW 1

Raphael, Frederic (Michael) 1931-
CLC 2, 14
See also CA 1-4R; CANR 1; DLB 14
Ratcliffe, James P.
See Mencken, H(enry) L(ouis)
Rathbone, Julian 1935- .... **CLC 41**
See also CA 101; CANR 34, 73
Rattigan, Terence (Mervyn) 1911-1977
CLC 7; DAM DRAM
See also CA 85-88; 73-76; CDBLB 1945-
1960; DLB 13; MTCW 1
Ratushinskaya, Irina 1954- ....**CLC 54**
See also CA 129; CANR 68
Raven, Simon (Arthur Noel) 1927-...**CLC 14**
See also CA 81-84
Ravenna, Michael
See Welty, Eudora
Rawley, Callman 1903-
See Rakosi, Carl
See also CA 21-24R; CANR 12, 32
Rawlings, Marjorie Kinnan 1896-1953
TCLC 4
See also AAYA 20; CA 104; 137; CANR 74;
DLB 9, 22, 102; DLBD 17; JRDA; MAICYA;
SATA 100; YABC 1
Ray, Satyajit 1921-1992 ... **CLC 16, 76; DAM
MULT**
See also CA 114; 137
Read, Herbert Edward 1893-1968 ..... **CLC 4**
See also CA 85-88; 25-28R; DLB 20, 149
Read, Piers Paul 1941- .... **CLC 4, 10, 25**
See also CA 21-24R; CANR 38; DLB 14; SATA
21
Reade, Charles 1814-1884 .... **NCLC 2, 74**
See also DLB 21
Reade, Hamish
See Gray, Simon (James Holliday)
Reading, Peter 1946- .... **CLC 47**
See also CA 103; CANR 46; DLB 40
Reaney, James 1926-...**CLC 13; DAC;
DAM MST**
See also CA 41-44R; CAAS 15; CANR 42; DLB
68; SATA 43
Rebreanu, Liviu 1885-1944 ...... **TCLC 28**
See also CA 165
Rechy, John (Francisco) 1934-...**CLC 1, 7,
14, 18, 107; DAM MULT; HLC**
See also CA 5-8R; CAAS 4; CANR 6, 32, 64;
DLB 122; DLBY 82; HW; INT CANR-6
Redcam, Tom 1870-1933 .... **TCLC 25**
Reddin, Keith ....**CLC 67**
Redgrove, Peter (William) 1932-...**CLC 6,
41**
See also CA 1-4R; CANR 3, 39; DLB 40
Redmon, Anne ....**CLC 22**
See also Nightingale, Anne Redmon
See also DLBY 86
Reed, Eliot
See Ambler, Eric
Reed, Ishmael 1938-...**CLC 2, 3, 5, 6, 13,
32, 60; BLC 3; DAM MULT**
See also BW 2; CA 21-24R; CANR 25, 48, 74;
DLB 2, 5, 33, 169; DLBD 8; MTCW 1
Reed, John (Silas) 1887-1920 .... **TCLC 9**
See also CA 106
Reed, Lou .... **CLC 21**
See also Firbank, Louis
Reeve, Clara 1729-1807 .... **NCLC 19**
See also DLB 39
Reich, Wilhelm 1897-1957 .... **TCLC 57**
Reid, Christopher (John) 1949- ....**CLC 33**
See also CA 140; DLB 40

Reid, Desmond
See Moorcock, Michael (John)
Reid Banks, Lynne 1929-
See Banks, Lynne Reid
See also CA 1-4R; CANR 6, 22, 38; CLR 24;
JRDA; MAICYA; SATA 22, 75
Reilly, William K.
See Creasey, John
Reiner, Max
See Caldwell, (Janet Miriam) Taylor (Hol-
land)
Reis, Ricardo
See Pessoa, Fernando (Antonio Nogueira)
Remarque, Erich Maria 1898-1970...**CLC
21; DA; DAB; DAC; DAM MST, NOV**
See also AAYA 27; CA 77-80; 29-32R; DLB
56; MTCW 1
Remington, Frederic 1861-1909 .... **TCLC 89**
See also CA 108; 169; DLB 12, 186, 188;
SATA 41
Remizov, A.
See Remizov, Aleksei (Mikhailovich)
Remizov, A. M.
See Remizov, Aleksei (Mikhailovich)
Remizov, Aleksei (Mikhailovich) 1877-
1957 ....**TCLC 27**
See also CA 125; 133
Renan, Joseph Ernest 1823-1892
NCLC 26
Renard, Jules 1864-1910 .... **TCLC 17**
See also CA 117
Renault, Mary .... **CLC 3, 11, 17**
See also Challans, Mary
See also DLBY 83
Rendell, Ruth (Barbara) 1930-...**CLC 28,
48; DAM POP**
See also Vine, Barbara
See also CA 109; CANR 32, 52, 74; DLB 87;
INT CANR-32; MTCW 1
Renoir, Jean 1894-1979 .... **CLC 20**
See also CA 129; 85-88
Resnais, Alain 1922- .... **CLC 16**
Reverdy, Pierre 1889-1960 .... **CLC 53**
See also CA 97-100; 89-92
Rexroth, Kenneth 1905-1982...**CLC 1, 2,
6, 11, 22, 49, 112; DAM POET; PC 20**
See also CA 5-8R; 107; CANR 14, 34, 63;
CDALB 1941-1968; DLB 16, 48, 165;
DLBY 82; INT CANR-14; MTCW 1
Reyes, Alfonso 1889-1959 .... **TCLC 33**
See also CA 131; HW
Reyes y Basoalto, Ricardo Eliecer Neftali
See Neruda, Pablo
Reymont, Wladyslaw (Stanislaw) 1868(?)-1925
TCLC 5
See also CA 104
Reynolds, Jonathan 1942- .... **CLC 6, 38**
See also CA 65-68; CANR 28
Reynolds, Joshua 1723-1792 .... **LC 15**
See also DLB 104
Reynolds, Michael Shane 1937- .... **CLC 44**
See also CA 65-68; CANR 9
Reznikoff, Charles 1894-1976 .... **CLC 9**
See also CA 33-36; 61-64; CAP 2; DLB 28, 45
Rezzori (d'Arezzo), Gregor von 1914-1998
CLC 25
See also CA 122; 136; 167
Rhine, Richard
See Silverstein, Alvin
Rhodes, Eugene Manlove 1869-1934
TCLC 53

Rhodius, Apollonius c. 3rd cent. B.C.-
CMLC 28
See also DLB 176

R'hoone
See Balzac, Honore de

Rhys, Jean 1890(?)-1979...CLC 2, 4, 6, 14,
19, 51; DAM NOV; SSC 21
See also CA 25-28R; 85-88; CANR 35, 62;
CDBLB 1945-1960; DLB 36, 117, 162;
MTCW 1

Ribeiro, Darcy 1922-1997 .... CLC 34
See also CA 33-36R; 156

Ribeiro, Joao Ubaldo (Osorio Pimentel)
1941- .... CLC 10, 67
See also CA 81-84

Ribman, Ronald (Burt) 1932- .... CLC 7
See also CA 21-24R; CANR 46

Ricci, Nino 1959- .... CLC 70
See also CA 137

Rice, Anne 1941-............ CLC 41; DAM POP
See also AAYA 9; BEST 89:2; CA 65-68; CANR
12, 36, 53, 74

Rice, Elmer (Leopold) 1892-1967...CLC 7,
49; DAM DRAM
See also CA 21-22; 25-28R; CAP 2; DLB 4, 7;
MTCW 1

Rice, Tim(othy Miles Bindon) 1944-
CLC 21
See also CA 103; CANR 46

Rich, Adrienne (Cecile) 1929-...CLC 3, 6,
7, 11, 18, 36, 73, 76; DAM POET; PC 5
See also CA 9-12R; CANR 20, 53, 74; DLB
5, 67; MTCW 1

Rich, Barbara
See Graves, Robert (von Ranke)

Rich, Robert
See Trumbo, Dalton

Richard, Keith .... CLC 17
See also Richards, Keith

Richards, David Adams 1950-...CLC 59;
DAC
See also CA 93-96; CANR 60; DLB 53

Richards, I(vor) A(rmstrong) 1893-1979
CLC 14, 24
See also CA 41-44R; 89-92; CANR 34, 74;
DLB 27

Richards, Keith 1943-
See Richard, Keith
See also CA 107

Richardson, Anne
See Roiphe, Anne (Richardson)

Richardson, Dorothy Miller 1873-1957
TCLC 3
See also CA 104; DLB 36

Richardson, Ethel Florence (Lindesay) 1870-
1946
See Richardson, Henry Handel
See also CA 105

Richardson, Henry Handel .... TCLC 4
See also Richardson, Ethel Florence (Lindesay)
See also DLB 197

Richardson, John 1796-1852...NCLC 55;
DAC
See also DLB 99

Richardson, Samuel 1689-1761 .. LC 1,
44; DA; DAB; DAC; DAM MST, NOV;
WLC
See also CDBLB 1660-1789; DLB 39

Richler, Mordecai 1931-...CLC 3, 5, 9, 13,
18, 46, 70; DAC; DAM MST, NOV
See also AITN 1; CA 65-68; CANR 31, 62; CLR
17; DLB 53; MAICYA; MTCW 1; SATA 44,
98; SATA-Brief 27

Richter, Conrad (Michael) 1890-1968
CLC 30
See also AAYA 21; CA 5-8R; 25-28R; CANR
23; DLB 9; MTCW 1; SATA 3

Ricostranza, Tom
See Ellis, Trey

Riddell, Charlotte 1832-1906 .. TCLC 40
See also CA 165; DLB 156

Riding, Laura .... CLC 3, 7
See also Jackson, Laura (Riding)

Riefenstahl, Berta Helene Amalia 1902-
See Riefenstahl, Leni
See also CA 108

Riefenstahl, Leni .... CLC 16
See also Riefenstahl, Berta Helene
Amalia

Riffe, Ernest
See Bergman, (Ernst) Ingmar

Riggs, (Rolla) Lynn 1899-1954 .... TCLC 56;
DAM MULT
See also CA 144; DLB 175; NNAL

Riis, Jacob A(ugust) 1849-1914 ..... TCLC 80
See also CA 113; 168; DLB 23

Riley, James Whitcomb 1849-1916
TCLC 51; DAM POET
See also CA 118; 137; MAICYA; SATA 17

Riley, Tex
See Creasey, John

Rilke, Rainer Maria 1875-1926...TCLC 1,
6, 19; DAM POET; PC 2
See also CA 104; 132; CANR 62; DLB 81;
MTCW 1

Rimbaud, (Jean Nicolas) Arthur 1854-1891
NCLC 4, 35; DA; DAB; DAC; DAM
MST, POET; PC 3; WLC

Rinehart, Mary Roberts 1876-1958
TCLC 52
See also CA 108; 166

Ringmaster, The
See Mencken, H(enry) L(ouis)

Ringwood, Gwen(dolyn Margaret) Pharis
1910-1984 ....CLC 48
See also CA 148; 112; DLB 88

Rio, Michel 19(?)- .... CLC 43

Ritsos, Giannes
See Ritsos, Yannis

Ritsos, Yannis 1909-1990 .... CLC 6, 13, 31
See also CA 77-80; 133; CANR 39, 61; MTCW
1

Ritter, Erika 1948(?)- .... CLC 52

Rivera, Jose Eustasio 1889-1928
TCLC 35
See also CA 162; HW

Rivers, Conrad Kent 1933-1968...CLC 1
See also BW 1; CA 85-88; DLB 41

Rivers, Elfrida
See Bradley, Marion Zimmer

Riverside, John
See Heinlein, Robert A(nson)

Rizal, Jose 1861-1896 .... NCLC 27

Roa Bastos, Augusto (Antonio) 1917-
CLC 45; DAM MULT; HLC
See also CA 131; DLB 113; HW

Robbe-Grillet, Alain 1922-...CLC 1, 2, 4,
6, 8, 10, 14, 43
See also CA 9-12R; CANR 33, 65; DLB 83;
MTCW 1

Robbins, Harold 1916-1997...CLC 5; DAM
NOV
See also CA 73-76; 162; CANR 26, 54;
MTCW 1

Robbins, Thomas Eugene 1936-
See Robbins, Tom
See also CA 81-84; CANR 29, 59; DAM
NOV, POP; MTCW 1

Robbins, Tom .... CLC 9, 32, 64
See also Robbins, Thomas Eugene
See also BEST 90:3; DLBY 80

Robbins, Trina 1938- .... CLC 21
See also CA 128

Roberts, Charles G(eorge) D(ouglas)
1860-1943 .... TCLC 8
See also CA 105; CLR 33; DLB 92; SATA
88; SATA-Brief 29

Roberts, Elizabeth Madox 1886-1941
TCLC 68
See also CA 111; 166; DLB 9, 54, 102; SATA
33; SATA-Brief 27

Roberts, Kate 1891-1985 .... CLC 15
See also CA 107; 116

Roberts, Keith (John Kingston) 1935-
CLC 14
See also CA 25-28R; CANR 46

Roberts, Kenneth (Lewis) 1885-1957TCLC 23
See also CA 109; DLB 9

Roberts, Michele (B.) 1949-............. CLC 48
See also CA 115; CANR 58

Robertson, Ellis
See Ellison, Harlan (Jay); Silverberg, Robert

Robertson, Thomas William 1829-1871
NCLC 35; DAM DRAM

Robeson, Kenneth
See Dent, Lester

Robinson, Edwin Arlington 1869-1935
TCLC 5; DA; DAC; DAM MST, POET;
PC 1
See also CA 104; 133; CDALB 1865-1917;
DLB 54; MTCW 1

Robinson, Henry Crabb 1775-1867
NCLC 15
See also DLB 107

Robinson, Jill 1936- .... CLC 10
See also CA 102; INT 102

Robinson, Kim Stanley 1952-........... CLC 34
See also AAYA 26; CA 126

Robinson, Lloyd
See Silverberg, Robert

Robinson, Marilynne 1944-............. CLC 25
See also CA 116

Robinson, Smokey .... CLC 21
See also Robinson, William, Jr.

Robinson, William, Jr. 1940-
See Robinson, Smokey
See also CA 116

Robison, Mary 1949- .... CLC 42, 98
See also CA 113; 116; DLB 130; INT 116

Rod, Edouard 1857-1910 .... TCLC 52

Roddenberry, Eugene Wesley 1921-1991
See Roddenberry, Gene
See also CA 110; 135; CANR 37; SATA 45;
SATA-Obit 69

Roddenberry, Gene .... CLC 17
See also Roddenberry, Eugene Wesley
See also AAYA 5; SATA-Obit 69

Rodgers, Mary 1931- .... CLC 12
See also CA 49-52; CANR 8, 55; CLR 20; INT
CANR-8; JRDA; MAICYA; SATA 8

Rodgers, W(illiam) R(obert) 1909-1969CLC 7
See also CA 85-88; DLB 20

Rodman, Eric
See Silverberg, Robert

Rodman, Howard 1920(?)-1985 .... CLC 65
See also CA 118

Rodman, Maia
See Wojciechowska, Maia (Teresa)
Rodriguez, Claudio 1934- .... **CLC 10**
See also DLB 134
Roelvaag, O(le) E(dvart) 1876-1931
TCLC 17
See also CA 117; 171; DLB 9
Roethke, Theodore (Huebner) 1908-1963
**CLC 1, 3, 8, 11, 19, 46, 101; DAM
POET; PC 15**
See also CA 81-84; CABS 2; CDALB 1941-
1968; DLB 5; MTCW 1
Rogers, Samuel 1763-1855 .... **NCLC 69**
See also DLB 93
Rogers, Thomas Hunton 1927-...**CLC 57**
See also CA 89-92; INT 89-92
Rogers, Will(iam Penn Adair) 1879-1935
TCLC 8, 71; DAM MULT
See also CA 105; 144; DLB 11; NNAL
Rogin, Gilbert 1929- .... **CLC 18**
See also CA 65-68; CANR 15
Rohan, Koda .... **TCLC 22**
See also Koda Shigeyuki
Rohlfs, Anna Katharine Green
See Green, Anna Katharine
Rohmer, Eric .... **CLC 16**
See also Scherer, Jean-Marie Maurice
Rohmer, Sax .... **TCLC 28**
See also Ward, Arthur Henry Sarsfield
See also DLB 70
Roiphe, Anne (Richardson) 1935-
CLC 3, 9
See also CA 89-92; CANR 45, 73; DLBY 80;
INT 89-92
Rojas, Fernando de 1465-1541 .... **LC 23**
**Rolfe, Frederick (William Serafino Austin
Lewis Mary)** 1860-1913 .... **TCLC 12**
See also CA 107; DLB 34, 156
Rolland, Romain 1866-1944 .... **TCLC 23**
See also CA 118; DLB 65
Rolle, Richard c. 1300-c. 1349...**CMLC 21**
See also DLB 146
Rolvaag, O(le) E(dvart)
See Roelvaag, O(le) E(dvart)
Romain Arnaud, Saint
See Aragon, Louis
Romains, Jules 1885-1972 .... **CLC 7**
See also CA 85-88; CANR 34; DLB 65; MTCW
1
Romero, Jose Ruben 1890-1952 ..... **TCLC 14**
See also CA 114; 131; HW
Ronsard, Pierre de 1524-1585 ..**LC 6;
PC 11**
Rooke, Leon 1934- ... **CLC 25, 34; DAM
POP**
See also CA 25-28R; CANR 23, 53
Roosevelt, Theodore 1858-1919 ..... **TCLC 69**
See also CA 115; 170; DLB 47, 186
Roper, William 1498-1578 .... **LC 10**
Roquelaure, A. N.
See Rice, Anne
Rosa, Joao Guimaraes 1908-1967 ... **CLC 23**
See also CA 89-92; DLB 113
Rose, Wendy 1948-...**CLC 85; DAM MULT;
PC 13**
See also CA 53-56; CANR 5, 51; DLB 175;
NNAL; SATA 12
Rosen, R. D.
See Rosen, Richard (Dean)
Rosen, Richard (Dean) 1949- .... **CLC 39**
See also CA 77-80; CANR 62; INT CANR-30
Rosenberg, Isaac 1890-1918 .... **TCLC 12**
See also CA 107; DLB 20

Rosenblatt, Joe .... **CLC 15**
See also Rosenblatt, Joseph
Rosenblatt, Joseph 1933-
See Rosenblatt, Joe
See also CA 89-92; INT 89-92
Rosenfeld, Samuel
See Tzara, Tristan
Rosenstock, Sami
See Tzara, Tristan
Rosenstock, Samuel
See Tzara, Tristan
Rosenthal, M(acha) L(ouis) 1917-1996
CLC 28
See also CA 1-4R; 152; CAAS 6; CANR 4,
51; DLB 5; SATA 59
Ross, Barnaby
See Dannay, Frederic
Ross, Bernard L.
See Follett, Ken(neth Martin)
Ross, J. H.
See Lawrence, T(homas) E(dward)
Ross, John Hume
See Lawrence, T(homas) E(dward)
Ross, Martin
See Martin, Violet Florence
See also DLB 135
Ross, (James) Sinclair 1908-...**CLC 13;
DAC; DAM MST; SSC 24**
See also CA 73-76; DLB 88
Rossetti, Christina (Georgina) 1830-1894
**NCLC 2, 50, 66; DA; DAB; DAC; DAM
MST, POET; PC 7; WLC**
See also DLB 35, 163; MAICYA; SATA 20
Rossetti, Dante Gabriel 1828-1882
**NCLC 4; DA; DAB; DAC; DAM MST,
POET; WLC**
See also CDBLB 1832-1890; DLB 35
Rossner, Judith (Perelman) 1935-...**CLC
6, 9, 29**
See also AITN 2; BEST 90:3; CA 17-20R;
CANR 18, 51, 73; DLB 6; INT CANR-18;
MTCW 1
Rostand, Edmond (Eugene Alexis) 1868-1918
**TCLC 6, 37; DA; DAB; DAC; DAM
DRAM, MST; DC 10**
See also CA 104; 126; DLB 192; MTCW 1
Roth, Henry 1906-1995 ..... **CLC 2, 6, 11, 104**
See also CA 11-12; 149; CANR 38, 63; CAP 1;
DLB 28; MTCW 1
Roth, Philip (Milton) 1933-...**CLC 1, 2, 3,
4, 6, 9, 15, 22, 31, 47, 66, 86; DA; DAB;
DAC; DAM MST, NOV, POP; SSC 26;
WLC**
See also BEST 90:3; CA 1-4R; CANR 1, 22,
36, 55; CDALB 1968-1988; DLB 2, 28, 173;
DLBY 82; MTCW 1
Rothenberg, Jerome 1931- .... **CLC 6, 57**
See also CA 45-48; CANR 1; DLB 5, 193
Roumain, Jacques (Jean Baptiste) 1907-1944
TCLC 19; BLC 3; DAM MULT
See also BW 1; CA 117; 125
Rourke, Constance (Mayfield) 1885-1941
TCLC 12
See also CA 107; YABC 1
Rousseau, Jean-Baptiste 1671-1741 ..... **LC 9**
Rousseau, Jean-Jacques 1712-1778
**LC 14, 36; DA; DAB; DAC; DAM MST;
WLC**
Roussel, Raymond 1877-1933 .... **TCLC 20**
See also CA 117
Rovit, Earl (Herbert) 1927- .... **CLC 7**
See also CA 5-8R; CANR 12

Rowe, Elizabeth Singer 1674-1737
LC 44
See also DLB 39, 95
Rowe, Nicholas 1674-1718 .... **LC 8**
See also DLB 84
Rowley, Ames Dorrance
See Lovecraft, H(oward) P(hillips)
Rowson, Susanna Haswell 1762(?)-1824
NCLC 5, 69
See also DLB 37, 200
Roy, Arundhati 1960(?)- .... **CLC 109**
See also CA 163; DLBY 97
Roy, Gabrielle 1909-1983 ...**CLC 10, 14;
DAB; DAC; DAM MST**
See also CA 53-56; 110; CANR 5, 61; DLB 68;
MTCW 1
Royko, Mike 1932-1997 .... **CLC 109**
See also CA 89-92; 157; CANR 26
Rozewicz, Tadeusz 1921- ...**CLC 9, 23; DAM
POET**
See also CA 108; CANR 36, 66; MTCW 1
Ruark, Gibbons 1941- .... **CLC 3**
See also CA 33-36R; CAAS 23; CANR 14,
31, 57; DLB 120
Rubens, Bernice (Ruth) 1923- .... **CLC 19, 31**
See also CA 25-28R; CANR 33, 65; DLB 14;
MTCW 1
Rubin, Harold
See Robbins, Harold
Rudkin, (James) David 1936- .... **CLC 14**
See also CA 89-92; DLB 13
Rudnik, Raphael 1933- .... **CLC 7**
See also CA 29-32R
Ruffian, M.
See Hasek, Jaroslav (Matej Frantisek)
Ruiz, Jose Martinez .... **CLC 11**
See also Martinez Ruiz, Jose
Rukeyser, Muriel 1913-1980...**CLC 6, 10,
15, 27; DAM POET; PC 12**
See also CA 5-8R; 93-96; CANR 26, 60; DLB
48; MTCW 1; SATA-Obit 22
Rule, Jane (Vance) 1931- .... **CLC 27**
See also CA 25-28R; CAAS 18; CANR 12; DLB
60
Rulfo, Juan 1918-1986 .... **CLC 8, 80; DAM
MULT; HLC; SSC 25**
See also CA 85-88; 118; CANR 26; DLB 113;
HW; MTCW 1
Rumi, Jalal al-Din 1297-1373...**CMLC 20**
Runeberg, Johan 1804-1877 ... **NCLC 41**
Runyon, (Alfred) Damon 1884(?)-1946
TCLC 10
See also CA 107; 165; DLB 11, 86, 171
Rush, Norman 1933- .... **CLC 44**
See also CA 121; 126; INT 126
Rushdie, (Ahmed) Salman 1947-....**CLC
23, 31, 55, 100; DAB; DAC; DAM MST,
NOV, POP; WLCS**
See also BEST 89:3; CA 108; 111; CANR 33,
56; DLB 194; INT 111; MTCW 1
Rushforth, Peter (Scott) 1945- .... **CLC 19**
See also CA 101
Ruskin, John 1819-1900 .... **TCLC 63**
See also CA 114; 129; CDBLB 1832-1890;
DLB 55, 163, 190; SATA 24
Russ, Joanna 1937- .... **CLC 15**
See also CANR 11, 31, 65; DLB 8; MTCW 1
Russell, George William 1867-1935
See Baker, Jean H.
See also CA 104; 153; CDBLB 1890-1914;
DAM POET

Shiel, M(atthew) P(hipps) 1865-1947
TCLC **8**
See also Holmes, Gordon
See also CA 106; 160; DLB 153

Shields, Carol 1935-...CLC **91, 113; DAC**
See also CA 81-84; CANR 51, 74

Shields, David 1956- .... CLC **97**
See also CA 124; CANR 48

Shiga, Naoya 1883-1971... CLC **33; SSC 23**
See also CA 101; 33-36R; DLB 180

Shikibu, Murasaki c. 978-c. 1014 ... CMLC **1**

Shilts, Randy 1951-1994 .... CLC **85**
See also AAYA 19; CA 115; 127; 144; CANR 45; INT 127

Shimazaki, Haruki 1872-1943
See Shimazaki Toson
See also CA 105; 134

Shimazaki Toson 1872-1943 ...... TCLC **5**
See also Shimazaki, Haruki
See also DLB 180

Sholokhov, Mikhail (Aleksandrovich) 1905-1984 ....CLC **7, 15**
See also CA 101; 112; MTCW 1; SATA-Obit 36

Shone, Patric
See Hanley, James

Shreve, Susan Richards 1939- .... CLC **23**
See also CA 49-52; CAAS 5; CANR 5, 38, 69; MAICYA; SATA 46, 95; SATA-Brief 41

Shue, Larry 1946-1985 .. CLC **52; DAM DRAM**
See also CA 145; 117

Shu-Jen, Chou 1881-1936
See Lu Hsun
See also CA 104

Shulman, Alix Kates 1932-....CLC **2, 10**
See also CA 29-32R; CANR 43; SATA 7

Shuster, Joe 1914- .... CLC **21**

Shute, Nevil .... CLC **30**
See also Norway, Nevil Shute

Shuttle, Penelope (Diane) 1947- .... CLC **7**
See also CA 93-96; CANR 39; DLB 14, 40

Sidney, Mary 1561-1621 .... LC **19, 39**

Sidney, Sir Philip 1554-1586...LC **19, 39; DA; DAB; DAC; DAM MST, POET**
See also CDBLB Before 1660; DLB 167

Siegel, Jerome 1914-1996 .... CLC **21**
See also CA 116; 169; 151

Siegel, Jerry
See Siegel, Jerome

Sienkiewicz, Henryk (Adam Alexander Pius) 1846-1916 .... TCLC **3**
See also CA 104; 134

Sierra, Gregorio Martinez
See Martinez Sierra, Gregorio

Sierra, Maria (de la O'LeJarraga) Martinez
See Martinez Sierra, Maria (de la O'LeJarraga)

Sigal, Clancy 1926-.............................. CLC **7**
See also CA 1-4R

Sigourney, Lydia Howard (Huntley) 1791-1865
NCLC **21**
See also DLB 1, 42, 73

Siguenza y Gongora, Carlos de 1645-1700
LC **8**

Sigurjonsson, Johann 1880-1919
TCLC **27**
See also CA 170

Sikelianos, Angelos 1884-1951 .... TCLC **39**

Silkin, Jon 1930- .... CLC **2, 6, 43**
See also CA 5-8R; CAAS 5; DLB 27

Silko, Leslie (Marmon) 1948-...CLC **23, 74, 114; DA; DAC; DAM MST, MULT, POP; WLCS**
See also AAYA 14; CA 115; 122; CANR 45, 65; DLB 143, 175; NNAL

Sillanpaa, Frans Eemil 1888-1964 ....CLC **19**
See also CA 129; 93-96; MTCW 1

Sillitoe, Alan 1928-...CLC **1, 3, 6, 10, 19, 57**
See also AITN 1; CA 9-12R; CAAS 2; CANR 8, 26, 55; CDBLB 1960 to Present; DLB 14, 139; MTCW 1; SATA 61

Silone, Ignazio 1900-1978 ....CLC **4**
See also CA 25-28; 81-84; CANR 34; CAP 2; MTCW 1

Silver, Joan Micklin 1935- ....CLC **20**
See also CA 114; 121; INT 121

Silver, Nicholas
See Faust, Frederick (Schiller)

Silverberg, Robert 1935- ..CLC **7; DAM POP**
See also AAYA 24; CA 1-4R; CAAS 3; CANR 1, 20, 36; DLB 8; INT CANR-20; MAICYA; MTCW 1; SATA 13, 91

Silverstein, Alvin 1933- .... CLC **17**
See also CA 49-52; CANR 2; CLR 25; JRDA; MAICYA; SATA 8, 69

Silverstein, Virginia B(arbara Opshelor) 1937-
CLC **17**
See also CA 49-52; CANR 2; CLR 25; JRDA; MAICYA; SATA 8, 69

Sim, Georges
See Simenon, Georges (Jacques Christian)

Simak, Clifford D(onald) 1904-1988
CLC **1, 55**
See also CA 1-4R; 125; CANR 1, 35; DLB 8; MTCW 1; SATA-Obit 56

Simenon, Georges (Jacques Christian) 1903-1989...CLC **1, 2, 3, 8, 18, 47; DAM POP**
See also CA 85-88; 129; CANR 35; DLB 72; DLBY 89; MTCW 1

Simic, Charles 1938-...CLC **6, 9, 22, 49, 68; DAM POET**
See also CA 29-32R; CAAS 4; CANR 12, 33, 52, 61; DLB 105

Simmel, Georg 1858-1918 .... TCLC **64**
See also CA 157

Simmons, Charles (Paul) 1924-...CLC **57**
See also CA 89-92; INT 89-92

Simmons, Dan 1948-.......CLC **44; DAM POP**
See also AAYA 16; CA 138; CANR 53

Simmons, James (Stewart Alexander) 1933-
CLC **43**
See also CA 105; CAAS 21; DLB 40

Simms, William Gilmore 1806-1870
NCLC **3**
See also DLB 3, 30, 59, 73

Simon, Carly 1945- ....CLC **26**
See also CA 105

Simon, Claude 1913-1984 ..CLC **4, 9, 15, 39; DAM NOV**
See also CA 89-92; CANR 33; DLB 83; MTCW 1

Simon, (Marvin) Neil 1927-...CLC **6, 11, 31, 39, 70; DAM DRAM**
See also AITN 1; CA 21-24R; CANR 26, 54; DLB 7; MTCW 1

Simon, Paul (Frederick) 1941(?)-......CLC **17**
See also CA 116; 153

Simonon, Paul 1956(?)- ....CLC **30**

Simpson, Harriette
See Arnow, Harriette (Louisa) Simpson

Simpson, Louis (Aston Marantz) 1923-
CLC **4, 7, 9, 32; DAM POET**
See also CA 1-4R; CAAS 4; CANR 1, 61; DLB 5; MTCW 1

Simpson, Mona (Elizabeth) 1957-
CLC **44**
See also CA 122; 135; CANR 68

Simpson, N(orman) F(rederick) 1919-
CLC **29**
See also CA 13-16R; DLB 13

Sinclair, Andrew (Annandale) 1935-
CLC **2, 14**
See also CA 9-12R; CAAS 5; CANR 14, 38; DLB 14; MTCW 1

Sinclair, Emil
See Hesse, Hermann

Sinclair, Iain 1943- .... CLC **76**
See also CA 132

Sinclair, Iain MacGregor
See Sinclair, Iain

Sinclair, Irene
See Griffith, D(avid Lewelyn) W(ark)

Sinclair, Mary Amelia St. Clair 1865(?)-
1946
See Sinclair, May
See also CA 104

Sinclair, May 1863-1946 .... TCLC **3, 11**
See also Sinclair, Mary Amelia St. Clair
See also CA 166; DLB 36, 135

Sinclair, Roy
See Griffith, D(avid Lewelyn) W(ark)

Sinclair, Upton (Beall) 1878-1968...CLC **1, 11, 15, 63; DA; DAB; DAC; DAM MST, NOV; WLC**
See also CA 5-8R; 25-28R; CANR 7; CDALB 1929-1941; DLB 9; INT CANR-7; MTCW 1; SATA 9

Singer, Isaac
See Singer, Isaac Bashevis

Singer, Isaac Bashevis 1904-1991
CLC **1, 3, 6, 9, 11, 15, 23, 38, 69, 111; DA; DAB; DAC; DAM MST, NOV; SSC 3; WLC**
See also AITN 1, 2; CA 1-4R; 134; CANR 1, 39; CDALB 1941-1968; CLR 1; DLB 6, 28, 52; DLBY 91; JRDA; MAICYA; MTCW 1; SATA 3, 27; SATA-Obit 68

Singer, Israel Joshua 1893-1944
TCLC **33**
See also CA 169

Singh, Khushwant 1915-....................CLC **11**
See also CA 9-12R; CAAS 9; CANR 6

Singleton, Ann
See Benedict, Ruth (Fulton)

Sinjohn, John
See Galsworthy, John

Sinyavsky, Andrei (Donatevich) 1925-1997
CLC **8**
See also CA 85-88; 159

Sirin, V.
See Nabokov, Vladimir (Vladimirovich)

Sissman, L(ouis) E(dward) 1928-1976
CLC **9, 18**
See also CA 21-24R; 65-68; CANR 13; DLB 5

Sisson, C(harles) H(ubert) 1914-....CLC **8**
See also CA 1-4R; CAAS 3; CANR 3, 48; DLB 27

Sitwell, Dame Edith 1887-1964...CLC **2, 9, 67; DAM POET; PC 3**
See also CA 9-12R; CANR 35; CDBLB 1945-1960; DLB 20; MTCW 1

Siwaarmill, H. P.
See Sharp, William

Sjoewall, Maj 1935- .... **CLC 7**
See also CA 65-68; CANR 73
Sjowall, Maj
See Sjoewall, Maj
Skelton, John 1463-1529 .... **PC 25**
Skelton, Robin 1925-1997 .... **CLC 13**
See also AITN 2; CA 5-8R; 160; CAAS 5;
CANR 28; DLB 27, 53
Skolimowski, Jerzy 1938- .... **CLC 20**
See also CA 128
Skram, Amalie (Bertha) 1847-1905
TCLC 25
See also CA 165
Skvorecky, Josef (Vaclav) 1924-...**CLC 15,
39, 69; DAC; DAM NOV**
See also CA 61-64; CAAS 1; CANR 10, 34,
63; MTCW 1
Slade, Bernard .... **CLC 11, 46**
See also Newbound, Bernard Slade
See also CAAS 9; DLB 53
Slaughter, Carolyn 1946- .... **CLC 56**
See also CA 85-88
Slaughter, Frank G(ill) 1908- ... **CLC 29**
See also AITN 2; CA 5-8R; CANR 5; INT
CANR-5
Slavitt, David R(ytman) 1935- ..... **CLC 5, 14**
See also CA 21-24R; CAAS 3; CANR 41; DLB
5, 6
Slesinger, Tess 1905-1945 .... **TCLC 10**
See also CA 107; DLB 102
Slessor, Kenneth 1901-1971 ...... **CLC 14**
See also CA 102; 89-92
Slowacki, Juliusz 1809-1849 .... **NCLC 15**
Smart, Christopher 1722-1771...**LC 3;
DAM POET; PC 13**
See also DLB 109
Smart, Elizabeth 1913-1986 .... **CLC 54**
See also CA 81-84; 118; DLB 88
Smiley, Jane (Graves) 1949-...**CLC 53, 76;
DAM POP**
See also CA 104; CANR 30, 50, 74; INT CANR-
30
Smith, A(rthur) J(ames) M(arshall) 1902-
1980 .... **CLC 15; DAC**
See also CA 1-4R; 102; CANR 4; DLB 88
Smith, Adam 1723-1790 .... **LC 36**
See also DLB 104
Smith, Alexander 1829-1867 .... **NCLC 59**
See also DLB 32, 55
Smith, Anna Deavere 1950- .... **CLC 86**
See also CA 133
Smith, Betty (Wehner) 1896-1972
CLC 19
See also CA 5-8R; 33-36R; DLBY 82; SATA 6
Smith, Charlotte (Turner) 1749-1806
NCLC 23
See also DLB 39, 109
Smith, Clark Ashton 1893-1961 .... **CLC 43**
See also CA 143
Smith, Dave .... **CLC 22, 42**
See also Smith, David (Jeddie)
See also CAAS 7; DLB 5
Smith, David (Jeddie) 1942-
See Smith, Dave
See also CA 49-52; CANR 1, 59; DAM POET
Smith, Florence Margaret 1902-1971
See Smith, Stevie
See also CA 17-18; 29-32R; CANR 35; CAP 2;
DAM POET; MTCW 1
Smith, Iain Crichton 1928-1998 ...... **CLC 64**
See also CA 21-24R; 171; DLB 40, 139
Smith, John 1580(?)-1631 .... **LC 9**
See also DLB 24, 30

Smith, Johnston
See Crane, Stephen (Townley)
Smith, Joseph, Jr. 1805-1844 .... **NCLC 53**
Smith, Lee 1944- .... **CLC 25, 73**
See also CA 114; 119; CANR 46; DLB 143;
DLBY 83; INT 119
Smith, Martin
See Smith, Martin Cruz
Smith, Martin Cruz 1942-...**CLC 25; DAM
MULT, POP**
See also BEST 89:4; CA 85-88; CANR 6, 23,
43, 65; INT CANR-23; NNAL
Smith, Mary-Ann Tirone 1944-...**CLC 39**
See also CA 118; 136
Smith, Patti 1946- ....**CLC 12**
See also CA 93-96; CANR 63
Smith, Pauline (Urmson) 1882-1959
TCLC 25
Smith, Rosamond
See Oates, Joyce Carol
Smith, Sheila Kaye
See Kaye-Smith, Sheila
Smith, Stevie .... **CLC 3, 8, 25, 44; PC 12**
See also Smith, Florence Margaret
See also DLB 20
Smith, Wilbur (Addison) 1933-.........**CLC 33**
See also CA 13-16R; CANR 7, 46, 66; MTCW
1
Smith, William Jay 1918-.............**CLC 6**
See also CA 5-8R; CANR 44; DLB 5;
MAICYA; SAAS 22; SATA 2, 68
Smith, Woodrow Wilson
See Kuttner, Henry
Smolenskin, Peretz 1842-1885 .... **NCLC 30**
Smollett, Tobias (George) 1721-1771
LC 2, 46
See also CDBLB 1660-1789; DLB 39, 104
Snodgrass, W(illiam) D(e Witt) 1926-
CLC 2, 6, 10, 18, 68; DAM POET
See also CA 1-4R; CANR 6, 36, 65; DLB 5;
MTCW 1
Snow, C(harles) P(ercy) 1905-1980
CLC 1, 4, 6, 9, 13, 19; DAM NOV
See also CA 5-8R; 101; CANR 28; CDBLB
1945-1960; DLB 15, 77; DLBD 17; MTCW
1
Snow, Frances Compton
See Adams, Henry (Brooks)
Snyder, Gary (Sherman) 1930-...**CLC 1,
2, 5, 9, 32; DAM POET; PC 21**
See also CA 17-20R; CANR 30, 60; DLB 5,
16, 165
Snyder, Zilpha Keatley 1927-.... **CLC 17**
See also AAYA 15; CA 9-12R; CANR 38;
CLR 31; JRDA; MAICYA; SAAS 2; SATA
1, 28, 75
Soares, Bernardo
See Pessoa, Fernando (Antonio Nogueira)
Sobh, A.
See Shamlu, Ahmad
Sobol, Joshua ....**CLC 60**
Socrates 469B.C.-399B.C. .... **CMLC 27**
Soderberg, Hjalmar 1869-1941 ..... **TCLC 39**
Sodergran, Edith (Irene)
See Soedergran, Edith (Irene)
Soedergran, Edith (Irene) 1892-1923
TCLC 31
Softly, Edgar
See Lovecraft, H(oward) P(hillips)
Softly, Edward
See Lovecraft, H(oward) P(hillips)
Sokolov, Raymond 1941- ....**CLC 7**
See also CA 85-88

Solo, Jay
See Ellison, Harlan (Jay)
Sologub, Fyodor .... **TCLC 9**
See also Teternikov, Fyodor Kuzmich
Solomons, Ikey Esquir
See Thackeray, William Makepeace
Solomos, Dionysios 1798-1857**NCLC 15**
Solwoska, Mara
See French, Marilyn
Solzhenitsyn, Aleksandr I(sayevich)
1918-...**CLC 1, 2, 4, 7, 9, 10, 18, 26, 34,
78; DA; DAB; DAC; DAM MST, NOV;
SSC 32; WLC**
See also AITN 1; CA 69-72; CANR 40, 65;
MTCW 1
Somers, Jane
See Lessing, Doris (May)
Somerville, Edith 1858-1949 ... **TCLC 51**
See also DLB 135
Somerville & Ross
See Martin, Violet Florence; Somerville, Edith
Sommer, Scott 1951- .... **CLC 25**
See also CA 106
Sondheim, Stephen (Joshua) 1930-
CLC 30, 39; DAM DRAM
See also AAYA 11; CA 103; CANR 47, 68
Song, Cathy 1955- .... **PC 21**
See also CA 154; DLB 169
Sontag, Susan 1933-...**CLC 1, 2, 10, 13, 31,
105; DAM POP**
See also CA 17-20R; CANR 25, 51, 74; DLB
2, 67; MTCW 1
Sophocles 496(?)B.C.-406(?)B.C. .. **CMLC 2;
DA; DAB; DAC; DAM DRAM, MST; DC
1; WLCS**
See also DLB 176
Sordello 1189-1269 .... **CMLC 15**
Sorel, Julia
See Drexler, Rosalyn
Sorrentino, Gilbert 1929-...**CLC 3, 7, 14,
22, 40**
See also CA 77-80; CANR 14, 33; DLB 5,
173; DLBY 80; INT CANR-14
Soto, Gary 1952-...**CLC 32, 80; DAM MULT;
HLC**
See also AAYA 10; CA 119; 125; CANR 50,
74; CLR 38; DLB 82; HW; INT 125; JRDA;
SATA 80
Soupault, Philippe 1897-1990 ... **CLC 68**
See also CA 116; 147; 131
Souster, (Holmes) Raymond 1921-
CLC 5, 14; DAC; DAM POET
See also CA 13-16R; CAAS 14; CANR 13,
29, 53; DLB 88; SATA 63
Southern, Terry 1924(?)-1995 ....**CLC 7**
See also CA 1-4R; 150; CANR 1, 55; DLB 2
Southey, Robert 1774-1843 .... **NCLC 8**
See also DLB 93, 107, 142; SATA 54
Southworth, Emma Dorothy Eliza Nevitte
1819-1899 .... **NCLC 26**
Souza, Ernest
See Scott, Evelyn
Soyinka, Wole 1934-... **CLC 3, 5, 14, 36,
44; BLC 3; DA; DAB; DAC; DAM
DRAM, MST, MULT; DC 2; WLC**
See also BW 2; CA 13-16R; CANR 27, 39; DLB
125; MTCW 1
Spackman, W(illiam) M(ode) 1905-1990
CLC 46
See also CA 81-84; 132
Spacks, Barry (Bernard) 1931-...**CLC 14**
See also CA 154; CANR 33; DLB 105
Spanidou, Irini 1946- .... **CLC 44**

Spark, Muriel (Sarah) 1918-...**CLC 2, 3, 5, 8, 13, 18, 40, 94; DAB; DAC; DAM MST, NOV; SSC 10**
See also CA 5-8R; CANR 12, 36; CDBLB 1945-1960; DLB 15, 139; INT CANR-12; MTCW 1

Spaulding, Douglas
See Bradbury, Ray (Douglas)

Spaulding, Leonard
See Bradbury, Ray (Douglas)

Spence, J. A. D.
See Eliot, T(homas) S(tearns)

Spencer, Elizabeth 1921- .... **CLC 22**
See also CA 13-16R; CANR 32, 65; DLB 6; MTCW 1; SATA 14

Spencer, Leonard G.
See Silverberg, Robert

Spencer, Scott 1945-..................... **CLC 30**
See also CA 113; CANR 51; DLBY 86

Spender, Stephen (Harold) 1909-1995
CLC 1, 2, 5, 10, 41, 91; DAM POET
See also CA 9-12R; 149; CANR 31, 54; CDBLB 1945-1960; DLB 20; MTCW 1

Spengler, Oswald (Arnold Gottfried) 1880-1936
TCLC 25
See also CA 118

Spenser, Edmund 1552(?)-1599...**LC 5, 39; DA; DAB; DAC; DAM MST, POET; PC 8; WLC**
See also CDBLB Before 1660; DLB 167

Spicer, Jack 1925-1965...**CLC 8, 18, 72; DAM POET**
See also CA 85-88; DLB 5, 16, 193

Spiegelman, Art 1948- .... **CLC 76**
See also AAYA 10; CA 125; CANR 41, 55, 74

Spielberg, Peter 1929-.....................**CLC 6**
See also CA 5-8R; CANR 4, 48; DLBY 81

Spielberg, Steven 1947-..................... **CLC 20**
See also AAYA 8, 24; CA 77-80; CANR 32; SATA 32

Spillane, Frank Morrison 1918-
See Spillane, Mickey
See also CA 25-28R; CANR 28, 63; MTCW 1; SATA 66

Spillane, Mickey .... **CLC 3, 13**
See also Spillane, Frank Morrison

Spinoza, Benedictus de 1632-1677...**LC 9**

Spinrad, Norman (Richard) 1940-
CLC 46
See also CA 37-40R; CAAS 19; CANR 20; DLB 8; INT CANR-20

Spitteler, Carl (Friedrich Georg) 1845-1924
TCLC 12
See also CA 109; DLB 129

Spivack, Kathleen (Romola Drucker) 1938-
CLC 6
See also CA 49-52

Spoto, Donald 1941- .... **CLC 39**
See also CA 65-68; CANR 11, 57

Springsteen, Bruce (F.) 1949- .... **CLC 17**
See also CA 111

Spurling, Hilary 1940-...................... **CLC 34**
See also CA 104; CANR 25, 52

Spyker, John Howland
See Elman, Richard (Martin)

Squires, (James) Radcliffe 1917-1993
CLC 51
See also CA 1-4R; 140; CANR 6, 21

Srivastava, Dhanpat Rai 1880(?)-1936
See Premchand
See also CA 118

Stacy, Donald
See Pohl, Frederik

Stael, Germaine de 1766-1817
See Stael-Holstein, Anne Louise Germaine Necker Baronn
See also DLB 119

Stael-Holstein, Anne Louise Germaine Necker Baronn 1766-1817 .... **NCLC 3**
See also Stael, Germaine de
See also DLB 192

Stafford, Jean 1915-1979...**CLC 4, 7, 19, 68; SSC 26**
See also CA 1-4R; 85-88; CANR 3, 65; DLB 2, 173; MTCW 1; SATA-Obit 22

Stafford, William (Edgar) 1914-1993
CLC 4, 7, 29; DAM POET
See also CA 5-8R; 142; CAAS 3; CANR 5, 22; DLB 5; INT CANR-22

Stagnelius, Eric Johan 1793-1823
NCLC 61

Staines, Trevor
See Brunner, John (Kilian Houston)

Stairs, Gordon
See Austin, Mary (Hunter)

Stannard, Martin 1947- .... **CLC 44**
See also CA 142; DLB 155

Stanton, Elizabeth Cady 1815-1902**TCLC 73**
See also CA 171; DLB 79

Stanton, Maura 1946-.....................**CLC 9**
See also CA 89-92; CANR 15; DLB 120

Stanton, Schuyler
See Baum, L(yman) Frank

Stapledon, (William) Olaf 1886-1950
TCLC 22
See also CA 111; 162; DLB 15

Starbuck, George (Edwin) 1931-1996
CLC 53; DAM POET
See also CA 21-24R; 153; CANR 23

Stark, Richard
See Westlake, Donald E(dwin)

Staunton, Schuyler
See Baum, L(yman) Frank

Stead, Christina (Ellen) 1902-1983
CLC 2, 5, 8, 32, 80
See also CA 13-16R; 109; CANR 33, 40; MTCW 1

Stead, William Thomas 1849-1912...**TCLC 48**
See also CA 167

Steele, Richard 1672-1729 ....**LC 18**
See also CDBLB 1660-1789; DLB 84, 101

Steele, Timothy (Reid) 1948- .... **CLC 45**
See also CA 93-96; CANR 16, 50; DLB 120

Steffens, (Joseph) Lincoln 1866-1936...**TCLC 20**
See also CA 117

Stegner, Wallace (Earle) 1909-1993
CLC 9, 49, 81; DAM NOV; SSC 27
See also AITN 1; BEST 90:3; CA 1-4R; 141; CAAS 9; CANR 1, 21, 46; DLB 9; DLBY 93; MTCW 1

Stein, Gertrude 1874-1946...**TCLC 1, 6, 28, 48; DA; DAB; DAC; DAM MST, NOV, POET; PC 18; WLC**
See also CA 104; 132; CDALB 1917-1929; DLB 4, 54, 86; DLBD 15; MTCW 1

Steinbeck, John (Ernst) 1902-1968
CLC 1, 5, 9, 13, 21, 34, 45, 75; DA; DAB; DAC; DAM DRAM, MST, NOV; SSC 11; WLC
See also AAYA 12; CA 1-4R; 25-28R; CANR 1, 35; CDALB 1929-1941; DLB 7, 9; DLBD 2; MTCW 1; SATA 9

Steinem, Gloria 1934- ....**CLC 63**
See also CA 53-56; CANR 28, 51; MTCW 1

Steiner, George 1929- ..... **CLC 24; DAM NOV**
See also CA 73-76; CANR 31, 67; DLB 67; MTCW 1; SATA 62

Steiner, K. Leslie
See Delany, Samuel R(ay, Jr.)

Steiner, Rudolf 1861-1925 .... **TCLC 13**
See also CA 107

Stendhal 1783-1842...**NCLC 23, 46; DA; DAB; DAC; DAM MST, NOV; SSC 27; WLC**
See also DLB 119

Stephen, Adeline Virginia
See Woolf, (Adeline) Virginia

Stephen, SirLeslie 1832-1904 .... **TCLC 23**
See also CA 123; DLB 57, 144, 190

Stephen, Sir Leslie
See Stephen, SirLeslie

Stephen, Virginia
See Woolf, (Adeline) Virginia

Stephens, James 1882(?)-1950...**TCLC 4**
See also CA 104; DLB 19, 153, 162

Stephens, Reed
See Donaldson, Stephen R.

Steptoe, Lydia
See Barnes, Djuna

Sterchi, Beat 1949- .... **CLC 65**

Sterling, Brett
See Bradbury, Ray (Douglas); Hamilton, Edmond

Sterling, Bruce 1954- .... **CLC 72**
See also CA 119; CANR 44

Sterling, George 1869-1926 ..... **TCLC 20**
See also CA 117; 165; DLB 54

Stern, Gerald 1925-..................... **CLC 40, 100**
See also CA 81-84; CANR 28; DLB 105

Stern, Richard (Gustave) 1928- ... **CLC 4, 39**
See also CA 1-4R; CANR 1, 25, 52; DLBY 87; INT CANR-25

Sternberg, Josef von 1894-1969...**CLC 20**
See also CA 81-84

Sterne, Laurence 1713-1768 ... **LC 2, 48; DA; DAB; DAC; DAM MST, NOV; WLC**
See also CDBLB 1660-1789; DLB 39

Sternheim, (William Adolf) Carl 1878-1942
TCLC 8
See also CA 105; DLB 56, 118

Stevens, Mark 1951- ....**CLC 34**
See also CA 122

Stevens, Wallace 1879-1955...**TCLC 3, 12, 45; DA; DAB; DAC; DAM MST, POET; PC 6; WLC**
See also CA 104; 124; CDALB 1929-1941; DLB 54; MTCW 1

Stevenson, Anne (Katharine) 1933-
CLC 7, 33
See also CA 17-20R; CAAS 9; CANR 9, 33; DLB 40; MTCW 1

Stevenson, Robert Louis (Balfour) 1850-1894
NCLC 5, 14, 63; DA; DAB; DAC; DAM MST, NOV; SSC 11; WLC
See also AAYA 24; CDBLB 1890-1914; CLR 10, 11; DLB 18, 57, 141, 156, 174; DLBD 13; JRDA; MAICYA; SATA 100; YABC 2

Stewart, J(ohn) I(nnes) M(ackintosh) 1906-1994 .... **CLC 7, 14, 32**
See also CA 85-88; 147; CAAS 3; CANR 47; MTCW 1

Stewart, Mary (Florence Elinor) 1916-
CLC 7, 35, 117; DAB
See also CA 1-4R; CANR 1, 59; SATA 12

Stewart, Mary Rainbow
See Stewart, Mary (Florence Elinor)

Stifle, June
See Campbell, Maria
Stifter, Adalbert 1805-1868 .... **NCLC 41;**
SSC 28
See also DLB 133
Still, James 1906- .... **CLC 49**
See also CA 65-68; CAAS 17; CANR 10, 26;
DLB 9; SATA 29
Sting 1951-
See Sumner, Gordon Matthew
See also CA 167
Stirling, Arthur
See Sinclair, Upton (Beall)
Stitt, Milan 1941- .... **CLC 29**
See also CA 69-72
Stockton, Francis Richard 1834-1902
See Stockton, Frank R.
See also CA 108; 137; MAICYA; SATA 44
Stockton, Frank R. .... **TCLC 47**
See also Stockton, Francis Richard
See also DLB 42, 74; DLBD 13; SATA-Brief
32
Stoddard, Charles
See Kuttner, Henry
Stoker, Abraham 1847-1912
See Stoker, Bram
See also CA 105; 150; DA; DAC; DAM MST,
NOV; SATA 29
Stoker, Bram 1847-1912...**TCLC 8; DAB;**
WLC
See also Stoker, Abraham
See also AAYA 23; CDBLB 1890-1914; DLB
36, 70, 178
Stolz, Mary (Slattery) 1920- ...... **CLC 12**
See also AAYA 8; AITN 1; CA 5-8R; CANR
13, 41; JRDA; MAICYA; SAAS 3; SATA 10,
71
Stone, Irving 1903-1989 .. **CLC 7; DAM POP**
See also AITN 1; CA 1-4R; 129; CAAS 3;
CANR 1, 23; INT CANR-23; MTCW 1;
SATA 3; SATA-Obit 64
Stone, Oliver (William) 1946-...**CLC 73**
See also AAYA 15; CA 110; CANR 55
Stone, Robert (Anthony) 1937-**CLC 5, 23, 42**
See also CA 85-88; CANR 23, 66; DLB 152;
INT CANR-23; MTCW 1
Stone, Zachary
See Follett, Ken(neth Martin)
Stoppard, Tom 1937-...**CLC 1, 3, 4, 5, 8, 15,**
29, 34, 63, 91; DA; DAB; DAC; DAM
DRAM, MST; DC 6; WLC
See also CA 81-84; CANR 39, 67; CDBLB
1960 to Present; DLB 13; DLBY 85; MTCW
1
Storey, David (Malcolm) 1933-...**CLC 2, 4,**
5, 8; DAM DRAM
See also CA 81-84; CANR 36; DLB 13, 14;
MTCW 1
Storm, Hyemeyohsts 1935- ...... **CLC 3; DAM**
MULT
See also CA 81-84; CANR 45; NNAL
Storm, Theodor 1817-1888 .... **SSC 27**
Storm, (Hans) Theodor (Woldsen) 1817-1888
NCLC 1; SSC 27
See also DLB 129
Storni, Alfonsina 1892-1938...**TCLC 5;**
DAM MULT; HLC
See also CA 104; 131; HW
Stoughton, William 1631-1701 .... **LC 38**
See also DLB 24
Stout, Rex (Todhunter) 1886-1975 ..... **CLC 3**
See also AITN 2; CA 61-64; CANR 71

Stow, (Julian) Randolph 1935-...**CLC 23,**
48
See also CA 13-16R; CANR 33; MTCW 1
Stowe, Harriet (Elizabeth) Beecher 1811-
1896 ..**NCLC 3, 50; DA; DAB; DAC;**
DAM MST, NOV; WLC
See also CDALB 1865-1917; DLB 1, 12, 42,
74, 189; JRDA; MAICYA; YABC 1
Strachey, (Giles) Lytton 1880-1932
TCLC 12
See also CA 110; DLB 149; DLBD 10
Strand, Mark 1934-...**CLC 6, 18, 41, 71;**
DAM POET
See also CA 21-24R; CANR 40, 65; DLB 5;
SATA 41
Straub, Peter (Francis) 1943-...**CLC 28,**
107; DAM POP
See also BEST 89:1; CA 85-88; CANR 28, 65;
DLBY 84; MTCW 1
Strauss, Botho 1944- ....**CLC 22**
See also CA 157; DLB 124
Streatfeild, (Mary) Noel 1895(?)-1986
CLC 21
See also CA 81-84; 120; CANR 31; CLR 17;
DLB 160; MAICYA; SATA 20; SATA-Obit
48
Stribling, T(homas) S(igismund) 1881-
1965 .... **CLC 23**
See also CA 107; DLB 9
Strindberg, (Johan) August 1849-1912
TCLC 1, 8, 21, 47; DA; DAB; DAC;
DAM DRAM, MST; WLC
See also CA 104; 135
Stringer, Arthur 1874-1950 .... **TCLC 37**
See also CA 161; DLB 92
Stringer, David
See Roberts, Keith (John Kingston)
Stroheim, Erich von 1885-1957...**TCLC 71**
Strugatskii, Arkadii (Natanovich) 1925-
1991 .... **CLC 27**
See also CA 106; 135
Strugatskii, Boris (Natanovich) 1933-
CLC 27
See also CA 106
Strummer, Joe 1953(?)- .... **CLC 30**
Stuart, Don A.
See Campbell, John W(ood, Jr.)
Stuart, Ian
See MacLean, Alistair (Stuart)
Stuart, Jesse (Hilton) 1906-1984...**CLC 1,**
8, 11, 14, 34; SSC 31
See also CA 5-8R; 112; CANR 31; DLB 9,
48, 102; DLBY 84; SATA 2; SATA-Obit
36
Sturgeon, Theodore (Hamilton) 1918-1985
CLC 22, 39
See also Queen, Ellery
See also CA 81-84; 116; CANR 32; DLB 8;
DLBY 85; MTCW 1
Sturges, Preston 1898-1959 .... **TCLC 48**
See also CA 114; 149; DLB 26
Styron, William 1925-...**CLC 1, 3, 5, 11,**
15, 60; DAM NOV, POP; SSC 25
See also BEST 90:4; CA 5-8R; CANR 6, 33,
74; CDALB 1968-1988; DLB 2, 143; DLBY
80; INT CANR-6; MTCW 1
Su, Chien 1884-1918
See Su Man-shu
See also CA 123
Suarez Lynch, B.
See Bioy Casares, Adolfo; Borges, Jorge Luis
Suckow, Ruth 1892-1960 .... **SSC 18**
See also CA 113; DLB 9, 102

Sudermann, Hermann 1857-1928
TCLC 15
See also CA 107; DLB 118
Sue, Eugene 1804-1857 .... **NCLC 1**
See also DLB 119
Sueskind, Patrick 1949- .... **CLC 44**
See also Suskind, Patrick
Sukenick, Ronald 1932-...**CLC 3, 4, 6, 48**
See also CA 25-28R; CAAS 8; CANR 32;
DLB 173; DLBY 81
Suknaski, Andrew 1942- .... **CLC 19**
See also CA 101; DLB 53
Sullivan, Vernon
See Vian, Boris
Sully Prudhomme 1839-1907 .... **TCLC 31**
Su Man-shu .... **TCLC 24**
See also Su, Chien
Summerforest, Ivy B.
See Kirkup, James
Summers, Andrew James 1942-...**CLC 26**
Summers, Andy
See Summers, Andrew James
Summers, Hollis (Spurgeon, Jr.) 1916-
CLC 10
See also CA 5-8R; CANR 3; DLB 6
Summers, (Alphonsus Joseph-Mary Augustus)
Montague 1880-1948 .... **TCLC 16**
See also CA 118; 163
Sumner, Gordon Matthew .... **CLC 26**
See also Sting
Surtees, Robert Smith 1803-1864
NCLC 14
See also DLB 21
Susann, Jacqueline 1921-1974 ....**CLC 3**
See also AITN 1; CA 65-68; 53-56; MTCW 1
Su Shih 1036-1101 .... **CMLC 15**

Suskind, Patrick
See Sueskind, Patrick
See also CA 145
Sutcliff, Rosemary 1920-1992...**CLC 26;**
DAB; DAC; DAM MST, POP
See also AAYA 10; CA 5-8R; 139; CANR 37;
CLR 1, 37; JRDA; MAICYA; SATA 6, 44,
78; SATA-Obit 73
Sutro, Alfred 1863-1933 .... **TCLC 6**
See also CA 105; DLB 10
Sutton, Henry
See Slavitt, David R(ytman)
Svevo, Italo 1861-1928...**TCLC 2, 35; SSC**
25
See also Schmitz, Aron Hector
Swados, Elizabeth (A.) 1951- .... **CLC 12**
See also CA 97-100; CANR 49; INT 97-100
Swados, Harvey 1920-1972 ....**CLC 5**
See also CA 5-8R; 37-40R; CANR 6; DLB 2
Swan, Gladys 1934- .... **CLC 69**
See also CA 101; CANR 17, 39
Swarthout, Glendon (Fred) 1918-1992
CLC 35
See also CA 1-4R; 139; CANR 1, 47; SATA
26
Sweet, Sarah C.
See Jewett, (Theodora) Sarah Orne
Swenson, May 1919-1989...**CLC 4, 14, 61,**
106; DA; DAB; DAC; DAM MST, POET;
PC 14
See also CA 5-8R; 130; CANR 36, 61; DLB 5;
MTCW 1; SATA 15
Swift, Augustus
See Lovecraft, H(oward) P(hillips)
Swift, Graham (Colin) 1949- ...... **CLC 41, 88**
See also CA 117; 122; CANR 46, 71; DLB 194

Swift, Jonathan 1667-1745...**LC 1, 42; DA; DAB; DAC; DAM MST, NOV, POET; PC 9; WLC**
See also CDBLB 1660-1789; CLR 53; DLB 39, 95, 101; SATA 19

Swinburne, Algernon Charles 1837-1909 **TCLC 8, 36; DA; DAB; DAC; DAM MST, POET; PC 24; WLC**
See also CA 105; 140; CDBLB 1832-1890; DLB 35, 57

Swinfen, Ann .... **CLC 34**

Swinnerton, Frank Arthur 1884-1982 **CLC 31**
See also CA 108; DLB 34

Swithen, John
See King, Stephen (Edwin)

Sylvia
See Ashton-Warner, Sylvia (Constance)

Symmes, Robert Edward
See Duncan, Robert (Edward)

Symonds, John Addington 1840-1893 **NCLC 34**
See also DLB 57, 144

Symons, Arthur 1865-1945 ...... **TCLC 11**
See also CA 107; DLB 19, 57, 149

Symons, Julian (Gustave) 1912-1994 **CLC 2, 14, 32**
See also CA 49-52; 147; CAAS 3; CANR 3, 33, 59; DLB 87, 155; DLBY 92; MTCW 1

Synge, (Edmund) J(ohn) M(illington) 1871-1909 .. **TCLC 6, 37; DAM DRAM; DC 2**
See also CA 104; 141; CDBLB 1890-1914; DLB 10, 19

Syruc, J.
See Milosz, Czeslaw

Szirtes, George 1948- .... **CLC 46**
See also CA 109; CANR 27, 61

Szymborska, Wislawa 1923- ..... **CLC 99**
See also CA 154; DLBY 96

T. O., Nik
See Annensky, Innokenty (Fyodorovich)

Tabori, George 1914- .... **CLC 19**
See also CA 49-52; CANR 4, 69

Tagore, Rabindranath 1861-1941 **TCLC 3, 53; DAM DRAM, POET; PC 8**
See also CA 104; 120; MTCW 1

Taine, Hippolyte Adolphe 1828-1893 **NCLC 15**

Talese, Gay 1932- .... **CLC 37**
See also AITN 1; CA 1-4R; CANR 9, 58; DLB 185; INT CANR-9; MTCW 1

Tallent, Elizabeth (Ann) 1954- ...... **CLC 45**
See also CA 117; CANR 72; DLB 130

Tally, Ted 1952- .... **CLC 42**
See also CA 120; 124; INT 124

Talvik, Heiti 1904-1947 .... **TCLC 87**

Tamayo y Baus, Manuel 1829-1898 **NCLC 1**

Tammsaare, A(nton) H(ansen) 1878-1940 **TCLC 27**
See also CA 164

Tam'si, Tchicaya U
See Tchicaya, Gerald Felix

Tan, Amy (Ruth) 1952- ... **CLC 59; DAM MULT, NOV, POP**
See also AAYA 9; BEST 89:3; CA 136; CANR 54; DLB 173; SATA 75

Tandem, Felix
See Spitteler, Carl (Friedrich Georg)

Tanizaki, Jun'ichiro 1886-1965...**CLC 8, 14, 28; SSC 21**
See also CA 93-96; 25-28R; DLB 180

Tanner, William
See Amis, Kingsley (William)

Tao Lao
See Storni, Alfonsina

Tarassoff, Lev
See Troyat, Henri

Tarbell, Ida M(inerva) 1857-1944 **TCLC 40**
See also CA 122; DLB 47

Tarkington, (Newton) Booth 1869-1946 **TCLC 9**
See also CA 110; 143; DLB 9, 102; SATA 17

Tarkovsky, Andrei (Arsenyevich) 1932-1986 **CLC 75**
See also CA 127

Tartt, Donna 1964(?)- .... **CLC 76**
See also CA 142

Tasso, Torquato 1544-1595 .... **LC 5**

Tate, (John Orley) Allen 1899-1979 **CLC 2, 4, 6, 9, 11, 14, 24**
See also CA 5-8R; 85-88; CANR 32; DLB 4, 45, 63; DLBD 17; MTCW 1

Tate, Ellalice
See Hibbert, Eleanor Alice Burford

Tate, James (Vincent) 1943-...**CLC 2, 6, 25**
See also CA 21-24R; CANR 29, 57; DLB 5, 169

Tavel, Ronald 1940- .... **CLC 6**
See also CA 21-24R; CANR 33

Taylor, C(ecil) P(hilip) 1929-1981 ....**CLC 27**
See also CA 25-28R; 105; CANR 47

Taylor, Edward 1642(?)-1729 ..... **LC 11; DA; DAB; DAC; DAM MST, POET**
See also DLB 24

Taylor, Eleanor Ross 1920- .... **CLC 5**
See also CA 81-84; CANR 70

Taylor, Elizabeth 1912-1975 ..... **CLC 2, 4, 29**
See also CA 13-16R; CANR 9, 70; DLB 139; MTCW 1; SATA 13

Taylor, Frederick Winslow 1856-1915 **TCLC 76**

Taylor, Henry (Splawn) 1942-.... **CLC 44**
See also CA 33-36R; CAAS 7; CANR 31; DLB 5

Taylor, Kamala (Purnaiya) 1924-
See Markandaya, Kamala
See also CA 77-80

Taylor, Mildred D. .... **CLC 21**
See also AAYA 10; BW 1; CA 85-88; CANR 25; CLR 9; DLB 52; JRDA; MAICYA; SAAS 5; SATA 15, 70

Taylor, Peter (Hillsman) 1917-1994 **CLC 1, 4, 18, 37, 44, 50, 71; SSC 10**
See also CA 13-16R; 147; CANR 9, 50; DLBY 81, 94; INT CANR-9; MTCW 1

Taylor, Robert Lewis 1912-1998 ....**CLC 14**
See also CA 1-4R; 170; CANR 3, 64; SATA 10

Tchekhov, Anton
See Chekhov, Anton (Pavlovich)

Tchicaya, Gerald Felix 1931-1988...**CLC 101**
See also CA 129; 125

Tchicaya U Tam'si
See Tchicaya, Gerald Felix

Teasdale, Sara 1884-1933 .... **TCLC 4**
See also CA 104; 163; DLB 45; SATA 32

Tegner, Esaias 1782-1846 ....**NCLC 2**

Teilhard de Chardin, (Marie Joseph) Pierre 1881-1955 .... **TCLC 9**
See also CA 105

Temple, Ann
See Mortimer, Penelope (Ruth)

Tennant, Emma (Christina) 1937- **CLC 13, 52**
See also CA 65-68; CAAS 9; CANR 10, 38, 59; DLB 14

Tenneshaw, S. M.
See Silverberg, Robert

Tennyson, Alfred 1809-1892...**NCLC 30, 65; DA; DAB; DAC; DAM MST, POET; PC 6; WLC**
See also CDBLB 1832-1890; DLB 32

Teran, Lisa St. Aubin de .... **CLC 36**
See also St. Aubin de Teran, Lisa

Terence 195(?)B.C.-159B.C....**CMLC 14; DC 7**

Teresa de Jesus, St. 1515-1582 ...... **LC 18**

Terkel, Louis 1912-
See Terkel, Studs
See also CA 57-60; CANR 18, 45, 67; MTCW 1

Terkel, Studs .... **CLC 38**
See also Terkel, Louis
See also AITN 1

Terry, C. V.
See Slaughter, Frank G(ill)

Terry, Megan 1932- ....**CLC 19**
See also CA 77-80; CABS 3; CANR 43; DLB 7

Tertullian c. 155-c. 245 .... **CMLC 29**

Tertz, Abram
See Sinyavsky, Andrei (Donatevich)

Tesich, Steve 1943(?)-1996 .... **CLC 40, 69**
See also CA 105; 152; DLBY 83

Tesla, Nikola 1856-1943 .... **TCLC 88**

Teternikov, Fyodor Kuzmich 1863-1927
See Sologub, Fyodor
See also CA 104

Tevis, Walter 1928-1984 .... **CLC 42**
See also CA 113

Tey, Josephine .... **TCLC 14**
See also Mackintosh, Elizabeth
See also DLB 77

Thackeray, William Makepeace 1811-1863 **NCLC 5, 14, 22, 43; DA; DAB; DAC; DAM MST, NOV; WLC**
See also CDBLB 1832-1890; DLB 21, 55, 159, 163; SATA 23

Thakura, Ravindranatha
See Tagore, Rabindranath

Tharoor, Shashi 1956- .... **CLC 70**
See also CA 141

Thelwell, Michael Miles 1939-...**CLC 22**
See also BW 2; CA 101

Theobald, Lewis, Jr.
See Lovecraft, H(oward) P(hillips)

Theodorescu, Ion N. 1880-1967
See Arghezi, Tudor
See also CA 116

Theriault, Yves 1915-1983 .... **CLC 79; DAC; DAM MST**
See also CA 102; DLB 88

Theroux, Alexander (Louis) 1939- **CLC 2, 25**
See also CA 85-88; CANR 20, 63

Theroux, Paul (Edward) 1941-...**CLC 5, 8, 11, 15, 28, 46; DAM POP**
See also BEST 89:4; CA 33-36R; CANR 20, 45, 74; DLB 2; MTCW 1; SATA 44

Thesen, Sharon 1946- .... **CLC 56**
See also CA 163

Thevenin, Denis
See Duhamel, Georges

Thibault, Jacques Anatole Francois 1844-1924
See France, Anatole
See also CA 106; 127; DAM NOV; MTCW 1

Tremblay, Michel 1942- ..... **CLC 29, 102;**
DAC; DAM MST
See also CA 116; 128; DLB 60; MTCW 1

Trevanian .... **CLC 29**
See also Whitaker, Rod(ney)

Trevor, Glen
See Hilton, James

Trevor, William 1928- ...**CLC 7, 9, 14, 25,**
71, 116; SSC 21
See also Cox, William Trevor
See also DLB 14, 139

Trifonov, Yuri (Valentinovich) 1925-1981
CLC 45
See also CA 126; 103; MTCW 1

Trilling, Lionel 1905-1975 ...... **CLC 9, 11, 24**
See also CA 9-12R; 61-64; CANR 10; DLB 28,
63; INT CANR-10; MTCW 1

Trimball, W. H.
See Mencken, H(enry) L(ouis)

Tristan
See Gomez de la Serna, Ramon

Tristram
See Housman, A(lfred) E(dward)

Trogdon, William (Lewis) 1939-
See Heat-Moon, William Least
See also CA 115; 119; CANR 47; INT 119

Trollope, Anthony 1815-1882...**NCLC 6,**
33; DA; DAB; DAC; DAM MST, NOV;
SSC 28; WLC
See also CDBLB 1832-1890; DLB 21, 57, 159;
SATA 22

Trollope, Frances 1779-1863 .... **NCLC 30**
See also DLB 21, 166

Trotsky, Leon 1879-1940 .... **TCLC 22**
See also CA 118; 167

Trotter (Cockburn), Catharine 1679-1749
LC 8
See also DLB 84

Trout, Kilgore
See Farmer, Philip Jose

Trow, George W. S. 1943- .... **CLC 52**
See also CA 126

Troyat, Henri 1911- .... **CLC 23**
See also CA 45-48; CANR 2, 33, 67; MTCW 1

Trudeau, G(arretson) B(eekman) 1948-
See Trudeau, Garry B.
See also CA 81-84; CANR 31; SATA 35

Trudeau, Garry B. .... **CLC 12**
See also Trudeau, G(arretson) B(eekman)
See also AAYA 10; AITN 2

Truffaut, Francois 1932-1984...**CLC 20,**
101
See also CA 81-84; 113; CANR 34

Trumbo, Dalton 1905-1976 .... **CLC 19**
See also CA 21-24R; 69-72; CANR 10; DLB
26

Trumbull, John 1750-1831 ...... **NCLC 30**
See also DLB 31

Trundlett, Helen B.
See Eliot, T(homas) S(tearns)

Tryon, Thomas 1926-1991**CLC 3, 11; DAM**
POP
See also AITN 1; CA 29-32R; 135; CANR 32;
MTCW 1

Tryon, Tom
See Tryon, Thomas

Ts'ao Hsueh-ch'in 1715(?)-1763 ..... **LC 1**

Tsushima, Shuji 1909-1948
See Dazai Osamu
See also CA 107

Tsvetaeva (Efron), Marina (Ivanovna) 1892-
1941 .... **TCLC 7, 35; PC 14**
See also CA 104; 128; CANR 73; MTCW 1

Tuck, Lily 1938- .... **CLC 70**
See also CA 139

Tu Fu 712-770 .... **PC 9**
See also DAM MULT

Tunis, John R(oberts) 1889-1975...**CLC 12**
See also CA 61-64; CANR 62; DLB 22, 171;
JRDA; MAICYA; SATA 37; SATA-Brief 30

Tuohy, Frank .... **CLC 37**
See also Tuohy, John Francis
See also DLB 14, 139

Tuohy, John Francis 1925-
See Tuohy, Frank
See also CA 5-8R; CANR 3, 47

Turco, Lewis (Putnam) 1934- ...... **CLC 11, 63**
See also CA 13-16R; CAAS 22; CANR 24, 51;
DLBY 84

Turgenev, Ivan 1818-1883 .... **NCLC 21; DA;**
DAB; DAC; DAM MST, NOV; DC 7; SSC
7; WLC

Turgot, Anne-Robert-Jacques 1727-1781
LC 26

Turner, Frederick 1943- .... **CLC 48**
See also CA 73-76; CAAS 10; CANR 12, 30,
56; DLB 40

Tutu, Desmond M(pilo) 1931-...**CLC 80;**
BLC 3; DAM MULT
See also BW 1; CA 125; CANR 67

Tutuola, Amos 1920-1997...**CLC 5, 14, 29;**
BLC 3; DAM MULT
See also BW 2; CA 9-12R; 159; CANR 27, 66;
DLB 125; MTCW 1

Twain, Mark ...**TCLC 6, 12, 19, 36, 48, 59;**
SSC 6, 26; WLC
See also Clemens, Samuel Langhorne
See also AAYA 20; DLB 11, 12, 23, 64, 74

Tyler, Anne 1941-...**CLC 7, 11, 18, 28, 44,**
59, 103; DAM NOV, POP
See also AAYA 18; BEST 89:1; CA 9-12R;
CANR 11, 33, 53; DLB 6, 143; DLBY 82;
MTCW 1; SATA 7, 90

Tyler, Royall 1757-1826 .... **NCLC 3**
See also DLB 37

Tynan, Katharine 1861-1931 .... **TCLC 3**
See also CA 104; 167; DLB 153

Tyutchev, Fyodor 1803-1873 .... **NCLC 34**

Tzara, Tristan 1896-1963 ...... **CLC 47; DAM**
POET
See also CA 153; 89-92

Uhry, Alfred 1936-...**CLC 55; DAM DRAM,**
POP
See also CA 127; 133; INT 133

Ulf, Haerved
See Strindberg, (Johan) August

Ulf, Harved
See Strindberg, (Johan) August

Ulibarri, Sabine R(eyes) 1919-...**CLC 83;**
DAM MULT
See also CA 131; DLB 82; HW

Unamuno (y Jugo), Miguel de 1864-1936
TCLC 2, 9; DAM MULT, NOV; HLC;
SSC 11
See also CA 104; 131; DLB 108; HW;
MTCW 1

Undercliffe, Errol
See Campbell, (John) Ramsey

Underwood, Miles
See Glassco, John

Undset, Sigrid 1882-1949...**TCLC 3; DA;**
DAB; DAC; DAM MST, NOV; WLC
See also CA 104; 129; MTCW 1

Ungaretti, Giuseppe 1888-1970...**CLC 7,**
11, 15
See also CA 19-20; 25-28R; CAP 2; DLB 114

Unger, Douglas 1952- .... **CLC 34**
See also CA 130

Unsworth, Barry (Forster) 1930-...**CLC 76**
See also CA 25-28R; CANR 30, 54; DLB
194

Updike, John (Hoyer) 1932-...**CLC 1, 2, 3,**
5, 7, 9, 13, 15, 23, 34, 43, 70; DA; DAB;
DAC; DAM MST, NOV, POET, POP;
SSC 13, 27; WLC
See also CA 1-4R; CABS 1; CANR 4, 33, 51;
CDALB 1968-1988; DLB 2, 5, 143; DLBD
3; DLBY 80, 82, 97; MTCW 1

Upshaw, Margaret Mitchell
See Mitchell, Margaret (Munnerlyn)

Upton, Mark
See Sanders, Lawrence

Upward, Allen 1863-1926 .... **TCLC 85**
See also CA 117; DLB 36

Urdang, Constance (Henriette) 1922-
CLC 47
See also CA 21-24R; CANR 9, 24

Uriel, Henry
See Faust, Frederick (Schiller)

Uris, Leon (Marcus) 1924-...**CLC 7, 32;**
DAM NOV, POP
See also AITN 1, 2; BEST 89:2; CA 1-4R;
CANR 1, 40, 65; MTCW 1; SATA 49

Urmuz
See Codrescu, Andrei

Urquhart, Jane 1949- .... **CLC 90; DAC**
See also CA 113; CANR 32, 68

Ustinov, Peter (Alexander) 1921-........ **CLC 1**
See also AITN 1; CA 13-16R; CANR 25, 51;
DLB 13

U Tam'si, Gerald Felix Tchicaya
See Tchicaya, Gerald Felix

U Tam'si, Tchicaya
See Tchicaya, Gerald Felix

Vachss, Andrew (Henry) 1942-...**CLC 106**
See also CA 118; CANR 44

Vachss, Andrew H.
See Vachss, Andrew (Henry)

Vaculik, Ludvik 1926- .... **CLC 7**
See also CA 53-56; CANR 72

Vaihinger, Hans 1852-1933 .... **TCLC 71**
See also CA 116; 166

Valdez, Luis (Miguel) 1940- .. **CLC 84; DAM**
MULT; DC 10; HLC
See also CA 101; CANR 32; DLB 122; HW

Valenzuela, Luisa 1938- ...**CLC 31, 104;**
DAM MULT; SSC 14
See also CA 101; CANR 32, 65; DLB 113; HW

Valera y Alcala-Galiano, Juan 1824-1905
TCLC 10
See also CA 106

Valery, (Ambroise) Paul (Toussaint Jules)
1871-1945 .... **TCLC 4, 15; DAM**
POET; PC 9
See also CA 104; 122; MTCW 1

Valle-Inclan, Ramon (Maria) del 1866-
1936 .... **TCLC 5; DAM MULT; HLC**
See also CA 106; 153; DLB 134

Vallejo, Antonio Buero
See Buero Vallejo, Antonio

Vallejo, Cesar (Abraham) 1892-1938
TCLC 3, 56; DAM MULT; HLC
See also CA 105; 153; HW

Valles, Jules 1832-1885 .... **NCLC 71**
See also DLB 123

Vallette, Marguerite Eymery
See Rachilde

Valle Y Pena, Ramon del
See Valle-Inclan, Ramon (Maria) del

Van Ash, Cay 1918- .... CLC 34
Vanbrugh, Sir John 1664-1726 ... LC 21;
    DAM DRAM
    See also DLB 80
Van Campen, Karl
    See Campbell, John W(ood, Jr.)
Vance, Gerald
    See Silverberg, Robert
Vance, Jack... CLC 35
    See also Kuttner, Henry; Vance, John Holbrook
    See also DLB 8
Vance, John Holbrook 1916-
    See Queen, Ellery; Vance, Jack
    See also CA 29-32R; CANR 17, 65; MTCW 1
Van Den Bogarde, Derek Jules Gaspard
    Ulric Niven 1921-
    See Bogarde, Dirk
    See also CA 77-80
Vandenburgh, Jane .... CLC 59
    See also CA 168
Vanderhaeghe, Guy 1951- .... CLC 41
    See also CA 113; CANR 72
van der Post, Laurens (Jan) 1906-1996
    CLC 5
    See also CA 5-8R; 155; CANR 35
van de Wetering, Janwillem 1931- .. CLC 47
    See also CA 49-52; CANR 4, 62
Van Dine, S. S. .... TCLC 23
    See also Wright, Willard Huntington
Van Doren, Carl (Clinton) 1885-1950
    TCLC 18
    See also CA 111; 168
Van Doren, Mark 1894-1972 .... CLC 6, 10
    See also CA 1-4R; 37-40R; CANR 3; DLB 45;
    MTCW 1
Van Druten, John (William) 1901-1957
    TCLC 2
    See also CA 104; 161; DLB 10
Van Duyn, Mona (Jane) 1921-...CLC 3, 7,
    63, 116; DAM POET
    See also CA 9-12R; CANR 7, 38, 60; DLB 5
Van Dyne, Edith
    See Baum, L(yman) Frank
van Itallie, Jean-Claude 1936- ....CLC 3
    See also CA 45-48; CAAS 2; CANR 1, 48;
    DLB 7
van Ostaijen, Paul 1896-1928 . TCLC 33
    See also CA 163
Van Peebles, Melvin 1932-... CLC 2, 20;
    DAM MULT
    See also BW 2; CA 85-88; CANR 27, 67
Vansittart, Peter 1920- .... CLC 42
    See also CA 1-4R; CANR 3, 49
Van Vechten, Carl 1880-1964 .... CLC 33
    See also CA 89-92; DLB 4, 9, 51
Van Vogt, A(lfred) E(lton) 1912- . CLC 1
    See also CA 21-24R; CANR 28; DLB 8; SATA
    14
Varda, Agnes 1928- .... CLC 16
    See also CA 116; 122
Vargas Llosa, (Jorge) Mario (Pedro) 1936-
    CLC 3, 6, 9, 10, 15, 31, 42, 85; DA;
    DAB; DAC; DAM MST, MULT, NOV;
    HLC
    See also CA 73-76; CANR 18, 32, 42, 67; DLB
    145; HW; MTCW 1
Vasiliu, Gheorghe 1881-1957
    See Bacovia, George
    See also CA 123
Vassa, Gustavus
    See Equiano, Olaudah
Vassilikos, Vassilis 1933- .... CLC 4, 8
    See also CA 81-84; CANR 75

Vaughan, Henry 1621-1695 .... LC 27
    See also DLB 131
Vaughn, Stephanie .... CLC 62
Vazov, Ivan (Minchov) 1850-1921
    TCLC 25
    See also CA 121; 167; DLB 147
Veblen, Thorstein B(unde) 1857-1929
    TCLC 31
    See also CA 115; 165
Vega, Lope de 1562-1635 .... LC 23
Venison, Alfred
    See Pound, Ezra (Weston Loomis)
Verdi, Marie de
    See Mencken, H(enry) L(ouis)
Verdu, Matilde
    See Cela, Camilo Jose
Verga, Giovanni (Carmelo) 1840-1922
    TCLC 3; SSC 21
    See also CA 104; 123
Vergil 70B.C.-19B.C. .... CMLC 9; DA; DAB;
    DAC; DAM MST, POET; PC 12; WLCS
Verhaeren, Emile (Adolphe Gustave) 1855-1916
    TCLC 12
    See also CA 109
Verlaine, Paul (Marie) 1844-1896
    NCLC 2, 51; DAM POET; PC 2
Verne, Jules (Gabriel) 1828-1905
    TCLC 6, 52
    See also AAYA 16; CA 110; 131; DLB 123;
    JRDA; MAICYA; SATA 21
Very, Jones 1813-1880 .... NCLC 9
    See also DLB 1
Vesaas, Tarjei 1897-1970 .... CLC 48
    See also CA 29-32R
Vialis, Gaston
    See Simenon, Georges (Jacques Christian)
Vian, Boris 1920-1959 .... TCLC 9
    See also CA 106; 164; DLB 72
Viaud, (Louis Marie) Julien 1850-1923
    See Loti, Pierre
    See also CA 107
Vicar, Henry
    See Felsen, Henry Gregor
Vicker, Angus
    See Felsen, Henry Gregor
Vidal, Gore 1925-...CLC 2, 4, 6, 8, 10, 22,
    33, 72; DAM NOV, POP
    See also AITN 1; BEST 90:2; CA 5-8R; CANR
    13, 45, 65; DLB 6, 152; INT CANR-13;
    MTCW 1
Viereck, Peter (Robert Edwin) 1916-
    CLC 4
    See also CA 1-4R; CANR 1, 47; DLB 5
Vigny, Alfred (Victor) de 1797-1863
    NCLC 7; DAM POET
    See also DLB 119, 192
Vilakazi, Benedict Wallet 1906-1947
    TCLC 37
    See also CA 168
Villa, Jose Garcia 1904-1997 .... PC 22
    See also CA 25-28R; CANR 12
Villaurrutia, Xavier 1903-1950 ...... TCLC 80
    See also IIW
Villiers de l'Isle Adam, Jean Marie
    Mathias Philippe Auguste, Comte de
    1838-1889 .... NCLC 3; SSC 14
    See also DLB 123
Villon, Francois 1431-1463(?) .... PC 13
Vinci, Leonardo da 1452-1519 .... LC 12
Vine, Barbara ....CLC 50
    See also Rendell, Ruth (Barbara)
    See also BEST 90:4

Vinge, Joan (Carol) D(ennison) 1948-
    CLC 30; SSC 24
    See also CA 93-96; CANR 72; SATA 36
Violis, G.
    See Simenon, Georges (Jacques Christian)
Virgil
    See Vergil
Visconti, Luchino 1906-1976 ..... CLC 16
    See also CA 81-84; 65-68; CANR 39
Vittorini, Elio 1908-1966 .... CLC 6, 9, 14
    See also CA 133; 25-28R
Vivekananda, Swami 1863-1902 .... TCLC 88
Vizenor, Gerald Robert 1934-...CLC 103;
    DAM MULT
    See also CA 13-16R; CAAS 22; CANR 5, 21,
    44, 67; DLB 175; NNAL
Vizinczey, Stephen 1933-........... CLC 40
    See also CA 128; INT 128
Vliet, R(ussell) G(ordon) 1929-1984
    CLC 22
    See also CA 37-40R; 112; CANR 18
Vogau, Boris Andreyevich 1894-1937(?)
    See Pilnyak, Boris
    See also CA 123
Vogel, Paula A(nne) 1951- .... CLC 76
    See also CA 108
Voigt, Cynthia 1942- .... CLC 30
    See also AAYA 3; CA 106; CANR 18, 37, 40;
    CLR 13, 48; INT CANR-18; JRDA;
    MAICYA; SATA 48, 79; SATA-Brief 33
Voigt, Ellen Bryant 1943- .... CLC 54
    See also CA 69-72; CANR 11, 29, 55; DLB 120
Voinovich, Vladimir (Nikolaevich) 1932-CLC
    10, 49
    See also CA 81-84; CAAS 12; CANR 33, 67;
    MTCW 1
Vollmann, William T. 1959- .... CLC 89;
    DAM NOV, POP
    See also CA 134; CANR 67
Voloshinov, V. N.
    See Bakhtin, Mikhail Mikhailovich
Voltaire 1694-1778...LC 14; DA; DAB;
    DAC; DAM DRAM, MST; SSC 12;
    WLC
von Aschendrof, BaronIgnatz
    See Ford, Ford Madox
von Daeniken, Erich 1935-......... CLC 30
    See also AITN 1; CA 37-40R; CANR 17, 44
von Daniken, Erich
    See von Daeniken, Erich
von Heidenstam, (Carl Gustaf) Verner
    See Heidenstam, (Carl Gustaf) Verner von
von Heyse, Paul (Johann Ludwig)
    See Heyse, Paul (Johann Ludwig von)
von Hofmannsthal, Hugo
    See Hofmannsthal, Hugo von
von Horvath, Odon
    See Horvath, Oedoen von
von Horvath, Oedoen
    See Horvath, Oedoen von
von Liliencron, (Friedrich Adolf Axel) Detlev
    See Liliencron, (Friedrich Adolf Axel) Detlev
    von
Vonnegut, Kurt, Jr. 1922-...CLC 1, 2, 3,
    4, 5, 8, 12, 22, 40, 60, 111; DA; DAB;
    DAC; DAM MST, NOV, POP; SSC 8;
    WLC
    See also AAYA 6; AITN 1; BEST 90:4; CA 1-
    4R; CANR 1, 25, 49, 75; CDALB 1968-
    1988; DLB 2, 8, 152; DLBD 3; DLBY 80;
    MTCW 1
Von Rachen, Kurt
    See Hubbard, L(afayette) Ron(ald)

von Rezzori (d'Arezzo), Gregor
See Rezzori (d'Arezzo), Gregor von
von Sternberg, Josef
See Sternberg, Josef von
Vorster, Gordon 1924- .... **CLC 34**
See also CA 133
Vosce, Trudie
See Ozick, Cynthia
Voznesensky, Andrei (Andreievich) 1933-
CLC 1, 15, 57; DAM POET
See also CA 89-92; CANR 37; MTCW 1
Waddington, Miriam 1917- .... **CLC 28**
See also CA 21-24R; CANR 12, 30; DLB 68
Wagman, Fredrica 1937- .... **CLC 7**
See also CA 97-100; INT 97-100

Wagner, Linda W.
See Wagner-Martin, Linda (C.)
Wagner, Linda Welshimer
See Wagner-Martin, Linda (C.)
Wagner, Richard 1813-1883 ...... **NCLC 9**
See also DLB 129
Wagner-Martin, Linda (C.) 1936- ... **CLC 50**
See also CA 159
Wagoner, David (Russell) 1926-...**CLC 3, 5, 15**
See also CA 1-4R; CAAS 3; CANR 2, 71; DLB 5; SATA 14
Wah, Fred(erick James) 1939- .... **CLC 44**
See also CA 107; 141; DLB 60
Wahloo, Per 1926-1975 .... **CLC 7**
See also CA 61-64; CANR 73
Wahloo, Peter
See Wahloo, Per
Wain, John (Barrington) 1925-1994
CLC 2, 11, 15, 46
See also CA 5-8R; 145; CAAS 4; CANR 23, 54; CDBLB 1960 to Present; DLB 15, 27, 139, 155; MTCW 1
Wajda, Andrzej 1926-.................. **CLC 16**
See also CA 102
Wakefield, Dan 1932-...................... **CLC 7**
See also CA 21-24R; CAAS 7
Wakoski, Diane 1937-...**CLC 2, 4, 7, 9, 11, 40; DAM POET; PC 15**
See also CA 13-16R; CAAS 1; CANR 9, 60; DLB 5; INT CANR-9
Wakoski-Sherbell, Diane
See Wakoski, Diane
Walcott, Derek (Alton) 1930-...**CLC 2, 4, 9, 14, 25, 42, 67, 76; BLC 3; DAB; DAC; DAM MST, MULT, POET; DC 7**
See also BW 2; CA 89-92; CANR 26, 47, 75; DLB 117; DLBY 81; MTCW 1
Waldman, Anne (Lesley) 1945- ....**CLC 7**
See also CA 37-40R; CAAS 17; CANR 34, 69; DLB 16

Waldo, E. Hunter
See Sturgeon, Theodore (Hamilton)
Waldo, Edward Hamilton
See Sturgeon, Theodore (Hamilton)

Walker, Alice (Malsenior) 1944-...**CLC 5, 6, 9, 19, 27, 46, 58, 103; BLC 3; DA; DAB; DAC; DAM MST, MULT, NOV, POET, POP; SSC 5; WLCS**
See also AAYA 3; BEST 89:4; BW 2; CA 37-40R; CANR 9, 27, 49, 66; CDALB 1968-1988; DLB 6, 33, 143; INT CANR-27; MTCW 1; SATA 31
Walker, David Harry 1911-1992...**CLC 14**
See also CA 1-4R; 137; CANR 1; SATA 8; SATA-Obit 71

Walker, Edward Joseph 1934-
See Walker, Ted
See also CA 21-24R; CANR 12, 28, 53
Walker, George F. 1947- ..... **CLC 44, 61; DAB; DAC; DAM MST**
See also CA 103; CANR 21, 43, 59; DLB 60
Walker, Joseph A. 1935- ....**CLC 19; DAM DRAM, MST**
See also BW 1; CA 89-92; CANR 26; DLB 38
Walker, Margaret (Abigail) 1915-
CLC 1, 6; BLC; DAM MULT; PC 20
See also BW 2; CA 73-76; CANR 26, 54; DLB 76, 152; MTCW 1
Walker, Ted ....**CLC 13**
See also Walker, Edward Joseph
See also DLB 40
Wallace, David Foster 1962- .....**CLC 50, 114**
See also CA 132; CANR 59
Wallace, Dexter
See Masters, Edgar Lee
Wallace, (Richard Horatio) Edgar 1875-1932 .... **TCLC 57**
See also CA 115; DLB 70
Wallace, Irving 1916-1990.... **CLC 7, 13; DAM NOV, POP**
See also AITN 1; CA 1-4R; 132; CAAS 1; CANR 1, 27; INT CANR-27; MTCW 1
Wallant, Edward Lewis 1926-1962
CLC 5, 10
See also CA 1-4R; CANR 22; DLB 2, 28, 143; MTCW 1
Walley, Byron
See Card, Orson Scott
Walpole, Horace 1717-1797 .... **LC 2**
See also DLB 39, 104
Walpole, Hugh (Seymour) 1884-1941
TCLC 5
See also CA 104; 165; DLB 34
Walser, Martin 1927- ....**CLC 27**
See also CA 57-60; CANR 8, 46; DLB 75, 124
Walser, Robert 1878-1956...**TCLC 18; SSC 20**
See also CA 118; 165; DLB 66
Walsh, Jill Paton .... **CLC 35**
See also Paton Walsh, Gillian
See also AAYA 11; CLR 2; DLB 161; SAAS 3
Walter, William Christian
See Andersen, Hans Christian
Wambaugh, Joseph (Aloysius, Jr.) 1937-
CLC 3, 18; DAM NOV, POP
See also AITN 1; BEST 89:3; CA 33-36R; CANR 42, 65; DLB 6; DLBY 83; MTCW 1
Wang Wei 699(?)-761(?).................. **PC 18**
Ward, Arthur Henry Sarsfield 1883-1959
See Rohmer, Sax
See also CA 108
Ward, Douglas Turner 1930- ....**CLC 19**
See also BW 1; CA 81-84; CANR 27; DLB 7, 38
Ward, Mary Augusta
See Ward, Mrs. Humphry
Ward, Mrs. Humphry 1851-1920**TCLC 55**
See also DLB 18
Ward, Peter
See Faust, Frederick (Schiller)
Warhol, Andy 1928(?)-1987 .... **CLC 20**
See also AAYA 12; BEST 89:4; CA 89-92; 121; CANR 34
Warner, Francis (Robert le Plastrier) 1937-
CLC 14
See also CA 53-56; CANR 11
Warner, Marina 1946- .... **CLC 59**
See also CA 65-68; CANR 21, 55; DLB 194

Warner, Rex (Ernest) 1905-1986...**CLC 45**
See also CA 89-92; 119; DLB 15
Warner, Susan (Bogert) 1819-1885
NCLC 31
See also DLB 3, 42
Warner, Sylvia (Constance) Ashton
See Ashton-Warner, Sylvia (Constance)
Warner, Sylvia Townsend 1893-1978
CLC 7, 19; SSC 23
See also CA 61-64; 77-80; CANR 16, 60; DLB 34, 139; MTCW 1
Warren, Mercy Otis 1728-1814 .....**NCLC 13**
See also DLB 31, 200
Warren, Robert Penn 1905-1989
CLC 1, 4, 6, 8, 10, 13, 18, 39, 53, 59; DA; DAB; DAC; DAM MST, NOV, POET; SSC 4; WLC
See also AITN 1; CA 13-16R; 129; CANR 10, 47; CDALB 1968-1988; DLB 2, 48, 152; DLBY 80, 89; INT CANR-10; MTCW 1; SATA 46; SATA-Obit 63
Warshofsky, Isaac
See Singer, Isaac Bashevis
Warton, Thomas 1728-1790...**LC 15; DAM POET**
See also DLB 104, 109
Waruk, Kona
See Harris, (Theodore) Wilson
Warung, Price 1855-1911 .... **TCLC 45**
Warwick, Jarvis
See Garner, Hugh
Washington, Alex
See Harris, Mark
Washington, Booker T(aliaferro) 1856-1915...**TCLC 10; BLC 3; DAM MULT**
See also BW 1; CA 114; 125; SATA 28
Washington, George 1732-1799 .... **LC 25**
See also DLB 31
Wassermann, (Karl) Jakob 1873-1934
TCLC 6
See also CA 104; DLB 66
Wasserstein, Wendy 1950-...**CLC 32, 59, 90; DAM DRAM; DC 4**
See also CA 121; 129; CABS 3; CANR 53; INT 129; SATA 94, 75
Waterhouse, Keith (Spencer) 1929-
CLC 47
See also CA 5-8R; CANR 38, 67; DLB 13, 15; MTCW 1
Waters, Frank (Joseph) 1902-1995
CLC 88
See also CA 5-8R; 149; CAAS 13; CANR 3, 18, 63; DLBY 86
Waters, Roger 1944-...................... **CLC 35**
Watkins, Frances Ellen
See Harper, Frances Ellen Watkins
Watkins, Gerrold
See Malzberg, Barry N(athaniel)
Watkins, Gloria 1955(?)-
See hooks, bell
See also BW 2; CA 143
Watkins, Paul 1964- ....**CLC 55**
See also CA 132; CANR 62
Watkins, Vernon Phillips 1906-1967
CLC 43
See also CA 9-10; 25-28R; CAP 1; DLB 20
Watson, Irving S.
See Mencken, H(enry) L(ouis)
Watson, John H.
See Farmer, Philip Jose
Watson, Richard F.
See Silverberg, Robert

Waugh, Auberon (Alexander) 1939-
CLC 7
See also CA 45-48; CANR 6, 22; DLB 14,
194
Waugh, Evelyn (Arthur St. John) 1903-
1966...CLC 1, 3, 8, 13, 19, 27, 44, 107;
DA; DAB; DAC; DAM MST, NOV,
POP; WLC
See also CA 85-88; 25-28R; CANR 22; CDBLB
1914-1945; DLB 15, 162, 195; MTCW 1
Waugh, Harriet 1944- .... CLC 6
See also CA 85-88; CANR 22
Ways, C. R.
See Blount, Roy (Alton), Jr.
Waystaff, Simon
See Swift, Jonathan
Webb, (Martha) Beatrice (Potter) 1858-
1943 ....TCLC 22
See also Potter, (Helen) Beatrix
See also CA 117; DLB 190
Webb, Charles (Richard) 1939-...CLC 7
See also CA 25-28R
Webb, James H(enry), Jr. 1946- ...... CLC 22
See also CA 81-84
Webb, Mary (Gladys Meredith) 1881-1927
TCLC 24
See also CA 123; DLB 34
Webb, Mrs. Sidney
See Webb, (Martha) Beatrice (Potter)
Webb, Phyllis 1927-.......................... CLC 18
See also CA 104; CANR 23; DLB 53
Webb, Sidney (James) 1859-1947...TCLC
22
See also CA 117; 163; DLB 190
Webber, Andrew Lloyd .... CLC 21
See also Lloyd Webber, Andrew
Weber, Lenora Mattingly 1895-1971
CLC 12
See also CA 19-20; 29-32R; CAP 1; SATA 2;
SATA-Obit 26
Weber, Max 1864-1920 .... TCLC 69
See also CA 109
Webster, John 1579(?)-1634(?) ... LC 33; DA;
DAB; DAC; DAM DRAM, MST; DC 2;
WLC
See also CDBLB Before 1660; DLB 58
Webster, Noah 1758-1843 .... NCLC 30
Wedekind, (Benjamin) Frank(lin) 1864-
1918 .... TCLC 7; DAM DRAM
See also CA 104; 153; DLB 118
Weidman, Jerome 1913-1998 ...... CLC 7
See also AITN 2; CA 1-4R; 171; CANR 1;
DLB 28
Weil, Simone (Adolphine) 1909-1943
TCLC 23
See also CA 117; 159
Weininger, Otto 1880-1903 .... TCLC 84
Weinstein, Nathan
See West, Nathanael
Weinstein, Nathan von Wallenstein
See West, Nathanael
Weir, Peter (Lindsay) 1944-....... CLC 20
See also CA 113; 123
Weiss, Peter (Ulrich) 1916-1982...CLC 3,
15, 51; DAM DRAM
See also CA 45-48; 106; CANR 3; DLB 69, 124
Weiss, Theodore (Russell) 1916-...CLC 3,
8, 14
See also CA 9-12R; CAAS 2; CANR 46; DLB
5
Welch, (Maurice) Denton 1915-1948
TCLC 22
See also CA 121; 148

Welch, James 1940-...CLC 6, 14, 52; DAM
MULT, POP
See also CA 85-88; CANR 42, 66; DLB 175;
NNAL
Weldon, Fay 1931-...CLC 6, 9, 11, 19, 36,
59; DAM POP
See also CA 21-24R; CANR 16, 46, 63; CDBLB
1960 to Present; DLB 14, 194; INT CANR-
16; MTCW 1
Wellek, Rene 1903-1995 .... CLC 28
See also CA 5-8R; 150; CAAS 7; CANR 8; DLB
63; INT CANR-8
Weller, Michael 1942- .... CLC 10, 53
See also CA 85-88
Weller, Paul 1958- .... CLC 26
Wellershoff, Dieter 1925- .... CLC 46
See also CA 89-92; CANR 16, 37
Welles, (George) Orson 1915-1985
CLC 20, 80
See also CA 93-96; 117
Wellman, John McDowell 1945-
See Wellman, Mac
See also CA 166
Wellman, Mac 1945- ....CLC 65
See also Wellman, John McDowell; Wellman,
John McDowell
Wellman, Manly Wade 1903-1986
CLC 49
See also CA 1-4R; 118; CANR 6, 16, 44;
SATA 6; SATA-Obit 47
Wells, Carolyn 1869(?)-1942... TCLC 35
See also CA 113; DLB 11
Wells, H(erbert) G(eorge) 1866-1946
TCLC 6, 12, 19; DA; DAB; DAC; DAM
MST, NOV; SSC 6; WLC
See also AAYA 18; CA 110; 121; CDBLB
1914-1945; DLB 34, 70, 156, 178;
MTCW 1; SATA 20
Wells, Rosemary 1943- .... CLC 12
See also AAYA 13; CA 85-88; CANR 48;
CLR 16; MAICYA; SAAS 1; SATA 18, 69
Welty, Eudora 1909-...CLC 1, 2, 5, 14, 22,
33, 105; DA; DAB; DAC; DAM MST,
NOV; SSC 1, 27; WLC
See also CA 9-12R; CABS 1; CANR 32, 65;
CDALB 1941-1968; DLB 2, 102, 143;
DLBD 12; DLBY 87; MTCW 1
Wen I-to 1899-1946 .... TCLC 28
Wentworth, Robert
See Hamilton, Edmond
Werfel, Franz (Viktor) 1890-1945 ... TCLC 8
See also CA 104; 161; DLB 81, 124
Wergeland, Henrik Arnold 1808-1845
NCLC 5
Wersba, Barbara 1932- .... CLC 30
See also AAYA 2; CA 29-32R; CANR 16, 38;
CLR 3; DLB 52; JRDA; MAICYA; SAAS 2;
SATA 1, 58
Wertmueller, Lina 1928- ....CLC 16
See also CA 97-100; CANR 39
Wescott, Glenway 1901-1987 ....CLC 13
See also CA 13-16R; 121; CANR 23, 70; DLB
4, 9, 102
Wesker, Arnold 1932-...CLC 3, 5, 42; DAB;
DAM DRAM
See also CA 1-4R; CAAS 7; CANR 1, 33;
CDBLB 1960 to Present; DLB 13; MTCW 1
Wesley, Richard (Errol) 1945- ....CLC 7
See also BW 1; CA 57-60; CANR 27; DLB 38
Wessel, Johan Herman 1742-1785...LC 7
West, Anthony (Panther) 1914-1987
CLC 50
See also CA 45-48; 124; CANR 3, 19; DLB 15

West, C. P.
See Wodehouse, P(elham) G(renville)
West, (Mary) Jessamyn 1902-1984
CLC 7, 17
See also CA 9-12R; 112; CANR 27; DLB 6;
DLBY 84; MTCW 1; SATA-Obit 37
West, Morris L(anglo) 1916- .... CLC 6, 33
See also CA 5-8R; CANR 24, 49, 64; MTCW 1
West, Nathanael 1903-1940 TCLC 1, 14,
44; SSC 16
See also CA 104; 125; CDALB 1929-1941;
DLB 4, 9, 28; MTCW 1
West, Owen
See Koontz, Dean R(ay)
West, Paul 1930- ....CLC 7, 14, 96
See also CA 13-16R; CAAS 7; CANR 22, 53;
DLB 14; INT CANR-22
West, Rebecca 1892-1983 ... CLC 7, 9, 31, 50
See also CA 5-8R; 109; CANR 19; DLB 36;
DLBY 83; MTCW 1
Westall, Robert (Atkinson) 1929-1993
CLC 17
See also AAYA 12; CA 69-72; 141; CANR
18, 68; CLR 13; JRDA; MAICYA; SAAS
2; SATA 23, 69; SATA-Obit 75
Westermarck, Edward 1862-1939 .TCLC
87
Westlake, Donald E(dwin) 1933-...CLC 7,
33; DAM POP
See also CA 17-20R; CAAS 13; CANR 16, 44,
65; INT CANR-16
Westmacott, Mary
See Christie, Agatha (Mary Clarissa)
Weston, Allen
See Norton, Andre
Wetcheek, J. L.
See Feuchtwanger, Lion
Wetering, Janwillem van de
See van de Wetering, Janwillem
Wetherald, Agnes Ethelwyn 1857-1940
TCLC 81
See also DLB 99
Wetherell, Elizabeth
See Warner, Susan (Bogert)
Whale, James 1889-1957 .... TCLC 63
Whalen, Philip 1923- .... CLC 6, 29
See also CA 9-12R; CANR 5, 39; DLB 16
Wharton, Edith (Newbold Jones) 1862-
1937...TCLC 3, 9, 27, 53; DA; DAB;
DAC; DAM MST, NOV; SSC 6; WLC
See also AAYA 25; CA 104; 132; CDALB
1865-1917; DLB 4, 9, 12, 78, 189; DLBD
13; MTCW 1
Wharton, James
See Mencken, H(enry) L(ouis)
Wharton, William (a pseudonym)
CLC 18, 37
See also CA 93-96; DLBY 80; INT 93-96
Wheatley (Peters), Phillis 1754(?)-1784
LC 3; BLC 3; DA; DAC; DAM MST,
MULT, POET; PC 3; WLC
See also CDALB 1640-1865; DLB 31, 50
Wheelock, John Hall 1886-1978 ...... CLC 14
See also CA 13-16R; 77-80; CANR 14; DLB 45
White, E(lwyn) B(rooks) 1899-1985 CLC
10, 34, 39; DAM POP
See also AITN 2; CA 13-16R; 116; CANR 16,
37; CLR 1, 21; DLB 11, 22; MAICYA;
MTCW 1; SATA 2, 29, 100; SATA-Obit 44
White, Edmund (Valentine III) 1940-
CLC 27, 110; DAM POP
See also AAYA 7; CA 45-48; CANR 3, 19,
36, 62; MTCW 1

White, Patrick (Victor Martindale) 1912-
1990 .... **CLC 3, 4, 5, 7, 9, 18, 65, 69**
See also CA 81-84; 132; CANR 43; MTCW
1
White, Phyllis Dorothy James 1920-
See James, P. D.
See also CA 21-24R; CANR 17, 43, 65; DAM
POP; MTCW 1
White, T(erence) H(anbury) 1906-1964
CLC 30
See also AAYA 22; CA 73-76; CANR 37;
DLB 160; JRDA; MAICYA; SATA 12
White, Terence de Vere 1912-1994 .. **CLC 49**
See also CA 49-52; 145; CANR 3
White, Walter F(rancis) 1893-1955**TCLC
15**
See also White, Walter
See also BW 1; CA 115; 124; DLB 51
White, William Hale 1831-1913
See Rutherford, Mark
See also CA 121
Whitehead, E(dward) A(nthony) 1933-
CLC 5
See also CA 65-68; CANR 58
Whitemore, Hugh (John) 1936- .... **CLC 37**
See also CA 132; INT 132
Whitman, Sarah Helen (Power) 1803-1878
NCLC 19
See also DLB 1
Whitman, Walt(er) 1819-1892 **NCLC 4,
31; DA; DAB; DAC; DAM MST, POET;
PC 3; WLC**
See also CDALB 1640-1865; DLB 3, 64; SATA
20
Whitney, Phyllis A(yame) 1903- ..... **CLC 42;
DAM POP**
See also AITN 2; BEST 90:3; CA 1-4R; CANR
3, 25, 38, 60; JRDA; MAICYA; SATA 1, 30
Whittemore, (Edward) Reed (Jr.) 1919-**CLC 4**
See also CA 9-12R; CAAS 8; CANR 4; DLB 5
Whittier, John Greenleaf 1807-1892
NCLC 8, 59
See also DLB 1
Whittlebot, Hernia
See Coward, Noel (Peirce)
Wicker, Thomas Grey 1926-
See Wicker, Tom
See also CA 65-68; CANR 21, 46
Wicker, Tom ....**CLC 7**
See also Wicker, Thomas Grey
Wideman, John Edgar 1941- **CLC 5, 34, 36,
67; BLC 3; DAM MULT**
See also BW 2; CA 85-88; CANR 14, 42, 67;
DLB 33, 143
Wiebe, Rudy (Henry) 1934-**CLC 6, 11, 14;
DAC; DAM MST**
See also CA 37-40R; CANR 42, 67; DLB 60
Wieland, Christoph Martin 1733-1813**N C L C
17**
See also DLB 97
Wiene, Robert 1881-1938 .... **TCLC 56**
Wieners, John 1934-............................**CLC 7**
See also CA 13-16R; DLB 16
Wiesel, Elie(zer) 1928- **CLC 3, 5, 11, 37; DA;
DAB; DAC; DAM MST, NOV; WLCS**
See also AAYA 7; AITN 1; CA 5-8R; CAAS 4;
CANR 8, 40, 65; DLB 83; DLBY 87; INT
CANR-8; MTCW 1; SATA 56
Wiggins, Marianne 1947- .... **CLC 57**
See also BEST 89:3; CA 130; CANR 60
Wight, James Alfred 1916-1995
See Herriot, James
See also CA 77-80; SATA 55; SATA-Brief 44

Wilbur, Richard (Purdy) 1921-...**CLC 3,
6, 9, 14, 53, 110; DA; DAB; DAC; DAM
MST, POET**
See also CA 1-4R; CABS 2; CANR 2, 29; DLB
5, 169; INT CANR-29; MTCW 1; SATA 9
Wild, Peter 1940-................................**CLC 14**
See also CA 37-40R; DLB 5
Wilde, Oscar (Fingal O'Flahertie Wills)
1854(?)-1900...**TCLC 1, 8, 23, 41; DA;
DAB; DAC; DAM DRAM, MST, NOV;
SSC 11; WLC**
See also CA 104; 119; CDBLB 1890-1914;
DLB 10, 19, 34, 57, 141, 156, 190; SATA 24
Wilder, Billy ....**CLC 20**
See also Wilder, Samuel
See also DLB 26
Wilder, Samuel 1906-
See Wilder, Billy
See also CA 89-92
Wilder, Thornton (Niven) 1897-1975
**CLC 1, 5, 6, 10, 15, 35, 82; DA; DAB;
DAC; DAM DRAM, MST, NOV; DC 1;
WLC**
See also AITN 2; CA 13-16R; 61-64; CANR
40; DLB 4, 7, 9; DLBY 97; MTCW 1
Wilding, Michael 1942-.....................**CLC 73**
See also CA 104; CANR 24, 49
Wiley, Richard 1944-...................**CLC 44**
See also CA 121; 129; CANR 71
Wilhelm, Kate ....**CLC 7**
See also Wilhelm, Katie Gertrude
See also AAYA 20; CAAS 5; DLB 8; INT
CANR-17
Wilhelm, Katie Gertrude 1928-
See Wilhelm, Kate
See also CA 37-40R; CANR 17, 36, 60; MTCW
1
Wilkins, Mary
See Freeman, Mary Eleanor Wilkins
Willard, Nancy 1936- ....**CLC 7, 37**
See also CA 89-92; CANR 10, 39, 68; CLR
5; DLB 5, 52; MAICYA; MTCW 1; SATA
37, 71; SATA-Brief 30
Williams, Ben Ames 1889-1953 ...... **TCLC 89**
See also DLB 102
Williams, C(harles) K(enneth) 1936-
CLC 33, 56; DAM POET
See also CA 37-40R; CAAS 26; CANR 57;
DLB 5
Williams, Charles
See Collier, James L(incoln)
Williams, Charles (Walter Stansby) 1886-1945
TCLC 1, 11
See also CA 104; 163; DLB 100, 153
Williams, (George) Emlyn 1905-1987
CLC 15; DAM DRAM
See also CA 104; 123; CANR 36; DLB 10,
77; MTCW 1
Williams, Hank 1923-1953 .... **TCLC 81**
Williams, Hugo 1942-.........................**CLC 42**
See also CA 17-20R; CANR 45; DLB 40
Williams, J. Walker
See Wodehouse, P(elham) G(renville)
Williams, John A(lfred) 1925-...**CLC 5,
13; BLC 3; DAM MULT**
See also BW 2; CA 53-56; CAAS 3; CANR 6,
26, 51; DLB 2, 33; INT CANR-6
Williams, Jonathan (Chamberlain) 1929-
CLC 13
See also CA 9-12R; CAAS 12; CANR 8; DLB
5
Williams, Joy 1944- ....**CLC 31**
See also CA 41-44R; CANR 22, 48

Williams, Norman 1952-............**CLC 39**
See also CA 118
Williams, Sherley Anne 1944-...**CLC 89;
BLC 3; DAM MULT, POET**
See also BW 2; CA 73-76; CANR 25; DLB 41;
INT CANR-25; SATA 78
Williams, Shirley
See Williams, Sherley Anne
Williams, Tennessee 1911-1983...**CLC 1,
2, 5, 7, 8, 11, 15, 19, 30, 39, 45, 71, 111;
DA; DAB; DAC; DAM DRAM, MST;
DC 4; WLC**
See also AITN 1, 2; CA 5-8R; 108; CABS 3;
CANR 31; CDALB 1941-1968; DLB 7;
DLBD 4; DLBY 83; MTCW 1
Williams, Thomas (Alonzo) 1926-1990
CLC 14
See also CA 1-4R; 132; CANR 2
Williams, William C.
See Williams, William Carlos
Williams, William Carlos 1883-1963
**CLC 1, 2, 5, 9, 13, 22, 42, 67; DA; DAB;
DAC; DAM MST, POET; PC 7; SSC 31**
See also CA 89-92; CANR 34; CDALB 1917-
1929; DLB 4, 16, 54, 86; MTCW 1
Williamson, David (Keith) 1942- ......**CLC 56**
See also CA 103; CANR 41
Williamson, Ellen Douglas 1905-1984
See Douglas, Ellen
See also CA 17-20R; 114; CANR 39
Williamson, Jack ....**CLC 29**
See also Williamson, John Stewart
See also CAAS 8; DLB 8
Williamson, John Stewart 1908-
See Williamson, Jack
See also CA 17-20R; CANR 23, 70
Willie, Frederick
See Lovecraft, H(oward) P(hillips)
Willingham, Calder (Baynard, Jr.) 1922-
1995 ....**CLC 5, 51**
See also CA 5-8R; 147; CANR 3; DLB 2, 44;
MTCW 1
Willis, Charles
See Clarke, Arthur C(harles)
Willy
See Colette, (Sidonie-Gabrielle)
Willy, Colette
See Colette, (Sidonie-Gabrielle)
Wilson, A(ndrew) N(orman) 1950- **C L C
33**
See also CA 112; 122; DLB 14, 155, 194
Wilson, Angus (Frank Johnstone) 1913-
1991 ...... **CLC 2, 3, 5, 25, 34; SSC 21**
See also CA 5-8R; 134; CANR 21; DLB 15,
139, 155; MTCW 1
Wilson, August 1945-...**CLC 39, 50, 63;
BLC 3; DA; DAB; DAC; DAM DRAM,
MST, MULT; DC 2; WLCS**
See also AAYA 16; BW 2; CA 115; 122;
CANR 42, 54; MTCW 1
Wilson, Brian 1942-.........................**CLC 12**
Wilson, Colin 1931-......................**CLC 3, 14**
See also CA 1-4R; CAAS 5; CANR 1, 22, 33;
DLB 14, 194; MTCW 1
Wilson, Dirk
See Pohl, Frederik
Wilson, Edmund 1895-1972...**CLC 1, 2, 3,
8, 24**
See also CA 1-4R; 37-40R; CANR 1, 46; DLB
63; MTCW 1
Wilson, Ethel Davis (Bryant) 1888(?)-1980
CLC 13; DAC; DAM POET
See also CA 102; DLB 68; MTCW 1

Poetry Criticism
Cumulative Nationality Index

Nationality Index

PC Cumulative Title Index

Title Index

Title Index

Title Index

Title Index

Title Index

ISBN 0-7876-3073-X

90000